Experiencing The Lifespan

Cross sequential study

Experiencing The Lifespan

THIRD EDITION

JANET BELSKY

MIDDLE TENNESSEE STATE UNIVERSITY

WORTH PUBLISHERS

For David

A world-class intellectual and the world's best possible husband.

Vice President, Editorial and Production: Catherine Woods
Publisher: Kevin Feyen
Senior Acquisitions Editor: Christine M. Cardone
Marketing Manager: Lindsay Johnson
Marketing Development Assistant: Stephanie Ellis
Developmental Editor: Elaine Epstein
Director of Print and Digital Development: Tracey Kuehn
Senior Media Editor: Christine Burak
Editorial Assistant and Supplements Editor: Eric Dorger
Photo Editor: Bianca Moscatelli
Photo Researcher: Deborah Anderson
Art Director: Babs Reingold
Cover Designer: Lyndall Culbertson
Interior Designers: Charles Yuen and Lyndall Culbertson
Chapter-opening Layouts: Lyndall Culbertson
Associate Managing Editor: Lisa Kinne
Project Editor: Julio Espin
Illustrations: cMPreparé, Dragonfly Media Group, Christy Krames
Production Manager: Sarah Segal
Composition: cMPreparé
Printing and Binding: RR Donnelley

Credit is given to the following sources for permission to use the part- and chapter-opening photos: cover, p. xxxii, BLOOM WORKS Inc./age fotostock; pp. 2, 454, Ali Johnson Photography/Getty Images, George Doyle/Stockbyte/Getty Images, Purestock/Alamy, Blend Images/Getty Images, APlights/Design Pics/Corbis, Ronnie Kaufman/Larry Hirshowitz/Blend Images/Corbis, i love images/Alamy, Rubberball/Rubberball/Corbis, Stockbyte/Getty Images, Dimitri Vervitsiotis/Getty Images, Jon Feingersh/Blend Images/Corbis, Radius/SuperStock p. 36, Ali Johnson Photography/Getty Images; p. 74, Blend Images/Getty Images; p. 76, George Doyle/Stockbyte/Getty Images; p. 110, Purestock/Alamy; p. 138, Rob Lewine/Tetra Images/Corbis; p. 140, Blend Images/Getty Images; p. 172, APlights/ Design Pics/Corbis; p. 202, Ronnie Kaufman/Larry Hirshowitz/Blend Images/Corbis; p. 234, Gabriela Medina/Blend Images/Corbis; p. 236, i love images/Alamy; p. 264, Rubberball/Rubberball/Corbis; p. 296, Radius Images/Alamy; p. 298, Stockbyte/Getty Images; p. 330, Dimitri Vervitsiotis/Getty Images; p. 362; Jon Feingersh/Blend Images/Corbis; p. 392, David Sacks/Digital Vision/Getty Images; p. 394, Westend61 GmbH/Alamy; p. 422, Radius/SuperStock; p. 452, Image Source/Alamy

Library of Congress Control Number: 2012945704

ISBN-13: 978-14292-9922-0
ISBN-10: 1-4292-9922-3

Printed in the United States of America

First printing

Worth Publishers
41 Madison Avenue
New York, NY 10010

ABOUT THE AUTHOR

BORN IN NEW YORK, JANET BELSKY always wanted to be a writer but was also very interested in people. After receiving her undergraduate degree from the University of Pennsylvania, she deferred to her more practical and people-loving side and got her Ph.D. in clinical psychology at the University of Chicago. After years in New York teaching at Lehman College and doing clinical work in nursing homes and city hospitals, she moved to Tennessee in 1991 to teach full time. In between teaching several sections of lifespan development every semester, Janet found the time to write a few textbooks in adult development and aging and one trade book, *Here Tomorrow: Making the Most of Life After 50*. Her son Thomas is now an "emerged" adult working in Key West, Florida. Janet lives in Murfreesboro, Tennessee, with her husband, David, to whom she has been married for more than 35 years. In writing *Experiencing the Lifespan*, she has been able to merge her three enduring life passions—writing, teaching undergraduates about the lifespan, and interviewing people from age 3 to 103. Following her own personal optimally aging (and, hopefully, stimulating neurogenesis!) program, Janet has now developed a new later life passion—acting in community theater.

BRIEF
CONTENTS

CONTENTS

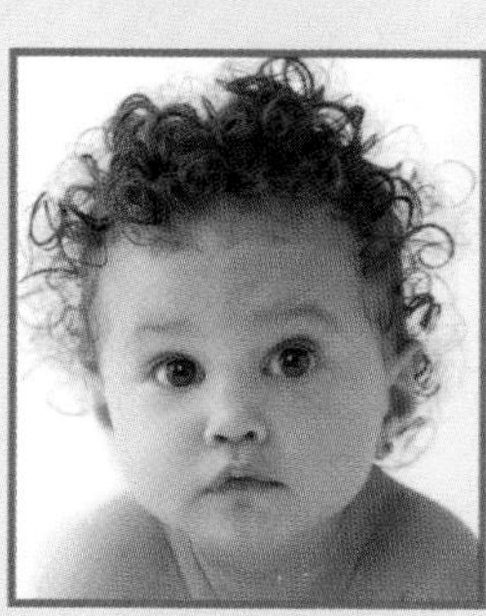

PREFACE

I spent my thirties and forties writing textbooks on adult development and aging. I've spent almost 15 years writing and revising this book. I've spent thirty-five years (virtually all of my adult life!) joyously teaching this course. My mission in this book is simple: to excite students in this marvelous field!

Because I want to showcase the most cutting-edge research, in this edition of *Experiencing the Lifespan*, you will find roughly 800 citations dating just from 2010. I've added new sections to almost every chapter, covering topics as varied as the economics of attending college, to cohort differences in aging rates. I've constructed roughly two dozen new tables and figures and even included a few classic theories that were missing or minimized in previous versions of the book. But, readers who have used *Experiencing the Lifespan* in the past will be comforted to know that this edition has the same familiar structure and plan. It reflects my enduring commitment to convey the beauty of our science in the same compelling way. What *exactly* makes this book compelling? What makes each chapter special? What makes this edition stand out?

What Makes This Book Compelling?

- ***Experiencing the Lifespan* unfolds like a story.** The main feature that makes this book compelling is the writing style. *Experiencing the Lifespan* reads like a conversation rather than a traditional text. Each chapter begins with a vignette constructed to highlight the material I will be discussing. I've designed my narrative to flow from topic to topic; and I've planned every chapter to interconnect. In this book, the main themes that underlie developmental science flow throughout the *entire* book. I want students to have the sense that they are reading an exciting, ongoing story. Most of all, I want them to feel that they are learning about a coherent, *organized* field.
- ***Experiencing the Lifespan* is uniquely organized to highlight development.** A second mission that has been driving my writing is to highlight how our lives evolve. What exactly makes an 8-year-old mentally different from a 4-year-old, or a 60-year-old different from a person of 85. In order to emphasize how children develop, I decided to cover all of childhood in a single three-chapter part. This strategy has allowed me to fully explore the magic of Piaget's preoperational and concrete operational stages and to trace the development of aggression, childhood friendships, and gender-stereotyped play. It permits me to show *concretely* how the ability to think through their actions changes as children travel from preschool through elementary school. I decided to put early and middle adulthood in one unit (Part IV) for similar reasons: It simply made logical sense to discuss important topics that transcend a single life stage, such as marriage, parenting, and work (Chapter 11) and adult personality and cognitive development (Chapter 12), together in the same place.

B. Tanaka/Getty Images

For this grandmother, mother, and daughter, getting dressed up to visit this Shinto family shrine and pay their respects to their ancestors is an important ritual. It is one way that the lesson "honor your elders" is taught to children living in collectivist societies such as Japan from an early age.

In fact, I've designed this *whole* text to highlight development. I follow the characters in the chapter-opening vignettes throughout each several-chapter book part. I've planned each life stage segment to flow in a developmental way. In the first infancy chapter, I begin with a discussion of newborn states. The second chapter in this sequence (Infancy: Socioemotional Development) ends with a discussion of toddlerhood. My three-chapter Early and Middle Adulthood book part starts with an exploration of the challenges of emerging adulthood (Chapter 10), then tackles marriage, parenthood, and career (Chapter 11), and culminates with a chapter tracking adult personality and intelligence through midlife and exploring "older" family roles such as parent care and grandparenthood (Chapter 12). In Part VI, Later Life, I begin with a chapter devoted to topics, such as retirement, that typically take place during the young-old years. Then I focus on physical aging (Chapter 14, The Physical Challenges of Old Age) because sensory-motor impairments, dementing diseases, and interventions for late-life frailty become crucial concerns mainly in the eighties and beyond. Yes, this textbook does—for the most part—move through the lifespan stage by stage. However, it's targeted to highlight the aspects of development—such as constructing an adult life in the 20s or physical disabilities in the 80s—that become salient at particular times of life. I believe that my textbook captures the best features of the chronological and topical approaches.

AP Photo/Watertown Daily Times/John Hart

Families come in many forms, and the love you have for your adopted children is no different than if you gave birth. Take it from me as an adoptive mom!

- ***Experiencing the Lifespan* is both shorter and more in-depth.** Adopting this flexible, development-friendly organization makes for a more manageable, teacher-friendly book. With 15 chapters and at roughly 500 pages, my textbook *really* can be mastered in a one-semester course! Not being locked into covering each slice of life in defined bits also gives me the freedom to focus on what is most important in special depth. As you will discover while reading my comprehensive discussions of central topics in our field, such as attachment, parenting, puberty, and adult personality consistency and change, omitting superficial coverage of "everything" allows time to explore the core issues in developmental science in a deeper, more thoughtful way.

- ***Experiencing the Lifespan* actively fosters critical thinking.** Guiding students to reflect on what they are reading is actually another of my writing goals. A great advantage of engaging readers in a conversation is that I can naturally embed critical thinking into the actual narrative. For example, as I move from discussing Piaget's ideas on cognition to Vygotsky's theory to the information-processing approach in Chapter 5, I point out the gaps in each perspective and highlight *why* each approach offers a unique contribution to understanding children's intellectual growth. On a policy-oriented level, after discussing the research relating to day care or teenage storm and stress, I ask readers to think critically about how to improve the way the twenty-first-century world cares for young families and treats normal adolescent acting out.

VStock/Alamy

It's a pleasure to see these newlyweds on this special day. Plus, this young husband may discover to his delight that choosing this wife will give him a deeper, richer appreciation of his own ethnic roots.

- ***Experiencing the Lifespan* has a global orientation and pays special attention to the issues facing immigrants and ethnic groups.** Intrinsic to getting students to evaluate their own cultural practices is the need to highlight alternate perspectives on our developing life. Therefore, *Experiencing the Lifespan* is a firmly international book. I introduce this global orientation in the first chapter when I spell out the differences between collectivist and individualistic cultures and the developed and developing worlds. In the childhood chapters, when discussing topics such as parenting, constructing a self, and adolescent parent-child relations, I have special heads devoted to cultural variations and immigrant issues. In the adulthood sections, standard "Setting the Context" heads, preceding the research, offer snapshots of love and marriage in different nations, discuss retirement in other world regions, and explore different societal practices and attitudes toward death.

(In fact, "How do other groups handle this?" is a question that crops up when I talk about practically every topic in the book!)

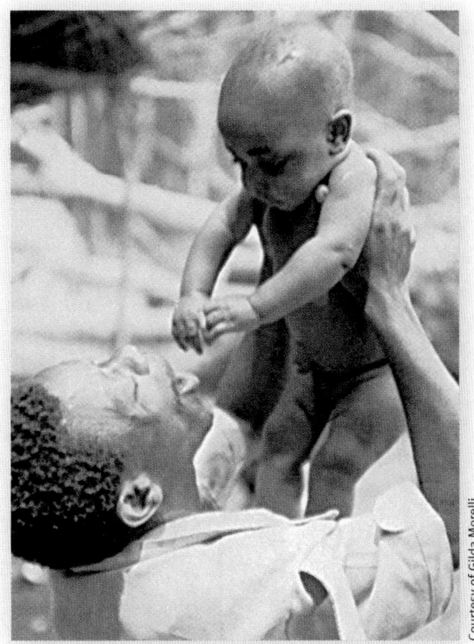

Courtesy of Gilda Morelli

This new member of the Efé people of central Africa will be lovingly cared for by the whole community, males as well as females, from his first minutes of life. Because he sleeps with his mother, however, at the "right" age he will develop his primary attachment to her.

- ***Experiencing the Lifespan* highlights the multiple forces that shape development.** Given my emphasis on cultural variations within our universal human experience, it should come as no surprise that the main theoretical framework I've used to organize this book is the developmental systems approach. Throughout the chapters, I explore the many influences that interact to predict core life milestones—from puberty to physical aging. Erikson's stages, attachment theory, behavioral genetics, evolutionary theory, self-efficacy, and, especially, the importance of looking at nature *and* nurture and providing the best person–environment fit—all are concepts that I introduce in the first chapter and continue to stress as the book unfolds. Another theme that runs through this text is the impact of socioeconomic status, both internationally and in the United States, on shaping everything from breast-feeding practices to the rate at which we age and die. In this new edition, I spend special time exploring how the Great Recession of 2008 is changing our adult pathway in the United States.

- ***Experiencing the Lifespan* is applications-oriented, and focused on how to construct a satisfying life.** Because of my background as a clinical psychologist, my other passion is to concretely bring home how we can use the scientific findings to improve the quality of life. So *each* topic in this text ends with an "Interventions" section spelling out practical implications of the research. With its varied Interventions, such as "How Can You Get Babies to Sleep Through the Night?" or "Using Piaget's Theory at Home and at Work," to its adulthood tables, such as "How to Flourish During Adulthood" and full sections devoted to "Aging Optimally," *Experiencing the Lifespan* is designed to show how the science of development can make a difference in people's lives.

- ***Experiencing the Lifespan* is a person-centered, hands-on textbook.** This book is also designed to bring the experience of the lifespan home in a personal way. Therefore, in "Experiencing the Lifespan" boxes, I report on interviews I've conducted with people ranging from a 16-year-old (a student of mine last semester) who was charged as an adult with second-degree murder to a 70-year-old man with Alzheimer's disease. To entice readers to empathize with the challenges of other life stages, I continually ask students to "imagine you are a toddler" or "a sleep-deprived mother" or "an 80-year-old struggling with the challenges of driving in later life."

Another strategy I use to make the research vivid and personal are questionnaires (often based on the chapter content) that get readers to think more deeply about their *own* lives: the checklist to identify your parenting priorities in Chapter 7; a scale for "using selective optimization with compensation at home and work" in Chapter 12; surveys for "evaluating your relationships" in Chapters 10 and 11; true/false quizzes at the beginning of my chapters on adolescence (Chapter 9), adult roles (Chapter 11), and later life (Chapter 13) that provide a hands-on preview of the content and entice students into reading the chapter so that they can assess the scientific accuracy of their ideas.

Jupiterimages/Brand X Pictures/Getty Images

If you can relate to this photo, the next time you are tempted to text during that not-so- interesting class, keep this message in mind: *Divided attention tasks* make memory worse!

- ***Experiencing the Lifespan* is designed to get students to learn the material while they read.** The chapter-opening vignettes, the applications sections with their summary tables, the hands-on exercises, and the end-of-section questionnaires (such as "A Research-based Guide for Evaluating Your Relationship" in Chapter 10) are part of an overall pedagogical plan. As I explain in my introductory letter to students on page 2, I want this to be a textbook you don't have to struggle to decode—one that helps you *naturally* cement the concepts in mind. The centerpiece of this effort is the "Tying It All Together" quizzes, which follow each major section. These mini-tests, involving multiple-choice, essay, and critical-thinking questions, allow students to test themselves on what they have absorbed. I've also planned the photo program in *Experiencing the Lifespan* to illustrate the major terms and concepts. As you page through the text, you may notice that the pictures and their captions feel organically connected to the writing. They visually bring the main text messages home. When it's important for students to learn a series of terms or related concepts, I provide a summary series of photos. You can see examples in the photographs illustrating the different infant and adult attachment styles on pages 116 and 324, and in Table 3.7 on page 100, highlighting Jean Piaget's infant circular reactions.

As you scan this book, you will see other special features: "**How do we know . . . ?**" boxes in some chapters delve more deeply into particular research programs; "**In Focus**" sections in the text showcase "hot topics," from ADHD to age discrimination at work; timelines pull everything together at the end of complex sections (such as the chart summarizing the landmarks of pregnancy and prenatal development on pages 60–61).

What will make this text a pleasure to teach from? How can I make this book a joy to read? These are questions I have been grappling with as I've been glued to my computer—often seven days a week—during this almost decade-and-a-half-long labor of love.

What Makes Each Chapter Special?

Now that I've spelled out my general writing missions, here are some highlights of each chapter, and a detailed preview of *exactly* what's new.

PART I: The Foundation

CHAPTER 1: The People and the Field

- Outlines the basic contexts of development: social class, culture, ethnicity, and cohort.
- Traces the evolution of the lifespan over the centuries and explores the classic developmental science theories that have shaped our understanding of life.
- Spells out the concepts, the perspectives, and the research strategies I will be exploring in each chapter of the book.

WHAT'S NEW?

- Discussion of the Great Recession of 2008, accompanied by a figure showing increasing income inequality and the rise in underemployment and unemployment. This introduction sets students up for this edition's special focus on the recession's wide-ranging effects.
- "In Focus" feature describing psychoanalytic theory is tailored to emphasize the Freudian concepts that will really resonate with students, such as the idea that self-knowledge is the key to a successful life.
- Theories section introduces the Flynn effect to illustrate how nurture (the environment) is changing our human nature, and includes a graphic of Bronfenbrenner's model for instructors who want to cover that specific theory in greater depth.

TEH ENG KOON/AFP/Getty Images

Imagine being this terrified woman as she surveys the rubble of her collapsed house. What is the impact of disasters, like this Malaysian landslide, on babies in the womb? Stay tuned for fascinating answers, as we explore *fetal programming research.*

CHAPTER 2: Prenatal Development, Pregnancy, and Birth

- Discusses pregnancy rituals and superstitions around the world.
- Highlights the latest research on fetal brain development.
- Fully explores the experience of pregnancy from both the mother's and father's points of view.
- Looks at the experience of birth historically and discusses policy issues relating to pregnancy and birth in the United States and around the world.

WHAT'S NEW?

- "In Focus" section explores that hot new topic, fetal programming. This discussion—tracking how traumas during pregnancy, such as famines or severe stress, can affect development into old age—sets students up for research linking low birth weight to obesity (described in Chapter 5) and the timing of puberty (in Chapter 8).

- Provides an updated account of smoking and alcohol's effects; assisted reproductive techniques; and a discussion of the ethics of birth interventions at the cusp of viability.

PART II: Infancy

CHAPTER 3: Infancy: Physical and Cognitive Development

- Covers the latest research on brain development.
- Focuses in depth on basic infant states such as eating, crying, and sleep.
- Explores breast-feeding and scans global undernutrition.
- Provides an in-depth, personal, and practice-oriented look at infant motor development, Piaget's sensorimotor stage, and beginning language.
- Explores the cutting-edge findings on infant social cognition.

WHAT'S NEW?

- Features a new table entitled "Brain Busting Facts to Wrap Your Head Around." (Similar summary brain-busting facts tables will appear in Chapters 5 and 9.)
- Basic states section focuses on physical deterrents to breast-feeding, offers recent data on U.S. food insecurity and global stunting, showcases research suggesting a brain stem abnormality may be at the root of SIDS, and describes new findings relating to getting infants to sleep.
- Language discussion traces the earliest roots of this core ability, while the vision section includes a new, delightful finding relating to what babies learn not to see. (In general, I'm tying the brain-pruning principle presented early in the chapter to emerging vision and language.)
- Social cognition section features a study suggesting 6 month olds may have a rudimentary understanding of morality, accompanied by images of the "mean" and "nice" puppets used in this innovative research.

CHAPTER 4: Infancy: Socioemotional Development

- Provides unusually in-depth coverage of attachment theory.
- Offers an honest, comprehensive look at day care in the United States and discusses early childhood poverty.
- Highlights exuberant and shy toddler temperaments, explores research on the genetics of temperament, and stresses the need to promote the right temperament–environment fit for each child.

WHAT'S NEW?

- Streamlined attachment discussion includes an "In Focus" feature exploring the fascinating studies of newborns exposed to the most severe attachment deprivation: being placed in Ceausescu's horrific Romanian orphanages, accompanied by other recent research exploring the causes and consequences of insecure attachments.
- Discusses the impact the wider neighborhood makes on school readiness, the latest NICHD findings, and the cost of day care in the United States.
- Concluding section (following the discussion of toddler temperaments) describes tentative findings suggesting that we may inherent a plasticity gene that either makes us more or less responsive to environmental events. This end-of-chapter material is designed to highlight a core message I want to bring home to readers: Labeling children (or people) as "difficult" or "easy" may not be appropriate. With the right person-environment fit, what looks like a liability can be a gift.

PART III: Childhood

CHAPTER 5: Physical and Cognitive Development

- Begins by exploring why we have childhood, illustrating what makes human beings qualitatively different from other species.

- Covers childhood obesity, including its emotional aspects, in depth.
- Showcases Piaget's, Vygotsky's, and the information-processing models of childhood cognition—with examples that stress the practical implications of these landmark perspectives for parents and people who work with children.
- Discusses ADHD, autobiographical memory, and theory of mind.

WHAT'S NEW?

- Explores cultural variations in emerging motor skills.
- Rewritten obesity discussion covers everything from the epidemic's possible prenatal roots, to the weight-gain ages that predict later obesity, to why contemporary parents are (naturally) reluctant to make their children's intake a main priority. A new concluding table outlines weight control interventions adults might make *without* explicitly focusing on weight and describes an intriguing survey suggesting that this cohort of young people is responding to the twenty-first-century overweight epidemic by seeing their size as "just fine" at higher weights.
- ADHD discussion highlights this condition's bewildering array of risk factors and paths, explores problematic issues related to medication use, and features environmental strategies, such as gaming, to enhance focus.
- Autobiographical memory section longitudinally tracks how our ability to reflect on the past coalesces into an identity in the teens, while the theory-of-mind discussion features a study suggesting that in difficult situations adults also fail false-belief tasks (demonstrating that theory of mind abilities depend on adequate working memory capacities).
- The above discussion is accompanied by an interesting fMRI "brain-busting table" suggesting that growing up in a collectivist versus individualistic society influences the actual brain regions that are activated when we reflect on our own and others' mental states.

CHAPTER 6: Socioemotional Development

- Discusses the development of self-understanding, prosocial behavior, aggression, and fantasy play, and explores friendships and popularity throughout childhood.
- Clearly spells out the developmental pathway to becoming an aggressive child.
- Highlights the challenge of emotion regulation, and focuses on internalizing and externalizing disorders.
- Covers the causes and consequences of bullying in older childhood.

SW Productions/Getty Images

It's a familiar scenario. Someone starts to harass an unpopular kid while a few friends egg that bully on and others passively stand by. But what do you think would happen if a bystander or two (let's say the boy or girl on the right) decided to angrily walk away or tell the instigator off?

WHAT'S NEW?

- Includes a description of Erikson's initiative versus guilt.
- "In Focus" feature entitled "Praise, Academic Self-Efficacy, and the Racial Self" documents how awareness of academic racial stereotypes affects the way Black students interpret teachers' praise and can generally erode minority children's school self-efficacy and school performance.
- Popularity discussion offers further data documenting the shift to peer-group norms favoring aggression during early adolescence.
- Rewritten bullying section introduces students to the term *bully-victim*, explores the pitfalls of standing up to a bully, and showcases findings illustrating that when the peer and school norms favor aggression, the nicest kids bully—emphasizing the message that 1) bullying is normal human behavior at *every age* and 2) the key to minimizing this unfortunate human activity lies in changing the social norms.

CHAPTER 7: Settings for Development: Home and School

- This final childhood chapter shifts from the process of development to the major settings for development—home and school—and tackles important controversies in the field, such as the influence of parents versus peers versus genetics in shaping development and the pros and cons of intelligence testing.
- Offers extensive discussions of ethnic variations in parenting styles and describes the latest research on how to stimulate intrinsic motivation.
- Showcases schools that beat the odds and targets the core qualities involved in effective teaching.

WHAT'S NEW?

- Updates the research on effective childrearing and explores a new study showing that in certain cultures a more authoritarian style works best.
- Provides a historical view of changing attitudes towards corporal punishment, tracks the trend to outlaw spanking in many nations, and further elaborates on group differences in attitudes towards spanking in the United States.
- Child abuse section alerts readers to the specific signs of physical abuse and focuses on why adults may be naturally reluctant to report this behavior.
- The discussion of intelligence in this chapter includes a thorough discussion of the Flynn effect.

PART IV: Adolescence

CHAPTER 8: Physical Development

- Offers an in-depth look at puberty, including the multiple forces that program the timing of this life transition, and looks at historical and cultural variations in puberty timetables.
- Explores the emotional experience of puberty (an "insider's" view) and the emotional impact of maturing early for girls.
- Provides up-to-date coverage of teenage body image issues, eating disorders, and emerging sexuality.

WHAT'S NEW?

- Offers the most cutting-edge research on puberty, exploring—among other topics—an example of a male puberty ritual; data relating to the remarkable differences in the rate of pubertal change among girls; tantalizing evidence suggesting infant weight gain (and early life stress) pushes the puberty timetable to an earlier age, but *only* for girls; new studies providing a more nuanced take on the standard ideas that early maturing sets girls up for trouble and that moving to middle school is bad for preteens.
- Updates the body image section with: a definition of "the thin ideal"; a clear account of the DSM criteria for anorexia and bulimia; a more in-depth look at the emotional correlates of eating disorders; an exploration of how girls with a positive body image think.
- Added to the sexuality discussion: updated statistics on U.S teenage sexual practices; delightful quotations from a qualitative study suggesting that male teens are interested in love as much as sex.

CHAPTER 9: Cognitive and Socioemotional Development

- Covers the latest developmental science research on teenage brain development and various facets of adolescent "storm and stress."
- Spells out the forces that enable adolescents to thrive and explains what society can do (and also may not be doing!) to promote optimal development in teens.
- Explores parent–child relationships and discusses teenage peer groups.

WHAT'S NEW?

- Critiques Kohlberg's theory by spelling out Gilligan's ideas.
- Showcases a study suggesting that the push for social status is a top priority during early adolescence and describes Steinberg's recent laboratory studies, accompanied by a summary table highlighting the major neuroscience findings relating to the teenage brain.
- Examines the female teenage increase in depression in more depth and spells out the emotional correlates of cutting.
- "In Focus" feature entitled "Possible Pubertal Problem: Popularity" makes the case that the push for social status—described earlier—may explain some of the rise in externalizing and internalizing behaviors in the early teens.
- Explores new data suggesting that risk-taking is part of the normal, healthy adolescent experience and examines both sides of the "brain deficit hypothesis" by featuring Robert Epstein's provocative idea that adolescent "storm and stress" is caused by a poor teen–society fit.
- *Most important,* discusses the alarming U.S. trend to try teenagers as adults, accompanied by a powerful first-person interview with a student of mine who spent his adolescent years in prison.
- Examines parent-child issues unique to second-generation immigrant teens.

PART V: Early and Middle Adulthood

CHAPTER 10: Constructing an Adult Life

- Devotes a whole chapter to the concerns of emerging adulthood.
- Offers extensive coverage of diversity issues during this life stage, such as forming an ethnic and biracial identity, interracial dating, and issues related to coming out gay.
- Gives students tips for succeeding in college and spells out career issues for non-college emerging adults.
- Introduces career-relevant topics, such as the concept of "flow," and provides extensive coverage of the research relating to selecting a mate and adult attachment styles.
- Focuses on current social policy issues such as the impact socioeconomic status makes on attending and completing college, and discusses "nest residing," given that so many twenty-somethings now live at home.

WHAT'S NEW?

- Features six new tables/figures! " A Twenty-Something Body at Its Physical Peak" explores age declines in height, the heart, the lungs, and muscles; "Tips for Getting Along as Co-residing Adults" offers advice for parents and children in this increasingly common situation; "Fun Research Findings Relating to Love and Sex" provides scientific answers to burning questions such as "How does a high female-to-male ratio affect undergraduates dating attitudes?" and "Who says I love you first, men or women?"; a revealing figure documents the widening earnings gap between college and high school graduates and vividly shows that low-income, high-ability students are far less likely to graduate from college than their affluent counterparts.
- Accompanying the above, rewritten chapter discussions explore staying in the nest and the economic hurdles to finishing college—featuring advice for parents and children, college freshmen, universities, and society.
- Includes William Perry's classic study tracking the undergraduate experience, and explores new research on interracial dating and the predictors of relationship success.

CHAPTER 11: Relationships and Roles

- Focuses directly on the core issues of adult life: work and family.

- Provides an extensive discussion of the research relating to how to have happy, enduring relationships, the challenges of parenting, and women's and men's work and family roles.
- Looks at marriage, parenthood, and work in their cultural and historical contexts.
- Offers research-based tips for having a satisfying marriage and career.
- Discusses job insecurity in our more fragile economy.

This photograph shows the reality of motherhood today. Young working mothers are spending much *more* time teaching their children than their own, stay-at-home mothers did in the past!

WHAT'S NEW?

- Table entitled "Cohabitation and Marriage, Stereotypes, and Realities" summarizes the research on this topic.
- Includes explicit discussions of happily married elderly couples and more on stepparent–stepchild relationships.
- Career part of the chapter features a totally rewritten exploration of gender differences in career attitudes and workforce participation, accompanied by a figure documenting how average salaries of women and men vary from profession to profession.
- Concluding "In Focus" feature at the end of this section directly tackles the experience of unemployment.

CHAPTER 12: Midlife

- Describes the complexities of measuring adult personality development, and organizes the discussion according to the "we don't change" and "we do change" points of view.
- Anchors the research on adult intellectual change (the fluid and crystallized distinctions) to lifespan changes in creativity and careers.
- Offers thorough coverage of the research on generativity and adult well-being.
- Provides research-based advice for constructing a fulfilling adult life.
- Covers age-related changes in sexuality, menopause, grandparenthood, and parent care.

WHAT'S NEW?

- Highlights the distinction between eudemonic and hedonic happiness and showcases the latest studies exploring emotional growth in midlife.
- Features exciting new research showing that wisdom does increase after age 60.
- Provides an evolutionary perspective on grandparenthood and updated studies exploring parent-care stress.

PART VI: Later Life

CHAPTER 13: Later Life: Cognitive and Socioemotional Development

- Offers an extensive discussion of Carstensen's socioemotional selectivity theory.
- Helps decode our contradictory stereotypes about later life emotional states, the core qualities that make for a happy or unsatisfying old age, and offers a section on "aging optimally."
- Describes the research on aging memory, retirement, and widowhood.
- Discusses salient social issues such as age discrimination in hiring and intergenerational equity.
- Looks at later life developmentally by tracing changes from the young-old to the old-old years.

WHAT'S NEW?

- Offers vivid examples of the looming age boom and—to further bust old-age attitudes and stereotypes—features a poll suggesting that emerging adults in collectivist cultures such as Japan have *more* negative attitudes towards old people than their counterparts in the West.

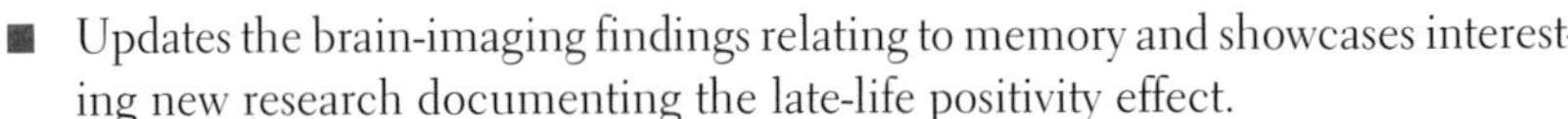

Martin Barraud/Getty Images

Although his main goal is to greet this woman in a warm, personal way, in order to remember his new friend's name, this elderly man might want to step back and use the mnemonic strategy of forming a mental image, thinking, "I'll remember it's Mrs. Silver because of her hair."

- Updates the brain-imaging findings relating to memory and showcases interesting new research documenting the late-life positivity effect.
- Highlights the trend to retiring later and generally stresses the economic constraints to retiring for baby boomers and women in our current economy.
- Tackles the topic of intergenerational equity in discussing possible retrenchments in Medicare and Social Security.

CHAPTER 14: The Physical Challenges of Old Age

- Offers a clear developmental look at how normal aging shades into chronic disease and ADL impairments and looks at the impact of gender, ethnicity, socioeconomic status (and now cohort) on physical aging.
- Focuses on how to change the environment to compensate for sensorimotor declines.
- Provides an in-depth look at dementia, accompanied by compelling firsthand descriptions of their inner experience by people with Alzheimer's disease.
- Explores alternatives to institutionalization and provides a full description of nursing home care.
- Strives to provide a realistic, honest, and yet action-oriented and uplifting portrait of the physical frailties of advanced old age.

WHAT'S NEW?

- Features a new section entitled "Cohort Differences in Aging" showing that baby boomers' are traveling into older midlife more disabled than the previous cohort (and that the ideal of "disease-free aging" applies to a small fraction of older people), as well as discussing the Hispanic health paradox, and the impact education plays in late-life disability.
- Includes an alarming a new figure showing that obesity rates among college graduates have quadrupled and concludes with preventative lifespan suggestions focusing on reducing child poverty and building less car-dependent communities.
- Focuses more explicitly on the emotional consequences of vision loss and describes that new intervention for the impaired hearing, the hearing loop.
- Explores the trend to providing person-centered institutional care but also looks at recent surveys suggesting that the average nursing home still provides far from optimal care.

© Stuart Monk/Alamy

The huge domed ceilings are awe inspiring, but—combined with bare floors and the clatter of commuters—they make New York City's Grand Central Station an acoustic nightmare. However, thanks to the miracle of the hearing loop, people can now bypass that background noise via loudspeaker train announcements beamed directly to their hearing aids.

PART VII: Epilogue

CHAPTER 15: Death and Dying

- Explores cross-cultural variations in dying and offers a historical look at death practices from the Middle Ages to today.
- Discusses the pros and cons of the hospice movement, with its focus on dying at home.
- Offers a look at the pros and cons of different types of advance directives and explores controversial topics such as physician-assisted suicide.

WHAT'S NEW?

- New Experiencing the Lifespan box, "Heart Disease Is a Family Affair," explores my own day-to-day experience with my husband, who has congestive heart failure, as well as showcasing equally personal quotations from studies exploring how family members cope with a child's death.
- Updates information on palliative care units and hospice, as well as health-care workers' continuing trouble predicting and discussing death.

- Explores new research on the best advance directives and predicts that age-based rationing of care is poised to become center stage as baby boomers flood into old age.

Final Thoughts

This edition ends with a wrap-up section entitled "Final Thoughts" in which I pull together and summarize five main underlying themes of this research tour.

What Media and Supplements Come with this Book?

When you decide to use this book, you're adopting far more than just this text. You have access to an incredible learning system—everything from tests to video clips that bring the material to life. The Worth team and several dozen dedicated instructors have worked to provide an array of supplements to my text to foster student learning and make this course memorable: Video clips convey the magic of prenatal development, clarify Piaget's tasks, highlight child undernutrition, and showcase the life stories of active and healthy people in their ninth and tenth decades of life. Lecture slides and clicker questions make class sessions more visual and interactive. My publisher has amassed a rich archive of developmental science materials. For additional information, please contact your Worth Publishers sales consultant or look at the Worth Web site at www.worthpublishers.com/belsky3e. Here are descriptions of the supplements:

DevelopmentPortal for *Experiencing the Lifespan*

Created *by* psychologists *for* psychologists, DevelopmentPortal is a breakthrough on-line learning space. Specifically built around the new edition, DevelopmentPortal combines:

- A Multimedia-Enhanced e-Book. The e-Book fully integrates the text and its images with a rich assortment of media resources and customization features for students and instructors. The e-Book is also available in a stand-alone version outside DevelopmentPortal.
- Diagnostic Quizzing and Study Plans. Students take a quiz before starting a new chapter. The results are translated into a personalized study plan, with links to specific sections and resources to help with the questions they missed.
- LearningCurve. Combining adaptive question selection and personalized study plans, LearningCurve provides students with a unique learning experience. LearningCurve quizzing activities have a game-like feel that keeps students engaged in the material while helping them learn key concepts.
- Assignment Center. Instructors can easily construct and administer tests and quizzes based on the Test Bank or their own questions. Quizzes are randomized and timed, and instructors can receive summaries of student results in reports that follow the section order of the chapters.
- Course Materials. In this convenient location, students can access all media associated with the book, and instructors will find a variety of videos and pre-made PowerPoint presentations for classroom and on-line presentation.
- DevelopmentPortal contains all the standard functionality you expect from a site that can serve as an independent on-line course, but it is the core teaching and learning components—developed with an advisory board of master teachers and learning experts—that make DevelopmentPortal truly unique.

Now Exclusively On-Line for Students! Video Tool Kit for Human Development

The student version of this edition's Video Tool Kit is now available exclusively on-line. It spans the full range of standard topics for the child development course, with over 40 student video activities that contain brief clips of research and news footage from the BBC Motion video activities that contain brief clips of research and news footage from the BBC Motion Library, UNICEF, and other sources. These activities are easily assignable and accessible by an instructor.

For instructors, in addition to the student activities, the Video Tool Kit offers hundreds of additional clips—over 350 in total, all closed captioned and easily downloadable in QuickTime and MPEG formats for easy integration into a PPT presentation. Clips can be used to introduce central topics, stimulate class discussions, or challenge students' critical thinking skills—either in class or via out-of-class assignments.

The Book Companion Site at www.worthpublishers.com/belsky3e

My Web site provides students with a ***virtual study guide, 24 hours a day, seven days a week***. Best of all, these resources are free and do not require any special access codes or passwords. The tools on the site include: ***on-line quizzes*** offering multiple-choice practice tests (for every chapter) that allow students to test their knowledge of chapter concepts; ***interactive flashcards*** that tutor students on all chapter terminology and allow them to then quiz themselves on the terms; and ***frequently asked questions about developmental psychology*** that permit students to think critically about lifespan development and that explore such topics as how understanding human development can help students in their careers and lives and how to pursue an advanced degree in developmental psychology.

A password-protected Instructor's Site offers a full array of teaching resources, including Illustration and Lecture slides, clicker questions, the Instructor's Resources, an on-line quiz grade book, and links to additional tools (Faculty Guides).

NEW! Developing Lives: An Interactive Simulation

The study of child development fully enters the digital age with ***Developing Lives***. Using this interactive program, each student raises his or her own unique "child." Students make decisions about common parenting issues (nutrition choices, parenting style, type of schooling) and respond to realistic events (divorce, temperamental variations, and social and economic diversity) that shape a child's physical, cognitive, and social development. At the heart of this program is interactivity—between students and the simulation but also with their classmates. While the core experience happens on the computer, students can get notices or check in with their child "on the go" on a variety of mobile devices, or even share photos of their baby with friends, family, and classmates. ***Developing Lives*** has a student-friendly "game-like" feel that not only engages students in the program, but also encourages them to learn. ***Developing Lives*** features these helpful resources to reinforce and assess student learning: Integrated links to the e-Book version of your Worth text; readings from *Scientific American*; more than 400 videos and animations (many of them newly filmed for *Developing Lives*); and links to easy-to-implement assessment tools, including assignable quizzes on core topics, discussion threads, and journal questions.

NEW! Interactive Presentation Slides

A new extraordinary series of "next generation" interactive presentation lectures give instructors a dynamic, yet easy-to-use, new way to engage students during classroom presentations of core developmental psychology topics. Each lecture provides opportunities for discussion and interaction and enlivens the psychology classroom with an unprecedented number of embedded video clips and animations from Worth's Video Tool Kit for Human Development Psychology.

PowerPoint Presentation Slides

There are two slide sets for each chapter of *Experiencing the Lifespan* (one featuring a full chapter lecture, the other featuring all chapter art and illustrations). In addition, Video PowerPoint Presentation Slides (on the Instructor's Resource Flash Drive) provide an easy way to integrate the Instructor's video clips into these PowerPoint slide sets. For every video clip, PowerPoint slides tie chapter concepts to the selected clip, present explanatory slides introducing each segment, and then follow each clip with discussion questions designed to promote critical thinking and foster the student discussion that is so critical to making this course a success.

Instructor's Resource Flash Drive and the Worth Publishers Video Collection

Each features a "best of" collection of 100 of the most popular and compelling clips from the collection. In addition to the videos, the Instructor Resource Flash Drive includes:

- All figures and tables from the text
- Illustration Slides
- Lecture Slides
- Clicker questions
- Video Collection for Human Development (in MPEG format)
- Video Presentation Slides that make it easy to integrate every video clip from the Instructor's Resource Flash Drive
- Faculty Guide to accompany the Video Collection for Human Development

Video/DVD Resources

***Journey Through the Lifespan* Developmental Video Series.** *Journey Through the Lifespan* illustrates the story of human growth and development from birth to old age in nine narrated segments. It includes vivid footage of people of all ages from around the world (North America, Europe, Africa, Asia, South America) in their normal environments (homes, hospitals, schools, office buildings) and at major life transitions (birth, marriage, divorce, becoming grandparents). More than one hour of unedited video footage helps students sharpen their observational skills. Interviews with prominent developmentalists, including Charles Nelson, Ann Peterson, Steven Pinker, and Barbara Rogoff, are integrated throughout this video to help show students exactly how researchers approach questions. Interviews with social workers, teachers, and nurses who work with children, adults, and older adults offer students insights into the challenges and rewards of these human service careers.

Assessment

- **NEW! LearningCurve: Formative Quizzing Engine**. Developed by a team of psychology instructors with extensive backgrounds in course design and online education, LearningCurve combines adaptive question selection, personalized study plans, and state-of-the-art question analysis reports. LearningCurve is based on the simple yet powerful concept of testing-to-learn, with game-like quizzing activities that keep students engaged in the material while helping them learn key concepts. A team of dedicated instructors have worked closely to develop more than 3,000 quizzing questions developed specifically for this edition of *Experiencing the Lifespan*.
- **Printed Test Bank.** Prepared by Janet Belsky, this Test Bank includes multiple-choice, fill-in, true-false, and essay questions for each chapter of *Experiencing the Lifespan*. Each question is keyed to the textbook by topic, page number, and level of difficulty.
- **Diploma Computerized Test Bank (Windows and Macintosh on one CD-ROM)**. This CD-ROM offers an easy-to-use test-generation system that guides you through the process of creating tests. The CD allows you to add an unlimited number of questions, edit questions, format a test, scramble questions, and include pictures, equations, or multimedia links. The CD-ROM will also allow you to export into a variety of formats that are compatible with

many Internet-based testing products. For more information on Diploma, visit: http://www.brownstone.net/publishers/products/dip6.asp

- **Online Quizzing at www.worthpublishers.com/belsky.** Using Worth Publishers' on-line quizzing engine, you can easily and securely quiz students on-line using prewritten multiple-choice questions (not from the Test Bank) for each text chapter. Students receive instant feedback and can take the quizzes multiple times. You can view results by quiz, student, or question and get weekly results via e-mail.

Course Management

Worth's E-Packs for Blackboard and WebCT provide you with cutting-edge on-line materials that facilitate critical thinking and learning. Best of all, this material is preprogrammed and fully functional in your course management system. Pre-built materials based on my text eliminate hours of work and offer you significant support as you develop on-line courses. This package includes preprogrammed quizzes, links, activities, interactive flashcards, and a wide array of other materials.

Print

- **Instructor's Resources.** Prepared by Beth Bigler, Pellisippi State Community College, the Instructor's Resources include chapter outlines, chapter objectives, springboard topics for discussion and debate, handouts for student projects, ideas for term projects, and a guide to integrating audiovisual material and software into the course. They also include activities and worksheets from our **Teaching Tips Booklet**, a collection of creative activities, worksheets, classroom or small-group discussions, and writing assignments that the Worth team has gathered from instructors across the nation.
- **Study Guide.** Prepared by Lisa Hager, Spring Hill College. Each chapter includes a review of key concepts, guided study questions, and section reviews that encourage students' active participation in their learning. Practice tests help students assess their mastery of the material.

Who Made This Book Possible?

This book was a completely collaborative endeavor engineered by the finest publishing company in the world: Worth (and not many authors can make that statement)! Firstly, heartfelt thanks go to my primary editor, Elaine Epstein, for meticulously poring over every sentence of this manuscript, helping select the photos, preparing everything for production, guiding this book through production, and in general being a terrific support and unseen full partner on this book.

I owe a lifelong debt to Catherine Woods, who took time from her busy schedule to oversee most of this edition and the previous one and to Jessica Bayne, my original editor, for putting me on this new life track. I'm thrilled to welcome Chris Cardone, my accomplished new Senior Acquisitions Editor, who has been carefully guiding this book into production and beyond.

This brings me to the actual production team. Thanks go to Julio Espin, Project Editor, for coordinating this intricate process, to Eric Dorger, Editorial Assistant and Supplements Editor, and to Sarah Segal, my world class Production Manager, for helping ensure everything fit together and pushing everyone to get things out on time. It's been my great fortune to rely on the advice of Worth's accomplished Director of Development for Print and Digital Tracey Kuehn, and of Anthony Calcara, my eagle-eyed copy editor, to check the manuscript for accuracy. At the final stage of this process, Sharon Kraus meticulously picked through the manuscript to place my commas correctly and make sure each sentence made grammatical sense.

Then there are the talented people who make *Experiencing the Lifespan* look like a breathtaking work of art. As you delight in looking at these fabulous pictures, you can thank Deborah Anderson for her outstanding photo research and Bianca Moscatelli for coordinating the photo program. Babs Reingold, Worth's resident artistic genius, along with designer Lyndall Culbertson, are responsible for planning and orchestrating this book's gorgeous design.

Thanks go to the Worth people who developed and coordinated the supplements and developed the media package: Christine Burak, my media editor, to Eric Dorger, Editorial Assistant and Supplements Editor, Beth Bigler, who wrote the Instructor's Resource Manual, and Lisa Hager, who wrote the terrific Student Study Guide. Because I realized just how crucial decent supplements can be, I've decided to prepare the new Test Bank for this edition of *Experiencing the Lifespan* myself.

Without good marketing, no one would read this book. And, as usual, this arm of the Worth team gets my A+ rating. Kate Nurre, our Executive Marketing Manager and Lindsay Johnson, Marketing Manager, do an outstanding job. They go to many conferences and spend countless hours in the field advocating for my work. Although I may not meet many of you personally, I want take this chance to thank all the sales reps for working so hard to get "Belsky" out in the real world.

This edition has benefited from the insights of many instructor reviewers. Special thanks go to Suzy Horton for having the fortitude to thoughtfully review several incarnations of my book and for being such a great enduring support. I am grateful for those student readers who took the time to personally e-mail and tell me "You did a good job," or "Dr. Belsky, I like it; but here's where you went wrong." These kinds of comments really make an author's day! Here are the names of *all* the instructors who helped make my writing and thinking so much better during the past 14 years:

Heather Adams, *Ball State University*

Daisuke Akiba, *Queens College*

Cecilia Alvarez, *San Antonio College*

Andrea S. Anastasiou, *Mary Baldwin College*

Emilie Aubert, *Marquette University*

Pamela Auburn, *University of Houston Downtown*

Tracy Babcock, *Montana State University*

Harriet Bachner, *Northeastern State University*

Carol Bailey, *Rochester Community and Technical College*

Thomas Bailey, *University of Baltimore*

Shelly Ball, *Western Kentucky University*

Mary Ballard, *Appalachian State University*

Lacy Barnes-Mileham, *Reedley College*

Kay Bartosz, *Eastern Kentucky University*

Laura Barwegen, *Wheaton College*

Jonathan Bates, *Hunter College, CUNY*

Don Beach, *Tarleton State University*

Lori Beasley, *University of Central Oklahoma*

Martha-Ann Bell, *Virginia Tech*

Daniel Bellack, *Trident Technical College*

Jennifer Bellingtier, *University of Northern Iowa*

Karen Bendersky, *Georgia College and State University*

Keisha Bentley, *University of La Verne*

Robert Billingham, *Indiana University*

Kathi J. Bivens, *Asheville-Buncombe Technical Community College*

Jim Blonsky, *University of Tulsa*

Cheryl Bluestone, *Queensborough Community College, CUNY*

Greg Bonanno, *Teachers College, Columbia University*

Aviva Bower, *College of St. Rose*

Marlys Bratteli, *North Dakota State University*

Bonnie Breitmayer, *University of Illinois, Chicago*

Jennifer Brennom, *Kirkwood Community College*

Tom Brian, *University of Tulsa*

Sabrina Brinson, *Missouri State University*

Adam Brown, *St. Bonaventure University*

Kimberly D. Brown, *Ball State University*

Donna Browning, *Mississippi State University*

Janine Buckner, *Seton Hall University*

Ted Bulling, *Nebraska Wesleyan University*

Holly Bunje, *University of Minnesota, Twin Cities*

Melinda Burgess, *Southwestern Oklahoma State University*

Barbara Burns, *University of Louisville*

Marilyn Burns, *Modesto Junior College*

Joni Caldwell, *Spalding University*

Norma Caltagirone, *Hillsborough Community College, Ybor City*

Lanthan Camblin, *University of Cincinnati*

Debb Campbell, *College of Sequoias*

Lee H. Campbell, *Edison Community College*

Robin Campbell, *Brevard Community College*

Kathryn A. Canter, *Penn State Fayette*

Peter Carson, *South Florida Community College*

Michael Casey, *College of Wooster*

Kimberly Chapman, *Blue River Community College*

Tom Chiaromonte, *Fullerton College*

Yiling Chow, *North Island College, Port Albernia*

Toni Christopherson, *California State University, Dominguez Hills*

Wanda Clark, *South Plains College*

Judy Collmer, *Cedar Valley College*

David Conner, *Truman State University*

Deborah Conway, *University of Virginia*

Diana Cooper, *Purdue University*

Ellen Cotter, *Georgia Southwestern State University*

Deborah M. Cox, *Madisonville Community College*

Kim B. Cragin, *Snow College*

Charles P. Cummings, *Asheville-Buncombe Technical Community College*

Karen Curran, *Mt. San Antonio College*

Antonio Cutolo-Ring, *Kansas City (KS) Community College*

Leslie Daniels, *Florida State College at Jacksonville*

Nancy Darling, *Bard College*

Paul Dawson, *Weber State University*

Janet B. Dean, *Asbury University*

Lynda De Dee, *University of Wisconsin, Oshkosh*

David C. Devonis, *Graceland University*

Charles Dickel, *Creighton University*

Darryl Dietrich, *College of St. Scholastica*

Stephanie Ding, *Del Mar College*

Lugenia Dixon, *Bainbridge College*

Benjamin Dobrin, *Virginia Wesleyan College*

Delores Doench, *Southwestern Community College*

Melanie Domenech Rodriguez, *Utah State University*

Sundi Donovan, *Liberty University*

Lana Dryden, *Sir Sanford Fleming College*

Gwenden Dueker, *Grand Valley State University*

Bryan Duke, *University of Central Oklahoma*

Trisha M. Dunkel, *Loyola University, Chicago*

Robin Eliason, *Piedmont Virginia Community College*

Traci Elliot, *Alvin Community College*

Frank Ellis, *University of Maine, Augusta*

Kelley Eltzroth, *Mid Michigan Community College*

Marya Endriga, *California State University, Stanislaus*

Kathryn Fagan, *California Baptist University*

Daniel Fasko, *Bowling Green State University*

Nancy Feehan, *University of San Francisco*

Meredyth C. Fellows, *West Chester University of Pennsylvania*

Gary Felt, *City University of New York*

Martha Fewell, *Barat College*

Mark A. Fine, *University of Missouri*

Roseanne L. Flores, *Hunter College, CUNY*

John Foley, *Hagerstown Community College*

James Foster, *George Fox University*

Geri Fox, *University of Illinois, Chicago*

Thomas Francigetto, *Northampton Community College*

James Francis, *San Jacinto College*

Doug Friedrich, *University of West Florida*

Lynn Garrioch, *Colby-Sawyer College*

Bill Garris, *Cumberland College*

Caroline Gee, *Palomar College*

C. Ray Gentry, *Lenoir-Rhyne College*

Carol George, *Mills College*

Elizabeth Gersten, *Victor Valley College*

Linde Getahun, *Bethel University*

Afshin Gharib, *California State University, East Bay*

Nada Glick, *Yeshiva University*

Andrea Goldstein, *Kaplan University*

Arthur Gonchar, *University of La Verne*

Helen Gore-Laird, *University of Houston, University Park*

Tyhesha N. Goss, *University of Pennsylvania*

Dan Grangaard, *Austin Community College, Rio Grande*

Julie Graul, *St. Louis Community College, Florissant Valley*

Elizabeth Gray, *North Park University*

Stefanie Gray Greiner, *Mississippi University for Women*

Erinn L. Green, *Wilmington College*

Dale D. Grubb, *Baldwin-Wallace College*

Laura Gruntmeir, *Redlands Community College*

Lisa Hager, *Spring Hill College*

Michael Hall, *Iowa Western Community College*

Andre Halliburton, *Prairie State College*

Laura Hanish, *Arizona State University*

Robert Hansson, *University of Tulsa*

Richard Harland, *West Texas A&M University*

Gregory Harris, *Polk CommunityCollege*

Virginia Harvey, *University of Massachusetts, Boston*

Margaret Hellie Huyck, *Illinois Institute of Technology*

Janice L. Hendrix, *Missouri State University*

Gertrude Henry, *Hampton University*

Rod Hetzel, *Baylor University*

Heather Hill, *University of Texas, San Antonio*

Elaine Hogan, *University of North Carolina, Wilmington*

Judith Holland, *Hawaii Pacific University*

Debra Hollister, *Valencia Community College*

Heather Holmes-Lonergan, *Metropolitan State College of Denver*

Rosemary Hornak, *Meredith College*

Suzy Horton, *Mesa Community College*

Rebecca Hoss, *College of Saint Mary*

Cynthia Hudley, *University of CaliforniaSanta Barbara*

Alycia Hund, *Illinois State University*

David P. Hurford, *Pittsburgh State University*

Elaine Ironsmith, *East Carolina University*

Jessica Jablonski, *Richard Stockton College*

Sabra Jacobs, *Big Sandy Community and Technical College*

David Johnson, *John Brown University*

Emilie Johnson, *Lindenwood University*

Mary Johnson, *Loras College*

Mike Johnson, *Hawaii Pacific University*

Peggy Jordan, *Oklahoma City Community College*

Lisa Judd, *Western Wisconsin Technical College*

Tracy R. Juliao, *University of Michigan Flint*

Elaine Justice, *Old Dominion University*

Steve Kaatz, *Bethel University*

Jyotsna M. Kalavar, *Penn State New Kensington*

Chi-Ming Kam, *City College of New York, CUNY*

Richard Kandus, *Mt. San Jacinto College*

Skip Keith, *Delaware Technical and Community College*

Michelle L. Kelley, *Old Dominion University*

Richie Kelley, *Baptist Bible College and Seminary*

Robert Kelley, *Mira Costa College*

Jeff Kellogg, *Marian College*

Colleen Kennedy, *Roosevelt University*

Sarah Kern, *The College of New Jersey*

Marcia Killien, *University of Washington*

Kenyon Knapp, *Troy State University*

Cynthia Koenig, *Mt. St. Mary's College of Maryland*

Steve Kohn, *Valdosta State University*

Holly Krogh, *Mississippi University for Women*

Martha Kuehn, *Central Lakes College*

Alvin Kuest, *Great Lakes Christian College*

Rich Lanthier, *George Washington University*

Peggy Lauria, *Central Connecticut State University*

Melisa Layne, *Danville Community College*

John LeChapitaine, *University of Wisconsin, River Falls*

Barbara Lehmann, *Augsburg College*

Rhinehart Lintonen, *Gateway Technical College*

Nancey Lobb, *Alvin Community College*

Carol Ludders, *University of St. Francis*

Dunja Lund Trunk, *Bloomfield College*

Vickie Luttrell, *Dury University*

Nina Lyon Jenkins, *University of Maryland, Eastern Shore*

Christine Malecki, *Northern Illinois University*

Marlowe Manger, *Stanly Community College*

Pamela Manners, *Troy State University*

Kathy Manuel, *Bossier Parish Community College*

Howard Markowitz, *Hawaii Pacific University*

Jayne D. B. Marsh, *University of Southern Maine, Lewiston Auburn College*

Esther Martin, *California State University, Dominguez Hills*

Jan Mast, *Miami Dade College, North Campus*

Pan Maxson, *Duke University*

Nancy Mazurek, *Long Beach City College*

Christine McCormick, *Eastern Illinois University*

Jim McDonald, *California State University, Fresno*

Clark McKinney, *Southwest Tennessee Community College*

George Meyer, *Suffolk County Community College*

Barbara J. Miller, *Pasadena City College*

Christy Miller, *Coker College*

Mary Beth Miller, *Fresno City College*

Al Montgomery, *Our Lady of Holy Cross College*

Robin Montvilo, *Rhode Island College*

Peggy Moody, *St. Louis Community College*

Michelle Moriarty, *Johnson County Community College*

Ken Mumm, *University of Nebraska, Kearney*

Joyce Munsch, *Texas Tech University*

Jeannette Murphey, *Meridian Community College*

Lori Myers, *Louisiana Tech University*

Lana Nenide, *University of Wisconsin, Madison*

Margaret Nettles, *Alliant University*

Gregory Newton, *Diablo Valley College*

Barbara Nicoll, *University of La Verne*

Nancy Nolan, *Nashville State Community College*

Harriett Nordstrom, *University of Michigan, Flint*

Wendy North-Ollendorf, *Northwestern Connecticut Community College*

Elizabeth O'Connor, *St. Mary's College*

Susan O'Donnell, *George Fox University*

Jane Ogden, *East Texas Baptist University*

Shirley Ogletree, *Texas State University*

Claudius Oni, *South Piedmont Community College*

Randall E. Osborne, *Texas State University, San Marcos*

John Otey, *Southern Arkansas University*

Carol Ott, *University of Wisconsin, Milwaukee*

Patti Owen-Smith, *Oxford College*

Heidi Pasek, *Montana State University*

Margaret Patton, *University of North Carolina, Charlotte*

Julie Hicks Patrick, *West Virginia University*

Evelyn Payne, *Albany State University*

Ian E. Payton, *Bethune Cookman University*

Carole Penner-Faje, *Molloy College*

Michelle L. Pilati, *Rio Hondo College*

Meril Posy, *Touro College, Brooklyn*

Shannon M. Pruden, *Temple University*

Ellery Pullman, *Briarcrest Bible College*

Samuel Putnam, *Bowdoin College*

Jeanne Quarles, *Oregon Coast Community College*

Mark Rafter, *College of the Canyons*

Cynthia Rand-Johnson, *Albany State University*

Janet Rangel, *Palo Alto College*

Jean Raniseski, *Alvin Community College*

Frances Raphael-Howell, *Montgomery College*

Celinda Reese, *Oklahoma State University*

Ethan Remmel, *Western Washington University*

Paul Rhoads, *Williams Baptist College*

Kerri A. Riggs, *Lourdes College*

Mark Rittman, *Cuyahoga Community College*

Jeanne Rivers, *Finger Lakes Community College*

Wendy Robertson, *Western Michigan University*

Richard Robins, *University of California, Davis*

Millie Roqueta, *Miami Dade College*

June Rosenberg, *Lyndon State College*

Christopher Rosnick, *University of South Florida*

Trisha Rossi, *Adelphi University*

Rodger Rossman, *College of the Albemarle*

Lisa Routh, *Pikes Peak Community College*

Stephanie Rowley, *University of Michigan, Ann Arbor*

Randall Russac, *University of North Florida*

Dawn Ella Rust, *Stephen F. Austin State University*

Tara Saathoff-Wells, *Central Michigan University*

Traci Sachteleben, *Southwestern Illinois College*

Douglas Sauber, *Arcadia University*

Chris Saxild, *Wisconsin Indianhead Technical College*

Barbara Schaudt, *California State University, Bakersfield*

Daniela E. Schreier, *Chicago School of Professional Psychology*

Pamela Schuetze, *SUNY College at Buffalo*

Donna Seagle, *Chattanooga State Technical Community College*

Bonnie Seegmiller, *Hunter College, CUNY*

Chris Seifert, *Montana State University*

Susan Shapiro, *Indiana University, East*

Elliot Sharpe, *Maryville University*

Lawrence Shelton, *University of Vermont*

Shamani Shikwambi, *University of Northern Iowa*

Denise Simonsen, *Fort Lewis College*

Penny Skemp, *Mira Costa College*

Peggy Skinner, *South Plains College*

Barbara Smith, *Westminster College*

Valerie Smith, *Collin County Community College*

Edward Sofranko, *University of Rio Grande*

Joan Spiegel, *West Los Angeles College*

Jason S. Spiegelman, *Community College of Baltimore County*

Carolyn I. Spies, *Bloomfield College*

Scott Stein, *Southern Vermont College*

Stephanie Stein, *Central Washington University*

Sheila Steiner, *Jamestown College*

Jacqueline Stewart, *Seminole State College*

Robert Stewart, Jr., *Oakland University*

Cynthia Suarez, *Wofford College*

Joshua Susskind, *University of Northern Iowa*

Josephine Swalloway, *Curry College*

Emily Sweitzer, *California University of Pennsylvania*

Chuck Talor, *Valdosta State University*

Jamie Tanner, *South Georgia College*

Norma Tedder, *Edison Community College*

George Thatcher, *Texas Tech University*

Shannon Thomas, *Wallace Community College*

Donna Thompson, *Midland College*

Vicki Tinsley, *Brescia University*

Eugene Tootle, *Barry University*

David Tracer, *University of Colorado, Denver*

Stephen Truhon, *Austin Peay Centre, Fort Campbell*

Dana Van Abbema, *St. Mary's College of Maryland*

Mary Vandendorpe, *Lewis University*

Janice Vidic, *University of Rio Grande*

Steven Voss, *Moberly Area Community College*

William Walkup, *Southwest Baptist University*

Anne Weiher, *Metropolitan State College of Denver*

Robert Weis, *University of Wisconsin, Stevens Point*

Lori Werdenschlag, *Lydon State College*

Noel Wescombe, *Whitworth College*

Andrea White, *Ithaca College*

Meade Whorton, *Louisiana Delta Community College*

Wanda A. Willard, *Monroe Community College*

Joylynne Wills, *Howard University*

Nancy A. Wilson, *Haywood Community College*

Steffen Wilson, *Eastern Kentucky University*

Bernadette Wise, *Iowa Lakes Community College*

Steve Wisecarver, *Lord Fairfax Community College*

Alex Wiseman, *University of Tulsa*

Rebecca Witt Stoffel, *West Liberty State College*

Nanci Woods, *Austin Peay State University*

Stephanie Wright, *Georgetown University*

David Yarbrough, *Texas State University*

Nikki Yonts, *Lyon College*

Ling-Yi Zhou, *University of St. Francis*

On the home front, I am indebted to my students at Middle Tennessee State University. As any teacher will tell you, I learn as much—or more—from you each semester as you do from me. I want to thank my students, Jac Mitchell and Agnes Thomas, for helping me with the references, and my interviewees for sharing their lives. My department deserves my gratitude for being such a special group of people that it's a joy to come to Jones Hall at 7 A.M. I'm grateful to my baby, Thomas, for being born, giving my life such meaning, and who now is, *astonishingly*, about to move to Key West for a "real" adult job and leave the emerging adult stage!! But most of all, I want to thank my life love David, for putting this book and my happiness center stage and for giving me the best possible life.

Janet Belsky
April 16, 2012

P.S. As textbook writing is a continual work in progress, I'd like to regularly update you on what I've been reading and, especially, in the next semesters, share insights I've been getting while teaching this course. With that goal in mind, I've set up a Web site (www.janetbelsky.com) to offer teaching and reading tips. And I urge everyone—both instructors and students—to feel free to add your own insights to this discussion (or just email me) as we journey through the lifespan in the next few years!

The Foundation

This two-chapter part offers you the foundations for understanding the lifespan journey.

Chapter 1—**The People and the Field** introduces *all* the major concepts and themes in this course. In this chapter, I'll describe our discipline's basic terminology, provide a bird's-eye view of the evolving lifespan, offer a framework for how to think about world cultures, and highlight some new twenty-first-century life stages. Most important, in this chapter you will learn about the themes, theories, and research strategies that have shaped our field. Bottom line: Chapter 1 gives you the tools you will need for understanding this book.

Chapter 2—**Prenatal Development, Pregnancy, and Birth** lays the foundation for our developing lives. Here, you will learn about how a baby develops from a tiny clump of cells, and get insights into the experience of pregnancy from the point of view of mothers- and fathers-to-be. This chapter describes pregnancy rituals in different cultures, discusses problems (including infertility) that may lie on the prenatal pathway, and offers an in-depth look at the miracle of birth.

PART I

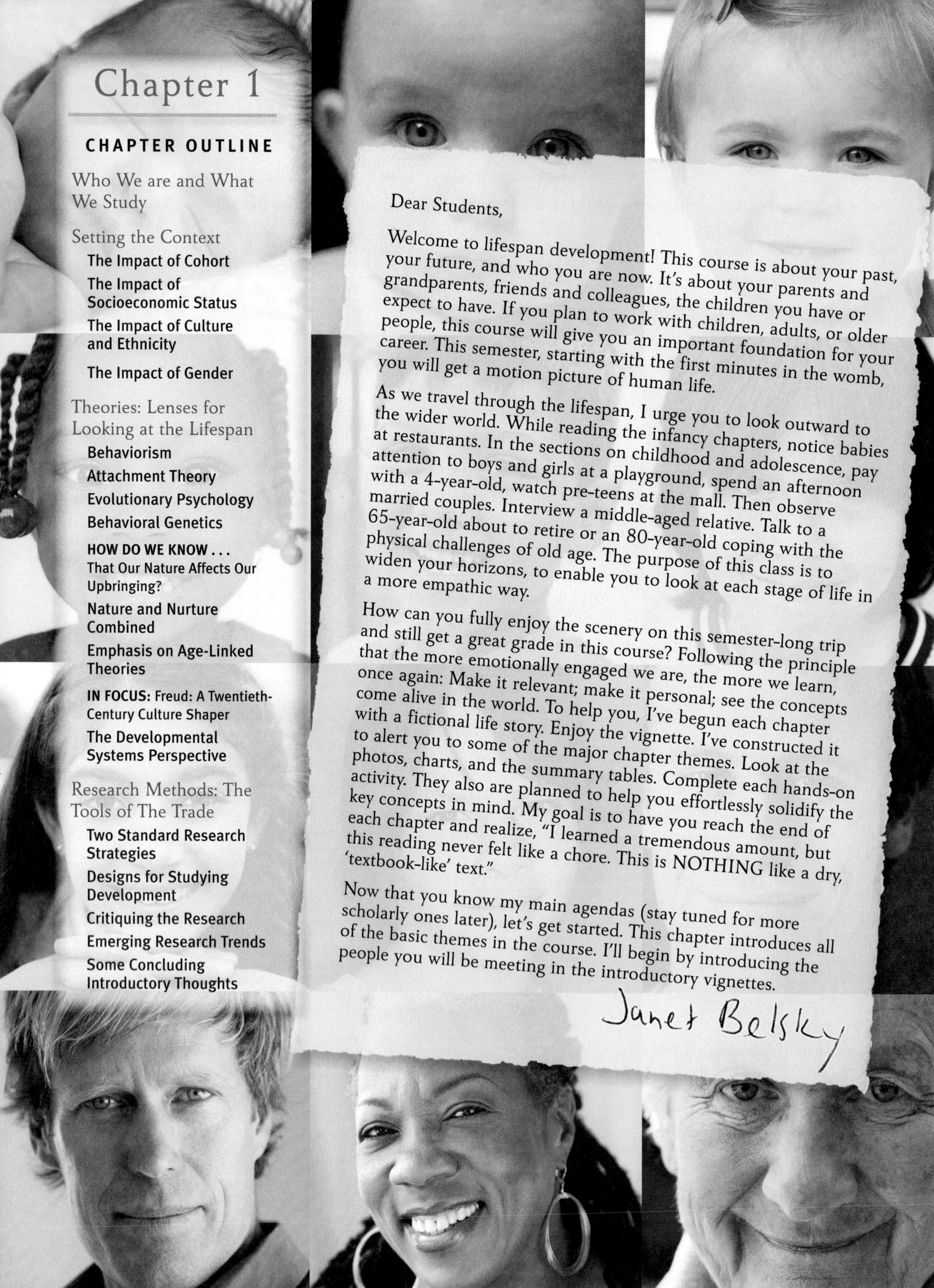

Chapter 1

CHAPTER OUTLINE

Dear Students,

Welcome to lifespan development! This course is about your past, your future, and who you are now. It's about your parents and grandparents, friends and colleagues, the children you have or expect to have. If you plan to work with children, adults, or older people, this course will give you an important foundation for your career. This semester, starting with the first minutes in the womb, you will get a motion picture of human life.

As we travel through the lifespan, I urge you to look outward to the wider world. While reading the infancy chapters, notice babies at restaurants. In the sections on childhood and adolescence, pay attention to boys and girls at a playground, spend an afternoon with a 4-year-old, watch pre-teens at the mall. Then observe married couples. Interview a middle-aged relative. Talk to a 65-year-old about to retire or an 80-year-old coping with the physical challenges of old age. The purpose of this class is to widen your horizons, to enable you to look at each stage of life in a more empathic way.

How can you fully enjoy the scenery on this semester-long trip and still get a great grade in this course? Following the principle that the more emotionally engaged we are, the more we learn, once again: Make it relevant; make it personal; see the concepts come alive in the world. To help you, I've begun each chapter with a fictional life story. Enjoy the vignette. I've constructed it to alert you to some of the major chapter themes. Look at the photos, charts, and the summary tables. Complete each hands-on activity. They also are planned to help you effortlessly solidify the key concepts in mind. My goal is to have you reach the end of each chapter and realize, "I learned a tremendous amount, but this reading never felt like a chore. This is NOTHING like a dry, 'textbook-like' text."

Now that you know my main agendas (stay tuned for more scholarly ones later), let's get started. This chapter introduces all of the basic themes in the course. I'll begin by introducing the people you will be meeting in the introductory vignettes.

Janet Belsky

The People and the Field

It's Theresa and Sal's anniversary and they are having a party. They've been spending a fabulous retirement meeting people while traveling and cruising. Now, it's time to get their new friends together for "our celebration of twenty-first-century American life."

One invitation is for Maria and baby Manuel, whom Theresa and Sal met on a cross-country drive to Las Vegas five years ago. What will that precious child be like now that he's in third grade?

David and Doreen, that lovely couple on last year's Caribbean cruise, get another invitation. There is nothing like sharing a dinner table for a week to cement new friendships for life. For Sal, those dinnertime talks offered a vivid lesson in how the world has changed. Sal married Theresa, his life love, at age 21. During the late 1950s, his family would never have tolerated divorcing or waiting until the late twenties to begin adult life. David took until almost age 30 to "find himself," and, after his divorce even selected a spouse of a different race. Actually, Sal can't help but be impressed by his "young" forty-something friends. Sal was blessed to reach adult life in an easier economy, when gender roles were clearly defined. How—in spite of their hectic lives—have David and Doreen mastered the secret of staying in love for more than ten years?

A final invitation goes to Kim, her husband Jeff, and baby Elissa. Will Theresa and Sal even recognize that adorable 6-month-old now that she's almost one-and-a-half? Theresa's kept up with everyone by e-mail. Now it's time to reconnect.

Let's start with the children. Kim reports that, since Elissa started walking, her baby does not slow down for a second. Actually, it's kind of depressing. Last year, Elissa went to Theresa with a smile. Now, all she wants is Mom. The changes in Manuel are equally astonishing. At age 8, that child can talk to you like an adult. Still, Theresa sees the same boy she first fell in love with five years ago: sunny, kind, and just as gifted mechanically as he was at age 3.

At their celebration feast, the talk turns to deeper issues: Kim shares her anxieties about putting Elissa in day care; Maria opens up about the challenges of being a single parent, an immigrant, and ethnic minority in the United States. Everyone bonds over the frustrations, but unparalleled meaning, children bring to life, as well as their worries for the future in these tough economic times. Doreen informs the group that she wants to make a difference. She is returning to school for a public policy Ph.D. But can she make it academically at age 53?

Theresa and Sal confess that they don't have many worries. In fact, what they half jokingly call "old age" is the happiest time of life. Still, there is the slowness, Theresa's vision problems, and Sal's heart disease. So this joking has a dark side, and today's celebration is a bit bittersweet. The eighties won't be like the seventies. There isn't much time left.

Could Sal be right that "old age" is life's happiest stage? If you met Sal and Theresa at age 30 or 50, would they be the same upbeat, outgoing people as today? Are Doreen's worries about her mental abilities realistic, and what *are* some secrets for staying passionately in love with your spouse? Why do 1-year-olds such as Elissa get clingy just as they begin walking, and what mental leaps make children at age 8, such as Manuel, seem so grown up? How might economic turmoil really affect children and adults?

Developmentalists, also called **developmental scientists**—researchers who study the lifespan—are about to answer these questions and hundreds of others about our unfolding life.

developmentalists Researchers and practitioners whose professional interest lies in the study of the human lifespan.

lifespan development The scientific field covering all of the human lifespan.

child development The scientific study of development from birth through adolescence.

gerontology The scientific study of the aging process and older adults.

adult development The scientific study of the adult part of life.

normative transitions Predictable life changes that occur during development.

non-normative transitions Unpredictable or atypical life changes that occur during development.

Who We Are and What We Study

Lifespan development, the scientific study of human growth throughout life, is a latecomer to psychology. Its roots lie in **child development,** the study of childhood and the teenage years. Child development traces its origins back more than a century. In 1877, Charles Darwin published an article based on notes he had made about his baby during the first years of life. In the 1890s, a pioneering psychologist named G. Stanley Hall established the first institute in the United States devoted to research on the child. Child development began to take off between World Wars I and II (Lerner, 1998). It remains the passion of thousands of developmental scientists working in every corner of the globe.

Gerontology, the scientific study of aging—the other core discipline in lifespan development—had a slower start. Researchers began to really study the aging process only after World War II (Birren & Birren, 1990). Gerontology and its related field, **adult development,** underwent their phenomenal growth spurt during the final third of the twentieth century.

Lifespan development puts it all together. It synthesizes what researchers know about our unfolding life. Who works in this huge mega-discipline, and what passions drive developmentalists?

- **Lifespan development is multidisciplinary.** It draws on fields as different as neuroscience, nursing, psychology, and social policy to understand every aspect of human development. A biologically oriented developmentalist interested in day care might examine toddlers' output of salivary cortisol (a stress hormone) when they first arrive at day care in the morning. An anthropologist might look at cultural values shaping the day-care choice. A social policy expert might explore the impact of offering universal government-funded day care in Finland and France. A biochemist who studies Alzheimer's disease might decode what produces the plaques and tangles that ravage the brain. A nurse might head an innovative Alzheimer's unit. A research-oriented psychologist might construct a scale to measure the behavioral impairments produced by this devastating disease.

Chris Hondros/Getty Images

This woman working with youth in Palestine is one of thousands of developmental scientists whose mission it is to help children around the world.

- **Lifespan development explores the predictable milestones on our human journey,** from walking to working, to Elissa's sudden shyness and attachment to her mother. Are people right to worry about their learning abilities in their fifties? What is physical aging, or puberty, or menopause all about? Are there specific emotions we feel as we approach that final universal milestone, death?

- **Lifespan development focuses on the individual differences that give spice to human life.** Can we really see the person we will be at age 8 (or 83) by age 3? How much does personality or intelligence change as we travel through life? Developmentalists want to understand what *causes* the striking differences between people in temperament, talents, and traits. They are interested in exploring individual differences in the timing of developmental milestones, too; examining, for instance, why people reach puberty earlier or later or age more quickly or slowly than their peers.

- **Lifespan development explores the impact of life transitions and practices.** It deals with **normative,** or predictable, **transitions,** such as retirement, becoming parents, or beginning middle school. It focuses on **non-normative,** or atypical, **transitions,** such as divorce, the death of a child, or how recent declines in the economy affect how we approach the world. It explores more enduring life practices, such as smoking, spanking, or sleeping in the same bed with your child.

Developmentalists realize that life transitions that we consider normative, such as retiring or starting middle school, are products of living in a particular time in history. They understand that life practices such as smoking or sleeping in bed with a child vary, depending on our social class and cultural background. They know that our travels through the lifespan are affected by several very basic markers, or overall conditions of life.

Now it's time to introduce several basic **contexts of development,** or broad general influences, which I will be continually discussing throughout this book.

Karen Kasmauski/National Geographic Image Collection

Our cultural background affects every aspect of development. So, culturally oriented developmentalists might study how this East Asian wedding ceremony expresses this society's messages about family life.

Setting the Context

How does being born in a particular historical time affect our lifespan journey? What about our social class, cultural and ethnic background, or that basic biological difference, being female or male?

The Impact of Cohort

Cohort refers to our birth group, the age group with whom we travel through life. In the vignette, you can immediately see the heavy role our cohort plays in influencing adult life. Sal reached his late teens in the 1950s, when men married in their early twenties and typically stayed married for life. David, who came of age 30 years later, faced a dazzling array of lifestyle choices in a time when divorce had become common. As an interracial couple, David and Doreen are taking a life path unusual even for today! Because they are in their forties, this couple is at an interesting cutting point. They are traveling through life right after that huge bulge in the population called the baby boom.

The **baby boom cohort,** defined as people born from 1946 to 1964, has made a huge impact on the Western world as it moves through society. The reason lies in size. When soldiers returned from World War II and got married, the average family size ballooned to almost four children. When this huge group was growing up during the 1950s, families were traditional, with the two-parent, stay-at-home-mother family being our national ideal. Then, as rebellious adolescents during the 1960s and 1970s, the baby boomers helped usher in a radical transformation in these attitudes and roles (more about this lifestyle revolution soon). Society, as we know, is currently experiencing an old-age explosion as the baby boom cohort floods into later life.

The cohorts living in the early twenty-first century are part of an endless march of cohorts stretching back thousands of years. Let's now take a brief historical tour to get a sense of the dramatic changes in childhood, old age, and adulthood during just the past few centuries, and pinpoint what our lifespan looks like today.

Changing Conceptions of Childhood

> At age ten he began his work life helping his father manufacture candles and soap. He hated dipping wicks into wax and wanted to go to sea, but his father refused and apprenticed him to a master printer. At age 17 he ran away from Boston to Philadelphia to search for work.
>
> His father died when he was 11, and he left school. At 17 he was appointed official surveyor for Culpepper County in Virginia. By age 20 he was in charge of managing his family's plantation.
>
> (Mintz, 2004)

Who were these boys? Their names were Benjamin Franklin and George Washington.

Imagine you were born in Colonial times. In addition to reaching adulthood at a much younger age, your chance of having *any* lifespan would have been far from

contexts of development Fundamental markers, including cohort, socioeconomic status, culture, and gender, that shape how we develop throughout the lifespan.

cohort The age group with whom we travel through life.

baby boom cohort The huge age group born between 1946 and 1964.

secure. In seventeenth-century Paris, roughly 1 in every 3 babies died in early infancy (Ariès, 1962; Hrdy, 1999). As late as 1900, almost 3 of every 10 U.S. children did not live beyond age 5 (Konner, 2010; Mintz, 2004).

The incredible childhood mortality rates, plus dire poverty, may have partly explained why child-rearing practices that we would view as abusive used to be routine. In eighteenth- and nineteenth-century Europe, middle-class babies were farmed out to be nursed by country women. They were separated from their parents during the first two years of life. Children were often beaten and, at their parents' whim, might be abandoned at birth (Konner, 2010; Pinker, 2011). In the early 1800s in Paris, about 1 in 5 newborns was "exposed"—placed in the doorways of churches, or simply left outside to die. In cities such as St. Petersburg, Russia, the statistic might have been as high as 1 in 2 (Ariès, 1962; Hrdy, 1999).

Library of Congress, Prints & Photographs Division, National Child Labor Committee Collection

In the nineteenth century, if you visited factories such as this cannery, you would see many young children at work—showing how far we have come in just a century in our attitudes about childhood.

In addition, for most of history, people did not have our feeling that childhood is a special life stage (Ariès, 1962; Mintz, 2004). Children, as you saw above, began to work at a very young age. During the industrial revolution, in British and U.S. mills, poor boys and girls made up more than a third of the labor force. They worked from dawn till dark (Mintz, 2004).

In the seventeenth and eighteenth centuries, enlightenment philosophers such as John Locke and Jean Jacques Rousseau spelled out a strikingly different vision of childhood and human life (Pinker, 2011). Locke believed that human beings are born a *tabula rasa,* a blank slate on which anything could be written, and that the way we treat children shapes their adult lives. Rousseau argued that babies enter life totally innocent; he felt we should shower these dependent creatures with love. However, this message could fully penetrate society only when the medical advances of the early twentieth century dramatically improved living standards, and we entered our modern age.

Bill Aron/Photo Edit

While we might imagine that adolescence has always been a life stage, teenagerhood only became a separate "age" during the twentieth century, when mandatory high school attendance helped postpone our entry into adulthood.

One force producing this kinder, gentler view of childhood was universal education. During the late nineteenth century in Western Europe and much of the United States, attendance at primary school became mandatory (Ariès, 1962). School kept children from working and insulated these years as a protected, dependent life phase. As one influential psychologist has argued, universal education, with its emphasis on reasoning, may *generally* explain why we are currently living in a far more caring and peaceful world than at previous historical times (Pinker, 2011). (Yes, in contrast to our media stereotypes, that's true!) Still, as late as 1915, only 1 in 10 U.S. children attended high school; most entered their work lives after seventh or eighth grade (Mintz, 2004).

At the beginning of the twentieth century, the developmentalist G. Stanley Hall (1904/1969) identified a stage of "storm and stress," located between childhood and adulthood, which he named *adolescence.* However, it was during the Great Depression of the 1930s, when President Franklin Roosevelt signed a bill making high school attendance mandatory, that adolescence became a standard U.S. life stage (Mintz, 2004). Our famous teenage culture has existed for only 70 or 80 years!

In recent decades, with so many of us going to college and graduate school, we have delayed the beginning of adulthood to an older age. Developmentalists (see Tanner & Arnett, 2010) have identified a new in-between stage of life in affluent countries. **Emerging adulthood,** lasting from age 18 to roughly the late twenties, is devoted to exploring our place in the world. One reason why twenty-first-century adults feel comfortable about postponing marriage or settling down to a career is that today we can expect to live for an amazingly long time.

emerging adulthood The phase of life that begins after high school, tapers off toward the late twenties, and is devoted to constructing an adult life.

Changing Conceptions of Later Life

In every culture, a few people always lived to "old age." However, for most of history, largely due to the high rates of infant and childhood mortality, **average life expectancy,** our fifty-fifty chance at birth of living to a given age, was shockingly low. In the New England colonies, average life expectancy was about age 30. In Maryland during Colonial times, it was under age 20, for both masters and their slaves (Fischer, 1977).

Toward the end of the nineteenth century, life expectancy in the United States rapidly improved. By 1900, it was 46. Then, in the next century, it shot up to 76.7. During the twentieth century, life expectancy in North America and Western Europe increased by almost 30 years! (Centers for Disease Control and Prevention [CDC], Health United States, 2007.)

The **twentieth-century life expectancy revolution** is perhaps the most important milestone that has occurred in the history of our species. The most dramatic increases in longevity occurred during the early decades of the last century, when public health improvements and medical advances, such as antibiotics, wiped out deaths from many *infectious diseases.* Since these illnesses, such as diphtheria, killed both the young and old, their conquest allowed us to live past mid-life. In the last 50 years, our progress has been slower because we are waging war against another category of disease. The illnesses we now die from, called *chronic diseases*—such as heart disease, cancer, and stroke—are tied to the aging process itself.

The outcome is that today life expectancies have zoomed into the upper seventies in North America, Western Europe, New Zealand, Israel, and Japan. As you can see in Figure 1.1, a baby born in affluent parts of the world, especially if that child is female, has a good chance of making it close to our **maximum lifespan,** the biological limit of human life (about age 105).

This extension of the lifespan has changed how we think about *every* life stage. It has moved grandparenthood, once a sign of being "old," down into middle age. If you become a grandparent in your late forties, expect to be called grandma or grandpa for roughly half of your life! Women can start new careers in their fifties, given that today females can expect to live on average for roughly 30 more years (CDC, Health United States, 2010). For well-off older people, retirement—until recently—has been as long a life stage as childhood and adolescence combined. Most important, we have moved the beginning of old age beyond age 65.

Today, people in their sixties and even seventies are often active and relatively healthy. But in our eighties, our chance of being disabled by disease increases dramatically. Because of this, developmentalists make a distinction between two groups of older adults. The **young-old,** defined as people in their sixties and seventies, often look and feel middle-aged. They reject the idea that they are old (Lachman, 2004). The **old-old,** people in their eighties and beyond, seem in a different class. Since they are more likely to have physical and mental disabilities, they are more prone to fit the stereotype of the frail, dependent older adult. In sum, Sal in the vignette was right: Today the eighties are a very different stage of life!

average life expectancy A person's fifty-fifty chance at birth of living to a given age.

twentieth-century life expectancy revolution The dramatic increase in average life expectancy that occurred during the first half of the twentieth century in the developed world.

maximum lifespan The biological limit of human life (about 105 years).

young-old People in their sixties and seventies.

old-old People age 80 and older.

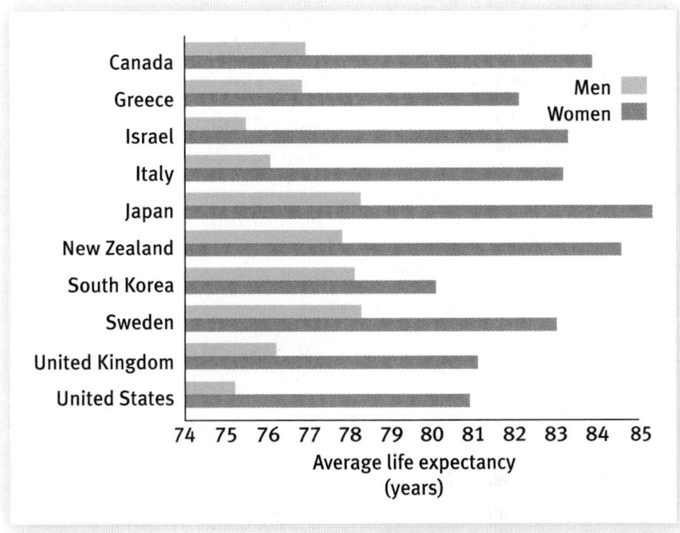

FIGURE 1.1: **Average life expectancy of men and women in some affluent nations:** Women today can expect to live close to the maximum lifespan in affluent countries. Notice, for instance, the astonishingly high life expectancy for women in Japan. (FYI: As of 2007, the United States ranked 45th globally in average life expectancy.)

Source: CIA World Factbook (2007 estimates).

Changing Conceptions of Adult Life

If the medical advances of the early twentieth century made it possible for us to survive to old age, during the last third of the previous century, a revolution in lifestyles transformed the way we live our adult lives. This change in society, which started in

George Shellye/Masterfile

Myrleen Ferguson Cate/Photo Edit, Inc.

The healthy, active couple in their 60s *(left)* have little in common with the disabled 90-year-old man living in a nursing home *(right)*—showing why developmentalists divide the elderly into the *young-old* and the *old-old*.

Western countries and has spread around the globe, occurred when the baby boomers moved into their teenage years.

The 1960s "Decade of Protest" included the civil rights and women's movements, the sexual revolution, and the "counterculture" movement that emphasized liberation in every area of life (Bengtson, 1989). People could have sex without being married. Women were free to fulfill themselves in a career. We encouraged husbands to share the housework and child care equally with their wives. Divorce became an acceptable alternative to living in an unfulfilling marriage. To have a baby, women no longer needed to be married at all.

Today, with women making up roughly half the labor force, only a minority of couples fit the traditional 1950s roles of breadwinner husband and homemaker wife. With roughly one out of two U.S. marriages ending in divorce, we can no longer be confident of staying together for life. While divorce rates may be stabilizing, the Western trend toward having children without being married continues to rise. In 2009, for instance, more than 2 in 5 U.S. babies were born to single moms (Amato, 2010).

The timeline at the bottom of this page visually illustrates the twentieth-century revolutionary shifts in life expectancy and family life, as well as charting the passage of the mammoth baby boom as it moves through life. In this book, I'll pay special attention to exploring the wide-ranging effects of the late-twentieth-century lifestyle revolution—highlighting the challenges single mothers face; tracing the impact of divorce; exploring contemporary women's and men's family roles. While this text does divide development into its standard categories (infancy, childhood, adolescence, adulthood, and later life), I'll also devote a whole chapter to emerging adulthood—that new life stage many of you are in right now. In the later-life section, I'll continually emphasize the distinction between the young-old and old-old (being 60 is miles different physically and mentally from being 80 or 95) and focus on the issues facing society as the baby boomers flood into their older years.

But, as history is always advancing, let's end this section by touching on a recent event that has the potential to cloud our lives in the United States, the West, and around the world.

TIMELINE Selected Twentieth-Century Milestones and The Progress of The Huge Baby Boom

	1900	1910	1920	1930	1940	1950	1960	1970	1980	1990	2000	2010	2020	2030
MAJOR SOCIETAL CHANGE	Life Expectancy Takes Off Deaths shift from infectious to chronic diseases							Lifestyle Revolution Women's movement/rise in divorce and single parenthood/more lifestyle freedom						
BABY BOOM COHORT						Born	Teenagers					Young-old	→	Old-old

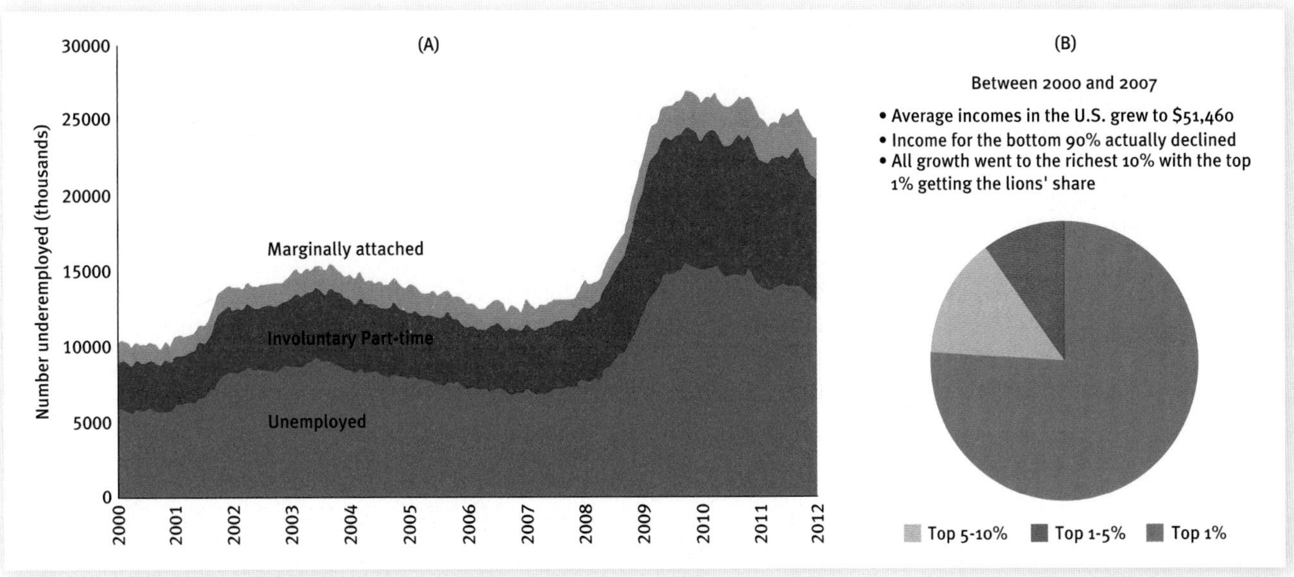

FIGURE 1.2: **Snapshots of the Great Recession of 2008 and widening U.S. income inequality as of 2012:** (A) After the Great Recession of 2008 hit, unemployment and underemployment skyrocketed. The red area indicates part-time workers wanting full-time jobs; the blue area indicates those who are unemployed. (B) Even before the Great Recession—from 2000-2007—the rich were getting richer, while everyone else was left behind.
Sources: Economic Policy Institute; State of Working America, 2012.

The Great Recession of 2008: Temporary Tsunami or Lasting Event?

> After 40 years of an uncompromising work-ethic, I've been unemployed for nearly 18 months. The weight of failure . . . and helplessness has taken a huge toll. When I lose my home . . . I will have lost the American Dream
>
> (Kevin, unemployed 80 weeks)

> I was laid off from my job on April 1st. This is my third major layoff. I've used up all my retirement funds and savings. I have never seen anything this bad in this country.
>
> (Sandra K, Cleveland Heights, Ohio)

Welcome to tales from the **Great Recession of 2008**, which began with the bursting of an 8-trillion-dollar-housing bubble, produced sharp cutbacks in U.S. consumer spending, and followed up with a loss of 8.4 million jobs within the following two years (Economic Policy Institute, 2011). The Great Recession has caused us to rethink standard adult markers, from retirement to leaving home for college (see Chapters 10 and 13). It has weakened our historic American faith in constructing a secure middle-class life. As this storm rolled in, it uncovered a festering problem called **income inequality**—the widening gap between the super rich and everyone else (Economic Policy Institute [EPI], 2011; Wilkinson & Pickett, 2009).

Figure 1.2 offers snapshots relating to these twin economic storms. Will this cloud linger later into the century or turn sunny and become an unpleasant memory by the time you are reading this book? Whatever the answer, it is clear that our economic situation is another vital marker that shapes how we think, develop, and behave. How *exactly* does being affluent or poor affect our passage through life?

The Impact of Socioeconomic Status

This question brings up the impact of **socioeconomic status (SES)**—a term referring to our education and income—on our unfolding lives. As you will vividly see throughout this book, living in poverty makes people vulnerable to a cascade of problems—

Great Recession of 2008 Dramatic loss of jobs (and consumer spending) that began with the bursting of the U.S. housing bubble in late 2007.

income inequality The gap between the rich and poor within a nation. Specifically, when income inequality is wide, a nation has a few very affluent residents and a mass of disadvantaged citizens.

socioeconomic status (SES) A basic marker referring to status on the educational and—especially—income rungs.

developed world The most affluent countries in the world.

developing world The more impoverished countries of the world.

collectivist cultures Societies that prize social harmony, obedience, and close family connectedness over individual achievement.

individualistic cultures Societies that prize independence, competition, and personal success.

from being born less healthy, to attending lower-quality schools; from living in more dangerous neighborhoods, to dying at a younger age. Not only do developmentalists rank individuals by socioeconomic status, but they rank nations, too.

Developed-world nations are defined by their wealth, or high median per-person incomes. In these countries, life expectancy is high (Central Intelligence Agency [CIA], 2007). Technology is advanced. People have widespread access to education and medical care, and can enjoy the latest advances of twenty-first-century life. Traditionally, the United States, Canada, Australia, New Zealand, and Japan, as well as every Western European nation, have been classified in this "most affluent" category, although its ranks *may* be expanding as the economies of nations such as China, India, and Brazil explode.

Developing-world countries stand in sharp contrast to these most affluent or advancing regions of the world. Here, poverty is rampant and income inequalities are extreme. In the least developed nations, residents may not have indoor plumbing, clean running water, or access to education. People may die at a young age from "curable" infectious disease. Babies born in the most disadvantaged regions of the globe face a twenty-first-century lifespan that has striking similarities to the one developed-world children faced more than a century ago.

The Impact of Culture and Ethnicity

Residents of developing nations often have shorter, more difficult lives. Still, if you visited these places, you might be struck by a shared sense of community and family commitment that we might not find in the West. Can we categorize societies according to their basic values, apart from their wealth? Developmentalists who study culture answer yes.

Collectivist cultures place a premium on social harmony. The family generations expect to live together, even as adults. Children are taught to obey their elders, to suppress their feelings, to value being respectful, and to subordinate their needs to the good of the wider group.

Individualistic cultures emphasize independence, competition, and personal success. Children are encouraged to openly express their emotions, to believe in their own personal power, to leave their parents, to stand on their own as self-sufficient and independent adults. Traditionally, Western nations score high on indices of individualism. Nations in Asia, Africa, and South America rank higher on collectivism scales (Hofstede, 1981, 2001; Triandis, 1995).

Imagine how your perspective on life might differ if becoming independent from your parents or honestly sharing your feelings was viewed as an inappropriate way to behave. How would you treat your children, choose a career, or select a spouse? What concerns would you have as you were facing death?

As we scan development around the world, I will regularly distinguish between collectivist and more individualistic societies. I'll highlight the issues families face when they move from these traditional cultures to the West, and explore research relating to the major U.S. ethnic groups listed in Figure 1.3. How does being an ethnic minority affect everything from emerging adult attitudes to the chance of developing age-related diseases?

B. Tanaka/Getty Images

For this grandmother, mother, and daughter, getting dressed up to visit this Shinto family shrine and pay their respects to their ancestors is an important ritual. It is one way that the lesson "honor your elders" is taught to children living in collectivist societies such as Japan from an early age.

As you read this information, keep in mind that what unites us as people far outweighs any distinctions based on culture, ethnicity, or race. Moreover, making diversity generalizations is hazardous because of the diversity that exists *within* each nation and ethnic group. In the most traditionally individualistic country (no surprise, that's the United States), people have a mix of collectivist and individualistic worldviews. As their economies have flourished, residents of classic collectivistic cultures, such as China and Japan, have developed more individualistic, Western worldviews.

If the census labels you as "Hispanic American" or "Asian American," you also are probably aware that this broad label masks more than it reveals. As a third-generation Cuban American, do you really have much in common with a recent immigrant from Mexico or Belize? Given that people arrive in the United States from hundreds of culturally different countries, does it really make sense to lump our citizens into a small number of ethnic groups? There is, however, one distinction that we can agree on. It's called being female or male.

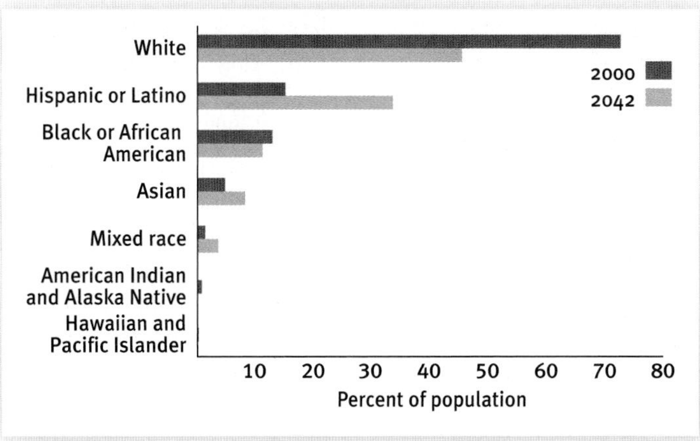

FIGURE 1.3: The major ethnic groups in the United States, their percentages in the 2000 census, and a few mid-twenty-first-century projections: By 2042, more than half of the U.S. population is projected to be ethnic minorities. Notice, in particular, the huge increase in the fraction of Hispanic Americans, and the fact that by the mid-twenty-first century the percentage of people who label themselves as "mixed race" is expected to double.

Sources: United States, Factsheet, American Factfinder (U.S. Census Bureau, 2006 community survey; U.S. Census Bureau, AFP, U.S. White Population a Minority by 2042).

The Impact of Gender

Obviously, our culture's values shape our life path as males and females. Are you living in a society or at a time in history when men are encouraged to be househusbands and women to be corporate CEOs? But biology is crucial in driving at least one fundamental difference in the pathways of women and men: Throughout the developed world, females outlive males by more than 4 years. Because they must survive childbearing and carry an extra X chromosome, women are the physiologically hardier sex.

Are boys more aggressive than girls? When we see male/female differences in caregiving, in career interests, and in childhood play styles, are these differences mainly due to the environment (societal pressures or the way we are brought up) or to inborn, biological forces? Throughout this book, I'll examine these questions as we explore the scientific truth of our gender stereotypes and spell out other fascinating facts about sex differences, too. To set you up for this ongoing conversation, you might want to take the "Is It Males or Females?" quiz in Table 1.1. Keep a copy handy. As we travel through the lifespan, you can check the accuracy of your ideas.

Now that you understand that our lifespan is a continuing work in progress that varies across cultures and historical times, let's get to the science. After you complete this section's Tying It All Together review quiz on page 12, I will introduce the main theories, research methods, concepts, and scientific terms in the chapters to come.

TABLE 1.1: **Is It Males or Females?**

1. Who are more likely to survive the hazards of prenatal development, male or female fetuses? (You will find the answer in Chapter 2.)
2. Who are more likely to be diagnosed with ADHD, girls or boys? (You will find the answer in Chapter 5.)
3. Who are more aggressive, boys or girls? (You will find the answer in Chapter 6.)
4. Who are more likely to be diagnosed with learning disabilities in school, boys or girls? (You will find the answer in Chapter 7.)
5. Who, when they reach puberty at an earlier-than-typical age, are more at risk of developing problems, boys or girls? (You will find the answer in Chapter 8.)
6. Who are likely to stay in the "nest" (at home) longer during the emerging-adult years, men or women? (You will find the answer in Chapter 10.)
7. Who tend to earn more today, women or men? (You will find the answer in Chapter 11.)
8. Who are more at risk of having enduring emotional problems after being widowed, men or women? (You will find the answer in Chapter 13.)
9. Who are apt to live longer, sicker men or women? (You will find the answer in Chapter 14.)
10. Who care more about being closely attached, males or females—or both sexes? (You will find the answer throughout this book.)

TYING IT ALL TOGETHER

1. Tuan, a historian, is arguing that over this century, conditions for children changed dramatically in very positive ways. He should mention all of the following examples *except* (check the statement that is *false*):
   a. Child mortality used to be high. Today, it is low in the developed world.
   b. Children used to be beaten and abandoned. Today, these practices are severely condemned.
   c. Children used to start their work lives at a young age. Today, childhood extends through (and even beyond) the adolescent years.
   d. Children are more likely to grow up in two-parent families today than a half-century ago.
2. Maria just became a grandmother; Sara just retired from her job; Rosa just entered a nursing home. If these women live in the United States and are middle class, roughly how old are they likely to be?
3. Jim and Joe are arguing about the impact of the 1960s lifestyle revolution. Jim believes that life is much better now that we have more freedom. Joe says that actually we are worse off. Argue Jim's position, then Joe's, backing up your points by using the information in this section.
4. Pablo says, "I would never think of leaving my parents or living far from my brothers and sisters. A person must take care of his extended family before satisfying his own needs." Peter says, "My primary commitment is to my wife and children. A person needs, above all, to make an independent life." Pablo has a(n) ________ worldview, while Peter's worldview is more ________.
5. List and (possibly discuss with the class) some ways the Great Recession of 2008 may have changed your own or your family's life plans.

Answers to the Tying It All Together questions can be found at the end of this chapter.

Theories: Lenses for Looking at the Lifespan

During his twenties, David was searching for his identity. Manuel's mechanical talents must be hereditary. If Elissa's mother gives her a lot of love during her first years of life, she will grow up to be a loving, secure adult. If any of these thoughts entered your mind while reading about the people in the opening chapter vignette, you were using a major theory that developmentalists use to understand human life.

Theories offer insights into that crucial *why* question. They attempt to explain what causes us to act as we do. They may allow us to predict the future. Ideally, they give us information about how to improve the quality of life. Theories in developmental science may offer broad general explanations of behavior that apply to people at every age. Or they may focus on describing specific changes that occur at particular ages. This section provides a preview of both kinds of theories.

theory Any perspective explaining why people act the way they do. Theories allow us to predict behavior and also suggest how to intervene to improve behavior.

nature Biological or genetic causes of development.

nurture Environmental causes of development.

Let's begin by outlining some very broad theories (one is actually a research discipline) that offer general explanations of behavior. I've organized these theories somewhat chronologically—based somewhat on *when* they appeared during the twentieth century—but mainly according to their position on that core issue in our field: Is it the environment, or the wider world, that determines how we develop? Are our personalities, talents, and traits shaped mainly by biological or genetic forces? This is the famous **nature** (biology) versus **nurture** (environment) question.

Behaviorism: The Original Blockbuster "Nurture" Theory

B.F. Skinner Foundation

This photo shows B. F. Skinner with his favorite research subject for exploring operant conditioning—the pigeon. By charting how often pigeons pecked to get reinforced by food and varying the patterns of reinforcement, this famous behaviorist was able to tell us a good deal about how humans act.

> Give me a dozen healthy infants . . . and I'll guarantee to take any one at random and train him to be any specialist I might select—doctor, lawyer, artist, merchant-chief, and yes, even beggar man and thief.
>
> (Watson, 1930, p. 104)

So proclaimed the early-twentieth-century psychologist John Watson as he spelled out the nurture-is-all-important position of traditional behaviorism. Intoxicated by the scientific advances that were transforming society and allowing most people to live to old age, Watson and his fellow behaviorist B. F. Skinner (1960, 1974) dreamed of a science of human behavior that would be as rigorous as physics. These pioneering theorists believed that psychologists could not study feelings and thoughts because inner experiences could not be observed. In their view, it was vital to chart only measurable, observable responses. Moreover, according to these **traditional behaviorists,** a few general laws of learning explain behavior in every life situation at every time of life.

Exploring Reinforcement

According to Skinner, the general law of learning that causes each voluntary action, from forming our first words to mastering higher math, is **operant conditioning.** Responses that we reward, or reinforce, will be learned. Responses that are not reinforced go away or are *extinguished.* So what accounts for Watson's beggar men and thieves, the out-of-control kids, all of the marriages that start out so loving and then fall apart? According to Skinner, the reinforcements are operating as they should. The problem is that instead of reinforcing positive behavior, we often reinforce the wrong things.

©UpperCut Images/Alamy

Imagine wheeling this whining toddler through your Walmart grocery aisle. Wouldn't you be tempted to reinforce this unpleasant behavior by silencing the child with an enticing object on the shelf?

One excellent place to see Skinner's point in action is to take a trip to your local Walmart or your favorite restaurant. Notice how when children act up at the store parents often buy them a toy to quiet them down. At dinner, as long as a toddler is playing quietly, adults ignore her. When she starts to hurl objects off the table, they pick her up, kiss her, and take her outside. Then, they complain about their child's difficult personality, not realizing that its source is really them. Their *own* reinforcements have produced these responses!

One of Skinner's most interesting concepts, derived from his work with pigeons, relates to *variable reinforcement schedules.* This is the type of reinforcement that typically occurs in daily life: We get reinforced at unpredictable times, so we learn to keep responding, realizing that if we continue, *at some point* we will be reinforced. Readers with children will understand just how difficult it is to follow the basic behavioral principle to be consistent or not let a negative variable schedule emerge. At Walmart, even though you vow, "I won't give in to bad behavior!" as your toddler's tantrums escalate, you end up caving in. It simply is more reinforcing to you to avoid the other shoppers' disapproving stares ("What an out-of-control mother and bratty kid!"). Unfortunately, your child has learned a valuable lesson: "If I keep whining, *eventually* I'll get what I want."

Reinforcement (and its opposite process, *extinction*) is a powerful force for both good and bad. It explains why, if a child starts out succeeding early in elementary school (being reinforced by receiving A's), he's likely to study and become more connected to academics. If a kindergartner begins failing socially (does not get positive reinforcement from her peers), she is at risk for becoming incredibly shy or

traditional behaviorism The original behavioral worldview that focused on charting and modifying only "objective," visible behaviors.

operant conditioning According to the traditional behavioral perspective, the law of learning that determines any voluntary response. Specifically, we act the way we do because we are reinforced for acting in that way.

reinforcement Behavioral term for reward.

cognitive behaviorism (social learning theory) A behavioral worldview that emphasizes that people learn by watching others and that our thoughts about the reinforcers determine our behavior. Cognitive behaviorists focus on charting and modifying people's thoughts.

modeling Learning by watching and imitating others.

self-efficacy According to cognitive behaviorism, an internal belief in our competence that predicts whether we initiate activities or persist in the face of failures, and predicts the goals we set.

highly aggressive in third or fourth grade (see Chapter 6). When you are not being reinforced by people, wouldn't you withdraw or generally start acting in socially inappropriate ways?

Behaviorism makes sense of why, after starting out so loving, marriages can end in divorce court. As newlyweds, couples are continually reinforcing each other with expressions of love. Then, over time, husbands and wives tend to ignore the good parts of their partner and pay attention when there is something wrong. Actually, as you will read in Chapter 11, one psychologist finds that he can predict which marriages will break up, simply by charting the ratio of positive to negative comments spouses make while discussing an issue in their lives.

Behaviorism even offers an optimistic environmental explanation for the physical and mental impairments of old age. If you were in a nursing home and weren't being reinforced for remembering or walking, wouldn't your memory or physical abilities decline? The key to producing well-behaved children, enduring, loving marriages, and fewer old-age disabilities is simple. According to traditional behaviorists, we simply need to reinforce the right things.

However, things are not quite that simple. Human beings *do* think and reason. People do not need to be personally reinforced to actually learn.

Taking a Different Perspective: Exploring Cognitions

Enter **cognitive behaviorism (social learning theory)**, launched by Albert Bandura (1977; 1986) and his colleagues in the 1970s, in studies demonstrating the power of **modeling**, or learning by watching and imitating what other people do.

Because we are a social species, modeling (both imitating other people, and others reciprocally imitating us) is endemic in daily life. Given that we are always modeling everything, from the expressions of the person we are talking with, to the latest hairstyle, who are we most likely to *generally* model as children and adults?

Bandura's (1986) studies suggest that we tend to model people who are nurturing, or relate to us in a caring way. (The good news here is that being a loving, hands-on parent is the best way to naturally embed your values and ideas.) We model people whom we categorize as being like us. At age 2, you probably modeled anything from the vacuum cleaner to the behavior of the family dog. As we grow older, we tailor our modeling selectively, based on our understanding of who we are.

Modeling similar people partly explains why, after children understand their gender label (girl or boy) at about age 2 1/2, they separate into sex-segregated play groups and prefer to play with their "own group" (see Chapter 6). It makes sense of why at-risk teenagers gravitate to the druggies group at school, and then model the leader who most embodies the group norms (see Chapter 9). While I will use modeling to explain behavior at several points in this book, another concept—also devised by Bandura—will be a *genuine* foundation in the chapters to come: self-efficacy.

Digital Vision/Getty Images

This student is obviously far from thrilled at getting a humiliating grade. But if he has *high self-efficacy*, he should view this failure as a challenge: "If I study twice as hard, I'll get an A next time." How would you react if you failed the first exam in this class?

Self-efficacy refers to our belief in our competence, our sense that we can be successful at a given task. According to Bandura (1989, 1992, 1997), efficacy feelings determine the goals we set. They predict which activities we engage in as we travel through life. When self-efficacy is low, we decide not to tackle that difficult math problem. We choose not to ask a beautiful stranger for a date. When self-efficacy is high, we not only take action but continue to act long after the traditional behavioral approach suggests that extinction should occur.

Let's imagine that your goal is to be a nurse or psychologist, but you get an F on this first test. If your "academic self-efficacy" is low, you might conclude: "I'm a terrible student. I'll never make it. I'm basically not smart." You might not put forth any effort on the next exam. You might even drop out of school. But if you have high self-efficacy, your reaction will be the opposite: "I just need to work harder. I can do it. I'm *going* to get a good grade in this class!"

How do children develop low or high self-efficacy? Can efficacy feelings predict success decades later in life? What role does self-efficacy play in our happiness as adults? These are the kinds of questions we will explore in examining the role that efficacy feelings play from elementary school to old age.

By now, you may be impressed with the power of behaviorism's simple, action-oriented concepts. Be consistent. Don't reinforce negative behavior. Reinforce positive things (from traditional behaviorism). Draw on the principles of modeling and stimulate efficacy feelings to help children and adults succeed (from cognitive behaviorism).

Still, many developmentalists, even people who believe that nurture (or the environment) is important, find behaviorism unsatisfying. Aren't we more than just a collection of efficacy feelings or reinforced responses? Isn't there a basic core to personality, and aren't the lessons we learn in childhood vital in shaping adult life? Notice that behaviorism doesn't address that core question: What *really* motivates us as people? To illustrate the problems that we run into when we don't consider basic human motivations, let's listen to John Watson (1924/1998) lashing out at what he calls pathological "love conditioning" destined to produce a whiny, dependent adult: "The child is alone putting blocks together and the mother comes in. . . . The child crawls . . . to the mother . . . climbs into her lap, puts its arms around her neck. The mother fondles her child, kisses it and holds it" (p. 78). Wait a second! Isn't that the way parents and children are supposed to behave?

attachment theory Theory formulated by John Bowlby centering on the crucial importance to our species' survival of being closely connected with a caregiver during early childhood and being attached to a significant other during all of life.

Attachment Theory: Focus on Nurture, Nature, and Love

According to **attachment theory**, the answer is yes. Attachment theory, put forth by British psychiatrist John Bowlby during the mid-twentieth century, has the same basic theme as traditional Freudian psychoanalytic theory. As you will learn in (a bit) more depth on page 20, Sigmund Freud revolutionized our culture by arguing that the way our parents treat us during early childhood determines our lifelong mental health. Bowlby agreed that our early experiences with caregivers shape our adult ability to love, but he focused on what he called the *attachment response*.

In observing young children separated from their mothers, Bowlby noticed that babies need to be physically close to a caregiver during the time when they are beginning to walk (Bowlby, 1969, 1973; Karen, 1998). Disruptions in this biologically programmed attachment response, he argued, if prolonged, can cause serious problems later in life. Moreover, our impulse to be close to a "significant other" is a basic human need during every stage of life.

How does the attachment response develop during infancy? Is Bowlby (and Freud) right that the quality of our early attachments determines our adult mental health? How can we draw on attachment theory to understand everything from adult love relationships to widowhood to our concerns as we approach death? Stay tuned for answers as we explore the principles of this influential theory throughout this book.

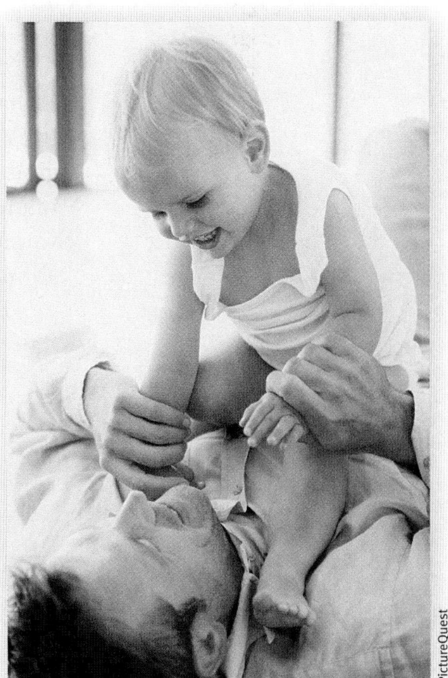
PictureQuest

Bowlby believes that the intense, loving bond between this father and his infant son will set the baby up for a fulfilling life. Do you agree with this basic principle of attachment theory?

Today, Freud's theory is seen as outdated (more about this later). But researchers draw on attachment theory as a major perspective for understanding human beings. One reason is that Bowlby's ideas fit with a seismic late-twentieth-century shift in

evolutionary psychology Theory or worldview highlighting the role that inborn, species-specific behaviors play in human development and life.

behavioral genetics Field devoted to scientifically determining the role that hereditary forces play in determining individual differences in behavior.

twin study Behavioral genetic research strategy, designed to determine the genetic contribution of a given trait, that involves comparing identical twins with fraternal twins (or with other people).

the way developmentalists conceptualize human motivations. Yes, Bowlby did believe in the power of caregiving (nurture), but he firmly anchored his theory in nature (genetics). Bowlby (1969, 1973, 1980) argued that the attachment response is genetically programmed into our species to promote survival. Bowlby, as it turns out, was an early evolutionary psychologist.

Evolutionary Psychology: Theorizing About the "Nature" of Human Similarities

Evolutionary psychologists are the mirror image of behaviorists. They look to nature, or inborn biological forces that have evolved to promote survival, to explain how we develop and behave. Why do pregnant women develop morning sickness just as the fetal organs are being formed, and why do newborns prefer to look at attractive faces rather than ugly ones? (That's actually true!) According to evolutionary psychologists, these reactions cannot be changed by modifying the reinforcers. They are based in the human genetic code that we all share.

Evolutionary psychology lacks the practical, action-oriented approach of behaviorism, although it does alert us to the fact that we need to pay close attention to basic human needs. Still, as I describe how far-flung topics—from birth weight (Chapter 2), to the timing of puberty (Chapter 8), to the purpose of grandparents (Chapter 12)—can be viewed through an evolutionary psychology lens, you will realize just how influential this "look to the human genome" perspective has become in our field. What *first* convinced developmentalists that genetics is important in determining the person we become? . . . . A simple set of research techniques.

Behavioral Genetics: Scientifically Exploring the "Nature" of Human Differences

Behavioral genetics is the name for research strategies devoted to examining the genetic contribution to the *differences* we see between human beings. How genetic is the tendency to bite our nails, develop bipolar disorders, have specific talents and attitudes about life? To answer these kinds of questions relating to the variations that make us special, scientists typically use two strategies: twin and adoption studies.

In **twin studies**, researchers typically compare identical (monozygotic) twins and fraternal (dizygotic) twins on the trait they are interested in (playing the oboe, obesity,

How "genetic" are these children's friendly personalities? To answer this question, researchers compare identical twins, such as these two girls *(left)*, with fraternal twins, like this girl and boy *(right)*. If the identicals (who share exactly the same DNA) are much more similar to each other than the fraternals in their scores on friendliness tests, friendliness is defined as a highly heritable trait.

Grace/Zefa/Corbis

John-Francis Bourke/Getty Images

and so on). Identical twins develop from the same fertilized egg (it splits soon after the one-cell stage) and are genetic clones. Fraternal twins, like any brother or sister, develop from separate conceptions and so, on average, share 50 percent of their genes. The idea is that if a given trait is highly influenced by genetics, identical twins should be much more alike in that quality than fraternal twins. Specifically, behavioral geneticists use a statistic called *heritability* (which ranges from 1 = totally genetic, to 0 = no genetic contribution) to summarize the extent to which a given behavior is shaped by genetic forces.

For instance, suppose you decided to conduct a twin study to determine the heritability of friendliness. First, you would select a large group of identical and fraternal twins and give both sets of twins various tests measuring their outgoing attitudes. You would then compare the strength of the test score relationships you found for each twin group. Let's say the identical twins' scores tended to be incredibly similar—almost like the same person taking the tests twice—and the fraternal twins' test scores tended to vary much more from each other. Your heritability statistic would be high, and you then would conclude: "Friendliness is a mainly genetically determined trait."

In **adoption studies,** researchers compare adopted children with their biological and adoptive parents. Here, too, they evaluate the impact of heredity on a trait by looking at how closely these children resemble their birth parents (with whom they share only genes) and their adoptive parents (with whom they share only environments).

Twin studies of children growing up in the same family and simple adoption studies are not difficult to carry out. The most striking evidence for the power of genetics comes from the rare **twin/adoption studies,** in which identical twins are separated in childhood and reunited in adult life. If Joe and James, who have exactly the same DNA, have very similar abilities, traits, and personalities, even though they grew up in *different families,* this would be strong evidence that genetics plays a crucial role in making us who we are.

Consider, for instance, the Swedish Twin/Adoption Study of Aging. Researchers combed national registries to find identical and fraternal twins adopted into different families in that country—where birth records of every adoptee are kept. Then they reunited these children in late middle age and gave the twins a battery of tests (Finkel & Pedersen, 2004; Kato & Pedersen, 2005).

While specific qualities varied in their heritabilities, you might be surprised to know that perhaps the most genetically determined quality was overall IQ (Pedersen, 1996). In fact, if one twin took the standard intelligence test, statistically speaking we could predict that the other twin would have an almost identical IQ despite living apart for almost an entire lifetime!

Behavioral genetic studies such as these have opened our eyes to fact that nature (genetics) plays a role in determining virtually every aspect of who we are (Turkheimer, 2004). Our tendencies to be religious, vote for conservative Republicans (Bouchard and others, 2004), drink to excess (Agrawal & Lynskey, 2008), or get divorced—qualities we thought *must* be due to how our parents raised us—are all somewhat shaped by genetic forces (Plomin and others, 2003b).

These studies have given us tantalizing insights into the meaning of nurture. It's tempting to assume that children growing up in the same family share the same nurture, or environment. But as you can see in the How Do We Know research box on page 18, that assumption is wrong. We inhabit very different life spaces than our brothers and sisters, even when we eat at the same dinner table and share the same room. These environments are shaped in part by our genes (Rowe, 2003).

The bottom line is that there is no such thing as nature *or* nurture. To really understand human development, we need to explore how nature *and* nurture combine. That is exactly how developmental scientists conceptualize the lifespan today.

adoption study Behavioral genetic research strategy, designed to determine the genetic contribution to a given trait, that involves comparing adopted children with their biological and adoptive parents.

twin/adoption study Behavioral genetic research strategy that involves comparing the similarities of identical twin pairs adopted into different families, to determine the genetic contribution to a given trait.

evocative forces The nature-interacts-with-nurture principle that our genetic temperamental tendencies and predispositions evoke, or produce, certain responses from other people.

bidirectionality The crucial principle that people affect one another, or that interpersonal influences flow in both directions.

active forces The nature-interacts-with-nurture principle that our genetic temperamental tendencies and predispositions cause us to actively choose to put ourselves into specific environments.

HOW DO WE KNOW . . .

that our nature affects our upbringing?

For much of the twentieth century, developmentalists assumed that parents treated all of their children the same way. We could classify mothers as either nurturing or rejecting, caring or cold. Then the Swedish Twin/Adoption Study turned these basic parenting assumptions upside down (Plomin, 1991).

Researchers asked middle-aged identical twins who had been adopted into different families as babies to rate their parents along dimensions such as caring, acceptance, and discipline styles. They were astonished to find similarities in the ratings, even though the twins were evaluating different families!

What was happening here? The answer, the researchers concluded, was that the genetic similarities in the twins' personalities *created* similar family environments. If Joe and Jim were both easy, kind, and caring, they evoked more loving parenting. If they were both temperamentally difficult, they caused their adoptive parents to react in more rejecting, less nurturant ways.

I vividly saw this *evocative*, child-shapes-parenting relationship in my own life. Because my adopted son has dyslexia and is very physically active, in our house we ended up doing active things like sports. As Thomas didn't like to sit still for story time, I probably would have been described as a "less than optimally stimulating" parent had some psychologist come into my home to rate how much I read to my child.

And now, the plot thickens. When I met Thomas's biological mother, I found out that she also has dyslexia. She's tremendously energetic and peppy. It's one thing to see the impact of nature in my son, as his mother revealed. But I can't help wondering. . . . Maureen is a very different kind of person than I am (although we have a terrific time together—traveling and doing active things). Would Thomas have had the *same* kind of upbringing (at least partly) that I gave my son if he had *not* been adopted—and had grown up with his biological mom?

Nature and Nurture Combined

Now let's look at two nature-plus-nurture principles that I will be drawing on again and again in this book.

Our Nature (Genetic Tendencies) Shapes Our Nurture (Life Experiences)

Developmentalists now understand that it doesn't make sense to separate nature and nurture into independent entities (see Diamond, 2009; Turkheimer, 2004). Our genetic tendencies mold and shape our wider world experiences in two distinctive ways.

Evocative forces refer to the fact that our inborn talents and temperamental tendencies naturally evoke, or produce, certain responses from the human world. A joyous child elicits smiles from everyone. A child who is temperamentally irritable, hard to handle, or has trouble sitting still is unfortunately set up to get the kind of harsh parenting she least needs to succeed. Human relationships are **bidirectional.** Just as you get grumpy when with a grumpy person, fight with your difficult neighbor, or shy away from your colleague who is paralyzingly shy, who we are as people causes other people to react to us in specific ways, driving our development for the good and the bad.

Active forces refer to the fact that we *actively select* our environments based on our genetic tendencies. A child who is talented at reading will gravitate toward devouring books, and so become an even better reader. His brother, who is well coordinated, may play baseball three hours a day and become a star athlete in

Photodisc Green/Getty Images

Imagine how you (and other people) would respond to this grumpy boy versus a sunny, upbeat child and you will understand how *evocative* influences work to make us more like ourselves genetically and why all human relationships are *bidirectional*.

his teenage years. Because we tailor our activities to fit our biologically based interests and skills, what start out as minor differences between people in early childhood tend to snowball—ultimately producing huge gaps in talents and traits. The unusually high heritabilities for IQ in the Swedish Twin/Adoption Study are consistently lower in similar behavioral genetic studies conducted during childhood (Plomin & Spinath, 2004). The reason is that, like heat-seeking missiles, our nature causes us to gravitate toward specific life experiences, so we literally become *more like ourselves* genetically as we travel into adult life (Scarr, 1997).

Nicole Katano/PictureQuest

Because this musically talented girl is choosing to spend hours playing the piano, she is likely to become even more talented as she gets older, illustrating the fact that we actively shape our environment to fit our genetic tendencies and talents.

We Need the Right Nurture (Life Experiences) to Fully Express Our Nature (Genetic Talents)

Developmentalists understand that even if a quality is mainly genetic, its expression can be 100 percent dependent on the outside world. Let's illustrate by returning to the high heritabilities for overall intelligence. Suppose you lived in an impoverished developing country, were malnourished, and forced to work as a laborer in a field. In this environment, having a genius-level IQ might be irrelevant, as there would be little chance to demonstrate your hereditary gifts.

Actually, the most fascinating example that we need "nurture," or a high-quality environment, to bring out our human genetic potential relates specifically to IQ. You might be astonished to know that, based on performance on the IQ test, our species has been getting much more intelligent. As with any test graded on a curve, in determining the IQ score, psychologists rank a given child or adult as average or gifted (and so on) according to how that person performs compared to other people of that age (see Chapter 7).

But in each successive cohort, the competition is getting stiffer. The same number of correct items a twenty-first-century teenager needs to get an "average" IQ (meaning a score of 100) on the test would have boosted that same child into the top third of the population in 1950. If that adolescent time-traveled back a century to take the test and got the identical number of items correct, he would have been labeled as gifted (with an IQ of *130*), in the top 2 percent of his peers (Pinker, 2011)!

Library of Congress

If this 17-year-old Civil War soldier took an intelligence test, compared to twenty-first-century teens, he would probably be labeled "mentally slow"—showing the role our environment (growing up in an advanced society) makes on the most biologically determined traits.

What is responsible for this remarkable upward shift in test performance, called the *Flynn effect*? Obviously, our basic "genetic" intellectual potential can't have changed over the past 100 years. It's just that as human beings have become better nourished, more educated, and far more technologically adept, they generally perform better, especially on the kinds of abstract-reasoning items on the IQ test (see Flynn, 2007; Pinker, 2011). So even when individual differences in IQ are "genetic," the environment makes a dramatic difference in how people perform.

My discussion brings home the fact that to promote our species-specific genetic human potential, we need to provide the best possible overall environment (that is, society). On a personal (or behavioral-genetic) level, we also need to provide the environment that best promotes our unique capacities, talents, and traits. Therefore, a core goal of developmental science is to foster the correct **person–environment fit**—making the wider world bring out our human "best."

person–environment fit The extent to which the environment is tailored to our biological tendencies and talents. In developmental science, fostering this fit between our talents and the wider world is an important goal.

Actually, rather than making what we do—as parents, teachers, and health-care professionals—irrelevant, our appreciation of the importance of genetics makes the environment we provide *more* crucial. From the studies that show exceptionally sensitive caregiving can help *lessen* the impact of a child's being born genetically "at risk" (Diamond, 2009; Rowe and others, 2009) to emerging research suggesting that we may inherit a gene form that either makes us highly responsive to wider-world events or relatively immune to life's blows (more about these fascinating, tentative findings in Chapter 4), the more we know about the power of nature (genetics) in shaping behavior, the better we can act to tailor the environment to enhance the quality of *each* of our lives.

Emphasis on Age-Linked Theories

Now that I've spelled out this book's basic "nature combines with nurture" message, it's time to explore two theories I'll repeatedly highlight that view development in defined stages. First, however, as promised, let's take a detour to focus on the world-class genius who devised the earliest stage theory of all.

IN FOCUS: Freud: A Twentieth-Century Culture Shaper

As I mentioned earlier, Freud's theory is mainly a historical footnote in contemporary developmental science. However, no one can dispute the fact that Sigmund Freud (1856–1939) singlehandedly transformed the way we think about human beings. Anytime you say, "I must have done that unconsciously" or "My problems are due to my childhood," you are loosely drawing on this genius's ideas. Freud, a Viennese Jewish physician, wrote more than 40 books and monographs in a burst of brilliance during the early twentieth century. His ideas revolutionized our understanding of everything from religion to anthropology to the arts, in addition to jump-starting the modern field of mental health. Freud's mission, however, was simple: to decode why his patients were in emotional pain.

Freud's theory is described as *psychoanalytic* because it analyzes the psyche or our inner life. By listening to his patients, Freud became convinced that our actions are dominated by feelings and motivations of which we are not aware. The roots of emotional problems lay in repressed (made unconscious) feelings from early childhood. Moreover, "mothering," during the first five years of life, determines adult mental health.

Specifically, Freud posited three hypothetical structures. The *id*, present at birth, is the mass of instincts, needs, and feelings we have when we arrive in the world. During early childhood, from these primitive needs and feelings, the conscious, rational part of our personality—called *the ego*—emerges. Ego functions involve thinking, reasoning, planning, and fulfilling our id desires in adaptive and realistic ways. Finally, a structure called the *superego*—the moral arm of our personality—exists in opposition to the id's desires.

According to Freud and his followers, if our parents are excellent caregivers, we will develop a strong ego, which sets us up to master the challenges of life. If they are insensitive or their caregiving is impaired, our behavior will be id driven, and our lives will be out of control. The purpose of his therapy, called *psychoanalysis*, was to enable his patients to become aware of the repressed early childhood experiences causing their symptoms and liberate them from the tyranny of the unconscious to live rational, productive lives. (As Freud famously put it, where *id* there was, *ego* there will be.)

In sum, according to Freud: 1) Human beings are basically irrational; 2) lifelong mental health depends on our parents' caregiving during early life; and 3) self-awareness is the key to living a fulfilling adult life.

So far, many of you might be on the same page as Freud. Where you are apt to part serious company with the theory relates to Freud's stages of sexuality. Freud argued that sexual feelings (which he called *libido*) are the motivation driving human life, and he put forth the shocking idea—especially in that puritanical time—that babies are sexual human beings. As the infant develops, he argued, sexual feelings are centered on specific areas of the body called *erogenous zones*. During the first year of life, the erogenous zone is the mouth (the famous *oral stage*). Around age 2, with toilet training, sexual feelings center on elimination (the *anal stage*). Finally, around ages 3 and 4, sexual feelings shift to the genitals (the *phallic stage*). During this time, the child develops sexual fantasies relating to the parent of the opposite sex (the *Oedipus complex*), and the same-sex parent becomes a threatening rival. Then, sexuality is violently repressed, the child identifies with that parent, the superego is formed, and we enter *latency*—an asexual stage that lasts through elementary school. At puberty, mature sexuality emerges.

Couldn't there be other basic motivations driving development, and can't we change, as people, after age 5? Erik Erikson answered yes.

Erik Erikson's Psychosocial Tasks

Erik Erikson, born in Germany in 1904, was an analyst who adhered to most tenets of psychoanalytic theory, but disagreed with the classical Freudians' in specific ways. Rather than emphasizing sexuality, Erikson (1963) saw issues related to becoming an independent self and having high-quality relationships as our basic motivations (which explains why Erikson's theory is called *psychosocial* to distinguish it from Freud's psychosexual stages). Erikson, however, is often labeled the father of lifespan development because he believed we continue to develop throughout life. He set out to chart the core challenges or developmental tasks we face at different ages.

Ted Streshinsky/Time Life Pictures/Getty Images

With his powerful writings on identity and, especially, his concept of age-related psychosocial tasks, Erik Erikson (shown here with his wife, Joan) has become a father of our field.

You can see these **psychosocial tasks,** or challenges, listed in Table 1.2. Each successive task, Erikson argued, builds on another because we cannot master the issue of a later stage unless we have accomplished the developmental milestones of the previous ones.

Notice how parents take incredible joy in lovingly satisfying their baby's needs and you will understand why Erikson believed that *basic trust* (the belief that the human world is caring) is our fundamental life task in the first year of life. Erikson's second psychosocial task, *autonomy*, makes perfect sense of the infamous "*no* stage" and "terrible twos." It tells us that we need to *celebrate* this not-so-pleasant toddler behavior as the blossoming of a separate self! Think back to elementary school, and you may realize why Erikson used the term *industry*, or learning to work—at friendships, sports, academics—as our basic challenge during our school years, from age 6 to 12.

Erikson's adolescent task, the search for *identity*, has now become a household word. Erikson was particularly interested in issues related to constructing

TABLE 1.2: Erikson's Psychosocial Stages

Life Stage	Primary Task
Infancy (birth to 1 year)	Basic trust versus mistrust
Toddlerhood (1 to 2 years)	Autonomy versus shame and doubt
Early childhood (3 to 6 years)	Initiative versus guilt
Middle childhood (6 years to puberty)	Industry versus inferiority
Adolescence (tens into twenties)	Identity versus role confusion
Young adulthood (twenties to early forties)	Intimacy versus isolation
Middle adulthood (forties to sixties)	Generativity versus stagnation
Late adulthood (late sixties and beyond)	Integrity versus despair

Erikson's psychosocial tasks In Erik Erikson's theory, each challenge that we face as we travel through the eight stages of the lifespan.

Piaget's cognitive developmental theory Jean Piaget's principle that from infancy to adolescence, children progress through four qualitatively different stages of intellectual growth.

an adult identity. As a young person, he wandered around Europe, thinking he wanted to be an artist before finding his career path as a teacher and psychoanalyst (Coles, 1970).

How have developmentalists expanded on Erikson's task of identity? Is Erikson right that nurturing the next generation, or *generativity*, is the key to a fulfilling adult life? These are just two of the questions I will be exploring as we draw on Erikson's psychosocial tasks to help us think more deeply about the challenges we face at each life stage.

Erikson offered a compelling roadmap to chart our developing lives. But—in brilliance and transformational thinking—there is only one human development rival to Freud: Jean Piaget.

Bill Anderson/Photo Researchers, Inc.

Jean Piaget, in his masterful studies spanning much of the twentieth century, transformed the way we think about children's thinking.

Piaget's Cognitive Developmental Theory

A 3-year-old tells you "Mr. Sun goes to bed because it's time for me to go to sleep." A toddler is obsessed with flushing different-sized wads of paper down the toilet and can't resist touching everything she sees. Do you ever wish you could get into the heads of young children and understand how they view the world? If so, you share the passion of our foremost genius in child development: Piaget.

Piaget, born in 1894 in Switzerland, was a child prodigy himself. As the teenaged author of several dozen published articles on mollusks, he was already becoming well known in that field (Flavell, 1963; Wadsworth, 1996). Piaget's interests shifted to studying children when he worked in the laboratory of a psychologist named Binet, who was devising the original intelligence test. Rather than ranking children according to how much they knew, Piaget became fascinated by children's *incorrect* responses. He spent the next 60 years meticulously devising tasks to map the minds of these mysterious creatures in our midst.

Piaget believed that as they travel from birth through adolescence, children progress through *qualitatively different* stages of cognitive growth (see Table 1.3). The term *qualitative* means that rather than simply knowing less or more (on the kind of scale we can rank from 1 to 10), infants, preschoolers, elementary-school-age children, and teenagers think about the world in *completely* different ways. However, Piaget also believed that there was a basic continuity to

TABLE 1.3: **Piaget's Stages of Development**

Age	Name of Stage	Description
0–2	Sensorimotor	The baby manipulates objects to pin down the basics of physical reality. This stage, ending with the development of language, will be described in Chapter 3.
2–7	Preoperations	Children's perceptions are captured by their immediate appearances. "What they see is what is real." They believe, among other things, that inanimate objects are really alive and that if the appearance of a quantity of liquid changes (for instance, if it is poured from a short, wide glass into a tall, thin one), the amount actually becomes different. You will learn about all of these perceptions in Chapter 5.
8–12	Concrete operations	Children have a realistic understanding of the world. Their thinking is really on the same wavelength as adults'. While they can reason conceptually about concrete objects, however, they cannot think abstractly in a scientific way.
12+	Formal operations	Reasoning is at its pinnacle: hypothetical, scientific, flexible, fully adult. Our full cognitive human potential has been reached. We will explore this stage in Chapter 9.

cognitive development. Human beings have a built-in hunger to learn and mentally grow. Mental growth occurs through **assimilation:** We fit the world to our capacities or existing cognitive structures (which Piaget calls *schemas*). And then **accommodation** occurs. We naturally change our thinking to fit the world (Piaget, 1971).

assimilation In Jean Piaget's theory, the first step promoting mental growth, involving fitting environmental input to our existing mental capacities.

accommodation In Piaget's theory, enlarging our mental capacities to fit input from the wider world.

Let's illustrate these two concepts by reflecting on your own thinking while you were reading the previous section. Before reading this chapter, you probably had certain ideas about heredity and environment. In Piaget's terminology, let's call them your "heredity/environment schemas." Perhaps you felt that if a trait is highly genetic, changing the environment doesn't matter; or you may have believed that genetics and environment were totally separate. While fitting (assimilating) your reading into these existing ideas, you entered a state of disequilibrium—"Hey, this contradicts what I've always believed"—and were forced to accommodate. The result was that your "nature/nurture" schemas became more complex and you developed a more advanced (intelligent) way of perceiving the world! Like a newborn who assimilates every new object to her small sucking schema, or a neuroscientist who incorporates each new finding into her huge knowledge-base mental slots, while assimilating each object or fact to what we already know, we must accommodate, and so—inch by inch—cognitively advance.

Piaget was a great advocate of hands-on experiences. He felt that we learn by acting on or physically operating in the world. Rather than using an adult-centered framework, he had the revolutionary idea that we need to understand how children experience life *from their own point of view.* As we explore the science of lifespan development, I hope you will adopt this Piagetian hands-on, person-centered perspective to understand the human experience from the perspective of 1-year-olds to people aged 101.

By now, you may be overwhelmed by all these theories and terms. But take heart. You already have the basic concepts you need for understanding this semester well in hand! Now, let's conclude by exploring a worldview that says, "Let's embrace *all* of these theories and influences on development and explore how they interact." (For a summary of the various theories, see Table 1.4.)

TABLE 1.4: **Summary of the Major Current Theories in Lifespan Development**

	Nature vs. Nurture Emphasis and Ages of Interest	Representative Questions
Behaviorism	Nurture (all ages)	What reinforcers are shaping this behavior? Who is this person modeling? How can I stimulate self-efficacy?
Attachment theory	Nature and nurture (infancy but also all ages)	How does the attachment response unfold in infancy? What conditions evoke this biologically programmed response at every life stage?
Evolutionary theory	Nature (all ages)	How might this behavior be built into the human genetic code?
Behavioral genetics	Nature (all ages)	To what degree are the differences I see in people due to genetics?
Erikson's theory	(all ages)	Is this baby experiencing basic trust? Where is this teenager in terms of identity? Has this middle-aged person reached generativity?
Piaget's theory	Children	How does this child understand the world? What is his thinking like?

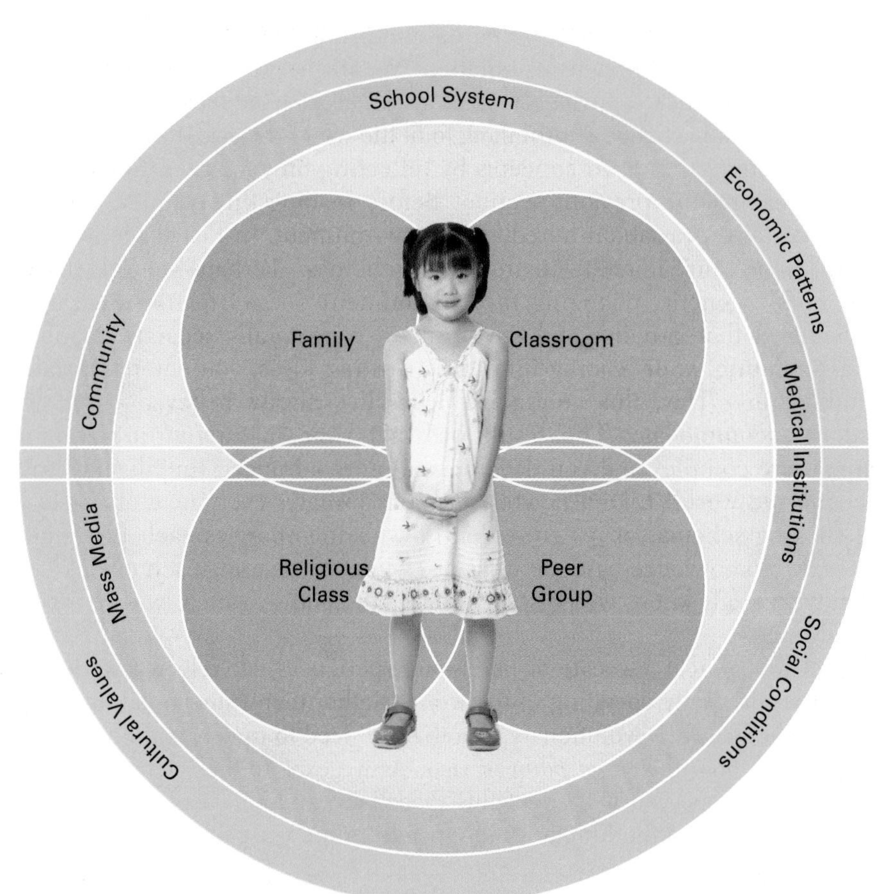

FIGURE 1.4: **Bronfenbrenner's ecological model:** This set of imbedded circles spells out the array of different forces that Bronfenbrenner believed shape development. First and foremost, there are the places that form the core of the child's daily life: family, church, peers, classroom (orange). What is the child's family, school, and religious life like? Who are his friends? How does the child interact with his siblings, his parents, his teacher, and his peers? Although its influence is more indirect, development also vitally depends on the broader milieu—the media, the school system, the community where the boy or girl lives (see blue circle). At the most macro—or broadest—level, we also need to consider that child's culture, the prevailing economic and social conditions of his society (green circle), and, of course, his cohort or the time in history in which he lives . Bottom line: Human behavior depends on multiple complex forces!

Red Chopsticks/Getty Images.

The Developmental Systems Perspective

An influential child psychologist named Urie Bronfenbrenner (1977) was among the earliest lifespan theorists to highlight the principle that real-world behavior has *many* different, complex causes. Bronfenbrenner, as you can see in Figure 1.4, viewed each of us at the center of an expanding circle of environmental influences. At the inner circle, development is shaped by the relationships between the child and people he relates to in his immediate setting, such as family, church, peers, and school. The next wider circles, that indirectly feed back to affect the child, lie in overarching influences such as his community, the media environment, the health-care community, and the whole school system itself. At the broadest levels, as you saw earlier in the chapter, the child's cultural values, the overall economic and social situation of his society, and his cohort, or the time in history when he travels through life, crucially shape behavior, too. Bronfenbrenner's plea to examine the total *ecology*, or life situation, of the child forms the heart of a contemporary scientific perspective called the **developmental systems approach** (Ford & Lerner, 1992; Lerner, 1998; Lerner, Dowling, & Roth, 2003). Specifically:

developmental systems perspective An all-encompassing outlook on development that stresses the need to embrace a variety of theories, and the idea that all systems and processes interrelate.

- **Developmental systems theorists stress the need to use many different approaches.** There are *many* valid ways of looking at behavior. Our actions *do* have many causes. To fully understand development, we need to draw on the principles of behaviorism, attachment theory, evolutionary psychology, and Piaget. At the widest societal level, to explain our actions, we need to look outward to our culture and cohort. At the tiniest molecular level, we need to look inward to focus on our genes. We have to embrace the input of everyone, from nurses to neuroscientists and from anthropologists to molecular biologists, to make sense of each individual life.

- **Developmental systems theorists emphasize the need to look at the interactions of processes.** As highlighted in Figure 1.4, Bronfenbrenner pointed out that we also need to be aware that every influence on development relates. Our genetic tendencies influence the cultures we construct; the cultures we live in affect the expression of our genes. In the same way that our body systems and processes are in constant communication, continual back-and-forth influences are what human development is all about (see Diamond, 2009).

For example, let's consider that basic marker: poverty. Growing up in poverty might affect your attachment relationships. You are less likely to get attention from your parents because they are under stress. You might not get adequate nutrition. Your neighborhood could be a frightening place to live. Each stress might combine to overload your body, activating negative genetic tendencies and setting you up physiologically for emotional problems.

But some children, because of their genetics, their cultural background, or their cohort, might be insulated from the negative effects of growing up poor. Others might thrive. In a classic study tracing the lives of children growing up during the Great Depression, researchers discovered that if this event occurred at the right time in the life cycle (adolescence, when the young person could take action to help support the family), it produced an enduring sense of self-efficacy. So, in special situations, this trauma might promote superior adult mental health (Elder & Caspi, 1988)! In sum, development occurs in surprising directions for good and for bad. Diversity of change processes and individual differences are the spice of human life.

TYING IT ALL TOGETHER

1. Hernando, a third grader, is having trouble sitting still and paying attention in class, so Hernando's parents consult developmentalists about their son's problem. Pick out which comments might be made by: (1) a traditional behaviorist; (2) a cognitive behaviorist; (3) an evolutionary psychologist; (4) a behavioral geneticist; (5) an Eriksonian; (6) an advocate of developmental systems theory.
   a. Hernando has low academic self-efficacy. Let's improve his sense of competence at school.
   b. Hernando, like other boys, is biologically programmed to run around. If the class had regular gym time, Hernando's ability to focus in class would improve.
   c. Hernando is being reinforced for this behavior by getting attention from the teacher and his classmates. Let's reward appropriate classroom behavior.
   d. Did you or your husband have trouble focusing in school? Perhaps your son's difficulties are hereditary.
   e. Hernando's behavior may have many causes, from genetics, to the reinforcers at school, to growing up in our twenty-first-century Internet age. Let's use a variety of different approaches to help him.
   f. Hernando is having trouble mastering the developmental task of industry. How can we promote the ability to work that is so important at this age?
2. In the above question, which suggestion involves providing the right person–environment fit?
3. Let's imagine your great-grandad was transported back to your current age and given today's IQ test. According to the Flynn effect, he would get *far fewer/more* items correct than you, mainly due to the poor quality of *his childhood environment/genetic potential* (pick one alternative each).
4. Billy, a 1-year-old, mouths everything—pencils, his favorite toy, DVDs—changing his mouthing to fit the object that he is "sampling." According to Piaget, the act of mouthing everything refers to ________, while changing the mouthing behavior to fit the different objects refers to ________.
5. Samantha, a behaviorist, is arguing for her worldview, while Sally is pointing up behaviorism's flaws. First, take Samantha's position, arguing for the virtues of behaviorism, and then discuss some limitations of the theory.

Answers to the Tying It All Together questions can be found at the end of this chapter.

Research Methods: The Tools of the Trade

Theories give us lenses for interpreting behavior. *Research* allows us to find the scientific truth. I already touched on the research technique designed to determine the genetic contributions to behavior. Now let's sketch out the general research strategies that developmental scientists use.

Two Standard Research Strategies: Correlations and Experiments

What impact does poverty have on relationships, personality, or physical health? What forces cause children to model certain people? Does a particular intervention to help improve self-efficacy really work? To answer any question about the impact one condition or entity (called a *variable*) has on another, developmentalists use two basic research designs: correlational studies and true experiments.

In a **correlational study,** researchers chart the relationships between the dimensions they are interested in exploring as they naturally occur. Let's say you want to test the hypothesis that providing a more cognitively stimulating environment at home—for instance, by extensively teaching or reading to your children—leads to better school performance. Your game plan is simple: Select a group of children by going to a class. Relate their academic skills to the reading and teaching their parents provide.

Immediately, however, you will be faced with decisions related to choosing your participants. Are you going to look at first or second graders, explore the practices of both parents or of mothers alone, get your group from a public or private school? You would need to get permission from the school system. You would need to get the parents to volunteer. Are you choosing a **representative sample**—meaning a group that reflects the characteristics of the population about whom you want to generalize?

Then you would face your most important challenge—accurately measuring your variables. Just as a broken thermometer can't tell us if we have a fever, if we don't have adequate indices of the concepts we are measuring, we can't conclude anything at all.

With regard to the adult dimension, one possibility might be to observe the parents with their children. This technique, called **naturalistic observation,** is appealing because it is concrete. You are seeing the behavior as it occurs in "nature," or real life. However, a minute's thought suggests this approach presents a huge practical challenge: the need to travel to each home to observe each family on many occasions for an extended time. Plus, when we watch parent–child interactions, or any socially desirable activity, people try to act their best. Wouldn't you be on good behavior if a psychologist arrived at your house to monitor your behavior with your child?

The most cost-effective strategy would be to give the parents a questionnaire with items such as: "How frequently do you read to your child?" or "How often do you go to museums?" This **self-report strategy,** in which people evaluate their behavior and ideas anonymously, is the main approach researchers use with adults. Still, it has its own biases. Do you think that people can report accurately on their activities? Is there a natural human tendency to magnify our positive behaviors and minimize our negative ones?

Now, turning to the child side of your question, a reasonable way to assess academic skills would be to give standard tests measuring abilities in areas such as reading or math (more about these measures, called *achievement tests,* in Chapter 7). Another strategy might be to ask the teacher to evaluate students' skills. Evaluations from expert observers, such as teachers or parents, are a very common approach that developmentalists use to assess behavior during the childhood years.

correlational study A research strategy that involves relating two or more variables.

representative sample A group that reflects the characteristics of the overall population.

naturalistic observation A measurement strategy that involves directly watching and coding behaviors.

self-report strategy A measurement strategy that involves having people report on their feelings and activities through questionnaires.

TABLE 1.5: Common Strategies Developmentalists Use to Measure Specific Variables (Behaviors or Concepts of Interest)

Type	Strategy	Commonly Used Ages	Pluses and Problems
Naturalistic observation	Observes behavior directly; codes actions, often by rating the behavior as either present or absent (either in real life or the lab)	Typically during childhood, but also used with impaired adults	**Pluses:** Offers a direct, unfiltered record of behavior **Problems:** Very time intensive; people behave differently when watched
Self-reports	Questionnaires in which people report on their feelings, interests, attitudes, and thoughts	Adults and older children	**Pluses:** Easy to administer; quickly provides data **Problems:** Subject to bias if the person is reporting on undesirable activities and behaviors
Ability tests	Tests evaluating mental (or physical) skills	Children and adults	**Pluses:** Offers an objective record of performance **Problems:** May not accurately measure that ability in the "real world"
Observer reports	Knowledgeable person such as a parent, teacher, or trained observer completes scales evaluating the person	Typically during childhood; also used during adulthood if the person is mentally or physically impaired	**Pluses:** Offers a structured look at the person's behavior **Problems:** Observers have their own biases

Table 1.5 spells out the uses, and the pluses and minuses, of these four frequently used ways of measuring concepts: naturalistic observation, self-reports, ability measures, and observer evaluations. Now, returning to our study, suppose you found a relationship, that is, a correlation, between the amount of cognitive stimulation at home and school performance. Could you infer that what parents do *causes* children to perform better in school? The answer is no!

- **With correlations, we may be mixing up the result with the cause.** Given that parent–child relationships are bidirectional, does parental cognitive stimulation really *cause* superior school performance, or do academically talented children provoke parents to act in more cognitively stimulating ways? "Mom, please read to me." "I want go to the science museum." (Remember the How Do We Know story about my son and his reading disability.) This chicken-or-egg argument applies to far more than child–parent relationships, cognition, and personality. Does exercising promote health in later life, or are some older adults likely to become physically active because they are *already* in good health?

- **With correlations, there may be another variable that explains the results.** In view of our discussion of the heritability of intelligence, with regard to the cognitive stimulation study, the immediate third force that comes to mind is genetics. Wouldn't parents who are genetically prone to be academic provide a more cognitively enriching home environment and also have children who are genetically more talented in school? In my exercise example above, wouldn't older adults who go to the gym or ski regularly also be likely to watch their diet and generally take better care of their health? Given that these other activities should naturally be associated with keeping physically fit, can we conclude that exercise *alone* accounts for the association we find?

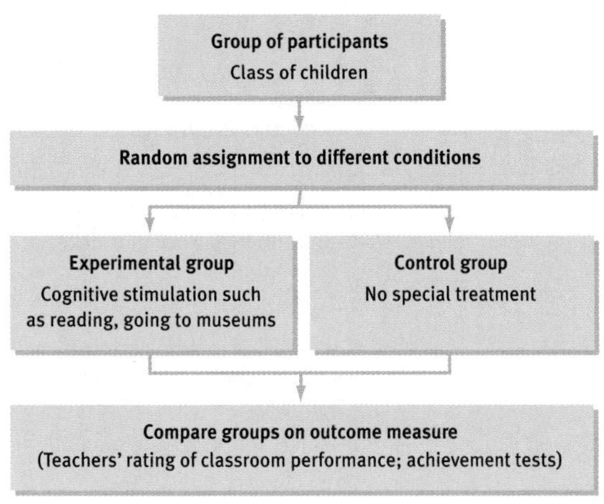

FIGURE 1.5: **How an experiment looks:** By randomly assigning our children to different groups and then giving an intervention (this is *called the independent variable*), we know that our treatment (cognitive stimulation) *caused* better school skills (this outcome is called *the dependent variable*).

To rule out these other forces, the solution is to conduct a **true experiment** (see Figure 1.5). Researchers take steps to isolate their variable of interest by manipulating that condition (called the *independent variable*), and then randomly assign people to either receive that treatment or another, *control* intervention. If we *randomly assign* people to different groups (say, like tossing a coin), there can't be any systematic, preexisting differences between our participants that would bias our results. If the group does differ in the way we predict, we have to say that our intervention *caused* the particular result.

The problem is that we could never assign children to cognitively stimulating parents! If a developmentalist decided to give some cognitively stimulating intervention to one group of children and withhold it from another, he could run into ethical problems. Would it be fair to deprive the control group of that treatment? In the name of science, is it right to take the risk of doing people genuine harm? Experiments are ideal for determining what causes behavior. But to tackle the most compelling questions about human development, we simply *have* to conduct correlational research.

Given that researchers need to take such care to "do no harm," you might think the scientific community would be attuned to the hazards of prescribing treatments based on correlational findings. You would be wrong. During the 1990s, U.S. physicians advocated that every older woman take postmenopausal hormone replacement therapy (HRT). HRT was touted as an intervention to stave off everything from cancer to heart attacks to Alzheimer's disease. But there was a problem. This advice was based on studies comparing the health of women who *chose* to take these supplements with that of the overall population. And who do you think these women were likely to be? You guessed it—a self-selected, upper-middle-class, health-aware group!

Once researchers at the National Institutes of Health conducted a *clinical trial*—an experiment in which they randomly assigned women to take hormones or not—they found that women taking HRT had a higher chance of developing breast cancer, blood clots, and heart disease. Furthermore, the therapy increased the risk of Alzheimer's disease! (See Alzheimer's Disease Education and Referral [ADEAR] Center, 2004; HealthLink, 2002.)

true experiments The only research strategy that can determine that something causes something else; involves randomly assigning people to different treatments and then looking at the outcome.

Designs for Studying Development: Cross-Sectional and Longitudinal Studies

Experiments and correlational studies are standard, all-purpose research strategies. In studying development, however, we have a special interest: "How do people change with age?" To answer this all-important question, scientists also typically use two research techniques—cross-sectional and longitudinal studies.

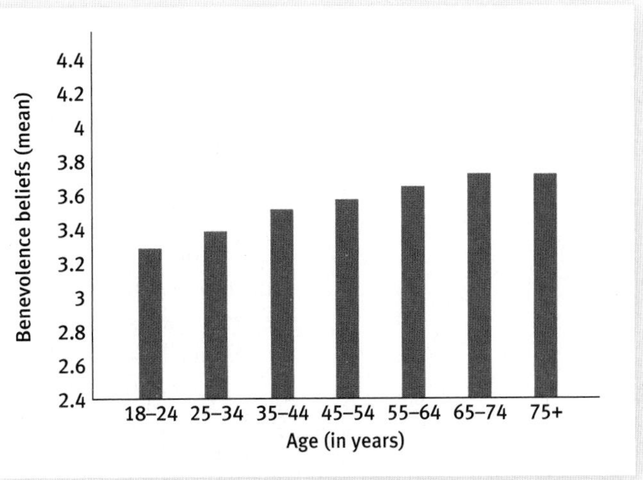

FIGURE 1.6: **"Benevolence beliefs," or faith in humanity across different age groups in a study of U.S. adults:** Notice that, while young people feel worst about human nature, the elderly have the most positive feelings about their fellow human beings.
Source: Poulin & Silver, 2008.

Cross-Sectional Studies: Getting a One-Shot Snapshot of Groups

Because cross-sectional research is relatively easy to carry out, developmentalists typically use this research strategy to explore changes over long periods of the lifespan (Hertzog, 1996). In a **cross-sectional study,** researchers compare *different age groups at the same time* on the trait or characteristic they are interested in, be it political attitudes, personality, or physical health. Consider a study that (among other questions) explored this interesting issue: "How do our feelings about human nature change with age?"

Researchers gave 2,138 U.S. adults a questionnaire measuring their beliefs in a benevolent world (Poulin & Silver, 2008). Presented with items such as "Human nature is basically good," people ranging in age from 18 to 101 ranked each statement on a scale from "agree strongly" to "disagree." As you scan the findings in Figure 1.6, notice that the youngest age group has the most negative perceptions about humanity. The elderly feel most optimistic about people and the world. If you are in your early twenties, does this mean you can expect to grow less cynical about human nature as you age?

Not necessarily. Perhaps your cohort has special reasons to feel suspicious about human motivations. After all, today the media delights in exposing the cheating and lying of authority figures, from senators to school principals. You've probably sat through hundreds of hours of *Big Brother* and *Jersey Shore*-like TV shows featuring two-faced human beings. Previous cohorts of young people were never exposed to this incessant drumbeat of messages highlighting human nature at its worst. In fact, if we conducted this same poll during the 1950s (in the Eisenhower era of *Leave it to Beaver* and *Father Knows Best*) we might find the opposite pattern: Positive feelings about human nature were highest among the young and declined with age!

The bottom-line message is that cross-sectional studies give us a current snapshot of differences among cohorts (or age groups); but they don't necessarily tell us about real *changes that occur as we grow old.*

Cross-sectional studies have a more basic problem. Because they measure only *group differences,* they can't reveal anything about the individual differences that give spice to life. If you are a real pessimist about people, compared to your friends, will your worldview stay the same as you age? What influences might make people feel better about humanity as they travel through adulthood, and what experiences might make people feel worse? To answer these important questions about how *individuals* develop, as well as to look at what forces make for specific kinds of changes, it's best to be on the scene to measure what is going on. This means doing longitudinal research.

Walter Sanders/Time & Life Pictures/Getty Images

Don't you think that these innocent 1950s-era twenty-somethings would have a more optimistic view of human nature than young people today? So could we really conclude from a cross-sectional study comparing these now elderly people with the young that "faith in humanity" grows with age?

cross-sectional study A developmental research strategy that involves testing different age groups at the same time.

longitudinal study A developmental research strategy that involves testing an age group repeatedly over many years.

Longitudinal Studies: The Gold-Standard Developmental Science Research Design

In **longitudinal studies,** researchers typically select a group of a particular age and periodically test those people over years (the relevant word here is *long*). Consider the Dunedin Multidisciplinary and Development Study: An international team of researchers descended on Dunedin, a city in New Zealand, to follow more than 1,000 children born between April 1972 and March 1973, examining them at two-year intervals from age 3 into adult life (Roberts and others, 2007). At each evaluation, they examined the participants' personalities. They looked at parenting practices and life events. The scientists are now tracking these babies as they move into middle age.

The outcome has been an incredible array of findings, especially related to psychological problems. Can we predict adult emotional difficulties as early as age 3? Do sleep problems in elementary school predict excessive anxiety in adulthood (Gregory and others, 2005)? If you smoke marijuana, would you want to know if you have a genetic vulnerability that puts you at an elevated risk of developing schizophrenic symptoms (Caspi and others, 2005)?

Because the researchers are using cutting-edge technology to examine participants' DNA, they can tackle these vital nature-plus-nurture questions. Plus, like other longitudinal research, this study offers a crystal ball into those questions at the heart of our field: "How will I change as I get older?" "When should we worry about children, and when should we *not* be concerned?"

Longitudinal studies are exciting, but they have their own problems. For one thing, they involve a tremendous amount of time, effort, and expense. Imagine the resources involved in planning this particular study. Think of the hassles involved in searching out the participants and getting them to return again and again to take the tests. The researchers must fly the overseas Dunedin volunteers back for each evaluation. They need to reimburse people for their time and lost wages. These logistical and financial problems become more serious the longer a study continues. For this reason, we have hundreds of studies covering infancy, childhood, or defined segments of adult life, such as the old-old years. The handful of studies that trace development from childhood to later life, described in the adulthood chapters of this book, are rare jewels.

The difficulty with getting people to return to be tested presents more than just practical hurdles. It leads to an important bias. Participating in a longitudinal study requires a special commitment. So people who agree to come back to be tested, particularly during adult life, tend to be highly motivated. Think of which classmates are going to come back to your high school reunion. Aren't they apt to be the people who are successful, versus those who have made a mess of their lives? Adults who stay in longitudinal studies, especially for the long haul, are an elite, much better than average group. While longitudinal studies offer us unparalleled information about life, these gold-standard studies have their biases, too.

Critiquing the Research

So to summarize our discussion, how would you go about being a good consumer of the research? When you are evaluating the findings in our field, keep these concerns in mind:

- Consider the study's participants. How were they selected? Ask yourself, "Can I generalize from this particular group to the wider world?"
- Examine the study's measures. Are they accurate? What biases might they have?
- In looking at the *many* correlational studies in this book, be attuned to the fact that their findings might be due to "other forces." What competing interpretations can you come up with to explain this researcher's results?
- With cross-sectional findings, beware of making assumptions that this is the way people *really* change with age.
- Look for longitudinal studies and welcome their insights. However, understand that—especially during adult life—these investigations are probably tracing the lives of the best and brightest people rather than the average adult.

Emerging Research Trends

Developmental scientists are attuned to these issues. In conducting correlational studies, they often try to control for other influences that might explain their findings. They may use several measures, such as teacher ratings and parent input, as well as direct observations, to make sure they are measuring their concepts accurately. Increasingly, they travel to different cultures to check out whether their results are limited to a particular society or apply to all human beings. Still, in addition to conducting better-designed, bigger, more global studies, developmentalists are getting up close and personal, too.

Quantitative research techniques—the strategies I have been describing, using groups of people and statistical tests—are the main approaches that researchers use to study human behavior. In order to make general predictions about people, we need to examine the behavior of different individuals. We need to pin down our concepts by using scales or ratings with numerical values that can be tallied and compared. Developmentalists who conduct **qualitative research** are not interested in making numerical comparisons. They want to understand the unique lives of people by conducting in-depth interviews. In this book, I will be focusing mainly on quantitative research because that is how we find out the scientific "truth." But I also will highlight the growing number of qualitative interview studies to put a human face on our developing life.

quantitative research Standard developmental science data-collection strategy that involves testing groups of people and using numerical scales and statistics.

qualitative research Occasional developmental science data-collection strategy that involves interviewing people to obtain information that cannot be quantified on a numerical scale.

Some Concluding Introductory Thoughts

This discussion brings me back to the letter on page 2 and my promise to let you in on my other agendas in writing this text. Because I want to teach you to critically evaluate the research findings, in the following pages I'll be analyzing individual studies and—in the "How Do We Know" features that appear in some chapters—I'll be focusing on research-related issues in more depth. To bring home the personal experience of the lifespan, I've filled each chapter with quotations and vignettes, and—in the "Experiencing the Lifespan" boxes—interviewed people myself. To bring home the principle that our human lifespan is a continuing work in progress, I'll be starting many chapters by setting the historical and cultural context before moving on to the research. To emphasize the power of research to improve lives, I'll conclude many sections by spelling out interventions that improve the quality of life.

This book is designed to be read like a story, with each chapter building on concepts and terms mentioned in the previous ones. It's planned to emphasize how our insights about earlier life stages relate to older ages. I will be discussing three major aspects of development—physical development, cognitive development, and personality and social relationships (*socioemotional development*)—separately. However, I'll be continually stressing how these aspects of development connect. After all, we are not just bodies, minds, and personalities, but whole human beings!

While I want you to share my excitement in the research, please don't read this book as "the final word." Science—like the lifespan—is always evolving. Moreover, with any research finding, take the phrase "it's all statistical" to heart. Yes, we developmentalists are passionate to make general predictions about life; but, because human beings are incredibly complex, at bottom, each person's lifespan journey can be a beautiful surprise.

Now, beginning with prenatal development and infancy (Chapters 2, 3, and 4); then moving on to childhood (Chapters 5, 6, and 7); adolescence (Chapters 8 and 9); early and middle adulthood (Chapters 10, 11, and 12); later life (Chapters 13 and 14); and, finally, that last milestone, death (Chapter 15), welcome to the lifespan and to the rest of this book!

TYING IT ALL TOGETHER

1. Craig and Jessica are taking a course in research methods at their university and want to test the hypothesis that children who eat excessive sugar at breakfast do poorly at school—but each student decides to tackle this question differently. Craig's plan is to go into children's homes to directly record their sugar consumption at breakfast and relate these data to scores on math and reading tests. Jessica decides to randomly assign one group of children to eat a sugary breakfast (for example, Cap'n Crunch) and another to eat a low-sugar alternative (such as Wheaties), and then have the first-grade teacher rate the math and reading skills of each group. Which student is conducting a correlational study, and which student is conducting a true experiment?
2. In question 1, which student, Craig or Jessica:
   a. will run into real ethical problems conducting the study?
   b. is employing naturalistic observation?
   c. is using expert observer ratings?
   d. will be able to prove that excess sugar consumption *causes* children to do more poorly at school?
   e. may run into the danger of people acting differently because they are being watched?
   f. is conducting a study that—although ethically acceptable—poses enormous practical hurdles in terms of actually carrying out the research?
3. Cecila and Jamel both want to test the hypothesis that people get wiser with age—but each student decides to use a different research strategy. Cecila gives young adults, middle-aged people, and older adults a wisdom questionnaire and compares their scores. Jamel solicits a large group of 20-year-olds, gives them the wisdom questionnaire, and then has them return every five years to take the questionnaire again. Which student is conducting a cross-sectional study, and which student is conducting a longitudinal study?
4. Plan a longitudinal study to test a developmental science question that interests you. Describe how you would select your participants, how your study would proceed, what measures you would use, and what practical problems and biases your study would have.

Answers to the Tying It All Together questions can be found at the end of this chapter.

SUMMARY

Who We Are and What We Study

Lifespan development is a huge mega-discipline encompassing **child development, gerontology,** and **adult development. Developmental scientists,** or **developmentalists,** chart the universal changes we undergo from birth to old age, explore individual differences in development, study the impact of **normative** and **non-normative** life transitions, and explore every other topic relevant to our unfolding life.

Several major **contexts of development** shape our lives. The first is our **cohort,** or the time in history in which we live. The huge **baby boom cohort,** born in the years following World War II, has dramatically affected society as it passes through the lifespan. Cohorts of babies born before the twentieth century faced a shorter, harsher childhood, and many did not survive. As life got easier and education got longer, we first extended the growing-up phase of life to include adolescence and, in recent years, with a new life stage called **emerging adulthood,** have extended the start date of full adulthood to our late twenties.

The early-**twentieth-century life expectancy revolution,** with its dramatic advances in curing ***infectious disease*** and shift to deaths from ***chronic illnesses,*** allowed us to survive to later life. Today, **average life expectancy** is within striking distance of the **maximum lifespan** in the most affluent parts of the world, and we distinguish between two groups of elderly, the healthy **young-old** (people in their sixties and seventies) and the frail **old-old** (people in and over their eighties). The second major twentieth-century lifespan change occurred in the 1960s with the sexual revolution, the women's movement, and the counterculture movement. While these lifestyle revolutions have given us incredible freedom to engineer our own adult path, the **Great Recession of 2008,** and widening **income inequalities,** are currently clouding the landscape of twenty-first-century life.

Socioeconomic status actually greatly affects our lifespan—with people who live in poverty in the United States and other Western nations facing a harsher, more stressful, shorter life. The gaps between **developed world** countries and **developing world**

countries are even more dramatic, with the least-developed countries lagging well behind in terms of health, wealth, and technology.

Our cultural and ethnic background also determines how we develop. Scientists distinguish between **collectivist cultures,** which place a premium on social harmony and close extended-family relationships, and **individualistic cultures,** which value independence and personal achievement. We need to make these distinctions cautiously, however. Residents of each nation have a mix of individualistic and collectivist worldviews. Although the census lumps the U.S. population into broad ethnic categories, these divisions mask diversity within each group. Finally, our gender dramatically influences our travels through life. Women outlive men by at least 4 years in the developed world.

Theories: Lenses for Looking at the Lifespan

Theories offer explanations about what causes people to act the way they do. The main theories in developmental science offering general explanations of behavior vary in their position on the **nature** versus **nurture** question. Behaviorists believe nurture is all-important. According to **traditional behaviorists,** in particular B. F. Skinner, **operant conditioning** and **reinforcement** determine all voluntary behaviors. According to **cognitive behaviorism/social learning theory, modeling** and **self-efficacy**—our internal sense that we can competently perform given tasks—predict how we act.

John Bowlby's **attachment theory** emphasizes both nature and nurture. According to Bowlby, the biological attachment response that develops during early childhood is genetically programmed to promote human survival, and the quality of our attachment relationships in our earliest years is crucial to later mental health. **Evolutionary psychologists** adopt a nature perspective, seeing actions and traits as genetically programmed into evolution to promote survival. **Behavioral genetic** research—in particular, **twin studies, adoption studies,** and occasionally **twin/adoption studies**—have convinced developmental scientists of the power of nature, revealing genetic contributions to almost any way we differ from each other as human beings.

Developmental scientists today, however, have gone beyond the nature *or* nurture question to explore how nature *and* nurture combine. Due to **evocative** and **active forces,** we shape our environments to go along with our genetic tendencies, and human relationships are **bidirectional**—our temperamental qualities and actions influence the responses of others, just as their actions influence us. A basic developmental science challenge is to foster an appropriate **person–environment fit.** We need to match our genetically based talents and abilities to the right environment. Advances in understanding genetics allow us to better arrange the environment to promote an optimal life.

Freud transformed our culture with his idea that human beings are motivated by unconscious drives and that adult mental health depends on the way our parents treated us during early childhood. Erik Erikson expanded on this theory (and Freud's controversial "stage view" of infantile sexuality) by spelling out eight **psychosocial tasks** that we must master as we travel from birth to old age. According Jean Piaget's **cognitive developmental theory,** children progress through four qualitatively different stages of intellectual development and all learning occurs through **assimilation** and **accommodation.**

Most developmental scientists today adopt the **developmental systems perspective.** They welcome input from every theory. They realize that many interacting influences shape who we are. They understand that diversity among people and change processes is the essence of development.

Research Methods: The Tools of the Trade

The two main research strategies scientists use are **correlational studies,** which relate naturally occurring variations among people, and **true experiments,** in which researchers take action to manipulate their variables of interest and randomly assign people to receive a given treatment or not. With correlational studies, there are always competing possibilities for the relationships we find. While experiments do allow us to prove causes, they are often unethical and impractical to carry out. In conducting research, it's best to strive for a **representative sample,** and it's essential to have accurate measures. **Naturalistic observation, self-reports,** tests of abilities, and expert observer evaluations are the main measurement strategies developmental scientists use.

The two major designs for studying development are longitudinal and cross-sectional research. **Cross-sectional studies,** which involve testing people of different age groups at the same time, are very easy to carry out. However, they may confuse differences between age groups with true changes that occur as people age, and they can't tell us about individual differences in development. **Longitudinal studies** are at the heart of our field because they can answer vital questions about how people develop. However, this informative research strategy—following people over years—is difficult to carry out and based on how atypical, elite volunteers behave and change.

Today our studies are getting more global and sophisticated. **Quantitative research**—studies involving groups of participants, and using statistical tests—is still the standard way we learn the scientific truth. But developmentalists are now occasionally conducting **qualitative research**—interviewing people in depth.

KEY TERMS

developmentalists (developmental scientists), p. 3
lifespan development, p. 4
child development, p. 4
gerontology, p. 4
adult development, p. 4
normative transitions, p. 4
non-normative transitions, p. 4
contexts of development, p. 5
cohort, p. 5
baby boom cohort, p. 5
emerging adulthood, p. 6
average life expectancy, p. 7
twentieth-century life expectancy revolution, p. 7
maximum lifespan, p. 7
young-old, p. 7
old-old, p. 7

Great Recession of 2008, p. 9
income inequality, p. 9
socioeconomic status (SES), p. 9
developed world, p. 10
developing world, p. 10
collectivist cultures, p. 10
individualistic cultures, p. 10
theory, p. 12
nature, p. 12
nurture, p. 12
traditional behaviorism, p. 13
operant conditioning, p. 13
reinforcement, p. 13
cognitive behaviorism (social learning theory), p. 14
modeling, p. 14
self-efficacy, p. 14
attachment theory, p. 15
evolutionary psychology, p. 16
behavioral genetics, p. 16
twin study, p. 16
adoption study, p. 17
twin/adoption study, p. 17
evocative forces, p. 18
bidirectionality, p. 18
active forces, p. 18
person–environment fit, p. 19
Erikson's psychosocial tasks, p. 21
Piaget's cognitive developmental theory, p. 22
assimilation, p. 23
accommodation, p. 23
developmental systems approach, p. 24
correlational study, p. 26
representative sample, p. 26
naturalistic observation, p. 26
self-report strategy, p. 26
true experiments, p. 28
cross-sectional study, p. 29
longitudinal study, p. 29
quantitative research, p. 31
qualitative research, p. 31

ANSWERS TO TYING IT ALL TOGETHER QUIZZES

Setting the Context

1. d. One unfortunate consequence of the late-twentieth-century family revolutions is that today's children are more likely to grow up in one-parent families.
2. Maria is probably in her late forties or early fifties; Sara is probably in her sixties; and Rosa is most likely in her eighties.
3. Jim might argue that life is better today because we have a more open society, with considerable individual freedom—especially for women and minority groups. Joe might counter that these same late-twentieth-century lifestyle changes have produced higher divorce rates and far more single-parent families.
4. Pablo has a collectivist worldview, while Peter's worldview is individualistic.
5. Your answers here will all vary.

Theories: Lenses for Looking at the Lifespan

1. (1) c, (2) a, (3) b, (4) d, (5) f, and (6) e.
2. b. As Hernando and other children need to run around, regular gym time would help to foster the best person-environment fit.
3. You should predict that your great-grandad would get *far fewer items* correct on the IQ test, mainly due to the poor quality of *his childhood environment.*
4. assimilation; accommodation
5. Samantha might argue that behaviorism is an ideal approach to human development because it is simple, effective, and easy to carry out. Behaviorism's easily mastered, action-oriented concepts—be consistent, reinforce positive behavior, draw on principles of modeling, and stimulate efficacy feelings—can make dramatic improvements in the

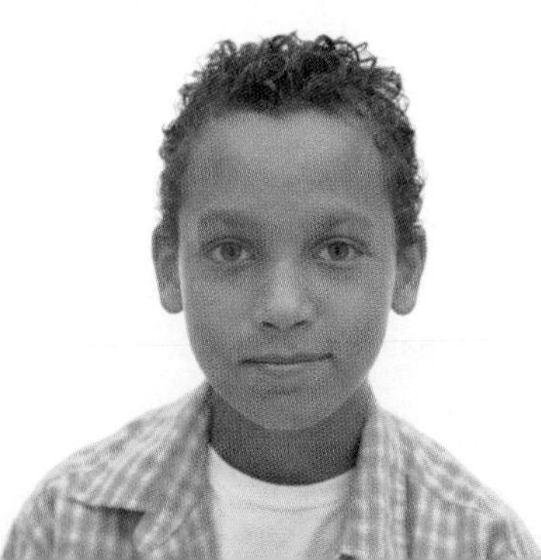

quality of life. Also, because behaviorism doesn't blame the person but locates problems in the learning environment, it has special appeal. Sally might argue that behaviorism's premise that nurture is all-important neglects the powerful impact genetic forces have in determining who we are. So the theory is far too limited—offering a wrongheaded view about development. We need the insights of attachment theory, evolutionary psychology, behavioral genetics, plus Piaget's and Erikson's theories to fully understand what motivates human beings.

Research Methods: The Tools of the Trade

1. Craig is conducting a correlational study; Jessica's is a true experiment.
2. (a) Jessica, (b) Craig, (c) Jessica, (d) Jessica, (e) Craig, and (f) Craig.
3. Cecila is conducting a cross-sectional study; Jamel's is a longitudinal study.
4. After coming up with your hypothesis, you would need to adequately measure your concepts—choosing the appropriate tests. Your next step would be to solicit a large representative sample of a particular age group, give them these measures, and retest these people at regular intervals over an extended period of time. In addition to the huge investment of time and money, it would be hard to keep track of your sample and entice participants to undergo subsequent evaluations. Therefore, a huge bias would relate to who stays in the study versus who drops out. Because the most motivated fraction of your original group will continue, your results will probably reflect how the "best people" behave and change over time (not the typical person).

Chapter 2

CHAPTER OUTLINE

Prenatal Development, Pregnancy, and Birth

It's hard to explain, different from anything that's happened before, Kim told me. Your whole self shifts. You are all about two people now. When you wake up, shop, or plan meals, this other person is always with you. You are always thinking, "What will be good for the baby? What will be best for the two of us?"

Feeling the first kick—like little feathers brushing inside me—was amazing. It was as if she woke up to tell me, "I'm here, Mommy." Another incredible thing was seeing the ultrasound. It's frightening when you go for that test. You wonder, "Will there be something wrong?" But when I saw her shape and heart, the feeling was unbelievable. At first I felt like I could never explain this to my husband. But Jeff is wonderful. I think he really gets it. So I feel very lucky. I can't imagine what this experience would be like if I was going through these nine months completely alone.

Now that it's the thirtieth week and I'm confident that my little girl can survive, there is another shift. I'm totally focused on the moment she will arrive: What will it be like to hold my baby in my arms? Will she be born healthy?

Actually, the downside has always been the fear that she will be born with some problem. I keep going back to the beginning. Did I do something that could have caused harm before the nausea and tiredness hit, which made me realize that I was pregnant? Could my baby have a birth defect?

Another downside is that, until recently, I still felt really nauseous and tired. Some days, I could barely make it to work. (Everything they told you about morning sickness only lasting through the first trimester is wrong—at least for me!)

But most amazing is what happens with strangers, when I'm at the store or walking around the mall. People light up and grin, wish me good luck, or give me advice. It's like the world is watching out for me, rooting for me, cherishing me.

Setting the Context

The concern and awe Kim is getting from the wider world seems built into our humanity. Many societies see pregnancy as a special time of life. Pregnant women are often pampered, kept calm and happy. Their desires and cravings are satisfied. But we also see pregnancy as a uniquely vulnerable time. In some cultures, pregnant women are shielded from funerals. Rituals—such as the nine-day Navajo Blessing Way ceremony—may be performed to ensure that all goes well. In previous eras, societies used good luck charms to keep evil spirits away—a pregnancy girdle in medieval England, a bell placed between the breasts in Brazil, a small sack of garlic worn in Guatemala (Aldred, 1997; Von Raffler-Engel, 1994), a cotton pregnancy sash in Japan (Ito & Sharts-Hopko, 2002).

AP Photo / Matt York

In this traditional southern Indian ceremony performed at the sixth or eighth month of pregnancy, family members and friends gather around to protect the woman and fetus from "the evil eyes." Rituals such as this one are common around the world and embody our fears about this special time of life.

We have the same uneasy feelings in the twenty-first-century developed West. Perhaps you have friends who refuse to tell anyone they are pregnant until after the first three months: "It might be bad luck." In traditional societies, the message—better hold off on celebrating—has been built into formal rituals. In Bulgaria, the first kick was the signal for a woman to bake bread and take it to the church. In Bali, at the seventh month, a prayer ceremony takes place to recognize that there is now, finally, a real person inside whom the spirits need to protect from harm (Kitzinger, 2000; Von Raffler-Engel, 1994).

As these thoughts and fears reveal, pregnancy is a uniquely exciting and frightening time of life. There can be wonderfully uplifting emotions, when women are totally absorbed with the baby and with their physical state. At the same time, there is a sense of danger and fear about the hazards that lie on the journey ahead. Let's keep these different feelings in mind as we turn to explore the science of what happens during the baby's nine months in the womb.

In the first part of this chapter, I'll trace prenatal development, describing what happens, stage by stage, as the baby grows. Then my focus shifts to the mother-to-be, as we examine the inner experience of being pregnant and the emotions of expectant dads. Next, I'll tackle the anxieties related to the baby, describing the external and internal threats to fetal development that, thankfully, only infrequently occur. Finally, we'll look at the event that Kim is anxiously awaiting: birth. What is this amazing experience really like? What was labor and delivery like in previous centuries, and what birth options do women in the developed world have today? I'll conclude this chapter by describing the newborn and exploring the major threats after birth—arriving in the world too soon and/or too small—and infant mortality.

The First Step: Fertilization

Before embarking on this chapter-long journey, however, it is vital to understand the starting point. What structures are involved in reproduction? What physiological process is involved in conceiving a child? What is taking place at the genetic level when a sperm and an egg unite to form a new human being?

The Reproductive Systems

The female and male reproductive systems are shown in Figure 2.1. As you can see, the female system has several basic parts:

uterus The pear-shaped muscular organ in a woman's abdomen that houses the developing baby.

- Center stage is the **uterus**, the pear-shaped muscular organ that will carry the baby to term. The uterus is lined with a velvety tissue, the *endometrium*, which thickens

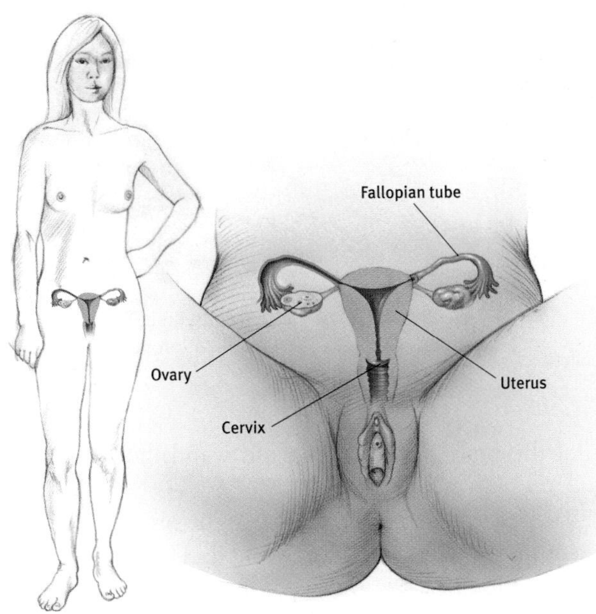

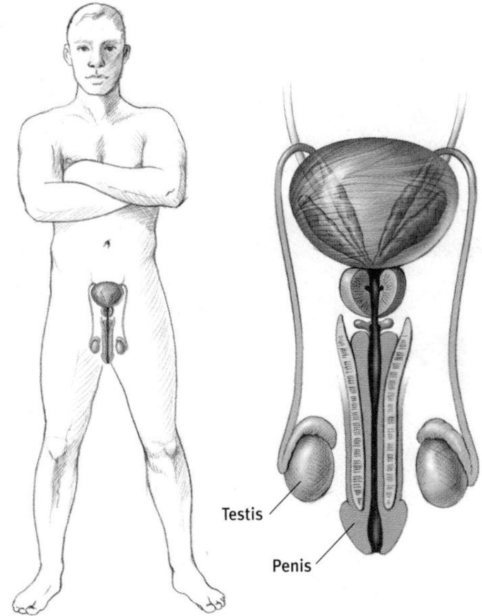

FIGURE 2.1: **The female and male reproductive systems**

in preparation for becoming pregnant and, if that event does not occur, is shed at the end of the monthly cycle, during menstruation.

- The lower section of the uterus, protruding into the vagina, is the **cervix.** During pregnancy, this thick uterine neck must perform an amazing feat: Be strong enough to stay intact for nine months under the pressure of the expanding uterus; be flexible enough to open fully at birth.
- Branching from the upper ends of the uterus are the **fallopian tubes.** These slim, pipe-like structures serve as conduits to the uterus.
- The feathery ends of the fallopian tubes surround the **ovaries,** the almond-shaped organs where the **ova,** the mother's egg cells, reside.

The Process of Fertilization

The pathway that results in **fertilization**—the union of sperm and egg—begins at **ovulation.** This is the moment, typically around day 14 of a woman's cycle, when a mature ovum erupts from the ovary wall. **Hormones**—chemical substances released into the bloodstream that target certain tissues and body processes and cause them to change—orchestrate the process of ovulation as well as the other events that program pregnancy.

At the moment of ovulation, the feathery ends of the fallopian tube, reacting to signals showing the site of the rupture, move to that location. As they suction the ovum in, the fallopian tube begins vigorous contractions that launch the ovum on its three-day journey toward the uterus.

Now the male's contribution to forming a new life arrives. In contrast to females, whose ova are all mainly formed at birth or early in life, the **testes**—the male structures comparable to the ovaries—are continually manufacturing sperm. An adult male typically produces several hundred million sperm a day. During sexual intercourse, these millions of cells, released at ejaculation, are expelled into the vagina,

cervix The neck, or narrow lower portion, of the uterus.

fallopian tube One of a pair of slim, pipe-like structures that connect the ovaries with the uterus.

ovary One of a pair of almond-shaped organs that contain a woman's ova, or eggs.

ovum An egg cell containing the genetic material contributed by the mother to the baby.

fertilization The union of sperm and egg.

ovulation The moment during a woman's monthly cycle when an ovum is expelled from the ovary.

hormones Chemical substances released in the bloodstream that target and change organs and tissues.

testes Male organs that manufacture sperm.

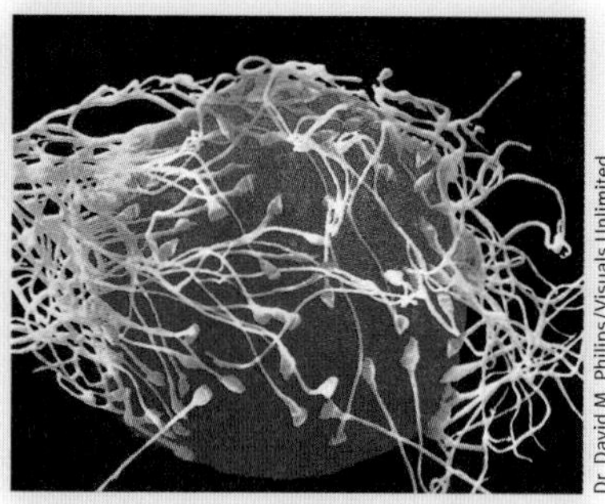

The sperm surround the ovum.

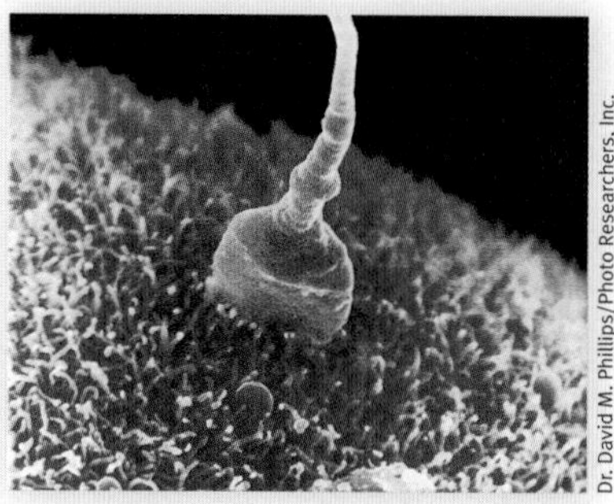

One sperm burrows in (notice the large head).

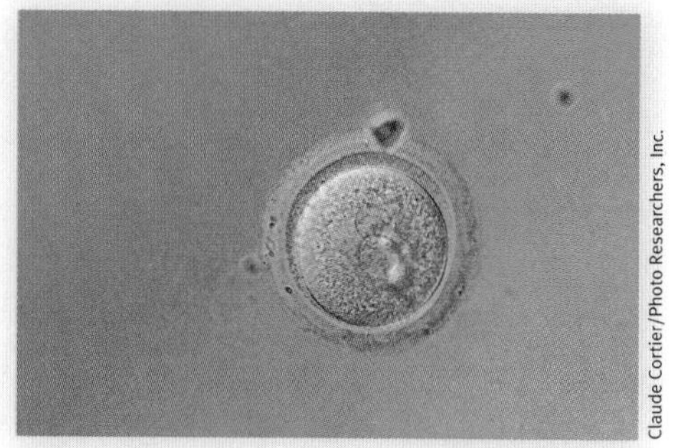

The nuclei of the two cells fuse. The watershed event called fertilization has occurred.

chromosome A threadlike strand of DNA located in the nucleus of every cell that carries the genes, which transmit hereditary information.

DNA (deoxyribonucleic acid) The material that makes up genes, which bear our hereditary characteristics.

gene A segment of DNA that contains a chemical blueprint for manufacturing a particular protein.

where a small proportion enter the body of the uterus and wend their way up the fallopian tubes.

To promote pregnancy, it's best to have intercourse right around ovulation. (Readers not interested in becoming pregnant, be forewarned: The hormones triggering ovulation are sensitive to erotic cues. So this event may occur in response to intense sexual arousal—at erratic times of the month.) The ovum is receptive for about 24 hours while in the tube's wide outer part. Sperm take a few hours to journey from the cervix to the tube. However, sperm can live almost a week in the recesses of the uterus and cervix, which means that intercourse several days prior to ovulation may also result in fertilization (Marieb, 2004).

Although the ovum emits chemical signals as to its location, the tiny tadpole-shaped travelers cannot easily locate the single cell or make the perilous journey upward into the tubes. So, of the estimated several hundred million sperm expelled at ejaculation, only 200 to 300 reach their destination, find their target, and begin to burrow in.

What happens now is a team assault. The sperm drill into the ovum, piercing its outer layers and penetrating through toward the center. Suddenly, one reaches the innermost part. Then the chemical composition of the ovum wall changes, shutting out the other sperm. The head of this sperm, containing its genetic blueprint, lies inside the nucleus of the ovum. The nuclei of the male and female cells move slowly together. When they meld into one cell, the landmark event called fertilization has occurred. What is taking place genetically when the sperm and egg combine?

The Genetics of Fertilization

The answer lies in looking at **chromosomes,** ropy structures composed of long ladder-like strands of the genetic material **DNA.** Arrayed along each chromosome are segments of DNA called **genes,** which function as the templates for creating the proteins responsible for carrying out all the physical processes of life (see Figure 2.2). Every cell in our body contains 46 chromosomes, with the exception of the sperm and ova, each of which has half this number, or 23. When the nuclei of these two cells, called *gametes,* combine at fertilization, their chromosomes align in pairs to again comprise 46. So nature has a marvelous mechanism to ensure that each new human life has an identical number of chromosomes and every new human being gets half of its genetic heritage from the parent of each sex.

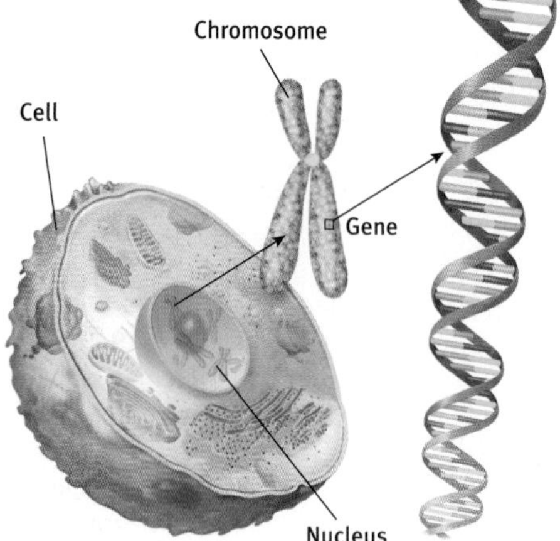

FIGURE 2.2: **The human building blocks:** The nucleus of every human cell contains chromosomes, each of which is made up of two strands of DNA connected in a double helix.

You can see the 46 paired chromosomes of a male in Figure 2.3. Notice that each chromosome pair (one member of which we get from our mother and one from our father) is a perfect match, with one exception—the sex chromosomes (X and Y). The X is far longer and heavier than the Y. Because each ovum carries

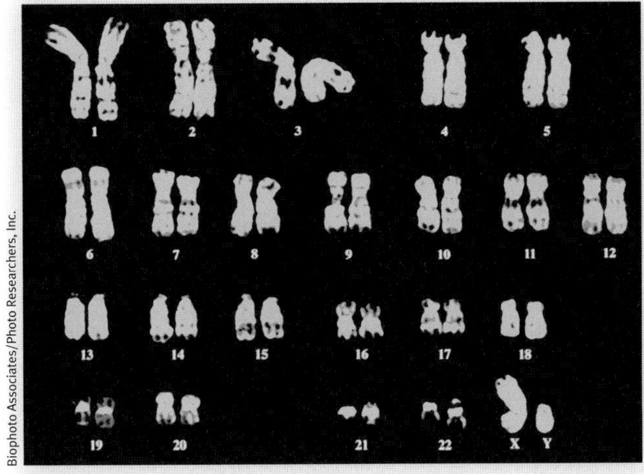

Biophoto Associates/Photo Researchers, Inc.

FIGURE 2.3: **A map of human chromosomes:** This magnified grid, called a karyotype, shows the 46 chromosomes in their matched pairs. The final pair, with its X and Y, shows that this person is a male. Also, notice the huge size of the X chromosome compared to the Y.

an X chromosome, our father's contribution to fertilization determines our sex. If a lighter, faster-swimming, Y-carrying sperm fertilizes the ovum, we get a boy (XY). If the victor is a more resilient, slower-moving X, we get a girl (XX).

In the race to fertilization, the Y's are statistically more successful; scientists estimate that 20 percent more male than female babies are conceived. But the prenatal period is particularly hard on developing males. If a family member learns that she is pregnant, the odds still favor her having a boy; but because more males die in the uterus, only 5 percent more boys than girls make it to birth (Werth, 2002). And throughout life, males continue to be the less hardy sex, dying off at higher rates at every age. Recall from our discussion in Chapter 1 that, throughout the developed world, women outlive men by at least four years.

TYING IT ALL TOGETHER

1. Match the following terms to the correct items: uterus, fallopian tubes, cervix, and ovaries.
   a. uterine neck; opens during labor to allow the baby to emerge
   b. slim pipeline conduit from ovaries to the uterus
   c. "expandable" structure housing the developing baby
   d. pea-shaped organs containing the ova (egg cells)
2. What is the parallel structure to the ovary in the male reproductive system?
3. Tiffany feels certain that if she has intercourse at the right time, she will get pregnant—but asks you, "What is the right time?" Give Tiffany your answer carefully, referring to the text discussion, and then tell her the chain of events that leads from ovulation to fertilization.
4. If your aunt is pregnant, statistically speaking, she is more likely to have a *girl/boy*, and your *aunt/ uncle* is responsible for the child's sex.

Answers to the Tying It All Together questions can be found at the end of this chapter.

Prenatal Development

Now that we have an overview of the starting point, let's chart prenatal development, tracing how the microscopic, fertilized ovum divides millions of times and differentiates into a living child. This miraculous transformation takes place in three distinct stages.

First Two Weeks: The Germinal Stage

The first approximately two weeks after fertilization—the time when the cell mass has not yet fully attached to the wall of the uterus—is called the **germinal stage**

germinal stage The first 14 days of prenatal development, from fertilization to full implantation.

FIGURE 2.4: **The events of the germinal stage:** The fertilized ovum divides on its trip to the uterus, then becomes a hollow ball called a blastocyst, and finally fully implants in the wall of the uterus at about 14 days after fertilization.

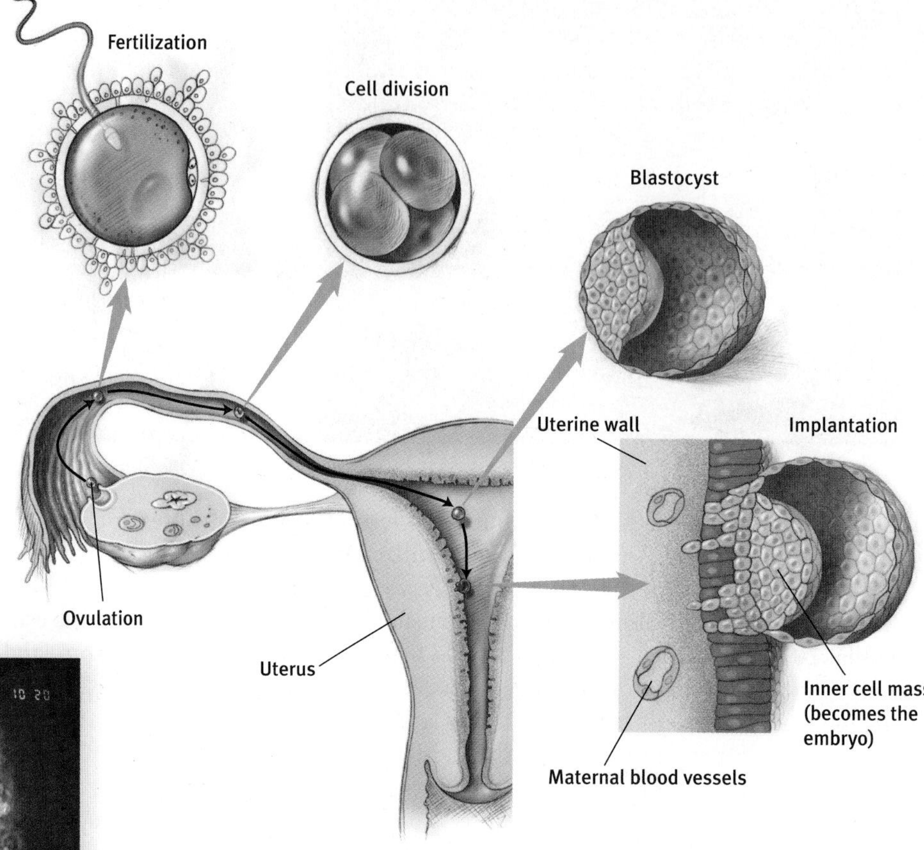

Andy Walker/Midland Fertility Services/Photo Researchers, Inc.

This is a photo of the blastocyst, the roughly 100-cell ball, soon to attach itself to the uterine wall. When implantation occurs, this event will signal the end of the germinal phase.

(see Figure 2.4 above). Within 36 hours, the fertilized ovum, now a single cell called the **zygote,** makes its first cell division. Then the tiny cluster of cells continues to divide every 12 to 15 hours as it wends its way on a roughly three-day trip down the fallopian tube. When the mass of cells passes into the uterine cavity, it sheds its outer wall and differentiates into layers—some destined to form the pregnancy support structures, others to comprise the cells of the child-to-be. Now called a **blastocyst,** this ball of roughly 100 cells faces its next vital challenge. This is **implantation**—the process of embedding into the uterine wall.

The blastocyst seeks a landing site on an upper section of the uterus. Meanwhile, hormones have prepared the uterus to receive the cell mass. The outer layer of the blastocyst develops projections. At about day 9, these tentacles burrow in. From this landing zone, blood vessels proliferate that will make up the **placenta,** the lifeline that passes nutrients from the mother's system to the developing baby. After implantation, the next stage of prenatal development begins. This is the all-important embryonic phase.

zygote A fertilized ovum.

blastocyst The hollow sphere of cells formed during the germinal stage in preparation for implantation.

implantation The process in which a blastocyst becomes embedded in the uterine wall.

placenta The structure projecting from the wall of the uterus during pregnancy through which the developing baby absorbs nutrients.

embryonic stage The second stage of prenatal development, lasting from week 3 through week 8.

Week 3 to Week 8: The Embryonic Stage

Although the **embryonic stage** lasts roughly only six weeks, it is the most fast-paced period of development. During this brief time, all the major organs are constructed. By the end of the embryonic stage, what began as an ill-defined clump of cells looks like a recognizable human being!

One early task after implantation is to form the mechanism that makes all future development possible. After the baby is hooked up to the maternal bloodstream—which will nourish the fetus as it grows—nutrients must be pumped to the rapidly differentiating cells. So by the third week after fertilization, the circulatory system (our body's transport system) forms, and its pump, the heart, starts to beat.

At around the same time, the rudiments of the nervous system appear. Between 20 and 24 days after fertilization, an indentation forms along the back of the embryo and closes up to form the **neural tube** (see Figure 2.5). The uppermost part of this cylindrical structure will become the brain. Its lower part will form the spinal cord. Although scientists now know we can "grow" new brain cells throughout life, almost all of those remarkable branching structures, called **neurons,** which cause us to think, to respond, and to process information, originated in cells formed in the neural tube during our first months in the womb.

Meanwhile, the body is developing at an astounding rate. At day 26, arm buds form; by day 28, swellings erupt where the legs will form. At day 37, rudimentary feet start to develop. By day 41, elbows, wrist curves, and the precursors of fingers can be seen. Several days later, ray-like structures that will turn into toes emerge. By about week 8, the embryo is only about the length of a thumb, but its internal organs are all in place. What started out looking like a curved stalk, then a strange outer-space alien, now appears like a distinctly *human* being.

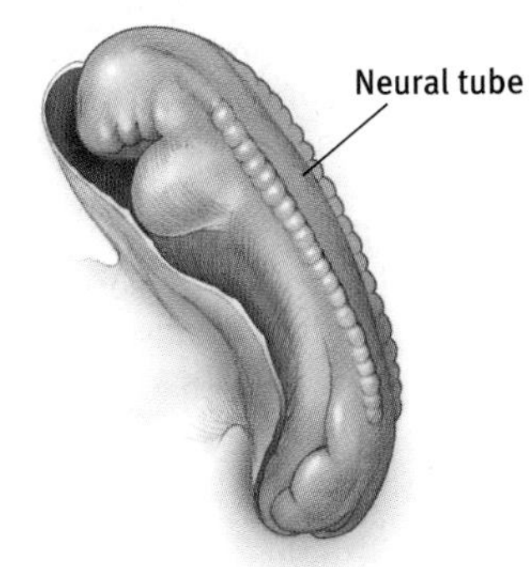

FIGURE 2.5: **The neural tube:** This structure is one of the first to form after implantation. The brain and spinal cord will develop from it.

Principles of Prenatal Development

Imagine that you wanted to spell out some guiding principles related to the sequence of development just described. In looking at the photographs of the developing embryo on this page, can you identify three basic patterns that underlie this rapid transformation to a fully formed human being?

- You might notice that from a core cylindrical shape, the arms and legs grow outward and then (not unexpectedly) the fingers and toes protrude. So the first principle is that growth follows the **proximodistal sequence,** from the most interior (proximal) part of the body to the outer (distal) sides.
- You might also notice that from the initial swelling that makes the embryo look mainly like a mammoth head, the arms emerge and the legs sprout. So development takes place according to the **cephalocaudal sequence,** meaning from top (*cephalo* = head) to bottom (*caudal* = tail).
- Finally, just as in constructing a sculpture, development begins with the basic building blocks and then fills in details. A head is formed before eyes and ears are carved; legs are constructed before feet and toes are chiseled. So the **mass-to-specific sequence,** or gross (large, simple) structures before smaller (complex) refinements, is the third basic principle of body growth.

neural tube A cylindrical structure that forms along the back of the embryo and develops into the brain and spinal cord.

neuron A nerve cell.

proximodistal sequence The developmental principle that growth occurs from the most interior parts of the body outward.

cephalocaudal sequence The developmental principle that growth occurs in a sequence from head to toe.

mass-to-specific sequence The developmental principle that large structures (and movements) precede increasingly detailed refinements.

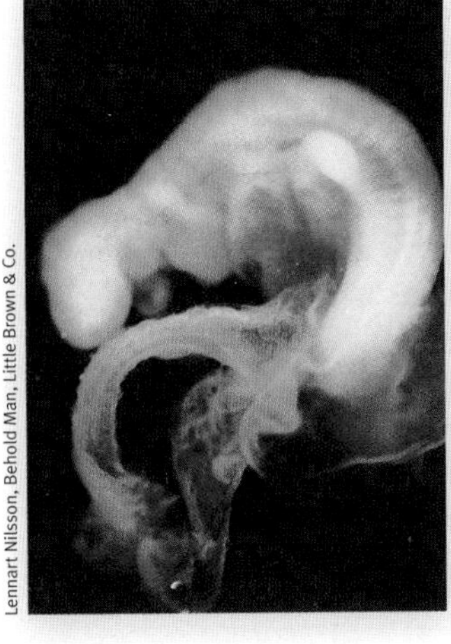

At about week 3, the embryo (the upside-down U across the top) looks like a curved stalk.

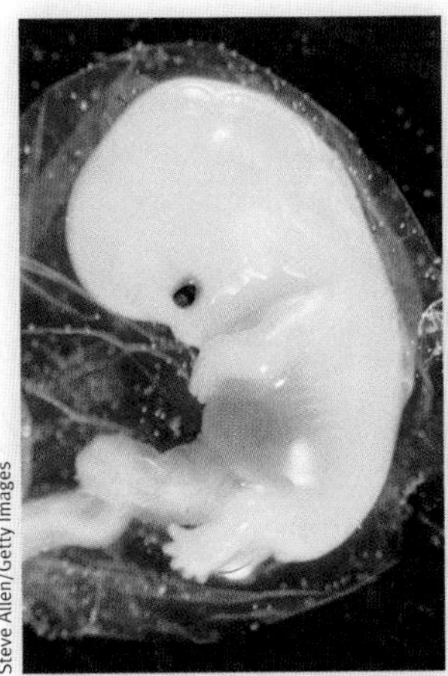

At week 4, you can see the indentations for eyes and the arms and legs beginning to sprout.

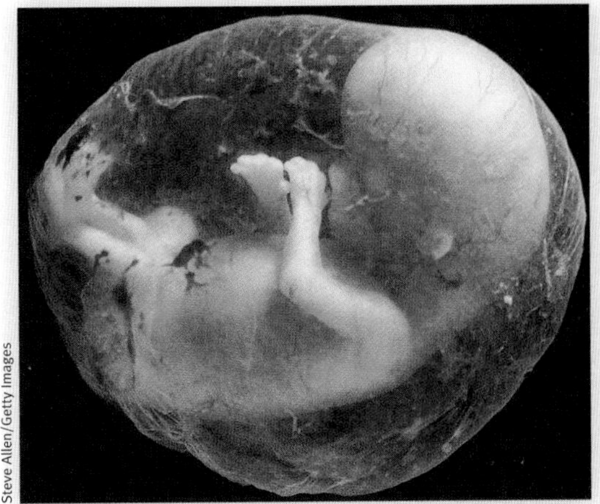

At week 9, the baby-to-be has fingers, toes, and ears. All the major organs have developed and the fetal stage has begun!

fetal stage The final period of prenatal development, lasting seven months, characterized by physical refinements, massive growth, and the development of the brain.

age of viability The earliest point at which a baby can survive outside the womb.

Keep these principles in mind. As you will see when I discuss physical development in infancy and childhood, the same patterns apply to growth and to our unfolding motor abilities *after* the baby leaves the womb.

Week 9 to Birth: The Fetal Stage

During the embryonic stage, basic body structures sprout almost daily. In the final period of prenatal growth—the **fetal stage**—development occurs at a more leisurely pace. From the eyebrows, fingernails, and hair follicles that develop from weeks 9 to 12 to the cushion of fat that accumulates during the final weeks before birth, it takes a full seven months to transform the fully formed embryo into a resilient baby ready to embrace life.

Why does our species need this prolonged period of refining that lasts for so many months? One reason is to allow time for the neurons composing that masterpiece organ—the human brain—to move into place. Let's now look at this crucial process of making a brain.

During the late embryonic stage, a mass of cells begins to form within the neural tube that will eventually produce the more than 100 billion neurons that compose our brain (Stiles & Jernigan, 2010). From this zone, the new neurons begin to migrate to a region just under the top of the differentiating tube. This phase of cell formation and migration, diagrammed in Figure 2.6, concludes when the neurons assemble in their "staging area" by the middle of the fetal period. Then, they assume their mature form. The cells lengthen and develop characteristic branches. They start to interlink. This process of interconnecting—responsible for every human thought and action—will continue until almost our final day of life.

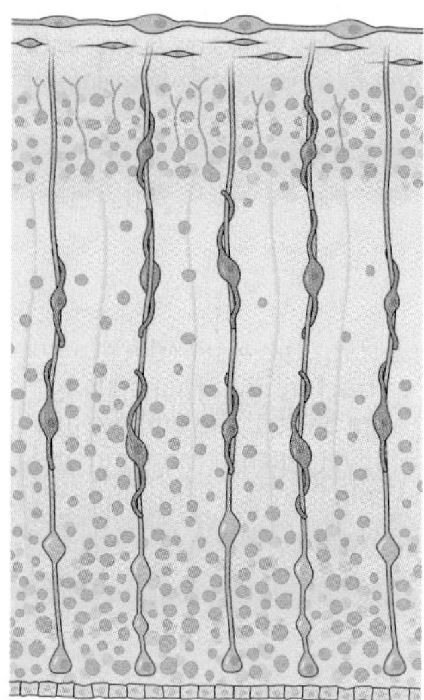

FIGURE 2.6: **Forming a brain: climbing neurons:** During the earlier part of the fetal period, the neurons destined to make up the brain ascend these ladder-like filaments to reach the uppermost part of what had been the neural tube.
Source: Huttenlocher, 2002.

Figure 2.7 shows the mushrooming brain. Notice that the brain almost doubles in size from month 4 to month 7. By now, the brain has already assumed the wrinkled structure of an adult.

This massive growth has a profound effect. At around month 6, the fetus can hear (Crade & Lovett, 1988). By month 7, should there be sufficient light, the fetus is probably able to see (Del Giudice, 2011). And by this time, with high-quality medical care, babies that are born typically survive. Today, the **age of viability**, or earliest date at which babies *possibly* can live, has dropped to a remarkable 22 to 23 weeks—almost halving the 38 weeks the fetus would normally spend in the womb. By week 25, the odds of survival are more than fifty-fifty, provided a baby is born in the affluent, developed word (Lawn and others, 2011).

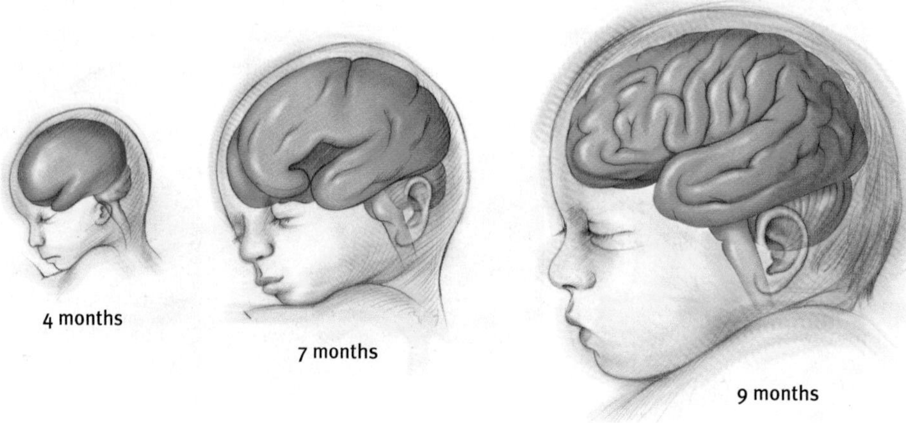

FIGURE 2.7: **The expanding brain:** The brain grows dramatically month by month during the fetal period. During the final months, it develops its characteristic folds.

However, it is *vitally* important that the fetus stay in the uterus as long as possible. As I will describe in depth later, being born too early (and too small) makes a tremendous difference in terms of health. During the last two months alone the fetus gains almost five pounds.

Figure 2.8 shows the fetus during the final month of pregnancy, when its prenatal nest becomes cramped and birth is looming on the horizon. Notice the support structures the baby requires: the placenta, projecting from the uterine wall, which supplies nutrients from the mother to the fetus; the **umbilical cord,** protruding from what will be the baby's bellybutton, the conduit through which nutrients flow; the **amniotic sac,** the fluid-filled chamber within which the baby floats. This tough, encasing membrane provides insulation from infection and harm.

At this stage of prenatal development, first-time mothers and fathers may be running around, buying the crib or shopping for baby clothes. In affluent countries, middle-class women may be marveling at the items their precious son or daughter "must have": a pacifier, a receiving blanket, a bassinet . . . and what else! Parents-to-be are anxiously focused on that upcoming event: birth. What is happening during *all* nine months from the mother's—and father's—point of view?

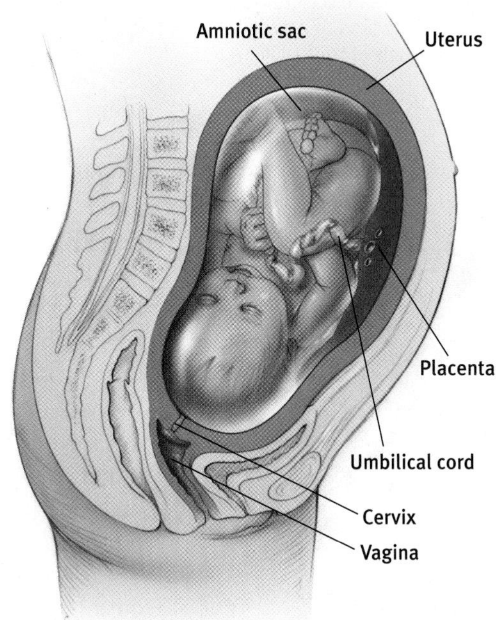

FIGURE 2.8: **Poised to be born:** This diagram shows the fetus inside the woman's uterus late in pregnancy. Notice the placenta, amniotic sac, and umbilical cord.

TYING IT ALL TOGETHER

1. Rapid organ formation; neural migration to the top of the brain; the blastocyst: Match each term or process to the appropriate prenatal stage.
   a. embryonic, fetal, germinal
   b. germinal, fetal, embryonic
   c. fetal, germinal, embryonic
   d. germinal, fetal, embryonic
2. A pregnant friend asks you, "How does my baby's brain develop?" Describe the process of neural migration—when it occurs, and when it is complete.
3. Give a concrete example of (a) the cephalocaudal sequence, (b) the proximodistal sequence, and (c) the mass-to-specific sequence.

Answers to the Tying It All Together questions can be found at the end of this chapter.

Pregnancy

The 266- to 277-day **gestation** period (or pregnancy) is divided into three segments. These phases, called **trimesters,** comprise roughly three months each. (Because it is difficult to know exactly when fertilization occurs, health-care professionals date the duration of pregnancy from the woman's last menstrual period.)

Pregnancy differs, however, from the carefully patterned process of prenatal development. Although there are some classic symptoms, there is no universal pregnancy experience at all.

To bring this point home, ask a few mothers to describe their pregnancies. One person might complain about being violently ill for nine months; another might feel physically better than ever. Some women adore looking pregnant and joyously look forward to the baby; others despise their bodies and feel demoralized and depressed.

Scanning the Trimesters

With the strong caution that variability—from person to person (and child to child)—is the norm, let's now offer a trimester-by-trimester overview of what pregnancy *can* be like.

umbilical cord The structure that attaches the placenta to the fetus, through which nutrients are passed and fetal wastes are removed.

amniotic sac A bag-shaped, fluid-filled membrane that contains and insulates the fetus.

gestation The period of pregnancy.

trimester One of the 3-month-long segments into which pregnancy is divided.

miscarriage The naturally occurring loss of a pregnancy and death of the fetus.

First Trimester: Often Feeling Tired and Ill

After the blastocyst implants in the uterus—a few days before the woman first misses her period—pregnancy often signals its presence through some unpleasant symptoms. Many women feel faint. (Yes, fainting can be an early sign of pregnancy!) They may get headaches or have to urinate frequently. Like Kim in the introductory chapter vignette, they may feel incredibly tired. Their breasts become tender, painful to the touch. So, many women do not need that definite tip-off—a missed menstrual period—to realize they are carrying a child.

The trigger for these varied symptoms is a flood of hormones. After implantation, the production of *progesterone* (literally *pro*, or "for," *gestation*)—the hormone responsible for maintaining the pregnancy—surges. The placenta produces its own unique hormone, *human chorionic gonadotropin (HCG)*, thought to prevent the woman's body from rejecting the "foreign" embryo.

Given this hormonal onslaught, the massive body changes, and the fact that the blood supply is being diverted to the uterus, the tiredness, dizziness, and headaches make perfect sense. What about that other classic symptom of early pregnancy—morning sickness?

Morning sickness—waves of nausea and sometimes vomiting—affects at least two out of every three women during the first trimester (Beckmann and others, 2002). This well-known symptom is not confined to the morning. Many women feel queasy on and off all day. A few get so ill that they cannot keep any food down. And men sometimes develop morning sickness along with their wives! This phenomenon, which occurs around the world, has its own name: *couvade* (Munroe, 2010).

But morning sickness seems senseless: Doesn't the embryo need all the nourishment it can get? Why, during the first months of pregnancy, might it be adaptive for women to feel revolted by particular foods?

Consider these clues: The queasiness is at its height during the period of intense organ formation, and, like magic, one day toward the end of the first trimester, usually (but not always) disappears. Munching on bread products is helpful. Strong odors also make many women gag. Evolutionary psychologists theorize that, in the days before refrigeration, morning sickness may have evolved to prevent the mother from eating spoiled meat or toxic plants, which could be especially dangerous to the baby while its basic body structures were being formed (Bjorklund & Pellegrini, 2002).

In support of this theory, crackers—the traditional treatment for morning sickness—do not spoil. To alleviate mothers' distress, health-care workers advise eating more frequently and consuming smaller (less potentially toxic) quantities of food. If you have a friend who is struggling with morning sickness, you can give her this heartening information: Some research suggests that women with morning sickness are more likely to carry their babies to term.

This brings up the topic of pregnancy anxieties. Why are some women reluctant to announce the news until after three months have elapsed? The reason is that during the first trimester, roughly 1 in 10 pregnancies ends in **miscarriage** (fetal death). For women in their late thirties, the chance of miscarrying during the first 12 weeks escalates to roughly 1 in 5. Many miscarriages are inevitable. They are caused by genetic problems in the developing embryo that are incompatible with life.

Second Trimester: Feeling Much Better and Connecting Emotionally

Another reason that the first months of pregnancy have a tentative quality is that mothers-to-be still don't feel the baby inside. But during the second trimester, the fetus makes its presence physically known.

By week 14, the uterus dramatically grows, often creating a need to shop for maternity clothes. The wider world may notice the woman's expanding body: "Are you pregnant?" "How wonderful!" "Take my seat."

Around week 18, an event called **quickening**—a sensation like bubbles that signals the baby kicking in the womb—appears. The woman feels viscerally connected to a growing human being:

quickening A pregnant woman's first feeling of the fetus moving inside her body.

> When I felt him move, I found myself fantasizing about this new person, visualizing what he would look like—seeing him growing up, getting married, becoming a wonderful person. That's when the magic really kicked in.

This mystical sense of connection varies from woman to woman. Some mothers-to-be are intensely bonded to their babies from the minute they learn they are pregnant. For many, however, the sense of being totally attached intensifies during the second trimester when they experience some watershed event such as feeling the baby move (Paul, 2010; Righetti and others, 2005). Whenever it happens, this feeling is vital. Although attachment can blossom at any point, feeling intensely connected to one's baby during pregnancy predicts being a sensitive, attuned mother after the child enters the world (Salisbury, 2003).

Another landmark event that alters the emotional experience of pregnancy occurs during the beginning of the third trimester, when the woman can actually give birth to a living child. This important late-pregnancy marker explains why some societies build in celebrations at month 6 or 7 to welcome the baby to the human community.

Third Trimester: Getting Very Large and Waiting for Birth

Look at a pregnant woman struggling up the stairs and you'll get a sense of her feelings during this final trimester: backaches (think of carrying a bowling ball); leg cramps; numbness and tingling as the uterus presses against the nerves of the lower limbs; heartburn, insomnia, and anxious anticipation as focus shifts to the birth ("When will this baby arrive?!"); uterine contractions occurring irregularly as the baby sinks into the birth canal and delivery draws very near.

Although women often do work up to the day of delivery, health-care workers advise taking time off to rest and relying on caring loved ones to help cook and clean during the final months. Actually, having caring loved ones is vital during all nine months!

Pregnancy Is Not a Solo Act

> I don't know what it's like for you and your partner to hear the baby's heartbeat, or see the ultrasound together, or feel the first kick. I lived through nine months of pregnancy by myself. No one understood how lonely I felt. I thought this was supposed to be the happiest time of your life. I found myself losing weight instead of gaining and being depressed most of the time.

> When I told my husband I was pregnant, he got furious, said he couldn't afford the baby and moved out. So now what do I do—I've been laid off from my job; I feel all alone. I'm frightened about how I can cope.

Robin Sachs/Photo Edit

Imagine what this woman is feeling while watching her husband paint the newborn's nursery during her final months of pregnancy. "Not only is my spouse a full partner in building our family nest, he is physically showing me his love."

As these quotations reveal, pregnancy has a very different emotional flavor depending on the wider world. What forces turn this joyous time of life into nine months of distress?

One influence, as suggested above, lies in economic concerns. Studies routinely show that low socioeconomic status puts pregnant women at risk of feeling demoralized and depressed (see, for example, Abdou and others, 2010). Imagine coping with the stresses associated with being poor—worrying about making ends meet, perhaps not getting adequate prenatal care—and you will understand why pregnancy is more likely to be one of life's great joys when an expectant mother is comfortably middle class.

Because she is being cherished and pampered by a huge loving family, this single mom is likely to find the pregnancy journey very fulfilling.

The main force, however, that predicts having a joyous pregnancy applies to both affluent and economically deprived women alike—feeling loved by one's mate (Rahman, Iqbal, & Harrington, 2003; Savage and others, 2007). In fact, in tracking pregnant Hispanic women, researchers found that the presence of a loving partner helped stave off postpartum depression even if a mother-to-be had suffered from depression before entering the pregnant state (Diaz and others, 2007).

Does this mean going through pregnancy without a partner is a terrible thing? The answer is no. What matters is whether a woman feels *generally* cared about and loved. When researchers gave pregnant women a questionnaire measuring what they called a "communal cultural orientation" ("Do you have nurturing family relationships? Can you reach out to friends when you need support?"), they found that this sense of connectedness was the most important predictor of emotional health. It *totally* compensated for the stresses associated with being poor (Abdou and others, 2010). Listen to this comment of an impoverished single woman whom researchers ranked as "thriving" during this time of life: "We've always been a close-knit family, and they were there to get me through.... They called me every night to make sure I was eating right" (Savage and others, 2007, p. 219).

Suppose, like the woman quoted at beginning of this section, you were married, but your spouse was hostile to your pregnancy. Wouldn't you rather be going through this journey with a loving family or good friends?

What About Dads?

This brings up the emotions of the standard partner in the pregnancy journey: dads. Given the attention we lavish on pregnant women, it should come as no surprise that fathers have been relatively ignored in the research exploring this transition of life. But fathers are also bonded to their babies-to-be. They can feel just as devastated when a pregnancy doesn't work out. Here are some comments about miscarriage from the male point of view:

Richard anguished,

> I keep thinking that my wife is still pregnant. Where is my little girl? I was so ready to spoil her and treat her like a princess...but now she is gone. I don't think I'll ever be the same again.
>
> (quoted in Jaffe & Diamond, 2011, p. 218)

And another grieving dad reported,

> I had to be strong for Kate. I had to let her cry on me and then I would . . drive up into the hills and cry to myself. I was trying to support her even though I felt my whole life had just caved in, you know, my whole life just ended then and there.
>
> (quoted in McCreight, 2004, p. 337)

As you saw in the quotation above, in coping with this trauma, men have a double burden. They may feel compelled to put aside their feelings to focus on their bereft wives (Jaffe & Diamond, 2011; Rinehart & Kiselica, 2010). Plus, because the loss of a baby is typically seen as a "woman's issue," the wider world tends to marginalize their pain. (One man in an interview study angrily reported having friends who called to ask: "How is your wife doing?" [McCreight, 2004].) These examples remind us that husbands are "pregnant" in spirit along with their wives. We should *never* thrust their feelings aside.

Is pregnancy normally a stressful time for men? While depression rates among new fathers are comparatively low (about 4 to 10 percent), these statistics slightly exceed the overall percentages for U.S. men (Paulson & Bazemore, 2010). Anxiety should be common, too (Dallos & Nokes, 2011). Put yourself in the place of a father-to-be. Perhaps you wonder: "Will the child take away from my relationship with my wife?" "Can I be an involved father and support the family?" "Will I be able to handle these two demanding roles?"

birth defect A physical or neurological problem that occurs prenatally or at birth.

Men usually don't have the safety valve of discussing their worries with friends and family. As you saw in the earlier discussion, our culture expects them to be strong on their own.

So, by returning to the beginning of the chapter, we now know that the widespread cultural practice of pampering pregnant women makes excellent psychological sense—for both the mother *and* her child. But we also need to realize that expectant fathers need cherishing, too!

Table 2.1 summarizes these points in a brief "stress during pregnancy" questionnaire. Now, let's return to the baby and tackle that common fear: "Will my child be healthy?"

TABLE 2.1: **Measuring Stress in Mothers-to-Be: A Short Section Summary Questionnaire**

1. Does this woman have serious financial troubles, or is she living in poverty?
2. Is this woman having marital problems, and does her husband want this baby?
3. Is the woman a single mother? If so, does she have a supportive network of friends and family?
4. If the woman is living in poverty, does she feel connected to others in loving, positive ways?

TYING IT ALL TOGETHER

1. Your friend Samantha just learned she is pregnant. Describe how she is likely to feel during each trimester.
2. You are interviewing a pregnant low-income, unmarried woman for a paper. What *single* question might best predict her emotional state?
3. As a clinic director, you are concerned that men are often left out of the pregnancy experience. Design a few innovative interventions to make your clinic responsive to the needs of fathers-to-be.

Answers to the Tying It All Together questions can be found at the end of this chapter.

Threats to the Developing Baby

In this section, we'll explore the prenatal reasons for **birth defects**, or health problems at birth. I'll also discuss exciting new research exploring how wider-world events while "in the womb" can potentially affect a fetus's lifelong health. In reading this catalogue of "things that can go wrong," keep these thoughts in mind: The vast majority of babies are born healthy. Only 4 percent have a genuine birth defect. Although the conditions described below do compromise health, many birth defects don't impair a baby's ability to have a rich, fulfilling life. Often birth defects result from a complex nature-plus-nurture interaction. Fetal genetic vulnerabilities combine with environmental hazards in the womb. However, in this section, we separate potential problems into two categories: toxins that flow through the placenta to impair development and genetic diseases.

Threats from Outside: Teratogens

The universal fears about the growing baby are expressed in mountains of cultural prohibitions: "Don't use scissors or your baby will have cut lips" (a cleft palate)

teratogen A substance that crosses the placenta and harms the fetus.

sensitive period The time when a body structure is most vulnerable to damage by a teratogen, typically when that organ or process is rapidly developing or coming "on line."

developmental disorders Learning impairments and behavioral problems during infancy and childhood.

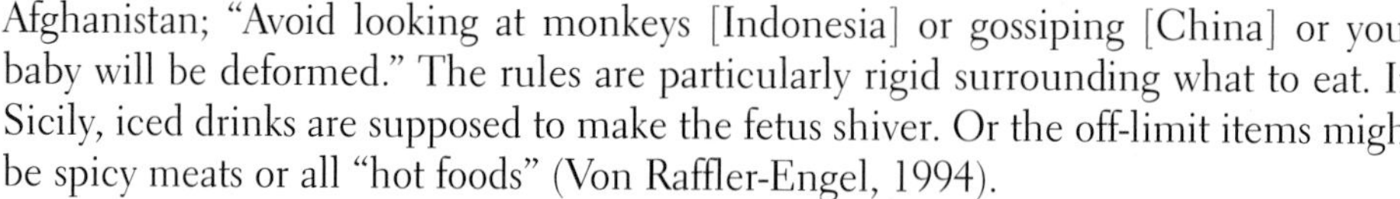

Afghanistan; "Avoid looking at monkeys [Indonesia] or gossiping [China] or your baby will be deformed." The rules are particularly rigid surrounding what to eat. In Sicily, iced drinks are supposed to make the fetus shiver. Or the off-limit items might be spicy meats or all "hot foods" (Von Raffler-Engel, 1994).

If you think these practices are strange, consider the standard mid-twentieth-century medical advice. Physicians put women in the United States on a strict diet if they gained over 15 pounds. They encouraged mothers-to-be to smoke and drink to relax and routinely prescribed medications to combat nausea, especially during the first trimester (Von Raffler-Engel, 1994; Wertz & Wertz, 1989). Today, these medical pronouncements might qualify as fetal abuse! What *can* hurt the developing baby? When during prenatal development is damage most apt to occur?

A **teratogen** (from the Greek word *teras*, "monster," and *gen*, "creating") is the name for any substance that crosses the placenta to harm the fetus. A teratogen may be an infectious disease; a medication; a recreational drug; environmental hazards, such as radiation or pollution; or the hormones produced by a pregnant woman who is under extreme stress. Table 2.2 describes potential teratogens in these categories.

Basic Teratogenic Principles

Teratogens typically exert their damage during the **sensitive period**—the timeframe when a particular organ or system is coming "on line." For example, the infectious disease called rubella (German measles) often damaged a baby's heart or ears, depending on the week during the first trimester when a mother contracted the disease. The sedative Thalidomide, prescribed in Europe during the late 1950s to prevent morning sickness, impaired limb formation, depending on which day after fertilization the drug was imbibed. In general, with regard to teratogens, the following principles apply:

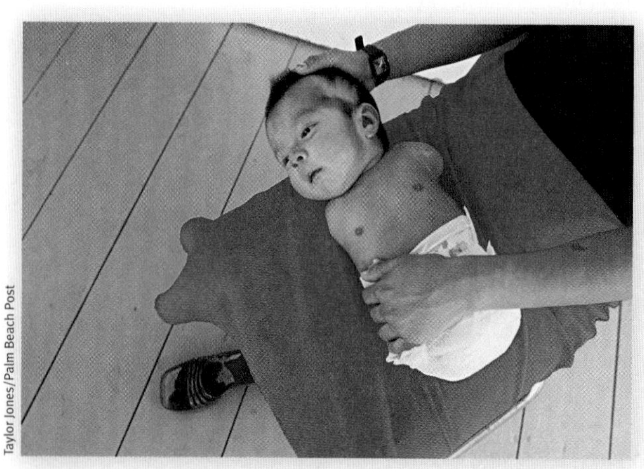

Taylor Jones/Palm Beach Post

This Honduran baby is a testament to the horrible damage teratogens can potentially cause during the embryonic period, as his condition was believed to be due to his mother's exposure to pesticides during early pregnancy.

1. **Teratogens are most likely to cause major structural damage during the embryonic stage.** Before implantation, teratogens have an all-or-nothing impact. They either inhibit implantation and cause death, or they leave the not-yet-attached blastocyst unscathed. It is during the time of organ formation (after implantation through week 8) that major body structures are most likely to be affected. This is why—unless expectant mothers have a chronic disease that demands they continue this practice—physicians advise women not to take any medications during the first trimester (American Academy of Pediatrics [AAP], Committee on Drugs, 2000).

2. **Teratogens can affect the developing brain throughout pregnancy.** As you saw earlier, because the brain is forming well into the second and third trimesters, the potential for neurological damage extends for all nine months. Japanese fetuses exposed during the second trimester to that incredibly severe teratogen, radiation from the World War II atomic bomb, were born with microcephaly (a small brain) and severe mental retardation (Huttenlocher, 2002). Typically, however, during the second and third trimesters, exposure to teratogens increases the risk of **developmental disorders.** This term refers to any condition that compromises normal development—from delays in reaching basic milestones, such as walking or talking, to serious learning problems and hyperactivity.

3. **Teratogens operate in a dose-response fashion.** With toxic substances, there is often a threshold level above which damage occurs. For instance, women who drink more than four cups of coffee a day throughout pregnancy have a slightly

TABLE 2.2: Examples of Known Teratogens and the Damage They Can Do

Teratogen	Consequences of Exposure
INFECTIOUS DISEASES	
Rubella (German measles)	If a pregnant woman contracts rubella during the embryonic stage, the consequence is, not infrequently, mental retardation, blindness, or eye, ear, and heart abnormalities in the baby—depending on the week the virus enters the bloodstream. Luckily, women of childbearing age are now routinely immunized for this otherwise minor adult disease.
Cytomegalovirus	About 25% of babies infected with this virus develop vision or hearing loss; 10% develop neurological problems.
AIDS	HIV-infected women can transmit the virus to their babies prenatally through the placenta, during delivery (when blood is exchanged between the mother and child), or after birth (through breast milk). Rates of transmission are much lower if infected mothers take the anti-AIDS drug AZT or if newborns are given a new drug that blocks the transmission of HIV at birth. If a mother takes these precautions, does not breast-feed, and delivers her baby by c-section, the infection rate falls to less than 1%. While mother-to-child transmission of HIV has declined dramatically in the developed world, it remains a devastating problem in sub-Saharan Africa and other impoverished regions of the globe (AVERT, 2005).
Herpes	This familiar sexually transmitted disease can cause miscarriage, growth retardation, and eye abnormalities in affected fetuses. Doctors recommend that pregnant women with active genital herpes undergo c-sections to avoid infecting their babies during delivery.
Toxoplasmosis	This disease, caused by a parasite found in raw meat and cat feces, can lead to blindness, deafness, and mental retardation in infants. Pregnant women should avoid handling raw meat and cat litter.
MEDICATIONS	
Antibiotics	Streptomycin has been linked to hearing loss; tetracycline to stained infant tooth enamel.
Thalidomide	This drug, prescribed in the late 1950s in Europe to prevent nausea during the first trimester, prevented the baby's arms and legs from developing if taken during the embryonic period.
Anti-seizure drugs	These medications have been linked to developmental delays during infancy.
Anti-psychotic drugs	These drugs may slightly raise the risk of giving birth to a baby with heart problems.
Antidepressants	Although typically safe, third-trimester exposure to selective serotonin reuptake inhibitors and tricyclic antidepressants has been linked to temporary jitteriness and excessive crying and to eating and sleeping difficulties in newborns. Rarely, these drugs can produce a serious syndrome involving seizures and dehydration, as well as higher rates of miscarriage.
RECREATIONAL DRUGS	
Cocaine	This drug is linked to miscarriage, growth retardation, and learning and behavior problems.
Methamphetamines	This drug may cause miscarriage and growth retardation.
ENVIRONMENTAL TOXINS	
Radiation	Japanese children exposed to radiation from the atomic bomb during the second trimester had extremely high rates of severe mental retardation. Miscarriages were virtually universal among pregnant women living within 5 miles of the blast. Pregnant women are also advised to avoid clinical doses of radiation such as those used in X-rays (and especially cancer treatment radiation).
Lead	Babies with high levels of lead in the umbilical cord may show impairments in cognitive functioning (Bellinger and others, 1987). Maternal exposure to lead is associated with miscarriage.
Mercury and PCBs	These pollutants are linked to learning and behavior problems.
STRESS	A vast array of studies suggest severe stress during pregnancy is linked to miscarriage, premature delivery, and learning and behavior problems—as well as possibly having long-term effects on adult health (see page 54 of text). But moderate stress during the second and third trimesters may accelerate prenatal growth and so promote *better* health at birth.
VITAMIN DEFICIENCIES	In addition to eating a balanced diet, every woman of childbearing age should take folic acid supplements. This vitamin, part of the B complex, protects against the incomplete closure of the neural tube during the first month of development—an event that may produce *spina bifida* (paralysis in the body below the region of the spine that has not completely closed) or *anencephaly* (failure of the brain to develop—and certain death) if the gap occurs toward the top of the developing tube.

General sources: Huttenlocher, 2002, and the references in this chapter. *Sources specifically correlating stress with child problems*: Bergman and others, 2010; Bregnab and others, 2010; Buss and others, 2010; Charil, and others, 2010; Davis & Sandman, 2010; Douglas, 2010; Figueiredo and others, 2010; Rice and others, 2010; and Schetter, 2011.

higher risk of miscarriage; but having an occasional Diet Coke is perfectly fine (Gilbert-Barness, 2000).

4. **Teratogens exert their damage unpredictably, depending on fetal and maternal vulnerabilities.** Still, mothers-to-be metabolize potential toxins differently, and babies differ genetically in susceptibility. So the damaging effects of a particular toxin can vary. On the plus side, you may know a child in your local school's gifted program whose mother drank heavily during pregnancy. On the negative side, we do not know where the teratogenic threshold lies in any particular case. Therefore, during pregnancy, erring on the side of caution is best.

Although the damaging impact of a teratogen can show up during infancy, not infrequently it manifests itself years later in learning difficulties during school or during the adult years. An unfortunate example of this teratogenic time bomb took place in my own life. My mother was given a drug called diethylstilbestrol (DES) while she was pregnant with me. (DES was routinely prescribed in the 1950s and 1960s to prevent miscarriage.) During my early twenties, I developed cancerous cells in my cervix—and, after surgery, had three miscarriages before ultimately being blessed by adopting my son.

The Teratogenic Impact of Medicines and Recreational Drugs

The fact that some medications are potentially teratogenic presents dilemmas for women. Do you cut down on your anti-epilepsy drugs and risk having a seizure that could hurt the baby because your normal dose is linked to infant developmental delays? (Thomas and others, 2008.) Or, suppose you are among the millions of women taking antidepressant drugs (Stolzer, 2010). You know that your medication slightly raises the risk of miscarriage (Nakhai-Pour, Broy, & Berard, 2010). But you also worry that stopping will cause excessive anxiety and, possibly a premature birth.

As these comments illustrate, with medications and pregnancy, it can be a difficult balancing act. Sometimes there are no perfect choices.

With recreational drugs, the choice is clear. Each substance is potentially teratogenic. So just say *no!*

Because tobacco and alcohol are woven into the fabric of daily life, let's now focus on these widely used teratogens. What *can* happen to the baby when pregnant women smoke and drink?

Gary Buss/Getty Images

As the wafting cigarette fumes enter this women's body, they can limit blood flow to the fetus and so compromise its growth—explaining why, if you saw this mother-to-be, you might get furious and say, "You are putting your child at risk!"

SMOKING Each time she reads the information on a cigarette pack, a pregnant woman gets a reminder that she may be doing her baby harm. Still, in polls, roughly one out of every nine pregnant women in the United States admits she still smokes (J.A. Martin and others, 2003). Because this practice is such a "no, no," these surveys underestimate the fraction of still-smoking mothers-to-be. When scientists in a national U.S. study measured blood levels of cotinine (a biological indicator of tobacco use), they discovered that roughly one in four pregnant smokers had earlier falsely reported: "Oh yes, I definitely quit!" (See Dietz and others, 2011.)

The main danger with smoking is giving birth to a smaller-than-normal baby, an event that, as you will see later, may compromise development throughout life (Dunkel Schetter, & Lobel, 2011). Nicotine constricts the mother's blood vessels, reducing blood flow to the developing fetus and so not allowing a full complement of nutrients to reach the child. Interestingly, smoking during the last trimester of pregnancy seems the riskiest, as it limits fetal growth most (Charil and others, 2010; Espy and others, 2010).

The good news is that one in four U.S. smokers takes the difficult step of quitting for the health of her baby, and almost all cut down. The bad news is that some studies show even six cigarettes a day can raise the risk of giving birth to a small child (Espy and others, 2010).

fetal alcohol syndrome (FAS) A cluster of birth defects caused by the mother's alcohol consumption during pregnancy.

ALCOHOL As you saw earlier, it used to be standard practice to encourage pregnant women to have a nightcap to relieve stress. In Italy, drinking red wine during pregnancy was supposed to produce a healthy, rosy-cheeked child! (See Von Raffler-Engel, 1994.) During the 1970s, as evidence mounted for a disorder called **fetal alcohol syndrome (FAS),** these prescriptions were quickly revised. Whenever you hear the word *syndrome,* it is a signal that the condition has a constellation of features that are present to varying degrees. The defining qualities of fetal alcohol syndrome include a far-smaller-than-normal birth weight; an abnormally small brain; facial abnormalities (such as a flattened face); and developmental disorders ranging from serious mental retardation to seizures and hyperactivity (Dean & Davis, 2007; Roussotte, Soderberg, & Sowell, 2010).

Women who binge-drink (have more than four drinks at a time) or who regularly consume several drinks throughout their pregnancies are at highest risk of giving birth to a baby with fetal alcohol syndrome. Their children, at a minimum, may be born with a less severe syndrome called *fetal alcohol spectrum disorders,* characterized by deficits in learning and impaired mental health (Wedding and others, 2007). As alcohol crosses the placenta, it causes genetic changes that impair neural growth (Hashimoto-Torii and others, 2011). Therefore, it makes sense that children exposed to this severe prenatal insult show abnormal brain activation when engaged in memory and self-regulation tasks (Godin and others, 2010; Hamilton and others, 2010; Roussotte, Soderberg, & Sowell, 2010). But granted that heavy drinking is dangerous, what about having one glass of wine a day?

Every U.S. public health organization recommends no alcohol during pregnancy. Interestingly, Europeans take a more permissive stance: "One drink per day is fine" (Paul, 2010; Royal College of Obstetricians and Gynaecologists [RCOG], 1999). Still, as fetal alcohol syndrome ranks as the number-one preventable birth defect in the United States (Wedding and others, 2007), when someone offers a pregnant woman a glass of wine, it's wise for her to just say no.

Measurement Issues

Why is there *any* controversy about the minimum safe level to smoke or drink? For answers, imagine the challenges you would face as a researcher exploring the impact of these teratogens on the developing child. You would have to ask thousands of pregnant women to estimate how often they indulged in these "unacceptable" behaviors. As you just saw, because of the natural tendency to lie (both to *oneself* and others), it would be hard to trust these *self-reports* (recall my discussion of this measurement issue in Chapter 1). You would then have to track the children for decades, looking for problems that might appear as late as adult life. Then, because your study is *correlational,* any problems you found might be due to a variety of influences. Wouldn't women who drink during pregnancy be likely to be poorly nourished? Might they not be more prone to smoke and/or be less committed mothers once their babies arrived? Could you really isolate the difficulties you found years later to a single teratogen given these many "at-risk" forces?

We cannot do an experiment to control for every confounding influence. Therefore, it's difficult to conclude, for instance, whether or not it was "just smoking" that "caused" a child to have problems at school. But one remarkable study used a creative experiment-like approach to tease out the influence of genetics (versus tobacco use) in explaining why children of pregnant smokers may lag behind academically.

Swedish scientists tracked each of the 654,707 babies (yes, you read that correctly) born in that nation from 1983 to 1991, into their teens (D'Onofrio and others, 2010). The researchers had a specific question in mind: If a woman reported smoking while carrying one child and not another, would there be differences in math performance

fetal programming research New research discipline exploring the impact of traumatic pregnancy events and intense stress on producing low birth weight, obesity, and long-term physical problems.

between the siblings at age 15? If differences did show up, notice we can tie this lower achievement more directly to smoking, as both children share their parent's genes. But, there were *no* differences—which raises a provocative issue. Granted, it's not a good idea to smoke while pregnant—because a smaller-than-normal baby *generally* has risks—but are the learning and behavior problems that children of smokers sometimes show (see Ekvlad and others, 2010) really due to their mother's tobacco use, or to something else?

Are you astonished by the commitment involved in this study? Then, take a deep breath as we explore studies tracking how events in the womb might affect development *into* old age!

IN FOCUS: Pregnancy as a Programmer of Adult Life

Imagine that while you are pregnant a disaster occurs—a war or an earthquake—or while you are carrying your baby, you are subjected to the stresses of being poor. Can these traumas have a lifelong impact on your child?

TEH ENG KOON/AFP/Getty Images

Imagine being this terrified woman as she surveys the rubble of her collapsed house. What is the impact of disasters, like this Malaysian landslide, on babies in the womb? Stay tuned for fascinating answers, as we explore *fetal programming research.*

The answer may be yes. In 1944, for instance, the Germans cut off the food supply to Holland, putting that nation in a semi-starvation condition for a few months. As you might imagine, miscarriages and stillbirths were far more frequent during this "Hunger Winter." But even the surviving babies carried a long-term toll. In searching out these particular fetuses (at the time, in later midlife), scientists found that heart disease rates were higher if a baby had been in the womb *specifically* during the Hunger Winter (Paul, 2010). Another landmark study had a similar result: Babies born in the most impoverished sections of England and Wales were more susceptible to dying from cardiovascular disease at a young age (Paul, 2010).

Why might deprivation in the womb be linked to premature, age-related disease? Speculations center on being born too small. When fetuses are deprived of nutrients and/or exposed to intense maternal stress, researchers hypothesize, the resulting impaired growth primes the baby to enter the world expecting "a state of deprivation" and to eat excessively or store more fat. But while this strategy promotes survival when nutrition is scarce, it boomerangs—promoting obesity and a potentially shorter life—when a baby arrives in the world in our contemporary era of overabundant food.

Is obesity (and adult chronic disease) caused just by personal lifestyle choices or partly promoted by a poor body-environment fit at birth? These tantalizing questions are driving **fetal programming research**—studies exploring how intrauterine events may affect everything from our temperament (Belsky & Pluess, 2011; Pluess & Belsky, 2011), to the timing of puberty (see Chapter 8), to premature aging and death (Dunkel Schetter, 2011; Harris & Seckl, 2011; Reissland & Hopkins, 2010; Thompson & Einstein, 2010). Freud revolutionized the twentieth century by arguing that childhood experiences shape adult life. Will twenty-first-century scientists go back further and trace the roots of adult development to experiences in the womb?

Fetal programming research is action oriented. Ideally, we can take steps before birth to influence a child's fate. With these next conditions, the problems are often more serious and permanent. They are frequently diagnosed at birth. This is because the child's condition is "genetic." It was sealed at conception with the union of a particular egg and sperm.

Threats from Within: Chromosomal and Genetic Disorders

Down syndrome The most common chromosomal abnormality, causing mental retardation, susceptibility to heart disease, and other health problems; and distinctive physical characteristics, such as slanted eyes and stocky build.

When a birth defect is classified as "genetic," there are two main causes. The child might have an unusual number of chromosomes, or the problem might be caused by a faulty gene (or set of genes).

Chromosomal Problems

As we know, the normal human chromosomal complement is 46. However, sometimes a baby with a missing or extra chromosome is conceived. The vast majority of these fertilizations end in first-trimester miscarriages, as the cells cannot differentiate much past the blastocyst stage.

Still, babies can be born with an abnormal number of sex chromosomes (such as an extra X or two, an extra Y, or a single X) and survive. In this case, although the symptoms vary, the result is often learning impairments and sometimes infertility.

Survival is also potentially possible when a child is born with an extra chromosome on a specific other pair. The most common example—happening in roughly 1 in every 2,000 births (EUROCAT, 2004)—produces a baby with Down syndrome.

Down syndrome typically occurs because a cell-division error, called *nondisjunction*, in the egg or sperm causes an extra chromosome or piece of that copy to adhere to chromosome pair 21. (If you turn back to Figure 2.3 on page 41, you will notice that this is the smallest matching set, and so the reason extra material adhering to chromosome 21 is not uniformly lethal is that this pair generally contains the fewest genes.) The child is born with 47 chromosomes instead of the normal human complement of 46.

This extra chromosome produces familiar physical features: a flat facial profile, an upward slant to the eyes, a stocky appearance, and an enlarged tongue. Babies born with Down syndrome are at high risk for heart defects and childhood leukemia. Here, too, there is a lifespan time-bomb impact. During midlife, many adults with Down syndrome develop Alzheimer's disease. The most well-known problem with this familiar disorder, however, is mild to moderate mental retardation.

A century ago, Down syndrome children rarely lived to adulthood. They were shunted to institutions to live severely shortened lives. Today, due to medical advances, infants with this condition in the United States have an average life expectancy of 58 (Bellenir, 2004). Ironically, this longevity gain can be a double-edged sword. Elderly parent caregivers may worry what will happen to their middle-aged child when they die or become physically impaired (Gath, 1993).

This is not to say that every Down syndrome baby is dependent on a caregiver's help. These children can sometimes learn to read and write. They can live independently, hold down jobs, marry and have children, construct fulfilling lives (Bellenir, 2004). Do you know a child with Down syndrome like the toddler in this photo who is the light of her loving extended family's life?

Although women of any age can give birth to Down syndrome babies, the risk rises exponentially among older mothers. Over age 40, the chance of having a Down syndrome birth is 1 in 100; over age 45, it is 1 in 25 (Bellenir, 2004). The reason is that, with more time "in storage," older ova are more apt to develop chromosomal faults.

Down syndrome is typically caused by a random event. A spontaneous genetic mistake has occurred in one ovum or, more rarely (in an estimated 5 percent of cases), in one sperm. Now let's look at a different category of genetic disorders—those passed down in the parents' DNA to potentially affect *every* child.

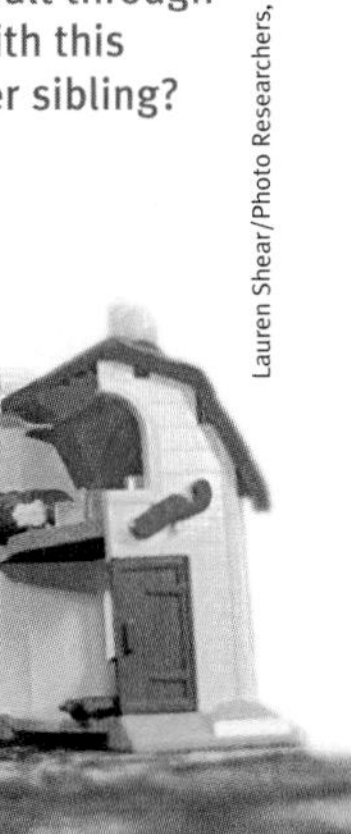

The birth of a Down syndrome child has a life-changing effect on every family member. Will this big sister become a more caring, sensitive adult through having grown up with this much-loved younger sibling?

Lauren Shear/Photo Researchers, Inc.

single-gene disorder An illness caused by a single gene.

dominant disorder An illness that a child gets by inheriting one copy of the abnormal gene that causes the disorder.

recessive disorder An illness that a child gets by inheriting two copies of the abnormal gene that causes the disorder.

sex-linked single-gene disorder An illness, carried on the mother's X chromosome, that typically leaves the female offspring unaffected but has a fifty-fifty chance of striking each male child.

Genetic Disorders

Most illnesses—from cancer to heart disease to schizophrenia—are caused by complex nature-plus-nurture interactions. They result from several, often unknown, genes acting in conjunction with murky environmental forces. The conditions we turn to now are different: These illnesses are caused by a *single,* known gene.

Single-gene disorders are passed down according to three modes of inheritance: They may be *dominant, recessive,* or *sex-linked.* To understand these patterns, you might want to look back again at the paired arrangement of the chromosomes in Figure 2.3 (page 41) and remember that we get one copy of each gene from our mother and one from our father. Also, in understanding these illnesses, it is important to know that one member of each gene pair can be dominant. This means that the quality will always show up in real life. If both members of the gene pair are not dominant (that is, if they are recessive), the illness will manifest itself only if the child inherits two of the faulty genes.

Dominant disorders are in the first category. A person who inherits one copy of the faulty gene always gets the disease. In this case, if one parent harbors the problem gene (and so has the illness), each child the couple gives birth to has a fifty-fifty chance of also getting ill.

Recessive disorders are in the second category. Unless a person gets two copies of the gene, one from the father and one from the mother, that child is disease free. In this case, the odds of a baby born to two carriers—that is, parents who each have one copy of that gene—having the illness are 1 in 4.

The mode of transmission for **sex-linked single-gene disorders** is more complicated. Most often, the woman is carrying a recessive (non-expressed in real life) gene for the illness on *one* of her two X chromosomes. Since her daughters have another X from their father (who doesn't carry the illness), the female side of the family is typically disease free. Her sons, however—with just one X chromosome that might code for the disorder—have a fifty-fifty chance of getting ill, depending on whether they get the normal or abnormal version of their mother's X.

Because their single X leaves them vulnerable, sex-linked disorders typically affect males. But as an intellectual exercise, you might want to figure out when females can get this condition. If you guessed that it's when the mother is a carrier (having one faulty X) and the dad has the disorder (having the gene on his single X), you are right!

Table 2.3 visually decodes these different modes of inheritance and describes a few of the best-known single-gene diseases. In scanning the first illness on the chart, Huntington's disease, imagine your emotional burden as a genetically at-risk child. People with Huntington's develop an incurable dementia in the prime of life. As a child you would probably have watched a beloved parent slowly lose his memory and bodily functions, and then slowly die. You would know that your odds of suffering the same fate are 1 in 2. (Although babies born with lethal dominant genetic disorders typically die before they can have children, Huntington's disease has remained in the population because it, too, operates as an internal time bomb, showing up during the prime reproductive years.)

With the other illnesses in the table—programmed by recessive genes—the fears relate to bearing a child. If both you and your partner have the Tay-Sachs carrier gene, you may have suffered the trauma of seeing a child die in infancy. With cystic fibrosis, your affected child would be subject to recurrent medical crises as his lungs filled up with fluid, and he would face a dramatically shortened life. Would you want to take the one-in-four chance of having this experience again?

The good news, as the table shows, is that the prognoses for some routinely fatal childhood single-gene disorders are no longer as dire. With hemophilia, the life-threatening episodes of bleeding can be avoided by supplying the missing blood factor through transfusions. While surviving to the teens with cystic

TABLE 2.3: Some Examples of Dominant, Recessive, and Sex-Linked Single-Gene Disorders

Dominant Disorders

- **Huntington's disease (HD)** This fatal nervous system disorder is characterized by uncontrollable jerky movements and irreversible intellectual impairment (dementia). Symptoms usually appear around age 35, although the illness can occasionally erupt in childhood and in old age. There is no treatment for this disease.

Recessive Disorders

- **Cystic fibrosis (CF)** This most common single-gene disorder in the United States is typically identified at birth by the salty character of the sweat. The child's body produces mucus that clogs the lungs and pancreas, interfering with breathing and digestion and causing repeated medical crises. As the hairlike cells in the lungs are destroyed, these vital organs degenerate and eventually cause premature death. Advances in treatment have extended the average life expectancy for people with CF to the early thirties. One in 28 U.S. Caucasians is a carrier for this disease.*
- **Sickle cell anemia** This blood disorder takes its name from the characteristic sickle shape of the red blood cells. The blood cells collapse and clump together, causing oxygen deprivation and organ damage. The symptoms of sickle cell anemia are fatigue, pain, growth retardation, ulcers, stroke, and, ultimately, a shortened life. Treatments include transfusions and medications for infection and pain. One in 10 African Americans is a carrier of this disease.*
- **Tay-Sachs disease** In this universally fatal infant nervous system disorder, the child appears healthy at birth, but then fatty material accumulates in the neurons and, at 6 months, symptoms such as blindness, mental retardation, and paralysis occur and the baby dies. Tay-Sachs is found most often among Jewish people of Eastern European ancestry. An estimated 1 in 25 U.S. Jews is a carrier.†

Sex-Linked Disorders

- **Hemophilia** These blood-clotting disorders typically affect males. The most serious forms of hemophilia (A and B) produce severe episodes of uncontrolled joint bleeding and pain. In the past, these episodes often resulted in death during childhood. Today, with transfusions of the missing clotting factors, affected children can have a fairly normal life expectancy.

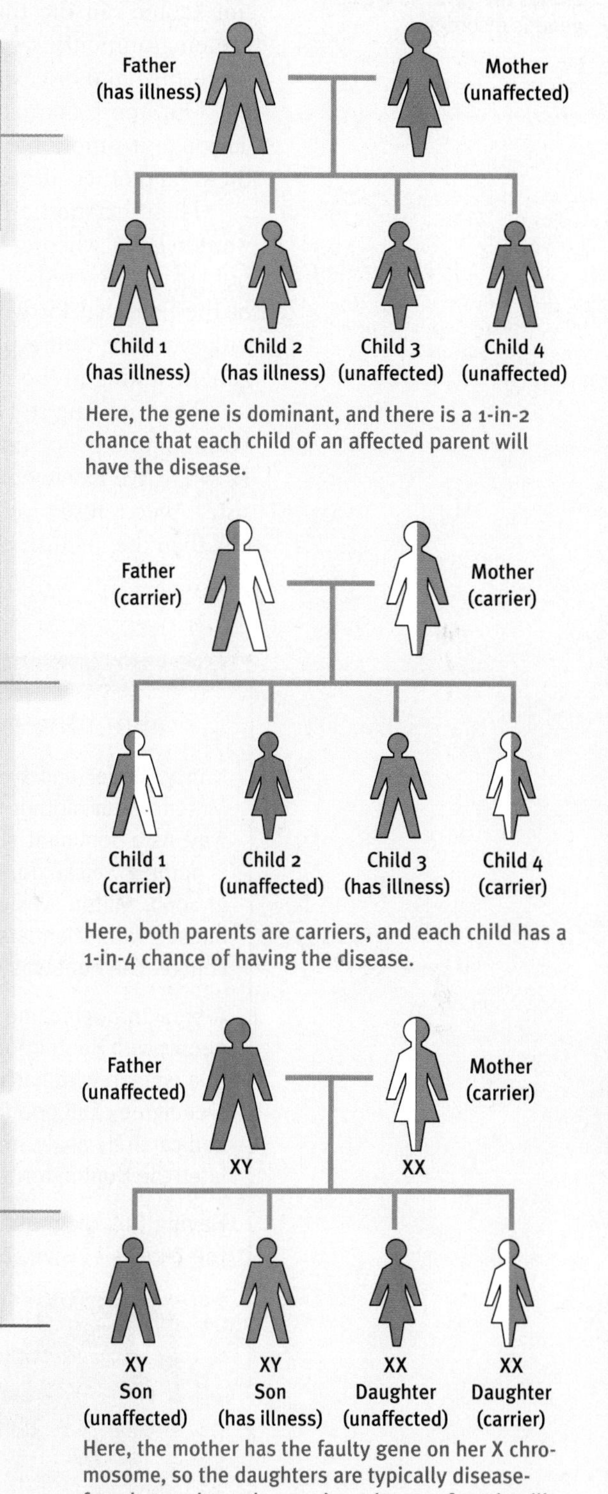

Here, the gene is dominant, and there is a 1-in-2 chance that each child of an affected parent will have the disease.

Here, both parents are carriers, and each child has a 1-in-4 chance of having the disease.

Here, the mother has the faulty gene on her X chromosome, so the daughters are typically disease-free, but each son has a 1-in-2 chance of getting ill.

*Sickle cell anemia may have remained in the population because having the trait (one copy of the gene) conferred an evolutionary advantage: It protected against malaria in Africa. Scientists also speculate that the cystic fibrosis trait may have conferred immunity to typhoid fever.

†Due to a vigorous public awareness program in the Jewish community, potential carriers are routinely screened and the rate of Tay-Sachs disease has declined dramatically.

fibrosis used to be a rare event, babies born with this disorder can now expect on average to live to their 20s and sometimes beyond (CysticFibrosis.com, n.d.). Still, with Tay-Sachs or Huntington's disease, there is *nothing* medically that can be done.

genetic testing A blood test to determine whether a person carries the gene for a given genetic disorder.

In sum, the answer to the question "Can single-gene disorders be treated and cured?" is "It depends." Although people still have the faulty gene—and so are not "cured" in the traditional sense—through advances in nurture (or changing the environment), we have made remarkable progress in treating what used to be uniformly fatal diseases.

Our most dramatic progress, however, lies in advances in **genetic testing.** Through a simple blood test, people can find out whether they carry the gene for these (and other) illnesses.

These diagnostic breakthroughs, however, bring up difficult issues. Would you want to know whether you have the gene for Huntington's? Suppose an employer got hold of your test results and, in view of your genetic profile, denied you a job? Because of the potential for workplace discrimination and because people have a right *not* to know their future physical fate, some advocates argue that Congress should ban genetic testing in the workplace (Krumm, 2002).

The inspiring story of Nancy Wexler, the psychologist who helped discover the Huntington's gene and whose mother died of the disease, is instructive here (see the How Do We Know box). While Nancy will not say whether she has been tested, her sister Alice refused to be screened because she felt not knowing was better emotionally than the anguish of living with a positive result.

How do we know . . .

about the gene for Huntington's disease?

Nancy Wexler and her sister got the devastating news from their physician father, Milton: "Your mother has Huntington's disease. She will die of dementia in a horrible way. As a dominant single gene disorder, your chance of getting ill is fifty-fifty. There is nothing we can do. (See Table 2.3.) But that doesn't mean we are going to give up." In 1969, Milton Wexler established the Hereditary Disease Foundation, surrounded himself with scientists, and put his young daughter, Nancy, a clinical psychologist, in charge. The hunt was on for the Huntington's gene.

A breakthrough came in 1979, when Nancy learned that the world's largest group of people with Huntington's lived in a small, inbred community in Venezuela—descendants of a woman who harbored the gene mutation that caused the disease. After building a pedigree of 18,000 family members, collecting blood samples from thousands more, and carefully analyzing the DNA for differences, the researchers hit pay dirt. They isolated the Huntington's gene.

Having this diagnostic marker is the first step to eventually finding a cure. So far the cure is elusive, but the hunt continues. Nancy still serves as the head of the foundation, vigorously agitating for research on the illness that killed her mother. She works as a professor in Columbia University's Neurology and Psychiatry Department. But every year, she comes back to the village in Venezuela to counsel and just visit with her families—her relatives in blood.

Courtesy of Nancy Wexler, http://www.hdfoundation.org

Interventions

The advantages of genetic testing are clearer when the issue relates to having a child. Let's imagine you and your spouse have been tested and know you are carriers of the gene for cystic fibrosis or another serious genetic disorder. If you are contemplating having children, what should you do?

genetic counselor A professional who counsels parents-to-be about their own or their children's risk of developing genetic disorders, as well as about available treatments.

ultrasound In pregnancy, an image of the fetus in the womb that helps to date the pregnancy, assess the fetus's growth, and identify abnormalities.

chorionic villus sampling (CVS) A relatively risky first-trimester pregnancy test for fetal genetic disorders.

amniocentesis A second-trimester procedure that involves inserting a syringe into a woman's uterus to extract a sample of amniotic fluid, which is tested for a variety of genetic and chromosomal conditions.

Sorting Out the Options: Genetic Counseling

Your first step would be to consult a **genetic counselor,** a professional skilled in both genetics and counseling, to help you think through your choices. Genetic counselors are experts in risk assessment. In addition to laying out the odds, they describe advances in treatment. For example, they would inform couples who are carriers for cystic fibrosis about life-prolonging biological strategies on the horizon, such as gene therapy. They would also highlight the interpersonal and economic costs of having a child with this disease. But they are trained never to offer specific advice. Their goal is to permit couples to make a *mutual decision* on their own (Bodenhorn & Lawson, 2003).

Now, suppose that, armed with this information, you and your partner go ahead and conceive. Let's briefly scan the major tests that are available to every woman carrying a child.

Tools of Discovery: Prenatal Tests

Blood tests performed during the first trimester can detect (with reasonable accuracy) various chromosomal conditions, such as Down syndrome. Brain scans (MRIs) offer a vivid prenatal window on the developing brain (Jokhi & Whitby, 2011). The standard fetal diagnostic test, however, has been available for over 30 years: the **ultrasound.**

Ultrasounds, which now can provide a crystal clear image of the baby in the womb (see the accompanying photo), are used to date the pregnancy and assess fetal growth, in addition to revealing physical abnormalities and answering interesting scientific questions such as, "Can the fetus learn?" (Emory, 2010; Hata, Dai, & Marumo, 2010).

This famous test has another side benefit. By making the baby visually real, ultrasound visits are emotional landmarks on the pregnancy journey itself (Paul, 2010). Have you ever had a friend proudly display a precious photograph of his baby's ultrasound? If you are a parent, perhaps you have shown your own child this priceless image of what he looked like before entering the world.

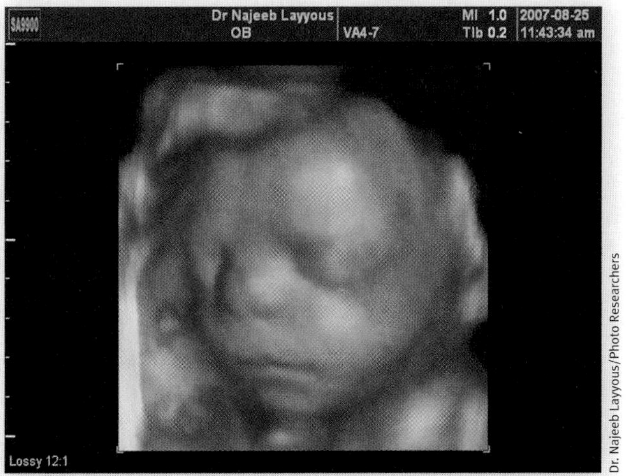

Dr. Najeeb Layyous/Photo Researchers

Due to the miracles of 3D ultrasound technology, when women visit their health-care provider, they can have the thrill of clearly seeing their baby's face. As they peer through this "window on the womb," doctors can get vital information about the health of this 26-week-old fetus, too.

Because these tests are noninvasive, advances in brain imaging and ultrasound technology may be the wave of the future in testing for fetal problems. The two procedures we turn to now, while usually safe, are a bit more risky, as they require entering the womb.

During the first trimester, **chorionic villus sampling** (CVS) can diagnose a variety of chromosomal and genetic conditions. A physician inserts a catheter into the woman's abdomen or vagina and withdraws a piece of the developing placenta for analysis. As this test carries a risk of miscarriage, and limb impairments, CVS is recommended only for couples at high risk of carrying a child with a particular disease.

During the second trimester, a safer test, called **amniocentesis**, can be used to determine the fetus's genetic fate. Aided by an ultrasound, the doctor inserts a syringe into the woman's uterus and extracts a sample of amniotic fluid. The cells can reveal a host of genetic and chromosomal conditions, as well as the sex of the fetus.

Amniocentesis is planned for a gestational age (typically week 14) when there is enough fluid to safely siphon out and time to decide whether or not to carry the baby

TIMELINE	Prenatal Development, Pregnancy, Prenatal Threats, Tools of Discovery		
	Germinal stage (weeks 1 and 2)	Embryonic stage (weeks 3–8)	Fetal stage (weeks 9–38)
PRENATAL DEVELOPMENT	Zygote → blastocyst, which implants in uterus.	All major organs and structures form.	Massive growth and refinements; brain develops; live birth is possible at 22–24 weeks.
THREATS	At fertilization: chromosomal and single-gene diseases.	Teratogens can cause basic structural abnormalities.	Teratogens can impair growth, affect the brain, and so cause developmental disorders. They can also produce miscarriage or premature labor.

to term. However, it, too, carries a small chance of infection and miscarriage, depending on the skill of the doctor performing the test. Moreover, as culturing the cells for analysis takes several weeks, by the time the results of the "amnio" arrive, quickening may have occurred. The woman must endure the trauma of labor should she decide to terminate the pregnancy at this late stage.

The summary timeline spanning these pages illustrates these tools of discovery, the threat zones for problems, and the landmarks of pregnancy from both the maternal and fetal points of view. Now that we have a good understanding of what normally occurs and what can go wrong, let's pause to look at what happens when the pregnancy journey is unfulfilled.

Infertility

> Been riding an emotional and financial roller coaster for the past five years. Had uterine surgery—Dr. took a cyst out. Had artificial insemination with my husband's sperm. Dr. gave me Clomid [a fertility drug], but I'm still not pregnant. All of my friends have babies. I know I was meant to be a mother. Why is this happening to me?

Some societies view a woman's ability to bear children as vital to the well-being of the whole community. When women are pregnant, the spirits will provide a bountiful harvest. Many cultures view bearing children as critical to the success of a marriage. In fact, the practice of throwing rice at a just-married couple is actually a fertility rite (Kitzinger, 2000). And as you can see in the quotation above, many people view having a child as critical to their own well-being.

Infertility, defined as the inability to conceive a child after a year of unprotected intercourse, affects an estimated 1 in 6 U.S. couples (Jaffe & Diamond, 2011). This event (no surprise) produces anxiety, depression, and often stress on other relationships. Imagine the pain of jealously witnessing friends and family members drift effortlessly into pregnancy, when your own dream of having a child is dashed month after month (Jaffe & Diamond, 2011).

Infertility can affect women (and men) of every age. However, just as with miscarriage and Down syndrome, female infertility rates tilt upward at older ages. Within the first six months of trying, roughly 3 out of 4 women in their twenties are able to conceive. At age 40, only 1 out of 5 achieves that goal (Turkington & Alper, 2001). Because of their more complicated anatomy, we assume infertility is usually a "female" problem. Not so! Male issues—which can vary from low sperm motility to varicose veins in the testicles—are *equally* likely to be involved (Turkington & Alper, 2001).

infertility The inability to conceive after a year of unprotected sex. (Includes the inability to carry a child to term.)

	First trimester (month 1–month 3)	Second trimester (month 4–month 6)	Third trimester (month 7–month 9)
PREGNANCY	Morning sickness, tiredness, and other unpleasant symptoms may occur; miscarriage is a worry.	Woman looks pregnant. Quickening occurs (around week 18). Mother can feel intensely bonded to baby.	Woman gets very large and anxiously waits for birth.
TOOLS OF DISCOVERY	Ultrasound Blood tests Chorionic villus sampling (CVS) around week 10	Ultrasound Amniocentesis (around week 15)	Ultrasound

To attack these varied male and female causes, we have a medical arsenal. To demonstrate the need for multiple weapons, Figure 2.9 offers another look at the woman's reproductive system, showing some places on the chain from ovulation to implantation where problems may arise.

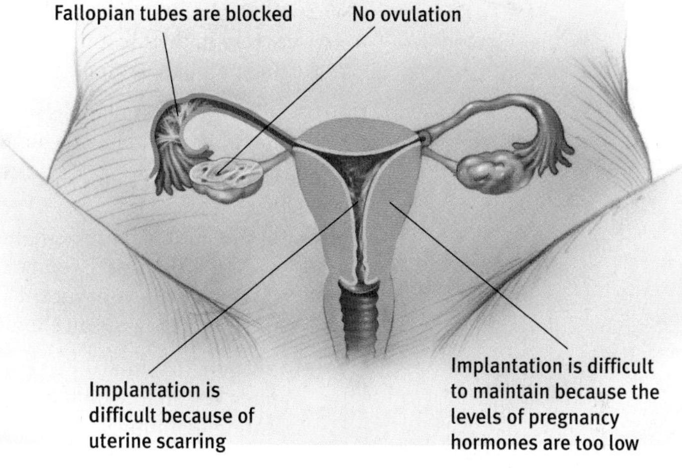

FIGURE 2.9: Some possible missteps on the path to reproduction: In this diagram, you can see some problems that may cause infertility in women. You can also use it to review the ovulation-to-implantation sequence.

INTERVENTIONS: Assisted Reproductive Technology

Each problem on the reproductive chain has its treatment—from fertility drugs to stimulate ovulation, to hormonal supplements to foster implantation; from surgery to help clean out the uterus and the fallopian tubes, to artificial insemination (inserting the sperm into the woman's uterus through a syringe). Then, some couples turn to that ultimate medical weapon: **assisted reproductive technology** (ART).

Assisted reproductive technology refers to any strategy in which the egg is fertilized outside the womb. The most widely used ART procedure is **in vitro fertilization (IVF).** After the woman is given fertility drugs (which stimulate multiple ovulations), her eggs are harvested and put in a laboratory dish, along with the partner's sperm, to be fertilized. A few days later, the fertilized eggs are inserted into the uterus. Then, the couple anxiously waits to find out if the cells have implanted in the uterine wall.

In vitro fertilization, initially developed to bypass blocked fallopian tubes, has spawned amazing variations. A sperm may be injected directly into the ovum if it cannot penetrate the surface on its own. The woman may use a donor egg—one from another woman— in order to conceive. Or the fertilized eggs may be inserted into a "carrier womb"—a surrogate mother, who carries the couple's genetic offspring to term.

Imagine the emotions that can arise when another person is carrying your baby, or if the child you are carrying has another woman's genes. And, consider the expense of these added "pregnancy players." As the cost of soliciting a donor egg can be as high as $30,000, and fees to the donor vary from $5,000 to $15,000, an ART investment can top $40,000—and that's *before* each roughly $12,000 round of treatments even begins! (See Jaffe & Diamond, 2011.)

Now, imagine enduring the invasive techniques used to harvest and insert the eggs, and managing your monthly anguish if a pregnancy doesn't occur. According to 2010 U.S. data, the overall odds of a woman getting pregnant after a round of in vitro

assisted reproductive technology (ART) Any infertility treatment in which the egg is fertilized outside the womb.

in vitro fertilization An infertility treatment in which conception occurs outside the womb; the developing cell mass is then inserted into the woman's uterus so that pregnancy can occur.

treatments was only 1 in 3. Over age 42, success rates slid down to 1 in 10 (Centers for Disease Control and Prevention [CDC] Assisted Reproductive Technology [ART] National Summary Report, 2010 National Summary).

The final insult is that some of these conceptions are doomed to end in miscarriage. Inserting several fertilized eggs into a woman's uterus increases the odds that one will implant. However, if all "take," there is the possibility that none of the tiny babies will survive. So a couple may have to decide whether to undergo a distressing in-utero procedure called "fetal reduction" to increase their odds of having a living child (Britt & Evans, 2007; Jaffe & Diamond, 2011).

What happens when *any* woman gives birth? The answer brings us to the final stop on the pregnancy pathway—labor and birth.

TYING IT ALL TOGETHER

1. Teratogen A caused limb malformations. Teratogen B caused developmental disorders. Teratogen A wreaked its damage during the__________ stage of prenatal development and was taken during the___________ trimester of pregnancy, while teratogen B probably did its damage during the __________stage and was taken during the _________ trimester.
2. Seto and Brandon's mothers contracted rubella (German measles) during different weeks in their first trimester of pregnancy. Seto has heart problems; Brandon has hearing problems. Which teratogenic principle is illustrated here?
3. Your friend Monique is planning to become pregnant and asks you if it will be OK for her to have a glass of wine with dinner each night. What should your answer be?
   a. Go for it! Teratogens operate in a dose-response fashion, and this is too low a dose to do harm.
   b. Go for it! The stress-reducing benefits of a glass would outweigh any harm.
   c. Absolutely not. Even one glass of wine per night is certain to harm the fetus.
   d. Don't press your luck. Even if one drink per night probably is not harmful, to be absolutely safe you should probably avoid alcohol completely.
4. Imagine that in 2014 a serious earthquake hits California. Based on the fetal programming research, which *two* predictions might you make about babies who were in-utero during that time?
   a. They might be at higher risk of being born small.
   b. They might be at higher risk of developing premature heart disease.
   c. They might be at higher risk of being very thin throughout life.
5. Latasha gives birth to a child with Down syndrome, while Jennifer gives birth to a child with cystic fibrosis. Which woman should be more worried about having another child with that condition, and why?
6. To a friend who is thinking of choosing between chorionic villus sampling (CVS) and amniocentesis, mention the advantages and disadvantages of each procedure.
7. Devise a checklist to help infertile couples determine whether in vitro fertilization might be an appropriate strategy.

Answers to the Tying It All Together questions can be found at the end of this chapter.

Birth

During the last weeks of pregnancy, the fetus's head drops lower into the uterus. On their weekly visits to the health-care provider, women, such as Kim in the opening chapter vignette, may be told, "It should be any minute now." The uterus begins to contract as it prepares for birth. The cervix thins out and softens under the weight of the child. Anticipation builds . . . and then—she waits!

> I am 39 weeks and desperate for some sign that labor is near, but so far NOTHING—no softening of the cervix, no contractions, and the baby has not dropped—the idea of two more weeks makes me want to SCREAM!!!

What sets off labor? One hypothesis is that the trigger is a hormonal signal that the fetus sends to the mother's brain. Once it's officially under way, labor proceeds through three stages.

Stage 1: Dilation and Effacement

This first stage of labor is the most arduous. The thick cervix, which has held in the expanding fetus for so long, has finished its job. Now it must *efface*, or thin out, and *dilate*, or widen from a tiny gap about the size of a dime to the width of a coffee mug or a medium-sized bowl of soup. This transformation is accomplished by *contractions*—muscular, wavelike batterings against the uterine floor. The uterus is far stronger than a boxer's biceps. Even at the beginning of labor, the contractions put about 30 pounds of pressure on the cervix to expand to its cuplike shape.

The contractions start out slowly, perhaps 20 to 30 minutes apart. They become more frequent and painful as the cervix more rapidly opens up. Sweating, nausea, and intense pain can accompany the final phase—as the closely spaced contractions reach a crescendo, and the baby is poised for the miracle of birth (see Figure 2.10).

Stage 2: Birth

The fetus descends through the uterus and enters the vagina, or birth canal. Then, as the baby's scalp appears (an event called *crowning*), parents get their first exciting glimpse of this new life. The shoulders rotate; the baby slowly slithers out, to be captured and joyously cradled as it enters the world. The prenatal journey has ended; the journey of life is about to begin.

Stage 3: The Expulsion of the Placenta

In the ecstasy of the birth, the final event is almost unnoticed. The placenta and other supporting structures must be pushed out. Fully expelling these materials is essential to avoid infection and to help the uterus return to its pre-pregnant state.

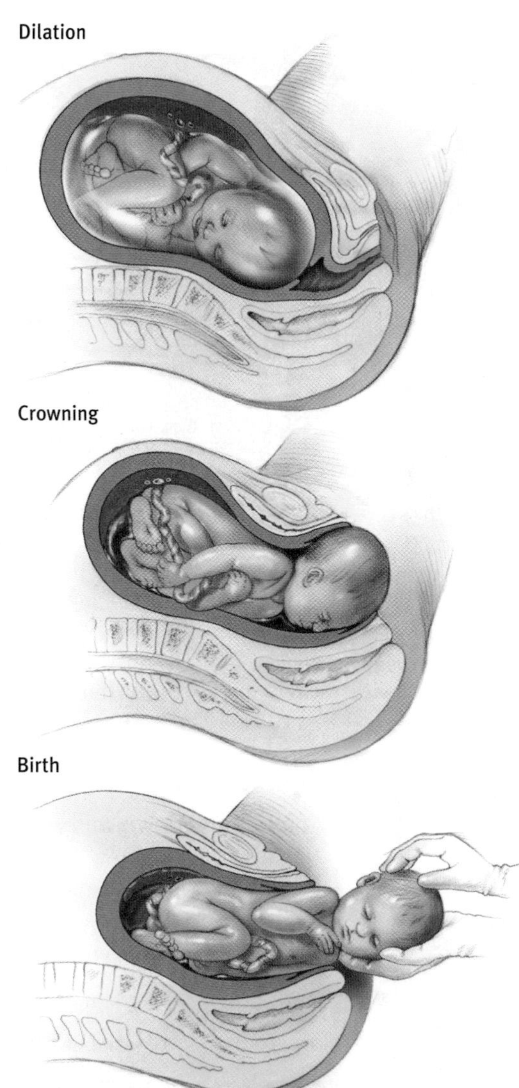

FIGURE 2.10: **Labor and childbirth:** In the first stage of labor, the cervix dilates; then in the second stage, the baby's head emerges and the baby is born.

Threats at Birth

Just as with pregnancy, a variety of missteps may happen during this landmark passage into life: problems with the contraction mechanism; the inability of the cervix to fully dilate; deviations from the normal head-down position as the fetus descends and positions itself for birth (this atypical positioning, with feet, buttocks, or knees first, is called a *breech birth*); difficulties stemming from the position of the placenta or the umbilical cord as the baby makes its way into the world. Today, these in-transit troubles are easily surmounted through obstetrical techniques. This was not true in the past.

Birth Options, Past and Present

For most of human history, pregnancy was a grim nine-month march to an uncertain end (Kitzinger, 2000; Wertz & Wertz, 1989). The eighteenth-

natural childbirth A general term for labor and birth without medical interventions.

century New England preacher Cotton Mather captured the emotions of his era perfectly when, on learning that a woman in his parish was pregnant, he darkly thundered, "Your death has entered into you!" Not only were there the hazards involved in getting the baby to emerge from the womb, but a raging infection called childbed fever could also quickly set in and kill a new mother (and her child) within days.

Public domain. In Richard W. Wertz and Dorothy C. Wertz, Lying-In: A History of Childbirth in America, 1977, p. 78

This classic nineteenth-century illustration shows just why early doctors were clueless about how to help pregnant women. They could not view the relevant body parts!

Women had only one another or lay midwives to rely on during this frightening time. So birth was a social event. Friends and relatives flocked around, perhaps traveling miles to offer comfort when the woman's due date drew near. Doctors were called to the scene in emergencies, but they were of little help. Because this age of modesty made it impossible to view the female anatomy directly, the training in "male midwifery" schools was all academic. In fact, due to their clumsiness (using primitive forceps to yank the baby out) and their tendency to unknowingly spread childbed fever by failing to wash their hands, eighteenth- and nineteenth-century doctors often made the situation worse (Wertz & Wertz, 1989).

Techniques gradually improved toward the end of the nineteenth century, but few wealthy women dared enter hospitals to deliver, as these institutions were hotbeds of contagious disease. Then, with the early-twentieth-century conquest of many infectious diseases, it became fashionable for affluent middle-class women to have a "modern" hospital birth. By the late 1930s, the science of obstetrics gained the upper hand, fetal mortality plummeted, and birth became genuinely safe (Leavitt, 1986). By the turn of this century, in the developed world, this conquest was virtually complete. In 1997, there were only 329 pregnancy-related maternal deaths in the United States (Miniño and others, 2002).

This watershed medical victory was accompanied by discontent. The natural process of birth had become an impersonal event. Women began to protest the assembly-line hospital procedures; for example, the fact that they were strapped down and sedated in order to give birth. They eagerly devoured books describing the new Lamaze technique, which taught controlled breathing, allowed partner involvement, and promised undrugged birth without pain. During the women's movement of the 1960s and early 1970s, the natural-childbirth movement fully arrived.

Natural Childbirth

Natural childbirth, a vague label for returning the birth experience to its "true" natural state, is now firmly embedded in the labor and birth choices available to women today. To avoid the medical atmosphere of a traditional maternity ward, some women choose to deliver in homelike birthing centers. They may use certified midwives rather than doctors in their quest for a less medical birth. They may avoid the epidural routinely ordered to ease labor pain, and instead draw on the help of a *doula,* a nonmedical pregnancy and labor coach. At the most daring end of the spectrum, mirroring the traditional practice in non-Western cultures, women may choose to give birth in their own homes. (Table 2.4 describes some natural birth options, as well as some commonly used medical procedures.)

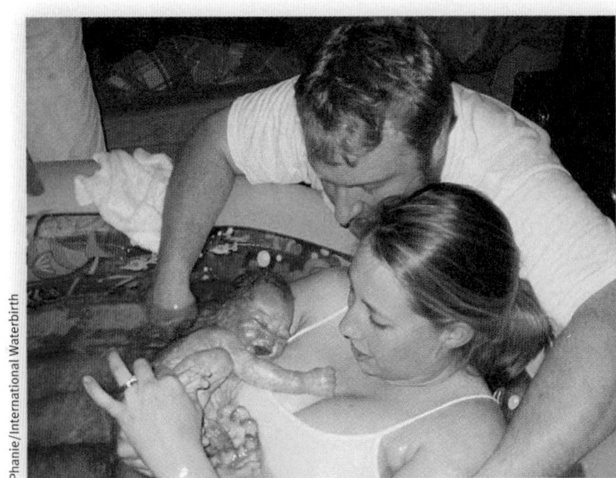

Phanie/International Waterbirth

Today, women have a variety of birth choices in the developed world. The woman in this photo is having a water birth.

At the medical end of the spectrum, as Table 2.4 shows, lies the arsenal of physician interventions designed to promote a less painful and safer birth. Let's now pause for a minute to look at the last procedure listed in the table: the cesarean section.

TABLE 2.4: The Major Players and Interventions in Labor and Birth

Natural-Birth Providers and Options

Certified midwife: Certified by the American College of Nurse Midwives, this health-care professional is trained to handle *low-risk* deliveries, with obstetrical backup should complications arise.

- ***Plus:*** Offers a birth experience with fewer medical interventions and more humanistic care.
- ***Minus:*** If the delivery suddenly becomes high risk, an obstetrician may be needed on the scene.

Doula: Mirroring the "old-style" female experience, this person provides loving emotional and physical support during labor, offering massage and help in breathing and relaxation, but not performing actual health-care tasks, such as vaginal exams. (Doulas have no medical training.)

- ***Plus:*** Provides caring support from an advocate.
- ***Minus:*** Drives up the birth expense.

Lamaze method: Developed by the French physician Ferdinand Lamaze, this popular method prepares women for childbirth by teaching pain management through relaxation and breathing exercises.

- ***Plus:*** Offers a shared experience with a partner (who acts as the coach) and the sense of approaching the birth experience with greater control.
- ***Minus:*** Doesn't necessarily work for pain control "as advertised"!

Bradley method: Developed by Robert Bradley in the 1940s, this technique is designed for women interested in having a completely natural, nonmedicated birth. It stresses good diet and exercise, partner coaching, and deep relaxation.

- ***Plus:*** Tailored for women firmly committed to forgoing any medical interventions.
- ***Minus:*** May set women up for disappointment if things don't go as planned and they need those interventions.

Medical Interventions

Episiotomy: The cutting of the perineum or vagina to widen that opening and allow the fetus to emerge (not recommended unless there is a problem delivery).*

- ***Plus:*** May prevent a fistula, a vaginal tear into the rectal opening, which produces chronic incontinence and pain.
- ***Minus:*** May increase the risk of infection after delivery and hinder healing.

Epidural: This most popular type of anesthesia used during labor involves injecting a painkilling medication into a small space outside the spinal cord to numb the woman's body below the waist. Epidurals are now used during the active stage of labor—effectively dulling much of the pain—and during c-sections, so that the woman is awake to see her child during the first moments after birth.

- ***Plus:*** Combines optimum pain control with awareness; because the dose can be varied, the woman can see everything, and she has enough feeling to push during vaginal deliveries.
- ***Minus:*** Can slow the progress of labor in vaginal deliveries, can result in headaches, and is subject to errors if the needle is improperly inserted. Concerns also center on the fact that the newborn may emerge "groggy."

Electronic fetal monitor: This device is used to monitor the fetus's heart rate and alert the doctor to distress. With an external monitor, the woman wears two belts around her abdomen. With an internal monitor, an electrode is inserted through the cervix to record the heart rate through the fetal scalp.

- ***Plus:*** Shown to be useful in high-risk pregnancies.
- ***Minus:*** Can give false readings, leading to a premature c-section. Also, its superiority over the lower-tech method of listening to the baby's heartbeat with a stethoscope has not been demonstrated.

C-section: The doctor makes an incision in the abdominal wall and the uterus and removes the fetus manually.

- ***Plus:*** Is life-saving to the mother and baby when a vaginal delivery cannot occur (as when the baby is too big to emerge or the placenta is obstructing the cervix). Also is needed when the mother has certain health problems or when the fetus is in serious distress.
- ***Minus:*** As a surgical procedure, it is more expensive than vaginal delivery and can lead to more discomfort after birth.

*Late-twentieth-century research has suggested that the once-common U.S. practice of routinely performing episiotomies had no advantages and actually hindered recovery from birth. Therefore, in recent decades, the episiotomy rate in the United States has declined.

The Cesarean Section

A **cesarean section** (or **c-section**), in which a surgeon makes incisions in the woman's abdominal wall and enters the uterus to remove the baby, is the lifesaving final solution for problems that occur during labor and delivery. This operation exploded in popularity during the 1970s, rising from 5 to 16 percent of all U.S. births (Wertz &

cesarean section (c-section) A method of delivering a baby surgically by extracting the baby through incisions in the woman's abdominal wall and in the uterus.

Wertz, 1989). By the turn of this century, c-sections accounted for an astonishing one in three U.S. deliveries (Martin and others, 2005).

Some c-sections are planned to occur before the woman goes into labor because the physician knows in advance that there will be dangers during a vaginal birth. Others are unexpected c-sections that occur after labor has begun. To what degree are these procedures unnecessary, due to fears of legal liability ("I might get sued unless I get this baby out") or prudent medical practice ("I want to take every precaution that this child is born healthy")? We don't know. What we do know is that rates of "optional" c-sections—those performed purely at the mother's request—are increasing. And, as the following example shows, even when a c-section is necessary, women can feel at bit let down if they had been avidly counting on having a child "the natural way" (Chalmers and others, 2010; Redshaw & Hockley, 2010).

> It all started on Sunday, April twenty-first. I arrived with my doula and was feeling contractions. Twelve hours later, my cervix had only dilated 1/2 centimeter, and I was given a Pitocin drip [a labor-stimulating drug]. Terrible, terrible contractions. But I only dilated to 4 centimeters by the next morning—and the doctor said that if things didn't change by 3 P.M. I needed a c-section. At first I freaked, as I had been planning a vaginal birth. Then . . . incredible relief . . . as I saw the most beautiful sight in the world emerge—and forgot everything else.

As a final comment, while developed-world critics bemoan the possible overuse of c-sections, the real tragedy is the horrifying *lack of access* to this operation in the least-developed regions of the world. In Haiti, only 2 percent of pregnant women have c-sections (Stanton, Ronsmans, & the Baltimore group on Cesareans, 2008). In many rural areas of Africa, women cannot get this lifesaving procedure at all (Lawn and others, 2011). This means billions of developing-world mothers-to-be approach birth with a more basic concern than their affluent counterparts. Their worries are not, "Should I *choose* a c-section?" It's not, "What birth method should I use?" Unfortunately, all too often, it's still: "Will I survive my baby's birth?" (Lester, Benfield, & Fathalla, 2010; Potts, Prata, & Sahin-Hodoglugil, 2010).

TYING IT ALL TOGETHER

1. Melissa says that her contractions are coming every 10 minutes now. Sonia has just seen her baby's scalp emerge. In which stages of labor are Melissa and Sonia?
2. To a friend interested in having the most natural birth possible, spell out some of these options.
3. C-sections may be sometimes *be over-/under* used in the developed world; but they are seriously *underutilized/overutilized* in poor areas of the globe.

Answers to the Tying It All Together questions can be found at the end of this chapter.

The Newborn

Now that we have examined how the baby arrives in the world, let's turn our attention to that tiny arrival. What happens after the baby is born? What are the main dangers that babies face after birth?

Apgar scale A quick test used to assess a just-delivered baby's condition by measuring heart rate, muscle tone, respiration, reflex response, and color.

Tools of Discovery: Testing Newborns

The first step after the newborn enters the world is to evaluate its health in the delivery room with a checklist called the **Apgar scale.** The child's heart rate, muscle tone, respiration, reflex response, and color are rated on a scale of 0 to 2 at one minute and then again at five minutes after birth. Newborns with five-minute Apgar scores over 7 are usually in excellent shape. However, if the score stays below 7, the child must be monitored or resuscitated and kept in the hospital for awhile.

low birth weight (LBW) A body weight at birth of less than 5 1/2 pounds.

very low birth weight (VLBW) A body weight at birth of less than 3 1/4 pounds.

neonatal intensive care unit (NICU) A special hospital unit that treats at-risk newborns, such as low-birth-weight and very-low-birth-weight babies.

Threats to Development Just After Birth

After their babies have been checked out medically, most mothers and fathers eagerly take their robust, full-term baby home. But other parents must hover at the hospital and anxiously wait. The reason, most often, is that their child has arrived in the world too small and/or too soon.

Born Too Small and Too Soon

In 2008, about one out of every eight U.S. babies were *preterm*, or premature—they arrived in the world more than three weeks early (Martin, Osterman, & Sutton, 2010). About one in every eleven U.S. babies were categorized as **low birth weight.** They entered the world weighing less than 5 1/2 pounds. Babies can be designated low birth weight because they either arrived before their due date or did not grow sufficiently in the womb. Earlier in this chapter, I highlighted smoking and intense maternal stress as risk factors for low birth weight. But often, uncontrollable influences—such as an infection that prematurely ruptures the amniotic sac, or a cervix that cannot withstand the pressure of the growing baby's weight—cause this too-early or excessively small arrival into life.

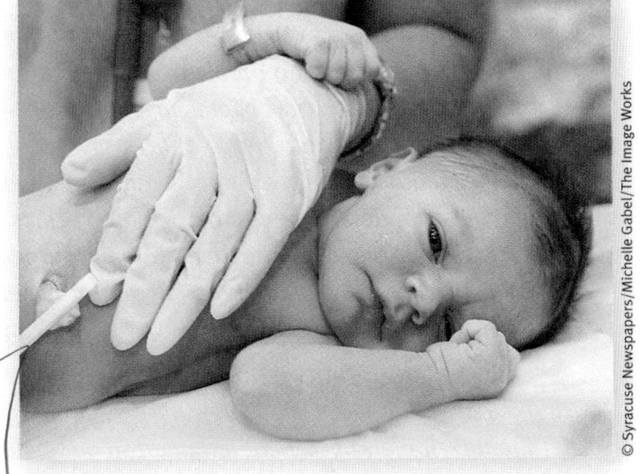

© Syracuse Newspapers/Michelle Gabel/The Image Works

This baby has an excellent Apgar score. Notice his healthy, robust appearance.

Many low-birth-weight babies are fine. The highly vulnerable newborns are the 1.4 percent classified as **very low birth weight,** babies weighing less than 3 1/4 pounds. When these infants are delivered, often *very* prematurely, they are immediately rushed to a major medical center to enter a special hospital unit for frail newborns—the **neonatal intensive care unit.**

> At 24 weeks my water broke, and I was put in the hospital and given drugs to stop the labor. I hung on, and then, at week 26, gave birth. Peter was sent by ambulance to Children's Hospital. When I first saw my son, he had needles in every point of his body and was wrapped in plastic to keep his skin from drying out. Peter's intestines had a hole in them, and the doctor had to perform an emergency operation. But Peter made it! A week later another surgery was needed to close a valve in Peter's heart. Now it's four months later, and my husband and I are about to bring our miracle baby home.

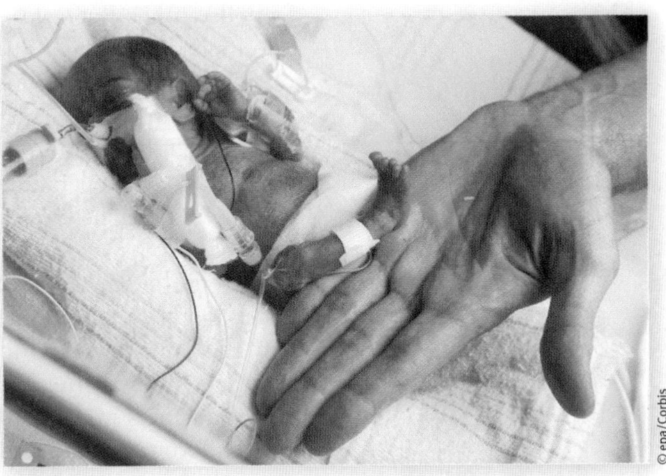

© epa/Corbis

This baby weighing less than one pound was incredibly lucky to make it out of the womb alive—but she is at high risk for having enduring problems as she travels through life.

Is this survival story purchased at the price of a life of pain? Enduring health problems are a serious risk with newborns such as Peter, born far too soon and excessively small. Study after study suggests low birth weight can lead to abnormalities in brain development (DiPietro and others, 2010; Mullen and others, 2010; Nagy, Lagercrantz, & Hutton, 2011). It may compromise intellectual abilities during childhood (Baron & Rey-Casserly, 2010; Cheadle & Goosby, 2010; Guarini and others, 2010; Loe and others, 2011; Rautava and others, 2010) and even later life (Erickson and others, 2010)—in addition, as you now know, to possibly promoting overweight and early age-related disease. And what about the costs? Astronomical sums are required to keep very frail babies such as Peter alive—expenses that can bankrupt families and are often borne by society as a whole (Caplan, Blank, & Merrick, 1992).

EXPERIENCING THE LIFESPAN: Marcia's Story

The service elevator at Peck Hall takes forever to get there, then moves in extra-slow motion up to the third floor. If, as sometimes happens, it's out of service, you are out of luck. It's about a 30-minute drive from my dorm in the motorized wheelchair, including the ramps. When it rains, there's the muck—slowing you up—keeping you wet. So I try to leave at least an hour to get to class.

My goal is to be at least five minutes early so I don't disrupt everything as I move the chair, back and forth, back and forth, to be positioned right in front. Because my bad eye wanders to the side, you may not think I can read the board. That's no problem, although it takes me weeks to get through a chapter in your book! The CP [cerebral palsy], as you know, affects my vocal cords, making it hard to get a sentence out. But I won't be ashamed. I am determined to participate in class. I have my note-taker. I have my hearing amplifier turned up to catch every sound. My mind is on full alert. I'm set to go.

I usually can take about two courses each semester—sometimes one. I'm careful to screen my teachers to make sure they will work with me. I'm almost 30 and still only a junior, but I'm determined to get my degree. I'd like to be a counselor and work with CP kids. I know all about it—the troubles, the physical pain, what people are like. I've got tons of experience starting from day one.

I'm not sure exactly what week I was born, but it wasn't really all that early; maybe two months at the most. My problem was being incredibly small. They think my mom might have gotten an infection that made me born less than one pound. The doctors were sure I'd never make it. They told Mom and Dad to prepare for the fact that I would die. But I proved everyone wrong. Once I got out of the ICU and, at about eight months, went into convulsions, and then had a stroke, everyone thought that would be the end again. They were wrong. I want to keep proving them wrong as long as I live.

I've had tons of physical therapy, and a few surgeries; so I can get up from a chair and walk around a room. But it took me until about age five to begin to speak or take my first step. The worst time of my life was elementary school—the kids who make fun of you; call you a freak. The parents were the meanest. When someone did invite me to their house, the answer was often, "You can't let that cripple come." In high school, and especially here at MTSU, things are much better. I've made close friends, both in the disability community and outside. Actually, I'm a well-known figure, especially since I've been here so long! Everyone on campus greets me with a smile as I scoot around.

In my future? I'd love to get married and adopt a kid. OK, I know that's going to be hard. Because of my speech problem, I know you're thinking it's going to be hard to be a counselor, too. But I'm determined to keep trying, and take every day as a blessing. Life is very special. I've always been living on borrowed time.

When a child is born at the cusp of viability—at around 22 weeks— doctors, not infrequently, refuse to vigorously intervene (Duffy & Reynolds, 2011; Ramsay & Santella, 2011). But one expert argues that it's unethical to make decisions about *any* threshold viability age. Survival rates vary, depending on the individual baby—and very important—that child's access to high-quality care (Sjörs, 2010). Plus, due to dramatic neonatal advances occurring during the 1980s, many more small babies are now living to adulthood unimpaired (Baron & Rey-Casserly, 2010). I have vividly seen these statistics in operation when, in recent years, a student or two proudly informed our class: "I weighed less than 2 pounds at birth" or "I was born at the twenty-sixth week of life."

Even when they do have serious disabilities, these tiny babies can have a full life. Listen to my former student Marcia, whose 15-ounce body at birth would have easily fit in the palm of your hand—and whom no doctor believed was capable of surviving. Marcia, as the Experiencing the Lifespan box describes, is partially deaf, blind in one eye, and suffers from the disorder cerebral palsy. But rarely have I met someone so upbeat, joyous, and fully engaged in the world.

The Unthinkable: Infant Mortality

infant mortality Death during the first year of life.

Some babies are not as lucky as Peter or Marcia or my very-low-birth-weight students. Premature deliveries and low birth weight rank as the most common causes of **infant mortality**, the term for deaths occurring within the first year of life. In the least-developed regions of the globe, where infant mortality rates are highest, infants may die soon after birth due to labor and delivery traumas (Lawn and others, 2011). Or they may succumb to infectious diseases such as pneumonia and diarrhea. In the developed world—where infant mortality is very low (see Figure 2.11)—babies who do not make it beyond their first year tend to be born around the age of viability, or have serious genetic disorders like Tay-Sachs disease.

The good news is that, in recent years, U.S. infant mortality is at a low ebb. By the early twenty-first century, of every 1,000 births, only roughly seven babies died before age 1 (CDC, 2007). The bad news is our dismal standing compared to many other industrialized countries. Why does the United States rank a humiliating forty-sixth in this basic marker of a society's health? (Central Intelligence Agency [CIA], 2011.) The main cause lies in income inequalities, stress, poor health practices, and unequal access to high-quality prenatal care.

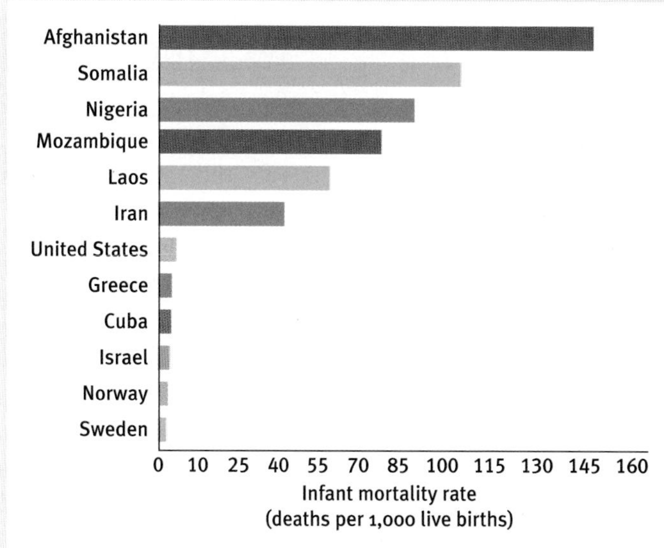

FIGURE 2.11: **Deaths of infants under one year of age in 2011, per 1000 live births in selected countries:** Infant mortality rates vary tremendously around the globe. Notice the disparities between affluent and least-developed countries. (Cuba, although relatively poor, is well known for its universal free medical care—and so boasts lower infant mortality rates than the United States.)

Source: World Factbook, Central Intelligence Agency, 2011.

The strong socioeconomic link to pregnancy and birth problems is particularly troubling. In every affluent nation, poverty puts women at higher risk of delivering prematurely or having their baby die before age 1 (Stanley, Langridge, & D'Antonie, 2011).

Specifically, what fraction of pregnant women in the United States is economically deprived? Alarming answers come from a statewide California survey conducted even before the Great Recession of 2008 hit. In 2006, *one in two* women who were carrying a child in that state qualified as low income, and so were eligible for special nutrition help (more about this government aid in Chapter 4). Moreover, this study uncovered high rates of stressful life events—such as divorce or job loss—among both economically strapped women as well as affluent mothers-to-be (Braveman and others, 2010). So, sadly, I must end this chapter on a downbeat note: The United States is falling far short of "cherishing" pregnant women and protecting them (and their babies) from harm.

A Few Final Thoughts on Biological Determinism and Biological Parents

But I also can't leave you with the downbeat impression that what happens during pregnancy is destiny. Yes, researchers now believe events "in-utero" play some role in how we develop. But a basic message of this book is that human beings are resilient. A quality environment matters greatly in shaping our life path (and even can change our biology) well into old age.

Now that we are on the topic of biology, I feel compelled to highlight a personal point, as an adoptive mom. In this chapter, you learned about the feelings of attachment (or mother-child bond) that often begin before birth. But I can assure you that to bond with a baby, you don't need to personally carry that child inside or share the same set of genes. So, just a reminder for later chapters when we scan the beautiful mosaic of families on our landscape today: The bottom-line blessing is being a parent, not being pregnant. Parenting is far different from personally giving birth!

AP Photo/Watertown Daily Times/John Hart

Families come in many forms, and the love you have for *all* your adopted children is no different than if you personally gave birth. Take it from me as an adoptive mom!

The next two chapters turn directly to the joys of babyhood itself, as we catch up with Kim and her daughter Elissa, and track the miraculous development that occurs during the first two years of life.

TYING IT ALL TOGETHER

1. Baby David gets a two-minute Apgar score of 8; at five minutes, his score is 9. What does this mean?
2. Bill says, "Pregnancy and birth are very safe today." George says, "Hey, you are very wrong!" Who is right?
   a. Bill, because worldwide maternal mortality is now very low.
   b. George, because birth is still unsafe around the world.
   c. Both are partly correct: Birth is typically very safe in the developed world, but maternal and infant mortality remains unacceptably high in the poorest regions of the globe.
3. If Latisha goes into labor at 26 weeks and has a very-low-birth-weight baby, what can you predict about this child's development?
   a. Due to medical advances, the baby will have no developmental problems.
   b. The baby will probably have developmental lags and *possibly* more enduring problems.
   c. The baby will certainly have severe impairments throughout life.
4. Sally brags about the U.S. infant mortality rate, while Samantha is horrified by it. First, make Sally's case and then Samantha's, referring to the chapter points.
5. You want to set up a program to reduce prematurity and neonatal mortality among low-income women and their babies. List some steps that you might take.

Answers to the Tying It All Together questions can be found at the end of this chapter.

SUMMARY

The First Step: Fertilization

Every culture cherishes pregnant women. Some build in rituals to announce the baby after a certain point during pregnancy, and many use charms to ward off fetal harm. Pregnancy is a time of intense mixed emotions—joyous expectations coupled with uneasy fears.

The female reproductive system includes the **uterus** and its neck, the **cervix;** the **fallopian tubes;** and the **ovaries,** housing the **ova.** To promote **fertilization** the optimum time for intercourse is when the egg is released. **Ovulation** and all of the events of pregnancy are programmed by **hormones.** At intercourse, hundreds of millions of sperm, produced in the **testes,** are ejaculated, but only a small fraction make their way to the fallopian tubes to reach the ovum. When the single victorious sperm penetrates the ovum, the two 23 **chromosome** pairs (composed of **DNA,** segmented into **genes**) unite to regain the normal complement of 46 that form our body's cells.

Prenatal Development

During the first stage of pregnancy, the two-week-long **germinal phase,** the rapidly dividing **zygote** travels to the uterus, becomes a **blastocyst,** and faces the next challenge—**implantation.** The second stage of pregnancy, the **embryonic stage,** begins after implantation and ends around week 8. During this intense six-week period, the **neural tube** forms and all the major body structures are constructed—according to the **proximodistal, cephalocaudal,** and **mass-to-specific** principles of development.

During the third stage of pregnancy, the **fetal stage,** development is slower paced. The hallmarks of this stage are enormous body growth and construction of the brain as the **neurons** migrate to the top of the tube and differentiate. Another defining landmark of this seven-month phase occurs around week 22, when the fetus can possibly be **viable,** that is, survive outside the womb if born.

Pregnancy

The nine months of **gestation,** or pregnancy, are divided into **trimesters.** The first trimester is often characterized by unpleasant symptoms, such as morning sickness, and a relatively high risk of **miscarriage.** The landmarks of the second trimester are looking clearly pregnant, experiencing **quickening,** and often feeling more intensely emotionally connected to the child. During the third trimester, the woman's uterus gets very large, and she anxiously awaits the birth.

The emotional experience of being pregnant varies, depending on socioeconomic status and, most importantly, social support. To really enjoy her pregnancy, a woman needs to feel cared about and loved. Fathers, the neglected pregnancy partners, also feel intensely bonded to their babies, and may find that pregnancy is a stressful time.

Threats to the Developing Baby

About 4 percent of babies are born with a **birth defect.** One cause is **teratogens,** toxins from the outside that exert their damage during the **sensitive period** for the development of a particular body part. In general, the embryonic stage is the time of greatest vulnerability, although toxins can affect the developing brain during the second and third trimesters also, producing **developmental disorders.** While there is typically a threshold level beyond which damage can occur, teratogens have unpredictable effects, depending on the vulnerabilities of the baby and mother and other forces. Damage may not show up until decades later.

Any recreational drug is potentially teratogenic. Smoking during pregnancy is a risk factor for having a smaller-than-optimal-size baby. Drinking excessively during pregnancy can produce **fetal alcohol syndrome,** or *fetal alcohol spectrum disorder*. **Fetal programming research** suggests that intense pregnancy stress (which leads to compromised fetal growth) can program babies to put on excessive weight and possibly develop premature age-related chronic diseases.

The second major cause of prenatal problems is genuinely "genetic"—chromosomal problems and single-gene diseases. **Down syndrome** is one of the few disorders in which babies born with an abnormal number of chromosomes survive. Although Down syndrome, caused by having an extra chromosome on pair 21, produces mental retardation and other health problems, people with this condition do live fulfilling lives.

With **single-gene disorders,** a specific gene passed down from one's parents causes the disease. In **dominant disorders,** a person who harbors a single copy of the gene gets ill, and each child born to this couple (one of whom has the disease) has a fifty-fifty chance of developing the condition. If the disorder is **recessive,** both parents carry a single copy of the "problem gene" that is not expressed in real life, but they have a 1-in-4 chance of giving birth to a child with that disease (that is, a son or daughter with two copies of the gene). With **sex-linked disorders,** the problem gene is recessive and lies on the X chromosome. If a mother carries a single copy of the gene, her daughters are spared (because they have two Xs), but each male baby has a fifty-fifty risk of getting the disease. Through advances in **genetic testing,** couples (and individuals) can find out if they harbor the genes for many diseases. Genetic testing poses difficult issues with regard to workplace discrimination, and whether people want to find out if they have incurable adult-onset diseases.

Couples at high risk for having a baby with a single-gene disorder (or any couple) may undergo **genetic counseling** to decide whether they should try to have a child. During pre[illegible] including the **ultrasound,** and more invasive procedures [illegible] **chorionic villus sampling** (during the first trimester) and **amnio[illegible] centesis** (during the second trimester) allow us to determine the baby's genetic fate.

Infertility is tackled by a variety of treatments, including **assisted reproductive technologies (ART),** such as **in vitro fertilization (IVF).** IVF, in which the egg is fertilized outside of the womb, is difficult, costly and offers no guarantee that a baby will result.

Birth

Labor and birth consist of three stages. During the first stage of labor, contractions cause the cervix to efface and fully dilate. During the second stage, birth, the baby emerges. During the third stage, the placenta and supporting structures are expelled.

For most of human history, childbirth was life-threatening to both the mother and the child. During the first third of the twentieth century, birth became much safer. This victory set the stage for the later-twentieth-century **natural childbirth** movement. Today women in the developed world can choose from a variety of birth options, including **cesarean sections.** Impoverished, developing-world women, do not have this kind of access or luxury of choices. Their main concern is surviving the baby's birth.

The Newborn

After birth, the **Apgar scale** and other tests are used to assess the baby's health. While most babies are healthy, **low birth weight** can compromise development. **Very-low-birth-weight** infants are most apt to have enduring problems and need careful monitoring in the **neonatal intensive care unit** during their early weeks or months of life.

Infant mortality is a serious concern in the developing world. While rates of infant mortality are generally very low in developed-world countries, the United States has a comparatively dismal standing compared to other affluent countries on this basic health parameter. The main cause is poverty, which affects a large number of pregnant women in the United States. Even though the environment in the womb (stress during pregnancy) may compromise babies' later health, providing a high-quality environment shapes our development at every life stage.

KEY TERMS

genetic counselor, p. 59
ultrasound, p. 59
chorionic villus sampling (CVS) , p. 59
amniocentesis, p. 59
infertility, p. 60
assisted reproductive technology (ART) , p. 61
in vitro fertilization (IVF) , p. 61
natural childbirth, p. 64
cesarean section (c-section), p. 65
Apgar scale, p. 66
low birth weight (LBW) , p. 67
very low birth weight (VLBW) , p. 67
neonatal intensive care unit (NICU) , p. 67
infant mortality, p. 68

ANSWERS TO TYING IT ALL TOGETHER QUIZZES

The First Step: Fertilization

1. a = cervix; b = fallopian tubes; c = uterus; d = ovaries
2. The testes
3. Tell Tiff that the best time to have intercourse is around the time of ovulation, as fertilization typically occurs when the ovum is in the upper part of the fallopian tube. The chain of events that lead to fertilization begins with sexual intercourse, during which millions of sperm are ejaculated. A few find their way to the fallopian tubes and drill into the ovum. When one sperm burrows to the nucleus the two nuclei merge to form a single 46-chromosome cell.
4. Your aunt is more likely to have *a boy. Your uncle* is responsible for the child's sex.

Prenatal Development

1. a. During the embryonic stage, organs rapidly form; the neurons migrate to the top of the brain during the fetal stage; in the germinal stage, the blastocyst forms.
2. From the neural tube, a mass of cells differentiates during the late embryonic phase. During the next few months, the cells ascend to the top of the neural tube, completing their migration by week 25. In the final months of pregnancy, the neurons elongate and begin to assume their mature structure.
3. (a) The head develops before the arms. (b) The arms develop before the hands. (c) The fingers develop before fingernails. (Now, see if you can come up with examples different from mine!)

Pregnancy

1. During the first trimester, Samantha will probably feel tired and have morning sickness. In the second trimester, she will feel better physically and experience an intense sense of emotional connectedness when she feels the baby move. During the third trimester, she is likely to feel uncomfortable and be excitedly waiting for labor and birth.
2. Do you feel supported and loved?
3. You may come up with a host of interesting possibilities. Here are a few of mine: Include fathers in all pregnancy and birth educational materials the clinic provides; strongly encourage men to be present during prenatal exams; alert female patients about the need to be sensitive to their partners; set up a clinic-sponsored support group for fathers-to-be.

Threats to the Developing Baby

1. Teratogen A most likely caused damage during *the embryonic stage* of development and was taken during *the first trimester* of pregnancy. Teratogen B probably did its damage during *the fetal stage* and was taken during the *second or third trimesters.*
2. Teratogens exert damage during the sensitive period for the development of a particular organ.

3. d. Although there should be no problem with one glass of wine, to be safe it's best to totally abstain.
4. a & b. They might be at higher risk of being born small and of developing premature heart disease.
5. Jennifer. Down syndrome is typically caused by an unlikely, random event. With cystic fibrosis, that single-gene recessive disorder, the mom (in this case, Jennifer) has a 1-in-4 chance of giving birth to another child with that disease.
6. Tell your friend that the plus of chorionic villus sampling is finding out a child's genetic fate in the first trimester. However, this procedure is more dangerous, carrying a slight risk of limb malformations and, possibly, miscarriage. Amniocentesis is much safer and can show a fuller complement of genetic disorders but must be performed in the second trimester—meaning you will have to undergo the trauma of a full labor should you decide to end the pregnancy.
7. You can devise your own checklist. Mine would include the following questions:

   Are you and your mate wealthy? Could you (women especially) spend time each month undergoing a physically and emotionally wrenching procedure? How important is it to you to have your own "biological child"? Could you live with a higher risk of miscarrying (or the difficult ethics of choosing fetal reduction)?

Birth

1. Melissa is in stage 1, effacement and dilation of the cervix. Sonia is in stage 2, birth.
2. "You might want to forgo any labor medications, and/or give birth in a birthing center under a midwife's (and doula's) care. Look into new options such as water births, and, if you are especially daring, consider giving birth at home."
3. C-sections may sometimes be ***overused*** in the developed world. But they are seriously ***underutilized*** in poor areas of the globe.

The Newborn

1. Baby David is in excellent health.
2. c. While birth is very safe in the developed world, maternal and infant mortality remain serious problems in the least-developed countries.
3. b. Developmental lags are predictable, and while many babies do outgrow their problems, some children do have enduring disabilities.
4. Sally: The United States—like other developed countries—has made tremendous strides in conquering infant mortality. Today, only 7 out of every 1,000 babies die in the first year of life. Samantha: The fact that the United States has higher infant mortality rates than many other developed countries is incredibly distressing. It's also very upsetting that stress and poverty characterize the lives of such a high fraction of U.S. moms-to-be.
5. You can come up with your own suggestions. Here are a few of mine: Increase the number of nurse-practitioners and obstetrician-gynecologists in poor urban and rural areas. Provide special monetary incentives to health-care providers to treat low-income women. Offer special "healthy baby" educational programs at schools, community centers, and local churches in low-income neighborhoods targeted for female teens. Make it easier for low-wage workers to actually see a health-care provider by providing incentives to employers. Set up volunteer programs to visit isolated pregnant single moms and provide social support. Target nutrition programs to low-income mothers-to-be (actually, this is the goal of the WIC program, described in the next chapter).

PART II

Infancy

This two-chapter part is devoted to infancy and toddlerhood (the period from birth through age 2). How does a helpless newborn become a walking, talking, loving child?

Chapter 3—**Infancy: Physical and Cognitive Development** starts by offering an overview of brain development, then explores those basic newborn states: feeding, crying, and sleeping. Next, I chart sensory and motor development: What do babies see? How do newborns develop from lying helplessly to being able to walk? What can caregivers do to keep babies safe as they travel into the world? Finally, I'll offer an overview of infants' evolving cognition and their first steps toward language, the capacity that allows us to really enter the human community.

Chapter 4—**Infancy: Socioemotional Development** looks directly at what makes us human: our relationships. First, I'll explore the attachment relationship between caregiver and child, then examine poverty and day care during the first years of life. The final part of this chapter focuses on toddlerhood—roughly from age 1 to 2 1/2. Toddlers are intensely attached to their caregivers and passionate to be independent. During this watershed time of life, when we are walking and beginning to talk, we first learn the rules of the human world.

Chapter 3

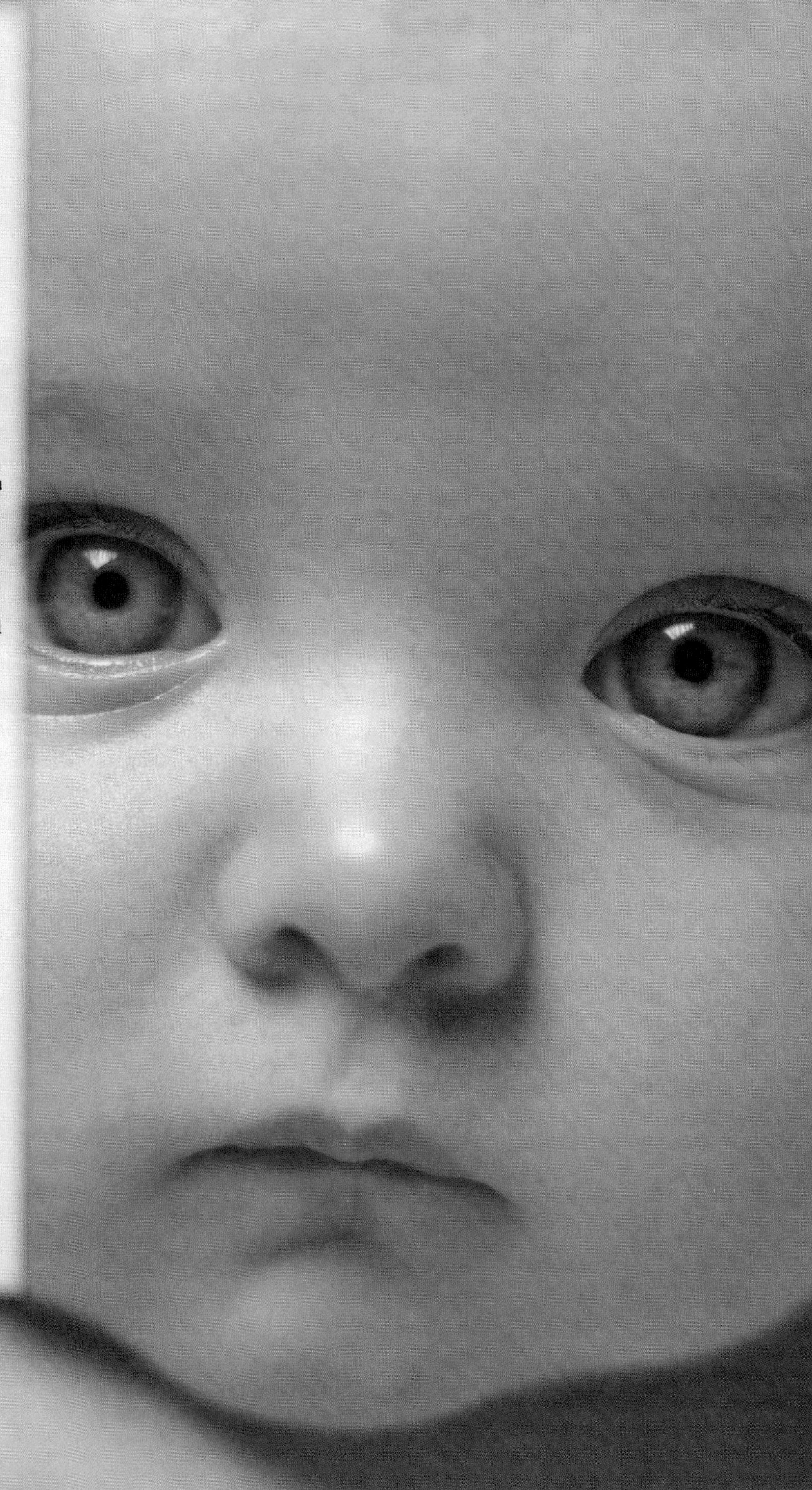

CHAPTER OUTLINE

Infancy: Physical and Cognitive Development

In Chapter 2 I talked to Kim at the beginning of the third trimester, anxiously waiting for her child's birth. Now, let's pay her a visit in the first months of new motherhood and meet Elissa, her baby girl.

She's been here for less than four months—fifteen weeks and two days, to be exact—and I feel like she's been here forever. For me, it was love at first sight and, of course, the same for Jeff. But the real thrill is watching a wonderful new person emerge day by day. Take what's happening now. At first, she couldn't care less, but since a few days ago, it's like, "Wow, there's a world out there!" See that baby seat? Elissa can make the colored buttons flash by moving her legs. Now, when I put her in it, she bats her legs like crazy. She can't get enough of those lights and sounds. Notice the way she looks at your face—like she wants to get into your soul. She really loves this blue smiley-face cushion I bought for 25 cents at a yard sale. Every time she sees it she starts to gurgle, reach, and laugh.

Elissa doesn't cry much—nothing like other babies during the first three months. Actually, I was worried. In the hospital, I asked the doctor whether there was something wrong. Crying is vital to communicating what you need! The same is true of sleeping. I'm almost embarrassed to tell you that I have the only baby in history who has been regularly giving her mom a good night's sleep since she was 2 months old.

Breast-feeding is indescribable. It feels like I am literally making her grow. But, here I also was concerned. Would I know how to do this? What helped me persevere through the rough first week was my supportive husband—and most important, the fact that Jeff makes enough money to let me take off work for five months. I feel so sad for my friend, Nora, who had to abandon this incredible experience when she needed to go back to her job at Walmart right after her son's birth.

Pick her up. Feel what it's like to hold her—how she melts into you. But lately she's starting to squirm more. See those push-ups, like a rocking machine? It's as if she's saying, "Mom, I can't wait to turn over—can't wait to get moving into the world." I plan to be there to video every step now that she's traveling into life.

Elissa is poised at a milestone. Past the first three months of life, she is fully waking up to the world. This chapter charts the transformation from lying helplessly to moving into the world and the other amazing physical and cognitive changes that occur during infancy—that magic first two years of life.

To set the context, I'll first spell out some remarkable brain changes (and principles) that program development throughout life. Then, returning to infancy, I'll chart those basic newborn states: eating, crying, and sleeping, as well as track babies' emerging vision and motor skills. The final sections of this chapter offer a tour of developing cognition and the pathway to mastering language, the capacity that makes our species unique.

What does this young baby see and understand about the tremendous loving object he is facing? That is the mystery we will be exploring in this chapter.

Setting the Context

What causes the remarkable changes—from seeing to walking to speaking—that unfold week by week during infancy? To get an answer, let's step back and explore what is happening in that masterpiece structure—the human brain—from birth to our adult years.

The Expanding Brain

The **cerebral cortex,** the outer, furrowed mantle of the brain, is the site of every conscious perception, action, and thought. With a surface area 10 times larger than the monkey's and 1000 times larger than the rat's, our cortex is what makes human beings stand apart from any other species on earth.

Because of our immense cortex, humans are also unique in the amount of brain growth that occurs outside of our womb. During the first four years of life, our brain volume quadruples (Stiles & Jernigan, 2010). It takes more than two decades for the brain to fully mature. Actually, the cortex really only starts taking over our behavior a few months *after* birth.

Recall from Chapter 2 that by the middle of the fetal period the cells that compose the brain have migrated to the top of the neural tube. During the final months of pregnancy, and especially the first year of life, they differentiate into their mature form. The cells form long **axons**—fibers that conduct impulses away from the cell body. They sprout **dendrites**—treelike, branching ends. As the dendrites proliferate at junctions, or **synapses,** the axons and dendrites interconnect (see Figure 3.1).

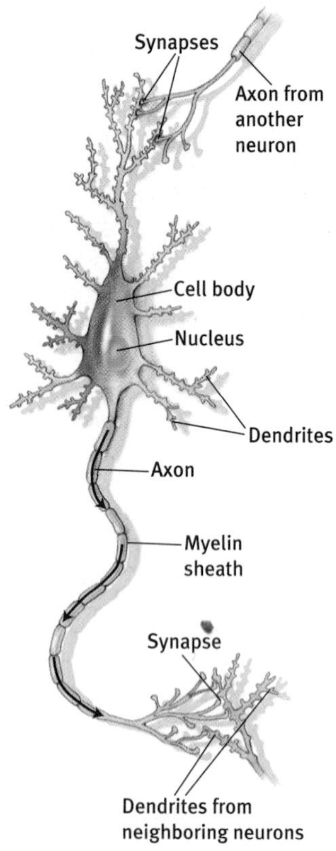

FIGURE 3.1: **The neuron and synapses:** Here is an illustration of the remarkable structure that programs every developing skill, perception, and thought. Notice the dendrites receiving information at the synapses and how impulses flow down the long axon to connect up with the dendrites of the adjoining cells.

Synaptogenesis, the process of making these myriad connections, programs every skill—from Elissa's vigorous push-ups to composing symphonies or solving problems in math. Another transformation that is critical for our abilities to emerge is called **myelination:** The axons form a fatty layer around their core. Just as a stream of water prevents us from painfully bumping down a water park slide, the myelin sheath serves as a lubricant that permits the neural impulses to speedily flow. This encasing layer, which insulates our neurons, may also determine which cells thrive (Stiles & Jernigan, 2010).

Synaptogenesis and myelination occur at different rates in specific regions of the brain. In the visual cortex, the part of the brain responsible for interpreting visual stimuli, the axons are myelinated by about age 1. In the frontal lobes, the region of the brain involved in higher reasoning, the myelin sheath is still forming into our twenties.

This makes sense. Seeing is a skill we need soon after birth. Visual abilities, as you will learn in this chapter, develop rapidly during our first year of life. But we won't need the skills to compose symphonies, do higher math, or competently make our way in the world until we become adults. So there are clear parallels between our unfolding real-world abilities and the way our brain matures.

Neural Pruning and Brain Plasticity

So far, you might imagine that the basic neural principle underlying development is that more extensive connections equal superior skills. Not so! Neural loss is critical to development, too. Following an initial phase of lavishly producing synapses, each region of the cortex undergoes a period of synaptic pruning and neural death. This shedding timetable also reflects our expanding abilities. It begins around age 1 in the visual cortex. It starts during late childhood in the frontal lobes. Just as weeding is critical to sculpting a beautiful garden, we need to get rid of the unnecessary neurons to permit the essential cells to flourish and flower.

Why does the brain undergo this frantic phase of overproduction, followed by cutting back? Neuroscientists believe that having this oversupply is essential, as it allows us to "recruit" surplus neurons and redirect them to perform other functions, should we have a major sensory deficit or experience a brain insult early in life (Fox, Levitt, & Nelson, 2010; Stiles & Jernigan, 2010). Actually, our cortex is amazingly malleable or **plastic** (able to be changed), particularly during infancy and the childhood years.

Using the fMRI, which measures the brain's energy consumption, researchers find that among people blind from birth, activity in the visual cortex is intense while reading Braille and localizing sounds in space. This suggests that, without early environmental stimulation from the eye, the neurons programmed for vision are captured, or taken over, to strengthen our abilities in hearing and touch (Collignon and others, 2011; Fox, Levitt, & Nelson, 2010).

A similar process occurs with language, which is normally represented in the left hemisphere of the brain. If an infant has a left-hemisphere stroke, with intense verbal stimulation, the right hemisphere takes over, and language develops normally (Rowe and others, 2009). Compare this to the outcome for someone who has a left-hemisphere stroke once pruning has occurred and language is located firmly in its appropriate places. For these unfortunate adults, the result can be devastating—a permanent loss in understanding speech or our ability to form words.

The bottom line is that our understanding of brain plasticity highlights the basic nature-combines-with-nurture principle that governs human life. Yes, the blueprint for our cortex is laid out at conception. But, environmental stimulation is vital in strengthening specific neural networks and determining which connections will be pruned (Fox, Levitt, & Nelson, 2010). Before the pruning phase, our brain is particularly malleable—permitting us to grow a somewhat different garden should disaster strike. Still, as synaptogenesis is a lifelong process, we continue to grow, to learn, to develop intellectually, from age 1 to age 101.

Table 3.1 on page 80 offers additional fascinating facts about neurons, synaptogenesis, and the pruning phase. Notice from the last item on the table that, in the same way as the houses in your subdivision look different—although they may have all had the same original plan (as each owner took charge of decorating his personal space)—scientists find remarkable variability in scanning the brains of *normally* developing girls and boys (Giedd and others, 2010). Actually, why should these variations on our universal brain blueprint be a surprise, given the diversity of interests and talents we develop in life!

cerebral cortex The outer, folded mantle of the brain, responsible for thinking, reasoning, perceiving, and all conscious responses.

axon A long nerve fiber that usually conducts impulses away from the cell body of a neuron.

dendrite A branching fiber that receives information and conducts impulses toward the cell body of a neuron.

synapse The gap between the dendrites of one neuron and the axon of another, over which impulses flow.

synaptogenesis Forming of connections between neurons at the synapses. This process, responsible for all perceptions, actions, and thoughts, is most intense during infancy and childhood but continues throughout life.

myelination Formation of a fatty layer encasing the axons of neurons. This process, which speeds the transmission of neural impulses, continues from birth to early adulthood.

plastic Malleable, or capable of being changed (used to refer to neural or cognitive development).

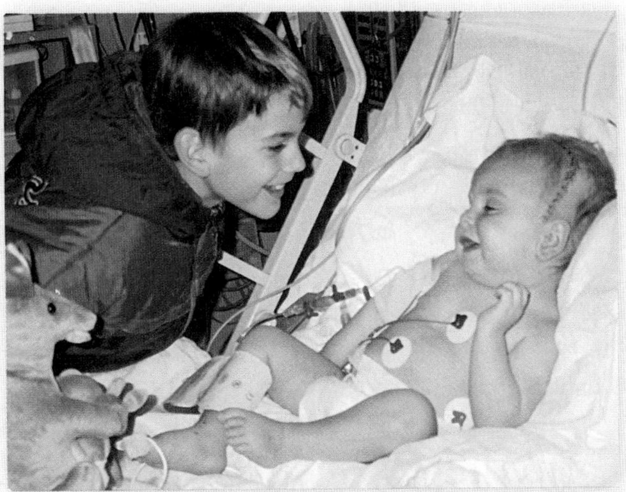

Sandy Lora

Sandy Lora

This resilient baby has survived three major surgeries in which large sections of his brain had to be removed. Remarkably—because the cortex is so *plastic* at this age—he is expected to be left with few, if any, impairments.

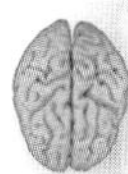

TABLE 3.1: Brain-Busting Facts to Wrap Your Head Around

- Our adult brain is composed of more than 1 billion neurons and, via synaptogenesis, makes roughly 60 trillion neural connections.
- As preschoolers, we have roughly double the number of synapses we have as adults—because, as our brain develops, roughly 40 percent of our synapses are ultimately pruned (see the text). So, ironically, the overall cortical thinning during elementary school and adolescence is a symptom of brain maturation.
- Boys' brains, on average, are 10 percent larger than girls' brains, even during childhood, when both sexes are roughly the same size, body-wise.
- The most amazing finding relates to the surprising, dramatic variability in brain size from child to child. Two normal 10-year-old boys might have a two-fold difference in brain volume, without showing any difference in intellectual abilities!

Sources: Giedd and others, 2010; Stiles & Jernigan, 2010.

Now keeping in mind the basic brain principles—(1) development unfolds "in its own neurological time" (you can't teach a baby to do something before the relevant part of the brain comes on-line); (2) stimulation sculpts neurons (our wider-world experiences physically change our brain); and (3) the brain is still "under construction" (and shaped by those same wider-world experiences) for as long as we live—it's time to explore how the expanding cortex works magic during the first two years of life.

TYING IT ALL TOGETHER

1. Cortez and Ashley are arguing about what makes our brain unique. Cortez says it's the immense size of our cortex. Ashley says it's the fact that we "grow" most of our brain after birth and that the cortex continues to mature for at least two decades. Who is right—Cortez, Ashley, or both students?
2. Latisha said she wouldn't bother reading this section on the developing brain because she learned that stuff in high school. She knows that the myelin sheath speeds neural impulses. She realizes that the more synaptic connections the neurons form, the higher the level of development. Is Latisha prepared for the test, and if not, where is she wrong?
3. When children with epilepsy have recurring life-threatening seizures, surgeons may remove the portion of the brain in which the seizures are taking place. Remarkably, these children go on to live normal lives. The concept describing this phenomenon is (choose one): *myelination/brain plasticity.*
4. Draw a neuron, labeling the axon, dendrites, myelin sheath, and synapses.

Answers to the Tying It All Together questions can be found at the end of this chapter.

Basic Newborn States

Visit a newborn and you will see a set of simple activities: She eats, she cries, she sleeps. In this section, I'll spotlight each basic state.

Eating: The Basis of Living

Eating undergoes amazing changes during infancy. Let's briefly scan these transformations and then discuss two nutritional topics that loom large in the first years of life.

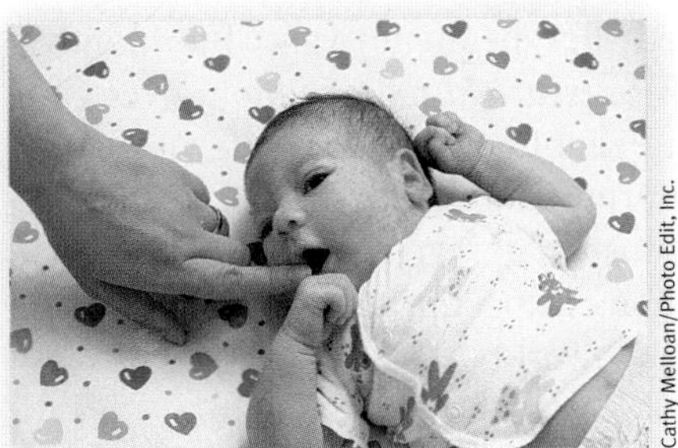
Cathy Melloan/Photo Edit, Inc.

Rooting: Whenever something touches their cheek, newborns turn their head in that direction and make sucking movements.

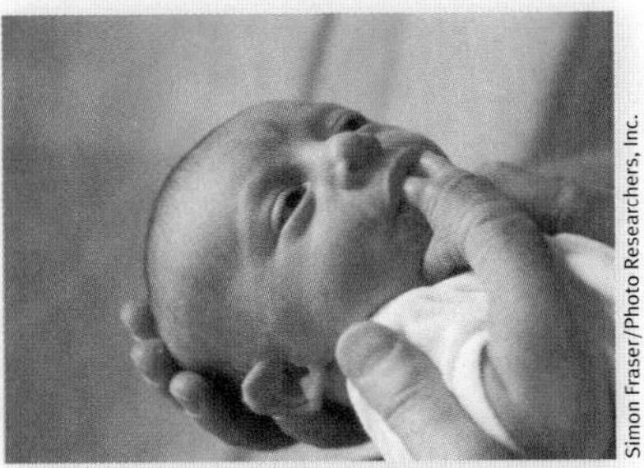
Simon Fraser/Photo Researchers, Inc.

Sucking: Newborns are programmed to suck, especially when something enters their mouth.

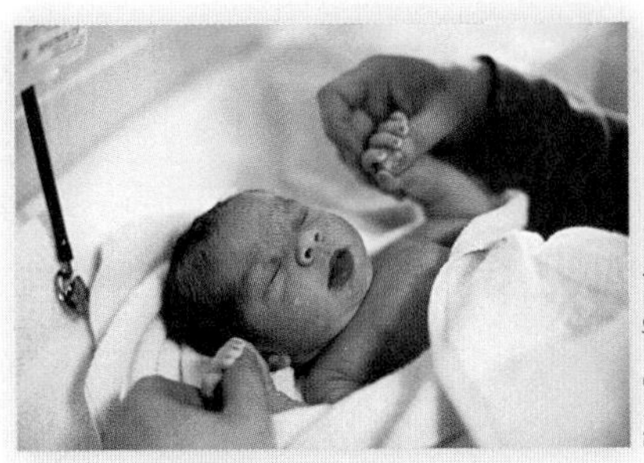
PicturePress/Getty Images

Grasping: Newborns automatically vigorously grasp anything that touches the palm of their hand.

FIGURE 3.2: **Some newborn reflexes:** If the baby's brain is developing normally, each of these reflexes is present at birth and gradually disappears after the first few months of life. In addition to the reflexes illustrated here, other newborn reflexes include the Babinski reflex (stroke a baby's foot and her toes turn outward), the stepping reflex (place a baby's feet on a hard surface and she takes small steps), and the swimming reflex (if placed under water, newborns can hold their breath and make swimming motions).

Developmental Changes: From Newborn Reflexes to Two-Year-Olds' Food Cautions

Newborns seem to be eating even when they are sleeping—a fact vividly brought home to me by the loud smacking noises that rhythmically erupted from my son's bassinet. The reason is that babies are born with a powerful **sucking reflex**—they suck virtually all the time. Newborns also are born with a **rooting reflex.** If *anything* touches their cheek, they turn their head in that direction and begin to suck.

Reflexes are automatic activities. Because they do not depend on the cortex, they are not under conscious control. It is easy to see why the sucking and rooting reflexes are vital to promoting survival the minute we leave the womb. If newborns had to learn to suck, they might die of starvation before they mastered that skill. Without having the rooting reflex built in at birth, babies might have trouble finding the breast.

Sucking and rooting have clear functions. What about the other infant reflexes shown in Figure 3.2? Do you think the grasping reflex may have helped newborns survive during hunter-gatherer times? Can you think of why newborns, when stood on a table, take little steps (the stepping reflex)? Whatever their value, these reflexes, and other characteristic ones, must be present at birth. They must disappear as the cortex grows.

As the cortex matures, voluntary processes replace these special newborn reflexes. By month four or five, babies no longer suck continually. Their sucking is governed by *operant conditioning*. When the breast draws near, they suck in anticipation of that delicious reinforcer: "Mealtime has arrived!" Still, Sigmund Freud named infancy the oral stage for good reason: During the first years of life, the basic theme is "Everything in the mouth."

This impulse to taste everything leads to scary moments as children begin to crawl and walk. There is nothing like the sickening sensation of seeing a baby put a forgotten pin in his mouth or taste your possibly poisonous plant. My personal heart-stopping experience occurred when my son was almost 2. I'll never forget the frantic race to the emergency room after Thomas toddled in to joyously share a new treasure, an open vial of pills!

Luckily, there is a mechanism that may help protect toddlers from sampling every potentially lethal substance during their first travels into the world. Between ages 1 1/2 and 2, children may revert to eating a few familiar foods, such as peanut butter sandwiches and apple juice. Evolutionary psychologists believe that, like morning sickness, this behavior is adaptive. By sticking to foods they know, children

sucking reflex The automatic, spontaneous sucking movements newborns produce, especially when anything touches their lips.

rooting reflex Newborns' automatic response to a touch on the cheek, involving turning toward that location and beginning to suck.

reflex A response or action that is automatic and programmed by noncortical brain centers.

reduce the risk of poisoning themselves when they begin to walk (Bjorklund & Pellegrini, 2002). Although it is temporary, this *2-year-old food caution* gives caregivers headaches. So it's important to reassure frantic parents: While not eating anything is a serious concern, picky eating is normal during the second year of life.

What is the best diet during the first months of life? When is poor childhood nutrition a widespread problem? These questions bring up two nutrition-oriented topics: breast-feeding and malnutrition around the world.

Breast Milk: Nature's First Food

During the late nineteenth century, U.S. babies faced enormous perils after birth. Paramount among these threats was diarrhea, which caused a spike in infant mortality in the teeming city tenements. The newborns of immigrant Eastern European Jews, however, were far less likely to develop diarrhea and other infectious diseases. The reason was that Jewish custom dictated exclusive breast-feeding for a prolonged time (Preston, 1991).

A century ago, because it protected babies against impure milk, breast-feeding was a life-saving act. That choice has an impact today. Breast milk provides immunities to middle ear infections and gastrointestinal problems. It makes toddlers more resistant to colds and the flu (McNeil, Labbok, & Abrahams, 2010). Breast-fed babies even tend to get higher scores on intelligence tests (Karns, 2001; Mortensen and others, 2002).

Still, we need to be cautious. These trends often don't quite reach statistical significance (McNiel, Labbok, & Abrahams, 2010). Plus they involve correlations. And, as we know, just because there is a relationship between two variables does not mean one causes the other. The research exploring breast milk's benefits rarely controls for that important "third variable"—social class. Western women who breast-feed for months tend to be well educated and affluent, and so may provide their children with optimum care in many other ways (Yeoh and others, 2007). Moreover, one U.S. study showed that mothers who breast-feed spend more time in hands-on infant care (Smith & Ellwood, 2011). Is it really breast *milk* that promotes health, or all the special nurturing that goes along with getting this natural first food?

As with pregnancy advice (recall Chapter 2), breast-feeding pronouncements have undergone fascinating twentieth-century shifts. During the 1950s, doctors recommended keeping infants on a tight feeding schedule, and pushed formula as the "scientific" best food. Since research revealed breast milk's benefits, public organizations such as the American Academy of Pediatrics (2005) and UNICEF (2009) mounted a vigorous campaign urging *exclusive* breast-feeding for the first six months of life.

Contemporary women have listened. Roughly three out of four new U.S. mothers, for instance, start out determined to breast-feed. But only a small percentage persist to the five- or sixth-month mark (Foss, 2010). Why?

One cause has to do with the need to work (Flower and others, 2008;Vaughn, 2010). Although U.S. worksites are mandated by law to permit new mothers to pump their milk, imagine the problems you would face following the six-month recommendation as a server or supermarket clerk, or anyone who had to return to work soon after delivery to a physically demanding job (Guendelman and others, 2009). Women complain that breast-feeding is not practical. They are embarrassed to nurse their babies in public, especially if men are around (Vaaler and others, 2010; Vaughn, 2010).

One advocate even blames medical experts: It's one thing for doctors to say, "Just do it," and another to provide the support a woman needs to stimulate milk production or position her infant in just the right way. How many new mothers abandon breast-feeding because they expect it to be easy (and it isn't), and they are left hanging without practical advice? (Foss, 2010.)

This suggests that to increase breast-feeding rates, we need to make this activity less difficult and—most important—genuinely welcome in the wider world. Imagine smiling at women who nurse on the subway rather than averting our eyes! But,

undernutrition A chronic lack of adequate food.

stunting Excessively short stature in a child, caused by chronic lack of adequate nutrition.

micronutrient deficiency Chronically inadequate level of a specific nutrient important to development and disease prevention, such as Vitamin A, zinc, and/or iron.

emphasizing a more personal benefit of breast-feeding might also help. Overweight women are less likely to nurse their babies than their slimmer counterparts (Liu and others, 2010). One study suggests these mothers tend to give up when they realize that this practice does not magically "make you slim" (Krause, Lovelady, & Ostbye, 2011). Still, research shows extended breast-feeding does reduce the odds of gaining weight from one pregnancy to the next (Ostbye and others, 2010). So, perhaps we need a new public health awareness slogan: "Breast-feeding is best for your baby and for your beauty, too!"

Alamy

Would you get uncomfortable—like this male rider on the subway—if a new mother sitting next to you suddenly popped out her breast to nurse?

Malnutrition: A Serious Developing-World Concern

Breast milk potentially gives *every* child around the world a chance to thrive. However, there comes a time—at around 6 months of age—when babies must be given some solid food. Then, the horrifying inequalities in global nutrition hit (Caulfield and others, 2006).

How many young children suffer from **undernutrition,** having a serious lack of adequate food? For answers, epidemiologists look at rates of **stunting,** the percentage of children under age 5 in a given region who rank below the fifth percentile in height, according to the norms for their age. This very short stature is a symptom of *chronic* inadequate nutrition, which takes a serious toll on cognition, on health, and on every activity of life (Abubakar and others, 2010; UNICEF, 2009).

The good news is that during the past 30 years, stunting rates have declined in poor regions of the world (UNICEF, 2002a). The tragedy is that as late as 2006, this sign of serious malnutrition still affected an alarming 195 million children, roughly *one in three* developing-world girls and boys (UNICEF, 2009). Notice from Figure 3.3 that in high stunting regions such as Africa and Asia, **micronutrient deficiencies**—inadequate levels of nutrients such as iron or zinc or Vitamin A—are rampant. Disorders, such as Kwashiorkor (described in the Experiencing the Lifespan box on page 84), can even strike when there is ample food.

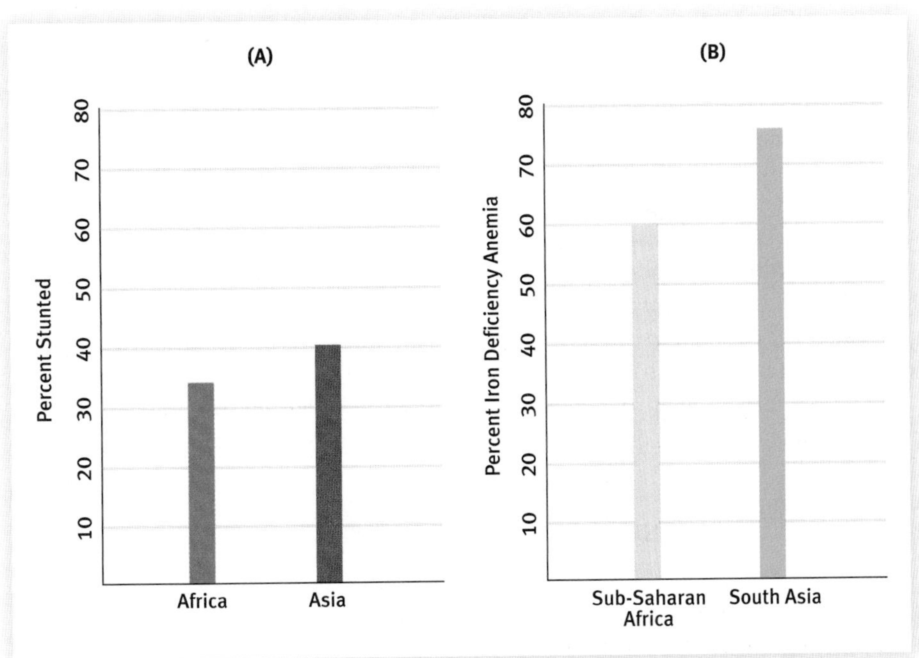

FIGURE 3.3: **Prevalence of two important indicators of undernutrition in poor regions of the world 2006:** Chart A shows that an incredible more-than-one-in-three-young-children in Asia and Africa are stunted. As you can see in chart B, in sub-Saharan Africa and South Asia the important micronutrient deficiency—iron-deficiency anemia—is rampant.

Sources: Caulfield and others, 2006; UNICEF, 2009.

EXPERIENCING THE LIFESPAN: A Passion to Eradicate Malnutrition: A Career in Public Health

What is it like to battle malnutrition in the developing world? Listen to Richard Douglass describe his life and career:

I grew up on the South Side of Chicago—my radius was maybe 4 or 5 blocks in either direction. Then, I spent my junior year in college in Ethiopia, and it changed my life. I lived across the street from the hospital, and every morning I saw a flood of people standing in line. The same people would wait all day and night, and in the mornings a cart would come and take away the dead. I had been Premed, but when I saw the lack of doctors I realized I needed a larger mission. I got my Master's and then my Ph.D. in public health.

In public health we focus on primary prevention, how to prevent diseases and save thousands of people from getting ill. So I've worked in Chicago to eradicate syphilis, helped pioneer the field of elder abuse. But my heart is still in Africa, where I spend much of my time. So let me tell you about my work in Ghana.

My focus for the past 10 years has been on Kwashiorkor, a disease that is responsible for 4 percent of deaths of African children under 5 years old. What it literally means is "the disease that happens when the second child is born." The first child is taken off the breast too soon and given a porridge that doesn't have amino acids, and so the musculature and the diaphragm break down. You get a bloated look (swollen stomach), and then you die. If a child does survive, he ends up stunted, and so looks maybe 5 years younger.

Once someone gets the disease, you can save their life. But it's a 36-month rehabilitation that requires the family to take that child to the clinic for treatment every week. It would be a terrible challenge in our country. In Ghana it can mean traveling a dozen miles by foot. So a single mom with two or three kids is going to drop out of the program as soon as the child starts to look healthy. Because of male urban migration, the African family is in peril. If a family has a grandmother or great-auntie, the child will make it because this woman can take care of the children. So the presence of a grandma is saving kids' lives.

Most malnutrition shows up after wars. The tragedy is that in Ghana there is tons of food. So it's a problem of ignorance, not poverty. The issue is partly cultural. First, among some groups, the men eat, then women, then older children, then the babies get what is left. So all the meat is gone, the fish is gone, and then you just have that porridge. We have been trying to impose a cultural norm that the mother is responsible for monitoring the family's education—and the way to do that is for everyone to sit around the dining table, thereby ensuring that the children get to eat. And we think it will work. The other issue is just pure public health education—teaching families "just because your child looks fat doesn't mean that he is healthy."

I feel better on African soil than anywhere else. There is a sincerity about the people. With poor people in the developing world who are used to being exploited, they are willing to write you off in a heartbeat if you give them a reason; but if you make a promise and follow through, then you are part of their lives forever. I keep going back forty years to my college experience in Ethiopia... watching those people standing at the hospital, just waiting to die. Making a difference for them is the reason why I was born. At age 62, I'm at the pinnacle of my life.

How many young children are stunted or chronically hungry in the United States? According to yearly polls sponsored by the U.S. Department of Agriculture, in 2010 roughly one in five U.S. households with children was designated as **food insecure.** This label means that people reported sometimes not having the money to provide a balanced diet, or worried that their money for food might run out at the end of the month. One in ten mother-headed families reported *severe food insecurity.* They sometimes went hungry due to lack of funds (United States Department of Agriculture, Economic Research Service, 2010). However, because the United States provides the life-saving nutrition-related entitlement programs described in Table 3.2, in our nation as well as in other developed countries, poor children are spared the *ongoing* hunger that limits the life chances of so many boys and girls around the globe.

food insecurity According to U.S Department of Agriculture surveys, the number of households that report needing to serve unbalanced meals, worrying about not having enough food at the end of the month, or having to go hungry due to lack of money (latter is *severe food insecurity*).

Crying: The First Communication Signal

At 2 months, when Jason started crying, I was clueless. I picked him up, rocked him, and kept a pacifier glued to his mouth; I called my mother, the doctor, even my local pharmacist, for advice. Since it immediately put Jason to sleep, my husband and I took

***TABLE 3.2:* Major U.S. Federal Nutrition Programs Serving Young Children**

Food Stamp Program (Now called SNAP, Supplemental Nutrition Assistance Program): This mainstay federal nutrition program provides electronic cards that participants can use like a debit card to buy food. To qualify, a family must have an income less than 130 percent of the federal poverty line and have no more than $2,000 in resources. Although families with young children make up the majority of food stamp recipients, others—single working adults, the homeless, and legal working immigrants who entered the United States before 1996—also qualify for this aid.*

Special Supplemental Nutrition Program for Women, Infants, and Children (WIC): This federally funded grant program is specifically for low-income pregnant women and mothers with children under age 5. To be eligible, a family must be judged nutritionally at risk by a health-care professional and earn below 185 percent of the poverty line. WIC offers a monthly package of supplements tailored to the family's unique nutritional needs (such as infant formula and baby cereals) plus nutrition education and breast-feeding support. In 2008, this program served over 8 million women, infants, and children.*

Child and Adult Care Food Program (CACFP): This program reimburses child-care facilities, day-care providers, after-school programs, and providers of various adult services for the cost of serving high-quality meals. Surveys show that children in participating programs have higher intakes of key nutrients and eat fewer servings of fats and sweets than do children who attend child-care facilities that do not participate.

Source: Food Research and Action Center, http://frac.org/federal-foodnutrition-programs/snapfood-stamps/, accessed September 28, 2011; U.S. Department of Agriculture (USDA), www.fns.usda.gov/fsp/faqs.htm, accessed November 7, 2005.

*As of this writing (2012) an incredible one in five U.S adults is on food stamps. This program and WIC are vital mainstays for families with children during these tough economic times.

car rides at three in the morning—the only people on the road were teenagers and other new parents like us. Now that my little love is 10 months old, I know exactly why he is crying, and those lonely countryside tours are long gone.

Crying, that vital way we communicate our feelings at any age, reaches its lifetime peak at around five weeks after birth (St. James-Roberts, 2007). However, a distinctive change in crying occurs at about month 4. As the cortex blossoms, crying rates decline, and babies selectively use this basic communication mode to express their needs.

It's tempting to think of crying as a negative state. However, because crying is as vital to survival as sucking, when babies cry too little, this can be a sign of a neurological problem (Zeskind & Lester, 2001). When babies cry, we pick them up, rock them, and give them loving care. So, up to a certain point, crying helps cement the infant–parent bond.

Still, there is a limit. When a baby cries continually and cannot be soothed, she may have that bane of early infancy—**colic.** Despite what some grandmas (unhelpfully) tell new mothers, it's a myth that inept or anxious parents produce colicky babies. The true cause of colic lies in an immature nervous system. After they exit the cozy womb, some babies react with intense distress when bombarded by challenging stimuli, such as being handled or fed (St. James-Roberts, 2007). So, we need to back off from blaming severely stressed-out moms and dads for this biological problem of early infant life.

The good news is that colic is short-lived. Most parents find, to their relief, that around month 4, their baby suddenly becomes a new, pleasant person overnight. For this reason, there is only cause for concern when a baby cries excessively after this age (Schmid and others, 2010).

Imagine having a baby with colic. You feel completely helpless. You cannot do anything to quiet the baby down. There are few things more damaging to parental self-efficacy than an infant's out-of-control crying (Keefe and others, 2006).

colic A baby's frantic, continual crying during the first three months of life; caused by an immature nervous system.

INTERVENTIONS: What Quiets a Young Baby?

What soothes a crying baby? One strategy is to provide a pacifier, a breast, a bottle, or anything that satisfies the need to suck. Another is clasping the baby to your body and rocking, or **swaddling** (wrapping) him.

An especially powerful soother is skin-to-skin human contact. And the practices of the !Kung San hunter-gatherers of Botswana offer Westerners a lesson here. In this collectivist culture, where mothers strap infants to their bodies and feed them on demand, babies still do get colic, but the frequency of this ailment is dramatically reduced. When researchers compared the babies of European women who adopted this strategy—carrying their babies around, offering the breast on demand—with a comparison group that practiced standard Western care, the continuously held and fed babies cried 50 percent less (St. James-Roberts, 2007).

Dean Conger/Corbis

Not only are these Mongolian babies getting protection from the intense winter cold, but by being lavishly swaddled, they may feel like they have re-entered their mother's cozy womb.

Kangaroo care, or using a baby sling, can even help premature infants grow (World Health Organization [WHO], 2003b). In one experiment, developmentalists had mothers with babies in an intensive care unit carry their infants in baby slings for one hour each day. They then compared these children's development with that of a comparable group given standard care. At 6 months of age, the kangaroo-care babies scored higher on developmental tests. Their parents were rated as providing a more nurturing home environment, too (Feldman & Eidelman, 2003).

Imagine having your baby whisked away at birth to spend weeks in the care of strangers. Now, think of being able to caress his tiny body, the sense of self-efficacy that would flow from helping him thrive. So it makes sense that any cuddling intervention can have a long-term impact on both the baby and the parent–child bond.

Another calming influence on babies is infant massage. From helping premature infants gain weight, to treating toddler (and adult) sleep problems, to reducing old-age pain, massage enhances well-being from the beginning to the end of life (Field, Diego, & Hernandez-Reif, 2007, 2011).

We all know the power of a cuddle or a relaxing massage to soothe our troubles. Can a good deal of holding and stroking in early infancy *generally* insulate us against stress? Consider this study with rats.

Because rodent mothers (like humans) differ in the "hands-on" contact they give their babies, researchers classified rats who had just given birth into high licking and grooming, average licking and grooming, and low licking and grooming groups. As adults, they discovered the lavishly licked and groomed rats were less agitated when exposed to stressful events (Menard & Hakvoort, 2007). We need to be cautious about generalizing this finding to humans. Advocating for the !Kung San approach to caregiving might be asking too much of modern moms. Still, the implication is clear: During the first months of life (or, for as long as you can), keep touching and loving 'em up!

Cuddles calm us from day 1 to age 101. However, the events that cause crying also undergo fascinating developmental changes. The same swaddling or long car ride that magically quieted a 2-month-old evokes agony in a toddler who cannot stand to be confined. First, it's swaddling, then watching a mobile, then seeing Mom enter the room that has the power to soothe. In preschool, it's monsters that cause wailing; during elementary school, it's failing or being rejected by our social group. As teenagers and emerging adults, we weep for lost love. Finally, among mature adults and old folks (as we reach Erikson's stage of generativity), we stop crying for ourselves and cry when our loved ones are in pain. Our crying shows just where we are developmentally throughout our lives!

swaddling Wrapping a baby tightly in a blanket or garment. This technique is calming during early infancy.

kangaroo care Carrying a young baby in a sling close to the caregiver's body. This technique is useful for soothing an infant.

Sleeping: The Main Newborn State

If crying is a crucial baby (and adult) communication signal, sleep is the quintessential newborn state. Visit a relative who has recently given birth. Will her baby be crying or eating? No, she is almost certain to be asleep. Full-term newborns typically sleep for 18 hours out of a 24-hour day. As Figure 3.4 shows, although they cycle through different stages of arousal, newborns are in the sleeping/drowsy phase about 90 percent of the time (Thoman & Whitney, 1990). And there is a reason for the saying, "She sleeps like a baby." Perhaps because it mirrors the whooshing sound in the womb, noise helps newborns zone out. The problem for parents, of course, is that babies wake up and start wailing, like clockwork, every three to four hours.

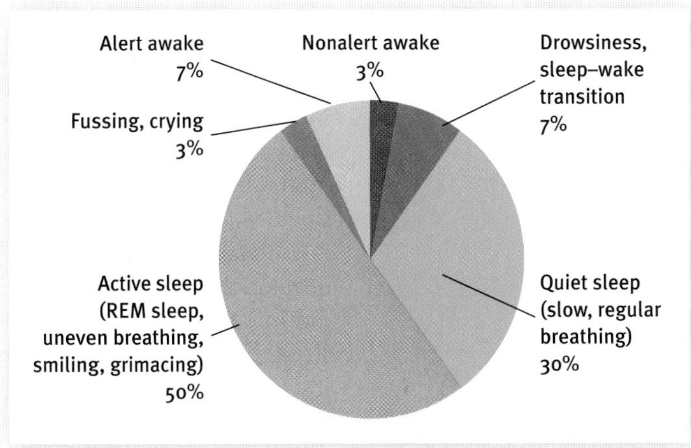

FIGURE 3.4: **Newborns sleep most of the time:** During each 24-hour period, newborns cycle through various states of arousal. Notice, however, that babies spend the vast majority of their time either sleeping or in the getting-to-sleep phase.

Source: Adapted from Thoman & Whitney, 1990.

Developmental Changes: From Signaling, to Self-Soothing, to Shifts in REM Sleep

During the first year of life, infant sleep patterns adapt to the human world. Nighttime awakenings become less frequent. Then, by about 6 months of age, there is a milestone. The typical baby sleeps for 6 hours a night. At age 1, the typical pattern is roughly 12 hours of sleep a night, with an additional morning and afternoon nap. During year two, the caretaker's morning respite to do housework or rest is regretfully lost, as children give up the morning nap. Finally, by late preschool, sleep often (although not always) occurs only at night (Anders, Goodlin-Jones, & Zelenko, 1998).

In addition to its incredible length and on-again-off-again pattern, infant sleep differs physiologically from our adult pattern. When we fall asleep, we descend through four stages, involving progressively slower brain-wave frequencies, and then cycle back to reach **REM sleep**—a phase of rapid eye movement, when dreaming is intense and our brain-wave frequencies look virtually identical to when we are in the lightest sleep stage (see Figure 3.5). When infants fall asleep, they immediately go into

REM sleep The phase of sleep involving rapid eye movements, when the EEG looks almost like it does during waking. REM sleep decreases as infants mature.

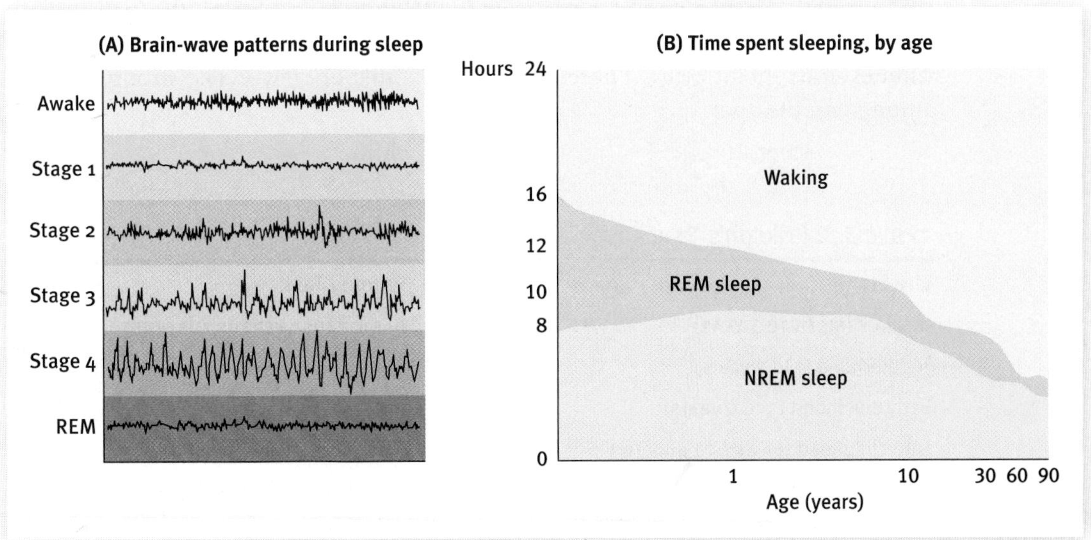

FIGURE 3.5: **Sleep brain waves and lifespan changes in sleep and wakefulness:** In chart A, you can see the EEG patterns associated with the four stages of sleep that first appear during adolescence. After we fall asleep, our brain waves get progressively slower (these are the four stages of non-REM sleep) and then we enter the REM phase during which dreaming is intense. Now, notice in chart B the time young babies spend in REM. As REM sleep helps consolidate memory, is the incredible time babies spend in this phase crucial to absorbing the overwhelming amount of information that must be mastered during the first years of life?

Source: Adapted from Roffwarg, Muzio, & Dement, 1966.

self-soothing Children's ability, usually beginning at about 6 months of age, to put themselves back to sleep when they wake up during the night.

the REM phase and spend most of their time in this state. It is not until adolescence that we have the adult sleep cycle shown in chart A, with four distinct stages (Anders, Goodlin-Jones, & Zelenko, 1998).

Parents are thrilled to say, "My child is sleeping though the night." This statement, surprisingly, is false. When developmentalists used time-lapse photography to monitor nightly sleep, they discovered that babies *never* sleep through the night. Most still wake up several times a night, even at age 2. However, by about 6 months of age, many develop the skills to become **self-soothing.** They can put themselves back to sleep when they do wake up (Goodlin-Jones, Burnham, & Anders, 2000).

Imagine that you are a new parent. Your first challenge is to get your baby to develop the skill of nighttime self-soothing. Around age 1, because your child is now put into the crib while still awake, there may be issues with getting your baby to *go* to sleep. During preschool and elementary school, the sleep problem shifts again. Now, it's concerns about getting the child *into* bed: "Mommy, can't I stay up later? Do I *have* to turn off the lights?"

As you might expect, during the first months of life, issues related to getting the baby to sleep through the night are the top-ranking parental concern (Smart & Hiscock, 2007). Although it may make them cranky, parents expect to be sleep-deprived with a very young baby; but once a child has passed the 5- or 6-month milestone, they get agitated if the infant has never permitted them a full night's sleep. Parents expect periodic sleep problems when their child is ill or under stress, but not the zombie-like irritability that comes from being chronically sleep-deprived for years. There is a poisonous bidirectional effect here: Children with chronic sleep problems produce irritable, stressed-out parents. Irritable, stressed-out parents produce childhood problems with sleep (Keller & El-Sheikh, 2010; Kelly & El-Sheikh, 2011; Schmid and others, 2011).

INTERVENTIONS: What Helps a Baby Self-Soothe?

What should parents do when their baby signals (cries out) from her crib? At one end of the continuum stand the traditional behaviorists: "Don't reinforce crying by responding—and be consistent. Never go in and comfort the baby lest you let a variable reinforcement schedule unfold, and the child will cry longer." At the other, we have John Bowlby with his emphasis on the attachment bond, or Erik Erikson with his concept of *basic trust* (see Table 3.3). During the first year of life, both Bowlby and Erikson imply that caregivers should sensitively respond whenever an infant cries. These contrasting points of view evoke strong passions among parents, too:

TABLE 3.3: Erikson's Psychosocial Stages

Life Stage	Primary Task
INFANCY (BIRTH TO 1 YEAR)	**BASIC TRUST VERSUS MISTRUST**
Toddlerhood (1 to 2 years)	Autonomy versus shame and doubt
Early childhood (3 to 6 years)	Initiative versus guilt
Late childhood (6 years to puberty)	Industry versus inferiority
Adolescence (teens into twenties)	Identity versus role confusion
Young adulthood (twenties to early forties)	Intimacy versus isolation
Middle adulthood (forties to sixties)	Generativity versus stagnation
Late adulthood (late sixties and beyond)	Integrity versus despair

According to Erikson, in the first year of life, our mission is to feel confident that the human world will lovingly satisfy our needs. Basic trust is the foundation for the challenges we face at every other life stage.

> I feel the basic lesson parents need to teach children is how to be independent, not to let your child rule your life, give him time to figure things out on his own, and not be attended to with every whimper.

> I am going with my instincts and trying to be a good, caring mommy. Putting a baby in his crib to "cry it out" seems cruel. There is no such thing as spoiling an infant!

co-sleeping The standard custom, in collectivist cultures, of having a child and parent share a bed.

Where do you stand on this "Teach 'em" versus "Give unconditional love" controversy? Based on the discussion of what quiets early crying, during a baby's first months, our bias should clearly be to respond. But, by about month 7 or 8, it may be better to hang back a bit, as one study showed that babies who are quickly picked up do have more trouble learning to self-soothe (St. James-Roberts, 2007). So for parents who care vitally about getting a good night's sleep, it's best not to react immediately to every nighttime whimper—but this advice only applies after the cortex has come on-line, when a baby theoretically can "learn" to get to sleep on her own.

The real bottom line, however, is that the choice is up to you because a more critical force outweighs any *specific* sleep practice: "Put a baby to bed with love." When researchers videoed the bedtime behavior of mothers with infants, they found that, apart from anything else, women who responded sensitively to their babies around bedtime (those who used gentle, loving, pre-bed soothing routines) had children with fewer sleep problems (Teti and others, 2010).

This finding makes excellent sense. Notice that when you feel disconnected from loved ones and anxious about your relationships, you have trouble sleeping. To sleep soundly at *any age*, we need to feel cushioned by love.

The same principle "do what works for you," applies to this next controversial topic: Having a baby sleep in your bed.

To Co-sleep or Not to Co-sleep: A Cultural and Personal Choice

> It was a standard nighttime routine in our house— one by one we'd wander in and say, "Mommy I'm afraid of witches and ghosts," and soon all four of us would be happily nestled in our parents' huge king-sized bed. I never realized that—in the 1950s, in our uptight, middle-class New York suburb—this family bed-sharing qualified as a radical act.

How do you feel about **co-sleeping** or sharing a bed with a child? If you live in the United States and feel queasy about my parents' decision, you are not alone. Until fairly recently, experts in our individualistic society vigorously cautioned parents against co-sleeping (see Ferber, 1985). Behaviorists warned that sharing a bed with a child could produce "excessive dependency." Freudian theorists implied that bed-sharing might place a child at risk for sexual abuse.

In collectivist cultures, where co-sleeping is routine, people would laugh at these ideas (Latz, Wolf, & Lozoff, 1999; Yang & Hahn, 2002). Japanese parents, for instance, often separate to give each child a sleeping partner, because they believe co-sleeping is crucial to babies developing into caring, loving adults (Kitahara, 1989).

Today, in the West, co-sleeping has come out of the closet. Surveys show that, yes, like my parents, many people do it (Ball, 2007; Germo and others, 2007). But, because some mothers and fathers are still reluctant to admit that fact, Table 3.4 on page 90 provides three typical anti-bed-sharing stereotypes and some relevant research so you can decide which choice works best for you.

This blissfully co-sleeping couple seems at peace with their decision—but they may be reluctant to advertise this behavior to potentially disapproving family members and friends.

TABLE 3.4: Classic Co-sleeping Stereotypes and Some Relevant Research

1. **Stereotype: Co-sleeping makes a child less independent and mature.**

   Relevant research: Among California parents of preschoolers, researchers looked at three groups: 1) people who actively chose to co-sleep with their child; 2) "reactive co-sleepers," who reluctantly brought a child into their bed because of sleep troubles; and 3) solitary sleepers—those who slept apart from their babies (Keller & Goldberg, 2004). The preschoolers whose parents had actively chosen to co-sleep were rated as more self-reliant (for example, able to dress themselves) and socially independent (for example, more able to make friends by themselves) compared to the other two groups. Although a variety of forces could explain this correlation, according to this finding, co-sleeping promotes greater maturity and independence, not less!

2. **Stereotype: Co-sleeping disrupts parents' and children's sleep.**

   Relevant research: Co-sleeping infants do awaken more often at night than solitary sleepers. However, co-sleeping babies get back to sleep in a shorter time (Latz, Wolf, & Lozoff, 1999; Mao and others, 2004). With regard to adults, one EEG sleep study found that parents who shared a bed with their infant spent a bit less time in the deepest sleep stages. However, because they did not have to go into the child's room, these parents did not spend fewer hours sleeping than the non-bed-sharing moms and dads (Mosko, Richard, & McKenna, 1997). Bottom line: Co-sleeping is not detrimental to sleep.

3. **Stereotype: Co-sleeping is dangerous because it can cause a baby to be smothered.**

   Relevant research: Here, there may be a few concerns. While some authors argue that co-sleeping helps regulate babies' breathing and so *may* help prevent suffocating at night (see St. James, 2007), bed-sharing infants spend a good fraction of their sleep time face down (Mao and others, 2004). This sleep position, as you can see in the In Focus feature, does not offer the best protection against the ultimate smothering tragedy, SIDS.

In this next section, we'll explore the topic raised by the third stereotype in the table: What causes a baby to die while sleeping, or succumb to that terrifying event called *sudden infant death syndrome (SIDS)?*

IN FOCUS: When Sleep Is Lethal

Sudden infant death syndrome (SIDS) refers to the unexplained death of an apparently healthy infant, often while sleeping, during the first months of life. Although it strikes only about 1 in 1,000 U.S. babies, SIDS is a top-ranking cause of infant mortality in the United States and the rest of the developed world (Karns, 2001).

What causes SIDS? In autopsying infants who died for no apparent reason during the peak risk zone for SIDS (about 1 to 10 months), researchers targeted abnormalities in a particular region of the brain. Specifically, compared to babies who died of other causes, a high percentage of SIDS infants had either too many or too few neurons in a section of the brain stem involved in coordinating tongue movements and maintaining the airway when we inhale (Lavezzi and others, 2010).

sudden infant death syndrome (SIDS) The unexplained death of an apparently healthy infant, often while sleeping, during the first year of life.

Interestingly, however, a significant fraction of the babies in the above study had mothers who smoked while pregnant, suggesting another reason to stop smoking during this vital time. But even if we can trace the origin of SIDS to biological pre-birth problems, this tragedy has clear post-birth environmental causes. SIDS deaths tend to spike on days when parental alcohol consumption is apt to be high, such as New Year's Eve (Phillips, Brewer, & Wadensweiler, 2011), implying that, sometimes, parental carelessness may be involved. Most important, SIDS is definitely linked to infants being inadvertently smothered, by being placed face down in a "fluffy" crib. During the early 1990s, this evidence prompted the American Academy of Pediatrics to urge parents to put infants to sleep on their backs. The Back to Sleep campaign worked, because from 1992 to 1997, there was a 43 percent reduction in SIDS deaths in the United States (Gore & DuBois, 1998).

The SIDS success story has a twenty-first-century postscript: It may have worked too well! With anxious caregivers refusing to give babies a minute on their stomachs, some experts worry that infants may not be getting the practice they need to reach motor milestones, such as creeping, at the appropriate age. So health professionals now urge people to also give babies "tummy time" (face-down minutes) during the day (Koren and others, 2010). Can't today's poor over-advised parents *ever* do anything right?

Table 3.5 offers a section summary in the form of practical tips for caregivers dealing with infants' eating, crying, and sleeping. Now it's time to move on to sensory development and moving into the world.

TABLE 3.5: Infants' Basic States: Summary Tips For Caregivers (and Others)

Eating

- Don't worry about continual newborn sucking and rooting. These are normal reflexes, and they disappear after the first months of life.
- As the baby becomes mobile, be alert to the child's tendency to put everything into the mouth and baby-proof the home (see the next section's discussion).
- Try to breast-feed exclusively for the first 6 months and reach out for help learning this skill. But if nursing becomes impossible, spend a lot of time with your baby, as the benefits breast-fed babies show may possibly result from more loving "bonding time."
- Employers should make efforts to support breast-feeding in the workplace. Society should celebrate women who nurse in public.
- After the child is weaned, provide a balanced diet. But don't get frantic if a toddler limits her intake to a few "favorite foods" at around age 1 1/2—this pickiness is normal and temporary.

Crying

- Appreciate that crying is crucial—it's the way babies communicate their needs—and realize that this behavior is at its peak during the first months of life. The frequency of crying declines and the reasons why the child is crying become far clearer after early infancy.
- If a baby has colic, hang in there. This condition typically ends at month 4. Moreover, understand that colic has nothing to do with insensitive mothering.
- During the day, carry a young infant around in a "baby sling" as much as possible, and if possible, feed the baby immediately. In addition, employ infant massage to soothe the baby.

Sleeping

- Expect to be sleep-deprived for the first few months, until the typical infant learns to self-soothe; meanwhile, try to take regular naps. After that, expect periodic sleep problems and understand that children will give up their daytime nap at around age 2.
- To promote self-soothing, after 4 months of age, don't go to the infant at the first whimper. But the choice is really up to you—as the best way to promote sleep is to put your baby to bed with love.
- Co-sleeping—having a child sleep in your bed—is a personal decision. Although most of the stereotypes about co-sleeping are wrong, this practice may not be completely safe with young infants, as bed-sharing may slightly increase the risk of SIDS.

TYING IT ALL TOGETHER

1. You're a nurse in the obstetrics ward, and new parents often ask you why their babies continually make sucking noises and turn their heads toward anything that touches their cheek and then suck. What should you say?
   a. The sucking noises are called the sucking reflex; the head-turning response is the rooting reflex.
   b. These behaviors are programmed by the lower brain centers to automatically occur at birth.
   c. These behaviors will start to disappear as the cortex matures.
   d. You should make all of these comments.
2. As a neonatal nurse, you want to design a questionnaire to predict which of your patients are most likely to abandon breast-feeding or persist. What questions might your survey include?
3. Your sister and her husband are under enormous stress because of their colicky 1-month-old's continual crying. Based on this section, give your sister and her husband two bits of advice for soothing their child. What encouraging information can you give your relatives about colic?
4. Jorge tells you that he's thrilled because last night his 6-month-old finally slept through the night. Is Jorge's child ahead of schedule, behind, or on time for this milestone? Is Jorge right in saying, "My child is sleeping *through* the night"?
5. Take a poll of your classmates, asking them if they believe in co-sleeping and whether they would immediately go in to quiet a crying infant. Do you find any differences in their answers by ethnicity, by gender, or by age?

Answers to the Tying It All Together questions can be found at the end of this chapter.

Sensory and Motor Development

Sleeping, eating, and crying are easy to observe; but what is it like to really *be* a newborn? Suppose you could time-travel back to your first days of life. What would you experience through your senses?

One sense is definitely operational before we leave the womb. Using ultrasound, researchers can see startle reactions in response to noise in fetuses, showing that rudimentary hearing capacities exist before birth. Recall from the previous chapter that the basics of vision may also be in place by about the seventh month of fetal life.

Table 3.6 lists other interesting facts about newborn senses. Now, let's focus directly on vision because the research in this area is so extensive, the findings are so astonishing, and the studies devised to get into babies' heads are so brilliantly planned.

TABLE 3.6: Some Interesting Facts About Other Newborn Senses

Hearing: Fetuses can discriminate different tones in the womb (Lecanuet and others, 2000). Newborns prefer women's voices, as they are selectively sensitive to higher-pitched tones. At less than 1 week of age, babies recognize their mother's voice (DeCasper & Fifer, 1980). By 1 month of age, they tune in to infant-directed speech (described on page 106) communications tailored to them.

Smell: Newborns prefer the odor of breast milk to that of amniotic fluid (Marlier, Schaal, & Soussignan, 1998). The smell of breast milk, unlike formula, increases blood flow in newborn's frontal lobes—which may be another benefit of nursing for 6 months (Aoyama and others, 2010). Plus, smelling breast milk has a soothing effect; newborns cry more vigorously when facing a scentless breast (one covered with a transparent film) (Doucet and others, 2007).

Taste: Newborns are sensitive to basic tastes. When they taste a bitter, sour, or salty substance, they stop sucking and wrinkle their faces. They will suck more avidly on a sweet solution, although they will stop if the substance grows too sweet. Having babies suck a sweet solution before a painful experience, such as a heel stick, reduces agitation and so can be used as a pain-management technique (Fernandez and others, 2003; Gibbins & Stevens, 2001).

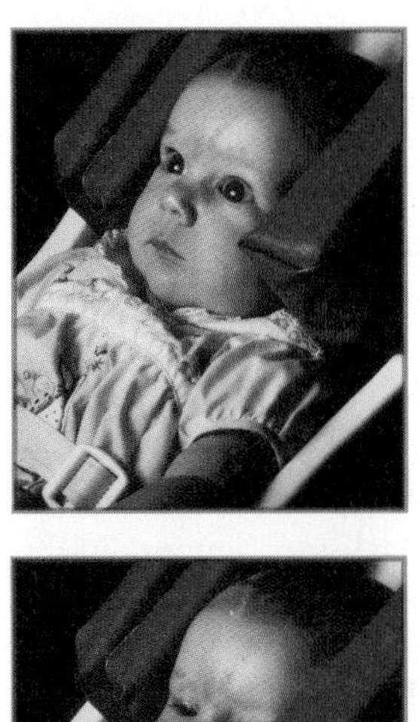
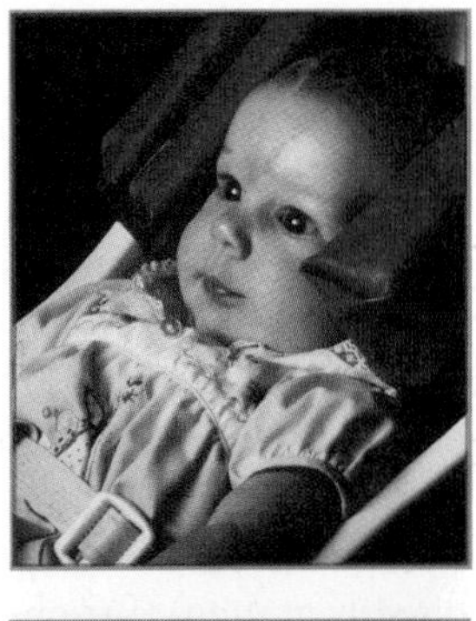
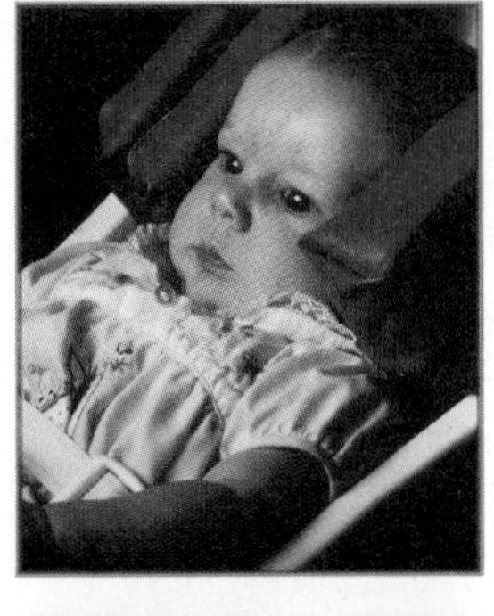
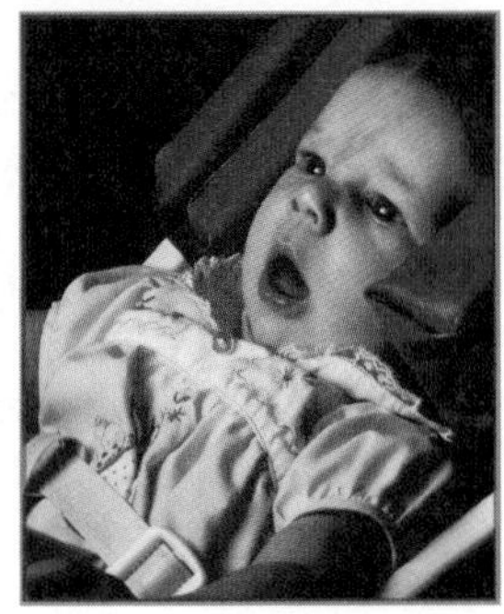

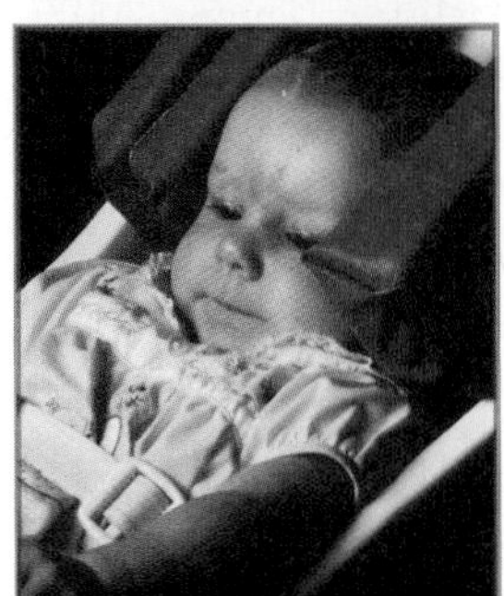
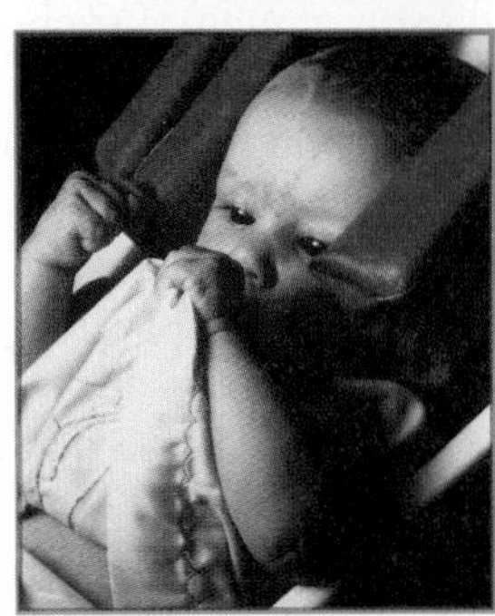
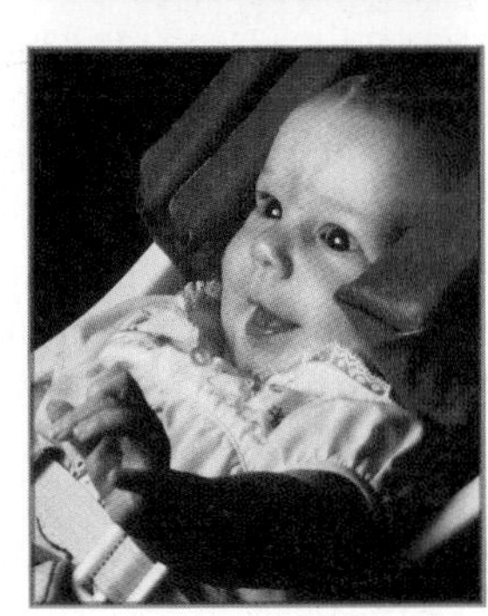

In this preferential-looking study, as an image pops up on the screen, this little girl is at first enthralled. She then *habituates* and gets interested in a new activity (picking at her dress). Finally (hooray!), another enticing new image appears on the screen.

preferential-looking paradigm A research technique to explore early infant sensory capacities and cognition, drawing on the principle that we are attracted to novelty and prefer to look at new things.

habituation The predictable loss of interest that develops once a stimulus becomes familiar; used to explore infant sensory capacities and thinking.

face-perception studies Research using preferential looking and habituation to explore what very young babies know about faces.

What Do Newborns See?

Imagine you are a researcher who wants to figure out what a newborn can see. What do you do? As the accompanying photo series reveals, you would put the baby into an apparatus, present images, and watch her eyes move. Specifically, researchers use the **preferential-looking paradigm**—the principle that human beings are attracted to novelty and look selectively at new things. As the photos show, they also draw on a process called **habituation**—the fact that we naturally lose interest in a new object after some time.

You can notice preferential looking and habituation in operation right now in your life. If you see or hear something new, you look up with interest. After a minute, you habituate and return to reading this book.

By showing newborns small- and large-striped patterns and measuring preferential looking, researchers have found that at birth our ability to see clearly at distances is very poor. With a visual acuity score of roughly 20/400 (versus our ideal adult 20/20), a newborn would qualify as legally blind in many states (Kellman & Banks, 1998). Because the visual cortex matures quickly, vision improves rapidly, and by about age 1, infants see just like adults.

What visual capacities *do* we have at birth? A century ago, the first American psychologist, William James, described the inner life of the newborn as "one buzzing, blooming confusion." In reading the following studies exploring **face perception** (making sense of human faces), you can judge whether or not James was correct.

Focusing on Faces

Face-perception research offers evidence that, from their first days out of the womb, babies selectively attend to the social world. When newborns are presented with the paired stimuli in Figure 3.6, they spend more time looking at the face pattern than at the scrambled pattern. They will track or follow that face-like stimulus longer when it is moved from side to side (Farroni, Massaccesi, & Simion, 2002; Slater and others, 2010).

The story gets more interesting. Newborns can make amazing distinctions. During their first week of life, they prefer to look at a photo of their mother compared to one of a stranger. They can pick out their mother's face from another face with similar features, although not if their mother's hair is covered by a scarf (Bushnell, 1998).

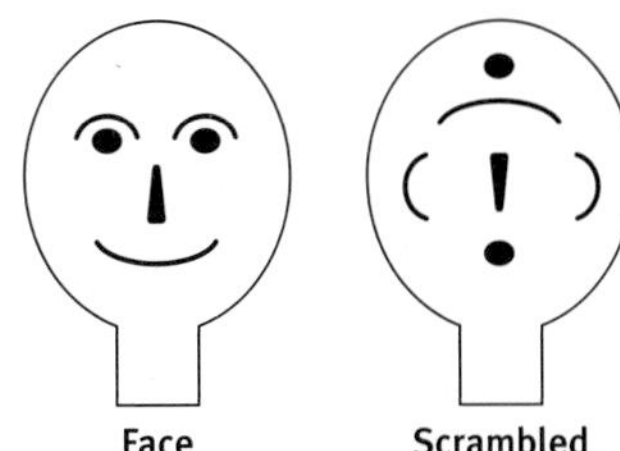

FIGURE 3.6: **Babies prefer faces:** When shown these illustrations, newborns looked most at the face-like drawing. Might the fact that infants are biologically programmed to selectively look at faces be built into evolution to help ensure that adults give babies loving care?

Most interesting, newborns prefer attractive-looking people! Researchers selected photos of attractive and unattractive women, then took infants from the maternity ward and measured preferential looking. The attractive faces got looked at significantly longer—61 percent of the time (Slater and others, 2010). By 3 to 6 months of age, this preference for good-looking people gets more sophisticated. Babies preferentially look at good-looking infants and children. They even prefer handsome men and pretty women of different racial groups (Slater, 2001). Unhappily, our tendency to gravitate toward people for their looks seems somewhat biologically built in. (In case you are interested, more symmetrical faces tend to be rated as better-looking.)

We also seem pre-wired to gravitate to *relationships*. Newborns look longer at faces when the "eyes" are gazing directly at them (Frischen, Bayliss, & Tipper, 2007). They can mimic facial expressions that an adult makes, such as sticking out the tongue (Meltzoff & Moore, 1977). So if you have wondered why you get uncomfortable when someone stares at you, or have agonized at your humiliating tendency to mimic everyone else's gestures and facial tics, this research offers answers. It's not a personal problem. It's built into our human biology, beginning from day one!

With experience, our sensitivity to faces—and the emotions they reveal—markedly improves. But fascinating research suggests that early experience also shapes what we learn *not* to see (Slater and others, 2010).

Developmentalists tested European American babies at different points during their first year of life for the infants' ability to discriminate between different faces within their own racial group and those belonging to other ethnicities (African American, Middle Eastern, and Chinese). While the 3-month-olds preferentially looked at "new faces" of every ethnicity, showing they could see the differences between individuals in each group, by 9 months of age, the babies could only discriminate between faces in their own ethnic group.

iStockphoto/ Thinkstock/Getty Images

While these monkeys look identical to us, you would have been able to see the differences in their faces at 6 months of age. Also, if your profession involved zoo keeping or researching primates, you would "relearn" to distinguish these faces! (See Slater and others, 2010.)

You might also be interested to know that during your first months of life, you could tell the difference between the two monkey faces shown in these photos—and you had the talent to link different monkey sounds, such as grunts, to their appropriate facial expressions, too (Lewkowicz, Leo, & Simon, 2010).

Why did these skills disappear? The cause, as you may have guessed, is cortical pruning—the fact that unneeded synapses in our visual system atrophy or are lost (Slater and others, 2010). So if you have wondered why "all Chinese look alike" (if you aren't Chinese) or have puzzled about why individual species at the zoo have identical faces, it's a misperception. You lost the connections to decode these differences during your first year of life!

In conclusion, William James was wrong. Newborns don't experience the world as a "blooming, buzzing confusion." We arrive in life with a remarkably well-developed sensory apparatus. We have a built-in antenna to tune into the human world. However, visual skills also change dramatically as we mature, in sometimes surprising ways.

Now let's trace another visual capacity as it gradually comes on-line—the ability to see and become frightened of heights.

Seeing Depth and Fearing Heights

Imagine you are a researcher facing a conundrum: How can I find out when babies develop **depth perception**—the ability to "see" variations in heights—without causing them harm? Elinor Gibson's ingenious solution: Develop a procedure called the **visual cliff**. As you can see in Figure 3.7, Gibson and her colleague placed infants on one end of a table with a checkerboard pattern while their mothers stood at the opposite end (Gibson & Walk, 1960). At the table's midpoint, the checkerboard design moved from table to floor level, so it appeared to the babies that if they crawled beyond that point, they would fall. Even when parents

depth perception The ability to see (and fear) heights.

visual cliff A table that appears to "end" in a drop-off at its midpoint; used to test for infant depth perception.

smiled and encouraged their children to crawl to them, 8-month-old infants refused to venture beyond what looked like the drop-off—showing that by this age depth perception exists. Do younger babies have this perception and fear?

To answer this question, other developmentalists dangled 2-month-old infants above the drop-off side of the table. The babies' heart rates declined (a sign of interest), showing that by this age they "saw" the difference in depth but were not afraid (Campos, Langer, & Krowitz, 1970). Babies start to fear heights about month 6 or 7, around the time they are ready to crawl. At this age, their heart rates accelerate (showing anxiety) when they are held near the drop-off side (Schwartz, Campos, & Baisel, 1973).

Mark Richards/ Photo Edit, Inc.

FIGURE 3.7: The visual cliff: Even though his mother is on the other side, this 8-month-old child gets anxious about venturing beyond what looks like the drop-off point in the table—demonstrating that by this age babies have depth perception. By using the strategies discussed in the text, researchers then use the same creative visual cliff apparatus to see if babies too young to crawl also see and fear heights.

In sum, while our ability to *see* differences in depth does appear soon after birth, the sick feeling we have when leaning over a balcony—"Wow, I'd better avoid falling into that space below"—only emerges later, when babies are getting mobile and really need that fear to protect them from getting hurt. How does mobility unfold?

Expanding Body Size

Our brain may expand dramatically after birth. Still, it's far out-paced by the blossoming of the envelope in which we live. Our bodies grow to 21 times their newborn size by the time we reach adulthood (Slater, 2001). This growth is most dramatic during infancy, drastically slows down during childhood, and increases in velocity again during the preadolescent years. Still, looking at overall height and weight statistics is not that revealing. This body sculpting occurs in a definite way.

Imagine taking time-lapse photographs of a baby's head from birth to adulthood and comparing your photos to snapshots of the body. You would not see much change in the overall size and shape of the head. In contrast, the body would elongate and thin out. Newborns start out with tiny "frog" legs timed to slowly straighten out by about month 6. Then comes the stocky, bowlegged toddler, followed by the slimmer child of kindergarten and elementary school. So during childhood, growth follows the same principle as it did inside the womb: Development proceeds according to the *cephalocaudal sequence*—from the head to the feet.

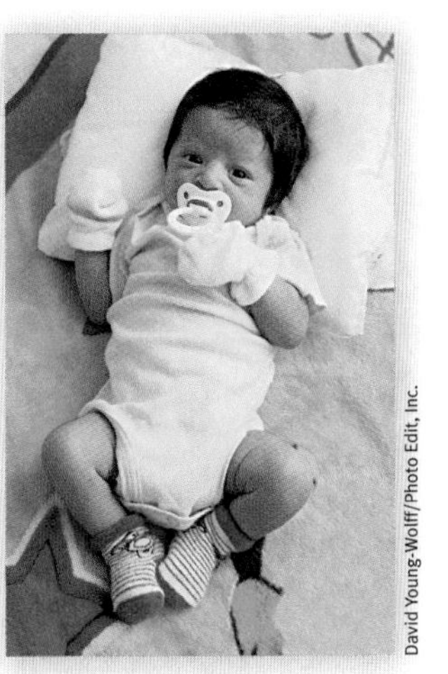

David Young-Wolff/Photo Edit, Inc.

Mark Harwood/Getty Images

The tiny frog legs of very early infancy straighten out by month 6 and then become longer and fully functional for carrying us around (as toddlers)—demonstrating the cephalocaudal principle of development.

Now think of Mickey Mouse, Big Bird, and Elmo. They, too, have relatively large heads and small bodies. Might our favorite cartoon characters be enticing because they mimic the proportions of a baby? Did the deliciously rounded infant shape evolve to seduce adults into giving babies special care?

Mastering Motor Milestones

Actually, all three growth principles spelled out in the previous chapter—*cephalocaudal*, *proximodistal*, and *mass-to-specific*—apply to infant *motor milestones*, the exciting progression of physical abilities during the first year of life. First, babies lift their head, then pivot their upper body, then sit up without support, and finally stand (the cephalocaudal sequence). Infants have control of their shoulders before they can make their arms and fingers obey their commands (proximodistal sequence, from interior to outer parts).

Royalty-Free/Corbis

Studio Forza/Getty Images

Jose Luis Pelaez, Inc./Corbis

Babies first joyously lift their heads and upper torsos, then sit up (at about month 5 or 6), and finally, at around age 1, take their first unforgettable steps—demonstrating that the cephalocaudal principle also applies to motor milestones.

But the most important principle programming motor abilities throughout childhood is the *mass-to-specific* sequence (large before small and detailed). From the wobbly first step at age 1 to the home run out of the ballpark during the teenage years—as the neurons gradually undergo myelination—big, uncoordinated movements are honed and perfected as we move from infancy to adult life.

Variations (and Joys) Related to Infant Mobility

Charting these milestones does not speak to the joy of witnessing them unfold—that landmark moment when your daughter finally masters turning over, after those practice "push-ups," or first connects with the bottle, grasps it, and awkwardly moves it to her mouth. I'll never forget when my own son, after what seemed like years of cruising around holding onto the furniture, finally ventured (so gingerly) out into the air, flung up his hands, and, *yes, yes,* took his ecstatic first step!

Nor do the standard motor milestone charts mention the hilarious glitches that happen when a skill is first being developed—the first days of creeping, when a baby can only move backward and you find him huddled in the corner in pursuit of objects that get steadily farther way. Or when a child first pulls herself to a standing position in the crib, and her triumphant expression changes to bewilderment: "Whoops, now tell me, Mom, *how do I get down?*"

Actually, rather than viewing motor development in static stages such as sitting, then crawling, then walking, researchers now stress the variability and ingenuity of babies' passion to get moving into life (Adolph, 2008). Consider the "creeping" or belly-crawling stage. Some babies scoot; others hunch over or launch themselves forward from their knees, roll from side to side, or scrape along with a cheek on the floor (Adolph & Berger, 2006). And can I *really* say that there was a day when my son definitely mastered walking? When walking, or any other major motor skill first occurs, children do not make steady progress (Adolph & Berger, 2006). They may take their first solo step on Monday and then revert to crawling for a week or so before trying, oh so tentatively, to tackle toddling again.

© Moodboard/Corbis

At 8 or 10 months of age, getting around is a challenge that babies approach in a variety of creative, unique ways.

But suppose a child is definitely behind schedule. Let's say your son is almost 15 months old and has yet to take his first solo step? And what about the fantasies that set in when an infant is ahead? "Only 8 months old, and he's walking. Perhaps my baby is special, a genius!"

What typically happens is that, within weeks, the worries become a memory and the fantasies about the future are shown to be completely wrong. Except in the case of children who have developmental disorders, the rate at which babies master motor milestones has no relation to their later intelligence. Since different regions of the cortex develop at different times, why should our walking or grasping-an-object timetable predict development in a complex function such as grasping the point of this book?

An interesting exception to the rule that early infant individual differences don't predict later cognition involves an ability that doesn't appear on the milestones chart. It concerns *habituation,* discussed in the earlier section exploring vision. In looking at infant abilities longitudinally, one researcher discovered that babies who quickly habituated to stimuli and then later preferentially looked at a new stimulus when it was paired with an "old" one (showing they remembered what they had seen before), had superior scores on elementary school intelligence tests (Fagan, 1988, 2000). The reason is that processing a stimulus quickly and remembering it is a general capacity that underlies a variety of intellectual skills, from mastering language to more effortlessly remembering the messages of this text.

But even if a baby's early locomotion (physically getting around) does not mean he will end up an Einstein, moving into the world does usher in many mental advances.

The Mind-Expanding Effects of Travel

Developmentalists have explored the mind-expanding changes linked to crawling, that classic sign of traveling into the world. Crawling provokes more interest in objects at distances (Anderson, Campos, & Barbu-Roth, 2004). Early crawlers—compared to other babies—are "mature" in the relationship area, too. They are more attuned to a caregiver's facial expressions. They get more upset when their parent leaves the room (Campos and others, 2000).

In interviewing mothers of newly crawling babies, developmentalists discovered that crawling is linked to changes in the parent–child bond (Campos and others, 2000). When their infants started crawling, women reported that they saw their children as more independent—people with a mind of their own. Many said this was the first time they got angry with and disciplined their child. So as babies get mobile, the basic parenting agenda emerges: A child's mission is to explore the world. A parent's job, for the next two decades, lies in setting limits to that exploration, as well as giving love.

INTERVENTIONS: Baby-Proofing, the First Person–Environment Fit

Mobility presents perils. Now safety issues become a major concern. How can caretakers encourage these emerging motor skills and still protect children from getting hurt? The answer is to strive for the right person–environment fit—that is, to **baby-proof** the house.

Get on the floor and look at life from the perspective of the child. Cover electrical outlets and put dangerous cleaning substances on the top shelf. Unplug countertop appliances. Take small objects off tables. Perhaps pad the furniture corners, too. The challenge is to anticipate possible dangers and to stay one step ahead. There will come a day when that child can pry out those outlet covers or ascend to the top of the cleanser-laden cabinet. Unfortunately, those exciting motor milestones have a definite downside, too!

baby-proofing Making the home safe for a newly mobile infant.

TYING IT ALL TOGETHER

1. You're watching through a one-way mirror as a researcher explores how well newborns can hear. The infant is wearing headphones, and the psychologist presents a tone and watches the baby's face to see if the child looks up with interest. The strategy the researcher is using is called the______________ paradigm.
2. Tania says, "Visual capacities improve dramatically during the first year of life." Thomas replies, "No, in some ways our vision gets worse." Who is correct: Tania, Thomas, or both students? Why?

sensorimotor stage Piaget's first stage of cognitive development, lasting from birth to age 2, when babies' agenda is to pin down the basics of physical reality.

3. If Alicia's 8-month-old daughter is participating in a visual cliff study, when she crawls near the drop-off she should (choose one): *look interested in the drop-off but show no fear/be frightened/not notice the drop-off.*
4. Charlie crawled and walked at a very young age, and grew bored before other babies in a habituation test at the local university. His excited parents are sure that Charlie is gifted and are saving up to send him to Harvard. Which, if any, of Charlie's behaviors might support his parents' dreams?
5. List some steps that you would take to baby-proof the room you are sitting in right now.

Answers to the Tying It All Together questions can be found at the end of this chapter.

Cognition

Why exactly *do* infants have an incredible hunger to explore, to touch, to get into every cleanser-laden cabinet and remove all those outlet plugs? For the same reason that, if you landed on a different planet, you would need to get the basics of reality down.

Imagine stepping out onto Mars. You would roam the new environment, exploring the rocks and the sand. While exercising your *walking schema*, or habitual way of physically navigating, you would need to make drastic changes. On Mars, with its minimal gravity, when you took your normal earthling stride, you would probably bounce up 20 feet. Just like a newly crawling infant, you would have to accommodate, and in the process reach a higher mental equilibrium, or a better understanding of life. Moreover, as a good scientist, you would not be satisfied to perform each movement only once. The only way to pin down the physics of this planet would be to repeat each action over and over again. Now you have the basic principles of Jean Piaget's **sensorimotor stage** (see Table 3.7).

Piaget's Sensorimotor Stage

Specifically, Piaget believed that during our first two years on this planet, our mission is to make sense of physical reality by exploring the world through our senses. Just as in the above Mars example, as they *assimilate*, or fit the outer world to what they are

TABLE 3.7: Piaget's Stages: Focus on Infancy

Age	Name of Stage	Description
0–2	Sensorimotor	The baby manipulates objects to pin down the basics of physical reality. This stage ends with the development of language.
2–7	Preoperations	Children's perceptions are captured by their immediate appearances. "What they see is what is real." They believe, among other things, that inanimate objects are really alive and that if the appearance of a quantity of liquid changes (for example, if it is poured from a short, wide glass into a tall, thin one), the amount actually becomes different.
8–12	Concrete operations	Children have a realistic understanding of the world. Their thinking is really on the same wavelength as adults. While they can reason conceptually about concrete objects, however, they cannot think abstractly in a scientific way.
12+	Formal operations	Reasoning is at its pinnacle: hypothetical, scientific, flexible, fully adult. Our full cognitive human potential has been reached.

already capable of doing, infants *accommodate* and so gradually mentally advance. (Remember my example in Chapter 1 of how, in the process of assimilating this information to your current knowledge schemas or mental slots, you are accommodating and so expanding what you know.)

Let's take the "everything into the mouth" schema that figures so prominently during the first year of life. As babies mouth each new object—or, in Piaget's words, assimilate everything to their mouthing schema—they realize that objects have different characteristics. Some are soft or prickly. Others taste terrible or great. Through continual assimilation and accommodation, by age 2, babies make a dramatic mental leap—from relying on their small set of reflexes, to reasoning and using symbolic thought.

circular reactions In Piaget's framework, repetitive action-oriented schemas (or habits) characteristic of babies during the sensorimotor stage.

primary circular reactions In Piaget's framework, the first infant habits during the sensorimotor stage, centered on the body.

secondary circular reactions In Piaget's framework, habits of the sensorimotor stage lasting from about 4 months of age to the baby's first birthday, centered on exploring the external world.

tertiary circular reactions In Piaget's framework, "little-scientist" activities of the sensorimotor stage, beginning around age 1, involving flexibly exploring the properties of objects.

Circular Reactions: Habits That Pin Down Reality

By meticulously observing his own three children, Piaget discovered that driving all these advances were what he called **circular reactions**—habits, or action-oriented schemas, which the child repeats again and again.

From the newborn reflexes, during months 1 to 4, **primary circular reactions** develop. These are repetitive actions that begin by accident, centered on the child's body. A thumb randomly makes contact with his mouth, and a 2-month-old removes that interesting object, observes it, and moves it back in and then out. Waving her legs captivates a 3-month-old for hours on end.

At around 4 months of age, **secondary circular reactions** appear. As the cortex begins to blossom and the child literally "wakes up" to life, action-oriented schemas become centered on the *outside* world. Here is how Piaget described his daughter Lucienne's first secondary circular reactions:

> Lucienne at 0:4 [4 months] is lying in her bassinet. I hang a doll over her feet which . . . sets in motion the schema of shakes. Her feet reach the doll . . . and give it a violent movement which Lucienne surveys with delight. . . . After the first shakes, Lucienne makes slow foot movements as though to grasp and explore. . . . When she tries to kick the doll, and misses . . . she begins again very slowly until she succeeds [without looking at her feet].
>
> (Piaget, 1950, p. 159 [as cited in Flavell, 1963, p. 103])

During the next few months, secondary circular reactions become better coordinated. By about 8 months of age, for instance, babies can simultaneously employ two circular reactions, using both grasping and kicking together to explore the world.

Then, around a baby's first birthday, **tertiary circular reactions** appear. Now, the child is no longer constrained by stereotyped schemas. He can operate just like a real scientist, flexibly changing his behavior to make sense of the world. A toddler gets captivated by toilet paper, unrolling sheets and throwing different-sized wads into the bowl. At dinner, he gleefully spits his food out at varying velocities and hurls his bottle off the high chair in different directions just to see where it lands.

How important are circular reactions in infancy? Spend time with a young baby, as she bats at her mobile or joyously pinwheels her legs. Try to prevent a 1-year-old from hurling plates from a high chair, flushing objects down the toilet, or inserting bits of cookie into a DVD slot. Then you will understand: Infancy is all about the insatiable drive to repeat interesting acts. (See Table 3.8 for a recap of the circular reactions, as well as a look at the sensorimotor substages.)

Piaget's concept of circular reactions offers a new perspective on those obsessions that drive adults crazy during what researchers call the **little-scientist phase** (and parents call the "getting into everything" phase). This is the time, around age 1, when the child begins experimenting with objects in a way that mimics how a scientist behaves:

***TABLE 3.8:* The Circular Reactions: A Summary Table (With a Look at Piaget's Substages)**

Primary Circular Reactions: 1–4 months

Description: Repetitive habits center around the child's own body.

Examples: Sucking toes; sucking thumb.

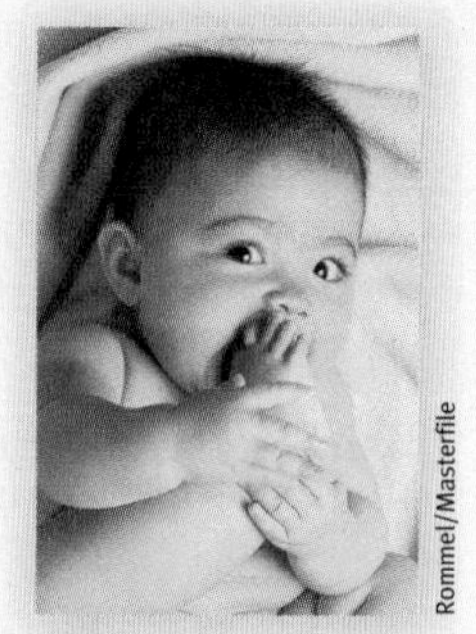
Rommel/Masterfile

Secondary Circular Reactions: 4 months–1 year

Description: Child "wakes up to wider world." Habits center on environmental objects.

Examples: Grabbing for toys; batting mobiles; pushing one's body to activate the lights and sounds on a swing.

Substages: From 4 to 8 months, children use single secondary circular reactions such as those above; from 8 to 12 months, they employ two circular reactions in concert to attain a goal (i.e., they may grab a toy in each hand, bat a mobile back and forth, coordinate the motions of toys).

Christina Kennedy/Photo Edit, Inc.

Tertiary Circular Reactions: 1–2 years

Description: Child flexibly explores the properties of objects, like a "little scientist."

Examples: Exploring the various dimensions of a toy; throwing a bottle off the high chair in different directions; flushing different objects down the toilet; putting different kinds of food in the computer.

Substages: From 12 to 18 months, the child experiments with concrete objects; from 18 to 24 months, his little-scientist behavior transcends what is observable and involves using symbols to stand for something else. (I'll be describing the many advances ushered in by this ability to reason symbolically in later chapters.)

David Young-Wolff/Photo Edit, Inc.

"Let me try this, then that, and see what happens." The reason it is impossible to derail a 1-year-old from putting oatmeal into the computer, or clogging the toilet with toys (making a plumber a parent's new best friend) is that circular reactions allow infants to pin down the basic properties of the world.

Why do *specific* circular reactions, such as flushing objects down the toilet, become irresistible during the little-scientist phase? This question brings me to Piaget's ideas about how babies progress from reflexes to the ability to reason and think.

Tracking Early Thinking

How do we know when infants begin to think? According to Piaget, one hallmark of thinking is deferred imitation—repeating an action that was witnessed at an earlier time. When Piaget saw Lucienne, at 16 months of age, mimic a tantrum she had seen another child have days earlier, he realized she had the mental skills to keep that image in her mind, mull it over, and translate it into action on her own. Another sign of reasoning abilities is the beginning of make-believe play. To pretend you are cleaning the house or talking on the phone like Mommy, you must realize that something *signifies*, or stands for, something else.

little-scientist phase The time around age 1 when babies use tertiary circular reactions to actively explore the properties of objects, experimenting with them like "scientists."

But perhaps the most important sign of emerging reasoning is **means–end behavior**—when the child is able to perform a totally separate, or different action, to get to a goal. Pushing the toilet lever to make the water swirl down, manipulating a switch to turn on the light, screwing open a bottle to extract the juice—all are examples of "doing something different" to reach a particular end.

If you have access to a 1-year-old, you might try to construct your own means–end task.

First, show the child something she really wants, such as a cookie or a toy. Then, put the object in a place where the baby must perform a different type of action to get the treat. For instance, you might put the cookie in a clear container and cover the top with Saran Wrap. Will the baby ineffectively bang the side of the container, or will she figure out the *different* step (removing the cover) essential to retrieving what she wants? If you conduct your test by putting the cookie in an opaque container, the baby must have another basic understanding: She must realize that—although she may not see it—the cookie is still there.

means–end behavior In Piaget's framework, performing a different action to get to a goal—an ability that emerges in the sensorimotor stage as babies approach age 1.

object permanence In Piaget's framework, the understanding that objects continue to exist even when we can no longer see them, which gradually emerges during the sensorimotor stage.

A-not-B error In Piaget's framework, a classic mistake made by infants in the sensorimotor stage, whereby babies approaching age 1 go back to the original hiding place to look for an object even though they have seen it get hidden in a second place.

Object Permanence: Believing in a Stable World

Object permanence refers to knowing that objects still exist even when we no longer see them—a perception that is, obviously, fundamental to our sense of living in a stable world. Suppose you felt that this book disappeared when you averted your eyes or that your house rematerialized out of nothing when you entered your driveway. Piaget believed that object permanence is not iborn. This perception develops gradually throughout the sensorimotor stage.

Piaget's observations suggested that during babies' first few months, life is a series of disappearing pictures. If an enticing image, such as her mother, passed her line of sight, Lucienne would stare at the place from which the image had vanished as if it would reappear out of thin air. (The relevant phrase here is "out of sight, out of mind.") Then, at around month 5, when the *secondary circular reactions* are first flowering, there was a milestone. An object dropped out of sight and Lucienne leaned over to look for it, suggesting that she knew it existed independently of her gaze. Still, this sense of a stable object was fragile. The baby quickly abandoned her search after Piaget covered that object with his hand.

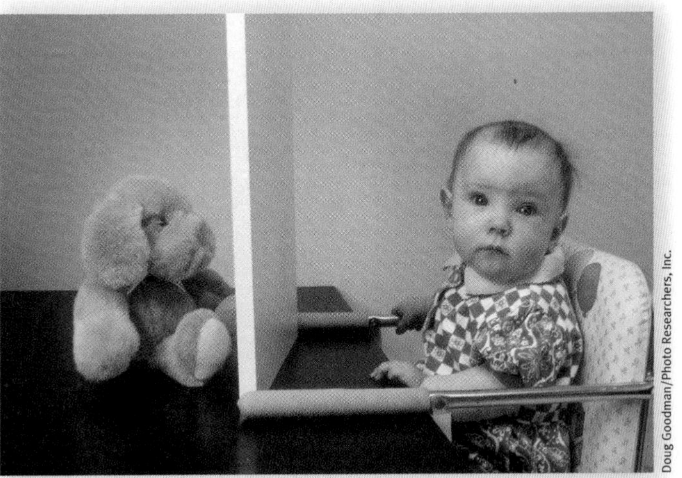

Doug Goodman/Photo Researchers, Inc.

A minute ago, this 4-month-old girl was delightedly grabbing this little bear; but, when this barrier blocked her image, it was "out of sight-out of-mind." If you have access to a young baby, can you perform this test to track the beginning of *object permanence?*

Hunting for hidden objects becomes a well-established activity as children approach their first birthday. Actually, for 9- or 10-month-olds, uncovering objects that adults hide underneath covers becomes a totally absorbing game. Still, around this age, children make a surprising mistake called the **A-not-B error.** If you put an object in full view of a baby into one out-of-sight location, have the baby get it, and then move it to another place while the child is watching, she will look for it in the initial place!

See if you can perform this classic test if you have access to a 10-month-old: Place an object, such as a toy, under a piece of paper (A). Then have the baby find it in that place a few times. Next, remove the toy as the infant watches and put it under a different piece of paper (B). What happens? Even though the child saw you put the toy in the new location, he will probably look under the A paper again, as if it had migrated unseen to its original place!

By about their first birthday, children seem to master the basic principle. Move an object to a new hiding place and they will look for it in the correct location. However, as Piaget found when he used this strategy but *covered* the object with his hand, object permanence does not fully emerge until children are almost 2 years old.

Emerging object permanence explains many puzzles about development. Why does peek-a-boo become an all-time favorite activity at around 8 months? The reason is that a child now thinks there is *probably* still someone behind those hands, but doesn't absolutely know for sure.

Emerging object permanence offers a wonderful perspective on why younger babies are so laid back when you remove an interesting object, and then become possessive by their second year of life. Those toddler tantrums about objects do not signal a new, awful personality trait called "the terrible twos." They simply show that children have become much smarter. They now have the cognitive skills to know that objects still exist when you take them away.

iStockphoto/Thinkstock/Getty Images

For this 1-year-old, pushing the buttons on the TV remote is more captivating than any possible toy—because he is in the *little scientist stage* of cognitive development.

Finally, the concept of object permanence, or fascination with disappearing objects, plus means–end behavior, makes sense of that passion to flush toys down the toilet or the compulsion to stick bits of cookie in a DVD slot. What could be more tantalizing during the little-scientist phase than taking a new action to get to a goal plus causing things to disappear and possibly reappear? It also explains why you can't go wrong if you buy your toddler nephew a pop-up toy.

But during the first year of life there is no need to arrive with any toy. Buy a toy for an infant and he will push it aside to play with the box. Your nephew probably much prefers fiddling with the TV remote to any object from Toys R Us. Toys only become interesting once we realize that they are different from real life. So, a desire for dolls or action figures—or for anything else that requires make-believe play—shows that a child is emerging from the sensorimotor period and making the transition to symbolic thought. With the concepts of circular reactions, emerging object permanence, and means–end behavior, Piaget masterfully made sense of the puzzling passions of infant life!

Critiquing Piaget

Piaget's insights have transformed the way we think about childhood. Research confirms the fact that children are, at heart, little scientists. They do form hypotheses about the way the world works and systematically test out these theories. The passion to decode the world is built into being human from our first months of life (Gopnik, 2010). However, the problem is that Piaget's timing was seriously off. Piaget's trouble was that he had to rely on babies' actions (for instance, taking covers off hidden objects) to figure out what they knew. He did not have today's creative strategies, like preferential looking and habituation, to decode what babies' understand before they can physically respond. Using these techniques, researchers realized that even young infants know far, far more about life than this master theorist ever believed.

Let's now look at two core criticisms of Piaget's ideas:

- **Infants grasp the basics of physical reality well before age one.** To demonstrate this point, developmentalist Renée Baillargeon (1993) presented young babies with physically impossible events such as showing a traveling rabbit that never appeared in a gap it had to pass through to reach its place on the other side (illustrated in Figure 3.8A). Even 5-month-olds looked astonished when they saw these impossible events. You could almost hear them thinking, "I know that's not the way objects should behave."

- **Infants' understanding of physical reality develops gradually.** For instance, while Baillargeon, discovered that the impossible event of the traveling rabbit in the figure provoked astonishment around month 5, other research shows it takes until age 1 for babies to master other basics about the world such as the fact that you cannot take a large rabbit

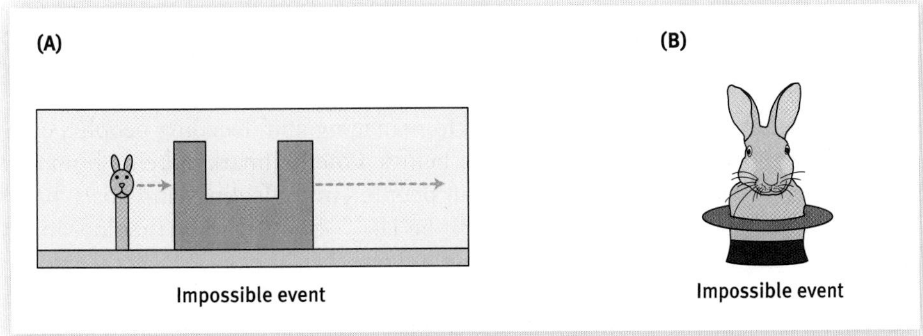

FIGURE 3.8: **Two impossible events:** At about 5 months of age babies were surprised by the physically impossible sequence in A—but they did not look surprised by the event in B till about age one. The bottom line: Infants understand the physical world far earlier than Piaget believed, but this knowledge occurs gradually.

Sources: Baillargeon, 1987; Baillargeon & DeVos, 1991; Baillargeon & Graber, 1987.

information-processing approach A perspective on understanding cognition that divides thinking into specific steps and component processes, much like a computer.

out of a little container (shown in Figure 3.8B). (As an aside, that explains why "magic" suddenly becomes interesting only around age 2 or 3.) Therefore, instead of adopting Piaget's framework of conceptualizing mental development in huge qualitative stages, many developmentalists adopt a more specific approach: focusing on core mental processes such as memory; decoding step by step how cognition *gradually* emerges.

Information-processing researchers use the metaphor of a computer with separate processing steps to help decode children's (and adults') intellectual skills. For instance, instead of seeing means–end behavior as a new capacity that suddenly emerges at age 1, a psychologist using this approach would isolate the specific talents involved in this milestone—memory, attention, the ability to inhibit your immediate perceptions—and then chart how each skill develops over time.

Table 3.9 shows some insights about babies' memories and emerging mathematical capacities, derived from using this more gradual, specific approach. Stay tuned for later chapters as we explore how an information-processing steps framework can help us understand how memory and thinking operate during elementary school and old age. Now, it's time to tackle another fascinating question: What do babies understand about human minds?

TABLE 3.9: Infant Memory and Conceptual Abilities: Some Interesting Findings

Memory: By using deferred imitation (see the text discussion), researchers find that babies as young as 9 months of age can "remember" events from the previous day. Infants will push a button if they saw an adult performing that act 24 hours earlier. In another study, most 10-month-olds imitated an action they saw one month earlier. There even have been cases where babies this age saw an action and then remembered it a year later.*

Forming categories: By 7 to 9 months of age, babies are able to distinguish between animals and vehicles. They will feed an animal or put it to bed, but even if they watch an adult put a car to bed, they will not model her action. So the first classification babies make is between something that moves by itself or cannot move on its own. (Is it alive, like an animal, or inanimate?) Then, categorization abilities get more refined depending on familiarity. Eleven-month-old infants, for example, can often distinguish between dogs and cats but not among dogs, rabbits, and fish.

Understanding numbers: By about 5 months of age, infants can make differentiations between different numbers—for instance, after seeing three dots on a screen, they will look preferentially at a subsequent screen showing four dots. They also have an implicit understanding of addition and subtraction. If they see someone add one doll to another, or take away a doll from a set, they look surprised when they see an image on a screen showing the incorrect number of dolls.

Source: Mandler, 2007.

*Because deferred imitation, like habituation, reflects the child's memory capacities, a preverbal baby's skill in this area predicts the rapidity of language development and later, IQ scores.

social cognition Any skill related to understanding feelings and negotiating interpersonal interactions.

joint attention The first sign of "getting human intentions," when a baby looks at an object an adult is pointing to or follows a person's gaze.

Tackling the Core of What Makes Us Human: Infant Social Cognition

Social cognition refers to any skill related to managing and decoding people's emotions, and getting along with other human beings. One hallmark of being human is that we are always making inferences about people's inner feelings and goals, based on their actions. ("He's running, so he must be late." "She slammed the door in my face, so she must be angry.") When do these judgments first occur? Piaget would say certainly not before age 2 (or much later) because infants in the sensorimotor period can't think conceptually. Here is one example that proves Piaget was wrong.

A nice tiger helps the dog open a box

PBS Courtesy of Karen Wynn

A mean dog slams the box door shut on the tiger

After seeing this video sequence of events, even infants under 6 months of age preferentially reached for the "nice" tiger rather than the "mean dog"—showing that the fundamental human *social-cognitive* awareness, "he's acting mean or nice" emerges at a remarkably young age.

Infants watched a video of a circle struggling to climb up a hill while a triangle and square looked on. They first saw the triangle push the square to the top, then watched the square push the circle down. After those images appeared, the babies saw the circle either approach the "helpful" triangle or the "mean" square. Even 5-month-old babies looked much longer when they saw the circle gravitate to the nasty square. They seemed to be thinking: "If Mr. Square treated you like that, why would you *ever, ever* choose him?" (Hamlin, Wynn, & Bloom, 2007.)

So at an incredibly young age, we begin to clue into human motivations. By the time they can reach for an object (at about month 5), for instance, babies preferentially choose a stuffed animal they previously saw being "helpful" versus one they witnessed acting "mean" (Hamlin & Wynn, 2011, also on this page, see the photos captured from the video of this interesting experiment). We intuitively grasp sophisticated social concepts like, "He shouldn't do that! or "She's not nice!" well before we can speak (Gopnik, 2010).

Another sign of decoding human intentions is a social landmark called **joint attention.** At around age 1, if a person points to something–or gazes in a specific direction—the baby will look at the object being pointed to, rather than the individual's hand or face (Harris, 2006; Mundy and others, 2007). Joint attention, understanding what people are communicating with gestures ("I want you to look at that"), sets the stage for that uniquely human milestone: understanding what people are communicating with words.

TYING IT ALL TOGETHER

1. You are working at a child-care center, and you notice Darien repeatedly opening and closing a cabinet door. Then Jai comes over and pulls open the door. You decide to latch it. Jai—undeterred—pulls on the door and, when it doesn't open, begins jiggling the latch. And then he looks up, very pleased, as he manages to figure out how to open the latch. Finally, you give up and decide to play a game with Sam. You hide a stuffed bear in a toy box while Sam watches. Then Sam throws open the lid of the box and scoops out the bear. Link the appropriate Piagetian term to each child's behavior: *circular reaction; object permanence; means–end behavior.*

2. Jose, while an avid Piaget fan, has to admit this master theorist went wrong. What two criticisms of the theory might Jose legitimately make?
   a. Infant cognition develops gradually, rather than in distinct stages.
   b. Infants understand far more than Piaget gave them credit for.
   c. Infant cognition occurs more slowly than Piaget thought.

3. Baby Sara watches her big brother hit the dog. Based on the research in this section, the baby might first understand her brother is being "mean" *months before/at/months after* age 1.

Answers to the Tying It All Together questions can be found at the end of this chapter.

Language: The Endpoint of Infancy

Piaget believed language signals the end of the sensorimotor period because its emergence showed that children could see that a symbol stands for something else. True, in order to master language, you must grasp the idea that the abstract word-symbol *textbook* refers to what you are reading now. But the miracle of language is that we can string together words in novel, understandable ways. What causes us to master this feat, and how does language evolve?

Nature, Nurture, and the Passion to Learn Language

The essential property of language is its elasticity. How can I come up with this totally new sentence, and why can you understand its meaning, although you have never seen it before? Why does every language have a **grammar**, with nouns, verbs, and rules for organizing words into sentences? According to linguist Noam Chomsky, the reason is that humans are biologically programmed to make "language." We possess a capacity in our genetic code, which Chomsky named the **language acquisition device (LAD).**

Chomsky developed his nature-oriented concept of a uniquely human LAD in reaction to the behaviorist B. F. Skinner's nurture-oriented proposition that we learn to speak through being reinforced for producing specific words (for instance, Skinner argued that we learn to say "I want cookie" by being rewarded for producing those sounds by getting that treat). This pronouncement was another example of the traditional behaviorist principle that "all actions are driven by reinforcement" run amok (see Chapter 1). It defies common sense to suggest that we can generate billions of new sentences by having people reinforce us for every word!

Still, Skinner is correct in one respect. I speak English instead of Mandarin Chinese because I grew up in New York City, not Beijing. So the way our genetic program for making language gets expressed depends on our environment. Once again, nature plus nurture work together to explain every activity of life!

Currently, developmentalists typically adopt a **social-interactionist view** on this core human skill. They focus on the social motivations that propel language (Hoff-Ginsberg, 1997). Babies are passionate to communicate. Adults are passionate to help babies learn to talk. How does the infant passion to communicate evolve?

Tracking Emerging Language

The pathway to producing language occurs in defined stages. Out of the reflexive crying of the newborn period comes *cooing* (*oooh* sounds) at about month 4. At around month 6, delightful vocal circular reactions called **babbling** emerge. Babbles are alternating consonant and vowel sounds, such as "da da da," that infants playfully repeat with variations of intonation and pitch.

The first word emerges out of the babble at around 11 months, although that exact landmark is difficult to define. There is little more reinforcing to paternal pride than when your 8-month-old genius continually repeats your name. But when does "da da da" really refer to Dad? In the first, **holophrase** stage of true speech, one word, accompanied by gestures says it all. When your son says "ja" and points to the kitchen, you know he wants juice . . . or was it a jelly sandwich, or was he referring to his sister Jane?

Children accumulate their first 50 or so words, centering on the important items in their world (people, toys, and food) slowly (Nelson, 1974). Then, typically between ages 1 1/2 and 2, there is a vocabulary explosion as the child begins to combine words. Because children pare communication down to its essentials, just like an old-style telegram ("Me juice"; "Mommy, no"), this first word-combining stage is called

grammar The rules and word-arranging systems that every human language employs to communicate meaning.

language acquisition device (LAD) Chomsky's term for a hypothetical brain structure that enables our species to learn and produce language.

social-interactionist view An approach to language development that emphasizes its social function, specifically that babies and adults have a mutual passion to communicate.

babbling The alternating vowel and consonant sounds that babies repeat with variations of intonation and pitch and that precede the first words.

holophrase First clear evidence of language, when babies use a single word to communicate a sentence or complete thought.

TABLE 3.10: Language Milestones from Birth to Age 2*

Age	Language Characteristic
2–4 months	Cooing: First sounds growing out of reflexes. Example: "oooo"
5–11 months	Babbling: Alternate vowel–consonant sounds. Examples: "ba-ba-ba," "da-da-da"
12 months	Holophrases: First one-word sentences. Example: "ja" ("I want juice.")
18 months–2 years	Telegraphic speech: Two-word combinations, often accompanied by an explosion in vocabulary. Example: "Me juice"

Babies vary a good deal in the ages at which they begin to combine words.

telegraphic speech. In Table 3.10, you can see a summary of these basic language landmarks, along with examples and the approximate time during infancy when each milestone occurs.

Just as with the other infant achievements described in this chapter, developmentalists are passionate to trace language to its earliest roots. It turns out, for instance, that newborns are "prewired" to gravitate to the sounds of living things—as they suck longer when reinforced by hearing monkey and/or human vocalizations (versus pure tones). By 3 months of age (notice the similarity to vision here), preferences get more selective. Now babies perk up *only* when they hear human speech (Vouloumanos and others, 2010). By 8 months of age, as irrelevant synapses are pruned, infants—like adults—lose the ability to hear sound tones that appear in other languages such as Hindi, but not their own (Gervain & Mehler, 2010). Simultaneously, as essential synapses strengthen, a remarkable sharpening occurs. When language starts to explode, toddlers can hear the difference between similar sounds like "bih" and "dih" and link them to objects after *just hearing this connection once*!

Caregivers foster these achievements by continually talking to babies. Around the world, they train infants in language by using *infant-directed speech.*

Infant-directed speech (IDS) (what you and I call *baby talk*) uses simple words, exaggerated tones, elongated vowels, and has a higher pitch than we use in speaking to adults (Hoff-Ginsberg, 1997). Although IDS sounds ridiculous ("Mooommy taaaaking baaaaby ooooout!" "Moommy loooves baaaaby!"), when babies are spoken to this way, they perk up (Santesso, Schmidt, & Trainor, 2007). So we naturally use infant-directed speech with babies, just as we are compelled to pick up and rock a child when she cries.

Parents beautifully pace their IDS communications to their child's emerging capacities. In an interesting qualitative study, at about 8 months of age—when her baby was poised to start speaking—one mother dramatically increased her IDS vocalizations and shifted to asking more questions (Rivero, 2010). Does IDS *really* help babies begin to master language? The answer is yes.

When developmentalists gave 10-month-old infants a string of nonsense words spoken either in adult or in infant-directed speech, babies picked up the individual words better when they were spoken in IDS (Thiessen, Hill, & Saffran, 2005). Listen carefully to someone speaking in "baby talk." Doesn't this mode of communication seem tailor-made to emphasize exactly where one word ends and another begins?

There is nothing more thrilling than being able to have a real father-to-daughter discussion for the first time when your toddler begins to combine words. But what might infant-directed speech sound like delivered in Japanese? Moreover, now that she is two, would this Japanese child even be able to identify sounds that are uniquely English?

Kayte M. Deioma/Photo Edit, Inc.

Babies "Connect" with the Human World

Have the studies in this chapter stimulated you to design your own "out of the box" research to get into infants' heads? As developmentalists continue to use their brainpower to design creative studies, what more will we know about babies' brains in the next 10 or 20 years?

Just as we arrive on earth equipped with a passion to master life, a basic message of this chapter is that—from face perception, to joint attention, to early language— our main agenda is to connect with the human world. The next chapter focuses on this number-one infant (and adult) agenda by exploring attachment relationships during our first two years of life.

telegraphic speech First stage of combining words in infancy, in which a baby pares down a sentence to its essential words.

infant-directed speech (IDS) The simplified, exaggerated, high-pitched tones that adults and children use to speak to infants that function to help teach language.

TYING IT ALL TOGETHER

1. "We learn to speak by getting reinforced for saying what we want." "We are biologically programmed to learn language." "Babies are passionate to communicate." Identify the theoretical perspective reflected in each of these statements: *Skinner's operant conditioning perspective; Chomsky's language acquisition device; a social-interactionist perspective on language.*
2. Baby Ginny is 4 months old; baby Jamal is about 7 months old; baby Sam is 1 year old; baby David is 2 years old. Identify each child's probable language stage by choosing from the following items: *babbling; cooing; telegraphic speech; holophrases.*
3. A friend makes fun of adults who use baby talk. Given the information in this section, is her teasing justified?

Answers to the Tying It All Together questions can be found at the end of this chapter.

SUMMARY

Setting the Context: Brain Blossoming and Sculpting

Because our uniquely large **cerebral cortex** develops mainly after birth, during the first two years of life, the brain mushrooms. **Axons** elongate and develop a fatty cover called myelin. **Dendrites** sprout branches and at **synapses** link up with other cells. **Synaptogenesis** and **myelination** program every infant ability and human skill. Although the brain matures for decades, we do not simply "develop more synapses." Each region undergoes rapid synaptogenesis, followed by pruning (or cutting back). Before pruning, the brain is particularly **plastic,** allowing us to compensate for early brain insults—but synaptogenesis and learning occur throughout life.

Basic Newborn States

Eating undergoes dramatic changes during infancy. We emerge from the womb with **sucking** and **rooting reflexes,** which jump-start eating, as well as a set of other special birth **reflexes,** which disappear after the early months of life. Although the "everything into the mouth" phase of infancy can make life scary for caregivers, a 2-year-old's food caution can partially protect toddlers from poisoning themselves.

Even though its specific health benefits are not always clear-cut, every public health organization advocates exclusive breast-feeding for the first 6 months of life. However, only a minority of women follows this recommendation. Mothers who must return to work may find it difficult to breast-feed. Experts may not give women the advice they need. The key to increasing breast-feeding rates is to actively teach this skill, make this practice far more acceptable in public, and emphasize that nursing helps control weight.

Undernutrition, both **stunting** (very short stature) and **micronutrient deficiencies,** are common in young children living in the developing world. Although families with children in the United States may suffer from **food insecurity,** due to government entitlement programs, severe, chronic hunger is very rare.

Crying is at its height during early infancy and declines around month 4 as the cortex develops. **Colic,** excessive crying that disappears after early infancy, is basically a biological problem. Strategies for quieting crying babies include rocking, holding, **swaddling,** and providing an outlet for the urge to suck. Providing intense skin-to-skin contact through infant massage and **kangaroo care** not only helps quiet babies; these practices also help infants—especially at-risk premature babies—grow.

Sleep is the basic newborn state, and from the 18-hour, waking-every-few hours newborn pattern, babies gradually adjust to falling asleep at night. **REM sleep** lessens and shifts to the end of the cycle. Babies, however, really do not ever sleep through the night. At about 6 months, many learn **self-soothing,** putting themselves back to sleep when they wake up. The decision about whether to "let a baby cry it out" or respond immediately at night is personal, because the best way to foster sleep is to provide a caring bedtime routine. **Co-sleeping** (or bed-sharing)—the norm in collectivist cultures—although still controversial in the West, is also a personal choice.

Sudden infant death syndrome (SIDS)—when a young baby stops breathing, often at night, and dies—is a main cause of developed-world infant mortality. Although SIDS may be caused by impairments in the developing fetal brain—it tends to occur most often when babies sleep face down. Therefore, a late-twentieth-century SIDS campaign urging parents to put babies to sleep on their backs (not stomachs) has been effective, although infants need a bit of "tummy time" too.

Sensory and Motor Development

The **preferential-looking paradigm** (exploring what objects babies look at) and **habituation** (the fact that we get less interested in looking at objects that are no longer "new") are used to determine what very young babies can see. Although at birth visual acuity is poor, it improves very rapidly. **Face-perception studies** show that newborns look at facelike stimuli, recognize their mothers, and even prefer good-looking people from the first weeks of life. At the same time that our visual capacities improve, due to neural pruning, we lose the ability to "see" facial differences we really don't need. **Depth perception** studies using the **visual cliff** show that although they notice differences in depth at a very young age, babies only get frightened of heights around the time they begin to crawl.

Infants' bodies lengthen and thin out as they grow. The cephalocaudal, proximodistal, and mass-to-specific principles apply to how the body changes and emerging infant motor milestones. Although they do progress through stages when getting to walking, babies show incredible creativity and variability when they first attain skills. There is no relationship between early motor development and later cognitive abilities, but habituation speed (signaling better memory for a stimulus) does correlate with later intelligence. Crawling is linked to widespread maturational changes, prompting the need to **baby-proof** the home.

Cognition

During Piaget's **sensorimotor stage,** babies master the basics of physical reality through their senses and begin to symbolize and think. **Circular reactions** (habits the baby repeats) help babies pin down the basics of the physical world. **Primary circular reactions**—body-centered habits, such as sucking one's toes—emerge first. **Secondary circular reactions,** habits centered on making interesting external stimuli last (for example, batting mobiles), begin around month 4. **Tertiary circular reactions,** also called **"little-scientist"** activities—like spitting food at different velocities just to see where the oatmeal lands—are the hallmark of the toddler years. A major advance in reasoning that occurs around age 1 is **means–end behavior**—understanding you need to do something different to get to a goal.

Piaget's most compelling concept is **object permanence**—knowing that objects exist when you no longer see them. According to Piaget, this understanding develops gradually during the first years of life. When this knowledge is developing, infants make the **A-not-B error,** looking for an object in the place where they first found it, even if it has been hidden in another location before their eyes.

Using preferential looking, and watching babies' expressions of surprise at impossible events, researchers now know that babies understand more about physical reality far earlier than Piaget believed. Because Piaget's stage model also does not fit the gradual way cognition unfolds, contemporary developmentalists sometimes adopt an **information-processing approach,** breaking thinking into separate components and steps. Scientists exploring **social cognition** find that **joint attention** and other signs of our ability to understand other peoples' motivations appears surprisingly early in life.

Language: The Endpoint of Infancy

Language, specifically our use of **grammar** and our ability to form infinitely different sentences, sets us apart from any other animal. Although B. F. Skinner believed that we learn to speak through being reinforced, the more logical explanation is Chomsky's idea that we have a biologically built-in **language acquisition device (LAD). Social-interactionists** focus on the mutual passion of babies and adults to communicate.

First, babies coo, then **babble,** then use one-word **holophrases,** and finally, at 1 1/2 or 2, progress to two-word combinations called **telegraphic speech.** Caregivers naturally use **infant-directed speech** (exaggerated intonations and simpler phrases) when they talk to babies. IDS helps teach infants to master this core human skill.

KEY TERMS

cerebral cortex, p. 78
axon, p. 78
dendrite, p. 78
synapse, p. 78
synaptogenesis, p. 78
myelination, p. 78
plastic, p. 79
sucking reflex, p. 81
rooting reflex, p. 81
reflex, p. 81
undernutrition, p. 83
stunting, p. 83
food insecurity, p. 84
colic, p. 85
swaddling, p. 86
kangaroo care, p. 86
REM sleep, p. 87
self-soothing, p. 88
co-sleeping, p. 89
sudden infant death syndrome (SIDS), p. 90
preferential-looking paradigm, p. 93
habituation, p. 93
face-perception studies, p. 93
depth perception, p.94
visual cliff, p. 94
baby-proofing, p. 94
sensorimotor stage, p. 98
circular reactions, p. 99
primary circular reactions, p. 99
secondary circular reactions, p. 99
tertiary circular reactions, p. 99
little-scientist phase, p. 99
means–end behavior, p. 101
object permanence, p. 101
A-not-B error, p. 101
information processing approach, p. 103
social cognition, p. 104
joint attention, p. 104
grammar, p. 105
language acquisition device (LAD), p. 105
social-interactionist view, p. 105
babbling, p. 105
holophrase, p. 105
telegraphic speech, p. 106
infant-directed speech (IDS), p. 106

ANSWERS TO TYING IT ALL TOGETHER QUIZZES

Setting the Context: Brain Blossoming and Sculpting

1. Both Cortez and Ashley are right. We are unique in our massive cerebral cortex, in growing most of our brain outside of the womb, and in the fact that the human cortex does not reach its adult form for more than two decades.
2. Latisha is partly right (with regard to the myelin sheath) and partly wrong. Synaptic loss and neural pruning are essential to fostering our emerging abilities.
3. The relevant concept here is "brain plasticity"— that remarkable neural flexibility permitting development to proceed normally, in that cells are captured and redirected to compensate for the part of the brain that the surgeons remove.
4. Make your drawing from memory, and then see how closely it mirrors the illustration in Figure 3.1 on page 78.

Basic Newborn States

1. d. All these statements are right. The sucking reflex (automatic sucking) and rooting reflex (head turning and sucking) are there at birth to help ensure the infant's survival. As the cortex matures, these reflexes disappear.
2. Your survey might include these questions: Do you plan to go back to work full-time right after the baby's birth—and if so, does your job/employer support breast-feeding? How much do you weigh? (Overweight is related to prematurely abandoning this practice.). Do you plan to seek out breast-feeding advice? Would you feel comfortable about nursing in public? How vital do you think breast-feeding is to infant health?
3. Tell your sister and her husband to get a baby sling and carry the child around (kangaroo care) and be sure to feed the baby on demand, as these techniques reduce excessive crying. (Also, they might make heavy use of a pacifier and learn baby massage!) Give your relatives the encouraging information that colic is short-lived—typically going away by month 4.
4. Jorge's child is right on schedule, but he's wrong to say his child is sleeping through the night. The baby has simply learned to self-soothe.
5. The answers here will depend on the class.

Sensory and Motor Development

1. The *preferential-looking paradigm.*
2. Both Tania and Thomas are right. In support of Tania's "dramatic improvement" position, while newborns are legally blind, vision improves to 20/20 by age 1. (Another example is the visual cliff research). Thomas is also correct that in some ways vision gets worse during infancy. He should mention the fact that by age one we have " unlearned" the ability to distinguish two monkey faces and become less sensitive to facial distinctions in people of other ethnic groups.
3. At 8 months of age, the child should *be frightened* of the cliff.
4. Charlie's early motor skills will have no relationship to his later cognitive abilities, although his parents are right that his rapid habituation does predict later high IQ.
5. Your answers might include installing electrical outlet covers; putting sharp, poisonous, and breakable objects out of a baby's reach; carpeting hard floor surfaces; padding furniture corners; installing latches on cabinet doors; and so on.

Cognition

1. Circular reaction = Darien; means–end behavior = Jai; object permanence = Sam.
2. a & b. Infant cognition develops gradually and babies "know more" than Piaget believed.
3. Baby Sara should pick up this idea, *months before* age 1.

Language: The Endpoint of Infancy

1. The idea that we learn language by getting reinforced reflects Skinner's operant conditioning perspective; Chomsky hypothesized that we are biologically programmed to acquire language; the social-interactionist perspective emphasizes the fact that babies and adults have a passion to communicate.
2. Baby Ginny is cooing; baby Jamal is babbling; baby Sam is speaking in holophrases (one-word stage); and baby David is using telegraphic speech.
3. NO, your friend is wrong!!! Baby talk—or in developmental science terms, infant-directed speech (IDS)—gets an infant's attention and helps promote early language.

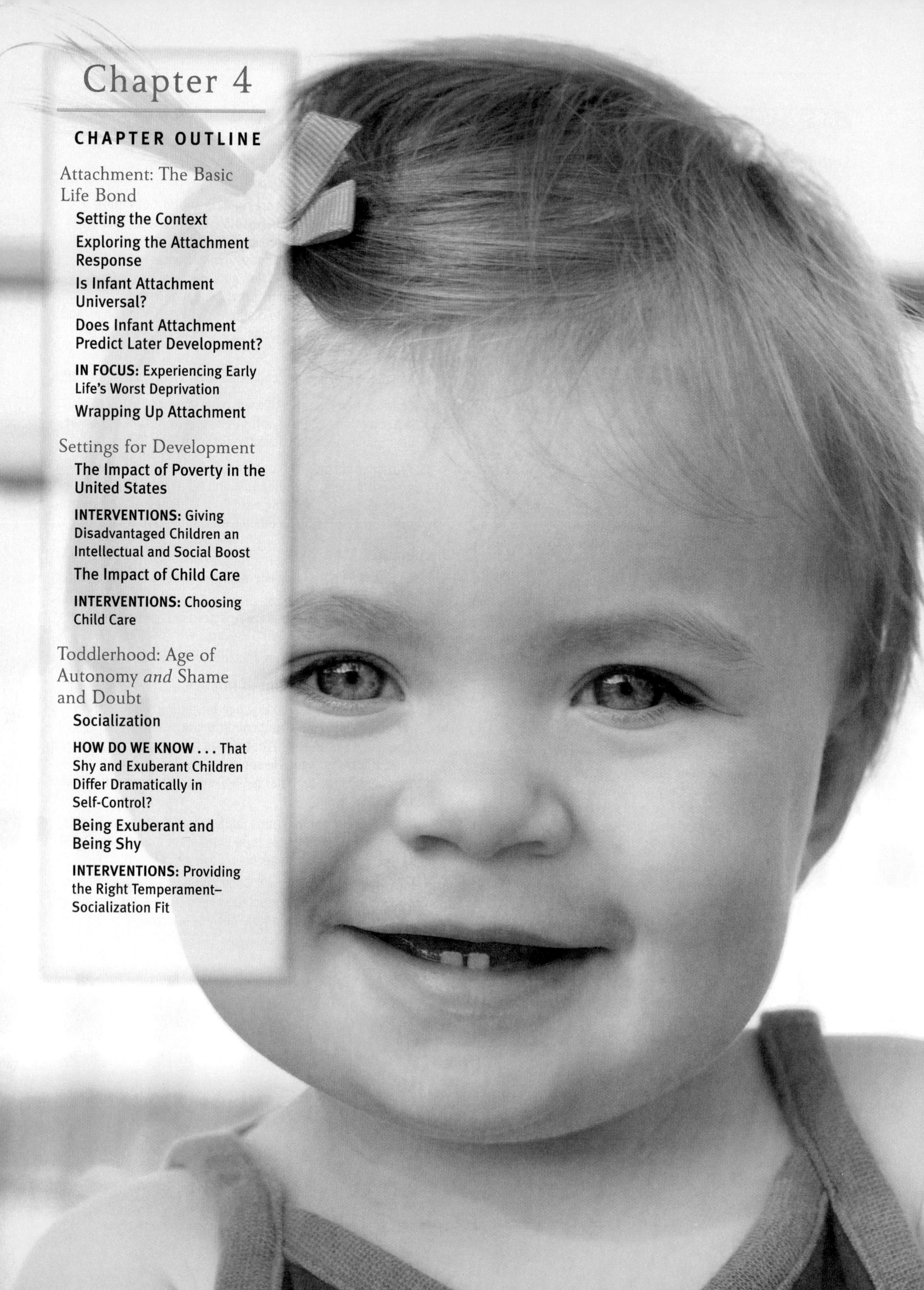

Chapter 4

CHAPTER OUTLINE

Infancy: Socioemotional Development

We've talked to Kim during pregnancy and visited when Elissa was a young baby, let's catch up with mother and daughter now that Elissa is 15 months old.

Elissa had her first birthday in December. She's such a happy baby, but now if you take something away, it's like, "Why did you do that?" Pick her up. For a second everything is fine, and then her face changes and she squirms and her arms go out toward me. She's really busy walking, busy exploring, but she's always got an eye on me. The minute I make a motion to leave, she stops what she is doing and races near. I think Elissa has a stronger connection to her dad, because now that I'm working, Jeff has arranged his schedule to watch the baby late in the afternoon . . . but when she's tired or sick, it's still Mom.

It was difficult to go back to work. You hear terrible things about day care, stories of babies being neglected. I looked at the center in town, but there were just so many kids. Finally I settled on a neighbor who watches a few toddlers in her home. I saw how much this woman loves children, and felt secure knowing who would be caring for my child. But you still get worried, feel guilty. The worst was Elissa's reaction—the way she screamed the first week when I left her off. But it's obvious that she's happy now. Every morning she runs smiling to Ms. Marie's arms.

It's bittersweet to see my baby separating from me, running into the world, becoming her own little person—with some very strong likes and dislikes. The clashes are becoming more frequent now that I'm turning up the discipline, expecting more in terms of behavior from my "big girl." But mainly it's so hard to be apart. I think about Elissa 50 million times a day. I speed home to see her. I can't wait to see her glowing face in the window, how she jumps up and down, and we run to kiss and cuddle again.

Imagine being Kim, with your child the center of your life. Imagine being Elissa, wanting to be independent but vitally needing your mother close. In this chapter, I'll focus on **attachment,** the powerful bond of love between caregiver and child.

My discussion of attachment—which takes up much of this chapter—starts a conversation that continues throughout this book. Attachment is not only at the core of infancy, but human life. After exploring this vital one-to-one relationship, I'll turn to the wider world, first examining how that basic marker, socioeconomic status, affects young children's development, then spotlighting day care, the setting where so many developed-world babies spend their days. The last section of this chapter focuses on **toddlerhood,** the famous time lasting roughly from age 1 to 2 1/2 years. (Your tip-off that a child is a toddler is that classic endearing "toddling" gait that characterizes the second year of life.)

attachment The powerful bond of love between a caregiver and child (or between any two individuals).

toddlerhood The important transitional stage after babyhood, from roughly 1 year to 2 1/2 years of age; defined by an intense attachment to caregivers and by an urgent need to become independent.

Attachment: The Basic Life Bond

Perhaps you remember being intensely in love. You may be in that wonderful state right now. You cannot stop fantasizing about your significant other. Your moves blend with your partner's. You connect in a unique way. Knowing that this person is there gives you confidence. You can conquer the world. You feel uncomfortable when you are separated. Your world depends on having your lover close. Now you have some sense of how Elissa feels about her mother and the powerful emotions that flow from Kim to her to child.

Mark Hall/Getty Images

The adoring expressions on the faces of parents and babies as they gaze at each other make it obvious why the attachment relationship in infancy is our basic model for romantic love in adulthood.

Setting the Context: How Developmentalists (Slowly) Got Attached to Attachment

During much of the twentieth century, U.S. psychologists seemed oddly indifferent to these feelings. In an age when psychology was dominated by behaviorist ideology, studying love, the province of the poets, seemed too unscientific. Behaviorists minimized our need for attachment, suggesting that the reason babies wanted to be close to their mothers was because this "maternal reinforcing stimulus" provided food. Worse yet, you may remember from Chapter 1 that the early behaviorist John Watson seemed *hostile* to attachment when he crusaded against the dangers of "too much" mother love:

> When I hear a mother say "bless its little heart" when it falls down, I . . . have to walk a block or two to let off steam. . . . Can't she train herself to substitute a kindly word . . . for . . . the pick up . . . the coddling? . . . Can't she learn to keep away from the child a large part of the day? [And then he made this memorable statement:] . . . I sometimes wish that we could live in a community of homes [where] . . . we could have the babies fed and bathed each week by a different nurse. (!)
>
> (Watson, 1928/1972, pp. 82–83)

European psychoanalysts, such as John Bowlby, felt differently. They were discovering that attachment was far from dangerous. It was crucial to infant life.

Nina Leen/Time Life Pictures

Ethologist Konrad Lorenz arranged to become the first living thing that newly hatched geese saw at their species-specific critical time for attachment. He then became the goslings' "mother," the object whom they felt compelled never to let out of their sight.

Consider a heart-rending mid-twentieth-century film that showed the fate of babies living in orphanages (Blum, 2002; Karen, 1998). In these clean, impeccably maintained institutions, Watson and the behaviorists would have predicted that infants should thrive. So why did babies lie listless on cots—unable to eat, withering away?

Now consider that ethologists—the forerunners of today's evolutionary psychologists—noticed that *every* species had a biologically programmed attachment response (or drive to be physically close to their mothers) that appeared at a specific point soon after birth. When the famous ethologist Konrad Lorenz (1935) arranged to become this attachment-eliciting stimulus for goslings, as this compelling photograph shows, Lorenz became the adored Pied Piper the baby geese tried to follow to the ends of the earth.

However, it took a rebellious psychologist named Harry Harlow, who studied monkeys, to convince U.S. psychologists that the behaviorist meal-dispenser model of mother love was wrong. In a classic study, Harlow (1958) separated baby monkeys from their mothers at birth and raised them in a cage with a wire-mesh "mother" (which offered food from a milk bottle attached to its chest) and a cloth "mother" (which was soft and provided contact comfort). The babies stayed glued to the cloth mother, making occasional trips to eat from the wire mom. In stressful situations, they scurried to the cloth mother for comfort. Love had won hands down over getting fed!

Moreover, there were serious psychological consequences for the monkeys raised without their moms. The animals couldn't have sex. They were frightened of their peers. After being artificially inseminated and giving birth, the "motherless mothers" were uncaring, abusive parents. One mauled her baby so badly that it later died (Harlow and others, 1966; Harlow, C. M., 1986).

Then, in the late 1960s, John Bowlby put the evidence together—the orphanage findings, Lorenz's ethological studies, Harlow's research, his own clinical work with children who had been hospitalized or separated from their mothers (Hinde, 2005). In a landmark series of books, Bowlby (1969, 1973, 1980) argued that there is no such thing as "excessive mother love." Having a loving **primary attachment figure** is crucial to our development. It is essential to living fully at any age. By the final decades of the twentieth century, attachment moved to the front burner in developmental science. It remains front and center today.

Harlow Primate Laboratory, University of Wisconsin

In Harlow's landmark study, baby monkeys clung to the cloth-covered "mother" (which provided contact comfort) as they leaned over to feed from the wire-mesh "mother"—vividly refuting the behaviorist idea that infants become "attached" to the reinforcing stimulus that feeds them.

Exploring the Attachment Response

Bowlby (1969, 1973) made his case for the crucial importance of attachment based on evolutionary theory. He believed that, as is true of other species, human beings have a critical period when the attachment response "comes out." As was true of Lorenz's ducks, attachment is built into our genetic code to allow us to survive. Although the attachment response is programmed to emerge during our first years of life, **proximity-seeking behavior**—our need to make contact with an attachment figure—is activated when our survival is threatened at *any* age.

Bowlby believed that threats to survival come in two categories. They may be activated by our internal state. When your three-year-old niece clings only to her mom, you know she must be ill or tired. When you go to the hospital, you make sure that your family is by your side. You immediately text your "significant other" when you have a fever or the flu.

They may be evoked by dangers in the external world. During childhood, it's a huge dog at the park that causes us to run anxiously into our parent's arms. As adults, it's a professor's nasty comment or a humiliating experience at work that provokes a frantic call to our primary attachment figure, be it our spouse, our father, or our best friend.

Although we all need to touch base with our significant others when we feel threatened, adults and older children can be separated from their attachment figures for some time. During infancy and early childhood, simply being apart from a caregiver causes distress. Now, let's trace step-by-step how human attachment unfolds.

Attachment Milestones

According to Bowlby, during their first three months of life, babies are in the **preattachment phase.** Remember that during this reflex-dominated time infants have yet to wake up to the world. However, at around 2 months there is a milestone called the **social smile.** Bowlby believed that this first real smile does not show attachment to *a* person. Because it pops up in response to any human face, it is just one example of an automatic reflex such as sucking or grasping that evokes care from adults.

Still, a baby's eagerly awaited first smile can be an incredible experience if you are a parent. Suddenly, your relationship with your child shifts to a different plane.

primary attachment figure The closest person in a child's or adult's life.

proximity-seeking behavior Acting to maintain physical contact or to be close to an attachment figure.

preattachment phase The first phase of John Bowlby's developmental attachment sequence, during the first three months of life, when infants show no visible signs of attachment.

social smile The first real smile, occurring at about 2 months of age.

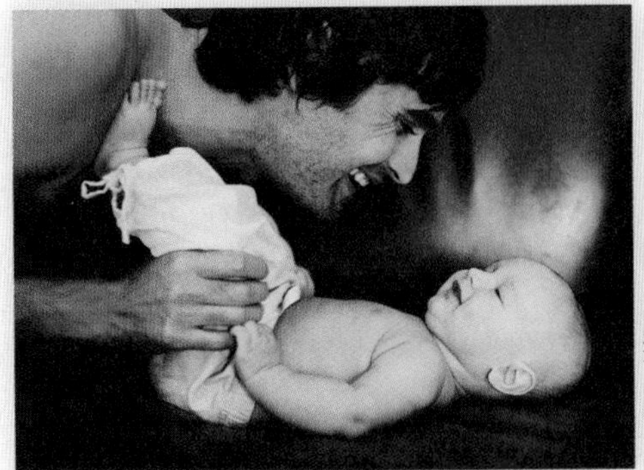

Kevin Fitzgerald/Getty Images

A baby's first social smile, which appears at the sight of any face at about 2 to 3 months of age, is biologically programmed to delight adults and charm them into providing love and care.

attachment in the making Second phase of Bowlby's attachment sequence, when, from 4 to 7 months of age, babies slightly prefer the primary caregiver.

clear-cut attachment Critical human attachment phase, from 7 months through toddlerhood, defined by separation anxiety, stranger anxiety, and needing a primary caregiver close.

separation anxiety Signal of clearcut attachment when a baby gets upset as a primary caregiver departs.

stranger anxiety Beginning at about 7 months of age, when a baby grows wary of people other than a primary caregiver.

Now, I have a confession to make: During my first two months as a new mother, I was worried, as I did not feel anything for this beautiful child I had waited so long to adopt. I date Thomas's first endearing smile as the defining event in my lifelong attachment romance.

At roughly 4 months of age, infants enter a transitional period, called **attachment in the making.** At this time, Piaget's environment-focused secondary circular reactions are unfolding (recall Chapter 3). The cortex is coming on-line. Babies may show a slight preference for their primary caregiver. But still, a 4- or 5-month-old can be the ultimate party person, happy to be cuddled by anyone—from Grandma, to a neighbor, to a stranger at the mall.

By around 7 or 8 months of age, this changes. At this age, as you saw in Chapter 3, babies are hunting for hidden objects—showing that they have the cognitive skills to miss their caregivers. Now that they can crawl, or walk holding onto furniture, children can really get hurt. The stage is set for **clear-cut** (or *focused*) **attachment**—the beginning of the full-blown attachment response. This phase of intense attachment will last throughout the toddler years.

© Christina Kennedy/PhotoEdit

A few weeks ago this 7-month-old boy would have happily gone to his new neighbor. But everything changes during the phase of clear cut attachment when stranger anxiety emerges.

Separation anxiety signals this milestone. When your baby is about 7 or 8 months old, she suddenly gets uncomfortable when you leave the room. Then, **stranger anxiety** appears. Your child gets agitated when any unfamiliar person picks her up. So, as children travel toward their first birthday, the universal friendliness of early infancy is a thing of the past. While they may still joyously gurgle at the world from their caregiver's arms, it's normal for babies to forbid any "stranger"—a nice day-care worker or even a loving Grandma who lives far away and flies in for a visit—to invade their space.

Between ages 1 and 2, the distress reaches a peak. A child may cling and cry when mom or dad makes a motion to leave. It's as if an invisible string connects the caregiver and the child. In one classic study at a park, 1-year-olds played within a certain distance from their mothers. Interestingly, this zone of optimum comfort (about 200 feet) was identical for both the parent and the child (Anderson, 1972).

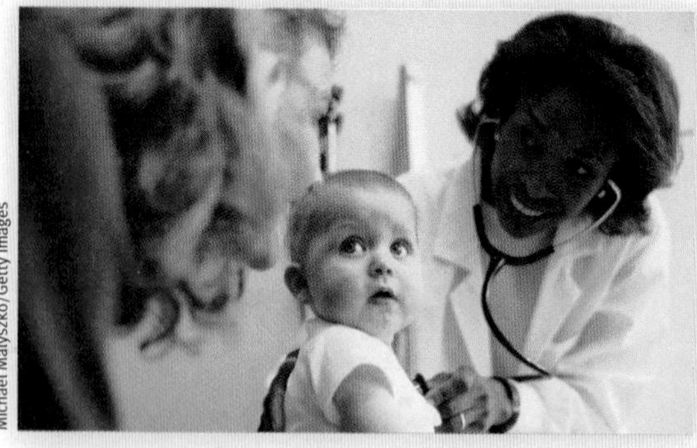

Michael Malyszko/Getty Images

As she socially references her mom this baby wants to know: Is that giant with the strange object really safe?

To see these changes, pick up a young baby (such as a 4-month-old) and an older infant (perhaps a baby about 10 months of age) and compare their reactions. Then, observe 1-year-olds at a local park. Can you measure this attachment zone of comfort? Do you notice the busy, exploring toddlers periodically checking back to make sure a caregiver is still there?

Social referencing is the term developmentalists use to describe this checking-back behavior. Social referencing helps alert the baby to which situations are dangerous and which ones are safe. ("Should I climb up this slide, Mommy?" "Does Daddy think this object is OK to explore?")

social referencing A baby's checking back and monitoring a caregiver for cues as to how to behave while exploring; linked to clear-cut attachment.

working model In Bowlby's theory, the mental representation of a caregiver, allowing children over age 3 to be physically apart from a caregiver.

Social referencing is not only the glue that permits babies to safely venture into the world; we depend on this vital relationship-oriented activity ("She is looking upset. I'd better not do that!") to pace our behavior from age 1 to 101. When does the infant attachment response—or need to be physically close to a caregiver—go away? Although the marker is hazy, babies typically leave this stage at about age 3. Children still care just as much about their primary attachment figure. But now, according to Bowlby, they have the cognitive skills to carry a **working model,** or internal representation, of this number-one person in their minds (Bretherton, 2005).

The bottom-line message is that our human critical period for attachment is timed to unfold during our most vulnerable time of life—when we first become mobile and are most in danger of getting hurt. Moreover, what compensates parents for the frustrations of having a Piagetian "little scientist" is enormous gratifications. Just when a toddler is continually messing up the house and saying "No!" parents know that their child's world revolves totally around them.

Do children differ in the way they express this priceless sense of connection? And if so, what might these differences mean about the quality of the infant–parent bond?

© Debbie Noda/ZUMA Press/Corbis

In kindergarten, this girl can say goodbye with minimal separation anxiety because she is in the working model phase of attachment.

Attachment Styles

Mary Ainsworth set out to answer these questions when she developed a classic test of attachment—the **Strange Situation** (Ainsworth, 1967; Ainsworth and others, 1978).

The Strange Situation procedure begins when a mother and a 1-year-old enter a room full of toys. After the child has time to explore, an unfamiliar adult enters the room. Then, the mother leaves the baby alone with the stranger and, a few minutes later, returns to comfort the child. Next, the mom leaves the baby totally alone for a minute; the stranger enters; and finally, the mother returns (see Figure 4.1). By observing the child's reactions to these separations and reunions through a one-way mirror, developmentalists categorize infants as either *securely* or *insecurely attached.*

Securely attached children use their mother as a secure base, or anchor, to venture out to explore the toys. When she leaves, they may or may not become highly distressed. Most important, when she returns, their eyes light up with joy. Their close relationship is apparent in the way they run and melt into their mothers' arms. **Insecurely attached** children react in one of these three ways:

- Infants classified as **avoidant** seem excessively detached. They rarely show separation anxiety or much emotion—positive or negative—when their primary attachment figure returns. They seem wooden, disengaged, without much feeling at all.
- Babies with an **anxious-ambivalent attachment** are at the opposite end of the spectrum—clingy, nervous, too frightened to explore the toys. Terribly distressed by their mother's departure, these infants may show contradictory emotions when she returns—clinging and then striking out in anger. Often, they are inconsolable, unable to be comforted when their attachment figure comes back.
- Children showing a **disorganized attachment** behave in a genuinely bizarre manner. They freeze, run around erratically, or even look frightened when the caregiver returns.

Mary D. Ainsworth

FIGURE 4.1: **The Strange Situation:** These scenes are from the original Strange Situation study. At left, the baby cries frantically after the mother and the stranger have left the room. At right, the baby is reunited with the mother as the stranger looks on.

Strange Situation Mary Ainsworth's procedure to measure attachment at age 1, involving planned separations and reunions with a caregiver.

secure attachment Ideal attachment response when a child responds with joy at being united with a primary caregiver; or, in adulthood, the genuine intimacy that is ideal in love relationships.

insecure attachment Deviation from the normally joyful response of being united with a primary caregiver, signaling problems in the caregiver-child relationship.

avoidant attachment An insecure attachment style characterized by a child's indifference to a primary caregiver at being reunited after separation.

anxious-ambivalent attachment An insecure attachment style characterized by a child's intense distress when reunited with a primary caregiver after separation.

Albert Normandin/Masterfile

Secure Attachment The child is thrilled to see the caregiver.

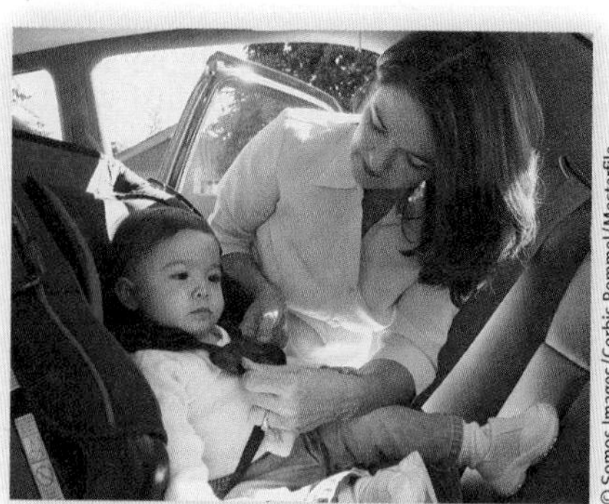

© Somos Images/Corbis Rommel/Masterfile

Avoidant Attachment The child is unresponsive to the caregiver.

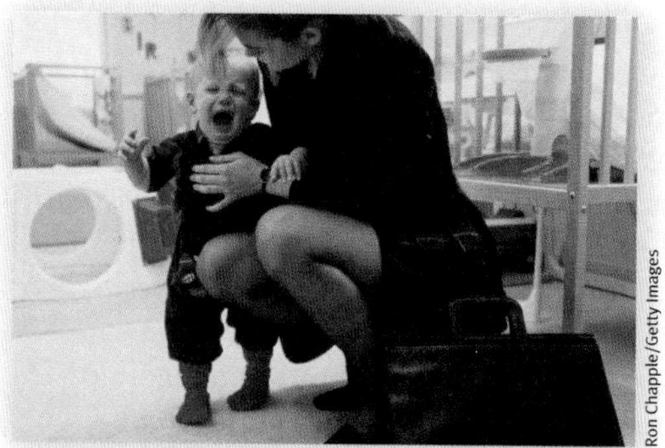

Ron Chapple/Getty Images

Anxious-Ambivalent Attachment The child cannot be calmed by the caregiver.

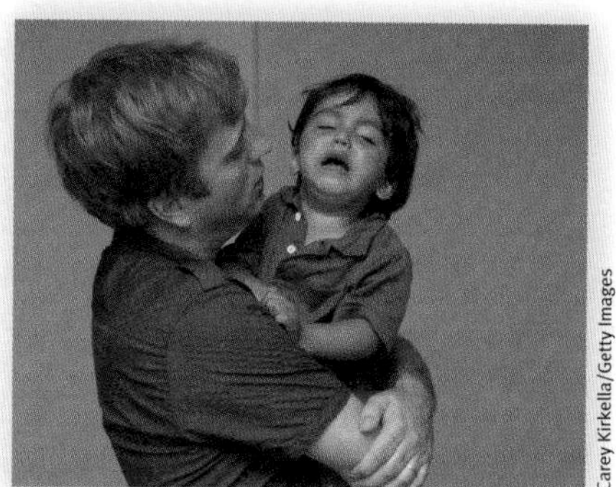

Carey Kirkella/Getty Images

Disorganized Attachment The child seems frightened and behaves bizarrely when the caregiver arrives.

FIGURE 4.2: **Secure and insecure attachments: A summary photo series**

Developmentalists point out that the insecure attachments illustrated in my summary in Figure 4.2 do not show a weakness in the *underlying* connection. Avoidant infants are just as bonded to their caregivers as babies ranked secure. Anxious-ambivalent infants are not more closely attached even though they show intense separation distress. To take an analogy from adult life, when a person who cares deeply about you pretends to be indifferent, is this individual less in love? Is a lover who can't let his partner out of sight more attached than a person who allows his significant other to have an independent life? Unless they endure the grossly abnormal rearing conditions described later in this section, *every infant* is closely attached (Zeanah, Berlin, & Boris, 2011).

Rick Gomez/Masterfile

The blissful rapture, the sense of being totally engrossed and in tune with each other, is the reason why developmentalists use the word *synchrony* to describe parent–infant attachment.

The Attachment Dance

Look at a baby and a caregiver and it is almost as if you are seeing a dance. The partners are alert to each other's signals. They know when to come on stronger and when to back off. They are absorbed and captivated, oblivious to the world. This blissful **synchrony,** or sense of being totally emotionally in tune, is what makes the infant–mother relationship our model for romantic love. Ainsworth and Bowlby believed that the parent's "dancing potential," or sensitivity to a baby's signals, produces secure attachments (Ainsworth and others, 1978). Were they correct?

THE CAREGIVER. Decades of studies suggest that the answer is yes. Sensitive caregivers tend to have babies who are securely attached. Parents who misread their baby's signals or are rejecting, disengaged, or depressed are more apt to have infants ranked insecure (see Behrens, Parker, & Haltigan, 2011 and Zeanah, Berlin, & Boris, 2011 for a review and recent example).

Moreover, a caregiver's working model of attachment predicts a baby's security, too (Bernier & Matte-Gagné, 2011; Pace & Zavattini, 2011). Imagine you are overly clingy or stiff and wooden, unable to relate. Wouldn't your own attachment insecurities hamper you from reacting to your child in an open, loving way? So, theorists suggest there may be an intergenerational component to the dance, with a parent transmitting her whole attachment worldview in the way she interacts with her child (Cowan, Cowan, & Mehta, 2009; Coyl, Newland, & Freeman, 2010; von der Lippe and others, 2010).

It seems logical that parents' "dancing style" implicitly trains babies to adopt a similar attachment worldview. By sensitively reacting to her infant's signals, isn't a caregiver offering her child lessons in responding in an open, empathic way? Conversely, aren't aloof, withdrawn parents implicitly giving their infants the message: "Don't reach out to people. The world is a harsh, unfriendly place" (notice how this perspective fits in with *both* the fetal programming research described in Chapter 2 and Erikson's infant task of "basic trust").

Still, because these are *correlations*, if we find that securely attached parents have open, loving children or that distant moms and dads have avoidant babies, couldn't these people be passing these styles of responding down in their genes? Furthermore, by blaming children's attachment issues on parents, aren't we neglecting the fact that there are *two* partners in the dance?

THE CHILD. Listen to any mother comparing her babies ("Sara was fussy; Matthew is easier to soothe") and you will realize that not all infants are born with the same dancing talent. Babies differ in their **temperament**—their characteristic, inborn behavioral styles of approaching the world.

In a pioneering study, developmentalists classified a group of middle-class babies into three temperamental styles: *Easy* babies—the majority of the children—had rhythmic eating and sleeping patterns; they were happy and easily soothed. More wary babies were labeled *slow to warm up*. One in 10 babies were ranked as *difficult*—hypersensitive, unusually agitated, reactive to every sight and sound (Thomas & Chess, 1977; Thomas, Chess, & Birch, 1968). Here is an example:

> My 5-month-old wakes up screaming from every nap. Everything seems to bother her—bright sunlight, a rough blanket, any sudden noise. I thought colic was supposed to go away by month 3. I'm getting discouraged and depressed.

Now, consider the stressful experiences a baby must go through during the Strange Situation. Do you see why some developmentalists have argued that biologically based differences in temperamental "reactivity"—not the quality of a mother's caregiving— determine attachment status at age 1? (See, for example, Kagan, 1984.)

Does a baby's biology (nature) or poor caregiving (nurture) produce insecure attachments? As you might imagine—given the nature-plus-nurture message of this book—the answer is, a little of both. Biologically, hardy babies—those who have a gene associated with resilience to stress (more about this later)—tend to be securely attached, even in the face of less sensitive parenting. However, when a child is fragile emotionally, he needs exceptionally nurturing caregiving to be classified as secure (Barry, Kochanska, & Philibert, 2008; Pace & Zavattini, 2011; Pluess and Belsky, 2010). So, a skillful dancer can sometimes shift a temperamentally "difficult" baby from insecure to secure.

But with extremely biologically vulnerable infants, there is a limit to how much the most sensitive parent can achieve. Suppose a child was extremely premature or autistic, or had some serious disease. Would it be fair to label the baby's attachment issues as the caregiver's fault?

Moreover, because "it takes two to tango" (that is, the dance is bidirectional), a child's temperament affects the parent's sensitivity, too. To use an analogy from real-life dancing, imagine waltzing with a partner who couldn't keep time with the music; or think of a time you tried to soothe a person who was too agitated to connect.

disorganized attachment An insecure attachment style characterized by responses such as freezing or fear when a child is reunited with the primary caregiver in the Strange Situation.

synchrony The reciprocal aspect of the attachment relationship, with a caregiver and infant responding emotionally to each other in a sensitive, exquisitely attuned way.

temperament A person's characteristic, inborn style of dealing with the world.

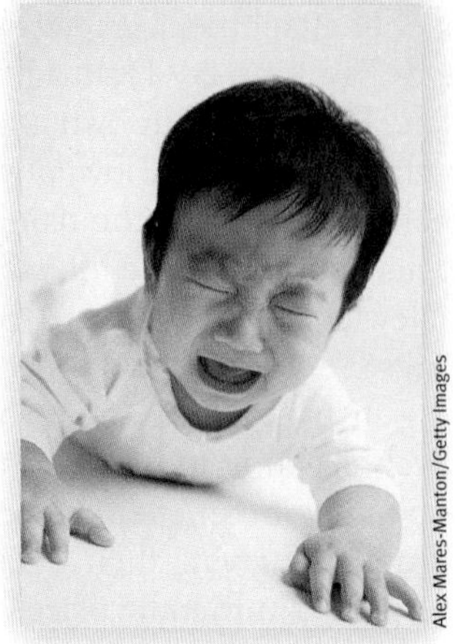

FIGURE 4.3: **Three pathways to insecure attachment:** Above left: The mother is too depressed to connect. Above center: The child has temperamental vulnerabilities. Above right: The caregiver's other attachment relationships make it difficult to "dance" with her baby.

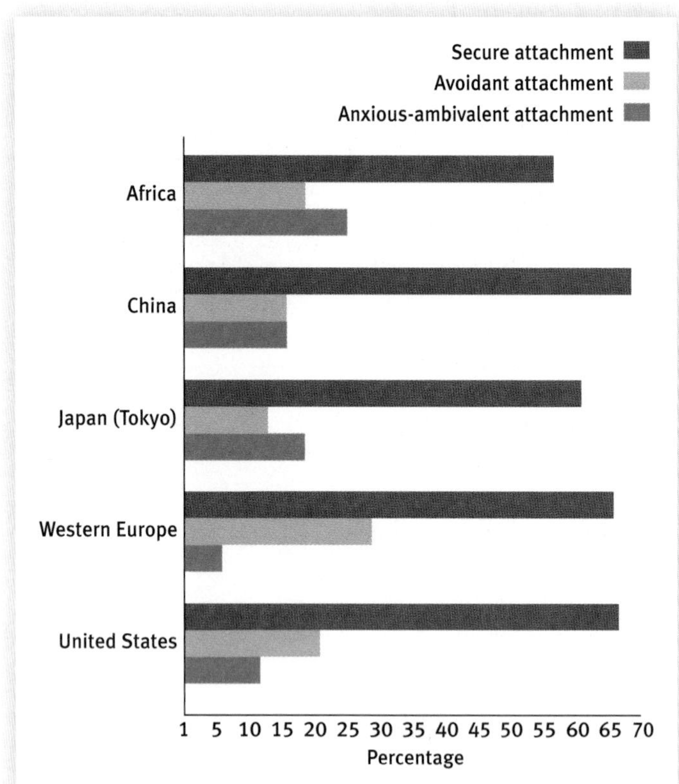

FIGURE 4.4: **Snapshots of attachment security (and insecurity) around the world:** Around the world, roughly 60 to 70 percent of 1-year-olds are classified as securely attached—although there are interesting differences in the percentages of babies falling into the different insecure categories.

Source: van IJzendoorn & Sagi, 1999, p. 729.

Even a prize-winning dancer or someone with world-class relationship skills would feel inept.

THE CAREGIVER'S OTHER ATTACHMENTS. And, to continue the analogy, it takes more than two to tango. Just as a woman's attitudes about being pregnant depend on feeling supported by the wider world (recall Chapter 2), it is difficult to be a sensitive caregiver if your other attachment relationships are not working out. When mothers (and fathers) are unhappily married, or don't dance well with each other, their babies are more likely to be rated as insecurely attached (Cowan, Cowan, & Mehta, 2009; Moss and others, 2005).

Figure 4.3—illustrating how the caregiver, the baby, and the parent's other relationships interact to shape attachment—brings home the need to adopt a *developmental systems approach*. The attachment dance is shaped by many different forces. By assuming that problems were due simply to the parent's personality, Bowlby and Ainsworth were taking an excessively limited view. What about the general theory? Is attachment to a primary caregiver universal? Do infants in different countries fall into the same categories of secure and insecure?

Is Infant Attachment Universal?

From Chicago to Capetown, from Naples to New York, Bowlby's and Ainsworth's ideas about attachment get high marks (van IJzendoorn & Sagi, 1999). Babies around the world do get attached to a primary caregiver at roughly the same age. As Figure 4.4 shows, the percentages of infants ranked secure in different countries are remarkably similar—clustering at roughly 60 to 70 percent (Sroufe, 2000; Tomlinson, Cooper, & Murray, 2005).

The most amazing validation of the universal quality of attachment comes from the Efé, a communal hunter-gatherer people living in Africa. Efé newborns freely nurse from any available lactating woman, even when their own parent is around.

They are dressed, bathed, and cared for by the whole community. But Efé babies still develop a primary attachment to their mothers at the typical age! (See van IJzendoorn & Sagi, 1999.)

So far you might be thinking that during the phase of clear-cut attachment, babies are connected to only one person. You would be wrong. A toddler may be attached to her father and day-care provider, as well as her mom. However, there is usually a single caregiver whom the child most prefers. This number-one attachment figure does *not* have to be the mother. It is typically the person the baby spends most time with, or the caregiver who seems most attentive to the infant's needs (Grossmann, Grossmann, & Zimmermann, 1999). And, just as you and I connect differently with each of our "significant others," a baby can be securely attached to his father and insecurely attached to his mom. The child's attachment to the primary caregiver predicts development best. How does infant attachment relate to the way we develop and behave?

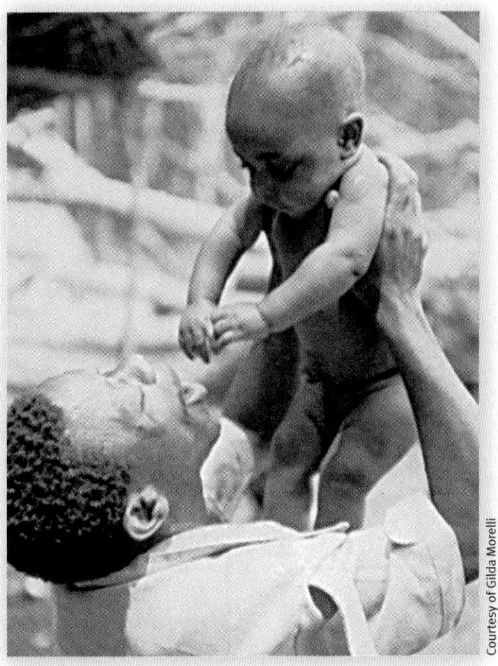

Courtesy of Gilda Morelli

This new member of the Efé people of central Africa will be lovingly cared for by the whole community, males as well as females, from his first minutes of life. Because he sleeps with his mother, however, at the "right" age he will develop his primary attachment to her.

Does Infant Attachment Predict Later Development?

Bowlby's core argument, in his working-model concept, is that our attachment relationships in infancy determine how we relate to other people and feel about ourselves (Bretherton, 2005). A baby who acts avoidant with his parents will be aloof and uncaring with friends; he may be unresponsive to a teacher's demands. An anxious-ambivalent infant will behave in a needy way in her other love relationships. A secure baby is set up to succeed socially.

Again, decades of research support Bowlby's prediction. Securely attached babies tend to be more socially competent and popular (for a recent example see McElwain, Booth-Laforce, & Wu, 2011). Insecure attachment foreshadows trouble with controlling one's emotions, and interpersonal problems, down the road (Fearon and others, 2010; Kochanska and others, 2010; von der Lippe and others, 2010).

Interestingly, the disorganized type of insecure attachment may be the most potent predictor of problems. This erratic, confused infant response style is a risk factor for "acting-out issues" (aggression, disobedience, difficulty controlling one's behavior) as children travel through elementary school (Bohlin and others, 2012; Fearon & Belsky, 2011).

However, the operative word here is "risk factor." As the following example shows, a child's negative pathway can change with highly sensitive caregiving in the wider world.

Dutch researchers measured parent–child attachment during preschool, and then evaluated each child's development a year later during kindergarten. They found that, if a particular kindergarten teacher was nurturing and went the extra mile to reach out to develop a secure attachment with an insecure child, that boy or girl was no longer at risk for having problems with his or her peers (Buyse, Verschueren, & Douman, 2011). So even in the face of an insecure attachment to a parent, a new, loving attachment can make a difference in how a child adjusts.

Exactly how much does infant attachment change as we travel into adult life? To answer this vital question, we have a remarkable set of studies in which researchers measure attachment at age 1 and then track babies into their adult years (Grossmann, Grossmann, and Kindler, 2005; Simpson and others, 2007; Sroufe and others, 2005). The basic message of this research is that, when the caregiving environment remains stable, so does a child's attachment style—with secure babies staying secure into early adult life (Zayas and others, 2011). But if dramatic changes occur in a child's life situation, attachment styles can change, for either the better or worse.

Consider, for instance, a boy named Tony, whom researchers ranked as securely attached during infancy. In preschool and early elementary school, Tony, like the other secure infants in this study, was succeeding at school and with friends. Then, as Tony entered his teenage years, he suffered a series of attachment blows. First, Tony's parents went through a difficult divorce. Then, Tony's mother was killed in a car accident and his father moved to another state, leaving Tony with his aunt. It should come as no surprise that as an adolescent, angry and depressed, Tony was classified as insecurely attached. But when Tony was retested at age 26, he was recovering. He met a wonderful woman and became a father. His status is slowly returning to secure (Sroufe and others, 2005).

So, the good news is that we can recover from rocky infant-attachment relationships. The bad news is that, although it gives us a beautiful beginning, being securely attached as a baby does not ensure being secure for one's whole life. But suppose there is a level of early deprivation that *can't* be overcome? What if a baby has experienced not just insensitive caregiving, but *no* caregiving at all?

IN FOCUS: Experiencing Early Life's Worst Deprivation

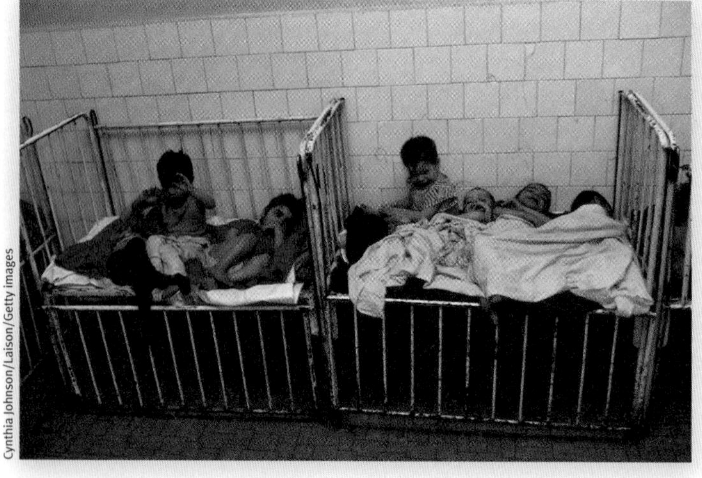

Cynthia Johnson/Laison/Getty images

Imagine visiting this orphanage in Romania and witnessing these terrible scenes. Now let's look at whether these infants, warehoused with no caring caregivers around, ever recover from this kind of deprivation.

"When I . . . walked into the . . . building (in 1990)," said a British school teacher . . . "what I saw was beyond belief . . . babies lay three and four to a bed, given no attention. . . . There were no medicines or washing facilities, and . . . physical and sexual abuse were rife . . . I particularly remember . . . the basement. There were kids there who hadn't seen natural light in years."

(McGeown, 2005, para. 4).

This scene was not from some horror movie. It was real. This woman had entered a Romanian orphanage, the bitter legacy of the dictator Ceausescu's decision to forbid contraception, which caused a flood of unwanted babies that destitute parents dumped on the state.

When the "Iron Curtain" fell and such grisly Eastern European scenes were revealed, British and American families rushed in to adopt these children. But then parents began to report distressing symptoms—sons and daughters who displayed a strange, indiscriminate friendliness and never showed interest in any specific adult (see Kreppner and others, 2011). These responses did not qualify as insecure attachment. They showed a *lack* of any attachment response.

Which institution-reared babies were most apt to show these problems? Can children recover from this terrible deprivation, and is there a specific age when help might come too late?

For answers, developmentalists descended on Bucharest, Romania, to conduct an actual experiment. (Yes, you read that right.) By lottery, they assigned institutionalized infants living in that city to either be cared for by trained local foster families or remain in institutional care. (Understand that this experiment was only ethically possible because there were no funds to pay families to take all of these children.) Given that the foster-care babies ranged in age from 6 months to 2 1/2 years, the researchers could look at the impact of "age at leaving" the institution on development, and compare these infants to non-movers as well as a never-institutionalized group.

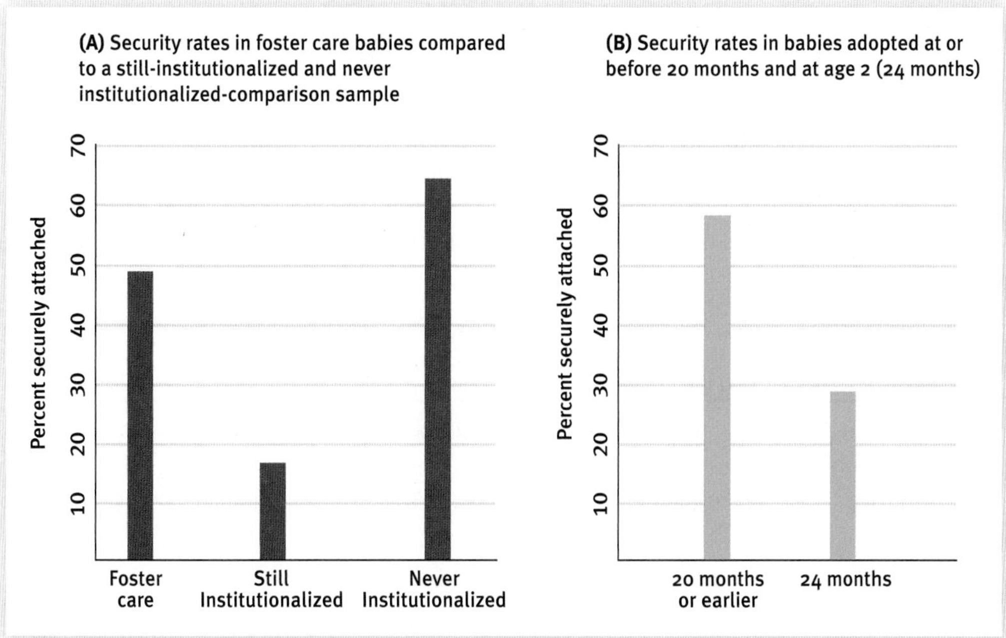

FIGURE 4.5: **Shapshots of security for orphanage babies after a year in foster care:** After a year in foster care, roughly half of the orphanage infants developed a secure attachment (see chart A)—but also notice that developing this connection was far less likely if a child was adopted at or after age 2 (see chart B).

Source: Smyke and others, 2010, pp. 218 and 219.

Figure 4.5 shows the differences in secure attachment rates a year later. Notice that the intervention made a *huge* difference. After a year in foster care, nearly half the babies were ranked secure. Chart B, however, shows "age at leaving" was crucial. If a child entered foster care by 20 months of age, his chance of forming a secure attachment was almost as high as if he had never been institutionalized. At age 2, the situation was less reversible. Roughly, only one in four older toddlers ended up secure. So following extreme deprivation, children can form secure attachments *if*—and that's a big *if*—the deprivation doesn't go on for too long (Smyke and others, 2010).

Actually, other research suggests that if a baby is adopted before 6 months of age (just prior to the zone of clear-cut attachment), there are no negative effects on development (Audet & LeMare, 2011). But after that age, problems—with learning, with relationships, with mental health—become a risk. A classic symptom of what scientists call the "institutionalization syndrome" is deficits in attention (McLaughlin and others, 2010; Wiik and others, 2011). Not unexpectedly, EEG studies suggest the reason for this impaired focusing ability is that lack of stimulation delays the normal maturation of the brain (McLaughlin and others, 2010).

As they track babies subjected to this horrendous "natural experiment" into their teens, scientists are finding out what intellectual abilities are apt to be permanently compromised (Pollak and others, 2010). They have discovered that, for some reason, institutionalized boys are more vulnerable to having enduring emotional problems because they are less likely than girls to develop secure attachments when placed in foster care (McLaughlin and others, 2012). They are getting lessons in resilience as, particularly in older childhood, an encouraging "catch up" development can occur (Sheridan and others, 2010). They are learning vital information about attachment, brain plasticity, and its limits in human beings.

Wrapping Up Attachment

To summarize, infancy is clearly a special zone of sensitivity for our ability to form relationships. The attachment response that unfolds during our first years of life lays down the foundation for healthy development in a variety of life realms. Still, attachment capacities (and human brains) are malleable, and negative trajectories can be altered provided the deprivation is not too profound and the wider world provides special help. How does the wider world affect development during infancy and beyond? To explore this question directly, let's turn to look at two crucial infant wider-world contexts: poverty and day care.

TYING IT ALL TOGETHER

1. List an example of "proximity-seeking in distress" in your own life within the past few months.
2. Baby Muriel is 1 month old, Baby Janine is 5 months old, and Baby Ted is 1 year old. List each infant's phase of attachment.
3. Match each of these terms to the correct definition: (1) social referencing; (2) working model; (3) synchrony; (4) Strange Situation.
   a. A researcher measures a child's attachment at age 1 in a series of separations and reunions with the mother.
   b. A toddler keeps looking back at the parent while exploring at a playground.
   c. An elementary school child keeps an image of her parent in mind to calm herself when she gets on the school bus in the morning.
   d. A mother and baby relate to each other as if they are totally in tune.
4. Your cousin is the primary caregiver of her 1-year-old son. On a recent visit to her house, you notice that the baby shows no emotion when his mother leaves the room, and—more important—seems indifferent when she returns. How might you classify this child's attachment?
5. Manuel is arguing for the validity of attachment theory as spelled out by Bowlby and Ainsworth. Manuel should say (pick one, neither, or both): *Infants around the world get attached to a primary caregiver at roughly the same age/a child's attachment status as of age 1 never changes.*
6. Jasmine is adopting a *12 month old* from an orphanage in Russia. You might caution Jasmine that (pick 2 items): *The infant is unlikely to ever get securely attached/The infant may show problems with attention/If the infant is a boy, it may be harder for him to get securely attached to you.*

You can find Answers to the Tying It All Together questions at the end of this chapter.

Settings for Development

What happens to children in the United States who spend their first years of life in poverty? And what about that crucial setting of early childhood—day care?

The Impact of Poverty in the United States

In Chapter 3, we examined the physical effects of extreme poverty—the high rates of stunting in the developing world. In the United States, we don't have the kind of poverty that causes undernutrition. Still, being poor during early childhood can compromise a developing life. How common is child poverty in the United States? How does poverty affect children's later well-being?

How Common Is Early-Childhood Poverty?

As Figure 4.6, shows, unfortunately, child poverty is alarmingly prevalent in the United States. In 2009, more than one in four children under age six was living

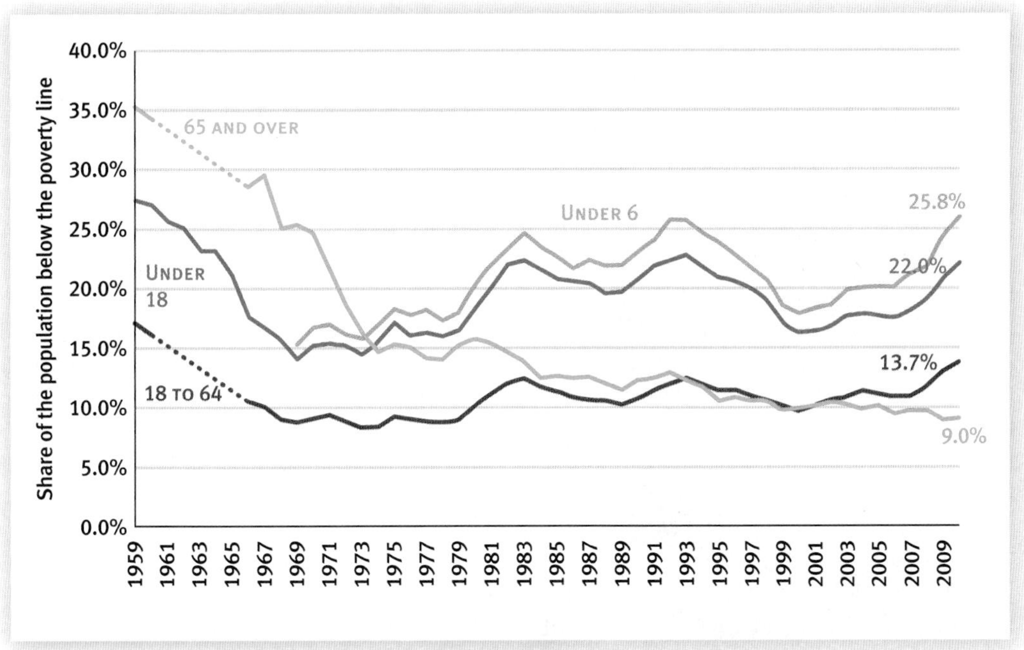

FIGURE 4.6: **Poverty rates by age, 1959–2010:** Notice that since the 1970s, children under 6 years of age have been more likely to live under the poverty line than other age groups in the United States. (FYI—Although the "poverty line" designation theoretically describes the minimum income needed to survive, experts feel that families really need twice that amount of money to really make ends meet.)
Source: State of Working America: Poor children, Economic Policy Institute, 2012.

under the poverty line. If we consider "low-income" families (those earning within 200 percent of the poverty line), the statistics rise to almost one in two (44 percent) (Miller, Sadegh-Nobari, & Lillie-Blanton, 2011). Moreover, notice that, since the 1970s, young children have been more likely to live in poverty than other age groups in the United States.

One cause is single motherhood. Imagine how difficult it would be as a woman raising a baby alone to work, pay for child care, and still have money to make ends meet. Now imagine how difficult it would be for *any* person—married or single—to support a family with a full-time job that paid $8 to $10 dollars an hour. So, with the kinds of jobs available to many young people at the brink of their careers, it's no wonder that economic disadvantage is a "fairly normal" consequence of starting a family if you are in your twenties today.

How Does Early-Childhood Poverty Affect Later Development?

Unfortunately, spending one's first years of life in poverty can have long-term effects. Poverty, not only compromises health during childhood, but the stresses associated with early economic disadvantage can take a long-term toll on the body, setting people up for adult illnesses and premature death (Miller, Chen, & Parker, 2011; recall also my discussion of deprivation in the womb, in Chapter 2).

The long-term educational impact is especially pronounced. You might be surprised to know that being poor specifically during the first four years of life makes it statistically less likely for a child to graduate from high school (Duncan & Brooks-Gunn, 2000). Experts estimate that for poverty-level families in the United States, a boost of *just* $3,000 dollars during each of a baby's first five years translates into roughly 19 percent higher wages when that child becomes an adult (Duncan, Ziol-Guest, & Kalil, 2010).

Why does early-childhood poverty, in particular, make such a difference in later academic and work success? One possibility is that it is difficult to make up for what you have lost if you enter school "left behind," not knowing your letters or numbers, without those basic building blocks required to succeed. Low-income children are less likely to go to museums, to have enriching toys, or books. As one social critic powerfully put it: Who is more likely to do well on reading and math tests, children who "spent the years from 2 to 4 in lovely Montessori schools . . . in which . . . attentive grown-ups read to them from story books, . . . or the ones who spent those years at home sitting in front of a TV . . . ?" (Kozol, 2005, p. 53.)

Janine Wiedel Photolibrary/Alamy

Relating in a sensitive, caring way to your baby (and other children) can be very difficult if you are an impoverished, stressed-out single mom.

Poverty also can impair the attachment dance, especially among at-risk children who need unusually sensitive care. Imagine you are a single mother arriving home, exhausted from a low-wage job, or are unemployed, *food insecure*, and worried about getting evicted because you can't pay the rent. How would you deal with the kind of temperamentally irritable infant I described in the previous section, a baby who was difficult to soothe? In summarizing more than 60 studies, developmentalists found that affluent mothers tended to react to the challenge of having a "difficult" baby by making special efforts to calm their child's distress. Stressed-out, low-income women were more prone to yell, to hit, and to scream (Paulussen-Hoogeboom and others, 2007). So although money cannot buy loving mothers, it can buy any mother breathing space to try to do her best.

Moreover, poor children may not have the *concrete* breathing space to learn (Leventhal & Newman, 2010). If a boy or girl lives in crowded, substandard housing or is among the roughly one in three low-income children in the United States whose family must repeatedly move (Miller, Sadegh-Nobari, & Lillie-Blanton, 2011), it's hard to focus on academics or get connected to school. And if a child lives in a dangerous area, she cannot escape the household chaos by venturing outside. Her neighborhood is likely to be a scary place.

As parents understand when they struggle to buy a house in a section of the city they can't quite afford, where families live make a difference in children's life chances. Growing up on a block blighted by poverty—one where your neighbors are poorly educated and out of work—is associated with lower performance on school-readiness tests (Hanson and others, 2011). Conversely, having more middle-class professionals on a street, *in and of itself*, relates to a child's scoring higher on academic tests. Interestingly, the neighborhood make its greatest impact at the low to medium end of the income spectrum, and then levels off (Dupree and others, 2010). Plus, these negative cognitive effects show up by age 3 or 4, *before* a child has entered school. So if parents live in an economically depressed area, it makes sense to move to a better neighborhood for their children's sake. But there's no academic benefit in abandoning a middle-class subdivision for the gated community across town.

So far, you may have impression that poor families with young children are totally left to flounder in the United States. Wrong! Well-established government programs exist to improve disadvantaged children's academic and social chances.

INTERVENTIONS: Giving Disadvantaged Children an Intellectual and Social Boost

The most famous U.S. government–sponsored program is **Head Start.** Head Start, established in 1965, aims to provide the kind of high-quality preschool experience to make poverty-level children as ready for kindergarten as their middle-class peers. In addition to this federal program, as of late 2011, 38 states also offered free pre-K (prekindergarten) programs targeted to children in economic need (Magnuson and Shager, 2010; Phillips & Lowenstein, 2011).

Early Head Start extends this help to infants and toddlers. This federal program focuses on training parents to be more effective caregivers, as well as supports low-income pregnant women with home visits and other services (Phillips & Lowenstein, 2011).

Head Start A federal program offering high-quality day care at a center and other services to help preschoolers aged 3 to 5 from low-income families prepare for school.

Early Head Start A federal program that provides counseling and other services to low-income parents and children under age 3.

Do these interventions work? The answer is "yes." *Provided they are high quality*, Head Start–like programs, as well as some other as infant and toddler interventions, make a documented difference in low-income children's lives (Bassok, 2010; Magnuson & Shager, 2010; Miller, Sadegh-Nobari, and Lillie-Blanton, 2011; Phillips & Lowenstein, 2011). In a genuine experiment, in which researchers randomly assigned disadvantaged children to a high-quality pre-K program, this one-shot intervention had an impact, decades later, in improved college graduation rates! (See Pungello and others, 2010.)

Unfortunately, however, excellent **preschools** (teaching-oriented group programs beginning at age 3) are most available to affluent young children. Disadvantaged children, and especially immigrant families, are less likely to participate (Magnuson & Shager, 2010). Moreover, no one-shot magic intervention at age 3 or 4 can really compensate for the academic barriers poor children face during their *entire* school careers. As you will learn in Chapter 7, low-income children typically attend the poorest-quality kindergartens. Their educational experiences—without adequate books, with mold-encrusted classrooms, and teachers who often quit just a few months into the school year—qualify as a national shame (Kozol, 1988, 2005).

Peter Byron/Photo Edit

This dispiriting photo of an inner-city elementary school powerfully brings home the fact that even the highest-quality preschool can't make up for the educational barriers that impoverished children face once they enter and move through real school.

Finally, I must emphasize that preschool doesn't work in isolation. Yes, attending a high-quality program can serve as a lifeline when a child's home environment is poor (Phillps & Lowenstein, 2011). But what matters most is *consistent stimulation* at school and home (Crosnoe and others, 2010).

This brings up the role of those primary educators: parents. Parents at *every* income level differ in their dancing skills and the teaching experiences they provide. Every study agrees: What happens at home matters most (Lugo-Gil & Tamis-LeMonda, 2008). Some affluent parents leave the dancing to others. Some poverty-level parents work overtime to nurture and stimulate their daughters and sons.

Can we identify some core qualities of these special low-income moms and dads? In one study, researchers found that if people felt good about their own childhoods and were optimistic, they could put aside their life problems and offer their children the ultimate in tender-loving care (Kochanska and others, 2007). As a student of mine commented, "I don't see my family in your description of poverty. My mom is my hero. We grew up very poor, but in terms of parenting, we were very rich."

The Impact of Child Care

Poverty issues can seem distant from life among parents who are comfortably well off. Child care affects every family, from millionaires, to middle-class urban mothers and fathers, to the rural poor. One in every two mothers in the United States returns to work during a baby's first year of life. With childcare costs currently ranging from $5,000 to 15,000 per year, the expense of putting even *one* baby in day care is daunting, even to couples who are clearly middle class (Palley & Shdaimah, 2011). When we combine these intense economic concerns ("This is taking up a huge chunk of my paycheck!") with anxieties about "leaving my baby with strangers," it makes sense that many new parents struggle to keep childcare in the family. They may rely on grandma or juggle work schedules so that one spouse is always home (Phillips & Lowenstein, 2011).

People who use paid caregivers have several options. Well-off families often hire a nanny or babysitter. Less-affluent parents, or those who want a more inexpensive option, often turn to **family day care,** where a neighbor or local parent cares for a small group of children in her home.

The big change on the childcare landscape has been the dramatic increase in licensed **day-care centers**—larger settings that cater to children of different ages. By the

preschool A teaching-oriented group setting for children aged 3 to 5.

family day care A day-care arrangement in which a neighbor or relative cares for a small number of children in her home for a fee.

day-care center A day-care arrangement in which a large number of children are cared for at a licensed facility by paid providers.

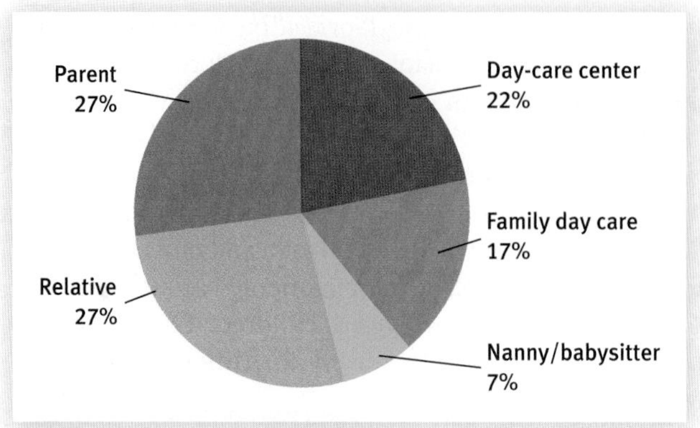

FIGURE 4.7: Day care arrangements for infants and toddlers with employed mothers, late 1990s: Notice that, while most infants and toddlers with working mothers are cared for by other family members, 1 in 5 attend licensed day-care centers.

Source: Shonkoff & Phillips 2000, p. 304.

late twentieth century, roughly than 1 in 2 U.S. preschoolers attended these facilities. The comparable figure for infants and toddlers was more than 1 in 5 (see Figure 4.7).

Child Care and Development

Imagine you are the mother of an infant and must return to work. You probably wonder, "Will my child be securely attached if I see her only a few hours a day?" You would also worry about finding a childcare provider and the quality of care your child would receive: "Will my baby get enough attention at the local day-care center?" "What is the *real* impact of putting my child in someone else's care?"

To answer these questions, in 1989, developmentalists began the National Institute of Child Health and Human Development (NICHD) Study of Early Child Care. They selected more than 1,000 newborns in 10 regions of the United States and tracked the progress of these children, measuring everything from attachment to academic abilities, from mental health, to mothers' caregiving skills. They looked at the hours each child spent in day care, and assessed the quality of the settings in which the children were placed. The NICHD newborns have now been regularly followed into their teens (Vandell and others, 2010).

The good news is that putting a baby in day care does not weaken the attachment bond. Most infants attending day care are securely attached to their parents. The important force that promotes attachment is the *quality* of the dance—whether a parent is a sensitive caregiver—not whether she works (Phillips & Lowenstein, 2011). Moreover, as I emphasized earlier, what happens at home is the crucial influence affecting how young children develop, outweighing long hours spent in day care during the first years of life (Belsky and others, 2007b).

However, when we look *just* at the impact of spending those long hours, the findings are less upbeat. As you saw in the previous section, attending an excellent preschool has clear cognitive benefits. At a recent evaluation, the NICHD researchers found that being sent to this kind of program offered children an academic boost that persisted into the teens (Vandell and others, 2010). But when we look at the impact of attending day care *throughout the first five years of life,* there is troubling news.

Earlier NICHD research raised alarm bells by reporting that children who spent long hours in "non-relative care" were slightly more likely to be rated as "difficult to control" by caregivers and kindergarten teachers (NICHD, Early Child Care Research Network, 2003, 2004, 2006). Now we have the findings through age 15. Long hours spent in day care, beginning early in life, still predict an elevated risk of "acting-out issues" as teens (Vandell and others, 2010).

These results do not offer comfort to the millions of parents who must rely heavily on day care for their babies. But luckily, the correlations are weak (Vandell and others, 2010). For certain at-risk infants and toddlers—those with difficult temperaments, boys living in poverty—*high-quality* day care can protect against behavior problems down the road (Pluess & Belsky, 2010; Votruba-Drzal and others, 2010). Moreover, the negative effects of day care apply mainly to children attending large centers, not smaller family care settings (Groeneveld and others, 2010).

What is the trouble specifically with day-care centers? For answers, let's scan the state of child care in the United States.

Exploring Childcare Quality in the United States

Visit several facilities and you will immediately see that U.S day care varies dramatically in quality. In some places, babies are warehoused and ignored. In others, every child is nurtured and loved.

Ellen B. Senisi/The Image Works

Can this day-care worker give enough attention to the babies and toddlers in her care? Unfortunately, with a caregiver–child ratio at over 3 to 1 at this center, the answer may be no.

The essence of quality day care again boils down to the dance—that is, the attachment relationship between caretakers and the children in their care. As I implied earlier in this chapter, children develop attachments to their day-care providers. If a particular caregiver is sensitive, a child in her care tends to be securely attached (Ahnert, Pinquart, & Lamb, 2006; De Schipper and others, 2008).

Child-care providers and parents agree: To be effective in this job, you need to be patient, caring, empathic, and child-centered (Berthelsen & Brownlee, 2007; Virmani & Ontai, 2010). It's not so much formal education that matters, but being able to reflect on your interactions (Virmani & Ontai, 2010) and being committed to this field (Martin and others, 2010).

You also need to work in a setting where you are respected as a professional (Martin and others, 2010) and can relate to children in a one-to-one way. To demonstrate this point, researchers videotaped teachers at 64 Dutch preschools, either playing with three children or with five. Teachers, they discovered, acted more empathic in the three-child group. They were more likely to criticize and get angry with the group of five (de Schipper, Riksen-Walraven, & Geurts, 2006). These differences in teachers' tone and style were especially pronounced with younger children (the 3-year-olds). So, group size matters; and the lower the child–teacher ratio, the better, especially earlier in life.

Another important dimension is consistency of care (Harrist, Thompson, & Norris, 2007). Forming an attachment takes time. Therefore, it is no surprise that children are more likely to be securely attached to a caregiver when that person has been there a longer time. (Ahnert, Pinquart, & Lamb, 2006).

However, partly because of the abysmal pay (in the United States, it's often close to the minimum wage), day-care workers are apt to quit. One parent bitterly commented: "We pay firefighters good money to sit around and hope there is not a fire . . . and what do we pay our childcare providers?. . . They are not *hoping* our kids are going to grow up . . . they are *helping* the kids grow up . . . and they get diddly squat!" (Harrist, Thompson, & Norris, 2007, p. 319.)

Combine these terrible salaries with burnout from feeling overwhelmed. While the recommended ratio is one caregiver to four toddlers, only eight states follow this guideline (Stebbins & Knitzner, NCCP, 2007). Some allow as many as one teacher per 12 children, even during the first year of life.

In sum, now we know why day-care centers are at risk of providing inadequate care. Their primary culprit is size. In family day care, there is a smaller number of children and often more stability (since the person is watching the children in her home) than in a large facility, where caregivers keep leaving and babies are warehoused in larger groups (Gerber, Whitebrook, & Weinstein, 2007). In fact, studies both in the United States and Europe suggest that children's well-being tends to be higher in family versus center-based care (Ahnert, Pinquart, & Lamb, 2006; Groeneveld and others, 2010).

TABLE 4.1: Choosing a Day-Care Center: A Checklist

Overall Considerations

- Consider the caregiver(s). Are they nurturing? Do they love babies? Are they interested in providing a good deal of verbal stimulation to children?
- Ask about stability, or staff turnover. Have caregivers left in the last few months? Can my infant have the same caregivers when she moves to the toddler room?
- Look for a low caregiver-to-baby ratio (and a small group). The ideal is one caregiver to every two or three babies.
- Look at the physical setting. Is it safe and clean, set up with children's needs in mind? (With toddlers, look for a variety of age-appropriate play materials, clearly defined social spaces and more private nooks, child-sized furniture, clear pathways for children to circulate, and sensitive placement of play areas, such as areas for painting situated near sinks.)

Additional Suggestions

- For infants and toddlers in full-time care, limit exposure by having a child take occasional vacations or building in special time with the child every day.
- Consider a child's temperament. Highly anxious babies—or very active toddlers—have special trouble coping with less-than-optimal care.
- Small family day care, however, may be really helpful to bring shy toddlers out of their shell.
- And finally, for society, pay day-care workers decently and make the qualities you are looking for in this checklist the norm!

Background sources: The authors cited in this section.

INTERVENTIONS: Choosing Child Care

Given these findings, what should parents do? The take-home message is not "avoid a day-care center," but rather "choose the best possible place." Look for a low staff turnover; check to see if the caregivers are empathic and warm; if you have an infant or toddler, make sure your baby will spend the day in a small group. You might find these conditions at your next-door neighbor's house. Perhaps you'll find these attributes at the largest childcare facility in town.

You also might look to your child. Just as they have more problems in the Strange Situation, highly anxious infants and extremely active toddlers are especially vulnerable to less-than-optimal day care (Crockenberg, 2003; Crockenberg & Leerkes, 2005). Still, sending a shy child to a small day-care setting with a supportive caregiver has special benefits, as it tends to *promote* social confidence down the road (Coplan, Findlay, & Schneider, 2010; Gunnar and others, 2011; also, see the toddler discussion at the end of this chapter).

Table 4.1 draws on these messages in a checklist. And if you are a parent who relies heavily on day care, keep these heartening thoughts in mind: There are *many* exceptional day programs. A silver lining of the Great Recession of 2008 may be less staff turnover and more incentive for people to make this crucial job their life career. Every study shows that *your* responsiveness is what matters most. You are your child's major teacher and the major force in making your child secure.

Now that we have examined attachment, poverty, and day care, it's time to turn directly to the topic I have been implicitly talking about all along—being a toddler.

TYING IT ALL TOGETHER

1. Hugo is discussing early-childhood poverty in the United States with Heloise. Which *two* statements should he make?
   a. Early-childhood poverty raises the risk of not graduating from high school.
   b. Young children are the poorest segment of the U.S. population.
   c. Head Start is the only U.S. program available to help poverty-level preschoolers succeed in school.

2. Nancy has just put her 6-month-old in day care, and she is anxious about her decision. Give a "good news" statement to ease Nancy's mind, and then be honest and give a "not such good news" statement about day care.

3. You are making a presentation to a Senate committee investigating early child care. What should you tell the senators about the impact of preschool on development? What improvements can you suggest with regard to day care itself?

Answers to the Tying It All Together questions can be found at the end of this chapter.

Toddlerhood: Age of Autonomy *and* Shame and Doubt

Imagine time-traveling back to when you were a toddler. Everything is entrancing—a bubble bath, the dishwasher soap box, the dirt and bugs in your backyard. You are just cracking the language barrier and finally (yes!) traveling on your own two feet. Passionate to sail into life, you are also intensely connected to that number-one adult in your life. So, during our second year on this planet, the two agendas that make us human first emerge: We need to be closely connected, and we want to be free, autonomous selves. This is why Erik Erikson (1950) used the descriptive word **autonomy** to describe children's challenge as they emerge from the cocoon of babyhood (see Table 4.2).

Autonomy involves everything from the thrill a 2-year-old feels when forming his first sentences, to the delight children have in dressing themselves. But it also involves those not-so-pleasant behaviors we associate with the "terrible twos." How common is difficult behavior at this special age? As you can see in Figure 4.8, very. Difficulties sitting still and "listening" and angry outbursts (Barry & Kochanska, 2010) are at their height during this magic age when children's life passion is to explore the world (recall Piaget's little scientist behaviors).

Erikson used the words *shame* and *doubt* to refer to the situation when a toddler's drive for autonomy is not fulfilled. But feeling shameful and doubtful is also vital to shedding babyhood and entering the human world. During their first year of

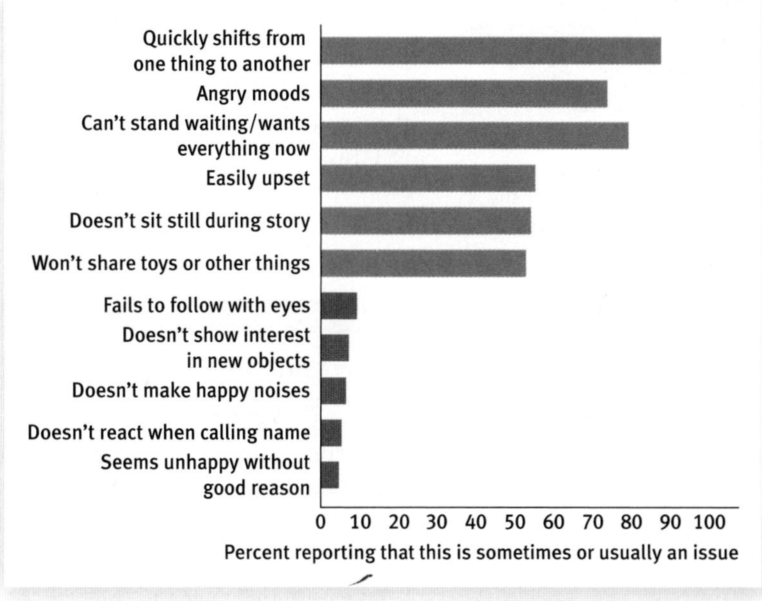

FIGURE 4.8: **Typical and unusual difficult toddler behaviors, based on a survey of Dutch parents of 6,491 infants aged 14 to 19 months:** Notice that it's normal for toddlers not to listen, have temper tantrums, and refuse to sit still or share—but the other difficult behaviors in red should be warning signs of a real problem.

Source: Beernick, Swinkels, & Buitelaar, 2007.

TABLE 4.2: **Erikson's Psychosocial Stages**

Life Stage	Primary Task
Infancy (birth to 1 year)	Basic trust versus mistrust
Toddlerhood (1 to 2 years)	**Autonomy versus shame and doubt**
Early childhood (3 to 6 years)	Initiative versus guilt
Late childhood (6 years to puberty)	Industry versus inferiority
Adolescence (teens into twenties)	Identity versus role confusion
Young adulthood (twenties to early forties)	Intimacy versus isolation
Middle adulthood (forties to sixties)	Generativity versus stagnation
Late adulthood (late sixties and beyond)	Integrity versus despair

autonomy Erikson's second psychosocial task, when toddlers confront the challenge of understanding that they are separate individuals.

SW Productions/Getty Images

This toddler has reached a human milestone: She can feel shame, which means that she is beginning to be aware that she has a separate self.

life, infants show joy, fear, and anger. At age 2, more complicated, uniquely human emotions emerge—pride and shame. The appearance of these **self-conscious emotions** is a milestone—showing that a child is becoming aware of having an actual self. The gift (and sometimes curse) of being human is that we are capable of self-reflection, able to get outside of our heads and observe our actions from an outsider's point of view. Children show signs of this uniquely human quality between age 2 and 3, when they feel ashamed and clearly are proud of their actions for the first time (Kagan, 1984).

Socialization: The Challenge for 2-Year-Olds

Shame and pride are vital in another respect. They are essential to **socialization**—being taught to live in the human community.

When do parents begin to seriously socialize their children—or turn up the heat on rules and discipline? For answers, developmentalists surveyed U.S. middle-class parents about their rules for their 14-month-olds and returned with the same questionnaire when the children just turned 2 (Smetana, Kochanska, & Chuang, 2000). While rules for 14-month-olds centered on safety issues ("Stay away from the stove!"), by age 2, parents were expecting their children to "share,"

HOW DO WE KNOW. . .

that shy and exuberant children differ dramatically in self-control?

How do researchers measure the toddler temperament discussed in the next section? How do they measure later self-control? Their first step is to design real-world situations tailored to elicit fear, anger, and joy and then observe how toddlers act.

In the situation specially designed to measure differences in fear, a child enters a room filled with frightening toy objects, such as the dinosaur with huge teeth shown below or a black box covered with spider webs. The experimenter asks that boy or girl to perform a mildly risky act, such as putting a hand into the box. To measure variations in anger, the researchers restrain a child in a car seat for a minute or two and then rate how frustrated the toddler gets. To tap into differences in exuberance, the researchers entertain a child with a set of funny puppets. Will the toddler respond with hysterical gales of laughter or be more reserved?

Several years later, the researchers set up a situation tailor-made to provoke noncompliance by asking the child, now age 4, to perform an impossible task (throw Velcro balls at a target from a long distance without looking) to get a prize. Then, they leave the room and watch through a one-way mirror to see if the boy or girl will cheat.

Courtesy of Graznya Kochanska

As it turns out, toddlers at the high end of the fearless, joyous, and angry continuum show less "morality" at age 4. Without the strong inhibition of fear, their exuberant "get closer" impulses are difficult to dampen down. So they succumb to temptation, sneak closer, and look directly at the target as they hurl the balls (Kochanska & Knaack, 2003).

self-conscious emotions Feelings of pride, shame, or guilt, which first emerge around age 2 and show the capacity to reflect on the self.

socialization The process by which children are taught to obey the norms of society and to behave in socially appropriate ways.

"sit at the table," "brush your teeth," and "don't disobey, bite, or hit." Therefore, the pressure to begin to act "like adults" comes on strong as children reach their second birthdays. No wonder 2-year-olds are infamous for those tantrums called "the terrible twos"!

Figure 4.8 on page 129 shows just how difficult it is for 1-year-olds to follow socialization rules when their parents are around. When do children have the self-regulating abilities to follow unwanted directions when a parent *isn't* in the room? To answer this question related to early *conscience*—the ability to adopt internal standards for our behavior, or have that little voice inside us that says, "even though I want to do this, it's wrong"—researchers devised an interesting procedure. Accompanied by their mothers, children enter a laboratory full of toys. Next, the parent gives an unwelcome instruction—telling the child either to clean up the toy area or not to touch another easily reachable set of enticing toys. Then, the mother leaves the room, and researchers watch the child through a one-way mirror.

Not unexpectedly, children's ability to "listen to a parent in their head" and stop doing what they want improves dramatically from age 2 to 4 (Kochanska, Coy, & Murray, 2001). Still, the really interesting question is: Which girls and boys are superior at this feat of self-control?

As some of you might guess, temperament is crucial. Fearful toddlers are more compliant at age 2. They are far less likely to cheat on a game at age 4 than more emotionally intense, uninhibited girls and boys (Aksan & Kochanska, 2004; see also the How Do We Know box). The bottom line is that the exuberant, joyful, fearless, intrepid toddler explorers (no surprise) are more difficult to socialize! (See Kochanska & Knaack, 2003.)

Being Exuberant and Being Shy

> Adam [was a vigorous, happy baby who] began walking at 9 months. From then on, it seemed as though he could never stop.
>
> (10 months) Adam . . . refuses to be carried anywhere. . . . He trips over objects, falls down, bumps himself.
>
> (12 months) The word osside appears. . . . Adam stands by the door, banging at it and repeating this magic word again and again.
>
> (16 months) Adam and his mother take a five-hour plane ride to visit his grandparents. . . . He is miserable unless he is going up and down the aisles.
>
> (19 months) Adam begins attending a toddler group. . . . The first day, Adam climbs to the highest rung of the climbing structure and falls down. . . . The second day, Adam upturns a heavy wooden bench. . . . The fourth day, the teacher [devastates Adam's mother] when she says, "I think Adam is not ready for this."
>
> . . .
>
> (13 months) (Erin begins to talk in sentences the same week as she takes her first steps.) . . . Rather suddenly, Erin becomes quite shy. . . . She cries when her mother leaves the room, and insists on following her everywhere.
>
> (15 months) Erin and her parents go to the birthday party of a little friend. . . . For the first half-hour, Erin stays very close to her mother, intermittently hiding her face on her mother's skirt.
>
> (16 months) Father and Erin go to a small grocery store where the friendly owner . . . praises her beautiful eyes and hair. . . . Erin bursts into tears.
>
> (18 months) Erin's mother takes her to a toddlers' gym. Erin watches the children . . . with a "tight little face." . . . Her mother berates herself for raising such a timid child.
>
> (Lieberman, 1993, pp. 83–87, 104–105)

Courtesy of Janet Belsky

My exuberant son—shown enjoying a sink bath at 9 months of age—began to have problems at 18 months, when his strong, joyous temperament collided with the need to "please sit still and listen, Thomas!"

Observe any group of 1-year-olds and you will immediately pick out the Erins and the Adams. Some children are wary and shy. Others are whirlwinds of activity, constantly in motion, bouncing off the walls. I remember my own first toddler group at the local Y, when—just like Adam's mother—I first realized how different my exuberant son was from the other children his age. After enduring the horrified expressions of the other mothers as Thomas whirled gleefully around the room while everyone else sat obediently for a snack, I came home and cried. How was I to know that the very qualities that made my outgoing, joyous, vital baby so charismatic during his first year of life might go along with his being so difficult to tame?

The classic longitudinal studies tracing children with shy temperaments, have been carried out by Jerome Kagan. Kagan (1994; see also Degnan, Almas, & Fox, 2010) classifies about one in five middle-class European American toddlers as inhibited. Although they are comfortable in familiar situations, these 1-year-olds, like Erin, get nervous when confronted with anything new. Inhibited 13-month-olds shy away from approaching a toy robot, a clown, or an unfamiliar person. They take time to venture out in the Strange Situation, get agitated when the stranger enters, and cry bitterly when their parent leaves the room.

Babies destined to be inhibited toddlers show precursors of their later shyness. At 4 months of age, they excessively fret and cry (Moehler and others, 2008; Marysko and others, 2010). At nine months of age, they are less able to ignore distracting stimuli such as flashing lights or background noise. Their attention wanders to any off-topic, irrelevant unpleasant event (Pérez-Edgar and others, 2010a).

Inhibited toddlers are more prone to be fearful throughout childhood (Degman, Almas, & Fox, 2010). They tend to over-focus on threatening stimuli in their teens (Pérez-Edgar and others, 2010 a). This temperamental sensitivity to threat shows up in adult life. Using brain scans, Kagan's research team found that his inhibited toddlers, now as young adults showed more activity in the part of the brain coding negative emotions when shown a stranger's face on a screen (Schwartz and others, 2003). So for all of you formerly very shy people (your author included) who think you have shed that childhood wariness, you still carry your physiology inside.

Still, if you think you have come a long way in conquering your *incredible* childhood shyness, you are probably correct. Many highly anxious toddlers (and exuberant explorers) get less inhibited as they move into elementary school and the teenage years (Degman, Almas, & Fox, 2010; Pérez-Edgar and others, 2010b).

INTERVENTIONS: Providing the Right Temperament–Socialization Fit

Faced with a temperamentally timid toddler such as Erin or an exuberant explorer like Adam or Thomas, what can parents do?

Socializing a Shy Baby

To see what works best for shy children, researchers compare different toddler childrearing strategies and then look longitudinally at social anxiety during preschool and elementary school.

As you might imagine, the studies suggest emotionally insulating a shy boy or girl tends to backfire. Parents of fearful children need to walk a difficult line. Be caring and responsive (Barnett and others, 2010; Degnan, Almas, & Fox, 2010), but avoid being overprotective and excessively anxious (Gartstein, 2010). ("Erin will get too upset, so day care wouldn't be right" [Edwards, Rapee, & Kennedy, 2010].) Gently exposing a shy toddler to *supportive* new social situations—such as a small, caring family day care—helps teach that child to cope.

power assertion An ineffective socialization strategy that involves yelling, screaming, or hitting out in frustration at a child.

Raising a Rambunctious Toddler

With fearless explorers, it's tempting for adults to adopt a socialization strategy called **power assertion**—yelling, screaming, and hitting a child who is bouncing off the walls (Verhoeven and others, 2010). Resist this impulse. Power assertion is linked to lower levels of conscience development and strongly predicts behavior problems down the road (Brotman and others, 2009; Kochanska & Knaack, 2003). To reduce the risk of later "acting-out problems," parents can't disengage emotionally (Leve and others, 2010) or use harsh discipline (Bakermans-Kranenburg and others, 2008; Gardner and others, 2007). Sensitive, positive parenting is the real route to socializing conscience—getting an exuberant toddler to *want* to be good for mom and dad (Kochanska and others, 2008). As my husband insightfully commented, "Punishment doesn't matter much to Thomas. What he does, he does for your love."

Finally, for readers who worry that this advice is destined to produce a spoiled, "out-of-control" child—consider this longitudinal study: Researchers found that new mothers whose main agenda was to never " spoil" their babies ("Let him know exactly who is boss") had children with the *most* pronounced social anxiety and acting-out problems at age 3! (Barnett and others, 2010)

Table 4.3 offers a summary of this discussion, showing these different toddler temperaments, their infant precursors, their pluses and potential later dangers, and lessons for socializing each kind of child. Now let's look at some general temperament-sensitive lessons for raising every child.

TABLE 4.3: Exuberant and Inhibited Toddler Temperaments: A Summary

Inhibited, Shy Toddler

- **Developmental precursor:** Responds with intense motor arousal to external stimulation in infancy.
- **Plus:** Easily socialized; shows early signs of conscience; not a discipline problem.
- **Minus:** Shy, fearful temperament can persist into adulthood, making social encounters painful.
- **Child-rearing advice:** Don't overprotect the child. Expose the baby to unfamiliar people, but gently and in a low-stress way.

Matt Carr/Getty Images

Exuberant Toddler

- **Developmental precursor:** Emotionally intense but unafraid of new stimuli.
- **Plus:** Joyous; fearless; outgoing; adventurous.
- **Minus:** Less easily socialized; potential problems with conscience development; at higher risk for later "acting-out" behavior problems.
- **Child-rearing advice:** Avoid power assertion and harsh punishment. Redirect the behavior and provide lots of positive reinforcement and love.

Andersen Ross/Getty Images

goodness of fit An ideal parenting strategy that involves arranging children's environments to suit their temperaments, minimizing their vulnerabilities and accentuating their strengths.

An Overall Strategy for Temperamentally Friendly Childrearing

Clearly, the main key to socializing children is to foster a secure, loving attachment. However, another key is to understand each child's specific temperament and work with that baby's unique behavioral style. This principle was demonstrated in the classic study I mentioned earlier, in which developmentalists classified babies as "easy," "slow-to-warm-up," and "difficult."

In following the difficult babies into elementary school, the researchers found that these highly intense infants were more likely to have problems with their teachers and peers (Thomas & Chess, 1977; Thomas, Chess, & Birch, 1968). However, some children did learn to compensate for their biology and to shine. The key, the researchers discovered, lay in a parenting strategy labeled **goodness of fit.** Parents who took steps to arrange their children's lives to minimize their vulnerabilities and accentuate their strengths had infants who later did well.

Understanding that their child was easily overwhelmed by stimuli, these parents kept the environment calm. They did not get hysterical when faced with their child's distress. They may have offered a quiet environment for studying and encouraged their child to do activities that took advantage of his or her talents. They went overboard to provide their child with a placid, nurturing, low-stress milieu.

Interestingly, emerging research, capitalizing on advances in genetics, suggests these parents may have been doing the right thing. Some developmentalists believe that a variation of a gene linked to the production of the neurotransmitter serotonin may predispose us to be either reactive or relatively immune to environmental events (Ellis and others, 2011). Specifically, several studies suggest that children and adults who have two long versions of this serotonin-producing gene cope well in difficult life situations. Their counterparts with two short gene-forms easily break down under stress. However, while having this long "immunity" gene promotes superior adaptation in adversity, it can be a disadvantage when the wider world is exceptionally supportive and stress free (for review, see Belsky & Pleuss, 2009). In fact, in one study, when temperamentally "high-reactive" children were in a nurturing, calm environment, they performed *better* than their more placid, laid-back peers! (Obradović, Burt & Masten , 2010)

I must emphasize that these findings are tentative. It's unlikely that *any* aspect of personality or temperament is programmed by a single gene. But the lesson here is that categorizing a baby (or person) as simply "difficult" or "easy" may not be totally appropriate. With the right person–environment fit, what looks like a liability might sometimes be a gift!

How can we foster goodness of fit, or person–environment fit, at every stage of life? What happens to babies who are shy or exuberant, difficult or easy, as they journey into elementary school and adolescence? How do Ainsworth's attachment styles play out in adult romance? Stay tuned for answers to these questions in the rest of this book.

TYING IT ALL TOGETHER

1. If Amanda has recently turned 2, what predictions are you *not* justified in making about her?
   a. Amanda wants to be independent, yet closely attached.
   b. Amanda is beginning to show signs of self-awareness and can possibly feel shame.
   c. Amanda's parents haven't begun to discipline her yet.
2. To a colleague at work who confides that he's worried about his timid toddler, what words of comfort can you offer?
3. Think back to your own childhood: Did you fit into either the shy or exuberant temperament type? How did your parents cope with your personality style?

Answers to the Tying It All Together questions can be found at the end of this chapter.

SUMMARY

Attachment: The Basic Life Bond

For much of the twentieth century, many psychologists in the United States—because they were behaviorists—minimized the mother–child bond. European psychoanalysts such as John Bowlby were finding, however, that **attachment** was a basic human need. Harlow's studies with monkeys convinced U.S. developmentalists of the importance of attachment, and Bowlby transformed developmental science by arguing that the need for a loving primary attachment figure is biologically built in, and satisfying that need is crucial to development. Although threats to survival at any age evoke **proximity-seeking behavior**—especially during **toddlerhood**—being physically apart from an attachment figure elicits distress.

According to Bowlby, life begins with a three-month-long **preattachment phase,** which is characterized by the first **social smile.** After an intermediate phase called **attachment in the making,** at about 7 months of age, the landmark phase of **clear-cut attachment** begins, signaled by **separation anxiety** and **stranger anxiety.** During this period spanning toddlerhood, children need their caregiver to be physically close, and they rely on **social referencing** to monitor their behavior. After age 3, children can tolerate separations, as they develop an internal **working model** of their caregiver—which they carry into life.

To explore individual differences in attachment, Mary Ainsworth devised the **Strange Situation.** Using this test, involving planned separations, and especially reunions, developmentalists label 1-year-olds as **securely** or **insecurely attached.** Securely attached 1-year-olds use their primary attachment figure as a secure base for exploration and are delighted when she returns. **Avoidant** infants seem indifferent. **Anxious-ambivalent** children are inconsolable and sometimes angry when their caregiver arrives. Children with a **disorganized attachment** react in an erratic way and often show fear when their parent reenters the room.

Caregiver–child interactions are characterized by a beautiful **synchrony,** or attachment dance. Although the caregiver's responsiveness to the baby is a major determinant of attachment security at age 1, infant attachment is also affected by the **temperament** of the child and depends on the quality of a caregiver's other relationships, too.

Cross-cultural studies support the idea that attachment to a primary caregiver is universal, with similar percentages of babies in various countries classified as securely attached. Although infants have one preferred attachment figure, they can become attached to other caregivers, too.

As Bowlby predicted in his working-model concept, securely attached babies have superior social and emotional skills. Infants with insecure attachments (especially disorganized attachments) are at risk for later problems. However, the good-news/bad-news finding is that, when the caregiving environment changes, attachment security can change for the better or worse. One "experiment" with foster-care children who began their lives in orphanages (in Romania) showed these infants could develop secure attachments, provided they left the institution before age 2. This research is shedding light on the effects of experiencing the most grossly abnormal caregiving environment, namely having no attachment figure during the first years of life.

Settings for Development

Early childhood poverty— widespread in the United States—can have long-lasting effects on health, emotional development, and, particularly, school success. Although **Head Start** and **Early Head Start,** as well as other high-quality **preschool** experiences, make a difference for disadvantaged children, they can't totally erase the impact of attending inadequate schools. Poverty-level parents can be excellent parents, and the quality of children's home life matters most.

Going back to work in a baby's first year of life is common, but due to day care's expense and anxieties about leaving their baby with strangers, parents in the United States ideally prefer to keep infant care in the family. Paid child-care options include nannies (for affluent parents), **family day care** (where a person takes a small number of children in her home), and larger **day-care centers.**

The NICHD Study of Early Child Care showed that the best predictor of being securely attached at age 1 is being a sensitive parent, not the number of hours a child spends in day care. Another piece of good news from this definitive U.S. child-care study is that attending preschool has enduring cognitive benefits. Unfortunately, however, children who spend many hours in day-care centers (versus family care) are at a slightly higher risk of having acting-out behaviors that continue into the teens.

Having loving, consistent care in a setting where caregivers can relate in a one-to-one way are the core components of quality "non family" care. Because day-care workers are so poorly paid in the United States, staff turnover is a serious problem. This issue, plus its large size, may explain why day-care centers can be problematic. Rather than avoiding day-care centers, parents should search for loving, consistent, one-to-one care. Although anxious and active babies are most vulnerable to poor-quality care, shy children may blossom in a small high-quality setting. No matter how many hours a child spends in day care, parents' care giving sensitivity matters most.

Toddlerhood: Age of Autonomy *and* Shame and Doubt

Erikson's **autonomy** captures the essence of toddlerhood, the landmark age when we shed babyhood, become able to observe the self, and enter the human world. **Self-conscious emotions** such as pride and shame emerge and are crucial to **socialization,** which begins in earnest at around age 2. Difficulties focusing and obeying are normal during toddlerhood. Temperamentally fearful children show earlier signs of "conscience," following adult prohibitions, when not being watched. Exuberant, active toddlers are especially hard to socialize.

As young babies, shy toddlers react with intense motor activity to stimuli. They are more inhibited in elementary school and adolescence and show neurological signs of social wariness as young adults. Still (with sensitive parenting), many shy toddlers and fearless explorers lose these extreme tendencies as they grow older.

To help an inhibited baby, be empathic, but don't overprotect the child. Socialize a fearless explorer by avoiding **power assertion**—yelling and screaming—and providing lots of love. While fostering secure attachments is essential in raising *all* children, another key is to promote **goodness of fit**—tailoring one's parenting to a child's temperamental needs. Interestingly, although these findings are tentative, there may be a gene form that makes us either more or less reactive to the quality of the environment. So temperamentally "reactive children," while prone to break down in stressful situations, may flower when their environment is exceptionally caring and calm.

KEY TERMS

attachment, p. 111
toddlerhood, p. 111
primary attachment figure, p. 113
proximity-seeking behavior, p. 113
preattachment phase, p. 113
social smile, p. 113
attachment in the making, p. 114
clear-cut attachment, p. 114
separation anxiety, p. 114
stranger anxiety, p. 114
social referencing, p. 114
working model, p. 114
Strange Situation, p. 115
secure attachment, p. 115
insecure attachment, p. 115
avoidant attachment, p. 115
anxious-ambivalent attachment, p. 115
disorganized attachment, p. 115
synchrony, p. 116
temperament, p. 117
Head Start, p. 124
Early Head Start, p. 124
preschool, p. 125
family day care, p. 125
day-care center, p. 125
autonomy, p. 129
self-conscious emotions, p. 130
socialization, p. 130
power assertion, p. 133
goodness of fit, p. 134

ANSWERS TO TYING IT ALL TOGETHER QUIZZES

Attachment: The Basic Life Bond

1. Your responses will differ, but any example you give, such as "I called Mom when that terrible thing happened at work," should show that in a stressful situation your immediate impulse was to contact your attachment figure.
2. Muriel = preattachment; Janine = attachment in the making; Ted = clear-cut attachment.
3. (1) b; (2) c; (3) d; (4) a
4. The child has an avoidant attachment.
5. Manuel should say: Infants around the world get attached to a primary caregiver at roughly the same age.
6. Caution Jasmine that her child may show problems with attention and may have special problems developing a secure attachment (especially if Jasmine is adopting a boy).

Settings for Development

1. a & b (there are pre-K programs targeted to low-income preschoolers besides Head Start).
2. The good news is that the quality of Nancy's parenting is the main force in determining her child's attachment (and emotional health). The bad news is that many day-care centers leave a good deal to be desired and long hours spent in these centers is associated with a slightly higher risk of having "acting-out issues" in school.
3. Tell the senate committee that 1) high-quality preschools can have a lasting effect on cognitive development. But 2) we have an imperative need to raise the quality of day care in the United States. Pass laws mandating (not simply recommending) small child-to-caregiver ratios; pay day-care workers decently; give this job the status it deserves! Also (when the economy recovers), consider providing government-funded toddler and infant child care and mandating paid family leave, so working parents can afford to stay home after a child's birth.

Toddlerhood: Age of Autonomy *and* Shame and Doubt

1. c. Parents typically start serious discipline around age 2.
2. You might tell him that most children grow out of their shyness, even if they do not completely shed this temperamental tendency. But be sure to stress the advantages of being shy: His baby will be easier to socialize, not likely to be a behavior problem, and may have a stronger conscience, too.
3. These answers will be totally your own.

Childhood

In this three-chapter book part covering childhood, the first two chapters trace children's unfolding abilities. In the final chapter, I'll explore the two settings within which children develop: home and school.

The first part of Chapter 5—**Physical and Cognitive Development** examines children's expanding motor skills and focuses on health issues such as obesity. Then comes the heart of this chapter: an exploration of children's minds. If you have ever wondered about the strange ways preschoolers think, want a basic framework for teaching, or would like to understand how memory and reasoning develop, this section is for you. This chapter also charts developing language and two types of social knowledge that evolve during childhood.

In Chapter 6—**Socioemotional Development** my focus shifts to personality and relationships. Here, I'll be tracing growing self-awareness, aggression, caring acts, play, friendships, and popularity from preschool through elementary school. A special focus of this chapter is on boys and girls who are having trouble relating to their peers and adults.

The first half of Chapter 7—**Settings for Development: Home and School** tackles children's family lives. Is there an ideal way of parenting? Why do some children thrive in spite of devastatingly dysfunctional early lives? What is the impact of spanking, child abuse, and divorce on the child? In the second section on school, you will learn all about intelligence tests, what makes schools successful, and how teachers can make every child eager to learn.

PART III

Chapter 5

CHAPTER OUTLINE

Physical and Cognitive Development

As the 3-year-olds drift in to Learning Preschool, Ms. Angela fills me in:

"We do free play, then structured games. Then we go outside. At 11 we have snack. We focus on the skills the kids need for school and life: Sit still; follow directions; listen; share. During free play, they need to remember three rules: Four kids to an activity center; clean up before you leave; don't take the toys from one center when you go to another place."

In the kitchen corner, Kanesha is pretending to scrub pots. "What is your name?" "You know!" says Kanesha, looking at me as if I'm totally dumb. "This is a picnic," Kanesha continues, giving me a plate: "Let's have psghetti and Nadia makeacake." We are having a wonderful time talking as she loads me up with plastic food. The problem is that we aren't communicating. Who is Nadia, that great cook? Then some girls run in with Barbies from the dress-up corner: "Our babies need some food!" We're happily feeding our toys when Ms. Angela pipes up: "No moving stuff from the play centers! Don't you remember our four kids to a center rule?" . . .

I move to the crafts table, where Moriah, a dreamy frail girl, and Manuel are surrounded by paper: "Hey!" Moriah yells, after Manuel cuts his paper into pieces, "Manuel has more than me!" Manuel tenderly gives Moriah his bunny, and gives me a heart-melting, welcoming smile: "I'm [holds up three fingers]." (Moriah and Manuel are obviously interested in what I'm doing.) "I'm taking notes for a book." "Taking nose," both children giggle and hold their noses. Moriah is making beautiful circles with paste. Manuel tries to copy her but can only make random lines. These children are so different in their physical abilities, even though they are the same age. But, oh, no, here come the kids from the kitchen corner with plastic vegetables, forgetting the "don't move the toys" and "four children to a center" rules! Luckily, it's time for structured games.

Ms. Angela shows the class cards picturing a sun, an umbrella with raindrops, and clouds, and asks: "What is the weather today?" Manuel proudly picks the umbrella. "How many people think Manuel is right?" Everyone raises a hand. "Who feels it's sunny?" Everyone yells: "Me!" "Who thinks it's cloudy?" Everyone agrees. Then Ms. Angela puts on a tape: "Dance fast, fast . . . slower slower . . . Now speed up!" The kids frantically dance around, and it's time to go outside. Soon the wind starts gusting (it really is about to rain), and everyone gets excited: "Let's catch the wind. . . . Oh, he ran away again!" And now (whew!) it's 11:00 and time for snack.

These 3-year-olds have amazing skills. They can cut, climb, follow directions, tell me about their lives, and (occasionally) remember the teacher's rules. But it will take at least another decade before they can reason like adults. What were the children thinking during the pretend feedings, and why was Kanesha sure I *had* to know her name? Why did Moriah assume Manuel had more paper when he cut his sheet into pieces, and why did *everyone* have so much trouble remembering the center's rules? In this chapter you'll find answers to these questions as we explore physical and cognitive development during **early childhood** (age 3 through kindergarten) and **middle childhood** (elementary school).

But before tackling these topics, let's pause to set the context by briefly exploring *why* our species needs so much time to mentally grow up.

early childhood The first phase of childhood, lasting from age 3 through kindergarten, or about age 5.

middle childhood The second phase of childhood, covering the elementary school years, from about age 6 to 11.

frontal lobes The area at the uppermost front of the brain, responsible for reasoning and planning our actions.

Setting the Context

The monkeys in this photo reached adulthood at roughly age seven or eight (Poirier & Smith, 1974). Why will it take human preschoolers twice as long to leave the childhood phase of life?

Special Mindreading Skills

The reason is that we humans have a capacity that no other animal possesses—the remarkable ability to build on each generation's intellectual advances. Three-year-olds born in biblical times had the same biology as today's preschoolers, but these twenty-first-century children will grow up using iPads and surfing online. They might even take vacations on the moon or Mars.

Markus Botzek/Zefa/Corbis

Imagine that these chimps could *really* share what insights were going on in each other's minds. Wouldn't they be inventing the Internet and traveling into outer space?

What talent allowed humanity to mentally take off? Evolutionary theorists believe at the core of our achievements is an effortless capacity to put ourselves in other people's heads and decode their intentions and thoughts. Scientists find that monkeys do have glimmers of this mindreading ability, as they demonstrate the rudimentary *joint attention* skills I described in Chapter 3 (see Buttlemann, Call, & Tomasello, 2009); but because they don't have our infinitely elastic language capacities (also described in that chapter), our closest mammal cousins never progressed to the point where they could draw on *each other's* insights to transform the wider world. ("Oh, yes, now I understand what you were trying to do. Let's work together to improve on that.") Capitalizing on these insights, in turn, demands a large, slow-growing brain.

Slow-Growing Frontal Lobes

Actually, our huge *cerebral cortex* takes more than two full decades to mature. The *myelin sheath*—the fatty neural cover—continues to grow into our twenties. *Synaptogenesis* (the process of making billions of connections between neurons) is on an extended blossoming and pruning timetable, too, especially in the region of the brain responsible for reasoning and thinking through our actions—the **frontal lobes.**

Figure 5.1, which compares the size of our cortex to that of other species, shows the huge frontal lobes positioned at the top of the brain. During early childhood,

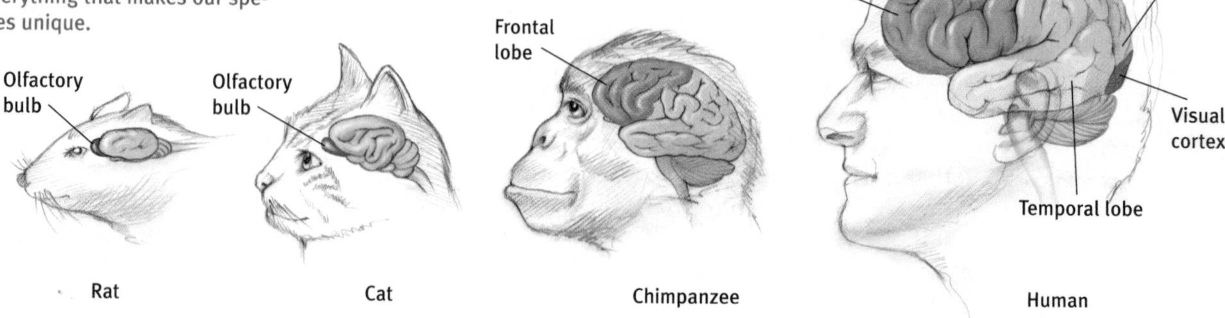

FIGURE 5.1: The human cortex and that of some other species: Notice the size of our cortex in comparison to other species. Also notice the dramatic increase in the size of our frontal lobes. It is our mammoth cortex and especially our huge frontal lobes that are responsible for everything that makes our species unique.

the neurons in the visual and motor cortices are in their pruning phase, which explains why vision develops rapidly and why we master basic physical milestones, such as walking, at a relatively young age. However, the frontal lobes are only in their early phase of synaptogenesis when we start toddling around. Pruning in this part of the brain will not start until about age 9.

Their slow frontal-lobe timetable helps account for why preschoolers have so much trouble controlling their behavior. It explains why our ability to plan, think through, and inhibit our actions improves throughout childhood and adolescence. It even accounts for the high expectations we have of children when the frontal lobes begin their pruning in late elementary school. We expect fourth and fifth graders to understand long division and take responsibility for completing their homework. After all, they can sometimes beat us at baseball and outscore us at the bowling alley, too.

In addition to allowing us to have the inner control to study (rather than watching TV) and the cognitive abilities to grasp long division, the frontal lobes are vital to mastering physical abilities, from tennis, to tight-rope walking, to inhibiting our immediate urges and getting to the toilet at about age 3.

So, understanding that *many* regions of the brain work in concert to program every action and thought, let's use our slow frontal-lobe timetable as a model to track how children's exciting physical and cognitive abilities unfold.

TYING IT ALL TOGETHER

1. Scientists often point to language as the core quality that differentiates us from other animals. See if you can list some other capacities that make our species unique.
2. When Steven played hide-and-seek with his 4-year-old nephew, he realized that while Ethan could run very well, the child was having a lot of trouble not betraying his hiding place and understanding the rules of the game. The reason is that Ethan's _________ cortex is on an earlier developmental timetable than his _________ lobes.
3. If you learn that a colleague was in an accident and has front-lobe damage, what kinds of impairments might you expect?

Answers to the Tying It All Together questions can be found at the end of this chapter.

Bob Daemmrich/The Image Works

Syracuse Newspapers/Michelle Gabel/The Image Works

What tips us off about the ages of the children in these two photographs relates to the *cephalocaudal principle* of development. We know that the children in the top photo are preschoolers because they have squat shapes and relatively large heads, while the longer bodies in the bottom photo are typical of the middle childhood years.

Physical Development

Look at children of different ages and you will immediately see the *cephalocaudal principle* of physical growth discussed in Chapters 2 and 3. Three-year-olds have large heads and squat, rounded bodies. As children get older, their limbs get longer and their bodies thin out. Although from age 2 to 12 children double their height and weight, after infancy growth slows down considerably (National Health and Nutrition Examination Survey, 2004). Because they grow at similar rates, boys and girls are roughly the same size until they reach the preadolescent years.

Now visit a playground or take out samples of your childhood artwork to see the *mass-to-specific* principle—the steady progression from clumsy to sure, swift movements year by year. Three-year-olds have trouble making circles; third graders can draw detailed bodies and faces. At age 4, children catch a ball with both hands; by fourth grade, they may be able to hit home runs. You can see the dramatic changes from mass to specific in a few skills in Table 5.1.

gross motor skills Physical abilities that involve large muscle movements, such as running and jumping.

fine motor skills Physical abilities that involve small, coordinated movements, such as drawing and writing one's name.

***TABLE 5.1:* Selected Motor Skill Milestones: Progression from Age 2 to Age 6**

At age 2	At age 4
Picks up small objects with thumb and forefinger, feeds self with spoon	Cuts paper, approximates circle
Walks unassisted, usually by 12 months	Walks down stairs, alternating feet
Rolls a ball or flings it awkwardly	Catches and controls a large bounced ball across the body
At age 5	**At age 6**
Prints name	Copies two short words
Walks without holding on to railing	Hops on each foot for 1 meter but still holds railing
Tosses ball overhand with bent elbows	Catches and controls a 10-inch ball in both hands with arms in front of body

Two Types of Motor Talents

Developmentalists divide physical skills into two categories. **Gross motor skills** refer to large muscle movements, such as running, climbing, and hopping. **Fine motor skills** involve small, coordinated movements, such as drawing faces and writing one's name.

Bob Daemmrich/Photo Edit, Inc.

Sean Sprague/The Image Works

While the boys in the top photograph may have an advantage in the gross motor skills needed to win a potato sack race, the girl in the lower photo might surpass many of the boys in the fine motor talents involved in forming handwritten words.

The stereotype that boys are better at gross motor abilities and girls at fine motor tasks is true—although often the differences are small. The largest sex difference in sports-related abilities occurs in throwing speed. During preschool and middle childhood, boys can typically hurl a ball much faster and farther than can girls (Geary, 1998; Thomas & French, 1985). Does this mean that girls can't compete with boys on a Little League team? Not necessarily. The boys probably will be faster pitchers and more powerful hitters. But the female talent at connecting with the ball, which involves fine motor coordination, may even things out.

Apart from their gender, what explains the variations between individual children in hurling balls or drawing faces? In our society, the main cause lies in genetics; by that I mean our differing biologically based timetables that program unfolding motor skills.

International comparisons suggest that the caregiving environment can play a heavy role. Mothers in some Middle Eastern countries treat infants as fragile and even dress their sons and daughters during the elementary school years, which may account for why these children are on a slower gross-motor skill timetable than in the West. Conversely, as a baby born in Hong Kong, your culture's intense fine-motor training would allow you to manage chopsticks as a toddler, write complex Chinese characters, and often read by age 4 (Venetsanou & Kambas, 2010).

This last example suggests that to improve "school readiness," Westerners might train preschoolers in fine motor skills. The problem, however, is that expecting 4-year-olds to write "just like adults," or master sports like baseball, is destined to produce frustration for parents and children alike. As young children don't have the physical or frontal-lobe capacities to write well or play organized games, the focus during preschool should be on providing activities—such as cutting paper or scaling the monkey bars—appropriate to young children's unfolding motor skills (Zaichkowsky & Larson, 1995). In early childhood, we need to walk a fine line: Allow preschoolers to exercise their physical talents, but don't push; and provide the right person–environment fit.

Now that we know what environments foster optimal physical development, let's look at what can go wrong.

body mass index (BMI) The ratio of weight to height; the main indicator of overweight or underweight.

childhood obesity A body mass index at or above the 95th percentile compared to the U.S. norms established for children in the 1970s.

Threats to Growth and Motor Skills

I discussed the main threat to growth and motor skills in Chapter 3: lack of food. In addition to causing stunting, undernutrition impairs gross and fine motor skills because it compromises the development of the bones, muscles, and brain. Most important, when children are hungry, they are too tired to move and so don't get the experience crucial to developing their physical skills.

During the 1980s, researchers observed how undernourished children in rural Nepal maximized their growth by cutting down on play (Anderson & Mitchell, 1984). Play does more than exercise our bodies. It can help prime neural development and is crucial in promoting *social cognition*, helping children learn how to get along with their peers. So, the lethargy that malnutrition produces is as detrimental to children's relationships as it is to their bodies and brains. Notice how, after skipping just one meal, you become listless, unwilling to talk, less interested in reaching out to people in a loving way.

Keeping in mind that undernutrition *remains* the top-ranking twenty-first-century global physical threat, let's now explore the condition that is ringing alarm bells in the developed world: childhood obesity.

Childhood Obesity

Have you ever wondered about the source of the numbers in the charts showing the ideal weights for people of different heights? These statistics come from a regular U.S. national poll called the National Health and Nutrition Examination Study (NHANES). Since the 1960s, the federal government has literally been measuring the size of Americans by charting caloric intakes, heights, and weights. The familiar statistic researchers use to monitor overweight is **body mass index (BMI)**—the ratio of a person's weight to height. If the BMI is at or over the 85 percentile for the norms in the first poll, a child is defined as "overweight." At the 95th percentile or above, the label is "obese."

Exploring the Epidemic's Size

Childhood obesity ballooned about 30 years ago. During the late 1980s, the NHANES researchers were astonished to find that the fraction of obese elementary school children had doubled over a decade (see Figure 5.2). By 2010, roughly two out of every five North American children was either overweight or obese—more than four times the number in the original poll (Gorden-Larson, The, & Adair, 2010). To bring this increase home, if you entered a second-grade classroom in the early 1970s, two children might stand out as overweight. *Eight or nine* would fit that category today.

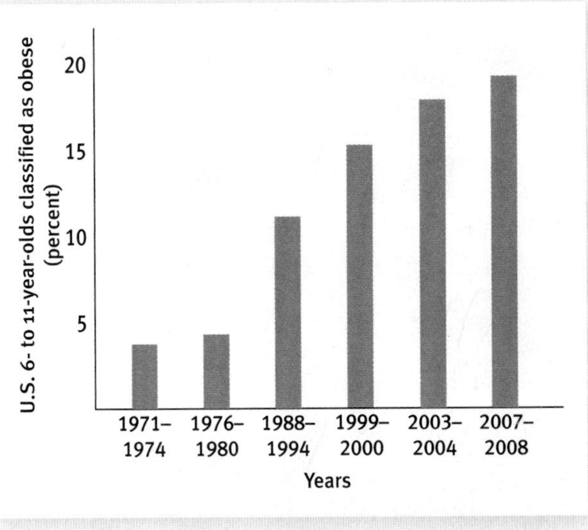

FIGURE 5.2: **Percentage of U.S. children aged 6–11 classified as obese, selected years:** This chart shows that the prevalence of child obesity almost tripled during the 1980s and has continued to rise, though, notice, at increasingly slower rates.

Source: Adapted from National Center for Health Statistics, CDC, Overweight prevalence among children and adults, through 2007–2008 (retrieved 10/14/11).

This late twentieth-century scourge has spread throughout the developed world. From Finland to France and Great Britain to Greece, governments have targeted child obesity as a serious public health threat (Stamatakis and others, 2010; Swinburn & de Silva-Sanigorski, 2010; Tambalis and others, 2010).

The shape of the threat, however, differs by nation. Obesity rates are lower in Scandinavia than in Mediterranean countries and the United States (Faeh & Bopp, 2010; Juliusson and others, 2010). In the developing world, childhood obesity is most prevalent in cities and among affluent boys and girls (Berkowitz & Stunkard, 2002). In the United States, obesity rates are higher in rural areas (Davis and others, 2011) and *far* more common among the poor. There is also an ethnic dimension to the epidemic. Obesity rates are highest among Latino and African American boys and girls (Gordon-Larson, The, & Adair, 2010).

The good news, as Figure 5.2 suggests, is that developed-world obesity may be starting to level off (Tambalis and others, 2010). The bad news is that we have stabilized at a high rate. Why, despite such vigorous attention, is obesity resistant to change?

Exploring the Epidemic's Causes

The reason lies in a perfect storm of societal "obesogenic" forces (Finegood, Merth, & Rutter, 2010; Swinburn & deSilva-Sanigorski, 2010): stressed out working parents who don't have time to prepare nutritious, sit-down meals (Morrissey, Dunifon, & Kalil, 2011); expanding restaurant portion sizes; and easy access to low-cost calorie-dense foods—such as chips and sugar-laced sodas—exquisitely tailored to tempt the palates of children (and adults) (Cornwell & McAlister, 2011). These tasty, low-priced items are especially alluring in an economy where people are watching every dime.

Image Sources/Getty Images

Since he is likely to be teased by the other kids for being "fat and clumsy" if he participates in this rope challenge, it makes sense that this boy would sit on the sidelines during gym, and so set himself up for gaining more weight.

Everyone agrees that lack of exercise plays an important role. With the Internet and TV, playing outside—that typical childhood vehicle for burning up calories—has sharply declined. Obese children are less physically active than their normal-weight peers (DuBose and others, 2008; Fusseneger, Pietrobelli, & Widhalm, 2008; Soric & Misigoj-Durakovic, 2010). Time spent snacking and watching television in itself predicts being overweight (Brown and others, 2011). There may be a poisonous *bidirectional* effect here. When children feel bad about their "big clumsy bodies" and are harassed by classmates ("Let's not choose fatty for the team"), they withdraw from physical activity, watch more TV, and snack more.

That overconsumption colliding with a sedentary lifestyle is the recipe for an overweight society is no surprise. The current epidemic, however, may have hidden prebirth roots. Recall from Chapter 2 that low birth weight primes babies to overeat and store fat. Scientists now speculate that "large" fetuses, those born to overweight women—being exposed to high levels of fat-associated hormones in the womb—also enter life at higher risk (Misra & Trudeau, 2011; Odaka and others, 2010). Given that this ailment of our age has entered its second generation, could obesity now have a self-perpetuating life of its own?

© Dennis Van Tine/Retna Ltd./Corbis

Many Republicans hoped the articulate governor of New Jersey could win his party's primaries and beat Obama in the election of 2012. But photos like this blocked Governor Christie at the starting gate, as he fell victim to the intense media weight bullying that—unlike with religion or race—is still "perfectly fine" in our modern cultural milieu.

Interestingly, the predisposition to pack on pounds does emerge soon after birth. There are two rapid-growth phases when children destined to be obese diverge from their peers—during infancy (from about 5 months to age 1 1/2) and around age 5 to 6 (Brune and others, 2010). So, by the brink of school, we can pretty much tell which child is apt to battle weight issues for life.

Exploring the Epidemic's Consequences

This lifelong battle takes a social toll. From being less likely to get hired (weight discrimination is one of the few U.S prejudices not against the law) (Puhl & Heuer, 2010) or finish college (Fowler-Brown and others, 2010) to having problems getting elected to public office (Miller & Lundgren, 2010), obesity can present serious barriers to living a successful life.

These barriers begin soon after babyhood (Puhl & Latner, 2007). In a classic study, elementary schoolers were shown pictures of an overweight child, a child in a wheelchair, another with facial disfigurements, and several others with disabilities. When asked, "Whom would you choose as a friend?" the children ranked the obese boy or girl last. By age 3, children describe chubby boys and girls as "mean" and "sloppy." So it's no wonder that, in the West, overweight children are at risk of suffering from depression and even have an elevated risk of suicide in their teens (Pitrou and others, 2010; Sánchez-Villegas and others, 2010; van Wijnen and others, 2010).

Attitudes are less harsh in other cultures. In Bangladesh, obesity actually promotes high self-worth (Asghar and others, 2010). There are differences by ethnicity, with African Americans more weight tolerant than their Caucasian counterparts (more about this in Chapter 8). And finally, of course, there are variations from family to family. Parents who care vitally about physical beauty hold especially negative stereotypes about overweight people, and are prone to nag their children about weight (Puhl & Latner, 2007).

Because nagging can backfire, causing family conflict and further impairing a child's sense of self-worth, many parents go in the opposite direction. They minimize weight issues in their child (Akerman, Williams, & Meunier, 2007; Luttikhuis, Stolk, & Sauer, 2010; Vuorela, Saha, & Salo, 2010). "My daughter may be chubby, but she's perfectly fine." Ironically, then, in one study, the very people who could most benefit from an obesity prevention program—mothers with overweight preschoolers—were *least* likely to enroll (Taveras and others, 2011).

Let's understand where these parents may be coming from. Society routinely blames mothers for children's obesity issues (Maher, Fraser, & Wright, 2010; Spivack and others, 2010). The real culprit lies in our obesogenic society itself. Family interventions, even when effective (see Bruss and others, 2010; Epstein & Wrotniak, 2010; Evans and others, 2010; Hesketh & Campbell, 2010; McAuley and others, 2010; Moens, Braet, & Van Winkel, 2010) often don't work in the long term. As a loving parent, wouldn't you be tempted to decide: "Why torture my daughter and ruin our caring relationship by monitoring her every pound?"

Society is making similar choices. Among contemporary U.S. young adults, weight norms have shifted upwards. Fewer people ages 17 to 35 now label themselves overweight at similar BMIs as in the past (Burke, Heiland, & Nadler, 2010). Do you think this new upwardly rescaled body–environment fit is a positive or negative thing?

Table 5.2 lists three *low-key* child weight-control interventions—ones that don't demand nagging—for caregivers to consider, as well as summarizes this section's messages for society as whole. Now, let's move from our developing bodies to our developing minds.

TABLE 5.2: Three Low-Stress, Research-based Obesity-Control Techniques for Parents and Three Research Messages for Society

Tips for parents:

- **For babies:** As the overweight pathway has its onset during infancy (see text), limit overconsumption at the youngest age. **Relevant study:** When researchers trained parents to minimize feeding for non-hunger related fussiness and introduce solid foods later and begin with vegetables, children gained less weight by age 1 (Paul and others, 2011).
- **For elementary schoolers:** Rather than restricting intake, load plates with low-calorie foods. **Relevant study:** When parents were told to double the portion size of fruits and vegitables on children's plates, overweight boys and girls ate far less of a high-calorie main dish (pasta).
- **For teenagers:** Have the child exercise for a half hour early each day. **Relevant study:** After 30 minutes of high-intensity morning exercise, obese teens ate significantly less during the next 24 hours, without feeling deprived (Thivel and others, 2011).

Tips for society:

- Heavily target obesity-prevention efforts to women of childbearing age to break this intergenerational cycle that may begin in the womb.
- Don't discriminate against overweight children (and adults).
- Hold off from blaming parents for their children's obesity issues!

Sources: Based on Paul and others, 2011; Thivel and others, 2010; and the chapter sources.

TYING IT ALL TOGETHER

1. You are astonished at the physical changes in your 7-year-old niece, Brittany, since you last saw her several years ago. Which example refers to the cephalocaudal principle and which to the mass-to-specific principle? (a) Brittany could barely draw a circle; now she can draw a detailed face; (b) Brittany's body has become much longer and skinnier.
2. Jessica has terrific gross motor skills but trouble with fine motor skills. Select the two sports from this list that Jessica would be most likely to excel at: long-distance running, tennis, water ballet, the high jump, bowling.
3. In a sentence—based on this section—explain why the public health effort to combat obesity has failed.
4. How do you feel about contemporary weight standards shifting upwards? Discuss the pros and cons of this development.

Answers to the Tying It All Together questions can be found at the end of this chapter.

Cognitive Development

In this section, we turn to the heart of this chapter: cognition. How do children develop intellectually as they travel from age 3 into elementary school? In our search for answers, we explore three perspectives on mental growth. Let's begin with the ideas of the master theorist Jean Piaget.

Piaget's Preoperational and Concrete Operational Stages

Recall from Chapter 1 that Piaget believed that through assimilation (fitting new information into their existing cognitive structures) and accommodation (changing those cognitive slots to fit input from the world), children undergo qualitatively different stages of cognitive growth. In Chapter 3, I discussed Piaget's sensorimotor stage. Now, it's time to tackle the next two stages, illuminated in Table 5.3: the preoperational and concrete operational stages.

As their names imply, we need to discuss these two stages together. **Preoperational thinking** is defined by what children are missing—the ability to step back from

preoperational thinking In Piaget's theory, the type of cognition characteristic of children aged 2 to 7, marked by an inability to step back from one's immediate perceptions and think conceptually.

TABLE 5.3: Piaget's Stages: Focus on Childhood

Age	Name of Stage	Description
0–2	Sensorimotor	The baby manipulates objects to pin down the basics of physical reality. This stage ends with the development of language.
2–7	Preoperations	Children's perceptions are captured by their immediate appearances. "What they see is what is real." They believe, among other things, that inanimate objects are really alive and that if the appearance of a quantity of liquid changes (for example, if it is poured from a short, wide glass into a tall, thin one), the amount becomes different.
8–12	Concrete operations	Children have a realistic understanding of the world. Their thinking is really on the same wavelength as adults'. While they can reason conceptually about concrete objects, however, they cannot think abstractly in a scientific way.
12+	Formal operations	Reasoning is at its pinnacle: hypothetical, scientific, flexible, fully adult. Our full cognitive human potential has been reached.

their immediate perceptions. **Concrete operational thinking** is defined by what children possess: the ability to reason about the world in a more logical, adult-like way.

When children leave infancy and enter the stage of preoperational thought, they have made tremendous mental strides. Still, they often seem on a different planet from adults in the way they reason about the world. The problem is that preoperational children take things at face value. They are unable to look beyond the way objects immediately appear. By about age 7 or 8, children can mentally transcend what first hits their eye. They have entered the concrete operational stage.

The Preoperational Stage: Taking the World at Face Value

You saw vivid examples of these "from another planet" ways of thinking in the preschoolers in my chapter-opening vignette. Now, let's enter the minds of young children and explore how they reason about physical substances and the social world.

STRANGE IDEAS ABOUT SUBSTANCES. The fact that preoperational children are locked into immediate appearances is illustrated by Piaget's (1965) famous **conservation tasks.** In Piaget's terminology, *conservation* refers to our knowledge that the amount of a given substance remains identical despite changes in its shape or form.

In the conservation of mass task, for instance, an adult gives a child a round ball of clay and asks that boy or girl to make another ball "just as big and heavy." Then she reshapes the ball so it looks like a pancake and asks, "Is there still the same amount now?" In the conservation of liquid task, the procedure is similar: Present a child with two identical glasses with equal amounts of liquid. Make sure he tells you, "Yes, they have the same amount of water or juice." Then, pour the liquid into a tall, thin glass while the child watches and ask, "Is there more or less juice now, or is there the same amount?"

Typically, when children under age 7 are asked this final question, they give a peculiar answer: "Now there is more clay" or "The tall glass has more juice." "Why?" "Because now the pancake is bigger" or "The juice is taller." Then, when the clay is remolded into a ball or the liquid poured into the original glass, they report: "Now it's the same again." The logical conflict in their statements doesn't bother them at all. In Figure 5.3 on page 150, I have illustrated these procedures as well as additional Piagetian conservation tasks to perform with children you know.

Why can't young children conserve? For two reasons, Piaget believes. First, children don't grasp a concept called **reversibility.** This is the idea that an operation (or procedure) can be repeated in the opposite direction. Adults accept the fact that we can change various substances, such as our hairstyle, or the color of our room, and reverse them to their original state. Young children lack this fundamental *schema*, or cognitive structure, for interpreting the world.

A second issue lies in a perceptual style that Piaget calls **centering.** Young children interpret things according to what first hits their eye, rather than taking in the entire visual array. In the conservation of liquid task, they get captivated by the height of the liquid. They don't notice that the width of the original container makes up for the height of the current one. When children reach concrete operations, they **decenter.** They can step back from the immediate appearance of a substance and scan the whole picture—understanding that an increase in one dimension makes up for a loss in the other one.

Centering—the tendency to fix on what is visually most striking—impairs **class inclusion.** This is the knowledge that a general category can encompass subordinate elements. Spread 20 Skittles and a few Gummi Bears on a plate and ask a 3-year-old, "Would you rather have the Skittles or the candy?" and she is almost certain to say, "The Skittles," even when you have determined beforehand that both types of candy have equal appeal. She gets mesmerized by the number of Skittles and does not notice that "candy" is the label for both.

Centering interferes with **seriation**—the child's capacity to put objects in order according to some principle, such as size. Place sticks of different lengths in various

concrete operational thinking In Piaget's framework, the type of cognition characteristic of children aged 8 to 11, marked by the ability to reason about the world in a more logical, adult way.

conservation tasks Piagetian tasks that involve changing the shape of a substance to see whether children can go beyond the way that substance visually appears to understand that the amount is still the same.

reversibility In Piaget's conservation tasks, the concrete operational child's knowledge that a specific change in the way a given substance looks can be reversed.

centering In Piaget's conservation tasks, the preoperational child's tendency to fix on the most visually striking feature of a substance and not take other dimensions into account.

decentering In Piaget's conservation tasks, the concrete operational child's ability to look at several dimensions of an object or substance.

class inclusion The understanding that a general category can encompass several subordinate elements.

seriation The ability to put objects in order according to some principle, such as size.

Type of conservation	Initial step and question	Transformation and next question	Preoperational child's answer
Number	Two equal rows of pennies.  "Are these two rows the same?" (Yes.)	Increase spacing of pennies in one line.  "Now is the amount of money the same?"	 "No, the longer row has more."
Mass	Two equal balls of clay. 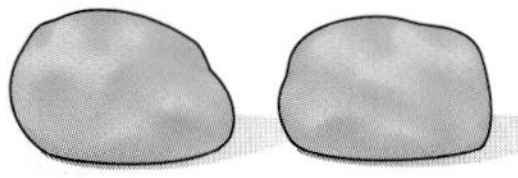 "Do these two balls have the same amount of clay?" (Yes.)	Squeeze one ball into a long pancake shape. 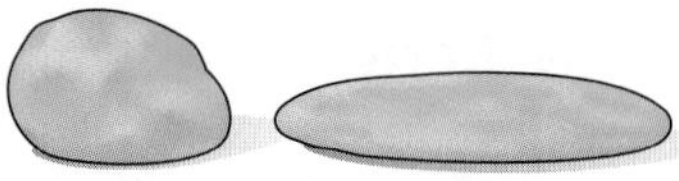 "Now is the amount of clay the same?"	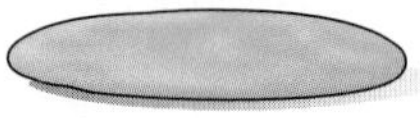 "No, the long, thin one has more clay."
Volume or liquid	Two glasses of the same size with liquid.  "Do these glasses have the same amount of juice?" (Yes.)	Pour one into a taller, narrower glass.  "Now do these glasses have the same amount of juice?"	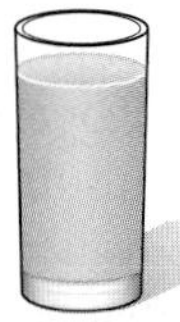 "No, the taller glass has more juice."
Matter*	Two identical cubes of sugar.  "Do these cubes have the same amount of sugar?" (Yes.)	Dissolve one cube in a glass of water. 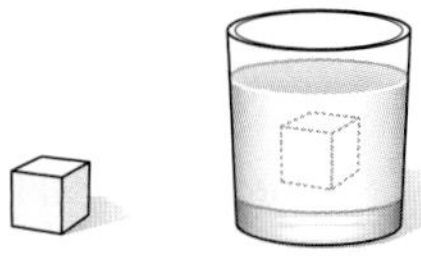 "Now is there the same amount of sugar?"	 "No, because you made one piece of sugar disappear."

*That is, the idea that a substance such as sugar is "still there" even though it seems to have disappeared (by dissolving).

FIGURE 5.3: **Four Piagetian conservation tasks:** Can you perform these tasks with a child you know?

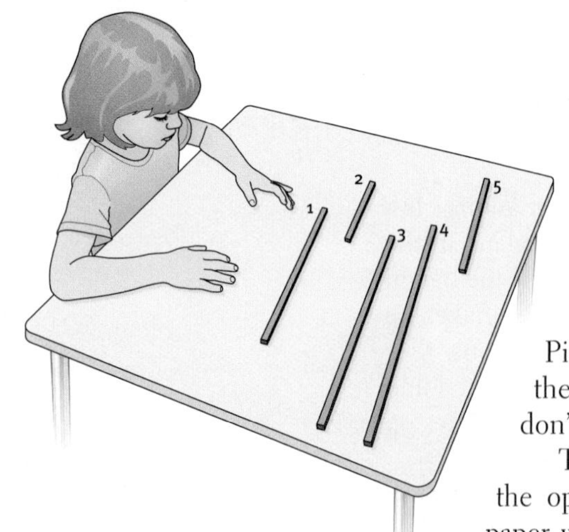

FIGURE 5.4: **A problem with seriation:** When asked to "put these sticks in order, from biggest to smallest," this kindergartner may center on the uppermost part of the table and identify the sticks numbered 2 and 5 as the biggest.

positions on a table and tell a 5-year-old to arrange them from the smallest to the biggest, and she is likely to pick the sticks that protrude farthest first. Because, as Figure 5.4 shows, she looks at (centers on) what first hits her eye, she doesn't consider the length of each stick.

These failures illustrate a basic cognitive difficulty. According to Piaget, young children don't have the abstraction skills to understand the concept of a category within which we can classify objects. They don't grasp the idea that it is possible to rank objects in a series at all.

This tendency to focus on immediate appearances explains why, in the opening chapter vignette, Moriah believed that Manuel had more paper when he cut his sheet into sections. Her attention was captured by the spread-out pieces, and she believed that now there must be more paper than before.

The idea that "bigger" automatically equals "more" extends to every aspect of preoperational thought. Ask a 3-year-old if he wants a nickel or a dime, and he will choose the first option. (This is a great source of pleasure to older siblings asked to equally share their funds.) Perhaps because greater height means "older" in their own lives, children even believe that a taller person has been on earth for a longer time:

> I was substitute teaching with a group of kindergarten children—at the time I was about 22—and when I met a student's mother at the end of the week, she was shocked. "When I asked Ben about you," she said, "he told me you were much older than his regular teacher." This teacher was in her mid- to late fifties and looked it. However, then we figured out the difference. This woman was barely 5 feet tall, whereas I am 6 feet two!

identity constancy In Piaget's theory, the preoperational child's inability to grasp that a person's core "self" stays the same despite changes in external appearance.

animism In Piaget's theory, the preoperational child's belief that inanimate objects are alive.

artificialism In Piaget's theory, the preoperational child's belief that human beings make everything in nature.

PECULIAR PERCEPTIONS ABOUT PEOPLE. Young children's tendency to believe that "what hits my eye right now is real" extends to people. It explains why a 3-year-old thinks her mommy is transformed into a princess when she dresses up for Halloween, or cries bitterly after her first visit to the beauty salon, believing that her short haircut has transformed her into a boy. It makes sense of why a favorite strategy of older sisters and brothers (to torture younger siblings) is to put on a mask and see the child run in horror from the room. As these examples show, young children lack a concept called **identity constancy.** They don't realize that people are still their essential selves despite changes in the way they visually appear.

I got insights into this identity constancy deficit at my son's fifth birthday party, when I hired a "gorilla" to entertain the guests (some developmental psychologist!). As the hairy 6-foot figure rang the doorbell, mass hysteria ensued—requiring the gorilla to take off his head. After the children calmed down, and the gorilla put on his head again to enact his skit, guess what? Pure hysteria again! Why did that huge animal cause such pandemonium? The reason is that the children believed that the gorilla, even though a costumed figure, was really alive.

Peter Hvizda/The Image Works

When her dad puts on a mask, he suddenly becomes a scary monster to this 4-year-old girl because she has not yet grasped the principle of identity constancy.

Animism refers to the difficulty young children have in sorting out what is really alive. Specifically, preschoolers see inanimate objects—such as dolls or costumed figures—as having consciousness, too. Look back at the beginning chapter vignette and you will notice several examples of animistic thinking—for example, the Barbies that were hungry or the wind that ran away. Now think back to when you were age 5 or 6. Do you remember being afraid the escalator might decide to suck you in? Or perhaps you recall believing, as in the Stephen King Experiencing the Lifespan box on page 152, that your dolls came alive at night.

Listen to young children talking about nature, and you will hear delightful examples of animism: "The sun gets sleepy when I sleep." "The moon likes to follow me in the car." The practice of assigning human motivations to natural phenomena is not something we grow out of as adults. Think of the Greek thunder god Zeus, or the ancient Druids who worshiped the spirits that lived within trees. Throughout history, humans have regularly used animism to make sense of a frightening world.

A related concept is called **artificialism.** Young children believe that everything in nature was made by human beings. Here is an example of this "daddy power" in action from Piaget's 3-year-old daughter, Laurent:

Jeff Greenberg/Photo Edit, Inc.

His animistic thinking causes this 4-year-old to believe that the bear is really going to enjoy the ride he is about to provide.

> L was in bed in the evening and it was still light: "Put the light out please" . . . (I switched the electric light off.) "It isn't dark"—"But I can't put the light out outside" . . . "Yes you can, you can make it dark." . . . "How?" . . . "You must turn it out very hard. It'll be dark and there will be little lights everywhere (stars)."
>
> (Piaget, 1951/1962, p. 248)

EXPERIENCING THE LIFESPAN: Childhood Fears, Animism, and the Power of Stephen King

There was one shadow that would constantly cast itself on my bedroom wall. It looked just like a giant creeping towards me with a big knife in his hand.

Our basement was a big hangout. But take away the kids and it was horrifying. I used to believe that Satan lived in my basement. The light switch was at the bottom of the steps, and whenever I switched off the light it was a mad dash to the top. I was so scared that Satan was going to stab my feet with knives.

Boy, do I remember my mom's doll that sat on the top of my dresser. I called it "Chatty Kathy." This doll came to life every night. She would stare at me, no matter where I went.

My mother used to take me when she went to clean house for Mrs. Handler, a rich lady. Mrs. Handler had this huge, shiny black grand piano, and I thought it came alive when I was not looking at it. It was so enormous, dark, and quiet. I remember pressing one of the bass keys, which sounded really deep and loud and it terrified me.

I remember being scared that there was something alive under my bed. I must tell you I sometimes still get scared that someone is under my bed and that they are going to grab me by my ankles. I don't think I will ever grow out of this, as I am 26.

Can you relate to any of these childhood memories collected from my students? Perhaps your enemy was that evil creature lurking in your basement, under your bed, or in the shadows in your room; the frightening stuffed animal on your wall; a huge object (with teeth) such as that piano; or your local garbage truck.

Now, you know where that master storyteller Stephen King gets his ideas. King's genius is that he taps into the preoperational kinds of thoughts that we have papered over, though not very well, as adults. When we read King's story about a toy animal that clapped cymbals to signal someone's imminent death, or about Christine, the car with a mind of its own, or about the laundry-pressing machine that loved human blood—these stories fall on familiar childhood ground. Don't you still get a bit anxious when you enter a dark basement? Even today, on a dark night, do you have an uneasy feeling that some strange monster might be lurking beneath your bed?

Animism and artificialism perfectly illustrate Piaget's concept of assimilation. The child knows that she is alive and so applies her "alive" schema to every object. Having seen adults perform heroic physical feats, such as turning off lights and building houses, a 3-year-old generalizes the same "big people control things" schema to the universe at large. Imagine that you are a young child taking a family vacation around the American West. After you visited that gleaming construction called Las Vegas, wouldn't it make sense that people carved out the Grand Canyon and the Rocky Mountains, too?

The sun and moon examples illustrate another core aspect of preoperational thought. According to Piaget, young children believe that they are the literal center of the universe, the pivot around which everything else revolves. Their worldview is characterized by **egocentrism**—the inability to understand that other people have different points of view.

By *egocentrism,* Piaget does not mean that young children are vain or uncaring, although they will tell you they are the smartest people on earth and the activities of the heavenly bodies are at their beck and call. Many of their most loving acts show egocentrism. There is nothing more touching than a 3-year-old's offer of a favorite "blankee" if he sees you upset. The child is egocentric, however, because he naturally assumes that what comforts *him* will automatically comfort you.

In Piaget's classic test of egocentrism, a child moves around a table that shows different views of three mountains, and then takes a seat. When shown photos of these differing perspectives and asked to pick "What the man on the opposite side sees," a preoperational child will select his view, rather than that of the adult. You can see delightful examples of egocentrism when having a conversation with a young child. Have you ever had a 3-year-old discuss an event at school without providing any background information, as if you *automatically* knew her teacher and the rest of the class?

egocentrism In Piaget's theory, the preoperational child's inability to understand that other people have different points of view from their own.

Piaget views egocentrism as a perfect example of centering in the human world. Young children are unable to decenter from their own mental processes. They don't realize that what is in their mind is not in everyone else's awareness, too.

The Concrete Operational Stage: Getting on the Adult Wavelength

Piaget discovered that the transition from preoperations to concrete operations happens gradually. First, children are preoperational in every area. Then, between ages 5 and 7, their thinking gets less static, or "thaws out" (Flavell, 1963). A 6-year-old, when given the conservation of liquid task, might first say the taller glass had more liquid, but then, after it is poured back into a wide glass, becomes unsure: "Is it bigger or not?" She has reached the tipping point where she is poised to reason on a higher cognitive plane.

By age 8, the child has reached this higher-level, concrete operational state: "Even though the second glass is taller, the first is wider" (showing decentering); "You can pour the liquid right back into the short glass and it would look the same" (illustrating reversibility). Now, she doesn't realize that she ever thought differently: "Are you silly? Of course it's the same!"

Piaget also found that specific conservations come in at different ages. First, children master conservation of number and then mass and liquid. They may not figure out the most difficult conservations until age 11 or 12. Imagine the challenge of understanding the last task in Figure 5.3 (see page 150)—realizing that when sugar is dissolved in water, it exists, but in a molecular form.

Still, according to Piaget, age 8 is a landmark for looking beyond immediate appearances, for understanding seriation and categories, for decentering in the physical and social worlds, for abandoning the tooth fairy and the idea that our stuffed animals are alive, and for entering the planet of adults.

Table 5.4 shows examples of different kinds of preoperational ideas. Now, test yourself by seeing if you can classify each statement in Piagetian terms.

INTERVENTIONS: Using Piaget's Ideas at Home and at Work

Piaget's concepts provide marvelous insights into the mysterious workings of young children's minds. For teachers, the theory explains why you need the same-sized cups at a kindergarten lunch table so that an argument won't erupt, even if you poured each drink from identical cans. Nurses understand that rationally explaining the purpose of a painful medical procedure to a 4-year-old may not be as effective as providing a magic doll to help the child cope.

TABLE 5.4: Can You Identify the Type of Preoperational Thought from These Real-World Examples?

Here are your possible choices: (*a*) no identity constancy, (*b*) animism, (*c*) artificialism, (*d*) egocentrism, (*e*) no conservation, and (*f*) inability to use classification.

_____ 1. Heidi was watching her father fix lunch. After he cut her sandwich into quarters, Heidi said, "Oh, Daddy, I only wanted you to cut it in two pieces. I'm not hungry enough to eat four!" (Bjorklund & Bjorklund, 1992, p. 168).

_____ 2. My 2-year-old son and I were taking our yearly trip to visit Grandma in Florida. As the plane took off and gained altitude, Thomas looked out the window and said with a delighted grin, "Mommy, TOYS!"

_____ 3. Melanie watched as her father, a professional clown, put on his clown outfit and then began applying his makeup. Before he could finish, Melanie suddenly ran screaming from the room, terrified of the strange clown.

_____ 4. Your child can't understand that he could live in his town and in his state at the same time. He tells you angrily, "I live in Newark, not New Jersey."

_____ 5. As you cross the George Washington Bridge over the Hudson River to New Jersey, your child asks, "Did the same people who built the bridge also make the river?"

Answers: 1 (*e*), 2 (*d*), 3 (*a*), 4 (*f*), 5 (*c*)

The theory makes sense of why forming a Little League team with a group of 4- or 5-year-olds is an impossible idea. Grasping the rules of a game requires abstract conceptualization—a skill that preoperational children do not possess. It tells us why young children are terrified of the dark and scary clowns at the amusement park. So for parents who feel uneasy about playing into their child's fantasies when they provide "anti-monster spray" to calm those bedtime fears, one justification is that, according to Piaget, when your child is ready, she will naturally grow out of her ideas.

Piaget's concepts also give us wonderful insights into children's passions at different ages. They explain the power of pretending in early childhood (more about this in Chapter 6) and the lure of that favorite holiday, Halloween. When a 4-year-old child dresses up as Batman, he may be grappling with the challenge of understanding that you can look different yet still remain your essential self. The theory accounts for why third or fourth graders become captivated with games such as soccer, and can be avid collectors of items such as baseball cards. Now that they can understand rules and categories, concrete operational children are determined to exercise their new conceptual and classification skills.

Suzanne Kreiter/The Boston Globe/The New York Times

In late elementary school, children take great pride in collecting, classifying, and trading items like Yu-Gi-Oh cards because they are practicing their new concrete operational skills.

The theory explains why "real school," the academic part, fully begins at about age 7. Children younger than this age often don't have the intellectual tools to understand reversibility, a concept critical to understanding mathematics (if 2 plus 4 is 6, then 6 minus 4 must equal 2). Even empathizing with the teacher's agenda is a concrete operational skill.

The fact that age 8 is a coming-of-age marker is represented by the classic movie *Home Alone.* The plot of this film would have been unthinkable if its hero were 5, or even 6. If the star was 11, the movie would be not be interesting because, by this age, a child could competently take care of himself. Eight is when we begin to make the transition to being able to make it "home alone." It is the age when we shift from worrying about monsters—things that are not real—to grappling with the dangers that we really face as adults.

Evaluating Piaget

Piaget has clearly transformed the way we think about young children. Still, as you saw with infancy, in important areas, Piaget was incorrect.

I described a major problem with Piaget's ideas in Chapter 3: Just as he minimized what babies know, Piaget underestimated preoperational children's capacities. In particular, Piaget overstated young children's egocentrism. If infants can decode other people's feelings, the first awareness that we live in "different heads" must dawn on children at a far younger age than 8! (At the end of this chapter, I'll trace exactly how this mindreading ability develops.)

We might also take issue with Piaget's idea that we grow out of animism by age 8 or 9. Maybe he was giving us too *much* credit here. Do you have a good luck charm that keeps the plane from crashing, or a place you go for comfort where you can hear the trees whispering to you?

Children around the world do learn to conserve (Dasen, 1977, 1984). But because nature interacts with nurture, the ages at which they master specific conservation tasks vary from place to place. An example comes from a village in Mexico, where weaving is the main occupation. Young children in this collectivist culture grasp conservation tasks involving spatial concepts when they are younger than age 7 or 8 because they have so much hands-on training in activities relating to this kind of skill (Maynard & Greenfield, 2003). This brings up a crucial dimension that Piaget's theory leaves out: the impact of teaching in promoting cognitive growth.

Lauren Greenfield/VII Photo

Because this girl growing up in Mexico gets so much practice at weaving, we might expect her to grasp concrete operational conservation tasks related to spatial concepts at a relatively early age.

Vygotsky's Zone of Proximal Development

Piaget implies that children naturally construct an adult view of the world. We can't convince preschoolers that their dolls are not alive or that the width of the glass makes up for the height. They must grow out of those ideas on their own. The Russian psychologist Lev Vygotsky (1962, 1978, 1986) had a different perspective: People propel mental growth.

Vygotsky was born in the same year as Piaget. He showed as much brilliance at a young age, but—unlike Piaget, who lived to a ripe old age—he died of tuberculosis in his late thirties. Still, Vygotsky's writings have given him towering status in developmental science today. One reason is that Vygotsky was, at heart, an educator. He believed that what *we* do helps children mentally advance.

zone of proximal development (ZPD) In Vygotsky's theory, the gap between a child's ability to solve a problem totally on his own and his potential knowledge if taught by a more accomplished person.

scaffolding The process of teaching new skills by entering a child's zone of proximal development and tailoring one's efforts to that person's competence level.

Vygotsky theorized that learning takes place within the **zone of proximal development,** which he defined as the difference between what the child can do by himself and his level of "potential development as determined through problem solving under adult guidance or in collaboration with more capable peers" (Vygotsky, 1978, p. 86; also, see the diagram in Figure 5.5). Teachers must tailor their instruction to a child's proximal zone. Then, as that child becomes more competent, they should slowly back off and allow the student more responsibility for directing that learning activity on his own. This sensitive pacing has a special name: **scaffolding** (Wood, Bruner, & Ross, 1976).

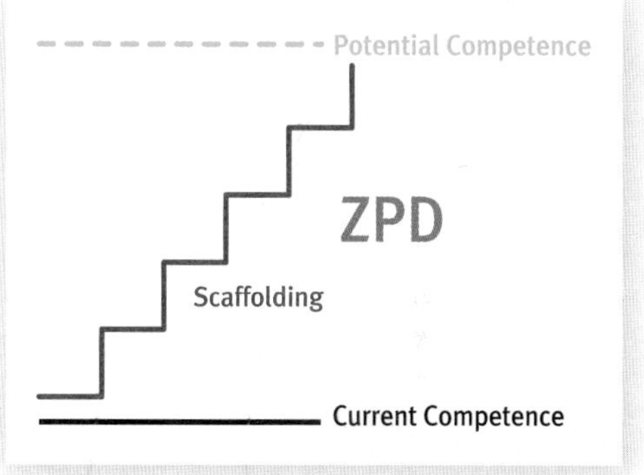

FIGURE 5.5: **Vygotsky's zone of proximal development:** These lines illustrate the ZPD—the gap between where a child is currently "at" intellectually and where he can potentially be. If a teacher sensitively teaches within this zone and employs scaffolding (see step-wise lines)—providing support, then backing off when help is no longer needed—students will reach their full intellectual potential.

You saw scaffolding in operation in Chapter 3 in my discussion of infant-directed speech, the simplified language that adults use when talking to babies. Recall that baby talk has a very adult function. It permits caregivers to penetrate a young child's proximal zone for language and so helps scaffold emerging speech. Now, let's explore scaffolding as we read about a mother teaching her 5-year-old daughter how to play her first board game, Chutes and Ladders:

> Tiffany threw the dice, then looked up at her mother. Her mother said, "How many is that?" Tiffany shrugged her shoulders. Her mother said, "Count them," but Tiffany just sat and stared. Her mother counted the dots aloud, and then said to her daughter, "Now you count them," which Tiffany did. This was repeated for the next five turns. Tiffany waited for her mother to count the dots, then modeled her mother's actions and moved her piece. On her sixth move, however, Tiffany counted the dots on the dice on her own after her mother's request. . . . During the next few moves, her mother still had to ask Tiffany to count how many dots she had. But eventually, Tiffany threw the dice and counted the dots herself and continued to do so, practicing counting and moving the pieces on both her own and her mother's turns.
>
> (Bjorklund & Rosenblum, 2001)

Notice that this mother was a superb scaffolder. By pacing her interventions to Tiffany's emerging capacities, she paved the way for her child to master the game. But this process did not just flow from parent to child. Tiffany was also teaching her mother how to respond. Just as your professor is getting new insights into lifespan development while teaching every class—or at this minute, as I struggle to write this page, I'm learning to better connect with Vygotsky's ideas—education is a *bidirectional,* mind-expanding duet (Scrimsher & Tudge, 2003).

This girl in Thailand is learning to weave just by observing her mother—a strategy that we might find unusual in our teaching-oriented culture.

In our culture, we have definite ideas about what makes a good scaffolder. Enter a child's proximal zone. Actively instruct, but be sensitive to a child's responses. However, in collectivist societies, such as among the Mayans living in Mexico's Yucatán Peninsula, children learn by observation. They listen. They watch. They are not explicitly taught the skills they need for adult life (Rogoff and others, 2003). So the qualities our culture sees as vital to socializing children are not necessarily part of the ideology of good parenting in other regions of the globe.

INTERVENTIONS: Becoming an Effective Scaffolder

In our teaching-oriented society, what do superior scaffolders do? Let's list a few techniques:

- They foster a secure attachment, as nurturing, responsive interactions are a basic foundation for learning (Laible, 2004).
- They break a larger cognitive challenge, such as learning Chutes and Ladders, into manageable steps (Berk & Winsler, 1999).
- They give nonthreatening (but clear) feedback about failure—for instance, hesitating and looking at the correct alternative when the child makes a mistake (Gallimore & Tharp, 1992; Rogoff, 1990).
- They continue helping until the child has fully mastered the concept before moving on, as Tiffany's mother did earlier.
- They set a framework for the learning task and build in motivation. So, in teaching reading, a first-grade teacher might say: "This is a book about lions. It's about how to make friends with a cub. Ooh, I can't wait to see what the author says!" (Clay & Cazden, 1992).

In Chapter 7, we'll be exploring these attributes as they relate to elementary school teaching. Now, think of a scaffolder, or teacher, who stood out in your life.

TABLE 5.5: Piagetian and Vygotskian Perspectives on Life and Learning

	Lev Vygotsky (1896–1934)	Jean Piaget (1896–1980)
	 www.davidsonfilms.com	 Bill Anderson/Photo Researchers, Inc.
Biography	Russian, Jewish, communist (reached teenage years during the Russian Revolution), believed in Marx	Swiss, middle-class family
Basic interests	Education, literature, literary criticism Wanted to know how to stimulate thinking	Biology, mollusks Wanted to trace the evolution of thought in stages
Overall orientation	Look at interpersonal processes and the role of society in cognition	Look for universal developmental processes
Basic ideas	1. We develop intellectually through social interactions.	1. We develop intellectually through physically acting on the world.
	2. Development is a collaborative endeavor.	2. Development takes place on our own inner timetable.
	3. People cause cognitive growth.	3. When we are internally ready, we reach a higher level of cognitive development.
Implications for education	Instruction is critical to development. Teachers should sensitively intervene within each child's zone of proximal development.	Provide ample materials to let children explore and learn on their own.

List that person's qualities. Keep your list handy to see if your items fit the teaching talents you'll read about two chapters from now.

Table 5.5 compares Vygotsky's and Piaget's perspectives and offers capsule summaries of the backgrounds that shaped these world-class geniuses' ideas (Vianna & Stetsenko, 2006). Although often described in opposing terms, these two theories form an ideal pair. Piaget gave us unparalleled insights into the developing structure of childhood cognition. Vygotsky offered us an engine to transform children's lives.

The Information-Processing Perspective

Vygotsky filled in the missing social pieces of Piaget's theory and provided us with a framework for stimulating mental growth. But he did not address the gaps in the theory itself. Why are children able to decenter? What *specific* skills allow children to understand that the width of the glass makes up for the height?

Piaget never mentions how crucial abilities such as memory, concentration, and planning develop. Was Ms. Angela, the teacher in the opening chapter vignette, asking too much of her 3-year-olds to remember those free-play rules? How can teachers best teach spelling to a third-grade class? Parents might want guidelines as to what to expect from a child at a particular age: "Can my 6-year-old daughter take responsibility for caring for a puppy?" "When will my son be able to get ready for school on his own?" Clinical psychologists and caregivers would want to understand why a particular child has so much trouble focusing and obeying at school and at home. To get this information, everyone would gravitate toward the *information-processing approach.*

Information-processing theorists, as you learned in Chapter 3, break cognitive processes into components and divide thinking into steps. Let's illustrate this approach by examining memory, the basis of all thought.

Making Sense of Memory

Information-processing theorists believe that on the way to becoming "a memory," information passes through different stores, or stages. First, we hold stimuli arriving from the outside world briefly in a sensory store. Then, features that we notice enter the most important store, called working memory.

Working memory is where the "cognitive action" takes place. Here, we keep information in awareness and act to either process it or discard it. Working memory is made up of limited-capacity holding bins. It also consists of an "executive processor," which allows us to focus on what we need to remember as well as to manipulate the material in working memory to prepare it for permanent storage (Baddeley, 1992; Best & Miller, 2010). Once we have moved information through working memory, it enters a more long-lasting store, and we can recall it at a later time.

You can get a real-life example of the fleeting quality of working memory when you get a phone number from information and call from a landline phone. You know that you can dial the seven-digit number without having to write it down, and your memory will not fail *if you get to finish.* If you are interrupted by a beep from another caller and lose focus, the number evaporates. In fact, for adults, the typical bin size of working memory is about the size of a local phone number: seven chunks (in this case, digits) of information.

Interestingly, by examining age changes in working memory, information-processing researchers have explained why young children can't conserve. Memory-bin capacity expands between ages 2 and 7—from about two to five bits of information (Dempster, 1981). During preschool, there are dramatic advances in children's ability to inhibit their responses (Best & Miller, 2010). These changes make sense of why children reach concrete operations at roughly age 8 (Case, 1999). Now, we finally have the memory capacities to step back from our first impressions and remember that what we saw previously (such as a wider glass) compensates for what we are seeing right now.

working memory In information-processing theory, the limited-capacity gateway system, containing all the material that we can keep in awareness at a single time. The material in this system is either processed for more permanent storage or lost.

executive functions Any frontal-lobe ability that allows us to inhibit our responses and to plan and direct our thinking.

rehearsal A learning strategy in which people repeat information to embed it in memory.

selective attention A learning strategy in which people manage their awareness so as to attend only to what is relevant and to filter out unneeded information.

Exploring Executive Functions

Executive functions refer to any skill related to managing our memory, controlling our cognitions, planning our behavior, and inhibiting our responses. Executive functions depend on the brain's master planner—the frontal lobes. Now, let's look at three examples of executive functions that make children in concrete operations very different thinkers than they were at age 4 or even 5.

OLDER CHILDREN REHEARSE INFORMATION. A major way we learn information is through **rehearsal.** We repeat material to embed it in memory. In a classic study, developmentalists had kindergarteners, second graders, and fifth graders memorize objects (such as a cat or a desk) pictured on cards (Flavell, Beach, & Chinsky, 1966). Prior to the testing, the research team watched the children's lips to see if they were repeating the names of the objects to themselves. Eighty-five percent of the fifth graders used rehearsal; only 10 percent of the kindergarteners did. So one reason why older children are superior learners is that they understand that they need to rehearse.

And, furthermore, as children get older, their rehearsal strategy becomes better thought out. Researchers asked third, fifth, and eighth graders to memorize a series of words (Ornstein, Naus, & Liberty, 1975). They presented each word individually and gave the children time in between each presentation to rehearse aloud. Third graders just repeated the previous word, for example, saying, *yard, yard, yard, yard.* Older children allotted their time strategically, saying, *yard, yard, man, desk,* to make sure they kept in mind all the words they needed to recall.

To bring home the message of this research: If your final exam in this class is cumulative, you know you need to spend most of your time memorizing the last section of this book but still go back and review what you learned for the other tests. In third grade, you *never* would have grasped this fundamental studying strategy.

OLDER CHILDREN UNDERSTAND HOW TO SELECTIVELY ATTEND. The ability to manage our awareness so we focus on what we need to know and filter out extraneous information is called **selective attention.** In a classic study illustrating young children's problems in this area, researchers presented boys and girls of different ages with cards. On one half of each card was an animal photo; on the other half was a picture of some household item (see Figure 5.6). The children were instructed to remember only the animals.

As you might expect, older children were better at recalling the animal names. But now comes the interesting part: When the children were asked how many irrelevant items they could recall, the performance differences evaporated—suggesting that the young children wasted effort looking at the objects they did not need to know (Bjorklund, 2005). This suggests that, in addition to having smaller memory

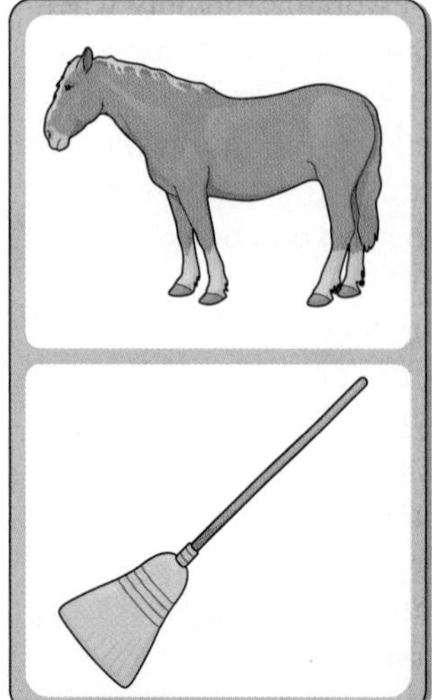

FIGURE 5.6: **A selective attention study:** In this study measuring selective attention, children were asked only to memorize the animals on the top half of the cards. Then researchers looked for age differences in their memory for the irrelevant household items.

bins, young children clog their existing bin space with irrelevant information. They can't focus their attention on what is relevant and filter out extraneous stimuli as well.

OLDER CHILDREN ARE SUPERIOR AT INHIBITION. Turn back to the vignette at the beginning of this chapter to vividly see the problems young children have inhibiting their impulses. Notice how the 3-year-olds ran into the different activity centers without thinking, "That's not what I'm supposed to do." The most fascinating example occurred during the weather report. Because the temptation to say yes was so strong, the children could not restrain themselves from agreeing when the teacher asked *any* question about the weather that day.

To measure differences in inhibition directly, researchers may ask children to perform some action that contradicts their immediate tendencies, such as instructing them to say the word *black* when they see the word *white* (Diamond, Kirkham, & Amso, 2002). Or, in *delay of gratification* studies, they may tell children, "you can get a small treat now or a larger one if you wait."

Performance on these tasks improves markedly during preschool, and gradually gets better with age (Best & Miller, 2010). Actually, fostering inhibition—not doing what you feel like doing—is a primary *socialization* goal. From following the preschool rules to having the self-control to study for this test and resist checking Facebook during class, inhibiting our responses is essential to succeeding at school and life.

Moreover, if you think these self-control feats are difficult, imagine being a young child. And never, ever tell a 4- or 5-year-old to keep a "big secret." Her automatic response will be to immediately blurt it out!

Gregor Schlaeger/VISUM/The Image Works

Given that the exciting news is on this child's mind and the frontal lobes are still under construction, there is no such thing as a secret!

INTERVENTIONS: Using Information-Processing Theory at Home and at Work

So, to bring us back to the beginning of this section, teachers *cannot* assume that third graders will automatically understand how to memorize spelling words. Scaffolding study skills, such as the need to rehearse, or teaching strategies to promote selective attention, such as putting large stars next to the relevant words for a test, should be an integral part of education, beginning in elementary school. Table 5-6 summarizes and amplifies on these tips and those you will read on page 160.

TABLE 5.6: Information-Processing Guidelines for Teachers and Parents

Early childhood

1. Don't expect a child to remember, without considerable prompting, regular chores such as feeding a pet, the details of a movie or show, or the name of the person who telephoned.
2. Expect the child to have a good deal of trouble with any situation that involves inhibiting a strong "prepotent impulse"—such as not touching toys, following unpleasant rules, or keeping a secret.

Middle childhood

1. Don't assume that the child knows how to best master school-related memorization tasks. Actively teach the need to rehearse information, selective attention strategies (such as underlining important points), and other studying skills.
2. Scaffold organizational strategies for school and life. For example, get the child to use a notebook for each class assignment and to keep important objects, such as eyeglasses, in a specific place.
3. Expect situations that involve many different tasks, such as getting ready for school, to present problems. Also expect activities that involve *ongoing* inhibition to give children trouble, such as refraining from watching TV or using the Internet before finishing their homework. Try to build in a regular structure for mastering these difficult executive-functioning tasks: "The rule is that at 8 or 9 P.M., it's time to get everything ready for school." "Homework must be completed by dinnertime, or the first thing after you get home from school."
4. To promote selective attention (and inhibition), have a child do homework, or any task that involves concentration, in a room away from tempting distractions such as the TV or Internet.

attention deficit/hyperactivity disorder (ADHD) The most common childhood learning disorder in the United States, disproportionately affecting boys, characterized by excessive restlessness and distractibility at home and at school.

Parents will probably need to regularly remind a child, even at age 6 or 7, to feed the dog. Expect activities requiring different information-processing tasks, such as getting dressed and remembering to take homework and pencils to class, to be difficult *throughout* elementary school (and beyond). Scaffold organizational strategies, such as helping a second grader get everything ready for school before bedtime and teaching that child to put important items in specific places. For everyone else, the information-processing research suggests that executive functions—from inhibiting yourself, to selectively attending—improve gradually over *many years* (Best & Miller, 2010; Zhan and others, 2011).

Now that we know how thinking normally develops, let's look at the insights information-processing research offers caregivers who want to understand children with problems focusing and obeying—boys and girls with attention deficit/hyperactivity disorder, or ADHD.

IN FOCUS: Attention Deficit/Hyperactivity Disorder

Attention deficit/hyperactivity disorder (ADHD), defined by inattentiveness, distractibility, and impulsivity, is the most widely diagnosed childhood disorder in the United States, affecting roughly one in ten girls and boys (Centers for Disease Control and Prevention [CDC], 2010). This condition is currently diagnosed in preschoolers and during the adult years. But since sitting still and focusing becomes mandatory at this age, boys and girls typically receive this label in elementary school. Actually, boys are several times more likely to receive this label than are girls (Sonuga-Barke & Halperin, 2010; Young & Amarasinghe, 2010).

ADHD has a bewildering array of risk factors—from prenatal smoking, to environmental toxins; from genetic predispositions, to orphanage life (recall the previous chapter). It follows a bewildering array of paths, from first appearing in preschool, to erupting during adulthood; from persisting for decades, to fading after months (Sonuga-Barke & Halperin, 2010).

ADHD has an equally bewildering array of possible "neural" causes. One widely accepted idea is that this condition results from a lower-than-normal output of dopamine, the neurotransmitter that modulates sensitivity to rewards (Williams, 2008). Some scientists feel ADHD is caused by the delayed maturation of the frontal lobes. Others speculate that impairments in lower brain centers are to blame. Neuropsychologists have linked symptoms to everything from smaller brain size to structural abnormalities in specific cortical regions, and documented a range of abnormal neural activation patterns when these children perform learning tasks (Groom and others, 2010; Halperin & Healey, 2011; Sonuga-Barke & Halperin, 2010).

The hallmark of ADHD, however, is deficits in executive functions (Halperin & Healey 2011). These children have problems with inhibition (Barkley, 1998, 2003; Roberts, Fillmore, & Milich, 2010; Wilson and others, 2011). When told, "Don't touch the toys," boys and girls diagnosed with ADHD have special trouble resisting this impulse.

These children have difficulties with selective attention. Researchers asked elementary schoolers to memorize a series of words. Some words were more valuable to remember (that is, worth more points), and others less. Boys and girls with ADHD memorized an equal number of words as a comparison group; but, like the preschoolers in the previous section, they got lower scores because they clogged their memory bins with less valuable words (Castel and others, 2010).

Ruth Jenkinson/Dorling Kindersley/Getty Images

Imagine mastering the skills involved in making sure you have the items you need for school, plus leaving the house on time while dealing with the distractions of a pesky brother, and you will understand why—for elementary schoolers with ADHD—"mornings" are an impossible trial.

As you might imagine, performing a sequence of tasks under time pressure, such as getting ready for school by 7:00 A.M., presents immense problems for boys and girls with ADHD. These children have more trouble estimating time (Gooch, Snowling, & Hulme, 2011; Hurks & Hendriksen, 2011; Hwang and others, 2010). Moreover, perhaps because of their dopamine deficit, they show less neural activation in the face of punishments and rewards (Stark and others, 2011). So, yelling, or threatening a child, simply may not work.

These issues explain why school is so problematic for boys and girls with ADHD. Sitting still and focusing on a teacher demands inhibitory and selective attention skills. Taking tests can involve exceptional time-management talents, too.

Because the same difficulties with inhibition, time management, and selective attention lead to problems at home, frustrated parents are apt to resort to *power-assertion* disciplinary techniques (Wymbs & Pelham, 2010). They lash out at a 9-year-old who seems incapable of getting his things in order. They scream at, hit, and punish a daughter who can't "just sit still." Therefore, due to an *evocative* process, boys and girls with ADHD are *least* likely to get the sensitive parenting that they most need. Their difficult behavior can provoke marital conflict (Wymbs & Pelham, 2010) and cause these children to fail with their peers (Andrade and others, 2009; Mrug and others, 2009; Ohan & Johnston, 2011; also, see the next chapter). Given these dangers, what should a caring adult do?

INTERVENTIONS: Helping Children with ADHD

The well-known treatment for ADHD is psycho-stimulant medications (Barkley & Murphy, 2006; Wender and others, 2011). Medications are most effective when combined with parent (and sometimes teacher) training. Behavioral programs using operant conditioning principles teach adults to target upsetting behaviors (rather than ineffectually yelling), pay attention to positive acts, consistently use time out, and offer children concrete rewards such as tokens to boost brain dopamine production (Ryan-Krause, 2011; Young & Amarasinghe, 2010). Caregivers are encouraged not to put pressure on their sons and daughters to complete demanding time-based tasks.

Interestingly, perhaps because it helps stimulate dopamine production, boys and girls with ADHD learn better in noisy environments. So, to enhance a school-aged child's ability to focus on his homework, it may help to provide "white" background noise (Soderlund, Sikstrom, & Smart, 2007). As providing regular recess also helps these children focus (Ridgway and others, 2003), schools should build more physical activity into the day (which, by the way, helps *every* child perform better in class!). Perhaps because it activates the brain's reward system, one study demonstrated that presenting learning tasks in a gaming format is especially beneficial for children with ADHD (Prins and others, 2011). Actually, you might be interested to know that one educational guru has advocated "gaming" as a key to generally enhancing the twenty-first-century relevance of school (Davidson, 2011).

Shannon Fagan/Photographer's Choice/Getty Images

Although he may regularly tune out in class, this boy clearly has no problem being riveted to this game. Therefore, it makes sense that providing high-intensity academics-related video games may help cure wandering school minds.

Students have told me that getting passionately involved in games or sports was the only treatment that "cured" a sibling's ADHD. Today, even some traditional medication-oriented experts are listening (see Halperin & Healey, 2011). Medicines, they admit, even when effective, don't get rid of all the symptoms. In addition, the pills have side effects, compliance is an issue (parents are, naturally, reluctant to "dope up" their child), and once a person stops the treatment, symptoms return (Graham and others, 2011; Sonuga-Barke & Halperin, 2010). Exercise, as you will see later in this book, helps stimulate neurogenesis and *may* reduce the risk of getting later-life Alzheimer's disease. Might intense exercise or even providing time for playing games help mend a child's brain?

But perhaps some brains don't need mending. ADHD symptoms appear on a continuum (Bell, 2011; Larsson and others, 2012). Where should we *really* put the cutting point between normal childhood inattentiveness and a diagnosed "disease"? The dramatic early twenty-first-century U.S. rise in the prevalence of ADHD (CDC, 2010) is troubling. So is the male tilt to this diagnosis, as boys are more physically active than girls. Without denying that ADHD can cause considerable heartache, what role might a poor elementary school child–environment fit play in this "disorder" at this moment in history?

Wrapping Up Cognition

Now that I have reached the end of our survey of cognition, it should be clear why our species needs a decade (or two) beyond infancy to master the intellectual challenges of the adult world. Now, imagine the insights we would be missing if we left out any theory. What if you wanted to make sense of the strange ideas preschoolers have, or needed a general strategy for stimulating intellectual growth? What if you were searching for guidance about what to expect from children in terms of listening, following directions, and sitting still? You would have to turn to Piaget, Vygotsky, and the information-processing perspective. Has a particular theory been especially valuable in helping you understand the children you know?

TYING IT ALL TOGETHER

1. While with your 3-year-old nephew Mark, you observe many examples of preoperational thought. Give the Piagetian label—egocentrism, animism, no conservation, artificialism, identity constancy—for each of the following:
   a. Mark tells you that the big tree in the garden is watching him.
   b. When you stub your toe, Mark gives you his favorite stuffed animal.
   c. Mark tells you that his daddy made the sun.
   d. Mark says, "There's more now," when you pour juice from a wide carton into a skinny glass.
   e. Mark tells you that his sister turned into a princess yesterday when she put on a costume.
2. In a sentence, explain the basic mental difference between an 8-year-old in the concrete operational stage and a preoperational 4-year-old.
3. Four-year-old Christopher can recognize every letter of the alphabet, and he is beginning to sound out words in books. Drawing on Vygotsky's theory, what should Chris's parents do?
   a. Buy only alphabet books because their son will succeed at recognizing all the letters.
   b. Buy some "easy-to-read" books just above their son's skill level.
   c. Challenge Chris by getting him books with more complicated stories.
4. Turn back to the opening chapter vignette on page 141. List three activities specifically tailored to help train these preschoolers in the skills of regulating and inhibiting their responses.
5. Laura's son has been diagnosed with ADHD. Based on this chapter, suggest some environmental strategies she might use to help her child.

Answers to the Tying It All Together questions can be found at the end of this chapter.

Language

So far, I have been discussing the cognitive and physical milestones in this chapter as if they occurred in a vacuum. But, as I highlighted at the beginning of this chapter, that uniquely human skill, language, is vital to every childhood advance. Vygotsky (1978) actually put using language—or speaking—front and center in everything we learn.

Inner Speech

According to Vygotsky, learning takes place when the words a child hears from parents and other scaffolders migrate inward to become talk directed at the self. For instance, using the earlier example of Chutes and Ladders, after listening to her mother say "Count them" a number of times, Tiffany learned the game by repeating "Count them" to herself. Thinking, according to Vygotsky, is really **inner speech.**

Support for this idea comes from listening to young children monitor their actions. A 3-year-old might say, "Don't touch!" as she moves near the stove; or she could remind herself to be "a good girl" at preschool that day (Manfra & Winsler, 2006). We may feel the same way as adults. If something is *really important*—and if no one is listening—have you ever given yourself instructions "Be sure to do X, Y and Z" out loud?

David Young-Wolff/Photo Edit

According to Vygotsky, by talking to her image in the mirror "out loud," this girl is learning to monitor her behavior. Have you ever done the same thing when no one was watching?

Developing Speech

How does language *itself* unfold? Actually, during early childhood language does more than unfold. It explodes.

By our second birthday, we are just beginning to put together words (see Chapter 3). By kindergarten, we basically have adult language nailed down. When we look at the challenges involved in mastering language, this achievement becomes more remarkable. To speak like adults, children must articulate word sounds. They must string units of meaning together in sentences. They must produce sentences that are grammatically correct. They must understand the meanings of words.

The word sounds of language are called **phonemes.** When children begin to speak in late infancy, they can only form single phonemes—for instance, they call their bottle *ba.* They repeat sounds that seem similar, such as calling their bottle *baba,* when they cannot form the next syllable of the word. By age 3, while children have made tremendous strides in producing phonemes, they still—as you saw in the introductory chapter vignette—have trouble pronouncing multisyllabic words (like *psghetti*). Then, early in elementary school, these articulation problems disappear—but not completely. Have you ever had a problem pronouncing a difficult word that you were able to read on a page?

The meaning units of language are called **morphemes** (for example, the word *boys* has two units of meaning: *boy* and the plural suffix *s*). As children get older, their average number of morphemes per sentence—called their **mean length of utterance (MLU)**—expands. A 2-year-old's sentence, "Me juice" (2 MLUs), becomes, "Me want juice" (3 MLUs), and then, at age 4, "Please give me the juice" (5 MLUS). Also around age 3 or 4, children are fascinated by producing long, jumbled-together sentences strung together by *and* ("Give me juice and crackers and milk and cookies and . . .").

This brings up the steps to mastering grammar, or **syntax.** What's interesting here are the classic mistakes that young children make. As parents are aware, one of the first words that children utter is *no.* First, children typically add this word to the beginning of a sentence ("No eat cheese" or "No go inside"). Next, they move the negative term inside the sentence, next to the main verb ("I no sing" or "He no do it"). A question starts out as a declarative sentence with a rising intonation: "I have a drink, Daddy?" Then it, too, is replaced by the correct word order: "Can I have a drink, Daddy?" Children typically produce grammatically correct sentences by the time they enter school.

The most amazing changes occur in **semantics**—understanding word meanings. Here, children go from three- or four-word vocabularies at age 1 to knowing about 10,000 words by age 6! (See Slobin, 1972; Smith, 1926) While we have the other core abilities basically under our belts by the end of early childhood, our vocabularies continue to grow from age 2 to 102.

inner speech In Vygotsky's theory, the way by which human beings learn to regulate their behavior and master cognitive challenges, through silently repeating information or talking to themselves.

phoneme The sound units that convey meaning in a given language—for example, in English, the *c* sound of *cat* and the *b* sound of *bat.*

morpheme The smallest unit of meaning in a particular language—for example, *boys* contains two morphemes: *boy* and the plural suffix *s.*

mean length of utterance (MLU) The average number of morphemes per sentence.

syntax The system of grammatical rules in a particular language.

semantics The meaning system of a language—that is, what the words stand for.

TABLE 5.7: Challenges on the Language Pathway: A Summary Table

Type of challenge	Description	Example
Phonemes	Has trouble forming sounds	*Baba, psghetti*
Morphemes	Uses few meaning units per sentence	*Me go home*
Syntax (grammar)	Makes mistakes in applying rules for forming sentences	*Me go home*
Semantics	Has problems understanding word meanings	*Calls the family dog a horsey*
Overregularization	Puts irregular pasts and plurals into regular forms	*Foots; runned*
Over/underextension	Applies verbal labels too broadly/narrowly	Calls every old man grandpa; tells another child he can't have a grandpa because grandpa is the name for his grandfather alone

One mistake young children make while learning language is called **overregularization.** Around age 3 or 4, they often misapply general rules for plurals or past tense forms even when exceptions occur. A preschooler will say *runned, goed, teached, sawed, mouses, feets*, and *cup of sugars* rather than using the correct irregular form (Berko, 1958).

Another error lies in children's semantic mistakes. Also around age 3, children often use **overextensions**—meaning they extend a verbal label too broadly. In Piaget's terminology, they assimilate the word *horsey* to all four-legged creatures, such as dogs, cats, and lions in the zoo. Or they use **underextensions**—making name categories too narrow. A 3-year-old may tell you that only her own pet is a dog and insist that all the other neighborhood dogs must be called something else. As children get older, through continual assimilation and accommodation, they sort these glitches out.

Table 5.7 summarizes these challenges. Now you might want to have a conversation with a 3- or 4-year-old child. Can you pick out examples of overregularization, overextensions or underextensions, problems with syntax (grammar), or difficulties pronouncing phonemes (word sounds)? Can you figure out the child's MLU?

TYING IT ALL TOGETHER

1. A 5-year-old is talking out loud and making comments such as "Put the big piece here," while constructing a puzzle. What would Vygotsky say about this behavior?
2. You are listening to a 3-year-old named Joshua. Pick out the example of overregularization and the overextension from the following comments.
   a. When offered a piece of cheese, Joshua said, "I no eat cheese."
   b. Seeing a dog run away, Joshua said, "The doggie runned away."
   c. Taken to a petting zoo, Joshua pointed excitedly at a goat and said, "Horsey!"

Answers to the Tying It All Together questions can be found at the end of this chapter.

overregularization An error in early language development, in which young children apply the rules for plurals and past tenses even to exceptions, so irregular forms sound like regular forms.

overextension An error in early language development in which young children apply verbal labels too broadly.

underextension An error in early language development in which young children apply verbal labels too narrowly.

Specific Social Cognitive Skills

Language makes us capable of uniquely human *social cognitive* understandings. We are the only species that reflects on our past and future (Fivush, 2011). The essence of being human, as I highlighted at the beginning of this chapter, is that we effortlessly transport ourselves into each other's heads, decoding what people are thinking from their own point of view. How do children learn they have an ongoing life history? When do we *fully* grasp that "other minds" are different from our own?

Constructing Our Personal Past

autobiographical memories Recollections of events and experiences that make up one's life history.

theory of mind Children's first cognitive understanding, which appears at about age 4, that other people have different beliefs and perspectives from their own.

Autobiographical memories refer to reflecting on our life histories: from our earliest memories at age 3 or 4, to that incredible experience we had at work last week (Fivush, 2011). Children's understanding that they have a unique autobiography is scaffolded through a specific kind of talk. Caregivers reminisce with young children: "Remember going on a train to visit Grandma?" "What did we do at the beach last week?" These *past-talk conversations* are teaching a basic lesson: "You have a past and future. You are an ongoing, enduring self."

Past-talk conversations typically begin with parents doing all the "remembering" when children first begin to speak (Harley & Reese, 1999). Then, during early preschool as their language skills improve, adults ask children about events that they shared: "What did we do at Grandma's?" "Whom did we see at the beach?" Gradually children become full partners in these mutual stories, and finally, at age 4 or 5, initiate past-talk conversations on their own (Nelson & Fivush, 2004). Listen to this vivid autobiographical memory produced by a 6-year-old:

INTERVIEWER TO 6-YEAR-OLD: Can you tell me about the ballet recital?

CHILD: It was driving me crazy.

INTERVIEWER: Really?

CHILD: Yes, I was so scared because I didn't know any of the people and I couldn't see mom and dad. They were way on top of the audience. . . . Ummm, we were on a slippery surface and we all did "Where the Wild Things Are" and we . . . Mine had horns sticking out of it . . . And I had baggy pants.

(adapted from Nelson & Fivush, 2004)

As this girl reaches adolescence, she will begin to link these kinds of memories to each other, and actively construct a timeline of her life (Habermas, Negele, & Mayer, 2010). By about age sixteen, she will use these events to reflect on her enduring personality ("This is the kind of person I am, as shown by how I felt at age 4 or 5 or 9"). Then she will have acheived that Eriksonian milestone—an *identity* she will carry through life (Fivush, 2011; more about this in Chapter 10).

Can parents take action during early childhood to promote identity formation in the teens? The fascinating answer may be yes. Caregivers, it turns out, differ in past-talk conversational styles. Some people do the minimum, either not talking about shared activities or just asking a question or two ("Where did we go yesterday?"). Others stimulate autobiographical memory by asking rich, open-ended questions: "What did we do at the park today?" " That's right, we went on the swing." "And who was with us?" "Did you have fun?" In one longitudinal study, adolescents whose mothers had been elaborate reminiscers a decade earlier had a richer autobiography and more memories of when they were young (Bauer & Fiviush, 2010; Fivush, 2011; Reese, Jack, & White, 2010).

As teenagers, our autobiographies become less external-fact oriented. We begin to describe important events in our life from other people's points of view (Pasupathi & Wainryb, 2010). When *does* the awareness that other people have different points of fully view lock in? Actually, this happens at around age 4, exactly when children first share events in their *own* lives!

Paul Avis/Getty Images

When they get home, this mother can help her daughter construct her "personal autobiography" by starting a dialogue about their wonderful day at the beach and—most important—encouraging the child to talk about her memories.

Making Sense of Other Minds

Listen to 3-year-olds having a conversation, and it's as if as if you are hearing two disconnected monologues, or mental ships passing in the night. Around age 4 or 5, children start relating in *give-and-take* ways. They have reached that human landmark called **theory of mind**, the understanding that we live in different heads (Lillard, 1998; Wellman, 1992). Developmentalists have a creative procedure to demonstrate this milestone—*the false-belief task*.

With a friend and a young child, see if you can perform this classic test for the presence of theory of mind in Figure 5.7 (Wimmer & Perner, 1983). Hide a toy in a place (location A) while the child and your friend watch. Then, have your friend leave the room. Once she is gone, move the toy to another hiding place (location

(1) Another adult and a young child watch while you hide a toy in a place like a desk drawer.

(2) The other adult [Ms. X] leaves the room.

(3) You hide the toy under the bed and then ask the child, "Where will Ms. X look for the toy?"

FIGURE 5.7: **The false-belief task:** In this classic test for *theory of mind,* when children under age 4 are asked, "Where will Ms. X look for the toy?" they are likely to say, "Under the bed," even though Ms. X could not possibly know the toy was moved to this new location.
Source: Based on Wimmer & Perner 1983.

B). Next, ask the child where *your friend* will look for the toy when she returns. If the child is under age 4, he will typically answer the second hiding place (location B), even though your friend could not possibly know the toy has been moved. It's as if the child doesn't grasp the fact that what *he* observed can't be in your friend's head, too.

What Are the Consequences and Roots of Theory of Mind?

Having a theory of mind is not only vital to having a give-and-take conversation, it is crucial to grasping a painful fact: Other people may not have your best interests at heart. One developmentalist had children play a game with "Mean Monkey," a puppet the experimenter controlled (Peskin, 1992). Beforehand, the researcher had asked the children which sticker they wanted. Then, she had Mean Monkey pick each child's favorite choice. Most 4-year-olds figured out how to play the game and told Mean Monkey the opposite of what they wanted. Three-year-olds never caught on. They always pointed to their favorite sticker and got the "yucky" one instead.

A remark from one of my students brings home the real-world message of this research. She commented that her 4-year-old nephew had reached the stage where he was beginning to tell lies. Under age 4, children don't fully have the mental abilities to understand that their parents don't know the thoughts in their head. So lying is an important cognitive advance! And, in fact, children who develop a theory of mind at a younger age do tell more sophisticated—less obvious—lies (Evans, Xu, & Lee, 2011).

The false-belief studies convinced developmentalists that Piaget's ideas about preoperational egocentrism had serious flaws. Although theory-of-mind abilities mature well into our teens (Dumontheil, Apperly, & Blakemore, 2010; Lagattuta, Sayfan, & Blattman, 2010; Samson & Apperly, 2010), children first grasp the principle that there are other minds out there far earlier than Piaget assumed. Even the age-4 marker is not accurate since children show signs of this vital ability before they can articulate their understanding in words (see Low, 2010).

To demonstrate this point, Renee Baillargeon and a colleague had toddlers watch two kinds of false-belief sequences (Onishi & Baillargeon, 2005). In one, the person who left and then returned looked for the hidden object in the place where she logically should have, in hiding place A. In the other, the person returned to look for the object in the second hiding place (location B). Even by 18 months of age, children appeared surprised when the adult looked in the second hiding place. It was as if they were thinking: "Hey, she wasn't in the room, so how could she know the object was moved?"

Actually, this finding comes as no surprise. Remember from Chapter 3, that even young infants grasp the basics of human motivations: "If that circle is mean to you, you shouldn't want to go to him!" Recall that *joint attention*—the tendency to follow a person's gaze or the direction of a pointing finger—occurs around age 1. So, mastering false-belief tasks is the end point of *gradual improvements* in the ability to "get into other people's heads," that begins during babyhood.

Do Individual Children (and Adults) Differ in Theory of Mind?

Interestingly, normally developing preschoolers around the world pass theory of mind tasks at roughly similar ages (around 4 or 5). However, perhaps because parent–child disagreements ("Mom, I won't do that!") are less acceptable in more collectivist cultures, Iranian and Chinese children take a bit longer to grasp the idea that people have conflicting opinions than do Western 4-year-olds (Shahaeian and others, 2011; see also Table 5.8 for some fascinating, neural findings related to theory of mind and the collectivist /individualistic distinction).

TABLE 5.8: Brain-Imaging Theory-of-Mind and Autobiographical-Memory Findings to Wrap your Head Around:

Reflecting on the self and others' mental states is a frontal-lobe activity involving slightly different brain regions: When people are asked to recall autobiographical memories or presented with self-referring stimuli such as their name, a brain region called the *medial frontal cortex* lights up. When given theory-of-mind–type tasks, a slightly different area of the medial frontal cortex is activated, which suggests that thinking about ourselves and other people's motivations involve distinctive (but closely aligned) brain areas.

Interesting cultural variation: While the above (slight) neural separation between self and other-person reflections applies to Westerners, the *identical* brain area lights up when Chinese adults think about themselves and their mothers. More astonishing, thinking about yourself and family members activates either the same or more separate brain regions, depending on whether you have a collectivist (interdependent) or individualistic (self-oriented) worldview.

Interesting variation from person to person: When you judge the mental state of someone you see as very much like you, such as a close friend, a closely aligned brain region lights up as when you are asked to reflect on yourself (as if you are drawing on your feelings about how you would respond in interpreting this person). But, inferring the mental states of dissimilar others—people you view as very different—activates truly separate brain areas. Imagining the feelings of disliked out-group members (e.g., as a Palestinian being asked to empathize with the perspective of a Jewish-Israeli West Bank settler) may elicit reduced activity in the "social" brain!

Conclusion: Our attitudes about the self in relationship to other human beings are mirrored in the physical architecture of our brain.

Sources: Abu-Akel & Shamay-Tsoory, 2011; Heatherington, 2011; Oddo and others, 2010; Rabin and others, 2010.

Conversely, perhaps because they have so much hands-on experience colliding (meaning arguing) with other minds—"Hey, I want that toy!" "No, I do!"—Western children with older siblings tend to pass theory-of-mind tasks at somewhat younger ages (Ruffman and others, 1998). Actually, as the youngest child in the family, you may need to develop your "mindreading" abilities to help you survive (Cummins & Allen, 1998). To illustrate, drawing on the Piaget discussion, after repeatedly being fooled, a 3-year-old might realize: "My big brother has a different agenda. When he tells me to take that big piece of money [the nickel], I'd better do the opposite of what he says!"

Being advanced intellectually, and having superior *executive functions,* also predicts earlier-than-average theory-of-mind skills (Samson & Apperly, 2010), which makes excellent sense because we need decent working-memory capacities to step back from our immediate perceptions and think, "OOPS, he has a different point of view." Most interestingly, bilingual preschoolers—because they must sensitively switch languages, depending on their conversation partner—also reach this social milestone at slightly younger ages. In fact—especially if a child is gifted—growing up bilingual or multilingual provides many cognitive benefits, from thinking more creatively to even *possibly* slowing the onset of Alzheimer's disease (Adi-Japha, Berberich-Artzi, & Libnawi, 2010; Chertkow and others, 2010; Cushen & Wiley, 2011).

Bill Aron/Photo Edit

For this intellectually advanced Latino girl, the challenge of switching to English to recite this poem to the class may provide a life-long cognitive boost.

On the other hand, having frontal-lobe damage (no surprise) can greatly impair theory- of-mind capacities (Geraci and others, 2010). But, the disorder most associated with "mind-blindness"—difficulties with theory of mind—is autism, that well-known impairment in the ability to socially relate (Baron-Cohen, 1999; Steele, Joseph, & Tager-Flusberg, 2003).

Does this mean that, in the absence of a pathological condition, our human mindreading abilities are firmly intact by age 4 or 5? The answer is no. Given the right conditions, you and I are apt to easily fail theory-of-mind tasks!

Imagine, for instance, being given instructions from the "director" on the opposite side of the display in Figure 5.8. You are shown his perspective, so you know he can't see the golf ball in the upper right hand corner because on his side that particular slot is obstructed. But when the director says, "Move the small ball left," almost half of all adult participants give an "egocentric" response. They move the ball only *they* can see rather than the correct tennis ball (Dumontheil, Apperly, & Blakemore, 2010).

Actually, whenever our working memory capacities are "otherwise engaged" (meaning, we are distracted), we all are prone to make mind-blind responses (Apperly and others, 2010; Lin, Keysar, & Epley, 2010). And, now, I must confess that yesterday I dismally failed the most basic theory-of-mind task. I left some tests to be copied in a secretary's box, but neglected to tell her whom the copies were for. I was in a hurry and automatically assumed that what was in my head (they're for me, of course) was in her head, too!

So far, we have just begun to explore our emerging sense of self and how we relate to other minds. Stay tuned for this next chapter, as I directly tackle these core human qualities by tracking personality and relationships as children move from preschool through elementary school.

FIGURE 5.8: **A task measuring theory of mind in adults:** In this study, adults are first shown the view of the man on the other side of this construction laden with objects that are sitting on partly occluded and fully open slots. Then they are told " Follow the director's instructions." When this man says, "Move the small ball left," many people make an egocentric response—moving the smallest golf ball that is only visible to them, rather than the tennis ball that only the director sees!
Source: Apperly and others, 2010.

TYING IT ALL TOGETHER

1. Andrew said to Madison, his 3-year-old son: "Remember when we went to Grandma and Grandpa's last year? . . . . It was your birthday, and what did Grandma make for you?" This ___________conversation will help scaffold Madison's _____________.
2. Pick the statement that would *not* signify that a child has developed a full-fledged theory of mind:
   a. He's having a real give-and-take conversation with you.
   b. He realizes that if you weren't there, you can't know what's gone on—and tries to explain to you what happened while you were absent.
   c. When he has done something he shouldn't do, he is likely to lie.
   d. He's learning to read.
3. Describe a recent example of mind-blindness in your own life.

Answers to the Tying It All Together questions can be found at the end of this chapter.

SUMMARY

Two Major Learning Challenges

Childhood comprises two phases—**early** and **middle childhood**—and this period of life lasts longer in our species than in any other animal. We need this time to absorb the lessons passed down by previous generations, and to take advantage of our finely tuned ability to decode intentions—the talent that has allowed us to advance. The **frontal lobes,** in particular, take two decades to become "adult." As this region of the brain—involved in reasoning and planning— develops, every childhood ability improves.

Physical Development

Physical growth slows down after infancy. Girls and boys are roughly the same height during preschool and much of elementary school. Boys are a bit more competent at **gross motor skills.** Girls are slightly superior in **fine motor skills.** Although cross-cultural studies suggest these biologically based skills can be accelerated through practice, we need to be careful not to push young children too hard. Undernutrition severely impairs motor skill development by making children too tired to exercise and play.

Rates of **childhood obesity**—defined by a high **body mass index (BMI)**—dramatically increased starting about 30 years ago, although the prevalence of this epidemic differs across nations and in specific demographic groups. The main cause for this modern scourge lies in toxic environmental forces (too little exercise, an abundance of tasty, calorie-dense foods, and so on). However, there also may be hidden prenatal influences involved in twenty-first-century child obesity, and later overweight can be predicted early in life. Prejudices against overweight children and adults are intense in the West. Today, parents (and young adults) may be responding by minimizing their children's weight issues and revising their own weight standards upward.

Cognitive Development

Piaget's preoperational stage lasts from about age 3 to 7. The concrete operational stage lasts from about age 8 to 11.

Preoperational thinkers focus on the way objects and substances (and people) immediately appear. **Concrete operational thinkers** can step back from their visual perceptions and reason on a more conceptual plane. In Piaget's **conservation tasks,** children in preoperations believe that when the shape of a substance has changed, the amount of it has changed. One reason is that young children lack the concept of **reversibility,** the understanding that an operation can be repeated in the opposite way. Another is that children **center** on what first captures their eye and cannot **decenter,** or focus on several dimensions at one time. Centering also affects **class inclusion** (understanding overarching categories) and **seriation** (putting objects in a series from small to big). Preoperational children believe that if something *looks* bigger visually, it always equals "more."

Preoperational children lack **identity constancy**—they don't understand that people are "the same" in spite of changes in external appearance. Their thinking is characterized by **animism** (the idea that inanimate objects are alive) and by **artificialism** (the belief that everything in nature was made by humans). They are **egocentric,** unable to understand that other people have different perspectives from their own. Although Piaget's ideas offer a wealth of insights into children's thinking, he underestimated what young children know. Children in every culture do progress from preoperational to concrete operational thinking—but the learning demands of the particular society make a difference in the age at which specific conservations are attained.

Lev Vygotsky, with his concept of the **zone of proximal development,** suggests that learning occurs when adults tailor instruction to a child's capacities and then use **scaffolding** to gradually promote independent performance. Education, according to Vygotsky, is a collaborative, bidirectional learning experience.

Information-processing theory provides another perspective on cognitive growth. In this framework on memory, material must be processed through a limited-capacity system, called **working memory,** in order to be recalled at a subsequent time. As children get older, their memory-bin capacity expands, and the executive processor fully comes on-line. These advances may explain why children reach concrete operations at age 7 or 8.

Executive functions—the ability to think through our actions and manage our cognitions—dramatically improve over time. Children adopt learning strategies such as **rehearsal.** They get better at **selective attention** and inhibiting their immediate responses. The research on rehearsal, selective attention, and inhibition provides a wealth of insights that can be applied in real life.

Attention deficit/hyperactivity disorder (ADHD), the most common childhood disorder in the United States, involves impairments in executive functions such as inhibition and selective attention, and presents widespread problems at home and school. This condition, usually diagnosed in elementary school (more often among boys), can have a bewildering array of pathways and possible brain causes. Treatments involve medication, parent training, providing white noise, exercise, and high-intensity games. Might the dramatic rise in ADHD be partly a product of a poor child and elementary school fit?

Language

Language makes every other childhood skill possible. Vygotsky believed that we learn everything through using **inner speech.** During early childhood, language abilities expand dramatically. **Phonemic** (sound articulation) abilities improve. As the number of **morphemes** in children's sentences increases, their **mean length of utterance (MLU)** expands. **Syntax,** or knowledge of grammatical rules, improves. **Semantic** understanding (vocabulary) shoots up. Common language mistakes young children make include **overregularization** (using regular forms for irregular verbs and nouns), **overextension** (applying word categories too broadly), and **underextension** (applying word categories too narrowly).

Specific Social Cognitive Skills

Autobiographical memories, the child's understanding of having a personal past, is socialized by caregivers through past-talk conversations during the first years of life. Questioning children about shared life events is key to putting them in touch with their personal autobiography. Specific autobiographical memories consolidate into a coherent identity during the teens.

Theory of mind, our knowledge that other people have different perspectives from our own, is measured by the false-belief task. Children around the world typically pass this milestone at about age 4 or 5, although the roots of this uniquely human ability appear before age 1. Cultural forces, having older siblings, superior intellectual abilities, and being bilingual predict the emergence of this vital skill. When our "working memory" is otherwise engaged, we adults are also prone to make mind-blind responses.

KEY TERMS

early childhood, p. 141
middle childhood, p. 141
frontal lobes, p. 142
gross motor skills, p. 144
fine motor skills, p. 144
body mass index (BMI), p. 145
childhood obesity, p. 145
preoperational thinking, p. 148
concrete operational thinking, p. 149
conservation tasks, p. 149
reversibility, p. 149
centering, p. 149
decentering, p. 149
class inclusion, p. 149
seriation, p. 149
identity constancy, p. 151
animism, p. 151
artificialism, p. 151
egocentrism, p. 152
zone of proximal development, p. 155
scaffolding, p. 155
working memory, p. 157
executive functions, p. 158
rehearsal, p. 158
selective attention, p. 158
attention deficit/hyperactivity disorder (ADHD), p. 160
inner speech, p. 163
phoneme, p. 163
morpheme, p. 163
mean length of utterance (MLU), p. 163
syntax, p. 163
semantics, p. 163
overregularization, p. 164
overextension, p. 164
underextension, p. 164
autobiographical memories, p. 165
theory of mind, p. 165

ANSWERS TO TYING IT ALL TOGETHER QUIZZES

Setting the Context

1. While your answers may be different, my thoughts include: Our sense of self-awareness and especially of having a continuous, enduring "self" and, of course, the related knowledge we will die; our sense of ethics and morality; our ability to use tools, walk on two feet, etc.
2. Ethan's *motor* cortex is on an earlier developmental timetable than his *frontal lobes*.
3. This is a disaster! Your colleague might have trouble with everything from regulating his physical responses, to analyzing problems, to inhibiting his actions.

Physical Development

1. (a) = mass-to-specific; (b) = cephalocaudal
2. Long-distance running and the high jump would be ideal for Jessica, as these sports heavily tap into gross motor skills.
3. The reason for this failure is that the whole environment today is overwhelmingly "obesogenic"!
4. Here, the answers are up to you: The pros, I believe, are emotional—no longer needing to adhere to unrealistic weight norms in the face of an obesogenic wider-world; the downside is accepting premature age-related disability, and a shorter lifespan (more about this topic in Chapter 14).

Cognitive Development

1. (a) = animism; (b) = egocentrism; (c) = artificialism; (d) = can't conserve; (e) = (no) identity constancy
2. Children in concrete operations can step back from their current perceptions and think conceptually, while preoperational children can't go beyond how things immediately appear.
3. b
4. 1) Following the play center rules to clean up, not take toys outside, and keep oneself from entering if there are four children; 2) having the class sit still and raise their hands to speak; 3) the dance slower and faster activity.
5. Don't put your son in demanding situations involving time management. When he studies, provide "white" background noise. Consistently use external rewards, such as prizes, to help your child focus. Get your son involved in sports or playing exciting games. Avoid power assertion (yelling and screaming), and go out of your way to provide lots of love.

Language

1. Vygotsky would say it's normal—the way children learn to think through their actions and control their behavior.
2. (b) = overregularization; (c) = overextension

Specific Cognitive Skills

1. This *past-talk* conversation will help stimulate Madison's *autobiographical memory.*
2. d
3. Here, your examples should involve times you forgot to explain things to someone that clearly needed explanations—given that this person was not in your head!

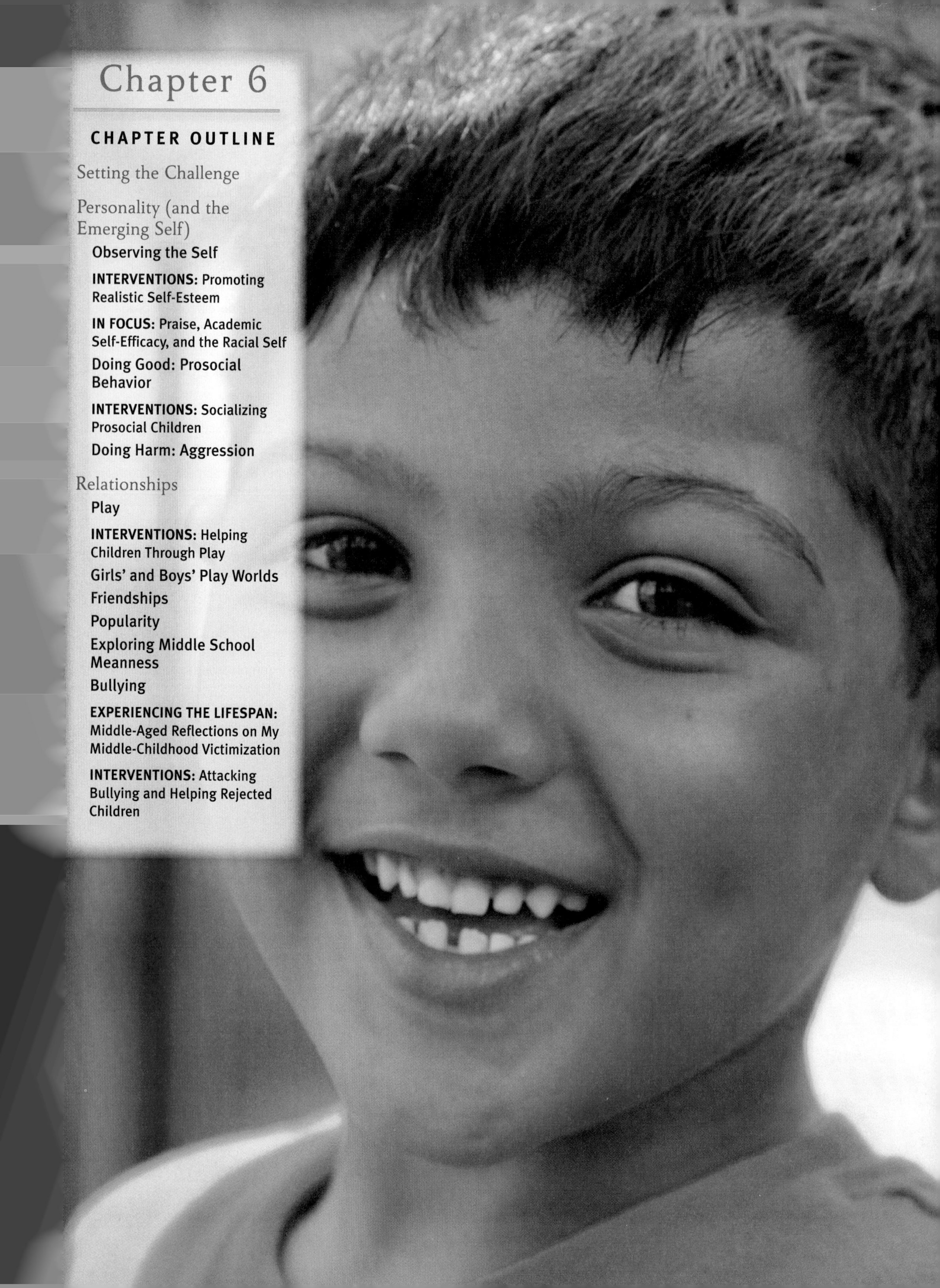

Chapter 6

CHAPTER OUTLINE

Setting the Challenge

Personality (and the Emerging Self)

- Observing the Self
- **INTERVENTIONS:** Promoting Realistic Self-Esteem
- **IN FOCUS:** Praise, Academic Self-Efficacy, and the Racial Self
- Doing Good: Prosocial Behavior
- **INTERVENTIONS:** Socializing Prosocial Children
- Doing Harm: Aggression

Relationships

- Play
- **INTERVENTIONS:** Helping Children Through Play
- Girls' and Boys' Play Worlds
- Friendships
- Popularity
- Exploring Middle School Meanness
- Bullying
- **EXPERIENCING THE LIFESPAN:** Middle-Aged Reflections on My Middle-Childhood Victimization
- **INTERVENTIONS:** Attacking Bullying and Helping Rejected Children

Socioemotional Development

It is recess at Black Fox Elementary School. Eight-year-old Manuel and his best friend Josh, the class leaders, burst into the yard and start a game of tag, with a ball. Soon six or seven other boys join in, having a great time, wrestling, jostling, chasing one another around. But then things get serious, changing fast and furiously. In comes Moriah, who had been hanging out with a small group of girls.

"Can I play?"

"No girls allowed!" say the boys.

Then Matt barges in, disrupting the game, shoving and hitting, taking over the ball. As usual, the children try to shut him out. A few minutes later, Jimmy, an anxious child who has few friends, tries to enter the group.

"Get out!" erupts Matt, "You wuss. You girl!"

Matt pushes Jimmy down and a few boys start to laugh. Jimmy starts to cry and slinks away. But suddenly, Manuel slows down.

"Hey, cool it, guys," he says. "Hey, man, are you all right? Come join us."

Manuel comforts Jimmy, manages to tell the other boys to lay off, and does his best to keep Matt from messing up the game without getting him too angry—as he knows from experience how that will turn out.

Have you ever wondered why some children, such as Manuel, are incredibly caring, while others, like Matt, seem insensitive, aggressive, and rude? Perhaps you are curious about what makes children popular or you want to help boys, like Jimmy and Matt, who are having problems with their peers. Have you puzzled over why boys love to wrestle or wondered why elementary schoolchildren love to hate the other sex? Maybe you simply want to understand your own and other people's behavior in a deeper way. If so, this chapter, covering children's emotional and social development, is for you.

In the following pages exploring personality and relationships, you'll be getting insights into the myriad challenges in *social cognition* that children face as they travel from preschool through elementary school. But this chapter has another purpose: To understand and help children such as Matt and Jimmy, who are having troubles relating in the world. With this goal in mind, let's begin by highlighting that fundamental human challenge—managing our emotions.

emotion regulation The capacity to manage one's emotional state.

externalizing tendencies A personality style that involves acting on one's immediate impulses and behaving disruptively and aggressively.

internalizing tendencies A personality style that involves intense fear, social inhibition, and often depression.

Setting the Challenge

In Chapter 5, you saw how the ability to inhibit and control our behavior underpins every childhood cognitive advance. We need the same *executive function* skills to succeed socially and emotionally, too. When we get angry, we must cool down our feelings, rather than lash out. We have to overcome our anxieties and talk to that scary professor, or conquer our shyness and go to a party because we might meet that special person who will be the love of our life. **Emotion regulation** is the term developmentalists use for the skills involved in managing our feelings so that they don't get in the way of a productive life.

Children with **externalizing tendencies** have special trouble with this challenge. Like Matt in the introductory chapter vignette, they act on their immediate emotions and often behave disruptively and aggressively. Perhaps you know a child who bursts into every social scene, fighting, bossing people around, wreaking havoc with his classmates and adults.

Children with **internalizing tendencies** have the opposite problem. They are flooded with intense anxiety. Like Jimmy, they may hang back in social situations. They are timid and self-conscious, frightened and depressed.

The beauty of being human is that we vary in our temperamental tendencies—to be shy or active, boisterous or reserved. In collectivist cultures such as India, that put a premium on being self-effacing, shyness is not necessarily a social liability (Bowker & Raja, 2011). In our individualistic society, being aggressive can be a real social plus. But having serious trouble *controlling* one's aggression or anxiety puts children around the world at a disadvantage (Chen & French, 2008; Prakash & Coplan, 2007). Externalizing and internalizing tendencies—at their extremes—present universal barriers to succeeding with people and in life.

In Chapter 4, you learned about the temperaments that put toddlers at risk for having these emotion regulation issues—being highly exuberant or inhibited. Now, let's look at what happens if these tendencies evolve to the point where they cause genuine suffering during the childhood years.

TYING IT ALL TOGETHER

1. Krista, a school psychologist, is concerned about two students: Paul, who bursts out in rage and is continually misbehaving; and Jeremy, who is timid, anxious, and sad. Krista describes Paul as having *internalizing/externalizing* tendencies and Jeremy as having *internalizing/externalizing tendencies*, and she says that issues with emotion regulation are a problem for *Paul/Jeremy/both boys*.

Answers to the Tying It All Together questions can be found at the end of this chapter.

Personality (and the Emerging Self)

As they get older, how do children's perceptions about themselves change and how do these changes affect self-esteem? What makes children (and adults) act in caring or hurtful ways?

Observing the Self

Developmentalist Susan Harter (1999) has explored the first questions in her research program examining how children view themselves. To make sense of her findings, Harter draws on Piaget's distinction between preoperational and concrete operational thinking—a difference I will be highlighting throughout this chapter. So let's take another look at the mental leap that Piaget believes takes place when children reach age 7 or 8.

Children in the concrete operational stage:

- Look beyond immediate appearances and think abstractly about inner states.
- Give up their egocentrism and realize they are but one person among many others in this vast world.

To examine how these changes affect **self-awareness**—the way children reflect on who they are as people—Harter asks boys and girls of different ages to describe themselves. Here are two examples illustrating the responses she finds:

> I am 3 years old and I live in a big house. . . . I have blue eyes and a kitty that is orange. . . . I love my dog Skipper. . . . I'm always happy. I have brown hair. . . . I'm really strong.
>
> I'm in fourth grade this year, and I'm pretty popular. . . .That's because I'm nice to people and can keep secrets, although if I get into a bad mood I sometimes say something that can be a little mean. At school I'm feeling pretty smart in . . . Language Arts and Social Studies. . . . But I'm feeling pretty dumb in Math and Science. . . . Even though I'm not doing well in those subjects I still like myself as a person.
>
> (adapted from Harter, 1999, pp. 37, 48)

Notice that the 3-year-old talks about herself in terms of external facts. The fourth grader's descriptions are internal and psychological, anchored in her feelings, abilities, and inner traits. The 3-year-old describes herself in totally unrealistic, positive ways as "always happy." The fourth grader lists her deficiencies and strengths in many areas of life. Moreover, while the younger child talks about herself as if she were living in a bubble, the older child focuses on how she measures up compared to her classmates. So Harter believes that when they reach concrete operations, children can realistically evaluate their abilities and decide whether they like or dislike the person they see. **Self-esteem**—the tendency to feel good or bad about ourselves—first becomes a *major issue* during elementary school.

Actually, studies around the world show that self-esteem tends to decline during early elementary school (Frey & Ruble, 1985, 1990; Harter & Pike, 1984; Super & Harkness, 2003). A mother may sadly notice this change when her 8-year-old daughter starts to make comments such as, "I am not pretty" or "I can't do math." ("What happened to that self-confident child who used to feel she was the most beautiful, intelligent kid in the world?") Caring teachers struggle with the same comparisons, the fact that their fourth graders are exquisitely sensitive to who is popular, which classmates are getting A's, and who needs special academic help.

Harter's research beautifully dovetails with Erik Erikson's early and middle childhood developmental tasks. Erikson, as you can see in Table 6.1, labeled the preschool psychosocial challenge as **initiative versus guilt.** Children's mission at this age, he believed, is to courageously test their abilities in the wider world. From risking racing

self-awareness The ability to observe our abilities and actions from an outside frame of reference and to reflect on our inner state.

self-esteem Evaluating oneself as either "good" or "bad" as a result of comparing the self to other people.

initiative versus guilt Erik Erikson's term for the preschool psychosocial task involving actively taking on life tasks.

TABLE 6.1: Erikson's Psychosocial Stages

Life Stage	Primary Task
Infancy (birth to 1 year)	Basic trust versus mistrust
Toddlerhood (1 to 2 years)	Autonomy versus shame and doubt
Early childhood (3 to 6 years)	**Initiative versus guilt**
Middle childhood (6 years to puberty)	**Industry versus inferiority**
Adolescence (teens into twenties)	Identity versus role confusion
Young adulthood (twenties to early forties)	Intimacy versus isolation
Middle adulthood (forties to sixties)	Generativity versus stagnation
Late adulthood (late sixties and beyond)	Integrity versus despair

In Erikson's framework, during preschool our agenda is to take the initiative to try out our skills in the wider world. During elementary school (see next page), our task is to learn to work for what we want.

© Robert Dant/Alamy

Maria Sweeney/Getty Images

Exuberantly taking off on your tricycle versus listening to the teacher and making sure you have finished your homework before raising your hand in class captures the essential difference between Erikson's *initiative* and *industry* tasks. It also shows why early childhood is a magical Garden of Eden interlude, before we enter the real world (a.k.a. concrete operations) and face the need to "work."

your tricycle in the street to scaling the school monkey bars, our challenge in early childhood is taking the initiative to confront life.

In middle childhood (from age 6 to 12) this agenda shifts. Now, our task is **industry versus inferiority**—the need to manage our emotions and work for what we want to achieve (industry). Now, we know that we are not just wonderful, and we are vulnerable to low self-esteem—or inferiority—having the painful sense that we don't measure up. In other words, the price of leaving the preoperational bubble, or early childhood Garden of Eden, is becoming realistically aware of our abilities and the demands of living in the "real world."

Still, all is not lost because this new, realistic understanding of ourselves and life produces another change. Notice how the fourth grader on page 175 compares her abilities in different areas such as personality and school. As they get older, this means children's self-esteem doesn't hinge on one quality. Even if they are not doing well in one area, they can take comfort in the places where they really shine.

According to Harter, children draw on five areas to determine their self-esteem: *scholastic competence* (academic talents); *behavioral conduct* (obedience or being "good"); *athletic skills* (performance at sports); *peer likeability* (popularity); and *physical appearance* (looks). To diagnose how a child feels in each domain, Harter devised the kinds of questions in Figure 6.1.

As you might expect, children who view themselves as "not so good" in several domains often report low self-esteem. However, to really understand a given child's self-esteem, it is important to know that person's priorities—the value that boy or girl attaches to doing well in a particular area of life.

To understand this point, take a minute to rate yourself in your people skills, politeness or good manners, your intellectual abilities, looks, and your physical abilities. If you label yourself "not so good" in an area you don't care about (for me, it would be physical skills), it won't make a dent in your self-esteem. If you care deeply about some area where you feel deficient, you would get pretty depressed.

This discounting process ("It doesn't matter if I'm not a scholar; I have great relationship skills") is vitally important. It lets us gain self-esteem from the areas in which we shine. The problem is that some children take this discounting to an extreme—minimizing their problems in *essential* areas of life.

Two Kinds of Self-Esteem Distortions

Normally, we base our self-esteem on the signals we receive from the outside world: "Am I succeeding or not doing so well?" However, when children with externalizing problems *are* failing—for instance, being rejected or performing poorly at school—they may deny reality (Chung-Hall & Chen, 2010) and blame others to preserve their unrealistically high self-worth (Diamantopoulou, Rydell, & Henricsson, 2008; Miller & Daniel, 2007). Perhaps you know an adult whose anger gets him into regular trouble at home and at work, but who copes by taking the position, "I'm wonderful. It's all their fault." Because this person seems impervious to his flaws and has such difficulty regulating his emotions, he cannot change his behavior and so ensures that he continues to fail.

Children with internalizing tendencies have the opposite problem. Their hypersensitivity to negative environmental cues (recall Chapter 4) may cause them to read failure into benign events. ("My teacher obviously hates me because she looked at me the wrong way.") They are at risk of developing **learned helplessness** (Abramson, Seligman, & Teasdale, 1978), the feeling that they are powerless to affect their fate. They may give up at the starting gate, assuming, "I know I'm going to fail, so why should I try?"

So children and adults with externalizing and internalizing tendencies face a similar danger—but for different reasons. When people minimize their real-world

industry versus inferiority Erik Erikson's term for the psychosocial task of middle childhood involving managing our emotions and realizing that real-world success involves hard work.

learned helplessness A state that develops when a person feels incapable of affecting the outcome of events, and so gives up without trying.

An examiner points to a girl to a preschooler's right and says, "This girl isn't good at doing puzzles." She then points to a girl to the child's left and says, "This girl is good at doing puzzles." Then she asks the child to point to the appropriate circle under each girl. If "this really fits me," the child points to the large circle. If "this fits me a little bit," the child points to the small circle.

Really True for Me	Sort of True for Me				Sort of True for Me	Really True for Me
☐	☐	Some kids are often *unhappy* with themselves.	BUT	Other kids are pretty *pleased* with themselves.	☐	☐
☐	☐	Some kids feel like they are *just as smart* as other kids their age.	BUT	Other kids aren't so sure and *wonder* if they are as smart.	☐	☐

Here the elementary schoolchild reads the items and checks the box that applies to her.

FIGURE 6.1: **How do children view themselves?:** Harter has devised this questionnaire format to measure children's feelings of competence in her five different areas of life. The item in the top panel is derived from Harter's scale designed for young children; the questions in the bottom panel are from a similar scale for elementary school children.

Source: Harter, 1999, pp. 121–122.

difficulties or assume they are incompetent, they cut off the chance of working to change their behavior and so ensure that they *will* fail.

Table 6.2 summarizes these self-esteem problems and their real-world consequences. Then, Table 6.3 offers a checklist, based on Harter's five dimensions, for

TABLE 6.2: **Externalizing and Internalizing Problems, Self-Esteem Distortions, and Consequences—A Summary Table**

Description	Self-Esteem Distortion	Consequence
CHILDREN WITH EXTERNALIZING PROBLEMS		
Act out "emotions," are impulsive and often aggressive.	May ignore real problems and have unrealistically high self-esteem.	Continue to fail because they don't see the need to improve.
CHILDREN WITH INTERNALIZING PROBLEMS		
Are intensely fearful.	Can read failure into everything and have overly low self-esteem.	Continue to fail because they decide that they cannot succeed and stop working.

Nicholas Prior/Getty Images

According to Susan Harter, even when they are failing in other areas of life, children can sometimes derive their self-esteem from the skills in which they shine. Do you think this girl can use this science prize to feel good about herself, even if she understands that she is not very popular with the other kids?

TABLE 6.3: Identifying Your Self-Esteem Distortions: A Checklist Using Harter's Five Domains

You have externalizing issues if you regularly have thoughts like these:

1. **Academics:** "When I get poor grades, it's because my teachers don't give good tests or teach well." "I have very little to learn from other people." "I'm much smarter than practically everyone else I know."
2. **Physical skills:** "When I play baseball, soccer, etc., and my team doesn't win, it's my teammates' fault, not mine." "I believe it's OK to take physical risks, such as not wearing a seatbelt or running miles in the hot sun, because I know I won't get hurt." "It's all statistics, so I shouldn't be concerned about smoking four packs a day or about drinking a six-pack of beer every night."
3. **Relationships:** "When I have trouble at work or with my family, it's typically my co-workers' or family's fault." "My son (or mate, friend, mother) is the one causing all the conflict between us."
4. **Physical appearance:** "I don't think I have to work to improve my appearance because I'm basically gorgeous."
5. **Conduct:** "I should be able to come to work late (or turn in papers after the end of the semester, talk in class, etc.)." "Other people are too uptight. I have a right to behave any way I want to."

Diagnosis: You are purchasing high self-esteem at the price of denying reality. Try to look at the impact of your actions more realistically and take steps to change.

You have internalizing issues if you regularly have thoughts like these:

1. **Academics:** "I'm basically stupid." "I can't do well on tests." "My memory is poor." "I'm bound to fail at science." "I'm too dumb to get through college." "I'll never be smart enough to get ahead in my career."
2. **Physical skills:** "I can't play basketball (or some other sport) because I'm uncoordinated or too slow." "I'll never have the willpower to exercise regularly (or stick to a diet, stop smoking, stop drinking, or stop taking drugs)."
3. **Relationships:** "I don't have any people skills." "I'm doomed to fail in my love life." "I can't be a good mother (or spouse or friend)."
4. **Physical appearance:** "I'm basically unattractive." "People are born either good-looking or not, and I fall into the not category." "There is nothing I can do to improve my looks."
5. **Conduct:** "I'm incapable of being on time (or getting jobs done or stopping talking in class)." "I can't change my tendency to rub people the wrong way."

Diagnosis: Your excessively low self-esteem is inhibiting your ability to succeed. Work on reducing your helpless and hopeless attitudes and try for change.

evaluating yourself. Are there areas where you gloss over your deficiencies? Do you have pockets of learned helplessness that prevent you from living a full life?

Giving this child "good boy" stars just to boost his self-esteem is likely to backfire—making him think "I'm the greatest" no matter how he behaves!

Michael Newman/Photo Edit, Inc.

INTERVENTIONS: Promoting Realistic Self-Esteem

This discussion shows why school programs focused *just* on raising self-esteem—those devoted to instilling the message, "You are a terrific kid"—are missing the boat (Baumeister and others, 2003; Swann, Chang-Schneider, & McClarty, 2007). Drawing on Erikson's theory, true self-esteem is derived from "industry"—taking action to work for our goals. Therefore, when children are having difficulties in a vital life domain, it's important to 1) enhance *self-efficacy*, or the feeling, "I can succeed if I work" (Miller & Daniel, 2007) and 2) promote *realistic* perceptions about the self. As a caring adult, how might you carry out this two-pronged approach?

ENHANCING SELF-EFFICACY. Using Lev Vygotsky's terminology, one key to fostering self-efficacy is to enter a child's *proximal zone* and put success within striking distance of the developing self. So, if a fourth grader—let's say, like Jimmy in the introductory chapter vignette—is very shy, you might move him to a more nurturing, less competitive class. If a second grader has problems reading, you first would determine the child's actual skill level, and then tailor your teaching upward from that point, regularly reinforcing that boy or girl for each small success.

As developmentalist Carol Dweck has demonstrated, one key to enhancing academic self-efficacy is to praise children for effort ("You are trying so hard!"), rather than to make comments about basic ability ("You are incredibly smart!"). In her studies, elementary schoolers, who were praised for being "very intelligent" after successfully completing problems, later had *lower* self-efficacy. They were afraid to tackle other challenging tasks ("I'd better not try this or everyone might learn I'm really dumb!") (Molden & Dweck, 2006; Mueller & Dweck, 1998).

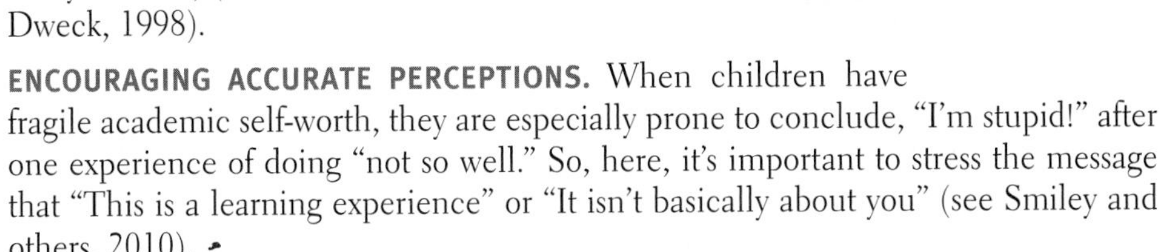

Bill Aron/ Photo Edit

How can this teacher get her fourth grader to tackle challenging new school tasks? Praise him for effort ("You are such a brave, hard worker") rather than making comments like "You are a basically brilliant kid."

ENCOURAGING ACCURATE PERCEPTIONS. When children have fragile academic self-worth, they are especially prone to conclude, "I'm stupid!" after one experience of doing "not so well." So, here, it's important to stress the message that "This is a learning experience" or "It isn't basically about you" (see Smiley and others, 2010).

For children with internalizing tendencies, who unrealistically see themselves as failing in *most* life realms, it's crucial to vigorously provide accurate feedback: "The teacher doesn't hate you. She was just in a bad mood yesterday." And, if a child with externalizing tendencies discounts his failures at the price of preserving an inflated sense of self-esteem, gently point out reality, too: Using the example of Matt in the chapter introductory vignette, for instance, you might say, "The kids don't like you when you barge in and take over those games" (Thomaes, Stegge, & Olthof, 2007).

There is a way of softening this painful "You are not doing so well message" that is the price of realistically seeing the self. Harter (1999, 2006) finds that feeling loved by their attachment figures provides a cushion when children understand they are having trouble in an important area of life. So, returning to the beginning of this section, school programs (and adults) that stress the message "I care about you," plus foster self-efficacy ("You can succeed if you work hard"), are the key to promoting *true* self-esteem (Miller & Daniel, 2007).

IN FOCUS: Praise, Academic Self-Efficacy, and the Racial Self

Until now, I've given you the impression that unless children have genuine externalizing or internalizing problems, being praised for real-world success promotes high (and realistic) self-worth. Sadly, this is not always true.

Researchers set up a situation in which African American and White college students succeeded at an academic task. Then, the White tester either gave the students praise ("Terrific job!") or neutral feedback ("Let's go on"). The White students interpreted praise in the way we would expect: "This person thinks I am smart. I like her." The Black students were apt to report: "She's only complimenting me because she believes that African Americans aren't smart. This person is condescending and impolite" (Lawrence, Crocker, & Blanton, 2011).

This depressing finding points up the double whammy Black children may face once becoming aware of negative racial academic stereotypes. Unable to trust feedback from nonminority adults thrusts people into a strange, non-reality-oriented, preoperational place ("Am I *really* doing well, or is she being kind because she thinks I'm dumb?"). Worse yet, minority children may develop learned helplessness if they apply the stereotypes to themselves: "African Americans (like me) are less intelligent. Why should I try in school?"

When does the awareness of negative racial stereotypes fully emerge? Not unexpectedly, stereotype knowledge rises dramatically during concrete operations and is solidly in place for most African American children by age 10. Moreover, if a given Black elementary schooler was aware of the stereotypes—this research showed—that child did perform more poorly on a test if it was labeled as measuring basic intellectual abilities (McKown & Strambler, 2009; see also Steele & Aronson, 1995, for related research).

Michael Newman/Photo Edit, Inc.

By emphasizing that our world-class intellectual role models often come from marginalized ethnic groups, this third-grade teacher is promoting academic self-efficacy in *all* of her students, no matter what their race. Plus, she is providing this teaching lesson at just the right age (early concrete operations).

The pressures promoting poor school performance can intensify during the teen years. If a Black or Mexican heritage adolescent attends a high-status, mainly nonminority school, there can be negative social consequences attached to getting good grades: "That kid is acting White"; "He's selling out" (Fuller-Rowell & Doan, 2010). Therefore, racial stereotypes can cause Black children to 1) distrust teachers' feedback, 2) develop learned helplessness (decide they are dumb), and 3) devalue their "academic selves."

This doesn't have to happen. Among African American third graders, one study showed, feeling good about one's racial identity correlated with *better* academic skills (Smith and others, 2009). Therefore, the best strategy may be to carefully teach about race in an inclusive, realistic, and positive way (Wegmann & Bowen, 2010). To foster self-efficacy in *all children*, emphasize those brilliant Black role models who overcame academic adversity through hard work!

Now that we've explored children's self-perceptions, it's time to focus on two qualities that make us human: our tendencies to act in caring and then hurtful ways.

Neville Elder/Corbis Sygma

What qualities made hundreds of New York City firefighters run into the burning Twin Towers on September 11, knowing that they might be facing death? This is the kind of question that developmentalists who study prosocial behavior want to answer.

Doing Good: Prosocial Behavior

On the morning of September 11, 2001, the nation was riveted by the heroism of the firefighters who ran into the World Trade Center buildings, risking almost certain death. We marveled at the "ordinary people" working in the Twin Towers, whose response to this emergency was to help others get out first.

Prosocial behavior is the term developmentalists use to describe such amazing acts of self-sacrifice as well as the minor acts of caring that people perform during daily life. Prosocial behaviors are fully in swing by preschool (Eisenberg, 2003; Kochanska and others, 2010a; Svetlova, Nichols, & Brownell, 2010): Children help the teacher clean up the blocks; they share their toys and give their cookie to a friend.

Prosocial activities become more frequent during elementary school (Fabes and others, 1996). Concrete operational children are more prone to act prosocially because they have better skills. They can get a bandage when their friend cuts her finger and immediately call a responsible adult for help. By this age, children also have the perspective-taking skills to understand who will best comfort their injured friend—deciding, for instance, "She'll feel better if I call her dad, rather than contacting my own father or even calling 911."

Individual and Cultural Variations

Amidst these normal developmental changes lie fascinating individual differences. Developmentalists measured how often preschoolers engaged in sharing and helping activities, then followed these boys and girls until they were adults. Children, they discovered, who showed high rates of spontaneous sharing at ages 3 and 4,

prosocial behavior Sharing, helping, and caring actions.

were ranked more prosocial in elementary school, adolescence, and also in young adulthood (Eisenberg and others, 1999). So, if your 4-year-old niece seems unusually caring, she may indeed grow up to be a caring adult.

If people differ in their prosocial tendencies, do cultures? Are children in less individualistic societies more prosocial than in the West? Making culture-by-culture comparisons is risky because, in some collectivist societies, children may be socialized to be prosocial within their family or group and incredibly callous (or genocidal) to "outsiders" (Eisenberg & Fabes, 1998). What we can say is that in non-Western cultures, specific kinds of prosocial behaviors, such as sacrificing one's own desires to help one's parents, are more of a norm (Chen & French, 2008; Eisenberg and others, 2006). In Asian nations that put a premium on modesty, it's less acceptable to take credit for one's prosocial acts.

Researchers revealed this enduring cultural difference when they gave Japanese and American children a scenario in which a boy did a good deed: "Because Timmy didn't have lunch money, Mark put his own cash in his classmate's desk". When asked how Mark should respond if the teacher asked the class,"Who did this kind thing?", Japanese students were more apt to say, "Mark should lie and say it wasn't me" (Heyman, Itakura, & Lee, 2011).

This study brings up an interesting point: Does broadcasting our prosocial acts ever *really* qualify as being prosocial?

altruism Prosocial behaviors that are carried out for selfless, non-egocentric reasons.

empathy Feeling the exact emotion that another person is experiencing.

sympathy A state necessary for acting prosocially, involving feeling upset *for* a person who needs help.

Mary Kate Denny/Photo Edit, Inc.

Will this caring 3-year-old become an especially prosocial adult? According to the research described in the text, her chances are good.

Decoding Altruism

Actually, we all act prosocially for very non-prosocial reasons: for praise ("I'll lend Timmy money because the teacher will think I am generous"); out of fear of punishment ("I'd better help Timmy because otherwise he'll be furious"); or for the well-known motive for adult "charitable donations," to show how successful we are ("If I give a Belsky Building to the college, everyone will know I'm very rich"). Genuinely prosocial behaviors involve **altruism.** They are motivated by the desire to help *apart* from getting external rewards. Acting altruistically, in turn, depends on experiencing a specific emotional state (Eisenberg, 1992, 2003).

Empathy is the term developmentalists use for directly feeling another person's emotion. You get anxious when you hear your boss berating a co-worker. You were overcome by horror as you saw a video of the Twin Towers go down.

Sympathy is the more muted feeling that we experience *for* another human being. You feel terrible *for* your co-worker, but don't feel her intense distress. Your heart went out to the people who were trapped in the Twin Towers that day. Rather than empathy, developmentalists argue, sympathy is related to behaving in an altruistic way (Eisenberg, 1992, 2003; Trommsdorff, Friedlmeier, & Mayer, 2007).

The reason is that experiencing another person's distress can provoke a variety of reactions, from becoming immobilized with fear to behaving in a far-from-caring way. We can vividly see this when, out of empathic embarrassment, we burst out laughing after a waiter spills a restaurant tray, or become paralyzed by terror as we see a highway crash. So to act altruistically, children need to use their emotion-regulating capacities to mute their empathic feelings into a sympathetic response (Eisenberg, 1992; Liew and others, 2011).

Behaving altruistically also involves having the *information-processing* skills to consider different alternatives and select a prosocial act. It requires feeling confident about being able to help. Just as

To respond altruistically to his injured playmate, this boy had to transform his empathy into sympathy, and, as you will see on the next page, also had to feel confident that he could take action to help.

Michael Newman/Photo Edit, Inc.

I would probably not run into a burning building unless I was a firefighter, the reason children in elementary school typically give for not acting prosocially is that they lack the skills (Denham, 1998; Eisenberg & Fabes, 1998). So, interestingly, children who are highly fearful (those prone to internalizing disorders), as well as those who are relatively non-empathic (children with externalizing problems), tend to be less prosocial than their peers (Liew and others, 2011; Saarni, 1999).

Finally, people act prosocially when they are happy; which explains why, when we are immersed in our own problems, we are unlikely to reach out to a friend. It gives us another reason why children with serious internalizing or externalizing problems are less likely to behave in prosocial ways (Eisenberg & Fabes, 1998).

To summarize, in predicting "Who will act prosocial?" we might ask: "Does this child have superior executive functions?" "Does he have the concrete skills to help?" "Is she a confident, upbeat human being?"

Actually, twin studies suggest that the tendency to be prosocial is somewhat "genetic." Children may be biologically predisposed to either act caring or to be callous and relatively immune to people's distress (Gregory and others, 2009; Rowe and others, 2010). What can adults do to help promote a prosocial self?

INTERVENTIONS: Socializing Prosocial Children

Giving concrete reinforcements, such as a big prize, for being helpful, as it turns out, is relatively ineffective. (In order to teach altruism, it doesn't make sense to provide a self-centered motive to be kind!) What works best is to pay attention to prosocial acts and attribute them to the child's personality—for instance, saying, "You really are a caring person for doing that," instead of "That was a nice thing you did" (Eisenberg, 2003). So if you regularly comment on the kind things your niece does *and* get her to define herself as a "kind person," you may help socialize her into becoming a caring adult (see Kochanska and others, 2010b).

Most studies exploring prosocial behavior center on a discipline style called **induction** (Hoffman, 1994, 2001). Caregivers who use induction scaffold altruism. When a child has done something hurtful, they point out the ethical issue and try to promote the development of an other-centered, sympathetic response. Now, imagine that classic situation when your 8-year-old daughter has invited everyone in class but Sara to her birthday party. Instead of punishing your child—or giving that other classic response "Kids will be kids"—here's what you should say: "It's hurtful to leave just Sara out. Think of how terrible she must feel!"

Induction has several virtues: It offers children concrete feedback about exactly what they did wrong and moves them off of focusing on their own punishment ("Now, I'm really going to get it!") to the *other* child's distress ("Oh, gosh, she must feel hurt"). Induction also allows for reparations, the chance to make amends. The bottom line is that induction works because it stimulates the emotion called guilt.

induction The ideal discipline style for socializing prosocial behavior, involving getting a child who has behaved hurtfully to empathize with the pain he has caused the other person.

shame A feeling of being personally humiliated.

guilt Feeling upset about having caused harm to a person or about having violated one's internal standard of behavior.

Shame Versus Guilt and Prosocial Acts

Think back to an event during childhood when you felt terrible about yourself. Perhaps it was the day you were caught cheating and sent to the principal. What you may remember was feeling so ashamed. Developmentalists, however, distinguish between feeling ashamed and experiencing guilt. **Shame** is the primitive feeling we have when we are *personally* humiliated. **Guilt** is the more sophisticated emotion we experience when we have violated a personal moral standard or hurt another human being.

I believe that Erikson may have been alluding to this maturity difference when he labeled "shame" as the emotion we experience as toddlers, and reserved "guilt" for the feeling that arises during preschool, when our drive to master the world causes other people distress (see Table 6.1 on page 175). While shame and guilt are both "self-conscious" relationship-oriented emotions, they have opposing effects. Shame causes us to withdraw from people, to slink away, and crawl into a hole (Thomaes, Stegge, & Olthof, 2007). We feel furious at being humiliated and want to strike back. Guilt connects us to people. We feel terrible about what we have done, and try to make amends. So, shame diminishes us. Guilt—*in moderation* (see Soenens & Vansteenkiste, 2010)—can cause us to emotionally enlarge (Tangney, 2003).

This suggests that socialization techniques involving shame are especially poisonous. If, when you arrived at the principal's office, he shamed you ("In the next school assembly, I'll announce what a terrible person you are!"), you might change your behavior, but at an emotional price. You would feel humiliated. You might decide you hated school. But if the principal induced guilt ("I feel disappointed because you're such a good kid"), you could act to enhance self-efficacy ("Dr. Jones, what can I do to make it up?"). You might end up feeling better about yourself and more connected to school. Has feeling guilty and apologizing ever made you feel closer to someone you love?

Table 6.4 summarizes these section messages and offers an additional tip. And, for readers who are thinking, "I'm prosocial, even though I didn't grow up in that kind of home," there is the reality that people can draw on intensely shaming childhood experiences to construct highly prosocial lives. Perhaps you have a friend who grew up in an abusive family whose mission it is to work with abused children or (like me) have been privileged to meet childhood survivors of Hitler's holocaust who have devoted their lives to teaching young people "never again!" Then you will realize that, while love is the best prosocial socializer, life's adversities can promote exceptional altruism, too (more about this compelling topic in Chapter 12).

Now that we have analyzed what makes us do good (the angel side of personality), let's enter the darker side of human nature: aggression.

China Tourism Press/Getty Images

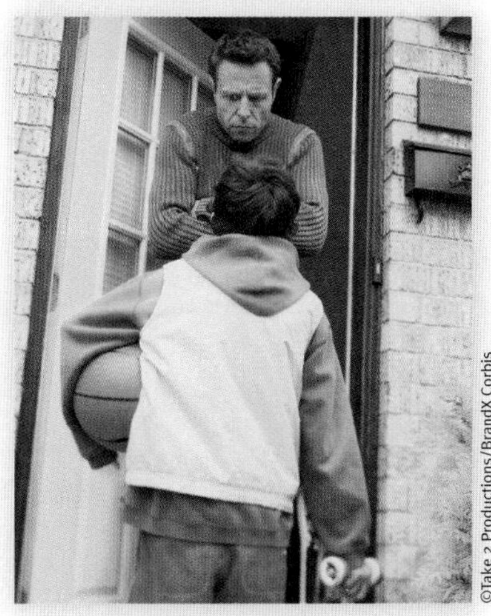

©Take 2 Productions/BrandX Corbis

When parents, like this father use *shame* to discipline, a child's impulse is to get furious. But by pointing out how disappointed she is in her "good girl," the mother in the photograph at the top can produce *guilt*—and so ultimately have a more prosocial child.

Doing Harm: Aggression

Aggression refers to acts designed to cause harm, from shaming to shoving, from gossiping to starting unprovoked wars. It should come as no surprise that physical aggression reaches its life peak at around age 2 1/2 (Dodge, Coie, & Lynam, 2006; van Aken and others, 2008). During this critical age for socialization, children are vigorously being disciplined but don't have the capacity to inhibit their responses. Imagine being a toddler continually ordered by giants to do impossible things, such as sharing and sitting still. Because being frustrated provokes aggression, it makes perfect sense that hitting, and throwing tantrums are normal during "the terrible twos."

TABLE 6.4: How to Produce Prosocial Children: A Summary Table

- Pay attention to kind behaviors. Then when a child has done something kind and considerate, tell him that he is "really a caring person."
- Avoid giving children treats or special privileges to reward prosocial acts. Instead, praise the child effusively and point out the positive impact of her behavior.
- When the child has hurt another person, use induction: Clearly point out the moral issue, and alert him to how the other person must feel.
- Avoid teasing and shaming. When the child has done something wrong, tell her you are disappointed and give her a chance to make amends.
- Don't think that you have fulfilled your responsibility to teach altruism by having a child participate in school or church drives to help the unfortunate. Morality isn't magically learned on Sunday. It must be taught in an ongoing way during *day-to-day* life.

aggression Any hostile or destructive act.

instrumental aggression A hostile or destructive act initiated to achieve a goal.

reactive aggression A hostile or destructive act carried out in response to being frustrated or hurt.

relational aggression A hostile or destructive act designed to cause harm to a person's relationships.

As preschoolers become more skilled at regulating their emotions and can make better sense of adults' rules, rates of open aggression (yelling or hitting) dramatically decline (Dishion & Tipsord, 2011). As children get older, the reasons for aggression change. Preschool fights center on objects, such as toys. During elementary school, when children have developed a full-fledged sense of self-esteem, aggression becomes personal. We strike out when we are wounded as human beings (Coie & Dodge, 1998). How do researchers categorize aggressive acts?

Types of Aggression

One way developmentalists classify aggression is by its motive. **Instrumental aggression** refers to hurtful behavior that is initiated to achieve a goal. Johnny kicks Manuel to gain possession of the block pile. Sally spreads a rumor about Moriah to replace her as Sara's best friend. **Reactive aggression** occurs in response to being hurt, threatened, or deprived. Manuel, infuriated at Johnny, kicks him back.

Its self-determined nature gives instrumental aggression a calculated, "cooler" emotional tone. When we behave aggressively to get something, we plan our behavior more carefully. We may feel a sense of self-efficacy as we carry out the act. Reactive aggression involves white-hot, disorganized rage. When you hear that your best friend has betrayed you, or even have a minor frustrating experience such as being caught in traffic, you may get furious and want to blindly lash out (Deater-Deckard and others, 2010).

Picture Partners/Alamy

As he lunges for his friend's book, the boy on the right may feel powerful (*instrumental aggression*). But his furious buddy is apt to react by bopping him on the head (*reactive aggression*).

This feeling is normal. According to a classic theory called the *frustration–aggression hypothesis*, when human beings are thwarted, we are biologically primed to retaliate or strike back.

In addition to its motive—instrumental or reactive—developmentalists distinguish between different forms of aggression. Hitting and yelling are direct forms of aggression. A more devious type of aggression is **relational aggression,** acts designed to hurt our relationships. Not inviting Sara to a birthday party, spreading rumors, or tattling on a disliked classmate qualify as relationally aggressive acts.

Because it targets self-esteem and involves more sophisticated social skills, relational aggression follows a different developmental path than openly aggressive acts. Just as rates of open aggression are declining, during middle childhood, relational aggression dramatically rises. In fact, the over-abundance of relational aggression during late elementary school and early adolescence (another intensely frustrating time) may explain why we tend to label these ages as the "meanest" times of life.

Most of us assume relational aggression is far more common in girls, but, in research, this "obvious" gender difference does not necessarily appear. Yes, overt aggression is severely sanctioned in females, so girls make relational aggression their major mode (Ostrov & Godleski, 2010; Smith, Rose, & Schwartz-Mette, 2010). But as spreading rumors and talking trash about your competitors can be vital to dethroning adversaries and climbing the social ranks (Neal, 2010), one study showed teenage boys were just as relationally aggressive as teenage girls! (Mayeux & Cillessen, 2008)

Masterfile Royalty Free

Excluding someone from your group is a classic sign of *relational aggression*—which really gets going in middle childhood. Can you remember being the target of the behavior shown here when you were in fourth or fifth grade?

Table 6.5 summarizes the different types of aggression and gives examples from childhood and adult life. While scanning the table, notice that we all behave in *every* aggressive way. Also, being aggressive is not "bad." As I just implied, it is vital to making our way in the world. Children, who are popular, as you will see later in this chapter, don't abandon being aggressive. They use aggression—especially the instrumental kind—to gain power and status (Guerra, Williams, & Sadek, 2011; Roseth and others, 2011). Without reactive aggression (fighting back when attacked), our species would never survive. Still, aggression can cause serious social problems when children make this behavior their *typical* life mode.

TABLE 6.5: Aggression: A Summary of the Types

What Motivated the Behavior?

Instrumental aggression: Acts that are actively instigated to achieve a goal.

Examples: "I'll hit Tommy so I can get his toys." "I'll cut off that car so I can get ahead of him." "I want my boss's job, so I'll spread a rumor that he is having an affair."

Characteristics: Emotionally cool and more carefully planned.

Reactive aggression: Acts that occur in response to being frustrated or hurt.

Examples: "Jimmy took my toy, so I'm going to hit him." "That guy shoved me to take my place in line, so I'm going punch him out." "Joe took my girlfriend, so I'm gonna get a gun and shoot him."

Characteristics: Furious, disorganized, impulsive response.

What Was Its Form?

Direct aggression: Everyone can see it.

Examples: Telling your boyfriend you hate his guts. Beating up someone. Screaming at your mother. Having a tantrum. Bopping a playmate over the head with a toy.

Characteristics: At its peak at about age 2 or 3; declines as children get older. More common in boys than in girls, especially physical aggression.

Relational aggression: Carried out indirectly, through damaging or destroying the victim's relationships.

Examples: "Sara got a better grade than me, so I'm going to tell the teacher that she cheated." "Let's tell everyone not to let Sara play in our group." "I want Sara's job, so I'll spread a rumor that she is stealing money from the company." "I'm going to tell my best friend that her husband is cheating on her because I want to break up their marriage."

Characteristics: Occurs mainly during elementary school and may be at its peak during adolescence, although—as we all know—it's common *throughout* adult life.

Understanding Highly Aggressive Children

You just saw that, as they get older, boys and girls typically get less openly aggressive. However, a percentage of children remain unusually aggressive into elementary school. These children are labeled with externalizing disorders defined by high rates of aggression. They are classified as defiant, antisocial kids.

THE PATHWAY TO PRODUCING PROBLEMATIC AGGRESSION. Longitudinal studies suggest that there may be a poisonous two-step, nature-plus-nurture pathway to being labeled as a highly aggressive child:

STEP 1: The toddler's exuberant (or difficult) temperament evokes harsh discipline. When toddlers are exuberant (Degnan, Almas, & Fox, 2010), temperamentally fearless (Gao and others, 2010), and have problems regulating their attention (Kim & Deater-Deckard, 2011)—recall from earlier chapters that caregivers often react by using *power-assertion* discipline. They shame, scream, and hit: "Shut up. You are impossible. You'll get a beating from mom." Physically punishing a "difficult" toddler is apt to backfire (Boden, Fergusson, & Horwood, 2010; Edwards and others, 2010). Notice, for instance, from scanning the study findings in Figure 6.2, that regularly spanking a difficult 15-month-old magnified that child's

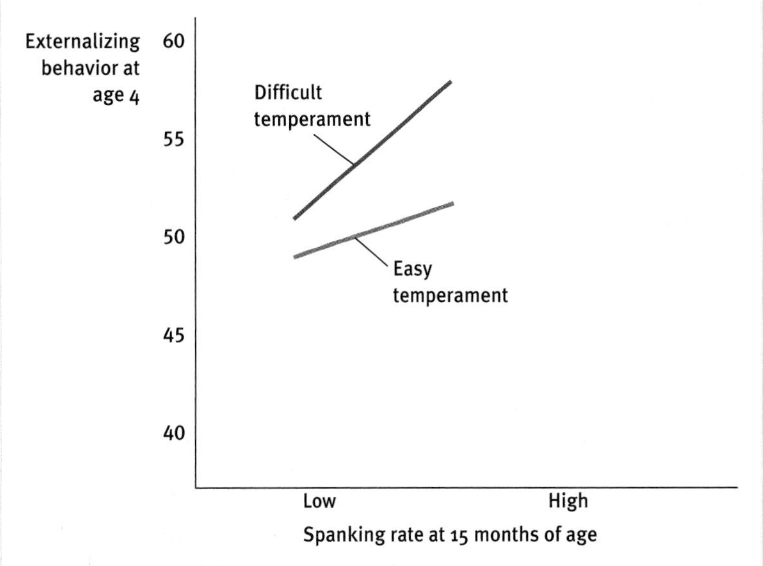

FIGURE 6.2: **The relationship between mothers' reports of spanking at 15 months and externalizing behavior at age 4, for temperamentally difficult and easy children, from a longitudinal study:** In this research, notice that if a child was temperamentally easy, being regularly spanked during toddlerhood slightly increased the risk of having later externalizing problems. However, this discipline style had a huge negative impact on development for toddlers with difficult temperaments. Bottom line: Power assertion is poisonous for a temperamentally at-risk child.

Source: Mulvaney & Mebert, 2007.

Regularly using power assertion to discipline an exuberant toddler (which makes him angry and defiant) and then having him be shunned by the other children for his disruptive behavior in elementary school—that's the two-step recipe for producing a highly aggressive child.

Michael Newman/Photo Edit, Inc.

Nicholas Prior/Getty Images

risk of developing externalizing problems at age 4. Therefore, unfortunately, the very toddlers who need sensitive, loving parenting the most can be set up to get the harshest, most punitive care.

STEP 2: The child is rejected by teachers and peers in school. Typically, the transition to being defined as an "antisocial child" occurs during early elementary school. As impulsive, by now clearly aggressive, children travel outside the family, they get rejected by their classmates. Being socially excluded is a powerful stress that provokes paranoia and aggression at any age (DeWall and others, 2009; Landsford and others, 2010). Moreover, because aggressive children *generally* have trouble inhibiting their behavior (Runions & Keating, 2010), during elementary school they may start failing in their academic work (Romano and others, 2010). This amplifies the frustration ("I'm not making it in any area of life!") and compounds the tendency to lash out ("Its their fault, not mine!").

A HOSTILE WORLDVIEW. As I just implied, aggressive children also think differently in social situations. They may have a **hostile attributional bias** (Crick & Dodge, 1996). They see threat in benign social cues. A boy gets accidentally bumped at the lunch table, and he sees a deliberate provocation. A girl decides that you are her enemy when you look at her the wrong way. So the child's behavior provokes a more hostile world.

To summarize, let's enter the mind of a highly aggressive child. As a toddler, your fearless temperament continually got you into trouble with your parents. You have been harshly disciplined for years. In school, you are failing academically and shunned by your classmates. So you never have a chance to interact with other children and improve your social skills. In fact, your hostile attributional bias makes perfect sense. You are living in a "sea of negativity" (Jenson and others, 2004). And yes, the world *is* out to do you in!

Finally, just as you saw in the Chapter 5 discussion of ADHD, there is a gender difference in the risk of being defined as "an acting-out, antisocial child." Because they are more "exuberant" and physical when they play, boys are several times more likely than girls to show the physically aggressive behavior that gets them labeled with an externalizing problem in elementary school (Vazsonyi & Chen, 2010).

How *do* boys and girls relate when they play? Now, I'll turn to this question and others as we move to part two of this chapter: relationships.

TYING IT ALL TOGETHER

hostile attributional bias The tendency of highly aggressive children to see motives and actions as threatening when they are actually benign.

1. You interviewed a 4-year-old and a fourth grader for your class project in lifespan development, but mixed up your interview notes. Which statement was made by the 4-year-old?
   a. "My friend Megan is better at math than me."
   b. "Sometimes I get mad at my friends, but maybe it's because I'm too stubborn."
   c. "I have a cat named Kit, and I'm the smartest girl in the world."

2. Identify which of the following boys has internalizing or externalizing tendencies and then, for one of these children, design an intervention using principles spelled out in this section: Ramon sees himself as wonderful, but he is having serious trouble getting along with his teachers and the other kids; Jared is a great student, but when he gets a B instead of an A, he decides that he's "dumb" and gets too depressed to work.

3. When the teacher yells at Zack, Austin and Gabriel both cringe and feel like crying. In addition, Gabriel feels really sorry for Zack. Although both children feel ______________ for Zack, Gabriel feels ________________. Who is more likely to comfort Zack?

4. A teacher wants to intervene with a student who has been teasing a classmate. Identify which statement is guilt-producing, which is shame-producing, and which involves the use of induction. Then, name which response(s) would promote prosocial behavior.
   a. "Think of how bad Johnny must feel."
   b. "If that's how you act, you can sit by yourself. You're not nice enough to be with the other kids."
   c. "I'm disappointed in you. You are usually such a good kid."

5. Alyssa wants to replace Brianna as Chloe's best friend, so she spreads horrible rumors about Brianna. Brianna overhears Alyssa dissing her and starts slapping Alyssa. Of the four types of aggression discussed in this section—*direct, instrumental, reactive, relational*—which two describe Alyssa's behavior, and which two fit Brianna's actions?

6. Mario, a fourth grader, feels that everyone is out to get him. Give the name for Mario's negative worldview.

Answers to the Tying It All Together questions can be found at the end of this chapter.

rough-and-tumble play Play that involves shoving, wrestling, and hitting, but in which no actual harm is intended; especially characteristic of boys.

fantasy play Play that involves making up and acting out a scenario; also called *pretend play*.

Relationships

Think back to your days pretending to be a superhero or supermodel, getting together with the girls or boys to play, your best friends, and whether you were popular at school. Now, beginning with play, moving on to the play worlds of girls and boys, then friendships and popularity, and finally tackling bullying—that important contemporary concern—let's explore each relationship-related topic one by one.

Play

Developmentalists classify children's "free play" (the non-sports-oriented kind) into different categories. **Rough-and-tumble play** refers to the excited shoving, wrestling, and running around that is most apparent with boys. Actually, rough-and-tumble play is classically boy behavior. It seems biologically built into being male (Bjorklund & Pellegrini, 2002; Pellegrini, 2006).

Rough-and-tumble play is not only tremendously exciting, but it seems to be genetically built into being "male."

Photodisc/Getty Images

Pretending: The Heart of Early Childhood

Fantasy play, or *pretending,* is different. Here, the child takes a stance apart from reality and makes up a scene, often with a toy or other prop. While fantasy play also can be immensely physical, this "as if" quality makes it unique. Children must pretend to be pirates or superheroes as they wrestle and run. Because fantasy play is so emblematic of early childhood, let's delve into pretending in depth.

THE DEVELOPMENT AND DECLINE OF PRETENDING. Fantasy play first emerges in toddlerhood, as children realize that a symbol can stand for something else. In a classic study, developmentalists watched 1-year-olds with their mothers at home. Although toddlers often initiated a fantasy episode, they needed

collaborative pretend play Fantasy play in which children work together to develop and act out the scenes.

a parent to expand on the scene (Dunn, Wooding, & Hermann, 1977). So a child would pretend to make a phone call, and his mother would pick up the real phone and say, "Hello, this is Mommy. Should I come home now?"

At about age 3, children transfer the skill of pretending with mothers to peers. **Collaborative pretend play,** or fantasizing *together* with another child, really gets going at about age 4 (Smolucha & Smolucha, 1998). Because they must work together to develop the scene, collaboratively pretending shows that preschoolers have a *theory of mind*—the knowledge that the other person has a different perspective. (You need to understand that your fellow playwright has a different script in his head.) Collaboratively pretending, in turn, helps teach young children the skill of making sense of different minds (Nicolopoulou and others, 2010).

Laura Dwight/Photo Edit, Inc.

For these 4-year-old girls (aka princesses who have dressed up to feed their baby dolls), their *collaborative pretend play* is teaching them vital lessons about how to compromise and get along.

Anyone with regular access to a young child can see these changes firsthand. When a 2-year-old has his "best friend" over, they play in parallel orbits—if things go well. More likely, a titanic battle erupts, full of instrumental and reactive aggression, as each child attempts to gain possession of the toys. By age 4, children can play *together.* At age 5 or 6, they can pretend together for hours—with only a few major fights that are usually quickly resolved.

Although fantasy play can continue into early adolescence, when children reach concrete operations, their interest shifts to structured games (Bjorklund & Pellegrini, 2002). At age 3, a child pretends to bake in the kitchen corner; at 9, he wants to bake a cake. At age 5, you ran around playing pirates; at 9, you tried to hit the ball like the Pittsburgh Pirates do.

THE PURPOSES OF PRETENDING. Interestingly, around the world, when children pretend, their play has similar plots. Let's eavesdrop at a U.S. preschool:

BOY 2: I don't want to be a kitty anymore.

GIRL: You are a husband?

BOY 2: Yeah.

BOYS 1 AND 2: Husbands, husbands! (Yell and run around the play house)

GIRL: Hold it, Bill, I can't have two husbands.

BOYS 1 AND 2: Two husbands! Two husbands!

GIRL: We gonna marry ourselves, right?

(adapted from Corsaro, 1985, pp. 102–104)

Why do young children play "family," and assume the "correct" roles when they play mommy and daddy? For answers, let's turn to Lev Vygotsky's brilliant insights again.

Play allows children to practice adult roles. Vygotsky (1978) believed that pretending allows children to rehearse being adults. The reason girls pretend to be mommy and baby is that women are the main child-care providers around the world. Boys play soldiers because this activity offers built-in training for the wars they face as adults (Pellegrini & Smith, 2005).

Play allows children a sense of control. As the following preschool conversation suggests, pretending has a deeper psychological function, too:

GIRL 1: Yeah, and let's pretend when Mommy's out until later.

GIRL 2: Ooooh. Well, I'm not the boss around here, though. 'Cause mommies are the bosses.

GIRL 1: (Doubtfully) But maybe we won't know how to punish.

GIRL 2: I will. I'll put my hand up and spank. That's what my mom does.

GIRL 1: My mom does too.

(adapted from Corsaro, 1985, p. 96)

While reading the previous two chapters, you may have been thinking that the so-called carefree early childhood years are hardly free of stress. We expect children to regulate their emotions when their frontal lobes aren't fully functional. We discipline toddlers and preschoolers when they really cannot make sense of the mysteries of adult rules. Vygotsky (1978) believed that, in response to this sense of powerlessness, young children enter "an illusory role" in which their desires are realized. In play, *you* can be the spanking mommy or the queen of the castle, even when you are small, and sometimes feel like a slave.

Courtesy of Dr. William Corsaro

Imagine that, like the supersized preschooler shown here (Professor William Corsaro), you could spend years going down slides, playing family, and bonding with 3- and 4-year-olds—and then get professional recognition for your academic work. What an incredible career!

To penetrate the inner world of preschool fantasy play, sociologist William Corsaro (1985, 1997) went undercover, entering a nursery school as a member of the class. (No problem. The children welcomed their new playmate, whom they called Big Bill, as a clumsy, enlarged version of themselves.) As Vygotsky would predict, Corsaro found that preschool play plots often centered on mastering upsetting events. There were separation/reunion scenarios ("Help! I'm lost in the forest." "I'll find you.") and danger/rescue plots ("Get in the house. It's gonna be a rainstorm!"). Sometimes, play scenarios centered on that ultimate frightening event, death:

CHILD 1: We are dead, we are dead! Help, we are dead! (Puts animals on their sides)

CHILD 2: You can't talk if you are dead.

CHILD 1: Oh, well, Leah's talked when she was dead, so mine have to talk when they are dead. Help, help, we are dead!

(adapted from Corsaro, 1985 p. 204)

Notice that these themes are basic to Disney movies and fairy tales. From *Finding Nemo, Bambi,* and *The Lion King* to—my personal favorite—*Dumbo,* there is nothing more heart-wrenching than being separated from your parent. From the greedy old witch in *Hansel and Gretel* to the jealous queen in *Sleeping Beauty,* no scenario is as sweet as triumphing over evil and possible death.

Play furthers our understanding of social norms. Corsaro (1985) found that death was a touchy play topic. When children proposed these plots, their partners might try to change the script. This relates to Vygotsky's third insight about play: Although children's play looks unstructured, it has boundaries and rules. Plots involving two husbands or dead animals waking up make children uncomfortable because they violate the rules of adult life. Children get especially uneasy when a play partner proposes scenarios with gory themes, such as cutting off people's heads (Dunn & Hughes, 2001). Therefore, play teaches children how to act and how not to behave. Wouldn't you want to retreat if someone showed an intense interest in decapitation while having a conversation with you?

Now that we know play has many benefits, let's look at how health-care professionals and teachers might use these insights in their work.

INTERVENTIONS: Helping Children Through Play

Based on the idea that play allows us to cope with our fears, nurses on a pediatric ward might be alert to a child's pretend play to get clues into a young patient's concerns about an operation. Then, they might enact their own pretend sequence to speak to the child's anxieties ("Little Joe Bear went to sleep, but when he woke up he felt much better, and you will, too").

Preschool teachers might see problems looming on the horizon if a 4-year-old is obsessed with playing "I'll cut off your head" or "My mom got killed" (see Wan & Green, 2010). They might try to help that child tone down his violent fantasies and encourage him to play in more appropriate ways (Bartolini & Lunn, 2002).

gender-segregated play Play in which boys and girls associate only with members of their own sex—typical of childhood.

Still, we have to be cautious about intervening in play. By managing (or micromanaging) make-believe, we may prevent children from learning important lessons on their own. If we decide how children *must* play, we might be going against nature. Many teachers get anxious about rough-and-tumble play. Misinterpreting this activity as true aggression, they tend to punish the very play that boys most love (Ardley & Ericson, 2002). Why do female teachers recoil from rough-and-tumble play? The reason will be clear as we explore that other fundamental play characteristic: Boys and girls live in separate play worlds.

Girls' and Boys' Play Worlds

> [Some] girls, all about five and a half years old, are looking through department store catalogues, . . . concentrating on what they call "girls' stuff" and referring to some of the other items as "yucky boys' stuff." . . . Shirley points to a picture of a couch . . . "All we want is the pretty stuff," says Ruth. Peggy now announces, "If you come to my birthday, every girl in the school is invited. I'm going to put a sign up that says, 'No boys allowed!'" "Oh good, good, good," says Vickie. "I hate boys."
>
> (adapted from Corsaro, 1997, p. 155)

Does this conversation bring back childhood memories of being 5 or 6? How does **gender-segregated play** develop? What are the differences in boy versus girl play, and what causes the sexes to separate into these different camps?

Exploring the Separate Societies

Visit a playground and observe children of different ages. Notice that toddlers show no sign of gender-segregated play. In preschool, children start to play mainly in sex-segregated groups (Martin, & Ruble, 2010). By elementary school, gender-segregated play is entrenched. On the playground, boys and girls do play in mixed groups (Fabes, Martin, & Hanish, 2003). Still, with friendships, there is a split: boys are typically best friends with boys and girls with girls (Maccoby, 1998).

Ellen B. Senisi/The Image Works

A visit to this elementary school lunchroom vividly brings home the fact that middle childhood is traditionally defined by *gender-segregated play*.

Now, go back to the playground and look at the *way* boys and girls relate. Do you notice that boy and girl play differs in the following ways?

BOYS EXCITEDLY RUN AROUND; GIRLS CALMLY TALK. Boys' play is more rambunctious. Even during physical games such as tag, girls play together in calmer and more subdued ways (Maccoby, 1998; Pellegrini, 2006). The difference in activity levels is striking if you have the pleasure of witnessing one gender playing with the opposite sex's toys. In one memorable episode, after my son and a friend invaded a girl's stash of dolls, they gleefully ran around the house bashing Barbie into Barbie and using their booty as swords.

BOYS COMPETE IN GROUPS; GIRLS PLAY COLLABORATIVELY, ONE-TO-ONE. Their exuberant, rough-and-tumble play explains why boys tend to burst on the scene, running and yelling, dominating every room. Another difference lies in playgroup *size*. Boys get together in packs. Girls play in smaller, more intimate groups (Maccoby, 1990, 1998; Ruble, Martin, & Berenbaum, 2006).

Boys and girls also differ in the *way* they relate. Boys try to establish dominance and compete to be the best. This competitive versus cooperative style spills over into children's talk. Girl-to-girl collaborative play really sounds collaborative ("I'll be the doctor, OK?"). Boys give each other bossy commands ("I'm doing the operation. Lie down, now!") (Maccoby, 1998). Girl-to-girl fantasy play involves nurturing themes. Boys prefer the warrior, superhero mode.

The intensely stereotypic quality of girls' fantasy play came as a shock when I spent three days playing with my visiting 7-year-old niece. We devoted day one to setting up a beauty shop, complete with nail polishes and shampoos. We had a table for massages and a makeover section featuring all the cosmetics I owned. Then, we opened for business for the visiting relatives and, (of course!)—by charging for our services—made money for toys. We spent the last day playing with a "pool party" Barbie combo my niece had selected at Walmart that afternoon.

Boys' and girls' different play interests show why the kindergartners in the vignette at the beginning of this section came to hate those "yucky" boys. Another reason why girls turn off to the opposite sex is the unpleasant reception they get from the other camp. In observing at a preschool, researchers found that while active girls played with the boys' groups early in the year, they eventually were rejected and forced to play with their own sex (Pellegrini and others, 2007a). Therefore, boys are the first to erect the barriers: "No girls allowed!" Moreover, the gender barriers are *generally* more rigid for males.

BOYS LIVE IN A MORE EXCLUSIONARY, SEPARATE WORLD. My niece did choose to buy Barbies, but she also plays with trucks. She loves soccer and baseball, not just doing her nails. So, even though they may dislike the opposite sex, girls do cross the divide. Boys are more likely to avoid that chasm—refusing to venture down the Barbie aisle or consider buying a toy labeled "girl." So boys live in a more roped-off gender world (Boyle, Marshall, & Robeson, 2003).

Now, you might be interested in what happened during my final day pretending with the pool party toys. After my niece said, "Aunt Janet, let's pretend we are the popular girls," our Barbies tried on fancy dresses ("What shall I wear, Jane?") in preparation for a "popular girls" pool party, where the dolls met up to discuss—*guess what*—where they shopped and who did their hair!

What Causes Gender-Stereotyped Play?

Why do children, such as my niece, play in gender-stereotyped ways? Answers come from exploring three forces: biology (nature), socialization (nurture), and cognitions (or thoughts).

A BIOLOGICAL UNDERPINNING. Ample evidence suggests that gender-segregated play is biologically built in. Children around the world form separate play societies (Maccoby, 1998). Troops of juvenile rhesus monkeys behave *exactly* like human children. The males segregate into their own groups and engage in rough-and-tumble play (Pellegrini, 2006). Grooming activities similar to my niece's beauty-shop behaviors are prominent among young female monkeys, too (Bjorklund & Pellegrini, 2002; Suomi, 2004).

Actually, when pregnant rhesus monkeys are injected with the male sex hormone testosterone, their female offspring also engage in rough-and-tumble play (Udry, 2000). Could a similar effect apply to females in our species, too?

To answer this fascinating question, one developmentalist measured the naturally occurring testosterone levels of women pregnant with female fetuses (Udry, 2000). He took maternal blood samples during the second trimester—the time, you may recall from Chapter 2, when the neurons are being formed. Then, years later, when the daughters were about age 17, he asked them to fill out sex-role questionnaires.

Girls who had been exposed to comparatively high levels of prenatal testosterone were more interested in traditionally male occupations, such as engineering, than the lower-hormone-level prenatal group. They were less likely to wear makeup. Even in their twenties, they showed more stereotypically male interests (such as race-car driving). So, depending on the dose, prenatal exposure to testosterone may program us to have more "feminized" or "masculinized" brains.

THE AMPLIFYING EFFECT OF SOCIALIZATION. The wider world helps biology along. From the images displayed in preschool coloring books (Fitzpatrick & McPherson, 2010) to parents' different toy selections for daughters and sons; from the messages beamed out in television sitcoms (Collins, 2011; Paek, Nelson, & Vilela, 2011) to teachers' differen-

Courtesy of Bella Malvania

Imagine the messages this five-year-old girl is absorbing while reading this preschool story book: Girls are "pinkalicious princesses" and act in dainty, female ways!

tial treatment of boys and girls in school (Chen & Rao, 2011)—everything brings home the message: Males and females act in different ways.

Peers play a powerful role in this programming. When they play in mixed-gender groups, children act in less gender-stereotyped ways (Fabes, Martin, & Hanish, 2003); boys tone down their rough-and-tumble activities when girls arrive; girls are less apt to play quietly with dolls when they are pretending with boys. Therefore, the act of splitting into separate play societies trains children to behave in ways typical of their own sex (Martin & Fabes, 2001).

Same-sex playmates reinforce one another for selecting gender-stereotyped activities ("Let's play with dolls." "Great!"). They model one another as they play together in "gentle" or "rough" ways. The pressure to toe the gender line is promoted by social sanctions. Children who behave in "gender atypical ways" (girls who hit a lot or boys who play with dolls) are rejected by their peers (Coplan, Closson, & Arbeau, 2007; Lee & Troop-Gordon, 2011; Smith, Rose, & Schwartz-Mette, 2010).

THE IMPACT OF COGNITIONS. A cognitive process reinforces these external messages. According to **gender schema theory** (Bem, 1981; Martin & Dinella, 2002), once children understand their category (girl or boy), they selectively attend to the activities of their own sex.

When do we first grasp our gender label and start this lifelong practice of modeling our group? The answer is at about age 2 1/2, right after we begin to talk (Martin, & Ruble, 2010)! Although they may not learn the real difference until much later (here it helps to have an opposite-sex sibling to see naked), 3-year-olds can tell you that girls have long hair, and cry a lot, while boys fight and play with trucks. At about age 5 or 6, when they are mastering the similar concept of identity constancy (the knowledge that your essential self doesn't change when you dress up in a gorilla costume), children grasp the idea that once you start out as a boy or girl, you stay that way for life (Kohlberg, 1966). However, mistakes are common. I once heard my 5-year-old nephew ask my husband, "Was that jewelry from when you were a girl?"

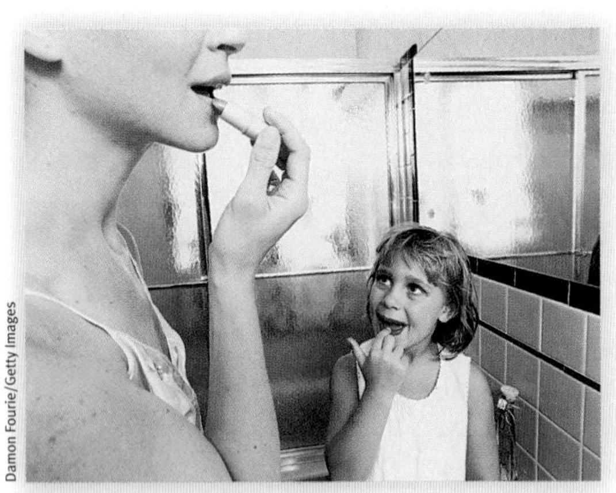

Damon Fourie/Getty Images

Children spend hours modeling their own sex, demonstrating why *gender schema theory* (the idea "I am a boy" or "I am a girl") also encourages behaving in gender-stereotyped ways.

In sum, my niece's beauty-shop activities had a biological basis, although a steady stream of nurture influences from adults and playmates helped this process along. Her behavior was also promoted by identifying herself as "a girl" and then spending hours modeling the women in her life.

But are the gender norms loosening? U.S. children now feel it's "unfair" to exclude boys from ballet class (Martin & Ruble, 2010). My students today often describe having had good friends of the other sex in elementary school, something that would *never* have occurred when I was a child. Do you think our less gender-defined adult world is reducing the childhood pressures to "act like a girl or boy"? Who were your best friends when you were age 7 or 9?

gender schema theory Explanation for gender-stereotyped behavior that emphasizes the role of cognitions; specifically, the idea that once children know their own gender label (girl or boy), they selectively watch and model their own sex.

Friendships

This last question brings me to the topic of friends. *Why* do children choose specific friends, and what benefits do childhood friendships provide?

The Core Qualities: Similarity, Trust, and Emotional Support

The essence of friendship is feeling similarity (Poulin & Chan, 2010). As I just described, children gravitate toward people who are "like them" in gender, as well

Mel Yates/Getty Images

Windsor & Wiehahn/Getty Images

Left: Preschool best friends connect through their shared passion for physical activities such as going down slides.
Right: In late elementary school, best friends bond by sharing secrets and plans.

as social status (Peters and others, 2010) and general worldview (Dishion & Tipsord, 2011). So in preschool, an active child will tend to make friends with a classmate who likes to run around. A 4-year-old who loves the slide will most likely become best buddies with a child who shares this passion, too (Rubin, Bukowski, & Parker, 2006).

Mirroring the way they describe themselves, however, young children describe their friendships in external fact-oriented ways: "She's my friend because we go down the slide together." As children enter concrete operations, they shift to talking about inner qualities: "Josh and I are buddies because he is funny and such a great guy." Around this age, children also develop the concept of loyalty ("I can trust Josh to stand up for me") and the sense that friends share their inner lives (Hartup & Stevens, 1997; Newcomb & Bagwell, 1995). Listen to these fourth and fifth graders describing their best friend:

> He is my very best friend because he tells me things and I tell him things.
>
> Me and Tiff share our deepest, darkest secrets and we talk about boys, when we grow up, and shopping.
>
> Jessica has problems at home and with her religion and when something happens she always comes to me and talks about it. We've been through a lot together.
>
> (quoted in Rose & Asher, 2000, p. 49)

These quotations would resonate with the ideas of personality theorist Harry Stack Sullivan. Sullivan (1953) believed that a chum (or best friend) fulfills the developmental need for self-validation and intimacy that emerges at around age 9. Sullivan also believed that this special relationship serves as a stepping-stone to adult romance.

The Protecting and Teaching Functions of Friends

In addition to offering emotional support and validating us as people, friends stimulate children's personal development in two other ways:

FRIENDS PROTECT AND ENHANCE THE DEVELOPING SELF. Perhaps you noticed this protective function in the quotation above in which the fourth grader spoke about how she helped her best friend when she had problems at home. Friends help insulate children from being bullied at school (Scholte, Sentse, & Granic, 2010). They become especially important safe zones of comfort as we become teenagers and begin separating from our parents and moving into the wider world (Rubin, Bukowski, & Parker, 2006). You also may have noticed that the reasons for shedding a friendship often center on not being protected: The person we *thought* was a friend let us down in our hour of need.

FRIENDS TEACH US TO MANAGE OUR EMOTIONS AND HANDLE CONFLICTS. Your parents will love you no matter what you do, but the love of a friend is contingent. So to relate to a friend, children must be able to modulate their emotions and attune themselves to the other person's needs (Bukowski, 2001; Denham and others, 2003).

This is not to say that friends are always positive influences. They can bring out a child's worst self by encouraging relational aggression ("We are best friends, so you can't play with us") and daring one another to engage in dangerous behavior ("Let's sneak out of the house at 2 A.M."). I will be exploring the dark side of friendship in this next section and also in Chapter 9. However, in general, Sullivan seems to be right: Friends do help teach us how to relate as adults.

Popularity

Friendship involves relating with a single person in a close one-to-one way. Popularity is a group concern. It requires rising to the top of the social totem pole.

Although children differ in social status in preschool, you may remember from childhood that "Who is popular?" becomes an absorbing question during later elementary school. Entering concrete operations makes children highly sensitive to making social comparisons. The urge to rank classmates according to social status is heightened by the confining conditions of childhood itself. In adulthood, popularity fades more into the background because we select our own social circles. Children must make it on a daily basis in a classroom full of random peers.

Who Is Popular and Who Is Unpopular?

How do children vary in popularity during the socially stressful later elementary school years? Here are the main categories researchers find when they ask third, fourth, or fifth graders to list the two or three classmates they like most and really dislike:

- *Popular children* are frequently named in the most-liked category and never appear in the disliked group. They stand out as being really liked by everyone.
- *Average children* receive a few most-liked and perhaps one or two disliked nominations. They rank around the middle range of status in the class.
- *Rejected children* land in the disliked category often and never appear in the preferred list. They stand out among their classmates in a negative way.

What qualities make children popular? Most importantly, what traits make children disliked by their peers?

Popular children—at least in elementary school—are friendly and outgoing, prosocial, and kind (Mayberry & Espelage, 2007). But, starting early on, there is a subset of popular children who are both prosocial and highly instrumentally aggressive (Hawley, Little, & Card, 2008; Rodkin & Roisman, 2010). They ascend the social hierarchy by vigorously competing for status, and then reach out to enlist the group in a caring way (Roseth and others, 2011). Rejected children are *simply* highly aggressive. Or, they shrink back from competing at all. Specifically:

Michael Newman/Photo Edit, Inc.

His shyness may set this boy up for social rejection in first grade because his anxiety will make the other children uneasy and he may not have the courage to reach out to his classmates.

REJECTED CHILDREN HAVE EXTERNALIZING (AND OFTEN INTERNALIZING) PROBLEMS. Children with severe externalizing tendencies quickly fall into the rejected category. These are the boys and girls who make aggression their major life mode (Hawley and others, 2007; Putallaz and others, 2007; Sturaro and others, 2011). Highly anxious children—those prone to internalizing disorders—may or may not be rejected. However, a *socially inept*, anxious child is apt to be avoided as early as first grade (Degnan, Almas, & Fox, 2010).

Moreover, a poisonous nature-evokes-nurture interaction can set in when a child enters school extremely shy. As children pick up on the fact that people are avoiding them, their shyness gets more intense. So they become less socially competent—and increasingly likely to be rejected (and, as you will see, victimized)—as they advance from grade to grade (Booth-LaForce & Oxford, 2008).

An unfortunate bidirectional process is also occurring. The child's anxiety makes other children nervous. They get uncomfortable and want to retreat when they see this person approach. In response to your own awkward encounters, have you ever been tempted to walk in the opposite direction when you saw a very shy person approaching in the hall?

REJECTED CHILDREN DON'T FIT IN WITH THE DOMINANT GROUP. Children who stand out as different are also at risk of being rejected: boys and girls who don't fit the gender stereotypes (Lee & Troop-Gordon, 2011); low-income children in middle-class schools (Zettergren, 2007); immigrant children in ethnically homogenous societies (Strohmeier, Kärnä & Salmivalli, 2010)—any child whom classmates label as "different," "weird," or "not like us."

Relationship between being liked and being thought popular

.70
.60
.50
.40
.30
.20
.10

5 7 9

Grade

FIGURE 6.3: **How being popular relates to being personally liked for girls in middle school:** In this study, children in different grades were asked which classmates were popular and which classmates they liked the most. Notice that, by ninth grade, there was little relationship between being viewed as in the "popular" group and being seen as well liked. Did you *really* like the kids in the "in-crowd" at your school?

Source: Cillessen & Mayeux (2004), p. 153.

Exploring Middle School Meanness

In elementary school, popular children are typically well liked by their teachers and peers. In middle school, being rebellious is an "in thing," and highly aggressive children can end up in the most popular group (Werner & Hill, 2010; Witvliet and others, 2010).

When researchers follow children from year to year, they are able to pinpoint this shift toward peer-group values favoring aggression—especially the relational kind—that peaks between ages 12 and 14 (Smith, Rose, & Schwartz-Mette, 2010; Werner & Hill, 2010; see also Tokunaga, 2010). Therefore, as children travel into their teens, no longer is being "popular" as closely tied to being well liked (Schwartz and others, 2010; see also the example in Figure 6.3). In fact, sometimes kids in the "in-crowd" are disliked by much of the class! (see Dishion & Tipsord, 2011; Neal, 2010)

Why does rebellion and relational aggression become linked to social status especially among younger teens? Stay tuned for interesting reasons as I explore this question in Chapter 9. But the bottom-line message is that the middle school "mean girls" (and "mean boys") phenomenon can really occur—which may explain why sixth-grade popularity has *no* relation to being well adjusted during adult life (Modin, Östberg, & Almquist, 2011).

Exploring the Fate of the Rejected

What about being unpopular? Is childhood rejection a prelude to poor adult mental health? The answer is "sometimes." Highly physically aggressive children are at risk for getting into trouble—at home, in school, and with the law—during adolescence and in their early adult years (Vazsconyi & Chen, 2010; also, more about this pathway in Chapter 9). Unfortunately, one longitudinal study suggested that women who were very unpopular as preteens had high rates of anxiety disorders and depression during midlife (Modin, Östberg, & Almquist, 2011).

Daniel Atkin/Alamy

Because he prefers to hang back and observe the group scene from afar, this boy is not winning any popularity contests in fourth or fifth grade. But, the same qualities that are giving him problems in elementary school might produce a world-class author or brilliant psychologist during adult life.

But there is great variability, especially if a child has been rejected due to being "different" from the group. Consider an awkward little girl named Eleanor Roosevelt, who was socially rejected at age 8, or a boy named Thomas Edison, whose preference for playing alone got him defined as a "problem" child. Because they were so different, these famous adults were dismal failures during elementary school. To get insights into the fleeting quality of childhood peer status, you might organize a reunion of your fifth- or sixth-grade class. You might be surprised at how many unpopular classmates flowered during their high school or college years.

bullying A situation in which one or more children (or adults) harass or target a specific child for systematic abuse.

bully-victims Exceptionally aggressive children (with externalizing disorders) who repeatedly bully and get victimized.

Bullying: A Core Contemporary Childhood Concern

> You can get bullied because you are weak or annoying or because you are different. Kids with big ears get bullied. Dorks get bullied. . . . Teacher's pet gets bullied. If you say the right answer in class too many times, you can get bullied.
>
> (quoted in Guerra, Williams, & Sadek, 2011, p. 306)

Children who are different can excel in the proving ground of life. This is not the case on the proving ground of the playground. As you just read, being different, weak, socially awkward, or even "too good" is a recipe for **bullying**—being teased, made fun of, and verbally or physically abused by one's peers.

As I implied earlier, some bullying is "normal" as children jockey for power and status in the group. But the roughly 10 to 20 percent of children subject to chronic harassment fall into two categories. The first—the less common type—are **bully-victims.** These children are highly aggressive boys and girls who bully, get harassed, then bully again in an escalating cycle of pain (Deater-Deckard and others, 2010; Waasdorp, Bradshaw, & Duong, 2011). The classic victim, however, has internalizing issues (Crawford & Manassis, 2011). These children are anxious, shy, low on the social hierarchy, and unlikely to fight back (Cook and others, 2010; Degnan, Almas, & Fox, 2010; Scholte, Sentse, & Granic, 2010; also, see my personal confession in the Experiencing the Lifespan box).

Being chronically bullied has devastating effects. As they travel through elementary school, in response to failing with their peers and teachers, aggressive bully-victims may become anxious and withdrawn (Boivin and others, 2010). Their *comorbid*—or simultaneous—externalizing and internalizing problems put them at high risk for having serious troubles during their teens (Burk and others, 2011).

EXPERIENCING THE LIFESPAN: Middle-Aged Reflections on My Middle-Childhood Victimization

It was a hot August afternoon when the birthday present arrived. As usual, I was playing alone that day, maybe reading or engaging in a favorite pastime, fantasizing that I was a princess while sitting in a backyard tree. The gift, addressed to Janet Kaplan, was beautifully wrapped—huge but surprisingly light. This is amazing! I must be special! Someone had gone to such trouble for me! When I opened the first box, I saw another carefully wrapped box, and then another, smaller box, and yet another, smaller one inside. Finally, surrounded by ribbons and wrapping paper, I eagerly got to the last box and saw a tiny matchbox—which contained a small burnt match.

Around that time, the doorbell rang, and Cathy, then Ruth, then Carol, bounded up. "Your mother called to tell us she was giving you a surprise birthday party. We had to come over right away and be sure to wear our best dresses!" But their excitement turned to disgust when they learned that no party had been arranged. My ninth birthday was really in mid-September—more than a month away. It turned out that Nancy and Marion—the two most popular girls in class—had masterminded this relational aggression plot directed at me.

Why was I selected as the victim among the other third-grade girls? I had never hurt Nancy or Marion. In fact, in confessing their role, they admitted to some puzzlement: "We really don't dislike Janet at all." Researching this chapter has offered me insights into the reasons for this 50-year-old wound.

Although I did have friends, I was fairly low in the classroom hierarchy. Not only was I shy, but I was that unusual girl—a child who genuinely preferred to play alone. But most important, I was the perfect victim. I dislike competitive status situations. When taunted or teased, I don't fight back.

As an older woman, I still dislike status hierarchies and social snobberies. I'm not a group (or party) person. I far prefer talking one-to-one. I am happy to spend hours alone. Today, I consider these attributes a plus (after all, having no problem sitting by myself for many thousands of hours was a prime skill that allowed me to write this text!), but they caused me anguish in middle childhood. In fact, today, when I find myself in status-oriented peer situations, I can still catch glimmers of my long-ago, nervous, third-grade self!

SW Productions/Getty Images

It's a familiar scenario. Someone starts to harass an unpopular kid while a few friends egg that bully on and others passively stand by. But what do you think would happen if a bystander or two (let's say the boy or girl on the right) decided to angrily walk away or tell the instigator off?

Traditional victims—boys and girls who are very socially anxious—find that their poor self-esteem snowballs (Boulton, Smith, & Cowie, 2010) and leaks out to poison their academic lives (see Véronneau and others, 2010).

So, what can bullied children do? Unfortunately, studies show that each course of action has downsides (Visconti & Troop-Gordon, 2010). Seeking support from adults may backfire. You run the risk of retaliation from your tormenters when others intervene. The traditional advice to "stand up for yourself!" can be counterproductive. That is the very action a highly anxious child *cannot* take. Yes, retaliating does decrease anxiety, but it can mean becoming physically or relationally aggressive yourself (see Ostrov, 2010). Avoiding the bully may cut you off socially from the group.

What does buffer a child is a sense of self-efficacy ("I can control this!"), or—among children being bullied for their ethnicity—strongly identifying with their cultural group (Hunter and others, 2010). Just as it insulates children from other life "failures," a loving family relationship also mutes the pain (Bowes and others, 2010).

But the real solution lies in the wider world. Bullying often demands an audience. One person (or a few people) does the harassing, while others provide the perpetrator with positive reinforcement by laughing or appreciatively standing by. Therefore, children are less likely to be bullied when bystanders ignore the bully or, better yet, tell that person to stop (Kärnä and others, 2010). Conversely, when bullying is frequent in a given classroom, or the class norm supports relational aggression, *everyone* is prone to bully *regardless of whether or not people personally believe this behavior is wrong* (Scholte, Sentse, & Granic, 2010; Werner & Hill, 2010).

In other words, bullying is a normal social phenomenon. The nicest children are apt to do it if the atmospheric conditions are right (Guerra, Williams, & Sadek, 2011). So, interventions to prevent bullying emphasize not changing the person, but reversing the peer-group norms.

INTERVENTIONS: Attacking Bullying and Helping Rejected Children

In the *Olweus Bully Prevention Program*, for example, administrators plan a school assembly to discuss bullying early in the year. Then, they form a bullying-prevention committee composed of children from each grade. Teachers and students are kept on high alert for bullying in their classes. The goal is to develop a schoolwide norm to not tolerate peer abuse (Olweus, Limber, & Mihalic, 1999).

Do the many bullying-prevention programs now in operation work? The answer is: " Yes, to some extent." But, as bullying or relational aggression is such an effective way of gaining status (Witvliet and others, 2010), this phenomenon, present at *every age*, is a bit like bad weather—not in our power to totally control (Guerra, Williams, & Sadek, 2011).

What was this incredibly brave prosocial Iraq War soldier really like at age 1 or 2? Probably a fearless handful!

That's why I'd like to conclude this chapter by returning to the classic recipients of this unfortunate, universal human activity—children who are socially shy. How can we help these boys and girls succeed?

In following a group of shy 5-year-olds, researchers found that if a child developed friends in kindergarten or first grade, that boy or girl became less socially anxious over time (Gazelle & Ladd, 2003). So, to help a temperamentally anxious child, parents need to immediately connect their son or daughter—preferably in preschool—with a playmate who might become a close friend. They can't be overly controlling (Soenens & Vansteenkiste, 2010). Parents must foster a secure attachment, the real foundation for venturing confidently into life.

With toddlers at risk for externalizing disorders, as I've stressed earlier, providing loving, sensitive parenting is just as vitally important (see Kochanska and others, 2010b). Adults also need to understand that, with active explorers, the same traits that *can* spell trouble can also be potential life assets. In an amazing decades-long study, when researchers measured temperament during infancy and then looked at personality during adulthood, the *one* quality that predicted being highly competent at age 40 was having been rated fearless during the first year of life (Blatny, Jelinek, & Osecka, 2007). So with the right person-environment fit, a "difficult to tame" toddler may turn into a caring soldier or a true prosocial hero, like the firefighters on 9/11!

How important are peer groups versus parents in shaping our behavior as we travel through childhood into adult life? What can schools do to *generally* help children thrive? Stay tuned as I delve into these questions—and related topics—in the next chapter, which is devoted to home and school.

TYING IT ALL TOGETHER

1. When Melanie and Miranda play, they love to make up pretend scenes together. Are these two girls likely to be about age 2, age 5, or age 9?
2. In watching boys and girls at recess in an elementary school, which two observations are you likely to make?
   a. The boys are playing in larger groups.
   b. Both girls and boys love rough-and-tumble play.
   c. The girls are quieter and they are doing more negotiating.
3. Erik and Maria are arguing about the cause of gender-stereotyped behavior. Erik says the reason why boys like to run around and play with trucks is biological. Sophia argues that gender-stereotyped play is socialized by adults and other children. First, argue Erik's position and then, make Sophia's case by referring to specific data in this section.
4. You are fondly remembering your best friend in later elementary school. Which of the following statements is *not* likely to fit this relationship?
   a. You and your best buddy were very different in social status.
   b. You and your best buddy were very similar in interests.
   c. You and your best buddy supported and protected each other.
5. If Madison is popular in third grade, she is apt to be *well liked/personally disliked* by her classmates. If she is popular in sixth grade, she may be *well liked/personally disliked* by much of the class.
6. Which of the following children is at risk of being rejected in elementary school?
   a. Miguel, a very shy, socially anxious child
   b. Lauren, a tomboy who hates "girls' stuff"
   c. Nicholas, a highly aggressive child
   d. All of these children
7. (a) If a child (or adult) is being regularly bullied, name the core qualities that may be making this person an easy target. (b) Then, based on what you just read, describe in a sentence what you personally might do to change this situation. (*Note:* Using the principles in this chapter, I'll tell you in the answers section how I intervened to break up in-group bullying in my own academic society this year.)

Answers to the Tying It All Together questions can be found at the end of this chapter.

SUMMARY

Setting the Challenge: Emotion Regulation

Emotion regulation, the ability to manage and control our feelings, is crucial to having a successful life. Children with **externalizing tendencies** often "act out their emotions" and behave aggressively. Children with **internalizing tendencies** have problems managing intense fear. Both temperamental tendencies, at their extreme, cause problems during childhood.

Personality (and the Emerging Self)

Self-awareness changes dramatically as children move into middle childhood. Concrete operational children think about themselves in psychological terms, realistically scan their abilities, and evaluate themselves in comparison with peers. These realistic self-perceptions explain why **self-esteem** normally declines during elementary school. Comparing Erikson's early childhood task **(initiative versus guilt)** with **industry** and **inferiority** highlights the message that, in middle childhood, we fully wake up to the realities of life. Relationships, academics, behavior, sports, and looks are the five areas from which elementary schoolchildren derive their self-esteem.

Children with externalizing tendencies minimize their difficulties with other people and may have unrealistically high self-esteem. Children with internalizing tendencies may develop **learned helplessness,** the feeling that they are incapable of doing well. Because both attitudes keep children from improving their behavior, the key to helping *every* child is to focus on enhancing self-efficacy, promote realistic views of the self, and offer love. Unfortunately, negative racial-group stereotypes about "intelligence" can cause African American children to distrust teachers' feedback and lose self-efficacy at school.

Prosocial behaviors—caring, helpful acts—become more varied and mature as children develop. There also is consistency, with prosocial preschoolers tending to be prosocial later on. In Japan, children are taught that it's inappropriate to openly advertise prosocial acts.

Altruism—prosocial behavior that is genuinely non-self-serving—involves transforming one's **empathy** (directly experiencing another's feelings) into **sympathy** (feeling for another person); being self-confident (not overly anxious); and being happy. The best way to socialize altruism is to use **induction** (getting a child who has behaved hurtfully to understand the other person's feelings) and to induce **guilt.** Child-rearing techniques involving **shame** (personal humiliation) backfire, making children angry and less likely to act in prosocial ways.

Aggression, or hurtful behavior, is also basic to being human. Rates of open aggression (hitting, yelling) dramatically decline as children get older. **Instrumental aggression** is hurtful behavior we initiate. **Reactive aggression** occurs in response to being frustrated or hurt. **Relational aggression** refers to acts of aggression designed to damage social relationships. Relational aggression increases during late elementary school and middle school, and is present in girls and boys.

A two-step pathway may produce a highly aggressive child. When toddlers are very active (exuberant) or difficult, caregivers may respond harshly and punitively—causing anger and aggression. Then, during school, the child's "bad" behavior causes social rejection which leads to more aggression. Highly aggressive children may have a **hostile attributional bias.** This "the world is out to get me" outlook is understandable since aggressive children may have been living in a rejecting environment since their earliest years. Because boys tend to act out their feelings, they are more likely to be diagnosed as having "problematic aggression" than are girls.

Relationships

Play is at the heart of childhood. **Rough-and-tumble play** (play fighting and wrestling), is typical of boys. **Fantasy play** or pretending—typical of all children—begins in later infancy and becomes mutual at about age 4, with the beginning of **collaborative pretend play.** Fantasy play declines during concrete operations, as children become interested in organized activities.

Fantasy play may help children practice adult roles; offer a sense of control; and teach the need to adhere to norms and rules. Through examining fantasy play, adults can get insights into children's inner concerns.

Gender-segregated play unfolds during preschool, and in elementary school girls and boys typically play mainly with their own sex. Boy-to-boy play is rambunctious, while girls play together in quiet, collaborative ways. Boys tend to compete in groups; girls play one to one. Boys' play is more excluding of girls. Gender-stereotyped play seems to have a strong biological basis, but it is also socialized by society and, especially, by peers as children play together in same-sex groups. According to **gender schema theory,** once children understand that they are a boy or a girl, they attend to and model behaviors of their own sex.

In childhood (and adulthood) we select friends who are similar to ourselves, and when children get older, inner qualities such as personality, loyalty, and sharing feelings become important. Friends provide children with vital emotional support and teach them to get along with others.

Popular children are ranked as most well liked by their classmates—especially in elementary school. Rejected children are actively disliked—either because of serious externalizing or internalizing problems, or because they are different from the group. While in elementary school, children in the high-status group tend to be generally well liked; in middle school, kids in "the in-crowd" can sometimes be highly relationally aggressive, and so, paradoxically, disliked by much of the class. Although unpopular children are at risk for later problems, children who are rejected for being different may flower as adults.

Children who are unpopular—either aggressive **bully-victims** or, more typically, shy, anxious kids—are vulnerable to chronic **bullying.** The best way to help these children is to change the group norms favoring relational aggression. While relational aggression (and bullying) is "normal" to some degree, its frequency can be reduced if bystanders don't reinforce this behavior.. To help socially anxious children, connect timid preschoolers with a friend. Give at-risk exuberant toddlers lots of love, and understand that these "difficult" girls and boys may sometimes be incredibly successful adults.

KEY TERMS

ANSWERS TO TYING IT ALL TOGETHER QUIZZES

Setting the Challenge: Emotion Regulation

1. Paul has *externalizing tendencies*; Jeremy has *internalizing tendencies*; and issues with emotion regulation are problems for *both* boys.

Personality (and the Emerging Self)

1. c
2. Ramon = externalizing tendencies. Jared = internalizing tendencies. *Suggested intervention for Ramon:* Point out his realistic problems ("You are having trouble in X, Y, Z areas."), but cushion criticisms with plenty of love. *Suggested intervention for Jared*: Continually point out reality ("No one can always get A's. In fact, you are a fabulous student."). Get Jared to identify his "hopeless and helpless" ways of thinking, and train him to substitute more accurate perceptions.
3. Empathy; sympathy. Gabriel is more likely to reach out and comfort Zack.
4. a. = induction; good for promoting prosocial behavior; b. = shame; bad strategy; and c. = guilt; good for promoting prosocial behavior
5. Alyssa = instrumental, relational. Brianna = direct, reactive
6. Mario has a hostile attributional bias.

Relationships

1. About age 5
2. a and c
3. Erik can argue that gender-stereotyped play must be biologically built in, as this behavior occurs in primates and appears in societies around the world. He can also mention

the study showing masculine-type interests during adulthood may be programmed by prenatal testosterone. Sophia can say differing gender roles are strongly socialized by parents, teachers, and media messages from a young age. Most important, peers powerfully reinforce traditional "girl" or "boy" behavior as they segregate into same-sex play groups. Children are highly motivated to conform to these "correct" ways of acting or risk being socially excluded.

4. a
5. If Madison is popular in third grade, she is apt to be *well liked* by her classmates, If she is popular in sixth grade, she may be *personally disliked* by much of the class.
6. d
7. (a) She may be highly aggressive, and is bullied, then victimized. Or, more typically, she is anxious, has few friends, and has trouble standing up for herself. (b) Speak up against the perpetrators while the group is around. In my academic society, when members of an "in-group" repeatedly made fun of an out-group member via emails, I composed a message to "send all," saying in effect, "Lay off X. He is a real prince."

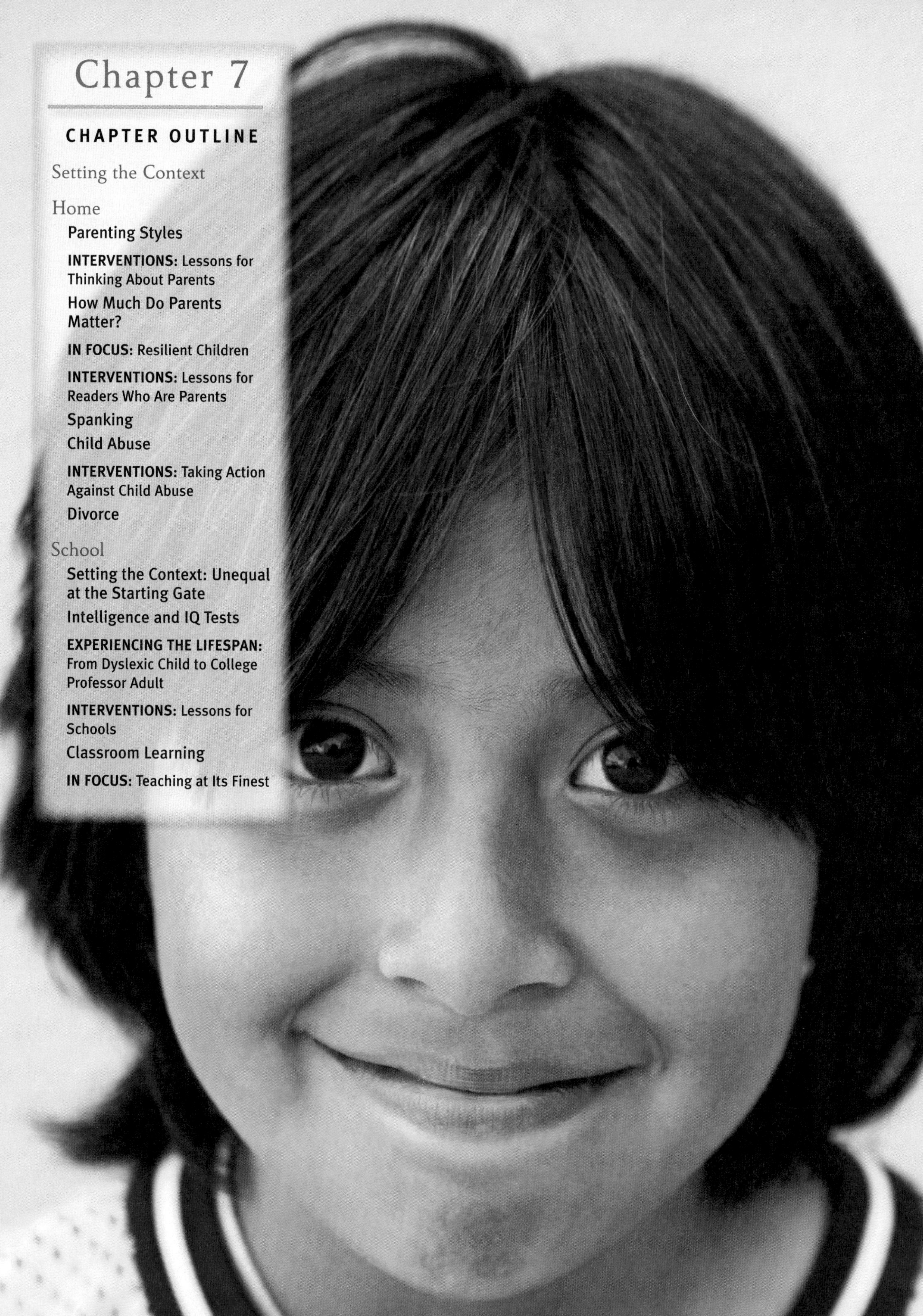

Chapter 7

CHAPTER OUTLINE

Settings for Development: Home and School

Manuel's parents migrated from Mexico to Las Vegas when he was a baby. Leaving their close extended family was painful, but they knew their son would not have a future in their small rural town.

At first, life was going well. The Las Vegas economy was booming. José joined the Culinary Workers' Union. Maria got a housekeeping job at Caesar's Palace. They sent money to relatives and made a down payment on a condo—carefully chosen to be in the best school district in town. Most important, their baby was turning into an exceptional boy. At age 5, Manuel could repair household appliances. He put together puzzles that would stump a 10-year-old child. He was picking up English beautifully, even though his parents, who only spoke Spanish, could not help him much with reading and preparing for school.

Then, when Manuel was 7, the economy tanked. José was laid off. He started to drink heavily. He came home late to regularly yell at his wife. Maria fell into a depression. This totally involved mother, who had been so strict but very loving—managing her son's activities, teaching him values—was barely able to pay any attention to her child. Although Manuel's first-grade teacher recommended he be tested for the gifted program, when the district psychologist got around to performing the evaluation, Manuel didn't make the cutoff. His performance IQ was off the charts. But growing up in a Spanish-speaking family was a real handicap. His verbal IQ was only 95. And this was the worst time for Manuel to be tested: Maria had recently taken her belongings, moved out, sent for her mother, and filed for divorce.

It's three years later and life is back to normal. Maria's becoming the caring mother she used to be. Manuel is returning to his old terrific self. Maria credits some "relationship therapy" she got at a local clinic for her son's self-confidence. She sings the praises of the fourth-grade teacher, too—for giving the class responsibility, understanding Manuel's talents, and having the courage to be creative and go beyond teaching to the standardized tests. The thorn in Maria's side is Grandma—or, to be exact, Manuel's attitude toward Grandma. Having her mother in the house has been a godsend. Manuel doesn't have to stay home alone at night when Maria works double shifts to keep the family above the poverty line. But Manuel is beginning to be ashamed to bring friends home to see that "Old World" lady. He wants to be a regular American boy. The downside of seeing your baby blossom beautifully in this country is watching your heritage get lost.

Is it typical for children, like Manuel, to have a few difficult years after their parents get divorced? Given that we vitally need to succeed in the wider world, how important are the lessons we learn from our parents as opposed to our peers? What was that test Manuel took, and what strategies can teachers use to make every child eager to learn? Now, we tackle these questions, and others, as I focus on the main settings within which children develop: home and school.

While my discussion applies to all children, in every home and school, in this chapter, I'll pay special attention to children such as Manuel, whose families differ from the traditional two-parent, middle-class, European American norm. So let's begin our exploration of home- and school-related topics by scanning the tapestry of families in the twenty-first-century United States.

Parenting grandmothers, such as this woman helping her grandson with his homework, show that strong, loving families in the United States come in many forms. What *exactly* is this grandma doing right? This is the question we will explore in this section.

Setting the Context

In 2010, two out of three U.S. families with children were categorized as "two-parent" (childstats.gov, 2010). That umbrella category covers varied family types. There is the *traditional two-parent family*—never-divorced couples with biological children. There are *blended families*—spouses have divorced and remarried, so children grow up with stepparents and, often, stepsiblings. There are *adoptive parents, gay parents, foster parents*, and *grandparent-headed families*.

Then there are the legions of *one-parent families*. With regard to this category, as you can see in Figure 7.1, we can make two generalizations. The vast majority of single-parent families are headed by mothers. With almost one in two single-parent families living under the poverty line, for children growing up with single moms in the United States, economic hardship is often a fact of life (childstats.gov, 2010).

Finally, there is the beautiful mosaic of U.S. ethnic families—people who vary in immigration status and everything else. What is your country of origin? What generation American are you? (Check out the stereotypes in Table 7.1 for statistics relating to this immigrant flood.)

TABLE 7.1: Stereotypes About "Immigrant America" and Some Statistical Facts

Stereotype #1: Immigrants are taking over the country.

Fact: While the phrase "taking over the country" may be too strong, as I suggested in Chapter 1, the United States is experiencing a remarkable influx of immigrants from every corner of the globe. In 2008, 70 million people were first- or second-generation immigrants, roughly 1 in 4 Americans. When we look at Hispanic Americans—currently 14 percent of the population and the largest minority group in the United States—the phrase "becoming more numerous" rings especially true. With a median age of 27, compared to 41 for European Americans, the face of the United States is poised to become far more Latino. By the mid-twenty-first century, this major minority group may outnumber whites.

Stereotype #2: Immigrants are poorly educated.

Fact: True and false, depending on their region of origin. Only half of all first-generation Hispanic Americans are high school graduates. However, with a whopping 1 in 4 Asian immigrants arriving with graduate degrees (versus 8.4 percent for Whites), new immigrants from the Far East are educationally miles ahead of native-born Americans.

Stereotype #3: Immigrants—particularly Hispanics—commit a disproportionate share of crimes.

Fact: Definitely false! Less than 1 percent of first-generation Hispanics are in prison (compared to more than 1 in 10 native-born African Americans and roughly 2 percent of Whites)—making newly arrived Latinos an incredibly law-abiding group. Unfortunately, however, over time, comparisons become less upbeat. Although incarceration rates never reach the alarming levels for African Americans, the percentage of second- and third-generation Hispanic Americans who have been in prison equals that of native-born Whites.

Stereotype #4: Immigrants don't want to learn the language or customs of the United States.

Fact: Once again, this (racist) stereotype is totally false. Even when they are raised in non–English-speaking families, more than half of all immigrant children say they prefer to speak English. By the third generation, English has become everyone's native tongue. Unfortunately, however, as I suggested above, the second and third generation also pick up some less-positive American customs. While the overwhelming majority of first-generations Mexican American children grow up in two-parent families, by the third generation, only slightly more than half make that claim. Among second-generation Asian Americans, rates of single motherhood are double that of their parents.

Sources: Fuller & García Coll, 2010; Rumbaut, 2008; Thai, Connel, & Tebes, 2010.

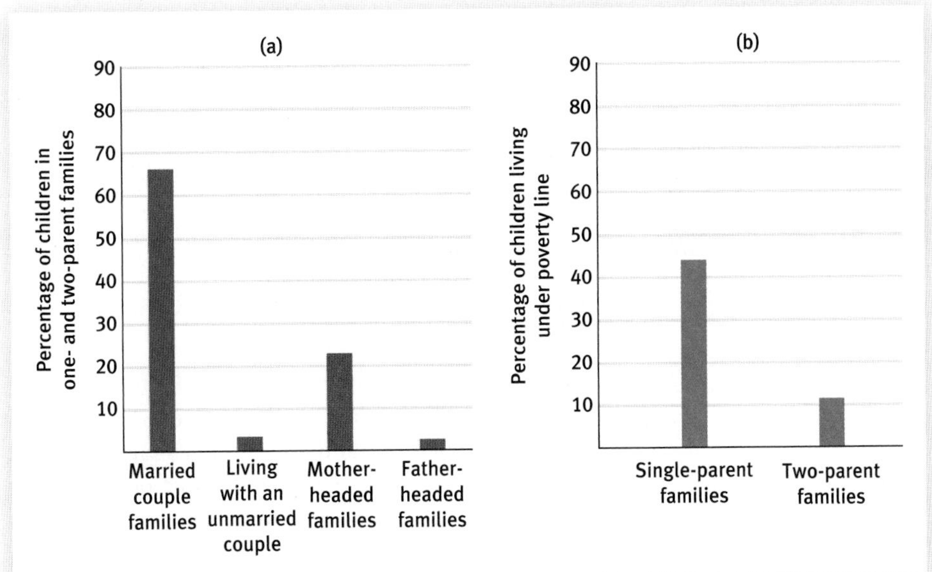

FIGURE 7.1: **Living arrangements of children in U.S. families:** (a) shows that the two-parent family is still the most common one—although this family form includes a wide variety of "traditional" and more nontraditional families. The second chart (b) shows that children who live in single-parent families have roughly four times the odds of living under the poverty line as those whose parents are married.

Source: childstats.gov, 2010.

Home

Can children thrive in every family? The answer is yes. The key lies in what parents do. We already know that parents need to promote a secure attachment and be sensitive to a child's temperamental needs. Can we outline an overall discipline style that works best? In a landmark series of studies conducted 40 years ago—by observing middle-class California parents interacting with their children—developmentalist Diana Baumrind (1971) decided that we could.

Parenting Styles

Think of a parent you admire. What is that mother or father doing right? Now think of parents who you feel are not fulfilling this job. Where are they falling short? Most likely, your list will center on two functions. Are these people loving and nurturing? Do they provide discipline or rules? By classifying parents on these two dimensions—being child-centered, and providing "structure" or rules—Baumrind (1971) and other researchers spelled out the following four **parenting styles:**

- **Authoritative parents** rank high on both nurturing and setting limits. They give their children reasonable freedom and lots of love but also have defined expectations and rules. These families set high standards for their children's behavior. There are specific bedtimes and homework times. However, if a daughter wants to watch a favorite TV program, these parents might relax the rule that homework must be finished before dinner. They could let a son extend his regular 9:00 P.M. bedtime for a special event. Although authoritative parents believe firmly in structure, they understand that rules don't take precedence over human needs.
- **Authoritarian parents** are more inflexible. Their child-rearing motto is, "Do just what I say." In these families, rules are not negotiable. While authoritarian parents may love their children deeply, their upbringing can appear to be inflexible, rigid, and cold.
- **Permissive parents** are at the opposite end of the spectrum from authoritarian parents. Their parenting mantra is, "Provide total freedom and unconditional love." In these households, there may be no set bedtimes and no homework demands. The child-rearing principle here is that children's wishes rule.
- **Rejecting-neglecting parents** are the worst of both worlds—low on structure and low on love. Their child-rearing motto is, "Minimize involvement with my

parenting style In Diana Baumrind's framework, how parents align on two dimensions of child-rearing: nurturance (or child-centeredness) and discipline (or structure and rules).

authoritative parents In the parenting-styles framework, the best possible child-rearing style, in which parents rank high on both nurturance and discipline, providing both love and clear family rules.

authoritarian parents In the parenting-styles framework, a type of child-rearing in which parents provide plenty of rules but rank low on child-centeredness, stressing unquestioning obedience.

permissive parents In the parenting-styles framework, a typ e of child-rearing in which parents provide few rules but rank high on child-centeredness, being extremely loving but providing little discipline.

rejecting-neglecting parents In the parenting-styles framework, the worst child-rearing approach, in which parents provide little discipline and little nurturing or love.

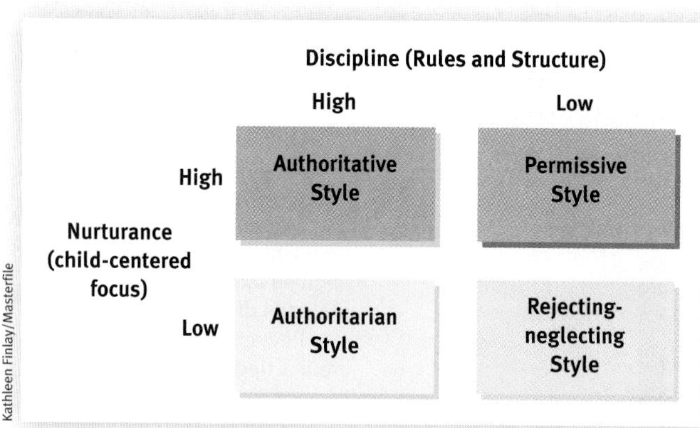

FIGURE 7.2: **Parenting styles:** A summary diagram.
Source: Adapted from Baumrind, 1971.

child." In this house, children are neglected, ignored, and emotionally abandoned. They are left to literally raise themselves (see Figure 7.2 for a recap).

In relating the first three discipline studies to children's behavior (the fourth was added later), Baumrind found that the children of "authoritative" parents were more successful and socially skilled. Hundreds of twentieth-century studies confirmed this finding: Authoritative parenting works best (Maccoby & Martin, 1983).

Decoding Parenting in a Deeper Way

At first glance, Baumrind's authoritative category offers a wonderful blueprint for the right way to raise children: Provide firm structure and lots of love. However, if you classify your parents along these dimensions, you may find problems. Perhaps one parent was permissive and another authoritarian. Or, perhaps, in some areas, your parents didn't allow for *any* disagreements (were authoritarian) and, in others, acted permissive. Maybe, over time, the rules in your house randomly veered from permissive to rigid.

To explore the impact of these inconsistencies, one researcher polled adolescents in nine countries. He related teens' reports of the three mismatches described above to the adolescents' mental distress (Dwairy, 2010).

Interestingly, the worst inconsistency—in every nation—occurred when parents' rules in a given area changed dramatically over time. Adolescents did sometimes report more trouble when mothers and fathers disagreed on discipline, with one parent being strict and the other loose. But being relatively permissive or rigid in different situations was no problem at all.

This finding makes good sense. Imagine how disoriented you would be if your parents sometimes came down very hard on you and later, in *similar situations*, seemed not to care. When one parent is more authoritarian and the other permissive, you do have predictability ("I can get away with things with mom, but not with dad"), although you might feel a bit upset. But isn't being strict in some areas and looser in others what parenting is all about? Rather than simply adhering to a single style, parents should provide a *consistent* roadmap for their child.

This more nuanced study makes sense of why many twenty-first-century developmentalists view Baumrind's styles perspective as too simplistic. Specifically, they argue:

Because this Chinese mom expects obedience and won't tolerate any "back talk" from her daughter, many of us would see her child-rearing style as rigid, according to Western norms. But, because collectivist cultures put a premium on respecting parents, this *authoritarian parenting strategy* may be highly effective for her child.

CHILD-REARING INVOLVES MANY DIFFERENT BEHAVIORS. Think back to previous chapters, and you will immediately realize that parents do far more than provide love and discipline (Grusec & Davidov, 2010). They scaffold learning (recall Chapter 5); coach their children about relationships (Mounts, 2011). They rearrange the environment by carefully selecting the right preschool or moving to a different neighborhood (recall Chapter 4) or nation (as in the introductory vignette in this chapter). Spend a day with parents and their children. How many of these mothers' and fathers' child-rearing activities have nothing to do with *any* defined style?

During that day, you may also notice how different these people's parenting decisions are from those you might make. But before making negative judgments, let's consider these choices through a cultural lens.

CHILD-REARING APPROACHES VARY BY CULTURE AND ETHNICITY. Baumrind's conclusion, that "ideal parenting" involves being authoritative, reflects middle-class, individualistic Western cultural priorities: Our society prizes being assertive and independent.

TABLE 7.2: Checklist for Identifying Your Parenting Priorities

Rank the following goals in order of their importance to you, from 1 (for highest priority) to 8 (for lowest priority). It's OK to use the same number twice if two goals are equally important to you.

_____ Producing an obedient, well-behaved child

_____ Producing a caring, prosocial child

_____ Producing an independent, self-sufficient child

_____ Producing a child who is extremely close to you

_____ Producing an intelligent, creative thinker

_____ Producing a well-rounded child

_____ Producing a happy, emotionally secure child

_____ Producing a spiritual (religious) child

What do your rankings reveal about the qualities you most admire in human beings?

So it makes sense that many North American and European parents adopt flexible, negotiable child-rearing rules. Residents of collectivist cultures such as China, or U.S. ethnic minorities such as Latinos, have different agendas: "Be obedient"; "Respect my rules" (Fuller & García Coll, 2010; Mistry, Chaudhuri, & Diez, 2003).

Might an authoritarian child-rearing style work best in a culture that prioritizes obedience and respect? A study comparing two groups of Israeli parents—Palestinians (who have more collectivistic ideas) with Jewish couples (a group with Western individualistic values)—suggests the answer is yes (Feldman & Masalha, 2010). Interestingly, while the Jewish preschoolers with highly authoritarian dads were apt to be labeled "less socially competent," for Palestinian boys and girls, having an authoritarian father was tied to superior social skills!

How important is it to you to raise an independent child? What priority do you put on your sons and daughters being respectful?

Table 7.2 offers you a chance step back and rank your child-rearing priorities, and think more deeply about how your values might be shaped by your family background or cultural group. If you compare your answers with those of other class members, you will vividly see that we can legitimately differ a great deal in the qualities we most admire in children (and human beings).

CHILD-REARING APPROACHES CHANGE, DEPENDING ON THE ENVIRONMENT. The fact that parenting practices legitimately differ is especially striking when we look throughout history. Recall from Chapter 1 that, during the eighteenth and nineteenth centuries, affluent parents in cities such as Paris sent their newborns away to be nursed by women in the countryside. Today, we would consider these practices abusive. In that era, they were vital to ensuring that babies would survive.

Difficult life conditions affect child-rearing decisions today. When parents believe their neighborhood is dangerous, they naturally react by laying down more rigid rules. And, some research suggests that among inner-city African Americans, this more authoritarian approach to parenting predicts children's success (Dearing, 2004). Think of how your parenting style would change if you moved to a war-torn country or a crime-ridden area in your city. Safety would be your *first* priority, before anything else.

Does this mean we should totally discard the styles framework? The answer is no! Rejecting-neglecting parenting is poisonous for children in every culture (Dwairy and others, 2010; Sturge-Apple, Davies, & Cummings, 2010). In every society, good parents provide consistent discipline and love. But parents also need to be flexible, varying their child-rearing strategies to provide the best discipline–environment fit.

INTERVENTIONS: Lessons for Thinking About Parents

How can you use this section's insights to relate to parents in a more empathic way in your daily life?

- Be culture-friendly. Don't impose your own parenting priorities on other people. Understand that there are a variety of valid child-rearing goals.
- Be aware that dangerous environments demand a more vigilant, rule-oriented kind of parenting—one that may look rigid and less child-centered from a traditionally middle-class Western view.
- Before you blame a mother or father for being too strict (or too lax), try to understand the pressures this family is facing. Rather than being judgmental, it is best to be caring and work to provide parents with support.

How Much Do Parents Matter?

My discussion, however, assumes that parents are in the driver's seat—that what happens at home is the crucial force in determining how children turn out. Why then do so many wonderful parents have children with terrible problems? Why do some children with terrible early lives succeed brilliantly as adults?

IN FOCUS: Resilient Children

> His aristocratic parents spent their time gallivanting around Europe; they never appeared at the nursery doors. At age 7, he was wrenched from the only person who loved him—his nanny—and shipped off to boarding school. Insolent, angry, refusing to obey orders or sit still, he was regularly beaten by the headmaster and teased by the other boys. Although gifted at writing, he was incapable of rote memorization; he couldn't pass a test. When he graduated at the bottom of his boarding school class, his father informed him that he would never amount to anything. His name was Winston Churchill. He was the man who stood up to Hitler and carried England to victory in the Second World War.

Churchill's upbringing was a recipe for disaster. He had neglectful parents, behavior problems, and was a total failure at school. But this dismal childhood produced the leader who saved the modern world.

Resilient children, like Churchill, confront terrible conditions such as parental abuse, poverty, and the horrors of war and go on to construct successful, loving lives. What qualities allow these children to thrive? Developmentalists who study these unusual boys and girls find that resilient children often have special talent, such as Churchill's gift for writing, or superior cognitive skills. They are adaptable and able to regulate their emotions. They have a high sense of self-efficacy and an optimistic worldview (Brodhagan & Wise, 2008; Pitzer & Fingerman, 2010). They possess a strong faith or sense of meaning in life (Wright & Masten, 2005).

Being resilient depends on inner resources—having an "easy" temperament and superior intellectual and social skills (Deater-Deckard, Ivy, & Smith, 2005a,b). But the *quantity* of environmental setbacks also matters (Greenfield, 2010). If you are exposed to a series of tragedies—for instance, having your parents get divorced after recently becoming homeless, due to experiencing a natural disaster such as a hurricane—it's more difficult to preserve your efficacy feelings or rebound to construct a happy life (Becker-Blease, Turner, & Finkelhor, 2010; Kronenberg and others, 2010).

resilient children Children who rebound from serious early life traumas to construct successful adult lives.

Not only is the quantity of life stress important, so is the presence of "social supports." Children who succeed against incredible odds typically have at least one close, caring relationship with a parent or another adult (such as Churchill's nanny). Like a plant that thrives in the desert, resilient children have the internal resources to to extract love from their parched environment. But they cannot survive without any water at all.

Might these children have specific resilience-promoting genes? Emerging neuroscience research suggests they may (Diamond, 2009). Remember, from Chapter 4, that people with two long forms of a gene that regulates the production of the neurotransmitter serotonin seem relatively insulated from breaking down under stress; but that this same "environmental immunity" gene form may be a liability when the wider world is nurturing and calm (Ellis and others, 2011; see Belsky & Pluess, 2009, for review). So, some of us may indeed be biologically blessed specifically to weather the hurricanes of human life (see also Fox and others, 2011).

The Library of Congress

Abandoned by his father at about age 9 to be cared for by a teenaged sister for several years after his mother's premature death, raised in a dirt-floor Kentucky shack without any chance to attend school—Abraham Lincoln grew up to become our most beloved president and perhaps the greatest man of the nineteenth century. What qualities made this incredibly resilient child thrive? The answer: towering intellectual gifts, a remarkable drive to learn, optimism, self-efficacy, and—most of all—a world-class talent for understanding human motivations and connecting with people in a caring, prosocial way. By the way, while he guided a battered nation, "father Abraham"—shown here with his son—also made time to be a totally *permissive*, hands-on dad.

Making the Case that Parents Don't Matter (Much)

How important is our biology (nature) versus our upbringing (nurture) in determining the adult we will become? Twin and adoption studies, you may remember from Chapter 1, come down firmly on the "a good deal is genetic" side. In fact, because Baumrind's findings involve correlations, behavioral geneticists have severely criticized them. Couldn't the link between authoritative parenting and successful children be explained by shared genetic tendencies? Parents who handle child-rearing competently pass down the same biological predispositions for competence that cause their children to succeed (Rowe, 2003; Scarr, 1997). Or, through an *evocative process* (recall Chapter 1), because children's inborn temperament causes specific caregiving reactions, wouldn't easy babies produce authoritative parents? (Think of how hard it would be for you to act authoritative with a child who was bouncing off the walls. Your main impulse would probably be to hit and yell or give up!) Therefore, don't children's personalities drive parenting styles, rather than the reverse? (See Deater-Deckard, 1996; Plomin & Bergeman, 1991)

Almost two decades ago, a rebel psychologist named Judith Harris proposed the most interesting twist on the "parents don't matter" argument. Harris (1995, 1998, 2002, 2006) believes that the environment has a dramatic impact on our development. But she makes the case that—rather than our parents—our peers (or social group) socialize us to become adults.

Harris begins by taking aim at the main principle underlying attachment theory—that the lessons we learn from our parents transfer to our other relationships. Learning, Harris believes, is context-specific. We cannot use the same *working model* with our mother and with the classroom bully, or we would never survive. Furthermore, because we live our lives in the wider world, she argues, the messages we absorb from the culture of our contemporaries must take precedence over the lessons we are taught at home.

Any parent can relate to Harris's peer-power principle when she witnesses, in horror, her three-year-old picking up every bad habit from the other children the first week after entering preschool. You saw a chilling example of a similar group infection in the last chapter, when I described how aggressive middle-school norms are apt to evoke bullying in the "nicest kids." The most compelling evidence for Harris's theory,

Skjold Photographs/The Image Works

Look at these exuberant boys, passionate to fit in with their friends. Then, ask yourself whether these children are acting the same way they were taught to behave at home. Suddenly, doesn't Judith Harris's theory that "peer groups shape our development" make a good deal of sense?

however, comes from looking at immigrant children Turn back to the stereotypes discussed in Table 7.1 on page 204, and you will notice that girls and boys who move to the United States prefer English—the language of the wider society—to the tongue they speak at home. From divorce, to non-marital parenthood, to the tendency to break the law, by the second generation, immigrants blend in with the American norm. So the rapidity with which **acculturation,** assimilation to *any* new culture, occurs is a vivid testament to the fact that Harris has an important point.

These arguments that genetics and the values of the wider culture shape development alert us to the fact that, when you see children "acting out" at a restaurant or at school, you cannot leap to the assumption that "it's all the parents' fault." As developmental systems theory predicts, a variety of influences—from genetics, to peer groups, to everything else—affect how children behave. But you may be thinking that the idea that parents are *not* important goes too far.

Many experts agree. For children to realize their genetic potential, parents should try to provide the *best* possible environment (Ceci and others, 1997; Kagan, 1998; Maccoby, 2002). In fact, when children are temperamentally vulnerable, as I've been pointing out in previous chapters, superior parenting is required.

Making the Case for Superior Parenting

Imagine, for instance, that your toddler is very active and has trouble regulating his emotions. You know from reading this book that your child's temperament puts him at risk of having externalizing problems as he travels into school. You are determined not to let that pattern unfold. So you inhibit your use of *power assertion.* You take care to provide lots of love. You arrange the environment to minimize your child's vulnerabilities and highlight his strengths.

Actually, when a child is temperamentally fragile, developmentalists find again and again that sensitive caregiving can make a critical difference. From studies that show loving touch helps premature infants grow (recall Chapter 3), to my earlier child-rearing suggestions to use with highly fearful or exuberant kids, the message is the same: When children are "at risk," superior parenting matters most.

So yes, biologically resilient children can flower in the face of difficult life conditions and less-than-ideal parenting styles. But when a baby needs special nurturing, the importance of high-quality nurture shines out.

INTERVENTIONS: Lessons for Readers Who Are Parents

Now let's summarize our discussion by shifting gears and talking to the parent readers of this book:

There are no firm guidelines about how to be an effective parent—except to be loving, set high standards, and provide consistent rules. But it also is critical to adapt your discipline to your life situation and especially to your unique child. You will face special challenges if you live in a dangerous neighborhood (where you may have to exert more control) or have children who are "harder to raise" (where you may have to work harder to stay loving and attached). Your ultimate power is limited at best.

Try to see this message as liberating. Children cannot be massaged into having an idealized adult life. Your child's future does not totally depend on you. Focus on the quality of your relationship, and enjoy these wonderful years. And if your son or daughter is having difficulties, draw inspiration from Winston Churchill's history. Predictions from childhood to adult life can be hazy. Your unsuccessful child may grow up to save the world!

Now that I've covered the general territory, let's turn to specifics. First, we'll examine that controversial practice, spanking; then, focus on the worst type of parenting, child abuse; and finally, explore that common family transition, divorce.

acculturation Among immigrants, the tendency to become more similar in terms of attitudes and practices to the mainstream culture after time spent living in a new society.

Spanking

corporal punishment The use of physical force to discipline a child.

Poll your friends and family about their opinions relating to **corporal punishment**—any discipline technique using physical measures such as spanking—and you are likely to get strong reactions. Some people believe in the biblical principle, "Spare the rod and spoil the child." They may blame the decline in spanking for every social problem. Others blame corporal punishment for *creating* those social problems. They believe that parents who rely on "hitting" are implicitly teaching children the message that it is OK to respond in a violent way. To put these positions into perspective, let's take a brief tour of a total turnaround in corporal punishment attitudes in recent times.

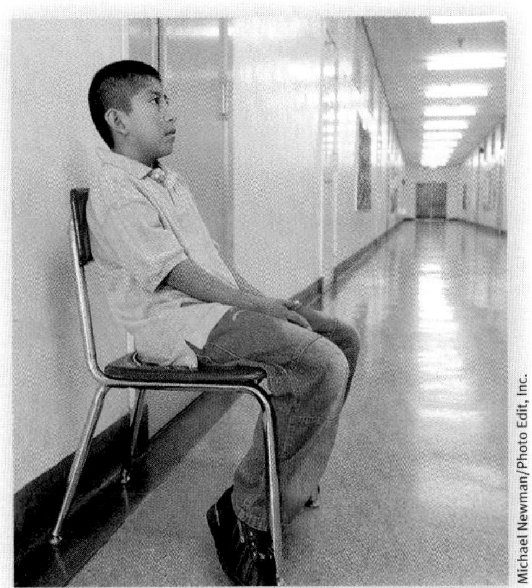

Michael Newman/Photo Edit, Inc.

In the not-so-distant past, this boy, who has misbehaved in school, would have been paddled by the principal or teacher. Today, because attitudes about corporal punishment have totally changed, his punishment is to have a "time-out" in the hall.

Throughout human history, corporal punishment used to be standard practice. Flogging was routine in prisons (Gould & Pate, 2010), in the military, and other places (Pinker, 2011). Until the late nineteenth century, in the United States, it was perfectly legal for men to "physically chastise" their wives (Knox, 2010). Today, while these practices still occur in less developed nations, in Western democracies they are widely condemned (Knox, 2010).

Although attitudes about child corporal punishment are more ambivalent, you might be interested to know that in recent years—from Spain to Sweden or Croatia to Costa Rica—a remarkable 24 nations have passed laws totally banning spanking. Organizations from the American Academy of Pediatrics, to the United Nations, to the Methodist Church have also passed resolutions calling corporal punishment "inhumane" (Knox, 2010).

In the United States, we've been listening—a bit. Spanking is illegal at schools and day- care centers in most states. But any person proposing a bill to universally ban this behavior would be laughed off the Congressional floor. Not only is our individualistic society wary about government intrusion in family life, but *most* U.S. parents do spank their daughters and sons.

Still, with surveys showing only one in ten parents saying they "often spank," corporal punishment is not the preferred U.S. discipline mode. Today, the most frequent punishments parents in the United States report are "time-outs" and removal of privileges and, to a lesser extent, getting sent to one's room (Barkin, 2007).

Who is most likely to spank? Corporal punishment is widely accepted in the African American community (Burchinal, Skinner, & Reznick, 2010; Lorber, O'Leary, & Smith Slep, 2011). As one Black woman in a poverty-level neighborhood reported: "I would rather me discipline them than (the police)" (Taylor, Hamvas, & Paris, 2011, p. 65). As you might imagine from the "spare the rod, spoil the child" injunction, people who believe the Bible is literally true and put high priority on having obedient children tend to strongly advocate this disciplinary technique (Rodriguez & Henderson, 2010).

Adults who were spanked as children see more value in this child-rearing approach (Simons & Wurtele, 2010). (In my classes, I often hear students report: "I was spanked and it helped; so I plan to do the same with my kids.") But there is a caution. If you feel that physical punishment got out of hand during your childhood, you are probably passionate about *never* hitting your own daughter or son (Gagne and others, 2007).

What do experts advise? Here, there is considerable debate. Many psychologists argue that physical punishment is *never* appropriate (Gershoff, 2002; Knox, 2010). They believe that hitting a child conveys the message that it is acceptable for big people to give small people pain. Yes, spanking, these psychologists point out, does produce compliance. But, it impairs the development of conscience because it gets children to only focus on themselves (Andero & Stewart, 2002; Benjet & Kazdin, 2003; Knox, 2010).

Other experts believe that mild spanking is not detrimental (Baumrind, Larzelere, & Cowan, 2002; Larzelere & Kuhn, 2005; Oas, 2010). They suggest that, if we rule out corporal punishment, caregivers may resort to more damaging, shaming responses such as saying, "I hate you. You will never amount to anything."

This "spanking can be acceptable" position now has interesting research as ammunition. One recent study suggests spanking may not result in negative consequences (Morris & Gibson, 2011). (But others—I must emphasize—offer a more negative view). So, for my parent readers who don't want to totally rule out corporal punishment, psychologists have the following guidelines as to how and when this type of discipline might be used:

- Never hit an infant. *Babies can't control their behavior. They don't know what they are doing wrong.* For a preschooler, a few light swats on the bottom can be an effective disciplinary technique when a child is engaging in dangerous activities—such as running into the street—that need to be immediately stopped (Larzelere & Kuhn, 2005).
- When you use physical punishment, accompany this action with a verbal explanation ("What you did was wrong because . . ."). Preferably, use other techniques such as time-outs or removing the child from the scene. Reserve a spanking as a backup technique when other strategies, such as time-outs, fail.

The problem is that spanking is often not a backup strategy—particularly among the very children whom physical punishment clearly *does* harm—namely boys and girls at risk for externalizing problems (recall Chapter 6). Therefore, parent training is crucial. We need to emphasize the behavioral principle that positive reinforcement (giving rewards for good behavior) is more effective than *any* punishment, be it spanking or being sent to a room. We must *vigorously* dispel the misconception that it's possible to spoil a baby, and that spanking produces a well-behaved child (Burchinal, Skinner, & Reznick, 2010).

Frequent spanking actually has the opposite effect. It tends to promote the very behavior it is supposed to cure. To take one example, researchers found that parents who believed strongly in spanking had kids who said it was fine, during disagreements with a playmate, to "hit" that other child (Simons & Wurtele, 2010). Worse yet, what might start out as a normal spanking can escalate as a parent "gets into it," the child cries more, and soon you have that worst-case scenario: child abuse.

Child Abuse

Child maltreatment—the term for acts that endanger children's physical or emotional well-being—comprises four categories. *Physical abuse* refers to bodily injury that leaves bruises. It encompasses everything from overzealous spanking to battering that may lead to a child's death. *Neglect* refers to caregivers' failure to provide adequate supervision and care. It might mean abandoning the child, not providing sufficient food, or failing to enroll a son or daughter in school. *Emotional abuse* refers to continual shaming or serious acts such as terrorizing or exploiting a child. *Sexual abuse* covers the spectrum from rape and incest to fondling and exhibitionistic acts.

Everyone can identify serious forms of maltreatment, but there is a gray zone as to what activities cross the line (Greenfield, 2010). Does *every* spanking that leaves bruises qualify as physical abuse? If a single mother is forced to leave her toddler in an 8-year-old sibling's care when she goes to work, is she neglectful? Are parents who walk around naked in the house guilty of sexual abuse? Emotional abuse is inherently murky to define, although this form of maltreatment may be the most common of all (Foster and others, 2010).

child maltreatment Any act that seriously endangers a child's physical or emotional well-being.

Even if we had the best definitions, it would be impossible to pin down the actual incidence of child abuse. Rates of maltreatment in the United States have declined in recent years, but as this documented disaster strikes roughly 1 in 100 children, its prevalence is still unacceptably high (childstats.gov, 2010). Worse yet, most cases are not reported to the authorities (Greenfield, 2010). They may be found "accidentally" when a child is discovered with welts, or stunted and near death. What provokes this kind of violence, and how might caring adults intervene?

Exploring the Risk Factors

As developmental systems theory would predict, several categories of influence combine to cause child abuse to flare up (Wolfe, 2011):

PARENTS' PERSONALITY PROBLEMS ARE IMPORTANT. People who abuse their children tend to suffer from psychological disorders such as depression and externalizing problems (Annerbäck, Svedin, & Gustafsson, 2010). They often have hostile attributional biases (Berlin, Appleyard, & Dodge, 2011; Crouch and others, 2010), assuming "bad" behavior from benign activities, like a toddler's running around. Their determination not to "spoil" their babies is accompanied by other unrealistic expectations. They may believe that 3-month-olds can be taught not to cry or that 8-month-olds can be totally toilet trained (Bissada & Briere, 2001).

LIFE STRESS ACCOMPANIED BY SOCIAL ISOLATION CAN BE CRUCIAL. Abusive parents are often coping with an overload of upsetting life events, from domestic violence to severe poverty (Annerbäck, Svedin, & Gustafsson, 2010). Most important, they feel cut off from other people. Just as lack of social support is a recipe for depression among poor pregnant single mothers (remember Chapter 2), social isolation, plus severe economic distress, researchers find, is the match that is most apt to ignite child abuse (Berlin, Appleyard, & Dodge, 2011; Li, Godinet, & Arnsberger, 2011).

CHILDREN'S VULNERABILITIES ARE IMPORTANT. Having a child who is "difficult" can fan this fire—caring for a baby who cries excessively (Reijneveld and others, 2004), has a medical problem (Svensson, Bornehag, & Janson, 2011), or is premature. Not only do these children need extra attention, their "noncompliant" behavior is apt to be viewed as a personal threat (Bugental and others, 2010). The fact that abusive parents may target just one child was brought home to me when I was working as a clinical psychologist at a city hospital in New York. A mother was referred for treatment for abusing her "spiteful" 10-year-old, although she never harmed his "sweet" 3-year-old brother. So disturbances in the attachment relationship are often a core ingredient in the poisonous recipe for producing a battered child.

As you learned in Chapter 4, maltreated children often have insecure attachments (Stronach and others, 2011). They may suffer from depression and anxiety (van Harmelen and others, 2010a), and have problems regulating their emotions (Kim & Cicchetti, 2010). They tend to be highly aggressive (Teisl and others, 2012) and get rejected by their peers (Kim & Cicchetti, 2010). Just as with the orphanage-reared babies discussed in Chapter 4, brain-imaging studies also suggest child maltreatment may compromise the developing frontal lobes (van Harmelen and others, 2010b).

Maltreated children (no surprise) can carry their attachment problems into dating relationships (Riggs, Cusimano, & Benson, 2010). At midlife, they earn less than their contemporaries (Currie & Widom, 2011) and suffer from comparatively poor physical health (Pitzer & Fingerman, 2010). And yes, adults who were abused are at higher risk of maltreating their own children.

But there is tremendous variability. Some abused children develop normally (Woodruff and Lee, 2011). Others are passionate to become the best possible parents, and never, ever hit their daughters and sons (Berlin, Appleyard, & Dodge, 2011). As one woman described: "I made a vow to protect my children no matter what.... It was almost like a mantra, that I'm never going to strike (my child) (quoted in Hall, 2011, p. 38).

INTERVENTIONS: Taking Action Against Child Abuse

What should you do if you suspect child abuse? Teachers, social workers, and health-care professionals are required by law to report the abuse to child protec-

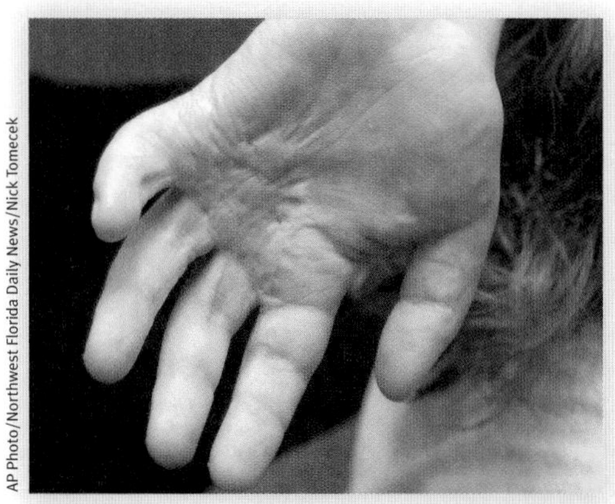

Imagine you are a teacher who sees these kinds of suspicious burns on a student's hands. You know that unusual injuries like this can signal child abuse, but you aren't absolutely sure. Would you immediately report the situation to the authorities? Would you talk to the parents first? What *exactly* would you do?

tive services. In 18 states as well as most Canadian provinces, the law impels *any* concerned citizen to speak up. Children in imminent danger are removed from the home, and the cases are referred to juvenile court. Judges do not have the power to punish abusive parents, but they can place their children in foster care and limit or terminate their parental rights.

Imagine you are a teacher or health-care worker who suspects a child is being abused. If you make a "mistake" and falsely report that case, you run the risk of ruining a family's life. You may feel that you don't have the training to make a difficult judgment call or fear your life would be in danger from a vengeful parent if you make a report (see Chen and others, 2010; Osofsky and Lieberman, 2010): "Are those injuries normal accidents, or the patterned bruises characteristic of being hit by a cord or belt?" (Harris, 2010.) "Will the hospital social worker listen to my report?" (See Feng and others, 2010.)

Then, imagine you are a judge who must make the heart-wrenching decision to put a child in foster care. If you leave the child in an abusive home, that boy or girl may be reinjured. But you also know that being separated from a primary attachment figure can leave emotional scars. This is why, if possible, it's best to keep the child in the family and provide parents with intensive support. The good news is that mental health interventions targeted to improving parent-child relationships in abusive families *do* work (Falconer, Clark, and Parris, 2011; Swenson and others, 2010). The same message—counseling helps—is true of that family situation we turn to now: divorce.

Divorce

Child abuse affects a small fraction of children. Millions of children each year, however, see their parents' marriage break up. How does divorce affect children, and what forces affect how children adjust?

Let's start with the bad news. Studies comparing children of divorce with their counterparts in intact married families show that children of divorce are at a statistical disadvantage—academically, socially, and in terms of mental health (Amato, 2010; Potter, 2010). However, these general comparisons are misleading because they paint an overly grim picture. Three out of four children whose parents divorce don't have major mental health problems (Kelly, 2003). Moreover, while some children show enduring scars after divorce, others have no problems or thrive (Amato, 2010).

Also, the psychological difficulties children do have may begin before the couple splits up (Amato, 2010; Kelly, 2003). Imagine your parents are continually fighting. The family atmosphere is tense. Your mother (or father) is depressed and angry. She cannot give you the attention you need. Around the time of the separation, researchers find, child-rearing tends to become more disorganized as couples struggle with their feelings and try to rearrange their lives (Hetherington, 1999). Because of their own inner turmoil, many parents have trouble talking about their situation—leaving their children confused, angry, and sad. Fortunately, however, most parents do regroup and regain their equilibrium after a year or two (Kelly, 2003).

What forces help children rebound from this trauma? One key is to keep life as consistent as possible. Unfortunately, after a couple divorces, families tend to move. But relocation can deprive a child of contact with a much loved, nonresident parent (Stein & Oler, 2010), as well as placing that boy or girl under added strain (Austin, 2008). Another key is to empower older children by giving them some say in what happens with regard to visitation and custody. In one poll of divorced parents and their children, everyone agreed that having child input was important, but that it might be too threatening for sons and daughters to have total control. As a teenager named Sophie commented, "I don't think they should have the final decision… but they should be able to say, 'I would prefer this and this'" (quoted in Cashmore & Parkinson, 2008, p. 94).

The main key to adjustment, however, lies in the care the parent who gets custody provides. Can the custodial mother or father be an effective parent? (See Amato, 2010.) It is also important to look at the relationship between the ex-spouses. When husbands and wives battle over visitation rights, continually bad-mouth each other, or turn the children against a former partner, children suffer most (Amato, 2010; Baker, 2005).

Would it be better for couples to stay together for the sake of the children? If the marriage is what researchers label "high conflict," the answer is no. For children subjected to continual marital fighting—and especially domestic violence—ending the marriage improves children's well-being (Amato, 2010). As one of my students commented, "Because the atmosphere at home was terrible, I felt much happier after my parents divorced."

Moreover, while for "low-conflict" marriages, joint custody makes good sense (Symons, 2010), if a father is antisocial—or if there are questions about maltreatment—there is a good case for limiting access to that particular dad (or mom) (see DeGarmo, 2010; Lessard and others, 2010). So, again, in understanding divorce, we need to adopt a developmental systems approach: "What are the unique conditions of that family's life?"

Figure 7.3 illustrates these issues on a timeline and suggests some interventions that counselors might make (see also Vélez and others, 2011). In Chapter 11, I'll explore divorce from the adult point of view. Now, it's time to turn to that other setting within which children develop—school.

Royalty-Free/Masterfile

Should this unhappy couple stay together "for the sake of their daughter"? The answer, as you can see in the text, depends on whether they can stop continually getting into these terrible arguments.

Timeline

Family arguments → Separation, chaotic parenting → Divorce → Reorganizing life

Interventions

Family arguments	Separation, chaotic parenting	Divorce / Reorganizing life
Couple counseling	Offer emotional support to children. Minimize other life changes.	Foster authoritative custodial parenting.
	Encourage open discussion with children about what is happening; give them some voice in visitation.	Discourage parents from using their children as pawns to express their anger.
	Support parents as they adjust to their new lives.	Discourage parents from fighting over custody.

FIGURE 7.3: Timeline of divorce, with counseling interventions to minimize problems for children.

Sources: Pedro-Carroll, 2005; Pruett, Insabella, & Gustafson, 2005; Wolshik and others, 2005.

TYING IT ALL TOGETHER

1. Montana's parents make firm rules but value their children's input about family decisions. Pablo's parents have rules for everything and tolerate no *ifs, ands,* or *buts*. Sara's parents don't really have rules. At their house it's always playtime and time to indulge the children. Which parenting style is being used by Montana's parents? By Pablo's parents? By Sara's parents?
2. Chloe grew up in a happy middle-class family, but Amber and Sierra both had difficult childhoods. Sierra is struggling in college and often feels very unhappy, but both Amber and Chloe are doing well at school. To which student does the term *resilient* best apply?
3. Melissa's son Jared, now in elementary school, was premature and has a difficult temperament. What might Judith Harris advise about fostering this child's development, and what might this chapter recommend?
4. Your sister is concerned about a friend who uses corporal punishment with her baby and her 4-year-old. She asks you what the experts say. Pick the following *two* positions developmentalists might take.
   a. Never spank children of any age.
   b. Mild spanking is OK for the infant.
   c. Mild spanking is OK for the 4-year-old, as a backup.
   d. If the child has a difficult temperament, regular corporal punishment might help.
5. As an elementary school teacher, you are worried about a student who has been coming to school without a coat this winter. You've also seen what you're pretty sure are burn marks on the child's arms. What kinds of abuse may be involved? What should you do? What should the ideal goal be?
6. Your friend Crystal recently had the courage to leave her abusive husband after years of fighting. Crystal is feeling good about the separation, but she is worried that maybe she should have stayed with her spouse for the sake of their daughter. Did Crystal make the right decision? What advice can you give Crystal about helping her child?

Answers to the Tying It All Together questions can be found at the end of this chapter.

School

What was that test Manuel (in the introductory chapter vignette) took, and what does intelligence really mean? What makes for good teaching and superior schools? Before looking at these school-related topics, let's begin by setting the framework—stepping back and, once again, exploring the impact of that basic marker, poverty, on young children's cognitive skills.

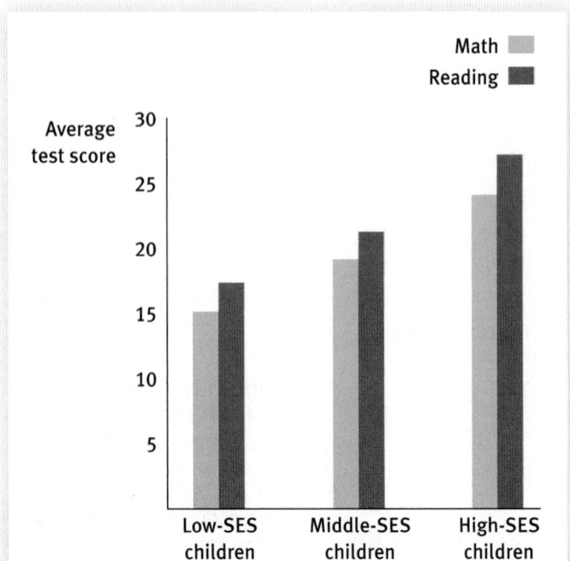

FIGURE 7.4: Socioeconomic status and kindergartners' scores on tests of readiness for reading and math: As children's socioeconomic status rises, so do average scores on tests of math and reading readiness. Notice the dramatic differences between low-income and affluent children.

Source: Lee & Burkam, 2002, p. 18.

Setting the Context: Unequal at the Starting Gate

In Chapter 4, you learned that living in poverty for the first years of life has damaging effects on cognition. Figure 7.4 reveals that devastation directly by offering sobering statistics with regard to an entering U.S. kindergarten class (Lee & Burkam 2002). Notice that children from low-income families, on average, do markedly worse than their upper-middle-class counterparts on tests of reading readiness and math. When we compare poverty-level Latino and African American children to the wealthiest European Americans, the test score gap widens to a chasm. The most disadvantaged children enter school academically several years behind their most affluent counterparts.

The reasons for these inequalities become apparent when developmentalists visit young children's homes to rate their family life. As one national survey showed, children growing up in poverty-level U.S. families had few books. Their parents infrequently read to them. They rarely had home computers. They practically never went to museums (Bradley and others, 2001).

I must emphasize that low-income parents may care just as much about their sons' and daughters' education as do corporate CEOs. But when you are working long hours to provide the bare necessities, children's basic needs—and safety—take priority. Here is how one parent at an inner-city school described the situation:

> I mean some of us are scraping to put food on the table, clothes on their backs . . , keeping the kids off of the street corner. That's our job, you know, taking care of business and making sure that they have the opportunity to go to school each day. 'Cause with no clothes, or if they wind up in trouble with the system, then school ain't a possibility for them.
>
> (quoted in Lawson, 2003, pp. 91–92)

Immigrant children face special stresses. They need to grapple with the challenges of poverty plus learn a new language (Suárez-Orozco and others, 2010). Among second-generation children of Mexican heritage, for instance, fewer than one in ten have parents who speak English "very well" (Rumbaut, 2008).

You would think that when children start a race miles behind, they should be given every chance to catch up. The reality is the reverse. From class size, to the quality of teacher training, to the attractiveness of the physical building—kindergartens serving poor children rank at the bottom of the educational heap. Here is the dismal—but not unexpected—conclusion that one group of researchers reached:

> The consistency of these findings across aspects of school quality that are themselves very different from one another is both striking and troubling. The least advantaged of America's children, who also begin their formal schooling at a substantial cognitive disadvantage, are systematically mapped into our nation's worst schools.
>
> (Lee & Burkam, 2002, p. 77)

Now, let's keep these inequalities in mind as we explore the controversial topic of intelligence tests.

Intelligence and IQ Tests

What does it mean to be intelligent? Ask classmates the question, and they will probably mention both academic and "real life" skills (Sternberg, Grigorenko, & Kidd, 2005). Conceptions of what it means to "be intelligent" also differ from society to society, and among different ethnic groups. Latino parents, for instance, focus more on social competence (getting along with people), while our mainstream culture views intelligence in terms of cognitive traits (Sternberg, 2007).

Traditional intelligence tests reflect the mainstream view. They measure only cognitive abilities. Intelligence tests, however, differ from **achievement tests,** the yearly evaluations children take to measure their knowledge in various subjects. The intelligence test is designed to predict a person's general academic potential, or ability to master *any* school-related task. Do the tests measure mainly genetic capacities? Do they have any relevance beyond school? To approach these hot-button issues, let's examine the intelligence test that children typically take today: the WISC.

achievement tests Measures that evaluate a child's knowledge in specific school-related areas.

WISC (Wechsler Intelligence Scale for Children) The standard intelligence test used in childhood, consisting of a Verbal Scale (questions for the child to answer), a Performance Scale (materials for the child to manipulate), and a variety of subtests.

Examining the WISC

The **WISC (Wechsler Intelligence Scale for Children),** now in repeated revisions, was devised by David Wechsler and is the current standard intelligence test. As you can see

mentally retarded The label for significantly impaired intellectual functioning, defined as when a child (or adult) has an IQ of 70 or below accompanied by evidence of deficits in learning abilities.

specific learning disability The label for any impairment in language or any deficit related to listening, thinking, speaking, reading, writing, spelling, or understanding mathematics; diagnosed when a score on an intelligence test is much higher than a child's performance on achievement tests.

***TABLE* 7.3: The WISC-III Subtests and Sample Kinds of Items**

Subtest	Sample (simulated) Item
Verbal Scale	
Information (tests factual knowledge)	Who is George Bush?
Similarities (analogies)	Cat is to kitten as dog is to ______________.
Vocabulary (defining words)	What is a table?
Comprehension (social judgment)	What do you do if you are lost in Manhattan?
Arithmetic	Mary has five apples and gives two away. How many does she have left?
Digit span (memory)	Repeat these seven digits forward . . . backward . . . .
Performance Scale	
(involves manipulating, arranging, or identifying materials within a time limit)	
Picture completion	What is missing in this picture?
Block design	Arrange these blocks to look like the photograph on the card.
Picture arrangement	Arrange these pictures in the correct sequence to tell a story.
Object assembly	Put these puzzle pieces together.
Coding	Using the key above, put each symbol in the correct space below.

Source: WISC-III, Psychological Corporation (Wechsler, 1991).

in Table 7.3, the WISC samples a child's performance in a variety of areas. However, it is divided into two sections—one involving answering questions (the Verbal Scale), and the other involving manipulating materials (the Performance Scale). This allows testers to give a child a separate IQ score for each part.

Achievement tests are administered to groups. The WISC is given individually to a child by a trained psychologist, a process that includes several hours of testing and concludes with a written report. If the child scores at the 50th percentile for his age group, his IQ is defined as 100. If that child's IQ is 130, he ranks at roughly the 98th percentile, or in the top 2 percent of children his age. If a child's score is 70, he is at the opposite end of the distribution, performing in the lowest 2 percent of children that age. Put on a graph, this score distribution, as you can see in Figure 7.5, looks like a bell-shaped curve.

When do children take this time-intensive test? The answer, most often, is during elementary school when there is an issue about classroom work. School personnel then use the IQ score as one component of a multifaceted assessment, which also includes achievement test scores, teachers' ratings, and parents' input, to determine whether a boy or girl needs special help (Sattler, 2001). If a child's low score (under 70) and other behaviors warrant this designation, she may be classified as **mentally retarded.** If a child's IQ is far higher than would be expected, compared to her performance on achievement tests, she is classified as having a **specific learning disability**—an umbrella term for any impairment in language or difficulties related to listening (such as ADHD), thinking, speaking, reading, spelling, or math.

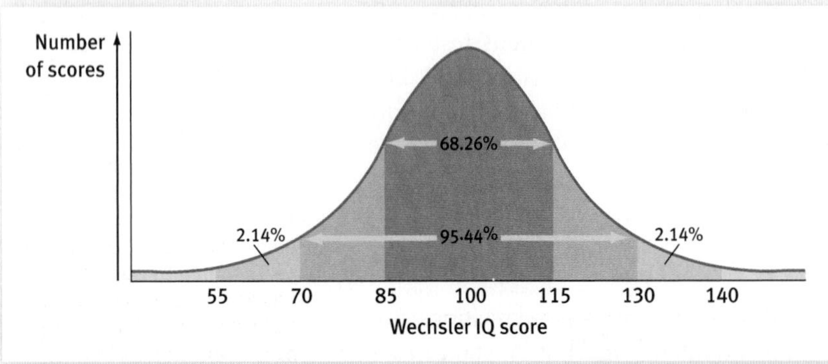

FIGURE 7.5: **The bell-shaped curve:** The WISC scores are arranged to align in a normal distribution. Notice from the chart that about 68 percent of the population has scores between 85 and 115 and about 95 percent of the scores are between 70 and 130.

Although children with learning disabilities often score in the average range on IQ tests, they have trouble with schoolwork. Many times, they have a debilitating impairment called **dyslexia** that undercuts every academic skill. Dyslexia, a catchall term referring to any reading difficulty, may have multiple causes (Nicolson & Fawcett, 2011; Zoccolotti and Friedmann, 2010). What's important, however, is that despite having good instruction and doing well on tests of intelligence, a dyslexic child is still struggling to read (Shaywitz, Morris, & Shaywitz, 2008).

My son, for instance, has dyslexia, and our experience shows just how important having a measure of general intelligence can be. Because Thomas was falling behind in the third grade, my husband and I arranged to have our son tested. Thomas was defined as having a learning disability because his IQ score was above average but his achievement scores were well below the norm for his grade. Although we were aware of our son's reading problems, the testing was vital in easing our anxieties. Thomas—just as we thought—was capable intellectually. Now we just had to get our son through school with his sense of self-efficacy intact!

Bob Daemmrich/The Image Works

This second grader, taking a subtest of the WISC Performance Scale, will be tested for at least an hour and a half. Then, the examiner will write a report and compare his scores with those of other children his age. If this boy's IQ is at least 130—ranking him at roughly the top 2 percent of his age group—he will be eligible for his school's gifted program.

Often, teachers and parents urge testing for a happier reason: They want to confirm their impression that a child is intellectually advanced. If the child's IQ exceeds a certain number, typically 130, or in the top 2 percent (see Figure 7.5), she is labeled **gifted** and eligible for special programs. In U.S. public schools, intelligence testing is mandated by law before children can be assigned to a gifted program or remedial class (Canter, 1997; Sattler, 2001).

Table 7.4 offers a fact sheet about dyslexia. The Experiencing the Lifespan box on the next page provides a firsthand view of what it is like to deal with—and triumph over—this debilitating condition. Now that we have explored the measure and when it is used, let's turn to that vital issue—what the scores really mean.

TABLE 7.4: Some Interesting Facts About Dyslexia

- Reading difficulties are shockingly prevalent among U.S. children. According to one 2005 survey, more than 1 in 4 high school seniors were reading below the most basic levels. The figures were higher for fourth graders—over 1 in 3 had trouble grasping the basic points of a passage designed for their grade.
- Specific learning disabilities (including dyslexia) are a mainly male diagnosis—affecting roughly three times as many boys as girls around the world. However, because a referral bias favors boys, there may be more undiagnosed females with dyslexia than had previously been thought.
- Many studies suggest that dyslexia is inherited and "genetic" in origin. However, multiple genes are involved in this condition, and, as I mentioned in the text, problems learning to read have a variety of different causes.
- Late-appearing language (entering the word-combining phase of speech at an older-than-typical age, such as close to age 2 1/2 [see Chapter 3]) and phonemic deficits (the inability to differentiate sounds [see Chapter 5]) are early predictors of dyslexia.
- Children prone to dyslexia may even be identified during their first weeks after birth—by looking at the pattern of their brain waves evoked by different sounds. These newborns have a slightly slower shift from positivity to negativity on "event-related potentials" when exposed to noises of different frequencies
- Although many children with dyslexia eventually learn to read, this condition persists to some extent into adulthood. Early interventions—involving massive instruction in teaching "at-risk" kindergartners and first graders to identify phonemes—are quite effective. After second or third grade, however, it is more challenging to bring children up to grade level.
- Boys and girls with dyslexia unfortunately perform more poorly on general tests of executive functions. They are also at higher risk for developing other mental health problems—such as depressive and anxiety disorders. About 15 to 50 percent also have ADHD.

Sources: Beneventi and others, 2010; Gooch, Snowling, & Hulme, 2011; Henry, Messer, & Nash, 2012: Hensler and others, 2010; Landerl & Moll, 2010; Leppänen and others, 2010; Shaywitz, Morris, & Shaywitz, 2008.

dyslexia A learning disability that is characterized by reading difficulties, lack of fluency, and poor word recognition that is often genetic in origin.

gifted The label for superior intellectual functioning characterized by an IQ score of 130 or above, showing that a child ranks in the top 2 percent of his age group.

EXPERIENCING THE LIFESPAN: From Dyslexic Child to College Professor Adult

Aimee Holt, a colleague of mine who teaches our school psychology students, is beautiful and intelligent, the kind of golden girl you might imagine would have been a great childhood success. When I sat down to chat with Amy about her struggles with dyslexia and other learning disabilities, I found first impressions can be very misleading:

In first grade, the teachers at school told my parents I was mentally retarded. I didn't notice the sounds that went along with the letters of words. I walked into walls and fell down a lot. My parents refused to put me in a special school and finally got me accepted at a private school, contingent on getting a good deal of help. I spent my elementary school years being tutored for an hour before school, an hour afterwards, and all summer.

Socially, elementary school was a nightmare . . . I remember kids laughing at me, calling me stupid. There was a small group of people that I was friendly with, but we were all misfits. One of my closest friends had an inoperable brain tumor. Because of my problems coordinating my vision with my motor skills, I couldn't participate in normal activities, such as sports or dance. By seventh grade, after years of working every day with my wonderful reading teacher, I was reading at almost grade level.

Then when we moved to Tennessee in my freshman year of high school, I felt like a completely new person. Nobody knew that I had learning difficulties. We moved to a rural community, so I got to be a top student, because I'd had the same classes in my Dallas private school the year before. In the tenth and eleventh grades, I was making A's and B's. I got a scholarship to college, where I was a straight-A student (with a GPA of 3.9).

My mom is the reason I've done so well. She always believed in me, always felt I could make it; she never gave up. Plus, as I mentioned, I had an exceptional reading teacher who ended up working as a leader in the field. My goal was always to be an elementary school teacher, but, after teaching for years and realizing that a lot of the kids in my classes were not being accurately diagnosed, I decided to go to graduate school to get my Ph.D.

Today, in addition to teaching, I do private tutoring with children like me. First, I get kids to identify word sounds (phonemes) because children with dyslexia have a problem decoding the specific sounds of words. I'll have the children identify how many sounds they hear in a word. . . . "Which sounds rhyme, which don't?" . . . "If I change the word from cat to hat, what sound changes?" Most children naturally pick up on these reading cues. Kids with dyslexia need to have these skills directly taught.

Many children I tutor are in fourth or even sixth grade and have had years of feeling like a failure. They develop an attitude of "Why try? I'm going to be a failure anyway." I can tell them that I've been there and that they can succeed. So I work on academic self-efficacy—teaching them to put forth effort. Most of these kids are intelligent, but as they progress through school, their verbal IQ drops because they are not being exposed to written material at their grade level. I try to get them to stay in the regular classroom, with modifications such as books on tape and oral testing, to prevent that false drop in their knowledge base. I was so fortunate—with a wonderful mother, an exceptional reading teacher, getting the help I needed at exactly the right time—that I feel my mission is to give something back.

Decoding the Meaning of the IQ Test

The first question we need to grapple with in looking at the meaning of the test relates to a measurement criterion called **reliability**. When people take a test thought to measure a basic trait, such as IQ, more than one time, their results should not really vary. Imagine that your IQ score randomly shifted from gifted to average, year by year. Clearly, this test score would be worthless. It would not tell us anything about a stable attribute called intelligence.

The good news is that, in elementary school, IQ test performance does typically remain stable (Ryan, Glass, & Bartels, 2010). In one amazing study, people's scores remained fairly similar when they first took the test in childhood and then were retested more than a half-century later (see Deary and others, 2000). Still, among individual children, the IQ can change dramatically. Scores are most likely to shift when children have undergone life stresses.

This research tells us that we should never evaluate a child's IQ during a family crisis such as a divorce. But being reliable is only the first requirement. The test must be **valid**. This means it must predict what it is supposed to be measuring. Is the WISC a valid test?

reliability In measurement terminology, a basic criterion of a test's accuracy that scores must be fairly similar when a person takes the test more than once.

validity In measurement terminology, a basic criterion for a test's accuracy involving whether that measure reflects the real-world quality it is supposed to measure.

If our predictor is academic performance, the answer is yes. A child who gets an IQ score of 130 will tend to perform well in the gifted class. A child whose IQ is 80 will probably need remedial help. But now we turn to the controversial question: Does the test measure genetic learning potential or biological smarts?

Flynn effect Remarkable and steady rise in overall performance on IQ tests that has been occurring around the world over the past century.

"g" Charles Spearman's term for a general intelligence factor that he claimed underlies all cognitive activities.

ARE THE TESTS A GOOD MEASURE OF GENETIC GIFTS? When we are evaluating children living in poverty (or boys and girls growing up in immigrant families who may not be familiar with our cultural norms), logic tells us that the answer should be no. The test score cannot offer a good portrait of a child's innate abilities. Look back at the items on the WISC Verbal Scale (Table 7.3 on p. 218), and you will immediately see that if parents stimulate a child's vocabulary, she will be at a clear advantage. If a family cannot afford to buy books and learning toys, their children will be handicapped on the test.

We can make an excellent logical argument that the quality of a child's environment must weigh heavily in predicting IQ by referring to the remarkable century-long general increase in intelligence test scores described in Chapter 1 (see page 19). This steady, worldwide rise in IQ scores, called the **Flynn effect** (named for its discoverer James Flynn) is dramatic. More years of education, plus the modern media, have made twenty-first-century children and adults far better "thinkers" than their parents and grandparents were at the same age. Incredibly, Flynn (2007) calculates that the average-scoring child taking the WISC in 1900 would rank at "mentally retarded" if using today's IQ norms!

Actually, we have a recent study that confirms the fact that disadvantaged and affluent children are definitely not equal at the test-taking gate today. For low-income children, the IQ score mainly reflects environmental forces. For upper-middle-class children, the test score is more reflective of genetic gifts (Turkheimer and others, 2003). So if an elementary schooler comes from a poverty-level family and attends a low-quality school, yes, his IQ score may indeed predict his current school performance well. But we should not assume that score reflects true intellectual potential unless a child has been exposed to the incredible learning advantages upper-middle-class life provides.

Now, imagine that you are an upper-middle-class child. You were raised by attentive parents, regularly read to, and taken to museums. You attended high-quality schools. Your IQ score is only 95 or 100. Is your intellectual potential *really* totally limited for life?

DO IQ SCORES PREDICT REAL-WORLD PERFORMANCE? When, as often happens, a student comes up after this class lecture and proudly admits that his IQ is 130 or 140, he is not thinking of school learning. He is assuming that his score measures a basic "smartness" that carries over to every life activity. In measurement terminology, this student would agree with theorist Charles Spearman. Spearman believed that a score on an IQ test reflects a general underlying, all-encompassing intelligence factor called **"g."**

Psychologists debate the existence of "g." Many strongly believe that the IQ test *generally* predicts intellectual capacities. They argue that we can use the IQ score as a summary measure of a person's cognitive potential for all life tasks (Herrnstein & Murray, 1994; Rushton & Jensen, 2005). Others believe that people have unique intellectual talents. There is no one-dimensional quality called "g" (Eisner, 2004; Schlinger, 2003; Sternberg, 2007). These critics argue that it is inappropriate to rank people on a single continuum from highly intelligent to not very smart (Gould, 1981; Sternberg, Grigorenko & Kidd, 2005).

Tantalizing evidence for "g" lies in the fact that people differ in the speed with which they process information (Brody, 2006; Rushton & Jensen, 2005). You may remember from Chapter 3 that infants who easily grasp the essence of a stimulus and habituate more quickly later perform at high levels on intelligence tests. Intelligence test scores also correlate with various indicators of life success, such as occupational status. However, the problem is that the gateway to high-status professions, such as law and medicine, is school performance, which is what the tests predict (Sternberg, 1997; Sternberg, Grigorenko, & Bundy, 2001).

One problem with believing that IQ tests offer a *total* X-ray into intellectual capacities is that people may carry around their test-score ranking as an inner wound. A psychologist supervisor once confessed to me that he was really not that intelligent because his IQ was only 105. He devalued the criterion the scores were supposed to predict—his many years of real-life success—by accepting what, in his case, was an invalid score!

A high test score can produce its own problems. Suppose the student who told me his IQ was 140 decided he was so intelligent he didn't have to open a book in my class. He might be in for a nasty surprise when he found out that what *really* matters is your ability to work. Or that person might worry: "I'd better not try in Dr. Belsky's class because, if I do put forth effort and *don't* get an A, I will discover that my astronomical IQ score was wrong." (Recall the research in Chapter 6 that showed how telling elementary schoolers "you are smart" made them afraid to tackle challenging academic tasks.)

Even the firmest advocate of "g" would admit that people have different talents. Some of us are marvelous mechanically and miserable at math, wonderful at writing but hopeless at reading maps. If a child, such as Manuel in the chapter-opening vignette, is gifted mechanically, shouldn't we nurture that skill even though he does not qualify as exceptional in every area of life?

Toward a Broader View of Intelligence

But if intelligence involves different abilities, such as mechanical talents, perhaps we should really go beyond the IQ test to measure those skills in a broader way. Psychologists Robert Sternberg and Howard Gardner have devoted their careers to providing this broader view of what it means to be smart.

STERNBERG'S SUCCESSFUL INTELLIGENCE. Robert Sternberg (1984, 1996, 1997) is a man on a mission. In hundreds of publications, this contemporary psychologist has transformed the way we think about intelligence. Sternberg's passion comes from the heart. He began his school career with a problem:

> As an elementary school student, I failed miserably on the IQ tests. . . . Just the sight of the school psychologist coming into the classroom to give a group IQ test sent me into a wild panic attack. . . . You don't need to be a genius to figure out what happens next. My teachers in the elementary school grades certainly didn't expect much from me. . . . So I gave them what they expected. . . . Were the teachers disappointed? Not on your life. They were happy that I was giving them what they expected.
>
> (Sternberg, 1997, pp. 17–18)

Sternberg actually believes that traditional intelligence tests can do damage in the school environment. As I implied earlier in discussing the Flynn effect, the relationship between IQ scores and schooling is somewhat bidirectional. Children who attend inferior schools, or who miss months of classroom work due to illness, perform more poorly on intelligence tests (Sternberg, 1997). Worse yet, Sternberg argues, when schools assign children to lower-track, less demanding classes on the basis of their low test scores, their IQs gradually decline year by year.

Most importantly, Sternberg (1984) believes that conventional intelligence tests are too limited. Although they do measure one type of intelligence, they do not cover the total terrain.

IQ tests, according to Sternberg, measure **analytic intelligence.** They test how well people can solve academic-type problems with a defined solution. They do not measure **creative intelligence,** the ability to "think outside the box," or to formulate problems in new ways. Nor do they measure a third type of intelligence called **practical intelligence,** common sense, or "street smarts."

analytic intelligence In Robert Sternberg's framework on successful intelligence, the facet of intelligence involving performing well on academic-type problems.

creative intelligence In Robert Sternberg's framework on successful intelligence, the facet of intelligence involved in producing novel ideas or innovative work.

Being a math wiz (*analytic intelligence*) demands different skills than deftly cooking and serving a complicated dish (*practical intelligence*). That's why Robert Sternberg believes that IQ tests, which mainly measure school type analytic skills, do not tap into many of the abilities that make people successful in the real world.

Brazilian street children who make their living selling flowers and don't have any formal education show impressive levels of practical intelligence. They understand how to handle money in the real world. However, they do poorly on measures of traditional IQ (Sternberg, 1984, 1997). Others, such as Winston Churchill, can be terrible scholars who flower after they leave their academic careers. Then, there are the people who excel at IQ test-taking and traditional schooling but fail abysmally once they enter the real world. Sternberg argues that to be **successfully intelligent** in life requires a balance of all three "intelligences." (As a postscript, Sternberg has now added a fourth type of intellectual gift—that rare attribute called *wisdom*. See Sternberg, 2010.)

practical intelligence In Robert Sternberg's framework on successful intelligence, the facet of intelligence involved in knowing how to act competently in real-world situations.

successful intelligence In Robert Sternberg's framework, the optimal form of cognition, involving having a good balance of analytic, creative, and practical intelligence.

multiple intelligences theory In Howard Gardner's perspective on intelligence, the principle that there are eight separate kinds of intelligence—verbal, mathematical, interpersonal, intrapersonal, spatial, musical, kinesthetic, naturalist—plus a possible ninth form, called spiritual intelligence.

GARDNER'S MULTIPLE INTELLIGENCES. Howard Gardner (1998) did not have Sternberg's problem with intelligence tests:

> As a child I was a good student and a good test taker . . . but . . . music in particular and the arts were important parts of my life. Therefore when I asked myself what optimal human development is, I became more convinced that [we] had to . . . broaden the definition of intelligence to include these activities, too.
>
> (Gardner, 1998, p. 3)

Gardner is not passionately opposed to standard intelligence tests. Still, he believes that using the single IQ score is less informative than measuring children's unique talents and gifts. (Gardner's motto is: "Ask not *how* intelligent you are, but *how are* you intelligent?") According to Gardner's (2004, 2006) **multiple intelligences theory,** human abilities come in eight, and possibly nine, distinctive forms.

In addition to the verbal and mathematical skills measured by traditional IQ tests, people may be gifted in *interpersonal intelligence*, or skillful at understanding other people. Their talents may lie in *intrapersonal intelligence*, the skill of understanding oneself, or in *spatial intelligence*, the ability to grasp where objects are arranged in space. (You might rely on a friend who is gifted in spatial intelligence to beautifully arrange the furniture in your house by quickly scanning a room.) Some people have

Being a terrific guitarist (*musical intelligence*) or a world-class gymnast (*kinesthetic intelligence*) doesn't necessarily mean that you will also shine in reading or math. That's why Howard Gardner believes that schools need to broaden their focus to teach to the *different* kinds of intelligences that we all possess.

high levels of *musical intelligence*, *kinesthetic intelligence* (the ability to use the body well), or *naturalist intelligence* (the gift for dealing with animals or plants and trees). There may even be an *existential (spiritual) intelligence*.

EVALUATING THE THEORIES. These perspectives on intelligence are exciting. Some of you may be thinking, "I'm gifted in practical or musical intelligence. I always knew there was more to being smart than success at school!" But let's use our practical intelligence to critique these approaches. Why did Gardner select these particular eight abilities and not others? (Barnett, Ceci, & Williams, 2006; White, 2006) Yes, parents may marvel at a 6-year-old's creative or kinesthetic intelligence. But, it is analytic intelligence that will get this child into the gifted program at school, not his artistic productions or how well his body moves (Eisner, 2004).

We can also criticize Sternberg's ideas. Is there really such a thing as creative or practical intelligence apart from a particular field? For instance, adopting the idea that there is a single "creative" intelligence might lead to the conclusion that Michelangelo would also be a talented musician or that Mozart could beautifully paint the Sistine Chapel.

The bottom line is that neither Gardner nor Sternberg has developed replacements for our current IQ test. But this does not matter. Their mission is larger than changing the way we test. They want to transform the way schools teach (Gardner, 2006; Sternberg,2010).

INTERVENTIONS: Lessons for Schools

Gardner's theory has been enthusiastically embraced by teachers who understand that intelligence involves more than having traditional academic skills. However, to implement his ideas requires revolutionizing the way we structure education. Therefore, the main use of multiple intelligences theory has been in helping "non-traditional learners" succeed in traditional schools (Schirduan & Case, 2004). Here is how Mark, a dyslexic teenager, describes how he uses his spatial intelligence to cope with the maze of facts in history:

> I'll picture things; for example, if we are studying the French revolution . . . Louis the 16th . . . . I'll have a picture of him in my mind [and I'll visualize] the castle and peasants to help me learn.
>
> (quoted in Schirduan & Case, 2004, p. 93)

Sternberg's research team has conducted an experiment demonstrating that teaching with every type of intelligence in mind produces better classroom performance. The researchers divided third-grade classes at a public school into two groups. One was taught social studies by standard methods. The other was given instruction balanced among the three types of intelligence. The children taught according to Sternberg's theory performed at a higher level even on standard multiple-choice tests (Sternberg, Torff, & Grigorenko, 1998).

So the real potential of these ideas is to enrich the way classrooms operate. How do classrooms operate?

Classroom Learning

The diversity of intelligences, cultures, and educational experiences at home is matched by the incredible diversity of American schools. There are small rural schools and large urban schools, public schools and private schools, highly traditional schools where students wear uniforms and schools that teach to Gardner's intelligences. There are single-sex schools, charter schools, religious schools, magnet schools that cater to gifted students, and alternative schools for children with behavior problems or learning disabilities.

Can students thrive in every kind of school? The answer is yes, *provided* schools have an intense commitment to student learning and teachers can excite students to learn. The rest of this chapter focuses on these challenges.

Examining Successful Schools

What qualities make a school successful? We can get insights from surveying elementary schools that are beating the odds. These schools, while located in low-income areas and serving mainly children whose parents do not speak English, have students who are thriving.

In the Vista School, located on a Native American reservation, virtually all the children are eligible for a free lunch. However, Vista consistently boasts dramatic improvements on statewide reading and math tests. According to Ms. Thompson, the principal, "Our job is not to make excuses for students, but just to give them every possible opportunity. At Vista, teachers refuse to dumb down the curriculum. We offer tons of high-level conceptual work" (quoted in Borko and others, 2003, p. 177).

Tony Cenicola/The New York Times/Redux

A school's physical appearance can also make a real difference in whether children "beat the odds." This boy attends a model public school, designed and built by a well-known architect and located in an impoverished section of New York City.

At Beacon Elementary School, two out of every three students exceed state-mandated writing standards despite coming from impoverished backgrounds. Here, Susie Murphy, the principal, comments: "You can … say, these kids are poor. You just need to love them. Or you can come to a school like this where the philosophy is that the best way to love them is to give them an education so they can make choices in their life" (quoted in Borko and others, 2003, p. 186). Beacon teachers, she continues, "are here … by choice. They are committed to proving that kids who live in poverty can learn every bit as well as other kids" (p. 192). At Beacon, teachers are also committed to providing challenging work. The school builds in opportunities for the teachers to share ideas: "We have mini-workshops in geometry, or problem solving. Our whole staff talks about the general focus and where math is going" (p. 194).

Committed teachers, continual professional collaboration, and a strong mission to "deliver for our kids" explain why another school serving disadvantaged children boosted language arts proficiency scores from less than 1 in 5 fourth graders to an astonishing 100 percent (Martin, Fergus, & Noguera, 2010). Washington Elementary, however, achieved this miracle by rethinking the traditional concept of school. Because half the students attending this school have "limited English," teachers provide a laserlike focus on language that spills over beyond the traditional day. Afterschool activities foster literacy by offering exciting programs in theater arts as well as intense traditional writing help. This total English immersion is accompanied by activities that continue all summer long.

But the unique aspect of this school is that it's not for children alone. Parents are enticed to become full school participants, by being offered everything from English classes to child health care. When ethnic-minority or poverty-level parents feel isolated from that alien culture called school, an "us against them" dynamic can develop, and all is lost (Wegmann & Bowen, 2010). But when home and school "speak the same language," all is won. Washington Elementary embodies the basic developmental systems message: Children's success depends on the *total* environment in which learning occurs.

To summarize, successful schools set high standards and believe that every child can succeed. Teachers offer an excess of nurture—to students, to one another, and, ideally, to families, too (Lumpkin, 2010). In terms of Baumrind's parenting-styles framework, these schools are *authoritative* in their approach.

Now that we have the general outlines for what is effective, let's tackle the challenge *every* teacher faces: getting students eager to learn.

intrinsic motivation The drive to act based on the pleasure of taking that action in itself, not for an external reinforcer or reward.

extrinsic motivation The drive to take an action because that activity offers external reinforcers such as praise, money, or a good grade.

Producing Eager Learners

But to go to school in a summer morn,

O! it drives all joy away;

Under a cruel eye outworn,

The little ones spend the day

In sighing and dismay.

—William Blake, from "The Schoolboy" (1794)

Jean Piaget believed that the hunger to learn is more important than food or drink. Why then do children over the centuries lament, "I hate school"? The reason is that learning loses its joy when it becomes a requirement instead of an activity we choose to engage in for ourselves.

THE PROBLEM: AN EROSION OF INTRINSIC MOTIVATION. Developmentalists divide motivation into two categories. **Intrinsic motivation** refers to self-generated actions, those we take from our inner desires. When Piaget described our hunger to learn, he was referring to intrinsic motivations. **Extrinsic motivation** refers to activities that we undertake in order to get external reinforcers, such as praise or pay, or a good grade.

Unfortunately, the learning activity you are currently engaged in falls into the extrinsic category. You know you will be tested on what you are reading. Worse yet, if you decided to pick up this book for an intrinsic reason—because you wanted to learn about human development—the very fact that you might be graded would make your basic interest fall off.

Numerous studies show that when adults give external reinforcers for activities that are intrinsically motivating, children are less likely to want to perform those activities for themselves (Patall, Cooper, & Robinson, 2008; Stipek, 1996). In one classic example, researchers selected preschoolers who were intrinsically interested in art. When they gave a "good player" award (an outside reinforcer) for the art projects, the children later showed a dramatic decline in their interest in doing art for fun (Lepper, Greene, & Nisbett, 1973). This research makes sense of the question you may have wondered about: "Why, after taking that literature class, am I less interested in reading on my own?"

Young children enter kindergarten brimming with intrinsic motivation. When does this love affair with school turn sour? Think back to your childhood, and you will realize that the enchantment often ends during the early years of elementary school, when teachers provide those external reinforcers—grades (Stipek, 1997). Moreover, during first or second grade, classroom learning often becomes abstract and removed from life. Rote activities, like filling in worksheets and memorizing multiplication tables, have replaced the creative hands-on projects of kindergarten. Ironically, then school may be the very setting where Piaget's little-scientist activities are *least* likely to occur.

Randi Sidman-Moore/Masterfile

Ellen B. Senisi/The Image Works

Compare the activities of the kindergarten class of "little scientists" at the left with those of the second graders in the photograph at the right and you will immediately understand why by about age 8 many children begin to say, "I hate school."

Then, as children enter concrete operations—at around age 8—they begin comparing their performance to that of their peers. This competitive orientation erodes intrinsic motivation (Dweck, 1986; Self-Brown & Mathews, 2003). The focus shifts from "I want to improve for myself" to "I want to do *better* than my friends."

In sum, several forces explain why many children dislike school: School involves extrinsic reinforcers (grades). School learning, because it often involves rote memorization, is not intrinsically interesting. In school, children are not free to set their own learning goals. Their performance is judged by a fixed outside standard: how they measure up to the rest of the class.

It is no wonder, therefore, that studies in Western nations document an alarming decline in intrinsic motivation as children travel through school (Katz, Kaplan, & Gueta, 2010; Spinath & Steinmayr, 2008). Susan Harter (1981) asked children to choose between two statements: "Some kids work really hard to get good grades" (referring to extrinsic motivation) or "Some kids work really hard because they like to learn new things" (measuring intrinsic motives). When she gave her measure to hundreds of California public school children, intrinsic motivation scores fell off from third to ninth grade.

Still, external reinforcers can be vital hooks that get us intrinsically involved. Have you ever reluctantly read a book for a class and found yourself captivated by the subject? Perhaps you enrolled in this course because it was required for graduation but are now so interested in the material that you want to make some aspect of developmental science your career. Given that extrinsically motivating activities are basic to school and life, how can we make them work best?

THE SOLUTION: MAKING EXTRINSIC LEARNING PART OF US. To answer this question, Edward Deci and Richard Ryan (1985, 2000) make the point that extrinsic learning tasks vary on a continuum. We engage in some types of extrinsic learning unwillingly: "I have to take that terrible anatomy course because it is a requirement for graduation." We enthusiastically embrace other extrinsic tasks, which may not be inherently interesting, because we identify with their larger goal: "I want to memorize every bone of the body because that information is vital to my nursing career." In the first situation, the learning activity is irrelevant. In the second, the task has become intrinsic because it is connected to our inner self. Therefore, the key to transforming school learning from a chore into a pleasure is to make extrinsic learning relate to children's goals and desires.

Masterfile

Computers in the classroom can draw on children's basic interest in video games to make academics intrinsically more interesting. But in order to make this learning *truly* intrinsic, this teacher cannot micromanage or hover over her students, or be overly critical. These boys need to feel that they can control their learning and master the concepts at their own pace.

The most boring tasks take on an intrinsic aura when they speak to children's passions. Imagine, for instance, how a first grader's motivation to sound out words might change if a teacher, knowing that a particular student was captivated by dinosaurs, gave that boy the job of sounding out dinosaur names. Deci and Ryan believe that learning becomes intrinsic when it satisfies our basic need for relatedness (attachment). Think back to the discussion of schools that beat the odds. Imagine how motivated those children were to learn to read when they understood that their success would make their beloved school proud. Finally, extrinsic tasks take on an intrinsic feeling when they foster our need for autonomy, or offer us choices of *how* to do our work (Patall, Cooper, & Robinson, 2008; Ryan and others, 2006).

Studies around the globe suggest that when teachers and parents take away children's autonomy—by controlling, criticizing, or micromanaging learning tasks—they erode intrinsic motivation (see Jang, Reeve, & Deci, 2010; Soenens & Vansteenkiste, 2010). We can see this principle in our own lives. By continually denigrating our work, or hovering over every move, a controlling supervisor has the uncanny ability to turn us off to the most intrinsically interesting job.

TABLE 7.5: Lessons for Teachers: A Recap of This Chapter's Insights

1. **Foster relevance.** For instance, in teaching reading, tailor the books you are assigning so that they fit children's passions. And entice students to learn to read in other ways, such as getting first and second graders energized by telling them that they will now be able to break a code that the world uses, just like a detective!
2. **Foster relatedness.** Develop a secure, loving attachment with every student. Continually tell each child how proud you are when that person tries hard or succeeds.
3. **Foster autonomy.** As much as possible, allow your students to select among several equivalent assignments (such as choosing which specific books to read). Don't give time limits, such as "It's 9:30 and this has to be done by 10:00," or hover, take over tasks, or make negative comments. Stand by to provide informational comments and careful scaffolding (see Chapter 5) when students ask. Build in assignments that allow high-level thinking, such as using essays in preference to rote work such as copying sentences or filling out worksheets.

Teaching Tips Based on Gardner's and Sternberg's Theories

1. Offer balanced assignments that capitalize on students' different kinds of intelligence—creative work such as essays; practical-intelligence activities such as calculating numbers to make change at a store; single-answer analytic tasks (using Sternberg's framework); and classroom time devoted to music, dance, the arts, and caring for plants (capitalizing on Gardner's ideas).
2. Explicitly teach students to use their different intelligences in mastering classroom work.

Additional Teaching Tips

1. Don't rely on IQ test scores, especially in assessing the abilities of low-income and ethnic-minority students.
2. Avoid praising children for being "brilliant." Compliment them for hard work.
3. Go beyond academics to teach children interpersonal skills.
4. Strive for excellence. Expect all students to succeed.
5. Foster collaborative working relationships with your colleagues and students' parents.
6. Minimize grade-oriented comparisons (such as who got A's, B's, C's, etc.). Emphasize the importance of personal improvement to students. Experiment with giving grades for individual progress.

Our need for autonomy offers clues as to why high-level conceptual learning tasks might be effective with every child. One researcher asked third-grade teachers to have students write creative essays and not to worry about specific learning objectives for the year. This change produced a shift from extrinsic to intrinsic motivations, with children now saying, "I really like this stuff!" Furthermore, especially the low-achieving boys and girls got *higher* scores on the standard end-of-year exam than if they had been drilled in material that would appear on the test! (Miller, 2003) So, teaching in a creative way, or embedding literacy into high-interest activities, like theater arts, may be the most intelligent strategy for student success across the board.

Table 7.5 summarizes these three messages for teachers: Focus on relevance, enhance relatedness, and provide autonomy. The table also pulls together other teaching tips based on Gardner's and Sternberg's perspectives on intelligence and our look at what makes schools successful. Now, let's conclude by paying a visit to a class that embodies all of these lessons.

IN FOCUS: Teaching at Its Finest

When you enter Cindy Jones's fourth-grade classroom in Murfreesboro, Tennessee, you immediately realize that this teacher is special. You see a corner cluttered with letters and gifts from former students now living around the world, and provocative sayings that dot the walls: "Teachers are united mind workers." "Fair means everyone gets what they need. Not everyone gets the same." There are creative projects on display, and canned goods stacked to be delivered to families in need. Offering caring, making learning intrinsically motivating, and teaching to different intelligences is clearly what this class is about.

To foster Gardner's interpersonal and intrapersonal intelligences, Cindy has divided the class into teams: the Red Hot Patriots, the Shooting Stars, and the Lightning Bolts. Here, Cindy strives for a balance. She puts students with learning problems together with children who are reading at the twelfth-grade level; pairs popular children with those who are rejected or very shy. Children get points for taking responsibility and for doing something positive for another child. Cindy tells me:

> Don't let them know, but I arrange the points so that every team wins each third week. I also tone down the competition by giving points for rooting for and helping the other teams. When children say they want to switch to be with a friend, I never say yes. Life involves relating to all kinds of people. That's an important lesson I want to instill. When conflicts come up, they take the responsibility to have a group pow-wow to work things out.

The teams are the subtext that keeps the year humming along. But each day unfolds according to a specific plan:

8:30–9:30 (CURRENT EVENTS)

The morning begins with a high-intensity curtain raiser, combining relevance and autonomy: Cindy has the children bring in some interesting fact they learned from reading the newspaper or watching the news. Her goal here is "to seize the teachable moment," or to relate this material to the academic content in class. So, when a girl reports that she heard that a woman died at age 107, Cindy says, "Let's calculate her birth date. What events were happening when she was a little girl?"

9:30–10:30 (CENTERS)

During this hour, the students circulate among areas designated for reading, computer activities, and using worksheets to practice for the statewide exams. How, I wonder, will Cindy handle this extrinsic task? The answer is to connect this activity to children's feelings of autonomy and relatedness: "Slow and steady." "You can do it." "Josh, I'm going to put a tattoo on your hand so when you invite me to your wedding, it will say 'Josh, slow up.'" For a girl with serious reading problems: "Brittany, would you be the class role model for a child in kindergarten this year?"

10:30–11:30 (GRAMMAR)

Now comes a hilarious exercise in understanding punctuation, showing how the most rote learning can be fun: "I bought PAPER . . . BAGS . . . FISH . . . GLUE . . . paper bags . . . fish . . . glue . . . Suppose I bought two things? . . . three things? . . . Or, suppose I decided to buy fish glue?" "Who got that one right, and who had trouble?" "David, I'm glad you are explaining that to Jason, just like he helped you with spelling last week."

Then there is some downtime before lunch listening to classical music, followed by an afternoon seminar discussing how the children feel about the piece: "Was the composer successful in conveying his ideas?" The day ends with the test, during which Cindy and I *leave the room*. Cindy explains, "I make it clear to the children that I trust them . . . but they also work to earn my trust."

Jenny Sevcik

Because this class—like any other—has students who are hard to manage, at the end of the day Cindy has a few children fill out a sheet listing goals for improvement, which they take home. The difference is that the children assume responsibility for monitoring their *own* behavior: Cindy asks questions like, "Think carefully: Do you give yourself a smiley-face sticker for focusing today?" Then, in the evening, she calls parents to brainstorm: "I try to call or e-mail when there is good news to report, not just when something goes wrong." Using the terminology describing what has made Washington elementary school "beat the odds" (see page 225), Cindy strives to get parents to talk "the same language" at home as she does at school.

Perhaps the most defining moment of my day occurred at 3 P.M. when Cindy reminded these fourth graders that there would be a holiday the next Monday and the students groaned and said, "Oh, no!" Outstanding teachers make school so exciting that children hate vacation time!

Throughout this chapter, you may have noticed that outstanding teachers like Cindy, as well as outstanding parents, have clear priorities. They provide consistent standards. They understand each child's gifts and weaknesses. They tailor their behavior to the needs of a given child.

I also hope that this discussion has encouraged you to think more deeply about the *many* forces involved in development and the crucial role that cultural and social context plays in shaping our lives. Other societies have a good deal to teach us about the child-rearing values we hold dear. Children who grow up in poverty have more trouble performing well on intelligence tests or in school. We need to provide the kind of environment that allows parents to effectively parent and school systems to teach in a way that permits *every* child to succeed.

TYING IT ALL TOGETHER

1. If Devin, from an upper-middle-class family, and Adam, from a low-income family, are starting kindergarten this fall, you can predict that (pick one):
   a. Both children will perform equally well on school readiness tests, but Adam will fall behind because he is likely to go to a poor-quality kindergarten.
   b. Devin will outperform Adam on school readiness tests, and the gap will probably widen because Adam will go to a poor-quality kindergarten.
2. Malik hasn't been doing well in school, and his achievement test scores have consistently been well below average for his grade. On the WISC, Malik gets an IQ score of 115. What is your conclusion?
3. You are telling a friend about the deficiencies of relying on a child's IQ score. Pick out the *two* arguments you might make.
   a. The tests are not reliable; children's scores *typically* change a lot during the elementary school years.
   b. The tests are not valid predictors of school performance.
   c. As people have different abilities, a single IQ score may not tell us much about a child's unique gifts.
   d. As poor children are at a disadvantage in taking the test, you should not use the IQ scores as an index of "genetic school-related talents" for low-income children.
4. Josh doesn't do well in reading or math, but he excels in music and dance, and he gets along with all kinds of children. In terms of Sternberg's theory of successful intelligence, Josh is not good in ____________, but he is skilled in _____________ and _______________. In terms of Gardner's theory of _________________, Josh is strong in which intelligences?
5. A principal of a school asks for some tips to help her children succeed. Based on this section, you can give all of the following suggestions *except*:
   a. Have your teachers meet to work together and share ideas.
   b. Be sure your teachers make the material simple so that all students experience success.
   c. Make sure that your teachers share a commitment to having every child learn.
   d. Encourage your teachers to give the children high-level creative work.
6. (a) Define intrinsic and extrinsic motivation. (b) Give an example of a task in your life right now that is driven by each kind of motivation. (c) From reading the chapter, can you come up with some ways to make the unpleasant extrinsic tasks you do feel more intrinsic?

Answers to the Tying It All Together questions can be found at the end of this chapter.

SUMMARY

Home

The composition of two-parent families varies dramatically, from the never-divorced two-parent family to different types of blended families. Most single-parent families are headed by women, and boys and girls growing up in these families are often poor. There are dramatic variations by ethnicity and immigrant status, too. Children, however, can thrive in any kind of family, depending on the care parents provide.

According to Diana Baumrind's **parenting styles** approach, based on providing rules and nurturing, parents are classified as **authoritative, authoritarian, permissive,** and **rejecting-neglecting.** Although middle-class Western parents who provide clear rules and are highly child-centered tend to raise the most well-adjusted children, we need to look beyond this framework. Parents should provide consistent discipline. They do more than just provide rules and love. Parenting practices differ by culture. Difficult environments demand a stricter, more authoritarian child-rearing approach.

Resilient children, boys and girls who do well in the face of traumatic experiences, tend to have an adaptable temperament; other talents; one close, secure attachment; and to not be faced with an overload of life blows. There may be a specific gene form that promotes resilience in the face of stress.

Behavioral-genetic researchers argue that children's biologically based temperament shapes parenting. Judith Harris believes that peer groups (and the wider society)—not parents—are the main socializers in children's lives. Although statistics related to **acculturation** support Harris's theory, high-quality parenting can matter greatly when children are biologically and socially "at risk." Parents need to be flexible, tailoring their child-rearing to their environment and to their children's needs. They should relax and enjoy these fleeting years.

Attitudes about **corporal punishment** have changed dramatically, with many developed nations now outlawing spanking. Passing similar bans however is unlikely in the United States. Although physical punishment is not the preferred discipline, it is still used by many U.S. parents and strongly endorsed by certain groups. Experts disagree as to whether corporal punishment can be appropriate, but we do know that spanking is detrimental with "at-risk" children, that it is not appropriate to hit a baby, and that positive reinforcement is preferable to punishment of any kind.

The behaviors that constitute **child maltreatment**—physical abuse, neglect, emotional abuse, and sexual abuse—can *sometimes* be hard to classify and their prevalence is unclear. However, in general, parents' personality problems, environmental stress, plus low social support, and having a "difficult child" are the main factors that can provoke abuse. Abused children often have a variety of emotional and social problems that can persist into adult life. Although teachers and health care professionals are required to report suspected abuse, this judgment call can be hard to make. All things being equal, it is best not to break up the family, but give parents the help they need to parent more effectively.

Although children of divorce are at risk for negative life outcomes, most boys and girls survive this childhood transition without serious emotional scars. The key to making divorce less traumatic lies in minimizing other changes in the child's life, giving children some say in custody arrangements, not having parents fight over the children and, especially, promoting high-quality custodial parenting. Living in a conflict-ridden two-parent home may be as bad—or worse—for children as divorce.

School

Many children from low-income families enter kindergarten well behind their affluent counterparts in basic academic skills. These inequalities at the starting gate are magnified by the fact that poor children are likely to attend the poorest-quality kindergartens.

Achievement tests measure a child's body of knowledge. IQ tests measure a child's basic potential for classroom work. The **Wechsler Intelligence Scale for Children (WISC),** with its Verbal and Performance Scales, is the main childhood IQ test. This time-intensive test, involving a variety of subtests, is given individually to a child. If the child's IQ score is below 70—and if other indicators warrant this designation—that boy or girl may be labeled **mentally retarded.** If the child's score is much higher than his performance on achievement tests, he is classified as having a **specific learning disability,** such as **dyslexia.** If a child's IQ score is at or above 130, she is considered **gifted** and is eligible to be placed in an accelerated class.

IQ scores satisfy the measurement criterion called **reliability,** meaning that people tend to get roughly the same score if the test is taken more than once. However, stressful life experiences can artificially lower a child's score. The test is also **valid,** meaning that it predicts what it was devised to measure: performance in school. Some psychologists claim that the test score reflects a single quality called **"g"** that relates to cognitive performance in every area of life; others feel that intelligence involves multiple abilities and argue that it is inappropriate to rank people as intelligent or not based on a single IQ score. The remarkable **Flynn effect** (century-long test performance increase due to improved environments), suggests that, for disadvantaged children, the IQ score cannot not be viewed as an index of genetic gifts.

Robert Sternberg and Howard Gardner argue that we need to expand our measures of intelligence beyond traditional tests. Sternberg believes that there are three types of intelligence: **analytic intelligence** (academic abilities), **creative intelligence,** and **practical intelligence** (real-world abilities, or "street smarts"). **Successful intelligence** requires having a balance among all three of these skills. Gardner, in his **multiple intelligences theory,** describes eight (or possibly nine) distinct types of intelligences. Although neither of these psychologists has developed alternatives to conventional IQ tests, their ideas have generated excitement and have been used to change some schools.

Schools that serve disadvantaged but high-achieving children share a mission to have every child succeed. They assume that children can do well at high-level work. Teachers support and mentor one another. Schools work best if they reach out to the wider community and embed parents in the life of the school.

Why do many children come to dislike school? The reason is that classroom learning is based on **extrinsic motivation** (external reinforcers such as grades), which impairs **intrinsic motivation** (the desire to learn for the sake of learning). School learning is inherently less interesting because it often involves rote memorization. Being evaluated in comparison to the class also erodes a child's interest in learning for its own sake. Studies show a disturbing decline in intrinsic motivation as children progress through elementary school.

Teachers (and parents) can make extrinsic learning tasks more intrinsic by offering material relevant to children's interests, fostering relatedness (or a close attachment), and giving students choices about how to do their work. Creative work not only stimulates intrinsic motivation, but it can sometimes promote better scores on end-of-year achievement tests. With exceptional teaching, students can love school!

KEY TERMS

parenting style, p. 205
authoritative parents, p. 205
authoritarian parents, p. 205
permissive parents, p. 205
rejecting-neglecting parents, p. 205
resilient children, p. 208
acculturation, p. 210
corporal punishment, p. 211
child maltreatment, p. 212
achievement tests, p. 217
WISC (Wechsler Intelligence Scale for Children), p. 217
mentally retarded, p. 218
specific learning disability, p. 218
dyslexia, p. 219
gifted, p. 219
reliability, p. 220
validity, p. 220
Flynn effect, p. 221
"g," p. 221
analytic intelligence, p. 222
creative intelligence, p. 222
practical intelligence, p. 222
Sternberg's successful intelligence, p. 223
Gardner's multiple intelligences theory, p. 223
intrinsic motivation, p. 226
extrinsic motivation, p. 226

ANSWERS TO TYING IT ALL TOGETHER QUIZZES

Home

1. Montana's parents = authoritative. Pablo's parents = authoritarian. Sara's parents = permissive
2. Amber
3. Judith Harris's advice = Get your son in the best possible peer group. This chapter's recommendation = Provide exceptionally sensitive parenting.
4. a and c
5. These are possible symptoms of neglect and physical abuse. You should report the problem to child protective services. The goal is to teach the parents to parent more effectively so that this student can remain with his family or be reunited with the family if he must be removed from home.
6. Tell Crystal she made the right decision as living in an atmosphere poisoned by chronic fighting might have devastating consequences for her child's mental health. *Your advice:* Encourage your child to express her feelings,

and try to give her *some* input into custody decisions. Minimize other life disruptions (e.g., see if you can keep your daughter in the same neighborhood or school). Don't bad-mouth your former spouse or continually battle over custody arrangements.

School

1. b
2. Malik has a learning disability.
3. c and d
4. Analytic intelligence . . . creative intelligence and practical intelligence . . . multiple intelligences . . . Josh's strengths are in musical, kinesthetic, and interpersonal intelligence.
5. b
6. (a) Intrinsic motivation is self-generated—we work at something simply because it gives us joy. Extrinsic motivation refers to activities propelled by external reinforcers like grades. (b) Ask yourself: Am I doing this because I love it or only because this activity results in an external reward? (c) 1. Make disliked, extrinsic tasks relevant to a larger personal goal. ("Cleaning the house will help me become a more organized person. Plus, it's great exercise, so I'll become healthier.") 2. Increase your sense of autonomy or feeling of having choices around this activity. ("I'll do my housecleaning at the time of day that feels least burdensome while I listen to my favorite CD.") 3. Enhance attachments ("If my significant other comes home to a clean house, she'll feel wonderful!")

Adolescence

PART IV

This two-chapter part dealing with the teenage years actually progresses a bit chronologically. That's because my first topic, puberty, can begin to take place as early as age 9 or 10.

In Chapter 8—**Physical Development**—I'll actually spend a good deal of time exploring puberty, that early adolescent total body change. However, I'll also be focusing on two other major teenage body-oriented topics: body image concerns (and eating disorders) and adolescent sexuality.

Chapter 9—**Cognitive and Socioemotional Development**—begins by examining the dramatic advances in reasoning and morality that take place during adolescence. Next, I'll be looking at teenagers' emotional states and offering insights into which children are at risk for having problems and flourishing during this special decade of life. The last part of this chapter is all about relationships—how teenagers behave with their parents; how they act with their peers.

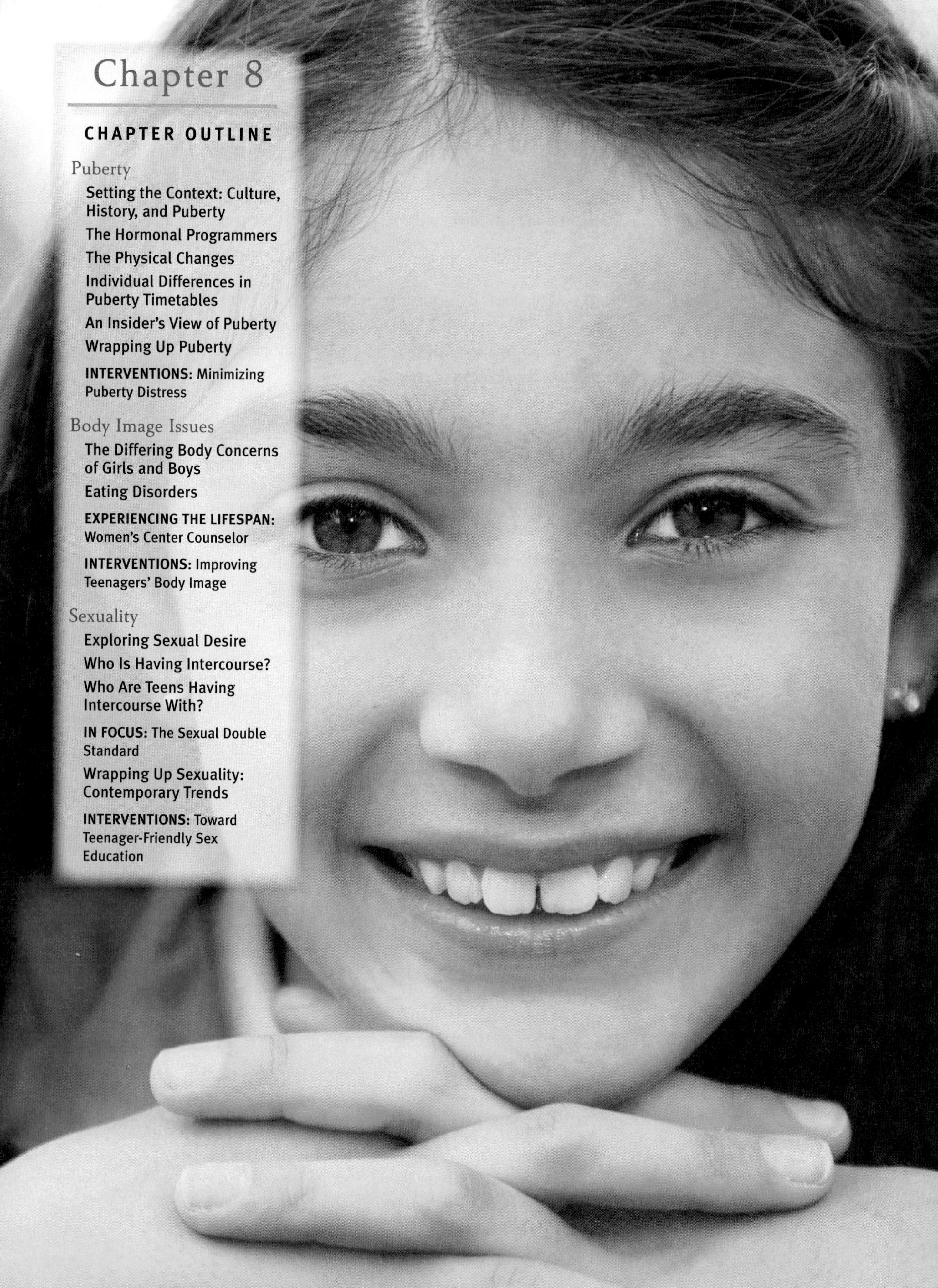

Chapter 8

CHAPTER OUTLINE

Physical Development

Samantha and her twin brother, Sam, were so much alike—in their physical features, their personalities, their academic talents. Except for the sex difference, they almost seemed like identical twins. Then, when Samantha was 10, she started to tower over Sam and the rest of the fifth-grade class.

Yes, there was a downside to being first to develop—needing to hide behind a locker when you dressed for gym; not having anyone to talk to when you got your period at age 10. But, oh, what fun! From being a neglected, pudgy elementary school child, by sixth grade, Samantha leaped into the ranks of most popular, especially with the older boys. At age 12, Samantha was smoking and drinking. By 14, she regularly defied her helpless parents and often left the house at 2 a.m.

Samantha's parents were frantic, but their daughter couldn't care less. Everything else was irrelevant compared to exploring being an adult. It took a life-changing tenth-grade trip to Costa Rica with Caroline, and a pregnancy scare, to get Samantha on track. Samantha had abandoned Caroline, her best friend during elementary school, for her new "mature" friends. But when the girls got close again that memorable summer, Caroline's calming influence woke Samantha up. Samantha credits comments like "Why are you putting yourself in danger by having unprotected sex?" with saving her life. Plus, her lifelong competition with her brother didn't hurt. Although Sam was also an early developer, when he shot up to 6 feet in the spring of seventh grade, he was great at sports and also an academic star.

Now that Samantha is 30, married, and expecting her first child, it's interesting for the three of them to get together and really talk (for the first time) about the teenage years. Sam remembers the thrill of getting so much stronger and his first incredible feelings of being in love. Samantha recalls being excited about her changing body, but she also remembers constantly dieting and obsessively worrying about being too fat. Then, there is Caroline, who says she sailed through middle school because she didn't begin to menstruate until age 14. Everyone goes through puberty, but why does everyone react in such different ways?

How do children feel during **puberty**, the name for all of the internal and external changes related to physically becoming adult? This chapter focuses on this question and many others as we explore physical development during the teenage years. I'll begin by tracking puberty—examining what sets off this transformation, exploring how the changes unfold, focusing on how teens react to their changing bodies. Why did Samantha—but not Sam—have trouble coping with being an "early-maturing" child? How can we make puberty a less stressful, more exciting experience for every boy and girl?

Next, I'll discuss body image issues such as Samantha's dieting frenzy and, finally, offer a look at sexuality during this watershed time of life. As you read though this chapter, think back to when you were 10 or 12 or 14. How did you feel about your body during puberty? When did you begin dating and fantasizing about having sex?

puberty The hormonal and physical changes by which children become sexually mature human beings and reach their adult height.

puberty rite A "coming of age" ritual, usually beginning at some event such as first menstruation, held in traditional cultures to celebrate children's transition to adulthood.

secular trend in puberty A century-long decline in the average age at which children reach puberty in the developed world.

menarche A girl's first menstruation.

spermarche A boy's first ejaculation of live sperm.

Olivier Ribardiere/Getty Images

Mooboard/Corbis

These photographs of fourth graders and high school juniors at the prom offer a vivid visual reminder of the total body transformation that takes place as children travel through puberty during early adolescence.

Puberty

Compare photos of yourself from late elementary school and high school to get a vivid sense of the incredible changes that occur during puberty. From the size of our thighs to the shape of our nose, we become a different-looking person during the early teenage years. Although children's timetables vary, today puberty—which lasts about five years from start to finish—typically is a pre-teen and early adolescent change (Archibald, Graber, & Brooks-Gunn, 2003). Moreover, today, as you saw with Samantha, who started menstruating at age 10 and has just gotten pregnant at age 30, the gap between being physically able to have children and actually *having* children can be twice as long as infancy and childhood combined.

This lack of person–environment fit, when our body is passionately saying "have sex" and society is telling us to "just say no" to intercourse, explains why issues relating to teenage sexuality provoke such anxiety among Western adults. Our concerns are fairly recent. They are a product of living in the twentieth-century developed world.

Setting the Context: Culture, History, and Puberty

For this rural Vietnamese boy, reaching puberty means it's time to assume his adult responsibilities as a fisherman. This is the reason why having *puberty rites* to mark the end of childhood makes excellent sense in less-industrialized cultures, but not in our own.

> As my sisters and I went about doing our daily chores, we choked on the dust stirred up by the herd of cattle and goats that had just arrived in our compound. . . . These animals were my bride wealth, negotiated by my parents and the family of the man who had been chosen as my husband. . . . I am considered to be a woman, so I am ready to marry, have children, and assume adult privileges and responsibilities. My name is Telelia ole Mariani. I am 14 years old.
>
> (quoted in Wilson, Ngige, & Trollinger, 2003, p. 95)

Keren Su/Getty Images

As you can see in this quotation from a girl in rural Nigeria, throughout most of history and even today in a few agrarian cultures, having sex as a teenager was "normal." The reason is that puberty was often society's signal to find a spouse (Schlegel, 1995; Schlegel & Barry, 1991). The fact that a young person's changing body meant entering a new adult stage of life produced a different attitude toward the physical changes. In our culture, we downplay puberty because we don't want teenagers to act on their sexual feelings for years. In traditional societies, people might celebrate the changes in a coming-of-age ceremony called the **puberty rite.**

Celebrating Puberty

Puberty rites were more than parties. They were intensely emotional events, carefully scripted to highlight a young person's entrance into adult life. Often, children were removed from their families and asked to perform challenging tasks. There was anxiety ("Can I really do this thing?") and feelings of awe and self-efficacy, as the young person returned to joyfully enter the community as an adult (Feixa, 2011; Weisfeld, 1997).

So at puberty, boys in one Amazonian hunter-gatherer society were required to prove their manhood by killing a large animal and then metaphorically "die"—by drinking a potent hallucinogen and spending time in isolation to "be born again" as a man. Among the Masai of Africa, male children first faced the challenge of undergoing a painful circumcision without showing distress. After passing this test, they were called "warriors," and entered a segregated compound to learn military maneuvers before proudly returning to the community and taking wives (Feixa, 2011).

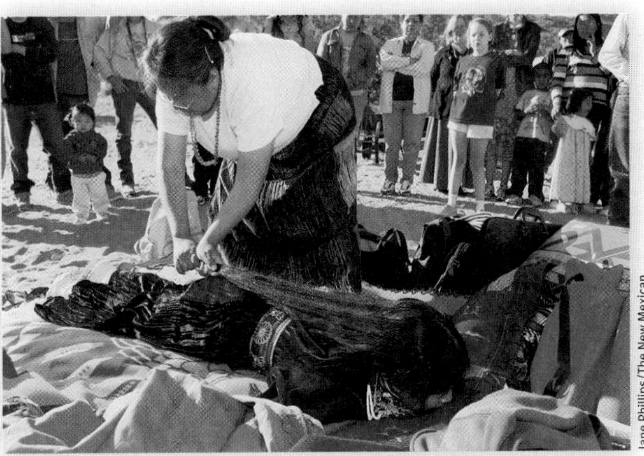

Jane Phillips/The New Mexican

As the female mentor symbolically welcomes her into adulthood, this newly menstruating Navajo girl is undergoing a traditional cultural ritual that will be an unforgettable highlight of her life. Plus, the female tourists watching this ceremony are getting insights into a very different, positive way of looking at menarche!

For girls, menstruation was the standard marker to celebrate one's arrival into womanhood. In the traditional Navajo Kinaalda ceremony, for instance, girls in their first or second menstrual cycle, guided by a female mentor, performed the long-distance running ritual, sprinting for miles. (Imagine your motivation to train for this event, when you understood that the length of your run symbolized how long you would live!) The female role model massaged the girl's body, painted her face, and supervised her by preparing a huge cake of corn (a symbol of fertility) that was then served to the community during a joyous, all-night community sing. The Navajo believe that when females begin menstruating, they possess special spiritual powers, so everyone would gather around for the girl's blessings as they gave her a new adult name.

Today, however, girls may menstruate at age 10 or even 9. At that age—in *any* society—could people be ready for adult life? The answer is no. In the past, we reached puberty at an older age.

The Declining Age of Puberty

You can see this fascinating decline, called the **secular trend in puberty,** illustrated in Figure 8.1. In the 1860s, the average age of **menarche,** or first menstruation, in northern Europe was over 17 (Tanner, 1978). In the 1960s, in the developed world, it dropped to under 13 (Parent and others, 2003). A century ago, girls could not get pregnant until their late teens. Today, many girls can have babies *before* they enter their teenage years.

Researchers typically use menarche as their marker for charting the secular trend in puberty because it is an obvious sign of being able to have a child. The male signal of fertility, **spermarche,** or first ejaculation of live sperm, is a hidden event. But at least through the mid-twentieth century, the age of puberty has also been declining for boys.

In addition, because it reflects better nutrition, in the same way as you saw with stunting

FIGURE 8.1: **The secular trend in puberty:** Notice that the average age of menarche dramatically declined in developed countries during the first half of the twentieth century. Is this decline continuing? Stay tuned for surprising answers later in this chapter.

Source: Tanner 1978, p. 103.

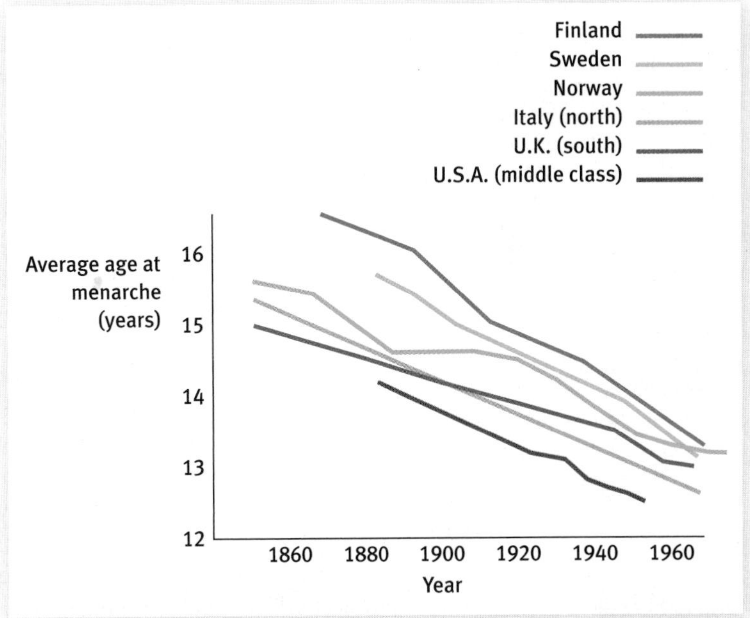

Peter Hvizdak/The Images Works

If they had grown up a century ago, these seventh graders at a summer computer camp would really have looked like girls. Due to the *secular trend in puberty*, they look like women today.

in early childhood (remember Chapter 3), we can use the secular trend in puberty as an index of a nation's economic development. In the United States, African American girls begin to menstruate at close to age 12. In impoverished African nations, such as Senegal, the average age of menarche is over 16! (Parent and others, 2003)

Given that nutrition is intimately involved, what *exactly* sets puberty off? For answers, let's focus on the hormonal systems that program the physical changes.

The Hormonal Programmers

Puberty is programmed by two command centers. One system, located in the adrenal glands at the top of the kidneys, begins to release its hormones at about age 6 to 8, several years before children show any observable signs of puberty. The **adrenal androgens,** whose output increases to reach a peak in the early twenties, eventually produce (among other events) pubic hair development, skin changes, body odor, and, as you will read later in this chapter, our first feelings of sexual desire (McClintock & Herdt, 1996).

About two years later, the most important command center kicks in. Called the **HPG axis**—because it involves the hypothalamus (in the brain), the pituitary (a gland at the base of the brain), and the **gonads** (the *ovaries* and the *testes*)—this system produces the major body changes.

As you can see in Figure 8.2, puberty is set off by a three-phase chain reaction. At about age 9 or 10, pulsating bursts of the hypothalamic hormone stimulate the pituitary gland to step up production of its hormones. This causes the ovaries and testes to secrete several closely related compounds called *estrogens* and the hormone called **testosterone.**

As the blood concentrations of estrogens and testosterone float upward, these hormones unleash a physical transformation. Estrogens produce females' changing shape by causing the hips to widen and the uterus and breasts to enlarge. They set in motion the cycle of reproduction, stimulating the ovaries to produce eggs. Testosterone causes the penis to lengthen, promotes the growth of facial and body hair, and is responsible for a dramatic increase in muscle mass and other internal masculine changes.

Boys and girls *both* produce estrogens and testosterone. Testosterone and the adrenal androgens are the desire hormones. They are responsible for sexual arousal in females and males. However, women produce mainly estrogens. The concentration of testosterone is roughly eight times higher in boys after puberty than it is in girls; in fact, this classic "male" hormone is responsible for *all* the physical changes in boys.

Now, to return to our earlier question: What primes the triggering hypothalamic hormone? Many genes control puberty (Ojeda and others, 2010). But the signal is set off when the body reaches a certain level of maturation or growth (Sisk & Foster, 2004). This explains why children with retarded growth—boys and girls whose bodies are stunted due to poor nutrition—reach puberty at older ages.

A critical chemical stimulating puberty in animals—and possibly humans—is a hormone called *leptin*, which acts as a sensor of body fat (Oswal & Yeo, 2010). Underfeeding laboratory rats inhibits the concentration of leptin, keeping them in a prolonged infantile state (Parent and others, 2003). As you will see later in this chapter, severe dieting and reaching a low level of body fat also provokes a loss of adult fertility in humans, as it causes women to stop menstruating and ovulating.

But in making sense of the puzzle of puberty, we need to take into account more than simply the amount of body fat. As Figure 8.2 illustrates, the hypothalamic

adrenal androgens Hormones produced by the adrenal glands that program various aspects of puberty, such as growth of body hair, skin changes, and sexual desire.

HPG axis The main hormonal system programming puberty; it involves a triggering hypothalamic hormone that causes the pituitary to secrete its hormones, which in turn cause the ovaries and testes to develop and secrete the hormones that produce the major body changes.

gonads The sex organs—the ovaries in girls and the testes in boys.

testosterone The hormone responsible for the maturation of the organs of reproduction and other signs of puberty in men, and for hair and skin changes during puberty and for sexual desire in both sexes.

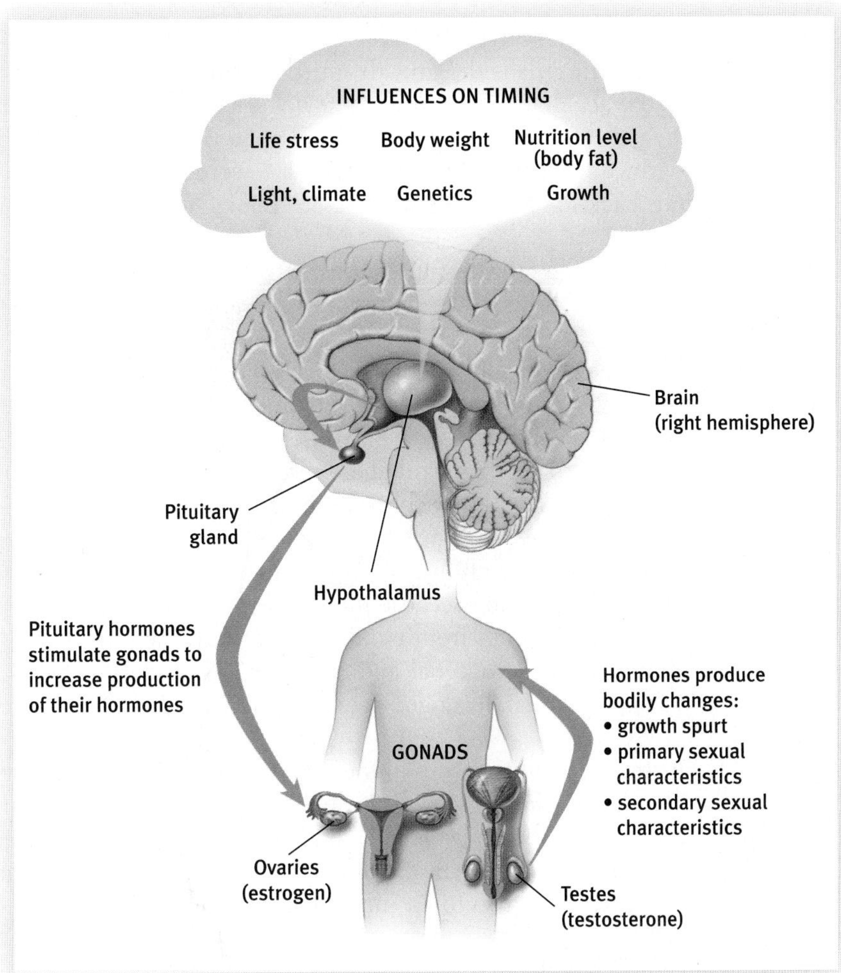

FIGURE 8.2: **The HPG axis: The three-phase hormonal sequence that triggers puberty:** As you can see here, in response to various genetic and environmental influences, the hypothalamus releases a hormone that stimulates the pituitary gland to produce its own hormones, which cause the ovaries in girls and the testes in boys to grow and secrete estrogens and testosterone, producing the physical changes of puberty.

Source: Tanner, 1978, p. 103.

trigger is sensitive to many signals—from leptin levels, to exposure to heat and light (given comparable nutrition, children who live in warmer climates tend to reach puberty comparatively early), to environmental stress (more about this fascinating force later) (Ebling, 2005). This complexity is mirrored by the diversity of the physical changes.

The Physical Changes

Puberty causes a total *psychological* as well as physical transformation. As the hormones flood the body, they affect specific brain regions, making teenagers more emotional and interested in taking risks (as you will read in Chapter 9). Scientists divide the physical changes into three categories:

- **Primary sexual characteristics** refers to the body changes directly involved in reproduction. The growth of the penis and menstruation are examples of primary sexual characteristics.
- **Secondary sexual characteristics** is the label for the hundreds of other changes that accompany puberty, such as breast development, the growth of pubic hair, voice changes, and alterations in the texture of the skin.
- The **growth spurt** merits its own special category. At puberty—as should come as no surprise—there is a dramatic increase in height and weight.

Now, let's offer a motion picture of these changes, first in girls and then in boys.

primary sexual characteristics Physical changes of puberty that directly involve the organs of reproduction, such as the growth of the penis and the onset of menstruation.

secondary sexual characteristics Physical changes of puberty that are not directly involved in reproduction.

growth spurt A dramatic increase in height and weight that occurs during puberty.

For Girls

The first sign of puberty in girls is the growth spurt. During late childhood, girls' growth picks up speed, accelerates, and then a few years later begins to decrease (Abbassi, 1998). On a visit to my 11-year-old niece, I got a vivid sense of this "peak velocity" phase of growth. Six months earlier, I had towered over her. Now, she insisted on standing back-to-back to demonstrate: "Look, Aunt Janet, I'm taller than you!"

About six months after the growth spurt begins, girls start to develop breasts and pubic hair. On average, girls' breasts take about four years to grow to their adult form (Tanner, 1955, 1978).

Interestingly, menarche typically occurs relatively late in this process, in the middle to final stages of breast and pubic hair development (Christensen and others, 2010), when girls' growth is winding down. So you can tell your 12-year-old niece, who has just begun to menstruate, that, while her breasts are still "works in progress," she is probably about as tall today as she will be as an adult.

When they reach menarche, can girls get pregnant? Yes, but there is often a window of infertility until the system fully gears up. Does puberty unfold in the same way for every girl? The answer is no. Because the hormonal signals are so complex, the timing of specific changes varies from child to child. In some girls, pubic hair development (programmed by the adrenal androgens) is well underway before the breasts begin to enlarge. Occasionally, a girl does grow much taller after she begins to menstruate.

The most fascinating variability relates to the *rate* of change. Some children are developmental "tortoises." Their progression through puberty is slow-paced. Others are hares. They speed through the body changes at an accelerated rate. For instance, while breast development *on average* takes four years, the process—from start to finish—can range from less than two to an incredible nine years! (see Mendle and others, 2010)

In tracking puberty in females, researchers focus on charting pubic hair and breast development because they can measure these external secondary sexual changes in stages. But the internal changes are equally dramatic. During puberty the uterus grows, the vagina lengthens, and the hips develop a cushion of fat. The vocal cords get longer, the heart gets bigger, and the red blood cells carry more oxygen. So, in addition to looking very different after puberty, girls become much stronger (Archibald, Graber, & Brooks-Gunn, 2003). The increases in strength, stamina, height, and weight are even more astonishing in boys.

Michael Newman/Photo Edit, Inc.

Because that landmark change, shaving, occurs fairly late in the sequence of puberty, we can be sure that this 14-year-old boy has been looking like a man for some time in the ways that you and I can't see.

For Boys

In boys, researchers also chart how the penis, testicles, and pubic hair develop in stages. However, because these organs of reproduction begin developing first, boys still look like children to the outside world for a year or two after their bodies start changing. Voice changes, the growth of body hair, and that other visible sign of being a man—needing to shave—all take place after the growth of the testes and penis are well underway (Tanner, 1978). Now, let's pause to look at the most obvious signals that a boy is becoming a man—the mammoth alterations in body size, shape, and strength.

You may recall from Chapter 5 that elementary school boys and girls are roughly the same size. Then, during the puberty growth spurt, males shoot up an incredible average of 8 inches, compared to 4 inches for girls (Tanner, 1978). Boys also become far stronger than the opposite sex.

One reason lies in the tremendous increase in muscle mass. Another lies in the dramatic cardiovascular changes. At puberty, boys' hearts increase in weight by more than one-third. In particular, notice in Figure 8.3 that, compared to females, after puberty, males have many more red blood cells and a much greater capacity for carrying oxygen in their blood. The visible signs of these changes are a big chest, wide shoulders, and a muscular frame. The real-world consequence is that after puberty males get a boost in gross motor skills that give them a biological edge in everything from soccer to sprinting; from cycling to carrying heavy loads.

Do you have access to seventh- or eighth-grade boys? If so, you might notice that growth during puberty takes place in the opposite pattern to the one that occurs earlier in life. Rather than following the *cephalocaudal* and *proximodistal* sequences (from the head downward and from the middle of the body outward), at puberty, the hands, feet, and legs grow first. While this happens for both sexes, because their growth is so dramatic, these changes are especially obvious in boys.

Their long legs and large feet explain why, in their early teens, boys look so gawky (and unattractive!). Adding to the problem is the crackly voice produced by the growing larynx, the wispy look of beginning facial hair, and the fact that during puberty a boy's nose and ears grow before the rest of his face catches up. Plus, the increased activity of the sweat glands and enlarged pores leads to the condition that results in so much emotional agony: acne. Although girls also suffer from acne, boys are more vulnerable to this condition because testosterone, which males produce in abundance, produces changes in the hair and skin.

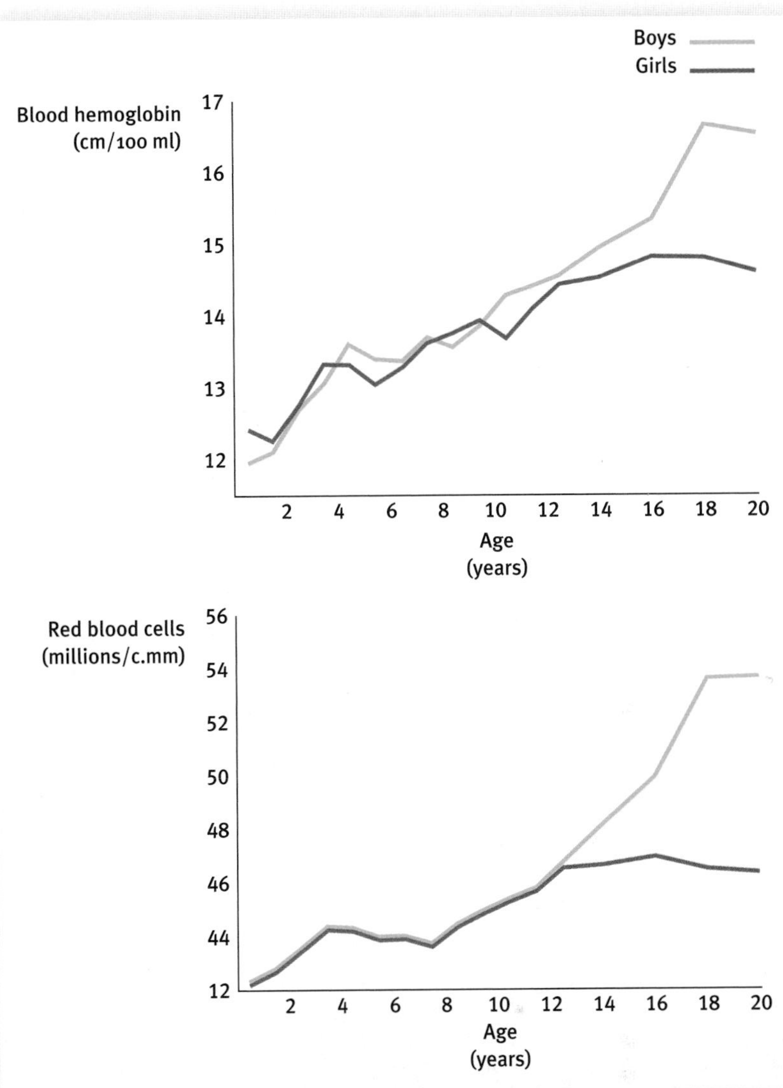

FIGURE 8.3: **Changes in blood hemoglobin and red blood cells during puberty in males and females:** At puberty, increases in the amount of hemoglobin in the blood and in the number of red blood cells cause children of both sexes to get far stronger. But notice that these changes are more pronounced in boys than in girls.
Source: Tanner, 1955, p. 103.

Are Boys on a Later Timetable? A Bit

Now, visit a middle school and you will be struck by the fact that boys, on average, appear to reach puberty two years later than girls. But appearances can be deceiving. In girls, as I mentioned earlier, the externally visible signs of puberty, such as the growth spurt and breast development, take place toward the beginning of the sequence. For boys, the more hidden developments, such as the growth of the testes, are the first changes to occur (Huddleston & Ge, 2003).

If we look at the *real* sign of fertility, interestingly, the timetables of girls and boys are not very far apart. In one study, boys reported that spermarche occurred at an average of roughly 13, only about six months later than the average age of menarche (Stein & Reiser, 1994).

Figure 8.4 on the next page graphically summarizes a few of the changes I have been discussing. Now, let's explore the numbers inside the chart. Why do children undergo puberty at such different ages?

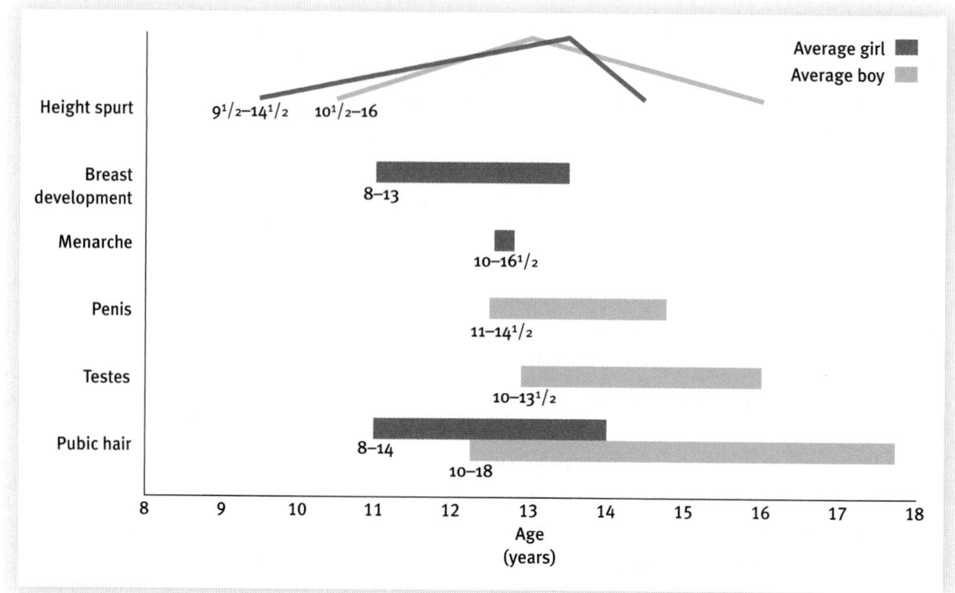

FIGURE 8.4: **The sequence of some major events of puberty:** This chart shows the ages at which some important changes of puberty occur in the average boy and girl. The numbers below each change show the range of ages at which that event begins. Notice that girls are on a slightly earlier timetable than boys, that boys' height spurt occurs at a later point in their development, and that there are dramatic differences from child to child in the timing of puberty.

Source: Adapted from Tanner, 1978, pp. 23, 29.

Individual Differences in Puberty Timetables

> I'm seventeen already. But I still look like a kid. I get teased a lot, especially by the other guys. . . . Girls aren't interested in me, either, because most of them are taller than I am. When will I grow up?
>
> (adapted from an on-line chat room)

The gender difference in puberty timetables can cause anxiety. As an early-maturing girl, I vividly remember slumping to avoid the humiliation of having my partner's head encounter my chest in sixth-grade dancing class! But nature's cruelest blow may relate to the individual differences in timing. What accounts for the five-year difference in puberty timetables between children who live in the same environment? (Parent and others, 2003)

Look at female middle school friends—such as these girls getting ready for a dance—and you will be struck with the differences in puberty timetables. In this section, you will find out why children mature earlier or later than their peers.

Not unexpectedly, genetics is important. Identical twins, for instance, go through puberty at roughly the same ages (Silventoinen and others, 2008).

There are also interesting genetic ethnic differences. Asian Americans tend to be slightly behind other U.S. children in puberty timetables (Sun and others, 2002). African American boys and girls are ahead of other North American groups (Rosenfield, Lipton, & Drum, 2009). In one turn-of-the-century survey, the average African American girl reached menarche at about her twelfth birthday, a full six months earlier than the typical European American girl (Wu, Mendola, & Buck, 2002).

But remember that in impoverished African countries—where children are poorly nourished—girls begin to menstruate, on average, as late as age 16. You might also recall from Chapter 5 that, in the United States, obesity rates are skyrocketing among African American elementary school girls and boys. This brings up an interesting question: Given that body fat is linked to the onset of puberty, does childhood "obesity" generally affect when children physically mature?

Overweight and Early Puberty (It's All About Girls)

If a third grader is seriously overweight, will that boy or girl tend to reach puberty at a younger age? Can we predict the onset of puberty by weight-related events even earlier in life?

The fascinating answer to both questions is yes—but *only* for girls. Controlling for other forces, having a high BMI (body mass index) during elementary school does predict entering puberty earlier for girls (Rosenfeld, Lipton, & Drum, 2009). Most tantalizing, rapid weight gain in the *first nine months of life* is strongly linked to menstruating at a younger age! (See Walvoord, 2010.)

Recall that this finding dovetails with the research I described in Chapter 5, suggesting that our overweight path is set in motion early in life. Now—in addition to foreshadowing later obesity—weight gain during infancy may even relate to when we sexually mature. What I find strangest, however, is that overweight boys *don't* reach puberty earlier. Some research even suggests they may reach this milestone later than their normal-weight peers! (See Walvoord, 2010.)

Although we might think there couldn't be any danger in pushing food on this adorable 8-month-old girl, we would be wrong, as rapid weight gain at this age predicts both early puberty and later struggles with weight. (NOTE: You NEVER, EVER want to put a baby on a diet, so readers might check out Table 5.2 on page 147 for a low-key suggestion to prevent overfeeding during infancy.)

So is the secular trend described earlier in Figure 8.1 continuing into the twenty-first century? If a female child is overweight, we can say yes. But for a male child the jury is out (Walvoord, 2010).

If you think these findings are complicated, now let's turn to a more astonishing environmental influence predicting puberty specifically in girls—the quality of family life.

Family Stress and Early Puberty (Again, It's About Girls)

Drawing on an *evolutionary psychology* perspective, about two decades ago, several developmentalists devised a compelling hypothesis. When family stress is intense, they argued, it would make sense to build in a mechanism to accelerate sexual maturity and free a child from the inhospitable nest (Belsky, Steinberg, & Draper, 1991). Furthermore, just as intense stress in the womb "instructs" the baby to store fat (recall the fetal programming hypothesis in Chapter 2), an unhappy childhood signals the body to expect a short life, and so pushes adult fertility to a younger age (Belsky, Houts & Pasco Fearon, 2010).

I must emphasize that "genetics" is by far the most important force predicting your puberty timetable (when your mother or father reached that marker). But, when a girl is temperamentally vulnerable to stress, *controlling for every other influence* (genetics, body weight, and so on), her family life makes its small, tantalizing contribution, too (Ellis and others, 2011). Early-maturing girls are more apt to grow up in mother-headed households (Graber, Nichols, & Brooks-Gunn, 2010; Neberich and others, 2010) and report intense childhood stress (Ellis, 2004; Moffitt and others, 1992). In one longitudinal study, mothers' use of *power assertive* discipline during preschool—yelling, shaming, rejecting—was associated with earlier menstruation (Belsky and others, 2007a, 2010). Even being insecurely attached at age 1 predicts reaching menarche at a younger age (Belsky, Houts, & Pasco Fearon, 2010).

Why—specifically in girls—is the hypothalamic timer sensitive to body weight and family stress? We do not know. But, these surprising studies emphasize the developmental-systems theory message that underlies this book: To understand *every* aspect of who we are, look to a variety of influences—from genetics to gender, from physiology to parenting, to everything else that combines in complex, unpredictable ways.

Table 8.1 summarizes these points by spelling out questions that would predict a female child's chance of reaching puberty at a younger-than-average age. If you were an early maturer, how many—if any—of these forces applied to you?

TABLE 8.1: Predicting a Girl's Chances of Early Puberty: Some Questions

1. Did this girl's parents reach puberty early?
2. Is this girl African American?
3. Is this girl overweight? Did she gain weight rapidly during her first year of life?
4. Has this girl's family life been stressful and unhappy? Did she have an insecure attachment?

FIGURE 8.5: **Getting your first bra:** To measure how girls undergoing puberty feel around their parents—without asking them directly—researchers used this specially constructed card and asked children of different ages to describe what was happening and asked "How do the mother, the father, and the girl feel?"

Source: Brooks-Gunn and others, 1994, p. 549.

Now that I've described the physical process, let's shift to an insider's perspective; first exploring how children feel about three classic signs of puberty—breast development, menstruation, and first ejaculation—and then looking at whether it *really* matters if a boy or girl reaches puberty relatively early or late.

An Insider's View of Puberty

If you think back to how you felt about your changing body during puberty, you probably remember a mixture of emotions: fear, pride, embarrassment, excitement. Now, imagine how you would react if a researcher asked you to describe your inner state. Would you want to talk about how you *really* felt? The reluctance of pre-teens to discuss what is happening ("Yuck! Just don't go there!") explains why, when researchers study reactions to puberty, they often ask adults to remember this time of life. When developmentalists do explore young teenagers' feelings, they tend to use indirect measures, such as having children tell stories about pictures, to reveal their inner concerns.

The Breasts

In a classic study, researchers used this indirect strategy to explore how girls feel in relation to their parents while undergoing that most visible sign of becoming a woman—breast development (Brooks-Gunn and others, 1994). They asked a group of girls to tell a story about the characters in a drawing that showed an adult female (the mother) taking a bra out of a shopping bag while an adolescent girl and an adult male (the father) watched (see Figure 8.5). While girls often talked about the mother in the picture as being excited and happy, they typically described the teenager as humiliated by her father's presence in the room. Moreover, girls in the middle of puberty told the most negative stories about the fathers, suggesting that body embarrassment is at its height when children are actually undergoing the physical changes.

Because society strongly values this symbol of being a woman (and our contemporary culture sees bigger as better!), other research suggests that U.S. girls feel proud of their developing breasts (Brooks-Gunn & Warren, 1988). However, among girls in ballet schools, where there are strong social pressures to look prepubescent, breast development evokes distress (Brooks-Gunn & Warren, 1985). The same principle—that children's reactions to puberty depend on the messages they get from the wider world—also holds true for menstruation.

Menstruation

Think of being a Navajo girl and being taught that, when you begin to menstruate, you enter a special spiritual state. Compare this with the less-than-glowing portrait

Imagine how these girls auditioning at a premier ballet academy in New York City will feel when they develop breasts and perhaps find that their womanly body shape interrupts their career dreams, and you will understand why children's reactions to puberty depend totally on their unique environment.

Chris Hondros/Getty Images

Western societies paint about "that time of the month" (Brooks-Gunn & Ruble, 1982; Costos, Ackerman, & Paradis, 2002). From the advertisements for pills strong enough to handle *even* menstrual pain to its classic description as "the curse," there's no wonder that previous cohorts of girls approached this milestone with feelings of dread (Brooks-Gunn & Ruble, 1982).

Luckily, contemporary upper-middle-class, baby boom mothers may be changing these cultural scripts. When 18- to 20-year-old students at Oregon State University were asked in 2006 to write about their "first period experiences," 3 out of 4 women recalled their moms as being supportive or thrilled ("She was incredibly excited"; "She treated me like a princess"). One person wrote that, the day after she told her mother, "I saw an expensive box of chocolates and a card addressed to me. It said 'Congrats on becoming a woman'" (quoted in Lee, 2008, p. 1332).

Positive responses make a difference. In contrast to the findings of earlier studies, about half of these young women described menarche as positive or "no big deal." But negative emotions linger on. Even when they described their mothers as supportive, 1 in 3 students remembered feeling "disgusted" or, more likely, ambivalent—both ashamed and happy—when menarche arrived.

First Ejaculation

Daughters must confide in their mothers about menarche because this change demands specific coping techniques. Spermarche, as I mentioned earlier, is hidden, because this event doesn't require instructions from the outside world. Who talks to male adolescents about first ejaculation, and how do teenagers feel about their signal of becoming a man? Listen to these memories from some 18-year-olds (Stein & Reiser, 1994):

> I woke up the next morning and my sheets were pasty. . . . After you wake up your mind is kind of happy and then you realize: "Oh my God, this is my wet dream!"
>
> (quoted in Stein & Reiser, 1994, p. 380)

> My mom, she knew I had them. It was all over my sheets and bedspread and stuff, but she didn't say anything, didn't tease me and stuff. She never asked if I wanted to talk about it—I'm glad. I never could have said anything to my mom.
>
> (quoted in Stein & Reiser, 1994, p. 377)

Most of these boys reported that they needed to be secretive. They didn't want to let *anyone* know. And notice from the second quotation—as you saw earlier with fathers and pre-teen girls—that boys also view their changing bodies as especially embarrassing around the parent of the opposite sex.

Is this tendency for children to hide the symptoms of puberty around the parent of the other gender programmed into evolution to help teenagers emotionally separate from their families? We can only speculate about this interesting idea. Where we do have scientific information is on the emotional impact of being early or late.

Being Early: It Can Be a Problem for Girls

Imagine being an early-maturing girl. How would you feel if you looked like an adult while everyone else in your class still looked like a child? Now imagine being a late maturer and thinking, "What's wrong with my body? Will I *ever* grow up?"

Actually, the timing of development matters, but again for girls, not boys. Hundreds of studies in the developed world agree: *Early-maturing girls are vulnerable to having difficulties during their adolescent years.*

EARLY-MATURING GIRLS ARE AT SPECIAL RISK OF DEVELOPING ACTING-OUT, EXTERNALIZING PROBLEMS. Because we choose friends who are "like us," early-maturing girls may gravitate toward becoming friends with older girls and boys. So they tend to

Lauren Greenfield/VII Photo

This 13-year-old cheerleader is getting a lot of attention from the 18-year-old football star. Unfortunately, she may be too young to assert herself and say no if they start to date and he pressures her to have sex.

get involved in "adult activities" such as smoking and drinking at a younger age. (Alert readers may realize this is yet another example of an *active* genetic-environment interaction. Our "biology"—in this case, our puberty timetable—shapes the particular environment we choose.)

Because they are so busy exploring adulthood, the result can be a disconnect from school. In one classic study, early-maturing girls tended to get worse grades than their classmates in the sixth and seventh grades (Simmons & Blyth, 1987). Once set in motion, this poor performance can be difficult to reverse. In another classic longitudinal study, by their twenties, early-maturing girls were several times less likely to have graduated from high school than their later-developing peers (Stattin & Magnusson, 1990).

Then, there is the main concern with having a mature body early on: having unprotected sex. Because they may not have the cognitive abilities to resist this social pressure and often have older boyfriends, early-maturing girls are more likely to have intercourse at a younger age (Graber, Nichols, & Brooks-Gunn, 2010). They are less likely to use contraception, making them more vulnerable to becoming pregnant as teens (Ellis, 2004). Imagine being a sixth- or seventh-grade girl thrilled to be pursued by the high school boys. Would you have the presence of mind to "just say no"?

EARLY-MATURING GIRLS ARE AT RISK OF GETTING ANXIOUS AND DEPRESSED. As if this were not enough, early-maturing girls are also more apt to feel bad about themselves (Blumenthal and others, 2011; Graber, Nichols, & Brooks-Gunn, 2010; Lien, Haavet, & Dalgard, 2010). During the teens, body dissatisfaction and depression are closely entwined (Markey, 2010)—and early maturers are more prone to struggle with their weight. Not only are these girls apt to be heavier before puberty, but they also tend to end up shorter and stockier because their height spurt occurs at an earlier point in their development (Adair, 2008; Must and others, 2005). Late-maturing girls are more prone to fit the tall ultra-slim model shape. Reaching puberty early sets girls up for a poor body image and low self-esteem.

So far, I've been painting a dismal portrait of early-maturing girls. But, as with any aspect of development, it's important to look at the *whole* context of a person's life. Early maturation may not pose body image problems for African American girls, because black women (and men) have a healthier, more inclusive idea about the ideal female body size (more about this later).

Most important, these negative effects happen only when there are other risk factors in a child's life. If a girl's family life is already stressful or if she is living in poverty, then, yes, early maturation can be the straw that breaks the camel's back (Lynne-Landsman, Graber, & Andrews, 2010). But, when a child has close relationships with her parents, strong religious values, and doesn't get involved with older "at-risk" friends, her puberty timetable will not matter at all (Stattin & Magnusson, 1990).

Another influence that affects a girl's chances of getting into trouble, can relate to the school she attends. In a classic study exploring puberty, developmentalists traced the lives of two groups of pre-teens in Milwaukee: boys and girls in school districts with separate junior high schools (what we now call middle school) and those who attended a K–8 (kindergarten through eighth grade) school (Simmons & Blyth, 1987).

You might think that the early-maturing girls in K–8 schools would have more problems because they look so different from everyone else. You would be wrong. Girls who transferred to a junior high school had more troubles. In fact, for *every child* who moved to the larger, more anonymous junior high, academic performance tended to decline and self-confidence typically became shakier.

Based on this research, as well as one large-scale twenty-first-century investigation (see Weiss & Baker-Smith, 2010), developmentalists (see Eccles & Roeser, 2003) have argued that it's best not to have children change to a larger, more anonymous middle school at this vulnerable time of life. But, the following study suggests, we may need to rethink the traditional scientific advice that "middle schools are worse."

In tracking students in 36 rural school systems that did and did not have a transition to middle school, the researchers were surprised to find that bullying was less frequent among the sixth graders who attended middle schools. Moreover, students who moved to middle schools generally reported more supportive class environments than children who remained at their original K-8 or K-12 schools (Farmer and others, 2011).

This study highlights the fact that with pre-teens (and every child), what's really essential is to move beyond a school's structure to consider more basic questions: Is this a nurturing, *authoritative* environment (see Chapter 7)? Does this school have caring peer norms (see Chapter 6)? Moreover, imagine being locked into the calcified status-hierarchies that can solidify, based on spending your whole childhood with the same group of peers. The great advantage of middle school is that it offers you (and everyone else) a liberating new start!

Wrapping Up Puberty

Now, let's summarize the messages of our discussion:

- **Children's reactions to puberty depend on the environment in which they physically mature.** Negative feelings are more likely to occur when society looks down on a given sign of development (as with menstruation) or when the physical changes are not valued in a person's particular group (as with breast development in ballerinas). Changing to a non-nurturing school during puberty may magnify the stress of the body changes (Eccles & Midgley, 1989; Eccles & Roeser, 2003).
- **With early-maturing girls, we need to take special steps to arrange the right body–environment fit.** Having an adult body at a young age is dangerous for girls, but only when the changes happen in a high-risk environment. Therefore, when a girl reaches puberty early, it's important to arrange her life with special care.
- **Communication about puberty should be improved—especially for boys.** While some contemporary mothers may be doing a fine job discussing menstruation with their daughters, boys, in particular, seem to enter puberty without any guidance about what to expect (Omar, McElderry, & Zakharia, 2003).

INTERVENTIONS: Minimizing Puberty Distress

Given these findings, what are the lessons for parents? What changes should society make?

LESSONS FOR PARENTS. It's tempting for parents to avoid discussing puberty because children are so sensitive about their changing bodies. This reluctance is a mistake. Developmentalists urge parents to make an effort to discuss what is happening with a same-sex child. They advise beginning these discussions when the child is at an age when talking is emotionally easier, before the actual changes take place (Graber, Nichols, & Brooks-Gunn, 2010). Fathers, in particular, need to make special efforts to talk about puberty with their sons (Paikoff & Brooks-Gunn, 1991).

Finally, parents of early-maturing daughters should try to get their child involved in positive activities, especially with friends her own age (more about this topic in Chapter 9) and, if possible, carefully pick the best school environment.

LESSONS FOR SOCIETY. No matter what a child's puberty timetable, the implicit message of this section is that the school environment matters *tremendously* at this often neglected gateway-to-adulthood age. Rather than viewing what happens in sixth or seventh grade as relatively unimportant (compared, let's say, to high school), let's understand that providing nurturing schools can be vital to setting young teens on the right path.

It also seems critical to provide more adequate puberty education. Think back to what you wanted to know about your changing body ("My breasts don't look right"; "My penis has a strange shape"), and you will realize that the current practice of offering a few fifth-grade health lectures at school is not enough. Actually, most formal sex education in the United States occurs in high school, after puberty has occurred (Guttmacher Institute, 2011a). (That's like locking the barn door after the horses have been stolen!) Programs focused heavily on abstinence warn teenagers, "Don't have intercourse" (Guttmacher Institute, 2011a). Teen health websites designed to answer "everything you wanted to know about sex" are not filling the gap. Boys and girls are (legitimately) wary of this information (Jones and Biddlecom, 2011). As one 17-year-old (accurately) reported, the Internet is not trustworthy because it's "like a giant billboard for sex" (quoted in Jones and others, 2011, p. 436). Suppose our culture really *celebrated* our blossoming sexual body, as the Navajo do? Perhaps this might cause a revolution where we celebrated *every* body size.

TYING IT ALL TOGETHER

1. Reading about traditional puberty rites, Luis thinks that they sound like an awesome idea but that they wouldn't make much sense in the twenty-first century. Give the *main* reason why our culture would find it difficult to celebrate puberty today?
2. You notice that your 11-year-old cousin is going from looking like a child to looking like a young woman. (a) Outline the three-phase hormonal sequence that is setting off the physical changes; (b) name the three classes of hormones involved in puberty; (c) identify which change is happening first.
3. Both Kendra and Anthony are 12 years old. Kendra recently shot up in height and is just beginning to develop breasts. Anthony still looks physically like a child. Statistically speaking, you can predict that Kendra [*is already menstruating/is not yet menstruating*] and that Anthony [*has not yet reached puberty/may or may not have reached puberty*].
4. All of the following facts about Brianna suggest that she may be on an earlier puberty timetable *except:*
   a. She is African American.
   b. She experienced "harsh," rejecting parenting.
   c. Her mother was an early maturer.
   d. She is a dancer and she is very thin.
5. Spell out what child is most at risk of getting into trouble (e.g., with drugs or having unprotected sex) if that person matures at an "off-time age"?
6. You are on a national advisory committee charged with developing programs to help children deal better with the changes of puberty. Based on this chapter, what recommendations might you make?

Answers to the Tying It All Together questions can be found at the end of this chapter.

Norman Parkinson Limited/Corbis

Exactly when did our culture develop the idea that women should be unrealistically thin? Historians trace this change to the 1960s and 1970s, when extremely slim actresses like Audrey Hepburn became our cultural ideal.

Body Image Issues

What do you daydream about?

Being skinny.

—Amanda (quoted in Martin, 1996, p. 36)

Puberty is a time of intense physical preoccupations, and there is hardly a teenager who isn't concerned about some body part. How important is it for young people to be *generally* satisfied with how they look?

Consider this finding: Susan Harter (1999) explored how feeling competent in each of her five "self-worth" dimensions—scholastic abilities, conduct, athletic skills, peer likeability, and appearance (recall Chapter 6)—related to teenagers' overall self-esteem. She found that being happy about one's looks outweighed *anything else* in determining whether adolescents generally felt good about themselves.

This finding is not just true of teenagers in the United States. It appears in surveys that Harter and her colleagues have conducted in a variety of Western countries among people at various stages of life. If we are happy with the way we look, we are likely to be happy with who we are as human beings.

thin ideal Media-driven cultural idea that females need to be abnormally thin.

Feeling physically appealing is important to everyone—for boys, surprisingly, one study suggested, more than for girls (Mellor and others, 2010). But, girls (no surprise) are prone to be especially unhappy with their looks (Lawler and Nixon, 2011; Warren, Schoen, & Schafer, 2010). One reason for the pervasive body dissatisfaction among teenage girls comes as no surprise—the intense cultural pressure for women to be thin.

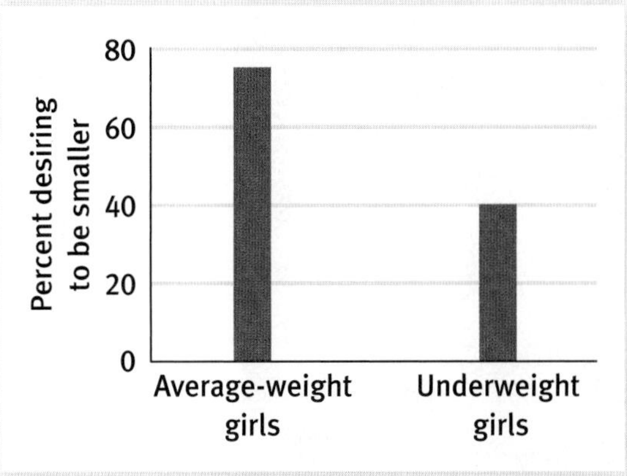

FIGURE 8.6: **The desire to be "smaller" among average and underweight Irish girls, aged 12 to 19:** Notice that with 3 out of 4 "average weight" girls wanting to be thinner and a significant proportion of underweight girls still wanting to shed pounds, female teens in Ireland are clearly buying into the destructive messages of *the thin ideal.*

Source: Lawler & Nixon, 2011, p. 67.

The Differing Body Concerns of Girls and Boys

You can vividly see the impact of the **thin ideal,** or pressure to be abnormally thin, in Figure 8.6. Notice in this survey, conducted in Ireland, that 3 out of 4 female teens with average BMIs felt they were too fat. An alarming percentage of *underweight* girls also wanted to shed pounds (Lawler & Nixon, 2011). While some boys (those who were genuinely heavy in this study, for instance) also worried about being too large, males tend to have another concern: They want to build up their muscles—spending hours at the gym, sometimes using dangerous anabolic steroids to increase their body mass (Parent & Moradi, 2011; Smolak & Stein, 2010).

These preoccupations may be promoted in part by biological forces. As you will see in the next chapter, the hormonal changes of puberty may make children highly sensitive to how they look. Another force that sets off the obsession to be thin is peer pressure: Pre-teens love to tease one another about their weight ("Ha ha. You are getting fat!") (Compian, Gowen, & Hayward, 2004; Jackson & Chen, 2008; Lawler & Nixon, 2011). When children are already unhappy with their bodies, this teasing can slide into depression—and, among emotionally fragile children provoke eating disorders– for either sex (Benas, Uhrlass, & Gibb, 2010; Hutchinson, Rapee, & Taylor, 2010).

A primary culprit is the media, for its regular drumbeat advocating the thin ideal. As early as preschool, one study showed, girls have internalized the message, "You need to be thin" (Harriger and others, 2010). Digitally altered images beamed from TV, the Internet, and magazines set body-size standards that are often impossible to attain (López-Guimerà and others, 2010). So it's no wonder that being shown snapshots of ultra-thin women activates body dissatisfaction in temperamentally vulnerable teens and adults (Anschutz and others, 2011; Roberts & Good, 2010).

Pressures to mirror that model-perfect male body have clearly infected this vulnerable eighth-grade boy. Worse yet, in his struggle to remake his recalcitrant skinny shape, he may be tempted to take dangerous anabolic steroids to attain the ideal Abercrombie and Fitch chest he craves.

Although the thin ideal specifically targets females, media-driven, body-oriented pressures on males are on the rise (Smolak & Stein, 2010). In examining past issues of *Sports Illustrated*, researchers found a recent trend to more male photos highlighting appearance (Abercrombie and Fitch ads are a good example). This emphasis on the body-as-external-object takes a toll. When boys see body-oriented advertisements targeting performance-oriented qualities such as "how to increase

© Sayre Berman/Corbis

Queen Latifa embodies the fact that bodies are beautiful at *every* size. Not only is she a role model for women of color, but for every woman in our culture.

your energy"—versus ads discussing strategies to "make better abs"—they feel better about themselves (Farquhar & Wasylkiw, 2007).

Still, some children are less susceptible to the traditional media messages. In Albert Bandura's social learning framework, for instance, African American and Latino girls should be more insulated from the thin ideal because their media role models, such as Queen Latifah and Beyonce, demonstrate that beauty comes in ample sizes. As one young Black woman in an interview study explained: "I feel like . . . for the woman of color . . . the look is like thick thighs, you know fat butt . . . (men) like, like want you to have meat on your body" (quoted in Hesse-Biber and others, 2010, p. 704).

Does this mean that, unless they are genuinely obese, Latino and African American teens don't worry about their weight? No! The real predictor of body dissatisfaction and depression is whether a minority female identifies with the mainstream, Western beauty ideal (Sabik, Cole, & Ward, 2010). Therefore, it should be no surprise that rates of body dissatisfaction are comparatively higher among acculturated Latino girls (Warren, Schoen, & Schafer, 2010). Unfortunately, one international poll showed, even in non-Western cultures that have appreciated ample-sized women, contemporary young people now prefer a "modern," slim female shape (Swami and others, 2010). So, in this era of globalization, we are in danger of exporting that debilitating, developed-world mental-health problem around the world: eating disorders.

Eating Disorders

> In the morning I'll have a black coffee. At noon I have a mix of shredded lettuce, carrots and cabbage. At around dinnertime I have 9 mini whole-wheat crackers. On a bad day I may have.... with my (morning) black coffee an egg white,...
>
> (adapted from Juarascio, Shoaib, & Timko, 2010, p. 402)

> Scales are evil! But I'm obsessed with them! I'm on the damn thing like 3 times a day!
>
> (adapted from Gavin, Rodham, & Poyer, 2008, pp. 327–328)

As these quotations from "pro-anorexia" social network sites show, **eating disorders** differ qualitatively from "normal" dieting. Here, being thin is the *sole* focus of life. Imagine waking up and planning each day around eating (or not eating). You monitor every morsel. You are obsessed with checking and rechecking your weight. Let's now look at two classic forms this obsession can take: anorexia and bulimia.

eating disorder A pathological obsession with getting and staying thin. The two best-known eating disorders are *anorexia nervosa* and *bulimia nervosa.*

anorexia nervosa A potentially life-threatening eating disorder characterized by pathological dieting (resulting in severe weight loss and, in females, loss of menstruation) and by a distorted body image.

bulimia nervosa An eating disorder characterized by at least biweekly cycles of binging and purging (by inducing vomiting or taking laxatives) in an obsessive attempt to lose weight.

Anorexia nervosa, the most serious eating disorder, is defined by self-starvation—specifically to the point of being 85 percent of one's ideal body weight or less. (This means that if 110 pounds is the ideal weight for your height, you would now weigh less than 95 pounds.) Another diagnostic feature of this primarily female disorder is that leptin levels have become too low to support adult fertility and the girl has stopped menstruating. A hallmark of eating disorders—among both girls and boys—is a distorted body image (Espeset and others, 2011). Even when people look skeletal, they feel fat. Sometimes they deny reality, and literally don't "see" their body size: As one girl named Sarah revealingly commented: "I remember … passing an open door and saw myself in the mirror . . . and thought "Oh gosh, she is thin!" but then when I understood that it was actually me, I didn't see me as thin anymore" (quoted in Espeset and others, 2011, p. 183).

Anorexia is a dangerous, life-threatening disease. When people reach two-thirds of their ideal weight or less, they need to be hospitalized and fed—intravenously, if necessary—to stave off death (Diamanti and others, 2008). A student of mine who runs a self-help group for people with eating disorders provided a vivid reminder of the enduring physical toll anorexia can cause. Alicia informed the class that she had permanently damaged her heart muscle during her teenage bout with this devastating disease.

Bulimia nervosa is typically not as life threatening because the person's weight often stays within a normal range. However, because this disorder involves frequent binging (at least twice-weekly eating sprees in which thousands of calories may be consumed in a matter of hours) and either purging (getting rid of the food by vomiting or misusing laxatives and diuretics) and/or fasting, bulimia can seriously compromise health. In addition to producing deficiencies of basic nutrients, the purging episodes can cause mouth sores, ulcers in the esophagus, and the loss of enamel in the teeth due to the throat and mouth being exposed to stomach acid.

How prevalent are these predominately female teen and young-adult problems? Adopting the stringent criteria used in the psychiatric diagnostic manual (DSM) (anorexia requires having every symptom above; bulimia requires binging and purging twice a week), these disorders affect roughly 1 to 4 percent of U.S. teens and adults (Hudson and others, 2007). But, possibly as many as one in ten girls have some of these symptoms—bingeing and purging less frequently; purging but not bingeing; obsessively exercising; regularly bingeing and then feeling an intense sense of shame; or suffering from *body dismorphia*, feeling intensely preoccupied and ashamed of some normal body part (Roberto and others, 2010).

EXPERIENCING THE LIFESPAN: Women's Center Counselor

Now that we know the diagnostic categories, lets get an insider's view. Here is what Mary, a counselor, told me when we sat down to chat about her clients with eating disorders. On the next page, I'll be summarizing the scientific research on what causes these debilitating diseases.

With eating disorders, denial is big. A lot of times, people won't bring their problem in as the issue that troubles them but, after talking for a while, they finally feel comfortable enough to say that they abuse laxatives or exercise incessantly. Sometimes, a person talks seemingly innocently and I'm thinking: "Hmm, sounds like you have an eating disorder."

You won't find it in the standard diagnostic criteria, but to me the key is, "Is this person's self-worth defined by how much she weighs?" Also, with eating disorders, the whole day focuses around what the person is going to eat. Because secrecy is involved, a fair amount of planning goes into a binge. A person might go to the drive-through at six fast food restaurants to hide the fact that she is buying six meals that she will eat right now.

So there's the obsession about obtaining the food, the obsession about what the food is going to be, and the obsession about weight. Gaining half a pound becomes a crisis. Losing half a pound makes the person's day. People often have a magic number where everything in life is going to fall into place. Sometimes, I get a call from a client who says, "I always thought if I weighed such-and-such everything would be OK." Then they do a reality check and say, "I think I need help."

It's a progressive disease. You start out binging and purging once every few weeks. Somebody who is pretty well into the illness will be doing it several days a week. A good day is when you fight the urge. A bad day is when you skip class or put your kid at the babysitter so you can binge and purge all day. Every case is individual, but I feel at the core of all eating disorders is the sense that "I'm not good enough." I frequently find people have controlling parents who don't let them make decisions, telling them exactly what to wear, exactly what to eat: "You have to make 'our family' look good, get the highest grades, be in such-and-such activity." You are not allowed to have problems. "Everything's OK in this family." These are people who are used to being controlled by everyone—parents, boyfriends. They don't have the concept of directing their life. They come in saying, "I hate to take up your time but my boyfriend wants me to be here."

Lauren Greenfield/VII Photo

At this clinic in Florida, teenagers and women with eating disorders participate in group therapy to learn how to cope with their anxiety and reduce the feelings of low self-efficacy that are at the root of their debilitating symptoms.

My goal is to have them take control of their life. We work on self-esteem issues, a sense of having value. Most people are more than willing to talk about how worthless a person they are. So that's my opening. It's a slow process. The most gratifying experience is seeing people grow, become assertive, take responsibility for their lives.

David Young-Wolff/Photo Edit

A temperamental tendency to be anxious, low self-efficacy, a great need for approval, and the inability to express your legitimate needs. These poisonous forces, plus a commitment to *the thin ideal*, may have produced this child's eating disorder. Moreover, because whenever she feels bad about herself, she automatically thinks, "I'm too fat"—self-starvation has become her main mode of dealing with stress.

What causes eating disorders to erupt? Twin studies suggest these conditions have a hereditary component (Striegel-Moore & Bulik, 2007). One nonspecific risk factor is prior internalizing symptoms—a tendency during middle childhood to be self-critical, anxious, and depressed (Touchette and others, 2011). At puberty, if these "I hate myself"" attitudes translate into a commitment to the *thin ideal*, an eating disorder can result (Espinoza, Penelo, & Raich, 2010; Stice, Ng, & Shaw, 2010).

Researchers find teens and young adults with eating disorders have other qualities: insecure attachments, an extreme need for approval (Abbate-Degas and others, 2010), rigidity (Masuda, Boone, & Timko, 2011), and great trouble admitting to anger or expressing their needs (Norwood and others, 2011). As I just suggested, they typically report incredibly low feelings of self-worth, thinking, "I'm terrible, worthless, a disgusting human being" (Fairchild & Cooper, 2010). At the root of many eating disorders (as the interview in the Experiencing the Lifespan box suggests) may be low *self-efficacy*—feeling out of control of one's life.

How specifically do these feelings get channeled into an obsession with one's body? Hints come from a revealing experiment in which researchers told girls with an eating disorder and a comparison group to think about an event in which they felt useless or incapable. After the "feeling incompetent" instructions, the girls with an eating disorder alone automatically focused on their body flaws (McFarlene, Urbszat, & Olmsted, 2011). So when girls are temperamentally prone to excessively low self-esteem, and believe that the key to happiness is being ultrathin, negative emotions and events may be displaced into feeling "I'm too fat," and warded off by extreme measures to control one's weight.

Once entrenched, this addiction to extreme weight control (self-starvation, binging and purging, and so on) can be highly reinforcing. Even years after "successful" treatment, people still may not be fully cured (Ackard and others, 2011; Helverskov and others, 2010). Still, if you know a young person who is struggling with these symptoms, there is brighter news. One 20-year-long study suggested that most adolescents grow out of eating problems as they age (Keel and others, 2007). Marriage, parenting, and grappling with the challenges of adult life tend to lessen the fixation on thinness that can be a toxic by-product of living in our Western cultural milieu.

But is our Western cultural milieu changing? Recall from Chapter 5, young adults in the United States now view their weight as "normal" at higher BMIs. Do you think the media popularity of more-than-ample-sized teens (such as Snookie from MTV's *Jersey Shore*) is symbolic of a new cohort's revolt against the rigid restrictions of the traditional baby-boom thin ideal? If so, might we see a heartening decline in U.S eating disorder rates as the twenty-first century unfolds?

Table 8.2 offers a section summary checklist for determining if a teenager is at risk for serious body dissatisfaction. If these forces ring true for you or someone you love, here are a few strategies that might help.

TABLE 8.2: Is a Teenager at Risk for Serious Body Dissatisfaction? A Checklist

(Background influences: Has this child reached puberty? Is this child female?)

1. Is this child temperamentally prone to anxiety and depression?
2. Does this child vigorously subscribe to the thin ideal?
3. Is this child becoming obsessed with dieting (or, if male, becoming obsessed with building up his muscles)?
4. Does this child have insecure attachments, trouble expressing her feelings, and excessively low self-efficacy and self-esteem?
5. When this child gets rejected or experiences a negative event, does she automatically think, "I feel fat"?

INTERVENTIONS: Improving Teenagers' Body Image

Perhaps the first place to begin to intervene with young people prone to eating disorders is to examine how teens who accept and embrace their bodies reason and think. As one interview study suggested, these young people do not deny their "imperfections," but they discount negative comments and focus on their physical pluses. Yes, they do care deeply about their looks, but they view being beautiful as taking care of their physical health—eating nutritious foods, exercising, appreciating what their bodies can do (Frisén & Holmqvist, 2010). Needless to say, these adolescents have high self-efficacy. Most important, they understand what *really* makes people beautiful in life. As one woman named Heather put it: "You have to remind yourself that even though (the thin ideal) is what (the media are)... promoting, self-esteem really looks the best" (Wood-Barcalow, Tylka, & Augustus-Horvath, 2010, p. 115).

Heather's remarks explain why teenage eating-disorder prevention programs focus mainly on raising self-efficacy (you are in control of your life!) and promoting true self-esteem. Interventions, experts emphasize, should target at-risk girls—those prone to depression and low self-worth, who already subscribe to the thin ideal (Stice, Ng, & Shaw, 2010). Programs are most effective when they demand genuine effort—for instance, involving readings and mandatory homework exercises, rather than just lectures—while simultaneously encouraging autonomy by telling teens, "It's your choice to get involved" (McMillan, Stice, & Rohde, 2011).

This need to empower children of *both* sexes to resist outside pressures—and make their own choices—looms large as we turn now to the final topic in this chapter: sexuality.

TYING IT ALL TOGETHER

1. Kimberly, an eleventh grader, tells you, "I am ugly," but knows she is terrific in sports and academics. According to Harter's studies, is Kimberly likely to have high or low self-esteem?
2. Daniel works out at the gym, trying to build up his muscle mass. Amy is regularly on a diet, trying for that Barbie-doll figure. Jasmine, who is far below her ideal body weight, is always exercising and has cut her food intake down to virtually nothing. Sophia, whose weight is normal, goes on eating sprees followed by purges every few days. Identify which *two* of these teenagers have a genuine eating disorder, and name each person's specific problem.
3. Your cousin Laura is reaching puberty. Pick the symptoms that might suggest she could be at risk for serious body dissatisfaction, and possibly symptoms of an eating disorder.
   a. Laura is anxious and depressed.
   b. Laura is heavily involved in sports.
   c. Laura wants desperately to look like the ultrathin models in magazines.
   d. Laura loves MTV's *Jersey Shore*!
4. Check out the sizes of the contemporary teenage media icons. Do you (and your classmates) think our society may be rebelling against the traditional thin ideal?

Answers to the Tying It All Together questions can be found at the end of this chapter.

Sexuality

548: Immculate ros: Sex sex sex that all you think about?

559: Snowbunny: people who have sex at 16 r sick:

560: Twonky: I agree

564: 00o0CaFfEinNe; no sex until ur happily married—Thtz muh rule

566: Twonky: I agree with that too.

567: Snowbunny: me too caffine!

(quoted in Subrahmanyam, Greenfield, & Tynes, 2004, p. 658)

Sex is the elephant in the room of teenage life. Everyone knows it's a top-ranking issue, but the adult world often shies way from even mentioning it. Celebrated in the media, ignored (or condemned) by U.S. society, the issue of when and whether to have sex is left for teenagers to decide on their own as they filter through the conflicting messages and—as you can see above—vigorously stake out their positions in on-line chats.

It is a minefield issue that contemporary young people negotiate in different ways. Take a poll of your classmates. Some people, as with the teenagers quoted above, may advocate abstinence, believing that everyone should remain a virgin until marriage. Others probably believe that having sex within a loving relationship is fine. Some students, if they are being honest, will admit, "Although I want to try out the sexual possibilities, I promise to use contraception!"

This increasing acceptability (within limits) of carving out our own sexual path was highlighted in a survey polling sexual attitudes of the seniors at a U.S. high school in 1950, 1972, and 2000 (Caron & Moskey, 2002). Over the years, as you might imagine, the number of seniors who decided "It's okay for teenagers to have sex" shot up from a minority to more than 70 percent. But in the turn-of-the-century poll, more teens than ever agreed with the idea that a person could decide to *not* have sex and still be popular. The majority of students felt confident they would always use birth control when they were sexually active, and could resist the pressure from romantic partners and wait to have intercourse until they got married—if they desired. How are these efficacious attitudes being translated into action? Let's begin our exploration of teenage sexual practices in the United States at the starting gate—with desire.

Exploring Sexual Desire

David, age 14: Since a year or so ago, I just think about sex and masturbation ALL THE TIME! I mean I just think about having sex no matter where I am and I'm aroused all the time. Is that normal?

Expert's reply: Welcome to the raging hormones of adolescence!

(adapted from a teenage sexuality on-line advice forum)

Why are these delicious, erotic feelings flaring up in this seventh-grade Romeo? One reason is that he is getting a lot of attention from the middle-school girls!

At what age does sexual desire begin? Although scientists had long assumed that the answer was probably in the middle of puberty, when testosterone is pumping through the body, research with homosexual adults caused them to rethink this idea. When gay women and men were asked to recall a watershed event in their lives—the age when they first realized that they were physically attracted to a person of the same sex—their responses centered around age 10. At that age the output of the adrenal androgens is rising but testosterone production has not yet fully geared up (McClintock & Herdt, 1996). So our first sexual feelings seem to be programmed by the adrenal androgens and appear before we undergo the visible changes of puberty, by about fourth grade!

How do sex hormone levels relate to the intensity of teenagers' sexual interests? According to researchers, we need a threshold androgen level to prime our initial feelings of sexual desire (Udry, 1990; Udry & Campbell, 1994). Then, signals from the environment feed back to heighten our interest in sex. As children see their bodies changing, they begin to think of themselves in a new, sexual way. Reaching puberty evokes a different set of signals from the outside world. A ninth-grade boy finds love notes in his locker. A seventh-grade girl notices men looking at her differently as she walks down the street. It is the physical changes of puberty and how outsiders react to those changes that usher us fully into our lives as sexual human beings. Which young people act on those desires by having intercourse as teens?

Who Is Having Intercourse?

Today, the average age of first intercourse in the United States is about 17. But about 1 out of 10 girls and 1 out of 7 boys make their "sexual debut" by age 15 (Guttmacher Institute, 2011b).

As developmental systems theory suggests, a variety of forces predict making what researchers call an earlier *transition to intercourse*. One influence, for both boys and girls, is biological—being on an earlier puberty timetable. Ethnicity and SES also matter. African Americans and lower-income males are more apt to be sexually active at younger ages (Moilanen and others, 2010; Zimmer-Gembeck & Helfand, 2008).

Personality makes a difference. Teens who are more impulsive, that is, those with externalizing tendencies, are apt to make the transition earlier (Moilanen and others, 2010). For European American girls, one study has suggested, having a risk-taking personality plus low social self-worth (but not depression) correlates with being more advanced sexually—that is, engaging in pre-intercourse activities such as fondling at age 12 (Hipwell and others, 2010). Conversely, also for girls, having religious parents predicts staying a virgin because it makes it more likely that a teen will be religious and so have friends who agree that abstinence is the way to go (Landor and others, 2011).

Image Source/Getty Images

Is my teenage daughter having intercourse? Researchers can now offer this parent precise odds by determining how many people in this crowd of best buddies have gone "all the way."

This brings up the crucial role of peers. As I suggested earlier in the discussion of early-maturing girls, we can predict a teenager's chance of having intercourse by looking at the company she (or he) chooses. Having an older boyfriend, or girlfriend (no surprise), dramatically raises the chance of a child's becoming sexually active (Marin and others, 2006). In fact, scientists can make precise statistical calculations of a teen's intercourse odds based on the number of people in that child's social circle who have gone "all the way" (Ali & Dwyer, 2011). So, just as with other aspects of teenage behavior, to understand whether a teen you know is sexually active, look at the values and behaviors of his (or her) group.

You also might want to look at what a child watches on TV. In one fascinating study, researchers were able to predict which virgin boys and girls were likely to become sexually active from looking at their prior TV watching practices. Teens who reported watching a heavy diet of programs rated high in sexually oriented talk were twice as likely to have intercourse in the intervening year as the children who did not (Collins and others, 2004).

Since sexual experiences (affairs, and so on) are a common media theme, we might predict that simply watching a good deal of television would promote the transition to intercourse. We would be wrong. With any media, it's the content that matters—whether a child watches sexually explicit cable channels (Bersamin and others, 2008), gravitates to Internet porn, or avidly consumes adult magazines like *Cosmo* rather than sticking to *Seventeen* (Walsh, 2008).

Spencer Grant/Photo Edit

The image of this girl gleefully reading the sex-laden articles in *Cosmo* may be a tip-off that she is poised to make the transition to intercourse.

Should we blame *Cosmo* reports such as "101 Ways to Drive Him Wild in Bed" for *causing* teenagers to start having sex? A bidirectional influence is probably in operation here. If a teenager is *already* very interested in sex, that boy or girl will gravitate toward media that fit this passion. For me, the tip-off was raiding my parents' library to read the steamy scenes in that forbidden book, D.H. Lawrence's *Lady Chatterley's Lover*. Today, parents know that their daughter has entered a different mental space when she abandons the Discovery Channel in favor of *Jersey Shore*. (For boys, it's when your passion shifts from playing Internet games to watching Internet porn.) Swimming in this sea of media sex would then naturally further inflame a teenager's desires.

Who Are Teens Having Intercourse With?

Internet pornography celebrates anonymous sex. Many intercourse episodes on TV involve one-night stands (Grube and others, 2008). Are children imitating these models when they actually start having intercourse? With the majority of U.S. teens (72 percent of girls and 56 percent of boys) reporting they first had sex with a steady partner, the answer is no. But as roughly one in five teens report making the transition to intercourse outside of a committed relationship (Guttmacher Institute, 2011b), let's pause to look briefly at what these nonromantic encounters are like.

Do adolescents who have sex with a person they are not dating hook up with a stranger or a good friend? For answers, we have an interview study in which researchers asked high schoolers in Ohio about their experiences with "noncommitted" sex (Manning, Giordano, & Longmore, 2006).

Of the teens who admitted to a nonromantic sexual encounter, 3 out of 4 reported that their partner was a person they knew very well. One boy described the day he and his best friend decided it was "time" to lose their virginity in these words: "It's like I wouldn't really consider dating her … but I've known her so long … anytime I feel down or she feels down, we just talk to each other" (quoted in Manning, Giordano, & Longmore, 2006, p. 469). Sometimes, the goal of having sex was to change a friendship to a romance: "After we started sleeping together … having a relationship came up." Or, a teenager might fall into having sex with an ex-boyfriend or girlfriend: "Well, it (sex) kind of happened like towards the end when we were both friends" (quoted in Manning, Giordano, & Longmore, 2006, p. 470).

So far, I have painted a relatively benign portrait of these more casual, "friends with benefits" experiences. Wrong! For teenage girls, engaging in noncommitted sex—especially with a number of partners—is a risk factor for getting depressed. But in one study, boys who said they had a good deal of casual sex reported high self-esteem! (See Grello, Welsh, & Harper, 2006.) This brings me to that important topic: the supposedly clashing sexual agendas of women and men.

IN FOCUS: The Sexual Double Standard

> It's different for boys, it's like . . . if they have sex with somebody and then they are rewarded . . . and all the guys are just like "That's great!" You have sex, and you're a girl and it's like "Slut." That's how it is . . .
>
> (quoted in Martin, 1996, p. 86)

These complaints from a 16-year-old girl named Erin refer to the well-known **sexual double standard.** Boys are expected to want sex; girls are supposed to resist. Teenage boys get considerable reinforcement for "getting to home base." Intercourse is fraught with ambivalence and danger for girls: "Should I do it? Will he love me if I do it? Will he love me if I don't? Will I get pregnant? What will my friends and my parents think?"

sexual double standard A cultural code that gives men greater sexual freedom than women. Specifically, society expects males to want to have intercourse and expects females to remain virgins until they marry and to be more interested in relationships than in having sex.

Basic to the stereotype of the double standard is the idea that girls are looking for committed relationships and that boys mainly want sex. The Ohio study, discussed in the previous section, offered a different view. These in-depth interviews confirmed the statistics showing that teenage sex often happens within a committed relationship. In fact, feeling emotionally intimate, most teens reported, was the reason why *both* boys and girls decided to have sex. And, when a couple did take that step, the decision was often as difficult for guys as girls.

Listen to a boy named Tim:

> *That was something that I had been saving. I really wanted to save it for marriage, but I was curious and um she was special enough to me that I could give her this part of my life that I had been saving and um... She felt the same way because she wanted to wait till marriage, but we had decided and we was [were] both curious I guess and so it just happened"*
>
> (quoted in Giordano, Manning, & Longmore, 2010, p. 1007)

Moreover, when sex happened too quickly, as this next quotation shows, boys—as much as girls—were turned off:

> *She was like . . . moving too fast... like she wanted to have sex with me in the car and I'm like "No" and then she starts touching me and I'm like "I'm cool, I'm cool; I got to go" . . .. And I did that and I left . . .. I was just, I don't know; she wasn't the girl I wanted to have sex with . . .. She wasn't the right girl.*
>
> (quoted in Giordano, Manning, & Longmore, 2010, p. 1002)

Boys, just like girls, want to have sex within a caring close relationship. The adoring expressions on the faces of this couple tell us that adolescent boys' relationships involve far more than just physical desire.

And, if you think boys have the power in a relationship, think again. In this study, *both* male and female teens reported that the decision to have sex was mutual; no one was pressuring anyone else. Or, as another boy in the study delightfully put it:

> *So if a girl says yes and a boy says no; it's a maybe. If a guy doesn't know and a girl says yes, it's yes . . .. If a girl says yes and a guy says yes, it's yes . . .. So I think the women have more control because their opinion matters more in that situation.*
>
> (quoted in Giordano, Manning, & Longmore, 2010, p. 1007)

So, yes, the double standard still firmly may apply in the abstract, when male teens brag about their exploits or people make snide comments about "sluts and studs." I cannot whitewash this reality: National surveys show an alarming 7 percent of U.S. women report that their particular transition into intercourse was unwillingly forced—often by an older male (Guttmacher Institute, 2011b; see also Silverman and others, 2011). But, the reality on the ground is more complex. Boys aren't just in love with making random love. They want sex in a loving relationship—just like girls (Ott and others, 2006). Once in that loving relationship, with regard to sexual decision-making, if anything, an anti-double standard applies!

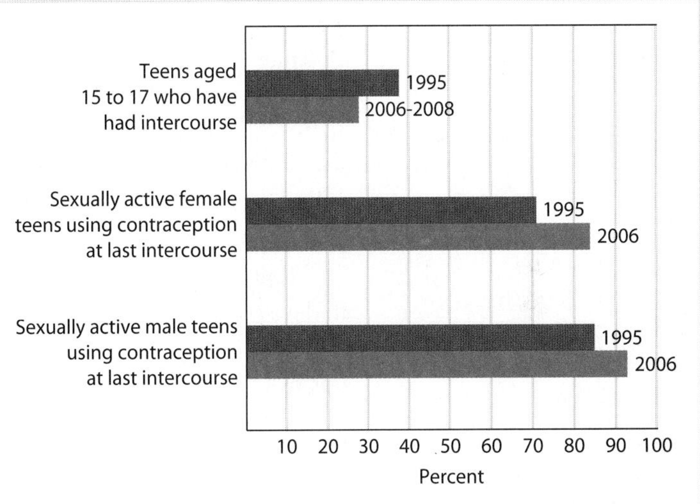

FIGURE 8.7: **Encouraging snapshots of twenty-first-century teenage sexuality in the United States:** This news about teenage sex is good! Fewer young people are having intercourse and more sexually active adolescents report using contraception.

Source: Guttmacher Institute, 2011a, 2011b; Mckay & Barrett, 2010.

Wrapping Up Sexuality: Contemporary Trends

In summary, the news about teenage sexuality is good. Teenagers today feel more confident about charting their sexual path. Most sexual encounters occur in committed love relationships. The decision to have teenage sex is not typically taken lightly, but in a climate of caring and mutual decision-making for both girls and boys.

These changes are mirrored in the encouraging statistics in Figure 8.7: fewer U.S. teenagers are having intercourse, and most teens report they use condoms when they do have sex. In fact, over a decade spanning the late 1990s to the early twenty-first century, teen pregnancy rates dipped from more than 5 to 4 per thousand girls.

Still, with regard to teenage pregnancy, the United States ranks near the pinnacle of the developed world (Guttmacher Institute, 2011b). The reality is that teen birth rates in the most "permissive" Western European nations, such as Sweden, put the United States to shame (Guttmacher Institute, 2011b; McKay & Barrett, 2010). Compared to Western Europe, the prevalence of gonorrhea and chlamydia among U.S. adolescents is very high (Guttmacher Institute, 2011b).

INTERVENTIONS: Toward Teenager-Friendly Sex Education

These less-than-flattering statistics bring us back to the issue I alluded to in the discussion of puberty: sex education. Clearly, in its mission to prevent teenage pregnancy, the United States is falling short. At a minimum, any anti-pregnancy program should be respectful of the legitimate differences in feelings and attitudes that contemporary teenagers bring to their exciting, emerging new sexual selves.

Unfortunately, however, as I mentioned earlier in this chapter, many sex education courses in the United States focus on urging teens to "just say no." In most states, public school sex education programs are required to stress abstinence—even though research demonstrates that abstinence programs don't work! (See Guttmacher Institute, 2011b.) What seem more effective are *comprehensive* programs that teach about contraception, and especially those that give young people the emotional tools to make their *own* sexual choices. Listen to a girl named Sophie discuss what she is yearning for from her sex education class:

> Umm what are the right circumstances and wrong circumstances to have sexual intercourse. . . . But umm, I think they should learn about what emotional steps they should go through to see if they are prepared to have sexual intercourse.
>
> (quoted in Martin, 1996, p. 124)

So, with sex education, what teenagers are really hungering for is information about *relationships*, not just information about sex.

Table 8.3 pulls together this section's insights by spelling out some considerations in devising a teenage sexuality program. Although contemporary young people in the United States are doing far better at negotiating sexual choices than teenagers were a few decades ago, clearly, the adult world can do more to help.

Any help we offer teenagers in coping with their changing bodies and new sexual feelings has to be based on knowing what teenagers are like "as people." In the next

TABLE 8.3: Designing a Teenager-Friendly Sex Education Program: A Summary Table

1. Know your group. Understand that sexual practices vary by SES, ethnicity, and family of origin. Then, tailor your interventions to your cultural group.
2. Be aware of peer influences—and try to foster a group norm of responsible sexuality. Bring home the message that even if your friends are having sex you can still remain a virgin. Stress that having an older boyfriend or girlfriend doesn't mean you "need to" have sex.
3. Assess your group's "media watching" practices and work to counter TV, Internet, or magazine images that celebrate random sex.
4. As every girl could benefit from interventions focused on increasing self-efficacy, build in the message that "you have control of your body." It's especially important to tell girls that often having sex outside of committed relationships is destined to produce low self-esteem.
5. Don't neglect boys. Pay special attention to teaching boys to resist peer pressure to be "players."
6. Design your program to provide information about contraception (rather than just stressing abstinence).+
7. Go beyond providing information just about sex. Teach teens about handling relationships.

+This research-based advice now is illegal in some states.

chapter, exploring teenage cognition and socioemotional development, we focus on penetrating the mysteries of the teenage mind.

TYING IT ALL TOGETHER

1. As a parent you are determined to talk to your children about sex when they are experiencing their *first* sexual feelings. What should your target age be?
   a. Around age 10, when the output of the adrenal androgens is rising
   b. Around age 12, when testosterone levels are rising
   c. Around age 10, when the output of testosterone is rising
2. Your friend thinks her teenage daughter may be having sex. So she asks for your opinion. All the following questions are relevant for you to ask *except*:
   a. Are your daughter's friends having sex?
   b. Is your daughter's school teaching abstinence?
   c. Is your daughter watching sexually explicit cable channels and reading *Cosmo*?
   d. Does your daughter have an older boyfriend?
3. Tom is discussing trends in teenage sex and pregnancy. Which *two* statements should he make?
   a. Today, sex often happens in a committed relationship.
   b. Today, the United States has lower teenage pregnancy rates than other Western nations.
   c. In recent decades, rates of teenage births in the United States have declined.
   d. Today, we know that abstinence programs work.
4. Based on what you have learned in this chapter, spell out in a sentence how you would make U.S. sex education classes genuinely responsive to teenagers' needs.

Answers to the Tying It All Together questions can be found at the end of this chapter.

SUMMARY

Puberty

Today, the physical changes of **puberty** occur during early adolescence, and there can be decades between the time children physically mature and the time they fully enter adult life. Because in traditional agrarian societies a person's changing body used to be the signal to get married, many cultures devised **puberty rites** to welcome the physical changes. The **secular trend in puberty** has magnified the separation between puberty and full adulthood, the fact that **menarche** (and **spermarche**) have been occurring at much younger ages.

Two hormonal command centers program puberty. The adrenal glands produce **adrenal androgens** starting in middle childhood. The **HPG axis**, the main system that sets the bodily changes in motion, involves the hypothalamus, the pituitary, and the **gonads** (ovaries and testes), which produce estrogens and **testosterone** (found in both males and females). Leptin levels and a variety of environmental influences trigger the initial hypothalamic hormone.

The physical changes of puberty are divided into **primary sexual characteristics, secondary sexual characteristics**, and **the growth spurt.** Although in females puberty begins with the growth spurt and menarche occurs late in the process, the rate and sequence of this total-body transformation varies from child to child. Because for males the externally visible changes of puberty occur later and the organs of reproduction are the first to start developing, the puberty timetables of the sexes are not as far apart as they appear to be.

The striking individual differences in the timing of puberty are mainly genetically programmed. African American children tend to reach puberty at a younger age. For girls, being overweight and having stressful family relationships are tied to reaching puberty earlier. These "environmental events" push up the hypothalamic timer, but strangely, only for females.

How children feel about their changing bodies varies, depending on the social environment. Breast development often evokes positive emotions. Feelings about menstruation seem more positive than in the past because today's mothers are more apt to celebrate this change. First ejaculation is rarely talked about. Children tend to be embarrassed about their changing bodies when they are around the parent of the opposite sex.

Girls who mature early are at risk of getting into trouble as teens (for example, taking drugs, getting pregnant, or doing poorly in school), but only if they reach puberty in a stressful environment and get involved with older friends. Because they often end up heavier and shorter, these girls tend to have a poor body image and are more prone to be anxious and depressed.

Although, based on older research, developmentalists have argued it's better not to move children undergoing puberty to a new school, there may be interesting pluses to moving to middle school. In general, our mission should be to provide nurturing schools to children at this vulnerable age. Parents need to talk about puberty with their children, especially their sons. We need to be alert to the potential for problems with early-maturing girls. We also need more sensitive education about puberty.

Body Image Issues

How children feel about their looks is closely tied to their overall self-esteem. Girls tend to feel worse about their looks than boys do, partly because society traditionally expects women to adhere to the **thin ideal.** Boys, however, feel increasingly pressured to build up their muscles. Media images play an important role in causing teenage body distress. African American and Latino girls seem more buffered from the need to be unrealistically thin. The bad news, however, is that globalization may be transmitting the Western thin ideal (and possibly eating disorders) around the world.

The two main **eating disorders** are **anorexia nervosa** (severe underweight and loss of menstruation, resulting from obsessive dieting) and **bulimia nervosa** (chronic binging and, often, purging) accompanied by body image distortions. Genetic vulnerabilities, prior internalizing tendencies, and adherence to the thin ideal may put girls at special risk. Children with eating disorders have low self-efficacy, and may cope with distressing feelings by "projecting" these emotions onto their body shape. Eating disorder interventions focus on promoting self-efficacy, and they use exercises and homework aimed toward at-risk teens.

Sexuality

Teenagers today feel freer to make their own sexual decisions, including whether or not to begin to have intercourse. While sexual desire is triggered by the adrenal androgens, and first switches on at around age 10, sexual signals from the outside world feed back to cause children to really become interested in sex.

Factors that predict making the transition to intercourse include, among others, race, SES, family and peer influences, and gravitating to sex-laden media. Most teens have their first intercourse experience in a romantic relationship. Noncommitted sex most often takes place with someone a teen knows well. Although the **sexual double standard** suggests that boys just want sex and girls are interested in relationships, both sexes are interested in having sex in a close relationship. The stereotype that boys are always the sexual aggressors may not apply in the "real world" of teenage love.

The good news about teenage sexuality in the United States is that children feel freer to make their own sexual choices, and teens typically report having sex in a committed relationship. Rates of teen pregnancies have dramatically declined, although they are still markedly higher in the United States than in other Western nations. Sex education in U.S. high schools should provide information about contraception and focus on helping teenagers deal with relationships, because we now know that the "abstinence only" programs don't work.

KEY TERMS

puberty, p. 237
puberty rite, p. 238
secular trend in puberty, p. 239
menarche, p. 239
spermarche, p. 239
adrenal androgens, p. 240
HPG axis, p. 240
gonads, p. 240
testosterone, p. 240
primary sexual characteristics, p. 241
secondary sexual characteristics, p. 241
growth spurt, p. 241
thin ideal, p. 251
eating disorder, p. 252
anorexia nervosa, p. 252
bulimia nervosa, p. 252
sexual double standard, p. 258

ANSWERS TO TYING IT ALL TOGETHER QUIZZES

Puberty

1. Today, puberty occurs a decade or more before we can fully reach adult life.
2. (a) The initial hypothalamic hormone triggers the pituitary to produce its hormones, which cause the ovaries and testes to mature and produce their hormones, which, in turn, produce the body changes. (b) Estrogens, testosterone, and the adrenal androgens. (c) Your cousin started growing taller.
3. Kendra is probably *not yet menstruating*. Anthony *may or may not* have reached puberty.
4. d
5. An early maturing girl
6. *Possible recommendations*: Pay special attention to providing nurturing schools in sixth and seventh grade. Push for more adequate, "honest" puberty education at a younger age, possibly in a format—such as on-line—where children can talk anonymously about their concerns. Institute a public awareness program encouraging parents to talk about puberty with a same-sex child. Encourage mothers to speak positively about menstruation and have dads discuss events such as spermarche with sons. Make everyone alert to the dangers associated with being an early-maturing girl and develop formal interventions targeted to this "at-risk" group.

Body Image Issues

1. Unfortunately, low self-esteem.
2. Jasmine and Sophia have eating disorders. Jasmine has the symptoms of anorexia nervosa; Sophia has the symptoms of bulimia nervosa.
3. a and c
4. While I believe that celebrities like the Kardashians, Snookie, and Lady Gaga are embodying (literally!) a cultural revolt against the confining dimensions of the thin ideal, obviously you might disagree; so the answers are up to you (and your class).

Sexuality

1. a
2. b
3. a and c
4. Sex education programs should focus on helping teens deal with relationships—and provide concrete information about contraception—rather than simply stressing abstinence.

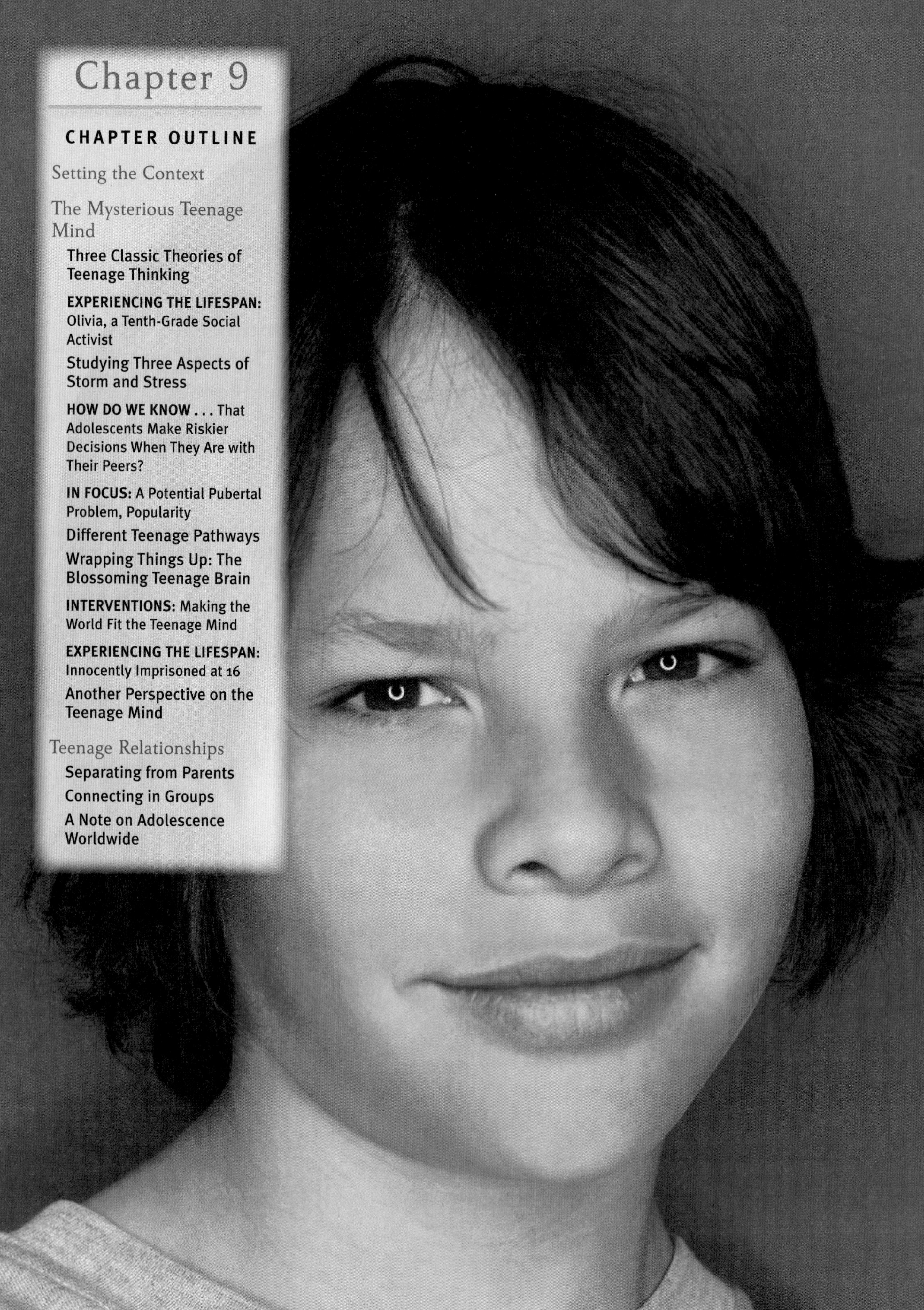

Chapter 9

CHAPTER OUTLINE

Cognitive and Socioemotional Development

Samantha's father began to worry when his daughter was in sixth grade. Suddenly, his sweet little princess was becoming so selfish, so moody, and so rude. She began to question everything, from her 10 o'clock curfew to why poverty exists. At the same time, she had to buy clothes with the right designer label and immediately download the latest music. She wanted to be an individual, but her clique shaped every decision. She got hysterical if anyone looked at her the wrong way. Worse yet, Samantha was hanging out with the middle school "popular" crowd—smoking, drinking, not doing her homework, cutting class.

Her twin brother, Sam, couldn't have been more different. Sam was obedient, an honor student, captain of the basketball team. He mellowly sailed into his teenage years. Actually, Sam defied the categories. He was smart and a jock; he really had heart. Sam volunteered with disabled children. He effortlessly moved among the brains to the popular kids to the artsy "Goth" groups at school. Still, this model child was also caught smoking and sampling the occasional joint. The most heart-stopping example happened when the police picked up Sam and a carload of buddies for drag racing on the freeway. Sam's puzzled explanation: "Something just took over and I stopped thinking, Dad."

If you looked beneath the surface, however, both of his children were great. They were thoughtful, caring, and capable of having the deepest discussions about life. They simply seemed to get caught up in the moment and lose their minds—especially when they were with their friends. What really *is going on in the teenage mind?*

Think of our contradictory stereotypes about the teenage mind. Teenagers are supposed to be idealistic, thoughtful, and introspective; concerned with larger issues; pondering life in deeper ways; but also impulsive, moody, and out of control. We expect them to be the ultimate radicals, rejecting everything adults say, and the consummate conformists, dominated by the crowd, driven by the latest craze, totally influenced by their peers. After I trace how adolescence became a defined life stage, the chapter you are about to read will make sense of these contradictory ideas.

"storm and stress" G. Stanley Hall's phrase for the intense moodiness, emotional sensitivity, and risk-taking tendencies that characterize the life stage he labeled adolescence.

Setting the Context

Youth are heated by nature as drunken men by wine.

Aristotle (n.d.)

I would that there were no age between ten and twenty-three . . . , for there's nothing in between but getting wenches with child, wronging the ancientry, stealing, fighting. . . .

William Shakespeare, *The Winter's Tale*, Act III

As the quotations above illustrate, throughout history, wise observers of human nature have described young people as being emotional, hotheaded, and out of control. When, in 1904, G. Stanley Hall first identified a new life stage characterized by **"storm and stress,"** which he called "adolescence," he was only echoing these timeless ideas. Moreover, as the mission of the young is to look at society in fresh, new ways, it makes sense that most cultures would view each new generation in ambivalent terms—praising young people for their energy and passion; fearing them as a menace and threat.

However, until fairly recently, young people never had years to explore life or rebel against society because they took on adult responsibilities at an early age. As you may remember from Chapter 1, adolescence only became a distinct stage of life in the United States during the twentieth century, when—for most children—going to high school became routine (Mintz, 2004; Modell, 1989; Palladino, 1996).

LOC/SSPL/The Image Works

As this famous 1930s photograph of a migrant family traveling across the arid Southwest to search for California jobs illustrates, during the Great Depression, there was no chance to go to high school and no real adolescence because children had, at a very young age, to work to help support their families.

Look into your family history and you may find a great-grandparent who finished high school or college. But a century ago, these events were fairly rare, as the typical U.S. child left school after sixth or seventh grade to find work (Mintz, 2004). Unfortunately, however, during the Great Depression of the 1930s, there was little work to actually find. Idle and at loose ends, young people took to roaming the countryside, angry, demoralized, and depressed. Alarmed by the situation, the federal government took action. At the same time that it instituted the Social Security system to provide for the elderly (to be discussed in Chapter 13), the Roosevelt administration implemented a national youth program to lure young people to school. The program worked. By 1939, 75 percent of all U.S. teenagers were attending high school.

High school boosted the intellectual skills of a whole cohort of Americans. But it produced a generation gap between these young people and their less educated, often immigrant parents and encouraged teens to spend their days together as an isolated, age-segregated group. Then, during the 1950s, when entrepreneurs began to target products to this new, lucrative "teen" market, we developed our familiar adolescent culture with its distinctive music and dress (Mintz, 2004; Modell, 1989). The sense of an adolescent society bonded together (against their elders) reached its height during the late 1960s and early 1970s. With "Never trust anyone over 30" as its slogan, the huge teenage baby boom cohort rejected the conventional rules related to marriage and gender roles and transformed the way we live our adult lives today.

In this chapter, we will explore the experience of being adolescent in the contemporary developed world—a time in history when we expect teenagers to go to high school (and now college) and society insulates young people from adult responsibilities for a decade or more. First, I'll enter the teenage mind, making sense of why

TABLE 9.1: Stereotypes About Adolescence: True or False?

T/F	1. Adolescents think about life in deeper, more thoughtful ways than children do.
T/F	2. Adolescence is when we begin to develop our personal moral code for living.
T/F	3. Adolescents are highly sensitive to what other people think.
T/F	4. Adolescents are unusually susceptible to peer influences.
T/F	5. Adolescents are highly emotional compared to other age groups.
T/F	6. Adolescents are prone to taking risks.
T/F	7. Most adolescents are emotionally disturbed.
T/F	8. Rates of suicide are at their peak during adolescence.
T/F	9. Adolescents reject their parents' basic ideas and worldviews.
T/F	10. Getting in with a bad crowd makes it more likely for teenagers to "go down the wrong path."

(Answers: 1. T, 2. T, 3. T, 4. T, 5. T, 6. T, 7. F, 8. F, 9. F, 10. T)

adolescents, like Samantha and Sam, seem both remarkably mature and immature. Then, I'll chart how teenagers separate from their parents and relate to one another in groups. This chapter ends by touching on some issues that affect the millions of young people living in impoverished regions of the world, who can't count on having a life stage called adolescence at all.

Before beginning your reading, you might want to take the "Stereotypes About Adolescence: True or False?" quiz in Table 9.1. In the following pages, I'll be discussing why each stereotype is right or wrong.

The Mysterious Teenage Mind

Thoughtful and introspective, but impulsive, moody, and out of control; peer-centered conformists and rebellious risk takers: Can teenagers *really* be all these things? In our search to explain these contradictions, let's first look at three classic theories of teenage thinking; then explore fascinating studies related to teenage storm and stress.

Three Classic Theories of Teenage Thinking

Have a thoughtful conversation with a 16-year-old and a 10-year-old and you will be struck by the remarkable mental growth that occurs during adolescence. It's not so much that teenagers know much more than they did in fourth or fifth grade, but that adolescents *think* in a different way. With an elementary school child in the concrete operational stage, you can have a rational talk about daily life. With a teenager, you can have a rational talk about *ideas*. This ability to reason abstractly about concepts is the defining quality of Jean Piaget's formal operational stage (see Table 9.2 on the next page).

Formal Operational Thinking: Abstract Reasoning at Its Peak

Children in concrete operations can look beyond the way objects immediately appear. They realize that when Mommy puts on a mask, she's still Mommy "inside." They understand that when you pour a glass of juice or milk into a different-shaped glass, the amount of liquid remains the same. Piaget believed that when children reach the **formal operational stage,** at around age 12, this ability to think abstractly takes a qualitative leap. Teenagers are able to reason logically in the realm of pure thought. Specifically, according to Piaget:

formal operational stage Jean Piaget's fourth and final stage of cognitive development, reached at around age 12 and characterized by teenagers' ability to reason at an abstract, scientific level.

TABLE 9.2: Piaget's Stages: Focus on Adolescence

Age	Name of Stage	Description
0–2	**Sensorimotor**	The baby manipulates objects to pin down the basics of physical reality.
2–7	**Preoperations**	Children's perceptions are captured by their immediate appearances. "What they see is what is real." They believe, among other things, that inanimate objects are really alive and that if the appearance of a quantity of liquid changes (for example, if it is poured from a short, wide glass into a tall, thin one), the amount actually becomes different.
8–12	**Concrete operations**	Children have a realistic understanding of the world. Their thinking is really on the same wavelength as adults'. While they can reason conceptually about concrete objects, however, they cannot think abstractly in a scientific way.
12+	**Formal operations**	Reasoning is at its pinnacle: hypothetical, scientific, flexible, fully adult. Our full cognitive human potential has been reached.

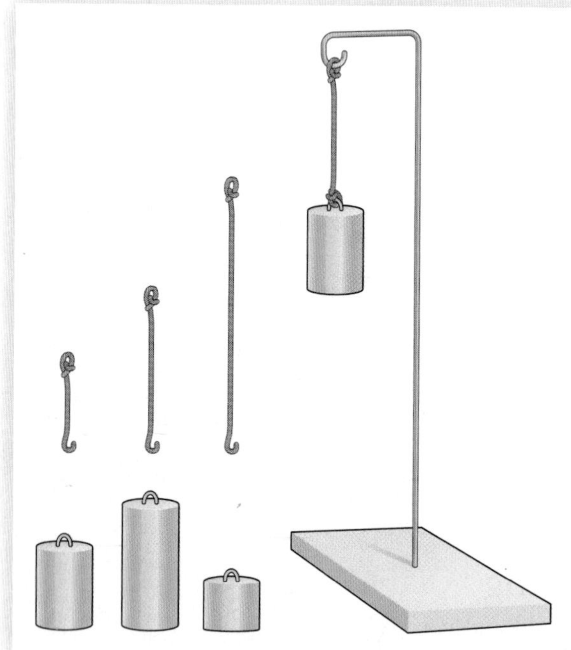

FIGURE 9.1: **Piaget's pendulum apparatus: A task to assess whether children can reason scientifically:** Piaget presents the child with the different weights and string lengths illustrated here and shows the boy or girl how to attach them to the pendulum (and to one another). Then he says, "Your task is to discover what makes the pendulum swing more or less rapidly from side to side—is it the length of the string, the heaviness of the weight, or the height (and force) from which you release the pendulum?" and watches to see what happens.

ADOLESCENTS CAN THINK LOGICALLY ABOUT CONCEPTS AND HYPOTHETICAL POSSIBILITIES. Ask fourth- or fifth-graders to put objects such as sticks in order from small to large, and they will have no problem performing this *seriation* task. But present a similar task verbally: "Bob is taller than Sam, and Sam is taller than Bill. Who is the tallest?" and the same children will be lost. The reason is that, during adolescence, we first become capable of logically manipulating concepts in our minds (Elkind, 1968; Flavell, 1963).

Moreover, if you give a child in concrete operations a reasoning task that begins, "Suppose snow is blue," she will refuse to go further, saying, "That's not true!" Adolescents in formal operations have no problem tackling that challenge because once our thinking is liberated from concrete objects, we are comfortable reasoning about concepts that may *not* be real.

ADOLESCENTS CAN THINK LIKE REAL SCIENTISTS. When our thinking occurs on an abstract plane, we can approach problems in a systematic way, devising a strategy to scientifically prove that something is true.

Piaget designed an exercise to reveal this new scientific thought: He presented children with a pendulum apparatus and unattached strings and weights (see Figure 9.1). Notice that the strings differ in their length and the weights vary in size or heaviness. Children's task was to connect the weights to the strings, then attach them to the pendulum, to decide which influence determined how quickly the pendulum swung from side to side. Was it the length of the string, the heaviness of the weight, or the height from which the string was released?

Think about how to approach this problem, and you may realize that it's crucial to be systematic—keeping everything constant but the factor whose influence you want to assess (remember my explanation of an experiment in Chapter 1). To test whether it's the heaviness of the weight, you must keep the string length and the height from which you drop it constant, varying only the weight. Then, you need to isolate another variable, keeping everything else the same. And when you vary the length of the string, keeping everything else the same, you will realize that the string length alone affects how quickly the pendulum swings.

Elementary school children, Piaget discovered, approach these problems haphazardly. Only adolescents adopt a scientific strategy to solve reasoning tasks (Flavell, 1963; Ginsburg & Opper, 1969).

HOW DOES THIS CHANGE IN THINKING APPLY TO REAL LIFE? This new ability to think hypothetically and scientifically explains why it's not until in high school that we can thrill to a poetic metaphor or comprehend chemistry experiments (Kroger, 2000). It's only during high school that we can join the debate team and argue the case for and against capital punishment, no matter what we *personally* believe. In fact, reaching the formal operational stage explains why teenagers are famous for debating *everything* in their lives. A 10-year-old who wants to stay up till 2 a.m. to watch a new movie will just keep saying, "I don't want to go to bed." A teenager will lay out his case point by point: "Mom, I got enough sleep last night. Besides, I only need six hours. I can sleep after school tomorrow."

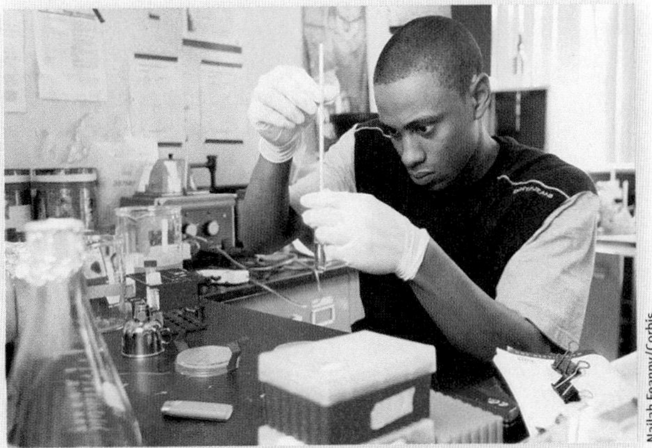

Najlah Feanny/Corbis

The advances in scientific thinking that allow teenagers to solve the pendulum problem are the core qualities that make it possible for this University of Maryland undergraduate to be a real research collaborator in his professor's chemistry lab.

But, do *all* adolescents really reach formal operations? The answer is definitely no. For one thing—rather than being universal—formal operational reasoning only occurs in scientifically oriented Western cultures. Worse yet, even in our society, most people don't make it to Piaget's final stage. In a classic study, one researcher discovered only a fraction of U.S adults approached the pendulum problem scientifically. More disheartening, when asked to debate a controversial issue, such as capital punishment, most people did not even realize that they needed to use logic to construct their case (Kuhn, 1989).

Still, even if many of us never reason like real scientists or master debaters, we can vividly see the qualities involved in formal operational thinking if we look at how adolescents—especially older teenagers—reason about their *own lives.*

If you are a traditional emerging-adult student, think back to the complex organizational skills it took to get into college. You may have learned about your options from an adviser, researched each possibility on the Internet, visited campuses, and constructed different applications to showcase your talents. Then, when you got accepted, you needed to reflect on your future self again: "This school works financially, but is it too large? How will I feel about moving far from home?" Would you have been able to mentally weigh these possibilities, and project yourself into the future in this way, at age 10, 12, or even 14?

James Marshall/The Image Works

Discussing your plans with an adviser, filling out college applications, and realistically assessing your interests and talents involve the kind of future-oriented adult thinking that only becomes possible in late adolescence. So, even if they don't reason at the formal operational level on Piaget's laboratory tasks, these Portland, Maine, high school seniors are probably firmly formal operational in terms of thinking about their own lives.

The bottom line is that reaching concrete operations allows us to be on the same wavelength as the adult world. Reaching formal operations allows us to *act* in the world like adults.

Kohlberg's Stages of Moral Judgment: Developing Internalized Moral Values

This new ability to reflect on ourselves as people allows us to reflect on our personal values. Therefore, drawing on Piaget's theory, developmentalist Lawrence Kohlberg (1981, 1984) argued that during adolescence we become capable of developing a moral code that guides our lives. To measure this moral code, Kohlberg constructed ethical dilemmas, had people reason about these scenarios, and asked raters to chart the responses according to the three levels of moral

TABLE 9.3: Kohlberg's Three Levels of Moral Reasoning, with Sample Responses to the Heinz Dilemma*

Preconventional level:

Description: Person operates according to a "Will I be punished or rewarded?" mentality.

Reasons given for acting in a certain way: (1) to avoid getting into trouble or to get concrete benefits. (2) person discusses what will best serve his own needs ("Will it be good for me?"), although he may also recognize that others may have different needs.

Examples: (1) Heinz shouldn't steal the drug because then the police will catch him and he will go to jail. (2) Heinz should steal the drug because his wife will love him more.

Conventional level:

Description: Person's morality centers on the need to obey society's rules.

Reasons given for acting in a certain way: (1) to be a thought of as a "good person"; (2) the idea that it's vital to follow the rules to prevent a breakdown in society.

Examples: (1) Heinz should steal the drug because that's what "a good husband" does; or Heinz should not steal the drug because good citizens don't steal. (2) Heinz can't steal the drug—even though it might be best—because, if one person decides to steal, so will another and then another, and then the laws would all break down.

Postconventional level:

Description: Person has a personal moral code that transcends society's rules.

Reasons given for acting in a certain way: (1) talks about abstract concepts, such as taking care of the welfare of all people; (2) discusses the fact that there are universally valid moral principles that transcend anything society says.

Examples: (1) Although it's wrong for Heinz to steal the drug, there are times when rules must be disobeyed to provide for people's welfare. (2) Heinz must steal the drug because the obligation to save a human life is more important than every other consideration.

*Within each general moral level, the reasons and examples numbered (1) reflect a slightly lower sub stage of moral reasoning than those numbered (2).

Source: Adapted from Reimer, Paolitto, & Hersh, 1983.

thought outlined in Table 9.3 above. Before looking at the table, take a minute to respond to the "Heinz dilemma," the most famous problem on Kohlberg's moral judgment test:

> A woman was near death from cancer. One drug might save her. The druggist was charging . . . ten times what the drug cost him to make. The . . . husband, Heinz, went to everyone he knew to borrow the money but he could only get together about half of what it cost. [He] asked the . . . druggist to sell it cheaper or let him pay later. But the druggist said NO! Heinz broke into the man's store to steal the drug. . . . Should he have done that? Why?

If you thought in terms of whether Heinz would be personally punished or rewarded for his actions, you would be classified at the lowest level of morality, the **preconventional level.** Responses such as "Heinz should not take the drug because he will go to jail," or "Heinz should take the drug because then his wife will treat him well," suggest that—because your focus is solely on external consequences, whether Heinz will get in trouble or be praised—you are not demonstrating *any* moral sense.

If you made comments such as "Heinz should [or shouldn't] steal the drug because it's a person's duty to obey the law [or to stick up for his wife]" or "Yes, human life is sacred, but the rules must be obeyed," your response would be classified at the **conventional level**—right where adults typically are. This shows your morality revolves around the need to uphold society's norms.

preconventional level of morality In Lawrence Kohlberg's theory, the lowest level of moral reasoning, in which people approach ethical issues by considering the personal punishments or rewards of taking a particular action.

conventional level of morality In Lawrence Kohlberg's theory, the intermediate level of moral reasoning, in which people respond to ethical issues by considering the need to uphold social norms.

People who reason about this dilemma using their own moral guidelines *apart* from the society's rules are operating at Kohlberg's highest **postconventional level.** As the table shows, a response showing postconventional reasoning might be, "No matter what society says, Heinz had to steal the drug because nothing outweighs the universal principle of saving a life."

postconventional level of morality In Lawrence Kohlberg's theory, the highest level of moral reasoning, in which people respond to ethical issues by applying their own moral guidelines apart from society's rules.

When he conducted studies with different age groups, Kohlberg discovered that at age 13, preconventional answers were universal. By 15 or 16, most children around the world were reasoning at the conventional level. Still, many of us stop right there. Although some of Kohlberg's adults did think postconventionally, using his *incredibly* demanding criteria, almost no person consistently made it to the highest moral stage (Reimer, Paolitto, & Hersh, 1983; Snarey, 1985).

HOW DOES KOHLBERG'S THEORY APPLY TO REAL LIFE? Kohlberg's categories get us to think deeply about our values. Do you have a moral code that guides your actions? Would you intervene, no matter what the costs, to save a person's life? These categories give us insights into other people's moral priorities, too. While reading about Kohlberg's preconventional level, you might have thought: "I know someone just like this. This person has no ethics. He only cares about whether or not he gets caught!"

However, Kohlberg's research has been severely criticized. For one thing, Kohlberg was wrong when he said that children can't go beyond a punishment and reward mentality. As with other *social cognitive skills* described earlier in this book, developmentalists have discovered that our intrinsic sense of fairness kicks in at a surprisingly young age. Three-year-olds get distressed when an experimenter distributes prizes, such as stickers, unequally. They may even object when *they* are getting most of the rewards (LoBue and others, 2011). Four-year-olds will say: "If you get an unfair prize, give it to the person who deserves it." They also realize that "stealing is wrong" (Nunner-Winkler, 2007).

In a classic late-twentieth-century critique, feminist psychologist Carol Gilligan has argued that Kohlberg's stages offer a specifically male-centered approach to moral thought. Recall that being classified at the postconventional stage requires abstractly weighing ideals of justice. People must verbalize the tension between societies' rules and universal ideals. Women's morality, Gilligan believes, revolves around concrete, caring-oriented criteria: "Hurting others is wrong"; " Moral people take responsibility to reach out in a nurturing way" (Gilligan & Attanucci, 1988).

Gilligan's criticisms bring up an interesting question: Is Kohberg's scale *valid?* Does the way people reason about his scenarios relate to the attitudes and behaviors, which, as you learned in Chapter 6, predict acting prosocially in life? Unfortunately, the answer is "not necessarily." When outstandingly prosocial teenagers—community leaders who set up programs for the homeless—took Kohlberg's test, researchers rated their answers at the same conventional level as non-prosocial teens! (See Reimer, 2003.)

Taking to the streets to stand in solidarity with the 99 percent is apt to be a life-changing experience for this teen. It also is a developmental landmark, as advances in moral reasoning make adolescents highly sensitive to social injustices.

Concerns about whether responses to artificial vignettes predict real-world morality are heightened when we look around. We all know people who can spout the highest ethical principles, but behave pretty despicably: the minister who lectures his congregation about the sanctity of marriage while cheating on his wife; the chairman of the ethics committee in the state legislature who has been taking bribes for years.

Still, when he describes the changes in moral reasoning that take place during adolescence, Kohlberg has an important point. Teenagers are famous for questioning society's rules, for seeing the injustice of the world, and for getting involved in idealistic causes (as you can read about in the Experiencing the Lifespan box on the next page). Unfortunately, this ability to step back and see the world as it should be, but rarely is, may produce the emotional storm and stress of teenage life.

EXPERIENCING THE LIFESPAN: Olivia, a Tenth-Grade Social Activist

In my niece Olivia's room there are no photos of teen idols, no cosmetics, no closet overflowing with clothes. The peace symbols and posters with titles such as "U.S. out of my uterus" show that this 16-year-old has a clear moral vision. Here's how Olivia explains the passions that dominate her life:

I volunteer at a soup kitchen. I am active in the Young People's Socialist League—that's a grassroots organization centering on social justice. I went to a couple of their protests at employers' workplaces. They pay illegal immigrants, like, $2 an hour and take advantage of the fact that they can't complain to the police.

My friends are wonderful, but a lot of the other kids at school are superficial. In our town, you have a lot of racial and class divisions. Everyone talks about what a diverse community it is, but the White kids live on the north end and the poor minority kids live on the south end. At school, there's a lot of separatism in the races. You might be friendly on the surface, but there's no real mixing. There's also this mad scramble to get into college. Parents are putting a lot of pressure on the kids. If they don't get a 95, there is going to be hell to pay. Some kids in the AP chemistry class were cheating . . . White kids from the north end. And they had already been inducted into the National Honor Society. So when these kids were caught, the department pretended like the thing never happened. If you are White and it looks like your parents have money, or if you are the kind of kid who looks like they are going to an Ivy League school, they are not interested in whether you cheat or not. It's a very Machiavellian system.

I try to do the best job I can, but I'm not interested in the "get the grade, get the grade" mentality. My plan is to apply to the United World College for my senior year. That's this real cool, rigorous academic program. They take high school students to places where you can make a difference, like in India and Africa. In Westchester we are the third richest county in the nation, so you don't get a chance to see real poverty. I'm trying to learn more about the inequality gap between nations. It's really of mammoth proportions. I want to spend these years taking time to read as much as I can.

Elkind's Adolescent Egocentrism: Explaining Teenage Storms

This was David Elkind's (1978) conclusion when he drew on Piaget's concept of formal operations to make sense of teenagers' emotional states. Elkind argues that, when children make the transition to formal operational thought at about age 12, they can see beneath the surface of adult rules. A sixth-grader realizes that his 10 o'clock bedtime, rather than being carved in stone, is an arbitrary number capable of being contested and changed. A socially conscious 14-year-old, like Olivia in the Experiencing the Lifespan Box above, becomes acutely aware of the difference between what adults *say* they do and how they really act. The same people who tell you to treat everyone equally let the rich kids cheat. The same parents and teachers who punish you for missing your curfew or being late to class can't get to the dinner table or a meeting on time.

The realization that the emperor has no clothes ("Those godlike adults are no better than me"), according to Elkind, leads to anger, anxiety, and the impulse to rebel. From arguing with a ninth-grade English teacher over a grade to testing the limits by drinking or driving fast, teenagers are well known for protesting anything just because it's "a rule."

More tantalizing, Elkind draws on formal operational thinking to make sense of the classic behavior we often observe in young teens—their incredible sensitivity to what other people think. According to Elkind, when children first become attuned to other people's flaws, this feeling turns inward to become an obsession with what others think about their *own* personal flaws. This leads to **adolescent egocentrism**—the distorted feeling that one's own actions are at the center of everyone else's consciousness.

adolescent egocentrism David Elkind's term for the tendency of young teenagers to feel that their actions are at the center of everyone else's consciousness.

So 13-year-old Melody drives her parents crazy. She objects to everything from the way they dress to how they chew their food. When her mother picks her up from school, she will not let this humiliating person emerge from the car: "Mom, I don't know you!" She does not spare herself: A minuscule pimple is a monumental misery; stumbling and spilling her food on the school lunch line is a source of shame for months ("Everyone is laughing at me! My life is over!"). According to Elkind, this intense self-consciousness is caused by one facet of adolescent egocentrism called the **imaginary audience.** By that term, he meant that young teens, such as Melody, literally feel that they are on stage, with everyone watching everything they do.

imaginary audience David Elkind's term for the tendency of young teenagers to feel that everyone is watching their every action; a component of adolescent egocentrism.

personal fable David Elkind's term for the tendency of young teenagers to believe that their lives are special and heroic; a component of adolescent egocentrism.

A second component of adolescent egocentrism is the **personal fable.** Teenagers feel that they are invincible and that their own life experiences are unique. So Melody believes that no one has *ever* had so disgusting a blemish. She has the *most* embarrassing mother in the world.

These mental distortions explain the exaggerated emotional storms we laugh about during the early adolescent years. Unfortunately, the "It can't happen to me" component of the personal fable may lead to tragic acts. Boys put their lives at risk by drag racing on the freeway because they imagine that they can never die. A girl does not use contraception when she has sex because, she reasons, "Yes, *other* girls can get pregnant, but not me. Plus, if I do get pregnant, I will be the center of attention, a real heroine."

Lauren Greenfield/VII

Look at the worried expressions on the faces of these freshmen cheerleaders and you can almost hear them thinking, "If I make a mistake during the game, everyone will laugh at me for my whole life!" According to David Elkind, the *imaginary audience* can make daily life intensely humiliating for young teens.

Studying Three Aspects of Storm and Stress

Are teenagers unusually sensitive to people's reactions? Is Elkind (like other observers, from Aristotle to Shakespeare to G. Stanley Hall) correct in saying that risk taking is intrinsic to being a "hotheaded youth"? Are adolescents really intensely emotional and/or likely to be emotionally disturbed? Now, let's turn to research related to these three core aspects of teenage storm and stress.

Are Adolescents Exceptionally Socially Sensitive?

In the last chapter, you learned that, when they reach puberty, children—especially girls—become self-critical (Oldehinkel, Verhulst, & Ormel, 2011) and attuned to their bodies' flaws. In Chapter 6, you saw how the passion to fit in socially (and target people who don't!) causes bullying to flare up during the early teens.

In one revealing study, when researchers asked middle schoolers to list their priorities, these pre-teens ranked socially succeeding as their top concern. Being in the "in crowd" was more important than being a scholar, being nice, or even having friends (LaFontana & Cillessen, 2011)! When scientists directly explored age differences in social sensitivity—by constructing a cyberball game and then arranging for people to get ostracized (no one threw them the ball)—as they predicted, adolescents reacted to this social slight more intensely than did adults (Sebastian and others, 2010).

This heightened social sensitivity makes sense of Laurence Steinberg's study described in the How Do We Know box on the next page. In emotionally charged situations, teens are apt to make risky decisions when with their friends—which explains why even the most levelheaded adolescents may get into trouble when the group atmosphere is right (Steinberg, 2005; 2008).

HOW DO WE KNOW . . .

that adolescents make riskier decisions when they are with their peers?

Their heightened sensitivity to social stimuli gives us strong indirect evidence that teenagers do more dangerous things in arousing situations with their friends. An ingenious laboratory study conducted by Steinberg and a colleague scientifically proved this point (Gardner & Steinberg, 2005). The researchers asked younger teenagers (aged 13 to 16), emerging adults (aged 18 to 22), and adults (aged 24-plus) to play a computer game in which they could earn extra points by taking risks, such as continuing to drive a car after a traffic light had turned yellow. They assigned the members of each age group to two conditions: Either play the game alone or in the presence of two friends.

The chart below shows the intriguingly different findings for young teenagers and for people over age 24. Notice that, while being with other people had no impact on risky decision making in the adults, it had an enormous effect on young teens, who were much more likely to risk crashing the car by driving farther after the yellow light appeared when with friends. The bottom line: Watch for risky behavior when groups of teenagers are together—a fact to consider the next time you see a car full of adolescents, barreling down the road with music playing full blast!

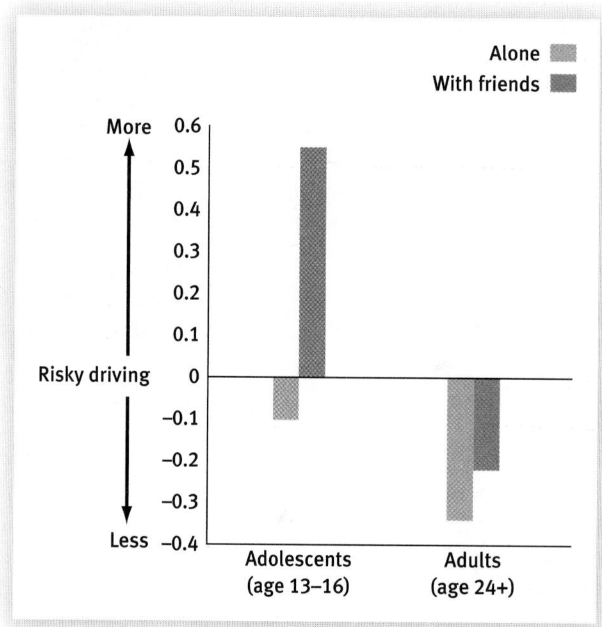

During early and middle adolescence, this risk-taking propensity is heightened by a tendency to prioritize immediate gratifications over future rewards. Steinberg's research team used a computer game in which people from age 10 through their twenties could choose to get a smaller amount of money right now or wait some time for a larger reward. Teens under age 16 accepted a smaller payoff to get a reward sooner than older players did (Steinberg and others, 2009). Or, as my student puzzled when he confessed to the class about a high-speed chase with the police that landed him in juvenile detention at age 15: "It's like I couldn't see that I might eventually end up in jail. All I thought of was the thrill of possibly getting away."

Are Adolescents Risk Takers?

> Doing something and getting away with it. . . . You are driving at 80 miles an hour and stop at a stop sign and a cop will turn around the corner and you start giggling. Or you are out drinking or maybe you smoked a joint, and you say "hi" to a police officer and he walks by. . . .
>
> (quoted in Lightfoot, 1997, p. 100)

This quotation from a teen in an interview study, plus Steinberg's laboratory findings, show that (no surprise) the second storm-and-stress stereotype is *definitely* true. From

TABLE 9.4: **Three Stereotypes and Surprising Facts About Alcohol and Teens**

Stereotype #1: Teenagers who drink heavily are prone to abuse alcohol later in life.

Research answer: "It depends." Beginning to drink at an atypically early age (under 16) is a risk factor for persistent problems (Pitkanen, Lyyra, & Pulkkinen, 2005). However, during the late teens and twenties, drinking—at least in Western societies—is normative. So we can't predict well from a person's consumption at these peak-use ages to the rest of adulthood.

Stereotype #2: Involvement in athletics protects a teen from abusing alcohol.

Research answer: "False." Actually, participation in high school sports is positively correlated with drinking (Barnes and others 2007; Peck, Vida, & Eccles, 2008)—especially for boys. In one study, identifying oneself as a jock predicted generally getting involved in delinquent acts! (Miller and others, 2007.) The best conclusion, however, is that sports neither promote nor discourage heavy drinking. We need to look at other core factors such as "aggressiveness" that may cause some teens to gravitate to athletics and also to abusing alcohol (Peck, Vida, & Eccles, 2008).

Stereotype #3: Middle childhood problems are risk factors for later excessive drinking.

Research answer: "Both true and surprisingly false." As you might expect, childhood externalizing problems are one predictor of adult problem drinking (Englund and others, 2008; Pitkanen and others, 2008). However, two longitudinal investigations—conducted in the United States and Great Britain—revealed that, for girls, high academic achievement was a risk factor for heavy drinking in the early twenties! (Englund and others, 2008; Maggs, Patrick, & Feinstein, 2008.) To explain away this uncomfortable finding, researchers suggest that girls who do well academically may be more likely to go to college, where, as many of you are well aware, the whole environment strongly encourages drinking to excess.

the thrill of taking that first drink to the lure of driving very fast, pushing the envelope is a basic feature of teenage life (Dahl, 2004; Steinberg, 2010).

Consider, for instance the findings of yearly nationwide University of Michigan-sponsored polls tracking U.S. young people's lives. In examining data spanning 1997 to 2008, researchers found that one in six teens had been arrested by age 18. By age 23, the arrest rate slid up to an astonishing almost 1 in 3! (See Brame and others, 2012.) In the 2010 survey, roughly, 2 in 10 high school seniors admitted to binge drinking (defined as having five or more drinks at a time for males and four or more drinks in a row for females) (Johnston and others, 2011). (Table 9.4 showcases some interesting research facts related specifically to alcohol and adolescents.)

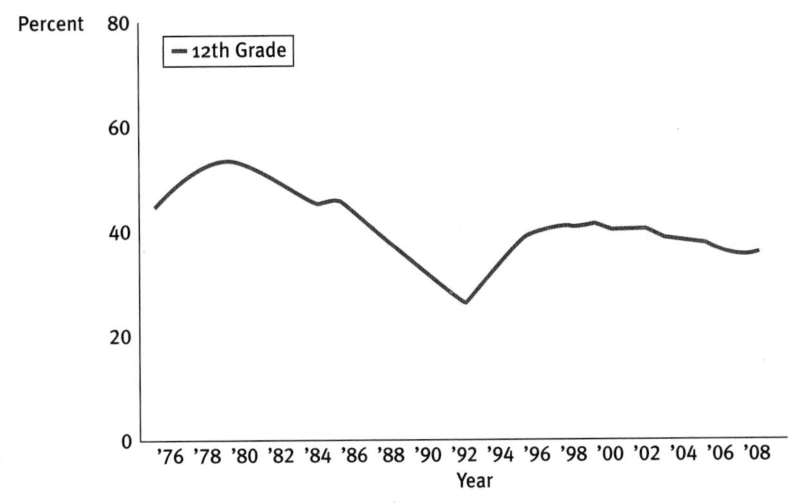

FIGURE 9.2: **Trends in prevalence of illicit drug use, reported by U.S. high school seniors from the mid-1970s to 2010:** Contrary to our stereotypes, only 2 in 5 U.S. high school seniors reports using any illicit drugs (including alcohol) over the past year. Notice also that drug use was actually somewhat more common during the late 1970s and early 1980s—among the parents of today's teens, during their own adolescence.

Source: Johnston and others, 2011.

The good news is that, as you can see in Figure 9.2, in contrast to our images of rampant teenage substance abuse, most high school seniors do not report using *any* drugs. The percent of adolescents who use any given illicit substance—other than marijuana and alcohol—has hovered in the single digits for years (Johnston and others, 2011). The bad news is that—for an alarming fraction of young people in the United States—encounters with the criminal justice system are a depressing feature of modern life.

Moreover, as I described earlier in discussing smoking and pregnancy (recall Chapter 2), we need to take *self-report* statistics with a grain of salt. Imagine, for instance, you are a teen being asked, "Do you drink to excess or use drugs?" Wouldn't you be tempted to report, " Oh no, not me!"—even if you occasionally did?

Younger children also rebel, disobey, and test the limits. But, if you have seen a group of teenage boys hanging from the top of a speeding car, you know that the risks adolescents take can be threatening to life. At the very age when they are most physically robust, teenagers—especially males—are most likely to die of preventable causes such as accidents (Dahl, 2004; Spear, 2008). So, yes, parents can worry about their children—particularly their sons—when they haven't made it home from a party and it's already 2 A.M.!

Are Adolescents More Emotional, More Emotionally Disturbed, or Both?

Given this information, it should come as no surprise that the third major storm-and-stress stereotype is also correct: Adolescents *are* more emotionally intense than adults. Developmentalists could not arrive at this conclusion by using surveys in which they

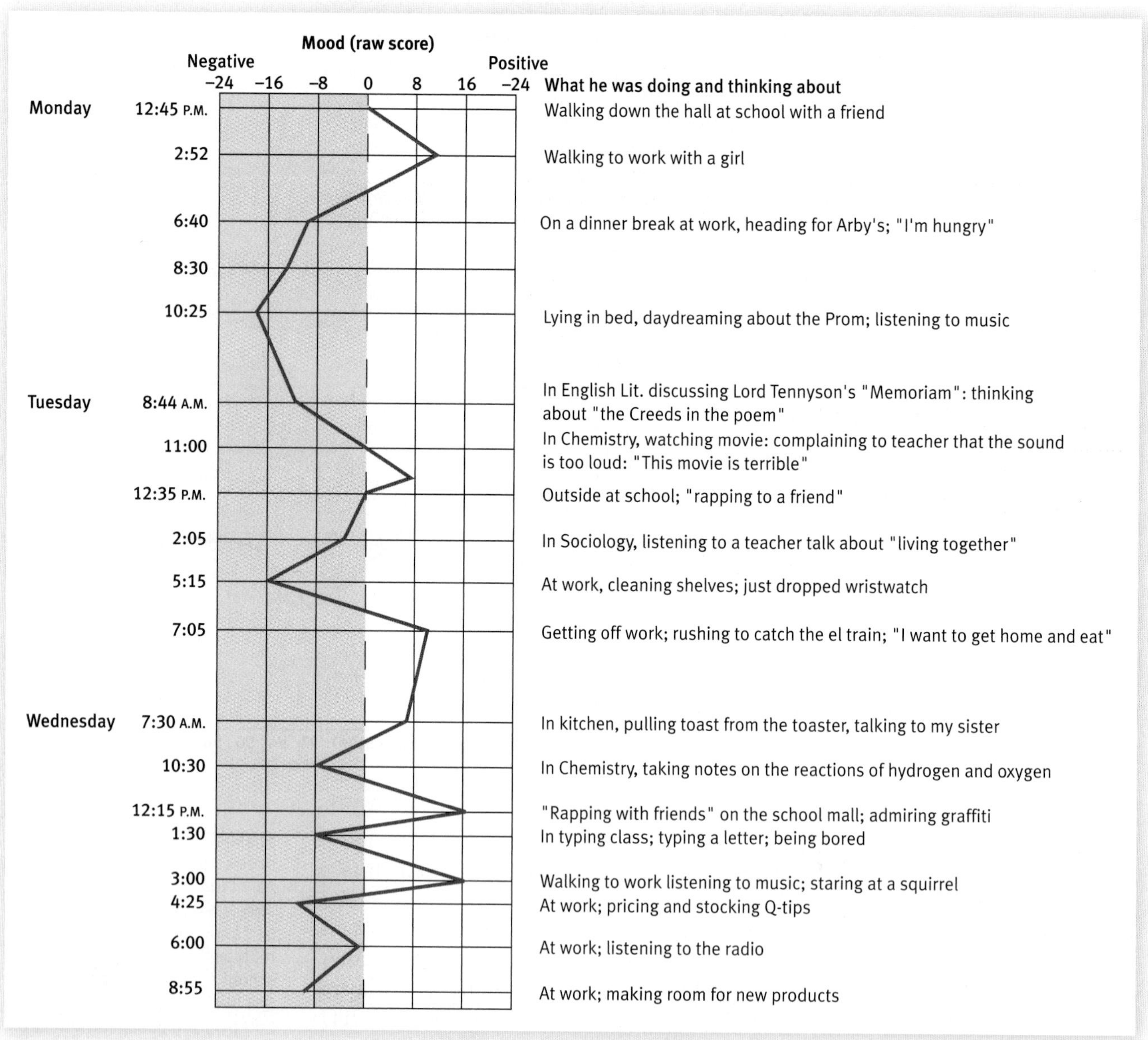

FIGURE 9.3: **Three days in the life of Gregory Stone: An experience-sampling record:** This chart is based on three days of self-reports by a teenager named Greg Stone, as he was randomly beeped and asked to rate his moods and what he was doing at that moment. By looking at the ups and downs of Greg's mood, can you identify the kinds of activities that he really enjoys or dislikes? Now, as an exercise, you might want to monitor your own moods for a few days and see how they change in response to your own life experiences. What insights does your internal mental checklist reveal about which activities are most enjoyable for you?

Source: Adapted from Csikszentmihalyi & Larson, 1984, p. 111.

asked young people to reflect on how they *generally* felt. They needed a method to chart the minute-to-minute ups and downs of teenagers' emotional lives.

experience-sampling technique A research procedure designed to capture moment-to-moment experiences by having people carry pagers and take notes describing their activities and emotions whenever the signal sounds.

Imagine that you could get inside the head of a 16-year-old as that person went about daily life. About 30 years ago, Mihaly Csikszentmihalyi and Reed Larson (1984) accomplished this feat through developing a procedure called the **experience-sampling technique.** The researchers asked students at a suburban Chicago high school to carry pagers programmed to emit a signal at random intervals during each day for a week. When the beeper went off, each teenager filled out a chart like the one you can see illustrated in Figure 9.3. Notice, if you scan Greg's record, that the experience-sampling procedure gives us insights into what experiences make teenagers (and people of other ages) feel joyous or distressed. Let's now look at what the charts revealed about the intensity of adolescents' moods.

The records showed that adolescents *do* live life on an intense emotional plane. Teenagers—both boys and girls—reported experiencing euphoria and deep depression far more often than a comparison sample of adults. Teenagers also had more roller-coaster shifts in their moods. While a 16-year-old was more likely to be back to normal 45 minutes after feeling terrific, an adult was likely to still feel happier than average hours after reporting an emotional high.

Does this mean that adolescents' moods are irrational? The researchers concluded that the answer was no. As Greg's experience-sampling chart shows, teenagers don't get excited or down in the dumps for no reason. It's hanging out with their friends that makes them feel elated. It's a boring class that bores them very, very much.

Does this mean that *most* adolescents are emotionally disturbed? Now, the answer is *definitely* no. Although the distinction can escape parents when their child wails, "I got a D on my chemistry test; I'll kill myself!" there is a difference between being highly *emotional* and being emotionally disturbed.

Actually, when developmentalists ask teenagers to step back and evaluate their lives, they get an upbeat picture of how young people generally feel. Most adolescents around the world are confident and hopeful about the future (Gilman and others, 2008; Lewin-Bizan and others, 2010). In one U.S. poll, researchers classified 4 out of 10 adolescents as "flourishing"—efficacious, zestful, connected to family and friends. Only 6 percent were "languishing," totally demoralized about life (Keys, 2007).

So the stereotypic impression that most teenagers are unhappy or suffer from serious psychological problems is false. Still, as you just read, the picture is far from totally rosy. Their risk-taking propensities make the late teens the peak crime years (Warr, 2007; see Figure 9.4). Teenagers' emotional storms can produce other distressing symptoms, too. Again, contrary to our stereotypes, adolescent suicide is rare (Males, 2009). For reasons to be explained in Chapter 13, the peak life stage for suicide is old

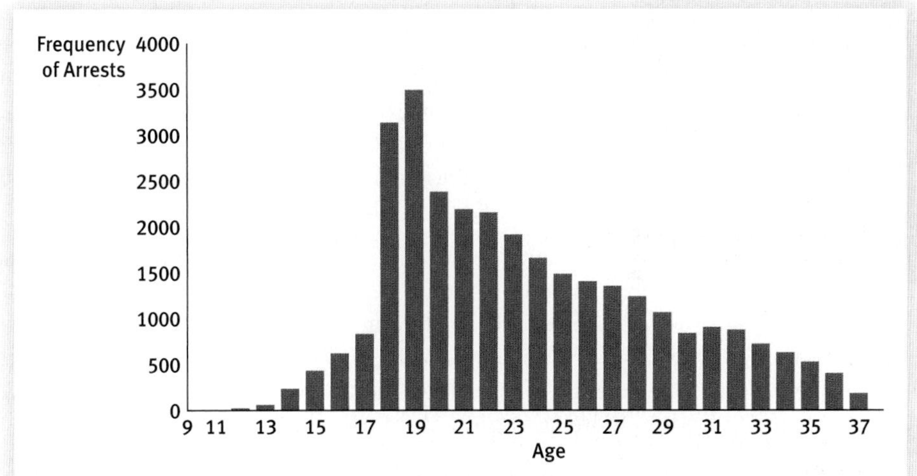

FIGURE 9.4: **Frequency of arrests by age in a California study of offenders (n 2350):** This chart shows the standard age pattern around the world.: The peak years for law breaking are the late teens, after which criminal activity falls off.
Source: Natsuaki, Ge, & Wenk, 2008.

nonsuicidal self-injury Cutting, burning, or purposely injuring one's body to cope with stress.

age! But, in one poll, one in three affluent high schoolers engaged in **nonsuicidal self-injury.** They reported cutting themselves, or performing other self-mutilation acts to deal with stress (Yates, Allison, & Luthar, 2008).

Peter Dazeley/Getty Images

Most teens are upbeat and happy, and suicide is very, very rare during the adolescent years. But specific signs of distress, such as this boy's *nonsuicidal self-injury* (cutting behavior), seem surprisingly prevalent among affluent adolescents, especially girls.

Teenagers who repeatedly cut or self-injure tend to be impulsive and have issues with emotion regulation (Baetens and others, 2012). They are often depressed (Muehlenkamp and others, 2011). Especially when female, they may be abetted in their behavior by their peer group (Prinstein and others, 2010). But this brings up a question. Given that externalizing behaviors, like breaking the law, accelerate during the teens, do internalizing problems, like depression, also rise during the adolescent years?

Unfortunately, the answer is yes. A multitude of studies show that depression rates shift upward during adolescence. Moreover, while the prevalence of this mental disorder is about equal for each sex during childhood, by the mid-teens, the adult gender pattern kicks in. Throughout life, women are roughly twice as susceptible to depression as are men. So, while they are worrying about their teenage sons, mothers might be a bit concerned about their daughters, too (see Oldehinkel & Bouma, 2011, for review).

Why does depression become a mainly female disorder during adult life? To explain this fascinating worldwide pattern, scientists have speculated about everything from evolutionary pressures (to promote our species' survival, when faced with stress, perhaps it makes sense for women to retreat from the world, thereby ensuring they are close to their children and able to protect them from harm), to the (yet unproven) role of estrogen in priming the physiological stress response (Oldenhinkel & Bouma, 2011). What we do know is that if a child's fate is to battle a serious mental health disorder such as a major depression, that condition often has its onset in late adolescence or the early emerging-adult years.

Moreover, I believe the push to be socially successful (or popular) may help explain some classic, distressing symptoms during the early teens.

IN FOCUS: A Potential Pubertal Problem, Popularity

Image Source/Getty Images

Being the center of adoring attention in her crowd is probably a wonderful experience for this girl. But, if she goes all out to chase social status (popularity), her quest may backfire, and she is apt to become *less* well liked by these friends.

Young teens' drive for social status, for instance, seems partly to blame for the fact that academic motivation often takes a nosedive in middle school (La Fontana & Cillessen, 2010; Li & Lerner, 2011). Worse yet—because at this age it can be "cool" to rebel (recall Chapter 6)—for children who are already somewhat instrumentally aggressive, being in the "popular group" is a risk factor for failing in school (Troop-Gordon, Visconti, & Kuntz, 2011). Therefore, chasing popularity can have academic costs. Plus, young teens may be faced with a difficult choice: "Either be in the 'in crowd' *or* do well in school" (Wilson, Karimpour, & Rodkin, 2011).

Making it into the in crowd can also have social costs. When pre-teens go all out for status (LaFontana & Cillessen, 2010), they are less respected by their peers (Dijkstra and others 2010; Neal, 2010; Witvliet and others, 2010). Furthermore, longitudinal studies suggest that, when a child enters a high-status, rebellious middle school crowd, this achievement leads to more aggression over time (Sijtsema and others, 2010).

Finally, because social standing is so important at this age (Molloy, Gest, & Rulison, 2011), getting isolated from the in crowd can lead to becoming depressed (Buck &

Dix, 2012; Witvliet and others, 2010). Popularity pressures may be implicated in *both* the upsurge in unhappiness and acting out during the early teens!

Different Teenage Pathways

So far, I seem to be sliding into stereotyping "adolescents" as a monolithic group. This is absolutely not true! Teenagers, as we all know, differ greatly—in their passion to be popular, in their school connectedness, in their tendencies to take risks or get depressed. As diversity at this life stage—and any other age—is the norm, the critical question is, "Who gets derailed and who thrives during this landmark decade of life?"

Which Teens Get into Serious Trouble?

Without denying that serious adolescent difficulties can unpredictably erupt, here are three thunderclouds that foreshadow stormy weather ahead:

AT-RISK TEENS TEND TO HAVE PRIOR EMOTION REGULATION DIFFICULTIES. It should come as no surprise that one thundercloud relates to elementary school externalizing tendencies and academic difficulties. Not only is the lure of getting into trouble overwhelming, when a child's problems regulating his behavior are already causing him to fail (Hirschfield & Gasper, 2011; Li & Lerner, 2011; Sibley and others 2011), as I will describe later, children who are not succeeding with the mainstream kids gravitate toward antisocial groups of friends, who then give each other reinforcement for doing dangerous things.

Therefore, tests of *executive functions*—measures charting whether girls and boys are having difficulties generally thinking through their behavior—strongly predict adolescent storms (Pharo and others, 2011). Moreover, the same self-regulation issues that lead to teenage turmoil are apt to appear earlier in life.

AT-RISK TEENS TEND TO HAVE POOR FAMILY RELATIONSHIPS. Feeling alienated from one's parents can also be a warning sign of developing storms. When researchers explored the emotions of teens who self-injured, these children often anguished: "My parents are way too critical"; "I can't depend on my mom or dad" (Bureau and others, 2010; Yates, Allison, & Luthar, 2008).

In essence, these young people were describing an insecure attachment. Teenagers want to be listened to and respected. They need to know they are unconditionally loved (Allen and others, 2007). So, to use the attachment metaphor spelled out in Chapter 4, with adolescents, parents must be skillful dancers. They should understand when to back off and when to stay close. In the terminology of Chapter 7, adolescents require an *authoritative* discipline style.

Still, when we see correlations between teenagers' reporting distant family relationships and their getting into trouble, is it *simply* parents who are at fault? Imagine that you are a teen who is having casual, unprotected sex or taking drugs. Wouldn't you lie to your parents about your activities? And when you lied, wouldn't you feel even more alienated: "My family knows nothing about my life"? (See Warr, 2007.)

Yes, it's easy to say that being authoritative is vital in parenting teens. But take it from me (I've been there!), when your teenager is on the road to trouble, confronting him about his activities—or snooping into his Facebook page, and then saying "you've been lying to me"—is apt to backfire. So, it can be difficult for frantic parents to understand how to *really* act authoritatively in a much-loved son or daughter's life.

Do children, who are *already* in trouble, cause parents to abandon acting authoritative and resort to harsh, power-assertive discipline or to emotionally withdraw? Given that human relationships are bidirectional, the answer is yes (Gault-Sherman, 2012; Willoughby & Hamza, 2011). More interesting, some adolescent specialists are

© David Deas/DK Stock/Corbis

How can this dad keep his beloved teen on the right path? Rather than simply monitoring what happens when the family is not around, make time to enjoy these kinds of exciting family events!

now questioning the standard advice that providing firm rules and careful monitoring prevents adolescents from going down the wrong path (Byrnes and others, 2011; Childs, Sullivan, & Gulledge, 2011; Gault-Sherman, 2012; Kerr, Stattin, & Burk, 2010). Keeping total tabs on teenagers is impossible—as every parent knows. The best strategy is to adopt a positive approach: Encourage activities that foster young people's passions (more about this later) and provide ample chances for shared "family fun" (Willoughby & Hamza, 2011).

AT-RISK TEENS LIVE IN A NON-NURTURING ENVIRONMENT. This brings me to the role the overall environmental atmosphere plays in teenage storms. If a school has stratified peer hierarchies that promote bullying (Wilson, Karimpour, & Rodkin, 2011), or a young person lives in a dangerous neighborhood (no surprise), the risk of problems accelerates. To rephrase the old saying: "It may take a village to raise a child, but it *really* takes a nurturing village to help an adolescent thrive." Now, let's look at who thrives during their teens.

Which Teens Flourish?

> In high school I really got it together. I connected with my lifelong love of music. I'll never forget that feeling when I got that special history prize my senior year.
>
> At about age 15, I decided the best to way to keep myself off the streets was to get involved in my church youth group. It was my best time of life.

© Hill Street Studios/Blend Images/Corbis

Suppose this 16-year-old chess wiz had no adult mentors to encourage and nurture his passion. He would probably never have a chance to express his talent and flourish during his teenage years.

As the quotations show, these attributes offer a mirror image of the qualities I just described: Teenagers thrive when they have superior executive functions and can thoughtfully direct their lives (Gestsdottir and others, 2010; Urban, Lewin-Bizan, & Lerner, 2010). They flourish when they are succeeding academically (Lewis and others, 2011) and are connected to school. Having a mentor or VIP (Very Important non-Parental adult) boosts young people's self-esteem (Haddad, Chen, & Greenberger, 2011)—and so does having a life interest, like music, provided your passion is nurtured by caring adults (Scales, Benson, & Roehlkepartain, 2011).

Thriving does not mean staying out of trouble. In one study, teens who were flourishing sometimes confessed to a good amount of risk taking during the early and middle adolescent years (Lerner and others, 2010). So again, we need to understand that testing of the limits is part of the *normal* adolescent experience even among the happiest, healthiest teens (more about the implications of this message later).

And let's not give up on children who *do* get seriously derailed. Developmentalists make a distinction between **adolescence-limited turmoil** (antisocial behavior during the teenage years) and **life-course difficulties** (antisocial behaviors that continue into adult life) (Moffitt, 1993). Perhaps you have a friend who used to stay out all night partying, drinking, or taking drugs, but later became a responsible parent. Or you may know an extremely "troubled teen" who is succeeding incredibly well after finding the right person–environment fit at college or work. (For a compelling example, stay tuned for my interview on the next page) If so, you understand a main message of the next chapter: We change the most during our emerging-adult years. (Table 9.5 offers a checklist so you can evaluate whether a child you love might have a stormy or sunny adolescence.)

adolescence-limited turmoil Antisocial behavior that, for most teens, is specific to adolescence and does not persist into adult life.

life-course difficulties Antisocial behavior that, for a fraction of adolescents, persists into adult life.

TABLE 9.5: Predicting Whether a Child Is at Risk for Teenage Storms or to Flourish: A Section Summary Checklist

Threatening Thunderclouds

1. Does this child have emotion regulation difficulties and academic problems?
2. Does this child have distant family relationships?
3. Does this child live in a "toxic" community or attend a school with stratified peer hierarchies?

Sunny Signs

4. Does this child have good executive functions and/or is she connected to academics?
5. Does this child have a mentor or close family relationships?
6. Does this child have a passion or talent that is being nurtured by caring adults?

Source: Adapted from Masten (2004), p. 315, and the sources in this section.

Wrapping Things Up: The Blossoming Teenage Brain

Now, let's put it all together: the mental growth; the morality; the emotionality; and sensitivity to what others think. Give teenagers an intellectual problem and they reason in mature ways. But younger teens tend to be captivated by popularity, and get overwhelmed in arousing situations when with their friends.

According to adolescence specialists, these qualities make sense when we look at the developing brain. During the teens, a dramatic pruning occurs in the frontal lobes (see Table 9.6). The insulating *myelin sheath* has years to go before reaching its

TABLE 9.6: Teenage Brain-Imaging Questions and Findings

Question #1: How does the brain change during adolescence?

Answer: *Dramatically, in different ways:* Frontal lobe grey matter (the neurons and synapses) peaks during the pre-teen years, and then declines due to pruning—meaning the cortex "gets thinner" over the teenage years. In the meantime, White matter (the myelin sheath) steadily grows into the twenties.

Question #2: Are there gender differences in this brain development?

Answer: *Yes.* Girls are on a slightly earlier timetable with regard to this grey-matter peak (it's age 10 for girls and 12 for boys)—meaning females are "advanced" in brain maturation. The genders also show different brain changes during puberty. For instance, in males, the volume of the amygdala (our "emotion center") increases; females show a rise in hippocampal volume (a brain region involved in memory). Might these differences relate to different peak ages for intense "storm and stress" in girls and boys? Might they have anything to do with teen gender differences in depression, or the tendency to take dangerous risks ? We do not know.

Question #3 Do the brain-imaging findings mirror the behavioral research in this section?

Answer. *Not really.* For instance, although as suggested above, the teen brain matures in definite ways from adolescence to adulthood, studies exploring *specific* activation pattern differences between teens and adults—as they relate to social sensitivities, risky decisions, and so on—have inconsistent, sometimes confusing, results.

Conclusion: While we do have good general data on teenage brain development, we still have far to go in neuroscientifically mapping the teenage (and adult!) mind.

Sources: Blakemore, Burnett, & Dahl, 2010; Bramen and others, 2011; Burnett and others, 2011; Lenroot & Giedd, 2010; Luciana, 2010; Negriff and others, 2011; Bava and others, 2010.

Note: The final statement here is based on my own impressions from reviewing the research cited above.

mature form. At the same time, puberty heightens the output of certain neurotransmitters, which provokes the passion to take risks (Guerri & Pascual, 2010; Steinberg, 2010) As Laurence Steinberg (2008) explains, it's like starting the engine of adulthood with an unskilled driver. This heightened activation of the "socioemotional brain," with a cognitive control center still "under construction," makes adolescence a potentially dangerous time.

But from an evolutionary standpoint, it is logical to start with an emotional engine in high gear. Teenagers' risk-taking tendencies propel them to venture into the world. Their passion to make it with their peers is vital to leaving their parents and forming new, close attachments as adults. The unique qualities of the adolescent mind are beautifully tailored to help young people make the leap from childhood to the adult world (Dahl, 2004; Steinberg, 2008).

INTERVENTIONS: Making the World Fit the Teenage Mind

Table 9.7 summarizes these section messages in a chart for parents. Now, let's explore our discussion's ramifications for society.

Don't punish adolescents as if they were mentally just like adults. If the adolescent brain is a work in progress, it doesn't make sense to have the same legal sanctions for teenagers who commit crimes that we have for adults. Rather than locking adolescents up, it seems logical that at this young age we focus on rehabilitation. As Laurence Steinberg (2008) and virtually every other adolescence expert suggest, with regard to the legal system, "less guilty by reason of adolescence" is the way to go.

Is the U.S. legal system listening to the adolescence specialists? The answer is absolutely no! As the Experiencing the Lifespan Box suggests, today officers and prosecutors have total leeway to transfer adolescents accused of violent crimes out of the Juvenile Justice system and have them tried as adults. Moreover, even though in 2005 the Supreme Court outlawed the death penalty for teens, the United States and Somalia share the dubious distinction of being the *only* two nations in the world where adolescents accused of murder can be jailed for life without parole. Yes, as my amazing interview with Jason suggests, with luck and a resilient temperament, a shockingly punitive approach can help turn a teen around. However, statistically speaking, there is *no evidence* that condemning adolescents to the gulag of dysfunctional adult prisons deters later criminal acts (Fabian, 2011). Do you believe that it's ever acceptable to try teenagers as adults?

TABLE 9.7: Tips for Parents of Teens

1. Understand that strong emotions may not have the same meaning for your teen that they do for you. So try not to take random comments like "I hate myself" or "I'm the dumbest person in the world" very seriously. Also, let negative comments such as "I hate you" roll off your back. Just because your child gets furious at you, don't think she doesn't love you!
2. Provide family-centered activities—but ensure they are ones your teen will enjoy.
3. Understand that laying down rules is less effective than encouraging your child's passions.
4. While sampling some forbidden activities is normal, if your teen is getting involved in clearly illegal activities or seems seriously depressed, you *do* need to be concerned.
5. Understand that your child's peer choices (and peer-group status) offer good hints about her behavior, and that striving to be in the "popular crowd"—while normal—can have unpleasant consequences.
6. Keep the lines of communication open and enjoy your teenager!

EXPERIENCING THE LIFESPAN: Innocently Imprisoned at 16

If you think our legal system protects 16-year-olds from adult jail and that U.S. citizens can't be falsely incarcerated without a trial, think again. Then, after reading Jason's story, you might link his horrific teenage years to the qualities involved in resilience I discussed in Chapter 7.

I grew up with crazy stuff. My mom was a drug dealer and my dad passed away so I was adopted by my grandparents. I was kicked out of four schools before ninth grade. By age 15, I was involved with a street gang and heavy gun trading in Birmingham, Alabama. I was in a car with some older guys during a drive-by shooting, got pulled over, and that was the last time I saw daylight for over 3 years.

The original charge was carrying a concealed weapon, and I was sent to a juvenile boot camp. Then, two days after being discharged to house arrest, detectives were knocking on my door with the full charges: three counts of attempted murder. Turns out, two guys in the car had committed suicide and another had left the state so I was the only one left and the arresting officers decided to transfer me to county jail, where I ended up for l9 months. If you go to trial and lose, you get the maximum sentence, 20 years to life, so—even though I was innocent—avoiding trial is the thing you want to do. What happens is that your lawyers keep negotiating plea bargains. First, I was offered 20 to life, with the idea I'd be out in 10 years; then 15 years, then 10. Not very appealing for a 16-year-old kid! Finally, by incredible good luck, I got a lawyer who takes kids from prisons and puts them into rehab facilities, and he convinced the judge that was best for me. I quickly had to take what they offered—being sent to the Nashville Rescue Mission and then a halfway house for 2 years—because my trial date was coming up very soon.

Jail was unbelievable. The ninth floor of the Jefferson County Jail is well known because that's where they send criminals from the penitentiary who have committed the most violent crimes to await trial. My first cellmate had cut a guy's head off. Inmates test you by challenging you to fight. Every time you get to know a group, the next week another group arrives and you have to fight again. The guards were no better. If they didn't like a prisoner, they would persuade inmates to beat the living daylights out of that person.

What helped me cope were my dreams, because you are not in jail in your dreams. I wrote constantly, read all the time. Reading helped the most. What ultimately helped was being sent out of state (so I couldn't get involved with my old friends) and, especially, my counselors at the mission. I never met guys so humble; such amazing people. Also, if I got into trouble again, I knew where I could be heading. Scared the heck out of me. Now, everything I do is dependent on being normal. I'm 22. I have good friends but I haven't told anyone anything about my past. I have a 3.5 average. I'm working two jobs. I'll be the first person in my family to graduate college. I want to go to grad school to get my psychology Ph.D.

Don't taint young people with a criminal record for minor teenage experimentation. Are you as disturbed as I am by the poll showing that, by their early twenties, almost one in three U.S. young people has been in trouble with the law? These statistics are especially galling because youth arrest rates (often for minor drug offenses) exploded during the *very* years when the United States experienced a dramatic decline in violent crimes (see Pinker, 2011). Given that risk taking is normal during adolescence—and employers routinely do criminal background checks in hiring—is our society's "zero tolerance" approach to youth experimentation impeding young people's travels into a productive adult life?

Provide activities that capitalize on adolescents' strengths. No matter what your position on these controversial issues (mine should be very clear!), many of you would agree that, rather than focusing on punishment, a positive strategy is best: Foster young people's passions and strengths.

Youth development programs fulfill this mission. They give adolescents safe places to explore their passions during the late afternoon hours, when teens are most prone to get into trouble while hanging out with their friends (Goldner and others, 2011). From 4-H clubs, to church groups, to high school plays, youth development programs ideally foster qualities that developmentalist Richard Lerner has named the five C's: *competence*, *confidence*, *character*, *caring*, and *connections*. They provide an

youth development program Any after-school program, or structured activity outside of the school day, that is devoted to promoting flourishing in teenagers.

environment that allows young people to thrive (Bowers and others, 2010; Lerner, Dowling, & Anderson, 2003).

I wish I could say that every youth program fostered flourishing. But as anyone who has spent time at a girls' club or the local Y knows, these settings can encourage group bullying and antisocial acts (Rorie and others, 2011). Therefore, programs must be structured and well supervised. They have to promote the 5 C's. Moreover, because of the teens who gravitate to these particular activities (testosterone-filled boys!), one study showed, heavy involvement in football and basketball was correlated with getting into *more* trouble as a teen (Wilson and others, 2010). So rather than just saying, "Afterschool activities are great," we need to consider the participants and the programs, too.

What we do know is that getting involved in a *range* of high school extracurricular activities predicts doing well in college (Fredricks & Eccles, 2010). Intense involvement, specifically in high school clubs, foreshadows work success years down the road (Gardner, Roth, & Brooks-Gunn, 2008; Linver, Roth, & Brooks-Gunn, 2009)—which brings me to that important issue: For the sake of *both* their present and future, how can we get more teens connected to school?

Change high schools to provide a better adolescent–environment fit. Adolescents who feel imbedded in a nurturing school tend to feel good about themselves (Hirschfield & Gasper, 2011; Lewis and others, 2011) and the world (Flanagan & Stout, 2010). School can offer at-risk teens a haven when they are having problems at home (Loukas, Roalson, & Herrera, 2010).

Unfortunately, however, many Western high schools are not very nurturing places. In one disheartening international poll, although teenagers were generally upbeat about other aspects of their lives, they rated their high school experience as only "so-so" (Gilman and others, 2008). How can we turn this situation around? Again, the experience-sampling method offers clues.

Bob Daemmrich/The Image Works

These high school girls are taking enormous pleasure in, and deriving a tremendous feeling of self-efficacy from, spending their Thanksgiving serving dinners to the homeless and impoverished elderly in their south Texas town. Was some teenage service learning experience life-changing for you?

In charting the emotions of students during various high school periods, Csikszentmihalyi and his colleagues found that passive activities, such as listening to lectures, almost always produced boredom. Teenagers were happiest when they were directing their own learning, either working on group projects or by themselves (Shernoff and others, 2003). Given that the main mode of instruction in traditional high schools (and, unfortunately, college) involves lectures, it makes sense for many young people to zone out in their classes and find school an unpleasant place.

In surveys, teenagers say that they are yearning for the experiences that characterize high-quality elementary schools (described in Chapter 7)—autonomy-supporting work that encourages them to think and teachers who respect their point of view (LaRusso, Romer, & Selman, 2008); courses that are relevant to their lives (Wagner, 2000).

Service-learning classes, involving volunteer activities, in particular, can make a lasting difference in later development (McIntosh, Metz, & Youniss, 2005). Here is what one African American young man had to say about his junior-year course in which he volunteered at a soup kitchen: "I was on the brink of becoming one of those hoodlums the world so fears. This class was one of the major factors in my choosing the right path" (quoted in Yates & Youniss, 1998, p. 509).

Finally, we might rethink the school day to take into account teenagers' unique sleep requirements. During early adolescence, the sleep cycle is biologically pushed back (Colrain & Baker, 2011; Feinberg & Campbell, 2010). Although adolescents often need at least nine hours of sleep to function at their best, because they tend to go to bed after 11 and must wake up for school at 6 or 7 A.M, the typical U.S. teen sleeps fewer than 7 hours each day (Colrain & Baker, 2011). Spending your days in a zombie-like state is destined to make even the most intrinsically motivating class torture. It is tailor-made to make any person irritable and depressed. Therefore, simply starting the school day a couple of hours later might go a long way toward reducing adolescent storm and stress!

Think back to your high school—what you found problematic; what helped you cope; what may have allowed you to thrive. Do you have other ideas about how we might change schools, or any other aspect of the environment, to help teenagers make the most of these special years?

Could this have been you in high school, particularly toward the end of the week? Did you decide not to take early-morning classes this semester because you realized the same thing would happen to you today? Do you think that we are making a mistake by resisting teenagers' biological clocks and insisting that their school day start at 8 A.M.?

Another Perspective on the Teenage Mind

Until this point, I've been highlighting the mainstream developmental science message: "Because of their brain immaturity, teens need special help." Now, let's consider some different views: Do we know enough about how the brain functions to make these kinds of neural attributions? (As I suggested in the brain imaging Table 9.6 on page 281, some developmental scientists legitimately could answer no) (Epstein, 2010; Sercombe, 2010). Doesn't the "brain deficit" label ignore the ways that adolescents are very mature? (Males, 2009.) In their push to invoke biology, might academics be overstating the vulnerabilities of the teenage mind?

Perhaps the most vocal critic of the immature adolescent brain position is psychologist Robert Epstein. Epstein (2010) reminds us that the life stage called adolescence is an artificial, twentieth-century construction. Nature intended us to enter adulthood at puberty. Now, he argues, young people may be forced into depression and dangerous risk taking by languishing for a full decade under the ill-fitting label of "child." How many "predictable" teenage symptoms of storm and stress have little to do with faulty frontal lobes and everything to do with a poor contemporary body-environment fit? Do teenagers *really* have immature brains, or is our culture to blame for shackling teenagers' newly adult minds?

Assuming adult responsibilities right after puberty, like fishing for a living, is what nature intended for our species (see Chapter 8). Therefore, Robert Epstein believes so-called teenage "dysfunction" is produced by a dysfunctional contemporary society.

TYING IT ALL TOGETHER

1. Robin, a teacher, is about to transfer from fourth grade to the local high school, and she is excited by all the things that her older students will be able to do. Based on what you have learned about Piaget's formal operational stage and Kohlberg's theory of moral reasoning, pick out which two *new* capacities Robin may find among her students.
   a. The high schoolers will be able to memorize poems.
   b. The high schoolers will be able to summarize the plots of stories.
   c. The high schoolers will be able to debate different ideas even if they don't personally agree with them.
   d. The high schoolers will be able to develop their own moral principles.
2. Eric is the coach of a basketball team. The year-end tournament is tomorrow, and the star forward has the flu and won't be able to play. Terry, last year's number one player, offers to fill in—even though this is a violation of the conference rules. Eric agonizes about the ethical issue. Should he deprive his guys of their shot at

the championship, or go against the regulations and put Terry in? How would you reason about this issue? Now, fit your responses into Kohlberg's categories of moral thought.

3. A 14-year-old worries that everyone is watching every mistake she makes; at the same time, she is fearless when her friends dare her to take life-threatening risks like bungee jumping off a cliff. According to Elkind, this feeling that everyone is watching her illustrates______________ ; the risk taking is a sign of _______________ ; and both are evidence of the overall process called_________________ .

4. Your 14-year-old nephew, Sanjay, is spending the Christmas holidays with you. If he is a typical teenager, you can expect which of the following symptoms:
   a. intense mood swings and social sensitivities.
   b. depression, as most adolescents have psychological problems.
   c. a tendency to engage in risky behavior when this normally level-headed kid is with his friends.
   d. few problems if Sanjay is in the popular crowd at school.

5. There has been a rise in teenage crimes in your town, and you are at a community meeting to explore solutions. Given what you know about the teenage mind, which interventions should you *definitely* support?
   a. Push the state legislature to punish teenage offenders as adults. Let them pay for their crimes!
   b. Encourage the local high school to expand its menu of exciting after-school clubs.
   c. Think about postponing the beginning of the school day to 10 A.M.

6. Imagine you are a college debater. Use your formal operational skills to argue first for and then against the proposition that society should try teens as adults.

Answers to the Tying It All Together questions can be found at the end of this chapter.

Teenage Relationships

What exactly are teenager/parent interactions like? Now, it's time to tackle this question, as I focus on those two agendas of adolescence—separating from parents; connecting with peers.

Separating from Parents

> When I'm with my dad fishing, or when my family is just joking around at dinner—it's times like these when I feel completely content, loved, the best about life and myself.

In their original experience-sampling study, Csikszentmihalyi and Larson (1984) discovered that teenagers' most uplifting experiences occurred when they were with their families—sharing a joke around the dinner table or having a close moment with mom or dad. Unfortunately, however, taken as a whole, those moments were few. In fact, when adolescents were with their families, unhappy emotions outweighed positive ones 10 to 1.

The Issue: Pushing for Autonomy

Why does family life produce a few peak moments and so many lows? As developmentalists point out, if our home life is good, our family provides our cocoon. Home is the place where we can relax, be totally ourselves, and feel completely loved. However, in addition to being our safe haven, our parents must be a source of pain. The reason is that parents' job is both to love us and to limit us. When this parental limiting function gets into high gear, teenage distress becomes acute. Consider this complaint from a child in the original experience-sampling study:

> Finally, I get a Sunday off..., so I can sleep a little later. But now I have to go to church. . . . They always wake you up, and they act like they are always cheerful . . . but they are

> really hostile if you don't want to go . . . [then on the way things get worse]. . . I asked them to change the channel—they were listening to some opera stuff. They just ignored me. . . . Jesus Christ, at least they could answer me!
>
> (quoted in Csikszentmihalyi and Larson, 1984, p. 141)

What do teenagers and their parents argue about? Studies dating from the Depression era, to the 1960s, to today agree: Conflicts do not typically occur over large concerns such as politics, the state of the world, or even the merits of being religious, but rather the minutiae of daily life—going to church, doing your homework, or cleaning your room (Daddis, 2011; Laursen & Collins, 1994; Montemayer, 1983; Smetana, Daddis, & Chuang, 2003). Conflicts relating to independence loom large ("Why can't I stay out late? Everyone at school is going to that party. You have too many rules!"). The most intense differences of opinion occur just when peer group popularity pressures reach their height—around the early to middle teens (De Goede, Branje, & Meeus, 2009). And just as parents suspect, young teens do often overestimate the freedoms their friends have! (See Daddis, 2011.)

The Process: Separating to Become Close in a New Way

Actually, parent–adolescent conflict tends to flare up while children are in the midst of puberty (Steinberg, 2005). When Steinberg and a colleague videotaped sons and mothers interacting, they found that if a boy was undergoing puberty, he was most likely to challenge, to contradict, and to argue with his parent's point of view (Steinberg & Hill, 1978). From an evolutionary perspective, the hormonal surges of puberty may propel this struggle for autonomy ("You can't tell me what do!") that sets in motion the dance of separation intrinsic to becoming an independent adult.

Even the physical changes of puberty may promote the impulse to separate. Parents are probably less interested in cuddling their suddenly shaving six-foot-tall son or having their 120-pound daughter sit on their lap. Being that pre-teens find the "symptoms" of puberty so embarrassing (recall Chapter 8), children may also put a halt to much of the kissing and hugging as they struggle to hide their developing bodies from their family's sight.

As teenagers push for freedom, they are given more decision-making opportunities and establish a new, more equal, adult-like relationship with their moms and dads. Although conflict may be intense through mid-adolescence, there is a dramatic shift toward freedom during the later teenage years (De Goede, Branje, & Meeus, 2009).

By late adolescence, parents simply trust their more responsible, less rebellious teens more (Wray-Lake, Crouter, & McHale, 2010). Now, it's important for young people to get it together and start preparing for college or a career. The agenda shifts to constructing an adult life. Even the major social markers of independence at around age 16 or 17 eliminate sources of family strain. Think about how getting your first job, or your license, removed an important area of family conflict. You no longer had to ask your parents for every dime or rely on mom or dad to get around.

These adult landmarks put distance between parents and teenagers in the most basic physical way. The experience-sampling charts showed that ninth-graders spent 25 percent of their time with family members. Among high school seniors, the figure dropped to 14 percent (Csikszentmihalyi and Larson, 1984).

Masterfile Royalty Free

Passing a driving test and *finally* getting the keys to the car is a joyous late-teenage transition into adult liberation. It's almost the developed-world equivalent of a puberty rite!

So the process of separating from our families makes it possible to have a more harmonious family life. The delicate task for parents, as I suggested earlier, is to give teens space to explore their new, adult selves and still remain closely

Randi Sidman-Moore/Masterfile

Being able to have a real woman-to-woman talk with your grown-up daughter can make the older teenage years a delight.

involved (Steinberg, 2001). One mother of a teenager explained what ideally should happen, when she said: "I don't treat her like a young child anymore, but we're still very, very close. Sort of like a friendship, but not really, because I'm still in charge. She's my buddy" (quoted in Shearer, Crouter, & McHale, 2005, p. 674).

Cultural Variations on a Theme

My parents won't let me date anyone who isn't Hindi—or go to parties. They never tell me they love me. I have to be at home right after school to do the grocery shopping and other family chores. Why can't they just let me be a normal American kid?

In individualistic societies, we strive for parent-child adult relationships that are less hierarchical, more like friends. What about teens—such as the young person quoted above—whose parents have collectivist values centered on obedience and putting family obligations first? How do these immigrant teens cope with separation issues?

AP Photo/Lincoln Journal Star, Krista Niles

As she translates an oath of naturalization to her non-English speaking Iraq mom, this daughter is engaging in a role reversal that can cause second generation immigrant teens (and their parents) considerable distress.

As researchers point out, with immigrant adolescents, the normal impulse to separate can be exacerbated by issues relating to *acculturation* (Kim & Park, 2011; Park and others, 2010; Wu & Chao, 2011). Teens want to become "real" Americans. They may think: "My parents have old-fashioned attitudes. Their values have nothing to do with my life." As Judith Harris's *peer group socialization theory* might predict (recall Chapter 7), with immigrant adolescents, parent–child disagreements may go beyond bickering about family rules to involve a fundamental difference in worldviews (Arnett, 1999).

Family pressures, as you saw in the example above, present special hurdles for immigrant teens. Heavy responsibilities at home make it difficult for any person to thrive at the most nurturing school (Wilkinson-Lee and others, 2011). In addition, straddling two cultures can upend the normal parent-child relationship—catapulting some second-generation children into becoming the family adults. As one teacher who works with Chinese immigrants commented, "The kids may be doing the interpreting and translating..., they may be the de facto parents" (quoted in Lim and others, 2009).

Given these strains, are immigrant teens at risk for poor parent-child relations? The answer is, "it depends." Rules that seem rigid to Western eyes have a different meaning when young people understand that their parents have sacrificed everything for their well-being (Wu & Chao, 2011). As one touching, international poll showed, the core quality that makes adolescents feel loved *worldwide* is feeling their parents have gone out of their way to do things that are rare and emotionally hard (McNeely & Barber, 2010).

So, knowing one's parents made a rare sacrifice ("giving up their happiness and moving for my future") has the potential to create unusually close parent-child bonds. This sense of family mission may help explain what researchers call the **immigrant paradox.** Despite coping with an overload of stresses (Cho & Haslam, 2010), many immigrant children living in poverty do better academically than their peers (van Geel & Vedder, 2011). But like all children, immigrant teens take different paths—some flourish and others flounder (Suárez-Orozco and others, 2010). One force can be critical in predicting failure or success—no surprise, it's a person's group of peers.

immigrant paradox The fact that despite living in poverty, going to substandard schools, and not having parents who speak the language, many immigrant children do far better than we might expect at school.

Connecting in Groups

Go to your local mall and watch sixth and seventh graders hanging out to get a first-hand glimpse of the group passion that takes over during the early teens. Now that we understand peer group's potentially destructive effects, let's turn to the vital positive functions pre-teen peer groups serve.

clique A small peer group composed of roughly six teenagers who have similar attitudes and who share activities.

crowd A relatively large teenage peer group.

Defining Groups by Size: Cliques and Crowds

Developmentalists classify teenage peer groups into categories. **Cliques** are intimate groups having a membership size of about six. Your group of closest friends would constitute a clique. **Crowds** are larger groupings. Your crowd comprises both your best buddies and a more loose-knit set of people you get together with less regularly.

In a 1960s observational study in Sydney, Australia, one researcher found that these groups serve a crucial purpose: They are the vehicles that convey teenagers to relationships with the opposite sex (Dunphy, 1963).

As you can see in the photos in Figure 9.5, children enter their pre-teen years belonging to unisex cliques, the close associations of same-gender best friends that I talked about in Chapter 6. Relationships start to change when cliques of boys and girls enter a public space and "accidentally" meet. At the mall, notice the bands of sixth- or seventh-grade girls who have supposedly arrived to check out the stores, but who really have another agenda: They know that Sam or José and his buddies will be there. A major mode of interaction when these groups meet is loud teasing. When several cliques get together to walk around the stores, they have melded into that larger, first genuinely mixed-sex group called a crowd (Cotterell, 1996).

The crowd is an ideal medium to bridge the gap between the sexes because there is safety in numbers. Children can still be with their own gender while they are crossing into that "foreign" land. Gradually, out of these large-group experiences, small heterosexual cliques form. You may recall this stage during high school, when your dating activities occurred in a small group of girls *and* boys. Finally, at the end of adolescence, the structure collapses. It seems babyish to get together as a group. You want to be with your romantic partner alone.

You might be surprised to know that the progression outlined in this 50-year-old research still rings true (Child Trends Data Bank, 2008): First, teenagers get together in large mixed-sex crowds; next, they align into smaller heterosexual groups; then, they form one-to-one relationships, or date.

What Is the Purpose of Crowds?

Crowds have other functions. They allow teenagers to connect with people who share their values. Just as we select friends who fit our personalities, we gravitate to the crowd that fits our interests. We disengage from a crowd when its values diverge from ours. As one academically focused teenager lamented: "I see some of my friends changing. . . . They are getting into parties and alcohol. . . . We used to be good friends . . . and now, I can't really relate to them . . . . That's kind of sad" (quoted in Phelan, Davidson, & Yu, 1998, p. 60).

At entry to middle school: **Unisex cliques** → Late middle school/early high school: **Crowds** | High school: **Mixed-sex cliques** → Late high school: **Romantic partners**

Anna Peisl / zefa / Corbis; Yellow Dog Productions / Getty Images; Masterfile Royalty Free; Val Loh / Jupiter Images

FIGURE 9.5: **The steps from unisex elementary cliques to adult romantic relationships: A visual summary:** Unisex cliques meld into large heterosexual crowds, then re-form as heterosexual cliques, and then break up into one-to-one dating relationships. Does this sequence match your own teen experience?

Brigitte Engl/PYMCA/Jupiter Images

As you pass this group of "punks" on the street, you may think, "Why do they dress in this crazy way?" But for this group, their outlandish hair and clothes are a message that "I'm very different, and I don't agree with what society says," and most important, they are a signal to attract other fellow minds: "I'm like you. I'm safe. I have the same ideas about the world."

Crowds, actually, serve as a roadmap, allowing teens to connect with "our kind of people" in an overwhelming social world (Smetana, Campione-Barr, & Metzger, 2006). Interestingly, it's mainly in large high schools that teens align into defined crowds such as "the Goths" or "the brains," who share activities, attitudes, and a special type of dress. Therefore, one developmentalist suggested that a school's size plays a vital role in promoting the teenage crowd (Cotterell, 1996). When your classes are filled with unfamiliar faces, it is helpful to develop a mechanism for finding a smaller set of people just like you. Teenagers adopt a specific look—like having blue hair and wearing grungy jeans—to signal: "I'm your type of person. It's okay to be friends with me."

What Are the Kinds of Crowds?

In affluent societies, there is consistency in the major crowd categories. The intellectuals (also called brains, nerds, grinds, or geeks), the popular kids (also known as hotshots, preppies, elites, princesses), the deviants (burnouts, dirts, freaks, druggies, potheads), and a residual type (Goths, alternatives, grubs, loners, independents) appear in high schools throughout the West (Sussman and others, 2007).

How much mixing occurs between different crowds? As it turns out, many teens straddle different crowds (Lonardo and others, 2009). However, adolescents typically tend to be friends with children in fairly similar groups. So a boy in the high-status jock crowd would tend to associate with the popular kids. He would have little to do with the groups that were socially very different, such as the deviants (or the bad kids).

Moreover, as should come as no surprise, the jocks and the popular kids are indeed the highest-status crowds. As I implied earlier in this chapter, because being brainy can involve going against the group norms, "intellectuality" (and advertising one's intelligence) does not gain teenagers kudos in their peer world, at least in the standard public high school (Sussman and others, 2007).

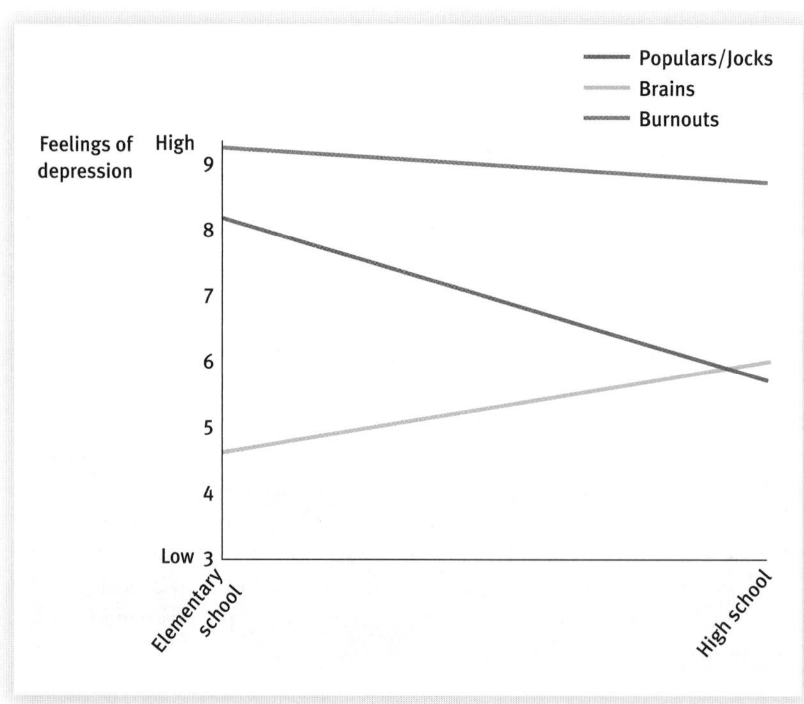

FIGURE 9.6: **Feelings of depression in late elementary school and high school, for children who ended up in three different high school crowds:** In this "follow-back" study, researchers tested children in grades four and six and then looked at their depression levels in high school and explored their particular high school crowds. Notice that the boys and girls in the high-status "popular" and "jocks" crowds became happier during high school. The children destined to be in the "brains" crowd felt happiest during elementary school. The teens who became "burnouts" were more depressed than any other group both in late elementary school and in high school. If you remember being in one of these high school crowds, how do these findings relate to your feelings in elementary school versus high school?

Source: Prinstein & La Greca, 2002, p. 340.

A study tracking children's self-esteem, as they moved from elementary school into high school, documents exactly how being brainy can be transformed from a plus to a greater teenage liability, and also charts the wider peer group scene (Prinstein & La Greca, 2002). Notice in Figure 9.6 that children who end up in the popular kids and jocks crowds became more self-confident during adolescence. (These are the people who would tell you, "I wasn't very happy in elementary school, but high school was my best time of life.") The brains group followed the opposite path—happiest during elementary school, less self-confident as teens.

Finally, notice that the teenagers in the deviant burnout group tend to be most depressed before adolescence and stay at the low end of the happiness continuum in high school (see also Heaven, Ciarrochi, & Vialle, 2008). We already know that failing in middle childhood predicts gravitating toward groups of "bad" peers. Now, let's explore why joining that bad crowd makes a teenager even more likely to fail.

"Bad Crowds"

The classic defense that parents give for a teenager's delinquent behavior is, "My child got involved with a bad crowd." Without ignoring the principle of selection (birds of a feather flock together), there are powerful reasons why bad crowds *do* cause kids to do bad things.

For one thing, as we know, teenagers are incredibly swayed by their peers. Moreover, each group has a leader, the person who most embodies the group's goals. So, if a child joins the brains group, his school performance is apt to improve because everyone is jockeying for status by competing for grades. (Cook, Deng, and Morgano, 2007; Molloy, Gest, & Rulison, 2011). However, in delinquent groups, the pressure is to model the most antisocial member. Therefore, the activities of this most acting-out leader set the standard for how the others want to behave.

So, in the same way you felt compelled to jump into the icy water at camp when the bravest of your bunkmates took the plunge, if one group member begins selling guns or drugs, the rest must follow the leader or be called "chicken." Moreover, when children compete for status by getting into trouble, this creates ever-wilder antisocial modeling and propels the group toward taking increasingly risky actions.

Combine this principle with the impact of just being in a group. When young people get together, a group high occurs. Talk gets louder and more outrageous. People act in ways that would be unthinkable if they were alone. From rioting at rock concerts to being in a car with your buddies during a drive-by shooting (recall the earlier Experiencing the Lifespan box), groups *do* cause people to act in dangerous ways (Cotterell, 1996).

Paul Underhil/PYMCA/Jupiter Images

As a group euphoria sets in and people start surging for the stage, these teenagers at a rock festival in England might trample one another—and then later be horrified that they could ever have acted this way.

By videotaping groups of boys, developmentalists have documented the **deviancy training,** or socialization into delinquency, that occurs as a function of simply talking with friends in a group (Dishion, McCord, & Poulin, 1999; Rorie and others, 2011). The researchers find that at-risk pre-teens forge friendships through specific kinds of conversations: They laugh; egg one another on; reinforce one another as they discuss committing antisocial acts. So peer interactions in early adolescence are a medium by which problem behavior gets established, solidified, and entrenched.

deviancy training Socialization of a young teenager into delinquency through conversations centered on performing antisocial acts.

gang A close-knit, delinquent peer group. Gangs form mainly under conditions of economic deprivation; they offer their members protection from harm and engage in a variety of criminal activities.

The lure of entering an antisocial peer group is especially strong for at-risk kids because they are already feeling "it's me against the world" (Veenstra and others, 2010). Put yourself in the place of a child whose executive function deficits are causing him to get rejected by the "regular" kids. You need to connect with other children like yourself because you have failed at gaining entry anywhere else. Once in the group, your *hostile attributional bias* is reinforced by your buddies. Your friends tell you that it's fine to go against the system. You are finally finding acceptance in an unfriendly world.

In middle-class settings, popular kids, as I mentioned earlier, can get into trouble, especially during the early teenage years. "Self-identifying" as a jock is actually a risk factor for abusing alcohol or having unprotected sex (Cook, Deng, & Morgano, 2007). (At this point, any reader who has lived through adolescence is probably saying, "Duh!") But in affluent communities, it tends to be children with prior problems who gravitate toward the druggy or delinquent groups. In economically deprived neighborhoods, however, there may be few achievers to hang out with. Flourishing is difficult because the community is a toxic place. The only major crowd may be the antisocial group called a gang.

Society's Nightmare Crowd: Teenage Gangs

The **gang**, a close-knit, delinquent peer group, embodies society's worst nightmares. Gang members share a collective identity, which they often express by adopting specific symbols and claiming control over a certain territory or turf (Shelden, Tracy, & Brown, 1997). This predominantly male group is found in different cultures and historical eras. However, with gangs, the socioeconomic context looms large: Adverse economic conditions promote gangs (again for a vivid example, turn back to the last Experiencing the Lifespan box).

Gangs provide teenagers with status. They offer physical protection in dangerous neighborhoods (Shelden, Tracy, & Brown, 1997). When young people have few options for making it in the conventional way, gangs offer a pathway to making a living (for example, by selling drugs or stealing). So, in dangerous neighborhoods, what starts as time-limited adolescent turmoil is more likely to turn into a life-course criminal career.

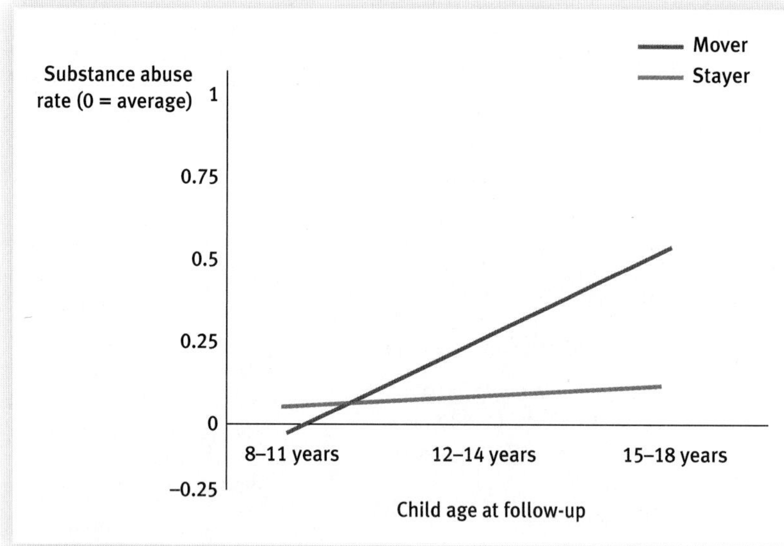

FIGURE 9.7: **Rates of substance abuse for inner-city children who moved to a middle-class community and those who stayed:** In the "moving to opportunity" study, children who were relocated from an inner-city neighborhood to an affluent community ended up worse off as teens than those who remained. This graph shows the upsetting findings with regard to substance abuse.

Source: Fauth, Leventhal, & Brooks-Gunn, 2007.

This suggests that moving inner city children to safe middle-class communities might turn them around. Not so fast! When impoverished ghetto families were randomly assigned by lottery to move to subsidized housing in an affluent suburban town, the "mover" teenagers actually did worse than the children who were left behind! (Fauth, Leventhal, & Brooks-Gunn, 2007; see Figure 9.7.) When we think more deeply, it makes sense that simply relocating disadvantaged children to a potentially unfriendly place might backfire. If a specific group is defined as "not like us"—in this case, rejected as "those scary kids who live in subsidized housing"—these young people will feel more isolated from a caring community than before. Again, it takes a whole *nurturing* village for adolescents to thrive.

A Note on Adolescence Worldwide

It also takes a kinder, gentler society for adolescence to exist. So, children growing up in impoverished areas of the world are less apt to have this extra decade insulated from adult life. Unfortunately, adolescence has been eliminated for the approximately 1 million children who enter the sex trade every year (United Nations Children's Fund [UNICEF], 2002a). Some of these boys and girls are street children, living in gangs in cities in Latin America and Southeast Asia. Or destitute parents may sell their daughters into the sex industry in order for the family to survive (Gajic-Veljanowki & Stewart, 2007).

Adolescence has been eliminated for the hundreds of thousands of child soldiers. Many combatants in the poorest regions of the globe are teenage boys. Some are coerced into fighting as young as age 10 or 8 (Child Soldiers Global Report, 2008; UNICEF, 2002a).

Yes, many teenagers in the world's affluent areas are flourishing. But children in the least-developed regions of the globe may not have the chance to be teenagers or construct a decent adult life. Although critics, such as Robert Epstein, bemoan the shackles of Western teens, having an extra decade liberated from grown-up responsibilities can be critical to flourishing during the adult years.

How can you personally flourish during your adult years? Stay tuned for a wealth of research relating to this question in the next part of the book.

AP Photo/Adam Butler

Miguel Rio Branco/Magnum Photos

This 14-year-old soldier in Sierra Leone and this teenage prostitute on a Rio de Janeiro street offer a stark testament that, in many areas of the world, young people still do not really have an adolescence.

TYING IT ALL TOGETHER

1. Chris and her parents are arguing again. If they're like most families, you can be pretty sure that their arguments concern which of the following topics?
   a. How their community treats the homeless
   b. How late Chris's curfew should be
   c. Issues such as Chris's cleaning her room and doing chores
2. Based on this chapter, at what age might arguments between Chris and her parents be most intense: age 14, 18, or 21?
3. Your niece Heather hangs around with a small group of girlfriends. You see them at the mall giggling at a group of boys. According to the standard pattern, what is the next step?
   a. Heather and her friends will begin going on dates with the boys.
   b. Heather and her clique will meld into a large heterosexual crowd.
   c. Heather and her clique will form another small clique composed of both girls and boys.
4. Mom #1 says, "Getting involved with the 'bad kids' makes teens get into trouble." Mom #2 disagrees: "It's the kid's personality that causes him to get into trouble." Mom #3 says, "You both are correct—but also partly wrong. "The kid's personality causes him to gravitate toward the 'bad kids,' and then that peer group encourages antisocial acts." Which mother is right?
5. You want to intervene to help prevent at-risk pre-teens from becoming delinquents. First, devise a checklist to assess who might be appropriate for your program. Then, applying the principles in this chapter, offer suggestions for how you would turn potentially "troublemaking teens" around.

Answers to the Tying It All Together questions can be found at the end of this chapter.

SUMMARY

The Mysterious Teenage Mind

Wise observers have described the "hotheaded" qualities of youth for millennia. However, adolescence, first identified by G. Stanley Hall in the early 1900s and characterized by **"storm and stress,"** became a life stage in the United States during the twentieth century, when high school became universal and "isolated" teens together as a group.

Jean Piaget believes that when teenagers reach the **formal operational stage,** they can think abstractly about hypothetical possibilities and reason scientifically. Although even most adults don't typically reason like scientists, older teenagers use the skills involved in formal operations to plan their adult futures.

According to Lawrence Kohlberg, reaching formal operations makes it possible for teenagers to develop moral values that guide their lives. By examining how they reason about ethical dilemmas, Kohlberg has classified people at the **preconventional level** (a level of moral judgment in which only punishment and reward are important); the **conventional level** (moral judgment that is based on obeying social norms); and the highest, **postconventional level** (moral reasoning that is based on one's own moral ideals, apart from society's rules). Despite the fact that Kohlberg's criteria for measuring morality has serious problems, adolescence is when we become attuned to society's flaws.

According to David Elkind, this ability to evaluate the flaws of the adult world produces **adolescent egocentrism.** The **imaginary audience** (the feeling that everyone is watching everything one does) and the **personal fable** (feeling invincible and utterly unique) are two components of this intense early-teenage sensitivity to what others think.

Studies suggest that many, but not all, storm-and-stress stereotypes about teenagerhood are true. Adolescents are highly socially sensitive and attuned to immediate reinforcements. In arousing situations, they are more influenced by their peers. This risk-taking (and sometimes law breaking) propensity, especially with friends, makes adolescence a potentially dangerous time. Research, using the **experience-sampling technique,** shows teens are more emotionally intense than adults. Contrary to our stereotypes, however, most adolescents are upbeat, and happy. Still, rates of **nonsuicidal self-injury** and depression rise during adolescence—especially among females. The push to be in the popular crowd may help explain both the upsurge in acting out and unhappiness during the tumultuous pubertal years.

The minority of teenagers who get into *serious* trouble tend to have prior emotional and school problems, feel distant from their families (and create more family distance), and live in nonnurturing communities. Being connected to academics and having personal and wider-world resources helps teens thrive. However, even adolescents who are succeeding experiment with forbidden activities, and even serious **adolescence-limited turmoil** may not lead to **life-course difficulties.** Many problem teens construct fulfilling adult lives.

The unique characteristics of the developing teenage brain may make early adolescence a relatively dangerous life stage. The frontal lobes are still maturing. Puberty heightens teenagers' social sensitivities and emotional states. The lessons for society are: Don't punish teenagers who break the law in the same ways that adult offenders are punished; rethink our contemporary U.S. zero-tolerance attitude to normal teenage experimentation; and, most of all, channel teenage passions in a positive way through *high-quality* **youth development programs.** We also need to make high school more appealing and adjust the school day to fit adolescent sleep needs. While the "immature brain" conception of adolescence is currently in vogue, critics suggest that it minimizes teenagers' strengths.

Teenage Relationships

Teenagers' conflicts with their parents tend to center on mundane issues (cleaning up their room, curfew, and so on), and struggles are most intense during puberty. In late adolescence, children ideally develop a more adult, friend-like relationship with their parents. Although the **immigrant paradox** suggests they can do remarkably well, some immigrant teens from families with collectivist values face unique issues relating to acculturation and family separation stresses.

Teenage peer groups comprise **cliques** and **crowds.** These different-sized groups convey adolescents, in stages, toward romantic involvement. Crowds, such as the jocks or the brains, give teenagers an easy way of finding people like themselves in large high schools. The popular kids and the jocks (in contrast to the lower-status brains) feel better about themselves in high school than during elementary school. Children who enter delinquent groups tend to be unhappy before high school and remain distressed during their teenage years.

Entering a "bad crowd" smoothes the way to antisocial behavior because group members model the most antisocial leader and compete for leadership by performing delinquent acts. **Deviancy training,** in which pre-teens egg one another on by talking about doing dangerous things, leads directly to delinquency as at-risk children travel into high school. **Gangs,** mainly male teenage peer groups that engage in criminal acts, are most common in impoverished communities. In poor regions of the world, young people may not have any adolescence at all.

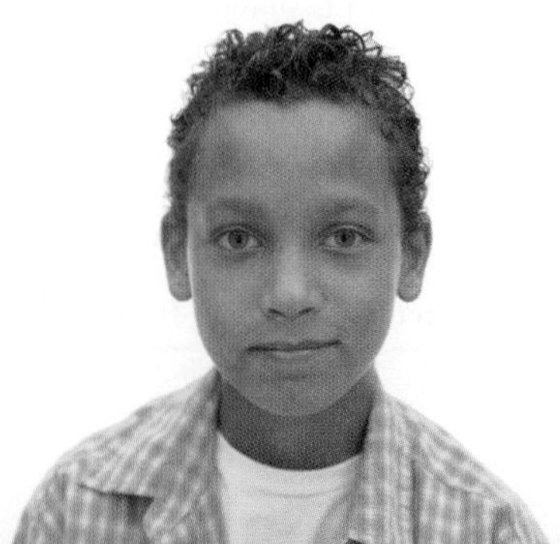

KEY TERMS

"storm and stress," p. 266
formal operational stage, p. 267
preconventional level of morality, p. 270
conventional level of morality, p. 270
postconventional level of morality, p. 271
adolescent egocentrism, p. 272
imaginary audience, p. 273
personal fable, p. 273
experience-sampling technique, p. 277
nonsuicidal self-injury, p. 278
adolescence-limited turmoil, p. 280
life-course difficulties, p. 280
youth development program, p. 283
immigrant paradox, p. 288
clique, p. 289
crowd, p. 289
deviancy training, p. 291
gang, p. 292

ANSWERS TO TYING IT ALL TOGETHER QUIZZES

The Mysterious Teenage Mind

1. c and d
2. If your arguments centered on getting punished or rewarded (the coach needs to put Terry in because that's his best shot at winning; or, the coach can't put Terry in because, if someone finds out, he will be in trouble), you are reasoning at the pre-conventional level. Comments such as "going against the rules is wrong" might be classified as conventional. If you argued, "Putting Terry in goes against my values, no matter what the team or the rules say," your response might qualify as post-conventional.
3. the imaginary audience; the personal fable; adolescent egocentrism
4. a and c
5. b and c
6. Trying teens as adults. Pro arguments: Kohlberg's theory clearly implies teens know right from wrong, so if teens knowingly do the crime, they should "do the time." Actually, the critical dimension in deciding on adult punishment should be a person's culpability— premeditation, seriousness of the infraction, etc., not age. Why is a person emotionally a child at 17 and suddenly "a responsible adult" on his l8th birthday? Con arguments: The research in this chapter suggests that teens are indeed biologically and behaviorally different, so it is cruel to judge their behavior by adult standards. Moreover, if society bars young people from voting or serving in the military until age 18, it's blatantly unfair to decide that adolescents are adult enough to be in prison at 16 or 15.

Teenage Relationships

1. b and c
2. At age 14
3. b
4. Mom #3 is correct.
5. Checklist: (1) Is this child unusually aggressive? (2) Is he failing at school and being rejected by the mainstream kids? (3) Does this child have poor relationships with his parents? (4) Does he live in a dangerous community? (Or, because he is poor, is he being defined as "dangerous" by the community?)

   Your possible program: Provide positive extracurricular activities and nurture each child's interests. Offer service-learning opportunities. Possibly, institute group sessions with parents to solve problems around certain issues. Definitely try to get these teens connected with caring mentors and a different set of (prosocial) friends.

Early and Middle Adulthood

This three-chapter book part spans the time from high school graduation (at roughly age 18) until society labels us as senior citizens (in our mid-sixties)—a lifespan chunk that covers almost 50 years!

Chapter 10—**Constructing an Adult Life** tackles the challenges of making it to full adulthood—a process that can take a decade or more after we reach age 18. In this chapter, among other topics, I'll tackle the challenges of college and give you tips for succeeding at your school, choosing a fulfilling career, and finding a mate. If you are a traditional college student or a twenty-something young adult, this chapter is about your life.

Chapter 11—**Relationships and Roles** continues this focus on work and love by exploring marriage, parenthood, and careers. In the marriage section, you will get insights into how different societies view this core relationship and how marriages change over time and, especially, get the benefit of the latest research findings related to how to have an enduring, satisfying relationship. In the parenthood section, you'll find out how becoming parents changes a marriage and learn what twenty-first-century motherhood and fatherhood is really like. The last section of the chapter addresses work: How have our career lives been changing? What makes for happiness in this vital role?

Chapter 12—**Midlife.** In much of this chapter, my focus is, "How do people change over the adult years?" Once again, as I survey the research on personality and intellectual change, you'll be getting a wealth of insights into what makes for a fulfilling adult life. The last sections of this chapter cover topics specific to middle age: grandparenthood, caring for elderly parents, and age-related changes in sexuality.

PART V

Chapter 10

CHAPTER OUTLINE

Constructing an Adult Life

After graduating from high school in the top third of his class, David looked forward to pursuing his dream of becoming a lawyer. But his freshman year at State U was a nightmare. His courses felt irrelevant. He zoned out during lectures. Compared to high school, the work seemed impossibly hard. Most important, with his full-time job at the supermarket, and five classes a semester, he lost his scholarship after the first year. The only rational solution seemed to be to drop out for a while and move back with his parents, so he could work his way up to management and then consider coming back.

Three years later, David was doing well. He had been promoted to store supervisor and moved out of the house. He met a terrific girl named Clara, and they got engaged. He re-enrolled at State U. Then, headquarters eliminated his local store, and at 27, David was suddenly unemployed.

David is an optimist. He is determined to achieve. But, he can't help getting jealous of his friend Josh, who doesn't have to worry about finances. Josh seems so unfocused, but he is having an easier time—breezing through college without needing a job, taking a few years off after graduation to travel the world. Adulthood can be thrilling—but the twenties are much, much harder than you'd expect!

Can you identify with David's financial troubles and his shock at the bumpy ups and downs involved in succeeding in the adult world? Perhaps, like Josh, you don't have money worries, but are struggling to figure out what to do with your life. No matter what your situation, if you are in your twenties, you might feel a bit "in between." You are clearly not a child, but you still haven't reached those classic goals of adulthood—marriage, parenthood, embarking on your "real" career. You fit into that new life category Jeffrey Arnett labels (2004, 2007a) *emerging adulthood.*

This chapter is devoted to this new life phase. It explores that time lasting roughly from age 18 through the late twenties, when we are constructing an adult life. First, I'll explore the features of emerging adulthood and describe the issues and challenges we face during this watershed, transitional life stage. The last half of this chapter focuses on three crucial emerging-adult concerns: career, college, finding love.

emerging adulthood The phase of life that begins after high school, tapers off toward the late twenties, and is devoted to constructing an adult life.

role The characteristic behavior that is expected of a person in a particular social position, such as student, parent, married person, worker, or retiree.

Emerging into Adulthood

As you learned in Chapter 1, **emerging adulthood** is not a universal life stage. It exists for a minority of young people—those living at this point in history in the developed world. Its function is exploration—trying out options before committing to adult **roles.** Emerging adults often are "not quite ready" to settle down. They don't feel financially or emotionally secure. They may be exploring trial pathways—moving from job to job, entering and then exiting college or a parent's home, testing out relationships before they commit (Arnett, 2007a; Arnett & Tanner, 2010 a &b).

Emerging adulthood is defined by testing out different possibilities and developing the self. Its other core quality, according to Arnett, is often exuberant optimism about what lies ahead (Tanner & Arnett, 2010). Emerging adults, as Table 10.1 shows, are at their physical peak. Their abilities to think and to reason are in top form. Still, the challenges of this age are perhaps more daunting than those we face at any time of life.

We need to totally re-center our lives. During adolescence, we are protected by our parents. Now, our task is to take control of ourselves and act like "real adults" (Tanner, 2006; Tanner & Arnett, 2010). We used to count on the standard roles of marriage or supporting a family to make us feel adult. No more! Today, people in Western nations view the top three characteristics of adulthood in internal terms. Being an adult means accepting responsibility, supporting yourself, and making your own independent decisions about life (Arnett, 2007a).

We have entered an unstructured, unpredictable path. During adolescence, high school organizes our days. We wake up, go to class; we are on an identical track. Then, at age 18, our lives diverge. Many of us go to college; others enter the world of work. Some people get married; others never enter that state. Emerging adults live alone or with friends, stay with their parents or move far away. For some emerging adults, constructing an adult life takes decades. For others—people who have children, get married, and enter the work world at age 18 or 19—there may be no life stage called emerging adulthood at all. So emerging adulthood is defined by variability—as we each set sail on our own. Why did this structure-free life stage emerge?

Setting the Context: Culture and History

Emerging adulthood was made possible because of our dramatic twentieth-century longevity gains. Imagine reaching adulthood a half-century ago. With a life expectancy in

TABLE 10.1: A Twenty-Something Body at Its Physical Peak, and Snapshots of How a Few Capacities Decline Over Time*†

The skeleton: Our height peaks at age 20 and then, due to the compression of the joint cartilage and bones, declines, especially after,midlife. So by age 70, we are roughly 2–5 percent shorter. (Erosion in the joint cartilage and fragile bones also produce classic age- related illnesses called osteoarthritis and osteoporosis, explained in Chapter 14.)

The muscles: The contracting skeletal muscle fibers allow us to perform physical tasks. As we age, these fibers atrophy and are replaced by fat, causing an average 30-40 percent decline in strength by the 70s.

The heart: During exercise, cardiac output, or our heart's pumping capacity, dramatically increases—delivering more oxygen to the muscles. With age the cardiac muscle weakens and thickens, so this maximum pumping ability declines, and we easily get winded. Fatty deposits and a loss of elasticity of the artery walls also compromise our strength and stamina over time.

The lungs: The lungs are the bellows that deliver oxygen to the blood. Our ability to breathe in deeply and exhale forcefully peaks in the twenties, and declines year by year, even for nonsmokers. This loss in vital capacity (and related measures) also explains why physical performance declines with age.

Source: Spense., 1989; Masoro, 1999.

* In general, losses accelerate after midlife.

† People differ greatly in the extent of these losses.

the mid-sixties, you could not have the luxury of spending almost a decade constructing an adult life. Now, with life expectancy floating up to the late seventies in industrialized nations, putting off adult commitments until an older age makes excellent sense.

Emerging adulthood was solidified by the need for more education. A half-century ago, high school graduates could climb to the top rungs in their careers. Today, in the United States, everyone agrees that college is crucial to adult success (Danziger & Ratner, 2010; Furstenberg, 2010). But, although most emerging adults enter college, it typically takes six years to get an undergraduate degree, especially because so many people need to work to finance school. If we add in graduate school, constructing a career can routinely take until the mid-twenties and beyond (Johnson, Crosnoe, & Elder, 2011).

Emerging adulthood was promoted by uniquely modern attitudes about what makes for a satisfying adult life (Cote & Levine, 2002). This life-stage took hold in an individualistic, late-twentieth-century Western culture that stressed self-expression and "doing your own thing," in which people make dramatic changes *throughout* their adult years.

Longevity, the need for education, and an ethic that stresses personal freedom made emerging adulthood possible. Still, the forces that drive this life stage vary from place to place. For snapshots of this variability, let's travel to southern Europe, Scandinavia, and then enter the United States.

The Mediterranean Model: Living with Parents and Having Trouble Making the Leap to Adult life

In Spain, Italy, and Greece, seriously sagging economies make it very difficult for young people to find jobs. The Italian and Spanish cultures, in particular, have norms against **cohabitation,** or living together and having babies before marriage. Students often attend universities close to home. So young people in these countries typically spend their emerging adult years in their parents' house (Furstenberg, 2010). Unfortunately, in the southern European nations, at the time of this writing (2012), family traditions, plus financial constraints, have seriously impeded young people's travels into an independent life.

Giani Giansanti/Corbis

Many Italian men in their twenties and thirties are still living with their parents because they cannot afford to leave the nest and construct an adult life. If you were in this situation, how would you react?

The Scandinavian Plan: Living Independently with Government Help

These impediments do not exist in Scandinavia, where the economy is better (again, as of this writing) and where promoting young people's independent adulthood has traditionally been a societal goal. In Norway, Sweden, and Denmark, the government subsidizes university attendance. Employers make a special effort to hire young workers. A strong social safety net provides free health care and other benefits to citizens of every age. So in Scandinavia, because young people can survive economically, **nest-leaving**—moving out of one's parents' home to live independently—routinely occurs at about age 18 (Furstenberg, 2010; Hendry & Kloep, 2010).

Moreover, because being married is not seen as important for having children, in Scandinavia, the traditional timing of these adult roles is reversed. Swedish women, on average, have their first baby at age 28; then later (in the early thirties), may decide to get married. In Northern Europe, the twenties are more apt to be a stress-free interlude—a time for exploring, for traveling the world, and for enjoying life (Buhl & Lanz, 2007).

The United States: Alternating Between Independence and Dependence

Emerging adulthood in the United States has features of both the Scandinavian and southern European scenes. As in Sweden, in the United States, young people often

cohabitation Sharing a household in an unmarried romantic relationship.

nest-leaving Moving out of a childhood home and living independently.

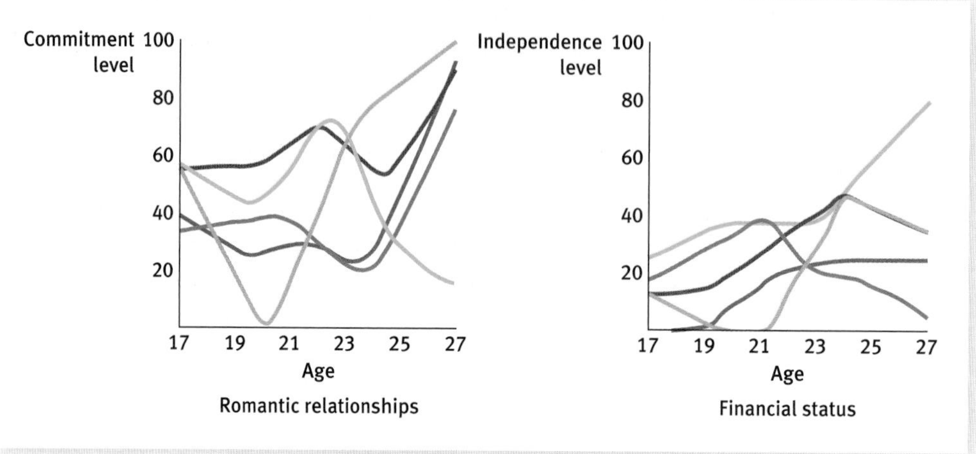

FIGURE 10.1: **The ups and downs of the emerging-adult years:** In a 10-year study tracing how young people develop from age 17 to 27, researchers discovered that many emerging adults move backward and forward on their way to constructing an adult life. These graphs illustrate the adult pathways of five different people in the areas of financial independence and romantic relationships.
Source: Cohen and others, 2003.

live together and have babies before they get married. However, unlike their Scandinavian counterparts, emerging adults who take this path in the United States are disproportionally young (often in their early twenties) and poor (Berzin & De Marco, 2010). As in Scandinavia, our individualistic culture has traditionally encouraged moving out of a parent's home at 18. However, as in southern Europe, the United States does not help young people find work and has its own sagging economy, so it can be difficult to actually exit the nest (more about this issue in the next section).

The reality is that our dramatic *income inequalities*, plus diversity of cultures, make U.S. young people emerging into adulthood very different at the starting gate (Furstenberg, 2010). We also have a more erratic passage to constructing an adult life (Settersten & Ray, 2010).

This bumpy path became evident even before the Great Recession when researchers tracked several hundred New York State young people from ages 17 to 27, looking at their progress toward reaching classic adulthood markers such as financial independence, marriage, and living on their own (Cohen and others, 2003). Yes, there was an overall shift to more mature adult status as people moved deeper into their twenties. But notice from Figure 10.1 that, when we look at individuals, we see variability and movement backward and forward toward the benchmarks of being adult.

So, at age 22, a man might be cohabiting with the idea of getting married. At 25, he might break up with his fiancée and begin dating again. A woman could be financially independent at 21, then slide backward, depending on her parents' help after losing her job and deciding to return to school.

If you are in your mid- or upper-twenties, take a minute to think about your progress to adulthood in terms of relationships, career, and becoming financially independent. Does your pathway also show these ups and downs? When do you expect to fully arrive at adulthood?

For this mother, being invited to her daughter's first apartment may be a thrilling experience: "My baby did grow up to become a responsible woman!"

Beginning and End Points

This last question brings up an interesting issue: When *does* emerging adulthood begin and end?

Exploring the "So-Called" Entry Point: Nest Leaving

If you are like many people, you might mark the event that launches emerging adulthood as moving out of a parent's home. Leaving home after high school for college, a job, or, if your parents are affluent, a gap year traveling the world, is often viewed as a rite of passage. It forces people to take that first step toward independent adulthood—

taking care of their needs on their own. It also causes a re-centering in family relationships, as parents see their children in a different, adult way. Listen to this British mother gushing about her 20-year-old daughter: "To be honest I'm real proud of her. . . She keeps her flat tidy which was a total shocker to me; I'd expected to be a laundry and maid service to her but fair play, she's done all her washing and cleaning" (quoted in Kloep & Hendry, 2010, p. 824).

This quotation hints at two possibly critical benefits of leaving home: It should produce more harmonious family relationships; it should force young people to "grow up."

DOES LEAVING HOME PRODUCE BETTER PARENT-CHILD RELATIONSHIPS? Longitudinal studies suggest the answer to this common perception is yes (Furstenberg, 2010). When researchers followed rural Pennsylvania families after a first-born left for college, both parents and this child reported less conflict compared to a stay-at-home group (Whiteman, McHale, & Crouter, 2010). In another study exploring parent-child discussions about sexuality, emerging adults reported more frank adult-to-adult conversations about this topic after they left home. Here, too, young people often traced this new level of sharing to being in college "and seeing that I'm responsible" (Morgan, Thorne, & Zurbiggen, 2010).

Physically leaving the house, I must emphasize, has nothing to do with becoming disconnected from parents. Close mother-child relationships—and, at least in one study, even calling each other frequently—is correlated with adjusting well to college and homing in on a satisfying career (Gentzler and others, 2011; Melendez & Melendez, 2010; Stringer & Kerpelman, 2010). Although they may not be making the meals or doing the laundry, mothers in particular remain a vital support as young people leave the nest and travel into the wider world.

DOES LEAVING HOME MAKE PEOPLE MORE ADULT? Here, European studies imply the answer *can* be yes. When Belgian researchers compared young people in their early twenties who never left home with a same-aged group who moved out, the "nest residers" were less likely to be in a long-term relationship, felt more emotionally dependent on their parents, and were less satisfied with life (Kins & Beyers, 2010; see also Seiffge-Krenke, 2010). Citing the statistic that roughly 2 out of 3 men and half of women aged 18 to 25 live at home in that nation, British researchers (Hendry & Kloep, 2010; Kloep & Hendry, 2010) agonized about an epidemic of "arrested adulthood" and used examples from their interviews to blame infantilizing moms: "He is my little boy, a mummy's boy if you like. . . . And 'cos he lives at home still. . . I do his clothes, his washing, tidy his room . . . and even still do packed lunch for him to take to work" (quoted in Kloep & Hendry, 2010, p. 826).

This quotation reinforces all of our negative images about emerging adults who stay in the nest (yes, in the developed world, they tend more often to be males): They are lazy, babyish, and unwilling to grow up. The problem is that, in our current economic climate, these stereotypes are no longer true! Nest leaving in the United States, after age 18, has a socioeconomic dimension. Lower-income young people are less apt to move out, because they cannot afford to live on their own (Berzin & DeMarco, 2010). Moreover, in 2010, of the 2 out of 3 entering college freshmen who reported major concerns about financing their education, many planned to live with their families to save money for school (Pryor and others, 2011).

AP/Wide World Photos

This 21-year-old college student is living at home to save money. How can she and her mother negotiate the difficult task of getting along as adults? Stay tuned for suggestions soon.

Actually, leaving the nest to be independent was always a luxury of living in an affluent late twentieth-century Western society. For most of human history and in many developing nations today, young people lived in multigenerational households. Even in America, until the mid-twentieth century, it was normal for people to stay at home until they married and fully made it into adult life (Furstenberg, 2010).

social clock The concept that we regulate our passage through adulthood by an inner timetable that tells us which life activities are appropriate at certain ages.

age norms Cultural ideas about the appropriate ages for engaging in particular activities or life tasks.

on time Being on target in a culture's timetable for achieving adult life tasks.

off time Being too late or too early in a culture's timetable for achieving adult life tasks.

TABLE 10.2: Tips for Getting Along as Co-residing Adults

1. **For parents:** Don't baby your child or micromanage or hover—texting or calling when your child comes home "late." Support and scaffold your child's passage into adulthood.
2. **For children:** Resist the lure of being babied, but lean on your parents for emotional support. Understand, if you are making progress to adulthood, that's the important issue—not that you are living "at home."
3. **For parents and children:** Talk openly about your living together concerns and set up shared rules if you think they will help: How will you divide household tasks? Is it important that your son or daughter stays in school or is looking for a job? Then, vow to treat each other like loving adults.

In addition to economic issues, there is another barrier to moving out for some immigrant and ethnic minority youth—values (Furstenberg, 2010; Kiang & Fuligni, 2009). If a young person's collectivist worldview says, "put family first," or if a family really needs help, children may stay in the nest for very adult-centered reasons—to help with the finances and the chores. As one Latino 20-year-old explained: "I can't leave my mom by herself, she is a single mother. The only person she's got is me. . . ." (quoted in Sánchez and others, 2010, p. 872).

So, does nest leaving qualify as the entry point of emerging adulthood? The answer is "less and less." Do young people *need* to live independently to act mature? As you can see above, the answer is no. The real challenge for families is to construct adult-to-adult relationships with their children no matter where the younger generation lives (see Table 10.2 for some suggestions). And the challenge for young people is to assemble the building blocks to construct a satisfying adult life. When should this constructing phase end and full adulthood arrive? The answer brings up a classic concept in adult development.

Exploring the Fuzzy End Point: The Ticking of the Social Clock

Our feelings about when we should get our adult lives in order reflect our culture's **social clock** (Neugarten, 1972, 1979). This phrase refers to shared **age norms** that act as guideposts to what behaviors are appropriate at particular ages. If our passage matches up with the normal timetable in our culture, we are defined as **on time**; if not, we are **off time**—either too early or too late in terms of where we should be at a given age.

David Young-Wolff/Photo Edit, Inc.

When this not-so-young man in his 40s *finally* proposed to his long-time, 38-year-old girlfriend, she and her family were probably thrilled. Feeling "off time" in the late direction in your social clock timetable can cause considerable distress.

So in the twenty-first-century developed world, exploring different options is considered "on time" during our twenties, but these activities become off time if they extend well into the next decade of life. A parent whose 35-year-old son is "just dating" and shows no signs of deciding on a career or moves back home for the third or fourth time may become impatient: "Will my child ever grow up?" A woman traveling through her thirties may get uneasy: "I'd better hurry up if I want a family," or "Do I still have time to go to medical school?"

Society sets the general social clock guidelines. Today, it's fine to get married in our thirties (or fifties). But in my mother's World War II cohort, any middle-class woman who didn't land a husband by her mid-twenties was labeled an "old maid."

Personal preferences make a difference, too. In one interesting undergraduate survey, developmentalists found that they could predict a given student's social clock timetable by asking a simple question: "Is having a family your main passion in life?" People who said that "marriage is my top-ranking agenda," or "I can't wait to be a mom or dad," were less interested in exploring different options. They often had an earlier timetable for entering adult life (Carroll and others, 2007). So, the limits of emerging adulthood are set both by the wider culture and shaped by our own priorities and goals.

The problem, however, is that our personal social clock agendas are not totally under our control. You cannot simply "decide" to marry the love of your life at a defined age. This sense of being "out of control," combined with the pressures to get our adult life in order, may partly explain why emerging adulthood is both an exhilarating *and* emotionally challenging time. On the positive side, most emerging adults, as I mentioned earlier, are optimistic about their futures (Frye & Liem, 2011; Pryor and others, 2011; Tanner & Arnett, 2010). On the minus side, during the early twenties, serious mental disorders such as alcoholism or debilitating depression are most apt to erupt. Nationwide yearly surveys of U.S. college freshmen showed that, in 2010, symptoms of emotional distress were at a 25-year high (Pryor and others, 2011).

Myrleen Ferguson Cate/Photo Edit

For a surprising number of people, coping with the demands of college can seem like an insurmountable challenge. You need to struggle with the anxious feeling of "can I make it academically?" plus take responsibility for handling all those fast-paced deadlines, all on your own. This shock of first bumping up against adult realities helps explain why today's college freshmen report high levels of emotional distress.

For some young people, the issue lies in failing at the task of taking adult responsibility. As one emerging adult anguished: "My life looks like a . . . gutter and effort to fight that gutter . . . then back in the gutter . . . I just don't have any control over myself" (quoted in Macek, Bejcek, & Vanickova, 2007, p. 466). For others, concerns center around balancing stressful multiple commitments, such as the need to work full time and go to school (Pryor and others, 2011; more about this soon). Or, some emerging adults may have the frightened feeling of not knowing where they are going in life: "We do have more possibilities . . . but that's why it's harder" . . . "You study and you wonder what it is good for" (quoted in Macek, Bejcek, & Vanickova, 2007, p. 468). The reason for this inner turmoil is that, during emerging adulthood, we undergo a mental makeover. We decide *who* to be as adults.

TYING IT ALL TOGETHER

1. You are giving a toast at your friend Sarah's twenty-first birthday party, and you want to offer some predictions on what the next years might hold for her. Given your new understanding of emerging adulthood, which of the following would *not* be a safe prediction?
   a. Sarah may not reach all the standard markers of adulthood until her late twenties.
   b. Sarah's pathway to adulthood will flow smoothly, with steady, predictable steps forward.
   c. Sarah might need to move back into the nest or might still be living at home.
2. Staying in the nest during the twenties today is typically a "symptom" of a child's refusing to grow up. (True or False)
3. Which person is most likely to be worrying about a social clock issue: Martha, age 50, who wants to apply to nursing school, or Lee, age 28, who has just become a father?
4. Statistically speaking, which college freshman might make the transition to adult life earlier—John, who can't wait to start a family, or Sam, whose main focus is establishing his career?

Answers to the Tying It All Together questions can be found at the end of this chapter.

Constructing an Identity

Erik Erikson was the theorist who highlighted the challenge of transforming our childhood self into the person we will be as adults. Recall he called this process the search for **identity** (see Table 10.3).

identity In Erikson's theory, the life task of deciding who to be as a person in making the transition to adulthood.

TABLE 10.3: Erikson's Psychosocial Stages

Life Stage	Primary Task
Infancy (birth to 1 year)	Basic trust versus mistrust
Toddlerhood (1 to 2 years)	Autonomy versus shame and doubt
Early childhood (3 to 6 years)	Initiative versus guilt
Late childhood (6 years to puberty)	Industry versus inferiority
Adolescence (teens into twenties)	**Identity versus role confusion**
Young adulthood (twenties to early forties)	Intimacy versus isolation
Middle adulthood (forties to sixties)	Generativity versus stagnation
Late adulthood (late sixties and beyond)	Integrity versus despair

Time spent wandering through Europe to find himself sensitized Erikson to the difficulties young people face in constructing an adult self. Erikson's fascination with identity as a developmental task, however, crystallized when he worked as a psychotherapist in a psychiatric hospital for troubled teens. Erikson discovered that many young patients suffered from a problem he labeled **role confusion.** They had no sense of *any* adult path. They found it impossible to move ahead:

> [The person feels as] if he were moving in molasses. It is hard for him to go to bed and face the transition into . . . sleep; and it is equally hard for him to get up . . . Such complaints as . . . "I don't know" . . . "I give up" . . . "I quit" . . . are often expressions of . . . despair.
>
> (Erikson, 1968, p. 169)

Some young people felt a frightening sense of falseness about themselves: "If I smoke a cigarette, if I tell a girl I like her, if I make a gesture . . . this third voice is at me all the time—'You're doing this for effect; you're a phony'" (quoted in Erikson, 1968, p. 173). Others could not cope with having any future and planned to end their lives on their eighteenth birthday or some other symbolic date.

This total derailment, which Erikson called confusion—an aimless drifting, or shutting down—differs from the active search process he labeled *moratorium* (1980). Taking time to explore various paths, Erikson argued, is crucial to forming a solid adult identity. Having witnessed Hitler's Holocaust, Erikson believed vehemently that young people must discover their *own* identities. He had seen a destructive process of identity formation firsthand. To cope with that nation's economic problems after World War I, many German teenagers leaped into pathological identities by entering totalitarian organizations such as the Hitler Youth.

Can we spell out the different ways people tackle the challenge of constructing an adult identity? Decades ago, James Marcia answered yes.

role confusion Erikson's term for a failure in identity formation, marked by the lack of any sense of a future adult path.

identity statuses Marcia's four categories of identity formation: identity diffusion, identity foreclosure, moratorium, and identity achievement.

identity diffusion An identity status in which the person is aimless or feels totally blocked, without any adult life path.

identity foreclosure An identity status in which the person decides on an adult life path (often one spelled out by an authority figure) without any thought or active search.

Marcia's Identity Statuses

Marcia (1966, 1987) actually devised four **identity statuses** to expand on Erikson's powerful ideas:

- **Identity diffusion** best fits Erikson's description of the most troubled teens—young people drifting aimlessly toward adulthood without any goals: "I don't know where I am going." "Nothing has any appeal."
- **Identity foreclosure** describes a person who adopts an identity without any self-exploration or thought. At its violent extreme, foreclosure might apply to a Hitler Youth member or a person who becomes a terrorist in his teens. In general, however, researchers define young people as being in foreclosure when they uncritically

Sky Bonillo/Photo Edit, Inc.

This young person may fit Marcia's category of *identity diffusion*. She seems listless and depressed.

Copyright Syracuse Newspapers/Stephen D. Cannerelli/The Image Works

The young man in the background plans to take over this barber shop when his father retires. People who follow their parents' career choices without exploring other possibilities are in *identity foreclosure*. (While Erikson and Marcia linked this status to poor mental health, young people "in foreclosure" can feel happy in this career identity if they explore their choice in depth.)

Michael J. Doolittle/The Image Works

This college student, volunteering as a tutor in a local public school to see if she wants a career as a teacher, is in *identity moratorium*.

Gideon Mendel/Corbis

South African singer Buddy Masondo (*left*), following his life's passion, is in *identity achievement*.

adopt a life path handed down by some authority: "My parents want me to take over the family business, so that's what I will do."

- The person in **moratorium** is engaged in the exciting, healthy search for an adult self. While this internal process may provoke anxiety, because it involves wrestling with different philosophies and ideas, Marcia (and Erikson) felt it is critical to arriving at the final stage.
- **Identity achievement** is the end point: "I've thought through my life. I want to be a musician and songwriter, no matter what my family says."

Marcia's categories offer a marvelous framework for pinpointing what is going wrong (or right) in a young person's life. Perhaps while reading these descriptions you were thinking, "I have a friend or co-worker in diffusion. Now, I understand exactly what this person's problem is!" How do these statuses *really* play out in life?

The Identity Statuses in Action

Marcia originally believed that, as we move through adolescence, we naturally pass from diffusion to moratorium to achievement. Who thinks much about adulthood in ninth or tenth grade? At that age, your agenda is to cope with puberty. You test the limits. You sometimes act in ways that seem tailor-made to undermine your adult life (see Chapter 9). Then, as older adolescents and emerging adults, we undertake a moratorium search as adulthood looms in full view. At some point during our twenties, we have reached achievement, finalizing our search for an adult identity.

moratorium An identity status in which the person actively searches out various possibilities to find a truly solid adult life path. A mature style of constructing an identity.

identity achievement An identity status in which the person decides on a definite adult life path after searching out various options.

moratorium in depth A focused real-world look at one's chosen career to confirm that decision.

ethnic identity How people come to terms with who they are as people relating to their unique ethnic or racial heritage.

biracial or multiracial identity How people of mixed racial backgrounds come to terms with who they are as people in relation to their heritage.

However, in real life, identity pathways are more erratic. People move backward and forward in statuses *throughout* their adult years (Côté & Bynner, 2008; Waterman, 1999). A woman might enter college exploring different faiths, then become a committed Catholic, start questioning her choice again at 30, and finally settle on her spiritual identity in Bahai at age 45. As many older students are aware, you may have gone through moratorium and firmly believed you were in identity achievement in your career, and now have shifted back to moratorium when you realized, "I need a more secure, fulfilling job."

This lifelong shifting is appropriate. It's unrealistic to think we reach a final identity as emerging adults. The push to rethink our lives, to change directions, to have plans and goals, is what makes us human. It is essential at any age. Moreover, revising our identity is vital to living fully since our lives are always prone to being disrupted—as we change careers, become parents, are widowed, or adapt to our children leaving the nest (McAdams, 2001b).

The bad news is that people can be stuck in unproductive places in their identity search. In some studies, an alarming 1 in 4 undergraduates is locked in diffusion (Côté & Bynner, 2008). They don't have *any* career goals. Or, as I see in my classes, students are sampling different paths, but without much Eriksonian moratorium joy. Is your friend who keeps changing his major and putting off graduation excitedly exploring his options, or is he afraid of entering the real world? Are the emerging adults who spend their twenties moving from low-wage job to low-wage job really in moratorium or randomly drifting into adult life?

Actually, Erikson and Marcia's assumption that we need to sample *many* fields in order to construct a solid career identity may not be accurate. Having a career goal in mind from childhood (the status Marcia dismisses as "foreclosure") may also be fine (see Schwartz and others, 2011). So, for readers who enter college determined to be psychologists or have known they wanted to be a nurse from age 9, experts advise conducting a targeted search called **moratorium in depth**—carefully exploring your chosen profession and confirming it is right. It doesn't matter *how* you got there. What's crucial is to feel confident about your choice (see Meeus, 2011, for review).

IN FOCUS: Ethnic Identity, a Minority Theme

As he wrestles to come to terms with his biracial background ("Should I identify with my African or European heritage?" "Where do I *really* fit in?"), this young man may be developing a crucial life strength—the capacity to think more deeply and thoughtfully about the world.

The fact that knowing where we fit (or our identity) can emerge during childhood and evolve for decades is highlighted by examining **ethnic identity**—our sense of belonging to an ethnic category such as "Asian American." If, like me, you are part of the mainstream culture, you rarely think of your ethnicity. For minority young people, labeling yourself as part of a group, with defined characteristics, tends to happen during concrete operations (recall Chapter 6), although the need to explore one's relationship to that label waxes and wanes at older ages. For instance, although ethnic identity issues often become intense during the teens, one study showed that in college, as people are solidifying other aspects of their identity, they intensely grapple with that consciousness again (Syed & Azmitia, 2009).

People cope with this consciousness in various ways. They may develop dual minority and mainstream identities (acting Black in one setting and not another), or reject one identity in favor of another ("I never think of myself as Black, just as American," or "I never think of myself as American, just Black") (Phinney, 2006). The best strategy is to see oneself as embedded in the universal human community (Tadmor, Tetlock, & Peng, 2009) and also feel proud of one's heritage (Smith and Silva, 2011) even in the face of discrimination in the wider world. As one 21-year-old Mexican American put it: "Even though a person may be racist . . . I'm not going to tell myself I shouldn't like myself because I'm Mexican" (Phinney, 2006, p. 125).

The challenges for **biracial** or **multiracial** emerging adults, people from mixed racial or ethnic backgrounds (like President Obama), are particularly poignant. These young people may feel adrift without *any* ethnic home (Literte, 2010). But, here, too, reaching identity achievement can have widespread benefits. Fascinating research suggests having a biracial or bicultural background pushes people to think in more creative, complex ways about life (Tadmor, Tetlock, & Peng, 2009). It can promote resilience, too. As one biracial woman in her early thirties put it: "When I was younger I felt I didn't belong anywhere. But now I've just come to the conclusion that my home is inside myself" (Phinney, 2006, p. 128).

Making sense of one's "place in the world" as an ethnic minority is literally a minority identity theme. But every young person has to grapple with those two universal identity issues: choosing a career and finding love. The rest of this chapter tackles those agendas.

TYING IT ALL TOGETHER

1. You overheard your psychology professor saying that his daughter Emma shows symptoms of Erikson's identity confusion. Emma must be __________ (drifting, actively searching for an identity), which in Marcia's identity status framework is a sign of __________ (diffusion, foreclosure, moratorium).
2. Joe said, "Because we Malloys have worked for generations on the family farm, I know that this must be my career." Kayla replied, "I don't know what my career will be. I'm searching out different possibilities." Joe's identity status is __________ (moratorium, foreclosure, diffusion, or achievement), while Kayla's status is __________ (moratorium, foreclosure, diffusion, or achievement).
3. After reading about the four identity statuses, Clara is thrilled that Marcia's categories fit in perfectly with the lives of her friends. Based on this section, you might caution Clara that (pick *two*):
   a. Friends in identity achievement may cycle back and forth out of this status throughout life.
   b. Friends in foreclosure may be perfectly fine.
   c. Friends in moratorium are probably emotionally disturbed.
4. Confronting the challenge of a biracial or multiracial identity tends to make people think in more rigid ways about the world. (True or False)

Answers to the Tying It All Together questions can be found at the end of this chapter.

Finding a Career

In a famous statement, Sigmund Freud, when asked to sum up the definition of ideal mental health, answered with the simple words, "the ability to love and work." Let's now look at finding ourselves in the world of work.

When did you begin thinking about your career? What influences are drawing you to psychology, nursing, or business—a compelling class, a caring mentor, or the conviction that this field would fit your talents best? How do young people feel about their careers, their futures, and working?

To answer these kinds of questions, Mihaly Csikszentmihalyi and Barbara Schneider (2000) conducted a pioneering study of teenagers' career dreams. They selected 33 U.S. schools and interviewed students from sixth to twelfth grade. To chart how young people felt—when at home, with friends, when working at school—they used the *experience-sampling method* (discussed in Chapter 9). Now, let's touch on their insights and other studies as we track young people entering and moving through the emerging adult years.

Entering with High (but Often Unrealistic) Career Goals

Almost every teenager, the researchers found, expects to go to college. Almost everyone wants to have a professional career. The tendency to aim high appears regardless of gender or social class. Whether male or female, rich or poor, adolescents have lofty career goals. Moreover, the stereotype about today's young people as "basically" unmotivated is completely wrong (see Arnett, 2010). In the 2010 survey of U.S. college freshmen I mentioned earlier, young people reported being *more* driven to achieve than their counterparts in previous years (Pryor and others, 2011).

The problem is that college freshmen are (naturally) often clueless about what it takes to implement their dream careers. Can someone who "hates reading" really spend a decade getting a psychology Ph.D.? What happens when my students learn they have to have a GPA close to 3.7 to enter our university's nursing program, or they can't go to law school because of the astronomical costs? Career disappointment can lurk right around the corner for young people as they emerge from the cocoon of high school and confront the real world. Who is apt to rise to these challenges and construct a fulfilling life?

Experiencing Emotional Growth

In their study, Csikszentmihalyi and Schneider (2000) targeted a group of adolescents that they labeled "workers," young people who delighted in mastering challenging tasks. So, for instance, if a teen thrived on balancing school responsibilities with a part-time job and had some compelling extracurricular passion, his "worker personality" would set him up to excel at the messy challenges of college life (see Busseri and others, 2010; Larson, 2011). However, let's not completely count out adolescents who are floundering or failing or depressed. As you vividly saw in Jason's story in the Chapter 9 Experiencing the Lifespan Box, emerging adulthood can offer a dramatic window for change.

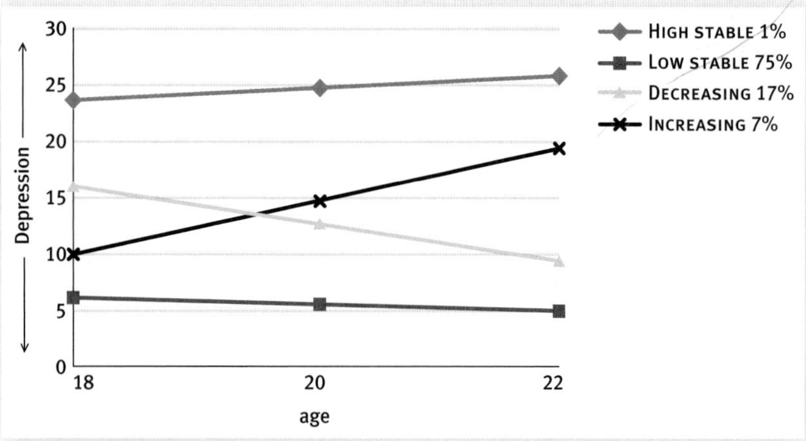

Do we have concrete research evidence that people can shed an unhappy childhood as they leave their teens behind? Consider the findings of the study illustrated in Figure 10.2 tracking depression rates in over 1000 young people from age 18 into their early twenties (Frye & Liem, 2011). Notice that, yes, the tiny minority of teens with the most debilitating symptoms tended to stay depressed over the years (blue line). However, as you can see in the yellow line, 1 in 6 moderately depressed teens became much less unhappy over the next three years (although admittedly a smaller group did get more depressed). Most interesting, the researchers found that the emerging adults whose mental health improved were just as likely to have endured poverty and other childhood traumas as their counterparts, whose symptoms remained or increased. Therefore, some—but not all—teens get it together emotionally as they make the leap to adult life.

FIGURE 10.2: **How rates of depression changed in an economically diverse sample of over 1000 young people traveling from age 18 to age 22:** Notice from this chart that the vast majority of 18-year-olds and early twenty-somethings are happy (red). Those teens with major depressive disorders is still battling their condition three years later (blue). But a reasonable percentage of moderately depressed teens become happier as they make the transition to adult life (yellow line).
Source: Frye & Liem (2011).

What inner quality is most apt to change for the better during the emerging adult years? Researchers target a broad temperamental dimension labeled *conscientiousness* (to be described in Chapter 12). As people move through their twenties, they become more reliable and develop better self-control (see Cramer, 2008; Donnellan, Conger, & Burzette, 2007; Johnson and others, 2007). Emerging adults are also capable of reasoning about real-world dilemmas in a complex, thoughtful way (Labouvie-Vief, 2006; also stay tuned for more about this attribute in Chapter 12).

flow Csikszentmihalyi's term for feeling total absorption in a challenging, goal-oriented activity.

To explain this rise in *executive functions* (or what you and I would call "maturity"), adolescent specialists like Laurence Steinberg might look to the fully developed frontal lobes (recall Chapter 9). But an equally plausible cause lies in the wider world. In one longitudinal study, researchers found that impulsive, troubled teens could be transformed into "workers" (in Mihaly Csikszentmihalyi's terms) after they got satisfying, responsible jobs (Dennissen, Asendorpf, & van Aken, 2008). A powerful inner state—also spelled out by Csikszentmihalyi—can help transform all of us into "workers" and lock people of any age into the right career.

Finding Flow

Think back over the past week to the times you felt energized and alive. You might be surprised to discover that events you looked forward to—such as relaxing at home or watching a favorite TV program—do not come to mind. Many of life's most uplifting experiences occur when we connect deeply with people. Others take place when we are immersed in some compelling task. Csikszentmihalyi names this intense task absorption **flow.**

Bob Daemmrich/Photo Edit

For this graduate student who is puzzling over the meaning of a difficult paper in his field, the hours may fly by. Challenging activities that fully draw on our talents and skills produce that marvelous inner state called "flow."

Flow is different from "feeling happy." We enter this state when we are immersed in an activity that stretches our capacities, such as the challenge of decoding a difficult academic problem, or (hopefully) getting absorbed in mastering the material in this class. People also differ in the kinds of activities that cause flow. For some of us, it's hiking in the Himalayas that produces this feeling. For me, it has been writing this book. When we are in flow, we enter an altered state of consciousness in which we forget the outside world. Problems disappear. We lose a sense of time. The activity feels infinitely worth doing for its own sake. Flow makes us feel completely alive.

Csikszentmihalyi (1990), who has spent his career studying flow, finds that some people rarely experience this feeling. Others feel flow several times a day. If you feel flow only during a rare mountain-climbing experience or, worse, when robbing a bank, Csikszentmihalyi argues that it will be difficult to construct a satisfying life. The challenge is to find flow in ways related to your career.

Flow depends on being *intrinsically motivated.* We must be mesmerized by what we are doing right now for its own sake, not for an extrinsic reward. But there also is a future-oriented dimension to feeling flow. Flow, according to Csikszentmihalyi, happens when we are working toward a goal.

For example, the idea that this book will be published two years from now is the ultimate goal that is pushing me to write this very page. But what really riveted me to my chair for hours this morning is the actual process of writing. Getting into a flow state is often elusive. On the days when I can't construct a paragraph, I get anxious. But if I could not regularly find flow in my writing, I would never be writing this book.

Figure 10.3 on page 312 shows exactly why finding flow can be difficult. Reaching that state depends on a delicate person–environment fit. When a task seems beyond our capacities, we become anxious. When an activity is too simple, we grow bored. Ideally, the activities in which we feel flow can alert us to the careers in which we want to spend our lives. Think about some situation in which you recently felt flow. If you are in moratorium or worry you may be in career diffusion, can you use this feeling to clue you in to a particular field?

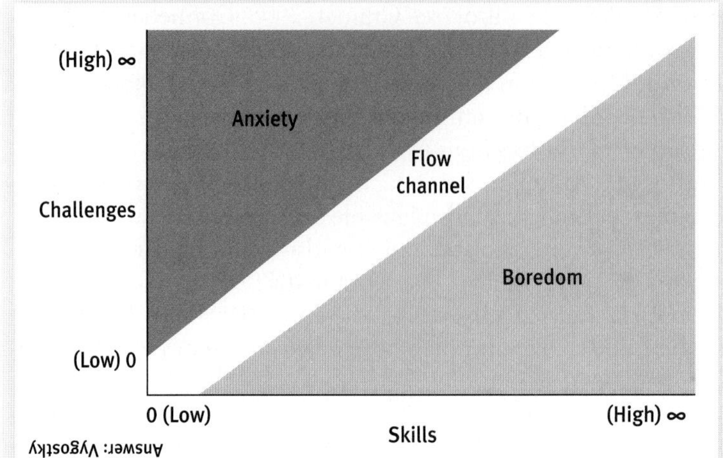

FIGURE 10.3: **The zone of flow:** Notice that the flow zone (white area) depends on a delicate matching of our abilities and the challenge involved in a particular real-world task. If the task is too difficult or beyond our capacities, we land in the upper red area of the chart and become anxious. If the task is too easy, we land in the lower, gray area of the chart and become bored. Moreover, as our skills increase, the difficulty of the task must also increase to provide us with the sense of being in flow. Which theorist's ideas about teaching and what stimulates mental growth does this model remind you of? (Turn page upside down for answer.)

Source: Adapted from Csikszentmihalyi (1990).

Drawing on the concept of flow, my discussion of identity, as well as our current U.S. economic concerns, let's now look at two career paths emerging adults follow.

Emerging into Adulthood Without a College Degree

"I never want this kind of job for my kids." This comment, from a 35-year-old high school graduate working at a construction job, sums up our contemporary feeling in the United States that college is vital for having a good life (Furstenberg, 2010). Actually, more than 2 of every 3 U.S. high school graduates enroll in college right after high school. However, as time passes, the ranks dramatically thin. By their mid-twenties, slightly less than one third (30.7 percent) of U.S. young people has completed a four-year degree (Radford and others, 2010).

People who don't go to college or who never get their degree can have fulfilling careers. Some may excel at Robert Sternberg's practical or creative intelligence (described in Chapter 7) but do not do well at academics. When they find their flow in the work world, they blossom. Consider the career of that college failure, the famous filmmaker named Woody Allen, or even that of Bill Gates, who found his undergraduate courses too confining and left Harvard to pioneer a new field.

Unfortunately, however, the famous billionaire dropouts are a minuscule statistical blip. The reality is that young people who enter the U.S. labor force with "only high school" have a hard time constructing a middle-class life (Settersten & Ray, 2010). As you can see in my snapshots of economic inequality in Figure 10.4, the wage gap between high school and college graduates widened to a chasm over the

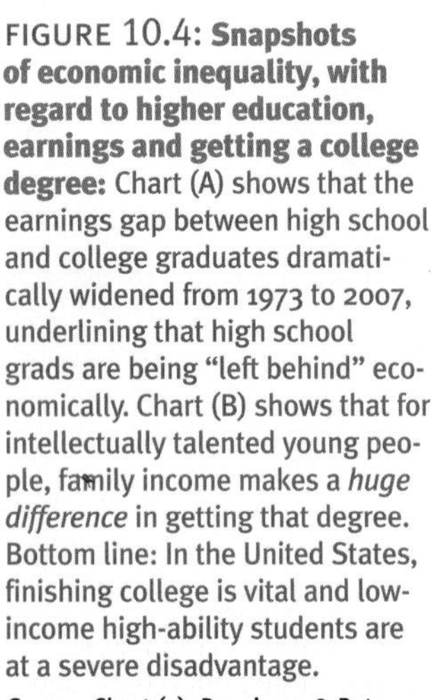

FIGURE 10.4: **Snapshots of economic inequality, with regard to higher education, earnings and getting a college degree:** Chart (A) shows that the earnings gap between high school and college graduates dramatically widened from 1973 to 2007, underlining that high school grads are being "left behind" economically. Chart (B) shows that for intellectually talented young people, family income makes a *huge difference* in getting that degree. Bottom line: In the United States, finishing college is vital and low-income high-ability students are at a severe disadvantage.

Source: Chart (a): Danzinger & Ratner, 2010. Chart (b) adapted from data in Carnevale & Strohl, 2010.

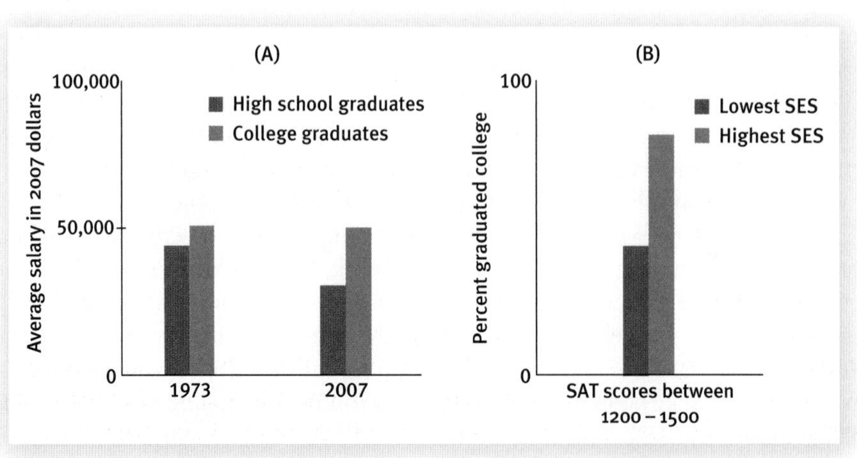

past 40 years. While the Great Recession of 2008 hit college graduates under age 25 hard—with 9 percent unemployed as of 2010—it's been devastating for their counterparts with "only high school." In that year, *1 in 4* male high school graduates ages 16 to 25 were out of work (Shierholz & Edwards, 2011).

Given these realities, why do many emerging adults drop out of school? Our first assumption is that most of these people are not "college material"—uninterested in academics, poorly prepared in high school, and/or can't do the work.

True, to succeed in college, prior academic aptitude is important. As a C student in your public school class, for instance, your odds of getting a B.A. are less than 1 in 5 (Engle. n.d). But, as Figure 10.4B shows, economic considerations matter greatly. The unfortunate reality is that talented, low-SES young people are far less likely to graduate from college than their affluent peers (Carnevale & Strohl, 2010).

When the Gates foundation commissioned a survey of more than 600 young adults ages 22 to 30, who had dropped out of college, they discovered the same message—money matters. Only 1 in 10 students said they left school because the courses were too difficult or that they weren't interested in the work. The main reason was that they had to work full time to finance school, and the strain became too much (Johnson & Rochkind, 2011).

Photodisc

This twenty-something high school graduate probably felt lucky to find this low wage job. For emerging adults who do not go to college, the current economic realities are bleak.

The silver lining was that most of these people did plan to return. And, as many nontraditional student readers are aware, there can be emotional advantages to leaving and then coming back. Young people who work, even at jobs not related to their career, have a firmer career identity (Stringer & Kerpelman, 2010). In Sweden, the social clock for college is programmed to start ticking a few years after high school has ended (Arnett, 2007a). The reasoning is that time spent in the wider world helps people home in on what to study in school.

Because conscientiousness shifts upward during the twenties, putting off college may improve academic performance. I can't tell you how many times students have told me, "I was too young to be in college. Now, I have the motivation to succeed." A recent prime example comes from a student of mine who flunked out of college two decades ago and returned last year. He is now making a 3.8, with plans to go to medical school—and that's while having a family and working full time!

What happens to people who don't return? Since the jobless rate for high school graduates *over age* 25 is far lower (10 percent in 2010) (Shierholz & Edwards, 2011), many (but clearly far from all) noncollege emerging adults do find steady jobs. Employers look for reliability and a good work ethic, virtues that can be demonstrated once someone gets his foot in the door. When British researchers explored the qualities that distinguished people who left school at 16 and had gone on to survive economically during midlife (granted, during better economies), the main predictor that stood out was prior academic skills (Schoon & Duckworth, 2010). So, if a non-college graduate is a "worker" and intellectually competent, that person can *sometimes* succeed against the odds.

INTERVENTIONS: Giving Economically Strapped Young People a Boost

Still, we can't let society off of the hook. The fact that financing college is so difficult for many U.S. young people is a national shame. If we can't reduce the tuition, the Gates Foundation respondents suggest: Make it possible for part-time students to get financial aid, and offer more classes on the weekends and evenings (and, of course, online). As many struggling students are parents, it would be terrific to have low-cost child care on campus and encourage employers to step up to the plate by providing students with flexible work hours (Johnson & Rochkind, 2011). I'll bet many readers can relate to this dilemma reported by a freshman in a focus group study: "I had to take off a shift from work because I had to take a test for my major. I got penalized" (quoted in Hornak, Farrell, & Jackson, 2010, p. 489).

In this survey, exploring the financial headaches of students at public universities, freshmen had several complaints: being overwhelmed by the need to search for a job, plus simultaneously negotiate the maze of college; not realizing what financial

school-to-work transition The change from the schooling phase of life to the work world.

Frances M. Roberts/Newscom

After joyously getting their degree, these new CUNY graduates now must face the dispiriting experience of feeling like a number as they wend their way through this impersonal job-fair line. Can you devise a better way to help contemporary young people handle the difficult *school-to-work transition*?

aid was available (several students didn't know about work-study opportunities on campus), not grasping the true added expense of college—fees for parking, joining clubs, buying textbooks. Therefore, it would help to provide the *total* ballpark costs of attending a given institution, prior to students' enrolling in that school. Moreover, it would be terrific to have a counselor/advisor assigned to incoming freshmen, who could consult about job possibilities and "everything else financial you should know" (Hornak, Farrell, & Jackson, 2010).

Finally, we need to rethink our contemporary emphasis on college as the *only* ticket to a decent life. As some people are skilled at working with their hands, or excel in practical intelligence, why force non-academically oriented emerging adults to suffer for years, enduring a poor talent–environment fit? Can't we develop the kinds of apprentice programs that have been successful in Germany? (See Cook & Furstenberg, 2002.) In that nation, employers partner with schools that offer on-the-job training. Graduates emerge with a *definite* position in that specific firm.

Actually, with an ethos stressing "personal responsibility," our individualistic nation does an abysmal job of helping even the most highly educated emerging adults negotiate the **school-to-work transition,** or make the leap from academics to work. Rather than leaving the anxiety-ridden, post-education job hunt to luck, random contacts, and putting the burden on the so-called "inner" talents of kids, let's devise creative, concrete conduits (preferably nationwide programs!) to smooth the way for young people confronting this crucial social-clock challenge of adult life.

Table 10.4 summarizes the main messages of this section, by offering suggestions for emerging adults and society at large. Now, it's time to immerse ourselves in the undergraduate experience.

TABLE 10.4: Succeeding in College/Finding a Career Identity Tips for Young People and Society: A Section Summary

For Young People

1. Focus on finding your flow in selecting a career. If you think you know what you want to do, conduct a moratorium-in-depth exploration; if you are still unsure, understand that it often takes time to formulate a career plan.
2. Be financially literate. Assess the probable costs, financial-aid options, and jobs available before beginning school. Try, if possible, to get a flexible job, one that allows you to study.
3. If you need to drop out for some time, understand it's not the end of the world. Having a year or two off may help you home in on a career identity and be a better student.

For Society

1. Provide spread sheets detailing the "real" costs of attending different institutions to help prospective students select wisely and be informed.
2. Assign counselors to incoming freshmen to clearly map out financial options and link students to community employers.
3. Reach out to low-income undergraduates and offer special services for students who are parents or working adults.
4. Set up apprenticeship programs linked to jobs—ones that offer a conduit to the work world without college.
5. Make negotiating young people's school-to-work transition a national priority!

Being in College

So far, I've been implying that the only purpose of college is to find a career. Thankfully, in surveys, large fractions of U.S. college graduates disagree. They report the main value of their undergraduate years was to help them "grow intellectually and personally" (Hoover, 2011).

How does this inner growth progress as people travel through college? According to William Perry (1999), freshmen come in blindly accepting the facts that authorities hand down, then they move to relativism (understanding that there are multiple truths); by senior year, they make their own ethical commitments in the face of appreciating diverse points of view.

Perry's longitudinal analyses were conducted with Harvard undergraduates 40 years ago. But another longitudinal study (granted, also at a selective university) confirms that this inner development does occur—and most important—it takes place *specifically* during the undergraduate years (Bauer & MacAdams, 2010).

If you are a traditional college student, here are some tips to make your college experience an inner-growth flow zone.

INTERVENTIONS: Making College an Inner-Growth Flow Zone

GET THE BEST PROFESSORS (AND TALK TO THEM OUTSIDE OF CLASS!). It's a no-brainer that exciting teachers loom large as factors in student success (Komarraju, Musulkin, & Bhattacharya, 2011; Pascarella, Salisbury, & Blaich, 2010; Schreiner and others, 2011). In U.S. surveys, private residential colleges—with their small classes and low student–faculty ratios—get the highest marks at providing challenging, exciting classes. But community college students are just as happy with their instructors (Seifert and others, 2010). (Why not? They are committed educators.) And, of course, large public universities have many outstanding professors, too (National Survey of Student Engagement, 2010). Outstanding professors adore their subject and can vividly communicate their passion to students (Bane, 2004). Just like their elementary school counterparts (see Chapter 7), they respect their students' talents and are committed to nurturing undergraduates' growth. So reach out and talk to your professors. Students from every end of the academic spectrum agree that feeling listened to can be a peak experience in one's academic life:

From a Harvard senior:

> He began by asking me which single book had the biggest impact on me. He was the first professor who was interested in what matters to me. . . . You can't imagine how excited I was.
>
> (quoted in Light, 2001, pp. 82–83)

From a community college student:

> You know, what he does more than anything else is that. . . he really listens. I was in his office last semester and I was telling him how I was struggling. . . . He really let me talk myself into doing what I needed to pass. It's like, you know he gives a damn.
>
> (quoted in Schreiner and others, 2011, p. 324)

CONNECT YOUR CLASSES TO POTENTIAL CAREERS. Professors' mission is to excite you about their field. But classes can't provide the hands-on experience you need to conduct your *moratorium-in-depth* career search. So, institute your personal school-to-work transition. Set up independent studies involving volunteer work. If you are interested in science, work in a professor's lab. If your passion is politics, do an internship with a local legislator. In one study, college seniors mentioned that the highlight of their undergraduate experience occurred during a mentored project in the real world (Light, 2001).

IMMERSE YOURSELF IN THE COLLEGE MILIEU. Following this advice is easier if you are attending a small residential school. The college experience is at your doorstep, ready to be embraced. At a large university, especially a commuter school, you'll need to make active efforts to get involved in campus life. If possible, spend your first year living in a

Photodisc

College is an ideal time to connect with people from different backgrounds. So go for it!

college dormitory. Join a college organization, or two, or three. Working for the college newspaper or becoming active in the drama club not only will provide you with a rich source of friends, but can help promote your career identity, too.

CAPITALIZE ON THE DIVERSE HUMAN CONNECTIONS COLLEGE PROVIDES. As you saw in previous chapters, the peer groups we select shape who we become. At college, it is tempting to find a single clique and then not reach out to other crowds. Resist this impulse. A major growth experience college provides is the chance to connect with people of different perspectives and points of view (Hu & Kuh, 2003; see also Leung & Chiu, 2011). Here's what another Harvard undergraduate had to say:

> I have re-evaluated my beliefs. . . . At college, there are people of all different religions around me. . . . Living . . . with these people marks an important difference. . . . [It] has made me reconsider and ultimately reaffirm my faith.
>
> (quoted in Light, 2001, p. 163)

But this community college student summed it up best:

> When I come home and have all these great stories; they think college is the most amazing thing in your life. . . and that's because of all the people I'm surrounded with.
>
> (quoted in Schreiner and others, 2011, p. 337)

Being surrounded by interesting people has another crucial benefit: It smoothes the way to Erikson's other emerging adult task: finding love.

TYING IT ALL TOGETHER

1. Your 15-year-old nephew continually gets into trouble at school and home, and his parents are concerned about what will happen when he enters the world of work. Based on the information in this section, what can you legitimately say to your relatives about how troubled teens fare, work-wise, as emerging adults?
2. Hannah confesses that she loves her server job—but only during busy times. When the restaurant is hectic, she gets energized. Time flies by. She feels exhilarated, at the top of her form, like a multitasking whiz! Hannah is describing a __________ experience.
3. Josiah says the reason why his classmates drop out of college is that they can't do the work. Jocasta says, "Sorry, it's the need to work incredible hours to pay for school." Make each person's case, using the information from this chapter.
4. You are testifying before a U.S. Senate committee about how to improve college completion rates. What might you suggest?
5. Your cousin Juan, who is about to enter his freshman year, asks you for tips about how to succeed in college. Based on the information in this section, pick the advice you should *not* give:
   a. Get involved in campus activities.
   b. Search out friends who have exactly the same ideas as you do.
   c. Select the best professors and reach out to make connections with them.

Answers to the Tying It All Together questions can be found at the end of this chapter.

Finding Love

intimacy Erikson's first adult task, involving connecting with a partner in a mutual loving relationship.

How do twenty-first-century emerging adults negotiate Erikson's first task of adult life (see Table 10.5)—**intimacy**, the search for enduring love? How do romantic relationships develop, and why do they sometimes fall apart? What insights does the social

TABLE 10.5: **Erikson's Life Stages and Their Psychological Tasks**

Life Stage	Primary Task
Infancy (birth to 1 year)	Basic trust versus mistrust
Toddlerhood (1 to 2 years)	Autonomy versus shame and doubt
Early childhood (3 to 6 years)	Initiative versus guilt
Late childhood (6 years to puberty)	Industry versus inferiority
Adolescence (teens into twenties)	Identity versus role confusion
Young adulthood (twenties to early forties)	**Intimacy versus isolation***
Middle adulthood (forties to sixties)	Generativity versus stagnation
Late adulthood (late sixties and beyond)	Integrity versus despair

***Although we began to tackle the early adult search for intimacy in this section, I'll be continuing this discussion in Chapter 11, when we discuss marriage.**

science research offer for finding an ideal mate? Let's now explore these questions one by one.

Setting the Context: Different Partner Choices

> Daolin Yang, 77, a grandfather, is retired and lives in Hebie Province, China. . . . At age 15, he married his wife Yufen, then 13, in a village. . . . A matchmaker proposed the marriage on behalf of the Yang family. They have been married for 62 years and reared three children. . . . He says that they married first and dated later. It is "cold at the start and hot in the end." The relationship gets better and better over the years.
>
> (Xia & Zhou, 2003, p. 231)

This long-lasting love story reminds us that searching for a mate on our own is a uniquely Western phenomenon. Throughout history, families have routinely taken over that responsibility. Even today in our multicultural nation (see the Experiencing the Lifespan box on the next page), among certain groups, mate-selection choices are carefully controlled. Still, the basic recent thrust in our society is for young people to have *much more* latitude than ever in the partners they select. Let's touch on two ways that mate-selection processes in the developed world have widened over the past thirty years.

The Growth of Interracial (and Inter-ethnic) Dating

During much of U.S. history, deciding to date outside of your "own kind" (even religiously) was a daring act. By the beginning of the twenty-first century, 1 in 3 European Americans reported getting romantically involved with someone of a different ethnicity or race. More than half of all African Americans, Hispanic Americans, and Asian Americans had also made that claim (Yancey & Yancey, 2002). How might a person's ethnic identity change after getting romantically involved with someone of another ethnicity or race?

VStock/Alamy

It's a pleasure to see these newlyweds on this special day. Plus, as you will see soon, this husband may discover that choosing this wife will give him a deeper, richer appreciation of his own ethnic roots.

To answer this question, researchers interviewed a common kind of inter-ethnic couple—European American men and Asian American women (AhnAllen & Suyemoto, 2011). You might predict that people become less identified with their own ethnic group when they date outside their race. You would be wrong. Yes, couples did report feeling more tolerant of other cultures. The men, in particular, became sensitized to the challenges facing minorities in America and felt passionate about

EXPERIENCING THE LIFESPAN: Another Perspective on U.S. Dating and Mating

To keep in mind that selecting love relationships on our own is far from universal, even in our choice-oriented society, listen to Alara, an immigrant from India:

Dating is not allowed in my religion. That is a strict rule. If I was to date someone and he was not Hindu, I couldn't marry him. If I met a Hindu, I might be allowed to see him, but it wouldn't be dating in the traditional sense. You can't date for the experience. It's always for the purpose of marriage.

We have loosened up a bit. My parents had an arranged marriage. My mother's and father's parents were best friends—and my two grandpas decided that my parents would marry each other when they were little children. Mom says if she had had a choice, she would not have married Dad. They used to argue all the time. Now that we are grown up, Mom moved back to Pittsburgh and teaches school there, and my dad still lives in Springfield. They still say they are married, but they really don't talk much.

When I was in kindergarten, we moved from India to Pittsburgh, where there is a large Indian community. Eight years ago, my dad got a better job offer, and we moved to western Massachusetts. In Pittsburgh, all my friends were Indian, either Hindu or Muslim; after we went to Springfield, I didn't have one Indian friend. They were all Americans. They were real cool, but I always felt their values were different.

My brother is 29 and about to get married. He met Shukla, his fiancée, at a friend's wedding. She lives in California. Every time he visits, her mom chaperones them. They are not allowed to be alone together. My sister is also engaged, but, once again, when they see each other, my mom always has to be there.

I did have a problem with our practices, but I've accepted them. When I lived at home, I didn't date. Then, when I went to college I went crazy for about a year. I fell in love with a Baptist guy, but after a while I realized I had to end the relationship. My mom, it would have broken her heart. I care too much about my family. People would look down on my parents if I married outside our religion. And, suppose I married my Baptist boyfriend, I mean, what religion would my children be? I want to give my children a firm sense of identity. So I'm comfortable waiting until I meet the right Hindu man.

Anthony Bolante/Reuters/Corbis

This cake decoration, created in Seattle for the first annual Gay Wedding Show, is a perfect sign of how the landscape of love has seriously widened in the United States.

homophobia Intense fear and dislike of gays and lesbians.

educating friends and family who (unfortunately) often held racist views. But these young people—once again, both men and women—reported feeling more in touch with their own heritage, too. As one interviewee named Curtis put it: ". . .there (isn't) too many special things about being White in America. But (now I) view it as different and special" (quoted in AhnAllen & Suyemoto, 2011, p. 69). Ironically, dating outside one's group can connect people (especially Whites who don't much think about it) to their own ethnic background in a stronger way!

More Acceptance of Same-Sex Romance

About 15 years ago at my Southern university, I remember being disturbed by the snickering that would erupt when I mentioned issues related to being gay. No more! Although the gay rights movement exploded on the scene in the late 1960s in New York's Greenwich Village, its most revolutionary strides took place within the twenty-first century's first years. As one expert put it, in a few years, the announcement of "I'm gay" has gone from evoking shock waves to producing yawns—"So what else is new?" (See Savin-Williams, 2001, 2008.)

This is not to say that **homophobia**, or intense fear and dislike of gays and lesbians, is absent. Discrimination is rampant, for instance, in Islamic nations, where coming out can mean death. Stereotypes, such as those described in Table 10.6, are far from rare in the Western world. Especially when they are struggling with their sexual orientation during adolescence—as the table shows—gay teens suffer from considerable emotional distress. As we know, sexual-minority adolescents remain vulnerable to being victimized at school (Saewyc, 2011). But, for a young person who is upper-middle-class European American, and in a liberal high school, coming out can be a teenage coming-of-age event. In an era in which hip college students define themselves as "mostly straight," "sometimes gay," or "occasionally

TABLE 10.6: Homosexual Stereotypes and Scientific Facts

Stereotype: *Overinvolved mothers and distant fathers "cause" boys to be homosexual.*

Scientific fact: There is no evidence that this or any other parenting problem causes homosexuality. The causes of homosexuality are unknown—however, recent research suggests that levels of prenatal testosterone may help program a fetus' later gender orientation (see Chapter 6).

Stereotype: *Homosexual couples have lower-quality relationships—their interactions are "psychologically immature."*

Scientific fact: Researchers compared the relationships of committed gay couples with their heterosexual counterparts via a variety of strategies. The finding: There were NO differences in the quality of heterosexual and homosexual relationships. There was one exception, however: Lesbian couples were rated as relating more harmoniously when being observed (Roisman and others, 2008).

Stereotype: *Homosexual parents have pathological family interactions and disturbed children.*

Scientific fact: When British researchers (Golombok and others, 2003) compared lesbian-mother, two-parent-heterosexual, and single-mother families, they found that children raised in lesbian families had no problems with their gender identity and had no signs of impaired mental health. In fact, the lesbian mothers showed signs of superior parenting—hitting their children less frequently and engaging in more fantasy play.

Stereotype: *Homosexuals are emotionally disturbed.*

Scientific fact: Unfortunately, as the text suggests, gay young people show elevated rates of psychological problems, such as suicidal thoughts, depression, and drug abuse. Emotional distress, however, seems most acute during the early and middle teens, when people are dealing with anxieties relating to coming out (Saewyc, 2010). I also must emphasize that gay teens can emerge into adulthood with exceptional levels of mental health (Ueno, 2010).

bisexual," even limiting one's sexual orientation to a certain category can be passé (Diamond & Savin-Williams, 2003; Thompson & Morgan, 2008).

Coming out to your friends or announcing your sexual orientation in school is different from telling Mom and Dad. What happens when young people make this announcement to their parents, and how is it received?

IN FOCUS: Coming Out to Mom and Dad

Imagine you are a parent and your child has just informed you that he is gay. You may have suspected the truth for years, but the revelation can hit like a bombshell. Believing that being gay is fine in the abstract but is different from feeling that it's fine for *your child.* You may worry about telling other family members or feel anxious about what "the neighbors" will think. Most importantly, you have fears for the future: Will your baby have trouble finding fulfilling love? In interviews with U.S. teenagers and emerging adults, Rich Savin-Williams explored what happened when young people deliver this news (Savin-Williams, 2001; Savin-Williams & Ream, 2003).

You may have heard stories of parents banishing gay offspring from the house. These events, according to Savin-Williams, are rare. Only 4 percent of the young people in his study described parental rejection or verbal abuse. Many parents did wrestle with intense feelings. However, after a period of adjustment, the majority rallied around their child. Few sons or daughters felt that their relationship with their parents deteriorated after coming out. Most reported that they felt either closer or just as close as before.

Coming to terms with one's sexual orientation can occur gradually, in fits and starts (Saewyc, 2011). When people are clear about their feelings, they typically confide in a good friend. Finally, they decide if and when to tell their family the news. Most people in Savin-Williams's study made the announcement to their parents at about age 19. There was considerable variability, however—from the people who came out as young as age 13 to those who said they would never tell.

Imagine you are a gay emerging adult who has yet to come out to your parents. How can you predict how they will respond? Studies show the key lies in knowing your family. If your parents are highly traditional (for instance, religious) and believe being gay is an individual choice that you can control, it's a good bet they may have trouble with the news (Heatherington & Lavner, 2008). According to Savin-Williams, if your family is highly homophobic and you feel that coming out may put you in jeopardy, you should trust your gut instincts and not tell. However, if you and your parents have a close, caring relationship, revealing your sexual orientation will not make a dent in that enduring bond.

The caution is that Savin-Williams's upbeat findings came only from young people who felt comfortable enough to tell their families, not from those who were reluctant to disclose. Still, this research makes an important point: Gay young people are like all young people. We cannot assume that they are alienated from their parents. We cannot assume that they relate in *any* stereotyped way. Diversity is a hallmark of family relationships among young people with same-sex orientations, just as it is with other teenagers and emerging adults (Savin-Williams, 2008).

This brief look at the changing social context of finding a mate tells us nothing about how people connect. Do opposites attract, or do we choose our mirror selves? How do relationships develop and progress?

Traditional Looks at Love: Similarity and Structured Relationship Stages

Bernard Murstein's now-classic **stimulus-value-role theory** (1970) views mate selection as a three-phase process. During the **stimulus phase,** we see a potential partner and make our first decision: "Could this be a good choice for me?" "Would this person want me?" Since we know nothing about the person, our judgment is based on superficial signs, such as looks or the way the individual dresses. In this assessment, we compare our own reinforcement value to the other person's along a number of dimensions (Murstein, 1999): "True, I am not as good-looking, but she may find me desirable because I am better educated." If the person seems of equal value, we decide to go on a date.

When we start dating, we enter the **value-comparison phase.** Here, our goal is to select the right person by matching up in terms of inner qualities and traits: "Does this person share my interests? Do we have the same values?" If this person seems "right," we enter the **role phase,** in which we work out our shared lives.

So, at a party, Michael scans the room and decides that Samantha with the tattoos and frumpy-looking Abigail are out of the question. He can do better than that! Erika, surrounded by all those men, may be *too* beautiful. He gravitates to Ashley, whose way of dressing and speaking suggests that she might be athletic or intellectual, and maybe—like him—a bit shy. As Michael and Ashley begin dating, he discovers, to his delight, that they are on the same wavelength. They enjoy the same movies; they both love the mountains; they have the same worldview. The romance could still end. On their third or tenth date, there may be a revelation that "this person is too different." But, if things go smoothly, Michael and Ashley begin planning their future. Should they move to California when they graduate? Will their wedding be small and intimate or big and expensive?

The "equal-reinforcement-value partner" part of Murstein's theory explains why we expect couples to be similar in their social status. We're not surprised if the best-looking girl in high school dates the captain of the football team. When we find serious partner status mismatches, we search for reasons to explain these discrepancies (Murstein, Reif, & Syracuse-Siewert, 2002): "That handsome young lawyer must have low self-esteem to have settled for that unattractive older woman." "Perhaps he chose that woman because she has millions in the bank."

Most important, Murstein's theory suggests that opposites definitely do *not* attract. In love relationships, as in childhood and adolescent friendships, the driving force is **homogamy** (similarity). We want to find a soul mate, a person

stimulus-value-role theory Murstein's mate-selection theory that suggests similar people pair up and that our path to commitment progresses through three phases (called the stimulus, value-comparison, and role phases).

stimulus phase In Murstein's theory, the initial mate-selection stage, in which we make judgments about a potential partner based on external characteristics such as appearance.

value-comparison phase In Murstein's theory, the second mate-selection stage, in which we make judgments about a partner on the basis of similar values and interests.

role phase In Murstein's theory, the final mate-selection stage, in which committed partners work out their future life together.

homogamy The principle that we select a mate who is similar to us.

who matches us, not just in external status, but also in interests and attitudes about life.

Our personal choices promote homogamy. We actively put ourselves in situations that give us a sense of flow. If your passion is politics, you might join the college Democrats and meet your soul mate. If you are devoted to your religion, you could find the love of your life at a local Bible study group. The fact that "birds of a feather" naturally flock together actually has a fascinating, not-so-obvious benefit. As you will see in the next chapter, sharing common passions helps keep marital passion alive.

Homogamy is also promoted by our need to have our partner mesh with our family and friends. It is an illusion that people choose a mate entirely on their own. Because we enter the landscape of adult love embedded in a network of other relationships, the input of family and friends weighs heavily in our romantic choices. So you actively select someone who will get along with your Mom and Dad (if you are close to your parents). It's certainly going to make things much easier if friends really like your significant other, too. Conversely, if your other attachment figures criticize your partner ("He's not right for you"), wouldn't you have second thoughts about your choice? (See Le and others, 2010.)

So far, I have stressed the importance of finding a similar mate. But the issue is deeper than that. Actually, it's best to choose a partner who is similar to "our ideal self"—the person we would like to be. In a fascinating series of studies, researchers found that, when people believe their significant other embodies key elements of their best self ("I fell in love with him because he's incredibly smart, and that's always been my goal"), they tend to grow emotionally as people, becoming more like their ideal. Moreover, prizing a mate's best qualities ("He's my intellectual role model") has another benefit. When couples idealize and value each other's strengths, relationships tend to grow more loving over time (Rusbult and others, 2009).

David Young-Wolff/Photo Edit

Admiring each other's talents in their shared life passion ("I love how brilliant my significant other is at science. I want to be just like that") predicts future happiness for this young couple. It also may make these people feel like they are becoming superior scientists, just from being together.

If you are currently in a relationship, you might list the specific qualities that attracted you to your significant other. What do these attributes say about your personal goals? Do you feel that being together is helping you grow as a human being in these important areas of life?

The bottom-line message is that, in love relationships, the main principle is "the more similar, the better." Along one dimension, however, it may be best to choose a partner who is the opposite of you. When psychologists asked unattached undergraduates to describe their ideal mate, in accordance with the homogamy principle, the young people selected someone with a similar personality. But when the researchers actually examined happiness among long-married couples, they found that people tended to get along best when one partner was more dominant and the other more submissive (Markey & Markey, 2007).

Logically, it makes sense that matching up two strong personalities might not be good for romantic bliss (you'd probably fight). Two passive partners might be destined to frustrate each other ("Why doesn't my lover take the lead?"). Yes, it's best to be similar in many ways, but not all!

New Looks at Love: Irrationality, Unpredictability, and Attachment Styles

So far, I have looked at love as a realistic process of matching up. We choose people based on homogamy. We get involved in stages. We select a person that embodies our ideal self. But romance is more irrational and unpredictable in the real world.

TABLE 10.7: Some Major Positive (+) and Negative (–) Turning Points in a Relationship

Personal Compatibility/Homogamy

We spent a lot of time together. +

We had a big fight. –

We had similar interests. +

Compatibility with Family and Friends

My friends kept saying that Sue was bad for me. –

I fit right in with his family. +

Her dad just hated me. –

Other Random Forces

I just turned 21, so I don't want to be tied down to anyone. –

The guy I used to date started calling me. –

If you are in a relationship, have you experienced any of these turning points?

Source: Surra, Hughes, & Jacquet, 1999.

Irrationality and Unpredictability

Actually, researchers find that, rather than seeing a realistic image, people in satisfying relationships view their mates through rose-colored glasses (Murray & Holmes, 1997). They inflate their partner's virtues (Murray and others, 2000). They overestimate the extent to which they and their mate are alike in values and goals (Murray and others, 2002). So science confirms George Bernard Shaw's classic observation: "Love is a gross exaggeration of the difference between one person and everyone else."

Moreover, the inner experience of commitment does not translate neatly into stages such as stimulus, value-comparison, and role phases. People have doubts and ups and downs; their feelings about the relationship and their partner fluctuate.

To get insights into this emotional ebb and flow, researchers asked couples who were seriously dating to graph their chances (from 0 to 100 percent) of marrying their partner (Surra & Hughes, 1997; Surra, Hughes, & Jacquet, 1999). They then had the young people return each month to chart changes in their commitment and asked them to describe the reasons for any dramatic relationship turning points, for better or worse.

You can see examples of these turning points in Table 10.7. Notice that relationships do often hinge on homogamy issues ("This person is really right for me") and the input of family and friends. Other causes may be turning points, too—from social comparisons ("Our relationship seems better than theirs") to the insight, "I'm too young to get involved."

Sometimes, people know when their relationship has reached a turning point. As one woman reported, "He told me to sit down and . . . and then he just looked at me and he said, 'I love you'" (quoted in Surra, Hughes, & Jacquet, 1999, p. 139). At other times, everything seems to be going according to schedule, when an event that has nothing to do with you or your partner intrudes: "I talked to my dad . . . who felt he got married too young so he was a little bit more encouraging against getting married" (quoted in Surra, Hughes, & Jacquet, 1999, p. 138).

Given that romances have normal ups and downs, what forces weigh *heaviest* in predicting whether a relationship survives? To provide this crystal ball, researchers summarized the results of an amazing 137 studies that followed dating couples over 30 years. A top ranking predictor, they found, was mentioned at the beginning of this section: idealizing your partner ("My mate is the greatest!"). Coming in a close second was the support of family and friends. But perhaps the strongest predictor was being intensely committed to one's mate (Le and others, 2010).

TABLE 10.8: Fun Research Findings Relating to Finding Love (and Sex)

Question 1: *Who tends to say, "I love you" first, males or females?*

Research answer: Surprisingly, one study suggests, it's men—and the authors believe, that's because males may say "I love you" because they want to have sex and hope this confession will get their partner to that place. In support of this idea, female "I love you" statements *after* a sexual relationship begins may make men (especially those not interested in having a serious relationship) nervous; while "I love you's" from men after sex make women feel more secure.

Question 2: *Does a high campus ratio of females to males affect women's dating practices and attitudes?*

Research answer: Unfortunately, it does. When women greatly outnumber men at a given college, female undergrads are more likely to be sexually active, but less apt to have a boyfriend. Women on that campus also evaluate the men at their college more negatively—probably because these guys are clearly calling the shots!

Question 3: *Who makes more promises to a romantic partner, and who is most apt to keep those "vows"?*

Research answer: No surprise, people who care deeply about their partners make more lavish promises in relationships. The problem, however, is that the main predictor of *keeping* promises is not how deeply you care, but the personality trait called *conscientiousness*. Therefore, the very lovers who impulsively promise their mate "the moon" may be least emotionally equipped to deliver on what they say!

Sources: Question 1: Brantley, Knox, & Zusman, 2002, and Ackerman, Griskevicious, & Li, 2011; Question 2: Uecker & Regnerus, 2010; Question 3: Peetz & Kammrath, 2011.

adult attachment styles The different ways in which adults relate to romantic partners, based on Mary Ainsworth's infant attachment styles. (Adult attachment styles are classified as secure, or preoccupied/ambivalent insecure, or avoidant/dismissive insecure.)

preoccupied/ambivalent insecure attachment An excessively clingy, needy style of relating to loved ones.

avoidant/dismissive insecure attachment A standoffish, excessively disengaged style of relating to loved ones.

secure attachment The genuine intimacy that is ideal in love relationships.

But if you now feel reassured that your relationship's fate depends mainly on the depth of your emotional connection, I must emphasize that "commitment" differs from being intensely in love. When I asked my brother why he broke up with a woman he dated throughout his twenties, he admitted, "Yes, she and I were deeply in love, but I married the first person I met when I was 35 and finally felt ready to settle down."

Table 10.8 lists additional, fun research findings relating to the realities of real-world love. Now, let's take a different perspective, as I shift from exploring relationships to examining the personalities of the partners in a romance.

Adult Attachment Styles

Think back to Chapter 4's discussion of the different infant attachment styles. Remember that Mary Ainsworth (1973) found that *securely attached* babies run to Mom with hugs and kisses when she appears in the room. *Avoidant* infants act cold, aloof, and indifferent in the Strange Situation when the caregiver returns. *Anxious-ambivalent* babies are overly clingy, afraid to explore the toys, and angry and inconsolable when their caregiver arrives. Now, think of your own romantic relationships, or the love relationships of family members or friends. Wouldn't these same attachment categories apply to adult romantic love? Cindy Hazan and Phillip Shaver (1987) had the same insight: Let's draw on Ainsworth's dimensions to classify people into different **adult attachment styles**.

People with a **preoccupied/ambivalent** type of insecure attachment fall quickly and deeply in love (see the How Do We Know box on the next page). But, because they are engulfing and needy, they often end up being rejected or feeling chronically unfulfilled. Adults with an **avoidant/dismissive** form of insecure attachment are at the opposite end of the spectrum—withholding, aloof, reluctant to engage. You may have dated this kind of person, someone whose main mottos seem to be "stay independent," "don't share," "avoid getting close" (Feeney, 1999).

Securely attached people are fully open to love. They give their partners space to differentiate, yet are firmly committed. Like Ainsworth's secure infants, their faces light up when they talk about their partner. Their joy in their love shines through. Decades of studies exploring these different attachment styles show that insecurely attached adults have trouble with relationships. Securely attached people are more successful in the world of love.

How do we know . . .

that a person is securely or insecurely attached?

How do developmentalists classify adults as either securely or insecurely attached? In the *current relationship interview*, they ask people questions about their goals and feelings about their romantic relationships; for example, "What happens when either of you is in trouble? Can you rely on each other to be there emotionally?" Trained evaluators then code the responses.

People are labeled securely attached if they coherently describe the pluses and minuses of their own behavior and of the relationship, if they talk freely about their desire for intimacy, and if they adopt an other-centered perspective, seeing nurturing the other person's development as a primary goal. Those who describe their relationship in formal, stilted ways, emphasize "autonomy issues," or talk about the advantages of being together in non-intimate terms ("We are buying a house"; "We go places"), are classified as avoidant/dismissive. Those who express total dependence ("I can't function unless she is nearby"), anger about not being treated correctly, or fears of being left are classified as preoccupied/ambivalent.

This in-depth interview technique is time intensive. But many attachment researchers argue that it reveals a person's attachment style better than questionnaires in which people simply check "yes" or "no" to indicate whether items on a scale apply to them.

Photodisc/Getty

Secure attachment

- **Definition:** Capable of genuine intimacy in relationships.
- **Signs:** Empathic, sensitive, able to reach out emotionally. Balances own needs with those of partner. Has affectionate, caring interactions. Probably in a loving, long-term relationship.

© Corbis/SuperStock

Avoidant/dismissive insecure attachment

- **Definition:** Unable to get close in relationships.
- **Signs:** Uncaring, aloof, emotionally distant. Unresponsive to loving feelings. Abruptly disengages at signs of involvement. Unlikely to be in a long-term relationship.

Bill Aron/Photo Edit, Inc.

Preoccupied/ambivalent insecure attachment

- **Definition:** Needy and engulfing in relationships.
- **Signs:** Excessively jealous, suffocating. Needs continual reassurance of being totally loved. Unlikely to be in a loving, long-term relationship.

Securely attached adults have happier marriages. They report more satisfying romances (Feeney, 1999; Mikulincer and others, 2002; Morgan & Shaver, 1999). Securely attached adults are more sensitive to their partner's signals. They freely support their partners during times of need (Davila & Kashy, 2009). Not being terrified about being "left," securely attached people are more forgiving (Burnette and others,

2009) and compassionate toward their mates (Sprecher & Fehr, 2010). Using the metaphor of mother–infant attachment, described in Chapter 4, people with secure attachments are wonderful dancers. They excel at being emotionally responsive and in tune.

Recall that Bowlby and Ainsworth believe that the dance of attachment between the caregiver and baby is the basis for feeling securely attached in infancy and for dancing well in other relationships in life. If you listen to friends anguishing about their relationship problems, you will hear similar ideas: "The reason I act clingy and jealous is that, during my childhood, I felt unloved." "It's hard for me to warm up and respond to kisses because my mom was rejecting and cold." How enduring are adult attachment styles, and how much can they change?

To answer this question, researchers measured the attachment styles of several hundred women at intervals over two years (Cozzarelli and others, 2003). They found that almost one-half of the women had changed categories over that time. So the good news is that we can change our attachment status from insecure to secure. And—as will come as no surprise to many readers—we can also move in the opposite direction, temporarily feeling insecurely attached after a terrible experience with love. The best way to understand attachment styles, then, is as somewhat enduring and consistent, arising, in part, from our current experiences in love.

One reason attachment styles stay stable is that they may operate as a self-fulfilling prophecy. A preoccupied, clingy person does tend to be rejected repeatedly. An avoidant individual remains isolated because piercing that armored shell takes such a heroic effort. A secure, loving person gets more secure over time because his caring behavior evokes warm, loving responses (Davila & Kashy, 2009).

By now, you are probably impressed with the power of the attachment-styles perspective to predict real-world love. But alert readers might notice that these *correlational* findings have conceptual flaws: Let's say, for instance, that a person labels his childhood as unhappy, is classified as having an insecure attachment style, and experiences relationship distress. It's tempting to say that "poor parenting" *caused* this insecure worldview, which then produced the current problems; but couldn't the causal chain go in the opposite way? "I'm not getting along with my partner, so I believe love can't work out, and it *must be* my parents fault." Or, couldn't these *self-reports* be caused by a third force having nothing to do with attachment: being depressed. If your general worldview is gloomy, wouldn't you see both your childhood and current relationship as dissatisfying, and also have an "avoidant" or "preoccupied" attachment style?

Still, as a framework for understanding people (and ourselves), the styles perspective has great appeal. Who can't relate to having had a lover (or friend or parent) with a "dismissing" or "preoccupied" attachment? Don't the defining qualities of secure attachment give us a beautiful roadmap for how we personally should relate to the significant others in our lives? Attachment theory allows us to look at *every* love relationship through a fascinating new lens.

INTERVENTIONS: Evaluating Your Own Relationship

How can you use *all* of the insights in this section to ensure smoother-sailing romance? Select someone who is similar in values and interests and be sensitive to how this person meshes with the people you really care about. Choose someone who embodies the person you want to be in important ways—but it's best if you each differ a bit on the need to take charge. Focus on the outstanding "special qualities" of your significant other. Be utterly committed to your mate (more about this in the next chapter). Look for a partner who is securely attached and secure as a human being. Take care, however, to note the message of the research on relationship turning points and the fact that sometimes "timing is all": If things don't work out, it easily may have *nothing* to do with you, your partner, or any problem basic to how well you get along! If you want to evaluate

TABLE 10.9: Evaluating Your Own Relationship: A Section Summary Checklist

	Yes	No
1. Are you and your partner similar in interests and values? You don't have to be clones of each other, but the research shows that the more similar you are in attitudes and basic worldviews, the greater your chances of a happy relationship.*	❒	❒
2. Do your other "attachment figures," such as close friends and family, like your partner? Not everyone needs to adore your partner, but if your most central attachment figures really dislike your partner, problems may arise.	❒	❒
3. Do you each believe that in key ways your partner embodies your ideal self? Seeing your partner as someone you want to be like predicts staying together happily as well as growing emotionally toward your ideal.	❒	❒
4. Do you see your partner as utterly wonderful and unique? Deciding that this person has no human flaws is not necessary—but seeing your partner as "unique and special" also predicts being happy together.	❒	❒
5. Are you committed to your mate? If you and you partner have minor arguments, that's fine, but you should both be invested in having the relationship last.	❒	❒
6. Is your partner able to fully reach out in love, neither intensely jealous nor aloof? Some jealousy or hesitation about commitment can be normal, but in general, your partner should be securely attached and able to love.	❒	❒

If you checked "yes" for all six of these questions, your relationship is in excellent shape. If you checked "no" for every question, your "relationship" does not exist! One or two no's mixed in with yes's suggest areas that need additional work.

***Recall that it may be best if one of you has a stronger, or more dominant, personality.**

your own relationship, you might take the questionnaire based on these chapter points in Table 10. 9.

So far, I have just begun my exploration into those adult agendas: love and work. In the next chapter, we'll focus directly on that core adult love relationship—marriage—and talk in far more depth about careers. Then stay tuned, in Chapter 12, for exciting findings exploring how we change as people during adulthood, and tips for constructing a fulfilling adult life.

TYING IT ALL TOGETHER

1. If Latoya is discussing with James how relationships have changed in recent decades, which statement should she *not* make?
   a. Today, there is more interracial and inter-ethnic dating.
   b. Today, same-sex relationships are much more acceptable.
   c. Today, people who date outside of their ethnic group lose contact with their own ethnic roots.

2. Natasha and Akbar met at a friend's New Year's Eve party and just started dating. They are about to find out whether they share similar interests, backgrounds, and world-views. This couple is in Murstein's (choose one) *stimulus/value-comparison/role* phase of romantic relationships.

3. Catherine tells Kelly, "To have a happy relationship, find someone as much like you as possible." In what ways might Catherine be somewhat wrong?

4. Kita is clingy and always feels rejected. Rena runs away from intimate relationships. Sam is affectionate and loving. Match the attachment status of each person to one of the following alternatives: *secure, avoidant-dismissive,* or *preoccupied.*

Answers to the Tying It All Together questions can be found at the end of this chapter.

SUMMARY

Emerging Adulthood

Psychologists have identified a new life phase called **emerging adulthood.** This in-between, not-quite-fully-adult time of life, beginning after high school and tapering off by the late twenties, involves testing out adult **roles.** The main challenge of this least-structured life stage is taking adult responsibility for our lives. This new, developed-world life stage differs from person to person and country to country. In southern Europe, young people typically live at home until they marry and have great trouble becoming financially independent. In Scandinavia, **cohabitation** and having babies before marriage are widespread. Here, government help, plus a norm stressing independence, make **nest-leaving** at age 18 routine. In the United States, with its income inequalities, there is tremendous variability, with people moving backward and forward on the way to constructing an adult life.

Today, we often think of the beginning of emerging adulthood as leaving the nest. But, although parent-child relationships often improve after emerging adults move out, the common idea that we must leave home to "act adult" is incorrect. Nest-leaving has become less common since the Great Recession. Ethnic-minority young people, in particular, may stay in the nest to help their families as "full adults."

Social clock pressures, or **age norms,** set the boundaries of emerging adulthood. Exploring is **on time,** or appropriate, in the twenties, but **off time** if it extends well into the thirties. Although society sets the overall social clock guidelines, people also have their own personal timetables for when to get married and reach other adult markers. Social clock pressures, plus other forces, make emerging adulthood both an exhilarating life stage and a time of special stress.

Constructing an Identity

Deciding on one's **identity,** Erikson's first task in becoming an adult, is the major challenge facing emerging adults. Erikson believed that exploring various possibilities and taking time to ponder this question is critical to developing a solid adult self. At the opposite pole lies **role confusion**—drifting and seeing no adult future.

James Marcia identified four **identity statuses: identity diffusion** (drifting aimlessly), **identity foreclosure** (leaping into an identity without any thought), **moratorium** (exploring different pathways), and **identity achievement** (settling on an identity). In contrast to Marcia's idea that we progress through these stages and reach achievement in the twenties, people shift from status to status throughout life. Emerging adults may not need to sample different fields to develop a secure career identity, as long as they conduct a **moratorium in depth** search. Finding a secure **ethnic** (or **biracial** or **multiracial identity)** is a special challenge for minority youth.

Finding a Career

Researchers find that teenagers have high career goals. The downside is that many people may not be able to fulfill these dreams. Young people who enjoy mastering challenges ("workers") seem best set up to cope with the bumpy realities of life. However, during emerging adulthood, people often get more conscientious and gain self-control. "Troubled teens," in particular, tend to grow emotionally if they lock into a satisfying job.

Flow is a feeling of total absorption in a challenging task. The hours seem to pass like minutes, intrinsic motivation is high, and our skills are in balance with the demands of a given task. Flow states can alert us to our ideal careers.

Although higher education is more necessary than ever to get a decent job, and most young people in the United States enroll in college, less than a third complete a degree. Economics looms large in who drops out, as high-performing young people from low-income backgrounds are less apt to finish school than their affluent counterparts. While there may be advantages to leaving college and coming back, we need to make it easier for financially strapped young people to get a B.A. and offer noncollege alternatives that lead directly to jobs. The absence of a real **school-to-work transition** in the United States is a national crisis.

Ideally, the college experience should be a time of inner growth. Get the best professors (and reach out to them); explore career-relevant work; become involved in campus activities; and reach out to students of different backgrounds to make the most of these special years.

Finding Love

Erikson's second emerging-adult task, **intimacy**—finding committed love—has changed dramatically in recent decades. Interethnic relationships are more common and can help solidify one's own ethnic identity. Same-sex relationships are "out in the open," although **homophobia** still exists, and teens grappling with this identity can suffer emotional turmoil. When gay young people come out to their families—if they generally have close, loving relationships with their parents—they are not in danger of losing that enduring love.

Stimulus-value-role theory spells out a three-stage process leading to marriage. First, we select a potential partner who looks appropriate (the **stimulus phase**); then, during the **value-comparison** phase, we find out whether that person shares our interests and worldview. Finally, during the **role phase,** we plan our lives together. **Homogamy,** people's tendency to choose similar partners and partners of equivalent status to themselves, is the main principle underlying this theory.

The chances of finding a homogamous partner are enhanced by the fact that people select activities where they find similar others and strive to have their social group (family and friends) approve of their mate. Actually, however, it's best to choose a partner who is similar to our "ideal self," and there is one exception to the principle that selecting by similarity is best: Relationships in which one person is dominant and the other partner is submissive make for the most harmonious romantic life. A good deal of irrationality is involved in romance. We tend to idealize a partner and exaggerate our similarities. Relationships have turning points rather than progressing in a smooth, patterned way. Idealizing a partner, support from other attachment figures, and feeling intensely committed are the main forces predicting which romances endure.

Researchers have spelled out three **adult attachment styles.** Adults ranked as insecurely attached—either **preoccupied/ambivalent** (overly clingy and engulfing) or **avoidant/dismissive** (overly aloof and detached)—have poorer-quality relationships. **Securely attached** adults tend to be successful in love and marriage. Although we can question the validity of this research, the adult attachment-styles framework offers fascinating insights into how people vary in their approach to love.

KEY TERMS

emerging adulthood, p. 300
role, p. 300
cohabitation, p. 301
nest-leaving, p. 301
social clock, p. 304
age norms, p. 304
on time, p. 304
off time, p. 304
identity, p. 305
role confusion, p. 306
identity statuses, p. 306
identity diffusion, p. 306
identity foreclosure, p. 306
moratorium, p. 307
identity achievement, p. 307
moratorium in depth, p. 308
ethnic identity, p. 308
biracial or multiracial identity, p. 308
flow, p. 311
school-to-work transition, p. 313
intimacy, p. 316
homophobia, p. 318
stimulus-value-role theory, p. 320
stimulus phase, p. 320
value-comparison phase, p. 320
role phase, p. 320
homogamy, p. 320
adult attachment styles, p. 323
preoccupied/ambivalent insecure attachment, p. 323
avoidant/dismissive insecure attachment, p. 323
secure attachment, p. 323

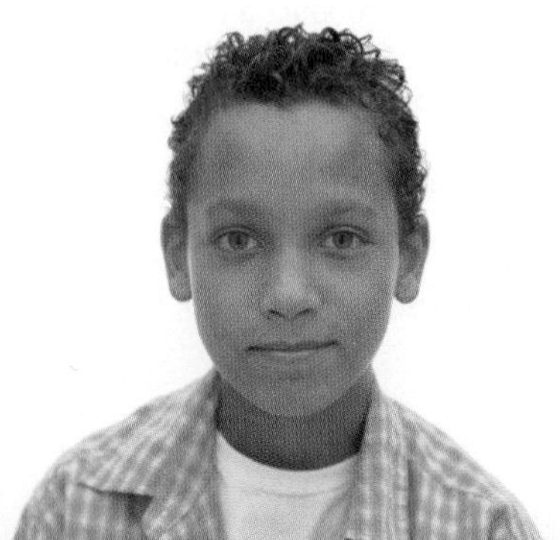

ANSWERS TO TYING IT ALL TOGETHER QUIZZES

Emerging into Adulthood

1. b
2. False
3. Martha, who is starting a new career at age 50; she will be most worried about the ticking of the social clock.
4. John, who can't wait to start a family

Constructing an Identity

1. drifting; diffusion
2. foreclosure; moratorium
3. a & b
4. False

Finding a Career

1. You should tell these parents that, realistically, their son may have more trouble constructing a work life. But, if he finds a satisfying job, chances are he will settle down and become more mature.
2. flow
3. Josiah might argue that prior academic performance predicts college completion, with low odds of finishing for high school graduates with a C-average or below. Jocasta should reply that money is crucial because academically talented low-income kids are far less likely to finish college than their affluent peers, and drop-outs cite "financial issues" as the main reason for leaving. She also might mention the survey showing that financing school is a major headache, beginning in freshman year.
4. As trouble paying for college (and juggling work with school) is the main reason people report dropping out, you might suggest: 1) Insisting colleges provide financial counseling and increase campus work study opportunities; 2) offering tax breaks to community employers that hire students; 3) widening financial-aid options, especially for low income, part-time students, and allowing their credits to widely transfer; and 4) the rest is up to you.
5. b

Finding Love

1. c
2. *value-comparison* phase
3. Actually, it's best to find a partner who is similar to our "ideal self." Also, people who have dominant personalities might be better off with more submissive mates (and vice versa).
4. Kita's status is preoccupied. Rena is avoidant/dismissing. Sam is securely attached.

Chapter 11

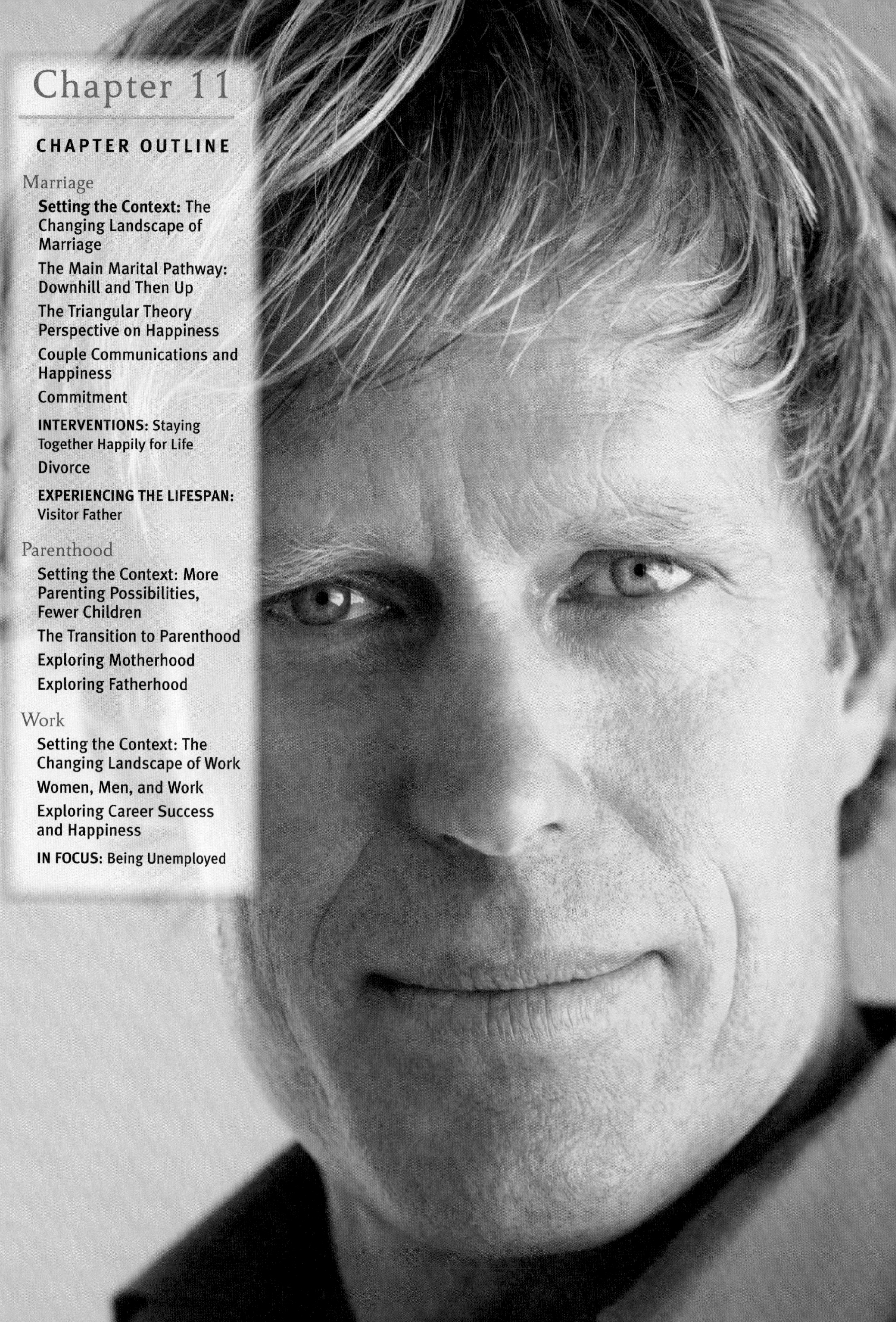

CHAPTER OUTLINE

Relationships and Roles

Home at 3 A.M. from closing the restaurant and hopefully to bed by 4. Then, Doreen wakes up and gets the kids ready for school to arrive at her accountant job at 9.

David's first marriage to Clara ended in a disastrous divorce. He feels blessed to have this second chance for happiness at age 35. David and Doreen met at a community-wide faith celebration. They share the same values. They understand that marriage involves commitment, sacrifice, and forgiveness. They are together in their passion for the Lord. David is trying to be the best possible stepdad—showing the twins massive affection, trying not to come on too strong. But his main mission, this time, is to be the best possible spouse. David wants to make enough money for Doreen to fulfill her dream of going back to school to get her master's in social work. He would love to have the funds to permit his wife to quit her high-stress job and be able to spend more time with the kids.

That's why David just "supplemented" his store manager position with a weekend shift running the local health food store. Yes, the 70-plus-hour workweeks will be exhausting, but having endured that debilitating year in his twenties unemployed, David is thrilled. What a blessing—in this economy—to find not just one, but two decently paying jobs. It's a 24/7 struggle, but this marriage must work for life!

Do you know someone like David who is struggling to be a caring husband, a sensitive father, and trying to support his family? Perhaps you know a woman like Doreen who feels overwhelmed by a high-pressure job, wants to spend more time with her children, and dreams of a more fulfilling career. If so, you know a twenty-first-century adult.

This chapter is devoted to the main role challenges involved in being adult. Here, I'll be building on last chapter's emerging adult love and career discussion by focusing directly on marriage, parenthood, and work. Before you begin your reading, you might want to take the family and work quiz in Table 11.1 on page 332. In the following pages, you will learn *why* each stereotype is right or wrong.

Although I will discuss them separately, I must emphasize that we cannot look at marriage, parenthood, and career as separate parts of life. Our work situation determines if we decide to get married. Having children changes a marriage and, as with Doreen in the vignette, affects our feelings about our career. As *developmental systems theory* suggests, marriage, parenthood, and career are tri-directional, interlocking roles. Moreover, how we approach these core adult roles depends on the time in history and the society in which we live.

TABLE 11.1: Stereotypes About Family and Work: A Quiz

Write "True" or "False" next to each of the following statements. To see how accurate your beliefs about family and work are, look at the correct answers, printed upside down below the table. As you read through the chapter, you'll find out exactly why each statement is true or false.

______ 1. Americans today are not as interested in getting married as they were in the past.

______ 2. Poor people often don't get married because they are basically less interested in having a permanent commitment.

______ 3. People are happiest in the honeymoon phase of a marriage.

______ 4. Having children brings married couples closer.

______ 5. People who don't have children are self-absorbed and narcissistic.

______ 6. Becoming a mother makes a woman more mature.

______ 7. Mothers used to spend more time with their children than they do today.

______ 8. The average workweek for full-time workers is 40 hours per week.

______ 9. Males and females are now totally equal in the world of work.

______ 10. People who are well educated and have wealthy parents "have it made" career-wise—even when they feel depressed and/or bad about themselves.

______ 11. The main reason unemployment is so difficult lies in economics—the challenge of having to survive without a salary.

Answers: 1. F, 2. F, 3. T, 4. F, 5. F, 6. F, 7. F, 8. T, 9. F, 10. F, 11. F

Marriage

Ask friends to describe their ideal marriage (or relationship) and you may hear phrases such as "soul mates," "equal sharing," and "someone who fulfills my innermost self" (Amato, 2007; Dew & Wilcox, 2011). This vision of "lovers for life," who work and share the housework equally, is a product of living in the contemporary, developed world.

Setting the Context: The Changing Landscape of Marriage

Throughout much of history, as I implied in Chapter 10, people often got married based on practical concerns. With many marriages being arranged by the brides' and grooms' parents, and daily life being so difficult, couples did not have the luxury of marrying for love. In addition, in the not-so-distant past, life expectancy was so low that the typical marriage only lasted a decade or two before one partner died.

Then, in the early twentieth century, as conditions improved and medical advances allowed people to routinely live into later life, in Western nations, we developed the idea that everyone should get married in their twenties and be lovers for a half-century or more. The traditional 1950s *Leave It to Beaver* marriage, with defined gender roles, reflected this idealized vision of enduring love (Amato, 2007; Cherlin, 2004; Coontz, 1992).

In the last third of the twentieth century, Western ideas about marriage took another dramatic turn. The women's movement told us that women should have careers and husbands and wives should share the child care. As a result of the 1960s lifestyle revolution, which stressed personal fulfillment, we rejected the idea that people should stay in an unhappy marriage. We could get divorced, decide to have babies without being married, and even choose not to get married at all.

H. Armstrong Roberts/Corbis

Ryan McVay/Getty Images

From the 1950s stay-at-home mom to the two-career marriage with fully engaged dads—over the last third of the twentieth century, a revolution occurred in our ideas about married life. How do you feel about these lifestyle changes?

deinstitutionalization of marriage The decline in marriage and the emergence of alternate family forms that occurred during the last third of the twentieth century.

The outcome was a late-twentieth-century change that social scientists call the **deinstitutionalization of marriage** (Cherlin, 2004, 2010). This phrase means that marriage has been transformed from the standard adult "institution" into a more optional choice.

Table 11.2 shows statistics related to this change in the United States: a tremendous rise in divorce and more people living alone. The most crucial shift relates to the standard idea that marriage comes before a baby carriage. During the 1950s, if a U.S. woman dared to reverse that order by getting pregnant without a spouse, her family might ship her off to a home for unwed mothers, or insist that she marry the dad (the infamously named "shotgun marriage"). A half-century later, with 2 in 5 women having babies "out of wedlock" and people taking longer to marry after giving birth (Gibson-Davis, 2011), the disconnect between motherhood and marriage—especially for less well-educated Americans—is a predictable path.

Still, marriage practices—including thoughts about whether it's OK to have a baby "out of wedlock"—vary from person to person and from culture to culture. To get global insights into this diversity, let's travel to the Middle East and then visit Scandinavia again.

Traditional Middle Eastern Model: Male-Dominated Marriage

As of this writing, the 1960s lifestyle revolution has not penetrated Islamic nations, such as Egypt and Iran, where getting married is still the *only* acceptable life path. Actually, Islam does not frown on highly educated women. In Iran—as in the West—more

TABLE 11.2: Some "Symptoms" of the Deinstitutionalization of Marriage in the United States

Sign	1960–1970 (percent)*	Early Twenty-First Century (percent)
Childbirths outside of marriage	5	39.6
Probability of marriage ending in divorce	about 14	about 50
Percentage of married couples	71	53
Children living with one parent	9	40
People living alone	17	27

*Rough data from 1960 and 1970.

Sources: Amato, 2010; U.S. Census Bureau, 2008; U.S. Department of Commerce, 2007.

AP Photo/Enric F. Marti

Jonathan Fernstrom/Getty Images

If you talked to this couple living in Cairo and then visited this Scandinavian family enjoying a picnic by a lake, the scenery change would be symbolic of a totally different approach to married life. In fact, there would be a fifty-fifty chance that the Swedish parents would not be married at all!

females enroll in universities than men (Abbas-Shavazi, Mohammad, & McDonald, 2008). However, according to Islamic law, when a woman gets married, she is expected to stay at home. In Iran and many Middle Eastern countries, people do not agree with the Western view that each sex should have equal rights (Moghadam, 2004). Husbands can forbid their wives to work if they feel that the woman's job will interfere with family life. While getting a divorce is difficult for females—involving lengthy court battles—until recently, if a man wanted to end his marriage, he could simply tell his partner, "I no longer want you around" (Abbas-Shavazi, Mohammad, & McDonald, 2008).

Given these conditions, it is no surprise that a young, unmarried Egyptian woman gave this unromantic answer when a researcher asked what she hoped for from married life: "I don't believe in love. The only kind of love [I know] is for my mother and sister . . . I want to marry a man who is rich, successful and able to take responsibility" (Amin & Al-Bassusi, 2004, p. 1295).

Scandinavian Social Norm: Marriage Doesn't Matter

In comparison, Scandinavian ideas about marriage seem to be from a different planet. With more than one-half of all babies being born to single mothers in Norway, Sweden, and Denmark, in these Northern European nations, having children is irrelevant to getting a wedding ring (Cherlin, 2004; Syltevik, 2010). With cohabitation rates outpacing marriage, in Sweden, the deinstitutionalization of marriage is complete (Thomson & Bernhardt, 2010). Scandinavian adults are not anti-marriage. Many do ultimately wed. It's just that in Northern Europe, living single and cohabiting are fully acceptable routes to a fulfilling life (Kiernan, 2002, 2004).

The United States: Dreaming of Marriage for Life

This is not true in the United States, where cohabitation and staying single are widely seen as far less appealing than having a wedding ring (check out Table 11.3 for the truth about some stereotypes related to cohabitation and marriage). Despite the dramatic rise in divorce, recent polls show roughly 8 out of 10 U.S. young people still plan to be married—the same fraction as in the past (Manning, Longmore, & Giordano, 2007). But developed-world young people are realists. Before planning a wedding, they want to have certain foundations in place.

Think about your requirements for getting married if you are single—or, if you are married, think of your personal goals before you were wed. In addition to finding the right person, if you are like most people, you probably believe that making this commitment demands reaching a certain place in your development. It's important to have a solid sense of identity (see Chapter 10) and to be financially secure (Gibson-Davis, 2009; Umberson, Pudrovska, & Reczek, 2010). Therefore, as you saw in Chapter 10, because we select partners according to *homogamy*, the marriage market for low-income adults—both male and female—is poor (Gibson-Davis, 2009). Even when couples have children and are committed to each other, they can find it difficult to move from living together to getting engaged.

Read what Candace, a 25-year-old, had to say about her marriage plans:

> Um, we have certain things that we want to do before we get married. We both want very good jobs. . . . He's been looking out for jobs everywhere and we— . . . we're trying. We just want to have—we gotta have everything before we say, "Let's get married."
>
> (quoted in Smock, Manning, & Porter, 2005, p. 690)

And 30-year-old Donald put it more bluntly:

> [I would marry her] if I was to hit the lottery and could take her somewhere and we wouldn't have to worry about no problems for the rest of our life.
>
> (quoted in Smock, Manning & Porter, 2005, p. 691)

TABLE 11.3: Cohabitation and Marriage: U.S. Stereotypes and Realities

Cohabitation

STEREOTYPE 1: YOUNG PEOPLE LIVE TOGETHER TO DECIDE IF THEY SHOULD MARRY THEIR PARTNER.

Research answer: Increasingly false. In a recent poll of emerging adult cohabitators, this "trial marriage" reason for deciding to live together was infrequently mentioned (Sassler & Miller, 2011). Cohabitating couples said they moved in together to "see each other more often" or for practical, non-romantic reasons, such as to pool expenses and/or get out of a parent's house. Interestingly, here there was a social class difference. Low-income cohabitators cited economic reasons for living together. Middle-class people were more apt to view cohabitation as a step on the pathway to marriage. Bottom line: Especially in this difficult economy, contemporary cohabitation motives are diverse.

STEREOTYPE 2: LIVING TOGETHER BEFORE MARRIAGE MAKES COUPLES LESS LIKELY TO GET DIVORCED.

Research answer: Wrong! Cohabitation is consistently correlated with a *higher* subsequent risk of divorce (see Stanley and others, 2011, for a recent example). But one cause may be "selection forces." Religious people, whose values prohibit cohabitation, are more apt to stay married for life. Moreover, when we just consider couples who move in because they are "almost engaged," living together has no impact—neither positive nor negative—on marital success (see Belsky, 2007, for a review). Bottom line: Instead of saying "cohabitation" is simply bad (or good) for marriage, look to the individual couple.

Marriage

STEREOTYPE 1: MARRIED PEOPLE ARE HEALTHIER AND THEY LIVE LONGER.

Research answer: Definitely true. (See Koball and others, 2010, for review.) However, in interpreting this well-documented correlation, we also need to consider "selection forces." Because—as the text suggests—low income adults are less likely to marry, this social class difference partly accounts for why marriage is linked to longevity and health. Still, from sharing sit-down meals, to watching each other's health, to offering emotional support, being in a *good* marriage is indeed probably life enhancing.

STEREOTYPE 2: GETTING MARRIED FORCES EMERGING ADULTS TO ABANDON RISKY, HEALTH-COMPROMISING BEHAVIORS.

Research answer: It's complicated. In studying people *under 26*, researchers (Harris, Lee, & DeLeone, 2010) found that, yes, white men did engage in less binge drinking after they got married. However, especially women tended to gain weight after they wed. So, being married increases the temptation to "let ourselves go" in this important health-related realm.

As these comments imply, rather than blaming a "culture of irresponsibility" (see Murray, 2012), the lack of decent jobs is a major reason why many low-income fathers and mothers never wed (Bianchi & Milkie, 2010). Today, for poverty-level women, having children and being the best possible mother is the main marker of adulthood. Getting married, although it is yearned for, can seem like a hazy, far-in-the-future, unattainable goal (Edin & Kefalas, 2005).

Another goal that can seem hard to reach—for everyone, rich or poor—is managing to stay married for life. I got insights into the awe young people feel about this achievement when a college-student server came up to my husband and me at a local restaurant and shyly asked for our secret when we said we had been married for over 30 years.

Is our dream of finding a soul mate for life too idealistic, given that we never expected people to stay madly in love for 50 or more years? How can we fulfill our dream of staying together for decades when there are so many alternatives to marriage and it is so easy to get divorced? In the next section, I'll focus on this question as I explore the insights that social science research offers about how to have enduring, happy relationships. Let's begin, however, by examining what *typically* happens over time, by tracing how marital happiness normally changes through the years.

The Main Marital Pathway: Downhill and Then Up

Many of us enter marriage (or any love relationship) with blissful expectations. Then, disenchantment sets in. Hundreds of studies conducted over the past 40 years in Western countries show that marital satisfaction is at its peak during the honeymoon and then decreases (Blood & Wolfe, 1960; Glenn, 1990; Lavner & Bradbury, 2010). As the decline—statistically speaking—is steepest during the first few years, some researchers believe that, if people make it beyond four years of marriage, they have passed the main divorce danger zone (Bradbury & Karney, 2004).

Notice the interesting similarity to John Bowlby's ideas about the different attachment phases. In the first year or two of their relationship, couples are in the phase of clear-cut attachment, when they are madly in love and see their significant other as the center of life. As they move into their relationship's *working model* phase—developing more separate lives, getting involved in the wider world—they risk disconnecting from their spouse.

Couples who pass the four-year mark are not out of the woods. During the next decade, as spouses cope with the pressures of work and the stresses of raising children, on average, there is a steady (but slower) decline in love. A first child's reaching puberty produces another dip in happiness, as parents wrestle with the emotional upheavals of the early teenage years (Whiteman, McHale, & Crouter, 2007; see also Chapters 8 and 9).

I must emphasize, however, that these are overall trends. Relationships differ in the way they change. Plus, for *many* married couples, there is a positive change to look forward to later on. According to the **U-shaped curve of marital satisfaction,** after it dips to a low point, couples get happier at the empty nest, when the children leave the house and husbands and wives have the luxury of focusing on each other again (Glenn, 1990; White & Edwards, 1990). And, at retirement, the curve can swing up even more. Compared to middle-aged couples, elderly spouses fight less. They relate in kinder, less combative ways (Carstensen, Gottman, & Levenson, 1995; Windsor & Butterworth, 2010).

Andrew Olney/Masterfile

The so-called "difficulties" of the empty nest are highly overrated. In fact, many couples find that, when the children leave, they can joyously rekindle marital love!

Happy elderly couples actually embody many of the good love-relationship principles spelled out in Chapter 10. They idealize their partners ("Your grandma is the best woman in the world!"); and, you might be interested to know, men who rank themselves as disagreeable are especially likely to display this trait ("How did I deserve this woman? I married a saint!") (O'Rourke and others, 2010). Elderly spouses are similar enough emotionally to literally feel each other's pain. Their blood pressure and heart rates rise when they see their partner in distress (Monin and others, 2010). And, not only is there a strong correlation between marriage and living longer (Koball and others, 2010; also recall Table 11.3), being old-old and *happily married* even mutes feelings of distress when old age disabilities strike (Waldinger & Schultz, 2010). So, we are right to yearn to stay married "till death do us part"—*if* (and this is a very important "if") our marriage is a happy one.

This brings up the topic of individual differences. Many of you may know miserable, long-married 80-year-olds who may be *making* each other ill. Moreover, a significant minority of newlyweds—one in five in a recent longitudinal survey—bucks the depressing happiness downswing to remain as blissful at year 5 as on their wedding day (Lavner & Bradbury, 2010). Why might marital happiness often, but not always, decline? What does the research tell us about staying together happily for life? For answers, let's start by spelling out a familiar psychologist's (that is, from his theory of intelligence, described in Chapter 7) conceptualizations about love—Robert Sternberg's *triangular theory.*

U-shaped curve of marital satisfaction The most common pathway of marital happiness in the West, in which satisfaction is highest at the honeymoon, declines during the child-rearing years, then rises after the children grow up.

triangular theory of love Robert Sternberg's categorization of love relationships into three facets: passion, intimacy, and commitment. When arranged at the points of a triangle, their combinations describe all the different kinds of adult love relationships.

The Triangular Theory Perspective on Happiness

According to Sternberg's (1986, 1988, 2004) **triangular theory of love,** we can break adult love relationships into three components: passion (sexual arousal), intimacy (feelings of closeness), and commitment (typically marriage, but also exclusive, lifelong cohabiting relationships). When we arrange them on a triangle, as you can see in Figure 11.1, we get a portrait of the different kinds of relationships in life.

With passion alone, we have a crush, the fantasy obsession for the girl down the street or a handsome professor we don't really know. With intimacy alone, we have the warm caring that we feel for a best friend. *Romantic love* combines these two qualities. Walk around your campus and you can see this type of relationship. Couples are passionate and clearly know each other well but have probably not made a commitment to form a lifelong bond.

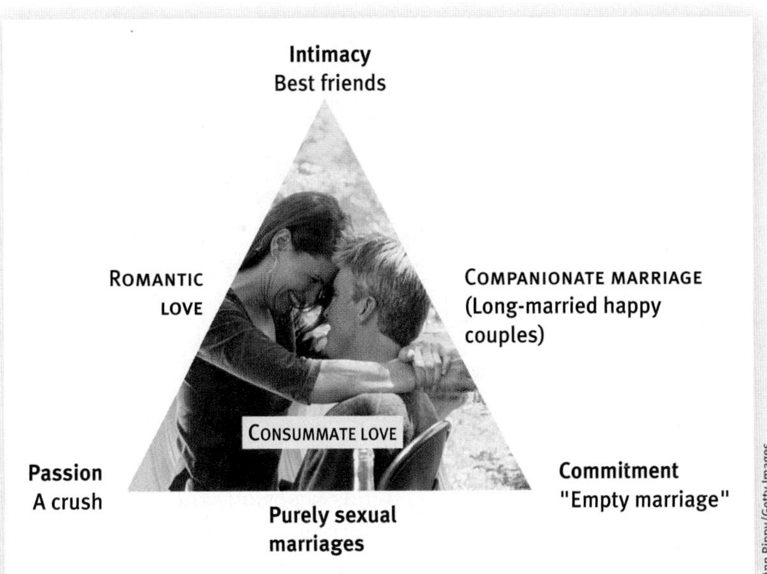

FIGURE 11.1: **Sternberg's triangle: The different types of love:** The three facets of love form the points of this triangle. The relationships along the triangle's sides reflect combinations of the facets. At the center is the ideal relationship: consummate love.

Source: Adapted from Sternberg, 1988.

On the marriage side of the triangle, commitment alone results in "empty marriages." In these emotionally barren, loveless marriages (luckily, fairly infrequent today), people stay together physically but live separate lives. Intimacy plus commitment produces *companionate marriages*, the best-friend relationships that long-married couples may have after passion is gone. Finally, notice from the bottom of the diagram that a few married couples stay together because they share sexual passion and nothing else. The ideal in our culture is the relationship at the triangle's center—one that combines passion, intimacy, and commitment. Sternberg calls this state **consummate love.**

Why is consummate love fragile? One reason, according to Sternberg, is that as familiarity increases, passion naturally falls off. It's hard to keep lusting after your mate when you wake up together day after day for years (Klusmann, 2002). As couples enter into the working-model phase of their marriage, and move out into the world, intimacy can also decline. You and your partner don't talk the way you used to. Work or the children are more absorbing. There is a danger of becoming "ships passing in the night."

Sternberg's theory beautifully alerts us to why marriages normally get less happy over time. But it does not offer clues as to how we can beat the odds and stay romantically connected for life. Actually, a fraction of couples (roughly 1 in 10 people) manage to stay passionate for decades (Acevedo & Aron, 2009). What are these marital role models doing right? For answers, researchers decided to decode the inner experience of falling in love.

When we fall in love, they discovered, our self-concept expands. Efficacy feelings are intense. We feel powerful, competent, special; capable of doing wonderful things (Aron and others, 2002). Given that romantic love causes a joyous feeling of self-expansion, couldn't we teach people to preserve passion and intimacy by encouraging couples to share exciting activities that expand the self?

To test this idea, the psychologists asked married volunteers to list their most exciting activities—the passions that gave them a sense of flow (see Chapter 10). Then, they instructed one group of husbands and wives to engage in the stimulating activities *both* partners had picked out (for example, going to concerts or skiing) frequently over 10 weeks. As they predicted, marital happiness rose dramatically among these couples compared to control groups who were told to engage in pleasant but not especially interesting activities (such as going out to dinner) or just to follow their normal routine (Reissman, Aron, & Bergen, 1993).

So, to stay passionate for decades, people may not need to take trips to Tahiti, or even have candlelit dinners with a mate. The secret is to simply *continue* to engage in the flow-inducing, self-expansion activities that brought couples together in the first place. If you connected through your commitment to your church, take mission trips with your mate. If you met through your passion for marine life, scuba dive with your spouse. The problem, however, is that during the working-model phase of a relationship, the activities that expand ourselves tend to migrate outside of married life. When work does become more compelling (or flow-inducing),

consummate love In Robert Sternberg's triangular theory of love, the ideal form of love, in which a couple's relationship involves all three of the major facets of love: passion, intimacy, and commitment.

Comstock Images/Jupiter Images

This couple is doing more than sharing a wonderful experience. They are actually "working" on their relationship. Engaging in mutually exciting activities helps preserve marital passion.

people may find their partner dull. Worse yet, they may fall in love with someone who is on the scene to promote their most efficacious self: "I feel so competent and powerful at my job. Hey, wait a second! It's my co-worker, not my wife, who is helping me emotionally grow!" Keeping "growth experiences" within a marriage helps keep marital passion alive.

Perceptive readers might notice that this research helps explain why we fall in love with people who embody our ideal selves—the person we want to be (recall Chapter 10). We implicitly count on our relationship to bring out our "best" possible self. But, this suggests that keeping marital passion alive may not demand sharing concrete activities. It might just involve being interested in growing as a person, and sharing your *flow states* with a mate. How can sharing flow experiences expand a partner's inner self? Listen to these quotations, from a study in which Israeli couples were asked, "What makes you feel especially close?"

> Wife (who had just gotten a job as a yoga teacher): *There are nights when I come home after class fully energized and excited. . . . I don't know why, but on those nights I just want to be with him. . . . I want him to be around me so I can share . . . my excitement."*
>
> Husband: *I love those Tuesday nights. I wait for them. I know she will come home so energetic. . . . It is contagious. It makes us like a couple on a honeymoon."*
>
> (quoted in Ben-Ari & Lavee, 2007, p. 635)

Couple Communications and Happiness

Watch happy couples, like this husband and wife, and you will be struck with the way they relate. Like mothers and babies enjoying the dance of attachment, happy couples share joyous experiences. They are playful, affectionate. They use humor to signal, "I love you," even when they disagree (Driver & Gottman, 2004). But have you ever spent an evening with newlyweds and had the uneasy feeling, "I don't think this marriage will work out"? By listening to couples talk, psychologist John Gottman (1994; 1999) can tell, with uncanny accuracy, whether a marriage will become unglued (see also Markman and others, 2010). Here are three communication styles that distinguish thriving relationships from those that are fated for serious problems down the road:

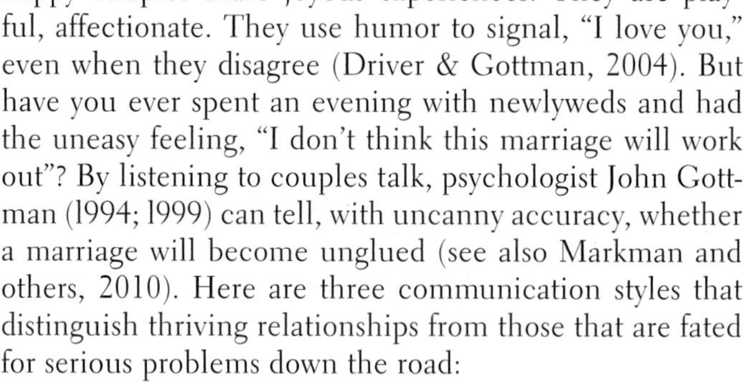

© moodboard/Corbis

Their delighted facial expressions tip us off that this young married man and woman are blissfully in love. But, *specifically*, how do happy couples communicate when they talk? (The answers are listed right here.)

- ***Happy couples engage in a high ratio of positive to negative comments.*** People can fight a good deal and still have a happy marriage. The key is to make sure that the number of caring, loving comments *strongly* outweighs the critical ones. In videotaping couples discussing problems in his "love lab," Gottman has discovered that when the ratio of positive to negative interactions dips well below 5 to 1, the risk of getting divorced escalates.
- ***Happy couples don't get personal when they disagree.*** When happily married couples fight, they confine themselves to the problem: "I don't like it when I come home and the house is messy. What can we do?" Unhappy couples personalize their conflicts: They use put-downs and sarcasm. They look disgusted. They roll their eyes. Expressions of contempt for a partner are poisonous to married life.

- ***Happy couples are sensitive to their partner's need for "space."*** Another classic way of interacting that signals a marriage is in trouble occurs when one person regularly pushes for more emotional involvement and the other tries to back off (Eldridge & Christensen, 2002; Noller and others, 2005). As this **demand–withdrawal interaction** escalates, it takes a bitter, personal turn:

demand–withdrawal interaction A pathological type of communication in which one partner, most often the woman, presses for more intimacy and the other person, most often the man, tends to back off.

WIFE (WORRIED VOICE): Is there something wrong, honey?

HUSBAND (DISTANT VOICE): Nope. Not a thing.

WIFE: I can tell that you are annoyed at me—I can see it in your face. What's wrong?

HUSBAND (SOUNDING ANNOYED): I already told you, there's nothing wrong. Will you lay off of me? I just need some time to myself.

WIFE (DISGUSTEDLY): Oh, you are impossible. You never talk to me.

HUSBAND (CONTEMPTUOUSLY): You are such a terrible nag!

(adapted from Gottman, 1994, p. 138)

You would not be surprised to learn that—as in the example above—women tend to be the "demanders." Wives want to talk about feelings; husbands withdraw and attempt to shut the discussion off (Eldridge & Christensen, 2002). But if we look more deeply, the real issue here is that the "demander"—whether male or female—is not responding sensitively to the other person's cues. This individual is hypersensitive to being rejected. She has a *preoccupied/ambivalent attachment style*. Her partner has an *avoidant/dismissive approach*.

The bottom line is that these unproductive ways of communicating signal that a lover has been transformed from an ally into a potential enemy. People who adopt these poisonous ways of relating are insecurely attached (Feeney & Noller, 2002; Murray and others, 2003).

Imagine how this father-to-be feels when he pampers his wife and you will understand why the thrill of "sacrificing" for a loved one helps relationships lovingly survive.

Andersen Ross/Getty Images/Blend Images

Commitment: A Core Quality in Relationship Success

Now that we know what behaviors signal secure and insecure attachments, can we target an inner attitude that keeps couples attached in the face of the natural pull toward less intimacy and passion over time? Actually, I also touched on that emotional glue in Chapter 10 while discussing romance: It's having a sense of commitment. Now, let's decode what specific qualities "being committed" involves.

According to Frank Fincham and his colleagues, again, the core sign of commitment is being dedicated to a partner's "inner growth" (Fincham, Stanley, & Beach, 2007; Overall, Fletcher, & Simpson, 2010). Specifically, commitment involves sacrifice, giving up one's own desires to further the other person's joy. Rather than seeing sacrifice as a negative thing (and, again, similar to the self-expansion studies), when people give up their needs for their partner, they are benefiting themselves. Sacrificing for the other person is essential in feeling happy (Kogan and others, 2010) and closely attached.

A final requirement for commitment is the ability to forgive. People have to be willing to let go of their anger when their partner, as in any human relationship, may not be sensitive or acts in a disappointing way.

Forgiveness—teaching people to "let go" of their hurt feelings—is a popular approach to helping promote better relationships and well-being (Bonach, 2007; Seligman, 2011; Wade, Johnson, & Meyer, 2008). Can forgiveness work? As one study showed, forgiveness has personal benefits. People who reported forgiving their significant other after an incident of being let down (provided they felt generally good about their partner and the person apologized!) felt better about their own lives (Bono, McCullough, & Root, 2008). Another study suggested that *not forgiving* had long-term consequences for how couples actually behaved.

Researchers asked husbands and wives to write about how they reacted after an incident when their spouse disappointed them. Did they "do something to even the score" or "forgive"? Then, they looked at these couples' conflict-resolution skills a year later. When wives, in particular, reported holding on to their anger, partners were more prone to engage in the kinds of counterproductive arguments in the previous section—even when they had been relating well before (Fincham, Beach, & Davila, 2007). So, at the root of those dysfunctional interactions, which escalate into destructive personal comments, may be "hurts" that are nursed and rehearsed and never forgiven—disappointments that lie simmering and waiting to re-erupt.

INTERVENTIONS: Staying Together Happily for Life

How can you draw on *all* of these research insights to have an enduring, happy relationship? Understand the natural time course of love. Preserve intimacy and passion by sharing exciting activities, or having your own compelling interests and discussing flow-inducing events (and ideas) with your mate. Be very, very positive after you get negative. Avoid getting personal when you fight. Be sensitive to your partner's need for space. Most important, be committed to your relationship. Act on that feeling by being devoted to the other person's development, sacrificing, and being predisposed to forgive. Table 11.4 offers a checklist based on these points to evaluate your current relationship or to keep on hand for the love relationships you will have as you travel through life.

As a final caution, however, I must emphasize that sacrifice or forgiveness is sometimes misplaced. One key to sacrificing is reciprocity. People need to know a partner will sacrifice for them. In fact, another family expert, Paul Amato (2007), believes a basic reason why Western marriages flounder is that one person, often the wife, feels she is doing all of the sacrificing: "My partner is not pulling his own weight."

Forgiveness is unwarranted if a person's violations are chronic and/or severe. Women in abusive relationships, for instance, tend to be *too* forgiving. As one battered

TABLE 11.4: Evaluating Your Close Relationship: A Checklist

Answer these questions as honestly as you can. The more "yes" boxes you check, the stronger your relationship is likely to be.

	Yes	No
1. Do you have realistic expectations about your relationship—realizing that passion and intimacy don't magically last forever?	❒	❒
2. Do you engage in activities that your partner feels as passionate about as you do?	❒	❒
3. Do you have compelling interests and talk about your flow states with your mate?	❒	❒
4. Are you affectionate and positive with your partner?	❒	❒
5. Do you solve differences of opinion in a constructive way—not getting personal when you fight?	❒	❒
6. Are you committed to your partner's self-development?	❒	❒
7. Does sacrificing your own needs to make your partner happy give you pleasure?	❒	❒
8. Are you both willing to let go and forgive, or do you hold on to hurts?	❒	❒

woman explained: "Every single time I thought: OK maybe . . . he's going through a bad patch . . . he will change" (quoted in Boonzaier, 2008, p. 93; see also Wade, Johnson, & Meyer, 2008). When couples engage in the contempt-filled arguments discussed in the previous section, forgiveness backfires and excusing destructive comments leads to further verbal abuse (McNulty, 2008). If a person is being degraded, treated with contempt, or being taken advantage of, it's time to reconsider one's commitment and contemplate divorce.

Divorce

Researchers stress that, just as we saw in Chapter 7 when I described its impact on children, we need to think of divorce as having specific phases.

When people consider this major life change, they weigh the costs of leaving against the benefits (Hopper, 1993; Kelly, 2000). You and your spouse are not getting along, but perhaps you should just hang on. One deterrent is financial: "Can I afford the loss in income after a divorce?" But if the couple has children, money issues are trumped by a more critical concern: "How will divorce affect my parenting?" "Will this damage my daughter or son?" (Poortman & Seltzer, 2007.)

Couples typically cite communication problems such as those I've been discussing, lack of "attachment," and life stress as the main reasons for their divorce (Bodenmann and others, 2007). Often, what tips the balance in favor of leaving, however, is an extramarital affair. In a national study tracking U.S. marriages, researchers found, among husbands and wives who eventually divorced, that 2 out of 3 people reported having had an affair around the time their relationship was breaking up (Amato and Hohmann-Marriott, 2007). But they also discovered that the stereotype that an affair breaks up an otherwise happy marriage is false. When people have an affair, they are often *already* unhappy in their married lives. However, there is a bidirectional process in operation here. An affair widens the emotional chasm that already exists.

Once a couple separates, they experience an overload of other changes. There is the need to move, perhaps find a different, better-paying job (Amato, 2010). There are the legal hassles, anxieties about the children, and telling other loved ones, "How will my friends and family feel?" As people adjust to their new lives, the stress does lessen (Mitchell-Flynn & Hutchinson, 1993). Support from one's "social network" eases the pain (Krumrei and others, 2007). But imagine regularly battling with your spouse over the children and you can see why psychologists have labeled divorce "a chronic stressor" in women's lives (Bursik, 1991).

Still, divorce can produce emotional growth and enhanced efficacy feelings as people learn they can make it on their own (Fahs, 2007; Hetherington & Kelly, 2002). And, of course, ending a terrible marriage can come as a welcome relief.

Who feels relieved, or better emotionally, after a divorce? Insights come from considering the reasons why people separate. In that national survey tracking U.S. married couples mentioned earlier in this section, researchers put the couples who later divorced into two categories: People who had reported being miserable in their marriage, and couples who divorced, even though they had previously judged their marital happiness as "fairly good" (Amato, 2010; Amato & Hohmann-Marriott, 2007).

People in very unhappy marriages did feel much better after divorcing. But relatively satisfied couples who later divorced, perhaps thinking, "I just don't find our

William Thomas Cain/Getty Images

Compare the body language of this man and woman with the joyous couples in the previous two photos and you can graphically see why the marital disconnect labeled in the text as "lack of attachment" can provoke an extramarital affair and a divorce.

Norbert/Schaffer/Corbis

The fact that their marriage is so full of conflict suggests that this couple may feel much better after they divorce—but simply splitting up because you find your relationship "somewhat unfulfilling" predicts feeling more depressed after a marriage breaks up.

relationship extremely fulfilling," reported subsequent declines in well-being! Given this finding, family expert Paul Amato (2007, 2010) suggests that perhaps our cultural fantasy of finding a life soul mate (or the sense that something is missing if we don't *automatically* have intimacy and passion for life) might lure people to leave a marriage who would be better off remaining with their spouse. And what happens to children when couples make this choice? If your house is a battleground, as I described in Chapter 7, it's probably better for the children's mental health to divorce. But imagine being shocked to learn that your beloved dad is moving out when you always believed your parents' marriage was perfectly fine.

This brings up the gender dimension of divorce. Because women still usually get primary custody of the children, there is a tendency for divorced dads to disengage from their families by not paying child support or perhaps not seeing the children at all (Amato, 2010; Graham & Beller, 2002; Lamb, 2002). While the temptation is to blame men for "opting out," the Experiencing the Lifespan box poignantly shows how difficult it can be to be a full-fledged father when you have the standard twice-a-week visitation schedule. Moreover, for some dads, as my interview reveals, arriving to get the children can be fraught with anxieties: "Will my daughter or son be there this time?"

What often happens is that, after a divorce, men remarry, have other children, and/or become stepfathers. They construct new relationships to make up for those they may have lost. However, as experts beautifully put it: "Stepparent and child meet as strangers. They may or may not find common ground" (quoted in Wallerstein & Lewis, 2007, p. 457).

Stepfather-stepchild connections actually vary from continuous struggle ("We fight all the time") or distance ("We have no relationship") to "He's more of a father to me than my biological dad" (quoted in Ganong, Coleman, & Jamison, 2011, p. 403). To really connect, research suggests, stepdads must tread carefully: They should "be there" to give support, but not step far into that landmine area for trouble—the

EXPERIENCING THE LIFESPAN: Visitor Father

Fatherhood is the critical experience of Henry's life. When Joanna was a preschooler, their destination was the zoo or the playground. As she grew older, Henry took Joanna for music lessons and taught her sports. His presence was hard won and, he feels, too rare. Henry had been demoted from father to person with visitation rights.

Henry and his wife separated when Joanna was almost 2. According to their divorce agreement, the child was supposed to be available every two weeks; but, often, Henry's ex-wife took off with the baby or gave him some excuse when he came to pick his daughter up. Henry never knew for sure if Joanna would be waiting there when he arrived.

Henry felt his only option was to sue for joint custody, the right to have Joanna on weekends and every other day. When they met in court, however, to Henry's astonishment, the judge ordered a psychiatric evaluation to determine if *he* was emotionally fit. One judge asked point blank: "Why would a man want to take care of a 2-year-old?" Eventually, Henry won the right to have Joanna one afternoon per week, every other weekend, alternate holidays, and the month of July.

Over the next 10 years, Henry went to court periodically to try to force a greater role in his daughter's life. Once, he sued for full custody. While no one denied that Henry was a good father, a psychologist testified that a child needed a mother during the early years.

For years, Henry felt terrible about not being able to see his daughter every day. His work suffered. He was often upset. Now that Joanna is 12, he has adjusted. His daughter has her own room in his apartment. He feels secure that she knows this is her second home. Henry feels he reached an emotional landmark when, during "his time" this past summer, he was able to let go and allow Joanna to attend sleep-away camp. Still, the heartache of not being on the scene to watch his child grow up never really goes away.

dad-as-disciplinarian role (Kinniburgh-White, Cartwright, & Seymour, 2010). They may desperately want to be "full fathers," but also feel somewhat shut out. As one man complained, "Sometimes I feel like I'm on the outside looking in because—sometimes I wish she was mine. . . . In my heart I feel like I'm her father" (quoted in Marsiglio, 2004, p. 31).

Stepmothers face similar boundary issues. For instance, one woman in another study reported asking her husband for guidelines: "Was . . . I supposed to be a mom or not a mom?" (Quoted in Whiting and others, 2007, p. 103.) But despite this lack of clarity, parental emotions can kick in. Another stepmother commented to the researchers: "I don't look at her as a stepdaughter because that implies they are not . . . your child . . . she's my only child and I just accept the fact that she has another mother as well" (quoted in Whiting and others, 2007, p. 102). And a stepfather put it more bluntly: "I don't introduce her as my stepdaughter because I didn't step on her. I introduce her, 'This is my daughter.' . . . I'd go crazy if something happened to her" (quoted in Marsiglio, 2004, p. 32).

David H. Wells/The Image Works

Because this stepfather wants his daughter to see him as her "real father," he needs to be exceptionally supportive. So when giving advice about this school play, he shouldn't say anything that this child might see as intrusive, pushy, or critical.

Now, let's explore the powerful feelings these men and women were experiencing by turning directly to parenthood, that second important adult role.

TYING IT ALL TOGETHER

1. Jared is making the case that, during the late twentieth century, there was an historic "deinstitutionalization of marriage." Which *two* of the following phenomena should Jared use to support this argument?
   a. Today, 1 of every 2 marriages ends in divorce.
   b. Today, unmarried motherhood is common, especially among poorly educated women.
   c. Today, marital satisfaction declines over the first few years of marriage.
2. Three couples are celebrating their silver anniversaries. Which relationship has followed the "classic" marital pathway?
   a. After being extremely happy with each other during the first three years, Ted and Elaine now find that their marriage has gone steadily downhill.
   b. Steve and Betty's marriage has had many unpredictable ups and downs over the years.
   c. Dave and Erika's marital satisfaction declined, especially during the first four years, but has dramatically improved now that their children have left home.
3. Describe the triangular theory to a friend and give an example of (a) romantic love, (b) consummate love, and (c) a companionate marriage. Can you think of couples who fit each category? At what stage of life are couples most likely to have companionate marriages?
4. Jennifer says, "I want to help my spouse grow and develop." Mark says, " I'm trying to be as interesting a person as possible in my marriage. " Based on this chapter, explain, in a sentence, why *both* strategies go along with each other to promote marital happiness.
5. You are a marriage counselor. Drawing on the research with regard to 1) keeping passion alive, 2) couple communications, and 3) commitment attitudes, formulate one suggestion for "homework" that you might give couples who come to your office for help.
6. Your best friend says, "I really like Kevin as a person, but I don't feel all that fulfilled in my marriage. Maybe I should get a divorce." Given the information in this section, what advice might you give?

Answers to the Tying It All Together questions can be found at the end of this chapter.

Rachel Epstein/Photo Edit, Inc.

In the past, gay couples such as these women could never have hoped to be parents. They would have had to hide their relationship from the outside world. Today, they proudly can fulfill their life dream.

Parenthood

I have never felt the joy that my daughter brings me when I wake up and see her . . . when you are laying there and . . . and feel this little hand tapping on your hand . . . that has been the most joyful thing I ever have experienced. . . . I've never been able to get that type of joy anywhere else.

(quoted in Palkovitz, 2002, p. 96)

Setting the Context: More Parenting Possibilities, Fewer Children

Take an informal poll of parents and you will hear similar comments: "The love and joy you have with children is impossible to describe." The great benefit of the 1960s lifestyle revolution is that more people than ever can participate in this life-changing experience, from stepparents, to gay couples, to never-married adults. Our twenty-first-century tapestry of nontraditional families, described in Chapter 7, offers many chances to fulfill this core identity of adult life.

At the same time, people have more freedom *not* to be parents—and, increasing numbers of adults are making that choice. One sign of the times is the dramatic decline in **fertility rates,** or the average number of births per woman, in many developed countries. And whatever happened to those huge Spanish, Italian or Greek families? As Figure 11.2 shows, adults in these southernmost European nations have some of the lowest fertility rates in the world.

Why has fertility dropped well below the level to keep the population constant (2.1 births) in every European nation, as well as in Russia and Asia? (See Li and others, 2011.) A major cause, in Europe, lies in the stalled progress people are making toward adulthood. Remember from Chapter 10 that, in Italy, Spain and Greece, due to the economic crisis, most twenty-somethings don't have the financial resources to get married and have children. Moreover, when a comparatively poor, developed nation has extreme income inequalities (such as exist in Russia), a government offers few social supports for new parents (such as in South Korea), or when a society (like Singapore) prizes material goods as the key to happiness (Li and others, 2011), young people are particularly unwilling to bring babies into the world.

Alarmed by their shrinking populations at the turn of the twenty-first century, a few elected officials in places like Italy resorted to giving "baby bonuses" (that is, money) to couples who conceived. (But Chapter 10 suggests that these nations might be better off if they promoted young people's transition to adulthood by providing jobs!) Newspapers in some European countries bombarded twenty-somethings with accusations of being self-indulgent, and offered warnings that choosing a childless life would lead to

fertility rate The average number of children a woman in a given country has during her lifetime.

FIGURE 11.2: **Fertility rates in selected developed countries, 2008:** This chart reveals just why declining fertility is a crucial concern in Western Europe, where fertility rates are now below the replacement level (2.1 children) in every country. Notice, also, that childbearing rates are especially low in the southernmost European nations, Russia, and several Asian countries.

Source: Central Intelligence Agency, World FactBook, 2008.

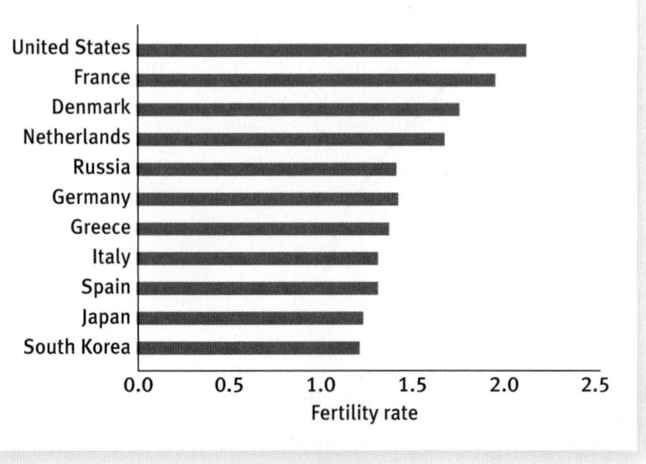

an unhappy old age (Brown & Ferree, 2005). Not true! People who decide not to have children are not more narcissistic (Gerson, Posner, & Morris, 1991). Childless adults—especially if they are female and have chosen this path—are just as happy as parents in midlife or old age (Umberson, Pudrovska, & Reczek, 2010). Moreover, the stereotype that having children makes a marriage stronger (or that having a child saves an unhappy marriage) is equally false. How does having a baby *really* change married life?

marital equity Fairness in the "work" of a couple's life together. If a relationship lacks equity, with one partner doing significantly more than the other, the outcome is typically marital dissatisfaction.

The Transition to Parenthood

To get a portrait of how becoming parents affects a marriage, researchers conduct longitudinal studies, selecting couples when the wife is pregnant and then tracking those families for a few years after the baby's birth. Understanding that parenthood arrives via many routes, social scientists have explored how having a child affects the bond between lesbian partners, too (Goldberg & Sayer, 2006). Here are the conclusions of these studies exploring *the transition to parenthood*:

- ***Parenthood makes couples less intimate and happy.*** Look back to the infancy chapters—especially the discussion of infant sleep in Chapter 3—and you will immediately see why a baby's birth is apt to change marital passion and intimacy for the worse. In fact, look at any couple struggling with an infant at your local restaurant and you will understand why researchers find that feelings about one's spouse shift from lover to "fellow worker" after the baby arrives (Belsky, Lang, & Rovine, 1985; Belsky & Rovine, 1990). One father summarized what happens when he commented: "Instead of channeling our love towards just each other . . . we have channeled our love together towards them" (adapted from Palkovitz, 2002, p. 176).
- ***Parenthood produces more traditional (and potentially conflict-ridden) marital roles.*** If the couple is heterosexual, having children tends to make gender roles more distinct (Katz-Wise, Priess & Hyde, 2010). Even when spouses have been sharing the household tasks fairly equally, women often take over most of the housework and child care after the baby arrives. Often, this occurs because, as you will see later in this chapter, after having children, a wife may leave her job or reduce her hours at work. However, even when both spouses work full time, mothers tend to do more of the diaper changing and household chores than fathers. This change can provoke conflicts centered on **marital equity**, or feelings of unfairness: Wives get angry at their husbands for not doing their share around the house (Dew & Wilcox, 2011; Feeney and others, 2001).

What compounds the sense of over-sacrificing are clashes centered on differing parenting styles (recall Chapter 7). One unhappy wife described this kind of disagreement when she informed her husband: "What's really getting to me . . . is that we hardly ever agree on how to handle [the baby]. I think you are too rough, and you think I'm spoiling her, and none of us wants to change" (quoted in Cowan & Cowan, 1992, p. 112).

These examples show how the stress of the baby's birth can poison the atmosphere between a husband and wife. However, most people adapt to this change in their relationship, although every study shows, *on average*, marital satisfaction does decline (Dew & Wilcox, 2011; Doss and others, 2009; Feeney and others, 2001; Houts and others, 2008). Still, about one in three couples reports that having a child has *increased* their feelings of love for their spouse (Belsky & Rovine, 1990).

Bruce Ayres/Getty Images

Will this young couple's relationship seriously deteriorate after the baby? Will it improve? To answer these questions, we need to look at what their marriage was like *before* having a child.

To predict which marriages completely deteriorate, decline slightly, or improve, our best clues come from looking at the pre-baby relationship. Are the parents-to-be securely attached? (See Feeney and others, 2001.) Did this husband and wife argue a good deal before the child arrived? (See Houts and others, 2008; Kluwer & Johnson, 2007.) In the words of pioneering researchers, "The transition to parenthood seems to act as an amplifier, tuning couples into their strengths and turning up the volume on existing difficulties in managing their . . . [love]" (Cowan & Cowan, 1992, p. 206).

Now that we've looked at its impact on a marriage, let's turn to the experience of parenthood from mothers' and fathers' points of view.

Exploring Motherhood

Marcy Malloy/Marcy Malloy Photography

Does becoming a mother really make people more tolerant, empathic, and mature? Just look at this photo and you will understand why— when a woman has young children—that stereotype definitely doesn't fit the facts!

I've already talked about the incredible love that mothers feel for their children, especially in the infancy section of this book. But motherhood has its downside. National surveys show that mothers of young children report the *lowest* levels of day-to-day happiness, compared to women who are not parents or those who are in the empty-nest stage of life (McLanahan & Adams, 1989). Moreover, unfortunately, it's a myth that becoming a parent makes us more mature. In fact, during the early childhood years—one longitudinal study showed—people become more distressed than before they were moms (Jokela and others, 2009). Now, let's look at some reasons why.

The Motherhood Experience

Motherhood, one classic poll showed, is tailor-made to destroy basic conceptions women have about themselves (Genevie & Margolies, 1987). In this U.S. study, 1 in 2 mothers admitted that they had trouble controlling their temper. Among the situations that made them most irate, challenges to their authority ranked first. Disobedience, disrespect, and even typical behaviors such as a child's whining might provoke reactions bordering on rage. When confronted with real-life children, these mothers found that their ideal of being calm, empathetic, and always in control came tumbling down (Genevie & Margolies, 1987).

Given the bidirectional quality of the parent–child bond, it should come as no surprise that a main force in this survey that affected how closely a woman fit her motherhood ideal lay in her attachment with a given child. Children who were temperamentally difficult provoked more irritation and lowered a mother's self-esteem. An easy child (recall Chapter 4) had the opposite effect, by evoking loving feelings and making that mother feel competent in her role. As one woman wrote:

> Lee Ann has been my godsend. My other two have given me so many problems and are rude and disrespectful. Not Lee Ann. . . . I disciplined her in the same way . . . except that she seemed to require less of it. Usually she just seemed to do the right thing. She is . . . my chance for supreme success after two devastating failures.
>
> (quoted in Genevie & Margolies, 1987, pp. 220–221)

These emotions destroy another ideal that we have about motherhood: Mothers love all their children equally. Although they tried not to let their preferences show, many women in this study did admit they had favorites. Typically, a favorite child was "easy" and successful in the wider world. However, what was most important, again, was the attachment relationship, the feeling of being totally loved by a particular child. As one woman reported:

> There will always be a special closeness with Darrell. He likes to test my word. . . . There are times he makes me feel like pulling my hair out. . . . But when he comes to "talk" to mom that's an important feeling to me.
>
> (quoted in Genevie & Margolies, 1987, p. 248)

Not only does the experience of motherhood vary dramatically from child to child, it shifts from minute to minute and day to day:

> Good days are getting hugs and kisses and hearing "I love you." The bad days are hearing "you are not my friend." Good days are not knowing the color of the refrigerator because of the paintings and drawings all over it. Bad days are seeing a new drawing on a just painted wall.
>
> (quoted in Genevie & Margolies, 1987, p. 412)

In sum, motherhood is wonderful and terrible. It evokes the most uplifting emotions *and* offers painful insights into the self. Now, drawing on this study, let's explore how outside influences—the media, friends, family members, and experts—amplify mothers' distress.

Bananastock/Jupiter Images

The blissful image of a mother and baby is nothing like contending with the reality of continual sleep deprivation and a screaming newborn—explaining why the idealized media images can make the first months of motherhood come as a total shock.

Expectations and Motherhood Stress

The world provides women with an airbrushed view of motherhood—from the movie stars who wax enthusiastic about the joys of having babies ("much better than that terrible old career") to the family members who gush at bleary-eyed, sleep-deprived new mothers: "How wonderful you must feel!" By portraying motherhood as total bliss, are we doing women a disservice when they realize that their own experience does not live up to this glorified image? (See Douglas & Michaels, 2004.)

What compounds the problem are unrealistic performance pressures. Good children, as you saw in the above quotation, make a mother feel competent. "Difficult" children can make a woman feel like a failure. Despite all we know about the crucial role of genetics, peers, and the wider society in affecting development, mothers still bear the weight of responsibility for the way their children turn out (Coontz, 1992; Crittenden, 2001; Douglas & Michaels, 2004; Garey & Arendell, 2001).

Single mothers face the most intense pressures as they struggle to cope with poverty, working full time, plus trying to fulfill the "blissful" mom ideal. But *every* woman is subject to the heavy demands of contemporary motherhood: the need to be infinitely patient, to cram in the right amount of reading, to take children to lessons—to produce a perfect child. Critics talk in anguished terms about how today's working mothers are not giving children the attention they received in "the good old days." Stressed-out mothers berate themselves for not spending enough time with their daughters and sons (Bianchi, Robinson, & Milkie, 2006). To what degree is the much-lamented epidemic of "helicopter" moms a byproduct of these intense performance demands, which force contemporary women to go overboard in their hovering to prove that they are not slacking off in the motherhood role?

Actually, our stereotypes about slacking-off mothers can be subjected to scientific scrutiny. And we have concrete data that *proves* the mother-bashing critics are wrong. When developmentalists compared diary reports of mothers' involvement over the past 40 years, they discovered that mothers today spend *more* time with their children than their counterparts did a generation ago (Bianchi, Robinson, & Milkie, 2006). In particular, notice from Figure 11.3 the dramatic increase in the amount of time mothers spent teaching and playing. This cohort of young-adult mothers—including

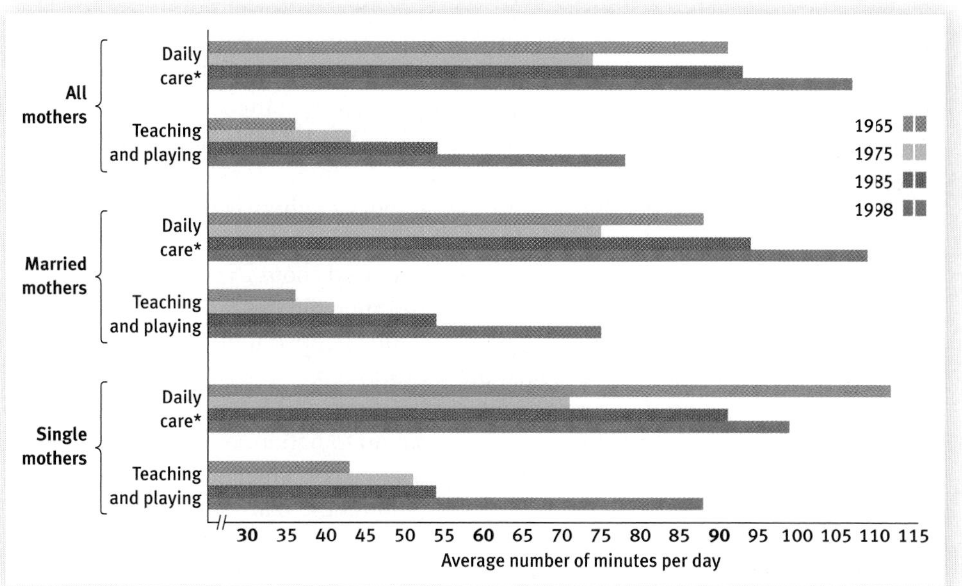

FIGURE 11.3: **Minutes per day devoted to hands-on child care by U.S. mothers:** Notice in particular that, in contrast to our myths, during the past 15 years, mothers are spending much more time teaching and playing with their children than in previous decades.

Source: Adapted from Sayer, Bianchi, & Robinson, 2004.

*Refers to routine kinds of care, such as helping the child get dressed.

breadwinner role Traditional concept that a man's job is to support a wife and children.

Daly & Newton/Getty Images

This photograph shows the reality of motherhood today. Young working mothers are spending much *more* time teaching their children than their own stay-at-home mothers did in the past!

those remarkable single moms—is spending almost *twice as much time* engaging in child cognition-stimulating activities as their own mothers spent with them!

Given that the average full-time working U.S. mother clocks in about 39 hours a week at a job, what is giving way? The diary studies show major cutbacks in hours spent at housework (that's probably a good thing!) and less time devoted to community activities and with friends. A more ominous casualty for married women is a loss of time spent with their spouse (Bianchi, Robinson, & Milkie, 2006; Glorieux, Minnen, & Tienoven, 2011). One cost of the heroic dual focus on mothering and working is that marriages are prone to suffer, as spouses become "ships passing in the night" (Dew & Wilcox, 2011).

Where are fathers in his picture? Earlier, when I talked about equity issues during the transition to parenthood, I might have given you the impression that contemporary dads are also slacking off. Not so! The diary studies suggest that when we count hours at work plus what they do at home, fathers spend just as much total time "sacrificing" for the family as do mothers (Bianchi, Robinson, & Milkie, 2006). Actually, today's fathers are often making valiant efforts to be involved parents, too (Halrynjo, 2009).

Exploring Fatherhood

When women first entered the workforce in large numbers in the 1970s, it became a badge of honor for fathers, in addition to fulfilling the traditional **breadwinner role,** to change the diapers and to be deeply involved in their children's lives. What social scientists called the *new nurturer father* became a masculine ideal. Furthermore, according to psychologists, we expect fathers to be good sex-role models, giving children a road map for how men should ideally behave. Sometimes, we even want them to be ultimate authority figures, the people responsible for laying down the family rules (as in the old saying: "Wait until your father gets home!").

The lack of guidelines leaves contemporary fathers with contradictory demands. "Should I be strict or nurturing, sensitive or strong? Should I work full time to feed my family or stay home to feed my child?" (See Perala-Littunen, 2007.) Given that there may be no "right" way to be a father, how do men carry out their parental role?

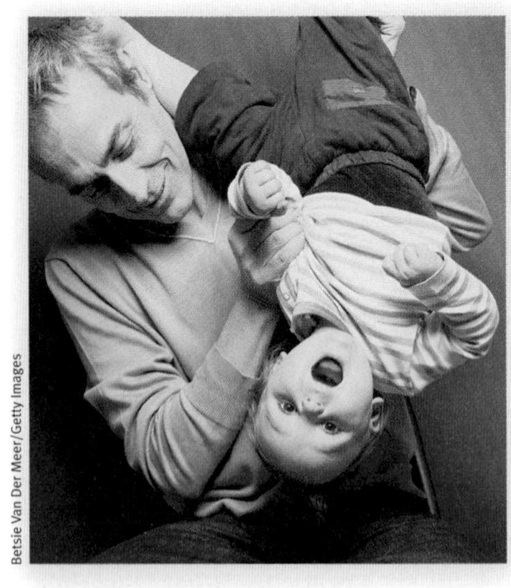

Betsie Van Der Meer/Getty Images

Think back to the thrilled expressions on the faces of the boys engaged in rough-and-tumble play in Chapter 6 and you can understand why this male "hang 'em upside down" play style is a compelling bonding experience for *both* fathers and their sons. It's also clear why "daddy play" is apt to give moms fits.

How Fathers Act

As you would expect from the principle that they should be good sex-role models, fathers, on average, spend more time with their sons than their daughters (Bronstein, 1988). They play with their children in classically "male," rough-and-tumble ways (see Chapter 6). Fathers run, wrestle, and chase. They dangle infants upside down (Belsky & Volling, 1987). Although children adore this whirl-the-baby-around-by-the-feet play (in our house we called it "going to Six Flags"), it can give mothers palpitations as they wonder: "Help! Is my baby going to be hurt?"

How much hands-on nurturing do today's fathers perform? As you can see in Figure 11.4, the diary studies show that, in many Western countries, a genuine father-as-caregiver revolution occurred about 25 years ago (Bianchi, Robinson, & Milkie, 2006). In the 1970s, men did not respond all that well to the call to be new nurturers. By the mid-1980s, they stepped in more. At the turn of the century, many fathers *fully* embraced the nurturer role.

Statistically speaking, however, twenty-first-century child care is still mainly a female job. Though the percentages vary from nation to nation, on average, Western women do roughly twice as much hands-on child care as do men (Bianchi, Robinson, & Milkie, 2006; Craig & Mullan, 2010). Furthermore, the diary studies don't tell us which parent is taking bottom-line responsibility for managing the children—making

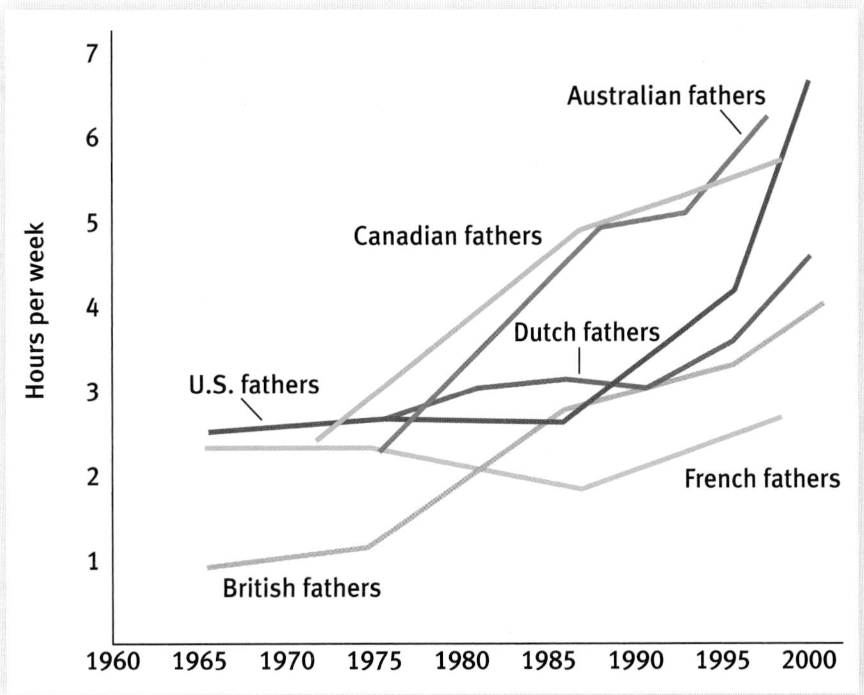

FIGURE 11.4: **Trends in father's primary activity time spent in child care in six countries:** Notice from this chart that, although the amount of time fathers spend in child care differs from nation to nation in interesting ways, in general, there was a dramatic increase in "hands-on" fathering during the last 15 years of the twentieth century.

Source: Adapted from Bianchi, Robinson, & Milkie, 2006, p. 160.

that dentist appointment, arranging for a babysitter, planning the meals, and being on call when a child is sick. Having bottom-line responsibility may not translate into many hours spent physically with a daughter or son, but the weight and worry make this aspect of parenting a 24/7 job.

Based on the earlier discussion of society's expectations, it seems likely that mothers typically continue to take bottom-line responsibility. When we look at where the parenting buck stops, the gender dimension of being a parent is fully revealed (Lamb, 1997).

In sum, although today's fathers are doing far more hands-on child care than in the past, their involvement still is skewed toward play activities, particularly of the rough-and-tumble, "Six Flags" kind. Dads are often more involved with their sons than their daughters. Mothers remain the caregivers of final resort.

Variations in Fathers' Involvement

If you look at the fathers you know, however, you will be struck by the variations from this generalized profile (Halrynjo, 2009). There are divorced men who never see their children, and traditional "I never touch a diaper" dads. There are househusbands who assume primary caregiving responsibilities, and men who take sole care of the kids (for instance, roughly 1 in 5 U.S. single-parent households is headed by a man). What statistical forces predict how involved a given father is likely to be?

In two-parent families, one clue comes from looking at the man's gender-role conceptions. As you might expect, highly religious dads with traditional views of women's roles avoid the "dirty work" of care such as diaper changing (DeMaris, Mahoney, & Pargament, 2011), although they are heavily involved in play-guy activities such as throwing baseballs or twirling babies in the air (Hofferth & Goldscheider, 2010). Another influence lies in the nonchild-care demands in a couple's lives. As women increase their hours at work, men often respond by doing more at home (Amato 2007). But there is a limit. When the gender balance tips far in the opposite direction—either a man is unemployed or works many fewer hours than his spouse—he may be *less* willing to assume traditional female roles such as diaper changing or cleaning the house (Hofferth & Goldscheider, 2010; more about this fascinating paradox later).

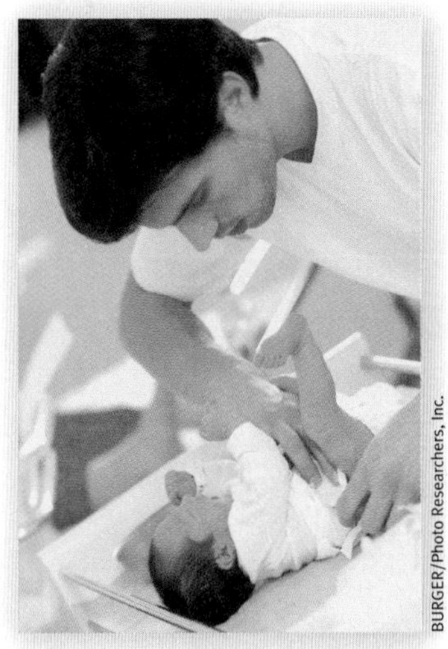

Contemporary fathers differ in how willing they are to change diapers. To explain this young man's behavior, we would predict that he has "father as hands-on caregiver" gender-role ideas and—as you will see on the next page a wife who praises him, rather than making fun of his diaper-changing skills.

And a third force depends on the attitudes of the partner in the parenthood duet: the woman. When a wife makes fun of her husband's diaper-changing skills, or gets angry with him for being too rough, or shows signs of being jealous of her husband's relationship with the children, the message gets across. Women can be crucial gatekeepers. If wives are discouraging or set impossibly high standards, they put up serious barriers to their husbands' hands-on care (Cowan & Bronstein, 1988; Schoppe-Sullivan and others, 2008).

So to understand how men approach being fathers, again, we need to adopt the *developmental systems* approach: Look at how a man views his role. See how his wife reacts when her husband assumes "female" child-care jobs. Expect heavier involvement when a man has sons and his wife is working full time. Understand, however, that when women are doing *all* the breadwinning, men may feel more uncomfortable taking on a full-time nurturing role.

This last consideration brings up the greatest barrier that keeps fathers from being completely involved: the need to be the primary breadwinner. As I implied earlier in the "who gets married discussion," for all our talk about equal family roles, supporting a family is at the core of many men's identities as adults (Miller, 2010; Willott & Griffin, 2004). How are things *really* changing with regard to work, women, and men? First, let's sum up the messages in this section in Table 11.5, then explore this question as we turn to the third vital adult role: work.

TABLE 11.5: Advice for Parents: A Checklist

Coping with the Transition to Parenthood

- Don't expect your romantic feelings about each other to stay the same—they won't.
- Try to agree on who is going to do what around the house, but understand that you may fall into more traditional roles.
- Work on your communication skills before the baby arrives.

For Mothers

- Understand that *you won't and can't be the perfect mother*—in fact, sometimes you will be utterly terrible—and accept yourself for being human!
- Don't buy into the fantasy of producing a perfect child. Children cannot be micromanaged into being perfect. Focus on enjoying and loving your child as he or she is (see also Chapter 7).
- Don't listen to people who say that working outside the home automatically means that you can't be an involved mother. Remember the findings discussed in this section.

For Fathers

- Understand that your role is full of contradictions—and that there is no "perfect" way to be a dad.
- Do what makes you feel comfortable, but also be flexible and responsive to the needs of your partner and the conditions of your life.
- Know your priorities. If—as may be common—fulfilling the breadwinner role is most important to you, don't beat yourself up for those feelings; but also take care to communicate your priorities to your spouse and children.

TYING IT ALL TOGETHER

1. Jenna and Charlie are expecting their first child, and Jenna plans to keep working full time. According to the research on the transition to parenthood, how is this couple prone to act after the baby is born?

2. Akisha, a new mother, is feeling unexpectedly stressed and unhappy. She and other mothers might cope better if they experienced which *two* of the following?

   a. Got a less rosy, more accurate picture about motherhood from the media
   b. Had more experts giving them parenting advice
   c. Had less pressure placed on them from the outside world to "be perfect"

3. Your grandmother is complaining that children today don't get the attention from their parents that they got in the "good old days." How should you respond, based on this chapter? Be specific with regard to both mothers and fathers.
4. Construct a questionnaire to predict how heavily involved in child care a particular man is likely to be, and give it to some fathers you know.

Answers to the Tying It All Together questions can be found at the end of this chapter.

traditional stable career A career path in which people settle into their permanent life's work in their twenties and often stay with the same organization until they retire.

boundaryless career Today's most common career path for Western workers, in which people change jobs or professions periodically during their working lives.

Work

What is the world of work *generally* like in the United States, and how do careers differ for women and men? Who tends to be successful at a job, and how can you construct a fulfilling work life?

Setting the Context: The Changing Landscape of Work

Let's begin our discussion by spelling out four shifts in the U.S. career landscape:

- ***More career (and job) changes.*** A half-century ago, careers had a secure, steady shape. Right after high school or college, men typically settled into a permanent job. Often, they stayed in that same organization until they retired (Super, 1957). Today, this **traditional stable career,** is atypical. People move from job to job, or change direction, starting new careers as they travel through life. In the twenty-first century, adults experience a shifting work pattern called **boundaryless careers** (DeFillippi & Arthur, 1994).

This variable career path has advantages. People are not locked into a single occupation. They have more freedom to flexibly shift their careers and find satisfying, flow-inducing work. Today, at least theoretically, our work lives are no longer tethered to being a certain age. We can get off the corporate track and shift to skydiving, or start a new career as a cake baker at 50 or 75 (Carstensen, 2009). But, as we are well aware, the boundaryless career has become common for a negative reason: job insecurity.

Courtesy of Jay Qualls, Nashville, TN

Courtesy of Jay Qualls, Nashville, TN

After being laid off from his health care job at 40, my friend Jay rolled up his sleeves and pursued his cake baking passion. With stints on TLC's *The Next Great Baker* and his concoctions featured in *Martha Stewart Living* magazine's wedding issue, Jay's midlife rise to prominence in this field is a sweet testament to the fact that—even when unwillingly forced—*a boundaryless career* can (occasionally) have its just desserts.

- ***More job insecurity (and, of course, unemployment).*** Job insecurity has been a concern for segments of the U.S. workforce since the late twentieth century, with outsourcing, globalization, and cutbacks in mid-twentieth-century corporations such as AT&T, which had previously hired many thousands of workers for life. Now, the worry, "Will I keep my job?" has migrated around the developed world, as the European economies have faced their own dramatic economic problems in recent years.

How do people react to the threat of being laid off? In part, these reactions depend on a nation's unique financial situation. In one comparative study, job insecurity provoked less anguish among Swiss adults than a comparable U.S. group because, as of this writing, unemployment in that nation has been relatively low (making it far easier to find a new job) (König and others, 2011).

Responses to the threat of losing a job also vary depending on a worker's unique life situation (Staufenbiel & König, 2010). People who are younger and better educated are apt to disengage mentally from their current position—coming in late, doing less, searching for other work. But, if someone's options are limited, let's say that person is older or has worked for the same employer for much of adult life, that individual may work harder in the hopes that his position will be saved (Carless & Arnup, 2011; Cheng & Chan, 2008; De Cuyper and others, 2008).

- ***Longer working hours.*** Actually, it's a myth that the U.S. work ethic has diminished and that Americans worked longer hours in the "good old days." When they can get full-time work, men (and, of course, women) are putting in more hours per week at their jobs than their parents or grandparents did.

Consider findings from the National Survey of the Changing Workforce (NSCW), a U.S. poll that has regularly monitored the hours that workers put in at their jobs (Families and Work Institute, 2009). The survey showed that by the beginning of the twenty-first century, the 40-hour workweek was a relic of the past. In 2002, the typical male worker spent an average of 49 hours a week on his so-called 40-hour-a-week job (Galinsky and others, 2005).

Photodisc/Getty Images

Having the flexibility to work at home is definitely a double-edged sword. Not only are you tempted to work on assignments when you should be putting your child to bed, but you are probably working far longer hours than if you had gone to the office.

Why has work expanded beyond 9 to 5? One reason is that, in a more cutthroat economy, the competitive pressures and reinforcements favor working longer hours. Your co-worker starts regularly staying at the office until 7 P.M. In order to keep your job, you then feel compelled to stay at your desk an extra hour or two. Soon, anyone who leaves the office at 5 is defined as slacking off (Schor, 1991). Furthermore, as companies continue to shed parts of their labor force, each individual worker has more to do. Since your company got rid of so many employees, everyone *must* work well into dinnertime to cover the job's demands.

The technology revolution has played a part, with people able to stay in touch with their work 24/7 via smart phones, pagers, and computers. In fact, in the NSCW survey, one in three people reported being contacted after hours at least once a week via one of these "labor saving devices" (Galinsky & others, 2005).

The benefit of technology, especially in high-level jobs, is that it offers flexibility. People can telecommute from an office that is halfway around the world; or, even if their office is around the corner, they can work on their "own time" at home. However, this blurring of work time and home time is a double-edged sword. Yes, not having to go into the office allows you to take the kids to the dentist or pick them up from school, but you are potentially on the job 24 hours a day. In fact, in several

U.S. polls, people who reported working 50-plus hours per week had the most flexible schedules of all (Golden, 2008; see also Bianchi & Milkie, 2010; DiRenzo, Greenhaus, & Weer, 2011)!

In working-class jobs—where employees must clock in at a specific time—the issue is different. If someone is earning minimum wage as a server or is working in a seasonal job at Six Flags, that person must pack in as many hours as possible to financially survive.

Women, Men, and Work: Variations on a Theme or Basic Differences?

Women face the same twenty-first-century work conditions that men do. But now that it has been 40 years since the women's movement urged career equality for both sexes, let's get a status report. What *really* is the situation with regard to gender and work?

Are women equal to men in the world of work? If we consider education, females are overtaking males. In addition to outnumbering men on college campuses by almost 10 percent, women are more likely than men to earn B.A.'s or graduate degrees (U.S. Bureau of labor Statistics, 2009). Another reason to think the work world is tilting toward females relates to layoffs. As traditionally female jobs such as nursing or secretarial work, have been relatively cushioned from the economic downturn, most positions, such as construction, lost in the Great Recession of 2008, were predominantly male. Still, a deeper look suggests that, *when they are married,* women continue to have a different relationship to work than men:

- ***Women have more erratic, less continuous "careers."*** Because, as you saw earlier, they are often the primary nurturers, women are more likely to move in and out of the workforce or to work part time for significant periods during their lives (Bianchi & Milkie, 2010). The first exit often occurs early in adulthood. As one U.S. longitudinal survey showed, a pregnant woman has three times higher odds of leaving work than her counterpart who is not planning to have a child (Shafer, 2011). So, a woman decides to give up teaching or to cut down on her hours at the law firm when she has her baby. Another exit may happen in midlife, when she takes off time to care for her elderly parents as they become physically frail (see the next chapter for more information). The problem is that these periodic "off ramps" to provide family care not only make women less apt to be promoted, they have long-term economic costs: increasing the risk of sliding into poverty in later life.

- ***Wives may see their work role as secondary to a spouse.*** To bring home this message, let's examine another off-ramp predictor derived from that national U.S. study above—called the Longitudinal Survey of Youth. If a wife earns significantly less than her husband (or her spouse is working more than 45 hours a week), she is more likely to quit her job (Shafer, 2011). Conversely, when her husband gets laid off, a wife tries to ramp up her hours at work (Mattingly & Smith, 2010).

This feeling that "My husband has the main job," or, put more strongly, "I'm filling in for him"—was explicitly spelled out when researchers interviewed working-class couples after the husband had been laid off. Even though they had been the sole breadwinners for more than a year, these women still saw their work as "temporary" or "until the situation turns around." Or, they misread reality to preserve their fantasies about how married life should go. As 56-year-old Mike described, "We . . . wouldn't get along so well if we reversed roles . . . she's pretty much a stay-a-home mom" (Legerski & Cornwall, 2010, p. 463). But Mike was wrong. His wife had worked full time as a teacher's aide since her children were young, and Mike was now out of the labor force and in school!

This research makes sense of the interesting finding I mentioned in the previous section. When men are unemployed, they are sometimes *less likely* to do the work at

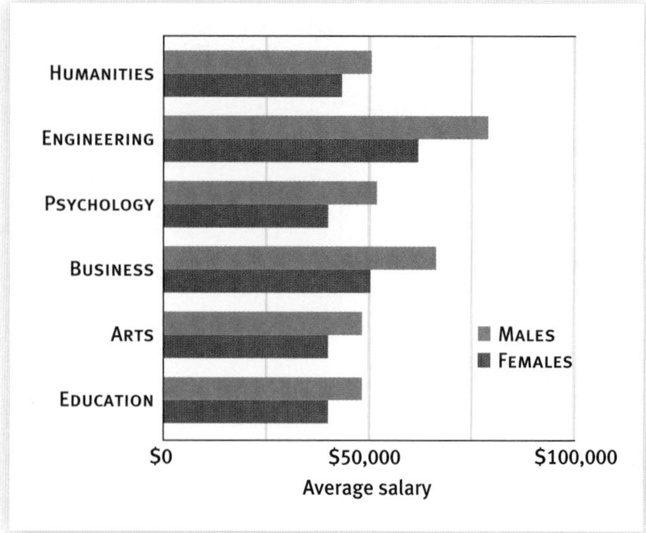

FIGURE 11.5: Snapshots of women's wage inequality: Notice that, while the salary gap varies, full-time female workers with B.A.'s in *every* major—both "female oriented" and "male oriented"—earn less than males.

Source: Center on Education and the Workforce, Georgetown University, 2011.

home. Even though these wives had become the sole breadwinners, many women in this study were averse to asking their demoralized husbands to help around the house. Louise explained it this way: " . . . It would be nice to . . . say well . . . honey, you'll do this . . . I can do this. . . . But . . . with his depression . . . it's like . . . I walk on eggshells. . . . Not sure if I say something he is going to take it wrong" (quoted in Legerski & Cornwall, 2010, p. 466).

If you think it's only "older cohorts" or working-class couples who feel that it's not quite kosher for a wife to bring in most of the bacon, consider this study: Researchers gave undergraduates fictitious scenarios in which they were asked to rate the qualifications of a person for promotion. When they arranged to have everything be equal, but made the main wage earner a wife (saying her salary was $100,000 in a household reporting an income of $150,000), *both* males and females rated this person as basically less qualified to advance (Triana, 2011).

- ***The work world is separated into women's and men's jobs.*** Now combine this information with **occupational segregation**—the fact that we still have classically "male" and "female" jobs. About 98 percent of secretaries and child-care workers are women (Charles, 1992; Cohen, 2004; Reskin, 1993). Statistically speaking, female-type jobs have lower wages. These pay differences, plus the forces I listed above, explain why, in 2011—with an average weekly wage standing at 82.4 percent of men's salaries—women who work full time still earn significantly less than men (U.S. Department of Labor, 2011). Moreover, notice from figure 11.5 that this wage gap applies *within* comparable college majors. So, as a female college graduate whose B.A. is in engineering, you can expect to earn considerably more than someone who majored in the arts; but you still will make, on average, a whopping $17,000 less than your male counterpart in that same field!

When the daycare teachers in this photo arrive at their jobs, they can expect to get lots of attention, from these 3-year-olds, their moms, and the staff. For males, there are special perks to being employed at a typically "female" workplace.

How do women feel when they are working as engineers or in another profession where most of their colleagues are male? Here, too, the news is not so good. In another U.S. poll, women working in mainly male job environments reported low levels of co-worker support compared to females employed in mixed or mainly same-sex groups. But, ironically, men working in female work environments—let's say, male child-care workers—reported the most collegial work conditions of all! (See Taylor, 2010.)

The bottom line is that, while the women's movement has blurred the twenty-first-century gender-role landscape, it definitely has *not* erased women's and men's traditional roles (Bianchi & Milkie, 2010). But, if you think I'm blaming discrimination for this situation, you would be wrong! For a variety of reasons (biological, psychological, social, and so on), family care remains a female priority, and succeeding at work is more emotionally vital for males. To emphasize this message: While for men having a well-paying, high-status job strongly predicts overall life-satisfaction, female CEOs are no happier than their counterparts who work as teachers or "household engineers" (aka., full-time moms) (Trzcinski & Holst, 2011).

Now, leaving the topic of gender, let's look *generally* at what forces predict success and happiness at work.

occupational segregation The separation of men and women into different kinds of jobs.

Exploring Career Success and Happiness

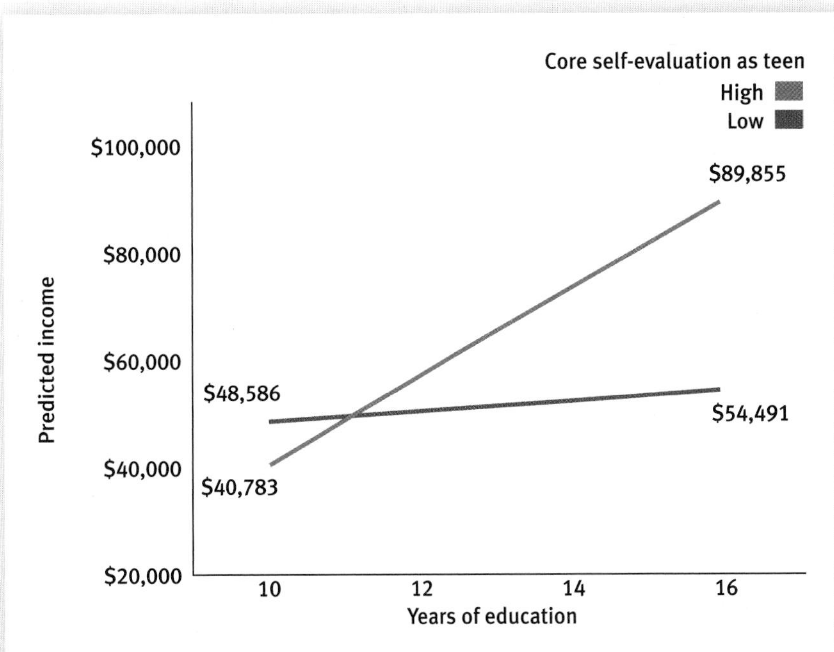

FIGURE 11.6: **How core self-evaluations measured in youth related to average income in early midlife for people with different amounts of education in the National Longitudinal Survey of Youth:** Notice that, as the number of years of schooling increases, feeling confident, efficacious, and happy as a teen translates into greater earning power. But, among people with low core self-evaluations, years of schooling make no difference. Bottom line: The best educational credentials only translate into economic success when people feel good about themselves and basically happy in life.

Source: Judge & Hurst 2007.

Suppose you wanted to predict which high school classmates would be most successful at their careers. It's a no-brainer that you might bet on the class valedictorian and/or your friend from an affluent family. But some of you may know Harvard Ph.D.'s or people with billionaire parents who are failing miserably to live up to their career potential. What might these people be missing in life?

Clues come, again, from the National Longitudinal Study of Youth. At their first evaluation, sampling teenagers in 1979, the researchers measured what they called "core self-evaluations": whether a person had high self-esteem; was optimistic or depressed; and whether that teenager felt in control of his life. For adolescents with life advantages, this *single* evaluation, decades earlier, predicted economic success by early midlife!

Figure 11.6 shows the findings for education. Notice that core self-evaluations did not translate into higher income for high school graduates—underlining, again, that in today's economy college is essential to succeed. But, as people got better educated, these inner attitudes had a powerful impact on wages. In fact, if a young person had poor self-esteem, felt depressed, and had low self-efficacy, there were *no* income advantages of finishing college at all.

Why do core self-evaluations matter so much, once we are on the college or graduate track? In exploring the self-esteem ratings, one researcher found that people who feel good about themselves gravitate to more rewarding fields (Drago, 2011). So, given equal GPAs, your college classmates with high self-esteem will tend to "go for" a more fulfilling job or career. Another study, with business majors, found that students with high core self-evaluations selected the most challenging classroom tasks (Srivastava and others, 2010). So, upbeat, efficacious young people may be successful because they generally adopt a "worker-like" approach to life's demands (recall the last chapter).

Yes, core self-evaluations, like optimism and self-efficacy, may be partly biologically built in or acquired during childhood. But, remember from Chapter 10, that most people do enter college optimistic, committed to succeed, and that personality can change a good deal during the emerging adult years. Moreover, another longitudinal study suggested this optimistic outlook might also be nurtured after a person leaves school.

In following business school graduates, researchers found that support from caring people—not specifically career mentoring, but general support—after students got their first post-graduation jobs, promoted optimism, which then snowballed and led to higher optimism down the road (Higgins, Dobrow, & Roloff, 2010). Just as at age 1, caring attachment figures *during* adulthood provide us with a platform to confidently venture into the world.

Now, let's say you have the basics—loving support, high self-efficacy, an optimistic world view, and a college degree—what *specifically* can you do to find your ideal person–environment fit at work?

Strategy 1: Match Career to your Personality

According to John Holland's (1997) classic theory, the key is to match your job to your personality. People who are sociable should not work in solitary cubicles. Someone strong

TABLE 11.6: Holland's Six Personality Types

Realistic type: These people enjoy manipulating machinery or working with tools. They like physical activity and being outdoors. If you fit this profile, your ideal career might be in construction, appliance repair, or car repair.

Investigative type: These people like to find things out through doing research, analyzing information, and collecting data. If you fit this pattern, you might get special satisfaction in some scientific career.

Artistic type: These people are creative and nonconforming, and they love to freely express themselves in the arts. If this is your type, a career as a decorator, dancer, musician, or writer might be ideal.

Social type: These people enjoy helping others and come alive when they are interacting with other human beings. If this description fits you, a career as a bartender, practicing physician, or social worker might be right.

Entrepreneurial type: These people like to lead others, and they enjoy working on organizational goals. As this kind of person, you might find special joy as a company manager or in sales.

Conventional type: These people have a passion for manipulating data and getting things organized. If you fit this type, you would probably be very happy as an accountant, administrative assistant, or clerk.

Take a minute to think about your three-letter code. Can you use this framework to come up with your ideal career?

in Howard Gardner's naturalistic intelligence (recall Chapter 7) should search for a profession that involves working with nature, perhaps choosing landscaping or working with animals, over slaving in a corporate tower. The closer we get to our ideal personality–career fit, as Holland argues, the more satisfied and successful we can be at our jobs.

To promote this fit, Holland classifies six personality types, described in Table 11.6, and fits them to occupations. Based on their answers to items on a career inventory, people get a three-letter code, showing the three main categories into which they fit, in descending order of importance. If a person's ranking is SAE (social, artistic, and entrepreneurial), that individual might find fulfillment directing an art gallery or managing a beautiful restaurant. If your code is SIE (social, investigative, and entrepreneurial), you might be better off marketing a new medicine for heart disease, or spending your work life as a practicing veterinarian.

Still, even when people have found work that fits their personality, there is no guarantee that they will be happy at a job. What if your gallery director job involves mountains of paperwork and little time exercising your creative or social skills? Suppose your gallery is in financial trouble, and you have a micromanaging owner in charge? To find work happiness, it's vital to consider the actual workplace, too.

Strategy 2: Find an Optimal Workplace

What constitutes an ideal job situation? U.S. workers agree on the following qualities: Jobs should give us autonomy to exercise our creativity. We want input into decision–making at work, caring colleagues, and organizations that are sensitive to our needs (Panaccio & Vandenbergehe, 2009; Simon, Judge, & Halvorsen-Ganepola, 2010). Remember from Chapter 7 that these same qualities—autonomy, nurturing, and relatedness—define ideal school environments. Ideally, we are looking for **intrinsic career rewards**—work that is fulfilling in itself.

intrinsic career rewards Work that provides inner fulfillment and allows people to satisfy their needs for creativity, autonomy, and relatedness.

extrinsic career rewards Work that is performed for external reinforcers, such as pay.

Extrinsic career rewards, or external reinforcers, such as salary, can also be crucial, depending on a person's situation. For instance, one longitudinal study showed intrinsic career rewards become less vital to work satisfaction as people (particularly men) moved through their twenties and had families—again suggesting that the breadwinner role remains a priority for twenty-first-century married men (Porfeli & Mortimer, 2010). Moreover, while money does not make for happiness, below a certain salary, family income has a dramatic impact on well-being. So, for the millions of U.S. workers who are struggling to make it from paycheck to paycheck, salary *is* a prime job concern. As I mentioned earlier, another extrinsic concern that ranks highly on U.S. workers' list of career priorities is job security (Meltzer and others, 2010). Unfortunately, having the luxury of viewing a job as an intrinsically gratifying, flow-inducing experience depends on having our "security needs" satisfied or knowing we can economically survive.

Remember from Chapter 10 that flow states require that our skills match the demands of a given task. Therefore, it should come as no surprise that the most poisonous job-related stress is "role ambiguity," or a lack of clear work demands (Gilboa and others, 2008). If you are unsure of what is expected at your job, or have no guidelines as to how you can be effective, there is simply no chance of feeling "in flow." Feeling a sense of unfairness—that other, less-competent people are getting ahead at your job—is tailor-made to produce burnout and frustration, too (Maslach & Leiter, 2008). Another problem that impairs flow states is **role overload**—having way too much to do to do an effective job. A related issue is **role conflict**—being torn between competing life demands.

This brings up the topic of **family–work conflict.** As hundreds of studies document, being pulled between the demands of a job and family is a major stress for women and men, especially during their prime childrearing years (the late twenties through the forties) (Bianchi & Milkie, 2010; Mathews, Bulger & Barnes-Farrell, 2010). But, without minimizing the fact that work-to-family conflict ("I feel guilty about not spending enough time with my son or daughter") and/or family-to-work interference ("If I stay home with my sick child, I might get fired") can cause anguish, a fulfilling job also energizes people to relate better as a parent or spouse (Bass & Grzywacz, 2011; Siu and others, 2010). The fact that work enriches our family life is very apparent when we look at the impact of being out of a job.

role overload A job situation that places so many requirements or demands on workers that it becomes impossible to do a good job.

role conflict A situation in which a person is torn between two or more major responsibilities—for instance, parent and worker—and cannot do either job adequately.

family–work conflict A situation in which people—typically parents—are torn between the demands of family and work.

© David Turnley/Corbis

Imagine what it's like to leave this screaming baby every morning and go to your job and you will understand why family–work conflict is a special torture, particularly when a couple has young children.

IN FOCUS: Being Unemployed

Do you know someone who is out of work? If you live in most places in the world today, your answer will almost certainly be yes. In recent years, with unemployment rates skyrocketing even in the "affluent" United States and many European nations, losing a job qualifies as a premier global life strain of our times.

It's a life strain that has effects that go beyond not earning a paycheck. Work gives people a place to go during the day. It offers social support. It provides purpose to our daily lives. From coping with financial hardships to—as you saw earlier in the gender discussion—handling a husband who is depressed, it's no wonder that marital conflict escalates and divorce rates rise when a spouse is out of work (Bianchi & Milkie, 2010; Falconier & Epstein, 2010; Hardie & Lucas, 2010, Kalil, Ziol-Guest, & Epstein, 2010). Based on my discussion of the male-provider identity, you might assume unemployment is more devastating for men. One study did suggest that for women with young children, being laid off *could* be viewed as an opportunity ("Now I can stay home!") (Forret, Sullivan, & Mainiero, 2010). But, the truth is that unemployment is a universal downer—impairing self-esteem for both sexes (Hammarstrom and others, 2011).

A main reason for the developed world demoralization lies in feelings of failure: "There must be something wrong with me because I've been 'downsized' and/or I can't find job." So, we might think that if everyone else is in the same boat—let's say, people live in a high-unemployment region—they would feel less depressed.

Ironically, neither regional nor national out-of-work rates matter (Pittau, Zelli, & Gelman, 2010), nor does a government's amount of unemployment aid. What seems most important is how a society *generally* views being out of work. If you live in a nation where people look down on the jobless as "failures," or "lacking personal responsibility," unemployment hurts the most (Stavrova, Schlösser, & Fetchenhauer, 2011).

This suggests that in our era of economic uncertainty, the best intervention we can make is to change our perceptions. Your jobless loved ones aren't lacking in self-efficacy or not trying "hard enough." And furthermore, the familiar, individualistic U.S. societal message of "You can be anything you want to be if you try hard" also has a serious downside. In one study, inner-city African American men, who adopted this individualistic "it's up to me; I can do anything" outlook were more depressed than people who felt their fate was less under their control (Angner, Hullett, & Allison, 2011). In trumpeting the virtues of inner traits, like core self-evaluations or self-efficacy in promoting achievement, might psychologists also be going too far? Could we, too, be inadvertently encouraging a blame-the-victim mentality, without considering the real-world work "facts" on the ground? How can you personally support the heroic (yes, I mean that) efforts of loved ones coping with this devastating contemporary life strain?

Unemployment (and divorce) are just two life strains we may encounter as we travel through adult life. In the next chapter, we'll generally explore how life stress affects development during the adult years. In that chapter, you'll also learn fascinating information about how we change intellectually and personality-wise as we move into middle age, and get tips for constructing a fulfilling adult life.

TYING IT ALL TOGETHER

1. Michael is unhappy about his job. His grandfather is trying to make him feel better by contrasting the career situation today with "the good old days." Which statement can this grandfather legitimately make?
   a. "Your problem isn't so bad! In my day, people had to stick with a single career."
   b. "Your problem isn't so bad! In my day, people worked longer hours than today."
   c. "Your problem isn't so bad! In my day, we had less job security."
2. Malia, age 26, just got married, and she and her husband are working full time. Based on this section, *statistically speaking*, you can make all of the following predictions *except:*
   a. Malia will be more likely to take time off from work for family caregiving.
   b. Malia will earn less than her spouse.
   c. Malia will be less well educated than her spouse.
   d. Malia will care less about having a high-status job than her spouse.
3. Vanessa, a bubbly, outgoing 30-year-old, has what her friends see as a perfect job: She's a researcher in a one-person office, with flexible hours; she has a large, quiet workspace; a boss who is often away; job security; and great pay. Yet Vanessa is unhappy with the job. According to Holland's theory, what is the problem?
4. Based on this chapter, in a sentence, mention how you might help a friend cope with the emotional strains of being unemployed.

Answers to the Tying It All Together questions can be found at the end of this chapter.

SUMMARY

Marriage

Marriages used to be practical unions often arranged by families. In the early twentieth century, as life expectancy increased dramatically, we developed the modern idea that couples should be best friends and lovers for 50 years. During the late twentieth century, with the women's movement, rising divorce rates, and especially the dramatic increase in unwed motherhood, marriage became **deinstitutionalized**—less of a standard path in the Western world. In contrast to the Middle East, with its male-dominated marriages, and Scandinavia, where not getting married is perfectly fine, in the United States we still care deeply about getting married—but are reluctant to enter that state unless we feel fairly financially secure. Couples can expect a decline in happiness, especially during the first four years of married life; but, for those who stay together, there is often a **U-shaped curve of marital satisfaction**, with happiness rising at the empty-nest stage to a peak in old age. Although elderly married couples can be exceptionally happy, it's important to understand that there are many miserable 50-plus year marriages, and some couples stay as content after 5 years as on their wedding day.

According to Robert Sternberg's **triangular theory of love,** married couples start out with **consummate love,** but passion and intimacy can decline as partners construct separate lives. To preserve passion and intimacy, foster your partner's inner development by being an interesting human being and sharing your flow states with your mate. Happy couples make a high ratio of positive to negative comments, don't get personally hurtful or engage in **demand–withdrawal interactions,** and are committed to the relationship and their partner's growth. Sacrifice and forgiveness—within reason—are important to commitment, too.

Divorce, that common adult event, has several phases. There is a pre-divorce phase of marital unhappiness—possibly accompanied by an affair—then the upheaval of the separation. Although divorce is very stressful, it can cause emotional growth, and lead to future happiness, but primarily if couples were very distressed earlier on (versus simply feeling "a bit" unfulfilled with their mates). Because mothers usually get custody of the children, divorced dads often face the problem of losing their children and go on to remarry and have new families. Both men and women struggle with the challenges and joys of step-parenthood.

Parenthood

Although many more people *can* become parents in our twenty-first-century society, a major concern in Europe and Asia is declining **fertility rates.** Despite our negative stereotypes, childless adults are not more self-centered or unhappy in old age.

The transition to parenthood tends to lessen romance and intimacy. Gender roles become more traditional. Conflicts centered on **marital equity** can arise. Still, some couples grow closer after the baby is born. The quality of a couple's relationship before becoming parents predicts how a marriage will fare after the baby arrives.

Motherhood has extreme lows as well as highs—and this experience is tailor-made to destroy women's idealized images of themselves. Society conveys a sanitized view of motherhood. We tend to blame mothers for their children's "deficiencies," and we sometimes berate working women for not spending enough time with their children. In contrast to our images of an epidemic of uninvolved mothers, twenty-first-century women spend much more time (especially teaching time) with their children than in the past. Contemporary mothers (and fathers) are giving their children unparalleled attention and love—even while they hold down jobs.

We expect fathers to be **breadwinners** and nurturers, as well as good sex-role models and, sometimes, disciplinarians. In recent decades, dads have stepped in to do far more child care, although, statistically speaking, women typically still do more. Fathers play with their children in traditionally male, active ways, and vary in their involvement, depending on their sex-role attitudes, their spouse, and the couple's work schedules. Despite all these changes, many men still vitally care about fulfilling the breadwinner role.

Work

We used to have **traditional stable careers.** Today, we often have **boundaryless careers.** Other contemporary trends are more job insecurity (and unemployment) and full-time workers working more than 40 hours a week. Technology, while it offers more flexibility with regard to physically being at a workplace, contributes to the current overwork trend.

Although they have outpaced men educationally, women have more erratic careers because of the need to provide family care and the fact that, among married couples, the husband is still often still viewed as "the primary breadwinner" (sometimes even when he is unemployed and his wife works full time). The gender gap in pay and **occupational segregation** also suggest that the traditional male breadwinner role endures.

Among college graduates, high core self-evaluations predict success at work. People who are basically happy and confident seek out challenging jobs. In addition to personality (and supportive attachments), work happiness can depend on choosing a job that fits one's personality and offers **intrinsic career rewards.** However, **extrinsic career rewards** such as pay become salient when people need to support a family or need a paycheck to economically survive.

Role overload (too much work to do) and **role conflict** (being pulled between family and work) impair career satisfaction. While **family–work conflict** is a major strain, unemployment can be devastating to self-esteem. As joblessness hurts most when it is seen as a personal failure, we need to support the many adults who are coping heroically with this societal challenge of modern times.

KEY TERMS

deinstitutionalization of marriage, p. 333
U-shaped curve of marital satisfaction, p. 336
triangular theory of love, p. 336
consummate love, p. 337
demand–withdrawal interaction, p. 339
fertility rate, p. 344
marital equity, p. 345
breadwinner role, p. 348
traditional stable career, p. 351
boundaryless career, p. 351
occupational segregation, p. 354
intrinsic career rewards, p. 356
extrinsic career rewards, p. 356
role overload, p. 357
role conflict, p. 357
family–work conflict, p. 357

ANSWERS TO TYING IT ALL TOGETHER QUIZZES

Marriage

1. a and b
2. c
3. According to Sternberg, by looking at three dimensions—passion, intimacy, and commitment—and exploring their combinations we can get a portrait of all the partner love relationships that exist in life. By exploring how these facets change over time, we can also understand why marital happiness might naturally decline over the years. (a) This couple is extremely emotionally involved (has intimacy and passion) but has not decided to get married or enter a fully committed relationship. (b) This couple has it all: intimacy, passion, and commitment. Most likely, they are newlyweds. (c) This couple is best friends (intimate) and married (committed) but no longer passionate. Couples who have been married for decades are most likely to have companionate marriages.

4. By having your own compelling interests and sharing these passions with a partner, you are helping your loved one grow and develop as a person.
5. (1) Spend time together doing exciting activities you both enjoy. (2) Keep disagreements to the topic. Never get personal when fighting. (3) Reach out and give to each other. If you are really committed, sacrificing for your partner should give you special joy.
6. You should advise *against* this!

Parenthood

1. Statistically speaking, Jenna will end up doing most of the childcare—which unfortunately may cause conflicts around marital equity.
2. a and c
3. Tell grandma that's not true! Parents are spending more time with their children than in the past. Moms do far more hands-on teaching—even when they have full-time jobs. And of course, fathers are also much more involved. Not only are dads spending more time teaching and playing with their daughters, and particularly sons, they are even doing more of the routine care.
4. My questions (but you can think of others!): (1) Do you think child care is basically a woman's job, or should couples share this responsibility? (2) Are females basically superior at childrearing than men? (3) Are you willing to change diapers and do the other "scut work" of child care? (4) Does your wife make fun of your caregiving skills and/or seem jealous when you step in to care for the kids? (5) How important is it to you to be the primary breadwinner, and how demanding is your job? (6) How much does your wife earn compared to you? (7) Are you currently out of work or working much less than your wife—and, if so, do you feel uncomfortable about that?

Work

1. a
2. c
3. Vanessa's isolated work environment doesn't fit her sociable personality. She needs ample chances to interact with people during the day.
4. Tell your friend she is really a hero and her situation is not her fault!

Chapter 12

CHAPTER OUTLINE

Midlife

At 20, I remember being so anxious about life. But there is nothing like 30-plus years of living to teach you who you really *are. I mainly credit the life-changing experience of having twins for making me mature. Children lock you into the fact that you have a mission larger than the self. The down times have made a difference in strengthening me too: raising my babies as a single mom before meeting my precious husband, helping Mom take care of Dad during his final years. At age 53, I have zero fears about physical aging. Getting through menopause was a problem, but now that it's over, I feel great. My anxiety relates to my mind. After getting my master's in social work, and seeing poverty up close "in the trenches," I want to return to school to get a Ph.D. in public policy. I now believe the best way to make a difference is to work in government to level the playing field a bit. But can I succeed in the classroom at my age? Am I too old to get a job?*

Then, there are the anxieties about time. I'm watching my new grandbaby a few days a week, while my daughter is at work. Not only is day care expensive, I can't let Joshua spend his first year of life with strangers. Child care is a grandma's job!

Still, I'm up for these challenges, especially since I can rely on my life love, David, to cheer me on. In most ways, I'm basically the same person I was at 20—just as outgoing, caring, and interested in exploring new ideas. And, it's now or never. I feel the clock ticking when I look around. My good friend Susan recently died of cancer. My baby brother Jay retired after having his stroke last year. I get my inspiration from Mom, at age 75, still running the beauty shop six days a week. Mom—well, she's supposed to be old, but she's really middle-aged.

When you think of middle age, what images come to your mind? As is true of Doreen, you might imagine adults at the peak of their powers: confident, mature, focused on what is important in life. You might envision people taking on new challenges, such as going back to school for a second or third career, but also think of menopause, sexual loss, and possible mental decline. You could imagine vigorous, happy grandparents, or midlife daughters overburdened by caring for their parents in old age. In this chapter, devoted to the long life stage that psychologist Carl Jung (1933) poetically labeled "the afternoon of life," we'll explore these joys and heartaches, challenges, and changes.

Let's start by setting some boundaries. When *are* people middle-aged?

Setting the Context

If you are like most people reading this chapter, you probably believe we enter middle age at about age 40 and exit this life stage at age 60 or 65 (Etaugh & Bridges, 2006; Lachman, 2004). Your parents or grandparents might not agree. In U.S. surveys, roughly *half* of all people in their late sixties and seventies call themselves middle-aged (Lachman, 2004). They may be right. When a woman, such as Doreen's mother, or the dance instructors in this photo, are healthy and working in their seventies, should we call them middle-aged or old? When someone is starting a family at age 45 or 50, is that individual middle-aged or a young adult?

Joel Rafkin/Photo Edit

Although the calendar would categorize these seventy-something dance instructors as "senior citizens," they would almost certainly say, "No, we are middle-aged." When people are healthy and active, middle age extends well into later life!

At the other extreme, you may know a middle-aged person who does qualify as "old": a relative in his fifties coping with heart disease; someone who was forced by poor health to retire at a too young, *off-time* age.

To complicate matters further, we might expect that people would have different perspectives about aging during early versus late middle age (the forties compared to the late fifties). We would be right—but in a surprising way. In one U.S. poll, people approaching 60 were just as prone to see the future as full of opportunities as adults in their early forties. But they also were more likely than the forty-somethings to agree with the statement "I feel that time is running out" (Cate & John, 2007).

So, just as with emerging adulthood, middle age is a hazy, ill-defined life stage, with different *social clock* feelings associated with its entry point and end. Moreover, people in this chronological category are a diverse group—in lifestyles, perceptions, and everything else. Diversity—of changes, and from person to person—*plus* consistency is the message of the chapter you are about to read.

The Evolving Self

Do we get more mature as we age, or are we the same people at age 50 as at 25? Should a person, like Doreen in the vignette, worry going back to school in her fifties, and how do our intellectual abilities really change during adult life? These questions have been hotly debated for decades. The reasons for the controversies will become clear as we explore these compelling questions: "How will I change as a person during adulthood?" "How can I have a happy, fulfilling adult life?"

Exploring Personality (and Well-Being)

We actually have *contradictory* views about how our personalities change over the years. One is that we basically don't change: "If Calista is bossy and self-centered in college, she will be bossy and self-centered in the nursing home." Another is that entering new stages of life, or having life-changing experiences, produces radical transformations in our inner self: "Since giving birth, I'm a different person." "Coming close to death in my car accident transformed how I think about the world." Then, there is the change that we hope for, the one many middle-aged and older women also report (Zucker, Ostrove, & Stewart, 2002). As we get older, we should become confident, happier, and more mature. Which point of view is true? The answer, as developmentalists have discovered, is *each* idea, depending on which aspect of personality we chart!

We Don't Change Much (on Average): Exploring the "Big Five"

Big Five: Five core psychological predispositions—neuroticism, extraversion, openness to experience, conscientiousness, and agreeableness—that underlie personality.

Today, the main way researchers measure personality is by ranking people according to five basic temperamental qualities. As you read this list, take a minute to think of where you stand on these partly genetically determined dimensions (see McCrae, Scally, & Terracciano, 2010), which Paul Costa and Robert McCrae have named the **Big Five** traits:

- *Neuroticism* refers to our general tendency toward mental health versus psychological disturbance. Are you resilient, stable, and well-adjusted, someone who bounces back after setbacks; or hostile, high-strung, and hysterical, a person who others might label as psychologically disturbed? (Children with serious externalizing and internalizing tendencies, for instance, would rank high on neuroticism.)
- *Extraversion* describes outgoing attitudes, such as warmth, gregariousness, activity, and assertion. Are you sociable, friendly, a real "people person," someone who thrives on meeting new friends and going to parties, or most comfortable curling up alone with a good book? Do you get antsy when you are by yourself, thinking "I've got to get out and be with people," or do you prefer living a reflective, solitary life?
- *Openness to experience* refers to our passion to seek out new experiences. Do you adore traveling the world, adopting different perspectives, having people shake up your preconceived ideas? Do you believe life should be a continual adventure and relish getting out of your comfort zone? Or are you cautious, rigid, risk averse, and comfortable mainly with what you already know?
- *Conscientiousness* describes having the kind of efficacious worker personality described in Chapter 10. Are you hardworking, self-disciplined, and reliable, someone others count on to take on demanding jobs and get things done? Or are you erratic and irresponsible, prone to renege on obligations and forget appointments, a person your friends and co-workers really can't trust?
- *Agreeableness* has to do with kindness, empathy, and the ability to compromise. Are you pleasant, loving, and easy to get along with; or stubborn, hot-tempered, someone who continually seems offended and gets into fights? (Agreeable people, for instance, have secure attachment styles.)

Decades of studies show that where we rank on the Big Five dimensions has consequences for our lives. Extroverts are upbeat and happy (Butkovic, Brkovic, & Bratko, 2011; Cox and others, 2010). People high on neuroticism are stressed out, anxious, and sad. Conscientious adults have fewer heart attack risk factors (Sutin and others, 2010) and live longer because they are more responsible and health aware. Being intellectually curious (Silva & Sanders, 2010), adults who are open to experience tend to stay cognitively sharp as they age (Gregory, Nettlebeck, & Wilson, 2010; Sharp & others, 2010). One longitudinal study even suggested that openness to experience and conscientiousness might help protect us against developing Alzheimer's disease (Duberstein and others, 2011).

Moreover, as you might expect, being conscientious, agreeable, extroverted and not neurotic makes for success in relationships. People who score high on these Big Five traits

Look at these exuberant women enjoying themselves at a party and you will understand why extroverts are *generally* happy (and also why simply being around a "people person" makes us feel more upbeat). How would you rank yourself on extraversion, and each of the other Big Five traits I just described?

Bob Daemmrich/Photo Edit

are more likely to be happily married, less prone to divorce. As one 45-year-long study showed, these dimensions even predict achieving at a high level in a career (reported in Roberts and others, 2007).

This brings up an interesting issue. How much do our Big Five rankings change during adult life? The good news is that positive traits like agreeableness and, as I implied in Chapter 10, conscientiousness, strengthen with age. Think "unreliable teenager" versus "responsible grandma" and you can see why, in one cross-sectional survey, the average difference in conscientiousness between 16-year-olds and 80-year-olds was huge (Allemand, Zimprich, & Hendriks, 2008). The bad news is that by roughly age 30, our relative rankings on all five dimensions stabilize. So, if your 35-year-old friend is very unreliable, he will probably grow *somewhat* more responsible as the years pass, but still fall short compared to his peers. After emerging adulthood, the bottom-line prediction, based on the Big Five, to the question "How much will my personality change?" is "not much" (Costa & McCrae, 2002; Schaie, Willis, & Caskie, 2004; Terracciano, McCrae, & Costa, 2010).

The idea that our basic personality doesn't change much may fit in with your personal experience. Contact a college acquaintance decades later, and you may be amazed at how much of the same person reemerges: "She's just as much a party animal at 60 as she was at 25!" "He's got the same problems with wife number three as with wife number one!"

Let's now follow the same approach I have been using throughout this book, exploring how *evocative* "nature produces nurture" forces work to solidify our basic personality tendencies and make us *more* like ourselves as we age.

Take Sara, in her mid-twenties, who ranks high on conscientiousness. Her hard-working personality ensures that she does well in college and gets an excellent first job. As she travels through her career, she is praised for her industriousness, and eventually lands an executive position at a firm. Sara is a committed, loyal friend who works hard on her marriage, and—because we match up by *homogamy*—has a conscientious mate. At age 55, Sara's life is a testament to the power of hard work in building a fulfilling life. She is the rock on which her family and employees depend.

Robert Brenner/Photo Edit

This temperamentally disagreeable, middle-aged man has probably been inciting these kinds of angry encounters for decades, explaining why our Big Five personality rankings tend to remain stable, and—in this particular case—showing that disagreeable people may get even angrier as they travel through life.

Now, imagine José, an emerging adult friend of yours, who ranked low on agreeableness at age 30. Because José is so hostile, he continually loses jobs and—over the decades—had several bitter divorces. At age 60, when you accidentally bump into José, he seems even more bitter, demoralized, and depressed.

But these are *average* tendencies. When developmentalists conduct longitudinal studies, they find some people change a good deal (Roberts and others, 2007). What causes these dimensions of personality to shift? In following men from late middle age into their sixties, researchers found that changes in basic temperamental traits often occur in response to *other* major changes (Mroczek & Spiro, 2003). A lifelong extrovert might become less outgoing after developing serious memory problems. A disagreeable 60-year-old could act mellower after finding a loving new mate (Small and others, 2003). So, yes, in general, you can predict that a 30-year-old extrovert will love to socialize at 65. But you could be very wrong.

Knowing that someone is extroverted, conscientious, or disagreeable gives us the basic outlines of personality. But it tells us nothing about the specifics of a person's life. Think of several friends who rank high on conscientiousness. One person might be a full-time mother; another might be a company manager; yet another might have found the outlet for her conscientiousness through being a nurse. In order to really understand what makes human beings tick, we have to move in closer and interview people about their lives. This is the strategy that Dan McAdams has used to explore personality during the adult years. Let's eavesdrop on one of McAdams's interviews:

> I was living in a rural North Dakota town and was the mother of a 4-year-old son. One summer afternoon . . . Jeff left without me and was hit by a car. When I got there, he was lying in the street unconscious . . . . I felt sure he was dying, and I didn't know of anything I could do .... My friend did, though, and today [Jeff] is 18 years old and very healthy. That feeling of being helpless... while I was sure I was watching my son die was a turning point. I decided I would never feel it again and I became an E.M.T.
>
> (quoted in McAdams, de St. Aubin, & Logan, 1993, p. 228)

When he listened to these kinds of life stories, McAdams came to different conclusions about how much our personality changes. Although this woman might have always ranked relatively high in conscientiousness, the *specific* path her life took was responsive to this life-changing event. In McAdams's opinion, once we fill in the rich details of human experience, we do see lives being transformed.

generativity In Erikson's theory, the seventh psychosocial task, in which people in midlife find meaning from nurturing the next generation, caring for others, or enriching the lives of others through their work. According to Erikson, when midlife adults have not achieved generativity, they feel stagnant, without a sense of purpose in life.

We Do Change: Examining Generative Priorities

In addition to exploring the twists and turns of our human journey through asking people to reflect on their lives, McAdams has devoted his career to testing the ideas of the pioneering theorist who *does* believe that we change at different life stages: Erik Erikson. Does **generativity**, or nurturing the next generation, become our main priority during midlife? Is Erikson (1969) correct that fulfilling our generativity is the key to feeling happy during "the afternoon" of life? When people in their forties or fifties don't feel generative, are they stagnant, demoralized, and depressed? (See Table 12.1.)

To capture Erikson's concept, McAdams's research team constructed a questionnaire to generally measure generative attitudes. (You can take the first ten items on this scale in Table 12.2 on page 368.) The researchers also explored people's generative priorities by telling them to "list the top ranking agendas in your life now" (see McAdams, 2001a).

When these developmentalists gave their measures to young, middle-aged, and elderly people, they found few age differences in generative attitudes. People were just as likely to care about making a difference in the world at age 20 or 50 or 85. The researchers did discover age differences in generative *priorities*—with emerging adults ranking very low on this scale (McAdams, Hart, & Maruna, 1998). Young people's goals were centered on identity issues. A 20-year-old might say, "I want to

TABLE 12.1: Erikson's Psychosocial Stages

Life Stage	Primary Task
Infancy (birth to 1 year)	Basic trust versus mistrust
Toddlerhood (1 to 2 years)	Autonomy versus shame and doubt
Early childhood (3 to 6 years)	Initiative versus guilt
Late childhood (6 years to puberty)	Industry versus inferiority
Adolescence (teens into twenties)	Identity versus role confusion
Young adulthood (twenties to early forties)	Intimacy versus isolation
Middle adulthood (forties to sixties)	**Generativity versus stagnation**
Late adulthood (late sixties and beyond)	Integrity versus despair

hedonic happiness Well-being defined as pure pleasure.

eudaimonic happiness Well-being defined as having a sense of meaning and life purpose.

TABLE 12.2: McAdams's Generative Concern Scale

True	False	
☐	☐	1. I try to pass along the knowledge I have gained through my experiences.
☐	☐	2. I do not feel that other people need me.
☐	☐	3. I think I would like the work of a teacher.
☐	☐	4. I feel as though I have made a difference to many people.
☐	☐	5. I do not volunteer to work for a charity.
☐	☐	6. I have made and created things that have had an impact on other people.
☐	☐	7. I try to be creative in most things that I do.
☐	☐	8. I think that I will be remembered for a long time after I die.
☐	☐	9. I believe that society cannot be responsible for providing food and shelter to all homeless people.
☐	☐	10. Others would say that I have made unique contributions to society.

Answers: 1. T, 2. F, 3. T, 4. T, 5. F, 6. T, 7. T, 8. T, 9. F, 10. T

Source: McAdams & de St. Aubin, 1992, pp. 1003–1015.

How do you score on this scale measuring overall generative motivations?

make it through college and get a good job" or "My plan is to figure out what I want to do with my life." Midlife and older adults were more likely to report: "My mission is to help my teenage son," or "My goal is to work for justice and peace in the world."

This makes sense. Remember from Chapter 6 that prosocial behaviors are in full swing by early childhood. There is no reason to think that our human drive to be nurturing changes at any particular life stage. But, just as Erikson would predict, we need to resolve issues related to our personal development before our primary concern shifts to giving to others in the wider world.

Is Erikson right that, as people *enter* midlife, generativity takes center stage? According to one study, "not necessarily." In following women from their forties into their sixties, researchers found that issues relating to identity ("developing as a person"; "expanding myself") remained strong well into middle age. But, as these women got older, generativity gradually grew. According to this research, priorities fully focused on giving to the next generation reach a crescendo in the early sixties, once we know exactly who we are (Newton & Stewart, 2010).

Adults of every age derive great pleasure from engaging in generative activities. But now that he is in his late sixties and has transcended self-oriented, identity concerns, cultivating a community garden to provide poor people with free vegetables qualifies as the generative center of this elderly man's life.

Michael Newman/Photo Edit, Inc.

Is Erikson correct that generativity is the key to happiness during adult life? Here, the answer is "it depends." If we define happiness as just "feeling good" (**hedonic happiness**) and then think of generative role models such as Martin Luther King, Jr., the word "happy" doesn't apply. But, if we consider happiness in its richer sense, as having purpose and meaning in life (**eudaimonic happiness**), then, yes, highly generative people do have exceptionally happy lives (Grossbaum & Bates, 2002; Zucker, Ostrove, & Stewart, 2002). And just as parent readers with children may choose to be miserable at the Magic Kingdom—rather than luxuriating in the hotel spa—our main mission (even when on vacation!), experts agree, is *not* chasing hedonic pleasure, but living meaningful, generative lives (McMahan & Estes, 2011; Seligman, 2011).

Actually, when people don't have generative goals, their lives lack meaning. As Erikson described, they feel *stagnant*—purposeless and at loose ends. Read what one researcher had to say about Deborah, who, in her late forties, scored very low on generativity in his study of women's lives:

> In reference to the birth of her first child, Deborah wrote, "All actions automatic. No emotional involvement . . . ; totally self-preserving but very unpleasant." After many years of marriage, Deborah underwent a difficult divorce. She began to work in a "blur of meaningless jobs."
>
> (adapted from Peterson, 1998, p. 12)

Tim Graham/Getty Images

The saintly life of the icon Mother Theresa (shown here with the poor children of Calcutta) is a testament (and reminder) that you can achieve the ultimate in generativity without being a parent.

As this case history suggests, having children does not automatically evoke generativity. You can give birth and be totally non-generative and uninvolved. But, becoming a parent, and relishing that role, can have long-term consequences for a person's life.

In one national U.S. study, researchers found that if a man became a father as a young adult and—very important—reported being emotionally engaged with his children (whether he was divorced and didn't live with his sons or daughters didn't matter), during late middle age, he was apt to be active in community service and altruistically involved with family and friends. So, while we definitely don't need to be parents to be generative, having children may give some people (particularly men) a platform to develop this aspect of their identity, and turn them on to the gratifications of a generative life (Eggebeen, Dew, & Knoester, 2010).

Moreover, in the longitudinal study I mentioned above, if a woman in her early fifties ranked as highly generative (unlike Deborah in the previous quote), in her sixties, she was likely to find being a grandmother a peak life experience: As one woman reported, "Falling in love is putting it too mildly." Unlike her less generative counterparts, she had no worries about growing old (Peterson & Duncan, 2007). So, just as Erikson predicts, generativity—for both men and women—can smooth the way to a fulfilling old age.

What about the early lives of highly generative people? Do their childhoods differ from more typical adults? To answer this question, McAdams's research team selected community leaders who scored at the upper ends of their Generative Concern Scale (see page 368) and asked them to tell their life stories. Would these autobiographies differ from those of adults such as Deborah in my earlier example, who ranked low on Erikson's midlife task?

The answer was yes. The life stories of highly generative adults had themes demonstrating what the researchers called a **commitment script.** They often described early memories of feeling "blessed": "I was my grandmother's favorite"; "I was a miracle child who should not have survived." They reported feeling sensitive to the suffering of others, from a young age. They talked about having an identity revolving around generative values that never wavered from their teenage years. A 50-year-old minister in one of McAdams's studies was a teenage prostitute, and then a con artist who spent two years in a federal prison; but, throughout her life, she reported, "I was always doing ministry."

The most striking characteristic of generative adults' life stories was **redemption sequences**—examples of devastating events that turned out in a positive way (McAdams, 2006; McAdams & Bowman, 2001). For instance, in the example I just mentioned, the woman minister might view the humiliation of being sent to prison as the

commitment script In Dan McAdams's research, a type of autobiography produced by highly generative adults that involves childhood memories of feeling special; being unusually sensitive to others' misfortunes; having a strong, enduring generative mission from adolescence; and redemption sequences.

redemption sequence In Dan McAdams's research, a characteristic theme of highly generative adults' autobiographies, in which they describe tragic events that turned out for the best.

Karen Kasmauski/Corbis

This group project to restore the oldest Black Baptist church in South Carolina is typical in the African American experience, where a mission to be of service—especially in a caring community that revolves around the church—is standard.

best thing that ever happened, the experience that turned her life around. According to McAdams (2008), early memories of feeling personally blessed, an enduring sensitivity to others' misfortunes, caring values, and, especially, being able to turn one's tragedies into growth experiences are the core ingredients of the commitment script and the main correlates a generative adult life (see also Lilgendahl & McAdams, 2011).

Exceptionally generative people have other attributes. Because taking action to improve society involves being confident and assertive (recall that this quality is also involved in acting prosocially during childhood), they have a strong sense of *self-efficacy*, as well as the motivation to do good. In fact, as McAdams (2008) insightfully points out, taking action to improve, or "repair," the world is our ultimate vehicle for *extending* the self. While they may be terribly troubled by humanity's disrepair, generative people are optimistic. They believe that change is possible and that human beings are basically good (McAdams, 2008; Walker & Frimer, 2007).

If you think of your own generative role models—from a favorite teacher to, hopefully, your mom or dad—these special people are apt to be sprinkled in every ethnic group. But, interestingly, McAdams' found that African American men and women were overrepresented among his sample of outstanding community activists (Hart and others, 2001; McAdams, 2006). Does coping with discrimination—plus their strong grounding in religion—make African Americans unusually sensitive to human suffering and so devote their lives to "repairing" the world? In support of this possibility, themes stressing progress toward overcoming adversity were central in highly generative African Americans' autobiographies (McAdams & Bowman, 2001).

Do you believe that dealing with adversity makes us more generative people? Did a painful experience in your own life change your priorities, transforming you into a stronger, more caring and mature human being?

The idea that life's setbacks cause emotional growth brings me to the third idea about how people change as adults: As we get older, we hope to become more self-confident and emotionally secure. Does coping with painful events promote resilience? Do we *really* get happier and more mature as the years pass?

Life Satisfaction: Optimally satisfied 0.3, 0.2, 0.1, Average 0, −0.1, −0.2, Most distressed −0.3

Traumatic life events: 0, 3, 6+

FIGURE 12.1: **The relationship between experiencing adverse life events and life satisfaction among a national sample of U.S. adults:** Notice from the chart that adults who report no upsetting events in their life history are more distressed than people who have experienced a few past traumas. But after a moderate "adversity level" threshold, happiness declines.

Source: Seery, Holman, & Silver, 2010. Adapted from p. 10.

Do We Get More Mature and Happier with Age?

McAdams' redemption sequence interviews imply that the answer to the first question above should be yes. But, to really test the idea that coping with adversity fosters inner growth (another way of putting it is, "What does not kill me makes me stronger"), we should go beyond the testimonials of a few generative people. And this is just what researchers did: they polled thousands of adults about major life stresses—from divorce, to death, to disasters (like floods)—and related the number of traumas to reports of well-being.

You can see the findings in Figure 12.1. Notice that the assumption that life stress strengthens us as human beings is partly true. People who report no major negative life events are more distressed than adults who have experienced a few traumatic events. But, after a certain stress threshold (about three major upsetting events), additional traumas do impair mental health. The bottom line is that, yes, experiencing life's blows *can* make us stronger—with this qualification: The stress must be tolerable and not too great (Seery, Holman, & Silver, 2010).

Do we get happier with age? Now the answer is an unqualified yes. In fact, you might be surprised to know, youth is overrated as life's happiest stage. Many studies in Western nations agree: The age of maximum life happiness is apt to be our early sixties! (See Angelini and others, 2012; Bergsma & Ardelt, 2011; George, 2010; Helson & Soto, 2005; Windsor & Anstey, 2010.)

Why would happiness peak in the early young-old years? Take a minute to list some possibilities. As I discuss this phenomenon in the next chapter, you'll see if your speculations agree with the ideas of a prominent gerontologist named Laura Carstensen. But, the good news is that we don't need to wait till our sixties to see positive developments in our emotional life. Using the *experience sampling* method, Carstensen and her colleagues discovered this change begins at far younger ages.

Think back to the experiencing sampling procedure in Chapter 9 and you may realize why using beepers to chart people's moment-to-moment feelings has considerable advantages, compared to *self-report* surveys that ask adults to "rate how generally satisfied you are with life." Not only can this beeper technique track the *ongoing* ebb and flow of happiness over time, it allows us to explore other common ideas we have about age and inner growth. As we get older, do our emotions become more stable and "under control"? How *exactly* do our emotional states change over the years?

To thoroughly answer these kinds of questions, Carstensen's research team first solicited over a hundred adults of different ages and collected experiencing sampling beeper data for each person for a week; then they returned to get additional experiencing sampling records three times over the next 10 years (Carstensen and others, 2011). Here are their main findings:

- *With age, the ratio of positive moods increasingly outweighs negative ones.* This is important because, as Table 12.3 on the next page illustrates, we need to experience roughly three positive emotions to one negative emotion to feel generally good about life. (Check out this table for other fascinating happiness research facts.)
- *With age comes greater emotional stability.* It's not that as people get older, their feelings get less intense; but, rather than simply feeling sad or happy, as the years pass, our inner life grows richer or more complex because we are more apt to feel mixed emotions—both happy and sad at the same time.

Norm Dettlaff/Las Cruces Sun-News/AP Photo

This young man is getting great satisfaction as he works to make a difference by registering new voters. According to the research, his youthful prosocial personality may also predict having a fulfilling life.

The bottom-line message is that, according to this beautifully constructed study, people *do* grow emotionally with age!

Obviously, these findings are averages. There are clearly many unhappy, "out-of-control" sixty-somethings. Perhaps you have a middle-aged friend, like Deborah in the earlier example of low generativity, who remains mired in stagnation. The teenage football hero or beauty queen who descends into depression and drug abuse in their forties are classic life stories, too.

Which emerging adults are most likely to grow in happiness—in the eudaimonic sense—as they approach midlife? Clues come from another longitudinal study, which explored men's values during college and followed them into their late thirties. And here the findings should come as no surprise. Emerging adults who had strong prosocial goals, versus priorities centered around making a lot of money, were most likely to be living emotionally meaningful, happy lives (Hill and others, 2011).

This brings me back to the power of enduring personality (and values) in shaping our development. Prosocial young people enter midlife most fulfilled. Men who get heavily involved in fatherhood tend to care for society in a wider way in their older years. Where we stand on the Big Five traits during emerging adulthood predicts succeeding with relationships and in careers. However, change is possible, and positive development occurs. The basic thrust is to get more mature during the adult years!

As a final note, I must re-emphasize that personality does not unfold in a vacuum. It's difficult to grow emotionally if you are mired in poverty or live in a society

TABLE 12.3: Happiness Perceptions and Interesting Research Facts

"Money can't buy happiness."

Answer: *That's true, but only once we are fairly comfortable economically.* Around the globe, poor people *are* significantly less happy than their more affluent counterparts. Once our basic survival needs are satisfied, the correlation between income and happiness becomes weaker—although it still exists. The main reason is probably not that getting more "things" matters, but that money can buy quality family time. And satisfying family relationships are *highly* related to reports of a happy life.

"I'll be happy when I get my career in order; become famous; achieve X, Y, Z goal."

Answer: *Sorry, not really.* According to a phenomenon called the *hedonic treadmill*, when we win the lottery, graduate from college, or (in my case) get a book published, we are thrilled at first, but then revert to our normal happiness set point ("So I got an Oscar last year. What else is new?"). The good news is that the hedonic treadmill also applies to negative events. We adjust and then, eventually, our "natural" happiness returns. Unfortunately, however, with major traumas such as chronic unemployment, we may never reach our prior happiness set point.

"You can't (1) measure happiness or (2) teach people to be happy."

Answer: *Point 1 is totally false; point 2 is probably false.* Research shows that we *can* concretely quantify what it takes to be happy. Once people get above a ratio of 2.9 positive to negative emotions, they generally feel good about life. Therefore, happiness experts (e.g., Seligman, 2011) have developed programs to teach people to savor the moment, count their blessings, or do gratitude exercises. Still, your author (me) believes the best strategy for achieving happiness is *not* to spend time monitoring that feeling. When we are generative, a natural by-product is a happy life.

Because happiness is an inner state, the nation we live in makes a minor impact on personal happiness.

Answer: *Wrong!* Our nation and its government greatly affects personal well-being (Ott, 2011; Pinker, 2011). As a resident of Denmark, for instance, you are probably very happy, with well-being scores topping the global charts at an average of 8 on a 10 point scale; in some African nations, the average person ranks fairly miserable (at below 4) (Wilkinson & Pickett, 2009). Check out the text below for a surprising society-wide characteristic that predicts happiness among *both* affluent and poor citizens.

Additional Sources: Jorgensen, Jamieson, & Martin, 2010; Ladis, Daniels, & Kawachi, 2009.

rife with conflict and corruption, where life traumas are intense and routine. The reason why Denmark clocks in with the world's highest well-being (see Table 12.3) is not just that this country is comparatively affluent. People are happiest in nations where they trust their government to be fair and effective (Ott, 2011) and income inequalities are relatively small (Wilkinson & Pickett, 2009). So our own happiness depends on living in a generative society, where life isn't a zero-sum game. We are most likely to flourish as people when everyone around us is flourishing, too.

Wrapping up Personality (and Well-Being)

Now, let's summarize *all* of these messages. Having read this section, here is what you might tell an emerging-adult friend who wants insights into the person she can expect to be at age 40 or 55:

- Expect to become somewhat more reliable and agreeable although, in general, your basic personality will probably not change much over the years.
- Expect your priorities to shift toward more generative concerns and to grow in generativity, especially during midlife.
- Expect to become more mature and grow happier if you have a few—but not too many—stressful life experiences, have prosocial values, and live in a trustworthy society that promotes human equality.

• Take each of these predictions with a grain of salt. Life-changing experiences, at any age, can set you on a different life path.

Consistency from youth to later life, diversity from person to person, and different pathways of change depending on how we measure personality—we can see these same themes as we explore how people develop intellectually during adult life.

Wechsler Adult Intelligence Scale (WAIS) The standard test to measure adult IQ, involving verbal and performance scales, each of which is made up of various subtests.

Exploring Intelligence (and Wisdom)

Remember from Chapter 7 that, when psychologists measure intelligence during childhood, they look mainly at how elementary schoolers perform on standard intelligence tests. Sometimes, they spell out different ideas about what it means to be smart, such as Gardner's multiple intelligences or Sternberg's successful intelligence. Developmentalists use standard IQ tests and nontraditional strategies to trace adult intelligence, too.

Stephen Marks/Corbis

How will this young woman's cognitive abilities change as she ages? Stay tuned for answers now.

Taking the Traditional Approach: Looking at Standard IQ Tests

Think of your intellectual role model. Most likely, your mind will immediately gravitate to someone who is 50 or 80—not a person who is 20 or 25. In fact, if you are like most adults, you probably assume that, in general, people get more intelligent over the years (Sternberg & Berg, 1992).

Mid-twentieth-century psychologists had a different idea: They believed that people reach their intellectual peak in their twenties, and then intelligence steadily declines (Botwinick, 1967). They based these disturbing conclusions on studies using the (at the time) newly developed Wechsler Adult Intelligence Scale.

The **Wechsler Adult Intelligence Scale (WAIS)**, the standard test measuring adult IQ, has the same format as the WISC, the parallel scale for children, described in Chapter 7. It has verbal and performance scales. The verbal scale measures different types of knowledge, such as vocabulary and adults' ability to solve math problems. The performance scale asks test-takers to perform relatively unfamiliar activities, such as putting together puzzles or arranging blocks. On this part of the test, speed is essential. People must complete the performance scale items within a limited time.

When psychologists tested adults to derive their standards for how people should normally perform on the WAIS at different ages, they discovered that, starting in the twenties, in each older age group, average scores declined. They also found the interesting pattern in Figure 12.2. While verbal scores stayed stable or declined to a lesser degree, average scores on the performance scale steadily slid down, starting in people's twenties (Botwinick, 1967).

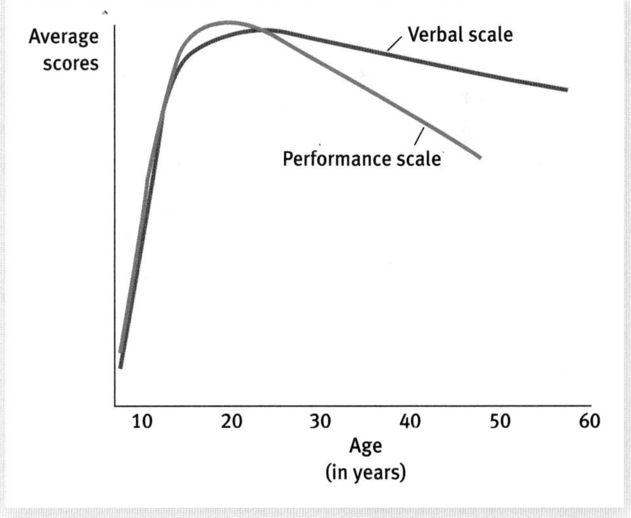

FIGURE 12.2: **Age-related changes in mean scores on the performance and verbal scales of the WAIS:** This chart shows the pattern of decline from a study using the early form of the WAIS. Notice how average scores on the performance scale regularly slid down starting in the twenties, while scores on the verbal scale remained more stable with age. *Source*: Botwinick, 1967.

These findings would not give any fifty-something student, like Doreen in the introductory chapter vignette, confidence about venturing into a college classroom full of 20-year-olds. Luckily, however, the researchers were not taking into account the huge educational differences between different cohorts at that time in U.S. history. While virtually all of the young people taking the test had gone to high school, many middle-aged or elderly people taking the original WAIS had probably left school in the seventh or eighth grade. So the psychologists were comparing apples to oranges—adults with far less education to those with much more.

Seattle Longitudinal Study The definitive study of the effect of aging on intelligence, carried out by K. Warner Schaie, involving simultaneously conducting and comparing the results of cross-sectional and longitudinal studies carried out with a group of Seattle volunteers.

How does our performance on standard intelligence tests *really* change as we travel through adult life? To answer this question, in the early 1960s, researchers began the **Seattle Longitudinal Study**—the definitive study of intelligence and age (Schaie, Willis, & Caskie, 2004; Schaie & Zanjani, 2006).

Imagine being a twentieth-century researcher interested in charting how people change intellectually during adulthood. If you were to carry out a cross-sectional study—comparing different age groups at the same time—your findings would be biased in a negative way. Older cohorts would be at a disadvantage, not having had as much experience taking tests, typically having gone to school for far fewer years. But if you carried out a longitudinal study, you would end up with a far-too-positive portrait of how the *average* person changes. The volunteers who enrolled in your study would probably be highly educated. Over the years, as people dropped out of your research, you would be left with an increasingly self-selected group, the fraction of older people who were proud of proving their intellectual capacities and—as they reached their seventies—those healthy enough to take your tests (Baltes & Smith, 1997).

Faced with these contrasting biases (longitudinal research will be too positive; cross-sectional research will be biased in a negative way), the researchers devised a brilliant solution: Combine the two kinds of studies, factor out the biases of each research method, and isolate the "true" impact of age on IQ.

First, the research team selected people enrolled in a Seattle health organization who were 7 years apart in age, tested them, and compared their scores. Then, they followed each group longitudinally, testing them at 7-year intervals. At each evaluation, the psychologists selected another cross-sectional sample, some of whom they also followed over time.

Using an IQ test that, unlike the WAIS, measured five basic cognitive abilities, the researchers got a more encouraging portrait of how we change intellectually—one that fits our intuitive sense of how we should perform. Notice in looking at Figure 12.3 that, on this measure—involving, for instance, tests of vocabulary and our ability to quickly think up words—we reach our intellectual peak during our forties and early fifties (Schaie, 1996; Schaie, Willis, & Caskie, 2004). Still, the Seattle study showed the same pattern researchers first found on the WAIS. On tests measuring people's store of knowledge, such as vocabulary, scores improve till at least age 60 or beyond (Larsen, Hartmann, & Nyborg, 2008). But when a test involves doing something new very fast (such as arranging puzzles within a time limit or the word fluency measure in Figure 12.3), losses start as early as the forties (Ardila, 2007). Now, let's look at a theory that makes sense of these findings and tells us a good deal about our intellectual abilities in the real world.

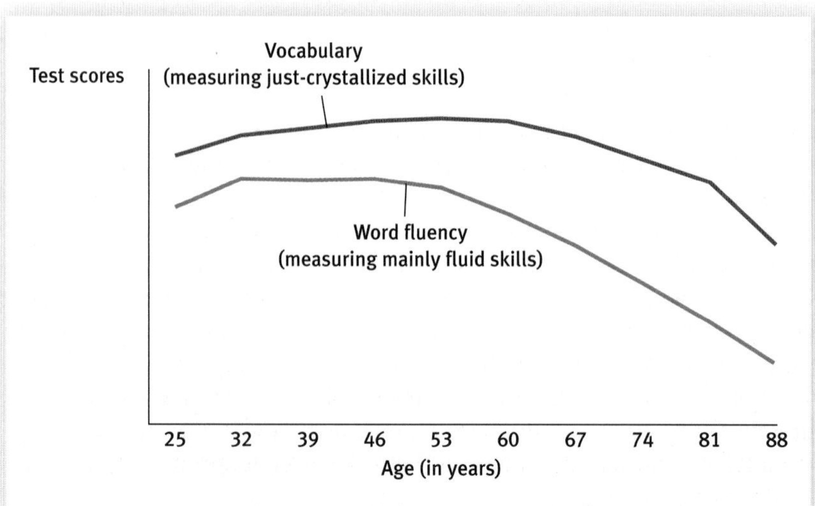

FIGURE 12.3: **Changes in two intellectual abilities over the decades in the Seattle Longitudinal Study:** Notice that scores on a test demanding a heavier component of fluid skills (word fluency, which asks people to name as many words as they can starting with a letter such as A, within a time limit) decrease after the late 40s; while those on a totally crystallized test (vocabulary) stay stable into the 60s. But in general, intellectual abilities are at their peak in the 50s and decline in old age.

Source: Schaie, 1996.

David Becker/Getty Images

AP Images

As his passion demands speedy mental processing, this gaming guru may feel "old" in his thirties. But this 60-year-old professor will probably see his teaching as better than ever today because his job depends almost exclusively on crystallized skills.

Two Types of Intelligence: Crystallized and Fluid Skills

Psychologists today typically divide intelligence into two categories. **Crystallized intelligence** refers to our knowledge base, the storehouse of information that we have accumulated over the years. The verbal scale of the WAIS, with its tests of vocabulary and math, mainly measures crystallized skills. **Fluid intelligence** involves our ability to reason quickly when facing new intellectual challenges. The WAIS performance scale, with its emphasis on putting together blocks or puzzles within a time limit, tends to measure fluid skills.

crystallized intelligence A basic facet of intelligence, consisting of a person's knowledge base, or storehouse of accumulated information.

fluid intelligence A basic facet of intelligence, consisting of the ability to quickly master new intellectual activities.

Fluid intelligence—because it depends on our nervous system being at its biological peak—is at its high point in our twenties and then declines. Because it measures the knowledge that we have amassed over years, crystallized intelligence tends to increase until about the late fifties, and then begins to slowly fall off (Kaufman, 2001). The reason is that, by this point in life, our rate of forgetting outpaces the amount of new knowledge that we can absorb.

The great news for baby boomers like me is that, with regard to the most vital crystallized skill—solving relationship-oriented problems—older adults do better than people of any other age (Grossmann and others, 2010; more about this later). Plus, the losses on fluid intelligence tests are not as great for my cohort as for my parents' generation (Zelinski & Kennison, 2007), suggesting that the *Flynn effect* (discussed in Chapters 1 and 7) also applies to the older years. Not only are we baby boomers "aging" mentally quicker, when your cohort arrives at middle and later life, you will probably outscore us on measures of fluid abilities, too. The bad news is that the inevitable age-related losses on fluid IQ tests reflect a slowing of information processing that extends to many areas of life.

So, in *any* situation requiring quick multitasking, people may notice their abilities declining at a relatively young age. In your late thirties it seems harder to dribble a basketball while keeping your attention on the opposing team. You are having more trouble juggling cooking and having conversations with guests at your dinner parties than at age 25. In old age, these steady fluid losses, as you will see in Chapter 14, progress to the point where they truly interfere with daily life.

The distinction between fluid and crystallized intelligence explains the lifespan path of specific careers. It accounts for why people in fast-paced jobs, such as air-traffic controllers, worry about being over the hill in their forties. It makes sense of why airline CEOs reach their professional peak in their early sixties (but not much beyond!). Anytime an activity depends heavily on quickness, being older presents problems. Whenever an intellectual challenge involves stored knowledge, people improve into their fifties and beyond.

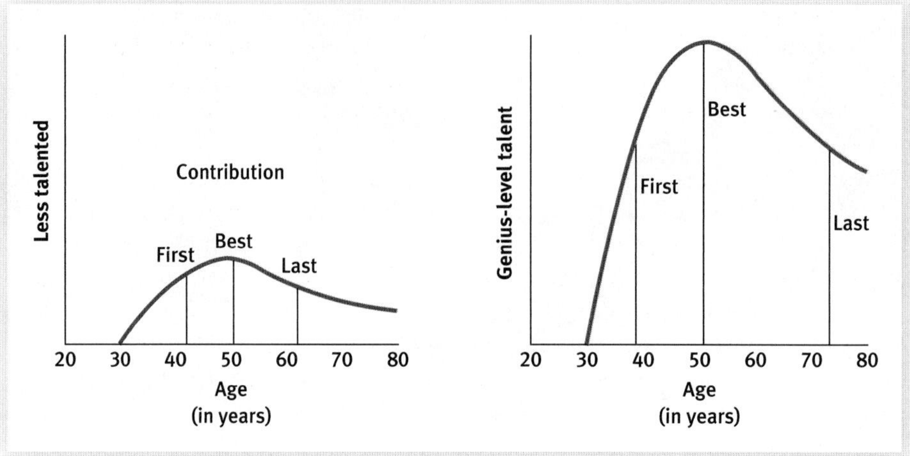

FIGURE 12.4: **Age-related changes in the career paths of geniuses and of less eminent creators:** This chart shows that people reach their peak period of creativity in midlife. However, the most gifted geniuses stand head and shoulders above their contemporaries at every age.
Source: Simonton, 1997.

Mike Powell/Getty Images

Is the middle-aged fashion designer on the left at his creative peak? According to the research, the answer is yes. How proficient will this young man watching ultimately be at designing suits? For answers, we would want to look at this person's creative talents right now.

Suppose you are an artist or a writer. When can you expect to do your finest work? Researchers also find that the age for peak creativity differs, depending on the specific art form. When a creative activity is dependent on being totally original, such as dancing or writing poetry, people tend to perform best in their thirties (see Simonton, 2007). If the form of creativity depends just on crystallized experience, such as writing nonfiction or, in my case, producing college textbooks (yes!), people perform at their best in their early sixties (Simonton, 1997, 2002). But in tracing the lives of people famous for their creative work, one researcher discovered that who we are *as people*, or our enduring abilities, outweighs the changes that occur with age. As Figure 12.4 shows, true geniuses outshine everyone else at *any* age (Simonton, 1997).

So, creatively or career-wise, expect to reach your peak in middle age (in most fields). Still, as you saw earlier with personality, expect to be the same person—to a large degree—as when you were younger. If you are exceptionally competent and creative at 30, you can stay exceptionally competent and creative at 70, or even 95. To illustrate this point, here are quotations from an interview study of creative people over age 60 (Csikszentmihalyi, 1996):

The poet Anthony Hecht, at age 70, commented:

> I'm not as rigid as I was. And I can feel this in the quality . . . of the poems . . . . They are freer metrically, . . . freer in general design. The earliest poems that I wrote were almost rigid in their eagerness not to make any errors. I'm less worried than that now.
>
> (p. 215)

And the historian C. Vann Woodward, at the time in his mid-eighties, said:

> Well, [today] I have . . . changed my mind and the . . . conclusions about what I have written. For example, that book on Jim Crow. I have done four editions of it and I am thinking of doing a fifth, and each time it changes. And they come largely from criticisms that I have received. I think the worst mistake you could make as a historian is to be . . . contemptuous of what is new. You learn that there is nothing permanent in history. It's always changing.
>
> (p. 216)

From Sigmund Freud, who put forth masterpieces into his eighties, to Frank Lloyd Wright, who designed world-class buildings into his ninth decade of life, history is full of examples showing that creativity can burn bright well into old age.

terminal drop A research phenomenon in which a dramatic decline in an older person's scores on vocabulary tests and other measures of crystallized intelligence predicts having a terminal disease.

Staying IQ Smart

Returning to normally creative people, such as you and me, what qualities help *any* person stay cognitively sharp? What causes our intellectual capacities to decline at a younger-than-normal age?

HEALTH MATTERS (BOTH MENTAL AND PHYSICAL). As our mind and our body are "all connected," the first key to staying intelligent with age lies in staying healthy and physically fit (see Brown and others, 2010). As I will describe in Chapter 14, physical and mental fitness are directly linked because cardiovascular problems in particular limit blood flow to the brain.

The most interesting evidence that illness affects IQ relates to an eerie phenomenon called **terminal drop.** While conducting the earliest longitudinal studies of intelligence, developmentalists were astonished to discover that they could predict which older people were more likely to die within the next few years by "larger than expected" losses in their verbal IQ (Cooney, Schaie, & Willis, 1988; Riegel & Riegel, 1972). If a person's scores on tests of vocabulary and other crystallized measures steeply declined, these changes were an ominous early warning sign of a soon-to-be-diagnosed life-threatening disease.

More recent studies suggest that changes in well-being can also be a barometer of approaching death. About 3 to 5 years before people die, happiness levels tend to dramatically decline (Gerstorf and others, 2010; Palgi and others, 2010). While this certainly doesn't mean becoming depressed *causes* us to die (that's like blaming the victim!), it is true that feeling optimistic and "younger than my age" predicts longevity among late middle-aged and older adults (Carstensen and others, 2011; Kotter-Gruhn and others, 2009). Conversely, unexplained dips in our mental state can signal something is seriously physically wrong.

These studies haunted me the summer when I noticed that my father had suddenly aged mentally. My dad, who was always an intellectual whiz, had lost interest in the world. He was disoriented and depressed. A few months later, my worst fears were confirmed: My father was diagnosed with liver cancer, the illness that was to quickly end his life.

MENTAL STIMULATION (WITH PEOPLE) MAY MATTER. Because, recall from Chapter 3, environmental stimulation promotes synaptogenesis, the second key to staying intelligent should be a no-brainer: Exercise your mind!

The studies showing "openness to experience" is linked to adult intelligence imply that stimulating mental activities keep the mind fine-tuned. Additional research reveals that people who work in complex jobs become more mentally flexible with age (Schooler, 1999, 2001; Schooler, Mulatu, & Oates, 2004). But, before we rush out to buy brain-busting gadgets, it's mainly complex jobs involving people—from hosting talk shows, to coaching teens—that predict staying cognitively sharp (Finkel and others, 2009). So, the best intellectual insurance policy is to follow my instructions in Chapter 11: Find a mentally stimulating partner (or surround yourself with interesting friends) that expand the self.

Julian Finney/FIFA/FIFA/Getty Images

Obviously, this fifty-something coach needs to take care of his health in order to do his job—but the interpersonal challenges involved dealing with these young athletes will keep him "on his toes" intellectually during his older years.

But wait a second! Aren't adults with stimulating mates, jobs, and friends, apt to be physically healthy and upper middle class? Couldn't these other forces account for why they tend to "get smarter" with age? To *prove* that interpersonal stimulation promotes cognitive growth, we might have to conduct an impossible (but fun) decades-long experiment: Assign young people to regularly participate in an intellectual version of the TV show *Survivor* (or to host National Public Radio's *All Things Considered*), and compare their IQs to those of a control group in later middle age.

The good news, however, is that while we can't carry out this study with our species, it's fine to experiment on rats. And, when researchers put a group of rats in a large cage with challenging wheels and swings and then compared their cortexes with control animals, this *Survivor*-like treatment produced thicker, heavier brains (Diamond, 1988, 1993). Let's tentatively accept the idea, then, that, just as physical exercise strengthens our muscles, mental exercise *may* produce a resilient mind.

selective optimization with compensation Paul Baltes's three principles for successful aging (and living): (1) selectively focusing on what is most important, (2) working harder to perform well in those top-ranking areas, and (3) relying on external aids to cope effectively.

In sum, people in their forties and fifties are at the peak of their mental powers. But they will have more trouble mastering new cognitive challenges (those involving fluid skills) when under time pressure. To preserve their cognitive capacities as they age, people need to take care of their health and search out stimulating interpersonal experiences. And you can tell any worried 50-year-old family member who is considering going back to school that she should definitely go for it!

INTERVENTIONS: Keeping a Fine-Tuned Mind

Now, let's look at the lessons the research offers for any person who wants to stay mentally sharp as the years pass.

- Develop a hobby or passion that challenges your mind—preferably when you are young. Keep intellectually involved with people as you age.
- Throughout life, search out interpersonal challenges—if not through a job, then through volunteer activities such as coaching or serving on a community board.
- As you age, watch your physical health. In particular, guard against developing cardiovascular disease.
- Understand that, as you get older, new activities involving complex information processing will be more difficult. To cope with these losses, you might adopt the following three-part strategy advocated by Paul Baltes called **selective optimization with compensation.**

Bill Aaron/Photo Edit, Inc.

What can this white-haired female college student do to ensure that she can keep up with her twenty-something classmates in this computer course? She can try to take just this one class, rather than four or five, this term (selection); spend more time studying (optimization); and perhaps tape the lectures, so she doesn't have to just rely on her notes (compensation).

As we move into the older years and notice we cannot function as well as we used to, Baltes believes that we need to (1) *selectively* focus on our most important activities, shedding less important priorities; (2) *optimize*, or work harder, to perform at our best in these most important areas of life; and (3) *compensate*, or rely on external aids, when we cannot cope on our own (Baltes, 2003; Baltes & Carstensen, 2003; Krampe & Baltes, 2003).

Let's take the example of Mrs. Fernandez, whose passion is gourmet cooking. As she reaches her fifties, she might decide to give up some less important interest such as gardening, conserving her strength for the hours she spends at the stove (*selection*). She would need to work harder to prepare complex dishes demanding split-second timing, such as her prize-winning soufflés (*optimization*). She might put a chair in the kitchen rather than stand while preparing meals, or give up preparing elaborate dinner party feasts all by herself, and rely on her guests to bring an appetizer or dessert (*compensation*).

Although Baltes originally spelled out these guidelines to apply to successful aging, they are relevant to anyone coping with the hectic demands of daily life—from parents struggling with *family–work conflict* (Young, Baltes, & Pratt, 2007; recall Chapter 11), to students, such as you, balancing the challenges of different courses. Because finding better life balance helps promote happiness at *any* age (Sheldon, Cummins, & Kamble, 2010), Table 12.4 offers a selective-optimization-with-compensation checklist to complete to help you enhance your life.

Taking a Nontraditional Approach: Examining Postformal Thought

So far, I have been mainly discussing the insights related to intelligence that we've derived from traditional IQ tests. But look back at the quotations from the older

TABLE 12.4: Using Selective Optimization with Compensation to Construct a Fulfilling Life

Selection: List your top-ranking priorities. Estimate how much time you spend on these agendas.

1. ______________________ hrs ______________

2. ______________________ hrs ______________

Can you increase the time you spend on these most critical agendas and decrease the time you spend on less important concerns?

Optimization: List strategies that you could use to perform better in your top-priority areas.

1. ______________________

2. ______________________

Compensation: List external aids that might help you be more successful in managing your time and/or family and friends you can rely on to take over some jobs when you feel overwhelmed.

1. ______________________

2. ______________________

3. ______________________

postformal thought A uniquely adult form of intelligence that involves being sensitive to different perspectives, making decisions based on one's inner feelings, and being interested in exploring new questions.

poet Anthony Hecht and the historian C. Vann Woodward, on page 376. The qualities these creative people were describing have nothing to do with putting together puzzles or blocks. What stands out about these men is their openness to experience and their sensitivity to their inner lives. Given that standard IQ tests were devised to predict performance in school, perhaps it would make sense to come up with a test to capture the qualities that define thinking intelligently during adult life.

Jean Piaget, as we know, devoted his career to describing qualitative changes in cognition that occur in children as they age. So developmentalists drew inspiration from this master theorist to construct an adult-relevant measure of IQ (Labouvie-Vief, 1992; Rybash, Hoyer, & Roodin, 1986; Sinnott, 2003).

Recall Piaget believed that we develop cognitively through hands-on experience with the world. Although Piaget believed that the pinnacle of mental development occurs when teens reach formal operations and reason like "real scientists," wouldn't years of living produce a more advanced kind of thinking called **postformal thought?** Let's look at what separates this adult intelligence from Piaget's formal operational stage:

POSTFORMAL THOUGHT IS RELATIVISTIC. As you saw in Chapter 9, adolescents in formal operations can argue rationally with their parents about rights and wrongs. With age and life experience, we realize that most real-world problems do not have clear-cut "right" answers. Postformal thinkers accept the validity of different perspectives. They embrace the ambiguities of life. This awareness that the truth is relative does not mean that postformal thinkers avoid making decisions or having strong beliefs. As with C. Vann Woodward, people who reason postformally make better decisions *because* they are open to changing their ideas when faced with the ambiguities of life.

POSTFORMAL THOUGHT IS FEELING-ORIENTED. Teenagers in formal operations feel that by using logic, they can make sense of the world. Postformal thinkers go beyond rationality to reason in a different way. Because there is often no objectively "right" answer to life's dilemmas, thinking postformally means relying more on one's gut feelings as the basis for making decisions. As with Anthony Hecht, people who reason postformally are less rigid, more open, fully in touch with their inner lives.

POSTFORMAL THOUGHT IS QUESTION-DRIVEN. Adolescents want to get the correct answers and finish or solve tasks. Postformal thinkers are less focused on solutions. They thrive on developing new questions and reconsidering their opinions. As you

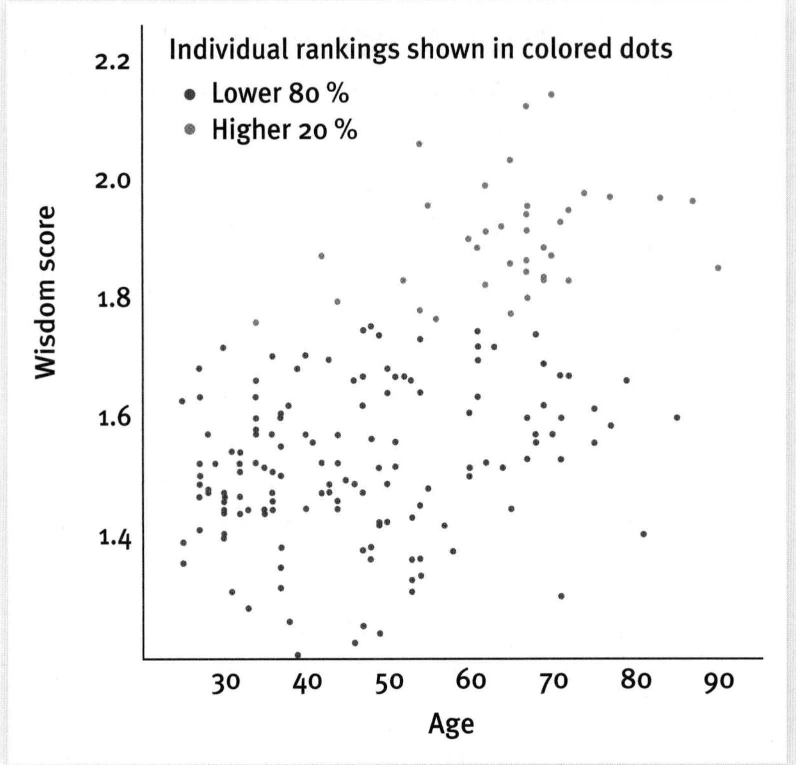

FIGURE 12.5: **Age distribution of "wisdom" scores as judged by the way a random sample of Michigan adults of different ages reasons about scenarios involving ethnic and social conflicts:** In this interesting study, notice that wisdom rates dramatically rise among the people in their sixties (blue dots), although about half of all elderly adults don't make it into the wise category (red dots).

Source: Grossmann and others, 2010, p. 7248.

saw with both Anthony Hecht and Prof. Woodward, people who think postformally enjoy coming up with new, interesting ways of looking at the world.

Clearly, we cannot measure this kind of intelligence by giving tests in which questions have a single correct answer. We need to adopt the strategy that Lawrence Kohlberg used with his moral dilemmas (recall Chapter 9): Present people with real-world situations and examine the *way* they think. How would you respond to this sample problem?

> John is known to be a heavy drinker, especially when he goes to parties. Mary, John's wife, warns him that if he gets drunk one more time, she will leave him and take the children. John goes to an office party and comes home drunk. Does Mary leave him? How sure are you of your answer?

Now that she is 60, this woman may qualify as truly wise.

If you answered this question rigidly ("Mary said she would leave, so she should; yes, I am sure I am right"), you are not thinking postformally. You must explore the consequences of leaving for Mary, for John, and for the children. You must understand that any answer you gave would be a judgment call.

Does this big-picture-oriented, person-centered reasoning increase as people get older and experience life's challenges? While the original studies suggested no (Sinnott, 1989), more recent research, measuring a similar concept called *wisdom*, offers a different view.

Psychologists (Grossmann and others, 2010) asked people of different ages to talk about social/ethnic conflicts: "The Issi want to preserve that nation's traditions, and the Assari want social change. What will happen? What would you advise?" They wanted to know: Would elderly people discuss this problem from each group's vantage point and realize that the outcome was uncertain? Would they emphasize that change comes gradually and stress the need for compromise?

As you can see by the blue dots in Figure 12.5, the answer was yes. Notice that a few middle-aged adults fit into the wise category. About half of elderly adults do not. But at the same age when we reach our well-being peak— the early sixties—wisdom takes off.

TABLE 12.5: How to Flourish During Adulthood: A Summary Table

1. Develop a generative mission. If you feel that your life lacks purpose, try volunteering or helping others—it's addictive!
2. Try to view your failures and upsetting life experiences as learning lessons. Understand life's disappointments offer us our best opportunities to grow.
3. To keep your mind fine-tuned, take care of your physical health and be open to experience—putting yourself in mentally stimulating situations involving people.
5. When you feel in role conflict—or that your life lacks balance—establish priorities, work hard in your most important areas, and rely on external aids to help you perform.
6. Think postformally: Be open to different perspectives; question your established ideas and ways of thinking; be aware of your inner feelings and use them as a guide to make wise life choices.

Now, returning to all of adulthood, what lessons does our general research tour have for constructing a fulfilling life? Table 12.5 summarizes *all* of this chapter's insights in a chart that offers tips for flourishing during adult life.

Until this point, I have been discussing issues that are relevant to everyone—people in their twenties, their forties and fifties, and even adults aged 95. In the next section, I'll explore transitions unique to the middle years.

TYING IT ALL TOGETHER

1. Tim is going to his thirtieth college reunion, and he can't wait to find out how his classmates have changed. Statistically speaking, which *two* changes might Tim find in his undergraduate friends?
   a. They will be less introverted and more outgoing.
   b. They will have different priorities, caring more about nurturing the next generation.
   c. They will be more confident and happier.
   d. They will be more depressed and burned out.
2. Kenyatta is giving Cory tips about growing emotionally with age. Pick the item that should *not* be on her list:
   a. Live a calm, stress-free life.
   b. Live a generative life.
   c. Develop prosocial goals as a young person.
   d. Live in a nation with a stable, responsive government.
3. Andres is an air traffic controller and Mick is a historian. Pick which man is likely to reach his career peak earlier, and explain the reasons why.
4. Your author is writing another textbook on lifespan development. She is also learning a new video game. Identify each type of intellectual skill involved and describe how my abilities in each of these areas are likely to change in my sixties.
5. Rick says, "I've got too much on my plate. I can't do anything well." Sara says, "I don't feel my life has meaning—I'm stagnating." Which theories discussed in this chapter would be most helpful in addressing each problem, and what might each theory advise?
6. Kayla is contemplating breaking up with her boyfriend, Mark, because, she says, "He doesn't give me the attention I need." Name the advice a postformal thinker would certainly *not* give to Kayla.
   a. "Leave the bum!"
   b. "Think of what is going on from Mark's perspective—for instance, is he overworked?"
   c. "Whatever choice you make, look at all the angles."
   d. "There may be no 'right decision.' Go with your gut."

Answers to the Tying It All Together questions can be found at the end of this chapter.

family watchdogs A basic role of grandparents, which involves monitoring the younger family member's well-being and intervening to provide help in a crisis.

Midlife Roles and Issues

As I mentioned at the beginning of this chapter, classic midlife events can be sources of joy and issues for concern. On the uplifting side, there is that unparalleled life experience called grandparenthood. The downside may be the need to care for disabled aged parents, and to face sexual decline. Let's now look at these "aging phase of life" joys and concerns one by one.

Grandparenthood

> The (Lakota) grandparents always took . . . ... the first grandchild to raise. They think that . . . they're more mature... and they could teach the children a lot more than the young parents . . . . I'm still trying to carry on that tradition because my grandmother raised me most of the time up until I was nine years old. . . .
>
> (quoted in Weibel-Orlando, 1999, p. 187)

This comment from Mrs. Big Buffalo, a Native American grandmother living in South Dakota, reminds us that every adult role, from spouse, to parent, to worker, to grandparent, is shaped by our society. In mainstream Western cultures, if people see grandparents raising a grandchild, they would (realistically) assume that there was a serious problem with the parents' ability to provide care.

Jon Feingesh/Masterfile

Still, as I implied in Chapter 4, even in developed nations offering extensive child care, many grandmothers see their mission as helping care for a young grandchild at least part-time while the parents work (Hank & Buber, 2009; Materne & Luszcz, 2010). Doesn't this universal impulse to watch over the youngest, most vulnerable family members suggest that there is a basic benefit built into grandparenthood?

Exploring the Grandparent Mission to Care

Because human beings are the only species with female bodies programmed to outlast the reproductive years, evolutionary theorists argue, the answer is yes. Menopause, they believe, evolved to offer an extra layer of mothers, without their own childrearing distractions, to care for the young (Coall & Hertwig, 2010). Put bluntly, grandmas function to help our species survive.

Jon Feingesh/Corbis

From jumping on trampolines to taking the grandchildren to the local lake, grandparents fulfill this joyous life role in their own distinctive, personal ways.

This lifesaving function is apparent in subsistence societies. Remember from reading the Experiencing the Lifespan box in Chapter 3 that, in Ghana, the grandma often steps in to take care of the family so her daughter can make the weekly trek to the clinic to stave off death in a young, malnourished child. Therefore, in Africa, the presence of a grandmother reduces mortality rates during the early years of life (Gibson & Mace, 2005).

In our culture, grandparents do their lifesaving selectively. As **family watchdogs,** they step in during a crisis to help the younger family members cope. At these times, their true value shines through. Grandparents are the family's safety net (Troll, 1983).

Can this extra layer of family members make a difference when the younger generations are at risk? The fact that baby-boom parents are putting off their retirements, to help their economically struggling children and grandchildren, suggests they may (see the next chapter).

Do grandparents make a personal difference in grandchildren's lives? The research, which shows "closeness to a grandparent" insulates "at risk" teens from mental health problems, suggests they can (Attar-Schwartz and others, 2009; Flouri and others, 2010). Anytime families are in trouble, generative watchdog grandparents play a vital, stabilizing role.

Even during normal times, grandparents help stabilize families. Grandparents can be mediators, helping parents and children resolve their differences (Kulik, 2007). They are the cement that keeps the extended family close and the command center for family news: "Hey, Mom. How are my sister Amy and her children *really* doing since the divorce? Is there anything I can do to help?" From Christmas get-togethers to Thanksgiving dinners, "Grandma's house" is often the focal meeting point—the place where brothers and sisters gather to regularly reconnect with one another during their adult years. As one developmentalist put it:

> Grandparents serve as symbols of connectedness within and between lives; as people who can listen and have the time to do so; as reserves of time, help, and attention; as links to the unknown past; as people who are sufficiently varied, flexible, and complex to defy easy categories and clear-cut roles.
>
> (Hagestad, 1985, p. 48)

You may notice this complexity and flexibility in your own family. One grandparent might be a shadowy figure; another may qualify as a second mother or best friend. Some grandparents love to jump on trampolines; others show their love in traditional, "baking cookies" ways. You may have an "intellectual grandma" who takes you to lectures and a "fishing grandpa" who takes you out on the lake.

Which Grandparents Are More or Less Involved?

What forces determine how involved a particular grandparent is likely to be? As I have been stressing, gender matters. Grandparenthood is often a more emotionally central role for women than men (Coall & Hertwig, 2010; Reitzes & Mutran, 2004). Physical proximity makes a difference. If you grow up in rural Iowa, your grandparents are more likely to be a major presence in your life because—living in a less mobile community—they may live nearby (King and others, 2003). Another predictor of involvement is age. Younger grandparents are more likely to be "very active." Grandparents who are elderly tend to be more peripherally involved (Coall & Hertwig, 2010).

Generative feelings are important. In fact, generativity is really what grandparenthood is all about (Hebblethwaite & Norris, 2011; Materne & Luszcz, 2010). As one woman gushed, "I cannot tell you how wonderful it is to take care of the grandchildren every Friday. My world lights up when they walk in the room. And the fact that I don't have to be there every day to discipline Karen and Matt makes being a grandma pure joy."

© Purestock/Alamy

For this grandma, spending the day with her grandson and her daughter-in-law is an absolute joy. Still, she has to be careful not to criticize this young woman's child-rearing skills or risk being cut off from future visits.

Grandparent Problems

Grandparents love their freedom to "spoil" the grandchildren and send them back to Mom and Dad. As you saw earlier, they view their mission as "being there" for the younger generation (the family watchdog role). But they also believe they shouldn't interfere with how the grandchildren are being raised (Mason, May, & Clarke, 2007).

This imperative to "never criticize," however, means that being a grandparent can demand considerable *emotion-regulation* skills. You can't be controlling or risk being cut off from visits. You must monitor your natural impulses to speak up. Therefore, grandparents are really vulnerable—and far from free. Their level of involvement depends on their relationship with the generation in between.

caregiving grandparents Grandparents who have taken on full responsibility for raising their grandchildren.

Imagine, for instance, your challenge as a paternal grandmother, the mother of a son. Because women are naturally closer to their own mothers (versus their mothers-in-law) and control the family's social relationships, maternal grandparents are often more heavily involved with the grandchildren (Bernal & Anuncibay, 2008; Monserud, 2008). Paternal grandparents are in danger of "not being there" as much as they would like.

Being in this situation produced heartache for a friend of mine. Her daughter-in-law decided to move across the country to be close to her own mother in Seattle, rather than stay in New York City—transforming my friend into the distant grandma she never wanted to be.

The allegiance to one's family of origin can have devastating effects after a divorce. When the wife gets custody, she can prevent her ex-husband's parents from seeing the grandchildren again. As one cut-off paternal grandmother anguished: "You are in no-man's-land—because (my grandson) is not missing, not dead. He is out there somewhere and you are looking for him in the crowd all the time, all the time" (Doyle, O'Dywer, & Timonen, 2010, p. 591). So, after a divorce, to preserve their access to the grandchildren, these grandmothers must sometimes attempt a heroic emotion-regulation feat: go out of their way to support their child's ex-spouse! (See Fingerman, 2004.)

Mothers of daughters may have the opposite problem. They may end up being there *too* much. Let's spell out a typical scenario: Your daughter wants you to watch the baby while she is at work. You don't want to disappoint your child, but you want your own life. The *role conflict* is especially intense when grandparents assume a more demanding job— becoming full-time parents again.

Caregiving grandparents take full responsibility for raising their grandchildren. In recent decades, the ranks of these grandparents have swelled. Of the 6.1 million U.S. grandparents who lived with their grandchildren as of 2006, roughly 40 percent, or 2.5 million, were responsible for a child's care. Although they span the socioeconomic spectrum, caregiving grandparents tend to be poor. Many are struggling to raise a grandchild plus work full time (U.S. Department of Commerce, 2008). In extreme cases, these front-line caregivers must petition the court for custody and formally adopt a granddaughter or grandson.

How does it feel to take this step? As you might expect, custodial grandparents are typically deeply distressed, mourning the fact that their own son or daughter—often because of drug or alcohol problems—is incapable of performing this job (Baird, 2003; Kelley & Whitley, 2003). They may feel angry at being forced into this "off-time" role. But they often feel a generative, "watchdog" mission to protect their flesh and blood (Hayslip & Patrick, 2003). Here is what one woman had to say to the police after her drug-abusing daughter took off with a grandchild and stole her car:

> [The police in a different state] said to me, "Ma'am, if you don't get here in 72 hours, then your grandson will be put in the [state protective services system] and you will have to fight to get him." I said, "I will fight from the moment I get there if my grandson is not there for me."
>
> (quoted in Climo, Terry, & Lay, 2002, p. 25)

And another woman summed up the general feeling of the custodial grandmothers in this study when she blurted out: "Nobody is going to take [my grandson] away from me. I have done everything except give birth to him" (quoted in Climo, Terry, & Lay, 2002, p. 25).

These women, mainly in their late fifties, complained about feeling physically drained: "Some days I feel really old, like I just can't keep up with him" (quoted in Climo, Terry, & Lay, 2002, p. 23). They had mixed emotions about their situation: "Some days I feel real blessed by it, other days I want to sit and cry" (p. 25). They sometimes described redemption sequences, too: "God has given me this wonderful little boy to raise and I'm thinking, 'How many people get the opportunity to do it a second time?'" (p. 26).

parent care Adult children's care for their disabled elderly parents.

Parent Care

Ask friends and family members and they will tell you that becoming a grandparent is one of the main joys of being middle-aged. Words such as *joy* and *fulfillment* do not come to mind when we imagine that second classic midlife role: caring for elderly parents. Researchers who study **parent care** speak of this family job using phrases like "burden," "hassles," and "strain" (Hunt, 2003; Son and others, 2007).

Caring for parents violates the basic principle in Western cultures that parents give to their children, not the reverse (Belsky, 1999). So, it makes sense that while older people may welcome help from siblings or a spouse, they prefer being the "givers" (or help providers) with an adult child. Moreover, as you might expect from the marriage vow "in sickness and in health," elderly spouses find caregiving far less stressful than daughters or sons do (Perrig-Chiello & Hutchison, 2010).

Actually, let me go further (and get personal). When older people are happily married, sacrificing (i.e., caring) for a chronically ill spouse is *not* a burden, but a source of fulfillment (Poulin and others, 2010; recall Chapter 11). It's definitely a "labor of love."

Unfortunately, this is often not true with parent care. Because caring for an ill parent is typically a female job, it can produce role conflict, as you saw in Chapter 11, when a daughter or daughter-in law must cut back her work hours, or "off ramp" from her career. If, as is increasingly true, a caregiving child is in her sixties or seventies, parent care may put a damper in that child's retirement plans or interfere with the need to care for her frail, disabled spouse. More rarely, a woman is pulled between two intergenerational commitments, caring for elderly parents and watching the grandchildren full time.

At this point, I need to set the record straight: The stereotype of a stressed-out "sandwich generation"—women pulled between caring for children and disabled parents—is a myth. Since parent care typically occurs in the fifties, that job usually occurs during empty nest, grandparent stage. Moreover, the popular concept of a "midlife crisis" is another myth. It doesn't exist for most adults.

Finally, the belief that in Asian cultures or in U.S. ethnic groups, such as African Americans, with more collectivist values, children are "happy" to care for aging parents is also untrue (Freeman and others, 2010; Hashizume, 2010). Firstly, in Japan, the tremendous growth of nursing homes demonstrates that today, in this society, the "rule" to care for aged family members is no longer a cultural norm. In one U.S. study, if children reported that helping their aged parent was "a family obligation," they felt under *more* stress when actually providing care (Sayegh & Knight, 2011). How stressful, generally, is parent care?

The answer—as *developmental systems theory* predicts—is "it varies" (Merz, Schulze, & Schuengel, 2010). If the person's needs are minimal, a daughter is not working, and/or she is providing intense care but getting a lot of support, caring for an aged parent is no problem (DiRosa and others, 2011). But coping with other stresses and feeling one's siblings are not doing their "fair share" is a recipe for depression and poor health (Koerner, Shirai, & Kenyon, 2010; Merrill, 1996).

The personality of the older person looms large. Parent care, as you will see in Chapter 14, poses particular challenges with Alzheimer's disease. According to one alarming study, if a caregiver perceived a parent as difficult and manipulative and became resentful, the situation could escalate to screaming, yelling, or threatening that person with a nursing home (Smith and others, 2011).

Still, caring for a disabled parent can have the opposite effect. It may offer its own *redemption sequence*, giving children the chance to repay a beloved mother

Dennis MacDonald/Photo Edit, Inc.

Will this middle-aged child find parent care an impossible stress? Keys lie in the amount of help she needs to provide, her other commitments and whether this daughter feels her siblings are doing their fair share.

or father for years of care (Kramer & Thompson, 2002). Moreover, as with other life stresses, dealing with an impaired parent—especially one with Alzheimer's disease—can make people more resilient and promote personal well-being (Leipold, Schacke, & Zank, 2008).

Balancing the need to respect a frail older parent's autonomy and knowing when to intervene (Funk, 2010); being generative with the grandchildren, but not intrusive, while balancing your own and your family's needs: These are the kinds of relationship-oriented challenges that explain why, in Jung's evocative words, the long "afternoon of life" may teach us to be wise.

Body Image, Sex, and Menopause

Jung famously believed, "We cannot live life's afternoon by the program of life's morning"—meaning that the key to growing more mature with age lies in giving up the quest for physical beauty in favor of more spiritual concerns. But judged by the developed-world passion for cosmetic surgery, how many contemporary adults fit Jung's idea of "wise"?

The (somewhat) good news is that while fifty-something females do love to catalog each sign of physical decay (see the Experiencing the Lifespan box), body dissatisfaction does not increase in midlife. This disease, while common at every age (Pruis & Janowsky, 2010), is at its peak when people are in college (Greenleaf, 2005; McKinley, 2006). Moreover, unless they are particularly age-phobic (Slevec & Tiggemann, 2011), middle-aged women take a kind of middle position with regard to Jung's advice: They reject extreme body-altering measures, such as facelifts, but want to age as beautifully as possible using creams and dyes (Muise & Desmarais, 2010).

EXPERIENCING THE LIFESPAN: Confronting an Aging Face

Letty Pogrebin, a feminist and founding editor of *Ms.* magazine, has written a humorous book exposing the female body on "the far side of 50." Here is her frank account of her 55-year-old image as witnessed in the mirror—and comments on what set her straight:

> Under my eyes are puffy fat pads surrounded by dark circles, each unfortunate feature trying its best to call attention to the other. My wrinkles materialized almost overnight when I was 49. Now the lines in my face remind me of my palms. When I raise my eyebrows, my forehead pleats, and when my eyebrows come down the pleats stay. . . .
>
> Just this year, my jaw, the Maginot Line of facial structure, surrendered to the force of gravity. . . . Once I had a right-angle profile; now there's a hypotenuse between my chin and neck. . . . Which brings me, regrettably, to my neck, with its double choker of lines; and my chest, creased like crepe paper; and my shoulders and arms, which are holding their own for now except for the elbows, which are rough enough to shred a carrot. I don't yet have loose skin on the underside of my upper arm—you know, the part that keeps waving after you've stopped—but I can see it coming.
>
> . . . the truth is I'm not crazy about my looks but I can live with them. . . . What jolted me out of my low-grade Body Image Blues was the death of friends felled by cancer in the prime of their lives. After the third funeral . . ., I saw my body, not as face, skin, hair, figure, but as the vehicle through which I could experience everything my friend would never know again. . . . Ordinary pleasures seemed so precious that I vowed to set my priorities straight before some fatal illness did it for me. Since then I . . . focus on the things that really matter. And I can assure you that being able to wear a bikini isn't one of them.
>
> (quoted in Pogrebin, 1996, pp. 128–129, 153)

The media appearance of a few fiftyish female sex symbols (granted, often White and slim) suggests that today we really don't have to give up our sexual selves until we move fairly far into life's afternoon (Weitz, 2010). What really happens sexually to *both* men and women as they age?

menopause The age-related process, occurring at about age 50, in which ovulation and menstruation stop due to the declining of estrogen.

The findings for middle-aged men are somewhat depressing. Older males need more time to develop an erection. They are more likely to lose an erection before ejaculation occurs. Their ejaculations become less intense. By their fifties, most men are not able to have another erection for 12 to 24 hours after having had sex (Masters & Johnson, 1966).

© Mark Savage/Corbis

In her mid-fifties, Sharon Stone is a glorious testament to the fact that youthful sex symbols can remain just as alluring (and natural looking!) well into the afternoon of life.

This slower arousal to ejaculation tempo has advantages. Because it blocks those infamous one-minute lovemaking events of youth, it can make men superior sexual partners as they age. But it also explains the popularity of the billion-dollar market for erection-stimulating drugs. Desire remains, but by late middle age, many men feel they need extra help to implement their plans.

In contrast, females reach their desire peak in their early thirties (Schmitt and others, 2002). But by late middle age, most women do report having less interest in sex than men (McHugh, 2007). One reason is not hard to guess: fewer sexual signals coming in from the outside world.

As they move into their fifties, more women are likely to be without a partner (due to widowhood or divorce). Or they may be in a long-term *companionate* relationship with an older spouse. (Recall from the last chapter that, over time, sexual desire tends to decline in any relationship.) Moreover, just as signals from the outside world accentuate our first feelings of sexual desire during puberty, when the outer world stops viewing older women as sexual human beings, desire tends to turn off (Kenrick and others, 1993). Menopause, as the stereotypes table 12.6 suggests, is supposed to take a toll on sexuality too.

Menopause typically occurs at about age 50, when estrogen production falls off dramatically and women stop ovulating. Specifically, the defining marker of menopause is not having menstruated for a year. As estrogen production declines and a

TABLE 12.6: Stereotypes and Facts About Menopause

1. **The stereotype:** Women have terrible physical symptoms while going through menopause.

   The facts: Researchers find that an upsurge of minor physical complaints does occur during the few years preceding menopause: lack of energy, backaches, and joint stiffness. Many women experience hot flashes and some sleeplessness. Still, there is variability from person to person, and complaints vary from culture to culture. In one study, while fewer than half the women in a Scandinavian poll reported difficult symptoms, 2 out of 3 U.S. women did (Nappi & Kokot-Kierepa, 2010).

2. **The stereotype:** Women are very moody while going through menopause.

   The facts: Statistically speaking, women do show a minor rise in anxiety and depression as they approach menopause, when estrogen levels are waning (Avis and others, 2004). However, these changes do not affect all people, and, after reaching menopause, many women report feeling better than ever.

3. **The stereotype:** Women feel empty, "dried up," old, and asexual after menopause.

   The facts: Many women find menopause a relief. For instance, one-third of the women in Taiwan and almost half of all Australian women in a cross-cultural study said that they were happy not to have to deal with a period every month (Fu, Anderson, & Courtney, 2003). In another Danish study, at menopause most women felt that they were entering a new, freer stage of life. Some said that their sex life was better now that they had no worries about getting pregnant (Hvas, 2001).

Yes, the secret is that this long-married couple is just as passionate now that they are middle-aged—because they have made staying sexy and interested in sex their shared priority!

woman approaches this milestone, the menstrual cycle becomes more irregular. During this sexual winding-down period, called *perimenopause,* as the stereotypes table suggests, many women experience minor mood changes and other physical symptoms, such as night sweats and hot flashes (sudden sensations of heat) (Lerner-Geva and others, 2010).

Although some women sail through menopause without symptoms, this estrogen loss produces changes in the reproductive tract. Normally, the walls of the vagina have thick folds that expand to admit a penis and to accommodate childbirth. After menopause, the vaginal walls thin out and become more fragile. The vagina shortens, and its opening narrows. The size of the clitoris and labia shrinks and blood flow tends to decrease. It takes longer after arousal for lubrication to begin (Masters & Johnson, 1966; Saxon, Etten, & Perkins, 2010). Women don't produce as much fluid as before. These changes can make having intercourse so painful that some women stop having sex.

When sexual desire declines after menopause (see Woods and others, 2010), is this due to pain during intercourse, the fact that society doesn't react to older women as sexual, or simply the passion-eroding effect of being married for decades? (Birnbaum, Cohen, & Werthemer, 2007; Hillman, 2008.) Whatever the answer, again, diversity is the message with regard to sexuality (McHugh, 2007). Some women find sex more exciting after menopause (Hillman, 2008). Some couples stay very sexually active well into their older years (Brecher and *Consumer Reports* editors, 1984). Table 12.7 summarizes the male/female changes described in this section and offers advice for staying passionate about sex.

TABLE 12.7: **Staying Passionate About Sex with Age**

For Men	
Problem	**Solutions**
Trouble maintaining or achieving an erection	1. Understand that some physiological slowing down is normal, and do not be alarmed by occasional problems performing. Sexual relations need to occur more slowly; manual stimulation may be necessary to achieve erection and orgasm.
	2. Stay healthy. Avoid sexually impairing conditions such as heart disease. If possible, avoid medications that have sexual side effects (such as antidepressants and blood pressure pills).
	3. If troubled by chronic problems performing, explore the medicines that are available for treating these issues.
For Women	
Problem	**Solutions**
No sexual signals coming from the outside world	1. Stay sexy, be conscious of your physical appearance
	2. Try to find a partner who appreciates you as a sexual human being.
Decline in estrogen levels makes having sexual intercourse painful	1. Consider using lubricants, such as K-Y Jelly, when having sex.
	2. Consider hormone replacement therapy (but discuss this with your doctor).

How do we change physically, cognitively, and personality-wise as we move through later life? Stay tuned for answers in the next part of the book, as I focus on that life stage we might call "the evening, or twilight, of life."

TYING IT ALL TOGETHER

1. Juanita has two grandmothers, Karen and Louisa. Grandma Karen is much more involved with Juanita than is Grandma Louisa. List several characteristics that might explain why Karen is the more active, hands-on grandmother.
2. Poll your class. Do most people report being closest to their maternal grandmother (or grandfather)? For the students who were closer to a paternal grandparent, explore why that might be.
3. Kim is caring for her elderly mother, who just had a stroke. Each of the following factors should make Kim's job feel easier *except*:
   a. Kim views this job as an opportunity to repay her mom for years of love.
   b. Kim's mom has a mellow personality.
   c. Kim has several siblings.
4. For the following "age and sexuality" statements, select the right gender: *Males/Females* decline the most physiologically, but *male/female* age changes in sexuality are most affected by social issues (such as not having a partner). As they reach their fifties, *males/females* report having less interest in sex. *Males/Females* have the most untapped sexual potential in later life.
5. If Joselyn is going through menopause, she will *definitely*:
   a. experience mood swings.
   b. lose interest in sex.
   c. undergo reproductive tract changes, such as a thinning of her vaginal walls.

Answers to the Tying It All Together questions can be found at the end of this chapter.

SUMMARY

The Evolving Self

Although the boundaries of middle age span about age 40 to the early sixties, many older adults describe themselves as middle aged. Diversity—among people and change processes—plus consistency are the defining characteristics of the middle years.

Research on the **Big Five** traits shows our scores on these core dimensions of personality predict a variety of life outcomes. Also, our relative rankings on these traits don't change much after age 30, unless we experience other major life changes. Interviews paint a different picture, suggesting that we change a good deal as we travel through life. Dan McAdams's research exploring Erikson's **generativity** shows that our priorities shift to "other-centered concerns" during midlife. Generativity grows into the sixties, can be "activated" by parenthood, and, while not necessarily related to **hedonic pleasure,** produces **eudaimonic happiness**—the sense of living a meaningful, fulfilling adult life.

In their autobiographies, highly generative adults produce a **commitment script** and describe **redemption sequences**—negative events that turned out for the best. African Americans may often be highly generative. Experiencing life adversity—in moderation— may produce emotional growth. We develop emotionally and get happier as we travel through life, into our sixties. Prosocial young people and people who live in generative societies are most likely to flourish emotionally as adults.

Early studies using the **Wechsler Adult Intelligence Scale (WAIS)** found that people reach their intellectual peak in their twenties—although scores on the timed performance scale tests declined more rapidly than did scores on the verbal scale. The **Seattle Longitudinal Study**—which controlled for the biases of this research—showed the same change pattern, but it also indicated that we reach our intellectual peak in midlife.

Fluid intelligence, the capacity to master unfamiliar cognitive challenges quickly, is at its height early in adulthood, and then it declines. **Crystallized intelligence,** our knowledge base, rises until well into middle age. In professions that heavily depend on crystallized knowledge—versus fast information processing—people do well into their sixties. Creativity reaches its peak in midlife, although our basic talents predict our real world performance (at any age) best.

Staying healthy and seeking out stimulating interpersonal activities (and jobs) can prevent age-related cognitive decline. **Terminal drop,** a significant loss in IQ, or decline in happiness, can indicate that a person is near death. Using **selective optimization with compensation** helps people successfully cope with age-related losses and live more successfully at any life stage.

Postformal thinkers are sensitive to diverse perspectives, interested in exploring questions, and attuned to their inner feelings in making life decisions. Encouraging new evidence suggests that "wisdom" (measured by superior reasoning about social conflicts) develops during the older years.

Midlife Roles and Issues

Grandmotherhood may have evolved to help our species survive. In our society, grandparents act as **family watchdogs,** stepping in when the younger family members need help. Gender, proximity to the grandchildren, age, and personality determine how people carry out this joyous but constrained life role. Because women tend to be closer to their own mothers, paternal grandmothers are at risk of being less involved with the grandchildren than they want to be. The problem for maternal grandparents lies in being pressured to do too much. The extreme case of taking "too much care" occurs with **caregiving grandparents,** especially those who must take full custody of a child.

Parent care is another family role that some middle-aged daughters may assume. While often stressful, a variety of forces affect how women feel when caring for a disabled parent, and this life role can sometimes promote emotional growth. Another midlife concern involves declining sexuality. For males, erectile capacity steadily declines. Although women tend to feel most passionate in their thirties, **menopause** has the side effect of making intercourse more painful. Because of this pain, as well as the fact that they may not have interested partners, many older women lose interest in sex. Still, women (and men) can stay very sexually active well into later life.

KEY TERMS

Big Five, p. 365
generativity, p. 367
hedonic happiness, p. 368
eudaimonic happiness, p. 368
commitment script, p. 369
redemption sequence, p. 369
Wechsler Adult Intelligence Scale (WAIS), p. 373
Seattle Longitudinal Study, p. 374
crystallized intelligence, p. 375
fluid intelligence, p. 375
terminal drop, p. 376
selective optimization with compensation, p. 378
postformal thought, p. 379
family watchdogs, p. 382
caregiving grandparents, p. 384
parent care, p. 385
menopause, p. 387

ANSWERS TO TYING IT ALL TOGETHER QUIZES

The Evolving Self

1. b and c
2. a
3. Andres will reach his career peak far earlier than Mick because his job is heavily dependent on fluid skills. A historian's job depends almost exclusively on crystallized skills.
4. Textbook writing is a crystallized skill, so I should be just as good at my life passion during my sixties—provided I don't get ill. Playing video games depends heavily on fluid skills, so I will be far worse now than when I was young.
5. The theory that applies to Rick's problem—"too much on his plate"—is Baltes's selective optimization with compensation: He needs to (1) prioritize and shed less important jobs, (2) work harder in his top-ranking areas, and (3) use external aids to help him cope. Sara's difficulty is a lack of generativity. She should get involved in activities that involve making a difference—volunteering, helping family and friends, and so on.
6. a

Midlife Roles and Issues

1. Karen may be younger, live closer to Emma, and be a more generative person. Most likely she is a maternal grandma.
2. Answers here will vary.
3. c
4. *Males* decline most physiologically at a younger age; *female* sexuality is most affected by social issues (such as the lack of a partner). As they reach their fifties, *females* report having less interest than males in sex. *Females* have the most untapped sexual potential in later life.
5. c

Later Life

This two-chapter book part, devoted to life's last stage, highlights how we develop and change as we move through senior citizenhood (the sixties and beyond). Chapter 13 covers issues relevant to both the young-old and old-old years. Chapter 14 emphasizes concerns that become pressing priorities in advanced old age.

Chapter 13—**Later Life: Cognitive and Socioemotional Development** begins with an overview of the historic twenty-first-century age boom, then turns to look at how memory changes as we age. During this discussion, you will not only learn a wealth of information about memory and aging, but also get insights into how to improve memory at any age. Then, we turn to the emotional side of life. I'll outline a creative theory explaining why happiness floats upward in later life, then decode whether (or when) late life is the worst or best life stage. Finally, you'll get tips about living meaningfully in old age. The second half of this chapter tackles those major later-life transitions: retirement and widowhood.

Chapter 14—**The Physical Challenges of Old Age** begins by describing the aging process and how it progresses into disease and disability. Then, I'll explore late-life sensory and motor changes and offer a detailed look at that most feared old-age disease: dementia. At the end of this chapter, you will learn about the living arrangements and health-care options available to people when old-age frailties strike. This chapter will open your eyes to the challenges of age-related disabilities and, hopefully, sensitize you to the need to change the wider world to promote an ideal older adult–environment fit.

PART VI

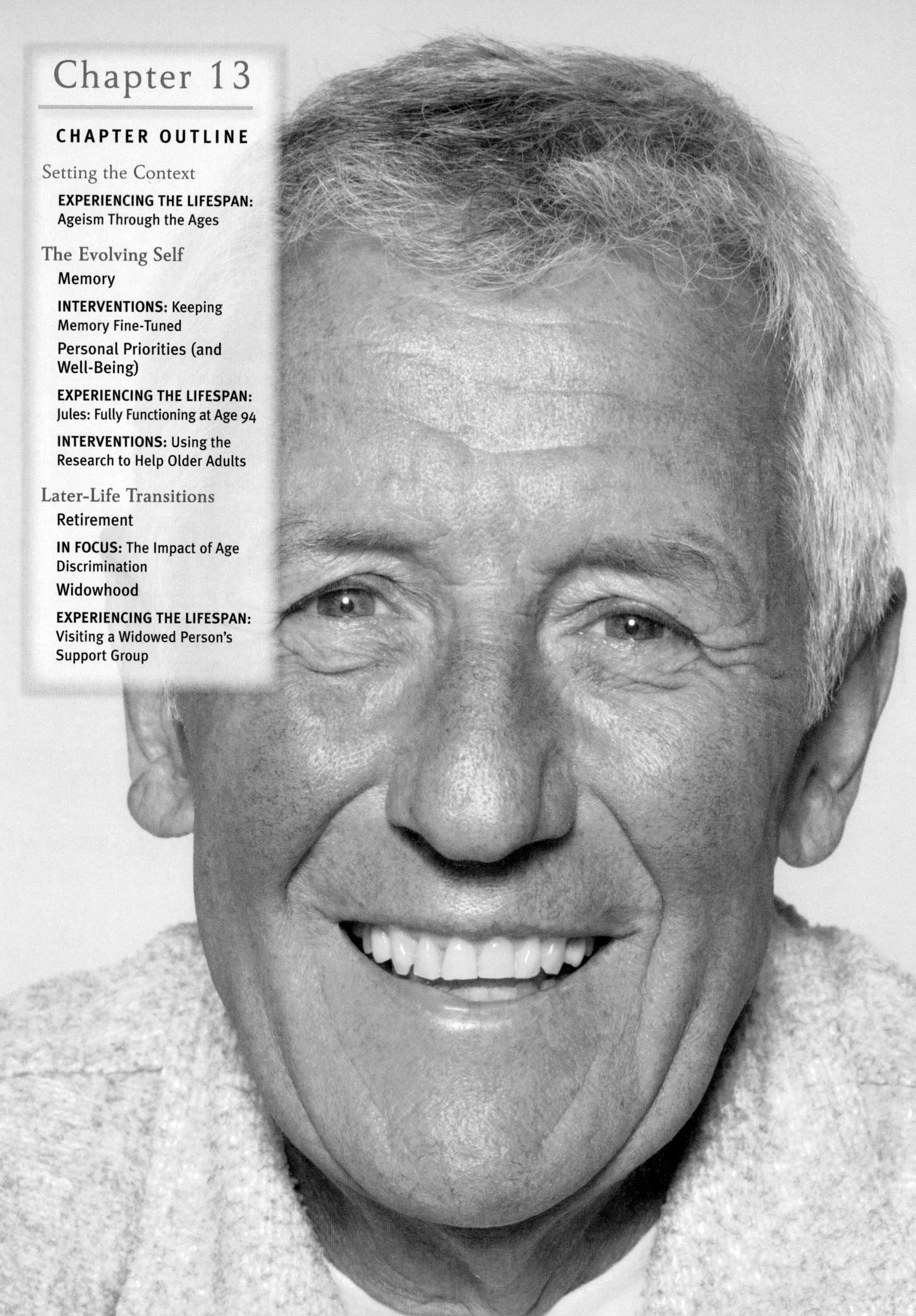

Chapter 13

CHAPTER OUTLINE

Later Life: Cognitive and Socioemotional Development

Ten years ago, at age 63, Theresa and Sal retired. They were healthy, active, and (at the time)—with Sal's investments and their pensions—well off. They were passionate to enjoy these final decades, to travel, to focus on the moment, to revel in this new phase of life. Theresa and Sal never had children, but they had their nieces and nephews and many friends. In particular, they had their second family in Jane, her children, and her grandkids. Theresa met Jane as a student teacher in the older woman's class. By now, she and her mentor have been best friends and "sisters in spirit" for more than 40 years.

For Theresa and Sal, retirement meant spending more time with their closest friends, like Jane. It involved devoting weekdays to volunteering at church, and especially, taking those well-loved cruises to Mexico, the Mediterranean, and Marrakesh. Most of all, it meant having the joy of just being together as a couple, free from the demands of work. Sal's heart disease—first diagnosed during his early sixties—lent poignancy to their shared life. As it turned out, their retirement years were priceless, but they were over too soon. At age 73, Sal died of a massive heart attack.

It has been hard for Theresa to function. How can you go on without your high school sweetheart, your life love for over 50 years? Theresa takes comfort from her widowed friends, particularly Jane. Theresa and Sal were there for Jane when she lost her husband, Carl, to cancer at age 61. Now, it is Jane's turn—spry and vigorous at age 83—to envelop Theresa in her loving family and serve as a sounding board for Theresa to talk (or not talk) about Sal.

Theresa feels Sal's comforting presence in the house. She even finds herself mentally consulting her husband for advice. But for the most part (bless the Lord), she's been amazed at her inner strength. After being hit with Sal's medical bills, Theresa found that her income was alarmingly low. She scoured the Internet for jobs, thinking, "Who would want to hire an "old lady" of 74?" She was wrong, and has just landed a 3-day-a-week consultant job at her old school. Tonight, she plans to celebrate by opening a bottle of champagne with Sal!

Theresa's life changed dramatically from the time she retired until after Sal became ill and died. These two chapters capture the developmental shifts people experience as they travel through the young-old (sixties and seventies) and old-old (over age 80) years. In the current chapter, I'll focus on cognition and the socioemotional side of later life. In Chapter 14, I'll be following Theresa as she moves into her eighties and faces the physical frailties of advanced old age.

Theresa and Sal's lives differ dramatically from those of elderly people around the world—in religion, in lifestyle, in having enough money to enjoy their older years. Still, in one way, they are the same as every person their age: They are early foot soldiers in a late-life army storming through the developed world.

median age The age at which 50 percent of a population is older and 50 percent is younger.

young-old People in their sixties and seventies.

old-old People age 80 and older.

Jens Lucking/Getty Images

Long life expectancies, declining fertility, the baby boomers reaching old age—all of these forces explain why the median age of the population is increasing and why, in the decades to come, more people will look closer in age to this elderly woman than her 22-year-old granddaughter.

Setting the Context

The well-known reason for this invasion is the baby boomers marching into their young-old years. Moreover, due to our remarkable twentieth-century advances in life expectancy, when people reach that magical sixty-fifth birthday, they can now expect, on average, to live for 18 more years (Adams & Rau, 2011).

Falling fertility is also producing this unique historic demographic change (Cherlin, 2010; recall Chapter 11). When birth rates decline, the **median age** of a nation—the cutoff age at which half of the population is older and half is younger—tends to rise. With childbearing rates dipping so sharply in Europe and Asia in recent decades, the median age of the population in most developed countries is now well into middle age.

The baby boomers, longevity, and low fertility are the trio of forces converging to produce our new, aging world. You can track this perfect demographic storm as it peaks in specific nations in Figure 13.1. In 2030 in Japan, where average life expectancy now tops age 81 and fertility rates are low, the median age of the population will be roughly age 50. In Italy, 1 out of *every* 2 people will be at least 52. And in that same year, roughly 1 in every 5 Americans and 1 in 4 Europeans will be over age 65 (National Center for Health Statistics, 2007).

How will you feel about living in a nation where the people with walkers may outnumber the babies in strollers on your streets? For hints, you might take a trip to a city in the United States where the age storm has already struck. In Sarasota, Florida, where the 65-plus population now tops 30 percent, residents view age 70 as "young." You aren't defined as elderly until you make it to age 80 and above (Fishman, 2010). In Sarasota, people really understand: Statistically speaking, there is a world of difference between being healthy and **young-old** and having physical frailties (or depending on those walkers) during the **old-old** years.

The health (and wealth) differences between the young-old and old-old may explain our contradictory stereotypes about later life. There is the image of the vital sixty-something embarking on an "encore" career and the vision of the lonely, aged person languishing in a nursing home; the portrait of an affluent, retired married couple traveling the world and the depressed institutionalized elder with a dementing disease.

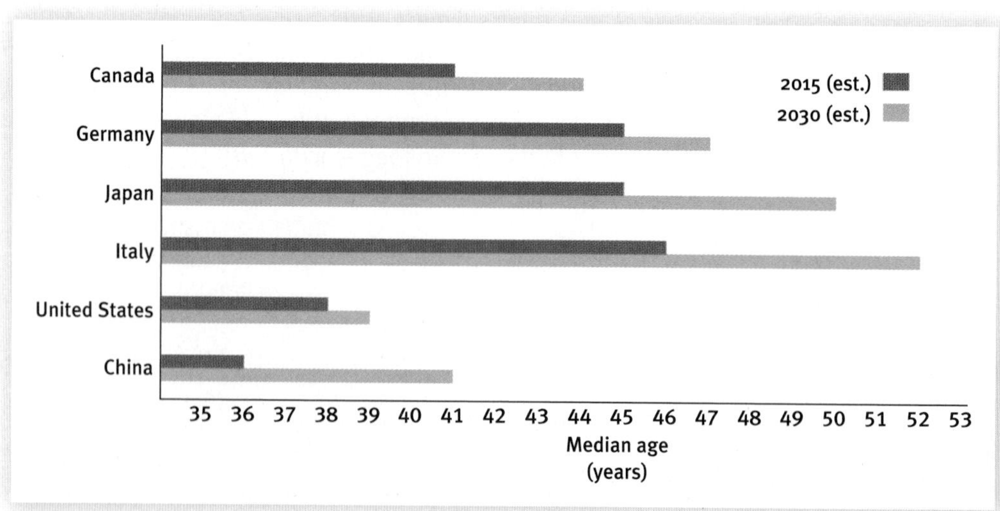

FIGURE 13.1: **Predicted median age of the population, selected countries, in 2015 and 2030:** Soon, the median age of the population—the point at which half the people are younger and half are older—will be 45-plus in Italy, Germany, and Japan. Also, notice how high the median ages in these nations will be in 2030. How do you think living in these "most-aged nations" will affect residents' daily lives?

Source**:** Kinsella & Velkoff, 2001.

But amidst this diversity lies considerable consensus about the general traits that define old age. In surveying college students in 26 nations, researchers found that worldwide, young people associate being old with looking unattractive, having trouble with everyday tasks, and learning new things. Luckily, in every culture, people also agree with the positive research findings highlighted in Figure 12.5 on page 380. In later life, wisdom is at its peak. Interestingly, with regard to life satisfaction, emerging adults take an ambivalent stance. They are not quite sure whether the elderly qualify as happy or demoralized and depressed (Löckenhoff, 2009).

© Randy Faris/CORBIS

Thomas Hoepker/Magnum Photos

The expressions on the faces of this joyous 65-year-old and dour 90-year-old say it all. In terms of lifestyle, personality, memory, health, and everything else, there is a world of difference between being young-old and old-old.

In these next two chapters, you'll be getting a wealth of insights into our negative stereotypes about old age. Why *exactly* can being old limit our ability to learn new things, and what *exactly* causes older people to have trouble functioning in the world? As we fully enter the emotional lives of the elderly, you will realize that the young people in the polls above are right to be on the fence about older people's mental health. Old age *can* be the happiest or most depressing life stage.

But before tackling these topics and others, I need to set the record straight (again). We might think that in Asia, with its collectivist values and tradition of respecting ones elders, young people would be most likely to view old people as wise. But interestingly, in this global survey, Western students more often equated age with wisdom than did their counterparts in China or Japan! We certainly would expect that, at earlier times in history, we respected the elderly more than in our current youth-obsessed society. But, as the Experiencing the Lifespan box suggests, that "obvious" fact also is false. In fact, because we are not killing off our frail elderly, we now may be living in the most age-friendly historical era of all!

EXPERIENCING THE LIFESPAN: Ageism Through the Ages

The hair is gray. . . . The brows are gone, the eyes are blear . . . The nose is hooked and far from fair. . . . The ears are rough and pendulous. . . . The face is sallow, dead and drear. . . . The chin is purs'd . . . the lips hang loose. . . . Aye such is human beauty's lot! . . . Thus we mourn for the good old days . . . , wretched crones, huddled together by the blaze. . . ..

(excerpted from an Old English poem called "Lament of the Fair Heaulmiere" [or Helmet-maker's girl], quoted in Minois, 1989, p. 230)

Many of us assume that people had better values and attitudes toward old age in "the good old days." Poems such as the one above show that we need to give that stereotype a closer look.

In ancient times, old age was seen as a miracle because it was so rare. Where there was no written language, older people were valued for their knowledge. However, this elevated status applied only to a few people—typically men—who were upper class. For slaves, servants, and women, old age was often a cruel time. Moreover, just as today, cultures made a distinction between active, healthy older people and those who were disabled and ill.

In many societies, for instance, the same person who had been revered was subjected to barbaric treatment once he outlived his usefulness—that is, became decrepit or senile. Samoans killed their elderly in elaborate ceremonies in which the victim was required to participate. Other cultures left their older people to die of neglect. Michelangelo and Sophocles, revered as old men, stand as symbols of the age-friendly attitudes of the nations in which they lived. However, the images portrayed in their creative works celebrated youth and beauty. Even in Classical Greece and Renaissance Italy—societies known for being enlightened—people believed old age was the worst time of life.

As historian Georges Minois (1989) concluded in a survey of how Western cultures treated their elders, "It is the tendency of every society to live and go on living: it extols the strength and fecundity that are so closely linked to youth and it dreads the . . . decrepitude of old age. Since the dawn of history . . . young people have regretted the onset of old age. The fountain of youth has always constituted Western man's most irrational hope" (p. 303).

(The information in this box is taken from Minois, 1989, and Fischer, 1977.)

TABLE 13.1: Is It True about the Elderly?

1. Memory stays stable through midlife, then declines in later life.
2. There is little that can be done to improve memory in old age.
3. Old people think about life more negatively than young people.
4. The typical retirement age is 65.
5. Older workers are more rigid and difficult to supervise.
6. Men tend to have more trouble adjusting to widowhood than women.
7. Due to advances in medical care, people are aging "healthier" today.
8. Compared to vision difficulties, hearing losses in old age are "a piece of cake."
9. No one who has Alzheimer's disease can live a meaningful life.
10. About 50 percent of people over 65 live in nursing homes.

(I'll be discussing items 1–6 in this chapter and items 7–10 in Chapter 14.)

Answers 1. F, 2. F, 3. F, 4. F, 5. F, 6. T, 7. F, 8. F, 9. F, 10. F

At this point, you might want to take the "Is It True about the Elderly" questionnaire (Table 13.1) to fully explore your own old-age perceptions. Now, let's start exploring the truth of your ideas where we left off in the last chapter—with the evolving self.

The Evolving Self

How might age impair our ability to learn new things? Do the inner lives of older people really differ from the young? Answers come from scanning memory, the basis of all learning and thought, and then exploring the emotional priorities of older adults.

Memory

When we think of our general intellectual abilities, as we get older, we can look forward to positive changes such as expanding our crystallized skills and growing wise (recall Chapter 12). These upbeat feelings do not extend to memory. With memory, when we look to the future, we see only decline. People worry about these losses well before they reach age 65. How often do you hear a 50-year-old say, "I'm having a senior moment," or, "Sorry, I forgot. . . . It's my Alzheimer's kicking in"? Virtually all elderly people agree that their memory has gotten worse (Slavin and others, 2010). The outside world is on high alert for late-life memory problems, too.

In a classic study, psychologists demonstrated this mindset by filming actors aged 20, 50, and 70 reading an identical speech. During the talk, each person made a few references to memory problems, such as "I forgot my keys." Volunteers then watched only the young, middle-aged, or older actor and wrote about what the person was like. Many of the people who saw the 70-year-old described him as forgetful. No one who heard the identical words read by the younger adults even mentioned memory! (See Rodin & Langer.)

So once someone is over age 65 or 75 or 80, we are especially attuned to memory lapses. We see memory failures in a more ominous light. When a young person forgets something, we pass off the problem as due to external forces: "He was distracted" or "She had too much else going on." When that person is old, we think: "Perhaps this is the beginning of Alzheimer's disease" (Erber & Prager, 1999). When you last were with an elderly family member and she forgot a name or appointment, did the idea that "Grandma is declining mentally" cross your mind?

Scanning the Facts

Are older people's memory abilities *really* worse than those of younger adults? Unfortunately, the answer, based on decades of studies, is yes. In testing everything from the ability to recall unfamiliar faces to the names of new places, from remembering the content of paragraphs to recalling where objects are located in space, the elderly perform more poorly than the young (see Dixon and others, 2007, for a review).

As a memory task gets more difficult, the performance gap between young and old people expands. When psychologists ask people to recognize a photograph they have previously seen, older people often do as well as the typical 20-year-old (Craik & McDowd, 1987). The elderly score comparatively worse when they need to come up with names of people pictured in those photos completely on their own. (The distinction here is analogous to taking a multiple-choice exam versus a short-answer test.) Older people perform even more dismally when they have to recall a face or name and link it to a specific context (Dennis and others, 2008; see also Craik, Luo, & Sakuta, 2010): "Yes, I recognize that guy . . . but was he the cable repairman or a guest at Claire's commencement party last month?"

Jupiterimages/Brand X Pictures/Getty Images

If you can relate to this photo the next time you are tempted to text during that not-so-interesting class, keep this message in mind: *Divided attention tasks* make memory worse!

While connecting names to places, or remembering exactly *where* we heard some bit of information, is especially difficult in old age, this task is not easy at any life stage. I'll never forget when a twenty-something student server blew me away with this comment: "I remember you very well, Dr. Belsky. I learned so much in your *English Literature class* three years ago."

The elderly have unusual trouble with **divided-attention tasks**—situations in which they need to memorize material or perform an activity while monitoring something else. Remembering to keep checking the clock so that you don't miss your 3 P.M. class, texting or spending time on Facebook while "listening" to a lecture—these activities impair memory performance at any age (Craik, Luo & Sakuta, 2010). Warning! This is a documented fact! But while young people can master these kinds of difficult divided-attention tasks, they are virtually impossible in old age (Gothe, Oberauer, & Kliegl, 2008).

More depressing, when researchers pile on the memory demands and add time pressures, deficits show up as early as the late *twenties* (Borella, Carretti, & De Beni, 2008). Returning to the previous chapter, it makes sense that when people have to remember completely new, random bits of information very fast, losses take place soon after youth. These requirements are prime examples of *fluid intelligence* tasks.

What is going wrong with memory as we age? Let's get insights from examining two different ways of conceptualizing "a memory": the information-processing and memory-systems approaches.

An Information-Processing Perspective on Memory Change

Remember from Chapters 3 and 5 that developmentalists who adopt an *information-processing theory* perspective on cognition see memory as progressing through stages. The gateway system, which transforms information into more permanent storage, is called *working memory*.

Working memory, as I mentioned in Chapter 5, contains a limited memory-bin space—the amount of information we can keep in our awareness. It includes an executive processor that controls our attention and transforms the contents of this temporary storage facility into material we can recall later on. Recall that, during childhood, as the frontal lobes mature, working memory-bin capacity dramatically improves. Unfortunately, as we travel through adulthood, working memory works worse and worse (McCabe and others, 2010).

divided-attention task A difficult memory challenge involving memorizing material while simultaneously monitoring something else.

What explains this decline? Today, experts target deficits with the executive processor, that hypothetical structure responsible for focusing our attention and manipulating

Jeff Greenberg/Photo Edit

Remembering the speaker's messages at this senior citizen center lecture is going to be especially hard—because being surrounded by all these other women is destined to produce high levels of distracting noise.

material into the permanent memory store (McCabe and others, 2010). As people age, this master controller doesn't filter out irrelevant information as well, and we have more trouble concentrating on what we need to learn (Rowe, Hasher, & Turcotte, 2008). One symptom of this *selective attention* deficit is that the elderly have unusual trouble memorizing information in noisy environments (Bell, Buchner, & Mund, 2008). Another is that, as you just saw, older people have so much trouble mastering divided-attention tasks.

When we think of *executive functions*, such as selective attention, a particular brain structure comes to mind. Later-life memory deficits, according to current thinking, mainly reflect age-related neural deterioration in the frontal lobes (Reuter-Lorenz & Park, 2010). Neuroscientists can "see" this cortical shrinkage, by using brain-imaging techniques (Rabins, 2011; Raz and others, 2010; Walhovd and others, 2010). How does the older brain adapt? Brain imaging techniques give us information about this issue, too.

Brain scans offer insights into the intensity of neural activity when adults are given different laboratory memory tasks. With easy memory challenges, such as remembering a few items, as Figure 13.2 shows, older adults show a broader pattern of frontal-lobe activity compared to young adults. But, as the task gets difficult, the older brain shifts to under-activation—suggesting it has totally maxed out (Reuter-Lorenz & Park, 2010)!

This finding is very depressing. Does the aging brain have to work on overdrive and then ultimately "give up" (neurologically speaking) in remembering everything? Luckily, the answer is no. Some memories are more indelibly carved in our mind.

A Memory-Systems Perspective on Change

Think of the amazing resilience of some memories and the incredible vulnerability of others. Why do you automatically remember how to hold a tennis racquet even though you have not been on a court for years? Why is "George Washington," the name of our first president, locked in your mind while you are incapable of remembering what you had for dinner three days ago? These kinds of memories seem to differ in ways that go beyond how much effort went into embedding them into our minds. They seem qualitatively different in a fundamental way.

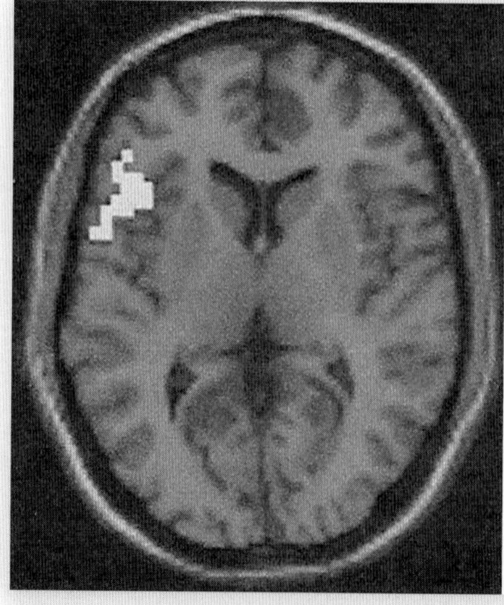

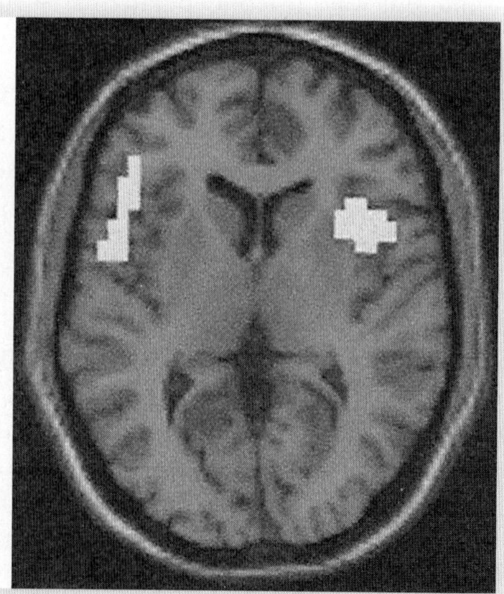

FIGURE 13.2: **Frontal lobe activation in young (left) and older adults (right) in a memory study:** In this fMRI study, researchers measured activation in the frontal lobes when older and younger adults were given a relatively easy laboratory memory task. Notice on the left photo that, while regions of the left hemisphere alone are activated in young adults, the older brains (right image) are working harder to master this task—as here activation occurs in both brain hemispheres.

Source: Reuter-Lorenz & Cappell, 2008.

According to the **memory-systems perspective** (Craik, 2000; Tulving, 1985), there are three basic types of memory:

- **Procedural memory** refers to information that we automatically remember, without conscious reflection or thought. A real-life example involves physical skills. Once we have learned a complex motor activity, such as how to ride a bike, we automatically remember how to perform that skill once we are in that situation again.
- **Semantic memory** is our fund of basic factual knowledge. Remembering that George Washington was our first president and knowing what a bike is, are examples of the kinds of information in this well-learned, crystallized database.
- **Episodic memory** refers to the ongoing events of daily life. When you remember going bike riding last Thursday or what you had for dinner last night, you are drawing on episodic memory.

As you can see in these examples and those described in Table 13.2, episodic memory is the most fragile system. A year from now you will still remember who George Washington is (semantic memory). You will recall how to get on the bike and use the handlebars to pace your speed (procedural memory). However, even a week later you are likely to forget what you had for dinner on a particular night. Remembering isolated events—from what day we last went bike riding, to what we ate last Tuesday, to the paragraph you are reading now—are especially vulnerable to time.

The good news is that on tests of semantic memory older people typically do as well as the young (Dixon and others, 2007). Procedural memory is amazingly long-lasting, as we know when we get on a bike after not having ridden for decades, and take off down the road. The real age loss occurs in episodic memory— remembering the ongoing details of daily life.

This decline in episodic memory is what people notice when they realize they are having more trouble remembering the name of a person at a party or where they parked the car. Our databank of semantic memories, or crystallized information, stays intact until well into later life, unless we have a fatal disease (recall my discussion of *terminal drop* in Chapter 12). People with Alzheimer's disease can retain procedural

memory-systems perspective A framework that divides memory into three types: procedural, semantic, and episodic memory.

procedural memory In the memory-systems perspective, the most resilient (longest-lasting) type of memory; refers to material, such as well-learned physical skills, that we automatically recall without conscious awareness.

semantic memory In the memory-systems perspective, a moderately resilient (long-lasting) type of memory; refers to our ability to recall basic facts.

episodic memory In the memory-systems perspective, the most fragile type of memory, involving the recall of the ongoing events of daily life.

TABLE 13.2: **Examples of the Differences Among Procedural, Semantic, and Episodic Memory**

Procedural Memory	Semantic Memory	Episodic Memory
You get into your blue Toyota and automatically know how to drive.	You know that you have a blue Toyota.	You memorize where you left your blue Toyota in the parking lot of the amusement park.
You automatically find yourself singing the words to "Jingle Bells" when the melody comes on the radio.	You remember that "Jingle Bells" is a song.	You remember the last time you heard "Jingle Bells."
You begin to get excited as you approach your college campus for the fall semester of your senior year.	You know that you are a student at *X* University and that you are a psychology major.	You memorize the room number of this class during the first week of the new semester.*
I unconsciously find the letters I am typing now on my computer.	I know that I am writing a book called *Experiencing the Lifespan*.	I remember that today I must go to the library and photocopy an article on memory that I will need in preparing this chapter.

*Now that it's late in the semester, the location of this class has migrated into procedural memory; so, although you automatically walk to the door, if a friend says, "I'll meet you at class. Just tell me the room number," you are apt to draw a blank!

Ralf Nau/Getty Images

Why can this elegant 85-year-old pianist still beautifully entertain you, even though she is beginning to forget basic facts about her life? Because her talents have migrated into *procedural memory*—the final memory system to go.

memories after the other memory systems are largely gone. They can walk, dress themselves, and even remember (to the horror of caregivers) how to turn on the ignition and drive after losing their ability to recall basic facts, such as where they live.

The incredible resilience of procedural memory explains why your 85-year-old aunt, who was a musician, can still beautifully play the piano, even though she is now incapable of remembering family members' names. Why is this particular system the last to go? The reason, according to neuropsychologists, is that the information in procedural memory resides in a different region of the brain. When we first learn a complex motor skill, such as driving or playing an instrument, our frontal lobes are heavily involved. Then, after we have thoroughly learned that activity, this knowledge becomes automatic and migrates to a lower brain center, which frees up our frontal cortex for mastering other higher-level thinking tasks (Friedman, 2003).

Actually, this is good. If I had to focus on remembering how to type these words on my computer, would I ever be able to simultaneously do the complicated mental work of figuring out how to describe the concepts I am explaining now?

In sum, the message with regard to age and memory is both worse and also far better than we might have thought: As we get older, we do not have to worry much about remembering basic facts. Our storehouse of crystallized knowledge is "really there." However, we will have more trouble memorizing bits of new information, and these losses in episodic memory show up at a surprisingly early age.

INTERVENTIONS: Keeping Memory Fine-Tuned

What should people do when they notice that their ability to remember life's ongoing details is worse? Let's look at three approaches:

USE SELECTIVE OPTIMIZATION WITH COMPENSATION. The first strategy is to use Baltes's three-step process, spelled out in Chapter 12: (1) Selectively focus on what you want to remember—that is, don't clog your working memory bins with irrelevant thoughts. (2) Optimize, or work hard to manipulate material in this system into permanent memory. (3) Use compensation, or external memory aids, when you do not feel confident about remembering information without help.

For example, to remember where you parked at the airport: (1) Focus on *where* you are parking when you slide your car into the spot. Don't daydream or get distracted by the need to catch the plane. (2) Work hard to encode that specific location in your brain. (3) Send yourself an e-mail on your smart phone ("G6, bus stop 4"), so you won't have to remember that place all on your own.

As two memory heads are better than one, older adults can extend Baltes's compensation step to their social partners (Dixon and others, 2007): "I'm going to write this down; but, if I forget, dear, could you remember where we parked?" Or, as my own social partner (husband) memorably pointed out: "It's 6 P.M., Janet. Don't you teach that Wednesday Aging class tonight?" (Whoops!) Now, let's look specifically at "optimization" (Baltes's step 2), by spelling out strategies for effortlessly sliding information into our memory bins.

USE MNEMONIC TECHNIQUES. Have you ever noticed that some episodic events are locked in memory (such as your wedding day or the time you and your significant other had that terrible fight), while others fade? Emotional events embed themselves solidly into memory because they activate wider regions of the brain (Dolcos & Cabeza, 2002). Therefore, the key to memorizing isolated bits of information is to make material stand out emotionally.

mnemonic technique A strategy for aiding memory, often by using imagery or enhancing the emotional meaning of what needs to be learned.

Mnemonic techniques are strategies to make information emotionally vivid. These approaches range from using the acronym OCEAN to help you recall the name of each Big Five trait in studying for the Chapter 12 test to, when introduced to the elderly woman in this photo, thinking, "I'll remember her name is Mrs. Silver because of her hair."

A good way of making random episodic material vivid is to conjure up a visual image. Using my earlier example—to remember where you parked at the airport—take a mental snapshot of the location: "Here's the marker G6, right over my head." Or, remember G6 by imagining Gina, your 6-year-old niece, driving your Toyota.

The fact that we learn emotionally salient information without much effort may explain why our memories vary in puzzling ways in real life. A history buff soaks up every detail about the Civil War but remains clueless about where he left his socks. Because your passion is developmental science, you do well with very little studying in this course, but it takes you hours to memorize a single page in your biology text. In fact, when asked to remember emotionally vivid material, older people perform almost as well as the young! (See Kensinger, Krendl, & Corkin, 2006.)

Martin Barraud/Getty Images

Although his main goal is to greet this woman in a warm, personal way, in order to remember his new friend's name, this elderly man might want to step back and use the mnemonic strategy of forming a mental image, thinking, "I'll remember it's Mrs. Silver because of her hair."

ENHANCE MEMORY SELF-EFFICACY. Because we learn emotionally relevant material best, this brings up the thought that standard laboratory memory tests may be unfair to older adults. These studies involve learning random bits of episodic information. So, they measure only the type of memory that dramatically declines with age. Furthermore, because older people have no hands-on experience memorizing meaningless items, they are less likely to spontaneously use mnemonic strategies than the college students to whom they are often compared. I must emphasize that everyone—old and young—benefits from being taught mnemonic techniques. But when different age groups are given tips such as "use imagery to remember that word," this training boosts older adults' performance most (Luo, Hendriks, & Craik, 2007; Naveh-Benjamin, Brav, & Levy, 2007).

Then, there is the poisonous, memory-impairing impact of self-doubt. If you were 70 or 80, imagine how you would feel during a memory study. Wouldn't you be frightened, thinking, "This test might show I have Alzheimer's disease!"

Therefore, a third strategy for improving memory in old age is to promote memory self-efficacy (Cavanaugh, 2000; West, Bagwell, & Dark-Freudeman, 2008). Take the data referring to neural loss lightly. Understand that with effort *anyone's* memory can improve. Just as believing that intelligence is a fixed genetic entity hurts children, when the elderly think they have a basic brain deficit—and so withdraw from learning situations—they *ensure* that their memory will be poor!

Actually, a rare, real-world memory study with older adults proved that motivation matters a great deal in daily life. Psychologists asked elderly and young adult groups to remember to perform an action in the future: "Call me on Sunday at three o'clock." Here, the more conscientious older people performed just as well as the young! (See Kvavilashvili & Fisher, 2007.) After all, despite believing that memory is "deficient" in old age, who would you trust more to remember to feed your cat when you are on vacation—the teenager next door or your elderly neighbor down the street?

Personal Priorities (and Well-Being)

Everyone believes that memory declines with age. But as I mentioned earlier, we have contradictory ideas about older people's emotional lives. On one hand, we believe that age brings self-confidence and inner security. But we equate old age with sadness and emotional fragility, too. You already know from the research described in Chapter 12 that happiness reaches its peak during the early sixties. Let's now look at why Laura Carstensen (whose encouraging "experiencing sampling" study was also highlighted in that chapter) argues we should generally look *forward* to later life.

socioemotional selectivity theory A theory of aging (and the lifespan) put forth by Laura Carstensen, describing how the time we have left to live affects our priorities and social relationships. Specifically, in later life people focus on the present and prioritize being with their closest attachment figures.

Focusing on Time Left to Live: Socioemotional Selectivity Theory

Imagine that you are elderly and aware that you have a limited time left to live. How might your goals and priorities change? The idea that our place on the lifespan changes our life agendas is the premise of Carstensen's **socioemotional selectivity theory.**

According to Carstensen (1995), during the first half of adult life, our push is to look to the future. We are eager to make it in the wider world. We want to reach a better place at some later date. As we grow older and realize that our future is limited, we refocus our priorities. We want to make the most of our present life.

Eri Morita/Getty Images

Socioemotional selectivity theory, with its principle that, in old age, we make the most of every moment explains why, at celebrations, older adults are often the life of the party.

Carstensen believes that this focus on making the most of every moment explains why late life is potentially the happiest life stage. When our agenda lies in the future, we often forgo our immediate desires in the service of a later goal. Instead of telling off the boss who insults us, we hold our tongue because this authority figure holds the key to getting ahead. We are nice to that nasty person, or go to that dinner party we would rather pass up in order to advance socially or in our career. We accept the anxiety-ridden months we face when we first move to an unfamiliar city because we expect to feel better than ever in a year or two.

In later life, we are less interested in where we *will* be going. So we refuse to waste time with unpleasant people, or enter anxiety-provoking situations because they may have a payoff at some later point. Almost unconsciously, we decide, "I don't have that long to live. I have to spend my time doing what makes me feel good emotionally *right now.*"

Furthermore, when our passion lies in making the most of the present, Carstensen believes, our social priorities shift. During childhood, adolescence, and emerging adulthood our mission is to leave our attachment figures. We want to expand our social horizons, form new close relationships, and connect with exciting new people who can teach us new things. Once we have achieved our life goals, we are less interested in developing new attachments. We already have our family and network of caring friends. So we center our lives on our spouse, our best friends, and our children—the people we love the most.

To test whether this age-related shift occurs, Carstensen's research team asked elderly and young people, "Who would you rather spend time with—a close family member, an acquaintance, or the author of a recent book?" Young people's choices were spread among the three possible partners. Older people chose overwhelmingly to be with the family member, their closest attachment figure in life (Fung, Lai, & Ng, 2001).

Eri Morita/Getty Images

Socioemotional selectivity theory, with its principle that, in old age, we choose to spend as much time as possible with our closest attachment figures, explains why simply spending time with each other and their grandchild is this elderly Japanese couple's passion in life.

When Do We Prioritize the Present Regardless of Our Life Stage?

But is this change in priorities *simply* a function of being old? The answer is no. People with fatal illnesses also voted to spend an evening with a familiar close person. So did people who were asked to imagine that they were about to move across the country alone. According to Carstensen, whenever we see our future as limited, we pare down our social contacts, spending as much time as possible with the people we care about the most.

Socioemotional selectivity theory explains why—although normally you are content to live a continent away—when you are in danger of losing a loved one, you want to be physically close. So, you fly in to spend time with your beloved grandma when she is seriously ill. You insist on spending a weekend with your high school friend who is leaving for a tour of duty in the military in some dangerous part of the world.

The theory accounts for the choices my cousin Clinton made when he was diagnosed with lymphoma in his early twenties. An exceptionally gifted architect, Clinton gave up his promising career and retired to rural New Hampshire to build houses, hike, and ski for what turned out to be another quarter-century of life. Clinton's funeral, at age 50, was an unforgettable celebration—a testament to a person who, although his life was shorter than most, lived fully for longer than many people who survive to twice this age. Have you ever seen the principles of socioemotional selectivity theory in operation in your own life?

Making the Case for Old Age as the Best Time of Life

This passion to make the most of every moment offers a compelling reason why happiness might soar in the early sixties. Here are two additional possible causes:

OLDER PEOPLE PRIORITIZE POSITIVE EMOTIONAL STATES. This bias to focus on positive experiences has been so well documented by now that it has its own label: the **positivity effect.** To take one example, imagine being at a casino and sitting next to an elderly adult. Carstensen's research suggests the older person will be just as happy as you when she expects to win. But, she probably won't be upset (or get far less disturbed) when she loses (Nielsen, Knutson, & Carstensen, 2008). People of every age, as I described in the previous section, remember emotional information best. However, the elderly perform especially poorly when asked to recall upsetting images, words, or facts (Murphy & Isaacowitz, 2008; Tomaszczyk, Fernandes, & MacLeod, 2008).

We can even document this tendency to shut out negative images by watching older people's eyes. When adults of different ages were shown a video of positive and negative scenes, the elderly group spent less time fixating on the upsetting photos than the young (Li, Fung, & Isaacowitz, 2011).

And, interestingly, the elderly may intuitively understand that their approach to life is different at their age. When Carstensen's research team had different age groups listen to stories about a 25-year-old and a 75-year-old, then asked these volunteers to retell the stories from the perspective of each person, the elderly participants used more positive statements when talking from the older person's point of view. The younger adults showed no signs of understanding that old people might think differently than the young (Sullivan, Mikels, & Carstensen, 2010). So, not only are older people adept at screening out negativity, they have a secret knowledge you only get from reaching later life. As one seventy-something woman confided: "I've never felt more authentically me, than ever… And it's just so cool" (quoted in Reichstadt and others, 2010, p. 570).

OLDER PEOPLE LIVE LESS STRESSFUL LIVES. Now, combine this inner security with the external reasons old age is more worry-free: no longer having the hassles of raising children or the gut-churning pressures to perform at work. Older people report fewer daily stresses than the young (Charles & Almeida, 2007; Charles and others, 2010; von Hippel, Henry, & Matovic, 2008). An added bonus is that the outside world treats you with special care (Luong, Charles, & Fingerman, 2010). In one study, when researchers asked adults how they would react in a difficult interpersonal situation, people said they would be prone to hold off confronting someone if that individual was old (Fingerman, Miller, & Charles, 2008). An elderly speaker alerted my class to this interesting perk when he mentioned, "The best thing about being 88 is that everyone is incredibly nice!" If strangers opened doors for you, people forgave your foibles, and everyone made a special effort to be kind, wouldn't you feel better about life and the human race?

positivity effect The tendency for older people to focus on positive experiences and screen out negative events.

Susan Van Etten/Photo Edit

Having help putting your jacket on is likely to be a new life experience for this man. How would you feel about "the goodness of humanity," if people started treating you in this unusually caring way?

So knowing your life will end, and many years spent living, provide surprising emotional bonuses. Moreover, in old age, people have the luxury to do just what they want, and the outside world hassles them less!

Making the Case for Old Age as the Worst Time of Life

But at this point, many of you may be thinking, "Something is wrong with this picture." What about the millions of miserable elderly people who the world doesn't treat so kindly, older adults left to languish, lonely and impoverished, in their so-called golden years? When I gave talks on successful aging at local senior centers in my thirties (some gall!), I vividly recall one 89-year-old woman who put me in my place: "Wait till you are my age, young lady. Then you will *really* know how terrible it is to be old!"

Looming Western-world economic cutbacks in elderly "entitlements" (to be described in the next section) are destined to impair the quality of old age. As "social connectedness" is critical to human happiness, losses like widowhood and outliving friends *must* take an emotional toll. Now combine this with the physical losses of advanced old age, and it should come as no surprise that there is an upsurge of depression as people travel into their mid-seventies and beyond (Dozeman and others, 2010; Rothermund & Brandstädter, 2003).

So, yes, late life can be wonderful when people can *enjoy* their present lives. Expect high levels of happiness among healthy, relatively affluent older people surrounded with family and friends. But, in advanced old age, when people are isolated, disabled, and death looms on the horizon, life can lose all purpose and joy. One 90-year-old nursing-home resident vividly described this lack of meaning when she anguished: "I want my life to end now..... I just lie here sick, and all I do is think of old times" (Dwyer, Nordenfelt, & Ternestedt, 2008, p. 102). Soon after this interview, this woman got her wish. She died in her sleep.

Still, let's not stereotype every 90-year-old person as in a dismal holding pattern, waiting for death. As my inspiring interview with Jules, in the Experiencing the Lifespan box shows, some people live exceptionally gratifying lives well into advanced old age.

Decoding Some Keys to Happiness in Old Age

Do you have an old-age role model such as Jules, someone who is living vigorously at age 90 or 94? What makes these people stand out? For one thing, notice that Jules doesn't define himself as "old." He believes that we keep developing until the day we die. Another striking quality about Jules is his incredible generativity and the fact that he has clearly reached Erikson's milestone of **integrity** (see Table 13.3). Jules knows he has lived according to the prophetic guidelines that he views at the core of having a meaningful life.

Erikson believed that, to reach integrity, older people must review their lives and make peace with what they have previously done. But, as you saw earlier with the demoralized nursing-home resident, happiness in old age does not involve dwelling on the past. As with Jules, it involves finding purpose and meaning in your *present* life (Burr, Santo, & Pushkar, 2011).

Older people need to use their *emotion regulation* talents to flexibly give up total control. In confronting an unchanging chronic disease, for instance, adopting an accepting, "I'll make the best of it" approach is better for one's mental health (Hall and others, 2010). (Here, the "God give me the strength to accept what I cannot change" part of the Serenity Prayer seems appropriate.) But preserving a sense of self-efficacy is crucial, too (George, 2010; Infurna and others, 2010; Windsor & Anstey, 2010). In one remarkable study of people over age 85, even in the face of very poor

integrity Erik Erikson's eighth psychosocial stage, in which elderly people decide that their life missions have been fulfilled and so accept impending death.

TABLE 13.3: Erikson's Psychosocial Stages and Tasks

Life Stage	Primary Task
Infancy (birth to 1 year)	Basic trust versus mistrust
Toddlerhood (1 to 2 years)	Autonomy versus shame and doubt
Early childhood (3 to 6 years)	Initiative versus guilt
Middle childhood (6 years to puberty)	Industry versus inferiority
Adolescence (teens into twenties)	Identity versus role confusion
Young adulthood (twenties to early forties)	Intimacy versus isolation
Middle adulthood (forties to sixties)	Generativity versus stagnation
Late adulthood (late sixties and beyond)	**Integrity versus despair**

According to Erikson, our task in later adulthood is to look back over our life to see if we accomplished what we set out to do. Older people who know they have lived fully are not afraid to die. But older adults, who have serious regrets about their lives, may be terrified of death and feel a sense of despair.

EXPERIENCING THE LIFESPAN: Jules: Fully Functioning at Age 94

It was a hot August morning at Vanderbilt University as friends, colleagues, and students gathered to celebrate the publication of his book. Their voices often cracked with emotion as they rose to testify: "You changed my life. You are an inspiration—the best therapist and supervisor I've ever had." Frail, bent over, beginning to doze—suddenly, 94-year-old Jules came to life. "My book traces the development of my ideas about ideal mental health. It's been a 60-year journey to identify the 'fully functional person' that I'm still trying to get right today." Who is this revered role model? What made Jules the person he is, and what is his philosophy about aging and life? Let's listen in to this interview.

My parents left Europe right before the First World War. So in 1915, I was lucky enough to arrive in this world (or be born). Growing up in Baltimore, my brothers and I were incredibly close because, as the only Jewish family in our Christian immigrant neighborhood, we were living in an alien world. I vividly remember the neighborhood kids regularly taunting us as Jesus killers as we walked to school. So we learned from an early age that the world can be a dangerous place. What this experience did was to take us in the opposite direction . . . to see every person as precious, to develop attitudes that were worldwide.

When I was a teenager, and asked myself, "What is important in life?" the answer was "relationships," . . . to have a fundamental faith in people. It was clear that human beings had a long way to go to reach maturity, but you need to act ethically and lovingly. I also looked to the Bible for guidance, asking myself, "What do the ancient prophets tell us about living an ethical life?" During the Second World War my brothers and I decided we could never participate in violence, and so we were conscientious objectors. I knew I could never kill another human being.

I started out my work life as a public school teacher in Baltimore. I had no desire to get a Ph.D., but when I read a paper by Carl Rogers* in 1948, who was developing his client-centered therapy, I was electrified: Understand the person from his own framework; don't be judgmental; look beyond the diagnosis to the real human being. By listening empathically and relating unconditionally, you can guide a person toward health. Those decades I spent collaborating with Carl ended up defining my life work.

I'm still the same person as always, the same adolescent hiding in the body of a 94-year-old man—but with much more experience in living! The difference is that, physically, I am handicapped [with congestive heart failure] and so I use a shorter horizon. Instead of thinking about a year ahead, I might think about a week. . . . I am well aware that I could die any time. But it's unthinkable to me not to do therapy. I'm incomplete if I am not expressing my passion in life.

It's important never to put life in the past tense. There is no such thing as "aging" or "retirement." You are always learning and developing. When I was younger and looked to the Bible for guidance, I gravitated to the prophet Micah. Micah sums up my philosophy for living in this one sentence: "What doeth the lord require of me but to do justly, to love mercy, and to walk humbly with thy god."

*Rogers was one of the premier twentieth-century psychologists.

health, if an older adult felt "efficacious" in a crucial life area—even one as simple as knowing he could still walk by himself—that person was highly satisfied with life (Berg and others, 2011).

Accepting reality, but feeling competent in an important life domain, being generative, staying "in relationship," continuing to see yourself as growing as a human being—these are some keys to aging happily into advanced old age (and living happily during any stage of adult life!).

© Radius Images/Corbis

Notice this man's quiet sense of pleasure at understanding: "Yes, I can get around on my own!" If older people feel "efficacious" in one important life domain, they can keep their *joie de vivre*, even when they are ill and need a walker to negotiate life.

INTERVENTIONS: Using the Research to Help Older Adults

Now, let's summarize *all* of these messages. How can we help older people improve their memory skills? How should you think about the relationship priorities of older loved ones, and when should you worry about their emotional states? Here are some suggestions:

- As late-life memory difficulties are most likely to show up in situations where there is "a lot going on," give older people ample time to learn material and provide them with a non-distracting environment (more about this environmental engineering in Chapter 14).
- Don't stereotype older adults as having a "bad" memory. Remember that semantic memory stays stable with age, and that teaching mnemonic strategies can work. Help older people develop self-efficacy by suggesting this chapter's memory tips. Also, however, be realistic. Tell the older person, "If you notice a decline in your ability to attend to life's details (episodic memory), that's normal. It does NOT mean you have Alzheimer's disease" (Dixon and others, 2007).
- Encourage older loved ones—even those with disabilities—to maintain a personal passion. Being "efficaciously" engaged not only helps slide information through our memory bins, but makes for a happy life.
- Using the insights that socioemotional selectivity theory offers, don't expect older people to automatically want to socialize or make new friends. When an elderly person says, "I don't want to go to the senior citizen center. All I care about is my family," she may be making an age-appropriate response.
- Don't imagine that older people are unhappy. Actually, assume the reverse is true, especially in the young-old years. However, be alert to depression in someone who is old-old, physically frail, impoverished, and socially isolated. Again, the key to warding off depression in old age is the same as at any age: being generative, feeling competent, and having a sense of meaning in life.

TYING IT ALL TOGETHER

1. Dwayne is planning on teaching lifespan development at the senior center. He's excited; but since, until now, he's taught only younger people, he's worried about how memory changes in his older students might affect their enjoyment of his class.. Based on your understanding of which memory situations give older people the most trouble, suggest some changes Dwayne might make in his teaching.
2. Classify each of the following memory challenges as involving episodic memory, semantic memory, or procedural memory:
   a. Someone asks you your street address.
   b. Someone asks you what you just read in this chapter.
   c. You go bike riding.
3. Which of the abilities in the previous question (1) will an older loved one retain the longest if she gets Alzheimer's disease and (2) will start to decline relatively early in life?

4. You are eavesdropping on three elderly friends at a local café as they discuss their feelings about life. According to socioemotional selectivity theory, which *two* comments might you expect to hear?
   a. Frances says, "Now that I'm older, I want to meet as many new people as possible."
   b. Allen reports, "I'm enjoying life more than ever today. I'm savoring every moment—and what a pleasure it is to do just what I want!"
   c. Milly mentions, "I've been spending as much time as possible with my family, the people who matter to me the most."
5. Based on this chapter, (a) give three reasons why happiness should peak in later life and then, (b) in a phrase, target the type of older adult who is most at risk of being seriously depressed.

Answers to the Tying It All Together questions can be found at the end of this chapter.

Later-Life Transitions

Now, let's look at how people find meaning as they confront the life transitions of retirement and widowhood.

Retirement

When we imagine the U.S. retirement age, we immediately think of 65. But, you might be surprised to know, the age for collecting full Social Security benefits is now 66 (and for people born after 1970, it will be 67); and, in recent decades, the "true" average U.S. retirement age has been closer to 60 than 65 (Cherlin, 2010; see also Social Security Fact Sheet, 2011). When we think of being retired, we tend to imagine a short life stage before death. But if you leave work in your early sixties—particularly if you are female—expect to be retired for about a quarter of your total life! (See Adams & Rau, 2011.)

What caused retirement to take up such a huge chunk of the lifespan, and why do people take this step? What is happening to this long life stage as the current Western economic bust collides with the age boom? Stay tuned for information about these questions after we tour the global retirement scene.

Setting the Context: Different Retirement Cushions

If you are like many young people, you probably aren't sure whether retirement will continue to exist once you reach later life. Actually, there are places where retirement doesn't exist today. In Bangladesh, Jamaica, and Mexico, where more than half of all people over 65 are in the labor force, the elderly must work till they get seriously ill (Kinsella & Velkoff, 2001). The reason is that these nations lack the government-financed programs that have propelled developed world retirement into a full life stage.

By the late twentieth century, government-sponsored programs (such as U.S. Social Security)—sometimes allowing retirement as young as the late fifties—were a fixture in more than 160 nations (Kinsella & Velkoff, 2001). But notice if you scan Figure 13.3 on the next page, that despite old-age supports, retirement anxieties differ from place to place. The reason for the country-by-country variations in this pre-European economic crisis poll relates to income inequalities and government trust (Hershey, Henkins, & van Dalen, 2010). In Scandinavia, with its strongly shared national goal to "help everyone cradle to grave," residents feel secure that they will be helped in old age. In Eastern Europe, where the gaps between rich and poor are wide and economic hardship is common earlier in life, people are intensely worried about their retirement years.

What kind of retirement programs can nations ideally provide? For answers, let's travel to Germany before exploring the economic retirement landscape in the United States.

FIGURE 13.3: **Retirement worries from polls taken in selected European nations, during the early twenty-first century:** The message here is that, during the first decade of the twenty-first century, retirement anxieties were intense in impoverished Portugal and Eastern European nations, where people can't count on their government to help float a decent old age—meaning that unfortunately, due to the current European economic crisis, these fears might be *generally* more intense today.

Source: Hershey, Henkins, & van Dalen, 2010.

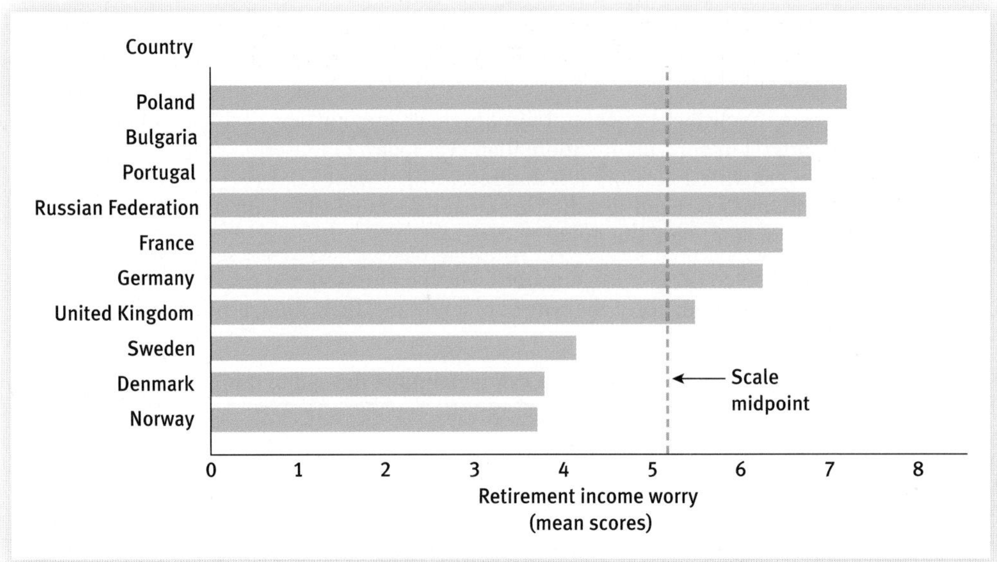

GERMANY: MERCEDES MODEL GOVERNMENT SUPPORT. As Figure 13.3 shows, Germans currently do worry about retirement because they live in a rapidly aging nation where the government may be forced to cut back on the lavish support citizens have long enjoyed—comfortable old-age income for life. Retirement in Germany is mainly financed by employee and employer payroll taxes, similar to the system we have in the United States. However, unlike in the United States, in Germany, the philosophy has traditionally been to keep people well-off during their older years. When the typical German worker retires, the government has replaced roughly three-fourths of that person's working income for life. Until recently, Germans have had no worries about falling into poverty in old age. Remarkably, German retirees have had *more* spending power as they traveled further into old age (Hungerford, 2003).

THE UNITED STATES: GOING IT ALONE WITH MODEST GOVERNMENT HELP. If Germany has offered a Mercedes-like model, government-funded U.S. retirement is more like a used car; it allows people to barely make it, but in not much comfort at all. The reason is that the famous, guaranteed old-age insurance program called Social Security operates as a safety net to keep people from being destitute in old age.

Social Security, the landmark government program instituted by President Franklin D. Roosevelt in 1935 at the height of the Great Depression, gets its financing from current workers. Employees and employers pay into this program to fund today's retirees; then, when it is their turn to retire, these adults get a lifelong stipend financed by the current working population. However, with an average monthly check of $1177, in early 2011, Social Security can only support the basics of life for the typical older adult (Social Security Online, 2011).

Social Security The U.S. government's national retirement support program.

private pensions The major source of nongovernmental income support for retirees, in which the individual worker and employer put a portion of each paycheck into an account to help finance retirement.

Private pensions (and personal savings) are supposed to take up the slack. Workers put aside a portion of each paycheck, and these funds, often matched by employer contributions, go into a tax-free account that accumulates equity. Then, at retirement, the person gets regular payouts, or a lump sum, on which to live (Johnson, 2009).

The central role of private pensions in financing retirement reflects the priority that the United States places on individual initiative. Just as with providing universal health care, we are leery about the welfare-state implications of a federal government plan, preferring to provide tax incentives that encourage workers to plan for retirement on their own.

The problem is that baby boomers haven't amassed the pension cushion (hundreds of thousands of dollars) to support a comfortable lifestyle for 20 or so years (Adams & Rau, 2011; Newman, 2011). Moreover, since pension investments depend on market fluctuations, they are risky (Feldman & Beehr, 2011)—which makes any reasonable person anxious: "Can I count on that income to 'be there' for decades?" When we add in the fact that during the Great Recession, people witnessed the value of their major asset—their homes—dramatically erode, it is no wonder that most baby boomers feel they don't have the funds to retire in their early sixties, much less at 65 (Johnson, 2009). Working-class adults, such as the cashiers at your local convenience store, are worse off. They enter retirement depending on Social Security, without pensions or savings at all.

These realities are translating into older average U.S. retirement ages (Ekerdt, 2010). Two decades ago, one in five people worked past age 65; in 2015, that number is expected to tilt upwards to 1 in 2 (Newman, 2011). Moreover, even after they retire, many people return to work. In, 2010, roughly 2 in 3 retirees did take a new post-retirement job, at least part time (Adams & Rau, 2011).

The fact that retiring is no longer "all or none" is terrific news if people can find less stressful jobs or start new, fulfilling late-life careers. The problem, however, is that Americans, who work into their late sixties, are probably *not* making this choice out of joy. Unfortunately, late retirement is most common among people who must keep working to economically survive (Raymo and others, 2011). (Actually, another reason why baby boomers—including your author—are putting off retirement is out of generative feelings. We want to help support our cash-strapped children and grandchildren.)

AP Photo/The Star Tribune, Courtney Perry

This 70-year-old clerk would probably much prefer basking at a beach to bending over a deli freezer. But given Social Security's meager allotment, and without a retirement nest egg, she must work during her so-called "golden" years.

Where do women fit into this picture? Here, we see an interesting split. Because marriage boosts a wife's economic status, divorced or single women are more likely to have to re-enter the labor market after they have retired (Pleau, 2010). Their less continuous work histories and lower-wage jobs (remember Chapter 11), plus longer life expectancies make it difficult to amass sufficient retirement funds ("How can I save for old age when I need my income to live?").

Still, even when women enter retirement married and upper-middle class, they are vulnerable to spending their nest eggs and ending their lives dependent just on Social Security. In fact, the U.S. age group most likely to live in poverty is females over 85.

The bottom-line message is that, yes, retirement is a shorter, more fragile phase of life. Moreover, the U.S. income inequalities highlighted throughout this book persist into the older years. Economic difficulties in earlier adulthood foreshadow economic difficulties in old age. Just as being single and female predicts earlier adult poverty, it spells financial trouble in later life. But, even for affluent women, poverty can be the unfortunate price of surviving to advanced old age.

Now that we know the financial hurdles to retiring, it's time to explore other influences that go into the decision to leave work.

Exploring the Complex Push/Pull Retirement Decision

Imagine that you are in your early sixties and considering leaving your job. Clearly, your primary consideration is economic: "Do I have enough money?" However, a second force that comes into play, particularly for low-income workers, is health: "Can I physically continue at work?" (See Feldman & Beehr, 2011.) There may be another, insidious influence prompting your decision: age discrimination.

IN FOCUS: The Impact of Age Discrimination

Age discrimination in the United States is illegal. People cannot get fired for being "too old." But, because it's acceptable to get rid of more expensive workers—who tend to be older—for "business reasons," it's difficult to prove that "age" was the reason why a fifty-something worker got laid off (Rothenberg & Gardner, 2011).

Rather than outright layoffs, employers may also use a one-shot pension bonus to lure long-standing employees into leaving (accompanied by an implicit threat): As one resentful late twentieth-century worker put it:

> They said if we didn't . . . tak(e) the early retirement incentive, they would . . . reduce the work force. . . . Ordinarily we were a two-man office, but when my boss retired . . . he was not replaced. . . . (and) you would have twice as much work because it wasn't being done by anyone else.
>
> (quoted in Williamson, Rinehart, & Blank, 1992, p. 43)

Encouraging retirement via a special buyout and/or making the job so onerous that older employees "want" to leave are standard techniques for propelling people to "go gently" into their retirement years (Ekerdt, 2010). But the most widespread form of age discrimination relates, not to getting rid of existing employees, but choosing *whom* to hire (Rothenberg & Gardner, 2011).

In many ways, older workers make superior employees. Studies show they are more ethical, more reliable, more safety conscious. Contrary to our stereotypes, they are even more compliant and less likely to take time off for being sick (Newman, 2011). Still, these traits may not matter much when it comes down to deciding whom to employ. It's impossible to prove that "too old" is the reason for a given applicant being consigned to the "won't hire" pile (Neumark, 2009). However, laboratory studies suggest that, given hypothetical older and younger job seekers, employers routinely go for the younger adult (Ekerdt, 2010; Rothenberg & Gardner, 2011).

How does this bias affect real people? Consider my friend Justine, fired from her sales manager job at age 50. Justine, a single mother with a teenager, has been unable to find work for more than a year, even in a lower-status job. Suppose you were a 30-year-old manager hiring a sales associate at your store. Be honest. Wouldn't you pass up Justine in favor of a job applicant your own age?

So far, I've been focusing on the dismal forces that affect retirement: Financial problems keep people in the labor force unwillingly; age discrimination or health issues push older workers to retire. I've been neglecting the fact that retirement is also a *positive* choice. Many baby boomers say they want to keep working after age 65 because they love their jobs (Adams & Rau, 2011; Galinsky, 2007). People may retire in order to enter an exciting, new phase of life.

Who is passionate to stay in the labor force until their seventies or up to age 85? As I implied earlier, these older adults are often healthy and highly educated workers, like Jules in the Experiencing the Lifespan box, who feel tremendous flow in their careers (Adams & Rau, 2011). What about adults who permanently retire? Are they depressed or thrilled after taking this step?

Life as a Retiree

The answer is "it depends." People who have left their jobs unwillingly are apt to feel unhappy after they retire (Calvo, Haverstick, & Sass, 2009). Having serious money or health worries also poisons the retirement years. Actually, the qualities that make for retirement happiness are identical to the attributes that make later life a *generally* happy life stage. Retirement smiles on people who are healthy, married, and have the economic resources to enjoy life (Pinquart & Schindler, 2007).

age discrimination Illegally laying off workers or failing to hire or promote them on the basis of age.

TABLE 13.4: Four Questions to Ask to Predict If a Relative Will Be Happy as a Retiree: A Section Summary

1. Did this person *want to* retire, or was he forced out of the workforce?
2. Is this person married (happily!), in good health, and does she have sufficient income?
3. Is this person generative and open to experience?
4. Does this person have an absorbing hobby, plan to use this time giving back to the community, or have fulfilling "bucket list" goals?

Personality matters, too. Just as earlier in life, being open to experience and generative (Burr, Santo, & Pushkar, 2011) sets people up for retirement happiness; having a serious leisure passion, such as playing the flute, also smoothes the way to a satisfying retirement life (Heo and others, 2010). In fact, you can predict whether a just-retired relative will end up happy by knowing two facts: Did this person *want* to leave work? What is she like as a human being? (See Table 13.4 for a summary of these forces.)

How can you expect your relative to spend her retirement years? Because "personality endures," one key is to look to her passions now (Atchley, 1989; Pushkar and others, 2010). So, a social activist joins the Peace Corps. A business executive volunteers at SCORE (Senior Corps of Retired Executives), advising young people about setting up small businesses. Others decide to take up new "bucket list" goals such as hiking the Himalayas or getting a history Ph.D. Or people open to experience might retire to pack in as much new learning as they possibly can.

Tom Wagner/Corbis

These older people are enrolled in an English class in a special senior citizens college in Japan. Because many people use their retirement years to devote themselves to the human passion for learning, special educational programs such as Elderhostel are flourishing in nations around the world.

A dazzling array of options is available to older adults who are passionate to expand their minds, from reduced fees at college (which, by the way, are standard at many universities) to older-adult institutes. Here is what one man had to say about his experience at a program called Elderhostel, in which, for one summer week, people age 55 and over can enroll in courses on campuses around the world.

> After my program at the University of Notre Dame ... I have an overwhelming memory. It was simply wonderful. . . . Dr. James Ellis . . . made mankind come alive, showed us how our species is swiftly and not wisely changing the world. His illustrations were stunning: "We Americans are using 75 percent of the world's calories." (And I didn't want to make him a liar as I passed through the cafeteria line.) . . . Next, Sandy Vanslinger put us through our paces in the aerobics class. . . . With my damaged ticker I was concerned, but . . . I felt great. . . . The quality of the program was so magnificent that I felt I was in heaven. . . . Notre Dame, I won't forget you!
>
> (quoted in Mills, 1993, pp. 108–111)

As these examples show, in our society retiring from work can be the opposite of retiring from life. These years are for vigorously connecting to the world (Ekerdt, 1986). However, there is a different cultural model of retirement. In the Hindu perspective, later life is a time to disengage from worldly concerns. Ideally, people become wandering ascetics, renouncing their connections to loved ones and earthly pleasures in preparation for death (Savishinsky, 2004). Although this goal is rarely followed in practice (after all, our need to be closely attached is a basic human drive!), let's not assume that our "do not go gently into the sunset," keep-active retirement ideal applies around the world.

old-age dependency ratio The fraction of people over age 60 compared to younger, working-age adults (ages 15 to 59). This ratio is expected to rise dramatically as the baby boomers retire.

intergenerational equity Balancing the needs of the young and old. Specifically, often referred to as the idea that U.S. government entitlements, such as Medicare and Social Security, "over-benefit" the elderly at the expense of other age groups.

Summing Things Up: Social Policy Retirement Issues

Now, let's summarize these section messages by focusing on some critical social issues with regard to retirement.

- **Retirement is an at-risk life stage.** In the United States, the decline in pension income and savings is the immediate threat to retiring at 60 or 65. But, the other issue lies in probable future cutbacks in Social Security (perhaps an increase until age 70 for receiving full benefits, or declining support levels). In 1950, there were about 16 workers for every U.S. retiree. Soon, the **old-age dependency ratio,** or proportion of working adults to retirees, will decline to almost 2 to 1 (Johnson, 2009). Social Security was never intended to finance a stage of life. It was instituted when life expectancy was far shorter as a stopgap, when health issues made it impossible to work. Now that the age of eligibility for full Social Security benefits is rising to 67, what other changes (retrenchments) will be on the horizon when the baby boomers have all stormed into later life?
- **Older workers are an at-risk group of employees.** From people being offered pension incentives to retire early to not hiring older workers—as you vividly saw—age discrimination at work is alive and well (Ekerdt, 2010; Neumark, 2009). But there is a silver lining. When the massive baby boom cohort are all over 65—and the general pool of workers shrinks—employers may feel compelled to hire more "aging" adults. If our economy improves, will employers change their negative attitudes toward older employees?
- **Older people are more at risk of being poor.** During the 1960s and 1970s, the United States took the landmark step of dramatically reducing poverty among older adults. Congress extended Social Security benefits. Our nation passed that crucial government-funded health-care program called Medicare. (You can see the incredible effects of these programs in cutting elderly poverty-rates by turning back to Figure 4.6, on page 123.) Old-age economic hardship is currently the fate for the roughly 1 in 3 retired Americans who currently survive on Social Security alone (Binstock, 2010), for low-wage workers who must keep working during their so-called golden years, and for an alarming percent of women as they reach advanced old age. Will poverty become *endemic* among the over-65 population in future years?

Finally, I can't leave the topic of old-age poverty without touching on the topic of **intergenerational equity**—balancing the needs of the young and the old. Given that the elderly get Medicare and Social Security and younger people don't, it's easy, during this time of economic duress, to argue that we are over-funding older Americans at the expense of the young. But, abandoning these programs leaves people dependent on their families. That hurts everyone, young and old (Binstock, 2010). Suppose you had to choose between helping your children and supporting your grandmother, and destitute older people roamed the streets? Again, we are in this together. Life is not a zero-sum game.

Widowhood

Although we worry about its future, most of us associate retirement with joy. That emotion does not apply to widowhood. In a classic study of life stress, researchers ranked the death of a spouse as life's most traumatic change (Holmes & Rahe, 1967). What multiplies the pain is that late-life marriages can be very happy (recall Chapter 11), and, today, widowhood still may strike a cohort who may have married in their early twenties and never lived alone.

Imagine losing your life partner after 50 or 60 years. You are unmoored and adrift, cut off from your main attachment figure. Tasks that may have been foreign, such as understanding the finances or fixing the food, fall on you alone. You must remake an

EXPERIENCING THE LIFESPAN: Visiting a Widowed Person's Support Group

What is it like to lose your mate? What are some of the hardest things to endure in the first year after a spouse dies? Here are the responses I got when I visited a local support group for widowed people and asked the women in the room these kinds of questions:

"I've noticed that even when I'm in a crowd, I feel lonely."

"I find the weekends and evenings hard, especially now that it gets dark so early."

"Sundays are my worst. You sit in church by yourself. People avoid you when you are a widow."

"I think the hardest thing is when you had a handyman and then you lose your handyman. You would be amazed at how much fixing there is that you didn't know about. My hardest jobs were George's jobs. For instance, every time I have a car problem I break down and cry."

"I was married to a handyman and a cook. He spoiled me rotten. You don't realize it until they are gone."

"For me, it's the incessant doctors' bills. I got one yesterday. It's that continual painful reminder of the death."

"And you get all this stuff from Medicare, from Social Security. This year will be the last I file with him."

"You just don't know what to do. I didn't know anything, didn't know how much money we had . . . didn't know about the insurance. . . . My friends would help me out but, you know, it's funny—you don't ask."

"You have friends, but you can't really talk to them. You don't bring him up, and neither does anyone else."

"The thing that upsets me is that I'm scared that no one but me will remember that he was alive."

identity whose central focus has been "married person" for all of adult life. Decades ago, British psychiatrist Colin Parkes (1987) beautifully described how the world tilts: "Even when words remain the same, their meaning changes. The family is no longer the same as it was. Neither is home or a marriage" (p. 93).

How do people mourn this loss? Who has special trouble with this trauma, and how can we help widowed loved ones cope? Let's look at these questions one by one.

Exploring Mourning

During the first months after a loved one dies, people are often obsessed with the events surrounding the final event (Lindemann, 1944; Parkes, 1972). Especially if the death was sudden, husbands and wives report repeatedly going over a spouse's final days or hours. They may feel the impulse to search for their beloved, even though they know intellectually that they are being irrational. Notice that these responses have similarities to those of a toddler who frantically searches for a caregiver when she leaves the room. With widowhood—as the poignant comments of the women in the Experiencing the Lifespan box show—John Bowlby's *clear-cut attachment response* reemerges at full force.

Experts dislike using the word "recovery" to describe bereavement, as it seems to imply that mourning, a normal life process, is a pathological state (Sandler, Wolchik, & Ayers, 2008). Morevover, when people lose a spouse, they do not simply "get better." They emerge as different, hopefully more resilient human beings (Balk, 2008a, 2008b; Tedeschi & Calhoun, 2008). Still, at some point, let's say after a year, we do expect widowed people to "improve" in the sense of remaking a satisfying new life (Rando, 1992–1993). People still care deeply about their spouses. Their emotional connection remains. However, this mental image is incorporated into the survivor's evolving identity as the widowed person continues to travel through life.

What Helps Widowed People Cope?

As they struggle to come to terms with their loss, across cultures people often say that they have the sense their spouse is still "really" there (Klass & Walter, 2001; Suhail and others, 2011). Experts believe that this feeling, called **continuing bonds**, helps mute the grief (Dannenbaum & Kinner, 2009). One widowed friend described this sense of solace when she wrote: "I am never lonely. . . . I feel that my husband is now part of my heart and inner self."

continuing bonds A widowed person's ongoing sense of the deceased spouse's presence "in spirit."

Chuck Savage/Corbis

Now that she is in the *working-model* phase of widowhood, this woman can take tremendous pleasure in this family party. But while enjoying a dance with her grandson, she might get sad as she thinks, "Wouldn't my husband be thrilled to be here?" Maybe she even believes that her husband is there "in spirit," looking down on everyone on this joyous day.

Continuing bonds may allow widows and widowers to disconnect gradually from their spouse and give them the strength to grapple with constructing a new life: "My husband would want me to be happy"; "I need to reach out to others for his sake." What else helps people adjust, and how do these influences change as men and women move from early bereavement into what attachment theorists might label the *working model*—or constructing an independent life—phase of widowhood?

To answer these questions, developmentalists evaluated the personalities of more than 1500 married couples, then followed the small subset of people who became widowed over the next four years (Brown & others, 2004; Ha, 2008).

THE IMPACT OF RELIGION. One force that the researchers felt might help people cope was faith in God. Do people become more religious after a spouse dies? Does religion help widows and widowers adjust?

Interestingly, during the first six months after the death, people did attend religious services more frequently. However, this rise in religiosity (or religious signs) was temporary. It declined to the pre-bereavement level at 24 months.

Did turning to religion mute the pain? The answer here was also a qualified yes. Widowed people who felt more spiritually connected to God did grieve less intensely although they were no less depressed than their counterparts who did not turn for comfort to their faith in a higher being.

THE IMPACT OF CHILDREN AND FRIENDS. A second influence the research team examined was "significant others." What roles do friends and family play at different time points in helping the bereaved? (See Ha, 2008.)

Here, too, there were tantalizing differences between early and later widowhood. At the six-month evaluation, people reported that they and their children had become especially close. Moreover, relationships with sons and daughters were more harmonious than before (Ha & Ingersoll-Dayton, 2008). At the 18-month point, there was a return to pre-bereavement levels in terms of closeness and parent/child harmony; but widowed people reported leaning more on their friends.

This makes sense. During the early phase of mourning, children rally around; families grieve together; they share memories. Sons and daughters make a special effort to shower their bereaved parent with love. But after a while, it's normal to think, "Mom or Dad should be feeling better. . . . It's time for me to return to my normal life." Now, widows and widowers need to reach out to friends—the people they will be counting on day to day to construct a new, satisfying life. Who may have special trouble constructing this satisfying new life?

Having Trouble Moving On

> It's been two years and I still can't get Joanne out of my mind. The children live miles away. I never see my old buddies from the plant . . . and after all, being men, we never were that close. How do you go on when everything you had is completely lost?

As the quotation above suggests, intuitively we might think one group of at-risk adults are men. Women are more emotionally embedded in relationships. They can use their attachments with their children and grandchildren and, especially, their closer connections with friends to construct new lives. The fact that friends play a unique, vital role in the lives of Western widows was showcased in this German finding: While satisfying "family attachments" predicted happiness among *married* elderly women, if a female was single, her happiness depended on having good friends (Albert, Labs, & Trommsdorff, 2010).

This gender split in close attachments may partly explain the **widowhood mortality effect.** While most women adapt fairly well to losing a spouse, the odds of dying—either through suicide or natural causes—are more than 10 times as great for widowers as for married men (Stroebe, Schut, & Stroebe, 2007). Because their remarriage options are limited and they are closer to dying, the most vulnerable group is old-old widowed men. Imagine losing your life mate at age 80 or 85 and you will understand why, for elderly widowers living alone, suicide is a major concern (Stroebe, Schut, & Stroebe, 2007).

Chuck Franklin/Alamy

Lost in loneliness, spending your days staring out at sea, this classic image of the elderly widower says it all. Men—especially when they are old-old—have special trouble after losing their life mate.

However, rather than making generalizations based on gender and age, in predicting who adjusts best, once again, we need to adopt a *developmental systems approach*—that is, consider a complex set of forces. How emotionally resilient is the widowed person? Does that individual have other attachments or a life passion to cushion the blow? (See Carr, 2004.) We also need to look at the person's married attachment style. People who are securely attached to their partner tend to have other secure attachments in the wider world. Men and women who are insecurely attached, because they generally have more trouble relating, may have trouble forming new close relationships to make up for their loss (Bonanno and others, 2002; Field, Gal-Oz, & Bonanno, 2003).

Ironically, this suggests that having a very close marriage might set people up to rebound from this trauma. And, in fact, in the longitudinal study following those couples into widowhood I have been highlighting, if a husband or wife reported that "my spouse is my closest confidant," that individual was more likely to develop another close one-to-one relationship after a partner died (Ha, 2008).

We also can't neglect the important role the wider environment plays in fostering adjustment. Widowhood is a more devastating economic blow for working-class women because they tend to be less well off prior to their husbands' death (Angel, Jimenez, & Angel, 2007). In one study, researchers found that, if older adults were living in an area with a high concentration of widowed people, their odds of dying after being widowed were reduced (Subramanian, Elwert, & Christakis, 2008). So moving as a couple to a senior-citizen community with all those widows and widowers may have an unexpected survivor bonus in later life!

Finally, we also need to look to the way a given culture treats widowed people. To take an extreme case, let's travel to a place where being widowed (for women) can have nightmarish aspects that go well beyond losing a spouse.

Among the Igbo of West Africa, new widows must "prove" that they did not kill their spouse by sleeping with their husband's corpse. Because property rights revert to the paternal side of the family, after the man's death, his relatives feel free to take the bereaved woman's possessions and force her off her land (Cattell, 2003; Sossou, 2002). Given this totally male-dominated tilt to their society, it is no wonder that an African widow in her sixties made this comment: "I've had so much of this bossing by men. I have my house, my garden. Why should I have a man take my money and spend it on drink and other women? I am the boss now" (quoted in Cattell, 2003, p. 59).

Widowed People Are Resilient

So far, I have highlighted the trauma of widowhood, except for this last ecstatic quote. However, we may be making an error in overemphasizing the pain (Bonanno, 2004). Most people who lose a spouse cope very well (Hahn and others, 2011). Support

widowhood mortality effect The elevated risk of death that occurs among surviving spouses—particularly men—after being widowed.

groups for widowed people, such as the one in the Experiencing the Lifespan box are not useful unless a person is unusually lonely and depressed (Bonanno & Lilienfeld, 2008; Onrust and others, 2010).

The most interesting evidence that widowhood has mixed effects comes once again from the longitudinal study that tracked older people from marriage through widowhood. In exploring personality, the researchers found, to their surprise, that wives with the lowest self-esteem during their marriage got *more* self-confident after their husbands died (Carr, 2004). Were these particular husbands infantilizing their wives or putting them down during their married lives? The answer is probably no. Women who have been married for their whole adult life may not realize how well they can cope on their own. When you discover that, yes, you *can* prepare the taxes or fix the faucet and you do not fall apart when finding yourself single after 50 or 60 years, you have learned an important lesson. As the Chinese proverb puts it: Within the worst crisis lies an opportunity (or, in Chapter 12's terminology, a potential redemption sequence). Once again, life traumas *can* promote emotional growth.

Steve Hamblin/Alamy

What should this young woman do to help her newly widowed grandma? Be there; listen; show she cares.

Furthermore, this study had a lesson for all of us. Widows who reported having the most help from friends and family did not feel better. They had lower self-worth (Carr, 2004). So perhaps we need to apply Chapter 5's childhood principles of *scaffolding* to widowhood: Give people support, but don't overprotect them. Don't rob widows or widowers of the chance to learn self-efficacy and connect with their confident, newly single selves. Table 13.5 summarizes these section messages by offering guidelines to surviving widowhood.

What can you say to a widowed loved one or any person who has been recently bereaved? Let's end this discussion with a study that offers answers to this delicate question, one that asked adults who had recently experienced a loved one's death, "What responses help most?" The answer: Listen openly; "be there"; express your care and concern; don't give advice (Rack & others, 2008). In other words, adopt Jules's strategy described in the Experiencing the Lifespan box on page 407 for living "in relationship" in a person-centered way.

In the next chapter, as we immerse ourselves in the physical challenges of later life, stay tuned for many tips about how to sensitively treat loved ones, especially during the old-old years.

TABLE 13.5: **Advice for Surviving Widowhood: A Summary Table**

1. Develop a network of friendships and fulfilling identities outside of marriage before being widowed, to cushion the loss of your life love.
2. You might want to draw on your faith in God, particularly in the first months, and use the feeling that your spouse is with you as you struggle to remake a new life.
3. Take comfort from your children, but understand that, after some time, they will need to go on with their own lives. Reach out to friends to help you construct meaning day by day.
4. Graciously accept emotional support—but don't let loved ones take over your life.
5. Try to see this tragedy as a challenge, an opportunity to understand that you can function on your own. You may find that you are more resilient than you thought.

TYING IT ALL TOGETHER

1. Joe, a 63-year-old baby boomer, is considering retiring from his job as a public school teacher. How might Joe's attitudes and situation differ from a teacher who retired from the same district a decade ago? (Here, pick out the *false* statement.)
   a. Joe is apt to have lower retirement assets, such as a pension (due to the 2008 recession).
   b. Joe is more likely to feel he needs to keep working until an older age.
   c. Joe's superintendent is more likely to urge him to stay at his job.
   d. After retiring, Joe is more likely to feel he needs go back to work in order to make ends meet.
2. Social Security provides a *lavish/meager* income that is *guaranteed by the government/ depends on personal investments.*
3. As I touched on in the text, to preserve Social Security, U.S. readers are apt to hear discussions about increasing the age of eligibility for getting full benefits to age 70. Discuss the pros and cons of this controversial idea.
4. Isabella's husband, Frank, just died, and her friends are especially worried because, during her 52-year marriage, Isabella was very dependent on Frank for practical things like handling the finances and doing home repairs. Should Isabella's friends (a) immediately step in to take over these jobs or (b) offer Isabella a good deal of emotional support but be careful to let her try to learn these tasks on her own?
5. An elderly relative has just been widowed. List the signals mentioned in the chapter that might set off alarm bells that this person is at risk for having a difficult time. Then, in a sentence, describe how your relative might want you to best approach her when discussing the loss.

Answers to the Tying It All Together questions can be found at the end of this chapter.

SUMMARY

Setting the Context: Scanning the New Older World

The **median age** of the population is rising due to declining fertility, longer life expectancies, and, of course, the baby boom. While our ideas about the defining qualities of "old age" are universal, we also have contradictory images about the elderly because there are such dramatic differences between being **young-old** and **old-old.** The stereotype that other cultures treated (or view) their elders more positively than we do is false.

The Evolving Self

Everyone believes that as people get older, memory declines. Elderly people do perform less well than the young on most memory tasks. Memory challenges that are more difficult—such as linking faces to specific situations, remembering bits of information quickly, and especially **divided-attention tasks**—produce the most severe deficits, and losses in these situations begin at a surprisingly young age.

Using the **information-processing perspective,** researchers find that as people age, working memory-bin capacity declines because the executive processor is less able to screen out task-irrelevant thoughts. Using the **memory-systems perspective,** studies reveal few age-related losses in **semantic memory** or **procedural memory** but dramatic declines in **episodic memory.** To improve memory in old age (or at any age), use selective optimization with compensation, employ **mnemonic techniques,** and foster memory self-efficacy.

Socioemotional selectivity theory suggests that in old age (or at any age), when people see their future as limited, they focus on maximizing the quality of their current life, and prefer to be with their closest attachment figures. This focus on enjoying the present, plus the late life **positivity effect** and lower daily stress, offer compelling reasons why old age can be an unusually satisfying life stage. Unfortunately, however, this upbeat emotional portrait applies mainly to affluent, healthy young-old people, but not the old-old. It also may not exist in the future if nations reduce their old age government support. Still, surveys show people live into their eighties and nineties highly satisfied if they reach **integrity** and feel a sense of meaning and control in life.

Later-Life Transitions

Until recently, most people retired in their early sixties and lived in that state for a large chunk of adult life. The reason was the explosion of government sponsored old-age programs offering developed-world older citizens income for life. Germany has historically been a model of the ultimate in guaranteed, comfortable government support.

In the United States, our main sources of retirement income are **Social Security, private pensions,** and savings. However, unlike in Germany, Social Security only provides a meager guaranteed income. Partly due to the economic crisis, baby boomers don't have pensions and other assets to fully float retirement. Therefore, the retirement age is drifting upward, with more U.S workers working after 65. While low-income older adults and single women are most apt to be forced to "work late," even married women who entered retirement affluent are vulnerable to falling into poverty in advanced old age.

Older workers mainly base their retirement decisions on financial considerations, but poor health can also force people to leave work. **Age discrimination,** although illegal, is another reason why middle-aged and older people are forced out of the work force. Even though they can be superior employees, biases against older workers clearly exist—especially when people are trying to find new jobs. Despite these negatives, the decision to retire (or not to retire) can be a positive choice. People who *choose* to keep working into their seventies or eighties are typically healthy and well-educated, with flow-inducing jobs.

Retirees are happy when they have freely chosen to leave work, have few health and money worries, are generative, open to experience, and have an enduring leisure passion. People also use these years to further their generativity, pursue other "bucket list" goals, and to learn. Baby boomers' inadequate pension and savings retirement cushion, and looming cuts to Social Security (partly due to the rising **old-age dependency ratio**), are serious threats to U.S. retirement. Expect issues relating to **intergenerational equity** (over-benefiting the elderly in our time of economic duress) to loom large as the baby boomers fully travel into later life.

Widowhood qualifies as a top ranking life stress, especially when it strikes old-old people who have been married for their entire adult lives. The early symptoms of bereavement have much in common with the separation response of an infant whose caregiver leaves the room, and then gradually over time, people recover, in the sense of constructing a satisfying new life. **Continuing bonds,** or having a sense of the deceased partner's presence, can offer people comfort. Religion and children's support seem particularly important in the early months; and friends help most during the later phases of widowhood.

Because they have a richer web of friends and are more connected to their children, women tend to cope better with the death of a spouse than men. Not only does the **widowhood mortality effect** hit males hard, but old-old men who lose a spouse are at especially high risk of suicide. Having a close marriage predicts resilience, as does having other attachments to cushion the blow. Socioeconomic status, the person's overall life situation, and cultural forces shape the experience of widowhood, too. Finally, we need to beware of seeing widowhood as an *impossible* trauma. Don't overprotect widowed people. Listen to them sensitively. Let them connect with their "efficacious" self.

KEY TERMS

median age, p. 396
young-old, p. 396
old-old, p. 396
divided-attention task, p. 399
memory-systems perspective, p. 401
procedural memory, p. 401
semantic memory, p. 401
episodic memory, p. 401
mnemonic technique, p. 402
socioemotional selectivity theory, p. 404
positivity effect, p. 405
integrity, p. 406
Social Security, p. 410
private pensions, p. 410
age discrimination, p. 412
old-age dependency ratio, p. 414
intergenerational equity, p. 414
continuing bonds, p. 415
widowhood mortality effect, p. 417

ANSWERS TO TYING IT ALL TOGETHER QUIZZES

The Evolving Self

1. Dwayne should present concepts more slowly (but not talk down to his audience) and refrain from presenting a good deal of information in a single session. He should tie the course content into older adults' knowledge base or crystallized skills and strive to make the material relevant personally. He must teach in a distraction-free environment. He might offer tips on using mnemonic techniques. He should continually stimulate self-efficacy: "With your life experience, learning this stuff should be a piece of cake!"
2. a. semantic memory b. episodic memory c. procedural memory
3. a. Bike riding, that automatic skill, is "in" procedural memory, so it can be maintained even into Alzheimer's disease. b. Remembering the material in this chapter, since it is in the most fragile system (episodic memory), is apt to decline at a relatively young age.
4. b and c
5. a. Older people (1) focus on enjoying the present, (2) selectively screen out negativity, and (3) live less stressful lives. b. An old-old person who is ill, socially isolated, impoverished, and has lost a sense of meaning in life.

Later-Life Transitions

1. c
2. meager/guaranteed
3. Pros: Raising the retirement age to 70 will keep Social Security solvent, encourage older people to be productive for longer, and get society used to the fact that people can be productive well into later life. Cons: No longer will retirement be a joyous *extended* life stage. VERY IMPORTANT: Keeping older people in the labor force longer makes it more difficult for young people to get jobs or advance at work. Many older adults do develop health problems in their sixties. Therefore, for these workers (who tend to be at the lower ends of the economic spectrum and so vitally depend on just Social Security), raising the retirement age will have devastating consequences.
4. b
5. Risk factors for a rocky bereavement: Being male, especially an old-old man; being socially isolated; having few interests or attachments outside of marriage; having an insecure married attachment style; in general, not having the internal or external resources to construct a satisfying new life. Best strategy for approaching your newly widowed relative: be there; show you care; listen; don't give advice.

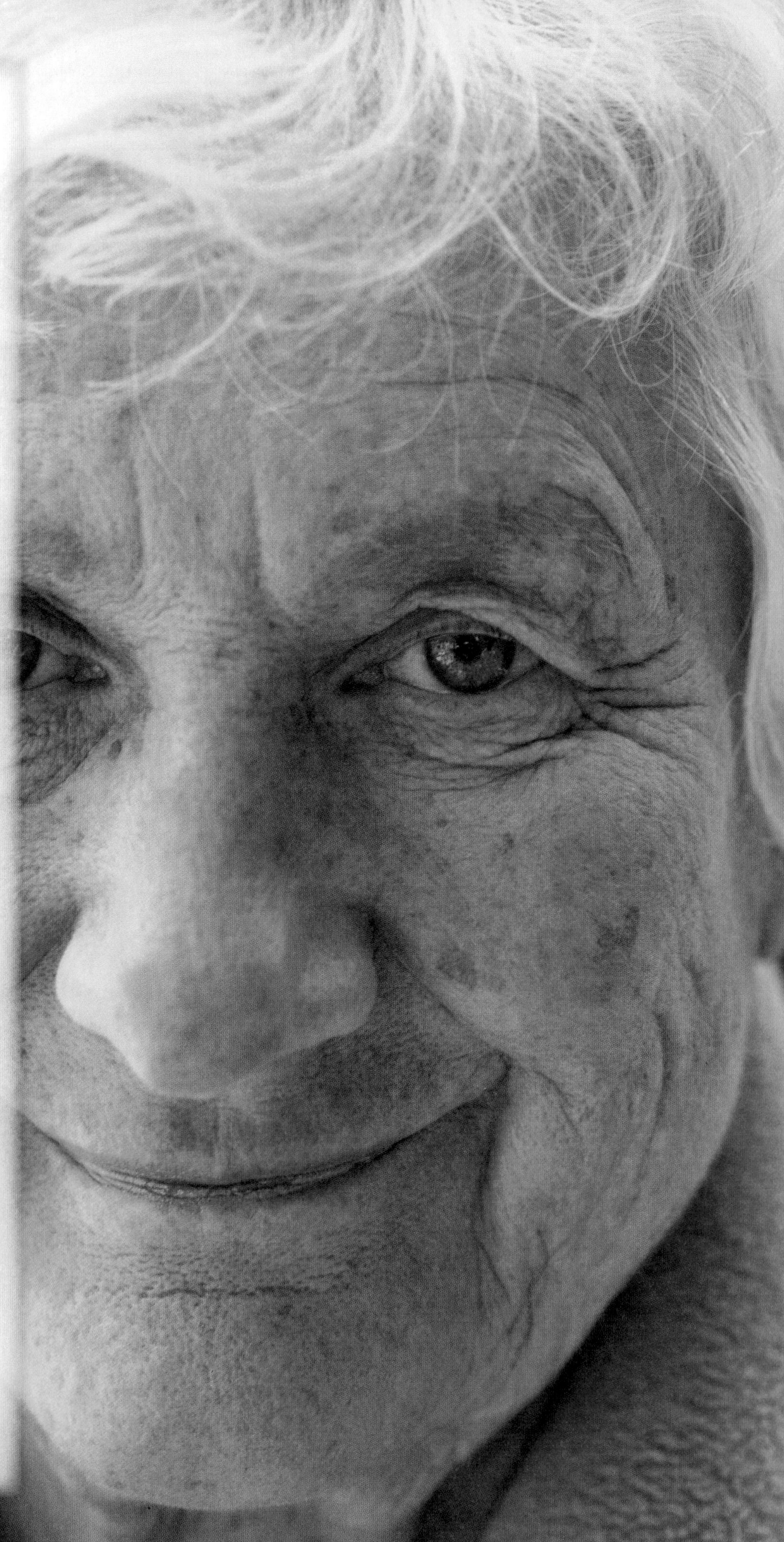

Chapter 14

CHAPTER OUTLINE

The Physical Challenges of Old Age

At age 76, Theresa was vigorous and fit. She walked a mile each day. In her new late-life job as a school mentor, everyone adored her, from the principal on down. However, because of her night vision problems, Theresa no longer drove after dusk. Medical checkups showed other ominous signs: Theresa's atherosclerosis was getting worse. The bone loss that had first shown up on the scan in her fifties had progressed to osteoporosis. By age 79, Theresa felt uncomfortable driving down Main Street in traffic. When she realized it was impossible to read the street signs, she knew it was time to quit her job.

Two years later, at age 81, Theresa was having trouble cooking and cleaning. She began to worry: "What will happen when I can't take care of myself?" Jane, now 90, still spry, and caring for a sister with Alzheimer's, plus a 59-year-old son with heart disease, suggested that Theresa move in with her. Jane's children and grandchildren agreed: "It's our mission to 'honor thy father and mother.' As Theresa is our second mom, we'd consider it a privilege to help." Theresa politely said no. She was determined to actively plan for her future, and that future did not involve burdening loved ones with her care. It was time to check out the new advances in long-term care. But after going online to scan the local assisted-living facilities, Theresa almost had a heart attack. The average rates at most facilities ($4000 a month) were higher than at a four-star hotel! Eventually, she found a nursing home at the forefront of geriatric care. The St. Mary Center was only 50 miles away and, best of all, had a priest on staff. Theresa immediately put her name on the waiting list—and none too soon. Three years later, she fell, breaking her hip, and could no longer live at home.

Today, Theresa uses a walker. She needs help getting dressed and using the toilet. However, when I visited her, she was surprisingly upbeat. True, Theresa admits that life at 84 can be difficult—not simply because of a person's physical state. The real problem is losing your life partner after 55 wonderful years. Still, the facility is wonderful. She loves the activities and many of her helpers. Ladies can hang onto their passions, too. The St. Mary's book club that Theresa formed—which uses books on tape—just won a national prize!

What enemy is Theresa battling? How does physical aging turn into disease, disability, and sometimes the need for a nursing home? This chapter offers answers to these compelling questions and many more.

In the following pages, I'll be exploring problems that some gerontologists (for example, Rowe & Kahn, 1998) have labeled as "unsuccessful aging," describing what *can* go seriously physically wrong during the old-old years. By now, you should realize that equating "successful aging" with walking miles at age 90 is wrong. Successful aging means drawing on what gives your life meaning to live fully, no matter how your body behaves. It is epitomized by 94-year-old Jules, described on page 407, who—although he can barely take a step without stumbling—is sensitively doing therapy and writing books.

Aging successfully means having Jules's sense of self-efficacy and generative mission. But, successful aging also depends on whether the wider world offers older people the support they need to function at their best. The real issue in later life is not so much being ill, but living fully in the face of chronic disease. The way people function in later life depends on their personal capacities (or nature) combined with nurture—having the right person–environment fit.

How can we engineer the right person–environment fit for older loved ones? Let's begin our search for answers by charting the aging process itself.

normal aging changes The universal, often progressive signs of physical deterioration intrinsic to the aging process.

chronic disease Any long-term illness that requires ongoing management. Most chronic diseases are age-related and are the endpoint of normal aging changes.

ADL (activities of daily living) problems Difficulty in performing everyday tasks that are required for living independently. ADLs are classified as either basic or instrumental.

instrumental ADL problems Difficulties in performing everyday household tasks, such as cooking and cleaning.

basic ADL problems Difficulty in performing essential self-care activities, such as rising from a chair, eating, and getting to the toilet.

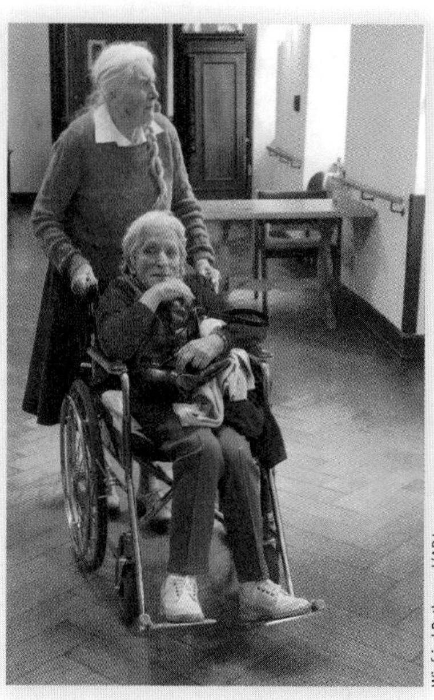

This alert, vigorous 93-year-old, enjoying a swim, seems to have little in common with the same-aged, confused, and wheelchair-bound woman suffering from Alzheimer's disease. However, their aging process is identical. Although aging progresses at different rates, normal aging changes are predictable, biologically programmed into being human, and advance in tandem with the advancing years.

Tracing Physical Aging

Theresa has atherosclerosis, or fatty deposits on her artery walls. She has trouble seeing at night and has lost density in her bones. These are just a few of the many body signs called **normal aging changes.**

Normal aging changes vary in their time of onset. Some, such as Theresa's bone density loss and night vision troubles, begin in midlife. Others, such as atherosclerosis and the losses in mental processing speed that I described in Chapters 12 and 13, become evident in our thirties or even before. But all normal aging changes have similar features: They are universal and genetically programmed into our DNA. They occur in every member of our species to some degree. They are progressive, growing more pronounced as the years pass.

Three Basic Principles of Age-Related Disease

Over time, as you can see below, normal aging shades into disease, then disability, and finally—by a specific barrier age—universal death.

CHRONIC DISEASE IS OFTEN NORMAL AGING "AT THE EXTREME." Many physical losses, when they occur to a moderate degree, are called normal. When these changes become more extreme, they have a different label: **chronic disease.** Bone density loss and atherosclerosis are perfect examples. These changes, as they progress, produce those familiar later-life illnesses—osteoporosis and heart disease.

The National Health Interview Survey (NHIS), an annual government poll of health conditions among the U.S. population, tells us other interesting illness facts. As you can see in Figure 14.1, arthritis is the top-ranking chronic illness in later life (Centers for Disease Control and Prevention [CDC], 2009). As we get older, our chance of having a variety of illnesses increases. Like arthritis, many age-related diseases are not fatal. They interfere with the ability to function in the world. So the outcome of chronic illness is not just death, but **ADL (activities of daily living) problems—difficulties handling life.**

ADL IMPAIRMENTS ARE A SERIOUS RISK DURING THE OLD-OLD YEARS. ADL limitations come in two categories. **Instrumental ADL problems** refer to troubles performing tasks important for living independently, such as being able to cook and clean or drive to the store. **Basic ADL limitations** refer to problems with basic self-care activities, such as standing or getting to the bathroom or feeding oneself. When people have these severe disabilities, they typically need full-time caregiving help.

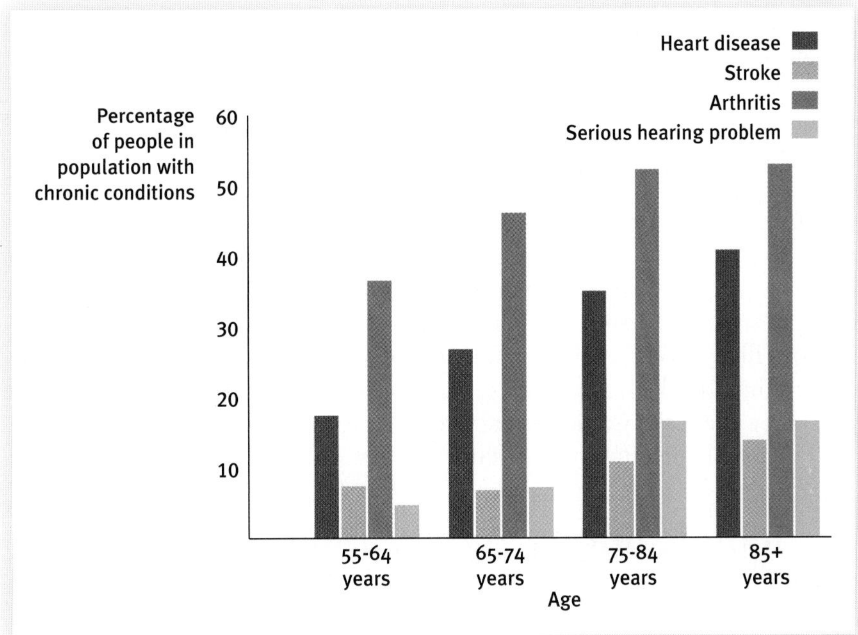

FIGURE 14.1: **Prevalence of selected chronic health conditions among U.S. adults in middle and later life (percentages):** As people travel into their seventies and eighties, the rates of common age-related chronic diseases rise. Although every chronic illness can impair the ability to fully enjoy life, many common chronic diseases don't actually result in death.

Source: CDC (2009); National Center for Health Statistics (2008).

Although ADL problems can happen at any age, notice from Figure 14.2 that the old-old years are when these problems really strike. Half of all people over 85 who are *living in their homes*, have instrumental ADL difficulties. Basic ADL limitations, or fundamental self-care impairments, such as walking to the toilet or dressing, affect 1 in 6 of the oldest old (CDC, 2009). These statistics minimize the true rate of problems because older adults with basic ADL impairments often have to enter a nursing home.

So, yes, people *can* arrive at age 85 or 90 virtually disability free. But as we travel further into later life, problems physically coping become a serious risk.

THE HUMAN LIFESPAN HAS A DEFINED LIMIT. A final fact about aging is that it has a fixed end. More people than ever are surviving past a century. Actually, the 100-plus group is the fastest-growing age group of all (Robine

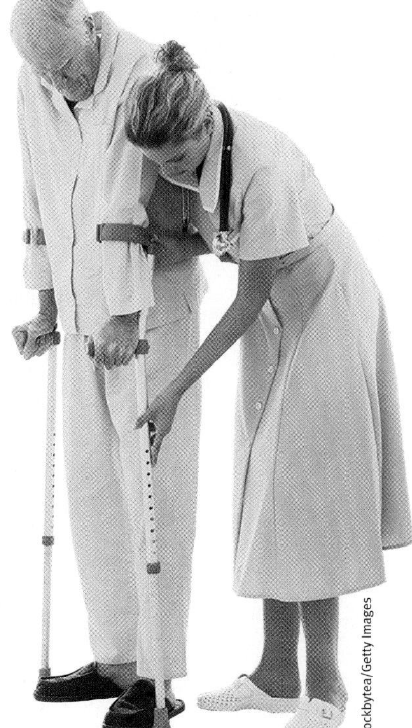

Here, you can see the real enemy in old age: It's ADL impairments, not specific illnesses. Moreover, if this 85-year-old man's difficulties walking independently to the toilet are permanent, he may be forced to enter a nursing home.

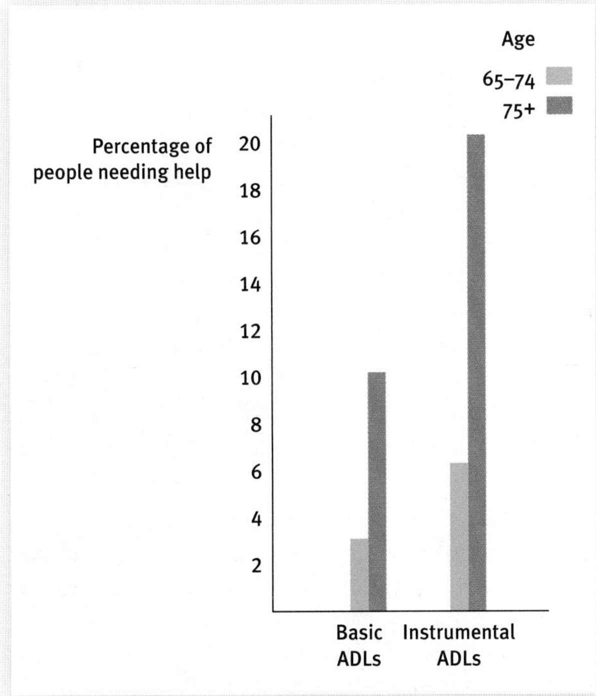

FIGURE 14.2: **Percentages of people needing assistance with instrumental ADLs and basic ADLs in the young-old years and over age 75:** Although in the sixties and early seventies the fraction of people with ADL difficulties is relatively small, the risk of having these problems escalates dramatically over age 75. (Over age 85, roughly 1 in 6 people living in the community has a basic ADL problem.)

Source: U.S. Department of Health and Human Services, 2009.

Jamal Saidi/Reuters/Corbis

Although our species-specific human maximum lifespan is about 100 to 105 years, a miniscule number of people (one out of many millions!) make it to super-centenarian status, living to 110. Here is a photograph of a Lebanese woman who in 2004 was working and—at an amazing 126 years old—qualified as the oldest person on earth.

& Michel, 2004). But few people make it much beyond that barrier age. In August 2011, worldwide, there were only 86 documented "super-centenarians"—people who lived until 110 and beyond (Supercentenarian Research Foundation, 2011). Unless scientists can tamper with our built-in, species-specific *maximum lifespan*, soon after a century on this planet, we all are fated to die.

The fact that our maximum lifespan lasts about a century makes our twentieth-century longevity strides more incredible. Remember from Chapter 1 that over the past century, *average life expectancies* zoomed into the upper seventies throughout the developed world. So, as an adult living in an affluent nation today, you have reasonable odds of surviving within striking distance of the limits of human life. But in examining your illness odds, we need to ask other questions: Are you affluent or poor? What is your ethnic background? Are you female or male? Exactly *when* were you born? Just as they affect every other aspect of development, our social class, ethnicity, gender, and cohort shape our physical aging path.

Socioeconomic Status, Aging, and Disease

How important is socioeconomic status in affecting aging rates? As should come as no surprise, very. Poverty-level U.S. adults tend to age faster and die more than five years earlier than their affluent counterparts (Manchester & Topoleski, 2008). Moreover, this **socioeconomic health gap** appears in each nation around the world. From Canada to Cameroon and from Sweden to Somalia, wealthier people live healthier and survive for a longer time.

When, during adulthood, does the health-wealth gap grow most pronounced? The answer, according to most (but not all) surveys, is during midlife, as normal age changes are progressing to chronic disease. For instance, in one study in Holland, only 5 percent of people in the top quarter of the income distribution reported being in poor health at age 55. For their bottom quarter counterparts, the odds were one in three (Kippersluis and others, 2010).

You may see these statistics in operation by just looking around. Notice how by the late thirties people show clear differences in their aging rates. Although there are many exceptions, notice also that people who appear to be poor often look physically older than their chronological age. In fact, for disadvantaged Americans, "old-age" illnesses, not infrequently, qualify as problems of midlife (CDC, 2009).

Comparing this elegant, well-dressed, 100-year-old San Francisco man to this impoverished sixty-something Polish woman, begging for change on the street, vividly brings home the basic message of this section: Statistically speaking, socioeconomic status is closely related to the rate at which we age and die.

Kevin Horan/Getty Images

© Peter Turnley/CORBIS

socioeconomic health gap The disparity, found in nations around the world, between the health of the rich and poor. At every step up on the socioeconomic ladder, people survive longer and enjoy better health.

How far back in development can we trace this accelerated aging path? Unfortunately, based on the *fetal programming* hypothesis, its roots might emerge in the womb. Remember from Chapter 2 that *low birth weight*—which is linked to poverty—is associated with premature heart disease and earlier death. Now, recall from Chapter 5 that obesity (that major risk factor for age-related illnesses) is more prevalent among boys and girls at the lower end of the socioeconomic scale. So, over time, according to experts, the *many* health-impairing forces linked to growing up poor—from diet, to illness, to life stress—accumulate to accelerate the path to chronic disease and death (Conroy, Sandel, & Zuckerman, 2010; Johnson and others, 2011).

These alarming figures, however, are correlations. They don't tell us about causes. Suppose you were frequently ill during childhood. Wouldn't you miss more school, be less likely to go to college, and tend to earn less during adult life? Or imagine developing heart disease in your forties. You could lose your job. You would have tremendous medical bills. You would slide down the socioeconomic scale. In addition to poverty causing illness, couldn't illness *cause* people to become poor?

But keeping in mind the fact that the poverty-illness relationship is *bidirectional* (Halleröd & Gustafsson, 2011), there are so *many* forces linked to socioeconomic status that might shorten our lives. From social-class differences in smoking (Boykin and others, 2011); to lack of exercise (who has time to work out if you are working two jobs to survive?); from poor eating habits (as high-fat foods are less expensive than fish or fresh fruit, what choices would you make if you had to save every dime?); to the stress-inducing impact of insecure jobs or living in crime-ridden neighborhoods (Beard and others, 2009)—poverty is a poisonous recipe for poor health.

Now combine this toxic cocktail with concerns about seeking medical care. At your hourly wage job, you won't get paid if you call in sick. You worry about being fired if you *do* take off work. You don't have the funds to pay for medicines even if you arrive at the clinic for care. Wouldn't you be cautious: "Even though I have that pain in my chest or lump in my breast, I *can't* visit the doctor now."

For immigrants and ethnic minorities, there are issues related to discrimination: "How can I talk to that White, upper-middle-class male doctor? The medical system is biased against people like me." (See Klonoff, 2009; Korda, Clements, & Dixon, 2011.) In fact, in one study, even upper-middle-class African American men complained about being given short shrift when they arrived for medical help (D'Anna, Ponce, & Siegel, 2010).

So far, I've spelled out a dismal scenario. But, remember that socioeconomic status involves both education and income. And, when researchers look longitudinally, and control for the economic component of SES, they find that it's mainly education and cognitive abilities that loom large in developing chronic disease. In one U.S. study, education alone predicted the transition time to ADL impairments (Taylor, 2010, 2011). High childhood IQ, British researchers discovered, was linked to low midlife levels of an inflammatory protein implicated in a range of chronic diseases (Calvin and others, 2011). So, the good news is that being well educated or intelligent may buffer us from the onslaught of health-eroding forces associated with being poor (Johnson and others, 2011).

Another illness buffer, according to one classic study, is social connectedness. In fact, in this path-breaking, late-twentieth-century longitudinal study, the researchers were shocked to find that close, nurturing relationships were as—or more—important than good health practices in predicting how long people survived (Berkman & Breslow, 1983).

Ethnicity, Aging, and Disease

This sense of being embedded in a caring community may help explain "the Hispanic paradox." In the face of poverty, discrimination, and high obesity rates, Hispanic Americans traditionally have fared better health-wise than we would expect.

Jamal Saidi/Reuters/Corbis

This compelling photo offers one reason for the "Hispanic paradox" (the fact that disadvantaged Latino-heritage adults tend to live a surprisingly long time): a culture immersed in intergenerational adoration and respect. The lesson: As a caring, involved grandchild of *any* cultural background, you might be "working" to help extend a beloved elderly family member's life!

At the lower ends of the socioeconomic spectrum, they actually outlive Whites (Turra & Goldman, 2007).

As one anthropologist discovered, when she entered a low-income Mexican neighborhood in Georgia to conduct interviews, Latina immigrant women followed a number of good health practices (Waldstein, 2010). They insisted on providing home-cooked meals. They offered everyone in the community—both family and neighbors—nourishing social support.

Unfortunately, these benefits don't apply to African Americans (see Beatty and others, 2011). At *every* economic level, Black men and women are more susceptible to age-related illnesses than other ethnic groups (Liang and others, 2010). The racial health gap is especially alarming with regard to cardiovascular diseases. African Americans—especially men—are roughly twice as likely to die of strokes as the U.S. population at large (Mays, Cochran, & Barnes, 2007).

When I worked in a nursing home, I saw these illness-odds firsthand in a 60-year-old African American patient, incapacitated by a stroke. The youngest person in our facility, this formerly vigorous, strapping railroad worker was angry and depressed. The staff was not sympathetic. Why didn't this man stop abusing alcohol? Why didn't he take the simple step of having his blood pressure checked? But my patient was recently divorced and had just lost his job. From biological susceptibility, to life stress, to losing his close attachments, the deck was stacked against this man.

Gender, Aging, and Disease

For women, the deck is stacked in the opposite way. Not only are females cushioned from late-life stressors by a network of family and friends (recall the widowhood mortality effect discussed in Chapter 13), their second X chromosome gives them a survival advantage from the time they are in the womb.

During adulthood, the main reason for this superior survival can be summed up in one phrase: fewer early heart attacks. Illnesses of the cardiovascular system (the arteries and their pump, the heart) are the top-ranking killers for both women and men. Heart disease alone accounts for more than one in four U.S. deaths (National Center for Health Statistics, 2009). However, because estrogen helps to slow the process by which fat deposits clog the arteries, men are roughly twice as likely as women to die of a heart attack in midlife (American Heart Association, 2001).

Their biological susceptibility to early heart attacks means men tend to "die quicker and sooner." For women, the pattern is "surviving longer but being more frail."

Years of experience with the medical system, being sensitive to her body's signals, understanding that "When I don't feel well, I need to go for tests such as this MRI"—all of these forces explain why this woman may be likely to have her cancer diagnosed at an early stage and so outlive the average man her age.

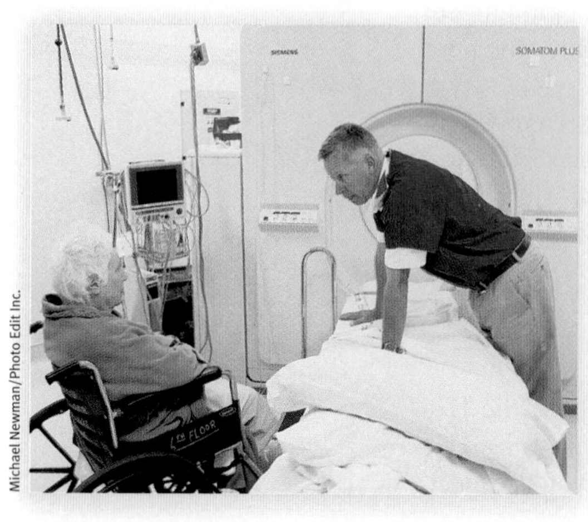

Michael Newman/Photo Edit Inc.

It makes sense that more disability is the price of traveling to the lifespan train's final stops. However, the phrase "living sicker" applies to women *throughout* adult life. At every stage of adulthood, females report being in poorer health than males (Jen, Jones, & Johnston, 2009; Zunzunegui and others, 2009).

To explain this paradox—higher life expectancy but more sickness—we can look to nature forces. During the first half of adulthood, only women experience the physical ailments related to pregnancy and menstruation. In their older years, females have far higher rates of arthritis, vision impairments, and obesity—illnesses that produce ADL problems but (except in the case of obesity) don't lead to death (Whitson and others, 2010).

We need to look to nurture forces, too. In their role as the family health protectors, women are more comfortable seeing doctors and more prone to go for medical care (von Bothmer & Fridlund, 2005). (Think of the stereotypical male "asking directions problem.") But being saved by that speedy doctor's visit can be a double-edged sword. How much extra life expectancy would you "purchase" if your final years were spent ADL-impaired?

Cohort, Aging, and Disease

This depressing question brings me to a final influence shaping our disability pathway, and it's also not a happy one. As a thoughtful observer of the late-twentieth-century obesity epidemic, you might wonder: "Are we seeing more age-related illness at younger ages"? Unfortunately, the answer is yes. Baby boomers *are* moving through midlife more disabled than the cohort that went before (Yang & Lee, 2010). In fact, during the early twenty-first century, the odds of successfully aging physically declined by a full 25 percent (McLaughlin and others, 2010).

Think obesity, and we imagine clogged arteries and weight-related troubles related to getting around. But the most devastating side effect of overweight may be diabetes, that disease of impaired sugar metabolism. Because diabetes accelerates vascular (blood vessel) decay, it attacks everything from the eyes, to the kidneys, to the heart. So this all-purpose ager really catapults late-life conditions into midlife (Cigolle and others, 2010).

Worse yet, with adult obesity rates quadrupling among college-aged men and women, as Figure 14.3 shows, this epidemic has expanded into the middle class

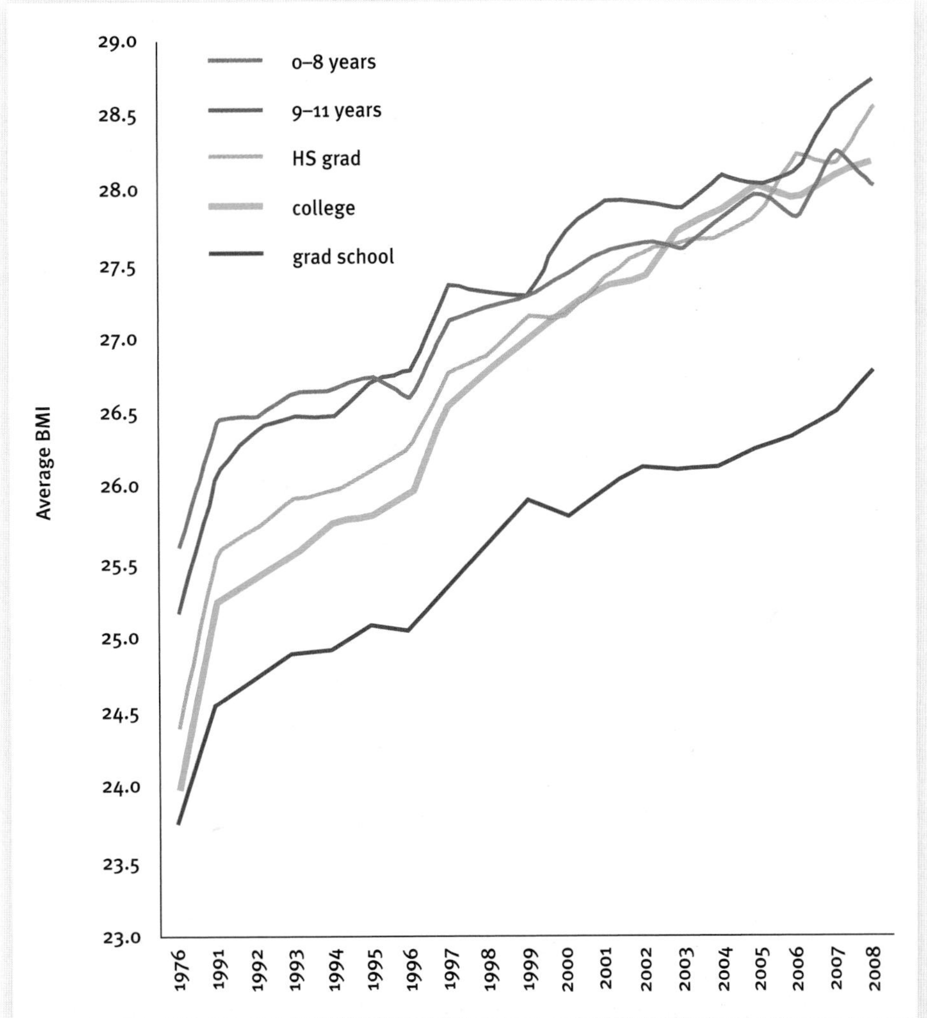

FIGURE 14.3: **Trends in obesity and overweight prevalence by educational attainment in U.S. adults, age 25 and over:** Notice the surprising message in the green line. Yes, overweight is linked to social class for people with graduate degrees (the red line). But, about 15 years ago, obesity rates for college-educated U.S. adults (the green line) expanded to reach "equality" with everyone else!

Source: Singh and others, 2011.

(Singh and others, 2011). I was hoping to see the wealth-health gap shrinking, with low SES people aging healthier. Will we be seeing less health inequality due to more affluent adults becoming ill?

INTERVENTIONS: Taking a Holistic Lifespan Disease-Prevention Approach

How can society make inroads in these toxic lifestyle forces? As I mentioned in Chapter 5, I believe blaming the victim won't work. Pinning total responsibility on the person for being obese—or, as you saw earlier, having a premature stroke—when the reinforcers *all* converge to promote unhealthy living, seems unfair. Ideally, the solution is to alter the health environment starting from day one. Specifically:

- *Focus on children.* As I've been stressing throughout this book, preventing premature births, making inroads in child poverty, and improving education yields dramatic health bonuses during adult life.
- *Focus on communities.* Make it easier for people to naturally exercise without going to a gym or getting on a treadmill, and to buy healthy, low-fat foods. Rather than concentrating stores within mammoth, faraway malls, have shopping located within biking distance or walking distance from homes. Encourage—and make it a badge of parental honor—for neighborhood children to play outside and, if reasonable, to walk from home to their neighborhood school. In fact, simply focusing on developing caring, nurturing neighborhoods alone will have health payoffs at every stage of life.

Finally, we need to face the facts about how we physically age. Only about 1 in 10 U.S. adults over 65 is defined as aging successfully, in the sense of being in perfect health (McLaughlin and others, 2010). Even in the healthiest, most lifestyle-conscious nations, such as Denmark, the label "disease-free aging" fits only 1 in 5 (Hank, 2011). Given that running for miles at age 90 is unrealistic, unless we tamper with our DNA, let's use our human ingenuity to make the world user-friendly for the millions of normally aging people marching into later life. With this goal in mind, it's time to confront the conditions causing ADL problems in the flesh—sensory-motor declines and dementia.

TYING IT ALL TOGETHER

1. In her late fifties, Edna's doctor found considerable bone erosion and atherosclerosis during a checkup. At 70, Edna's been diagnosed with osteoporosis and heart disease. Did Edna:
   a. suddenly develop these diseases, or
   b. have normal aging changes that slowly progressed into these chronic diseases? or
   c. did both events occur
2. Marjorie has problems cooking and cleaning the house. Sara cannot dress herself or get out of bed without someone's help. Marjorie has ________ problems and Sara has ________ problems.
3. Statistically speaking, which man will be most likely to die of a heart attack at the youngest age?
   a. a hard-driving, upper-middle-class executive
   b. a first-generation immigrant from Mexico, living in poverty
   c. an African American man
4. Nico and Hiromi are arguing about men's versus women's health. Nico says that women are basically "healthier"; Hiromi thinks that it's men. Explain why both Nico and Hiromi are each partly correct.
5. Your mom is a baby boomer born in 1950; your grandma was born in 1923. Statistically speaking, who is more likely to develop ADL problems at a younger age, and why?

Answers to the Tying It All Together questions can be found at the end of this chapter.

Sensory-Motor Changes

What happens to vision, hearing, and motor abilities as we grow old, and how can we take action to minimize sensory-motor declines?

presbyopia Age-related midlife difficulty with near vision, caused by the inability of the lens to bend.

lens A transparent, disk-shaped structure in the eye, which bends to allow us to see close objects.

Our Windows on the World: Vision

One way aging affects our sight becomes evident during midlife. By their late forties and fifties, people have trouble seeing close objects. The year I turned 50, this change struck like clockwork and I had to buy glasses to read.

Presbyopia, the term for age-related difficulties with seeing close objects, is one of those classic signs, like gray hair, showing that people are no longer young. When I squint to make out sentences, the fact of my age crosses my consciousness. I imagine my students have this same thought ("Dr. Belsky is older") when they see me struggle with this challenge in class.

Other age-related changes in vision progress gradually. Older people have special trouble seeing in dim light. They are more bothered by *glare*, a direct beam of light hitting the eye. They cannot distinguish certain colors as clearly or see visual stimuli as distinctly as before.

What is it like to be in the midst of this progression? It can be annoying to ask the server what the impossibly faint restaurant bill comes to or to fumble your way into a neighbor's seat at a darkened movie theater. For me, the most hair-raising experiences relate to driving at night. Once, a curve of the highway exit ramp loomed out of the dark and I was inches from death. But apart from my worries about night driving, especially on unfamiliar roads, these problems have virtually no effect on my life.

Unfortunately, this may not be true a decade or two from now. As Figure 14.4 illustrates, seeing in glare-filled environments such as a lighted medicine cabinet, or even making out the print on a white page, can be a real challenge during the old-old years.

FIGURE 14.4: **How an 85-year-old might see the world:** Age-related visual losses, such as sensitivity to glare, make the world look fuzzier at age 80 or 85. So, as these images show, everything from finding a bottle of pills in the medicine cabinet to reading the print in books such as this text can be a difficult task.

Nicole Villamora

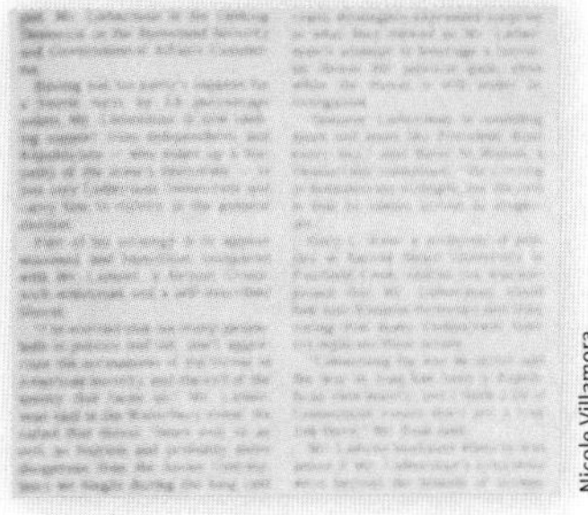

Nicole Villamora

These signs of normal aging—presbyopia, problems seeing in the dark, and increased sensitivity to glare—are mainly caused by changes in a structure toward the front of the eye called the **lens** (see Figure 14.5). The disk-shaped lens allows us to see close objects by bending or curving outward. As people reach midlife, the transparent lens thickens and develops impurities, and so can no longer bend. This clouding and thickening not only produces presbyopia, but also limits vision in dimly lit places where people need as much light as possible to see.

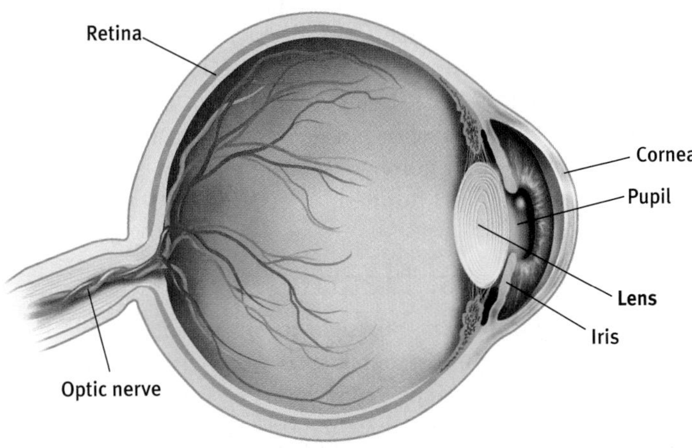

FIGURE 14.5: **The human eye:** Deterioration in many structures of the eye contributes to making older adults' vision poor. However, as I discussed in the text, changes in the lens, shown here, are responsible for presbyopia and also contribute greatly to impaired dark vision and sensitivity to glare—the classic signs of "aging vision."

These changes also make older adults far more sensitive to glare. Notice how, when sunlight hits a dirty window, the rays scatter and it becomes impossible for you to see out. Because they are looking at the world through a cloudier lens, older people see far less well when a beam of light shines in their eye. When this normal, age-related lens clouding becomes so pronounced that the person's vision is seriously impaired, the outcome is that familiar late-life chronic condition—a *cataract*.

The good news is that cataracts are curable. The physician simply removes the defective lens and inserts a contact lens. The bad news is that the other three top-ranking old-age vision conditions—*macular degeneration* (deterioration of the receptors promoting central vision), *glaucoma* (a buildup of pressure that can damage the visual receptors), and *diabetic retinopathy* (a leakage from the blood vessels of the retina into the body of the eye)—*can* sometimes permanently impair sight.

INTERVENTIONS: Clarifying Sight

To lessen the impact of the normal vision losses basic to getting old, once again, the key is to modify the wider world. People should make sure their homes are well lit but avoid overhead light fixtures, especially fluorescent bulbs shining down directly on a bare floor, as these produce glare. Appliances should be designed with nonreflective materials and adjustable lighting. Putting enlarged letters and numbers on appliances will make items such as the stove and computer keyboard easier to use.

Vision impairments are a prime cause of ADL problems because they make everything from cooking, to walking, to working, a challenging task (Whitson and others, 2007). So, when older adults have genuinely poor vision, it's tempting to withdraw from the world (Alma and others, 2011).

How do people respond, psychologically, when they face these permanent losses? Interestingly, there seems to be an adaptation process in which the older adult first gets depressed, and then, over time, regains her sense of well-being (remember the happiness set point research in Chapter 12) (Schilling and others, 2011). Interview studies show people adopt an array of coping techniques—from rearranging the wider world ("I make contrasts everywhere"; "I just bought new white mugs so I can see where the coffee is," said one woman), to using their late-life *positivity* skills to see the world with "new eyes": " I keep going to the ballet, but the ballerinas now have no feet… It's an interesting show, like angels floating" (quoted in Boerner and others, 2010, p. 29).

This is not to minimize the sadness (see Weber & Wong, 2010) and the pain at having to rely on loved ones: "I feel so embarrassed…" said one man. "I can't even change a fuse, and it's embarrassing, belittling" (quoted in Girdler, Packer, & Boldy, 2008, p. 113). But the danger in feeling "I must be independent" is that it may keep people from searching out the low-vision services that might make for an independent life ("Not me! Those places are for the blind!"). (See Spafford and others, 2010.)

This is a mistake. Consider Jim Vlock, a retired executive whose eyes were literally opened when he (reluctantly) visited a center for the visually impaired. After a thorough evaluation, Mr. Vlock emerged laden with devices, from a talking watch, to specialized glasses for different tasks, to a computer with an enlarged screen that can "read for him." As one center director put it, " Too often we get patients who … have lost their jobs, their wives, their home…. Our philosophy is to get patients to do things for themselves so they can feel fulfilled." (See Brody, 2010.)

Our Bridge to Others: Hearing

It's natural to worry most about losing our sight in old age. You might be surprised to know that hearing impairments present just as many barriers to living fully in later life. The reason is that, while poor vision limits our contact with the physical world, hearing losses prevent us from understanding language, our bridge to other minds. So when we lose the ability to hear, we are deprived of fully entering the human world.

presbycusis Age-related difficulty in hearing, particularly high-pitched tones, caused by the atrophy of the hearing receptors located in the inner ear.

Unfortunately, later-life hearing problems are very common—striking roughly one in three older adults (Hartley and others, 2010). The statistics are particularly alarming for men. Around the world, males are several times more likely than women to develop hearing losses in midlife (Belsky, 1999).

The main reason is that hearing impairments have an environmental cause: exposure to noise. Men are more likely to be construction workers, ride motorcycles, and go to NASCAR races. These high-noise environments set people up to develop hearing handicaps at an unusually young age. While government regulations mandate hearing protection devices for workers in noisy occupations, people must take responsibility for protecting their hearing on their own. Ominously, rates of age-associated hearing problems are increasing for *both* sexes (Wallhagen, 2010). From exposing ourselves to the roar of rock concerts to regularly embedding an iPod in our ear, the reason is that today we have noisier daily lives.

Presbycusis—the characteristic age-related hearing loss—is caused by the atrophy or loss of the hearing receptors, located in the inner ear (see Figure 14.6). So this condition is permanent. The receptors encoding our perception of high-pitched tones are most vulnerable. This means older people have special difficulties hearing tones that are of higher pitch. (For instance, if musicians are playing a guitar and a drum *equally* loudly, to an older person, the guitarist's melody will sound more faint.)

Put yourself in the place of someone with presbycusis. Because of your problem hearing higher-pitched sounds, listening to conversations feels a bit like hearing a radio filled with static. (That's why older people complain: "I can hear you, but I can't understand you.") Because your impairment has been progressing gradually, you may not be sure you *have* a problem, thinking, "Other people are talking too softly." If you are like roughly 8 in 10 hearing-impaired people, you won't be getting a hearing aid (Laplante-Levesque, Hickson, & Worrall, 2010). Hearing aids are hard to manage, and they do not work well—or so you have been told. Besides, these devices are for "old people" (Wallhagan, 2010). And, after all, you can hear fairly well in quiet situations. It's only when it gets noisy that you can't hear at all.

Being in a wheelchair seriously compromises anyone's quality of life. But this woman's hearing impairment, which makes having a conversation with her husband practically impossible, may be even more important in cutting her off from the outside world. Moreover, if she is like the vast majority of older people, she won't be using a hearing aid.

Lon C. Diehl/Photo Edit, Inc.

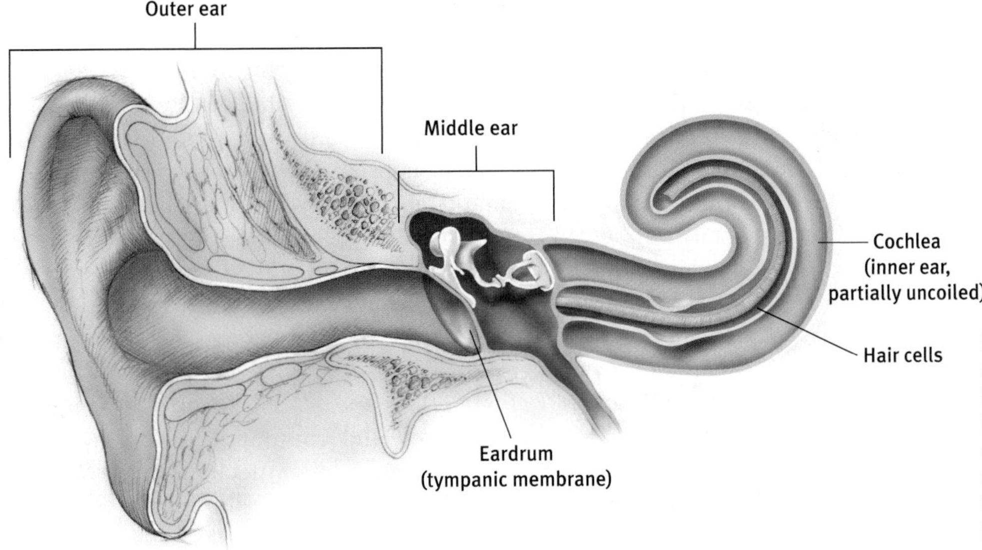

FIGURE 14.6: **The human ear:** Presbycusis is caused by the selective loss of the hearing receptors in the inner ear—called hair cells—that allow us to hear high-pitched tones—so these changes are permanent.

elderspeak A style of communication used with an older person who seems to be physically impaired, involving speaking loudly and with slow, exaggerated pronunciation, as if talking to a baby.

Think of the pitch of the background noises surrounding you right now: the hum of a computer, the sound of a car motor starting up. These sounds are all lower in pitch than speech. This explains why hearing-impaired people complain about "all that noise." Background sounds overpower the higher-pitched conversations they need to understand.

Imagine having a conversation with a relative who cannot hear well—having to repeat your sentences, needing to shout to make yourself understood. Although you love your grandpa dearly, you automatically cringe when he enters the room. Now, imagine that you are a hearing-impaired person who must continually say, "Please repeat that," and you will understand why this ailment can provoke isolation (Barlow and others, 2007). Hearing losses block our ability to participate in the human world.

INTERVENTIONS: Amplifying Hearing

Because background noise is crucially important in determining how well older people hear, the solution is to choose your social settings with special care. Don't go to a noisy restaurant. Avoid places with low ceilings or bare floors, as they magnify sound. Install wall-to-wall carpeting in the house to help absorb background noise. Get rid of noisy appliances, such as a rattling air conditioner or fan. If a loved one is somewhat receptive, you might mention that assistive devices such as flashing phones might really improve his life.

When talking to a hearing-impaired older adult, speak clearly. Face the person. Perhaps use gestures so the person can take advantage of multiple sensory cues (Diederich, Colonius, & Schomburg, 2008). But avoid *elderspeak*, the tendency to talk more slowly and in exaggerated tones ("HOW *ARE* YOU, *DARLING*? WHAT IS FOR *DINNER* TODAY?").

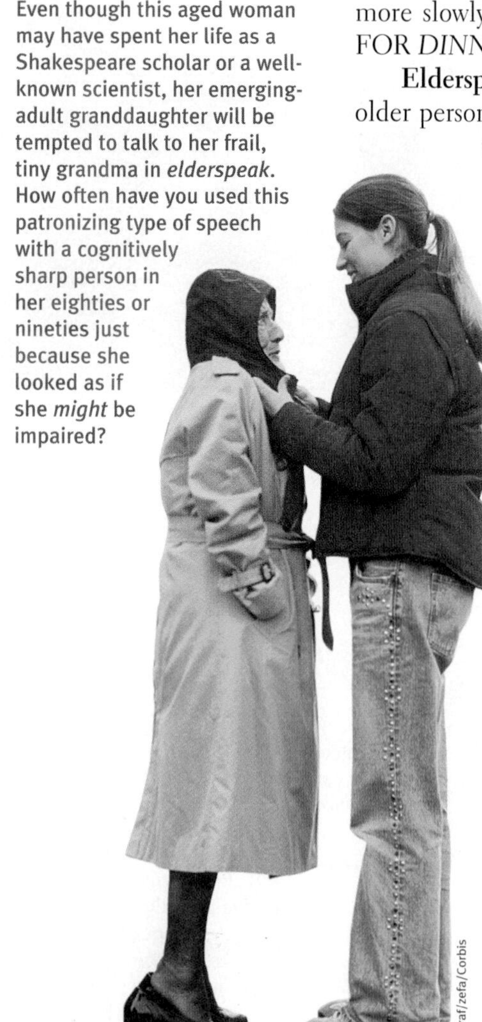

Even though this aged woman may have spent her life as a Shakespeare scholar or a well-known scientist, her emerging-adult granddaughter will be tempted to talk to her frail, tiny grandma in *elderspeak*. How often have you used this patronizing type of speech with a cognitively sharp person in her eighties or nineties just because she looked as if she *might* be impaired?

Ole Graf/zefa/Corbis

Elderspeak—a mode of communication we tend to naturally fall into when an older person looks physically (and so mentally) impaired—has unfortunate similarities to *infant-directed speech*. We use simpler phrases and grammar, and employ infantile "loving" words, such as *darling*, that we would never adopt when formally addressing a "real" adult (Kemper & Mitzner, 2001). I'll never forget going out to dinner with a friend in his late eighties who needed to use a walker, and cringing at how the 18-year-old server treated this intellectual man like a 2-year-old!

For your own future hearing, the message rings out loud and clear. *Avoid high-noise environments and cover your ears when you pass by noisy places*. Why do we hear so much about the need to exercise, and yet there is a deafening silence about the need to protect our hearing? How many of you religiously work out to prevent health problems like heart attacks but then attend rock concerts without a thought? Think of the noise level at your fitness center. Could the same place where you are going to improve your health be producing this very common age-related disease?

As a postscript, some of the same noise-filled public places contributing to late-life hearing problems now offer solutions for the hearing impaired. A remarkable assistive device has been installed in big city public venues—such as train, bus, and subway stations—that "delivers" loudspeaker announcements directly to a user's hearing aid. This microphone-attached advance, called the hearing loop, works miracles at making speech crystal clear by bypassing the cacophony of background noise. The good news for any hearing-impaired person is that, as we speak, this technology may have migrated to your local church and community theater, too. (See Hearing Loop, n.d.) And for any budding mechanical genius listening in: You'll benefit humankind (and possibly make billions) by inventing a hearing aid that actually works well!

© Stuart Monk/Alamy

The huge domed ceilings are awe-inspiring, but combined with bare floors and the clatter of commuters, they make New York City's Grand Central Station an acoustic nightmare. However, thanks to the miracle of the hearing loop, people can now bypass that background noise via loudspeaker train announcements beamed directly to their hearing aids.

Motor Performances

Poor hearing causes heartaches when we communicate with older people one-to-one. What bothers us when we imagine the general category "old person" lies in the motor realm. The elderly are so slow!

Slowness puts older people out of sync with the physical world. It can make driving or getting across the street a challenging feat. It causes missteps in relationships, too. If you find yourself behind an elderly person at the supermarket checkout counter or an older driver going 40 in a 65-mile-per-hour zone, notice that your reaction is to get annoyed. Age-related slowing alone may help explain why our fast-paced, time-oriented society has such negative prejudices against the old.

The slowness that is emblematic of old age is mainly caused by the loss in information-processing speed that starts decades earlier, in young adulthood (described in Chapters 12 and 13). This slowed **reaction time**—or decline in the ability to respond quickly to sensory input—affects every action, from accelerating when the traffic light turns green, to performing well on a fluid IQ test.

© Ball Miwako/Alamy

This British road sign perfectly symbolizes our image of "the old": ADL-impaired; needing special care; most of all, impossibly slow.

Age changes in the skeletal structures propelling action compound the slowness: With *osteoarthritis*, the joint cartilage wears away, making everything from opening a jar to running for the bus an endurance test. With **osteoporosis,** the bones become porous, brittle, and fragile, and break easily. Although men can also develop osteoporosis, women, as is well-known, are more susceptible to this disease. The main reason is that females—particularly slender women—have frailer, smaller bones. With this illness, the fragile bones break at the slightest pressure and cannot knit themselves back together. Hip fractures are a special danger. They are the primary reasons for needing to enter a nursing home (Jette and others, 1998). In fact, because they are aware of this debilitating cascade, more than half of the 70-plus females in one survey ranked "fear of falling" as a major concern (Oh-Park and others, 2011).

reaction time The speed at which a person can respond to a stimulus. A progressive increase in reaction time is universal to aging.

osteoporosis An age-related chronic disease in which the bones become porous, fragile, and more likely to break. Osteoporosis is most common in thin women and so most common in females of European and Asian descent.

INTERVENTIONS: Managing Motor Problems

What can insulate people from tripping and landing in a nursing home? As problems with balance and gait are apt to cause falls, older adults need to check out exercise programs focused on improving these specific skills (such as Tai Chi) (Gschwind, Bridenbaugh, & Kressig, 2010). Encourage the person to go outside, as retreating

Alamy

Medical scooters provide vital wheels to elderly and disabled adults like this man—keeping people fully, physically connected to life; putting off the need for a nursing home.

to one's home ensures further physical decline (Kono and others, 2007).

Take steps to remodel older adults' homes: provide high-quality indirect lighting (as I mentioned earlier); install low-pile, wall-to-wall carpeting; put grab bars in places, such as in the bathtub, where falls are likely to occur. Install cabinet doors that open to the touch, and place shelves within easy reach.

"Lower body" impairments—because they limit mobility—are the number-one barrier to living independently in later life (Pressler & Ferraro, 2010). Suppose you needed help standing, and getting to the toilet was a scary balancing act. Still, I know a man who cannot walk at all—and should be in a nursing home—whose life was transformed by that simple assistive device: the medical scooter. The scooter has permitted him to stay in his own home (with a lot of loving family support) and given him wheels to travel. It has also saved our government thousands of dollars in institutional care!

Table 14.1 summarizes the main points of this sensory-motor section, with special emphasis on highlighting what older adults can do to produce the right person–environment fit at home. How do the elderly handle that environmental challenge so important to staying independent: Driving?

TABLE 14.1: Age-Related Sensory-Motor Changes and Interventions: A Summary

Changes	Interventions
VISION	
Problems with seeing in dimly lit places, sensitivity to glare	• Use strong, indirect light, and avoid using fluorescent bulbs.
	• Look for home appliances with large letters, nonreflective surfaces, and adjustable lighting.
	• Consider giving up driving at night and in the rain.
	• If your eyesight becomes severely impaired, search out low-vision aids.
HEARING	
Loss of hearing for high-pitched tones	• Reduce background noise.
	• Speak distinctly while facing the person, but avoid elderspeak.
	• Install wall-to-wall carpeting and double-paned windows in a home.
MOTOR ABILITIES	
Slower reaction time	• Be careful in speed-oriented situations.
Osteoporosis and osteoarthritis	• Search out exercise programs focused on improving balance and gait.
Gait problems	• Install low-pile carpeting to prevent tripping, grab bars, and other assistive devices at home. (The lighting interventions suggested above will also help prevent falls.)

IN FOCUS: Driving in Old Age

Imagine that you are an elderly person whose vision problems or lower-body impairments are making driving dangerous. You first stop driving during rush hour. For years, you have been uncomfortable driving at night and in the rain. But even if you are aware of having problems, if you are like many older people, you cannot imagine giving up your car (Lindstrom-Forneri, Tuokko, & Rhodes, 2007). Abandoning driving means confronting the loss of independent selfhood that you first gained when you got your license as a teen. Giving up driving might even lead to abandoning your home and entering a nursing home.

Actually, driving is a special concern for the elderly because it involves many sensory and motor skills. In addition to demanding adequate vision, driving is affected by hearing losses because we become alert to the location of other cars partly by their sound (see Munro and others, 2010). To drive well demands having the muscle strength to push down the pedals and the joint flexibility to turn the wheel. And, as anyone behind an older driver when the light turns green knows, driving is especially sensitive to increases in reaction time.

The good news is that, when older people feel uncomfortable about their abilities, they limit how much they drive (Blanchard and Myers, 2010; Ross and others, 2009). The bad news is if an 80-plus driver gets into a two-car crash, his odds of being to blame are about 4 to 1! (See Clarke and others, 2010.) In other words, as Figure 14.7 shows, driving—*during the old-old years*—is a perilous practice indeed (Stamatiadis, 1996; see also Ross and others, 2009).

Imagine you are a passenger and your 90-year-old uncle is behind the wheel. When should you be most concerned? Expect special trouble at complex intersections—which demand *divided attention* and complex information processing. For similar reasons, expect making difficult left turns into traffic to be unusually hair-raising (Clarke and others, 2010). Obviously, the danger accelerates in poor visibility and with lots of traffic around (Trick, Toxopeus, & Wilson, 2010).

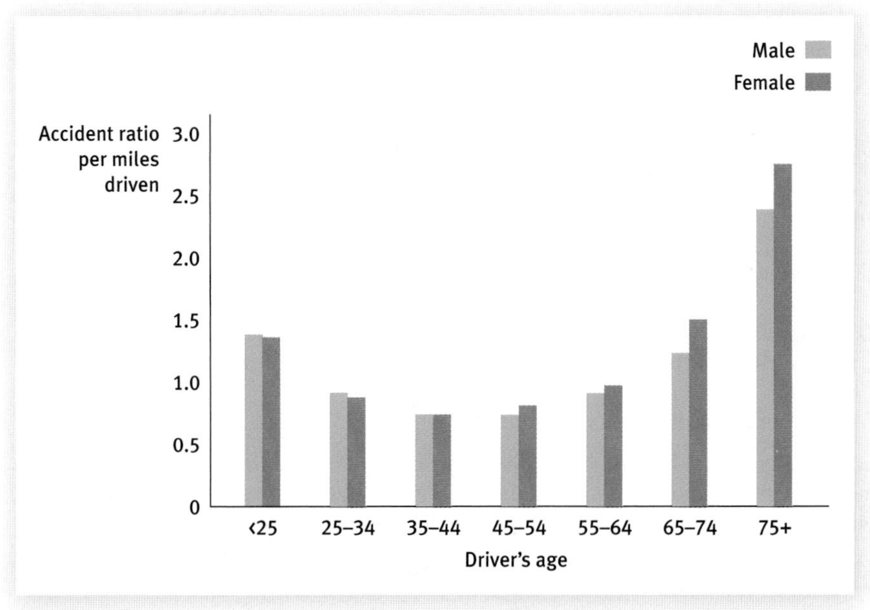

FIGURE 14.7: **Accident rates in U.S. urban areas, by age and gender:** Driving is especially dangerous for drivers age 75 and over. Notice that, if we look at per person miles driven, old-old drivers have accident rates that out pace those in the other highest-risk group—teenagers and emerging adults.
Source: Stamatiadis, 1996.

Jose Luis Pelaez, Inc./Blend Images/Getty Images

Vision problems, hearing difficulties, and slowed reaction time—all combine to make this 80-year-old a more dangerous driver. Can you think of some ways to change the environment so that this man can either drive more safely or be able to stay independent without having to engage in this stressful activity?

What should society do? Our first thought would be to require yearly license renewals, accompanied by vision tests for people over 75. Still, a simple eye test will not be enough. With late-life driving difficulties, reaction-time issues loom large (Martin and others, 2010). Because the elderly have trouble processing the changing array of stimuli on the road (Roenker and others, 2003), to really weed out dangerous drivers, we might need to give each older driver neuropsychological tests (Dawson and others, 2010). Should we rely on relatives or ask physicians to report impaired older drivers? Would you have the courage to rob your uncle of his adult status by taking away his keys?

None of these interventions speaks to the larger issue: "If I can't drive, I may have to leave my home." We need to redesign the driving environment by putting adequate lighting on road signs, streets, highways, and, especially, exit ramps. As most crashes occur at intersections, let's build more roundabouts (circular structures with traffic flowing in the same way).

Let's also construct fewer car-dependent communities: have stores located within walking distance (or scooter distance) of homes; invest in mass transportation. This mandate is mandatory to tackle our global energy problems, ballooning obesity, and the looming ADL crisis as the baby boomers move farther down the highway of later life.

On your way home tonight, think of how to change the driving environment to provide a better person–environment fit for older adults (and yourself!). This environmental engineering is crucial when dealing with the most feared condition of old age: dementia.

TYING IT ALL TOGETHER

1. Roy, who is 55, is having trouble seeing in the dark and in glare-filled environments. Roy's problem is caused by the clouding of his *cornea/iris/lens*. At age 80, when Roy's condition has progressed to the point where he can't see much at all, he will have a *cataract/diabetic retinopathy/macular degeneration*, a condition that *can/cannot* be cured by surgery.
2. Dr. Jones has just given a 45-year-old a diagnosis of presbycusis. All of the following predictions about this patient are accurate *except* (pick out the false statement):
   a. The patient is likely to be a male.
   b. The patient has probably been exposed to high levels of noise.
   c. The patient is at risk for becoming socially isolated.
   d. The patient will hear best in noisy environments.
3. Your 75-year-old grandmother asks for advice about how to remodel her home to make it safer. Which modifications should you suggest?
   a. Install low-pile carpeting and put grab bars in the bathroom.
   b. Put fluorescent lights in your ceilings.
   c. Buy appliances with larger numerals and nonreflective surfaces.
   d. Put a skylight in the bathroom that allows direct sunlight to shine down on the medicine cabinet.
   e. Get rid of noisy air conditioners and fans.
4. Your state legislature is considering a law to require annual eye exams for drivers over the age of 75. Explain to the lawmakers why this law may not be effective, and offer some alternate strategies that could minimize the dangers of needing to drive in old age.

Answers to the Tying It All Together questions can be found at the end of this chapter.

Dementia

dementia The general term for any illness that produces serious, progressive, usually irreversible cognitive decline.

Dementia is the general label for any illness that produces serious, progressive, and often irreversible cognitive decline. Dementia involves the total erosion of our personhood, the complete unraveling of the inner self. Younger people can also develop a dementing disease if they have a brain injury or an illness such as AIDS. However, because—as you will see later in our discussion—dementias are typically produced by two illnesses basic to the aging process, these conditions typically strike people in later life.

What are the general symptoms of *any* later-life dementia? As you can poignantly see in the Experiencing the Lifespan box, in the earlier stages of these diseases, people forget basic *semantic information*. They cannot recall core facts about their lives, such as the name of their town or how to get home. Impairments in *executive functions* are prominent. A conscientious person behaves erratically. An extrovert withdraws from the world. In fact, to qualify for the diagnosis of dementia, a person must have serious memory impairments plus difficulties managing daily life (Theis & Bleiler, 2011).

As the symptoms progress, every aspect of thinking is affected. Abstract reasoning becomes difficult. People can no longer think through options when making decisions. Their language abilities are compromised. People cannot name common objects, such as a shoe or a bed. Judgment is gone. Older adults may act inappropriately—undressing in public, running out in traffic,. They may wander aimlessly and behave recklessly, unaware that they are endangering their lives.

As these diseases reach their later stages, people may be unable to speak or move. Ultimately, they are bedridden, unable to remember how to eat or even swallow. At this point, complications such as infections or pneumonia often lead to death.

EXPERIENCING THE LIFESPAN: An Insider's Portrait of Alzheimer's Disease

Hal is handsome and elegant, a young-looking 69. He warmly welcomes me into his apartment at the assisted-living facility. Copies of National Geographic and Scientific American are laid out in stacks. Index cards list his daughters' names and phone numbers, and provide reminders about the city and the state where he lives.

Hall taught university chemistry for years. Then his mind began to unravel. In addition to the forgetfulness, there were the rambling conversations, the disorganized letters, and calls at all hours of the night. Concerned about Hal's ability to live on his own, his daughters planned to move him to Tennessee this fall. Their plans were cut short when Hal set out to drive to Nashville but could not remember where he was going or who he was going to see. Luckily, Hal checked himself into a hospital, where he learned that he had the illness whose symptoms he graciously consents to describe:

I first noticed that I had a problem giving short speeches. You have a blank and like . . . what do I put in there . . . . I can speak. You are listening to me and you don't hear any pauses, but if you get me into something. . . . I just had one of these little pauses. I knew what I wanted to say and I couldn't get into it, so I think a little bit and wait and try to get around to it. I know it's there . . . but where do I use it? . . . It's ups and downs; and then one day you are in a deep valley. You can't get tied up in the hills and valleys because they just lead you around and it makes you more frustrated than ever. . . . If I can't get things, I just give up and then try to calm down and come back to it. Like, when I read, I get confused; but then I just stop and try again a month later. Or the people here: I know them by face, by sight, but I cannot get that focus down to memorize any names. I remember things from when I was five. It's what's happening now that doesn't make a lot of sense. . . . .

As we walk to my car after this interview, Hal's daughter fills me in:

My father seems a lot happier now that he is here. The problem is the frustration, when he tries to explain things and I can't understand and neither of us connects. Then he gets angry, and I get angry. My father has always been a very intellectual person, so feeling out of control is overwhelming for him. . . . He has days where he gets paranoid, decides that there is a conspiracy out for him. It's tiny things. A letter came to the wrong place and he went down and exploded at the people at the desk. For me the worst thing is remembering how my father was. You expect a certain response from him and you get this strange response. It's like there's a different person inside.

The Dimensions of Dementia

How long does this devastating decline path take? As you will see later, there is an in-between period between experiencing moderate memory problems and having full-blown symptoms. So it's hard to clearly define when dementia actually begins. The deterioration progresses at different rates from person to person and also varies depending on the specific dementing disease. But in general, dementia deserves the label *chronic* disease. On average, the time from diagnosis until death is approximately four to ten years (Rabins, 2011; Theis & Bleiler, 2011).

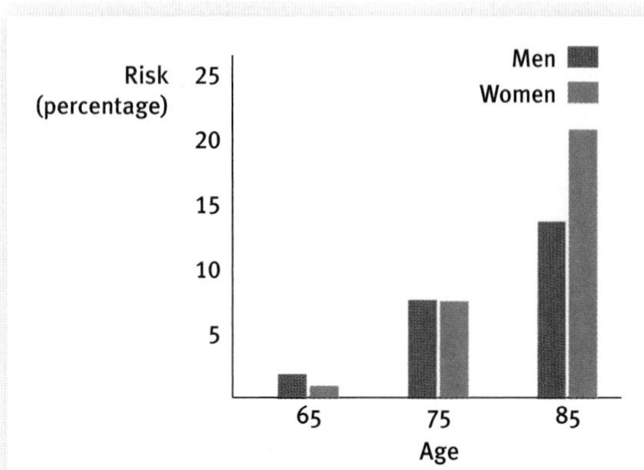

FIGURE 14.8: **Estimated risks for dementia in a major U.S. study, by age and sex:** The good news is that our chance of getting dementia by age 65 is minuscule. The bad news is that, by age 85—especially for females—the risk accelerates.
Source: Alzheimer's Association, 2009.

The good news is that dementias are typically illnesses of *advanced* old age. Among the young-old, the prevalence of these diseases is in the single digits. Over age 85, one in three people is destined to develop memory problems this severe (see Figure 14.8). While these statistics are alarming, notice the small silver lining here. Most older adults *do* survive sound in mind well into the old-old years.

Dementia's Two Main Causes

What illnesses produce these terrible symptoms? Although there is a host of rare dementing diseases, typically the older person will be diagnosed with *Alzheimer's disease* or *vascular dementia* or some combination of those two illnesses.

Vascular dementia involves impairments in the vascular (blood) system, or network of arteries feeding the brain. Here, the person's cognitive problems are caused by multiple small strokes.

Alzheimer's disease directly attacks the core structure of human consciousness, our neurons. With this illness, the neurons wither away and are replaced by strange wavy structures, called **neurofibrillary tangles,** and, as you can see in this photo, thick, bullet-shaped bodies of protein, called **senile plaques.**

Vascular problems—because they impair the brain's blood supply—accelerate this neural loss. So, when a very old person develops dementia, small strokes plus Alzheimer's changes often work together to produce the mental decline (Theis & Bleiler, 2011).

As you just saw, the number-one risk factor for developing dementia is being old-old. But there is a genetic marker that raises the chances of getting Alzheimer's disease. Roughly 15 percent of the U.S. population possesses two copies of the APOE-4 marker. Being in this unlucky group roughly doubles the chance of a person's getting ill during the young-old years (Blacker & Lovestone, 2006).

This breakthrough in the genetics of Alzheimer's poses a dilemma. Children who have witnessed a parent develop this illness are (no surprise) terrified of the disease. Knowing they don't have the genetic marker would ease their minds. But having the APOE-4 allele does not mean that a person will definitely get ill. It only shows that person is at higher risk. Would you decide to be tested? The answer, if you are like many people, might hinge on whether there are strategies to ward off the blow. Where *are* we in terms of preventing and treating Alzheimer's disease?

This magnified slice of the brain showing the senile plaques (dark circles) provides a disturbing window into the ravages of Alzheimer's disease.

Martin M. Rotker/ Photo Researchers, Inc.

Targeting the Beginnings: The Quest to Nip Alzheimer's in the Bud

The main front in the war to prevent Alzheimer's centers on a protein called amyloid, a fatty substance that is the basic constituent of the senile plaques. According to much—but not all—current scientific thinking, the amyloid-laden plaques are central to producing the cortical decay (Theis & Bleiler, 2011). Efforts to dissolve the plaques in Alzheimer's patients have not worked. The challenge is to stem this amyloid cascade before the damage has occurred and people show symptoms of the disease.

This means early diagnosis is crucial. But since scientists cannot look into the brain to see the individual neurons, as of this writing there is no definitive medical test showing the person is getting ill. The current way of diagnosing Alzheimer's is to: (1) Look for a history of steady mental deterioration (rapid mental confusion signals a state called *delirium* which, in the elderly, may be due to anything from medication side effects to a heart attack); (2) rule out other physical and psychological causes; and (3) explore performance on neuropsychological tests.

Older adults diagnosed with *mild cognitive impairment* are centrally important in this research goal. These people show serious learning impairments in the laboratory but have not crossed the line to Alzheimer's disease. Not everyone with mild cognitive impairment makes the transition to Alzheimer's. However, a good fraction (roughly 1 in 2 people) develops the illness within a few years (Theis & Bleiler, 2011). How does the neuropsychological test performance of these people differ from that of unimpaired older adults? And what about middle-aged adults with the APOE-4 marker? Do they manifest brain changes that may foreshadow the onset of the disease? Once we have specific "biomarkers" of incipient Alzheimer's, scientists can really get to work on developing medicines that might stop the disease in its tracks.

Joel Rafkin/Photo Edit

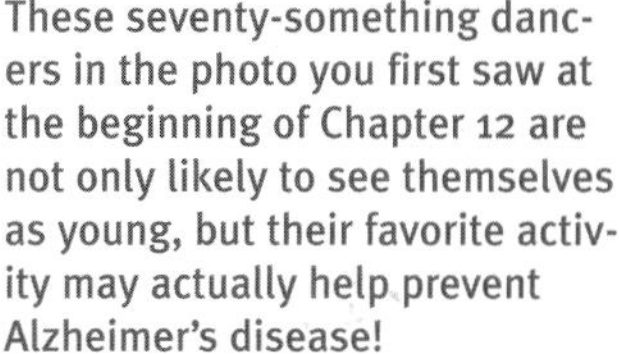

These seventy-something dancers in the photo you first saw at the beginning of Chapter 12 are not only likely to see themselves as young, but their favorite activity may actually help prevent Alzheimer's disease!

In the meantime, is there anything you and I can do? Adopting a heart-healthy diet is a good policy because it helps stave off the cardiovascular problems that are closely tied to cognitive loss. Although Alzheimer's is an equal-opportunity illness, affecting everyone from scholars on down, being well educated can offer people a cognitive reserve to buffer the decline when the illness strikes. However, as I mentioned in the last chapter, despite a blossoming, brain-stimulating gadget industry aimed at anxious baby boomers, there is *no evidence* that doing specific mental exercises is effective.

Still, longitudinal studies suggest that people who walk or work out regularly have a lower risk of declining cognitively in later life (Aichberger and others, 2010; Archer, 2011; Jedrziewski and others, 2010). Interestingly, exercise seems to slow the accelerated rate of plaque formation in the very group most susceptible to Alzheimer's—adults with the APOE marker (Head and others, 2012). Running laboratory rats on treadmills or wheels stimulates neuron formation (Lou and others, 2008; Pietropaolo and others, 2008). So, if I had to vote, my number-one candidate for an anti-Alzheimer's strategy would be *physical exercise*. Even if it doesn't help our species construct new brain cells, at a minimum, going to the gym or walking will help with the vascular component of a dementing illness (and, of course, help prevent the lower-body problems that are such a threat to independent living in later life).

vascular dementia A type of age-related dementia caused by multiple small strokes.

Alzheimer's disease A type of age-related dementia characterized by neural atrophy and abnormal by-products of that atrophy, such as senile plaques and neurofibrillary tangles.

neurofibrillary tangles Long, wavy filaments that replace normal neurons and are characteristic of Alzheimer's disease.

senile plaques Thick, bullet-like amyloid-laden structures that replace normal neurons and are characteristic of Alzheimer's disease.

INTERVENTIONS: Dealing with Dementing Diseases

What about those Alzheimer's drugs we always see advertised on TV? Unfortunately, their effects, put charitably, are minor at best (Rabins, 2011). With dementia, the main interventions are environmental. They involve providing the best disease–environment fit for the person and helping dementia's second casualty—caregivers.

FOR THE PERSON WITH DEMENTIA: USING EXTERNAL AIDS AND MAKING LIFE PREDICTABLE AND SAFE. Creative external aids such as using note cards can jog memory, when people are in the beginning stages of the illness. It helps to put shoes right next to socks or the coffee pot by the cup, and verbally remind the person what to do. A prime concern is safety. To prevent people from wandering off (or driving off!), double-lock or put buzzers on doors. Deactivate dangerous appliances, such as the stove, and put toxic substances, such as household cleaners, out of reach. Many nursing homes feature specialized "memory units," with living environments designed to promote cognitive capacities and staff skilled in dealing with dementing diseases. At every stage of the illness, the goals are to (1) protect people and keep them functioning as well as possible for as long as possible and (2) be caring and offer loving support.

So far, I have mainly discussed what others can do for dementia—as if the disease had magically evaporated a human being. This assumption is wrong. The real profiles in courage are the people in the early stages of these illnesses who get together to problem-solve and offer each other support. What does it feel like to be losing your basic anchor, your inner self? We already got insights from Hal in the Experiencing the Lifespan box on page 439. Now let's read what other people with early Alzheimer's have to say:

> Well, the first word that comes to my mouth is fear; becoming an infant, incontinence, not knowing who you are . . . I can go on and on, with those kinds of expressions.
>
> (quoted in MacRae, 2008, p. 400)

Outsiders can compound this terror when they develop their own kind of memory problem—centering on the label and forgetting the real human being inside. A woman named Bea vividly described this situation when she was first told her diagnosis:

> The last person who interviewed me was the neurologist. He was very indifferent and said it was just going to get worse. . . . Health-care professionals need to be compassionate. . . . There but for the grace of God go I.
>
> (quoted in Snyder, 1999, pp. 17–18)

Can people use their late-life *positivity* skills to act efficaciously in the face of their disease? Listen to a man named Ed:

> Life is a challenge . . . I am alive and I'm going to live life to the best I can. (If) people want to (say) oh what's the point in living? Well, they've stopped living. And I think you only get one chance and this is it. Make the most of it.
>
> (quoted in MacRae, 2008, p. 401)

Another man named Gorman went even further:

> This early diagnosis has given me time to enjoy the life I have now. . . .: A beautiful sunset, a tree in the spring, the rising sun . Yes, having Alzheimer's has changed my life; it has made me appreciate life more. I no longer take things for granted.
>
> (quoted in MacRae, 2008, p. 401)

Can older adults with dementia give us other insights into what it means to be genuinely wise? Judge for yourself, as you read what a loving dad named Booker has to say about the cycle of life:

> I'm blessed to have a wonderful daughter. I sent her to . . . school and college and now she takes care of all of my business. . . . I'm in her hands. I'm in my baby phase now, so to speak. So sometimes I call her "my mumma." . . . Yes, she's my mumma now. [Booker smiled appreciatively.] . . . She's my backbone. She's such a blessing to me.
>
> (quoted in Snyder, 1999, p. 103)

FOR THE CAREGIVER: COPING WITH LIFE TURNED UPSIDE DOWN. Imagine your beloved father or spouse has dementia. You know that the illness is permanent. You must helplessly witness your loved one deteriorate. As the disease progresses to its middle stage, your challenge is to deal with a human being who has turned alien, where the tools used in normal encounters no longer apply. The person may be physically and verbally abusive. She may be agitated and wake and wander in the night. When the older adult becomes incontinent and needs total care, you often suffer the guilt of putting your loved one in a nursing home. Or, you decide to put your own life on hold for years and care for the person every minute of the day.

What strategies do people use to cope? One study with African American caregivers revealed that people rely on their faith for solace: "This is my mission from God" (Dilworth-Anderson, Boswell, & Cohen, 2007). Others turn to the Alzheimer's caregiver support groups and Internet chat rooms for advice: "She seems to get worse during the night." "What works for you?" "My husband hit me the other day, and I was devastated." "Keep telling yourself it's the illness. People with dementia can't help how they act."

Another key lies in changing your orientation to the wider world:

> Accept the fact that the patient won't be able to live up to even minimum standards of behavior. . . . Let it go. . . . I realized I never knew what would happen but I . . . decided that wasn't a reason not to do things. He was happier and I was happier if the ordinary standards of life just didn't apply.
>
> (quoted in Aneshensel and others, 1995, p. 170)

And—most of all—you can simply relish the time together you have left:

> (Tom and Jane, married for 63 years, who were being interviewed about the illness) sat close to one another on the couch . . . and shared a great deal of smiles and giggles... and at times it felt they were the only people in the room . . . Although the stories Jane told did not always make sense, her eyes lit up whenever a question was asked about her marriage to Tom . . . What cannot be easily captured on paper were the warm interactions . . . The investigators felt privileged to be part of such a rich process in which one couple had the opportunity to share the story of their relationship together.
>
> (quoted in Daniels, Lamson, & Hodgson, 2007, p. 167)

Yes, dealing with a loved one with dementia is embarrassing (Montoro-Rodriguez and others, 2009). It's stressful and depressing, too. But this life experience offers its own *redemption sequence*. Dementia caregivers, as I suggested above, tend to grow emotionally and think about the world in more complex ways (Leipold, Schacke, & Zank, 2008). They also get a firsthand lesson in what is really important in life. One woman summed up her journey of self-awareness like this: "What it's done for me, Alzheimer's, is . . . to give me a whole new life" (quoted in Peacock and others, 2010, p. 648). (Table 14.2 on the next page summarizes these messages in a list of caregiving tips.)

Until this point, I've been exploring how older people and their loved ones can personally take action to promote the best person–environment fit when old-age frailties strike. Now, lets look at what society is doing to help.

TABLE 14.2: Tips for Helping People with Dementia

1. Provide clear cues to alert the person to the surroundings, such as using note cards and labeling rooms and objects around the home (for example, use a picture of the toilet and tub at the door to the bathroom); use strong, contrasting colors to highlight the difference between different rooms in the house.
2. Protect the person from getting injured by double-locking the doors, turning off the stove, and taking away the keys to the car.
3. Offer a highly predictable, structured daily routine.
4. Don't take insulting comments personally. Try to understand that "it's the disease talking."
5. *Remember that there is a real person in there.* Respect the individual's personhood.
6. Try to see the silver lining; this is a time to understand what's really important in life, to grow as a person and show your love.
7. Definitely join a caregiver support group—and contact the Alzheimer's Association (www.alz.org).

TYING IT ALL TOGETHER

1. Your grandmother has just been diagnosed with dementia. Describe the two disease processes that typically cause this condition.
2. Mary, age 50, is terrified of getting a dementing disease. Which statement can you make that is both accurate and comforting? (Pick one.) a. Don't worry. Dementia is typically an illness of the "old-old" years. b. Don't worry. Scientists can cure dementing illnesses when the illnesses are caught at their earliest stages.
3. You are giving a status report to a Senate Committee on biomedical efforts to prevent dementia. First, target the main research problem scientists face. Then, offer a tip to the worried elderly senators about a strategy that *might* help ward off the disease.
4. Mrs. Jones has just been diagnosed with early Alzheimer's disease. Her relatives might help by:
   a. taking steps to keep her safe in her home.
   b. encouraging her to attend an Alzheimer's patient support group.
   c. treating her like a human being.
   d. doing all of the above.

Answers to the Tying It All Together questions can be found at the end of this chapter.

Options and Services for the Frail Elderly

Imagine you are in your seventies, and cooking and cleaning are difficult. You have trouble walking to the mailbox or getting from your car to the store. You start out by using *selection and optimization*. You focus on your most essential activities. You spend more time on each important life task. You are determined to live independently for as long as possible. But you know that the time is coming when you will enter Baltes's full-fledged compensation mode. You will need to depend on other people for your daily needs. Where can you turn?

Setting the Context: Scanning the Global Elder-Care Scene

For most of human history and in many regions of the developing world today, older people would never confront this challenge. Families lived in multigenerational households. When the oldest generation needed help, caregivers were right on the scene.

Today, however, with women in the labor force and younger generations moving from the villages to cities to find work, this support network is fraying. So, especially residents of newly affluent nations such as South Korea and China are turning to Western society-wide models of providing elder care (Chow and others, 2004).

The Scandinavian countries offer excellent models of the services an advanced society can provide (Rodrigues & Schmidt, 2010). In Sweden, Norway, and Denmark, government-funded home health services swing into operation to help impaired older people "age in place"—meaning stay in their own homes. Residents can get cash grants to remodel their homes in the ways discussed earlier in this chapter (see Johansson, Josephsson, & Lilja, 2009). Innovative elderly housing alternatives dot the countryside—from multigenerational villages with a central community center providing health care to small nursing facilities with attractive private rooms (Johri, Beland, & Bergman, 2003). Because their care is free and government funded, Scandinavian older adults don't need to face that anxiety-ridden question of "can I afford to get help?"

Alternatives to Institutions in the United States

In the United States, we do have these worries. The reason is that **Medicare,** the U.S. health insurance system for the elderly, pays only for services defined as cure-oriented. It does not cover help with activities of daily living—the very services such as cooking or cleaning or bathing that might keep people out of a nursing home when they are having some trouble functioning in life.

What choices do older people in the United States (and people who love them) have *other* than going to a nursing home? Here are the main **alternatives to institutionalization** that exist today:

- A **continuing-care retirement community** is a residential complex that provides different levels of services from independent apartments to nursing home care. Continuing care aims to provide the ultimate person–environment fit. Residents arrive in relatively good health and then get the appropriate type of care as their physical needs change. With this type of housing, older adults are purchasing peace of mind. They know exactly where they will be going if and when they need nursing home care.
- An **assisted-living facility** is designed for people who have ADL limitations, but not the kinds of impairments that require full-time, 24-hour care. Assisted living—which has mushroomed in popularity—offers care in a less medicalized, homey setting. Residents often have private rooms with their own furniture. These settings

Medicare The U.S. government's program of health insurance for elderly people.

alternatives to institutionalization Services and settings designed to keep older people who are experiencing age-related disabilities that don't merit intense 24-hour care from having to enter nursing homes.

continuing-care retirement community A housing option characterized by a series of levels of care for elderly residents, ranging from independent apartments to assisted living to nursing home care. People enter the community in relatively good health and move to sections where they can get more care when they become disabled.

assisted-living facility A housing option providing care for elderly people who have instrumental ADL impairments and can no longer live independently but may not need a nursing home.

Jim Wilson/The New York Times/Redux

Assisted living has become an enticing option for upper-middle-class people with ADL impairments. The breathtaking atrium in this photo shows that top-of-the-line housing of this type often looks like a luxurious hotel.

day-care program A service for impaired older adults who live with relatives, in which the older person spends the day at a center offering various activities.

home health services Nursing-oriented and housekeeping help provided in the home of an impaired older adult (or any other impaired person).

nursing home/long-term-care facility A residential institution that provides shelter and intensive caregiving, primarily to older people who need help with basic ADLs.

do not have the overtones of an anonymous, institutional "old-age home" (Phillips & Hawes, 2005; Yamasaki & Sharf, 2011).

- **Day-care programs** are specifically for older people who live with their families. Much like its namesake for children, adult day-care provides activities and a place for an impaired older person to go when family members are at work. Because this service allows relatives to care for a frail parent at home without having to give up their other responsibilities—day care puts off the need for a nursing home (Cho, Zarit, & Chiriboga, 2009).
- **Home health services** help people age "in place" (at home). Paid caregivers come to the house to cook, clean, and help the older adult with personal care activities such as bathing.

With their homey atmosphere, planned activities, and other services, assisted-living and continuing-care facilities can be marvelous settings to spend your last years of life. (I'm planning on going to one of these places myself!) However, because these housing alternatives are expensive, they are mainly available to upper-income older adults (Ball and others, 2009). Can you devise some innovative, low-cost options for helping frail older people? We are in especially dire need of housing that bridges the gap from living independently to needing that setting tailored for people who *are* severely physically impaired—the nursing home.

Nursing Home Care

Nursing homes, or **long-term-care facilities,** provide shelter and services to people with basic ADL problems—individuals who really do require 24-hour caregiving help. Although adults of every age live in nursing homes, it should come as no surprise that the main risk factor for entering these institutions is being very old. The average nursing home resident is in his—or, I should say, her—late eighties and nineties. Because, as we know, females live sicker well into advanced old age, women make up the vast majority of residents in long-term-care (Belsky, 2001).

What causes people to enter nursing homes? Often, a person arrives after some incapacitating event, such as breaking a hip. Given that dementia requires such daunting 24/7 care, roughly half of the nursing home population has some dementing disease.

In predicting who ends up in a nursing home, both nature and nurture forces are involved. Yes, the person's biology (or physical state) does matter. But so does the environment, specifically, whether a network of attachment figures is available to provide care. Does the person have several family members and/or a friend willing to take the person in? The more places (and people) a frail older adult has "in reserve" to provide help, the lower the risk of that person's landing in long-term care (Kasper, Pezzin, & Rice, 2010).

Just as the routes by which people arrive differ, residents take different paths once they enter nursing homes. Sometimes, a nursing home is a short stop before returning home. Or it may be a short interlude before death. Some residents live for years in long-term care.

You might be surprised to learn who is paying for these residents' care. Because people start out paying the costs out of their own pockets and "spend down" until they are impoverished, *Medicaid*, the U.S. health-care system specifically for the poor, finances our nation's nursing homes.

Eye of Science/Photo Researchers

The simple act of going down steps can be an ordeal when people have ADL impairments. Imagine being this woman and knowing that, because of your osteoporosis (graphically shown in the small image at the lower left), any misstep might land you in a nursing home.

Evaluating Nursing Homes

Nursing homes are often viewed as dumping grounds where residents are abused or left to languish unattended until they die. How accurate are these stereotypes?

certified nurse assistant or aide The main hands-on care provider in a nursing home who helps elderly residents with basic ADL problems.

Many times, the generalizations are unfair. Some nursing homes are state-of-the-art, with perks such as private rooms and enriching activities tailored to residents' needs. Others have nurturing organizational cultures. "This is a family" (Tyler & Parker, 2011). "We act ethically" (McDaniel, Roche, & Veledar, 2011). "This place is committed to providing excellent care" (Lyons, 2010). Most experts feel long-term care is improving (Castle & Ferguson, 2010). A vigorous national movement is in place to make nursing homes truly person-centered, and attentive to residents' needs (Rahman & Schnelle, 2008).

But, we still have far to go. In one poll, more than one-half of industry experts ranked the quality of U.S. nursing homes as "fair" or "poor" (Miller, Mor, & Clark, 2010). In an alarming Michigan survey, 1 out of 5 family members reported that, yes, their impaired relative had suffered some nursing-home abuse (Conner and others, 2011). (As you might imagine, "difficult" residents—that is, those with behavior problems and/or the totally physically incapacitated—are most at risk here.)

Even the most loving nursing home can't erase the efficacy-eroding liabilities attached to entering institutional life. Imagine needing to share a small room with a stranger. You have to eat the food the facility serves at predetermined hours (Kane, 1995–1996). Nursing home residents can't just decide to lie in bed or refuse to take a medicine. Their every action—from sitting in a chair to being taken to the toilet—is dependent on the workers providing care.

This brings up the front-line care worker in the nursing home—the **certified nurse assistant or aide.** Just as during life's early years, caregiving at the upper end of the lifespan is low-status work. Nursing home aides, like their counterparts in day-care centers, make poverty-level wages. Facilities are chronically understaffed (Teeri and others, 2008). So, even when an aide loves what she does, the conditions of the job can make it difficult to provide adequate care. Having worked in long-term care, I can testify that residents are sometimes left lying in urine for hours. They wait inordinately long for help getting fed. One reason is that it can take hours to feed the eight or so people in your care when dinner arrives!

Still, although they hate the pay and complain about the low status (Teeri and others, 2008), people do get enormous satisfaction from this job. Listen to Jayson, a mellow, 6-foot-tall, 200-pound giant talking about his work as an activities director at a Philadelphia nursing home:

> At first I was put off by the smells. . . . Then I got moved to the Alzheimer's unit . . . and I found this to be like . . . the best task I ever had. . . . If you just come in here and say, "Okay, I got a job to do and I'm just doing my job," . . . then you're in the wrong field. . . . When somebody here dies, we all talk, we say how much we miss the person. . . . Some of them cry. . . . Some of them go to their funerals. . . . I actually spoke at some of the funerals. . . . I say how much this person meant to me.
>
> (quoted in Black & Rubinstein, 2005, pp. S-4–6)

For Jayson, who—after being shot and lingering near death—reported seeing an angel visit him in the form of a little old man, his career is a calling from God. At age 36, he is flourishing in this consummately generative job. What about nursing-home residents? Can people get it together within this most unlikely setting? For uplifting answers, check out the Experiencing the Lifespan box on the next page.

A Few Concluding Thoughts

Dealing with ADL impairments is a vital social challenge facing our rapidly aging world. One message of my discussion is that no medical miracles (or lifestyle changes) can magically erase the physical difficulties that are the downside of living until advanced old age. We need to prepare right now for the ADL crisis that will hit full force in about a decade as the baby boomers march into their old-old years.

EXPERIENCING THE LIFESPAN: Getting It Together in the Nursing Home

A few years ago, I attended an unforgettable memorial service at a Florida nursing home. Person after person rose to eulogize this woman, a passionate advocate who had worked with immense self-efficacy to make a difference in her fellow residents' lives. Then Mrs. Alonzo's son told his story. He said that he had never really known his mother. When he was young, she became schizophrenic and was shunted to an institution. Then, at age 68, Mrs. Alonzo entered the nursing home to await death. It was only in this place, where life is supposed to end, that she blossomed as a human being.

If you think that this story of emotional growth is unique, listen to this friend of mine, a psychologist who, like Jayson, finds her generativity in nursing home work:

My most amazing success entered treatment two years ago. This severely depressed resident had had an abusive marriage and suffered from enduring feelings of powerlessness and low self-esteem. I think that being sent to our institution allowed this woman to make the internal changes that she had been incapable of before. She began to look at her past and see how her experiences had shaped her poor sense of self and then to see her inner strengths. She and I formed a very close relationship.

So then she decided to work on becoming closer to her children. She had been aloof as a mother, and she told me that once her younger child had asked her to say that she loved her and she couldn't get the words out. Now, at age 89, she called this daughter, told her that she did love her and that she was sorry she couldn't say it before. Her daughters said that I had presented them with a miracle, the loving mother they always wanted. My patient made friends on the floor and became active in the residents' council. In the time we saw one another she used to tell me, "I never believed I could change at this age."

As she finished her story, my friend's eyes filled with tears: "My patient died a few months ago, and I still miss her so much."

Our personal challenge, as you learned in these later-life chapters, is to live fully as long as we are alive. The Experiencing the Lifespan box above highlights the fact—again—that yes, it is possible to flourish even in a nursing home. It underlines the importance of close attachments in promoting a meaningful life. Plus, the story of this woman who got it together in the nursing home enriches Erikson's masterful ideas that have guided our lifespan tour: It's never too late to accomplish developmental tasks that we may have missed. People can find their real identity (or authentic self), fulfill their generativity, and so reach integrity in their final months of life!

In the next chapter, I'll continue this theme of inner development and also stress the crucial importance of making connections with loved ones as I focus directly on life's endpoint—death.

TYING IT ALL TOGETHER

1. You are a geriatric counselor, and an 85-year-old woman and her family come to your office for advice about the best arrangement for her care. Match the letter of each item below with the number of the suggestion that would be most appropriate if this elderly client:
   a. is affluent, worried about living alone, and has no ADL problems.
   b. has ADL impairments and is living with her family—who want to continue to care for her at home.
   c. has instrumental ADL impairments (but can perform basic self-care activities), can no longer live alone, and has a good amount of money.
   d. has basic ADL impairments.
   e. is beginning to have ADL impairments, lives alone, and has very little money (but does not qualify for Medicaid).
      (1) a continuing-care retirement facility
      (2) an assisted-living facility
      (3) a day-care program
      (4) a nursing home
      (5) There are no good alternatives you can suggest; people in this situation must struggle to cope at home.

2. Joey and Jane realize that their mother needs to go a nursing home. Which two likely comments can you make about this mother's situation—and nursing homes in general?
   a. No one in the family is available to take their mom in.
   b. Medicare will completely cover their mom's expenses.
   c. The quality of the facilities to which their mom will go may vary greatly.
   d. The caregivers at their mom's nursing home will hate their jobs.
3. Devise some creative strategies to care for the frail elderly, other than the ones described in this chapter.

Answers to the Tying It All Together questions can be found at the end of this chapter.

SUMMARY

Tracing Physical Aging

Normal aging changes progress into **chronic disease** and finally, during the old-old years, may result in impairments in **activities of daily living (ADLs),** either less incapacitating **instrumental ADL problems** or **basic ADL problems**—troubles with basic self-care. Although living much beyond a century is impossible, the statistical odds of reaching the upper ends of the lifespan vary depending on our socioeconomic status, culture, gender, and cohort.

The **socioeconomic health gap** refers to the fact that—within each nation—people who are affluent live healthier for a longer time. A variety of forces, from health-compromising lifestyles, to inadequate medical care, make poverty a major risk factor for early disability and death. Still, education and close attachments can buffer us from the health consequences of being poor, and Latinos do better "illness-wise" than we might expect. Unfortunately, African Americans do worse—dying earlier (particularly from cardiovascular diseases) than other ethnic groups. Being male is also a risk factor for dying younger, especially of a heart attack. Women outlive men, but report more health problems at every stage of adult life. Depressing new research suggests that due to the obesity epidemic, the baby boomers may be emerging into their older years more "ill" than their parents' generation.

Sensory-Motor Changes

The classic age-related vision problems—**presbyopia** (impairments in near vision), difficulties seeing in dim light, and problems with glare—are caused by a rigid, cloudier **lens.** Modifying lighting can help compensate for these losses. Cataracts, the endpoint of a cloudy lens, can be easily treated, although the other major age-related vision impairments often result in a more permanent loss of sight. If vision losses are permanent people often rely on external aids and their own emotional resources to cope.

The old-age hearing impairment **presbycusis** presents special problems because it limits a person's contact with the human world. Because exposure to noise causes this selective loss for high-pitched tones, men are at higher risk of having hearing handicaps, especially at younger ages—although, in our noisy society, hearing problems are increasing for both sexes. To help a hearing-impaired person, limit low-pitched background noise and speak distinctly—but avoid **elderspeak,** the impulse to talk to the older person like a baby. For your own future hearing, protect yourself against excessive noise.

"Slowness" in later life is due to age-related changes in **reaction time** and skeletal conditions such as osteoarthritis and **osteoporosis** (thin, fragile bones). Osteoporosis is a special concern because falling and breaking a hip is a major reason for entering a nursing home. As mobility is crucial to late-life independence, older people must take care to exercise and modify their homes to reduce the risk of falls.

Although the elderly drive less often, accident rates rise sharply among drivers over age 75. Solutions to the problem, such as mandatory vision tests over a certain age, may not work so well, as driving involves many sensory and motor skills. Modifying the driving environment and especially developing a more car-free society is a critical challenge today.

Dementia

Dementia, the most feared old-age condition, is typically caused by **Alzheimer's disease** (neural atrophy accompanied by **senile plaques** and **neurofibrillary tangles**) and/or **vascular dementia** (small strokes). These diseases typically erupt during the old-old years and progress gradually, with the person losing all functions. Scientists are trying to prevent the accumulation of the plaques (the hallmark of Alzheimer's disease) by targeting this illness at its very earliest stage, and studying people with a genetic marker that makes them more prone to this disease. Today, Alzheimer's cannot be prevented or cured, although physical exercise *may* help ward off its onset. The key is to make environmental modifications to keep the person safe—and understand that older adults with dementia are still people. Caregivers' accounts and the testaments of people with early stage dementia offer profiles in human courage.

Options and Services for the Frail Elderly

In the past, and in many developing nations, older people lived in multigenerational households, with a built-in family support network for when they became frail. We now need formal (nonfamily) structures to help older people who are ADL impaired. In the United States, the major **alternatives to institutionalization—continuing-care retirement communities, assisted-living facilities, day-care programs,** and **home health services**—are typically fairly costly. These options are not covered by **Medicare.** We need creative services to keep frail older people from prematurely entering that setting for the most impaired older adults—the nursing home.

Being female, very old, and not having loved ones to take the person in are the main risk factors for entering **nursing homes,** or **long-term-care facilities.** While nursing homes vary in quality, and are improving, they still don't typically provide high-quality care. The **certified nursing assistant or aide,** the main caregiver, while poorly paid, can find a generative mission in nursing home work. Society needs to prepare for an onslaught of ADL problems as the baby boomers enter their old-old years. People can develop as human beings even in a nursing home, and reach every Eriksonian milestone during their final years—or months—of life.

KEY TERMS

normal aging changes, p. 424
chronic disease, p. 424
ADL (activities of daily living) problems, p. 424
instrumental ADL problems, p. 424
basic ADL limitations, p. 424
socioeconomic health gap, p. 426
presbyopia, p. 431
lens, p. 431
presbycusis, p. 433
elderspeak, p. 434
reaction time, p. 435
osteoporosis, p. 435
dementia, p. 439
vascular dementia, p. 440
Alzheimer's disease, p. 440
neurofibrillary tangles, p. 440
senile plaques, p. 440
Medicare, p. 445
alternatives to institutionalization, p. 445
continuing-care retirement community, p. 445
assisted-living facility, p. 445
day-care program, p. 446
home health services, p. 446
nursing home/long-term-care facility, p. 446
certified nurse assistant or aide, p. 447

ANSWERS TO TYING IT ALL TOGETHER QUIZZES

Tracing Physical Aging

1. b
2. Marjorie has *instrumental ADL* problems, and Sara has *basic ADL* problems.
3. c
4. Nico and Hiromi are both correct because although women live longer (meaning that they must be healthier), they also live "sicker" (meaning that they are more apt to be ill) throughout adulthood.
5. Your mom, because unfortunately—being a baby boomer—she is more apt to be overweight and so at higher risk of developing ADL impairments at a younger age.

Sensory-Motor Changes

1. lens; cataract; can
2. d
3. a, c, and e. (Suggestions b and d will make grandma's eyesight worse.)
4. Tell the lawmakers that relying just on an eye exam won't be effective because driving is dependent on many sensory and motor skills. Suggest sponsoring bills to change roads by putting adequate lighting on exit ramps, more traffic signals at intersections (especially left-turn signals), and exploring other ways to make the driving environment more age-friendly. Most important, foster initiatives that don't

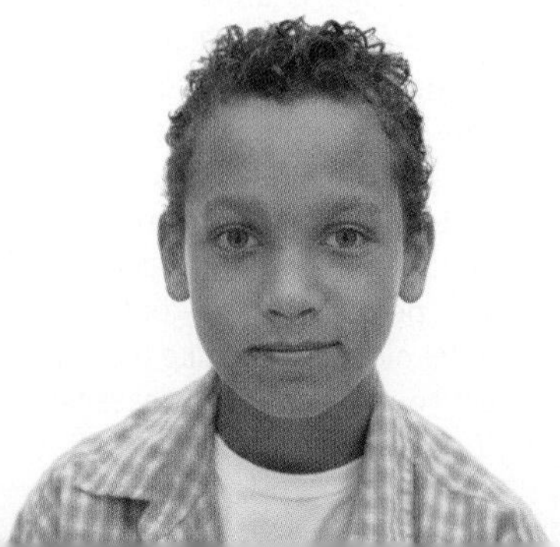

depend on driving: Invest in public transportation. Give tax incentives to developers to embed shopping in residential neighborhoods, and encourage creative alternatives to cars.

Dementia

1. The illnesses are Alzheimer's disease, which involves deterioration of the neurons and their replacement with senile plaques and tangles, and vascular dementia, which involve small strokes. (Grandma—not infrequently—may have both illnesses.)
2. a
3. The main problem scientists face is diagnosing incipient Alzheimer's before it progresses to the disease stage—so that we can develop treatments to ward off the illness. Tell the worried senators that they should start a fitness regimen now! While we don't have definitive evidence, there are strong hints that regular exercise may help stave off dementia.
4. d

Options and Services for the Frail Elderly

1. *a*, 1; *b*, 3; *c*, 2; *d*, 4; *e*, 5
2. a and c
3. Here, you can use your own creativity. My suggestions: (1) Institute a program whereby people get cash incentives to care for frail elders in their homes. (2) Build small, intergenerational living communities, with a centrally located home option specifically for the frail elderly. Residents who buy houses here would commit to taking care of the older adults in their midst. (3) Set up a Craigslist-type Web site, matching older people with a room to spare with area college students in need. Young people would live rent-free in exchange for helping the older person with cooking and shopping. (4) Establish a national scholarship program (perhaps called the "Belsky Grant"!) that would pay your tuition and living expenses if you commit to caring for frail elders in the community.

Epilogue

PART VII

Now that we have reached the end of our lifespan journey, it's time to focus on life's final chapter (death) and reflect on what we've learned.

Chapter 15—**Death and Dying** is actually a perfect finale to this lifespan tour, because not only does this milestone end our personal lives, but death is the one milestone that occurs at *every* life stage. How have death attitudes and practices changed throughout history and in different cultures, and what do people (and their loved ones) feel when approaching this final "act" of life? How is the health-care system approaching the terminally ill, and how can we make dying more humane? These issues lead us into that controversial contemporary ethical issue: strategies for taking control of when we die.

In **Final Thoughts,** I'll take a *very* short step back to scan the high points of the journey as whole. After your read the top five insights that stood out for me in surveying the research, take some time to think about the issues that struck you most forcefully in reading this book.

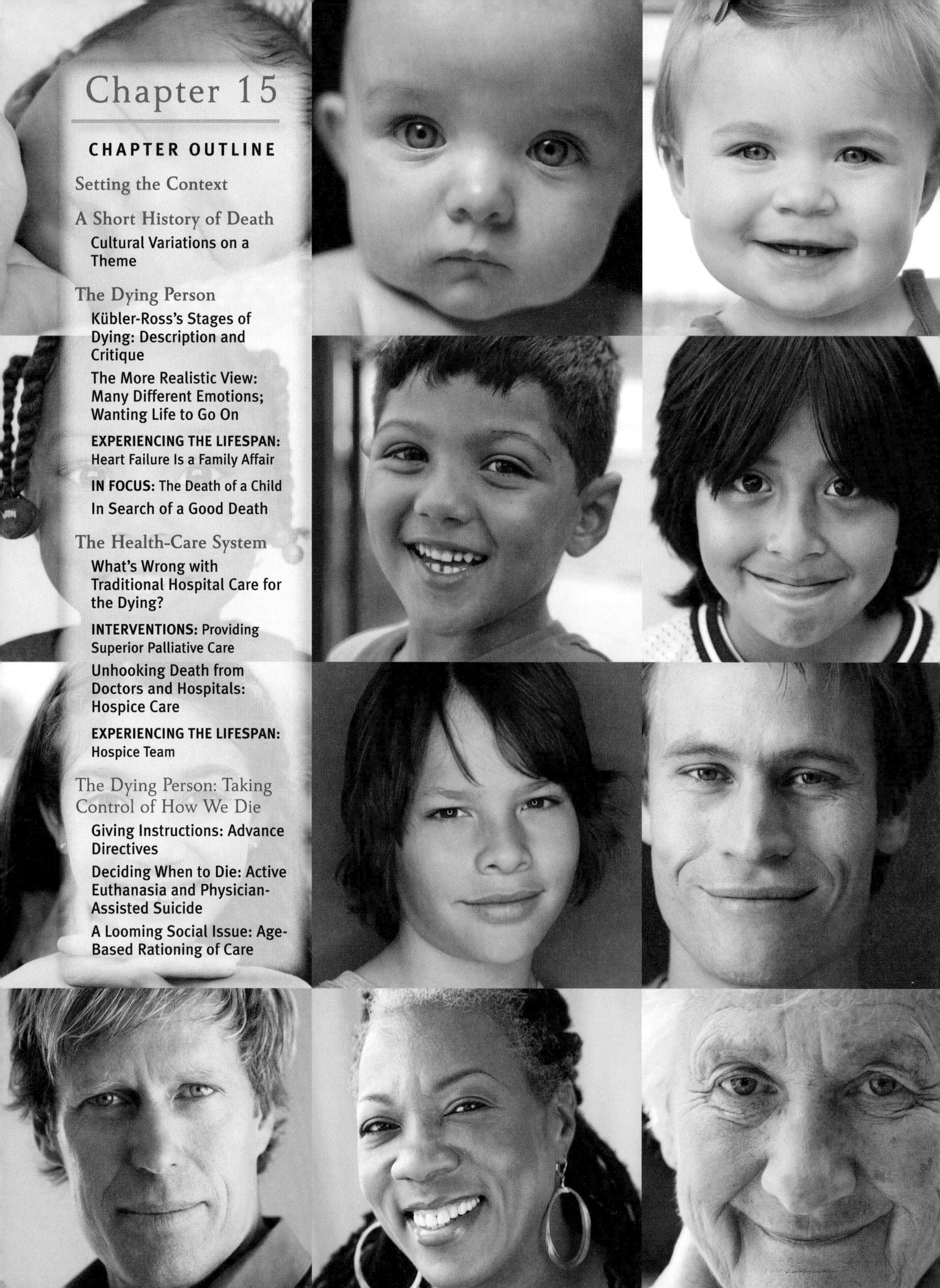

Chapter 15

CHAPTER OUTLINE

Death and Dying

I was getting in the car to drive to work when Amy screamed, "Stewart! Come listen to the news!" We figured out pretty quickly that it came in right about the floor where she worked, the 96th. By the time the tower came down, we knew for sure that she died. With a normal death, you prepare for the grieving process. With a shocking death, it hits you by surprise. My wife was about to give birth to our first child, and my mother had plane tickets to come down on Friday. You get into the part of it where you mentally play back the events. Mom (typical, for her) had gone into work early so she could leave for a dentist appointment. If she'd been a less responsible person, she would not have been there at 8:46. The other weird part of it is, like, the whole country feels they own pieces of this tragedy and need to constantly remind you about it. So it doesn't go away.

My mom didn't have young children, but she was looking forward to retirement, to being a grandmother, and so she was cheated of all those things. Not only did she die in this horrible way—she died at an unacceptably early age.

. . .

In his seventies, my father seemed immortal. While he often joked about being an "old man," he had no major infirmities. At age 81, mortality hit. For a few months, Dad had been listless—not his old self, suddenly looking old. Then came the unforgettable call: "The doctor says that it's cancer of the liver. Jan, I'm going to die."

Because medicine never admits defeat, the plan was three rounds of chemotherapy, punctuated by "recovery" at home. The doctor said, "Maybe we can lick this thing," but the treatments were agonizing. Worse yet, recovery never happened. My father got weaker. After a few months, he could barely walk. Then, before going into the hospital for the third round, my mother called: "Last night we cried together and decided not to continue. We're calling in hospice. I think it's time for you to come down." My father had two more weeks to live.

A day or two before you die, you slip into a coma. It's the preceding week or two that lasts for years. Everyone has been summoned to bustle around a train that cannot be derailed. Yes, you can talk, but what do you say? My father was never a verbal man. Then, as if on cue, the disease picks up speed. From the wheelchair to becoming bedridden, the voice that mutates into a whisper, followed by waiting . . . for what? You force yourself to be at the bedside when the breathing gets slow and rattled, but you are terrified. You have never seen a dying person. You don't know how things will go. Above all, you hope that things go quickly. You can't stand to see your father suffer anymore.

My father died in the "normal" late-twentieth-century way. Although we knew nothing about how exactly people die, we had plenty of time to plan for the event. Dad's death came at the "right" time, at the end of a long life. The kind of death Stewart's mother faced on September 11 was horrifying, unexpected— totally outside the norm. How does death *really* happen today? How did people die in centuries past?

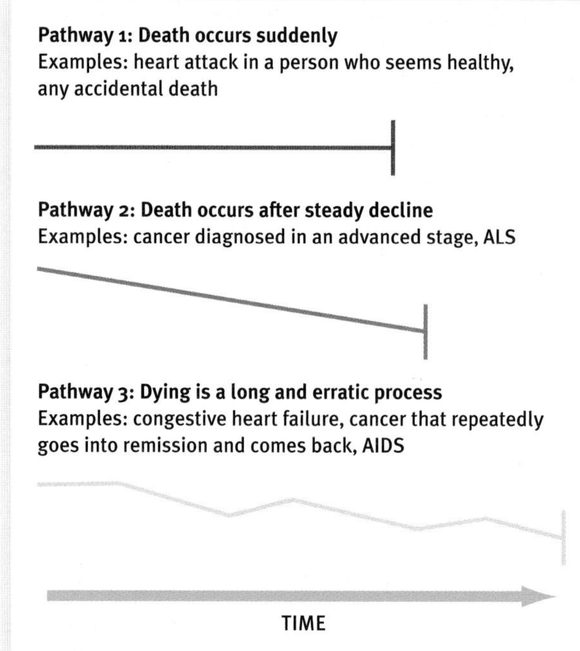

FIGURE 15.1: **Three pathways to death:** Although some people die suddenly, the pattern in blue and especially that in yellow are the most common pathways by which people die today.

Setting the Context

Today, as Figure 15.1 suggests, our pathways to death take different forms (Field, 2009). As happened most dramatically in the World Trade Center tragedy, roughly 1 out of every 6 or 7 people in developed nations dies without any warning—as a result either of an accident or, more often, of a sudden, fatal, age-related event, such as a heart attack or stroke (Enck, 2003; see the red line in Figure 15.1). My father's death fit the pattern when illnesses such as cancer are discovered at an advanced stage. Here, as you can see in the blue line, a person is diagnosed with a fatal disease and then steadily declines.

The prolonged, erratic pattern shown in yellow, however, is probably the most common dying pathway in our age of extended chronic disease. After developing cancer—or, like my husband, congestive heart failure (see the Experiencing the Lifespan Box, on page 461)—people battle that condition for years, helped by medical technology, until death eventually occurs.

So today, deaths in affluent countries typically occur slowly. They are dominated by medical procedures. They have a protracted, uncertain course (Field, 2009). For most of human history, people died in a different way.

A Short History of Death

> She contracted a summer cholera. After four days she asked to see the village priest, who came and waited to give her the last rites. "Not yet, M. le Curé, I'll let you know when the time comes." Two days later: "Go and tell M. le Curé to bring me Extreme Unction."
>
> (reported in Walter, 2003, p. 213)

Mary Evans Picture Library/The Image Works

For most of human history, death was ever present—"up close and personal"—and occurred in the midst of normal life. Here is an eighteenth-century painting entitled "The Dying Request," in which a dying young woman is offering her final words to her spouse.

As you can see in this nineteenth-century description of the death of a French peasant woman, before modern medicine, death arrived quickly. People let nature take its course. There was nothing they could do. Dying was familiar, predictable, and normal. It was embedded in daily life (Wood & Williamson, 2003).

According to the historian Philippe Ariès (1974, 1981), while life in the Middle Ages was horrid and "wild," death was often "tame." Famine, childbirth, and infectious disease ensured that death was an expected presence throughout the lifespan. People died, as they lived, in full view of the community and were buried in the churchyard in the center of town.

During the eighteenth and nineteenth centuries, death began to move off center stage when—because of fears about disease—villagers relocated burial sites to cemeteries outside of town (Kastenbaum, 2004). Then, a more dramatic change took place about a century ago, when doctors began to vigorously wage war against disease. The early-twentieth-century conquest of many infectious illnesses moved dying toward the end of the lifespan, relocating it to old age (Field, 2009). Today, with 3 out of 4 deaths in the United States occurring among people over age 65 (and often happening in our eighties and nineties), the actors in the death drama are often a marginal, atypical group—nothing like you or me.

Moreover, as medicine took over, the scene of dying shifted to hospitals and nursing homes, so the physical process was removed from view. Now, when a person dies, often in the inner recesses of the intensive care unit, we shroud the body and erase all signs of its presence as we ship it to the funeral home (Kastenbaum, 2004). According to one social critic, by the mid-twentieth century, death had become the new "pornography"—disgusting, abnormal, never to be seen or talked about (Gorer, 1965).

thanatology The study of death and dying.

The word pornographic still may fit our twenty-first-century feelings about confronting dying in the flesh. However, during the 1960s lifestyle revolutions, Western ideas related to *talking* about death changed. University courses on **thanatology** (death and dying) became the rage (Doka, 2003). Doctors did a total turnaround from the earlier practice of concealing a devastating diagnosis (never mentioning, for instance, the "C word") in favor of honestly telling people, "Yes, it's cancer, and there is not much we can do" (see Bradley & Brasel, 2008). Today, we no longer see planning the way people die as ghoulish. We urge everyone to document in writing their personal preferences for "a good, dignified death."

Cultural Variations on a Theme

But while our society stresses full disclosure and active planning for our "final act," death attitudes differ dramatically from person to person and culture to culture in the contemporary United States. To demonstrate this point, let's scan the practices of a group for whom dying remains *very* up close and personal, but among whom death is never openly discussed: the Hmong.

The Hmong, persecuted for centuries in China and Southeast Asia, migrated to North America after the Vietnam War and number close to a million U.S. residents today. According to Hmong tradition, discussing dying "will unlock the gate of evil spirits." So when a person enters the terminal phase of life, no one is permitted to discuss that fact. However, when death is imminent, the family becomes intimately involved. Relatives flock around and dress the ill person in the traditional burial garment—a black robe or suit. After death arrives, they lovingly wash and groom the corpse, preparing it to be viewed.

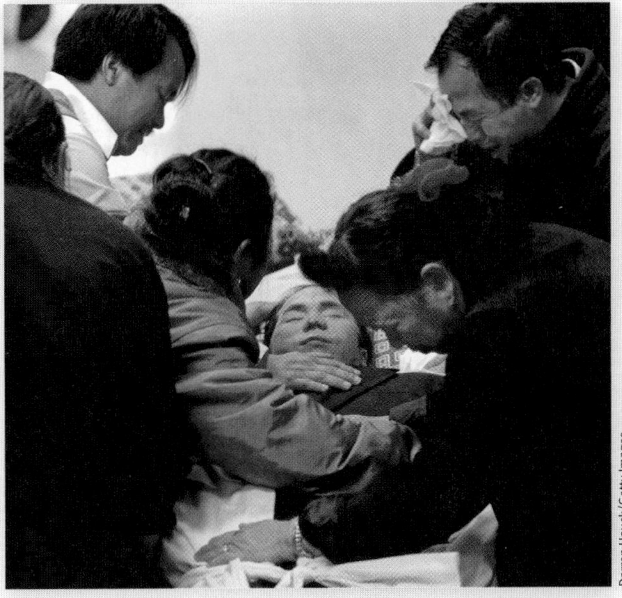

Darren Hauck/Getty Images

Even today, small pockets of the U.S. population adopt an intensely hands-on approach to death. Here, you can see phase one in the carefully orchestrated days-long Hmong funeral ceremony—the body, dressed in its traditional garments, being caressed by distraught family members.

If, contrary to Hmong custom, the person dies in a hospital, it's crucial that the body *not* be immediately sent to the morgue. The family congregates at the bedside to wail and caress the corpse for hours. Then, after a lavish four-day funeral ceremony, during which the body remains in view, the deceased is lovingly dressed in warm clothing to guard against the cold, and the feet are encased in special blue shoes for the journey to the next world. At the gravesite, the coffin is reopened for a final viewing before being permanently closed (Gerdner and others, 2007). Could you participate in these activities, by giving your relative the hands-on care that the Hmong and other societies routinely provided throughout history to prepare loved ones for the grave?

In this chapter, I'll explore what dying is like in the twenty-first-century West, an age of open communications, death-defying treatments, and extended chronic disease. First, I'll examine the feelings of the dying person; then, turn to the health-care system; and then, return to the person to tackle those touchy issues related to controlling the timing of when we die. As you just saw with the Hmong, however, it's crucial to remember that—just as dying pathways differ—with death and dying *in general*, diversity is the main theme. We all bring unique, *equally* valid perspectives to that ultimate event of human life.

TYING IT ALL TOGETHER

1. Imagine that you were born in the seventeenth or eighteenth century. Which of the following statements about your dying pathway would *not* be true?
   a. You would probably have died quickly of an infectious disease.
   b. You would have died in a hospital.
   c. You would have seen death all around you from a young age.
   d. You would probably have died at a relatively young age.
2. If you follow the typical twenty-first-century pattern, as you approach death, you can expect to decline (*quickly/slowly and erratically*) due to (*an accident/an age-related chronic disease*).
3. Margaret says that, today, we live in a death-denying society. Ella says, "No, that's not true. Today, we are more accepting of death than ever." First, make Ella's case and then Margaret's, referring to the information in this section.

Answers to the Tying It All Together questions can be found at the end of this chapter.

The Dying Person

How do people react when they are diagnosed with a fatal illness? What are their emotions as they struggle with this devastating news? The first person to scientifically study these topics was a young psychiatrist named Elisabeth Kübler-Ross.

Kübler-Ross's Stages of Dying: Description and Critique

While working as a consultant at a Chicago hospital during the 1960s, Kübler-Ross became convinced that the health-care system was neglecting the emotional needs of the terminally ill. As part of a seminar, she got permission to interview dying patients. Many people, she found, were relieved to talk about their diagnosis and knew that their condition was terminal, even though the medical staff and family members had made valiant efforts to conceal that fact. Kübler-Ross published her discovery that open communication was important to dying people in *On Death and Dying*, a slim best-seller that ushered in a revolution in the way we treat the terminally ill.

Kübler-Ross (1969), in her **stage theory of dying,** originally proposed that we progress through five emotions in coming to terms with death: *denial, anger, bargaining, depression*, and *acceptance*. Let's now briefly look at each emotional state:

When a person first gets some terrible diagnosis, such as "You have advanced lung cancer," her immediate reaction is denial. She thinks, "There must be a mistake," and takes trips to doctor after doctor, searching for a new, more favorable set of tests. When these efforts fail, denial gives way to anger.

In the anger stage, the person lashes out, bemoaning her fate, railing at other people. One patient may get enraged at a physician: "He should have picked up my illness earlier on!" Others direct their fury at a friend or family member: "Why did I get lung cancer at 55, while my brother, who has smoked a pack of cigarettes a day since he was 20, remains in perfect health?"

Kübler-Ross's stage theory of dying The landmark theory, developed by psychiatrist Elisabeth Kübler-Ross, that people who are terminally ill progress through five stages in confronting their death: denial, anger, bargaining, depression, and acceptance.

Eventually, this emotion yields to a more calculating one: bargaining. Now, the person pleads for more time, promising to be good if she can put off death a bit. Kübler-Ross (1969) gives this example of a woman who begged God to let her live long enough to attend the marriage of her oldest son:

> The day preceding the wedding she left the hospital as an elegant lady. Nobody would have believed her real condition. She . . . looked radiant. I wondered what her reaction would be when the time was up for which she had bargained. . . . I will never forget the

> moment she returned to the hospital. She looked tired and somewhat exhausted and before I could say hello, said, "Now don't forget I have another son."
>
> (1969, p. 83)

Then, once reality fully sinks in, the person gets depressed and, ultimately, reaches acceptance. By this time, the individual is quite weak and no longer feels upset, angry, or depressed. She may even look forward to the end.

Kübler-Ross deserves enormous credit for alerting us to the fact that there is a living, breathing person inside the diagnosis "terminal cancer" or "end-stage heart disease." The problem is that her original ideas were embraced in a rigid, simplistic way. Here are three reasons why we *cannot* take this theory as the final word about death:

TERMINALLY ILL PEOPLE DO NOT ALWAYS WANT TO DISCUSS THEIR SITUATION. Although she never intended this message, many people read into Kübler-Ross's theory the idea that all patients want to talk about impending death. This is emphatically not true (Baile, Aaron, & Parker, 2009; Carlander and others, 2011; Shih and others, 2009). When researchers ask fatally ill patients about how they feel about openly discussing death, they find that people broach this subject selectively and reluctantly. As one woman said: "They're scary subjects and . . . we don't want to touch on it too much. . . ." (quoted in McGrath, 2004, p. 836). Patients avoid these discussions because they believe others won't want to hear: "I try to be open but ... many people ... can't manage it. They withdraw" (quoted in Saeteren, Lindström, & Nåden, 2010, p. 815). Sometimes, they shy away from these conversations to protect loved ones and themselves: ". . . My sister is good but I couldn't load off onto her, she would just break.... I've got as much as I can cope with. So I can't get her upset . . . and then have ... to calm her down" (quoted in McGrath, 2004, pp. 837, 839).

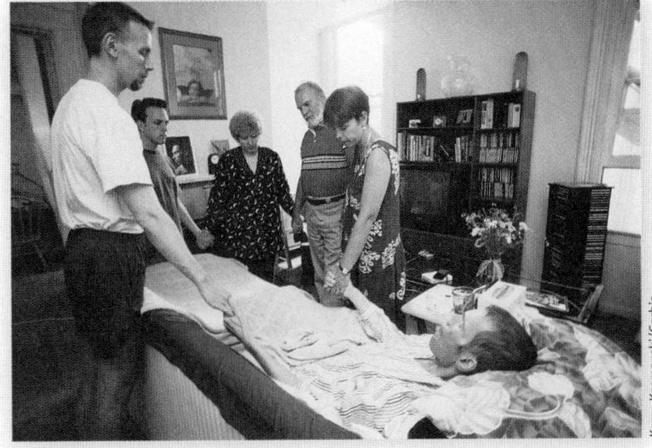
Karen Kasmauski/Corbis

Having members of a congregation praying by one's bedside can offer solace and a sense of connection during a person's final days. But to be really sensitive, this minister and church members would also need to respect this man's privacy, taking their cues from him as to whether he *really* wanted to discuss his impending death.

The bottom line is that people who are dying behave just as they do when they are fully living (which they are!). They are leery about bringing up painful subjects. People don't shed their sensitivity to others and feelings about what topics are appropriate to discuss when they have a terminal disease. Actually, as life is drawing to a close, preserving the quality of our attachment relationships is a *paramount* agenda—and this, as you will see, is a main message I will highlight throughout this chapter.

NOT EVERY CULTURE OR PERSON OR FAMILY FEELS IT'S BEST TO SPELL OUT "THE FULL TRUTH." As you saw earlier with the Hmong, the idea that we must inform terminally ill patients about their condition is also not universally accepted. So, in collectivist cultures that stress social harmony, such as China, doctors feel uncomfortable when asked to adhere to the Western practice of openly discussing death (Siu and others, 2010). Yes, in our individualistic society, people *say* they are interested in knowing the facts: "Information is important," said one Swedish woman with cancer. "Even if you have a short time left, you have to plan this time" (quoted in Saeteren, Lindström, & Nåden, 2010, p. 814). But they may not want doctors to get specific when the prognosis is dire (Baile, Aaron, & Parker, 2009; Innes & Payne, 2009). Families go further: "Don't tell my loved one anything at all!" Here is how one social worker described how she reacted when she received this plea from some loving sons:

> Hurting and sad (after learning their mom's diagnosis of inoperable cancer), . . . The older sons rushed to the clinic to make me privy to the decision. . . . "Our mother doesn't know anything and that's how we want to keep it." I could see their behavior as denial

middle knowledge The idea that terminally ill people can know that they are dying yet at the same time not completely grasp or come to terms emotionally with that fact.

and discuss the western ethic of patient responsibility. But ... I knew their children were protecting their mother from what they saw as worse than death: The expectation of nearing death.

(quoted in Kannai, 2008, pp. 146–147)

As this sensitive woman realized, the approach that Kübler-Ross and our contemporary culture spells out as caring can sometimes be unloving, insensitive, and rude.

PEOPLE DO NOT PASS THROUGH DISTINCTIVE STAGES IN ADJUSTING TO DEATH. Most important, Kübler-Ross's theory is wrong! People facing death do *not* progress emotionally in a stage-to-stage, cookie-cutter way. In fact, uncritically accepting Kübler-Ross's stages can be dangerous if it encourages us to distance ourselves from dying loved ones (Kastenbaum, 2004). Instead of understanding that becoming depressed is a reasonable reaction when facing a life-threatening illness, if friends and family see this feeling as "a phase," they might view this response as somehow not real. It's perfectly understandable for an ill person to get angry when others respond insensitively or don't call; but if we view this response through the lens of stage theory, we might dismiss these natural feelings of hurt as "predictable" signs of the anger stage.

Therefore, experts view Kübler-Ross's contributions with mixed emotions. Yes, she pioneered an important topic. But her theory encouraged its own kind of insensitivity to the terminally ill (Kastenbaum, 2004).

The More Realistic View: Many Different Emotions; Wanting Life to Go On

People who are dying *do* get angry, bargain, deny their illness, and become depressed. However, as one psychiatrist argues, it's more appropriate to view these feelings as "a complicated clustering of intellectual and affective states, some fleeting, lasting for a moment, or a day" (Schneidman, 1976, p. 6). Even when people "know" their illness is terminal, the awareness of "I am dying" may not penetrate in a definitive way (Groopman, 2004; Saeteren, Lindström, & Nåden, 2010). This emotional state, called **middle knowledge,** is beautifully highlighted in this description of Rachel, a 17-year-old who knew she had end-stage cystic fibrosis.

Rachel said... that when she is to die, she wanted to be here in Canuck Place (the hospice), surrounded by friends and family . . . and the nurses and doctors that can help her feel not scared. And then she said "but I have another way that I'd like to die . . . sitting on my front porch wrapped in an afghan in a rocking chair and my husband holding my hand."

(Liben, Papadatou, & Wolfe, 2008, p. 858)

Diagnosed with fatal pancreatic cancer in the prime of life (his mid-forties), beloved Carnegie Mellon Computer Science Professor Randi Pausch captivated the world with his Last Lecture, entitled "Fulfilling Your Childhood Dreams," viewed on YouTube by over six million people, and wrote a best-selling book in the months before he died. Pausch's final inspirational year of life is a testament that joy and future plans can remain very much alive when people know that they are dying. Here, you can see Pausch being granted a childhood dream—becoming a Pittsburgh Steeler for a day.

Steven Adams/Tribune-Review/AP Images

Moreover, as Rachel's final heart-wrenching comment suggests, when people realize that they are close to death, an emotion that often burns strong is hope (Groopman, 2004; Innes & Payne, 2009). If people are religious, their hopes may hinge on divine intervention: "God will provide a miraculous cure." Others pin their hopes on meditation, alternative therapies, or exercise. Another source of hope—as Kübler-Ross suggested—is the idea that the medical predictions can be wrong: "True, I have that diagnosis, but I know of cases where a doctor told a person with my illness she had six months left and she has been living for 10 years."

EXPERIENCING THE LIFESPAN: Heart Failure is a Family Affair

It started on a trip to Washington—David's favorite city—three summers ago. "Something is different with my body. I got out of breath when I took a walk around the mall." Then came the diagnosis: "You have congestive heart failure. Because your heart muscle is enlarged, fluid is accumulating around your lungs and legs. But with our medicines, you can almost certainly live—with restrictions—for some time." During the past two years, when a treatment got less effective, and my husband's body became bloated, we visited the doctor to increase the dosage or get a more effective cocktail of pills. But, as I know trouble walking to the mailbox is a serious sign, I panicked when, a few weeks ago, the *Times* still sat in our driveway when I got home from work. Now, David gasps for breath when he walks to the kitchen. He can't fit into his shoes, even *after* he takes that new miracle pill.

Last weekend, when he slept all morning and afternoon, I knew he decided, "It's the end." He donated his favorite paintings to the university; taught me how to decode the finances so I would know what to do after he was gone. Thomas called, worried, saying, "Dad must be in terrible shape. He phoned *just* to talk." But Tuesday, David was better. We went out to dinner. Maybe we'll have another two months together, or six. Maybe a miracle will happen and David will feel well enough to take that trip to Washington we planned for later this fall.

How do families feel when one member has a life-threatening illness? According to Swedish researchers, they feel just like me (Carlander and others, 2011). During periods of stability, you think you have infinite time. When things get worse, you go into a panic state. You are living your separate life, working (or, in my case, teaching classes) as if everything is fine—but your family life is on a different plane. You are living together as a normal, healthy family, getting closer to death.

Hope, as you can see in the Experiencing the Lifespan box, is a family affair. It doesn't mean hoping for a cure. It may mean wishing you have another six months together, or that your husband feels well enough to make it to Washington—a city he has always loved. It can mean hoping that your wife has no financial worries, or your love lives on in your family, or that your life work will make a difference in the world. (Remember, that's what being generative is all about.) Contrary to what Kübler-Ross implies, even reaching acceptance has nothing to do with abandoning hope. People can understand—"I'm dying"—and still have many future goals and plans.

Heart failure epitomizes that common twenty-first-century pathway to death. Patients have good days and bad days. They can live for years in the shadow of death. Although extended, ultimately fatal, chronic illnesses can strike at any age (recall, for instance, the earlier quote relating to cystic fibrosis), most often, as with my husband, they occur *on time* in terms of our social clock, in our older years.

AFP/Getty Images/Newscom

Deprived of life as a husband and father at an *off-time* age seems totally "against nature" and unfair—making this man's funeral in his thirties impossibly sad.

Drawing on Erik Erikson's theory, we might predict that facing death in our teens or early adult life is uniquely difficult. How can you reach integrity, or the sense you have fulfilled your life goals if you have not found your identity, mastered intimacy, or discovered your generative path? Although they worry about being dependent, older people often report they are not afraid of death itself (Waterworth & Jorgensen, 2010).

Still, while living a full lifespan may make our own death acceptable, it does not erase the fear of a loved one's dying. Because there is no event more distressing than the death of a child, let's now pause to look at this horrendous off-time event.

IN FOCUS: The Death of a Child

> My first son passed away at age 24 . It's been over 40 years since he died, but not a day goes by when I don't miss him. My younger boy just died from heart disease, last month, at age 62. I don't understand it. I'm 90. Why didn't the Lord take me instead?

When I worked in a nursing home, I realized that the death of a child outweighs any other loss. It doesn't matter whether their "baby" dies at age 6 or in his sixties; parents never fully come to terms with that unnatural event (Hayslip & Hansson, 2003). People do go on to construct a fulfilling life. However, when a child dies, it's harder to move on to the *working-model*, "recovery" stage of mourning described in Chapter 13 (Meert and others, 2011). In one study, even after 4 years, many bereaved parents still continually yearned for their child (McCarthy and others, 2010).

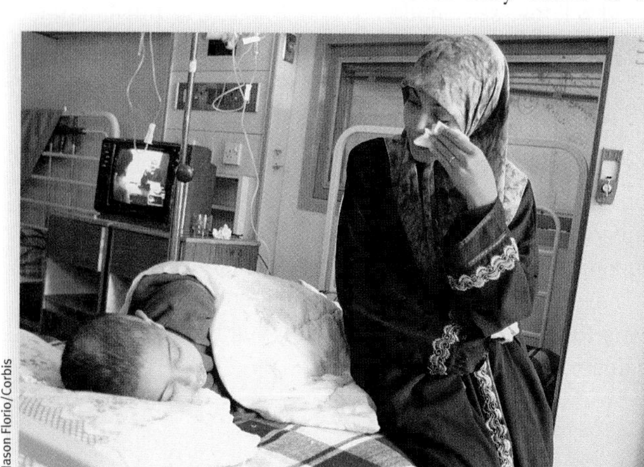

Jason Florio/Corbis

This grieving mother may pine for her baby for many of her remaining years—as the death of a child ranks as life's most devastating event.

As you just saw in the quotation above, a child's death may evoke powerful feelings of survivor guilt: "Why am I still alive?" If the death occurred suddenly due to an accident, there is disbelief and possibly guilt at having failed in one's mission as a parent: "I couldn't protect my baby!" (See Cole & Singg, 1998.) If the death was expected—for instance, a child died of an incurable genetic disorder such as cystic fibrosis—it seems easier to cope. But even when they are confident that medically everything possible has been done, mothers and fathers may still have concerns: "Maybe I *could* have done something else emotionally for my daughter or son."

When a child has inoperable cancer *and seems to understand that he is dying*, should parents talk about death? To explore this question, Swedish researchers interviewed *every* family who had lost a child to cancer in that country over several years (Kreicbergs and others, 2004). No parent who reported having a conversation about death with an ill daughter or son had any regrets. In contrast, more than half of the mothers and fathers who believed that their child understood what was happening but never discussed this topic felt guilty later on.

Other research has a similar message: If parents feel satisfied that they said goodbye to their child, this helps lessen the pain. Moreover, not discussing what is happening can produce enduring regrets:

> I wish I had him back so that we could hug and kiss and say goodby" (said one anguished mother). "We never said good-bye. We faked the whole thing. . . . I just feel there was no ending, no finish . . . Yet he never took the lead . . . he never said, 'Ma, I'm dying.'
>
> (quoted in Wells-di Gregorio, 2009, p. 252)

What else helps families cope? In one interview study, parents and surviving brothers and sisters stressed that it's vital to preserve *continuing bonds* (recall Chapter 13):

> Keep personal belongings (for when you need to smell them or need to remember).
>
> From a sibling: "I always sleep in his bed, 'cause he has this really cool mattress. It's nice and comfy."

The message from mothers went further: "Keep caring for your beloved child."

> I talk to her… every night… . I just say... I'm so sorry for what you had to go through, but mommy is so proud of you.
>
> I'd …. get his ashes and sit…. and rock. I'll… kiss his little container thing and try to say good night to him every night when I go to bed.
>
> (quoted in Foster and others, 2011, pp. 427, 428, 429, 432)

What can health professionals do to help? Attend the funeral. Write condolence letters to honor the struggle of the parents and the courage of the child (Liben, Papadatou, & Wolfe, 2008; Wolfe, 2004). Moreover, when death becomes imminent, invite parents to *actively* participate in the care. After watching a man pace the room helplessly as his son was dying of AIDS, here is how a nurse gave a father one last chance to be a parent in the final moments of his son's life:

> I adjusted the damp cloth on the young man's head and the father asked if he could do that. I handed him the cloth, and as he stroked his son's face with it, he told me about the times he had bathed his son when he was a little boy .... I asked if he would like to do this now. . . . He then proceeded to bathe his son, who died later that evening. At the wake, the father came up to me, smiled and said proudly that his son had died in clean pajamas. . . . [Along with his pain] he will always have [that] memory.
>
> (quoted in Brabant, 2003, pp. 480–481)

Because it is clearly off time, most of us would never see the death of a child as appropriate or right. What qualities are involved in having what psychologists call "a good death"?

In Search of a Good Death

We can get insights by turning to religious sources. From the Old Testament (Spronk, 2004) to Hindu traditions (Gupta, 2011), religions agree that death should be celebrated—but *only* after a long life. Death should be peaceful, explaining why violent deaths, like suicides or murders, are especially repellent and why people dislike the idea of dying after being "tortured" by medical technology (Long, 2004; Walter, 2003). Death is "best" when it occurs in the "homeland" (not far away), accounting for why—around the globe—people prefer to die surrounded by their loved ones, and reject the sanitized, impersonal dying that takes place in intensive care (Prevost & Wallace, 2009; Shih and others, 2009).

Mary Evans Picture Library/The Image Works

The principle that good deaths must occur "near the homeland" is embedded in many religious traditions. This nineteenth-century depiction shows a Hindu funeral ceremony, with the deceased making his final passage surrounded by loving community members while being carried ceremoniously to the grave.

My personal example of a good death came to my grandmother, Lillian Sheerr, one beautiful summer day. Grandma, at age 98, was just beginning to get slightly frail. One afternoon, before preparing dinner for her visiting grandchildren and great-grandchildren (which she insisted on doing), she got in her car to drive to the hairdresser and—on leaving the driveway—was hit by an oncoming car. Of the eight people involved in the accident, no one was hurt but Grandma, who was killed instantly. They said she never felt any pain. My grandma got the death she deserved—because we all believed she was a saint in her life.

Given that our chances of being killed instantly at our doorstep, without frailties at the limit of human life, are almost nil, how can we expand on the above criteria to spell out specific dimensions of a good death? One psychologist offers the following guidelines (Corr, 1991–1992):

1. We want to minimize our physical distress, to be as free as possible from debilitating pain.
2. We want to maximize our psychological security, reduce fear and anxiety, and feel in control of how we die.
3. We want to enhance our relationships and be as close as possible emotionally to the people we care about most.

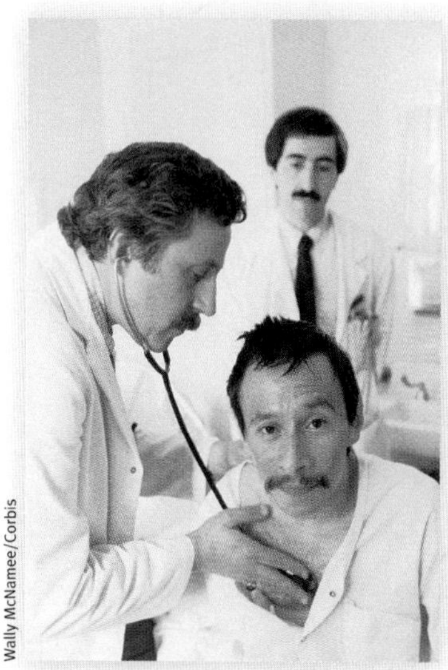

Did this relatively young cancer patient (who later died) have a "good death"? According to the research, much depended on whether he believed he had fulfilled his generative life-mission, and so reached Erikson's integrity, accepting the fact that his personal death was a natural part of the cycle of life.

4. We want to foster our spirituality and have the sense that there was integrity and purpose to our lives.

Minimize pain and fear; be close to loved ones; enhance spirituality; feel that life has meaning—these are the themes from the few studies that poll caregivers about the qualities involved in a loved one's "good death" (Downey and others, 2010; Karlsson & Berggren, 2011; Leung and others, 2010; Shih and others, 2009). Yes, one study suggested a strong religious faith does provide people with some peace in their final days (Braam, Klinkenberg, & Deeg, 2011). But it's not necessary to believe in an afterlife or any religion. Actually, in another study, the main dimension that was related to feeling comfortable about dying was having a sense of purpose in life (Ardelt & Koenig, 2006).

So again, Erikson seems right in saying that the key to accepting death is fulfilling our life tasks and, especially, our generative missions. And in Erikson's (1963) poetic words, appreciating that one's "individual life is the accidental coincidence of . . . one lifecycle within . . . history" (p. 268) can be important in embracing death, too:

> Barbara turned on the lamp.... Her eyes were sunken and her skin was pale. It would not be long, I thought. . . . "Are you afraid?" I asked. "You know, not really,. . . . I have strange comforting thoughts. . . . When fear starts to creep up on me, I conjure up the idea that millions and millions of people have passed away before me, and millions more will pass away after I do . . . I guess if they all did it, so can I."
>
> (Groopman, 2004, pp. 137–138)

What are your priorities for a good death? Table 15.1 offers an expanded checklist based on the principles in this section, to help you evaluate your top-ranking death goals. In the next section, we turn to how well the health-care system is doing at helping people fulfill their plans for a dignified death.

TABLE 15.1: Evaluating Your Priorities for a Good Death: A Checklist

When you think about dying, rank how important each of these criteria might be to you as: (1) of utmost importance; (2) important, but not primary; or (3) relatively unimportant.

_______ 1. Not being a burden to my family.

_______ 2. Being at peace with death—that is, not being anxious about dying.

_______ 3. Not being in physical pain.

_______ 4. Having control over where I die—that is, being able to choose whether to die at home or in the hospital.

_______ 5. Having control over how I die—that is, being able to choose whether to be kept alive through medical interventions or to die naturally. Being able to end my life if I am terminally ill and in great pain.

_______ 6. Feeling close to my loved ones.

_______ 7. Feeling close to God.

_______ 8. Feeling that I have fulfilled my mission on earth or made a difference in the world.

Do your top-ranking priorities for dying tell you anything about your priorities for living?

TYING IT ALL TOGETHER

1. Sara is arguing that Kübler-Ross's conceptions about dying are "fatally flawed." Pick out the argument she should *not* use to make her case (that is, identify the false alternative):
   a. People who are dying do not necessarily want to talk about that fact.
   b. People do not go through "stages" in adjusting to impending death.
   c. People who are dying simply accept that fact.

2. If your uncle has recently been diagnosed with advanced lung cancer, he should feel (*many different emotions/only depressed/only angry*), but in general, he should have (*hope/a lot of anger*).
3. You are a psychologist who works with the terminally ill and their families. All other things being equal, which client is likely to find it easiest to cope with impending death: a 16-year-old girl, a 30-year-old man, an 80-year-old woman, a parent of a dying 8-year-old child?
4. As a hospital administrator, outline some steps you might take to help patients have a good death by reducing their fear and increasing their feelings of having control over how they die.

Answers to the Tying It All Together questions can be found at the end of this chapter.

The Health-Care System

How does the health-care system deal with dying patients? Let's first take a critical look at standard hospital terminal care and then explore the new health-care options designed to tame twenty-first-century death.

What's Wrong with Traditional Hospital Care for the Dying?

Most of us, as mentioned earlier, will die in a hospital (Prevost & Wallace, 2009). But social scientists have known for a half-century that the traditional hospital approach to dying has flaws. Consider the findings of this groundbreaking 1960s study in which sociologists entered hospitals and observed how the medical staff organized "the work" of terminal care (Glaser & Strauss, 1968).

The researchers found that, when a person was admitted to the hospital, nurses and doctors set up predictions about what pattern that individual's dying was likely to follow. This implicit **dying trajectory** then governed how the staff acted.

There actually were several dying trajectories. In "the expected swift death," a patient would arrive (in the emergency room) whose death was imminent, perhaps from an accident or heart attack, and who had no chance of surviving. "Expected lingering while dying" was another pathway. In this case, a man or woman would enter the hospital with advanced cancer or end-stage heart disease and slowly decline. Or the patient might follow the "entry–reentry" path: admitted and stabilized medically, then discharged, to return periodically until the final crisis before death.

The problem, however, was that dying schedules could not always be predicted. When someone mistakenly categorized as "expected to linger" was moved to a unit in the hospital where she was not monitored, this mislabeling tended, not infrequently, to hasten death. An interesting situation happened when "expected swift death" changed to "lingering." Doctors would call loved ones to the bedside to say goodbye, only to find that the person began to improve. This "final goodbye" scenario could play out time and time again. The paradox, as you can see below, was that if it was "off schedule," *living* might be transformed into a negative event!

> One patient who was expected to die within four hours had no money, but needed a special machine in order to last longer. A private hospital... agreed to receive him as a charity patient. He did not die immediately but started to linger indefinitely, even to the point where there was some hope he might live. The money problem, however, created much concern among both family members and the hospital administrators.... The doctor continually had to reassure both parties that the patient (who lived for six weeks) would soon die; that is, to try to change their expectations back to "certain to die on time."
>
> (Glaser & Straus, 1968, pp. 11–12)

dying trajectory The fact that hospital personnel make projections about the particular pathway to death that a seriously ill patient will take and organize their care according to that assumption.

The bottom line is that deaths don't occur according to a programmed timetable. Hospitals are structured according to the assumption that they do. This incompatibility makes for an inherently messy dance of terminal care.

Unfortunately, since this research was conducted, conditions have not changed. According to one review of hospital records spanning 1996 to 2010, the odds of health-care workers accurately predicting the date of a patient's dying were only fifty-fifty (Phillips and others, 2011). This means that many families still suffer the trauma of being caught "off guard" when faced with that event (Wells-di Gregorio, 2009). When dying proceeds according to schedule (or as expected), health-care personnel classify the death as "good." As one resident in a study reported: "I felt good that he died in a comfortable way. . . . I guess I just knew it would happen in 24 hours so it doesn't come as a shock" (quoted in Good and others, 2004, p. 944). When trajectories are mislabeled, the death is defined as "bad": "She came in for a bone marrow transplant to cure her [cancer] . . . and got pulmonary toxicity and died" (p. 945). Good deaths happen when there is smooth communication between the medical team and patients' families. Bad deaths are rife with disagreements, anger, and hurt (see Wells-di Gregorio, 2009). In fact, because of the potential for miscommunication, traditional hospital dying may be more turbulent in the twenty-first century than ever before.

© Mark Richards/PhotoEdit

How can this doctor relate to this Spanish-speaking immigrant woman, anxiously waiting for news of her gravely ill son? Issues like these loom large as hospital personnel struggle to do the right thing for the families of dying patients in our contemporary multicultural society.

One reason is that, today, patients do not typically spend weeks or months in a hospital. They often enter this setting when they are within days of death. Therefore, the health-care professionals on the death scene may not be emotionally involved with the person (Good and others, 2004). They may have little understanding of patients' and families' needs.

Disagreements between members of the health-care team add to this problem. Physicians make the final decisions about treatments; but nurses, the frontline caregivers on the scene, know the patient's and family's wishes best. Nurses want to advocate for dying patients but may be afraid of being disciplined if they do speak up (Thacker, 2008; Yu & Chan, 2010). Compounding these professional conflicts are issues related to living in our multicultural society (Wells-di Gregorio, 2009). Suppose the attending doctor on the floor where your relative is dying is a recent immigrant from Beijing or Bangladesh, or your parents only speak Spanish or Swahili. How can everyone really communicate at this intensely emotional time?

What underlies many of these conflicts is the quantum leap in our death-defying technologies. Physicians can offer nutrition to people through a tube into the stomach, bypassing the body's normal signal to stop eating in preparation for death. They put critically ill patients on ventilators, machines that breathe for the person, after the lungs would have given out. Caring doctors may agonize about using these heroic measures. They worry about causing dying people unnecessary pain (Liben, Papadatou, & Wolfe, 2008). But their mission to cure makes it difficult to resist the lure of the machines:

> We were realizing that we were going to hurt him [a 40-year-old lung cancer patient who had had multiple surgeries and several strokes] if we . . . kept trying to keep a body alive that was not wanting to be alive. And everyone figured "what the heck, give it a shot."
>
> (quoted in Good and others, 2004, p. 945)

Today, health-care workers are faced with agonizing ethical choices: How long do you vigorously wage war against death, and when should you say, "enough is enough"? Shifting from the cure-at-all-costs mode can be very difficult. To paraphrase one expert, it's like "deciding to play baseball while the football game is in full swing" (Chapple, 1999). Understanding that we can never take the mess out of dying, just as we can never take the mess out of living, let's now look at how the traditional health-care system is taking action to tame death today.

INTERVENTIONS: Providing Superior Palliative Care

palliative care Any intervention designed not to cure illness but to promote dignified dying.

end-of-life care instruction Courses in medical and nursing schools devoted to teaching health-care workers how to provide the best palliative care to the dying.

palliative-care service A service or unit in a hospital that is devoted to end-of-life care.

Palliative care refers to any strategy designed, not to cure people, but to promote dignified dying. Palliative care includes educating health-care personnel about how to deal with dying patients; modifying the hospital structure; or providing that well-known alternative to dying in a hospital, hospice care. Let's scan these interventions one by one.

Educating Health-Care Providers

In recent decades, **end-of-life care instruction** has become a frequent component of medical and nursing training. Courses cover everything from the best drugs to control pain without "knocking the person out" to the ethics of withdrawing treatment—from tips on talking about death with patients to ways of providing sensitive end-of-life care to people from different cultural groups. Training may range from formal hospital "death" rounds (Smith & Hough, 2011) to experiential workshops in which student nurses personally imagine what it is like to die (Liu and others, 2011).

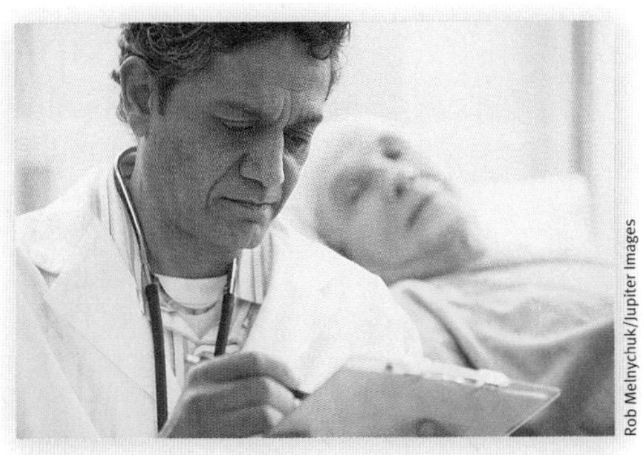

Rob Melnychuk/Jupiter Images

Imagine being this doctor and knowing the terminally ill patient whose chart you are reading is about to ask, "What is my prognosis?" Wouldn't it be helpful to have some end-of-life care instruction during your training to guide you about how best to respond?

Unfortunately, we need to do more (Smith & Hough, 2011). In one hospital survey, although nurses reported dealing with death on a daily basis, fewer than half said they had any training in end-of-life care within the previous three years (Thacker, 2008). Doctors want more guidance in how to discuss negative prognoses since they are, naturally, incredibly uncomfortable when conveying the message, "There isn't much we can do" (Smith & Hough, 2011).

The result of this anxiety is that we sometimes get physicians who (perhaps out of their own fear) decide to take Kübler-Ross's concept of "honesty" literally, saying, "Your illness is terminal," and then bolting from the room. Or—as you saw above—health-care providers persist in carrying out painful, futile treatments for far too long (Bonebrake and others, 2010). Luckily, however, we have a hospital structure designed to ease these difficult discussions, a new mainstream medical alternative devoted to promoting the best possible death.

Changing Hospitals: Palliative-Care Units

A **palliative-care service** is a special unit or service within a traditional hospital that is devoted to end-of-life care. Here, certain groups of inpatients—for instance, old-old people with multiple chronic illnesses and people with advanced cancer—have their care managed by a team of providers trained in when to shift from "football to baseball mode" (recall the analogy mentioned earlier). Patients enrolled in the palliative-care service are not denied cure-oriented interventions (Bonebrake and others, 2010). However, as their illness becomes terminal, the vigor of life-prolonging treatments shifts to providing the best possible "comfort care."

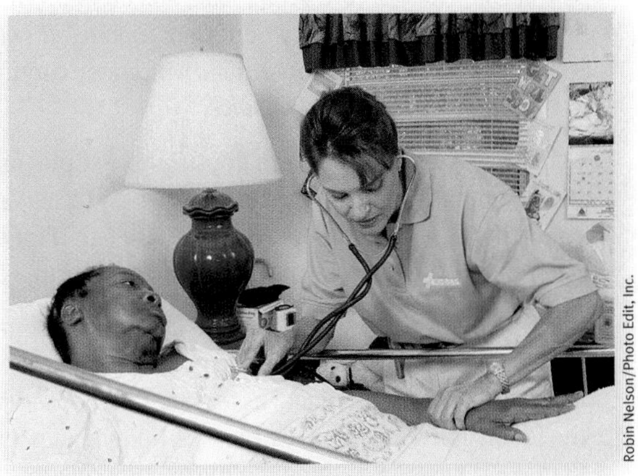

Robin Nelson/Photo Edit, Inc.

Palliative-care services, with their focus on pain control and letting patients spend their final days in a more natural setting, provide an alternative to dying in the medicalized recesses of intensive care. In this palliative-care unit, a nurse is taking the blood pressure of a patient who has had a stroke and is suffering from end-stage heart disease.

Families give palliative care high marks, compared to traditional end-of-life care (García-Pérez and others, 2009). These services are "cost-effective" (Meier & Beresford, 2009). Moreover—unlike what some readers may fear—having this unit at a hospital doesn't make death more likely when patients enter that institution's care (Cassel and others, 2010). So, by the first decade of the twenty-first century, many major medical centers in the United States provided specific palliative-care services (Dobbins, 2007).

The global view, however, is bleak. Even in affluent nations—such as Canada—experts estimate that only 1 in 4 terminally ill people has access to hospital-based palliative care (Shariff, 2011). Of the roughly one million human beings who die each week worldwide, a large fraction spend their final days in agony, without even over-the-counter medicines to control their pain (Clark, 2007).

hospice movement A movement, which became widespread in recent decades, focused on providing palliative care to dying patients outside of hospitals and especially on giving families the support they need to care for the terminally ill at home.

State-of-the art, hospital-based palliative-care services are a welcome trend. But it still seems unfair to ask health-care professionals to embrace the enemy. Physicians in particular may shy away from dying patients because it means they failed in their mission to cure—and they are human like the rest of us (Prevost & Wallace, 2009). As one resident admitted, because of his own feelings of failure and powerlessness, even "To go into the (dying) patient's room . . . becomes tough!" (Quoted in Luthy and others, 2009, p. 62.) Therefore, the best way to ensure dignified dying might be to remove that process completely from the doctors with their cure-oriented focus and death-defying machines.

Unhooking Death from Doctors and Hospitals: Hospice Care

This is the philosophy that underlies the **hospice movement**, which gained momentum in the 1970s, along with the natural childbirth movement. Like birth, hospice activists argued, death is a natural process. We need to let this natural process occur in the most personal, pain-free, natural way (Corr, 2007).

Hospice workers are skilled in techniques to minimize patients' physical discomfort. They are trained in providing a humanistic, supportive psychological environment, one that assures patients and family members that they will not be abandoned in the face of approaching death (Monroe and others, 2008).

Initially, hospice care was delivered only in an inpatient setting called a hospice, much like the palliative-care hospital services described above. Although there are still inpatient hospice facilities (Addington-Hall & O'Callaghan, 2009), the current emphasis of the hospice movement—at least in the United States—is on providing backup care that allows people to die with dignity at home (Connor, 2007). As you can see in the Experiencing the Lifespan box, multidisciplinary hospice teams go into the person's home, offering care on a part-time, scheduled, or daily basis. They provide

EXPERIENCING THE LIFESPAN: Hospice Team

What is hospice care really like? For answers, here are some excerpts from an interview I conducted with that team (nurse, social worker, and volunteer coordinator) who manages our local hospice.

Usually, we get referrals from physicians. People may have a wide community support system or be new to the area. Even when there are many people involved, there is almost always one primary caregiver, typically a spouse or adult child.

We see our role as empowering families, giving them the support to care for their loved ones at home. We go into the home as a team to make our initial assessment: What services does the family need? We provide families training in pain control, in making beds, in bathing. A critical component of our program is respite services. Volunteers come in for part of each day. They may take the children out for pizza, or give the primary caregiver time off, or just stay there to listen.

Families will say initially, "I don't think I can stand to do this." They are anxious because it's a new experience they have never been through. At the beginning, they call a lot. Then, you watch them gain confidence in themselves. We see them at the funeral and they thank us for helping them give their loved one this experience. Sometimes, the primary caregiver can't bear to keep the person at home to the end. We respect that, too.

The whole thing about hospice is choice. Some people want to talk about dying. Others just want you to visit, ask about their garden, talk about current affairs. We take people to see the autumn leaves, to see Santa Claus. Our main focus is: What are your priorities? We try to pick up on that. We had a farmer whose goal was to go to his farm one last time and say goodbye to his tractor. We got together a big tank of oxygen, and carried him down to his farm. We have one volunteer who takes a client to the mall.

We keep in close touch with the families for a year after, providing them counseling or referring them to bereavement groups in the community. Some families keep in contact with notes for years. We run a camp each summer for children who have lost a parent.

We have an unusually good support system among the staff. In addition to being with the families at 3 A.M., we call one another at all times of the night. Most of us have been working here for years. We feel we have the most meaningful job in the world.

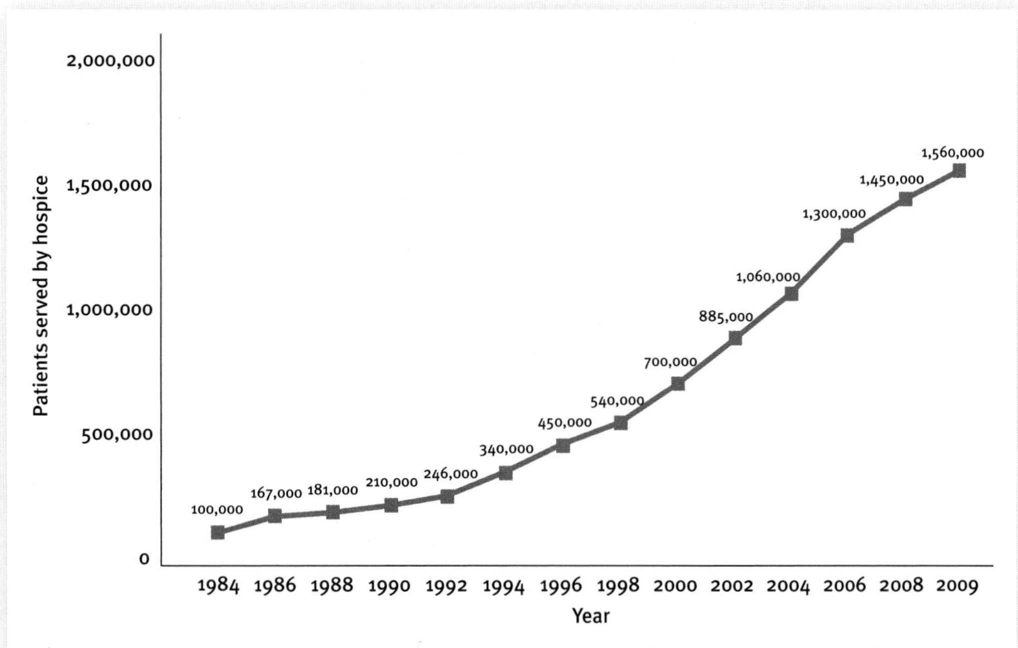

FIGURE 15.2: **Patients served by hospice in the United States, 1984–2009:** Notice that number of people enrolling in hospice grew exponentially, especially during the first decade of the twenty-first century.

Source: National Hospice and Palliative Care Organization, 2011.

24-hour help in a crisis, giving family caregivers the support they need to allow their relative to spend his final days at home. Their commitment does not end after the person dies: An important component of hospice care is bereavement counseling.

Hospice has struck a tremendous chord. As I mentioned earlier in this chapter, surveys show most people want to spend their final days of life at home. Since the first American hospice was established in Connecticut in 1974, the hospice movement has mushroomed (Casarett, 2011). Notice from Figure 15.2 that, by 2009, more than one and a half million people who died in the United States spent their final days in hospice care.

Entering a hospice program is simple: It merely requires a physician to certify that the person is within six months of death. As of 2011, a demonstration project has allowed people to enroll in U.S. hospices without abandoning curative care (Casarett, 2011). Moreover, as Medicare covers this service, hospice is available to people on every economic rung. Still, surveys routinely show that many eligible patients don't enroll (Vig and others, 2010). Ethnic and racial minorities, in particular, are less likely to use this service (Kreling and others, 2010; Lepore, Miller, & Gozalo, 2011). Why might people avoid hospice even when they say they want to die in a natural way?

Barriers to Hospice Care

One reason is that, as you saw earlier, it's natural for human beings to hold on to hope. Entering hospice still means confronting the reality, "I am going to die." People of color—those who have not always gotten the best curative care from the medical system (recall the previous chapter)—may have the perception that "I'll be abandoning my best shot at treatment if I enter hospice care" (Ardelt, 2003; Dresser, 2004). Because loved ones need to openly admit the person's condition is terminal, as I implied earlier, family members are naturally reluctant to bring up hospice (Kreling and others, 2010; Vig and others, 2010). In cultures such as the Hmong, talking about a dying person's condition is actually taboo.

Moreover, to enter hospice, a patient needs a strong family support system. Yes, today, it's possible to have this service at home if the person lives alone or has a spouse who cannot provide hands-on-care, provided a full-time home health aide (CNA) is on the scene. However, as you just saw in the Experiencing the Lifespan, people may not utilize this program unless they are living with loved ones who commit to providing the physically and emotionally draining tasks of the day-to-day care (Masucci and others, 2010; Nakamura and others, 2010).

Another barrier may lie in the hospice gatekeeper—the physician (Jenkins and others, 2011). Even when they are theoretically open to hospice, doctors often want to put a positive spin on terminal diagnoses (Baile, Aaron, & Parker, 2009). As one physician put it, "A tumor has not always read the textbook, and a treatment can have an unexpectedly dramatic effect" (quoted in Groopman, 2004, p. 210). The good news is that—because dying trajectories *are* unpredictable—providing hope is perfectly compatible with telling the truth!

For these reasons, as was true of my father in the chapter-opening vignette, people often enter hospice when death is imminent. The median time spent in hospice in the United States before death occurs is only about three weeks. One in three hospice enrollees dies within that very week (Casarett, 2011).

As you saw in the previous Experiencing the Lifespan box, hospice care can offer tremendous solace to the dying person and families, offering the backup that allows loved ones to be together fully during this final journey of life (Candy and others, 2011; Karlsson & Berggren, 2011; Kumar, Markert, & Patel, 2011). Without minimizing these benefits, so beautifully described by the hospice team, let's point out some cautions about actually dying at home.

The Case Against Dying at Home

Deciding to care for a loved one at home demands a daunting commitment. True, hospice volunteers do come to relieve the family periodically, but if you are a spouse or caregiving child, you are on call 24/7. You may need to take time off from work, perhaps for months. Even with the backup provided by the hospice team, it may be too anxiety-provoking to manage the crises associated with impending death, so you may need to transfer your loved one to an inpatient setting in his final days.

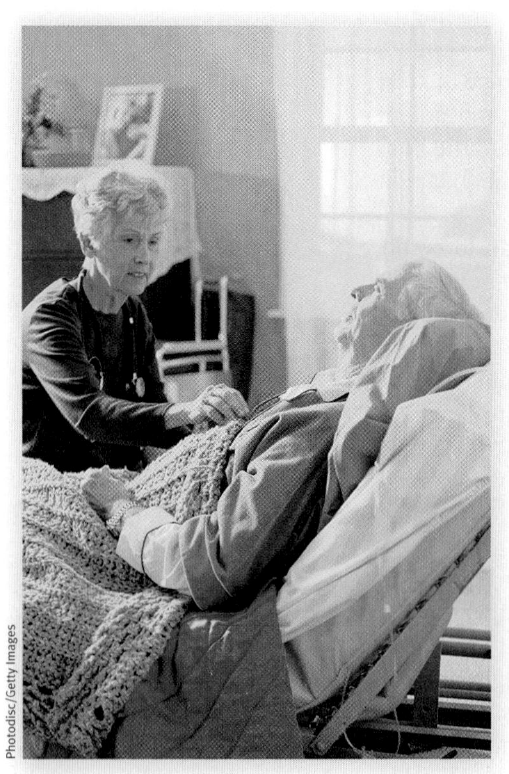

Photodisc/Getty Images

Although this wife probably would say she wouldn't have it any other way, caring for a beloved husband at home puts a tremendous burden on the caregiver and can be difficult from the perspective of the dying person as well.

There are problems from the patient's perspective, too. Imagine spending your final weeks of life being totally taken care of by your family. You don't have any privacy. Loved ones must bathe you and dress you; they must care for your every need. You may be embarrassed about being seen naked and incontinent; you may want time alone to vent your anguish and pain. In a hospital, care is impersonal. At home, there is the humiliation of having to depend on the people you love most for each intimate bodily act.

Most importantly, care by strangers equals care that is free from guilt. As I described earlier in this chapter, when people are approaching death, they often want to emotionally protect their loved ones—to shield them from pain. Witnessing the toll that your disease is taking on your family may multiply the pain of dying itself.

For these reasons, when researchers *ask* seriously ill people about their preferences, they find less-than-overwhelming enthusiasm about dying at home (Thomas, Morris, & Clark, 2004). In one interview study, when women with breast cancer were questioned, many people suggested they were ambivalent about taking that route (Hays and others, 2001). One patient said, "I guess it would depend on if you are not in great pain." Another was uncomfortable about the idea of blood—"Hemorrhaging concerns me. That would be so frightening [to my children]" (p. 9). A widow mentioned that she definitely wanted to die in the hospital because "I would not want my son to come into the bedroom one day and find me dead. That would be too traumatic for a 16-year-old" (p. 10).

Actually, when people are grappling with a fatal illness, concerns about feeling dependent loom large (Waterworth & Jorgensen, 2010). As I suggested above, terminally ill people worry about attachment-related issues—embarrassment over not being able to control their bodies, being a burden, leaving loved ones behind. (Now, you might want to see how this research compares with your responses to the death anxieties checklist you completed in Table 15.1 on page 464.) If preserving the quality of our relationships is vital at the end of life, the best choice may be to *not* die at home.

Table 15.2 summarizes these section points by comparing the pros and cons of home and hospital deaths. Now that I have surveyed the health-care possibilities, it's time to continue our search for a "good" twenty-first-century death by returning to the dying person.

TABLE 15.2: Hospital Death Versus Home Death: Pros and Cons

The case for dying in a hospital

1. Potential for better management of the physical aspects of dying.
2. No fear of burdening your family with your care.
3. Privacy to vent your feelings, without family members around.
4. Avoiding the embarrassment of depending on loved ones for help with your intimate body functions.

The case for dying at home

1. Avoiding having life-prolonging machines used on you.
2. Spending your final days surrounded by the people you care about most.
3. Spending your final days in the physical setting you love best.
4. Having freedom to follow your own cultural and religious preferences relating to dying.

Given these considerations, where would you prefer to meet death—in a hospital or at home?

TYING IT ALL TOGETHER

1. In a sentence, describe to a friend the basic message of the classic research describing the various dying trajectories discussed on page 465 and 466.
2. Based on this section, which statement most accurately reflects doctors' reactions to the terminally ill? (Pick one.) a. Doctors are insensitive to dying patients' needs or b. Doctors feel terribly upset when a patient is dying, but may feel forced to use modern technologies to "prolong" death.
3. Sara is arguing that we have made tremendous strides in improving end-of-life care in medical settings such as hospitals. Martha says no—we have a long way to go. First, make Sara's case and, then, make Martha's, citing the evidence discussed in this section.
4. Which patient are you *most* likely to find enrolled in a U.S. hospice program?
   a. an old-old man who lives alone
   b. a man with end-stage lung cancer living with his wife and daughters
   c. an ethnic minority, first-generation immigrant who has had a stroke
5. Melanie is arguing that there's no way she will die in a hospital. She wants to end her life at home, surrounded by her husband and children. Using the information in this section, convince Melanie that there may be a downside to spending her final days at home.
6. Your grandmother is dying. Her main priorities are likely to be (pick one): (a) feeling close to you and your parents or (b) dying at home.

Answers to the Tying It All Together questions can be found at the end of this chapter.

advance directive Any written document spelling out instructions with regard to life-prolonging treatment if individuals become irretrievably ill and cannot communicate their wishes.

living will A type of advance directive in which people spell out their wishes for life-sustaining treatment in case they become permanently incapacitated and unable to communicate.

durable power of attorney for health care A type of advance directive in which people designate a specific surrogate to make health-care decisions if they become incapacitated and are unable to make their wishes known.

Do Not Resuscitate (DNR) order A type of advance directive filled out by surrogates (usually a doctor in consultation with family members) for impaired individuals, specifying that if they go into cardiac arrest, efforts should not be made to revive them.

Do Not Hospitalize (DNH) order A type of advance directive put into the charts of impaired nursing home residents, specifying that in a medical crisis they should not be transferred to a hospital for emergency care.

The Dying Person: Taking Control of How We Die

In this section, I'll explore two strategies people can use to control their final passage and so promote a "good death." The first is an option that our society strongly encourages: People should make their wishes known in writing about their treatment preferences should they become permanently mentally incapacitated. The second approach is very controversial: People should be allowed to get help if they want to end their lives.

Giving Instructions: Advance Directives

An **advance directive** is the name for any written document spelling out instructions with regard to life-prolonging treatment when people are irretrievably ill and cannot communicate their wishes. There are four basic types of advance directives: two that the individual drafts and two that are filled out by other people, called *surrogates*, when the ill person is seriously mentally impaired.

- In the **living will**, mentally competent individuals leave instructions about their treatment wishes for life-prolonging strategies should they become comatose or permanently incapacitated. Although people typically fill out living wills in order to refuse aggressive medical interventions, it is important to point out that this document can also specify that every heroic measure be carried out.
- In a **durable power of attorney for health care**, individuals designate a specific surrogate, such as a spouse or a child, to make end-of-life decisions "in their spirit" when they are incapable of making those choices known.
- A **Do Not Resuscitate (DNR) order** is filled out when the sick person is already mentally impaired, usually by the doctor in consultation with family members. This document, most often placed in a nursing home or hospital chart, stipulates that, if a cardiac arrest takes place, health-care professionals should not try to revive the patient.
- A **Do Not Hospitalize (DNH) order** is specific to nursing homes. It specifies that, in case of a medical crisis, a mentally impaired resident should not be transferred to a hospital for emergency care.

Advance directives have an admirable goal. Ideally, they provide a road map so that family members and doctors are not forced to guess what care the permanently incapacitated person *might* want. However, there are serious issues, especially with regard to the most well-known advance directive—the living will (Cicirelli, 2007).

One difficulty is that people are reluctant to plan for their death in writing. Do you or your parents have a living will? Estimates suggest that only about 5 to 25 percent of the U.S. population does (Pevey, 2003). Doctors don't do better. In one survey of Finnish physicians, only 13 percent had filled out a living will (Hildén, Louhiala, & Palo, 2004).

The concept of putting one's personal plans in writing flies in the face of cultural norms to not talk about death. Therefore, urging advance directives on groups like the Hmong might be considered insulting, or worse. Other minorities may be leery of filling out these documents. Imagine, for instance, that you are an African American and well aware of the sordid history of health discrimination against your group. Would you want to write a living will telling medical personnel what *not* to do? So, in the United States, Blacks and Latinos are less likely to have advance directives in place than their affluent European American counterparts (Carr, 2011).

The main problem, however, is that the most well-known advance directive, the living will, does not really work! (See Cicirelli, 2007; Dobbins, 2007.) Somehow, Grandma's living will gets lost in the transition to the hospital, or family members override the document and say, "Grandma wanted (or didn't want) that particular intervention." The information in the typical living will is vague (Cicirelli, 2007). Does "no aggressive treatments" mean not putting in the feeding tube that has allowed my aunt to survive for a year after brain surgery? What exactly does "no heroic measures" mean?

While we might think the solution would be to come up with specific checklists (" I don't want to be on a ventilator, but I do want a feeding tube"), can we expect people to make these detailed decisions? How many of you *really* know what being on a ventilator or having a feeding tube entails? Moreover, while you might say "no heroic measures" while you are healthy, your decisions may be different when you are actually battling a fatal disease. Therefore, experts advocate having a series of evolving discussions with loved ones, and then choosing a designated family member, who in consultation with the physician, makes the final choice (Vogel, 2011).

This means the best advance directive is a durable power of attorney for health care (Hawkins and others, 2005; Silveira, Kim, & Langa, 2010). Granted, deciding on a single family member to carry out one's wishes can lead to jealousy ("Why did Mom give power of attorney to my brother and not me?"). It doesn't ensure mistakes won't occur. Interestingly, one study comparing the wishes of an older person to different family members showed accuracy was highest when the proxy was a spouse. Discrepancies were most likely to occur when the surrogate was a child and family conflict was high (Parks and others, 2011). Still, having a defined proxy—but making sure to sit down and discuss your wishes with the *whole* family—can reduce the sibling conflicts that crop up when there is no person in charge. Suppose you believe that Mom's suffering should not be prolonged, while your brother insists that treatment continue at all costs. Issues such as these can poison family relationships for years (or life).

Experts advise this elderly woman to regularly have these kinds of frank conversations, with *both* her daughter and son, as she prepares her *durable power of attorney* for health care.

By now, some readers may be getting uneasy, not about keeping people alive too long, but about the opposite problem—letting them die too soon. Let's ratchet up the anxiety as we move to the next step in the search for death with dignity: actively helping people take their own lives.

Deciding When to Die: Active Euthanasia and Physician-Assisted Suicide

> Dr. Cox, a British rheumatologist, had a warm relationship with Mrs. Boyles, who had been his patient for 13 years. Mrs. Boyles was terminally ill, in excruciating pain and begged Dr. Cox to end her life: "Her pain was . . . grindingly severe. . . . [It] did not respond to increasingly large doses of opioids. Dr. Cox had reassured her that she would not be allowed to suffer terrible pain during her final days but was unable to honor that pledge. . . . As an act of compassion, he injected two ampoules of potassium chloride (a fatal drug). . . . The patient died a few minutes later peacefully in the presence of her (grateful) sons. . . ." Then the ward sister, out of a sense of duty . . . reported the action to the police. Told to "disregard the doctor's motives" but only rule on his "intent to kill," a jury… convicted Dr. Cox "amid scenes of great emotional distress in the court."
>
> (as reported in Begley, 2008; quotes are from pp. 436 and 438)

How do you feel about this doctor's decision, the reaction of his nurse, and the jury's judgment? If you were like many people in Great Britain, you would have been outraged, believing that Dr. Cox was a hero because he acted on his mission to relieve human suffering rather than follow an unjust law (recall Kohlberg's *post-conventional stage*, in Chapter 9).

Let's first make some distinctions. **Passive euthanasia,** withdrawing potentially life-saving interventions, such as a feeding tube, is perfectly legal. (That's what advance directives specify.) But the step Dr. Cox took qualified as **active euthanasia**—taking *action* to help a person die. Active euthanasia is illegal in every nation except

passive euthanasia Withholding potentially life-saving interventions that might keep a terminally ill or permanently comatose patient alive.

active euthanasia A deliberate health care intervention that helps a patient die.

physician-assisted suicide A type of active euthanasia in which a physician prescribes a lethal medication to a terminally ill person who wants to die.

Belgium, Luxembourg, and the Netherlands. However, as of this writing (2012) a variation on active euthanasia called **physician-assisted suicide** is legal in Switzerland, Oregon, and Washington State. Under very strict conditions, at a terminally ill patient's request, physicians can prescribe a medication the individual can personally take to bring on death.

As the judge in the above trial spelled out, the distinction between the two types of euthanasia lies in intentions (Dickens, Boyle, & Ganzini, 2008). When we withdraw some heroic measure, we don't specifically wish for death. When doctors give a patient a lethal dose of a drug or, as in physician-assisted suicide, prescribe a lethal substance for a terminally ill person, they *want* that individual to die.

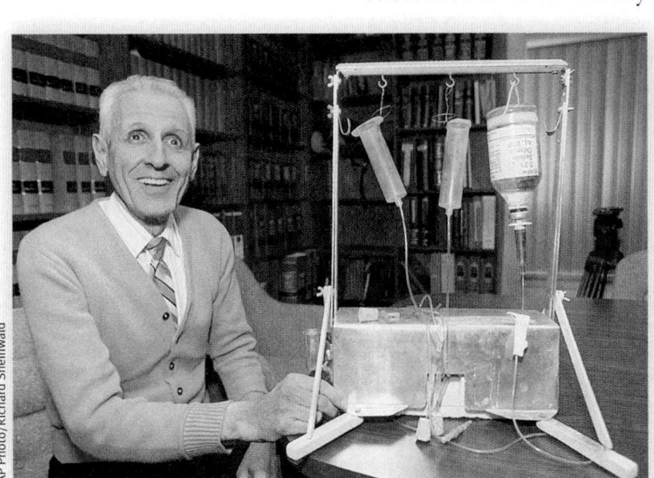

AP Photo/Richard Sheinwald

During the 1990s, Dr. Jack Kevorkian ignited a nationwide controversy when he reported having helped many terminally ill patients die and made numerous media appearances proudly showing off this "suicide machine." For the reasons discussed in the text, many people reacted with horror; Dr. Kevorkian was dubbed "Dr. Death" and he was sentenced to serve time in prison for second-degree murder!

Although active euthanasia is almost universally against the law, surveys routinely suggest practices that hasten death do occur (Chambaere and others, 2011; Seale, 2009). To take a classic example, doctors may sedate a dying patient beyond the point required for pain control, and so "accelerate" that person's death (Cellarius, 2011). Polls in the United States and other Western countries show that most people believe in "restricted" active euthanasia—if an individual is terminally ill and in great pain (Dickens, Boyle, & Ganzini, 2008). However, there is resistance to making these practices fully legal. Why?

One reason is that killing violates the principle that only God can give or take a life. This is why religious people—and particularly those living in predominately Catholic countries—passionately oppose both physician-assisted suicide and active euthanasia (Ardelt, 2003; Seale, 2009; Verbakel & Jaspers, 2010). Apart from religious considerations, there are other reasons we might be leery about taking this step.

By agreeing to legalize these practices, critics fear, we may be opening the gates to involuntary euthanasia, allowing doctors and families to "pull the plug" on people who are impaired but don't want to die (Verbakel & Jaspers, 2010). Even when someone requests help to end his life, we don't know whether the patient is being pressured into that decision by unscrupulous relatives who are anxious to get an inheritance or want to be spared the expense of waiting for the person to die.

Another issue relates to trusting the patient's *own* feelings and thoughts. People who request physician-assisted suicide, not infrequently, are depressed (Wilson and others, 2007). If the depression were treated, they might feel differently about ending their lives. One psychiatrist cited the case of a young man in his thirties diagnosed with leukemia and given a 25 percent chance of survival. Fearing both the side effects of the treatment and being a burden to his family, he begged for assistance in killing himself:

> Once the young man and I could talk about the possibility of his dying—what separation from his family and the destruction of his body meant to him—his desperation subsided. He accepted medical treatment and used the remaining months of his life to become closer to his wife and parents. Two days before he died, he talked about what he would have missed without the opportunity for a loving parting.
>
> (quoted in Hendin, 1994, Dec. 16, p. A19)

There are also excellent arguments on the other side. Should patients be forced to unwillingly endure the pain and humiliation of dying when physicians have the tools to mercifully end life? Knowing the agony that terminal disease can cause, is it humane to stand by and let nature take its course? Do you believe that legalizing active euthanasia or physician-assisted suicide is a true advance in caring for the dying or its opposite, the beginning of a "slippery slope" that might end in sanctioning the killing of anyone whose quality of life is impaired?

A Looming Social Issue: Age-Based Rationing of Care

age-based rationing of care The controversial idea that society should not use expensive life-sustaining technologies on people in their old-old years.

There is an age component to the "slippery slope" of withholding care. As I suggested earlier, people with DNR or DNH orders in their charts are typically elderly, near the end of their natural lives. We already use passive euthanasia at the upper end of the lifespan on a case-by-case basis, holding off from giving aggressive treatments to people we deem "too frail." Should we formally adopt the principle "don't use death-defying strategies" for people after they reach a certain age?

Daniel Callahan (1988), a prominent biomedical ethicist, argues that the answer must be yes. There is a time when "the never-to-be-finished fight against death" must stop. According to Callahan, waging total war for everyone might be acceptable if we all had equal access to health care. But as of this writing (2012) in the United States, Medicare pays for expensive life-prolonging strategies, while millions of younger Americans have no health insurance at all. Let's read Callahan's arguments in favor of **age-based rationing of care:**

1. *After a person has lived out a natural lifespan, medical care should no longer be oriented to resisting death.* While stressing that no precise cutoff age can be set, Callahan puts this marker at around the eighties. This does not mean that life at this age has no value, but rather that when people reach their old-old years, death in the near future is inevitable and this process cannot be vigorously defied.
2. *The existence of medical technologies capable of extending the lives of elderly persons who have lived out a natural lifespan creates no presumption that the technologies must be used for that purpose.* Callahan believes that the proper goal of medicine is to stave off premature death. We should not become slaves to our death-defying technology by blindly using each intervention on every person, no matter what that individual's age.

Is Callahan "telling it like it should be" from a logical, rational point of view, or do his proposals give you chills? As you consider this issue, you may recall from Chapter 2 that today many doctors won't vigorously intervene when a baby is born around the limit of viability—at around week 22 or 23. Age-based rationing of care applies to both the beginning and the very end of life!

Age-based rationing of health care is poised to become a national debate as I am writing this chapter and the U.S. Congress grapples with ways of limiting the explosive growth of Medicare. By the time you are reading this chapter, we may know whether every rapidly aging Western nation will be taking Callahan's advice to heart.

But the real heart of this chapter revolves around a timeless, universal human concern. As we approach death, notice that our life comes full circle, and we care only about what mattered during our first year of life—being connected to the people we most love. Okay, during most of the lifespan, self-efficacy is important. But when we come right down to it, attachment trumps everything else!

TYING IT ALL TOGETHER

1. Your mother asks you whether she should fill out an advance directive. Given what you now know from this chapter, what should your answer be?
   a. Go for it! The best thing to do is to fill out a living will so you can be sure your preferences will be fulfilled.
   b. Go for it! But you need to regularly discuss your preferences with each of us and complete a durable power of attorney.
   c. Avoid advance directives like the plague because your preferences will never be fulfilled.
2. Latoya and Jamal are arguing about legalizing physician-assisted suicide. Jamal is furious that this practice is not legal and feels that "people should have the right to die." Latoya is terribly worried about formally institutionalizing this practice. Using the points in this section, first make Jamal's case, and then support Latoya's argument.

3. Poll your class: How would your fellow students vote if they were on the jury deciding Dr. Cox's case? If you were the ward nurse, would you have reported this doctor's decision to the police?

Answers to the Tying It All Together questions can be found at the end of this chapter.

SUMMARY

The Dying Person

Today, we have three major pathways to death: We may die suddenly, without warning; we may steadily decline; and, most often, we may battle an ultimately fatal, chronic condition for a prolonged time. Before modern medicine, people died quickly and had a good deal of hands-on experience with death. Today, we have "moved" death to old age and keep the act of dying hidden from view. The physical process of dying is still "off the horizon"; but during the late twentieth century, studying **thanatology** became popular. Doctors now openly tell patients their illness may be terminal, and we urge people to discuss their dying preferences, although talking about death is still forbidden in some cultural groups.

Elisabeth Kübler-Ross, in her **stage theory of dying,** proposed that people pass through *denial, anger, bargaining, depression,* and *acceptance* when they learn they have a fatal disease. However, we cannot take this landmark theory as the final truth. Not every person wants to talk about impending death. Many people disagree with Kübler-Ross that we should be totally honest with dying loved ones. Furthermore, terminally ill people feel many different emotions—especially hope. Rather than emotionally approaching death in "stages," patients may experience a state called **middle knowledge,** both knowing and not fully comprehending their fate. Even in the face of accepting death, dying people still have life goals.

Parents have an enormously difficult time coping with that off-time event, the death of a child. When parents openly discuss death (if the child knows he or she is dying) and say goodbye to their child, they seem to adjust better to this trauma. Families recommend that keeping the child alive (in spirit) helps mute the pain. Health-care workers can help by inviting parents to share in the hands-on caregiving during a child's final hours.

The Old Testament and Hindu traditions agree that dying at peace after a long life while surrounded by our loved ones is best. Specifically, people want to die relatively free of pain and anxiety, feel in control of how they die, and end their lives feeling close to their attachment figures. Believing that we have fulfilled our purpose in living and appreciating that our death is part of the universal human cycle of life is also important in accepting death.

The Health-Care System

A classic study of **dying trajectories** showed that because dying doesn't proceed according to a "schedule" but medical personnel assume it does, the way hospitals manage death leaves much to be desired. Communication problems among patients, families, and medical personnel, along with the fact that medical technologies can extend life well beyond the time the body "wants" to die, increase the potential for undignified hospital deaths. Interventions to provide better **palliative care** include: (1) offering **end-of-life care instruction** to health-care personnel; (2) establishing hospital-based **palliative-care services;** and (3) removing the scene of dying from hospitals to the hospice.

The **hospice movement** offers backup services that allow families to let their loved ones spend their final months dying naturally, often at home. Although more people than ever use hospice care, this popular program has not caught on as much with ethnic minorities. Enrolling in hospice means labeling the patient as dying and typically having family members who can provide hands-on care. Home deaths may not always be the best choice when we understand that attachment-related issues such as not burdening loved ones matter most to people facing a fatal disease.

The Dying Person: Taking Control of How We Die

Advance directives—the **living will** and **durable power of attorney for health care,** filled out by the individual in health, and the **Do Not Resuscitate (DNR)** and **Do Not Hospitalize (DNH)** orders, filled out by surrogates when the person is mentally impaired—provide information about whether to use heroic measures when individuals cannot make their treatment wishes known. The best advance directive is the durable power of attorney, in which a person gives a specific family member decision-making power to decide on end-of life care.

With **active euthanasia** and **physician-assisted suicide,** physicians move beyond **passive euthanasia** (withdrawing treatments) to actively take steps that promote the death of seriously ill people who want to end their lives. Paramount among the objections to legalizing active euthanasia is the idea that we may be opening the door to killing people who don't really want to die.

A related issue is **age-based rationing of care,** whether to hold off on using expensive death-defying technologies with people who are in their old-old years. At this moment, age-based rationing of care is poised to move center stage in the United States and other Western nations, as the cost of providing end-of-life care to hordes of frail elderly balloons. The timeless message of this chapter—and the book—is that love (or, in developmental science terminology, our attachments) is at the core of human life.

KEY TERMS

thanatology, p. 457
Kübler-Ross's stage theory of dying, p. 458
middle knowledge, p. 460
dying trajectory, p. 465
palliative care, p. 467
end-of-life care instruction, p. 467
palliative-care service, p. 467
hospice movement, p. 468
advance directive, p. 472
living will, p. 472
durable power of attorney for health care, p. 472
Do Not Resuscitate (DNR) order, p. 472
Do Not Hospitalize (DNH) order, p. 472
passive euthanasia, p. 474
active euthanasia, p. 474
physician-assisted suicide, p. 475
age-based rationing of care, p. 475

ANSWERS TO TYING IT ALL TOGETHER QUIZZES

Setting the Context

1. b
2. slowly and erratically; an age-related chronic disease
3. Ella's case: Today, we openly discuss dying with seriously ill patients and try to get everyone to document their wishes for a dignified death. We also routinely offer death education classes and make active efforts to think about how to take good care of the terminally ill. Margaret's case: We still are disconnected from—and frightened about—the physical reality of death. Our euphemisms for death, like "passing away," clearly show that we still live in a death-denying culture.

The Dying Person

1. c
2. many different emotions; hope
3. an 80-year-old woman
4. Use your creativity here. My suggestions: provide counselors on call 24/7 so that terminally ill people on the units can express their fears and concerns. At entry to the hospital, ask seriously ill patients "what exactly do you want in terms of care?" and make sure that their preferences—with regard to family visits, pain control, and everything else—are fulfilled by the staff.

The Health-Care System

1. Although medical personnel set up predictions about how patients are likely to die, death doesn't always go according to schedule—so these prognostications are often wrong!
2. b
3. Sara's case: We now routinely provide death education courses to health professionals and, increasingly, have established hospital-based palliative-care services. Martha's case: We need far more education in end-of-life care. Most people, even in the developed world, don't have access to palliative services. Moreover, traditional medicine is cure-oriented, making it difficult to shift to palliative care.
4. b
5. Here's what you might say to Melanie: Would you feel comfortable about burdening your family 24/7 with the job of nursing you for months or having them manage the health crises that would occur? How would you feel having loved ones see you naked and incontinent—would you want that to be their last memory of you? Wouldn't it be better to be in a setting where trained professionals could manage your physical pain?
6. a

The Dying Person: Taking Control of How We Die

1. b
2. Jamal's case: We are free to make decisions about how to live our lives, so it doesn't make logical sense that we can't decide when our lives should end. Plus, it's cruel to torture fatally ill people, forcing them to suffer fruitless, unwanted pain when we can easily provide a merciful death. Latoya's argument: I'm worried that greedy relatives might pressure ill people into deciding to die "for the good of the family" (that is, to save the family money). I believe that legalizing physician-assisted suicide leaves the door open to society deciding to kill people when *we think* the quality of their life is not good. Furthermore, only God can take a life!
3. Here your answers may vary in interesting ways. Enjoy the discussion!

Final Thoughts

We are done! When I finish a book, I get to RELAX. But I also get to step back and reflect on what I've learned. What stands out from my survey of the science? Can I target specific, good-news messages and lifespan issues that need special work? Here—accompanied by advice—are my personal top five themes.

Theme 1: We evolve as we age (and are evolving as a species!).

I've always wanted to tell my classes that, yes, people do grow emotionally during adult life. But, until recently, developmental scientists haven't had research to back up that claim. Now, we do. Recall from Chapters 12 and 13 that many studies suggest we do tend to get better—happier, more positive, more "in control," and wiser—with age, especially into the sixties. Just as important, we now have a good grasp on the qualities most apt to make for personal growth: living in a generative society, being open to experience, having prosocial priorities, and experiencing a medium amount of stress. Take this positive message about your future development to heart. And keep in mind the remarkable Flynn effect. The steady cohort-by-cohort rise in IQ reasoning abilities shows that, due to nurture (or advances in society), human "nature" has been changing in a very positive way!

Theme 2: Pay attention to families at the starting point of life.

This does not mean that everything is rosy. A second, striking research message is that the roots of our adult pathway emerge astonishingly early in life. From the fetal programming findings, to the fact that weight gain during infancy predicts adult obesity, to the impact of early childhood poverty on high school graduation rates, events before birth and during our earliest years affect later development in far-ranging ways. Now, combine these data with the reality that infants and toddlers are the poorest segment of the U.S. population and that life stress is common among mothers-to-be (see Chapters 2 and 4). Recall how hard it can be for parents to pay for day care, get decently paying jobs, and balance family and work (see Chapters 10 and 11). Can the United States do a better job, for the sake of the next generation, to better support young families and parents-to-be?

Theme 3: Smooth the transition from childhood to adult life.

As today the time from puberty to "full adulthood" is such an extended, unstructured, fuzzy stage, these coming-of-age decades need more attention, too. At puberty, it is tempting for many parents (and society) to disengage. The rise in depression and negative popularity pressures spelled out in Chapter 9 suggest that pre-teens need *more* adult guidance, not less. Let's focus the gateway to adolescence to when puberty is in full bloom, social sensitivities can be acute, and young people are vulnerable to getting on the wrong path. Let's understand that, while most contemporary teens are doing incredibly well, some risk-taking is normal during adolescence. Let's not overreact by punishing 15-, 16-, or 17-year-olds as if they were adults (thereby undercutting young people's ability to succeed in life). And, above all, let's have society genuinely prioritize launching twenty-somethings into the work world so that—even in hard economic times—a whole cohort of young people do not lose the potential for an optimally productive, economically secure adult life. . Bottom line: The watershed time, from the preteens through emerging adulthood, could benefit from a better person–environment fit.

THEME 4: Society needs to look old age in the eye.

We also need to face the facts about life's final stage. The good news is that more of us are living close to the limits of human life. The bad news is that the baby boomers are reaching their later years less healthy and that disabilities are often the price of living to our eighties and beyond (see Chapter 14). From making the driving environment more user-friendly to constructing communities that don't depend on cars, we need to redesign the world specifically to make it more user-friendly for people with physical frailties. Today, housing for people with less-intense ADL impairments, such as continuing-care communities, are only available to affluent older adults. I believe that we can devise creative living alternatives—such as intergenerational housing, which is less costly—and put off the need for a nursing home. And here, we don't have time to spare. Can we put these structures in place before the very-old age boom hits full force about a decade from now?

THEME 5: Underneath all its complexity, human behavior is simple!

Throughout this book, I've been spelling out the complex forces that shape development. But, amidst the diversity, three core values run through this book. When developmentalists use the terms "executive functions," or "emotion regulation," or "postformal thought" (or even "theory of mind"), they really are saying the key to living successfully is being able to step back and reflect on our own and others' actions and emotions. When we boil down terms like "identity" or "industry" or "self-efficacy," we are referring to our human need to feel competent and productive in our lives. And whether we use the words "prosocial behavior," "generativity," or "attachment," our third fundamental need is to be connected to others in a nurturing way. All of this takes us back to that twentieth-century genius who jump-started our field: Sigmund Freud himself summed up mental health as self-understanding, work, and love!

As you have read this book, what top five themes stood out for you?

Glossary

A

accommodation: In Piaget's theory, enlarging our mental capacities to fit input from the wider world.

acculturation: Among immigrants, the tendency to become more similar in terms of attitudes and practices to the mainstream culture after time spent living in a new society.

achievement tests: Measures that evaluate a child's knowledge in specific school-related areas.

active euthanasia: A deliberate health care intervention that helps a patient die.

active forces: The nature-interacts-with-nurture principle that our genetic temperamental tendencies and predispositions cause us to actively choose to put ourselves into specific environments.

ADL (activities of daily living) problems: Difficulty in performing everyday tasks that are required for living independently. ADLs are classified as either basic or instrumental.

adolescence-limited turmoil: Antisocial behavior that, for most teens, is specific to adolescence and does not persist into adult life.

adolescent egocentrism: David Elkind's term for the tendency of young teenagers to feel that their actions are at the center of everyone else's consciousness.

adoption study: Behavioral genetic research strategy, designed to determine the genetic contribution to a given trait, that involves comparing adopted children with their biological and adoptive parents.

adrenal androgens: Hormones produced by the adrenal glands that program various aspects of puberty, such as growth of body hair, skin changes, and sexual desire.

adult attachment styles: The different ways in which adults relate to romantic partners, based on Mary Ainsworth's infant attachment styles. (Adult attachment styles are classified as secure, or preoccupied/ambivalent insecure, or avoidant/dismissive insecure.)

adult development: The scientific study of the adult part of life.

advance directive: Any written document spelling out instructions with regard to life-prolonging treatment if individuals become irretrievably ill and cannot communicate their wishes.

age-based rationing of care: The controversial idea that society should not use expensive life-sustaining technologies on people in their old-old years.

age discrimination: Illegally laying off workers or failing to hire or promote them on the basis of age.

age norms: Cultural ideas about the appropriate ages for engaging in particular activities or life tasks.

age of viability: The earliest point at which a baby can survive outside the womb.

aggression: Any hostile or destructive act.

alternatives to institutionalization: Services and settings designed to keep older people who are experiencing age-related disabilities that don't merit intense 24-hour care from entering nursing homes.

altruism: Prosocial behaviors that are carried out for selfless, non-egocentric reasons.

Alzheimer's disease: A type of age-related dementia characterized by neural atrophy and abnormal by-products of that atrophy, such as senile plaques and neurofibrillary tangles.

amniocentesis: A second-trimester procedure that involves inserting a syringe into a woman's uterus to extract a sample of amniotic fluid, which is tested for a variety of genetic and chromosomal conditions.

amniotic sac: A bag-shaped, fluid-filled membrane that contains and insulates the fetus.

analytic intelligence: In Robert Sternberg's framework on successful intelligence, the facet of intelligence involving performing well on academic-type problems.

animism: In Piaget's theory, the preoperational child's belief that inanimate objects are alive.

anorexia nervosa: A potentially life-threatening eating disorder characterized by pathological dieting (resulting in severe weight loss and, in females, loss of menstruation) and by a distorted body image.

A-not-B error: In Piaget's framework, a classic mistake made by infants in the sensorimotor stage, whereby babies approaching age 1 go back to the original hiding place to look for an object even though they have seen it get hidden in a second place.

anxious-ambivalent attachment: An insecure attachment style characterized by a child's intense distress when reunited with a primary caregiver after separation.

Apgar scale: A quick test used to assess a just-delivered baby's condition by measuring heart rate, muscle tone, respiration, reflex response, and color.

artificialism: In Piaget's theory, the preoperational child's belief that human beings make everything in nature.

assimilation: In Jean Piaget's theory, the first step promoting mental growth, involving fitting environmental input to our existing mental capacities.

assisted-living facility: A housing option providing care for elderly people who have instrumental ADL impairments and can no longer live independently but may not need a nursing home.

assisted reproductive technology (ART): Any infertility treatment in which the egg is fertilized outside the womb.

attachment in the making: Second phase of Bowlby's attachment sequence, when, from 4 to 7 months of age, babies slightly prefer the primary caregiver.

attachment: The powerful bond of love between a caregiver and child (or between any two individuals).

attachment theory: Theory formulated by John Bowlby centering on the crucial importance to our species' survival of being closely connected with a caregiver during early childhood and being attached to a significant other during all of life.

attention deficit/hyperactivity disorder (ADHD): The most common childhood learning disorder in the United States, disproportionately affecting boys, characterized by excessive restlessness and distractibility at home and at school.

authoritarian parents: In the parenting-styles framework, a type of child-rearing in which parents provide plenty of rules but rank low on child-centeredness, stressing unquestioning obedience.

authoritative parents: In the parenting-styles framework, the best possible child-rearing style, in which parents rank high on both nurturance and discipline, providing both love and clear family rules.

autobiographical memories: Recollections of events and experiences that make up one's life history.

autonomy: Erikson's second psychosocial task, when toddlers confront the challenge of understanding that they are separate individuals.

average life expectancy: A person's fifty-fifty chance at birth of living to a given age.

avoidant attachment: An insecure attachment style characterized by a child's indifference to a primary caregiver at being reunited after separation.

avoidant/dismissive insecure attachment: A standoffish, excessively disengaged style of relating to loved ones.

axon: A long nerve fiber that usually conducts impulses away from the cell body of a neuron.

B

babbling: The alternating vowel and consonant sounds that babies repeat with variations of intonation and pitch and that precede the first words.

baby boom cohort: The huge age group born between 1946 and 1964.

baby-proofing: Making the home safe for a newly mobile infant.

basic ADL problems: Difficulty in performing essential self-care activities, such as rising from a chair, eating, and getting to the toilet.

behavioral genetics: Field devoted to scientifically determining the role that hereditary forces play in determining individual differences in behavior.

bidirectionality: The crucial principle that people affect one another, or that interpersonal influences flow in both directions.

Big Five: Five core psychological predispositions—neuroticism, extraversion, openness to experience, conscientiousness, and agreeableness—that underlie personality.

biracial or multiracial identity: How people of mixed racial backgrounds come to terms with who they are as people in relation to their heritage.

birth defect: A physical or neurological problem that occurs prenatally or at birth.

blastocyst: The hollow sphere of cells formed during the germinal stage in preparation for implantation.

body mass index (BMI): The ratio of weight to height; the main indicator of overweight or underweight.

boundaryless career: Today's most common career path for Western workers, in which people change jobs or professions periodically during their working lives.

breadwinner role: Traditional concept that a husband's job is to support a wife and children.

bulimia nervosa: An eating disorder characterized by at least biweekly cycles of binging and purging (by inducing vomiting or taking laxatives) in an obsessive attempt to lose weight.

bullying: A situation in which one or more children (or adults) harass or target a specific child for systematic abuse.

bully-victims: Exceptionally aggressive children (with externalizing disorders) who repeatedly bully and get victimized.

C

caregiving grandparents: Grandparents who have taken on full responsibility for raising their grandchildren.

centering: In Piaget's conservation tasks, the preoperational child's tendency to fix on the most visually striking feature of a substance and not take other dimensions into account.

cephalocaudal sequence: The developmental principle that growth occurs in a sequence from head to toe.

cerebral cortex: The outer, folded mantle of the brain, responsible for thinking, reasoning, perceiving, and all conscious responses.

certified nurse assistant or aide: The main hands-on care provider in a nursing home who helps elderly residents with basic ADL problems.

cervix: The neck, or narrow lower portion, of the uterus.

cesarean section (c-section): A method of delivering a baby surgically by extracting the baby through incisions in the woman's abdominal wall and in the uterus.

child development: The scientific study of development from birth through adolescence.

childhood obesity: A body mass index at or above the 95th percentile compared to the U.S. norms established for children in the 1970s.

child maltreatment: Any act that seriously endangers a child's physical or emotional well-being.

chorionic villus sampling (CVS): A relatively risky first-trimester pregnancy test for fetal genetic disorders.

chromosome: A threadlike strand of DNA located in the nucleus of every cell that carries the genes, which transmit hereditary information.

chronic disease: Any long-term illness that requires ongoing management. Most chronic diseases are age-related and are the endpoint of normal aging changes.

circular reactions: In Piaget's framework, repetitive action-oriented schemas (or habits) characteristic of babies during the sensorimotor stage.

class inclusion: The understanding that a general category can encompass several subordinate elements.

clear-cut attachment: Critical human attachment phase, from 7 months through toddlerhood, defined by separation anxiety, stranger anxiety, and needing a primary caregiver close.

clique: A small peer group composed of roughly six teenagers who have similar attitudes and who share activities.

cognitive behaviorism (social learning theory): A behavioral worldview that emphasizes that people learn by watching others and that our thoughts about the reinforcers determine our behavior. Cognitive behaviorists focus on charting and modifying people's thoughts.

cohabitation: Sharing a household in an unmarried romantic relationship.

cohort: The age group with whom we travel through life.

colic: A baby's frantic, continual crying during the first three months of life; caused by an immature nervous system.

collaborative pretend play: Fantasy play in which children work together to develop and act out the scenes.

collectivist cultures: Societies that prize social harmony, obedience, and close family connectedness over individual achievement.

commitment script: In Dan McAdams's research, a type of autobiography produced by highly generative adults that involves childhood memories of feeling special; being unusually sensitive to others' misfortunes; having a strong, enduring generative mission from adolescence; and redemption sequences.

concrete operational thinking: In Piaget's framework, the type of cognition characteristic of children aged 8 to 11, marked by the ability to reason about the world in a more logical, adult way.

conservation tasks: Piagetian tasks that involve changing the shape of a substance to see whether children can go beyond the way that substance visually appears to understand that the amount is still the same.

consummate love: In Robert Sternberg's triangular theory of love, the ideal form of love, in which a couple's relationship involves all three of the major facets of love: passion, intimacy, and commitment.

contexts of development: Fundamental markers, including cohort, socioeconomic status, culture, and gender, that shape how we develop throughout the lifespan.

continuing bonds: A widowed person's ongoing sense of the deceased spouse's presence "in spirit."

continuing-care retirement community: A housing option characterized by a series of levels of care for elderly residents, ranging from independent apartments to assisted living to nursing home care. People enter the community in relatively good health and move to sections where they can get more care when they become disabled.

conventional level of morality: In Lawrence Kohlberg's theory, the intermediate level of moral reasoning, in which people respond to ethical issues by considering the need to uphold social norms.

corporal punishment: The use of physical force to discipline a child.

correlational study: A research strategy that involves relating two or more variables.

co-sleeping: The standard custom, in collectivist cultures, of having a child and parent share a bed.

creative intelligence: In Robert Sternberg's framework on successful intelligence, the facet of intelligence involved in producing novel ideas or innovative work.

cross-sectional study: A developmental research strategy that involves testing different age groups at the same time.

crowd: A relatively large teenage peer group.

crystallized intelligence: A basic facet of intelligence, consisting of a person's knowledge base, or storehouse of accumulated information.

D

day-care center: A day-care arrangement in which a large number of children are cared for at a licensed facility by paid providers.

day-care program: A service for impaired older adults who live with relatives, in which the older person spends the day at a center offering various activities.

decentering: In Piaget's conservation tasks, the concrete operational child's ability to look at several dimensions of an object or substance.

deinstitutionalization of marriage: The decline in marriage and the emergence of alternate family forms that occurred during the last third of the twentieth century.

demand–withdrawal interaction: A pathological type of communication in which one partner, most often the woman, presses for more intimacy and the other person, most often the man, tends to back off.

dementia: The general term for any illness that produces serious, progressive, usually irreversible cognitive decline.

dendrite: A branching fiber that receives information and conducts impulses toward the cell body of a neuron.

depth perception: The ability to see (and fear) heights.

developed world: The most affluent countries in the world.

developing world: The more impoverished countries of the world.

developmentalists: Researchers and practitioners whose professional interest lies in the study of the human lifespan.

developmental systems perspective: An all-encompassing outlook on development that stresses the need to embrace a variety of theories, and the idea that all systems and processes interrelate.

deviancy training: Socialization of a young teenager into delinquency through conversations centered on performing antisocial acts.

disorganized attachment: An insecure attachment style characterized by responses such as freezing or fear when a child is reunited with the primary caregiver in the Strange Situation.

dividend-attention task: A difficult memory challenge involving memorizing material while simultaneously monitoring something else.

DNA (deoxyribonucleic acid): The material that makes up genes, which bear our hereditary characteristics.

Do Not Hospitalize (DNH) order: A type of advance directive put into the charts of impaired nursing home residents, specifying that in a medical crisis they should not be transferred to a hospital for emergency care.

Do Not Resuscitate (DNR) order: A type of advance directive filled out by surrogates (usually a doctor in consultation with family members) for impaired individuals, specifying that if they go into cardiac arrest, efforts should not be made to revive them.

dominant disorder: An illness that a child gets by inheriting one copy of the abnormal gene that causes the disorder.

Down syndrome: The most common chromosomal abnormality, causing mental retardation, susceptibility to heart disease, and other health problems; and distinctive physical characteristics, such as slanted eyes and stocky build.

durable power of attorney for health care: A type of advance directive in which people designate a specific surrogate to make health-care decisions if they become incapacitated and are unable to make their wishes known.

dying trajectory: The fact that hospital personnel make projections about the particular pathway to death that a seriously ill patient will take and organize their care according to that assumption.

dyslexia: A learning disability that is characterized by reading difficulties, lack of fluency, and poor word recognition that is often genetic in origin.

E

early childhood: The first phase of childhood, lasting from age 3 through kindergarten, or about age 5.

Early Head Start: A federal program that provides counseling and other services to low-income parents and children under age 3.

eating disorder: A pathological obsession with getting and staying thin. The two best-known eating disorders are anorexia nervosa and bulimia nervosa.

egocentrism: In Piaget's theory, the preoperational child's inability to understand that other people have different points of view from his or her own.

elderspeak: A style of communication used with an older person who seems to be physically impaired, involving speaking loudly and with slow, exaggerated pronunciation, as if talking to a baby.

embryonic stage: The second stage of prenatal development, lasting from week 3 through week 8.

emerging adulthood: The phase of life that begins after high school, tapers off toward the late twenties, and is devoted to constructing an adult life.

emotion regulation: The capacity to manage one's emotional state.

empathy: Feeling the exact emotion that another person is experiencing.

end-of-life care instruction: Courses in medical and nursing schools devoted to teaching health-care workers how to provide the best palliative care to the dying.

episodic memory: In the memory-systems perspective, the most fragile type of memory, involving the recall of the ongoing events of daily life.

Erikson's psychosocial tasks: In Erik Erikson's theory, each challenge that we face as we travel through the eight stages of the lifespan.

ethnic identity: How people come to terms with who they are as people relating to their unique ethnic or racial heritage.

eudaimonic happiness: Well-being defined as having a sense of meaning and life purpose.

evocative forces: The nature-interacts-with-nurture principle that our genetic temperamental tendencies and predispositions evoke, or produce, certain responses from other people.

evolutionary psychology: Theory or worldview highlighting the role that inborn, species-specific behaviors play in human development and life.

executive functions: Any frontal-lobe ability that allows us to inhibit our responses and to plan and direct our thinking.

experience-sampling technique: A research procedure designed to capture moment-to-moment experiences by having people carry pagers and take notes describing their activities and emotions whenever the signal sounds.

externalizing tendencies: A personality style that involves acting on one's immediate impulses and behaving disruptively and aggressively.

extrinsic career rewards: Work that is performed for external reinforcers, such as pay.

extrinsic motivation: The drive to take an action because that activity offers external reinforcers such as praise, money, or a good grade.

F

face-perception studies: Research using preferential looking and habituation to explore what very young babies know about faces.

fallopian tube: One of a pair of slim, pipe-like structures that connect the ovaries with the uterus.

family day care: A day-care arrangement in which a neighbor or relative cares for a small number of children in her home for a fee.

family watchdogs: A basic role of grandparents, which involves monitoring the younger family member's well-being and intervening to provide help in a crisis.

family–work conflict: A situation in which people—typically parents—are torn between the demands of family and work.

fantasy play: Play that involves making up and acting out a scenario; also called pretend play.

fertility rate: The average number of children a woman in a given country has during her lifetime.

fertilization: The union of sperm and egg.

fetal alcohol syndrome (FAS): A cluster of birth defects caused by the mother's alcohol consumption during pregnancy.

fetal programming research: New research discipline exploring the impact of traumatic pregnancy events and intense stress on producing low birth weight, obesity, and long-term physical problems.

fetal stage: The final period of prenatal development, lasting seven months, characterized by physical refinements, massive growth, and the development of the brain.

fine motor skills: Physical abilities that involve small, coordinated movements, such as drawing and writing one's name.

flow: Csikszentmihalyi's term for feeling total absorption in a challenging, goal-oriented activity.

Fluid Intelligence: A basic facet of intelligence, consisting of the ability to quickly master new intellectual activities.

Flynn effect: Remarkable and steady rise in overall performance on IQ tests that has been occurring around the world over the past century.

food insecurity: According to U.S Department of Agriculture surveys, the number of households that report needing to serve unbalanced meals, worrying about not having enough food at the end of the month, or having to go hungry due to lack of money (latter is severe food insecurity).

formal operational stage: Jean Piaget's fourth and final stage of cognitive development, reached at around age 12 and characterized by teenagers' ability to reason at an abstract, scientific level.

frontal lobes: The area at the uppermost front of the brain, responsible for reasoning and planning our actions.

G

"g": Charles Spearman's term for a general intelligence factor that he claimed underlies all cognitive activities.

gang: A close-knit, delinquent peer group. Gangs form mainly under conditions of economic deprivation; they offer their members protection from harm and engage in a variety of criminal activities.

gender schema theory: Explanation for gender-stereotyped behavior that emphasizes the role of cognitions; specifically, the idea that once children know their own gender label (girl or boy), they selectively watch and model their own sex.

gender-segregated play: Play in which boys and girls associate only with members of their own sex—typical of childhood.

gene: A segment of DNA that contains a chemical blueprint for manufacturing a particular protein.

generativity: In Erikson's theory, the seventh psychosocial task, in which people in midlife find meaning from nurturing the next generation, caring for others, or enriching the lives of others through their work. According to Erikson, when midlife adults have not achieved generativity, they feel stagnant, without a sense of purpose in life.

genetic counselor: A professional who counsels parents-to-be about their own or their children's risk of developing genetic disorders, as well as about available treatments.

genetic testing: A blood test to determine whether a person carries the gene for a given genetic disorder.

germinal stage: The first 14 days of prenatal development, from fertilization to full implantation.

gerontology: The scientific study of the aging process and older adults.

gestation: The period of pregnancy.

gifted: The label for superior intellectual functioning characterized by an IQ score of 130 or above, showing that a child ranks in the top 2 percent of his age group.

gonads: The sex organs—the ovaries in girls and the testes in boys.

goodness of fit: An ideal parenting strategy that involves arranging children's environments to suit their temperaments, minimizing their vulnerabilities and accentuating their strengths.

grammar: The rules and word-arranging systems that every human language employs to communicate meaning.

Great Recession of 2008: Dramatic loss of jobs (and consumer spending) that began with the bursting of the U.S. housing bubble in late 2007.

gross motor skills: Physical abilities that involve large muscle movements, such as running and jumping.

growth spurt: A dramatic increase in height and weight that occurs during puberty.

guilt: Feeling upset about having caused harm to a person or about having violated one's internal standard of behavior.

H

habituation: The predictable loss of interest that develops once a stimulus becomes familiar; used to explore infant sensory capacities and thinking.

Head Start: A federal program offering high-quality day care at a center and other services to help preschoolers aged 3 to 5 from low-income families prepare for school.

hedonic happiness: Well-being defined as pure pleasure.

holophrase: First clear evidence of language, when babies use a single word to communicate a sentence or complete thought.

home health services: Nursing-oriented and housekeeping help provided in the home of an impaired older adult (or any other impaired person).

homogamy: The principle that we select a mate who is similar to us.

homophobia: Intense fear and dislike of gays and lesbians.

hormones: Chemical substances released in the bloodstream that target and change organs and tissues.

hospice movement: A movement, which became widespread in recent decades, focused on providing palliative care to dying patients outside of hospitals and especially on giving families the support they need to care for the terminally ill at home.

hostile attributional bias: The tendency of highly aggressive children to see motives and actions as threatening when they are actually benign.

HPG axis: The main hormonal system programming puberty; it involves a triggering hypothalamic hormone that causes the pituitary to secrete its hormones, which in turn cause the ovaries and testes to develop and secrete the hormones that produce the major body changes.

I

identity achievement: An identity status in which the person decides on a definite adult life path after searching out various options.

identity constancy: In Piaget's theory, the preoperational child's inability to grasp that a person's core "self" stays the same despite changes in external appearance.

identity: In Erikson's theory, the life task of deciding who to be as a person in making the transition to adulthood.

identity diffusion: An identity status in which the person is aimless or feels totally blocked, without any adult life path.

identity foreclosure: An identity status in which the person decides on an adult life path (often one spelled out by an authority figure) without any thought or active search.

identity statuses: Marcia's four categories of identity formation: identity diffusion, identity foreclosure, moratorium, and identity achievement.

imaginary audience: David Elkind's term for the tendency of young teenagers to feel that everyone is watching their every action; a component of adolescent egocentrism.

immigrant paradox: The fact that despite living in poverty, going to substandard schools, and not having parents who speak the language, many immigrant children do far better than we might expect at school.

implantation: The process in which a blastocyst becomes embedded in the uterine wall.

income inequality: The gap between the rich and poor within a nation. Specifically, when income inequality is wide, a nation has a few very affluent residents and a mass of disadvantaged citizens.

individualistic cultures: Societies that prize independence, competition, and personal success.

induction: The ideal discipline style for socializing prosocial behavior, involving getting a child who has behaved hurtfully to empathize with the pain he has caused the other person.

industry versus inferiority: Erik Erikson's term for the psychosocial task of middle childhood involving managing our emotions and realizing that real-world success involves hard work.

infant-directed speech (IDS): The simplified, exaggerated, high-pitched tones that adults and children use to speak to infants that function to help teach language.

infant mortality: Death during the first year of life.

infertility: The inability to conceive after a year of unprotected sex. (Includes the inability to carry a child to term.)

information-processing approach: A perspective on understanding cognition that divides thinking into specific steps and component processes, much like a computer.

initiative versus guilt: Erik Erikson's term for the preschool psychosocial task involving actively taking on life tasks.

inner speech: In Vygotsky's theory, the way by which human beings learn to regulate their behavior and master cognitive challenges, through silently repeating information or talking to themselves.

insecure attachment: Deviation from the normally joyful response of being united with a primary caregiver, signaling problems in the caregiver-child relationship.

instrumental ADL problems: Difficulties in performing everyday household tasks, such as cooking and cleaning.

instrumental aggression: A hostile or destructive act initiated to achieve a goal.

integrity: Erik Erikson's eighth psychosocial stage, in which elderly people decide that their life missions have been fulfilled and so accept impending death.

intergenerational equity: Balancing the needs of the young and old. Specifically, often referred to as the idea that U.S. government entitlements, such as Medicare and Social Security, "over-benefit" the elderly at the expense of other age groups.

internalizing tendencies: A personality style that involves intense fear, social inhibition, and often depression.

intimacy: Erikson's first adult task, involving connecting with a partner in a mutual loving relationship.

intrinsic career rewards: Work that provides inner fulfillment and allows people to satisfy their needs for creativity, autonomy, and relatedness.

intrinsic motivation: The drive to act based on the pleasure of taking that action in itself, not for an external reinforcer or reward.

in vitro fertilization: An infertility treatment in which conception occurs outside the womb; the developing cell mass is then inserted into the woman's uterus so that pregnancy can occur.

J

joint attention: The first sign of "getting human intentions," when a baby looks at an object an adult is pointing to or follows a person's gaze.

K

kangaroo care: Carrying a young baby in a sling close to the caregiver's body. This technique is useful for soothing an infant.

Kübler-Ross's stage theory of dying: The landmark theory, developed by psychiatrist Elisabeth Kübler-Ross, that people who are terminally ill progress through five stages in confronting their death: denial, anger, bargaining, depression, and acceptance.

L

language acquisition device (LAD): Chomsky's term for a hypothetical brain structure that enables our species to learn and produce language.

learned helplessness: A state that develops when a person feels incapable of affecting the outcome of events, and so gives up without trying.

lens: A transparent, disk-shaped structure in the eye, which bends to allow us to see close objects.

life-course difficulties: Antisocial behavior that, for a fraction of adolescents, persists into adult life.

lifespan development: The scientific field covering all of the human lifespan.

little-scientist phase: The time around age 1 when babies use tertiary circular reactions to actively explore the properties of objects, experimenting with them like "scientists."

living will: A type of advance directive in which people spell out their wishes for life-sustaining treatment in case they become permanently incapacitated and unable to communicate.

longitudinal study: A developmental research strategy that involves testing an age group repeatedly over many years.

low birth weight (LBW): A body weight at birth of less than 5 1/2 pounds.

M

marital equity: Fairness in the "work" of a couple's life together. If a relationship lacks equity, with one partner doing significantly more than the other, the outcome is typically marital dissatisfaction.

mass-to-specific sequence: The developmental principle that large structures (and movements) precede increasingly detailed refinements.

maximum lifespan: The biological limit of human life (about 105 years).

mean length of utterance (MLU): The average number of morphemes per sentence.

means–end behavior: In Piaget's framework, performing a different action to get to a goal—an ability that emerges in the sensorimotor stage as babies approach age 1.

median age: The age at which 50 percent of a population is older and 50 percent is younger.

Medicare: The U.S. government's program of health insurance for elderly people.

memory-systems perspective: A framework that divides memory into three types: procedural, semantic, and episodic memory.

menarche: A girl's first menstruation.

menopause: The age-related process, occurring at about age 50, in which ovulation and menstruation stop due to the declining of estrogen.

mentally retarded: The label for significantly impaired intellectual functioning, defined as when a child (or adult) has an IQ of 70 or below accompanied by evidence of deficits in learning abilities.

micronutrient deficiency: Chronically inadequate level of a specific nutrient important to development and disease prevention, such as Vitamin A, zinc, and/or iron.

middle childhood: The second phase of childhood, covering the elementary school years, from about age 6 to 11.

middle knowledge: The idea that terminally ill people can know that they are dying yet at the same time not completely grasp or come to terms emotionally with that fact.

miscarriage: The naturally occurring loss of a pregnancy and death of the fetus.

mnemonic technique: A strategy for aiding memory, often by using imagery or enhancing the emotional meaning of what needs to be learned.

modeling: Learning by watching and imitating others.

moratorium: An identity status in which the person actively searches out various possibilities to find a truly solid adult life path. A mature style of constructing an identity.

moratorium in depth: A focused real-world look at one's chosen career to confirm that decision.

morpheme: The smallest unit of meaning in a particular language—for example, "boys" contains two morphemes: boy and the plural suffix s.

multiple intelligences theory: In Howard Gardner's perspective on intelligence, the principle that there are eight separate kinds of intelligence—verbal, mathematical, interpersonal, intrapersonal, spatial, musical, kinesthetic, naturalist—plus a possible ninth form, called spiritual intelligence.

myelination: Formation of a fatty layer encasing the axons of neurons. This process, which speeds the transmission of neural impulses, continues from birth to early adulthood.

N

natural childbirth: A general term for labor and birth without medical interventions.

naturalistic observation: A measurement strategy that involves directly watching and coding behaviors.

nature: Biological or genetic causes of development.

neonatal intensive care unit (NICU): A special hospital unit that treats at-risk newborns, such as low-birth-weight and very-low-birth-weight babies.

nest-leaving: Moving out of a childhood home and living independently.

neural tube: A cylindrical structure that forms along the back of the embryo and develops into the brain and spinal cord.

neurofibrillary tangles: Long, wavy filaments that replace normal neurons and are characteristic of Alzheimer's disease.

neuron: A nerve cell.

non-normative transitions: Unpredictable or atypical life changes that occur during development.

nonsuicidal self-injury: Cutting, burning, or purposely injuring one's body to cope with stress.

normal aging changes: The universal, often progressive signs of physical deterioration intrinsic to the aging process.

normative transitions: Predictable life changes that occur during development.

nursing home/long-term-care facility: A residential institution that provides shelter and intensive caregiving, primarily to older people who need help with basic ADLs.

nurture: Environmental causes of development.

O

object permanence: In Piaget's framework, the understanding that objects continue to exist even when we can no longer see them, which gradually emerges during the sensorimotor stage.

occupational segregation: The separation of men and women into different kinds of jobs.

off time: Being too late or too early in a culture's timetable for achieving adult life tasks.

old-age dependency ratio: The fraction of people over age 60 to younger, working-age adults (ages 15 to 59). This ratio is expected to rise dramatically as the baby boomers retire.

old-old: People age 80 and older.

on time: Being on target in a culture's timetable for achieving adult life tasks.

operant conditioning: According to the traditional behavioral perspective, the law of learning that determines any voluntary response. Specifically, we act the way we do because we are reinforced for acting in that way.

osteoporosis: An age-related chronic disease in which the bones become porous, fragile, and more likely to break. Osteoporosis is most common in thin women and so most common in females of European and Asian descent.

ovary: One of a pair of almond-shaped organs that contain a woman's ova, or eggs.

overextension: An error in early language development in which young children apply verbal labels too broadly.

overregularization: An error in early language development, in which young children apply the rules for plurals and past tenses even to exceptions, so irregular forms sound like regular forms.

ovulation: The moment during a woman's monthly cycle when an ovum is expelled from the ovary.

ovum: An egg cell containing the genetic material contributed by the mother to the baby.

P

palliative care: Any intervention designed not to cure illness but to promote dignified dying.

palliative-care service: A service or unit in a hospital that is devoted to end-of-life care.

parent care: Adult children's care for their disabled elderly parents.

parenting style: In Diana Baumrind's framework, how parents align on two dimensions of child-rearing: nurturance (or child-centeredness) and discipline (or structure and rules).

passive euthanasia: Withholding potentially life-saving interventions that might keep a terminally ill or permanently comatose patient alive.

permissive parents: In the parenting-styles framework, a type of child-rearing in which parents provide few rules but rank high on child-centeredness, being extremely loving but providing little discipline.

person–environment fit: The extent to which the environment is tailored to our biological tendencies and talents. In developmental science, fostering this fit between our talents and the wider world is an important goal.

personal fable: David Elkind's term for the tendency of young teenagers to believe that their lives are special and heroic; a component of adolescent egocentrism.

phoneme: The sound units that convey meaning in a given language—for example, in English, the c sound of cat and the b sound of bat.

physician-assisted suicide: A type of active euthanasia in which a physician prescribes a lethal medication to a terminally ill person who wants to die.

Piaget's cognitive developmental theory: Jean Piaget's principle that from infancy to adolescence, children progress through four qualitatively different stages of intellectual growth.

placenta: The structure projecting from the wall of the uterus during pregnancy through which the developing baby absorbs nutrients.

plastic: Malleable, or capable of being changed (used to refer to neural or cognitive development).

positivity effect: The tendency for older people to focus on positive experiences and screen out negative events.

postconventional level of morality: In Lawrence Kohlberg's theory, the highest level of moral reasoning, in which people respond to ethical issues by applying their own moral guidelines apart from society's rules.

postformal thought: A uniquely adult form of intelligence that involves being sensitive to different perspectives, making decisions based on one's inner feelings, and being interested in exploring new questions.

power assertion: An ineffective socialization strategy that involves yelling, screaming, or hitting out in frustration at a child.

practical intelligence: In Robert Sternberg's framework on successful intelligence, the facet of intelligence involved in knowing how to act competently in real-world situations.

preattachment phase: The first phase of John Bowlby's developmental attachment sequence, during the first three months of life, when infants show no visible signs of attachment.

preconventional level of morality: In Lawrence Kohlberg's theory, the lowest level of moral reasoning, in which people approach ethical issues by considering the personal punishments or rewards of taking a particular action.

preferential-looking paradigm: A research technique to explore early infant sensory capacities and cognition, drawing on the principle that we are attracted to novelty and prefer to look at new things.

preoccupied/ambivalent insecure attachment: An excessively clingy, needy style of relating to loved ones.

preoperational thinking: In Piaget's theory, the type of cognition characteristic of children aged 2 to 7, marked by an inability to step back from one's immediate perceptions and think conceptually.

presbycusis: Age-related difficulty in hearing, particularly high-pitched tones, caused by the atrophy of the hearing receptors located in the inner ear.

presbyopia: Age-related midlife difficulty with near vision, caused by the inability of the lens to bend.

preschool: A teaching-oriented group setting for children aged 3 to 5.

primary attachment figure: The closest person in a child's or adult's life.

primary circular reactions: In Piaget's framework, the first infant habits during the sensorimotor stage, centered on the body.

primary sexual characteristics: Physical changes of puberty that directly involve the organs of reproduction, such as the growth of the penis and the onset of menstruation.

private pensions: The major source of nongovernmental income support for retirees, in which the individual worker and employer put a portion of each paycheck into an account to help finance retirement.

procedural memory: In the memory-systems perspective, the most resilient (longest-lasting) type of memory; refers to material, such as well-learned physical skills, that we automatically recall without conscious awareness.

prosocial behavior: Sharing, helping, and caring actions.

proximity-seeking behavior: Acting to maintain physical contact or to be close to an attachment figure.

proximodistal sequence: The developmental principle that growth occurs from the most interior parts of the body outward.

puberty: The hormonal and physical changes by which children become sexually mature human beings and reach their adult height.

puberty rite: A "coming of age" ritual, usually beginning at some event such as first menstruation, held in traditional cultures to celebrate children's transition to adulthood.

Q

qualitative research: Occasional developmental science data-collection strategy that involves interviewing people to obtain information that cannot be quantified on a numerical scale.

quantitative research: Standard developmental science data-collection strategy that involves testing groups of people and using numerical scales and statistics.

quickening: A pregnant woman's first feeling of the fetus moving inside her body.

R

reaction time: The speed at which a person can respond to a stimulus. A progressive increase in reaction time is universal to aging.

reactive aggression: A hostile or destructive act carried out in response to being frustrated or hurt.

recessive disorder: An illness that a child gets by inheriting two copies of the abnormal gene that causes the disorder.

redemption sequence: In Dan McAdams's research, a characteristic theme of highly generative adults' autobiographies, in which they describe tragic events that turned out for the best.

reflex: A response or action that is automatic and programmed by non-cortical brain centers.

rehearsal: A learning strategy in which people repeat information to embed it in memory.

reinforcement: Behavioral term for reward.

rejecting-neglecting parents: In the parenting-styles framework, the worst child-rearing approach, in which parents provide little discipline and little nurturing or love.

relational aggression: A hostile or destructive act designed to cause harm to a person's relationships.

reliability: In measurement terminology, a basic criterion of a test's accuracy that scores must be fairly similar when a person takes the test more than once.

REM sleep: The phase of sleep involving rapid eye movements, when the EEG looks almost like it does during waking. REM sleep decreases as infants mature.

representative sample: A group that reflects the characteristics of the overall population.

resilient children: Children who rebound from serious early life traumas to construct successful adult lives.

reversibility: In Piaget's conservation tasks, the concrete operational child's knowledge that a specific change in the way a given substance looks can be reversed.

role: The characteristic behavior that is expected of a person in a particular social position, such as student, parent, married person, worker, or retiree.

role conflict: A situation in which a person is torn between two or more major responsibilities—for instance, parent and worker—and cannot do either job adequately.

role confusion: Erikson's term for a failure in identity formation, marked by the lack of any sense of a future adult path.

role overload: A job situation that places so many requirements or demands on workers that it becomes impossible to do a good job.

role phase: In Murstein's theory, the final mate-selection stage, in which committed partners work out their future life together.

rooting reflex: Newborns' automatic response to a touch on the cheek, involving turning toward that location and beginning to suck.

rough-and-tumble play: Play that involves shoving, wrestling, and hitting, but in which no actual harm is intended; especially characteristic of boys.

S

scaffolding: The process of teaching new skills by entering a child's zone of proximal development and tailoring one's efforts to that person's competence level.

school-to-work transition: The change from the schooling phase of life to the work world.

Seattle Longitudinal Study: The definitive study of the effect of aging on intelligence, carried out by K. Warner Schaie, involving simultaneously conducting and comparing the results of cross-sectional and longitudinal studies carried out with a group of Seattle volunteers.

secondary circular reactions: In Piaget's framework, habits of the sensorimotor stage lasting from about 4 months of age to the baby's first birthday, centered on exploring the external world.

secondary sexual characteristics: Physical changes of puberty that are not directly involved in reproduction.

secular trend in puberty: A century-long decline in the average age at which children reach puberty in the developed world.

secure attachment: Ideal attachment response when a child responds with joy at being united with a primary caregiver; or, in adulthood, the genuine intimacy that is ideal in love relationships.

selective attention: A learning strategy in which people manage their awareness so as to attend only to what is relevant and to filter out unneeded information.

selective optimization with compensation: Paul Baltes's three principles for successful aging (and living): (1) selectively focusing on what is most important, (2) working harder to perform well in those top-ranking areas, and (3) relying on external aids to cope effectively.

self-awareness: The ability to observe our abilities and actions from an outside frame of reference and to reflect on our inner state.

self-conscious emotions: Feelings of pride, shame, or guilt, which first emerge around age 2 and show the capacity to reflect on the self.

self-efficacy: According to cognitive behaviorism, an internal belief in our competence that predicts whether we initiate activities or persist in the face of failures, and predicts the goals we set.

self-esteem: Evaluating oneself as either "good" or "bad" as a result of comparing the self to other people.

self-report strategy: A measurement strategy that involves having people report on their feelings and activities through questionnaires.

self-soothing: Children's ability, usually beginning at about 6 months of age, to put themselves back to sleep when they wake up during the night.

semantic memory: In the memory-systems perspective, a moderately resilient (long-lasting) type of memory; refers to our ability to recall basic facts.

semantics: The meaning system of a language—that is, what the words stand for.

senile plaques: Thick, bullet-like amyloid-laden structures that replace normal neurons and are characteristic of Alzheimer's disease.

sensitive period: The time when a body structure is most vulnerable to damage by a teratogen, typically when that organ or process is rapidly developing or coming "on line."

sensorimotor stage: Piaget's first stage of cognitive development, lasting from birth to age 2, when babies' agenda is to pin down the basics of physical reality.

separation anxiety: Signal of clearcut attachment when a baby gets upset as a primary caregiver departs.

seriation: The ability to put objects in order according to some principle, such as size.

sex-linked single-gene disorder: An illness, carried on the mother's X chromosome, that typically leaves the female offspring unaffected but has a fifty-fifty chance of striking each male child.

sexual double standard: A cultural code that gives men greater sexual freedom than women. Specifically, society expects males to want to have intercourse and expects females to remain virgins until they marry and to be more interested in relationships than in having sex.

shame: A feeling of being personally humiliated.

single-gene disorder: An illness caused by a single gene.

social clock: The concept that we regulate our passage through adulthood by an inner timetable that tells us which life activities are appropriate at certain ages.

social cognition: Any skill related to understanding feelings and negotiating interpersonal interactions.

social-interactionist view: An approach to language development that emphasizes its social function, specifically that babies and adults have a mutual passion to communicate.

socialization: The process by which children are taught to obey the norms of society and to behave in socially appropriate ways.

social referencing: A baby's checking back and monitoring a caregiver for cues as to how to behave while exploring; linked to clear-cut attachment.

Social Security: The U.S. government's national retirement support program.

social smile: The first real smile, occurring at about 2 months of age.

socioeconomic health gap: The disparity, found in nations around the world, between the health of the rich and poor. At every step up on the socioeconomic ladder, people survive longer and enjoy better health.

socioeconomic status (SES): A basic marker referring to status on the educational and—especially—income rungs.

socioemotional selectivity theory: A theory of aging (and the lifespan) put forth by Laura Carstensen, describing how the time we have left to live affects our priorities and social relationships. Specifically, Carstensen believes that as people reach later life, they focus on enhancing the quality of the present and place priority on spending time with their closest attachment figures.

specific learning disability: The label for any impairment in language or any deficit related to listening, thinking, speaking, reading, writing, spelling, or understanding mathematics; diagnosed when a score on an intelligence test is much higher than a child's performance on achievement tests.

spermarche: A boy's first ejaculation of live sperm.

stimulus phase: In Murstein's theory, the initial mate-selection stage, in which we make judgments about a potential partner based on external characteristics such as appearance.

stimulus-value-role theory: Murstein's mate-selection theory that suggests similar people pair up and that our path to commitment progresses through three phases (called the stimulus, value-comparison, and role phases).

"storm and stress": G. Stanley Hall's phrase for the intense moodiness, emotional sensitivity, and risk-taking tendencies that characterize the life stage he labeled adolescence.

stranger anxiety: Beginning at about 7 months of age, when a baby grows wary of people other than a primary caregiver.

Strange Situation: Mary Ainsworth's procedure to measure attachment at age 1, involving planned separations and reunions with a caregiver.

stunting: Excessively short stature in a child, caused by chronic lack of adequate nutrition.

successful intelligence: In Robert Sternberg's framework, the optimal form of cognition, involving having a good balance of analytic, creative, and practical intelligence.

sucking reflex: The automatic, spontaneous sucking movements newborns produce, especially when anything touches their lips.

sudden infant death syndrome (SIDS): The unexplained death of an apparently healthy infant, often while sleeping, during the first year of life.

swaddling: Wrapping a baby tightly in a blanket or garment. This technique is calming during early infancy.

sympathy: A state necessary for acting prosocially, involving feeling upset for a person who needs help.

synapse: The gap between the dendrites of one neuron and the axon of another, over which impulses flow.

synaptogenesis: Forming of connections between neurons at the synapses. This process, responsible for all perceptions, actions, and thoughts, is most intense during infancy and childhood but continues throughout life.

synchrony: The reciprocal aspect of the attachment relationship, with a caregiver and infant responding emotionally to each other in a sensitive, exquisitely attuned way.

syntax: The system of grammatical rules in a particular language.

T

telegraphic speech: First stage of combining words in infancy, in which a baby pares down a sentence to its essential words.

temperament: A person's characteristic, inborn style of dealing with the world.

teratogen: A substance that crosses the placenta and harms the fetus.

terminal drop: A research phenomenon in which a dramatic decline in an older person's scores on vocabulary tests and other measures of crystallized intelligence predicts having a terminal disease.

tertiary circular reactions: In Piaget's framework, "little-scientist" activities of the sensorimotor stage, beginning around age 1, involving flexibly exploring the properties of objects.

testes: Male organs that manufacture sperm.

testosterone: The hormone responsible for the maturation of the organs of reproduction and other signs of puberty in men, and for hair and skin changes during puberty and for sexual desire in both sexes.

thanatology: The study of death and dying.

theory: Any perspective explaining why people act the way they do. Theories allow us to predict behavior and also suggest how to intervene to improve behavior.

theory of mind: Children's first cognitive understanding, which appears at about age 4, that other people have different beliefs and perspectives from their own.

thin ideal: Media-driven cultural idea that females need to be abnormally thin.

toddlerhood: The important transitional stage after babyhood, from roughly 1 year to 2 1/2 years of age; defined by an intense attachment to caregivers and by an urgent need to become independent.

traditional behaviorism: The original behavioral worldview that focused on charting and modifying only "objective," visible behaviors.

traditional stable career: A career path in which people settle into their permanent life's work in their twenties and often stay with the same organization until they retire.

triangular theory of love: Robert Sternberg's categorization of love relationships into three facets: passion, intimacy, and commitment. When arranged at the points of a triangle, their combinations describe all the different kinds of adult love relationships.

trimester: One of the 3-month-long segments into which pregnancy is divided.

true experiments: The only research strategy that can determine that something causes something else;

involves randomly assigning people to different treatments and then looking at the outcome.

twentieth-century life expectancy revolution: The dramatic increase in average life expectancy that occurred during the first half of the twentieth century in the developed world.

twin/adoption study: Behavioral genetic research strategy that involves comparing the similarities of identical twin pairs adopted into different families, to determine the genetic contribution to a given trait.

twin study: Behavioral genetic research strategy, designed to determine the genetic contribution of a given trait, that involves comparing identical twins with fraternal twins (or with other people).

U

ultrasound: In pregnancy, an image of the fetus in the womb that helps to date the pregnancy, assess the fetus's growth, and identify abnormalities.

umbilical cord: The structure that attaches the placenta to the fetus, through which nutrients are passed and fetal wastes are removed.

underextension: An error in early language development in which young children apply verbal labels too narrowly.

undernutrition: A chronic lack of adequate food.

U-shaped curve of marital satisfaction: The most common pathway of marital happiness in the West, in which satisfaction is highest at the honeymoon, declines during the child-rearing years, then rises after the children grow up.

uterus: The pear-shaped muscular organ in a woman's abdomen that houses the developing baby.

V

validity: In measurement terminology, a basic criterion for a test's accuracy involving whether that measure reflects the real-world quality it is supposed to measure.

value-comparison phase: In Murstein's theory, the second mate-selection stage, in which we make judgments about a partner on the basis of similar values and interests.

vascular dementia: A type of age-related dementia caused by multiple small strokes.

very low birth weight (VLBW): A body weight at birth of less than 3 1/4 pounds.

visual cliff: A table that appears to "end" in a drop-off at its midpoint; used to test for infant depth perception.

W

Wechsler Adult Intelligence Scale (WAIS): The standard test to measure adult IQ, involving verbal and performance scales, each of which is made up of various subtests.

widowhood mortality effect: The elevated risk of death that occurs among surviving spouses— particularly men— after being widowed.

WISC (Wechsler Intelligence Scale for Children): The standard intelligence test used in childhood, consisting of a Verbal Scale (questions for the child to answer), a Performance Scale (materials for the child to manipulate), and a variety of subtests.

working memory: In information-processing theory, the limited-capacity gateway system, containing all the material that we can keep in awareness at a single time. The material in this system is either processed for more permanent storage or lost.

working model: In Bowlby's theory, the mental representation of a caregiver, allowing children over age 3 to be physically apart from a caregiver.

Y

young-old: People in their sixties and seventies.

youth development program: Any after-school program, or structured activity outside of the school day, that is devoted to promoting flourishing in teenagers.

Z

zone of proximal development (ZPD): In Vygotsky's theory, the gap between a child's ability to solve a problem totally on his own and his potential knowledge if taught by a more accomplished person.

zygote: A fertilized ovum.

References

Abbassi, V. (1998). Growth and normal puberty. *Pediatrics, 102*, 507–511.

Abbasi-Shavazi, J., Mohammad J., & McDonald, P. (2008). Family change in Iran: Religion, revolution, and the state. In R. Jayakody, A. Thornton, & W. Axinn (Eds.), *International family change: Ideational perspectives* (pp. 177–198). New York, NY: Taylor & Francis Group/Lawrence Erlbaum Associates.

Abbate-Daga, G., Gramaglia, C., Amianto, F., Marzola, E., & Fassino, S. (2010). Attachment insecurity, personality, and body dissatisfaction in eating disorders. *The Journal of Nervous and Mental Disease, 198*(7), 520–524.

Abdou, C. M., Dunkel, S. C., Campos, B., Hilmert, C. J., Dominguez, T. P., Hobel, C. J., … Sandman, C. A. (2010). Communalism predicts prenatal affect, stress, and physiology better than ethnicity and socioeconomic status. *Cultural Diversity and Ethnic Minority Psychology, 16*(3), 395–403.

Abramson, L. Y., Seligman, M. E., & Teasdale, J. D. (1978). Learned helplessness in humans: Critique and reformulation. *Journal of Abnormal Psychology, 87*, 49–74.

Abu-Akel, A., & Shamay-Tsoory, S. (2011). Neuroanatomical and neurochemical bases of theory of mind. *Neuropsychologia, 49*, 2971–2984.

Abubakar, A., Holding, P., Vijver, F. J. R., Newton, C., & Baar, A. V. (2010). Children at risk for developmental delay can be recognised by stunting, being underweight, ill health, little maternal schooling or high gravity. *The Journal of Child Psychology and Psychiatry, 51*(6), 652–659.

Acevedo, B. P., & Aron, A. (2009). Does a long-term relationship kill romantic love? *Review of General Psychology, 13*, 59–65.

Ackard, D. M., Cronemeyer, C. L., Franzen, L. M., Richter, S. A., & Norstrom, J. (2011). Number of different purging behaviors used among women with eating disorders: Psychological, behavioral, self-efficacy and quality of life outcomes. *Eating Disorders, 19*, 156–174.

Ackerman, J. M., Griskevicius, V., & Li, N. P. (2010). Let's get serious: Communicating commitment in romantic relationships. *Journal of Personality and Social Psychology, 100*(6), 1079–1094.

Adair, L. S. (2008). Child and adolescent obesity: Epidemiology and developmental perspectives. *Physiology & Behavior, 94*, 8–16.

Adams, G. A., & Rau, B. (2011). Putting off tomorrow to do what you want today: Planning for retirement. *American Psychologist, 66*(3), 180–192.

Addington-Hall, J. M., & O'Callaghan, A. C. (2009). A comparison of the quality of care provided to cancer patients in the UK in the last three months of life in inpatient hospices compared with hospitals, from the perspective of bereaved relatives: Results from a survey using the VOICES questionnaire. *Palliative Medicine, 23*, 190–197.

Adi-Japha, E., Berberich-Artzi, J., & Libnawi, A. (2010). Cognitive flexibility in drawings of bilingual children. *Child Development, 81*(5), 1356–1366.

Adolph, K. E. (2008). Learning to move. *Current Directions in Psychological Science 17*(3), 213–218.

Adolph, K., & Berger, S. E. (2006). Motor development. In D. Kuhn, R. S. Siegler, W. Damon, & R. M. Lerner (Eds.), *Handbook of child psychology: Vol. 2, cognition, perception, and language* (6th ed.), pp. 161–213. Hoboken, NJ: John Wiley & Sons, Inc.

Agrawal, A., & Lynskey, M. T. (2008). Are there genetic influences on addiction: Evidence from family, adoption, and twin studies. *Addiction, 103*, 1069–1081.

AhnAllen, J. M., & Suyemoto, K. L. (2011). Influence of interracial dating on racial and/or ethnic identities of Asian American women and White European American men. *Asian American Journal of Psychology, 2*(1), 61–75.

Ahnert, L., Pinquart, M., & Lamb, M. (2006). Security of children's relationships with nonparental care providers: A meta-analysis. *Child Development, 74*(3), 664–679.

Aichberger, M. C., Busch, M. A., Reischies, F. M., Strohle, A., Heinz, A., & Rapp, M. A. (2010). Effects of physical inactivity on cognitive performance after 2.5 years of follow-up: Longitudinal results from the survey of health, ageing, and retirement (SHARE). *GeroPsych, 23*(1), 7–15.

Ainsworth, M. D. S. (1967). *Infancy in Uganda: Infant care and the growth of love.* Baltimore: Johns Hopkins Press.

Ainsworth, M. D. S. (1973). The development of infant-mother attachment. In B. M. Caldwell & H. N. Ricciuti (Eds.), *Review of child development research* (Vol. 3, pp. 1–94). Chicago: University of Chicago Press.

Ainsworth, M. D. S., Blehar, M. C., Waters, E., & Wall, S. (1978). *Patterns of attachment: A psychological study of the strange situation.* Hillsdale, NJ: Erlbaum.

Akerman, A., Williams, M. E., & Meunier, J. (2007). Perception versus reality: An exploration of children's measured body mass in relation to caregivers' estimates. *Journal of Health Psychology, 12*(6), 871–882.

Aksan, N., & Kochanska, G. (2004). Links between systems of inhibition from infancy to preschool years. *Child Development, 75*, 1477–1490.

Albert, I., Labs, K., & Trommsdorff, G. (2010). Are older adult German women satisfied with their lives? On the role of life domains, partnership status, and self-control. *GeroPsych, 23*(1), 39–49.

Aldred, H. E. (1997). *Pregnancy and birth sourcebook: Basic information about planning for pregnancy, maternal health, fetal growth and development.* Detroit, MI: Omnigraphics.

Ali, M. M., & Dwyer, D. S. (2011). Estimating peer effects in sexual behavior among adolescents. *Journal of Adolescence, 34*, 183–190.

Allemand, M., Zimprich, D., & Hendricks, A. A. J. (2008). Age differences in five personality domains across the life span. *Developmental Psychology, 44*(3), 758–770.

Allen, J. P., Porter, M., McFarland, C., McElhaney, K. B., & Marsh, P. (2007). The relation of attachment security to adolescents' paternal and peer relationships, depression, and externalizing behavior. *Child Development, 78*(4), 1222–1239.

Alma, M. A., van der Mei, S. F., Melis-Dankers, B. M., van Tilburg, T. G., Groothoff, J. W., & Suurmeijer, T. M. (2011). Participation of the elderly after vision loss. *Disability and Rehabilitation: An International, Multidisciplinary Journal*, 33(1), 63–72.

Alzheimer's Association. (2009). 2009 *Alzheimer's disease, facts and figures*, p. 14. Retrieved from http://www.alz.org/national/documents/report_alzfactsfigures2009

Alzheimer's Disease Education & Referral Center [ADEAR]. (2004). Estrogen-alone hormone therapy could increase risk of dementia in older women. Retrieved January 13, 2006, from http://www.alzheimers.org/nianews/nianews66.html

Amato, P. R. (2007). Transformative processes in marriage: Some thoughts from a sociologist. *Journal of Marriage and Family, 69*(2), 305–309.

Amato, P. R. (2010). Research on divorce: Continuing trends and new developments. *Journal of Marriage and Family,* 72, 650–666.

Amato, P. R., & Hohmann-Marriott, B. (2007). A comparison of high- and low-distress marriages that end in divorce. *Journal of Marriage and Family, 69*(3), 621–638.

American Academy of Pediatrics [AAP], Committee on Drugs. (2000). Use of psychoactive medication during pregnancy and possible effects on the fetus and newborn. *Pediatrics, 105,* 880–887.

American Academy of Pediatrics [AAP], Section on Breastfeeding. (2005). Breastfeeding and the use of human milk. *Pediatrics, 115,* 496–506.

American Heart Association (2001). *2002 heart and stroke statistical update.* Dallas, TX: American Heart Association.

Amin, S., & Al-Bassusi, N. H. (2004). Education, wage work, and marriage: Perspectives of Egyptian working women. *Journal of Marriage and Family,* 66, 1287–1299.

Andero, A. A., & Stewart, A. (2002). Issue of corporal punishment: Re-examined. *Journal of Instructional Psychology, 29,* 90–96.

Anders, T., Goodlin-Jones, B., & Zelenko, M. (1998). Infant regulation and sleep-wake state development. *Zero to Three, 19*(2), 9–14.

Anderson, D. I., Campos, J. J., & Barbu-Roth, M. A. (2004). A developmental perspective on visual proprioception. In G. Bremner & A. Slater (Eds.), *Theories of infant development* (pp. 30–69). Malden, MA: Blackwell.

Anderson, J. W. (1972). Attachment behaviour out of doors. In N. Blurton Jones (Ed.), *Ethological studies of child behaviour* (pp. 199–215). Oxford, England: Cambridge University Press.

Anderson, R., & Mitchell, E. M. (1984). Children's health and play in rural Nepal. *Social Science & Medicine, 19,* 735–740.

Andrade, B. F., Brodeur, D. A., Waschbusch, D. A., Stewart, S. H., & Mcgee, R. (2009). Selective and sustained attention as predictors of social problems in chiildren with typical and disordered attention abilities. *Journal of Attention Disorders, 12*(4), 341–352.

Aneshensel, C. S., Pearlin, L. I., Mullan, J. T., Zarit, S. H., & Whitlatch, C. J. (1995). *Profiles in caregiving: The unexpected career.* San Diego, CA: Academic Press.

Angel, J. L., Jimenez, M. A., & Angel, R. J. (2007). The economic consequences of widowhood for older minority women. *The Gerontologist, 47(2),* 224–234.

Angelini, V., Cavapozzi, D., Corazzini, L., & Paccagnella, O. (2012). Age, health and life satisfaction among older Europeans. *Social Indicators Research, 105*(2), 293–308.

Angner, E., Hullett, S., & Allison, J.J. (2011). "I'll die with the hammer in my hand": John Henryism as a predictor of happiness. *Journal of Economic Psychology,* 32, 357–366.

Annerbäck, E.-M., Svedin, C.-G., & Gustafsson, P. A. (2010). Characteristic features of severe child physical abuse—A multi-informant approach. *Journal of Family Violence, 25,* 165–172.

Anschutz, D. J., Spruijt-Metz, D., Van Strien, T., & Engels, R. C. M. E. (2011). The direct effect of thin ideal focused adult television on young girls' ideal body figure. *Body Image,* 8, 26–33.

Aoyama, S., Toshima, T., Saito, Y., Konishi, N., Motoshige, K., Ishikawa, N., … Kobayashi M. (2010). Maternal breast milk odour induces frontal lobe activation in neonates: A NIRS study. *Early Human development,* 86, 541–545.

Apperly, I. A., Carroll, D. J., Samson, D., Humphreys, G. W., Qureshi, A., & Moffitt, G. (2010). Why are there limits on theory of mind use? Evidence from adults' ability to follow instructions from an ignorant speaker. *The Quarterly Journal of Experimental Psychology,* 63(6), 1201–1217.

Archer, T. (2011). Physical exercise alleviates debilities of normal aging and Alzheimer's disease. *ACTA Neurologica Scandanavia, 123,* 221–238.

Archibald, A. B., Graber, J. A., & Brooks-Gunn, J. (2003). Pubertal processes and physiological growth in adolescence. In G. R. Adams & M. D. Berzonsky (Eds.), *Blackwell handbook of adolescence* (pp. 24–47). Malden, MA: Blackwell.

Ardelt, M., & Koenig, C. S. (2006). The role of religion for hospice patients and relatively healthy older adults. *Research on Aging,* 28, 184–215.

Ardila, A. (2007). Normal aging increases cognitive heterogeneity: Analysis of dispersion in WAIS-III scores across age. *Archives of Clinical Neuropsychology,* 22, 1003–1011.

Ardley, J., & Ericson, L. (2002). "We don't play like that here!": Understanding aggressive expressions of play. In C. R. Brown & K. C. Marchant (Eds.), *Play in practice: Case studies in young children's play* (pp. 35–48). St. Paul, MN: Redleaf.

Ariès, P. (1962). *Centuries of childhood: A social history of family life.* New York: Knopf.

Ariès, P. (1974). *Western attitudes toward death: From the Middle Ages to the present* (P. M. Ranum, Trans.). Baltimore: Johns Hopkins University Press.

Ariès, P. (1981). *The hour of our death* (H. Weaver, Trans.). New York: Knopf.

Arnett, J. J. (1999). Adolescent storm and stress, reconsidered. *American Psychologist, 54,* 317–326.

Arnett, J. J. (2004). *Emerging adulthood: The winding road from the late teens through the twenties.* New York: Oxford University Press.

Arnett, J. J. (2007). The long and leisurely route: Coming of age in Europe today. *Current History: A Journal of Contemporary Affairs, 106,* 130–136.

Arnett, J. J. (2010). Oh, grow up! Generational grumbling and the new life stage of emerging adulthood—Commentary on Trzeniewski & Donnellan. *Perspectives on Psychological Sciences, 51*(1), 89–92.

Arnett, J. J., & Tanner, J. L. (2010). Themes and variations in emerging adulthood across social classes. In J. J. Arnett, M. Kloep, L.B. Hendry, & J. L. Tanner (Eds.), *Debating emerging adulthood: Stage or process?* (pp. 31–51). New York: Oxford University Press.

Aron, A., Norman, C. C., Aron, E. N., & Lewandowski, G. (2002). Shared participation in self-expanding activities: Positive effects on experienced marital quality. In P. Noller & J. A. Feeney (Eds.), *Understanding marriage: Developments in the study of couple interaction* (pp. 177–194). New York: Cambridge University Press.

Asghar, S., Magnusson, A., Khan, A., Ali, K., Hussain, A. (2010). In Bangladesh, overweight individuals have fewer symptoms of depression than nonoverweight individuals. *Obesity, 18*(6), 1143–1145.

Atchley, R. (1989). A continuity theory of normal aging. *The Gerontologist,* 29(2), 183–190.

Attar-Schwartz, S., Buchnan, A., Tan, J., Flouri, E., & Griggs, J. (2009). Grandparenting and adolescent adjustment in two-parent biological, lone parent, and step-families. *Journal of Family Psychology*, 23, 67–75.

Audet, K., & Le Mare, L. (2011). Mitigating effects of the adoptive caregiving environment on inattention/overactivity in children adopted from Romanian orphanages. *International Journal of Behavioral Development*, 35(2), 107–115.

Austin, W. G. (2008). Relocation, research, and forensic evaluation, part I: Effects of residential mobility on children on divorce. *Family Court Review*, *46*(1), 137–150.

AVERT. (2005, November 22, 2005). AIDS and HIV statistics for Sub-Saharan Africa. Retrieved January 24, 2006, from http://www.avert.org/subaadults.htm

Avis, N. E., Assmann, S. F., Kravitz, H. M., Ganz, P. A., & Ory, M. (2004). Quality of life in diverse groups of midlife women: Assessing the influence of menopause, health status and psychosocial and demographic factors. *Quality of Life Research*, *13*, 933–946.

Baddeley, A. D. (1992). Working memory: The interface between memory and cognition. *Journal of Cognitive Neuroscience*, *4*, 281–288.

Baetens, I., Claes, L., Muehlenkamp, J., Grietens, H., & Onghena, P. (2011). Differences in psychological symptoms and self-competencies in non-suicidal self-injurious Flemish adolescents. *Journal of Adolescence*, 35, 1–7.

Baile, W. F., Aaron, J., & Parker, P. A. (2009). Practitioner-patient communication in cancer diagnosis and treatment. In S. M. Miller, D. J. Bowen, R. T. Croyle, & J. H. Rowland (Eds.), *Handbook of cancer control and behavioral science: A resource for researchers, practitioners, and policymakers* (pp. 327–346). Washington, DC: American Psychological Association.

Baillargeon, R. (1993). The object concept revisited: New direction in the investigation of infants' physical knowledge. In C. Granrud (Ed.), *Visual perception and cognition in infancy* (pp. 265–315). Hillsdale, NJ: Erlbaum.

Baillargeon, R., & DeVos, J. (1991). Object permanence in young infants: Further evidence. *Child Development*, 62, 1227–1246.

Baillargeon, R., & Graber, M. (1987). Where's the rabbit? 5.5-month-old infants' representation of the height of a hidden object. *Cognitive Development*, 2, 375–392.

Baird, A. H. (2003). Through my eyes: Service needs of grandparents who raise their grandchildren, from the perspective of a custodial grandmother. In B. Hayslip, Jr. & J. H. Patrick (Eds.), *Working with custodial grandparents* (pp. 59–65). New York: Springer.

Baker, A. J. L. (2005). The long-term effects of parental alienation on adult children: A qualitative research study. *American Journal of Family Therapy*, 33, 289–302.

Bakermans-Kranenburg, M. J., van IJzendoorn, M. H., Pijlman, F. T. A., Mesman, J., & Juffer, F. (2008). Experimental evidence for differential susceptibility: Dopamine D4 Receptor Polymorphism (DRD4) moderates intervention effects on toddlers' externalizing behavior in a randomized controlled trial. *Developmental Psychology*, *44*(1), 293–300.

Balk, D. E. (2008a). A modest proposal about bereavement and recovery. *Death Studies*, 32, 84–93.

Balk, D. E. (2008b). Special issue on bereavement, outcomes, and recovery: Guest editor's opening remarks. *Death Studies*, 32, 1–5.

Ball, H. (2007). Bed-sharing practices of initially breastfed infants in the first 6 months of life. *Infant and Child Development*, *16*, 387–401.

Ball, M. M., Perkins, M. M., Hollingsworth, C., Whittington, F. J., & King, S. V. (2009). Pathways to assisted living: The influence of race and class. *Journal of Applied Gerontology*, 28, 81–108.

Baltes, M. M., & Carstensen, L. L. (2003). The process of successful aging: Selection, optimization and compensation. In U. M. Staudinger & U. Lindenberger (Eds.), *Understanding human development: Dialogues with lifespan psychology* (pp. 81–104). Dordrecht, Netherlands: Kluwer Academic.

Baltes, P. B. (2003). On the incomplete architecture of human ontogeny: Selection, optimization, and compensation as foundation of developmental theory. In U. M. Staudinger & U. Lindenberger (Eds.), *Understanding human development: Dialogues with lifespan psychology* (pp. 17–43). Boston: Kluwer Academic Publishers.

Baltes, P. B., & Smith, J. (1997). A systemic-wholistic view of psychological functioning in very old age: Introduction to a collection of articles from the Berlin Aging Study. *Psychology and Aging*, *12*, 395–409.

Bandura, A. (1977). *Social learning theory*. Englewood Cliffs, NJ: Prentice Hall.

Bandura, A. (1986). *Social foundations of thought and action: A social cognitive theory*. Englewood Cliffs, NJ: Prentice-Hall.

Bandura, A. (1989). Human agency in social cognitive theory. *American Psychologist*, *44*, 1175–1184.

Bandura, A. (1992). Exercise of personal agency through the self-efficacy mechanism. In R. Schwarzer (Ed.), *Self-efficacy: Thought control of action* (pp. 3–38). Washington, DC: Hemisphere.

Bandura, A. (1997). *Self-efficacy: The exercise of control*. New York: Freeman.

Bane, K. (2004). *What the best college teachers do*. Cambridge, MA: President and Fellows of Harvard College.

Barkin, S., Scheindlin, B., Ip, E. H., Richardson, I., & Finch, S. (2007). Determinants of parental discipline practices: A national sample from primary care practices. *Clinical Pediatrics*, *46*(1), 64–69.

Barkley, R. A. (1998). *Attention-deficit hyperactivity disorder: A handbook for diagnosis and treatment* (2nd ed.). New York: Guilford Press.

Barkley, R. A. (2003). Attention-deficit/hyperactivity disorder. In E. J. Mash & R. A. Barkley (Eds.), *Child psychopathology* (2nd ed., pp. 75–143). New York: Guilford Press.

Barkley, R. A., & Murphy, K. R. (2006). *Attention-deficit hyperactivity disorder: A clinical workbook* (3rd ed.). New York: Guilford Press.

Barlow, J. H., Turner, A. P., Hammond, C. L., & Gailey, L. (2007). Living with late deafness: Insight from between worlds. *International Journal of Audiology*, *46*, 442–448.

Barnes, G. M., Hoffman, J. H., Welte, J. W., Farrell, M. P., & Dintcheff, B. A. (2007). Adolescents' time use: Effects on substance use, delinquency and sexual activity. *Journal of Youth and Adolescence*, 36, 697–710.

Barnett, M. A., Shanahan, L., Deng, M., Haskett, M. E., & Cox, M. J. (2010). Independent and interactive contributions of parenting behaviors and beliefs in the prediction of early childhood behavior problems. *Parenting Science and Practice*, *20*, 43–59.

Barnett, S. M., Ceci, S. J., & Williams, W. M. (2006). Is the ability to make a bacon sandwich a mark of intelligence?, and other issues: Some reflections on Gardner's theory of multiple intelligences. In J. A. Schaler (Ed.) *Howard Gardner under fire: The rebel psychologist faces his critics* (pp. 95–114). Chicago, IL: Open Court Publishing Co.

Baron, I. S., & Rey-Casserly, C. (2010). Extremely preterm birth outcome: A review of four decades of cognitive research. *Neuropsychology Review, 20*(4), 430–425.

Baron-Cohen, S. (1999). The evolution of a theory of mind. In M. C. Corballis & S. E. G. Lea (Eds.), *The descent of mind: Psychological perspectives on hominid evolution* (pp. 261–277). New York: Oxford University Press.

Barry, R. A., & Kochanska, G. (2010). A longitudinal investigation of the affective environment in families with young children: From infancy to early school age. *Emotion, 10*(2), 237–249.

Barry, R. A., Kochanska, G., & Philibert, R. A. (2008). G × E interaction in the organization of attachment: Mother's responsiveness as a moderator of children's genotypes. *Journal of Child Psychology and Psychiatry, 49,* 1313–1320.

Bartolini, V., & Lunn, K. (2002). "Teacher, they won't let me play!": Strategies for improving inappropriate play behavior. In C. R. Brown & K. C. Marchant (Eds.), *Play in practice: Case studies in young children's play* (pp. 13–20). St. Paul, MN: Redleaf.

Bass, B. L., & Grzywacz, J. G. (2011). Job adequacy and work-family balance: Looking at jobs as a whole. *Journal of Family Issues,* 32(3), 317–345.

Bassok, D. (2010). Do black and Hispanic children benefit more from preschool? Understanding differences in preschool effects across racial groups. *Child Development, 81*(6), 1828–1845.

Bauer, J. J., & McAdams, D. P. (2010). Eudaimonic growth: Narrative growth goals predict increases in ego development and subjective well-being 3 years later. *Developmental Psychology, 46*(4), 761–772.

Bauer, P. J., & Fivush, R. (2010). Context and consequences of autobiographical memory development [Editorial]. *Cognitive Development,* 25(4), 303–308.

Baumeister, R. F., Campbell, J. D., Krueger, J. I., Vohs, K. D, (2003). Does high self-esteem cause better performance, interpersonal success, happiness, or healthier lifestyles? *Psychological Science in the Public Interest,* 4(1), 1–44.

Baumrind, D. (1971). Current patterns of parental authority. *Developmental Psychology,* 4(1, Pt. 2), 1–103.

Baumrind, D., Larzelere, R. E., & Cowan, P. A. (2002). Ordinary physical punishment: Is it harmful? Comment on Gershoff (2002). *Psychological Bulletin, 128,* 580–589.

Bava, S., Thayer, R., Jacobus, J., Ward, M., Jernigan, T. L., & Tapert, S. F. (2010). Longitudinal characterization of white matter maturation during adolescence. *Brain Research, 1327,* 38–46.

Beard, J. R., Blaney, S., Cerda, M., Frye, V., Lovasi, G. S., Ompad, D., … Vlahov, D. (2009). Neighborhood characteristics and disability in older adults. *Journals of Gerontology: Social Sciences, 64B,* 252–257.

Beatty, D. L., Kamarck, T. W., Matthews, K. A., & Shiffman, S. (2011). Childhood socioeconomic status is associated with psychosocial resources in African Americans: The Pittsburgh Healthy Heart Project. *Health Psychology,* 30(4), 472–480.

Becker-Blease, K. A., Turner, H. A., & Finkelhor, D. (2010). Disasters, victimization, and children's mental health. *Child Development, 81*(4), 1040–1052.

Beckmann, C. R. B., Ling, F. W., Laube, D. W., Smith, R. P., Barzansky, B. M., & Herbert, W. N. P. (2002). *Obstetrics and gynecology* (4th ed.). Baltimore: Lippincott Williams & Wilkins.

Beernick, A. C. E., Swinkels, S. H. N., & Buitelaar, J. K. (2007). Problem behavior in a community sample of 14- and 19-month-old children. *European Child and Adolescent Psychiatry, 16,* 271–280.

Begley, A. M. (2008). Guilty but good: Defending voluntary active euthanasia from a virtue perspective. *Nursing Ethics, 15*(4), 434–445.

Behrens, K. Y., Parker, A. C., & Haltigan, J. D. (2011). Maternal sensitivity assessed during the Strange Situation Procedure predicts child's attachment quality and reunion behaviors. *Infant Behavior & Development,* 34(2), 378–381.

Bell, A. S. (2011). A critical review of ADHD diagnostic criteria: What to address in the DSM-V. *Journal of Attention Disorders, 15*(1), 3–10.

Bell, R., Buchner, A., & Mund, I. (2008). Age-related differences in irrelevant-speech effects. *Psychology and Aging, 23(2),* 377–391.

Bellenir, K. (ed.). (2004). *Genetic disorders sourcebook* (3rd Ed.). Detroit, MI: Omnigraphics.

Bellinger, D., Leviton, A., Waternaux, C., Needleman, H., & Rabinowitz, M. (1987). Longitudinal analyses of prenatal and postnatal lead exposure and early cognitive development. *New England Journal of Medicine, 316,* 1037–1043.

Belsky, J. K. (1999). *The psychology of aging: Theory, research, and interventions* (3rd ed.). Pacific Grove, CA: Brooks/Cole.

Belsky, J. K. (2001). Aging. In J. Worell (Ed.), *Encyclopedia of women and gender: Sex similarities and differences and the impact of society on gender* (Vol. 1, pp. 95–108). San Diego, CA: Academic Press.

Belsky, J., Houts, R. M., & Pasco Fearon, R. M. (2010). Infant attachment security and the timing of puberty: Testing an evolutionary hypothesis. *Psychological Science, 21,* 1195–1201.

Belsky, J., Lang, M. E., & Rovine, M. (1985). Stability and change in marriage across the transition to parenthood: A second study. *Journal of Marriage and the Family, 47,* 855–865.

Belsky, J., & Pluess, M. (2009). Beyond diathesis stress: Differential susceptibility to environmental influences. *Psychological Bulletin, 135*(6), 885–908.

Belsky, J., & Pluess, M. (2011). Beyond adversity, vulnerability, and resilience: Individual differences in developmental plasticity. In Cicchetti, D & Roisman, G. I. (Eds.) *The Origins and Organization of Adaptation and Maladaptation,* pp. 379–422. Hoboken, NJ: Wiley.

Belsky, J., & Rovine, M. (1990). Patterns of marital change across the transition to parenthood: Pregnancy to three years postpartum. *Journal of Marriage & the Family, 52,* 5–19.

Belsky, J., Steinberg, L., & Draper, P. (1991). Childhood experience, interpersonal development, and reproductive strategy: An evolutionary theory of socialization. *Child Development, 62,* 647–670.

Belsky, J., Steinberg, L. D., Houts, R. M., Friedman, S. L., DeHart, G., Cauffman, E., … Susman, E. (2007). Family rearing antecedents of pubertal timing. *Child Development, 78*(4), 1302–1321.

Belsky, J., Steinberg, L., Houts, R. M., & Halpern-Felsher, B. L. (2010). The development of reproductive strategy in females: Early maternal → earlier menarche → increased sexual risk taking. *Developmental Psychology, 46*(1), 120–128.

Belsky, J., Vandell, D. L., Burchinal, M., Clarke-Stewart, K. A., McCartney, K., Owen, M. T., & The NICHD Early Child Care Research Network. (2007b). Are there long-term effects of early child care? *Child Development, 78*(2), 681–701.

Belsky, J., & Volling, B. L. (1987). Mothering, fathering, and marital interaction in the family triad during infancy: Exploring family system's processes. In

P. W. Berman & F. A. Pedersen (Eds.), *Men's transitions to parenthood: Longitudinal studies of early family experience* (pp. 37–63). Hillsdale, NJ: Erlbaum.

Bem, S. L. (1981). Gender schema theory: A cognitive account of sex typing. *Psychological Review, 88,* 354–364.

Ben-Ari, A., & Lavee, Y. (2007). Dyadic closeness in marriage: From the inside story to a conceptual model. *Journal of Social and Personal Relationships, 24*(5), 627–644.

Benas, J. S., Uhrlass, D. J., & Gibb, B. E. (2010). Body dissatisfaction and weight-related teasing: A model of cognitive vulnerability to depression among women. *Journal of Behavior Therapy and Experimental Psychiatry, 41*(4), 352–356.

Beneventi, H., Tønnessen, F. E., Ersland, L., & Hugdahl, K. (2010). Working memory deficit in dyslexia: Behavioral and fMRI evidence. *International Journal of Neuroscience, 120,* 51–59.

Bengtson, V. L. (1989). The problem of generations: Age group contrasts, continuities, and social change. In V. L. Bengtson & K. W. Schaie (Eds.), *The course of later life: Research and reflections* (pp. 25–54). New York: Springer.

Benjet, C., & Kazdin, A. E. (2003). Spanking children: The controversies, findings and new directions. *Clinical Psychology Review, 23,* 197–224.

Berg, A. I., Hassing, L. B., Thorvaldsson, V., & Johansson, B. (2011). Personality and personal control make a difference for life satisfaction in the oldest-old: Findings in a longitudinal population-based study of individuals 80 and older. *European Journal of Ageing, 8,* 13–20.

Bergman, K., Sarkar, P., Glover, V., & O'Conner, T. G. (2010). Maternal prenatal cortisol and infant cognitive development: Moderation by infant-mother attachment. *Biological Psychiatry,* 67(11), 1026–1032.

Bergsma, A., & Ardelt, M. (2011). Self-reported wisdom and happiness: An empirical investigation. *Journal of Happiness Studies,* 37(2), 1–19.

Berk, L. E., & Winsler, A. (1999). *NAEYC research into practice series: Vol. 7. Scaffolding children's learning: Vygotsky and early childhood education.* Washington, DC: National Association for the Education of Young Children.

Berkman, L., & Breslow, L. (1983). *Health and ways of living: The Alameda County study.* New York: Oxford University Press.

Berko, J. (1958). The child's learning of English morphology. *Word, 14,* 150–177.

Berkowitz, R. I., & Stunkard, A. J. (2002). Development of childhood obesity. In T. A. Wadden & A. J. Stunkard (Eds.), *Handbook of obesity treatment* (pp. 515–531). New York: Guilford Press.

Berlin, L. J., Appleyard, K., & Dodge, K. (2011). Intergenerational continuity in child maltreatment: Mediating mechanisms and implications for prevention. *Child Development,* 82(1), 162–176.

Bernal, J. G., & Anuncibay, R. D. (2008). Intergenerational grandparent/grandchild relations: The socio-educational role of grandparents. *Educational Gerontology, 34,* 67–88.

Bernier, A., & Matte-Gagné, C. (2011). More bridges: Investigating the relevance of self-report and interview measures of adult attachment for marital and caregiving relationships. *International Journal of Behavioral Development,* 35(4), 307–316.

Bersamin, M., Bourdeau, B., Fisher, D. A., Hill, D. L., Walker, S., Grube, J. W., & Grube, E. L. (2008). *Casual partnerships: Media exposure and relationship status at last oral sex and vaginal intercourse.* Paper presented at the Biennial Meeting, Society for Research in Adolescence, Chicago, 2008.

Berthelsen, D., & Brownlee, J. (2007). Working with toddlers in child care: Practitioners' beliefs about their role. *Early Childhood Research Quarterly,* 22, 347–362.

Berzin, S. C., & De Marco, A. C. (2010). Understanding the impact of poverty on critical events in emerging adulthood. *Youth & Society,* 43(2), 278–300.

Best, J. R., & Miller, P. H. (2010). A developmental perspective on executive function. *Child Development,* 81(6), 1641–1660.

Bianchi, S. M., & Milkie, M. A. (2010). Work and family research in the first decade of the 21st century. *Journal of Marriage and Family, 72,* 705–725.

Bianchi, S., Robinson, J. R., & Milkie, M. A. (2006). *Changing rhythms of American family life.* New York: Russell Sage Foundation.

Binstock, R. H. (2010). From compassionate ageism to intergenerational conflict? *The Gerontologist, 50*(5), 574–585.

Birnbaum, G. E., Cohen, O., & Wertheimer, V. (2007). Is it all about intimacy? Age, menopausal status, and women's sexuality. *Personal Relationships, 14,* 167–185.

Birren, J. E., & Birren, B. A. (1990). The concepts, models, and history of the psychology of aging. In J. E. Birren & K. W. Schaie (Eds.), *Handbook of the psychology of aging* (3rd ed., pp. 3–20). San Diego, CA: Academic Press.

Bissada, A., & Briere, J. (2001). Child abuse: Physical and sexual. In J. Worell (Ed.), *Encyclopedia of women and gender: Sex similarities and differences and the impact of society on gender* (pp. 219–232). San Diego, CA: Academic Press.

Bjorklund, D. F. (2005). *Children's thinking: Cognitive development and individual differences* (4th ed.). Belmont, CA: Wadsworth.

Bjorklund, D. F., & Bjorklund, B. R. (1992). *Looking at children: An introduction to child development.* Monterey, CA: Brooks-Cole.

Bjorklund, D. F., & Pellegrini, A. D. (2002). *The origins of human nature: Evolutionary developmental psychology.* Washington, DC: American Psychological Association.

Bjorklund, D. F., & Rosenblum, K. E. (2001). Children's use of multiple and variable addition strategies in a game context. *Developmental Science, 4,* 184–194.

Black, H. K., & Rubinstein, R. L. (2005). Direct care workers' response to dying and death in the nursing home: A case study. *Journals of Gerontology: Psychological Sciences, 60B,* S3–S10.

Blacker, D., & Lovestone, S. (2006). Genetics and dementia nosology. *Journal of Geriatric Psychiatry and Neurology, 19,* 186–191.

Blake, W. (1794). The schoolboy. Retrieved October 21, 2006, from University of Dundee Web site: http://www.dundee.ac.uk/english/wics/blake/blake2.htm#e25

Blakemore, S.-J., Burnett, S., & Dahl, R. E. (2010). The role of puberty in the developing adolescent brain. *Human Brain Mapping, 31,* 926–933.

Blanchard, R. A., & Myers, A. M. (2010). Examination of driving comfort and self-regulatory practices in older adults using in-vehicle devices to assess natural driving patterns. *Accident Analysis and Prevention, 42,* 1213–1219.

Blatney, M., Jelinek, M., & Osecka, T. (2007). Assertive toddler, self-efficacious adult: Child temperament predicts personality over forty years. *Personality and Individual Differences,* 43, 2127–2136.

Blood, R. O., & Wolfe, D. M. (1960). *Husbands and wives: The dynamics of family living.* Oxford, England: Free Press Glencoe.

Blum, D. (2002). *Love at Goon Park: Harry Harlow and the science of affection.* Cambridge, MA: Perseus.

Blumenthal, H., Leen-Feldner, E. W., Babson, K. A., Gahr, J. L., Trainor, C. D., & Frala, J. L. (2011). Elevated social anxiety among early maturing girls. *Developmental Psychology, 47*(4), 1133–1140.

Boden, J. M., Fergusson, D. M., & Horwood, J. (2010). Risk factors for conduct disorder and oppositional/defiant disorder: Evidence from a New Zealand birth cohort. *Journal of the American Academy of Child & Adolescent Psychiatry, 49*(11), 1125–1133.

Bodenhorn, N., & Lawson, G. (2003). Genetic counseling: Implications for community counselors. *Journal of Counseling & Development, 81,* 497–501.

Bodenmann, G., Charvos, L., Bradbury, T. N., Bertoni, A., Iafrate, R., Giuliani, C., … Behling, J. (2007). The role of stress in divorce: A three-nation retrospective study. *Journal of Social and Personal Relationships, 24*(5), 707–728.

Boerner, K., Brennan, M., Horowitz, A., & Reinhardt, J. P. (2010). Tackling vision-related disability in old age: An application of the life-span theory of control to narrative data. *Journals of Gerontology: Psychologocal Sciences, 65B1,* 22–31.

Bohlin, G., Eninger, L., Brocki, K. C., Karin C., & Thorell, L. B. (2012). Disorganized attachment and inhibitory capacity: Predicting externalizing problem behaviors. *Journal of Abnormal Child Psychology, 40*(3), 449–458.

Boivin, M., Petitclerc, A., Feng, B., & Barker, E. D. (2010). The developmental trajectories of peer victimization in middle to late childhood and the changing nature of their behavioral consequences. *Merrill-Palmer Quarterly, 56*(3), 231–260.

Bonach, K. (2007). Forgiveness intervention model: Application to coparenting post-divorce. *Journal of Divorce & Remarriage, 48*(1/2), 105–123.

Bonanno, G. A. (2004). Loss, trauma, and human resilience: Have we underestimated the human capacity to thrive after extremely aversive events? *American Psychologist, 59,* 20–28.

Bonanno, G. A., & Lilienfeld, S. O. (2008). Let's be realistic: When grief counseling is effective and when it's not. *Professional Psychology: Research and Practice, 39(3),* 377–380.

Bonanno, G. A., Wortman, C. B., Lehman, D. R., Tweed, R. G., Haring, M., Sonnega, J., … Nesse, R. M. (2002). Resilience to loss and chronic grief: A prospective study from preloss to 18-months postloss. *Journal of Personality and Social Psychology, 83,* 1150–1164.

Bonebrake, D., Culver, C., Call, K., & Ward-Smith, P. (2010). Clinically differentiating palliative care and hospice. *Clinical Journal of Oncology Nursing, 14*(3), 273–275.

Bono, G., McCullough, M. E., & Root, L. M. (2008). Forgiveness, feeling connected to others, and well-being: Two longitudinal studies. *Personality and Social Psychology Bulletin, 34*(2), 182–195.

Boonzaier, F. (2008). 'If the man says you must sit, then you must sit': The relationship construction of woman abuse: Gender, subjectivity and violence. *Feminism & Psychology, 18*(2), 183–206.

Booth-LaForce, C., & Oxford, M. L. (2008). Trajectories of social withdrawal from grades 1 to 6: Prediction from early parenting, attachment, and temperament. *Developmental Psychology, 44,* 1298–1313.

Borella, E., Carretti, B., & De Beni, R. (2008). Working memory and inhibition across the adult life-span. *Acta Psychologica, 128,* 33–44.

Borko, H., Wolf, S. A., Simone, G., & Uchiyama, K. P. (2003). Schools in transition: Reform efforts and school capacity in Washington state. *Educational Evaluation and Policy Analysis, 25,* 171–201.

Botwinick, J. (1967). *Cognitive processes in maturity and old age.* New York: Springer.

Bouchard, T. J., Segal, N. L., Tellegen, A., McGue, M., Keyes, M., & Kruger, R. (2004). Genetic influences on social attitudes: Another challenge to psychology from behavior genetics. In L. F. DiLalla (Ed.), *Behavior genetics principles: Perspectives in development, personality, and psychopathology.* Washington, DC.: American Psychological Association Press.

Boulton, M. J., Smith, P. K., & Cowie, H. (2010). Short-term longitudinal relationships between children's peer victimization/bullying experiences and self-perceptions: Evidence for reciprocity. *School Psychology International, 31*(3), 296–311.

Bowers, E. P., Li, Y., Kiely, M. K., Brittian, A., Lerner, J. V., & Lerner, R. M. (2010). The Five Cs model of positive youth development: A longitudinal analysis of confirmatory factor structure and measurement invariance. *Journal of Youth and Adolescence, 39,* 720–735.

Bowes, L., Maughan, B. Caspi, A., Moffitt, T. E., & Arseneault, L. (2010). Families promote emotional and behavioural resilience to bullying: Evidence of an environmental effect. *Journal of Child Psychology and Psychiatry, 51*(7), 809–817.

Bowker, J. C., & Raja, R. (2011). Social withdrawal subtypes during early adolescence in India. *Journal of Abnormal Child Psychology, 39,* 201–212.

Bowlby, J. (1969). *Attachment and loss: Vol. 1. Attachment.* New York: Basic Books.

Bowlby, J. (1973). *Attachment and loss: Vol. 2. Separation: Anxiety and anger.* New York: Basic Books.

Bowlby, J. (1980). *Attachment and loss: Vol. 3. Loss: Sadness and depression.* New York: Basic Books.

Boykin, S., Diez-Roux, A. V., Carnethon, M., Shrager, S., Ni, H., & Whitt-Glover, M. (2011). Racial/ethnic heterogeneity in the socioeconomic patterning of CVD risk factors in the United States: The multi-ethnic study of atherosclerosis. *Journal of Health Care for the Poor and Underserved, 22,* 111–127.

Boyle, D. E., Marshall, N. L., & Robeson, W. W. (2003). Gender at play: Fourth-grade girls and boys on the playground. *American Behavioral Scientist, 46,* 1326–1345.

Braam, A. W., Klinkenberg, M., & Deeg, D. J. H. (2011). Religiousness and mood in the last week of life: An explorative approach based on after-death proxy interviews. *Journal of Palliative Medicine, 14*(1), 31–37.

Brabant, S. (2003). Death in two settings: The acute care facility and hospice. In C. D. Bryant (Ed.), *Handbook of death & dying* (pp. 475–484). Thousand Oaks, CA: Sage.

Bradbury, T. N., & Karney, B. R. (2004). Understanding and altering the longitudinal course of marriage. *Journal of Marriage and Family, 66,* 862–879.

Bradley, C. T., & Brasel, K. J. (2008). Core competencies in palliative care for surgeons: Interpersonal and communication skills. *American Journal of Hospice & Palliative Medicine, 24*(6), 499–507.

Bradley, R. H., Corwyn, R. F., Burchinal, M., McAdoo, H. P., & Garcia Coll, C. (2001). The home environments of children in the United States Part II: Relations with behavioral development through age thirteen. *Child Development, 72,* 1868–1886.

Brame, R., Turner, M. C., Paternoster, R., & Bushway, S. (2012). Cumulative prevalence of arrest from ages 8 to 23 in a national sample. *Pediatrics, 129*(1), 21–27.

Bramen, J. E., Hranilovich, J. A., Dahl, R. E., Forbes, E. E., Chen, J., Toga, A. W., & ... Sowell, E. R. (2011). Puberty influences medial temporal lobe and cortical gray matter maturation differently in boys than girls matched for sexual maturity. *Cerebral Cortex, 21*(3), 636–646.

Brantley, A., Knox, D., & Zusman, M. E. (2002). When and why gender differences in saying 'I Love You' among college students. *College Student Journal, 36(4)*, 614–615.

Braveman, P., Marchi, K., Egerter, S., Kim, S., Meltzer, M., Stancil, T., & Libet M. al. (2010). Poverty, near-poverty, and hardship around the time of pregnancy. *Maternal and Child Health Journal, 14*(1), 20–35.

Brecher, E. M., & the editors of Consumer Reports books. (1984). *Love, sex, and aging: A Consumers Union report.* Boston: Little, Brown.

Bregnab., K. Glover., V., Sakar, P., Abbot, D. H., & O'Conner, T. G. (2010). In utero cortisol and testoterone exposure and fear reactivity in infancy [Electronic version]. *Hormones and Behavior, 57*(3). 306–312.

Bretherton, I. (2005). In pursuit of the internal working model construct and its relevance to attachment relationships. In K. E. Grossmann, K. Grossmann, & E. Waters (Eds.), *Attachment from infancy to adulthood: The major longitudinal studies* (pp. 13–47). New York: Guilford Press.

Britt, D. W., & Evans, M. I. (2007). Sometimes doing the right task sucks: Frame combinations and multi-fetal pregnancy reduction decision difficulty. *Social Science & Medicine, 65*, 2342–2356.

Brodhagen, A., & Wise, D. (2008). Optimism as a mediator between the experience of child abuse, other traumatic events, and distress. *Journal of Family Violence, 36*, 403–411.

Brody, J. E. (2010, December 27). Just because one's vision is waning, hope doesn't have to. *The New York Times*, p. D2. Retrieved Dec. 9, 2011.

Brody, N. (2006). Geocentric theory: A valid alternative to Gardner's theory of intelligence. In J. A. Schaler (Ed.), *Howard Gardner under fire: The rebel psychologist faces his critics* (pp. 73–94). Chicago, IL: Open Court Publishing Co.

Bronfenbrenner, U. (1977). Toward an experimental ecology of human development. *American Psychologist, 32*, 513–531.

Bronstein, P. (1988). Father-child interaction: Implications for gender-role socialization. In P. Bronstein & C. P. Cowan (Eds.), *Fatherhood today: Men's changing role in the family* (pp. 107–124). Oxford, England: Wiley.

Brooks-Gunn, J., Newman, D. L., Holderness, C. C., & Warren, M. P. (1994). The experience of breast development and girls' stories about the purchase of a bra. *Journal of Youth and Adolescence, 23*, 539–565.

Brooks-Gunn, J., & Ruble, D. N. (1982). The development of menstrual-related beliefs and behaviors during early adolescence. *Child Development, 53*, 1567–1577.

Brooks-Gunn, J., & Warren, M. P. (1985). The effects of delayed menarche in different contexts: Dance and nondance students. *Journal of Youth and Adolescence, 14*, 285–300.

Brooks-Gunn, J., & Warren, M. P. (1988). The psychological significance of secondary sexual characteristics in nine- to eleven-year-old girls. *Child Development, 59*, 1061–1069.

Brotman, L. M., O'Neal, C. R., Huang, K., Gouley, K. K., Rosenfelt, A., & Shrout, P. E. (2009). An experimental test of parenting practices as a mediator of early childhood physical aggression. *Journal of Child Psychology and Psychiatry, 50*(3), 235–245.

Brown, A. D., McMorris, A., Longman, R. S., Leigh, R., Hill, M. D., Friedenreich, C. M., & Poulin, M. J. (2010) Effects of cardiorespiratory fitness and cerebral blood flow on cognitive outcomes in older women. *Neurobiology of Aging, 31*(12), 2047–2057.

Brown, J. A., & Ferree, M. M. (2005). Close your eyes and think of England: Pronatalism in the British print media. *Gender & Society, 19*, 5–24.

Brown, J. E., Nicholson, J. M., Broom, D. H., & Bittman, M. (2011). Television viewing by school-age children: Associations with physical activity, snack food consumption and unhealthy weight. *Social Indicators Research, 101*(2), 221–225.

Brown, S. L., Nesse, R. M., House, J. S., & Utz, R. L. (2004). Religion and emotional compensation: Results from a prospective study of widowhood. *Personality and Social Psychology Bulletin, 30*, 1165–1174.

Brune, B. C., Gerlach, M. K., Seewald, M. J., & Brune, T. G. (2010). Early postnatal BMI adaptation is regulated during a fixed time period and mainly depends on maternal BMI. *Obesity, 18*(4), 798–802.

Bruss, M. B., Michael, T. J., Morris, J. R., Applegate, B., Dannison, L., Quitugua, J. A., & Klein, D. J. (2010). Childhood obesity prevention: An intervention targeting primary caregivers of school children. *Obesity, 18*(1), 99–107.

Buck, K. A., & Dix, T. (2012). Can developmental changes in inhibition and peer relationships explain why depressive symptoms increase in early adolescence? *Journal of Youth and Adolescence, 41*, 403–413.

Bugental, D. B., Ellerson, P. C., Lin, E. K., Rainey, B., Kokotovic, A., & O'Hara, N. (2010). A cognitive approach to child abuse prevention. *Psychology of Violence, 1*(S), 84–106.

Buhl, H. M., & Lanz, M. (2007). Emerging adulthood in Europe: Common traits and variability across five European countries. *Journal of Adolescent Research*, 22(5), 439–443.

Bukowski, W. M. (2001). Friendship and the worlds of childhood. In D. W. Nangle & C. A. Erdley (Eds.), *New directions for child and adolescent development: No. 91. The role of friendship in psychological adjustment* (pp. 93–105). San Francisco: Jossey-Bass.

Burchinal, M., Skinner, D., & Reznick, J. S. (2010). European American and African American mothers' beliefs about parenting and disciplining infants: A mixed-method analysis. *Parenting: Science and Practice, 10*, 79–96.

Bureau, J.-F., Martin, J., Freynet, N., Poirier, A. A., Lafontaine, M.-F., & Cloutier, P. (2010). Perceived dimensions of parenting and non-suicidal self-injury in young adults. *Journal of Youth and Adolescence*, 39, 484–494.

Burk, L. R., Armstrong, J. M., Park, J.-H., Zahn-Waxler, C., Klein, M. H., & Essex, M. J. (2011). Stability of early identified aggressive victim status in elementary school and associations with later mental health problems and functional impairments. *Journal of Abnormal Child Psychology*, 39, 225–238.

Burke, M. A., Heiland, F. W., & Nadler, C. M. (2010). From 'overweight' to 'about right': Evidence of a generational shift in body weight norms. *Obesity, 18*(6), 1226–1234.

Burnett, S., Thompson, S., Bird, G., & Blakemore, S. (2011). Pubertal development of the understanding of social emotions: Implications for education. *Learning and Individual Differences, 21*(6), 681–689.

Burnette, J. L., Davis, D. E., Green, J. D., Worthington Jr., E. L., & Bradfield, E. (2009). Insecure attachment and depressive symptoms: The mediating role of rumination, empathy, and forgiveness.

Personality and Individual Differences, 49, 276–280.

Burr, A., Santo, J. B., & Pushkar, D. (2011). Affective well-being in retirement: The influence of values, money, and mental health across three years. *Journal of Happiness Studies, 12,* 17–40.

Bursik, K. (1991). Adaptation to divorce and ego development in adult women. *Journal of Personality and Social Psychology, 60*(2), 300–306.

Bushnell, I. W. R. (1998). The origins of face perception. In F. Simion & G. Butterworth (Eds.), *The development of sensory, motor and cognitive capacities in early infancy: From perception to cognition* (pp. 69–86). Hove, England: Psychology Press.

Buss, C., Davis, E. P., Muftuler, L. T., Head, K., & Sandman, C. A. (2010). High pregnancy anxiety during mid-gestation is associated with decreased gray matter density in 6–9-year-old children [Electronic version]. *Psychoneuroendocrinology,* 35(1). 141–153.

Busseri, M. A., Rose-Krasnor, L., Pancer, S. M., Pratt, M. W., Adams, G. R., Birnie-Lefcovitch, S., Birnie-Lefcovitch, ... Wintre, M. G. (2010). A longitudinal study of breadth and intensity of activity involvement and the transition to university. *Journal of Research on Adolescence, 21*(2), 512–518.

Butkovic, A., Brkovic, I., & Bratko, D. (2011). Predicting well-being from personality in adolescents and older adults. *Journal of Happiness Studies, 21,* 1–13.

Buttelmann, D., Call, J., & Tomasello, M. (2009). Do great apes use emotional expressions to infer desires? *Developmental Science, 12*(5), 688–698.

Buyse, E., Verschueren, K., & Douman, S. (2011). Preschoolers' attachment to mother and risk for adjustment problems in kindergarten: Can teachers make a difference? *Social Development,* 20(1), 33–50.

Byrnes, H. F., Miller, B. A., Chen, M.-J., & Grube, J. W. (2011). The roles of mothers' neighborhood perceptions and specific monitoring strategies in youths' problem behavior. *Journal of Youth and Adolescence, 40,* 347–360.

Callahan, D. (1988). *Setting limits: Medical goals in an aging society.* New York: Simon and Schuster.

Calvin, C. M., Batty, G. D., Lowe, G. D. O., & Deary, I. J. (2011). Childhood intelligence and midlife inflammatory and hemostatic biomarkers: The National Child Development Study (1958) cohort. *Health Psychology,* 30(6), 710–718.

Calvo, E., Haverstick, K., & Sass, S. A. (2009) Gradual retirement, sense of control, and retirees' happiness. *Research on Aging, 31,* 112–135.

Campos, J. J., Anderson, D. I., Barbu-Roth, M. A., Hubbard, E. M., Hertenstein, M. J., & Witherington, D. (2000). Travel broadens the mind. *Infancy, 1,* 149–219.

Campos, J. J., Langer, A., & Krowitz, A. (1970, October 9). Cardiac responses on the visual cliff in prelocomotor human infants. *Science, 170,* 196–197.

Candy, B., Holman, A., Leurent, B., Davis, S., & Jones, L. (2011). Hospice care delivered at home, in nursing homes and in dedicated hospice facilities: A systematic review of quantitative and qualitative evidence. *International Journal of Nursing Studies, 48,* 121–133.

Canter, A. S. (1997). The future of intelligence testing in the schools. *School Psychology Review, 26,* 255–261.

Caplan, A. L., Blank, R. H., & Merrick, J. C. (Eds.). (1992). *Compelled compassion: Government intervention in the treatment of critically ill newborns.* Totowa, NJ: Humana Press.

Carlander, I., Ternestedt, B.-M., Sahlberg-Blom, E., Hellström, I., & Sandberg, J. (2011). Being me and being us in a family living close to death at home. *Qualitative Health Research, 21*(5), 683–695.

Carless, S. A., & Arnup, J. L. (2011). A longitudinal study of the determinants and outcomes of career change. *Journal of Vocational Behavior,* 78, 80–91.

Carnevale, A., & Strohl, J. (2010). How increasing college access is increasing inequality and what to do about it. In R. D. Kahlenberg (Ed.). *Rewarding strivers: Helping low-income students succeed in college.* New York: The Century Foundation Press.

Caron, S. L., & Moskey, E. G. (2002). Changes over time in teenage sexual relationships: Comparing the high school class of 1950, 1975, and 2000. *Adolescence, 37,* 515–526.

Carr, D. (2004). Gender, preloss marital dependence, and older adults' adjustment to widowhood. *Journal of Marriage and Family, 66,* 220–235.

Carr, D. (2011). Racial differences in end-of-life planning: Why don't Blacks and Latinos prepare for the inevitable? *Omega: The Journal of Death and Dying, 63*(1), 1–20.

Carroll, J. S., Willoughby, B., Badger, S., Nelson, L. J., Barry, C. M., & Madsen, S. D. (2007). So close, yet so far away: The impact of varying marital horizons on emerging adulthood. *Journal of Adolescent Research,* 22(3), 219–247.

Carstensen, L. (2009). *A long bright future: An action plan for a lifetime of happiness, health, and financial security.* New York: Broadway Books.

Carstensen, L. L. (1995). Evidence for a life-span theory of socioemotional selectivity. *Current Directions in Psychological Science, 4,* 151–156.

Carstensen, L. L., Graff, J., Levenson, R. W., & Gottman, J. M. (1996). Affect in intimate relationships: The developmental course of marriage. In C. Magai & S. H. McFadden (Eds.), *Handbook of emotion, adult development, and aging* (pp. 227–247). San Diego, CA: Academic Press.

Carstensen, L. L., Turan, B., Scheibe, S., Ram, N., Ersner-Hershfield, H., Samanez-Larkin, G. R., ... Nesselroade, J. R. (2011). Emotional experience improves with age: Evidence based on over 10 years of experience sampling. *Psychology and Aging, 26*(1), 21–33.

Casarett, D. J. (2011). Rethinking hospice eligibility criteria. *Journal of the American Medical Association,* 305(10), 1031–1032.

Case, R. (1999). Conceptual development. In M. Bennett (Ed.), *Developmental psychology: Achievements and prospects* (pp. 36–54). New York: Psychology Press.

Cashmore, J., & Parkinson, P. (2008). Children's and parents' perceptions on children's participation in decision making after parental separation and divorce. *Family Court Review, 46*(1), 91–104.

Caspi, A., Moffitt, T. E., Cannon, M., McClay, J., Murray, R., Harrington, H., ... Craig, I. W. (2005). Moderation of the effect of adolescent-onset cannabis use on adult psychosis by a functional polymorphism in the catechol-O-methyltransferase gene: Longitudinal evidence of a gene X environment interaction. *Biological Psychiatry, 57,* 1117–1127.

Cassel, J. B., Hager, M. A., Clark, R. R., Retchin, S. M., Dimartino, J., Coyne, P. J., ... Smith, T. J. (2010). Concentrating hospital-wide deaths in a palliative care unit: The effect of place on death and system-wide mortality. *Journal of Palliative Medicine, 13*(4), 371–374.

Castel, A. D., Lee, S. S., Humphreys, K. L., & Moore, A. N. (2010). Memory capacity, selective control, and value-directed remembering in children with and without attention-deficit/hyperactivity disorder (ADHD). *Neuropsychology,* 25(1), 15–24.

Castle, N. G., & Ferguson, J. C. (2010). What is nursing home quality and how is it measured? *The Gerontologist*, 50(4), 426–442.

Cate, R. A., & John, O. P. (2007). Testing models of the structure and development of future time perspective: Maintaining a focus on opportunities in middle age. *Psychology and Aging*, 22(1), 186–201.

Cattell, M. G. (2003). African widows: Anthropological and historical perspectives. *Journal of Women & Aging, 15*, 49–66.

Caulfield, L., Richard, S. A., Rivera, J. A., Musgrove, P., & Black, R. E. (2006). *Disease control priorities in developing countries* (2nd ed.). New York: Oxford University Press.

Cavanaugh, J. C. (2000). Metamemory from a social-cognitive perspective. In D. C. Park & N. Schwarz (Eds.), *Cognitive aging: A primer* (pp. 115–130). New York: Psychology Press.

Ceci, S. J., Rosenblum, T., de Bruyn, E., & Lee, D. Y. (1997). A bio-ecological model of intellectual development: Moving beyond h-sup-2. In R. J. Sternberg & E. L. Grigorenko (Eds.), *Intelligence, heredity, and environment* (pp. 303–322). New York: Cambridge University Press.

Cellarius, V. (2011). 'Early terminal sedation' is a distinct entity. *Bioethics*, 25(1), 46–54.

Center on Education and the Workforce, Georgetown University. (2011). The gender gap in earnings for college graduates varies across major disciplines. Retrieved from http://www.wiareport.com/2011/05

Centers for Disease Control and Prevention. (2007). Infant mortality statistics from the 2004 period: Linked birth/infant death data. Retrieved from National Vital Statistics Reports Web site: http://www.cdc.gov/nchs/data/nvsr/nvsr55/nvsr55_14.pdf

Centers for Disease Control and Prevention. (2009). Health data interactive, retrieved April 7, 2009.

Centers for Disease Control and Prevention. (2010). Assisted Reproductive Technology (ART) Report. National Summary Report.

Centers for Disease Control and Prevention. (2010). Increasing prevalence of parent-reported attention-deficit/hyperactivity disorder among children: United States, 2003–2007. *Morbidity and Mortality Weekly Report (MMWR)*, 59(44). Retrieved October 14, from http://www.ncbi.nlm.nih.gov/pubmed/21063274

Central Intelligence Agency. (2007). *The world factbook 2007*. Washington, DC: U.S. Government Printing Office.

Central Intelligence Agency. (2008). *The world factbook 2008*. Washington, DC: U.S. Government Printing Office.

Central Intelligence Agency. (2011). *The world factbook 2011*. Washington, DC: U.S. Government Printing Office.

Chalmers, B., Kaczorowski, J., Darling, E., Heaman, M., Fell, D. B., O'Brien, B., . . . Maternity Experiences Study Group of the Canadian Perinatal Surveillance System. (2010). Cesarean and vaginal birth in Canadian women: A comparison of experiences. *Birth Issues in Prenatal Care*, 37(1), 44–49.

Chambaere, K., Bilsen, J., Cohen, J., Onwuteaka-Philipsen, B. D., Mortier, F., & Deliens, L. (2011). Trends in medical end-of-life decision making in Flanders, Belgium 1998–2001–2007. *Medical Decision Making*, 31(3), 500–510.

Chapple. H. S. (1999). Changing the game in the intensive care unit: Letting nature take its course. *Critical Care Nurse, 19*, 25–34.

Charil, A., Laplante, D. P., Vaillancourt, C., & King, S. (2010). Prenatal stress and brain development. *Brain Research Reviews*, 65(1), 56–79.

Charles, M. (1992). Cross-national variation in occupational sex segregation. *American Sociological Review, 57*, 483–502.

Charles, S. T., & Almeida, D. M. (2007). Genetic and environmental effects on daily life stressors: More evidence for greater variation in later life. *Psychology and Aging*, 22(2), 331–340.

Charles, S. T., Luong, G., Almeida, D. M., Ryff, C., Sturm, M., & Love, G. (2010). Fewer ups and downs: Daily stressors mediate age differences in negative affect. *Journals of Gerontology: Psychological Sciences*, 65B(3), 279–286.

Cheadle, J. E., & Goosby, B. J. (2010). Birth weight, cognitive development, and life chances: A comparison of siblings from childhood into early adulthood. *Social Science Research, 39*, 570–584.

Chen, E. S. L., & Rao, N. (2011). Gender socialization in Chinese kindergartens: Teachers' contributions. *Sex Roles, 64*, 103–116.

Chen, W., Glasser, S., Benbenishty, R., Davidson-Arad, B., Tzur, S., & Lerner-Geva, L. (2010). The contribution of a hospital child protection team in determining suspected child abuse and neglect: Analysis of referrals of children aged 0–9. *Children and Youth Services Review*, 32(12), 1664–1669.

Chen, X., & French, D. C. (2008). Children's social competence in cultural context. *Annual Review of Psychology, 59*, 591–616.

Cheng, G. H-L., & Chan, D. K-S. (2008). Who suffers more from job insecurity? A meta-analytic review. *Applied Psychology: An International Review, 57*, 272–303.

Cherlin, A. J. (2004). The deinstitutionalization of American marriage. *Journal of Marriage and Family, 66*, 848–861.

Cherlin, A. J. (2010). Demographic trends in the United States: A review of research in the 2000s. *Journal of Marriage and Family*, 72(3), 403–419.

Chertkow, H., Whitehead, V., Phillips, N., Wolfson, C., Atherton, J., & Bergman, H. (2010). Multilingualism (but not always bilingualism) delays the onset of Alzheimer disease: Evidence from a bilingual community. *Alzheimer Disease and Associated Disorders*, 24(2), 118–125.

Child Soldiers Global Report. (2008). Coalition to stop the use of child soldiers. http://www.Childsoldiersglobalreport.org

Child Trends Data Bank. (2008). Retrieved on August 20, 2009, from www.childtrends.org

Childs, K. K., Sullivan, C. J., & Gulledge, L. M. (2011). Delinquent behavior across adolescence: Investigating the shifting salience of key criminal predictors. *Deviant Behavior*, 32(1), 64–100.

Childstats.gov. (2010). America's children: Key national indicators of well-being, 2010. Retrieved October 31, 2011, from http://www.childstats.gov

Cho, S., Zarit, S. H., & Chiriboga, D. A. (2009). Wives and daughters: The differential role of day care use in the nursing home placement of cognitively impaired family members. *The Gerontologist*, 49(1), 57–67.

Cho, Y., & Haslam, N. (2010). Suicidal ideation and distress among immigrant adolescents: The role of acculturation, life stress, and social support. *Journal of Youth and Adolescence*, 39(4), 370–379.

Chow, E. S. L., Kong, B. M. H., Wong, M. T. P., Draper, B., Lin, K. L., Ho, S. K. S., & Wong, C. P. (2004). The prevalence of depressive symptoms among elderly Chinese private nursing home residents in Hong Kong. *International Journal of Geriatric Psychiatry, 19*, 734–740.

Christensen, K. Y., Maisonet, M., Rubin, C., Holmes, A., Flanders, W. D., Heron, J., … Marcus, M. (2010). Progression through puberty in girls enrolled in a contemporary British cohort. *Journal of Adolescent Health, 47*(3), pp. 282–289.

Chung-Hall, J., & Chen, X. (2010). Aggressive and prosocial peer group functioning: Effects on children's social, school, and psychological adjustment. *Social Development, 19*, 659–680.

Cicirelli, V. G. (2007). End of life decisions: Research findings and implications. In A. Tomer, P. T. Wong, & G. Eliason (Eds.), *Existential and spiritual issues in death attitudes* (pp. 115–138). Hillsdale, NJ: Lawrence Erlbaum.

Cigolle, C. T., Lee, P. G., Langa, K. M., Lee, Y. Y., Tian, Z., & Blaum, C. S. (2010). Geriatric conditions develop in middle-aged adults with diabetes. *Journal of General Internal Medicine, 26*(3), 272–279.

Cillessen, A. H. N., & Mayeux, L. (2004). From censure to reinforcement: Developmental changes in the association between aggression and social status. *Child Development, 75*, 147–163.

Clark, D. (2007). End-of-life care around the world: Achievements to date and challenges remaining. *Omega, 56*(1), 101–110.

Clarke, D. D., Ward, P., Bartle, C., & Truman, W. (2010). Older drivers' road traffic crashes in the UK. *Accident Analysis and Prevention, 42*, 1018–1024.

Clay, M. M., & Cazden, C. B. (1992). A Vygotskian interpretation of Reading Recovery. In L. C. Moll (Ed.), *Vygotsky and education: Instructional implications and applications of sociohistorical psychology* (pp. 206–222). New York: Cambridge University Press.

Climo, J. J., Terry, P., & Lay, K. (2002). Using the double bind to interpret the experience of custodial grandparents. *Journal of Aging Studies, 16*, 19–35.

Coall, D. A., & Hertwig, R. (2010). Grandparental investment: Past, present, and future. *Behavioral and Brain Sciences, 33*, 1–59.

Cohen, P. N. (2004). The gender division of labor: "Keeping house" and occupational segregation in the United States. *Gender & Society, 18*, 239–252.

Cohen, P., Kasen, S., Chen, H., Hartmark, C., & Gordon, K. (2003). Variations in patterns of developmental transmissions in the emerging adulthood period. *Developmental Psychology, 39*, 657–669.

Coie, J. D., & Dodge, K. A. (1998). Aggression and antisocial behavior. In W. Damon (Series ed.) & N. Eisenberg (Vol. Ed.), *Handbook of child psychology: Vol 3. Social, emotional, and personality development* (5th ed., pp. 779–862). Hoboken, NJ: John Wiley & Sons Inc.

Cole, B., & Singg, S. (1998). *Relationship between parental bereavement reaction factors and selected psychosocial variables.* Paper presented at the Annual Meeting of the American Psychological Society, Washington, DC.

Coles, R. (1970). *Erik H. Erikson: The growth of his work.* Boston: Little, Brown.

Collignon, O., Vandewalle, G., Voss, P., Albouy, G., Charbonneau, G., Lassonde, M., & Lepore, F. (2011). Functional specialization for auditory-spatial processing in the occipital cortex of congenitally blind humans. *PNAS, 108 (11), 4435--4440.*

Collins, R. L. (2011). Content analysis of gender roles in media: Where are we now and where should we go? *Sex Roles, 64*, 290–298.

Collins, R. L., Elliott, M. N., Berry, S. H., Kanouse, D. E., Kunkel, D., Hunter, S. B., & Miu, A. (2004). Watching sex on television predicts adolescent initiation of sexual behavior. *Pediatrics, 114*, e280–289.

Colrain, I. M., & Baker, F. C. (2011). Changes in sleep as a function of adolescent development. *Neuropsychology Review, 21*, 5–21.

Compian, L., Gowen, L. K., & Hayward, C. (2004). Peripubertal girls' romantic and platonic involvement with boys: Associations with body image and depression symptoms. *Journal of Research on Adolescence, 14*, 23–47.

Conner, T., Prokhorov, A., Page, C., Fang, Y., Xiao, Y., & Post, L. A. (2011). Impairment and abuse of elderly by staff in long-term care in Michigan: Evidence from structural equation modeling. *Journal of Interpersonal Violence, 26*(1), 21–33.

Connor, S. R. (2007). Development of hospice and palliative care in the United States. *Omega, 56*(1), 89–99.

Conroy, K., Sandel, M., & Zuckerman, B. (2010). Poverty grown up: How childhood socioeconomic status impacts adult health. *Journal of Developmental & Behavioral Pediatrics, 31*(2), 154–160.

Cook, C. R., Williams, K. R., Guerra, N. G., Kim, T. E., & Sadek, S. (2010). Predictors of bullying and victimization in childhood and adolescence: A meta-analytic investigation. *School Psychology Quarterly, 25*(2), 65–83.

Cook, T. D., Deng, Y., & Morgano, E. (2007). Friendship influences during early adolescence: The special role of friends' grade point average. *Journal of Research on Adolescence, 17*(2), 325–356.

Cook, T. D., & Furstenberg, F. F. (2002). Explaining aspects of the transition to adulthood in Italy, Sweden, Germany, and the United States: A cross-disciplinary, case synthesis approach. *Annals of the American Academy of Political & Social Science, 580*, 257–287.

Cooney, T. M., Schaie, K. W., & Willis, S. L. (1988). The relationship between prior functioning on cognitive and personality dimensions and subject attrition in longitudinal research. *Journals of Gerontology, 43*, P12–P17.

Coontz, S. (1992). *The way we never were: American families and the nostalgia trap.* New York: Basic Books.

Coplan, R. J., Closson, L. M., & Arbeau, K. A. (2007). Gender differences in the behavioral associates of loneliness and social dissatisfaction in kindergarten. *Journal of Child Psychology and Psychiatry, 48*(10), 988–995.

Coplan, R., Findlay, L. C., & Schneider, B. H. (2010). Where do anxious children "fit" best? Childcare and the emergence of anxiety in early childhood. *Canadian Journal of Behavioral Science, 42*(3), 185–193.

Cornwell, T., & McAlister, A. R. (2011). Alternative thinking about starting points of obesity. Development of child taste preferences. *Appetite 56*(2), 428–439.

Corr, C. A. (1991–1992). A task-based approach to coping with dying. *Omega: Journal of Death and Dying, 24*, 81–94.

Corr, C. A. (2007). Hospice: Achievements, legacies, and challenges. *Omega, 56*(1), 111–120.

Corsaro, W. A. (1985). *Friendship and peer culture in the early years.* Norwood, NJ: Ablex.

Corsaro, W. A. (1997). *The sociology of childhood.* Thousand Oaks, CA: Pine Forge Press/Sage.

Costa, P. T., & McCrae, R. R. (2002). Looking backward: Changes in the mean levels of personality traits from 80 to 12. In D. Cervone & W. Mischel (Eds.), *Advances in personality science* (pp. 219–237). New York: Guilford Press.

Costos, D., Ackerman, R., & Paradis, L. (2002). Recollections of menarche: Communication between mothers and daughters regarding menstruation. *Sex Roles, 46*, 49–59.

Côté, J., & Bynner, J. M. (2008). Changes in the transition to adulthood in the UK and Canada: The role of structure and agency in emerging adulthood. *Journal of Youth Studies, 11*, 251–268.

Côté, J. E., & Levine, C. G. (2002). *Identity formation, agency, and culture: A social psychological synthesis*. Mahwah, NJ: Lawrence Erlbaum Associates Publishers.

Cotterell, J. (1996). *Social networks and social influences in adolescence*. New York: Routledge.

Cowan, C. P., & Bronstein, P. (1988). Fathers' roles in the family: Implications for research, intervention, and change. In P. Bronstein & C. P. Cowan (Eds.), *Fatherhood today: Men's changing role in the family* (pp. 341–347). Oxford, England: Wiley.

Cowan, C. P., & Cowan, P. A. (1992). *When partners become parents: The big life change for couples*. New York: Basic Books.

Cowan, P. A., Cowan, C. P., & Mehta, N. (2009). Adult attachment, couple attachment, and children's adaptation to school: An integrated attachment template and family risk model. *Attachment & Human Development, 11*(1), 29–46.

Cox, K. S., Wilt, J., Olson, B., & McAdams, D. P. (2010). Generativity, the big five, and psychosocial adaptation in midlife adults. *Journal of Personality*, 78(4), 1185–1208.

Coyl, D. D., Newland, L. A., & Freeman, H. (2010). Predicting preschoolers' attachment security from parenting behaviors, parents' attachment relationships and their use of social support. *Early Child Development and Care, 180*(4), 499–512.

Cozzarelli, C., Karafa, J. A., Collins, N. L., & Tagler, M. J. (2003). Stability and change in adult attachment styles: Associations with personal vulnerabilities, life events, and global construals of self and others. *Journal of Social & Clinical Psychology*, 22, 315–346.

Crade, M., & Lovett, S. (1988). Fetal response to sound stimulation: Preliminary report exploring use of sound stimulation in routine obstetrical ultrasound examinations. *Journal of Ultrasound in Medicine*, 7, 499–503.

Craig, L., & Mullan, K. (2010). Parenthood, gender and work-family time in the United States, Australia, Italy, France, and Denmark. *Journal of Marriage and Family*, 72(5), 1344–1361.

Craik, F. I. M. (2000). Age-related changes in human memory. In D. C. Park & N. Schwarz (Eds.), *Cognitive aging: A primer* (pp. 75–92). New York: Psychology Press.

Craik, F. I. M., Luo, L., & Sakuta, Y. (2010). Effects of aging and divided attention on memory for items and their contexts. *Psychology and Aging, 25*(4), 968–979.

Craik, F. I. M., & McDowd, J. M. (1987). Age differences in recall and recognition. *Journal of Experimental Psychology: Learning, Memory, and Cognition, 13*, 474–479.

Cramer, P. (2008). Identification and the development of competence: A 44-year longitudinal study from late adolescence to late middle age. *Psychology and Aging, 23*, 410–421.

Crawford, A. M., & Manassis, K. (2011) Anxiety, social skills, friendship quality, and peer victimization: An integrated model. *Journal of Anxiety Disorders*, 25(7), 924–937.

Crick, N. R., & Dodge, K. A. (1996). Social information-processing mechanisms on reactive and proactive aggression. *Child Development, 67*, 993–1002.

Crittenden, A. (2001). *The price of motherhood: Why the most important job in the world is still the least valued*. New York: Metropolitan Books.

Crockenberg, S. C. (2003). Rescuing the baby from the bathwater: How gender and temperament (may) influence how child care affects child development. *Child Development, 74*, 1034–1038.

Crockenberg, S. C., & Leerkes, E. M. (2005). Infant temperament moderates associations between childcare type and quantity and externalizing and internalizing behaviors at 2 1/2 years. *Infant Behavior & Development, 28*, 20–35.

Crosnoe, R., Wirth, R. J., Pianta, R. C., Leventhal, T., & Pierce, K. M. (2010). Family socioeconomic status and consistent environmental stimulation in early childhood. *Child Development, 81*(3), 972–987.

Crouch, J. L., Milner, J. S., Skowronski, J. J., Farc, M. M., Irwin, L. M., & Neese, A. (2010). Automatic encoding of ambiguous child behavior in high and low risk for child physical abuse parents. *Journal of Family Violence, 25*, 73–80.

Csikszentmihalyi, M. (1990). *Flow: The psychology of optimal experience*. New York: Harper & Row.

Csikszentmihalyi, M. (1996). *Creativity: Flow and the psychology of discovery and invention*. New York: HarperCollins.

Csikszentmihalyi, M., & Larson, R. (1984). *Being adolescent: Conflict and growth in the teenage years*. New York: Basic Books.

Csikszentmihalyi, M., & Schneider, B. L. (2000). *Becoming adult: How teenagers prepare for the world of work*. New York: Basic Books.

Cummins, D. D., & Allen, C. (Eds.). (1998). *The evolution of mind*. New York: Oxford University Press.

Currie, J., & Widom, C. S. (2010). Long-term consequences of child abuse and neglect on adult economic well-being. *Child Maltreatment, 15*(2), 111–120.

Cushen, P. J., & Wiley, J. (2011). Aha! Voila! Eureka! Bilingualism and insightful problem solving. *Learning and Individual Differences, 21*(4), 458–462.

CysticFibrosis.com. (n.d.). CysticFibrosis.com. Retrieved January 20, 2006, from http://www.cysticfibrosis.com/info/index.html

D'Anna, L. H., Ponce, N. A., & Siegel, J. M. (2010). Racial and ethnic health disparities: Evidence of discrimination's effects across the SEP spectrum. *Ethnicity & Health, 15*(2), 121–143.

D'Onofrio, B. M., Singh, A. L., Iliadou, A., Lambe, M., Hultman, C. M., Neiderhiser, J. M., … Lichtenstein, P. (2010). A quasi-experimental study of maternal smoking during pregnancy and offspring academic achievement. *Child Development, 81*(1), 80–100.

Daddis, C. (2011). Desire for increased autonomy and adolescents' perceptions of peer autonomy: "Everyone else can; why can't I?" *Child Development, 82*(4), 1310–1326.

Dahl, R. E. (2004). Adolescent brain development: A period of vulnerabilities and opportunities. In R. E. Dahl & L. P. Spear (Eds.), *Adolescent brain development: Vulnerabilities and opportunities* (Vol. 1021, p. 1–22). New York: New York Academy of Sciences.

Dallos, R., & Nokes, L. (2011). Distress, loss, and adjustment following the birth of a baby: A qualitative exploration of one new father's experiences. *Journal of Constructivist Psychology, 24*, 144–167.

Daniels, K. J., Lamson, A. L., & Hodgson, J. (2007). An exploration of the marital relationship and Alzheimer's disease: One couple's story. *Families, Systems, & Health, 25*(2), 162–177.

Dannenbaum, S. M., & Kinnier, R. T. (2009). Imaginal relationships with the dead: Applications for psychotherapy. *Journal of Humanistic Psychology, 49,* 100–113.

Danziger, S., & Ratner, D. (2010). Labor market outcomes and the transition to Adulthood, *The Future of Children, 20,* 1–24. Retrieved June 2, 2011, from http://futureofchildren.org/publications/journals/article/index.xml?journalid=72&articleid=524

Dasen, P. R. (1977). *Piagetian psychology: Cross-cultural contributions.* New York: Gardner Press.

Dasen, P. R. (1984). The cross-cultural study of intelligence: Piaget and the Baoule. *International Journal of Psychology, 19,* 407–434.

Davidson, C. (2011). *Now you see tt: How the brain science of attention will transform the way we live, work, and learn.* New York: Viking.

Davila, J., & Kashy, D. A. (2009). Secure base processes in couples: Daily associations between support experiences and attachment security. *Journal of Family Psychology, 23,* 76–88.

Davis, A. M., Bennett, K. J., Befort, C., Nollen, N. (2011). Obesity and related health behaviors among urban and rural children in the United States: Data from the National Health and Nutrition Examination Survey 2003–2004 and 2005–2006. *Journal of Pediatric Psychology, 36*(6), 669–676.

Davis, E. P., & Sandman, C. A. (2010). The timing of prenatal exposure to maternal cortisol and psychosocial stress is associated with human infant cognitive development. *Child Development, 81*(1), 131–148.

Dawson, J. D., Uc, E. Y., Anderson, S. W., Johnson, A. M., & Rizzo, M. (2010). Neuropsychology predictors of driving errors in older adults. *Journal of the American Geriatrics Society, 58*(6), 1090–1096.

De Cuyper, N., Bernhard-Oettel, C., Berntson, E., De Wiite, H., & Alarco, B. (2008). Employability and employees' well-being: Mediation by job insecurity. *Applied Psychology: An International Review, 57*(3), 488–509.

De Goede, I. H. D., Branje, S. J. T., & Meeus, W. H. J. (2009). Developmental changes in adolescents' perceptions of relationships with their parents. *Journal of Youth and Adolescence, 38,* 75–88.

de Schipper, E. J., Riksen-Walraven, J. M., & Geurts, S. A. E. (2006). Effects of child-caregiver ratio on the interactions between caregivers and children in child-care centers: An experimental study. *Child Development, 77*(4), 861–874.

De Schipper, J. C., Tavecchio, L. W. C., & van IJzendoorn, M. H. (2008). Children's attachment relationships with day care caregivers: Associations with positive caregiving and the child's temperament. *Social Development, 17*(3), 454–470.

Dean, R. S., & Davis, A. S. (2007). Relative risk of perinatal complications in common childhood disorders. *School Psychology Quarterly, 22*(1), 13–23.

Dearing, E. (2004). The developmental implications of restrictive and supportive parenting across neighborhoods and ethnicities: Exceptions are the rule. *Journal of Applied Developmental Psychology, 25,* 555–575.

Deary, I. J., Whalley, L. J., Lemmon, H., Crawford, J. R., & Starr, J. M. (2000). The stability of individual differences in mental ability from childhood to old age: Follow-up of the 1932 Scottish Mental Survey. *Intelligence, 28,* 49–55.

Deater-Deckard, K. (1996). Within family variability in parental negativity and control. *Journal of Applied Developmental Psychology, 17,* 407–422.

Deater-Deckard, K., Beekman, C., Wang, Z., Kim, J., Petrill, S., Thompson, L., & DeThorne, L. (2010). Approach/positive anticipation, frustration/anger, and overt aggression in childhood. *Journal of Personality, 78*(3), 991–1010.

Deater-Deckard, K., Ivy, L., & Smith, J. (2005). Resilience in gene-environment transactions. In S. Goldstein, & R. B. Brooks (Eds.), *Handbook of resilience in children* (pp. 49–63). New York: Kluwer Academic/Plenum Publishers.

DeCasper, A. J., & Fifer, W. P. (1980, June 6). Of human bonding: Newborns prefer their mothers' voices. *Science, 208,* 1174–1176.

Deci, E. L., & Ryan, R. M. (1985). The general causality orientations scale: Self-determination in personality. *Journal of Research in Personality, 19,* 109–134.

Deci, E. L., & Ryan, R. M. (2000). The "what" and "why" of goal pursuits: Human needs and the self-determination of behavior. *Psychological Inquiry, 11,* 227–268.

DeFillippi, R. J., & Arthur, M. B. (1994). The boundary-less career: A competency-based perspective. *Journal of Organizational Behavior, 15,* 307–324.

DeGarmo, D. S. (2010). Coercive and prosocial fathering, antisocial personality, and growth in children's postdivorce noncompliance. *Child Development, 81*(2), 503–516.

Degnan, K. A., Almas, A. N., & Fox, N. A. (2010). Temperament and the environment in the etiology of childhood anxiety. *Journal of Child Psychology and Psychiatry, 51*(4), 497–517.

Del Giudice, M. (2011). Alone in the dark? Modeling the conditions for visual experience in human fetuses. *Developmental Psychobiology, 53*(2), 214–219.

DeMaris, A., Mahoney, A., & Pargament, K.T. (2011). Doing the scut work of infant care: Does religiousness encourage father involvement? *Journal of Marriage and Family, 73,* 354–368.

Dempster, F. N. (1981). Memory span: Sources of individual and developmental differences. *Psychological Bulletin, 89,* 63–100.

Denham, S. A. (1998). *Emotional development in young children.* New York: Guilford Press.

Denham, S. A., Blair, K. A., DeMulder, E., Levitas, J., Sawyer, K., Auerbach-Major, S., & Queenan, P. (2003). Preschool emotional competence: Pathway to social competence. *Child Development, 74,* 238–256.

Dennis, N. A., Hayes, S. M., Prince, S. E., Madden, D. J., Huettel, S. A., & Cabeza, R. (2008). Effects of aging on the neural correlates of successful item and source memory encoding. *Journal of Experimental Psychology: Learning, Memory, and Cognition, 34*(4), 791–808.

Dennissen, J. J. A., Asendorpf, J. B., & van Aken, M. A. G. (2008). Childhood personality predicts long-term trajectories of shyness and aggressiveness in the context of demographic transitions in emerging adulthood. *Journal of Personality, 76*(1), 67–99.

Dew, J., & Wilcox, W. B. (2011). If momma ain't happy: Explaining declines in marital satisfaction among new mothers. *Journal of Marriage and Family, 73,* 1–12.

DeWall, C. N., Twenge, J. M., Gitter, S. A., & Baumeister R. F. (2009). It's the thought that counts: The role of hostile cognition in shaping aggressive responses to social exclusion. *Journal of Personality and Social Psychology, 96,* 45–59.

Diamanti, A., Basso, M. S., Castro, M., Bianco, G., Ciacco, E., Calce, A., . . . Gambarara, M. (2008). Clinical efficacy and safety of parental nutrition in adolescent girls with anorexia nervosa. *Journal of Adolescent Health, 42,* 111–118.

Diamantopoulou, S., Rydell, A., & Henricsson, L. (2008). Can both low and high self-esteem be related to aggression in children? *Social Development, 17*, 682–698.

Diamond, A. (2009). The interplay of biology and the environment broadly defined. *Developmental Psychology, 45*, 1–8.

Diamond, A., Kirkham, N., & Amso, D. (2002). Conditions under which young children can hold two rules in mind and inhibit a prepotent response. *Developmental Psychology, 38*, 352–362.

Diamond, L. M., & Savin-Williams, R. C. (2003). Explaining diversity in the development of same-sex sexuality among young women. In L. D. Garnets & D. C. Kimmel (Eds.), *Psychological perspectives on lesbian, gay, and bisexual experiences* (2nd ed., pp. 130–148). New York: Columbia University Press.

Diamond, M. C. (1988). *Enriching heredity: The impact of the environment on the anatomy of the brain.* New York: Free Press.

Diamond, M. C. (1993). An optimistic view of the aging brain. *Generations, 17*(1), 31–33.

Diaz, M. A., Le, H-N., Cooper, B. A., & Muñoz, R. F. (2007). Interpersonal factors and perinatal depressive symptomatology in a low-income Latina sample. *Cultural Diversity and Ethnic Minority Psychology, 13*(4), 328–333.

Dickens, B. M., Boyle, J. M., & Ganzini, L. (2008). Euthanasia and assisted suicide. In P. A. Singer, & A. M. Viens (Eds.), *The Cambridge textbook of bioethics* (pp. 72–77). New York, NY: Cambridge University Press.

Diederich, A., Colonius, H., & Schomburg, A. (2008). Assessing age-related multisensory enhancement with the time-window-of-integration model. *Neuropsychologia, 46*, 2556–2562.

Dietz, P. M., Homa, D., England, L. J., Burley, K., Tong, V. T., Dube, S. R., & Bernert, J. T. (2011). Estimates of nondisclosure of cigarette smoking among pregnant and nonpregnant women of reproductive age in the United States. *American Journal of Epidemiology, 173*(3), 355–359.

Dijkstra, J. K., Cillessen, A. H. N., Lindenberg, S., & Veenstra, R. (2010). Basking in reflected glory and its limits: Why adolescents hang out with popular peers. *Journal of Research on Adolescence, 20*(4), 942–958.

Dilworth-Anderson, P., Boswell, G., & Cohen, M. D. (2007). Spiritual and religious coping values and beliefs among African American caregivers: A qualitative study. *Journal of Applied Gerontology, 26*(4), 355–369.

DiPietro, J. A., Kivlighan, K. T., Costigan, K. A., Rubin, S. E., Shiffler, D. E., Henderson, J. L., & Pillion, J. P. (2010). Prenatal antecedents of newborn neurological maturation. *Child Development, 81*(1), 115–130.

DiRenzo, M. S., Greenhaus, J. H., & Weer, C. H. (2011). Job level, demands, and resources as antecedents of work-family conflict. *Journal of Vocational Behavior, 79*, 305–314.

DiRosa, M., Kofahl, C., McKee, K., Bién, B., Lamura, G., Prouskas, C., … Mnich, E. (2011). A typology of caregiving situations and service use in family carers of older people in six European countries. *GeroPsych, 24*(1), 5–18.

Dishion, T. J., McCord, J., & Poulin, F. (1999). When interventions harm: Peer groups and problem behavior. *American Psychologist, 54*, 755–764.

Dishion, T. J., & Tipsord, J. M. (2011). Peer contagion in child and adolescent social and emotional development. *Annual Review of Psychology, 62*, 189–214.

Dixon, R. A., Rust, T. B., Feltmate, S. E., & See, S. K. (2007). Memory and aging: Selected research directions and application issues. *Canadian Psychology, 48*(2), 67–76.

Dobbins, E. H. (2007). End-of-life decisions: Influence of advance directives on patient care. *Journal of Gerontological Nursing, 33*, 50–56.

Dodge, K. A., Coie, J. D., & Lynam, D. (2006). Aggression and antisocial behavior in youth. In N. Eisenberg, W. Damon, & R. M. Lerner (Eds.), *Handbook of child psychology: Vol. 3, Social, emotional, and personality development* (6th ed. pp. 719–788). Hoboken, NJ: John Wiley & Sons Inc.

Doka, K. J. (2003). The death awareness movement: Description, history, and analysis. In C. D. Bryant (Ed.), *Handbook of death & dying* (pp. 50–55). Thousand Oaks, CA: Sage.

Dolcos, F., & Cabeza, R. (2002). Event-related potentials of emotional memory: Encoding pleasant, unpleasant, and neutral pictures. *Cognitive, Affective & Behavioral Neuroscience, 2*, 252–263.

Donnellan, M. B., Conger, R. D., & Burzette, R. G. (2007). Personality development from late adolescence to young adulthood: Differential stability, normative maturity, and evidence for the maturity-stability hypothesis. *Journal of Personality, 75*(2), 237–263.

Doucet, S., Soussignan, R., Sagot, P., & Schaal, B. (2007). The "smellscape" of mother's breast: Effects of odor masking and selective unmasking on neonatal arousal, oral and visual responses. *Developmental Psychobiology, 49*, 129–138.

Douglas, A. J. (2010). Baby on board: Do responses to stress in the maternal brain mediate adverse pregnancy outcomes? *Frontiers in Neuroendocrinology, 31*, 359–376.

Douglas, S. J., & Michaels, M. W. (2004). *The mommy myth: The idealization of motherhood and how it has undermined women.* New York: Free Press.

Downey, L., Curtis, J. R., Lafferty, W. E., Herting, J. R., & Engelberg, R. A. (2010). The quality of dying and death questionnaire (QODD): Empirical domains and theoretical perspectives. *Journal of Pain and Symptom Management, 39*(1), 9–22.

Doyle, M., O'Dywer, C., & Timonen, V. (2010). "How can you just cut off a whole side of the family and say move on?" The reshaping of paternal grandparent-grandchild relationships following divorce or separation in the middle generation. *Family Relations, Interdisciplinary Journal of Applied Family Studies, 59*, 587–598.

Dozeman, E., van Marwijk, H. W., van Schaik, D. J. F., Stek, M. L., van der Horst, H. E., Beekman, A. T. F., & van Hout, H. P. (2010). High incidence of clinically relevant depressive symptoms in vulnerable persons of 75 years or older living in the community. *Aging & Mental Health, 14*, 828–833.

Drago, F. (2011). Self-esteem and earnings. *Journal of Economic Psychology, 32*, 480–488.

Dresser, R. (2004). Death with dignity: Contested boundaries. *Journal of Palliative Care, 20*, 201–206.

Driver, J., & Gottman, J. M. (2004). Daily marital interactions and positive affect during marital conflict among newlywed couples. *Family Process, 43*(3), 301–314.

Duberstein, P. R., Chapman, B. P., Sink, K. M., Tindle, H. A., Bamonti, P., Robbins, J., … Franks, P. (2011). Personality and risk for Alzheimer's disease in adults 72 years of age and older: A 6-year follow-up. *Psychology and Aging, 26*(2), 351–362.

DuBose, K. D., Mayo, M. S., Gibson, C. A., Green, J. L., Hill, J. O., Jacobsen, D. J., Smith, B. K., Sullivan, D. K., Washburn, R. A., & Donnelly, J. E. (2008). Physical activity across the curriculum (PAAC): Rationale and design. *Contemporary Clinical Trials, 29*(1), 83–93.

Duffy, D., & Reynolds, P. (2011). Babies born at the threshold of viability: Attitudes of paediatric consultants and trainees in South East England. *Acta Pædiatrica, 100*, 42–46.

Dumontheil, I., Apperly, I. A., & Blakemore, S.-J. (2010). Online usage of theory of mind continues to develop in late adolescence. *Developmental Science, 13*(2), 331–338.

Duncan, G. J., & Brooks-Gunn, J. (2000). Family poverty, welfare reform, and child development. *Child Development, 71*, 188–196.

Duncan, G. J., Ziol-Guest, K. M., & Kalil, A. (2010). Early-childhood poverty and adult attainment, behavior, and health. *Child Development, 81*(1), 306–325.

Dunkel Schetter, C., & Lobel, M. (2011). Pregnancy and birth: A multilevel analysis of stress and birthweight. In (A. Baum, T. A. Revenson, & Singer, J., Handbook of Health Psychology (2nd ed., pp. 431–464).). New York, NY: Psychology Press.

Dunn, J., & Hughes, C. (2001). "I got some swords and you're dead!": Violent fantasy, antisocial behavior, friendship, and moral sensibility in young children. *Child Development, 72*, 491–505.

Dunn, J., Wooding, C., & Hermann, J. (1977). Mothers' speech to young children: Variation in context. *Developmental Medicine & Child Neurology, 19*, 629–638.

Dunphy, D. C. (1963). The social structure of urban adolescent peer groups. *Sociometry, 26*, 230–246.

Dupree, V., Leventhal, T., Crosnoe, R., & Dion, E. (2010). Understanding the positive role of neighborhood socioeconomic advantage in achievement: The contribution of the home, child care, and school environments. *Developmental Psychology, 46*(5), 1227–1244.

Dwairy, M. (2010). Parental inconsistency: A third cross-cultural research on parenting and psychological adjustment of children. *Journal of Child and Family Studies, 19*, 23–29.

Dwairy, M., Achoui, M., Filus, A., Rezvan nia, P., Casullo, M. M., & Vohra, N. (2010). Parenting, mental health and culture: A fifth cross-cultural research on parenting and psychological adjustment of children. *Journal of Child and Family Studies, 19*, 36–41.

Dweck, C. S. (1986). Motivational processes affecting learning. *American Psychologist, 41*, 1040–1048.

Dwyer, L-L., Nordenfelt, L., & Ternestedt, B.-M. (2008). Three nursing home residents speak about meaning at the end of life. *Nursing Ethics, 15*(1), 97–109.

Ebling, F. J. P. (2005). The neuroendocrine timing of puberty. *Reproduction, 129*, 675–683.

Eccles, J. S., & Midgley, C. (1989). Stage-environment fit: Developmentally appropriate classrooms for young adolescents. In C. Ames & R. Ames (Eds.), *Research on motivation in education: Vol. 3. Goals and cognitions* (pp. 13–44). New York: Academic Press.

Eccles, J. S., & Roeser, R. W. (2003). Schools as developmental contexts. In G. R. Adams & M. D. Berzonsky (Eds.), *Blackwell handbook of adolescence* (pp. 129–148). Malden, MA: Blackwell.

Economic Policy Institute. (2011). *State of Working America*. Washington, DC: EP1.

Economic Policy Institute. (2012). *State of Working America*. Washington, DC: EP1.

Edin, K., & Kefalas, M. (2005). *Promises I can keep: Why poor women put motherhood before marriage*. Berkeley: University of California Press.

Edwards, A. C., Dodge, K. A., Latendresse, S. J., Lansford, J. E., Bates, J. E., Pettit, ... Dick, D. M. (2010). MAOA-uVNTR and early physical discipline interact to influence delinquent behavior. *Journal of Child Psychology and Psychiatry, 51*(6), 679–687.

Edwards, S. L., Rapee, R. M., & Kennedy, S. (2010). Prediction of anxiety symptoms in preschool-aged children: Examination of maternal and paternal perspectives. *The Journal of Child Psychology and Psychiatry, 51*(3), 313–321.

Eggebeen, D. J., Dew, J., & Knoester, C. (2010). Fatherhood and men's lives at middle age. *Journal of Family Issues, 31*(1), 113–130.

Eisenberg, N. (1992). *The caring child*. Cambridge, MA: Harvard University Press.

Eisenberg, N. (2003). Prosocial behavior, empathy, and sympathy. In M. H. Bornstein, L. Davidson, C. L. M. Keyes, & K. A. Moore (Eds.), *Well-being: Positive development across the life course* (pp. 253–265). Mahwah, NJ: Erlbaum.

Eisenberg, N., & Fabes, R. A. (1998). Prosocial development. In W. Damon (Series ed.) & N. Eisenberg (Vol. ed.), *Handbook of child psychology: Vol 3. Social, emotional, and personality development* (5th ed., pp. 701–778). Hoboken, NJ: John Wiley & Sons Inc.

Eisenberg, N., Guthrie, I. K., Murphy, B. C., Shepard, S. A., Cumberland, A., & Carlo, G. (1999). Consistency and development of prosocial dispositions: A longitudinal study. *Child Development, 70*, 1360–1372.

Eisenberg, N., Zhou, Q., Liew, J., Champion, C., Pidada, S. U. (2006). Emotion-related regulation, and social functioning. In X. Chen, D. C. French, & B. H. Schneider (Eds.), *Peer relationships in cultural context* (pp. 170–197). New York, NY: Cambridge University Press.

Eisner, E. W. (2004). Multiple intelligences: Its tensions and possibilities. *Teachers College Record, 106*, 31–39.

Ekerdt, D. J. (1986). The busy ethic: Moral continuity between work and retirement. *Gerontologist, 26*, 239–244.

Ekerdt, D. J. (2010). Frontiers of research on work and retirement. *Journals of Gerontology: Social Sciences, 65B*(1), 69–80.

Ekvlad, M., Gissler, M., Lehtonen, L., & Korkrila, J. (2010). Prenatal smoking exposure and the risk of psychiatric morbidity into young adulthood [Electronic version]. *Archives of General Psychiatry, 67*(8), 841–849.

Elder, G. H., & Caspi, A. (1988). Economic stress in lives: Developmental perspectives. *Journal of Social Issues, 44*, 25–45.

Eldridge, K. A., & Christensen, A. (2002). Demand-withdraw communication during couple conflict: A review and analysis. In P. Noller & J. A. Feeney (Eds.), *Understanding marriage: Developments in the study of couple interaction* (pp. 289–322). New York: Cambridge University Press.

Elkind, D. (1968). Cognitive development in adolescence. In J. F. Adams (Ed.), *Understanding adolescence* (pp. 128–158). Boston: Allyn and Bacon.

Elkind, D. (1978). Understanding the young adolescent. *Adolescence, 13*, 127–134.

Ellis, B. J. (2004). Timing of pubertal maturation in girls: An integrated life history approach. *Psychological Bulletin, 130*, 920–958.

Ellis, B. J., Boyce, W. T., Belsky, J., Bakermans-Kranenburg, M. J., & Van Ijzendoorn, M. H. (2011). Differential susceptibility to the environment: An evolutionary-neurodevelopmental theory. *Development and Psychopathology, 23*(1), 7–28.

Ellis, B. J., Shirtcliff, E. A., Boyce, W., Deardorff, J., & Essex, M. J. (2011). Quality of early family relationships and the timing and tempo of puberty: Effects depend on biological sensitivity to context. *Development and Psychopathology, 23*(1), 85–99.

Emory, E. K. (2010). A womb with a view: Ultrasound for evaluation of fetal neurobehavioral development. *Infant and Child Development, 19*, 119–124.

Enck, G. E. (2003). The dying process. In C. D. Bryant (Ed.), *Handbook of death & dying* (pp. 457–467). Thousand Oaks, CA: Sage.

Engle, S. (n.d.). Degree attainment rates at colleges and universities: College completion declining, taking longer, UCLA study shows. Retrieved September 6, 2006, from Higher Education Research Institute Web site: http://www.gseis.ucla.edu/heri/darcu_pr.html

Englund, M. M., Egeland, B., Olivia, E. M., & Collins, W. A. (2008). Childhood and adolescent predictors of heavy drinking and alcohol use disorders in early adulthood: A longitudinal development analysis. *Addiction, 103* (Suppl. 1), 23–35.

Epstein, L. H., & Wrotniak, B. H. (2010). Future directions for pediatric obesity treatment. *Obesity, 18*(Suppl 1), S8–S12.

Epstein, R. (2010). *Teen 2.0: Saving our children and families from the torment of adolescence.* New York: Linton Publishing.

Erber, J. T., & Prager, I. G. (1999). Age and memory: Perceptions of forgetful young and older adults. In T. M. Hess & F. Blanchard-Fields (Eds.), *Social cognition and aging* (pp. 197–217). San Diego, CA: Academic Press.

Erickson, K., Kritz-Silverstein, D., Wingard, D. L., & Barrett-Conner, E. (2010). Birth weight and cognitive performance in older women: The Rancho Berbardo study [Electronic version]. *Archives of Women's Mental Health, 13*(2). 141–146.

Erikson, E. H. (1950). *Childhood and society.* Oxford, England: Norton.

Erikson, E. H. (1963). *Childhood and society* (2nd ed.). New York: Norton.

Erikson, E. H. (1968). *Identity: Youth and crisis.* New York: Norton.

Erikson, E. H. (1969). *Gandhi's truth: On the origins of militant nonviolence.* New York: Norton.

Erikson, E. H. (1980). *Identity and the life cycle.* New York: Norton.

Espeset, E. M. S., Nordbø, R. H. S., Gulliksen, K. S., Skárderud, F., Geller, J., & Holte, A. (2011). The concept of body image disturbance in anorexia nervosa: An empirical inquiry utilizing patients' subjective experiences. *Eating Disorders, 19*(2), 175–193.

Espinoza, P., Penelo, E., & Raich, R. M. (2010). Disordered eating behaviors and body image in a longitudinal pilot study of adolescent girls: What happens 2 years later? *Body Image, 7*, 70–73.

Espy, K. A., Fang, H., Johnson, C., Stopp, C., Wiebe, S. A., & Respass, J. (2010). Prenatal tobacco exposure: Developmental outcomes in the neonatal period. *Developmental Psychology, 47*(1), 153–169.

Etaugh, C. A., & Bridges, J. S. (2006). Midlife transitions. In J. Worell & C. D. Goodheart (Eds.), *Handbook of girls' and women's psychological health: Gender and well-being across the lifespan* (pp. 359–367). New York: Oxford University Press.

EUROCAT. (2004). *EUROCAT special report: A review of environmental risk factors for congenital anomalies.* Newtownabbey, Northern Ireland: Author.

Evans, A. D., Xu, F., & Lee, K. (2011). When all signs point to you: Lies told in the face of evidence. *Developmental Psychology, 47*(1), 39–49.

Evans, W., Christoffel, K. K., Necheles, J. W., & Becker, A. B. (2010). Social marketing as a childhood obesity prevention strategy. *Obesity, 18*(Suppl 1), S23–S26.

Fabes, R. A., Eisenberg, N., Smith, M. C., & Murphy, B. C. (1996). Getting angry at peers: Associations with liking of the provocateur. *Child Development, 67*, 942–956.

Fabes, R. A., Martin, C. L., & Hanish, L. D. (2003). Young children's play qualities in same-, other-, and mixed-sex peer groups. *Child Development, 74*, 921–932.

Fabian, J. (2011). Applying Roper v. Simmons in juvenile transfer and waiver proceedings: A legal and neuroscientific inquiry. *International Journal of Offender Therapy and Comparative Criminology, 55*(5), 732–755.

Faeh, D., & Bopp, M. (2010). Increase in the prevalence of obesity in Switzerland 1982–2007: Birth cohort analysis puts recent slowdown into perspective. *Obesity, 18*(3), 644–646.

Fagan, J. F. (1988). Evidence for the relationship between responsiveness to visual novelty during infancy and later intelligence: A summary. *Cahiers de Psychologie Cognitive/Current Psychology of Cognition, 8*, 469–475.

Fagan, J. F. (2000). A theory of intelligence as processing: Implications for society. *Psychology, Public Policy, and Law, 6*, 168–179.

Fahs, B. (2007). Second shifts and political awakenings: Divorce and the political socialization of middle-aged women. *Journal of Divorce & Remarriage, 47*(3/4), 43-64.

Fairchild, H., & Cooper, M. (2010). A multidimensional measure of core beliefs relevant to eating disorders: Preliminary development and validation. *Eating Behaviors, 11*, 239–246.

Falconier, M. K., Clark, M. H., & Parris, D. (2011). Validity in an evaluation of Healthy Families Florida—A program to prevent child abuse and neglect. *Child and Youth Services Review, 33*, 66–77.

Falconier, M. K., & Epstein, N. B. (2010). Couples experiencing financial strain: What we know and what we can do. *Family Relations: Interdisciplinary Journal of Applied Family Studies, 60*, 303–317.

Families and Work Institute. (2009). Times are changing: Gender and generation at work and at home. http://familiesandwork.org/site/research/reports/Times_Are_Changing.pdf

Farmer, T. W., Hamm, J. V., Leung, M., Lambert, K., & Gravelle, M. (2011). Early adolescent peer ecologies in rural communities: Bullying in schools that do and do not have a transition during the middle grades. *Journal of Youth and Adolescence, 40*(9), 1106–1117.

Farquhar, J. C., & Wasylkiw, L. (2007). Media images of men: Trends and consequences of body conceptualization. *Psychology of Men & Masculinity, 8*(3), 145–160.

Farroni, T., Massaccesi, S., & Simion, F. (2002). La direzione dello sguardo di un'altra persona puo dirigere l'attenzione del neonato? [Can the direction of the gaze of another person shift the attention of a neonate?]. *Giornale Italiano di Psicologia, 29*, 857–864.

Fauth, R. C., Leventhal, T., & Brooks-Gunn, J. (2007). Welcome to the neighborhood? Long term impacts of moving to low-poverty neighborhoods on poor children's and adolescents' outcomes. *Journal of Research on Adolescence, 17*(2), 249–284.

Fearon, R. M. P., & Belsky, J. (2011). Infant-mother attachment and the growth of externalizing problems across the primary-school years. *The Journal of Child Psychology and Psychiatry, 52*(7), 782–791.

Fearon, R. P., Lapsely, A., Bakermans-Kranenburg, M. J., IJzendoorn, M. H., & Roisman, G. I. (2010). The significance of insecure attachment and disorganization in the development of children's externalizing behavior: A meta-analytic study. *Child Development, 81*(2), 435–456.

Feeney, J. A. (1999). Adult romantic attachment and couple relationships. In J. Cassidy & P. R. Shaver (Eds.), *Handbook of attachment: Theory, research, and clinical applications* (pp. 355–377). New York: Guilford Press.

Feeney, J. A., Hohaus, L., Noller, P., & Alexander, R. P. (2001). *Becoming parents: Exploring the bonds between mothers, fathers, and their infants.* New York: Cambridge University Press.

Feeney, J. A., & Noller, P. (2002). Allocation and performance of household tasks: A comparison of new parents and childless couples. In P. Noller & J. A. Feeney (Eds.), *Understanding marriage: Developments in the study of couple interaction* (pp. 411–436). New York: Cambridge University Press.

Feinberg, I., & Campbell, I. G. (2010). Sleep EEG changes during adolescence: An index of a fundamental brain reorganization. *Brain and Cognition, 72,* 56–65.

Feixa, C. (2011). Past and present of adolescence in society: The 'teen brain' debate in perspective. *Neuroscience and Biobehavioral Reviews,* 35(8), 1634–1643.

Feldman, D. C., & Beehr, T. A. (2011). A three-phase model of retirement decision making. *American Psychologist, 66*(3), 193–203.

Feldman, R., & Eidelman, A. I. (2003). Skin-to-skin contact (kangaroo care) accelerates autonomic and neurobehavioural maturation in preterm infants. *Developmental Medicine & Child Neurology, 45,* 274–281.

Feldman, R., & Masalha, S. (2010). Parent-child and triadic antecedents of children's social competence: Cultural specificity, shared process. *Developmental Psychology, 46*(2), 455–467.

Feng, J.-Y., Fetzer, S., Chen, Y.-W., Yeh, L., & Huang, M.-C. (2010). Multidisciplinary collaboration reporting child abuse: A grounded theory study. *International Journal of Nursing Studies, 47,* 1483–1490.

Ferber, R. (1985). Sleep, sleeplessness, and sleep disruptions in infants and young children. *Annals of Clinical Research,* 17(5). Special issue: Sleep research and its clinical implications. 227–234.

Fernandez, M., Blass, E. M., Hernandez-Reif, M., Field, T., Diego, M., & Sanders, C. (2003). Sucrose attenuates a negative electroencephalographic response to an aversive stimulus for newborns. *Journal of Developmental & Behavioral Pediatrics, 24,* 261–266.

Field, M. J. (2009). How people die in the United States. In J. L. Werth Jr. and D. Blevins (Eds.), Decision making near the end of life: Issues, developments, and future directions (pp. 63–75). New York: Routledge.

Field, N. P., Gal-Oz, E., & Bonanno, G. A. (2003). Continuing bonds and adjustment at 5 years after the death of a spouse. *Journal of Consulting and Clinical Psychology, 71,* 110–117.

Field, T., Diego, M., & Hernandez-Reif, M. (2007). Massage therapy research. *Developmental Review, 27,* 75–89.

Field, T., Diego, M., & Hernandez-Reif, M. (2011). Potential underlying mechanisms for greater weight gain in massaged preterm infants. *Infant Behavior & Development, 34*(3), 383–389.

Figueiredo, B., Pacheco, A., Costa, R., Conde, A., & Teixeira, C. (2010). Mother's anxiety and depression during the third pregnancy trimester and neonate's mother versus stranger's face/voice visual preference. *Early Human Development, 86,* 479–485.

Fincham, F. D., Beach, S. R. H., & Davila, J. (2007). Longitudinal relations between forgiveness and conflict resolution in marriage. *Journal of Family Psychology, 21*(3), 542–545.

Fincham, F. D., Stanley, S. M., & Beach, S. R. (2007). Transformative processes in marriage: An analysis of emerging trends. *Journal of Marriage and Family, 69*(2), 275–292.

Finegood, D. T., Merth, T. N., & Rutter, H. (2010). Implications of the Foresight Obesity System Map for solutions to childhood obesity. *Obesity, 18*(Suppl 1), S13–S16.

Fingerman, K. L. (2004). The role of offspring and in-laws in grandparents' ties to their grandchildren. *Journal of Family Issues, 25,* 1026–1049.

Fingerman, K. L., Miller, L., & Charles, S. (2008). Saving the best for last: How adults treat social partners of different ages. *Psychology and Aging, 23(2),* 399–409.

Finkel, D., & Pedersen, N. L. (2004). Processing speed and longitudinal trajectories of change for cognitive abilities: The Swedish Adoption/Twin Study of Aging. *Aging, Neuropsychology, and Cognition, 11,* 325–345.

Finkel, D., Andel, R., Gatz, M., & Pedersen, N. (2009). The role of occupational complexity in trajectories of cognitive aging before and after retirement. *Psychology and Aging, 24*(3), 563–573.

Fischer, D. H. (1977). *Growing old in America.* New York: Oxford University Press.

Fishman, T. (2010). *Shock of gray: The aging of the world's population and how it pits young against old, child against parent, worker against boss, company against rival, and nation against nation.* New York: Scribner.

Fitzpatrick, M. J., & McPherson, B. J. (2010). Coloring within the lines: Gender stereotypes in contemporary coloring books. *Sex Roles, 62,* 127–137.

Fivush, R. (2011). The development of autobiographical memory. *Annual Review of Psychology, 62,* 559–582.

Flanagan, C. A., & Stout, M. (2010). Developmental patterns of social trust between early and late adolescence: Age and school climate effects. *Journal of Research on Adolescence, 20*(3), 748–773.

Flavell, J. H. (1963). *The developmental psychology of Jean Piaget.* New York: Van Nostrand.

Flavell, J. H., Beach, D. R., & Chinsky, J. M. (1966). Spontaneous verbal rehearsal in a memory task as a function of age. *Child Development, 37,* 283–299.

Flouri, E., Tan, J., Griggs, J., & Attar-Schwartz, S. (2010). [Electronic version]. Adverse life events, area socioeconomic disadvantage, and adolescent psychopathology: The role of closeness to grandparents in moderating the effect of contextual stress. *The International Journal on the Biology of Stress, 13*(5), 402–412.

Flower, K. B., Willoughby, M., Cadigan, R. J., Perrin, E. M., & Randolph, G. (2008). Understanding breastfeeding initiation and continuation in rural communities: A combined qualitative/quantitative approach. *Maternal and Child Health Journal, 12*(3), 402–414.

Flynn, J. R. (2007). *What is intelligence?: beyond the flynn effect.* New York: Cambridge University Press.

Ford, D. H., & Lerner, R. M. (1992). *Developmental systems theory: An integrative approach.* Newbury Park, CA: Sage.

Forret, M. L., Sullivan, S. E., & Mainiero, L. A. (2010). Gender role differences in reactions to unemployment: Exploring psychological mobility and boundaryless careers. *Journal of Organizational Behavior, 31,* 647–666.

Foss, K. A. (2010). Perpetuationg "scientific motherhood": Infant feeding discourse in Parents Magazine 1930–2007. *Women & Health, 50*(3), 297–311.

Foster, R. E., Stone, F. P., Linkh, D. J., Besetsny, L. K., Collins, P. S., Saha, T., ... Milner, J. S. (2010). Substantiation of spouse and child maltreatment reports as a function of referral source and maltreatment type. *Military Medicine, 175*(8), 560–566.

Foster, T. L., Gilmer, M. J., Davies, B., Dietrich, M. S., Barrera, M., Fairclough, ... Gerhardt, C. A. (2011). Comparison of continuing bonds reported by parents and siblings after a child's death from cancer. *Death Studies, 35*, 420–440.

Fowler-Brown, A. G., Ngo, L. H., Phillips, R. S., & Wee, C. C. (2010). Adolescent obesity and future college degree attainment. *Obesity, 18*(6), 1235–1241.

Fox, E., Zougkou, K., Ridgewell, A., & Garner, K. (2011). The serotonin transporter gene alters sensitivity to attention bias modification: Evidence for a plasticity gene. *Biological Psychiatry, 70*(11), 1049–1054.

Fox, S. E., Levitt, P., & Nelson, C. A. (2010). How the timing and quality of early experiences ifluence the development of brain architecture. *Child Development, 81*(1), 28–40.

Fredricks, J. A., & Eccles, J. S. (2010). Breadth of extracurricular participation and adolescent adjustment among African-American and European-American youth. *Journal of Research on Adolescence, 20*(2), 307–333.

Freeman, S., Kurosawa, H., Ebihara, S., & Kohzuki, M. (2010). Caregiving burden for the oldest old: A population based study of centenarian caregivers in Northern Japan. *Archives of Gerontology and Geriatrics, 50*, 282–291.

Frey, K. S., & Ruble, D. N. (1985). What children say when the teacher is not around: Conflicting goals in social comparison and performance assessment in the classroom. *Journal of Personality and Social Psychology, 48*, 550–562.

Frey, K. S., & Ruble, D. N. (1990). Strategies for comparative evaluation: Maintaining a sense of competence across the life span. In R. J. Sternberg & J. Kolligian, Jr. (Eds.), *Competence considered* (pp. 167–189). New Haven, CT: Yale University Press.

Friedman, D. (2003). Cognition and aging: A highly selective overview of event-related potential (ERP) data. *Journal of Clinical and Experimental Neuropsychology, 25*, 702–720.

Frischen, A., Bayliss, A. P., & Tipper, S. P. (2007) Gaze cueing of attention: Visual attention, social cognition, and individual differences. *Psychological Bulletin, 133*(4), 694–724.

Frisén, A., & Holmqvist, K. (2010). What characterizes early adolescents with a positive body image? A qualitative investigation of Swedish girls and boys. *Body Image, 7*, 205–212.

Frye, A. A., & Liem, J. H. (2011). Diverse patterns in the development of depressive symptoms among emerging adults. *Journal of Adolescent Research, 26*(5), 570–590.

Fu, S.-Y., Anderson, D., & Courtney, M. (2003). Cross-cultural menopausal experience: Comparison of Australian and Taiwanese women. *Nursing & Health Sciences, 5*, 77–84.

Fuller, B., & García Coll, C. (2010). Learning from Latinos: Contexts, families, and child development in motion. *Developmental Psychology, 46*(3), 559–565.

Fuller-Rowell, T. E., & Doan, S. N. (2010). The social costs of academic success across ethnic groups. *Child Development, 81*(6), 1696–1713.

Fung, H. H., Lai, P., & Ng, R. (2001). Age differences in social preferences among Taiwanese and mainland Chinese: The role of perceived time. *Psychology and Aging, 16*, 351–356.

Funk, L. M. (2010). Prioritizing parental autonomy: Adult children's accounts of feeling responsible and supporting aging parents. *Journal of Aging Studies, 24*(1), 57–64.

Furstenberg, F. F. Jr. (2010). On a new schedule: Transitions to adulthood and family change. *The Future of Children, 20*, 67–87. Retrieved June 2, 2011, from http://futureofchildren.org/futureofchildren/publications/docs/20_01_04.pdf

Fussenegger, D., Pietrobelli, A., & Widhalm, K. (2007). Childhood obesity: Political developments in Europe and related perspectives for future action on prevention. *Obesity Reviews, 9*, 76–82.

Gagne, M. H., Tourigny, M., Joly, J., & Pouliot-Lapointe, J. (2007). Predictors of adult attitudes toward corporal punishment of children. *Journal of Interpersonal Violence, 22*(10), 1285–1304.

Gajic-Veljanoski, O., & Stewart, D. E. (2007). Women trafficked into prostitution: Determinants, human rights, and health needs. *Transcultural Psychiatry, 44*(3), 338–358.

Galinsky, E. (2007). The changing landscape of work. *Generations, 31*(1), 16–22.

Galinsky, E., Bond, J. T., Kim, S., Backon, L., Brownfield, E., & Sakai, K. (2005). *Overwork in America: When the way we work becomes too much.* New York: Families and Work Institute.

Gallimore, R., & Tharp, R. (1992). Teaching mind in society: Teaching, schooling, and literate discourse. In L. C. Moll (Ed.), *Vygotsky and education: Instructional implications and applications of sociohistorical psychology* (pp. 175–205). New York: Cambridge University Press.

Ganong, L. H., Coleman, M., & Jamison, T. (2011). Patterns of stepchild–stepparent relationship development. *Journal of Marriage and Family, 73*(2), 396–413.

Gao, Y., Raine, A., Venables, P. H., Dawson, M. E., & Mednick, S. A. (2010). Reduced electrodermal fear conditioning from ages 3 to 8 years is associated with aggressive behavior at age 8 years. *Journal of Child Psychology and Psychiatry, 51*(5), 550–558.

García-Pérez, L., Linertová, R., Martín-Olivera, P., Serrano-Aguilar, P., & Benítez-Rosario, M. P. (2009). A systematic review of specialised palliative care for terminal patients: Which model is better? *Palliative Medicine, 23*(1), 17–22.

Gardner, F., Shaw, D. S., Dishion, T. J., Burton, J., & Supplee, L. (2007). Randomized prevention *trial* for early conduct problems: Effects on proactive parenting and links to toddler disruptive behavior. *Journal of Family Psychology, 21*(3), 398–406.

Gardner, H. (1998). A multiplicity of intelligences. *Scientific American Presents, 9*(4), 18–23.

Gardner, H. (2004). *Frames of mind: The theory of multiple intelligences.* New York: Basic Books.

Gardner, H., & Moran, S. (2006). The science of multiple intelligences theory: A response to Lynn Waterhouse. *Educational Psychologist, 41*(4), 227–232.

Gardner, M., Roth, J., & Brooks-Gunn, J. (2008). Adolescents' participation in organized activities and developmental success 2 and 8 years after high school: Do sponsorship, duration, and intensity matter? *Developmental Psychology, 44*, 814–830.

Gardner, M., & Steinberg, L. (2005). Peer influence on risk taking, risk preference, and risky decision making in adolescence and adulthood: An experimental study. *Developmental Psychology, 41*, 625–635.

Garey, A. I., & Arendell, T. (2001). Children, work, and family: Some thoughts on "mother blame". In R. Hertz & N. L. Marshall (Eds.), *Working families:*

The transformation of the American home (pp. 293–303). Berkeley, CA: University of California Press.

Gartstein, M. A., Rothbart, M. K., Bridgett, D. J., Robertson, C., Iddins, E., Ramsay, K., & Schlect, S. (2010). A latent growth examination of fear development in infancy: Contributions of maternal depression and the risk for toddler anxiety. *Developmental Psychology, 46*(3), 651–668.

Gath, A. (1993). Changes that occur in families as children with intellectual disability grow up. *International Journal of Disability, Development and Education, 40*, 167–174.

Gault-Sherman, M. (2012). It's a two-way street: The bidirectional relationship between parenting and delinquency. *Journal of Youth and Adolescence, 41*, 121–145.

Gavin, J., Rodham, K., & Poyer, H. (2008). The presentation of "pro-anorexia" in online group interactions. *Qualitative Health Research, 18*(3), 325–333.

Gazelle, H., & Ladd, G. W. (2003). Anxious solitude and peer exclusion: A diathesis-stress model of internalizing trajectories in childhood. *Child Development, 74*, 257–278.

Geary, D. C. (1998). *Male, female: The evolution of human sex differences.* Washington, DC: American Psychological Association.

Genevie, L. E., & Margolies, E. (1987). *The motherhood report: How women feel about being mothers.* New York: Macmillan.

Gentzler, A. L., Oberhauser, A. M., Westerman, D., & Nardoff, D. K. (2011). College students' use of electronic communication with parents: Links to loneliness, attachment, and relationship quality. *CyberPsychology, Behavior, and Social Networking, 11*(1–2), 71–74.

George, L. K. (2010). Still happy after all these years: Research frontiers in subjective well-being in later life. *Journals of Gerontology: Social Sciences, 65B*(3), 331–339.

Geraci, A., Surian, L., Ferraro, M., & Cantagallo, A. (2010). Theory of mind in patients with ventromedial or dorsolateral prefrontal lesions following traumatic brain injury. *Brain Injury, 24*(7-8), 978–987.

Gerber, E. B., Whitebook, M., & Weinstein, R. S. (2007). At the heart of child care: Predictors of teacher sensitivity in center-based child care. *Early Childhood Research Quarterly, 22*, 327–346.

Gerdner, L. A., Cha, D., Yang, D., & Tripp-Reimer, T. (2007). The circle of life: End-of-life care and death rituals for Hmong-American elders. *Journal of Gerontological Nursing, 33*(5), 20–29.

Germo, G. R., Chang, E. S., Keller, M. A., & Goldberg, W. A. (2007). Child sleep arrangements and family life: Perspectives from mothers and fathers. *Infant and Child Development, 16*, 433–456.

Gershoff, E. T. (2002). Corporal punishment by parents and associated child behaviors and experiences: A meta-analytic and theoretical review. *Psychological Bulletin, 128*, 539–579.

Gerson, M.-J., Posner, J.-A., & Morris, A. M. (1991). The wish for a child in couples eager, disinterested, and conflicted about having children. *American Journal of Family Therapy, 19*, 334–343.

Gerstoff, D., Ram, N., Estabrook, R., Schupp, J., Wagner, G., & Lindenberger, U. (2008). Life Satisfaction shows terminal decline in old age: Longitudinal evidence from the German Socio-Economic Panel Study (SOEP). *Developmental Psychology, 44*, 1148–1159.

Gerstorf, D., Mayraz, G., Linfenberger, U., Ram, N., Hidajat, M., & Wagner, G. G. (2010). Late-life decline in well-being across adulthood in Germany, the United Kingdom, and the United States: Something is seriously wrong at the end of life. *Psychology and Aging, 25*(2), 477–485.

Gervain, J., & Mehler, J. (2010). Speech perception and language acquisition in the first year of life. *Annual Review of Psychology, 61*, 191–218.

Gestsdottir, S., Bowers, E., von Eye, A., Napolitano, C. M., & Lerner, R. M. (2010). Intentional self regulation in middle adolescence: The emerging role of loss-based selection in positive youth development. *Journal of Youth and Adolescence, 39*, 764–782.

Gibbins, S., & Stevens, B. (2001). Mechanisms of sucrose and nonnutritive sucking in procedural pain management in infants. *Pain Research & Management, 6*, 21–28.

Gibson-Davis, C. (2011). Mothers but not wives: The increasing lag between nonmarital births and marriage. *Journal of Marriage and Family, 73*, 264–278.

Gibson-Davis, C. M. (2009). Money, marriage, and children: Testing the financial expectations and family formation theory. *Journal of Marriage and Family, 71*, 146–160.

Gibson, E. J., & Walk, R. D. (1960). The "visual cliff." *Scientific American, 202*(4), 64–71.

Gibson, M. A., & Mace, R. (2005). Helpful grandmothers in rural Ethiopia: A study of the effect of kin on child survival and growth. *Evolution and Human Behavior, 26*, 469–482.

Giedd, J. N., Stockman, M., Weddle, C., Liverpool, M., Alexander-Bloch, A., Wallace, G. L., & Lenroot, R. K. (2010). Anatomic magnetic resonance imaging of the developing child and adolescent brain and effects of genetic variation. *Neuropsychology Review, 20*(4), 349–361.

Gilbert-Barness, E. (2000). Maternal caffeine and its effect on the fetus. *American Journal of Medical Genetics, 93*, 253.

Gilboa, S., Shirom, A., Fried, Y., & Cooper, C. (2008). A meta-analysis of work demand stressors and job performance: Examining main and moderating effects. *Personnel Psychology, 61*(2), 227–272.

Gilligan, C., Attanucci, J. (1988). Two moral orientations: Gender differences and similarities. *Merrill-Palmer Quarterly: Journal of Developmental Psychology, 34*(3), 223–237.

Gilman, R., Huebner, E. S., Tian, L., Park, N., O'Byrne, J., Schiff, . . . Langknecht, H. (2008). Cross-national adolescent multidimensional life satisfaction reports: Analysis of mean scores and response style differences. *Journal of Youth Adolescence, 37*, 142–154.

Ginsburg, H., & Opper, S. (1969). *Piaget's theory of intellectual development: An introduction.* Englewood Cliffs, NJ: Prentice-Hall.

Giordano, P. C., Manning, W. D., & Longmore, M. A. (2010). Affairs of the heart: Qualities of adolescent romantic relationships and sexual behavior. *Journal of Research on Adolescence, 20*(4), 983–1013.

Girdler, S., Packer, T. L., & Boldy, D. (2008). The impact of age-related vision loss. *OTJR: Occupation, Participation, and Health, 28*, 110–120.

Glaser, B. G., & Strauss, A. L. (1968). *Time for dying.* Chicago: Aldine.

Glazier, R., Elgar, F., Goel, V., & Holzapfel, S. (2004). Stress, social support and emotional distress in a community sample of pregnant women. *Journal of Psychosomatic Obstetrics & Gynecology, 25*, 247–255.

Glenn, N. (1990). Quantitative research on marital quality in the 1980s: A critical review. *Journal of Marriage and the Family, 52*, 818–831.

Glorieux, I., Minnen, J., & Tienoven, T. P. V. (2011). Spouse "time together": Quality time within the household. *Social Indicators Research, 101*(2), 281–287.

Godin, E., O'Leary-Moore, S. K., Khan, A. A., Parnell, S. E., Ament, J. J., Dehart, D. B., et al. (2010). Magnetic resonance microscopy defines ethanol-induced brain abnormalities in prenatal mice: Effects of acute insult on gestational day 7 [Electronic version]. *Alcoholism: Clinical and Experimental Research, 34*(1), 98–111.

Goldberg, A. E., & Sayer, A. (2006). Lesbian couples' relationship quality across the transition to parenthood. *Journal of Marriage and Family, 68,* 87–100.

Golden, L. (2008). Limited access: Disparities in flexible work schedules and work-at-home. *Journal of Family Economic Issues, 29,* 86–109.

Goldner, J., Peters, T. L., Richards, M. H., & Pearce, S. (2011). Exposure to community violence and protective and risky contexts among low income urban African American adolescents: A prospective study. *Journal of Youth and Adolescence, 40,* 174–186.

Golombok, S., Perry, B., Burston, A., Murray, C., Mooney-Somers, J., Stevens, M., & Golding, J. (2003). Children with lesbian parents: A community study. *Developmental Psychology, 39,* 20–33.

Gooch, D., Snowling, M., & Hulme, C. (2011). Time perception, phonological skills and executive function in children with dyslexia and/or ADHD symptoms. *Journal of Child Psychology and Psychiatry, 52*(2), 195–203.

Good, M.-J. D., Gadmer, N. M., Ruopp, P., Lakoma, M., Sullivan, A. M., Redinbaugh, E., Arnold, R. M., & Block, S. D. (2004). Narrative nuances on good and bad deaths: Internists' tales from high-technology work places. *Social Science & Medicine, 58,* 939–953.

Gopnik, A. (2010). How babies think: Even the youngest children know, experience and learn far more than scientists ever thought possible. *Scientific American, 303,* 76–81.

Gordon-Larsen, P., The, N. S., & Adair, L. S. (2010). Longitudinal trends in obesity in the United States from adolescence to the third decade of life. *Obesity, 18*(9), 1801–1804.

Gore, T., & Dubois, R. (1998). The "Back to Sleep" campaign. *Zero To Three, 19*(2), 22–23.

Gorer, G. (1965). *Death, grief, and mourning in contemporary Britain.* London: Cresset Press.

Gothe, K., Oberauer, K., & Kliegl, R. (2008). Age differences in dual-task performance after practice. *Psychology and Aging, 22*(3), 596–606.

Gottman, J. (1994). *Why marriages succeed or fail: And how you can make yours last.* New York: Simon & Schuster.

Gottman, J. M. (1999). *The marriage clinic: A scientifically based marital therapy.* New York: Norton.

Gould, L. A., & Pate, M. (2010). Discipline, docility, and disparity: A study of inequality and corporal punishment. *British Journal of Criminology, 50,* 185–205.

Gould, S. J. (1981). *The mismeasure of man.* New York: Norton.

Graber, J. A., Nichols, T. R., & Brooks-Gunn, J. (2010). Putting pubertal timing in developmental context: Implications for prevention. *Developmental Psychobiology, 52*(3), 254–262.

Graham, J. W., & Beller, A. H. (2002). Nonresident fathers and their children: Child support and visitation from an economic perspective. In C. S. Tamis-LeMonda & N. Cabrera (Eds.), *Handbook of father involvement: Multidisciplinary perspectives* (pp. 431–453). Mahwah, NJ: Erlbaum.

Graham, J., Banaschewski, T., Buitelaar, J., Coghill, D., Danckaerts, M., Dittmann, R. W., … Taylor, E. (2011). European guidelines on managing adverse effects of medication for ADHD. *European Child & Adolescent Psychiatry, 20,* 17–37.

Greenfield, E. A. (2010). Child abuse as a life-course social determinant of adult health. *Maturitas, 66,* 51–55.

Greenleaf, C. (2005). Self-objectification among physically active women. *Sex Roles, 52,* 51–62.

Gregory, A. M., Caspi, A., Eley, T. C., Moffitt, T. E., O'Connor, T. G., & Poulton, R. (2005). Prospective longitudinal associations between persistent sleep problems in childhood and anxiety and depression disorders in adulthood. *Journal of Abnormal Child Psychology, 33,* 157–163.

Gregory, A. M., Light-Häusermann, J. H., Rijsdijk, F., & Eley, T. C. (2009). Behavioral genetic analyses of prosocial behavior in adolescents. *Developmental Science, 12,* 165–174.

Gregory, T., Nettelbeck, T., & Wilson, C. (2010). Openness to experience, intelligence, and successful ageing. *Personality and Individual Differences, 48,* 895–899.

Grello, C. M., Welsh, D. P., & Harper, M. S. (2006). No strings attached: The nature of casual sex in college students. *The Journal of Sex Research, 43*(3), 255–267.

Groeneveld, M. G., Vermeer, H. J., van IJzendoorn, M. H., & Linting, M. (2010). Children's well-being and cortisol levels in home-based and center-based childcare. *Early Childhood Research Quarterly, 25*(4), 502–514.

Groom, M. J., Cahill, J. D., Bates, A. T., Jackson, G. M., Calton, T. G., Liddle, P. F., & Hollis, C. (2010). Electrophysiological indices of abnormal error-processing in adolescents with attention deficit hyperactivity disorder (ADHD). *Journal of Child Psychology and Psychiatry, 51*(1), 66–76.

Groopman, J. E. (2004). *The anatomy of hope: How patients prevail in the face of illness.* New York: Random House.

Grossbaum, M. F., & Bates, G. W. (2002). Correlates of psychological well-being at midlife: The role of generativity, agency and communion, and narrative themes. *International Journal of Behavioral Development, 26,* 120–127.

Grossmann, I., Na, J., Varnum, M. E. W., Park, D. C., Kitayama, S., & Nisbett, R. E. (2010). Reasoning about social conflicts improves into old age. *Psychological and Cognitive Sciences, 107*(16), 7246–7250.

Grossmann, K. E., Grossmann, K., & Zimmermann, P. (1999). A wider view of attachment and exploration: Stability and change during the years of immaturity. In J. Cassidy & P. R. Shaver (Eds.), *Handbook of attachment: Theory, research, and clinical applications* (pp. 760–786). New York: Guilford Press.

Grossmann, K., Grossmann, K. E., & Kindler, H. (2005). Early care and the roots of attachment and partnership representations: The Bielefeld and Regensburg longitudinal studies. In K. E. Grossmann, K. Grossmann, & E. Waters (Eds.), *Attachment from infancy to adulthood: The major longitudinal studies* (pp. 98–136). New York: Guilford Press.

Grube, J. W., Bourdeau, B., Fisher, D. A., & Bersamin, M. (2008). *Television exposure and sexuality among adolescents: A longitudinal survey study.* Paper presented at the Biennial Meeting, Society for Research in Adolescence, Chicago, 2008.

Grusec, J. E., & Davidov, M. (2010). Integrating different perspectives on socialization theory and research: A domain-specific approach. *Child Development, 81*(3), 687–709.

Gschwind, Y. J., Bridenbaugh, S. A., & Kressig, R. W. (2010). Gait disorders and falls. *GeroPsych, 23*(1), 21–32.

Guarini, A., Sansavini, A., Fabbri, C., Savini, S., Alessandroni, R., Faldella, G., et al. (2010). Long-term effects of preterm birth on language and literacy at eight years [Electronic version]. *Journal of Child Language, 37*(4), 865–885.

Guendelman, S., Kosa, J. L., Pearl, M., Graham, S., Goodman, J., & Kharrazi, M. (2009). Juggling work and breastfeeding: Effects of maternity leave and occupational characteristics. *Pediatrics, 123,* e38–e46.

Guerra, N. G., Williams, K. R., & Sadek, S. (2011). Understanding bullying and victimization during childhood and adolescence: A mixed methods study. *Child Development, 82*(1), 295–310.

Guerri, C., & Pascual, M. (2010). Mechanisms involved in the neurotoxic, cognitive, and neurobehavioral effects of alcohol consumption during adolescence. *Alcohol, 44*(1), 15–26.

Gunnar, M.R., Kryzer, E., Ryzin, M.J., & Phillips D.A. (2011). The import of the cortisol rise in child care differs as a function of behavioral inhibition. *Developmental Psychology, 47*(3), 792–803.

Gupta, R. (2011). Death beliefs and practices from an Asian Indian American Hindu perspective. *Death Studies, 35,* 244–266.

Guttmacher Institute. (2011a). *Facts on American Teens' Sources of Information About Sex.* New York: Guttmacher Institute.

Guttmacher Institute. (2011b). *In brief: facts on american teens' sexual and reproductive health.* New York: Guttmacher Institute.

Ha, J-H. (2008). Changes in support from confidants, children, and friends following widowhood. *Journals of Marriage and Family, 70,* 306–318.

Ha, J-H., & Ingersoll-Dayton, B. (2008). The effect of widowhood on international ambivalence. *Journals of Gerontology: Social Sciences, 63B*(1), S49–S58.

Habermas, T., Negele, A., & Mayer, F. B. (2010). "Honey, you're jumping about"—Mothers' scaffolding of their children's and adolescents' life narration. *Cognitive Development, 25,* 339–351.

Haddad, E., Chen, C., & Greenberger, E. (2011). The role of important non-parental adults (VIPs) in the lives of older adolescents: A comparison of three ethnic groups. *Journal of Youth and Adolescence, 40,* 310–319.

Hagestad, G. O. (1985). Continuity and connectedness. In V. L. Bengtson & J. F. Robertson (Eds.), *Grandparenthood* (pp. 31–48). Thousand Oaks, CA: Sage.

Hahn, E. A., Cichy, K. E., Almeida, D. M., & Haley, W. E. (2011). Time use and well-being in older widows: Adaptation and resilience. *Journal of Women and Aging, 23,* 149–159.

Hall, G. S. (1969). *Adolescence.* New York: Arno Press. (Original work published 1904.)

Hall, N. C., Heckhausen, J., Chipperfield, J. G., & Perry, R. P. (2010). Control striving in older adults with serious health problems: A 9-year longitudinal study of survival, health, and well-being. *Psychology and Aging, 25*(2), 432–445.

Hall, S. (2011). "It's going to stop in this generation": Women with a history of child abuse resolving to raise their children without abuse. *Harvard Educational Review, 81*(1), 24–49.

Halleröd, B., & Gustafsson, J. (2011). A longitudinal analysis of the relationship between changes in socio-economic status and changes in health. *Social Science & Medicine, 72*(1), 116–123.

Halperin, J. M., & Healey, D. M. (2011). The influences of environmental enrichment, cognitive enhancement, and physical exercise on brain development: Can we alter the developmental trajectory of ADHD? *Neuroscience and Biobehavioral Reviews, 35,* 621–634.

Halrynjo, S. (2009). Men's work-life conflict: Career, care, and self-realization: Patterns of privileges and dilemmas. *Gender, Work, and Organization, 16,* 98–125.

Hamilton, D. A., Candelaria-Cook, F. T., Akers, K. G., Rice, J. P., Maes, L. I., Rosenberg, M., … Savage, D. D. (2010). Patterns of social experience-related c-fos and arc expressions in the frontal cortices of rats exposed to saccharin or moderate levels of ethanol during prenatal brain development [Electronic version]. *Behavioral Brain Research, 214*(1), 66–74.

Hamlin, J. K., & Wynn, K. (2011). Young infants prefer prosocial to antisocial others. *Cognitive Development, 26,* 30–39.

Hamlin, J. K., Wynn, K., & Bloom, P. (2007). Social evaluation by preverbal infants. *Nature, 450,* 557–559.

Hammarstrom, A., Gustafsson, P. E., Strandh, M., Virtanen, P., & Janlert, U. (2011). It's no surprise! Men are not hit more than women by the health consequences of unemployment in the northern Swedish cohort. *Scandinavian Journal of Public Health, 39,* 187–193.

Hank, K. (2011). How "successful" do older Europeans age? Findings from SHARE. *Journals of Gerontology: Social Sciences, 66B*(2), 230–236.

Hank, K., & Buber, I. (2009). Grandparents caring for their grandchildren: Findings from the 2004 Survey of Health, Ageing, and Retirement in Europe. *Journal of Family Issues, 30,* 53–73.

Hanson, M. J., Miller, A. D., Diamond, K., Odom, S., Lieber, J., Butera, G., … Fleming, K. (2011). Neighborhood community risk influences on preschool children's development and school readiness. *Infants & Young Children, 24*(1), 87–100.

Hardie, J. H., & Lucas, A. (2010). Economic factors and relationship quality among young couples: Comparing cohabitation and marriage. *Journal of Marriage and Family, 72,* 1141–1154.

Harley, K., & Reese, E. (1999). Origins of autobiographical memory. *Developmental Psychology, 35,* 1338–1348.

Harlow, C. M. (Ed.). (1986). *From learning to love: The selected papers of H. F. Harlow.* New York: Praeger.

Harlow, H. F. (1958). The nature of love. *American Psychologist, 13,* 673–685.

Harlow, H. F., Harlow, M. K., Dodsworth, R. O., & Arling, G. L. (1966). Maternal behavior of rhesus monkeys deprived of mothering and peer associations in infancy. *Proceedings of the American Philosophical Society, 110,* 58–66.

Harriger, J. A., Calogero, R. M., Witherington, D. C., & Smith, J. E. (2010). Body size stereotyping and internalization of the thin ideal in preschool girls. *Sex Roles, 63,* 609–620.

Harris, A., & Seckl, J. (2011). Glucocorticoids, prenatal stress and the programming of disease. *Hormones and Behavior, 59,* 279–289.

Harris, J. R. (1995). Where is the child's environment? A group socialization theory of development. *Psychological Review, 102,* 458–489.

Harris, J. R. (1998). *The nurture assumption: Why children turn out the way they do.* New York: Free Press.

Harris, J. R. (2002). Beyond the nurture assumption: Testing hypotheses about the child's environment. In J. G. Borkowski, S. L. Ramey, & M. Bristol-Power (Eds.), *Parenting and the child's world: Influences on academic, intellectual, and social-emotional development* (pp. 3–20). Mahwah, NJ: Erlbaum.

Harris, J. R. (2006). *No two alike: Human nature and human individuality*. New York, NY: W. W. Norton & Co.

Harris, K., Lee, H., & DeLeone, F. (2010). Marriage and health in the transition to adulthood: Evidence for African Americans in the Add Health Study. *Journal of Family Issues, 31*(8), 1106–1143.

Harris, T. S. (2010). Bruises in children: Normal or child abuse?. *Journal of Pediatric Health Care, 24*(4), 216–221.

Harrist, A. W., Thompson, S. D., & Norris, D. J. (2007). Defining quality child care: Multiple stakeholder perspectives. *Early Education and Development, 18*(2), 305–336.

Hart, H. M., McAdams, D. P., Hirsch, B. J., & Bauer, J. J. (2001). Generativity and social involvement among African Americans and White adults. *Journal of Research in Personality, 35*, 208–230.

Harter, S. (1981). A new self-report scale of intrinsic versus extrinsic orientation in the classroom: Motivational and informational components. *Developmental Psychology, 17*, 300–312.

Harter, S. (1999). *The construction of the self: A developmental perspective*. New York: Guilford Press.

Harter, S. (2006). Developmental and individual difference perspectives on self-esteem. In D. K. Mroczek, & T. D. Little (Eds.), *Handbook of personality development* (pp. 311–334). Mahwah, NJ: Lawrence Erlbaum Associates Publishers.

Harter, S., & Pike, R. (1984). The pictorial scale of perceived competence and social acceptance for young children. *Child Development, 55*, 1969–1982.

Hartley, D., Roctchina, E., Newall, P., Golding, M., & Mitchell, P. (2010). Use of hearing aids and assistive listening devices in an older Australian population. *Journal of the American Academy of Audiology, 21*, 642–653.

Hartup, W. W., & Stevens, N. (1997). Friendships and adaptation in the life course. *Psychological Bulletin, 121*, 355–370.

Hashimoto-Torii, K., Kawasawa, Y. I., Kuhn, A., & Rakic, P. (2011). Combined transcriptome analysis of fetal human and mouse cerebral cortex exposed to alcohol. *Proceedings of the National Academy of Sciences of the United States of America, 108*(10), 4212–4217.

Hashizume, Y. (2010). Releasing from the oppression: Caregiving for the elderly parents of Japanese working women. *Qualitative Health Research, 20*(6), 830–844.

Hata, T., Dai, S., & Marumo, G. (2010). Ultrasound for evaluation of fetal neurobehavioral development: From 2-D to 4-D ultrasound. *Infant and Child Development, 19*, 99–118.

Hawkins, N. A., Ditto, P. H., Danks, J. H., & Smucker, W. D. (2005). Micromanaging death: Process preferences, values, and goals in end-of-life medical decision making. *Gerontologist, 45*, 107–117.

Hawley, P. H., Johnson, S. E., Mize, J. A., & McNamara, K. A. (2007). Physical attractiveness in preschoolers: Relationships with power, status, aggression, and social skills. *Journal of School Psychology, 45*, 499–521.

Hawley, P. H., Little, T. D., & Card, N. A. (2008). The myth of the alpha male: A new look at dominance-related beliefs and behaviors among adolescent males and females. *International Journal of Behavioral Development*, 32(1), 76–88.

Hays, J. C. G., Palmer, A., Tahira, A., McQuoid, D. R., Flint, E. P. (2001). Preference for place of death in a continuing care retirement community. *The Gerontologist, 41*(1), 123–128.

Hayslip, B., Jr., & Hansson, R. O. (2003). Death awareness and adjustment across the life span. In C. D. Bryant (Ed.), *Handbook of death & dying* (pp. 437–447). Thousand Oaks, CA: Sage.

Hayslip, B., Jr., & Patrick, J. H. (Eds.). (2003). *Working with custodial grandparents*. New York: Springer.

Hazan, C., & Shaver, P. (1987). Romantic love conceptualized as an attachment process. *Journal of Personality and Social Psychology*, 52, 511–524.

Head, D., Bugg, J. M., Goate, A. M, Fagan, A. M. Minton, M. A., Bensigner, T., … Morris, J. C. (2012) Exercise engagement as a moderator of the effects of APOE genotype on amyloid deposition. *Archives of Neurology, 69*(5), 636–643.

HealthLink. (2002). Bad news about hormone replacement therapy. Retrieved September 24, 2006, from Medical College of Wisconsin Web site: http://healthlink.mcw.edu/article/1025191125.html

Hearing Loop. Retrieved December 9, 2011, from http://www.hearingloop.com

Heatherington, L., & Lavner, J. A. (2008). Coming to terms with coming out: Review and recommendations for family systems-focused research. *Journal of Family Psychology*, 22(3), 329–343.

Heatherton, T. F. (2011). Neuroscience of self and self-regulation. *Annual Review of Psychology, 62*, 363–390.

Heaven, P. C. L., Ciarrochi, J., & Vialle, W. (2008). Self-nominated peer crowds, school achievement, and psychological adjustment in adolescents: Longitudinal analysis. *Personality and Individual Differences, 44*, 977–988.

Hebblethwaite, S., & Norris, J. (2011). Expressions of generativity through family leisure: Experiences of grandparents and adult grandchildren. *Family Relations: An Interdisciplinary Journal of Applied Family Studies, 60*(1), 121–133.

Helson, R., & Soto, C. J. (2005). Up and down in middle age: Monotonic and nonmonotonic changes in roles, status, and personality. *Journal of Personality and Social Psychology*, 89(2), 194–204.

Helverskov, J. L., Clausen, L., Mors, O., Frydenberg, M., Thomsen, P. H., & Rokkedal, K. (2010). Trans-diagnostic outcome of eating disorders: A 30-month follow-up study of 629 patients. *European Eating Disorders Review, 18*, 453–463.

Hendin, H. (1994, December 16). Scared to death of dying [Op-Ed]. *New York Times*, p. A19.

Hendry, L. B., & Kloep, M. (2010). How universal is emerging adulthood? An empirical example. *Journal of Youth Studies, 13*(2), 169–179.

Henry, L. A., Messer, D. J., & Nash, G. (2012). Executive functioning in children with specific language impairment. *Journal of Child Psychology and Psychiatry*, 53, 37–45.

Hensler, B. S., Schatschneider, C., Taylor, J., & Wagner, R. K. (2010). Behavioral genetic approach to the study of dyslexia. *Journal of Developmental and Behavioral Pediatrics*, 31(7), 525–532.

Heo, J., Lee, Y., McCormick, B. P., & Pedersen, P. M. (2010). Daily experience of serious leisure, flow, and subjective well-being of older adults. *Leisure Studies*, 29(2), 207–225.

Herrnstein, R. J., & Murray, C. A. (1994). *The bell curve: Intelligence and class structure in American life*. New York: Free Press.

Hershey, D. A., Henkens, K., & van Dalen, H. P. (2010). What drives retirement income worries in Europe? A multilevel analysis. *European Journal of Ageing, 7*, 301–311.

Hertzog, C. (1996). Research design in studies of aging and cognition. In J. E. Birren, K. W. Schaie, R. P. Abeles, M. Gatz, & T. A. Salthouse (Eds.), *Handbook of the psychology of aging* (4th ed., pp. 24–37). San Diego, CA: Academic Press.

Hesketh, K. D., & Campbell, K. J. (2010). Interventions to prevent obesity in 0–5 year olds: An updated systematic review of the literature. *Obesity, 18*(Suppl 1), S27–S35.

Hesse-Biber, S., Livingstone, S., Ramirez, D., Barko, E. B., & Johnson, A. L. (2010). Racial identity and body image among black female college students attending predominately white colleges. *Sex Roles, 63*, 697–711.

Hetherington, E. M. (1999). *Coping with divorce, single parenting, and remarriage: A risk and resiliency perspective*. Mahwah, NJ: Erlbaum.

Hetherington, E. M., & Kelly, J. (2002). *For better or for worse: Divorce reconsidered*. New York: Norton.

Heyman, G. D., Itakura, S., & Lee, K. (2011). Japanese and American children's reasoning about accepting credit for prosocial behavior. *Social Development, 20*, 171–184.

Hickman, S. E., Tilden, V. P., & Tolle, S. W. (2004). Family perceptions of worry, symptoms, and suffering in the dying. *Journal of Palliative Care, 20*, 20–27.

Higgins, M., Dobrow, S. R., & Roloff, K. S. (2010). Optimism and the boundaryless career: The role of developmental relationships. *Journal of Organizational Behavior, 31*, 749–769.

Hildén, H. M., Louhiala, P., & Palo, J. (2004). End of life decisions: Attitudes of Finnish physicians. *Journal of Medical Ethics, 30*, 362–365.

Hill, P. L., Jackson, J. J., Roberts, B. W., Lapsley, D. K., & Brandenberger, J. W. (2011). Change you can believe in: Changes in goal setting during emerging and young adulthood predict later adult well-being. *Social Psychological and Personality Science, 2*(2), 123–131.

Hillman, J. (2008). Sexual issues and aging within the context of work with older adult patients. *Professional Psychology: Research and Practice, 39*(3), 290–297.

Hinde, R. A. (2005). Ethology and attachment theory. In K. E. Grossmann, K. Grossmann, & E. Waters (Eds.), *Attachment from infancy to adulthood: The major longitudinal studies* (pp. 1–12). New York: Guilford Press.

Hipwell, A. E., Keenan, K., Loeber, R., & Battista, D. (2010). Early predictors of sexually intimate behaviors in an urban sample of young girls. *Developmental Psychology, 46*(2), 366–378.

Hirschfield, P. J., & Gasper, J. (2011). The relationship between school engagement and delinquency in late childhood and early adolescence. *Journal of Youth and Adolescence, 40*(1), 3–22.

Hoff-Ginsberg, E. (1997). *Language development*. Belmont, CA: Brooks/Cole.

Hofferth, S.L., & Goldscheider, F. (2010). Does change in young men's employment influence fathering? *Family Relations: Interdisciplinary Journal of Applied Family Studies, 59*, 479–493.

Hoffman, M. L. (1994). Discipline and internalization. *Developmental Psychology, 30*, 26–28.

Hoffman, M. L. (2001). Toward a comprehensive empathy-based theory of pro-social moral development. In A. C. Bohart & D. J. Stipek (Eds.), *Constructive & destructive behavior: Implications for family, school, & society* (pp. 61–86). Washington, DC: American Psychological Association.

Hofstede, G. (1981). Cultures and organizations. *International Studies of Management and Organization, 10*(4), 15–41.

Hofstede, G. (2001). *Culture's consequences: Comparing values, behaviors, institutions, and organizations across nations* (2nd ed.). Thousand Oaks, CA: Sage.

Holland, J. (1997). *Making vocational choices: A theory of vocational personalities and work environments* (3rd ed.). Odessa, FL: Psychological Assessment Resources.

Holmes, T. H., & Rahe, R. H. (1967). The social readjustment rating scale. *Journal of Psychosomatic Research, 11*, 213–218.

Hoover, E. (2011). The Chronicle of Higher Education: Surveys of the public and presidents. In *College's value goes deeper than the degree, graduates say*. Retrieved May 18, 2011, from http://chronicle.com/article/Its-More-Than-the/127534

Hopper, J. (1993). The rhetoric of motives in divorce. *Journal of Marriage & the Family, 55*, 801–813.

Hornak, A. M., Farrell, P., & Jackson, N. (2010). Making it (or not) on a dime in college: Implications for practice. *Journal of College Student Development, 51*(5), 481–495.

Houts, R. M., Barnett-Walker, K. C., Paley, B., & Cox, M. J. (2008). Patterns of couple interaction during the transition to parenthood. *Personal Relationships, 15*, 103–122.

Hrdy, S. B. (1999). *Mother nature: A history of mothers, infants, and natural selection*. New York: Pantheon Books.

Hu, S., & Kuh, G. D. (2003). Diversity experiences and college student learning and personal development. *Journal of College Student Development, 44*, 320–334.

Huddleston, J., & Ge, X. (2003). Boys at puberty: Psychosocial implications. In C. Hayward (Ed.), *Gender differences at puberty* (pp. 113–134). New York: Cambridge University Press.

Hudson, J. I., Hiripi, E., Pope, H. G., Jr., Kessler, R. C. (2007). The prevalence and correlates of eating disorders in the National Comorbidity Survey Replication. *Biological Psychiatry, 61*(3), 348–358.

Hungerford, T. L. (2003). Is there an American way of aging? Income dynamics of the elderly in the United States and Germany. *Research on Aging, 25*, 435–455.

Hunt, C. K. (2003). Concepts in caregiver research. *Journal of Nursing Scholarship, 35*, 27–32.

Hunter, S. C., Durkin, K., Heim, D., Howe, C., & Bergin, D. (2010). Psychosocial mediators and moderators of the effect of peer-victimization upon depressive symptomatology. *Journal of Child Psychology and Psychiatry, 51*(10), 1141–1149.

Hurks, P. P. M., & Hendriksen, J. G. M. (2011). Retrospective and prospective time deficits in childhood ADHD: The effects of task modality, duration, and symptom dimensions. *Child Neuropsychology, 17*(1), 34–50.

Hutchinson, D. M., Rapee, R. M., & Taylor, A. (2010). Body dissatisfaction and eating disturbances in early adolescence: A structural modeling investigation examining negative affect and peer factors. *Journal of Early Adolescence, 30*(4), 489–517.

Huttenlocher, P. R. (2002). *Neural plasticity: The effects of environment on the development of the cerebral cortex*. Cambridge, MA: Harvard University Press.

Hvas, L. (2001). Positive aspects of menopause: A qualitative study. *Maturitas, 39*, 11–17.

Hwang, S.-L., Gau, S. S.-F., Hsu, W.-Y., & Wu, Y.-Y. (2010). Deficits in interval timing measured by the dual-task paradigm among children and adolescents with attention-deficit/hyperactivity disorder. *Journal of Child Psychology and Psychiatry, 51*(3), 223–232.

Infurna, F. J., Gerstorf, D., Robertson, S., Berg, S., & Zarit, S. H. (2010). The nature and cross-domain correlates of subjective age in the oldest old: Evidence form the OCTO study. *Psychology and Aging, 25*(2), 470–476.

Innes, S., & Payne, S. (2009). Advanced cancer patients' prognostic information preferences: A review. *Palliative Medicine*, 23, 29–39.

Ito, M., & Sharts-Hopko, N. C. (2002). Japanese women's experience of childbirth in the United States. *Health Care for Women International*, 23, 666–677.

Jackson, T., & Chen, H. (2008). Predicting changes in eating disorder symptoms among Chinese adolescents: A 9-month prospective study. *Journal of Psychosomatic Research*, 64, 87–95.

Jaffe, J., & Diamond, M. O. (2011). *Reproductive trauma: Psychotherapy with infertility and pregnancy loss clients*. Washington DC.: American Psychological Association.

Jang, H., Reeve, J., & Deci, E. L. (2010). Engaging students in learning activities: It is not autonomy support or structure but autonomy support and structure. *Journal of Educational Psychology*, *102*(3), 588–600.

Jedrziewski, M. K., Ewbank, D. C., Wang, H., & Trojanowski, J. Q. (2010). Exercise and cognition: Results from the National Long Term Care Survey. *Alzheimer's & Dementia*, 6, 448–455.

Jen, M. H., Jones, K., & Johnston R. (2009). Global variations in health: Evaluating Wilkinson's income inequality hypothesis using the World Values Survey. *Social Science & Medicine*. 68, 643–653.

Jenkins, T. M., Chapman, K. L., Ritchie, C. S., Arnett, D. K., McGwin, G. Jr., Cofield, S. S., & Maetz, H. M. (2011). Barriers to hospice care in Alabama: Provider-based perceptions. *American Journal of Hospice & Palliative Medicine*, 28(3), 153–160.

Jenson, W. R., Olympia, D., Farley, M., & Clark, E. (2004). Positive psychology and externalizing students in a sea of negativity. *Psychology in the Schools*, 41, 67–79.

Jette, A. M., Assmann, S. F., Rooks, D., Harris, B. A., & Crawford, S. (1998). Interrelationships among disablement concepts. *Journals of Gerontology: Series A: Biological Sciences and Medical Sciences*, 53A, M395–M404.

Johansson, K., Josephsson, S., & Lilja, M. (2009). Creating possibilities for action in the presence of environmental barriers in the process of 'ageing in place.' *Ageing & Society*, 29, 49–70.

Johnson, J., & Rochkind, J. (2011). *With their whole lives ahead of them: Myths and realities about why so many students fail to finish college* (The Public Agenda Report). Retrieved from the Bill and Melinda Gates Foundation Web site: http://www.publicagenda.org/TheirWholeLivesAheadofThem

Johnson, M., Crosnoe, R., & Elder, G. R. (2011). Insights on adolescence from a life course perspective. *Journal of Research on Adolescence*, *21*(1), 273–280.

Johnson, R. W. (2009), Employment opportunities at older ages: Introduction to the special issue. *Research on Aging*, 31, 3–16.

Johnson, W., Corley, J., Starr, J. M., & Deary, I. J. (2011). Psychological and physical health at age 70 in the Lothian birth cohort 1936: Links with early life IQ, SES, and current cognitive function and neighborhood environment. *Health Psychology*, 30(1), 1–11.

Johnson, W., Hicks, B. M., McGue, M., & Iacono, W. G. (2007). Most of the girls are alright, but some aren't: Personality trajectory groups from ages 14 to 24 and some associations with outcomes. *Journal of Personality and Social Psychology*, 93(2), 266–284.

Johnston, L. D., O'Malley, P. M., Bachman, J. G., & Schulenberg, J. E. (2011). Marijuana use continues to rise among U.S. teens, while alcohol use hits historic lows. University of Michigan News Service: Ann Arbor, MI. Retrieved May 4, 2012, from http://www.monitoringthefuture.org

Johri, M., Beland, F., & Bergman, H. (2003). International experiments in integrated care for the elderly: A synthesis of the evidence. *International Journal of Geriatric Psychiatry*, 18, 222–235.

Jokela, M., Kivimaki, M., Elovainio, M., & Keltikangas-Jarvinen, L. (2009). Personality and having children: A two-way relationship. *Journal of Personality and Social Psychology*, 96, 218–230.

Jokhi, R. P., & Whitby, E. H. (2011). Magnetic resonance imaging of the fetus. *Developmental Medicine & Child Neurology*, 53, 18–28.

Jones, R. K., & Biddlecom, A. E. (2011). The more things change…: The relative importance of the Internet as a source of contraceptive information for teens. *Sexuality Research and Social Policy*, 8, 27–37.

Jones, R. K., Biddlecom, A. E., Hebert, L., & Mellor, R. (2011). Teens reflect on their sources of contraceptive information. *Journal of Adolescent Research*, 26(4), 423–446.

Jorgensen, B. S., Jamieson, R. D., & Martin, J. F. (2010). Income, sense of community and subjective well-being: Combining economic and psychological variables. *Journal of Economic Psychology*, *31*(4), 612–623.

Juarascio, A. S., Shoaib, A., & Timko, C. A. (2010). Pro-eating disorder communities on social networking sites: A content analysis. *Eating Disorders*, 18, 393–407.

Judge, T. A., & Hurst, C. (2007). Capitalizing on one's advantages: Role of core self-evaluations. *Journal of Applied Psychology*, 92(5), 1212–1227.

Júlíusson, P. B., Egil Eide, G., Roelants, M., Waaler, P. E., Hauspie, R., & Bjerknes, R. (2010). Overweight and obesity in Norwegian children: Prevalence and socio-demographic risk factors. *Acta Paediatrica*, 99(6), 900–905.

Jung, C. G. (1933). *Modern man in search of a soul*. Oxford, England: Harcourt.

Kagan, J. (1984). *The nature of the child*. New York: Basic Books.

Kagan, J. (1994). *Galen's prophecy: Temperament in human nature*. New York: Basic Books.

Kagan, J. (1998). *Galen's prophecy: Temperament in human nature*. Boulder, CO: Westview Press.

Kalil, A., Ziol-Guest, K. M., Epstein, J. L. (2010). Nonstandard work and marital instability: Evidence from the National Longitudinal Survey of Youth. *Journal of Marriage and Family*, 72, 1289–1300.

Kane, R. A. (1995–1996). Transforming care institutions for the frail elderly: Out of one shall be many. *Generations*, *14*(4), 62–68.

Kannai, R. (2008). Zohara. *Patient Education and Counseling*, 71, 145–147.

Karen, R. (1998). *Becoming attached: First relationships and how they shape our capacity to love*. London: Oxford University Press.

Karlsson, C., & Berggren, I. (2011). Dignified end-of-life care in the patients' own homes. *Nursing Ethics*, *18*(3), 374–385.

Karns, J. T. (2001). Health, nutrition, and safety. In G. Bremner & A. Fogel (Eds.), *Blackwell handbook of infant development* (pp. 693–725). Malden, MA: Blackwell.

Kasper, J. D., Pezzin, L. E., & Rice, J. B. (2010). Stability and changes in living arrangements: Relationship to nursing home admission and timing of placement. *Journals of Gerontology: Social Sciences*, 65B(6), 783–791.

Kastenbaum, R. (2004). *On our way: The final passage through life and death.*

Berkeley, CA: University of California Press.

Kato, K., & Pedersen, N. L. (2005). Personality and coping: A study of twins reared apart and twins reared together. *Behavior Genetics, 35,* 147–158.

Katz-Wise, S. L., Priess, A., & Hyde, J. S. (2010). Gender-role attitudes and behavior across the transition to parenthood. *American Psychological Association,* 46(1), 18–28.

Katz, I., Kaplan, A., & Gueta, G. (2010). Students' needs, teachers' support, and motivation for doing homework: A cross-sectional study. *Journal of Experimental Education,* 78(2), 246–267.

Kaufman, A. S. (2001). WAIS-III IQs, Horn's theory, and generational changes from young adulthood to old age. *Intelligence, 29,* 131–167.

Keefe, M. R., Karlsen, K. A., Lobo, M. L., Kotzer, A. M., & Dudley, W. N. (2006). Reducing parenting stress in families with irritable infants. *Nursing Research,* 55(3), 198–205.

Keel, P. K., Baxter, M. G., Heatherton, T. F., & Joiner, T. E. (2007). A 20-year longitudinal study of body weight, dieting, and eating disorder symptoms. *Journal of Abnormal Psychology, 116*(2), 422–432.

Keller, M. A., & Goldberg, W. A. (2004). Co-sleeping: Help or hindrance for young children's independence? *Infant and Child Development, 13,* 369–388.

Keller, P., & El-Sheikh, M. (2010). Children's emotional security and sleep: Longitudinal relations and directions of effects. *The Journal of Child Psychology and Psychiatry,* 52(1), 64–71.

Kelley, S. J., & Whitley, D. M. (2003). Psychological distress and physical health problems in grandparents raising grandchildren: Development of an empirically-based intervention model. In B. Hayslip, Jr. & J. H. Patrick (Eds.), *Working with custodial grandparents* (pp. 127–144). New York: Springer.

Kellman, P. J., & Banks, M. S. (1998). Infant visual perception. In W. Damon (Series ed.) & D. Kuhn & R. S. Siegler (Vol. eds.), *Handbook of child psychology: Volume 2: Cognition, perception, and language* (pp. 103–146). Hoboken, NJ: John Wiley & Sons Inc.

Kelly, J. B. (2000). Children's adjustment in conflicted marriage and divorce: A decade review of research. *Journal of the American Academy of Child & Adolescent Psychiatry, 39,* 963–973.

Kelly, J. B. (2003). Changing perspectives on children's adjustment following divorce: A view from the United States. *Childhood: A Global Journal of Child Research, 10,* 237–254.

Kelly, R. J., & El-Sheikh, M. (2011). Marital conflict and children's sleep: Reciprocal relations and socioeconomic effects. *Journal of Family Psychology,* 25(3), 412–422.

Kemper, S., & Mitzner, T. L. (2001). Language production and comprehension. In J. E. Birren & K. W. Schaie (Eds.), *Handbook of the psychology of aging* (5th ed., pp. 378–398). San Diego, CA: Academic Press.

Kenrick, D. T., Groth, G. E., Trost, M. R., & Sadalla, E. K. (1993). Integrating evolutionary and social exchange perspectives on relationships: Effects of gender, self-appraisal, and involvement level on mate selection criteria. *Journal of Personality and Social Psychology, 64,* 951–969.

Kensinger, E. A., Krendl, A. C., & Corkin, S. (2006). Memories of an emotional and a nonemotional event: Effects of aging and delay interval. *Experimental Aging Research,* 32, 23–45.

Kerr, M., Stattin, H., & Burk, W. J. (2010). A reinterpretation of parental monitoring in longitudinal perspective. *Journal of Research on Adolescence,* 20(1), 39–64.

Keys, C. L. (2007). Promoting and protecting mental health as flourishing: A complementary strategy for improving national mental health. *American Psychologist,* 61, 95–108.

Kiang, L., & Fuligni, A. J. (2009). Ethnic identity and family processes among adolescents from Latin American, Asian, and European backgrounds. *Journal of Youth and Adolescence,* 38, 228–241.

Kiernan, K. (2002). Cohabitation in Western Europe: Trends, issues, and implications. In A. Booth & A. C. Crouter (Eds.), *Just living together: Implications of cohabitation on families, children, and social policy* (pp. 3–31). Mahwah, NJ: Erlbaum.

Kiernan, K. (2004). Redrawing the boundaries of marriage. *Journal of Marriage and Family, 66,* 980–987.

Kim, J., & Cicchetti, D. (2010). Longitudinal pathways linking child maltreatment, emotion regulation, peer relations, and psychopathology. *Journal of Child Psychology and Psychiatry,* 51(6), 706–716.

Kim, J., & Deater-Deckard, K. (2011). Dynamic changes in anger, externalizing and internalizing problems: Attention and regulation. *Journal of Child Psychology and Psychiatry,* 52(2), 156–166.

Kim, M., & Park, I. J. K. (2011). Testing the moderating effect of parent-adolescent communication on the acculturation gap-distress relation in Korean American families. *Journal of Youth and Adolescence, 40,* 1661–1673.

King, V., Silverstein, M., Elder, G. H., Bengtson, V. L., & Conger, R. D. (2003). Relations with grandparents: Rural midwest versus urban Southern California. *Journal of Family Issues, 24,* 1044–1069.

Kinniburgh-White, R., Cartwright, C., & Seymour, F. (2010). Young adults' narratives of relational development with stepfathers. *Journal of Social and Personal Relationships,* 27(7), 890–907.

Kins, E., & Beyers, W. (2010). Failure to launch, failure to achieve criteria for adulthood. *Journal of Adolescence Research,* 25(5), 743–777.

Kinsella, K., & Velkoff, V. A. (2001). *An aging world: 2001* (Series P95/01-1). Washington, DC: U.S. Census Bureau.

Kippersluis, H., O'Donnell, O., Doorslaer, E., & Ourti, T. V. (2010). Socioeconomic differences in health over the life cycle in an egalitarian country. *Social Science and Medicine,* 70, 428–438.

Kitahara, M. (1989). Childhood in Japanese culture. *Journal of Psychohistory, 17,* 43–72.

Kitzinger, S. (2000). *Rediscovering birth.* New York: Pocket Books.

Klass, D., & Walter, T. (2001). Processes of grieving: How bonds are continued. In M. S. Stroebe, R. O. Hansson, W. Stroebe, & H. Schut (Eds.), *Handbook of bereavement research: Consequences, coping, and care* (1st ed., pp. 431–448). Washington, DC: American Psychological Association.

Kloep, M., & Hendry, L. B. (2010). Letting go or holding on? Parents' perceptions of their relationships with their children during emerging adulthood. *British Journal of Developmental Psychology,* 28(4), 817–834.

Klonoff, E. A. (2009). Disparities in the provision of medical care: An outcome in search of an explanation. *Journal of Behavioral Medicine,* 32, 48–63.

Klusmann, D. (2002). Sexual motivation and the duration of partnership. *Archives of Sexual Behavior, 31,* 275–287.

Kluwer, E. S., & Johnson, M. D. (2007). Conflict frequency and relationship quality across the transition to parenthood. *Journal of Marriage and Family,* 69(5), 1089–1106.

Knox, M. (2010). On hitting children: A review of corporal punishment in the United States. *Journal of Pediatric Health Care, 24*(2), 103–107.

Koball, H. L., Moiduddin, E., Henderson, J., Goesling, B., & Besculides, M. (2010). What do we know about the link between marriage and health? *Journal of Family Issues, 31*(8), 1019–1040.

Kochanska, G., Aksan, N., Penney, S. J., & Boldt, L. J. (2007). Parental personality as an inner resource that moderates the impact of ecological adversity on parenting. *Journal of Personality and Social Psychology*, 92(1), 136–150.

Kochanska, G., Barry, R. A., Aksan, N., & Boldt, L. J. (2008). A developmental model of maternal and child contributions to disruptive conducts: The first six years. *Journal of Child Psychology and Psychiatry, 49*, 1220–1227.

Kochanska, G., Coy, K. C., & Murray, K. T. (2001). The development of self-regulation in the first four years of life. *Child Development, 72*, 1091–1111.

Kochanska, G., & Knaack, A. (2003). Effortful control as a personality characteristic of young children: Antecedents, correlates, and consequences. *Journal of Personality, 71*, 1087–1112.

Kochanska, G., Koenig, J. L., Barry, R. A., Kim, S., & Yoon, J. E. (2010a). Children's conscience during toddler and preschool years, moral self, and a competent, adaptive developmental trajectory. *Developmental Psychology, 46*(5), 1320–1332.

Kochanska, G., Woodard, J., Kim, S., Koenig, J. L., Yoon, J. E., & Barry, R. A. (2010b). Positive socialization mechanisms in secure and insecure parent-child dyads: Two longitudinal studies. *Journal of Child Psychology and Psychiatry, 51*(9), 998–1009.

Koerner, S. S., Shirai, Y., & Kenyon, D. B. (2010). Sociocontextual circumstances in daily stress reactivity among caregivers for elder relatives. *Journals of Gerontology: Psychological Sciences, 65B*(5), 561–572.

Kogan, A., Impett, E. A., Oveis, C., Hui, B., Gordon, A. M., & Keltner, D. (2010). When giving feels good: The intrinsic benefits of sacrifice in romantic relationships for the communally motivated. *Psychological Science, 21*(12), 1918–1924.

Kohlberg, L. (1966). Moral education in the schools: A developmental view. *School Review, 74*, 1–30.

Kohlberg, L. (1981). *The meaning and measurement of moral development.* Worcester, MA: Clark University Press.

Kohlberg, L. (1984). *The psychology of moral development: The nature and validity of moral stages.* San Francisco: Harper & Row.

Komarraju, M., Musulkin, S., & Bhattacharya, G. (2010). Role of student-faculty interactions in developing college students' academic self-concept, motivation, and achievement. *Journal of College Student Development, 51*(1), 332–342.

König, C. J., Probst, T. M., Staffen, S., & Graso, M. (2011). A Swiss-US comparison of the correlates of job insecurity. *Applied Psychology: An International Review, 60*(1), 141–159.

Konner, M. (2010). *The evolution of childhood.* Cambridge, MA: Harvard University Press.

Kono, A., Kai, I., Sakato, C., & Rubenstien, L. Z. (2007). Frequency of going outdoors predicts long-range functional change among ambulatory frail elders living at home. *Archives of Gerontology and Geriatrics, 45*, 233–242.

Korda, R. J., Clements, M. S., & Dixon, J. (2011). Socioeconomic inequalities in the diffusion of health technology: Uptake of coronary procedures as an example. *Social Science & Medicine*, 72(2), 224–229.

Koren, A., Reece, S.M., Kahn-D'angelo, L., & Medeiros, D. (2010). Parental information and behaviors and provider practices related to tummy time and back to sleep. *Journal of Pediatric Health Care*, 24(4), 222–229.

Kotter-Gruhn, D., Klienspehn-Ammerlahn, A., & Gerstorf, D. (2009). Self-perceptions of aging predict mortality and change with approaching death: 16-year longitudinal results from the Berlin Aging Study. *Psychology and Aging*, 24(3), 654–667.

Kozol, J. (1988). *Rachel and her children: Homeless families in America.* New York: Crown.

Kozol, J. (2005). *The shame of the nation: The restoration of apartheid schooling in America.* New York: Crown.

Kramer, B. J., & Thompson, E. H. (2002). *Men as caregivers: Theory, research, and service implications.* New York: Springer.

Krampe, R. T., & Baltes, P. B. (2003). Intelligence as adaptive resource development and resource allocation: A new look through the lenses of SOC and expertise. In R. J. Sternberg & E. L. Grigorenko (Eds.), *The psychology of abilities, competencies, and expertise* (pp. 31–68). New York: Cambridge University Press.

Krause, K. M., Lovelady, C. A., & Ostbye, T. (2011). Predictors of breastfeeding in overweight and obese women: Data from active mothers postpartum (AMP). *Maternal and Child Health Journal, 15*, 367–375.

Kreicbergs, U., Valdimarsdóttir, U., Onelöv, E., Henter, J.-I., & Steineck, G. (2004). Talking about death with children who have severe malignant disease. *New England Journal of Medicine, 351*, 1175–1186.

Kreling, B., Selsky, C., Perret-Gentil, M., Huerta, E. E., & Mandelblatt, J. S. (2010). 'The worst thing about hospice is that they talk about death': Contrasting hospice decisions and experience among immigrant Central and South American Latinos with US-born White, non-Latino cancer caregivers. *Palliative Medicine*, 24(4), 427–434.

Kreppner, J., Rutter, M., Marvin, R., O'Conner, T., & Sonuga-Barke, E. (2011). Assessing the concept of the 'insecure-other' category in the Cassidy-Marvin scheme: Changes between 4 and 6 years in the English and Romanian Adoptee study. *Social development*, 20(1), 1–16.

Kroger, J. (2000). *Identity development: Adolescence through adulthood.* Thousand Oaks, CA: Sage.

Kronenberg, M. E., Hansel, T. C., Brennan, A. M., Osofsky, H. J., Osofsky, J. D., & Lawrason, B. (2010). Children of Katrina: Lessons learned about postdisaster symptoms and recovery patterns. *Child Development, 81*(4), 1241–1259.

Krumm, J. (2002). Genetic discrimination: Why Congress must ban genetic testing in the workplace. *Journal of Legal Medicine*, 23, 491–521.

Krumrei, E., Coit, C., Martin, S., Fogo, W., & Mahoney, A. (2007). Post-divorce adjustment and social relationships: A meta-analytic review. *Journal of Divorce & Remarriage*, 46(3/4), 145–166.

Kübler-Ross, E. (1969). *On death and dying.* New York: Macmillan.

Kuhn, D. (1989). Children and adults as intuitive scientists. *Psychological Review*, 96, 674–689.

Kulik, L. (2007). Contemporary midlife grandparenthood. In V. Muhlbauer, & J. C. Chrisler (Eds.), *Women over 50: Psychological perspectives* (pp. 131–146). New York, NY: Springer Science + Business Media.

Kumar, G., Markert, R. J., & Patel, R. (2011). Assessment of hospice patients' goals of care at the end of life. *American Journal of Hospice & Palliative Medicine*, 28(1), 31–34.

Kvavilashvili, L., & Fisher, L. (2007). Is time-based prospective remembering mediated by self-initiated rehearsals? Role of incidental cues, ongoing activity, age, and motivation. *Journal of Experimental Psychology: General, 136*(1), 112–132.

Labouvie-Vief, G. (1992). A neo-Piagetian perspective on adult cognitive development. In R. J. Sternberg & C. A. Berg (Eds.), *Intellectual development* (pp. 197–228). New York: Cambridge University Press.

Labouvie-Vief, G. (2006). Emerging structures of adult thought. In J. J. Arnett & J. L. Tanner (Eds.), *Emerging adults in America: Coming of age in the 21st century* (pp. 59–84). Washington, DC: American Psychological Association.

Lachman, M. E. (2004). Development in midlife. *Annual Review of Psychology, 55*, 305–331.

Ladis, K., Daniels, N., & Kawachi, I. (2009). Exploring the relationship between absolute and relative position and late-life depression: Evidence from 10 European countries. *The Gerontologist, 50*(1), 48–59.

LaFontana, K. M., & Cillessen, A. H. N. (2010). Developmental changes in the priority of perceived status in childhood and adolescence. *Social Development, 19*(1), 130–147.

Lagattuta, K., Sayfan, L., & Blattman, A. J. (2010). Forgetting common ground: Six- to seven-year-olds have an overinterpretive theory of mind. *Developmental Psychology, 46*(6), 1417–1432.

Laible, D. J. (2004). Mother-child discourse surrounding a child's past behavior at 30 months: Links to emotional understanding and early conscience development at 36 months. *Merrill-Palmer Quarterly, 50*, 159–180.

Lamb, M. E. (1997). *The role of the father in child development* (3rd ed.). Hoboken, NJ: John Wiley & Sons Inc.

Lamb, M. E. (2002). Infant-father attachments and their impact on child development. In C. S. Tamis-LeMonda & N. Cabrera (Eds.), *Handbook of father involvement: Multidisciplinary perspectives* (pp. 93–117). Mahwah, NJ: Erlbaum.

Landerl, K., & Moll, K. (2010). Comorbidity of learning disorders: Prevalence and familial transmission. *Journal of Child Psychology and Psychiatry, 51*(3), 287–294.

Landor, A., Simons, L. G., Simons, R. L., Brody, G. H., & Gibbons, F. X. (2011). The role of religiosity in the relationship between parents, peers, and adolescents in risky sexual behavior. *Journal of Youth and Adolescence, 40*, 296–309.

Lansford, J. E., Malone, P. S., Dodge, K. A., Pettit, G. S., & Bates, J. E. (2010). Developmental cascades of peer rejection, social information processing biases, and aggression during middle childhood. *Development and Psychopathology, 22*(3), 593–602.

Laplante-Levesque, A., Hickson, L., & Worrall, L. (2010). Rehabilitation of older adults with hearing impairment: A critical review. *Journal of Aging and Health, 22*(2), 143–153.

Larsen, L., Hartmann, P., & Nyborg, H. (2007). The stability of general intelligence from early adulthood to middle age. *Intelligence, 36*(1), 29–34.

Larson, R. W. (2011). Positive development in a disorderly world. *Journal of Research on Adolescence, 21*(2), 317–334.

Larsson, H., Andkarsater, H., Rastam, M., Chang, Z., & Lichtenstein, O. (2012). Childhood attention-deficit hyperactivity disorder as an extreme of a continuous trait: A quantitative genetic study of 8,500 twin pairs. *Journal of Child Psychology and Psychiatry, 53*(1), 73–80.

LaRusso, M. D., Romer, D., & Selman, R. L. (2008). Teachers as builders of respectful school climates: Implications for adolescent drug use norms and depressive symptoms in high school. *Journal of Youth and Adolescence, 37*, 386–398.

Larzelere, R. E., & Kuhn, B. R. (2005). Comparing child outcomes of physical punishment and alternative disciplinary tactics: A meta-analysis. *Clinical Child and Family Psychology Review, 8*, 1–37.

Latz, S., Wolf, A. W., & Lozoff, B. (1999). Cosleeping in context: Sleep practices and problems in young children in Japan and the United States. *Archives of Pediatrics & Adolescent Medicine, 153*, 339–346.

Laursen, B., & Collins, W. A. (1994). Interpersonal conflict during adolescence. *Psychological Bulletin, 115*, 197–209.

Lavezzi, A. M., Corna, M., Mingrone, R., & Matturri, L. (2010). Study of the human hypoglossal nucleus: Normal development and morpho-functional alterations in sudden unexplained late fetal and infant death. *Brain & Development, 32*, 275–284.

Lavner, J. A., & Bradbury, T. N. (2010). Patterns of change in marital satisfaction over the newlywed years. *Journal of Marriage and Family, 72*, 1171–1187.

Lawler, M., & Nixon, E. (2011). Body dissatisfaction among adolescent boys and girls: The effects of body mass, peer appearance culture and internalization of appearance ideals. *Journal of Youth and Adolescence, 40*, 59–71.

Lawn, J. E., Blencowe, H., Pattinson, R., Cousens, S., Kumar, R., Ibiebele, I., . . . Stanton, C. (2011). Stillbirths: Where? When? Why? How to make the data count? *The Lancet, 377*(9775), 1448–1463.

Lawrence, J. S., Crocker, J., & Blanton, H. (2011). Stigmatized and dominant cultural groups differentially interpret positive feedback. *Journal of Cross-Cultural Psychology, 42*(1), 165–169.

Lawson, M. A. (2003). School-family relations in context: Parent and teacher perceptions of parent involvement. *Urban Education, 38*, 77–133.

Le, B., Dove, N. L., Agnew, C. R., Korn, M. S., & Musto, A. A. (2010). Predicting nonmarital romantic relationship dissolution: A meta-analytic synthesis. *Personal Relationships, 17*, 377–390.

Leavitt, J. W. (1986). *Brought to bed: Childbearing in America, 1750 to 1950*. New York: Oxford University Press.

Lecanuet, J. P., Graniere-Deferre, C., Jacquet, A. Y., & DeCasper, A. J. (2000). Fetal discrimination of low-pitched musical notes. *Developmental Psychobiology, 36*, 29–39.

Lee, E. A. E., & Troop-Gordon, W. (2011). Peer processes and gender role development: Changes in gender atypicality related to negative peer treatment and children's friendships. *Sex Roles, 64*, 90–102.

Lee, J. (2008). "A kotex and a smile": Mothers and daughters at menarche. *Journal of Family Issues, 29*, 1325–1347.

Lee, V. E., & Burkam, D. T. (2002). *Inequality at the starting gate: Social background differences in achievement as children begin school.* Washington, DC: Economic Policy Institute.

Legerski, E., & Cornwall, M. (2010). Working-class job loss, gender, and the negotiation of household labor. *Gender & Society, 24*, 447–470.

Leipold, B., Schacke, C., & Zank, S. (2008). Personal growth and cognitive complexity in caregivers of patients with dementia. *European Journal of Ageing, 5*, 203–214.

Lenroot, R. K., & Giedd, J. N. (2010). Sex differences in the adolescent brain. *Brain and Cognition, 72*, 46–55.

Lepore, M. J., Miller, S. C., & Gozalo, P. (2011). Hospice use among urban Black and White U.S. nursing home decedents in 2006. *The Gerontologist, 51*(2), 251–260.

Leppänen, P. H. T., Hämäläinen, J. A., Salminen, H. K., Eklund, K. M., Guttorm, T. K., Lohvansuu, K., … Lyytinen, H. (2010). Newborn brain event-related potentials revealing atypical processing of sound frequency and the subsequent association with later literacy skills in children with familial dyslexia. *Cortex, 46*, 1362–1376.

Lepper, M. R., Greene, D., & Nisbett, R. E. (1973). Undermining children's intrinsic interest with extrinsic reward: A test of the "overjustification" hypothesis. *Journal of Personality and Social Psychology, 28*, 129–137.

Lerner-Geva, L., Boyko, V., Blumstein, T., & Benyamini, Y. (2010). The impact of education, cultural background, and lifestyle on symptoms of the menopausal transition: The women's health at midlife study. *Journal of Women's Health, 18*(5), 975–985.

Lerner, R. M. (1998). Theories of human development: Contemporary perspectives. In W. Damon (Series ed.) & R. M. Lerner (Vol. Ed.), *Handbook of child psychology: Vol. 1: Theoretical models of human development* (5th ed., pp. 1–24). Hoboken, NJ: John Wiley & Sons Inc.

Lerner, R. M., Dowling, E. M., & Anderson, P. M. (2003). Positive youth development: Thriving as the basis of personhood and civil society. *Applied Developmental Science, 7*, 172–180.

Lerner, R. M., Dowling, E., & Roth, S. L. (2003). Contributions of lifespan psychology to the future elaboration of developmental systems theory. In U. M. Staudinger & U. Lindenberger (Eds.), *Understanding human development: Dialogues with lifespan psychology* (pp. 413–422). Dordrecht, Netherlands: Kluwer Academic.

Lerner, R. M., von Eye, A., Lerner, J. V., Lewin-Bizan, S., & Bowers, E. P. (2010). Special issue introduction: The meaning and measurement of thriving: A view of the issues. *Journal of Youth and Adolescence, 39*, 707–719.

Lessard, G., Flynn, C., Turcotte, P., Damant, D., Vézina, J., Godin, M., & Rondeau-Cantin, S. (2010). Child custody issues and co-occurrence of intimate partner violence and child maltreatment: Controversies and points of agreement amongst practitioners. *Child & Family Social Work, 15*(4), 492–500.

Lester, F., Benfield, N., & Fathalla, M. M. F. (2010). Global women's health in 2010: Facing the challenges. *Journal of Women's Health, 19*(11), 2081–2089.

Leung, A. K., & Chiu, C. (2011). Multicultural experience fosters creative conceptual expansion. In A. K. Leung, C. Chiu, & Y. Y. Hong, (Eds.), *Cultural processes: A social psychological perspective* (pp. 263–285). New York, NY: Cambridge University Press.

Leung, K. K., Tsai, J. S., Cheng, S. Y., Liu, W. J., Chiu, T. Y., Wu, C. H., & Chen, C. Y. (2010). Can a good death and quality of life be achieved for patients with terminal cancer in a palliative care unit? *Journal of Palliative Medicine, 13*(12), 1433–1438.

Leve, L. D., Shaw, D., Neiderhiser, J. M., Reid, J. B., Kerr, D. C. R., Ge, X., Neiderhiser, J. M., Scaramella, L. V., … Reiss, D. (2010). Infant pathways to externalizing behavior: Evidence genotype x environmental interaction. *Child Development, 81*(1), 240–356.

Leventhal, T., & Newman, S. (2010). Housing and child development. *Children and Youth Services Review, 32*(9), 1165–1174.

Lewin-Bizan, S., Lynch, A. D., Fay, K., Schmid, K., McPherran, C., Lerner, J. V., & Lerner, R. M. (2010). Trajectories of positive and negative behaviors from early- to middle-adolescence. *Journal of Youth and Adolescence, 39*, 751–763.

Lewis, A. D., Huebner, E. S., Malone, P. S., & Valois, R. F. (2011). Life satisfaction and student engagement in adolescents. *Journal of Youth and Adolescence, 40*, 249–262.

Lewkowicz, D. J., Leo, I., & Simon, F. (2010). Intersensory perception at birth: Newborns match nonhuman primate faces and voices. *Infancy, 15*(1), 46–60.

Li, F., Godinet, M. T., & Arnsberger, P. (2011). Protective factors among families with children at risk of maltreatment: Follow up to early school years. *Children and Youth Services Review, 33*, 139–148.

Li, N. P., Patel, L., Balliet, D., Tov, W., & Scollon, C. N. (2011). The incompatibility of materialism and the desire for children: Psychological insights into the fertility discrepancy among modern countries. *Social Indicators Research, 101*(3), 391–404.

Li, T., Fung, H. H., & Isaacowitz, D. M. (2011). The role of dispositional reappraisal in the age-related positivity effect. *Journals of Gerontology: Psychological Sciences, 66B*(1), 56–60.

Li, Y., & Lerner, R. M. (2011). Trajectories of school engagement during adolescence: Implications for grades, depression, delinquency, and substance use. *Developmental Psychology, 4*(1), 233–247.

Liang, J., Quiñones, A. R., Bennett, J. M., Ye, W., Xu, X., Shaw, B. A., & Ofstedal, M. (2010). Evolving self-rated health in middle and old age: How does it differ across Black, Hispanic, and White Americans? *Journal of Aging and Health, 22*(1), 3–26.

Liben, S., Papadatou, D., & Wolfe, J. (2008). Paediatric palliative care: Challenges and emerging ideas. *Lancet, 371*, 852–864.

Lieberman, A. F. (1993). *The emotional life of the toddler.* New York: Free Press.

Lien, L., Haavet, O., & Dalgard, F. (2010). Do mental health and behavioural problems of early menarche persist into late adolescence? A three year follow-up study among adolescent girls in Oslo, Norway. *Social Science & Medicine, 71*(3), 529–533.

Liew, J., Eisenberg, N., Spinrad, T. L., Eggum, N. D., Haugen, R. G., Kupfer, A., & Baham, M. E. (2011). Physiological regulation and fearfulness as predictors of young children's empathy related reactions. *Social Development, 20*(1), 111–134.

Light, R. J. (2001). *Making the most of college: Students speak their minds.* Cambridge, MA: Harvard University Press.

Lightfoot, C. (1997). *The culture of adolescent risk-taking.* New York: Guilford Press.

Lilgendahl, J. P., & McAdams, D. P. (2011). Constructing stories of self-growth: How individual differences in patterns of autobiographical reasonings relate to well-being in midlife. *Journal of Personality, 79*(2), 392–425.

Lillard, A. S. (1998). Playing with a theory of mind. In O. N. Saracho & B. Spodek (Eds.), *Multiple perspectives on play in early childhood education* (pp. 11–33). Albany, NY: State University of New York Press.

Lim, S. L., Yeh, M., Liang, J., Lau, A. S., & McCabe, K. (2009) Acculturation gap, intergenerational conflict, parenting style, and youth distress in immigrant Chinese American families. *Marriage & Family Review, 45*, 84–106.

Lin, S., Keysar, B., & Epley, N. (2010). Reflexively mindblind: Using theory of mind to interpret behavior requires effortful attention. *Journal of Experimental Social Psychology, 46*, 551–556.

Lindemann, E. (1944). Symptomatology and management of acute grief. *American Journal of Psychiatry, 101*, 141–148.

Lindstrom-Forneri, W., Tuokko, H., & Rhodes, R. E. (2007). "Getting around town": A preliminary investigation of the theory of planned behavior and intent to change driving behaviors among older adults. *Journal of Applied Gerontology, 26*(4), 385–398.

Linver, M. R., Roth, J. L., & Brooks-Gunn, J. (2009). Patterns of adolescents' participation in organized activities: Are sports best when combined with other activities? *Developmental Psychology, 45*, 354–367.

Literte, P.E. (2010). Revising race: How biracial students are changing and challenging student services. *Journal of College Student Development, 51*(2), 115–135.

Liu, J., Smith, M. G., Dobre, M. A., Ferguson, J. E. (2010). Maternal obesity and breast-feeding practices among white and Black women. *Obesity, 18*(1), 175–182.

Liu, Y. C., Su, P. Y., Chen, C. H., Chiang, H. H., Wang, K. Y., & Tzeng, W. C. (2011). Facing death, facing self: Nursing students' emotional reactions during an experiential workshop on life-and-death issues. *Journal of Clinical Nursing, 20*(5–6), 856–863.

LoBue, V., Nishida, T., Chiong, C., DeLoache, J. S., & Haidt, J. (2011). When getting something good is bad: Even three-year-olds react to inequality. *Social Development, 20*(1), 154–170.

Löckenhoff, C. E., Fruyt, F. D., Terracciano, A., McCrae, R. R., Bolle, M. D., Costa, P. T., Jr., … Yik, M. (2009). Perceptions of aging across 26 cultures and their culture-level associates. *Psychology and Aging, 24*(4), 941–954.

Loe, I. M., Lee, E. S., Luna, B., & Feldman, H. M. (2011). Behavior problems of 9-16 year old preterm children: Biological, sociodemographic, and intellectual contributions. *Early Human Development, 87*(4), 247–252.

Lonardo, R. A., Giordano, P. C., Longmore, M. A., & Manning, W. D. (2009). Parents, friends, and romantic partners: Enmeshment in deviant networks and adolescent delinquency involvement. *Journal of Youth and Adolescence, 38*, 367–383.

Long, S. O. (2004). Cultural scripts for a good death in Japan and the United States: Similarities and differences. *Social Science & Medicine, 58*, 913–928.

López-Guimerà, G., Levine, M. P., Sánchez-carracedo, D., & Fauquet, J. (2010). Influence of mass media on body image and eating disordered attitudes and behaviors in females: A review of effects and processes. *Media Psychology, 13*(4), 387–416.

Lorber, M. F., O'Leary, S. G., & Smith Slep, A. M. (2011). An initial evaluation of the role of emotion and impulsivity in explaining racial/ethnic differences in the use of corporal punishment. *Developmental Psychology, 47*(6), 1744–1749.

Lorenz, K. (1935). Der Kumpan in der Umwelt des Vogels. Der Artgenosse als auslosendes Moment sozialer Verhaltungsweisen. [The companion in the bird's world. The fellow-member of the species as releasing factor of social behavior.]. *Journal fur Ornithologie. Beiblatt. (Leipzig), 83*, 137–213.

Lou, S., Liu, J., Chang, H., & Chen, P. (2008). Hippocampal neurogenesis and gene expression depend on exercise intensity in juvenile rats. *Brain Research, 1210*, 48–55.

Loukas, A., Roalson, L. A., & Herrera, D. E. (2010). School connectedness buffers the effects of negative family relations and poor effortful control on early adolescent conduct problems. *Journal of Research on Adolescence, 20*(1), 13–22.

Low, J. (2010). Preschoolers implicit and explicit false-belief understanding: Relations with complex syntactical mastery. *Child Development, 81*(2), 597–615.

Luciana, M. (2010). Adolescent brain development: Current themes and future directions Introduction to the special issue [Editorial]. *Brain and Cognition, 72*, 1–5.

Lugo-Gil, J., & Tamis-LeMonda, C. S. (2008). Family resources and parenting quality: Links to children's cognitive development across the first 3 years. *Child Development, 79*(4), 1065–1085.

Lumpkin, A. (2010). 10 school-based strategies for student success. *Kappa Delta Pi Record, 46*(2), 71–75.

Luo, L., Hendriks, T., & Craik, F. I. M. (2007). Age differences in recollection: Three patterns of enhanced encoding. *Psychology and Aging, 22*(2), 269–280.

Luong, G., Charles, S. T., & Fingerman, K. L. (2010). Better with age: Social relationships across adulthood. *Journal of Social and Personal Relationships, 28*(1), 9–23.

Luthy, C., Cedraschi, C., Pautex, S., Rentsch, D., Piguet, V., & Allaz, A. F. (2009). Difficulties of residents in training in end-of-life care: A qualitative study. *Palliative Medicine, 23*, 59–65.

Luttikhuis, H. G. M. O., Stolk, R. P., & Sauer, P. J. J. (2010). How do parents of 4- to 5-year-old children perceive the weight of their children? *Acta Paediatrica, 99*, 263–267.

Lynne-Landsman, S. D., Graber, J. A., & Andrews, J. A. (2010). Do trajectories of household risk in childhood moderate pubertal timing effects on substance initiation in middle school? *Developmental Psychology, 46*(4), 853–868.

Lyons, S. S. (2010). How do people make continence care happen? An analysis of organizational culture in two nursing homes. *The Gerontologist, 50*(3), 327–339.

Maccoby, E. E. (1990). Gender and relationships: A developmental account. *American Psychologist, 45*, 513–520.

Maccoby, E. E. (1998). *The two sexes: Growing up apart, coming together.* Cambridge, MA: Belknap Press of Harvard University Press.

Maccoby, E. E. (2002). Gender and group process: A developmental perspective. *Current Directions in Psychological Science, 11*, 54–58.

Maccoby, E. E., & Martin, J. A. (1983). Socialization in the context of the family: Parent-child interaction. In P. H. Mussen (Series ed.) & E. M. Hethenington (Vol. ed.), *Handbook of child psychology: Vol. 4. Socialization, personality, and social development* (4th ed., pp. 1–101). New York: John Wiley & Sons Inc.

Macek, P., Bejcek, J., & Vanickova, J. (2007). Contemporary Czech emerging adults: Generation growing up in the period of social changes. *Journal of Adolescent Research, 22*(5), 444–474.

MacRae, H. (2008). Making the best you can of it: Living with early-state Alzheimer's disease. *Sociology of Health & Wellness, 30*(3), 396–412.

Maggs, J. L., Patrick, M. E., & Feinstein, L. (2008). Childhood and adolescent predictors of alcohol use and problems in adolescence and adulthood in the National Child Development Study. *Addiction, 103* (Suppl. 1), 7–22.

Magnuson, K., & Shager, H. (2010). Early education: Progress and promise for children from low-income families. *Children and Youth Services Review, 32*, 1186–1198.

Maher, J., Fraser, S., & Wright, J. (2010). Framing the mother: Childhood obesity, maternal responsibility and care. *Journal of Gender Studies, 19*(3), 233–247.

Males, M. (2009). Does the adolescent brain make risk taking inevitable? *Journal of Adolescent Research 24*, 3–20.

Manchester, J., & Topoleski, J. (2008). *Growing disparities in life expectancy. Economic and Budget Issue Brief.* Washington, DC: Congressional Budget Office.

Mandler, J. M. (2007). On the origins of the conceptual system. *American Psychologist, 62*(8), 741–751.

Manfra, L., & Winsler, A. (2006). Preschool children's awareness of private speech. *International Journal of Behavioral Development, 30*(6), 537–549.

Manning, W. D., Giordano, P. C., & Longmore, M. A. (2006). Hooking up: The relationship contexts of "nonrelationship" sex. *Journal of Adolescent Research, 21*(5), 459–483.

Manning, W. D., Longmore, M. A., & Giordano, P. C. (2007). The changing institution of marriage: Adolescents' expectation to cohabit and to marry. *Journal of Marriage and Family, 69*(3), 559–575.

Mao, A., Burnham, M. M., Goodlin-Jones, B. L., Gaylor, E. E., & Anders, T. F. (2004). A comparison of the sleep-wake patterns of cosleeping and solitary-sleeping infants. *Child Psychiatry & Human Development, 35*, 95–105.

Marcia, J. E. (1966). Development and validation of ego-identity status. *Journal of Personality & Social Psychology, 3*, 551–558.

Marcia, J. E. (1987). The identity status approach to the study of ego identity development. In T. Honess & K. Yardley (Eds.), *Self and identity: Perspectives across the lifespan* (pp. 161–171). New York: Routledge.

Marieb, E. N. (2004). *Human anatomy & physiology* (6th ed.). New York: Pearson Education.

Markey, C. N. (2010). Invited commentary: Why body image is important to adolescent development. *Journal of Youth and Adolescence, 39*(12), 1387–1391.

Markey, P. M., & Markey, C. N. (2007). Romantic ideals, romantic obtainment, and relationship experiences: The complementarity of interpersonal traits among romantic partners. *Journal of Social and Personal Relationships, 24*(4), 517–533.

Markman, H. J., Rhoades, G. K., Whitton, S. W., Stanley, S. M., & Ragan, E. P. (2010). The premarital communication roots of marital distress and divorce: The first five years of marriage. *Journal of Family Psychology, 24*(3), 289–298.

Marlier, L., Schaal, B., & Soussignan, R. (1998). Neonatal responsiveness to the odor of amniotic and lacteal fluids: A test of perinatal chemosensory continuity. *Child Development, 69*, 611–623.

Marsiglio, W. (2004). When stepfathers claim stepchildren: A conceptual analysis. *Journal of Marriage and Family, 66*, 22–39.

Martin, C. L., & Dinella, L. M. (2002). Children's gender cognitions, the social environment, and sex differences in cognitive domains. In A. McGillicuddy-De Lisi & R. De Lisi (Eds.), *Biology, society, and behavior: The development of sex differences in cognition* (pp. 207–239). Westport, CT: Ablex.

Martin, C. L., & Fabes, R. A. (2001). The stability and consequences of young children's same-sex peer interactions. *Developmental Psychology, 37*, 431–446.

Martin, C. L., & Ruble, D. N. (2010). Patterns of gender development. *Annual Review of Psychology, 61*. 353–381.

Martin, J. A., Hamilton, B. E., Menacker, F., Sutton, P. D., & Mathews, T. J. (2005, November 15). *Preliminary births for 2004: Infant and maternal health.* Hyattsville, MD: National Center for Health Statistics.

Martin, J. A., Hamilton, B. E., Sutton, P. D., Ventura, S. J., Menacker, F., & Munson, M. L. (2003, December 17). Births: Final data for 2002. *National Vital Statistics Reports,* 52(10).

Martin, J. A., Osterman, M. J. K., & Sutton, P. D. (2010). Are preterm births on the decline in the United States? Recent data from the National Vital Statistics System. *NCHS Data Brief (39)*. Hyattsville, MD: Centers for Disease Control and Prevention, National Center for Health Statistics.

Martin, K. A. (1996). *Puberty, sexuality, and the self: Boys and girls at adolescence.* New York: Routledge.

Martin, M., Fergus, E., & Noguera, P. (2010). Responding to the needs of the whole child: A case study of a high-performing elementary school for immigrant children. *Reading & Writing Quarterly, 26*(3), 195–222.

Martin, P., Audet, T., Corriveau, H., Hamel, M., D'Amours, M., & Smeesters, C. (2010). Comparison between younger and older drivers of the effect of obstacle direction on the minimum obstacle distance to brake and avoid a motor vehicle accident. *Accident Analysis and Prevention, 42*(4), 1144–1150.

Martin, S., Meyer, J., Jones, R. C., Nelson, L., & Ting, L. (2010). Perceptions of professionalism among individuals in the child care field. *Child Youth Care Forum, 39*, 341–349.

Marysko, M., Finke, P., Wiebel, A., Resch, F., & Moehler, E. (2010). Can mothers predict childhood behavioral inhibition in early infancy? *Child and Adolescent Mental Health, 15*(2), 91–96.

Maslach, C., & Leiter, M. P. (2008). Early predictors of job burnout and engagement. *Journal of Applied Psychology,* 93(3), 498–512.

Mason, J., May, V., & Clarke, L. (2007). Ambivalence and the paradoxes of grandparenting. *Sociological Review,* 55(4), 687–706.

Masoro, E. (1999). *Challenges of biological aging.* New York: Springer.

Masten, A. S. (2004). Regulatory processes, risk, and resilience in adolescent development. In R. E. Dahl & L. P. Spear (Eds.), *Adolescent brain development: Vulnerabilities and opportunities* (Vol. 1021, pp. 310–319). New York: New York Academy of Sciences.

Masters, W. H., & Johnson, V. E. (1966). *Human sexual response.* Boston: Little, Brown.

Masucci, L., Guerriere, D. N., Cheng, R., & Coyte, P. C. (2010). Determinants of place of death for recipients of home-based palliative care. *Journal of Palliative Care, 26*(4), 279–286.

Masuda, A., Boone, M. S., & Timko, C. A. (2011). The role of psychological flexibility in the relationship between self-concealment and disordered eating symptoms. *Eating Behaviors, 12*, 131–135.

Materne, C. J., & Luszcz, M. A. (2010). Offering to provide child care for preschool grandchildren: Grandparents behaving generatively. *Australian Journal on Ageing, 29*(1), 47–48.

Matthews, R. A., Bulger, C. A., & Barnes-Farrell, J. L. (2010). Work, social supports, role stressors, and work-family conflict: The moderating effect of age. *Journal of Vocational Behavior, 72*, 78–90.

Mattingly, M. J., & Smith, K. E. (2010). Changes in wives' employment when husbands stop working: A recession-prosperity comparison. *Family Relations: Interdisciplinary Journal of Applied Family Studies, 59*, 343–357.

Mayberry, M. L., & Espelage, D. L. (2007). Associations among empathy, social competence, & reactive/proactive aggression subtypes. *Journal of Youth and Adolescence, 36*, 787–798.

Mayeux, L., & Cillessen, A. H. N. (2008). It's not just being popular, it's knowing it, too: The role of self-perceptions of status in the associations between peer status and aggression. *Social Development, 17*, 871–888.

Maynard, A. E., & Greenfield, P. M. (2003). Implicit cognitive development in cultural tools and children: Lessons from Maya Mexico. *Cognitive Development, 18*, 489–510.

Mays, V. M., Cochran, S. D., & Barnes, N. W. (2007). Race, race-based discrimination, and health outcomes among African Americans. *Annual Review of Psychology, 58*, 201–225.

McAdams, D. (2008). Generativity, the redemptive self, and the problem of a noisy ego in American life. In H. A. Wayment & J. J. Bauer (Eds.), *Transcending Self-Interest: Psychological Explorations of the quiet ego* (pp. 235–242). Washington, DC: American Psychological Association.

McAdams, D. P. (2001a). Generativity in midlife. In M. E. Lachman (Ed.), *Handbook of midlife development* (pp. 395–443). Hoboken, NJ: John Wiley & Sons Inc.

McAdams, D. P. (2001b). The psychology of life stories. *Review of General Psychology, 5*, 100–122.

McAdams, D. P. (2006). *The redemptive self: Stories Americans live by*. New York: Oxford University Press.

McAdams, D. P., & Bowman, P. J. (2001). Narrating life's turning points: Redemption and contamination. In D. P. McAdams, R. Josselson, & A. Lieblich (Eds.), *Turns in the road: Narrative studies of lives in transition* (pp. 3–34). Washington, DC: American Psychological Association.

McAdams, D. P., & de St. Aubin, E. (1992). A theory of generativity and its assessment through self-report, behavioral acts, and narrative themes in autobiography. *Journal of Personality and Social Psychology, 62*, 1003–1015.

McAdams, D. P., de St. Aubin, E., & Logan, R. L. (1993). Generativity among young, midlife, and older adults. *Psychology and Aging, 8*, 221–230.

McAdams, D. P., Hart, H. M., & Maruna, S. (1998). The anatomy of generativity. In D. P. McAdams & E. de St. Aubin (Eds.), *Generativity and adult development: How and why we care for the next generation* (pp. 7–43). Washington, DC: American Psychological Association.

McAuley, K. A., Taylor, R. W., Farmer, V. L., Hansen, P., Williams, S. M., Booker, C. S., & Mann, J. I. (2010). Economic evaluation of a community-based obesity prevention program in children: The Apple Project. *Obesity, 18*(1), 131–136.

McCabe, D. P., Roediger, H. L., McDaniel, M. A., Balots, D. A., & Hambrick, D. Z. (2010). The relationship between working memory capacity and executive functioning: Evidence for a common executive attention construct. *Neuropsychology, 24*(2), 223–243.

McCarthy, M. C., Clarke, N. E., Ting, C. L., Conroy, R., Anderson, V. A., & Heath, J. A. (2010). Prevalence and predictors of parental grief and depression after the death of a child from cancer. *Journal of Palliative Medicine, 13*(11), 1321–1326.

McClintock, M. K., & Herdt, G. (1996). Rethinking puberty: The development of sexual attraction. *Current Directions in Psychological Science, 5*, 178–183.

McCrae, R. R., Scally, M., & Terracciano, A. (2010). An alternative to the search for single polymorphisms: Toward molecular personality scales for the five-factor model. *Journal of Personality and Social Psychology, 99*(6), 1014–1024.

McCreight, B. S. (2004). A grief ignored: Narratives of pregnancy loss from a male perspective. *Sociology of Health and Illness, 26*, 326–350.

McDaniel, C., Roche, J. K., & Veledar, E. (2011). Ethics environment in long-term care. *Journal of Applied Gerontology, 30*(1), 67–84.

McElwain, N. L., Booth-LaForce, C., & Wu, X. (2011). Infant–mother attachment and children's friendship quality: Maternal mental-state talk as an intervening mechanism. *Developmental Psychology, 47*(5), 1295–1311.

McFarlane, T., Urbszat, D., & Olmsted, M. P. (2011). "I feel fat": An experimental induction of body displacement in disordered eating. *Behaviour Research and Therapy, 49*, 289–293.

McGeown, K. (2005). Life in Ceauseascu's institutions. Retrieved Febuary 6, 2011, from http://news.bbc.co.uk/2/hi/europe/4630855.stm

McGrath, P. (2004). Affirming the connection: Comparative findings on communication issues from hospice patients and hematology survivors. *Death Studies, 28*, 829–848.

McHugh, M. C. (2007). Women and sex at midlife: Desire, dysfunction, and diversity. In V. Muhlbauer, & J. C. Chrisler (Eds.), *Women over 50: Psychological perspectives* (pp. 26–52). New York, NY: Springer Science.

McIntosh, H., Metz, E., & Youniss, J. (2005). Community service and identity formation in adolescents. In J. L. Mahoney, R. W. Larson, & J. S. Eccles (Eds.), *Organized activities as contexts of development: Extracurricular activities, after-school and community programs* (pp. 331–351). Mahwah, NJ: Erlbaum.

McKay, A., & Barrett, M. (2010). Trends in teen pregnancy rates from 1996–2006: A comparison of Canada, Sweden, U.S.A., and England/Wales. *Canadian Journal of Human Sexuality, 19*(1–2), 43–52.

McKinley, N. M. (2006). The developmental and cultural contexts of objectified body consciousness: A longitudinal analysis of two cohorts of women. *Developmental Psychology, 42*, 679–687.

McKown, C., & Strambler, M. J. (2009). Developmental antecedents and social and academic consequences of stereotype-consciousness in middle childhood. *Child Development, 80*(6), 1643–1659.

McLanahan, S., & Adams, J. (1989). The effects of children on adults' psychological well-being: 1957–1976. *Social Forces, 68*, 124–146.

McLaughlin, K. A., Fox, N. A., Zeanah, C. H., Sheridan, M. A., Marshall, P., & Nelson, C. A. (2010). Delayed maturation in brain electrical activity partially explains the association between early environmental deprivation and symptoms of attention-deficit/hyperactivity disorder. *Biological Psychiatry, 68*(4), 329–336.

McLaughlin, K. A., Zeanah, C., Fox, N., & Nelson, C. (2012) Attachment security as a mechanism linking foster care placement to improved mental health outcomes in previously institutionalized children. *Journal of Child Psychology and Psychiatry, 53*(1), 46–55.

McLaughlin, S. J., Connell, C. M., Heeringa, S. G., Li, L. W., & Roberts, J. S. (2010). Successful aging in the United States: Prevalence estimates from a national sample of older adults. *Journal of Gerontology: Social Sciences, 65B*(2), 216–226.

McMahan, E. S., & Estes, D. (2011). Hedonic versus eudaimonic conceptions of well-being: Evidence of different associations with self-reported well-being. *Social Indicators Research, 103*, 93–108.

McMillan, W., Stice, E., & Rohde, P. (2011). High- and low-level dissonance-based eating disorder prevention programs with young women with body image concerns: An experimental trial. *Journal of Consulting and Clinical Psychology, 79*(1), 129–134.

McNeely, C. A., & Barber, B. K. (2010). How do parents make adolescents feel loved? Perspectives on supportive parenting from adolescents in 12 cultures. *Journal of Adolescent Research, 25*(4), 601–631.

McNiel, M. E., Labbok, M. H., & Abrahams, S. W. (2010). What are the risks associated with formula feeding? A re-analysis and review. *Birth: Issues in Prenatal Care, 37*(1), 50–58.

McNulty, J. K. (2008). Forgiveness in marriage: Putting the benefits into context. *Journal of Family Psychology, 22*, 171–175.

Meert, K. L., Shear, K., Newth, C. J. L., Harrison, R., Berger, J., Zimmerman, J., … Nicholson, C. (2011). Follow-up study of complicated grief among parents eighteen months after a child's death in the pediatric intensive care unit. *Journal of Palliative Medicine, 14*(2), 207–214.

Meeus, W. (2011). The study of adolescent identity formation 2000–2010: A review of longitudinal research. *Journal of Research on Adolescence, 21*(1), 75–94.

Meier, D. E., & Beresford, L. (2009). Palliative care cost research can help other palliative care programs make their case. *Journal of Palliative Medicine, 23*, 15–20.

Melendez, M. C., & Melendez, N. B. (2010). The influence of parental attachment on the college adjustment of White, Black, and Latina/Hispanic women: A cross-cultural investigation. *Journal of College Student Development, 51*(4), 419–435.

Mellor, D., Fuller-Tyszkiewicz, M., McCabe, M. P., & Ricciardelli, L. A. (2010). Body image and self-esteem across age and gender: A short-term longitudinal study. *Sex Roles, 63*(9–10), 672–681.

Meltzer, H., Bebbington, P., Brugha, T., Jenkins, R., McManus, S., & Stansfeld, S. (2010). Job insecurity, socio-economic circumstances and depression. *Psychological Medicine, 40*, 1401–1407.

Meltzoff, A. N., & Moore, M. K. (1977, October 7). Imitation of facial and manual gestures by human neonates. *Science, 198*, 75–78.

Menard, J. L., & Hakvoort, R. M. (2007). Variations of maternal care alter offspring levels of behavioral defensiveness in adulthood: Evidence for a threshold model. *Behavioral Brain Research, 176*, 302–313.

Mendle, J., Harden, K. P., Brooks-Gunn, J., & Graber, J. A. (2010). Development's tortoise and hare: pubertal timing, pubertal tempo, and depressive symptoms in boys and girls. *Developmental Psychology, 46*(5), 1341–1353.

Merrill, D. M. (1996). Conflict and cooperation among adult siblings during the transition to the role of filial caregiver. *Journal of Social and Personal Relationships, 13*(3), 399–413.

Merz, E. M., Schulze, H. J., & Schuengel, C. (2010). Consequences of filial support for two generations: A narrative and quantitative review. *Journal of Family Issues, 31*(11), 1530–1554.

Mikulincer, M., Florian, V., Cowan, P. A., & Cowan, C. P. (2002). Attachment security in couple relationships: A systemic model and its implications for family dynamics. *Family Process, 41*, 405–434.

Miller, B. J., & Lundgren, J. D. (2010). An experimental study of the role of weight bias in candidate evaluation. *Obesity, 18*(4), 712–718.

Miller, D., & Daniel, B. (2007). Competent to cope, worthy of happiness? How the duality of self-esteem can inform a resilience-based classroom environment. *School Psychology International, 28*(5), 605–622.

Miller, E. A., Mor, V., & Clark, M. (2010). Reforming long-term care in the United States: Findings from a national survey of specialists. *The Gerontologist, 50*(2), 238–252.

Miller, G. E., Chen, E., & Parker, K. J. (2011). Psychological stress in childhood and susceptibility to the chronic diseases of aging: Moving toward a model of behavioral and biological mechanisms. *Psychological Bulletin, 137*(6), 959–997.

Miller, K. E., Merrill, J. M., Barnes, G. M., Sabo, D., & Farrell, M. P. (2007). Athletic involvement and adolescent delinquency. *Journal of Youth and Adolescence, 36*, 711–723.

Miller, S. D. (2003). How high and low challenge tasks affect motivation and learning: Implications for struggling learners. *Reading & Writing Quarterly: Overcoming Learning Difficulties, 19*, 39–57.

Miller, T. (2010). "It's a triangle that's difficult to square": Men's intentions and practices around caring, work, and first-time fatherhood. *Fathering, 8*(3), 362–378.

Miller, W. D., Sadegh-Nobari, T., & Lillie-Blanton, M. (2011). Healthy starts for all: Policy prescriptions. *American Journal of Preventive Medicine, 40*(1), S19–S37.

Mills, E. S. (1993). *The story of Elderhostel.* Hanover, NH: University Press of New England.

Miniño, A. M., Arias, E., Kochanek, K. D., Murphy, S. L., & Smith, B. L. (2002, September 16). Deaths: Final data for 2000. *National Vital Statistics Reports, 50*(16).

Minois, G. (1989). *History of old age: From antiquity to the Renaissance* (S. H. Tenison, Trans.). Chicago: University of Chicago Press.

Mintz, S. (2004). *Huck's raft: A history of American childhood.* Cambridge, MA: Belknap Press of Harvard University Press.

Misra, V. K., & Trudeau, S. (2011). The influence of overweight and obesity on longitudinal trends in maternal serum leptin levels during pregnancy. *Obesity, 19*(2), 416–421.

Mistry, J., Chaudhuri, J., & Diez, V. (2003). Ethnotheories of parenting: Integrating culture and child development. In R. M. Lerner, F. H. Jacobs, & D. Wertlieb (Eds.), *Handbook of applied developmental science: Promoting positive child, adolescent, and family development through research, policies, and programs* (pp. 233–256). Thousand Oaks, CA: Sage.

Mitchell-Flynn, C., & Hutchinson, R. L. (1993). A longitudinal study of the problems and concerns of urban divorced men. *Journal of Divorce & Remarriage, 19*, 161–182.

Modell, J. (1989). *Into one's own: From youth to adulthood in the United States, 1920–1975.* Berkeley, CA: University of California Press.

Modin, B., Östberg, V., & Almquist, Y. (2011). Childhood peer status and adult susceptibility to anxiety and depression. A 30-year hospital follow-up. *Journal of Abnormal Child Psychology, 39*, 187–199.

Moehler, E., Kagan, J., Oelkers-Ax, R., Brunner, R., Poustka, L., Haffner, J., & Resch, F. (2008). Infant predictors of behavioural inhibition. *British Journal of Developmental Psychology, 26*(1), 145–150.

Moens, E., Braet, C., & Van Winkel, M. (2010). An 8-year follow-up of treated obese children: Children's process and parental predictors of successful outcome. *Behaviour Research and Therapy, 48*(7), 626–633.

Moffitt, T. E. (1993). Adolescence-limited and life-course-persistent antisocial behavior: A developmental taxonomy. *Psychological Review, 100*, 674–701.

Moffitt, T. E., Caspi, A., Belsky, J., & Silva, P. A. (1992). Childhood experience and the onset of menarche: A test of a sociobiological model. *Child Development, 63*, 47–58.

Moghadam, V. M. (2004). Patriarchy in transition: Women and the changing family in the Middle East. *Journal of Comparative Family Studies, 35*, 137–162.

Moilanen, K. L., Crockett, L. J., Raffaelli, M., & Jones, B. L. (2010). Trajectories of sexual risk from middle adolescence to early adulthood. *Journal of Research on Adolescence, 20*(1), 114–139.

Molden, D. C., & Dweck, C. S. (2006). Finding "meaning" in psychology: A lay theories approach to self-regulation, social perception, and social development. *American Psychologist, 61*, 192–203.

Molloy, L. E., Gest, S. D., & Rulison, K. L. (2011). Peer influences on academic motivation: Exploring multiple methods of assessing youths' most "influential" peer relationships. *The Journal of Early Adolescence, 31*(1), 13–40.

Monin, J. K., Schulz, R., Martire, L. M., Jennings, J. R., Lingler, J. H., & Greenberg, M. S. (2010). Spouses' cardiovascular reactivity to their partners' suffering. *Journals of Gerontology: Psychological Sciences, 65B*(3), 195–201.

Monroe, B., Hansford, P., Payne, M., & Sykes, N. (2008). St. Christopher's and the future. *Omega: Journal of Death and Dying. Special Issue: "Hospice heritage" In memory of Dame Cicely Saunders, 56*, 63–75.

Monserud, M. A. (2008). Intergenerational relationships and affectual solidarity between grandparents and young adults. *Journal of Marriage and Family, 70*(1), 182–195.

Montemayor, R. (1983). Parents and adolescents in conflict: All families some of the time and some families most of the time. *Journal of Early Adolescence, 3*, 83–103.

Montoro-Rodriguez, J., Kosloski, K., Kercher, K., & Montgomery, R. J. V. (2009). The impact of social embarrassment on caregiving distress in a multicultural sample of caregivers. *Journal of Applied Geontology, 28*, 195–217.

Morgan, E. M., Thorne, A., & Zubriggen, E. L. (2010). A longitudinal study of conversations with parents about sex and dating during college. *Developmental Psychology, 46*(1), 139–150.

Morgan, H. J., & Shaver, P. R. (1999). Attachment processes and commitment to romantic relationships. In J. M. Adams & W. H. Jones (Eds.), *Handbook of interpersonal commitment and relationship stability* (pp. 109–124). Dordrecht, Netherlands: Kluwer Academic.

Morris, S. Z., & Gibson, C. L. (2011). Corporal punishment's influence on children's aggressive and delinquent behavior. *Criminal Justice and Behavior, 38*, 818–839.

Morrissey, T. W., Dunifon, R. E., & Kalil, A. (2011). Maternal employment, work schedules, and children's body mass index. *Child Development, 82*(1), 66–81.

Mortensen, E. L., Michaelsen, K. F., Sanders, S. A., & Reinisch, J. M. (2002). The association between duration of breastfeeding and adult intelligence. *Journal of the American Medical Association, 287*, 2365–2371.

Mosko, S., Richard, C., & McKenna, J. (1997). Maternal sleep and arousals during bedsharing with infants. *Sleep: Journal of Sleep Research & Sleep Medicine, 20*, 142–150.

Moss, E., Cyr, C., Bureau, J.-F., Tarabulsy, G. M., & Dubois-Comtois, K. (2005). Stability of attachment during the preschool period. *Developmental Psychology, 41*, 773–783.

Mounts, N. S. (2011). Parental management of peer relationships and early adolescents' social skills. *Journal of Youth and Adolescence, 40*(4), 416–427.

Mroczek, D. K., & Spiro, A. (2003). Modeling intraindividual change in personality traits: Findings from the Normative Aging Study. *Journals of Gerontology: Series B: Psychological Sciences and Social Sciences, 58B*, P153–P165.

Mrug, S., Hoza, B., Gerdes, A. C., Hinshaw, S., Arnold, E. L., Hechtman, L., & Pelham, W. E. (2009). Discriminating between children with ADHD and classmates using peer variables. *Journal of Attention Disorders, 12*, 372–380.

Muehlenkamp, J. J., Ertelt, T. W., Miller, A. L., & Claes, L. (2011). Borderline personality symptoms differentiate nonsuicidal and suicidal self-injury in ethnically diverse adolescent outpatients. *The Journal of Child Psychology and Psychiatry, 52*(2), 148–155.

Mueller, C. M., & Dweck, C. S. (1998). Praise for intelligence can undermine children's motivation and performance. *Journal of Personality and Social Psychology, 75*(1), 33–52.

Muise, A., & Desmarais, S. (2010). Women's perceptions and use of "anti-aging" products. *Sex Roles, 63*, 126–137.

Mullen, K. M., Vohr, B. R., Katz, K. H., Schneider, K. C., Lacadie, C., Hampson, M., … Ment, L.R. (2010). Preterm birth results in alterations in neural connectivity at age 16 years [Electronic version]. *NeuroImage, 54*(4). 2563–2570.

Mulvaney, M. K., & Mebert, C. J. (2007). Parental corporal punishment predicts behavior problems in early childhood. *Journal of Family Psychology, 21*(3), 389–397.

Mundy, P., Block, J., Delgado, C., Pomares, Y., Van Hecke, A. V., & Parlade, M. V. (2007). Individual differences and the development of joint attention in infancy. *Child Development, 78*(3), 938–954.

Munro, C. A., Jefferys, J., Gower, E. W., Muñoz, B. E., Lyketsos, C. G., Keay, L., … West, S. K. (2010). Predictors of lane-change errors in older drivers. *Journal of the American Geriatrics Society, 58*, 457–464.

Munroe, R. L. (2010). Following the Whitings: The study of male pregnancy symptoms. *Journal of Cross-Cultural Psychology, 41*(4), 592–604.

Murphy, N. A., & Isaacowitz, D. M. (2008). Preferences for emotional information in older and younger adults: A meta-analysis of memory and attention tasks. *Psychology and Aging, 23*(2), 263–286.

Murray, C. (2012). *Coming apart: The state of White America, 1960–2010.* New York: Crown Forum.

Murray, S. L., Bellavia, G. M., Rose, P., & Griffin, D. W. (2003). Once hurt, twice hurtful: How perceived regard regulates daily marital interactions. *Journal of Personality and Social Psychology, 84*, 126–147.

Murray, S. L., & Holmes, J. G. (1997). A leap of faith? Positive illusions in romantic relationships. *Personality and Social Psychology Bulletin, 23*, 586–604.

Murray, S. L., Holmes, J. G., Bellavia, G., Griffin, D. W., & Dolderman, D. (2002). Kindred spirits? The benefits of egocentrism in close relationships. *Journal of Personality and Social Psychology, 82*, 563–581.

Murray, S. L., Holmes, J. G., Dolderman, D., & Griffin, D. W. (2000). What the motivated mind sees: Comparing friends' perspectives to married partners' views of each other. *Journal of Experimental Social Psychology, 36*, 600–620.

Murstein, B. I. (1999). The relationship of exchange and commitment. In J. M. Adams & W. H. Jones (Eds.), *Handbook of interpersonal commitment and relationship stability* (pp. 205–219). Dordrecht, Netherlands: Kluwer Academic.

Murstein, B. I., Reif, J. A., & Syracuse-Siewert, G. (2002). Comparison of the function of exchange in couples of similar and differing physical attractiveness. *Psychological Reports, 91*, 299–314.

Must, A., Naumova, E. N., Phillips, S. M., Blum, M., Dawson-Hughes, B., &

Rand, W. M. (2005). Childhood overweight and maturational timing in the development of adult overweight and fatness: The Newton Girls Study and its follow-up. *Pediatrics, 116*, 620–627.

Nagy, Z., Lagercrantz, H., & Hutton, C. (2011). Effects of preterm birth on cortical thickness measured in adolescence. *Cerebral Cortex, 21*(2), 300–306.

Nakamura, S., Kuzuya, M., Funaki, Y., Matsui, W., & Ishiguro, N. (2010). Factors influencing death at home in terminally ill cancer patients. *Geriatrics and Gerontology International, 10*, 154–160.

Nakhai-Pour, H. R., Broy, P., & Berard, A. (2010). Use of antidepressants during pregnancy and the risk of spontaneous abortion. *Canadian Medical Association Journal, 182*(10), 1031–1037.

Nappi, R. E., & Kokot-Kierepa, M. (2010). Women's voices in the menopause: Results from an international survey on vaginal atrophy. *Maturitas, 67*, 233–238.

National Center for Health Statistics (CDC Faststats). (2009). Hyattsville, MD. Retrieved April 2, 2009, from www.cdc.gov/cdc-info at cdcinfo[a]cdc.gov.

National Center for Health Statistics. (2008). *Health, United States, 2007: With chartbook on trends in the health of Americans.* Hyattsville, MD: U.S. Government Printing Office.

National Center for Health Statistics. (2011). *Health, United States, 2010: With special feature on death and dying.* Hyattsville, Maryland MD: U.S. Government Printing Office.

National Health and Nutrition Examination Survey. (2004). Clinical growth charts. Retrieved October 4, 2006, from National Center for Health Statistics (U.S. Department of Health & Human Services [USDHHS]) Web site: http://www.cdc.gov/nchs/about/major/nhanes/growthcharts/clinical_charts.htm

National Hospice and Palliative Care organization (2011). Patients served by hospice in the United States, 1984–2009: NHPCO. Retrieved from http://www.nhpco.org/files/public/Statistics_Research/Graph_of_hos pice_1982_2009.pdf

National Survey of Student Engagement. (2010). *Major Differences: Examining student engagement by fields of study. retrieved* from www.nsse.iub.edu 69

Natsuaki, M., Ge, X., & Wenk, E. (2008). Continuity and changes in the developmental trajectories of criminal career: Examining the roles of timing of first arrest and high school graduation. *Journal of Youth and Adolescence, 37*, 431–444.

Naveh-Benjamin, M., Brav, K. T., & Levy, O. (2007). The associative memory deficit of older adults: The role of strategy utilization. *Psychology and Aging, 22*(1), 202–208.

Neal, J. W. (2010). Social aggression and social position in middle childhood and early adolescence: Burning bridges or building them? *Journal of Early Adolescence, 30*(1), 122–137.

Neberich, W., Penke, L., Lehnart, J., & Asendorpf, J. B. (2010). Family of origin, age at menarche, and reproductive strategies: A test of four evolutionary-developmental models. *European Journal of Developmental Psychology, 7*(2), 153–177.

Negriff, S., Dorn, L. D., Pabst, S. R., & Susman, E. J. (2011). Morningness/eveningness, pubertal timing, and substance use in adolescent girls. *Psychiatry Research, 185*, 408–413.

Nelson, K. (1974). Concept, word, and sentence: Interrelations in acquisition and development. *Psychological Review, 81*, 267–285.

Nelson, K., & Fivush, R. (2004). The emergence of autobiographical memory: A social cultural developmental theory. *Psychological Review, 111*, 486–511.

Neugarten, B. (1972). Personality and the aging process. *Gerontologist, 12*(1, Pt. 1), 9–15.

Neugarten, B. L. (1979). Time, age, and the life cycle. *American Journal of Psychiatry, 136*, 887–894.

Neumark, D. (2009). The age discrimination in employment act and the challenge of population aging. *Research on Aging, 31*, 41–68.

Newcomb, A. F., & Bagwell, C. L. (1995). Children's friendship relations: A meta-analytic review. *Psychological Bulletin, 117*, 306–347.

Newman, K. L. (2011). Sustainable careers: Lifecycle engagement in work. *Organizational Dynamics, 40*, 136–143.

Newton, N., & Stewart, A. J. (2010). The midlife ages: Change in women's personalities and social roles. *Psychology of Women's Quarterly, 31*, 75–84.

NICHD Early Child Care Research Network. (2003). Does amount of time spent in child care predict socioemotional adjustment during the transition to kindergarten? *Child Development, 74*, 976–1005.

NICHD Early Child Care Research Network. (2004). Type of child care and children's development at 54 months. *Early Childhood Research Quarterly, 19*, 203–230.

NICHD Early Child Care Research Network. (2006). Child-care effect sizes for the NICHD Study of Early Child Care and Youth Development. *American Psychologist, 61*, 99–116.

Nicolopoulou, A., Barbosa de Sá, A., Ilgaz, H., & Brockmeyer, C. (2010). Using the transformative power of play to educate hearts and minds: From Vygotsky to Vivian Paley and beyond. *Mind, Culture, and Activity, 17*, 42–58.

Nicolson, R. I., & Fawcett, A. J. (2011). Dyslexia, dysgraphia, procedural learning and the cerebellum. *Cortex, 47*, 117–127.

Nielsen, L., Knutson, B., & Carstensen, L. L. (2008). Affect dynamics, affective forecasting, and aging. *Emotion, 8*(3), 318–330.

Noller, P., Feeney, J. A., Roberts, N., & Christensen, A. (2005). Withdrawal in couple interactions: Exploring the causes and consequences. In R. E. Riggio & R. S. Feldman (Eds.), *Applications of nonverbal communication* (pp. 195–213). Mahwah, NJ: Erlbaum.

Norwood, S. J., Bowker, A., Buchholz, A., Henderson, K. A., Goldfield, G., & Flament, M. F. (2011). Self-silencing and anger regulation as predictors of disordered eating among adolescent females. *Eating Behaviors, 12*, 112–118.

Nunner-Winkler, G. (2007). Development of moral motivation from childhood to early adulthood. *Journal of Moral Education, 36*(4), 399–414.

O'Rourke, N., Neufeld, E., Claxton, A., & Smith, J. A. Z. (2010). Knowing me – knowing you: Reported personality and trait discrepancies as predictors of marital idealization between long-wed spouses. *Psychology and Aging, 25*(2), 412–421.

Oas, P. T. (2010). Current status on corporal punishment with children: What the literature says. *The American Journal of Family Therapy, 38*(5), 413–420.

Obradovi , J., Burt, K. B., & Masten, A. S. (2010). Testing a dual cascade model linking competence and symptoms over 20 years from childhood to adulthood. *Journal of Clinical Child and Adolescent Psychology, 39*(1), 90–102.

Odaka, Y., Nakano, M., Tanaka, T., Kaburagi, T., Yoshino, H., Sato-Mito, N., & Sato, K. (2010). The influence of a high-fat dietary environment in the fetal period on postnatal metabolic and immune function. *Obesity, 18*(9), 1688–1694.

Oddo, S., Lux, S., Weiss, P. H., Schwab, A., Welzer, H., Markowitsch, H. J., & Fink, G. R. (2010). Specific role of medial prefrontal cortex in retrieving recent autobiographical memories: An fMRI study of young female subjects. *Cortex, 46,* 29–39.

Oh-Park, M., Xue, X., Holtzer, R., & Verghese, J. (2011). Transient versus persistent fear of falling in community-dwelling older adults: Incidence and risk factors. *Journal of the American Geriatrics Society, 59*(7), 1225–1231.

Ohan, J. L., & Johnston, C. (2011). Positive illusions of social competence in girls with and without ADHD. *Journal of Abnormal Child Psychology, 39*(4), 527–539.

Ojeda, S. R., Lomniczi, A., Loche, A., Matagne, V., Kaidar, G., Sandau, U. S., & Dissen, G. A. (2010). The transcriptional control of female puberty. *Brain Research, 1364,* 164–174.

Oldehinkel, A. J., & Bouma, E. C. (2011). Sensitivity to the depressogenic effect of stress and HPA-axis reactivity in adolescence: A review of gender differences. *Neuroscience and Biobehavioral Reviews,* 35(8), 1757–1770.

Oldehinkel, A. J., Verhulst, F. C., & Ormel, J. (2011). Mental health problems during puberty: Tanner stage-related differences in specific symptoms. The TRAILS study. *Journal of Adolescence, 34,* 73–85.

Olweus, D., Limber, S., & Mihalic, S. F. (1999). *Blueprints for violence prevention, Book 9: Bullying prevention program.* Boulder, CO: Center for the Study and Prevention of Violence, Institute of Behavioral Science, University of Colorado at Boulder.

Omar, H., McElderry, D., & Zakharia, R. (2003). Educating adolescents about puberty: What are we missing? *International Journal of Adolescent Medicine and Health, 15,* 79–83.

Onishi, K. H., & Baillargeon, R. (2005, April 8). Do 15-month-old infants understand false beliefs? *Science, 308,* 255–258.

Onrust, S., Willemse, G., VanDenBout, J., & Cuijpers, P. (2010). Effects of a visiting service for older widowed individuals: A randomized clinical trial. *Death Studies, 34*(9), 777–803.

Ornstein, P. A., Naus, M. J., & Liberty, C. (1975). Rehearsal and organizational processes in children's memory. *Child Development, 46,* 818–830.

Osofsky, J. D., & Lieberman, A. F. (2010). A call for integrating a mental health perspective into systems of care for abused and neglected infants and young children. *American Psychologist, 66*(2), 120–128.

Ostbye, T., Krause, K. M., Swamy, G. K., & Lovelady, C. A. (2010). Effect of breastfeeding on weight reduction from one pregnancy to the next: Results from the North Carolina WIC program. *Preventive Medicine, 51,* 368–372.

Ostrov, J. M. (2010). Prospective associations between peer victimization and aggression. *Child Development, 81*(6), 1670–1677.

Ostrov, J. M., & Godleski, S. A. (2010). Toward an integrated gender-linked model of aggression subtypes in early and middle childhood. *Psychological Review, 117*(1), 233–242.

Oswal, A., & Yeo, G. (2010). Leptin and the control of body weight: A review of its diverse central targets, signaling mechanisms, and role in the pathogenesis of obesity. *Obesity, 18*(2), 221–229.

Ott, J. C. (2011). Government and happiness in 130 nations: Good governance fosters higher level and more equality of happiness. *Social Indicators Research, 102*(1), 3–22.

Ott, M. A., Millstein, S. G., Ofner, S., & Halpern-Felsher, B. L. (2006). Greater expectations: Adolescents' positive motivations for sex. *Perspectives on Sexual and Reproductive Health, 38,* 84–89.

Overall, N. C., Fletcher, G. O., & Simpson, J. A. (2010). Helping each other grow: Romantic partner support, self-improvement, and relationship quality. *Personality and Social Psychology Bulletin, 36*(11), 1496–1513.

Pace, C. S., & Zavattini, G. C. (2011). 'Adoption and attachment theory' the attachment models of adoptive mothers and the revision of attachment patterns of their late-adopted children. *Child Care, Health and Development, 37*(1), 82–88.

Paek, H.-J., Nelson, M. R., & Vilela, A. M. (2011). Examination of gender-role portrayals in television advertising across seven countries. *Sex Roles, 64,* 192–207.

Paikoff, R. L., & Brooks-Gunn, J. (1991). Do parent-child relationships change during puberty? *Psychological Bulletin, 110,* 47–66.

Palgi, Y., Shrira, A., Ben-Ezra, M., Spalter, T., Shmotkin, D., & Kavé, G. (2010). Delineating terminal change in subjective well-being and subjective health. *Journals of Gerontology: Psychological Sciences, 65B*(1), 61–64.

Palkovitz, R. J. (2002). *Involved fathering and men's adult development: Provisional Balances.* Mahwah, NJ: Erlbaum.

Palladino, G. (1996). *Teenagers: An American history.* New York: Basic Books.

Palley, E., & Shdaimah, C. (2011). Child care policy: A need for greater advocacy. *Children and Youth Services Review, 33,* 1159–1165.

Panaccio, A., & Vandenberghe, C. (2009). Perceived organizational support, organizational committment and psychological well-being: A longitudinal study. *Journal of Vocational Behavior, 75,* 224–236.

Parent, A.-S., Teilmann, G., Juul, A., Skakkebaek, N. E., Toppari, J., & Bourguignon, J.-P. (2003). The timing of normal puberty and the age limits of sexual precocity: Variations around the world, secular trends, and changes after migration. *Endocrine Reviews, 24,* 668–693.

Parent, M. C., & Moradi, B. (2011). His biceps become him: A test of objectification theory's application to drive for muscularity and propensity for steroid use in college men. *Journal of Counseling Psychology, 58,* 246–256.

Park, Y. S., Kim, B. S. K., Chiang, J., & Ju, C. M. (2010). Acculturation, enculturation, parental adherence to Asian cultural values, parenting styles, and family conflict among Asian American college students. *Asian American Journal of Psychology, 1*(1), 67–79.

Parkes, C. M. (1972). *Bereavement: Studies of grief in adult life.* New York: International Universities Press.

Parkes, C. M. (1987). *Bereavement: Studies of grief in adult life* (2nd ed.). Madison, CT: International Universities Press.

Parks, S. M., Winter, L., Santana, A. J., Parker, B., Diamond, J. J., Rose, M., & Myers, R. E. (2011). Family factors in end-of-life decision-making: Family conflict and proxy relationship. *Journal of Palliative Medicine, 14*(2), 179–184.

Pascarella, E. T., Salisbury, M. H., & Blaich, C. (2011). Exposure to effective instruction and college student persistence: A multi-institutional replication and extension. *Journal of College Student Development, 52*(1), 4–19.

Pasupathi, M., & Wainryb, C. (2010). On telling the whole story: Facts and interpretations in autobiographical memory narratives from childhood through mid-adolescence. *Developmental Psychology, 46*(3), 735–746.

Patall, E. A., Cooper, H., & Robinson, J. C. (2008). The effects of choice on intrinsic motivation and related outcomes: A meta-analysis of research findings. *Psychological Bulletin, 134*(2), 270–300.

Paul, A. M. (2010). *Origins: How the nine months before birth shape our lives.* New York: Free Press.

Paul, I. M., Savage, J. S., Anzman, S. L., Beiler, J. S., Marini, M. E., Stokes, J. L., & Birch, L. L. (2011). Preventing obesity during infancy: A pilot study. *Obesity, 19*(2), 353–361.

Paulson, J. F., & Bazemore, S. D. (2010). Prenatal and postpartum depression in fathers and its association with maternal depression: A meta-analysis. *Journal of the American Medical Association, 303*(19), 1961–1969.

Paulussen-Hoogeboom, M. C., Stams, G. J. J. M., Hermanns, J. M. A., & Peetsma, T. T. D. (2007). Child negative emotionality and parenting from infancy to preschool: A meta-analytic review. *Developmental Psychology, 43*(2), 438–453.

Peacock, S., Forbes, D., Markle-Reid, M., Hawranik, P., Morgan, D., Jansen, L., & Henderson, S. R. (2010). The positive aspects of the caregiving journey with dementia: Using a strengths-based perspective to reveal opportunities. *Journal of Applied Gerontology,* 29(5), 640–659.

Peck, S. C., Vida, M., & Eccles, J. S. (2008). Adolescent pathways to adulthood drinking: Sport activity involvement is not necessarily risky or protective. *Addiction, 103* (Suppl. 1), 69–83.

Pedersen, N. L. (1996). Gerontological behavior genetics. In J. E. Birren, K. W. Schaie, R. P. Abeles, M. Gatz, & T. A. Salthouse (Eds.), *Handbook of the psychology of aging* (4th ed., pp. 59–77). San Diego, CA: Academic Press.

Pedro-Carroll, J. L. (2005). Fostering resilience in the aftermath of divorce: The role of evidence-based programs for children. *Family Court Review, 43,* 52–64.

Peetz, J., & Kammrath, L. (2011). Only because I love you:Why people make and why they break promises in romantic relationships. *Journal of Personality and Social Psychology, 100*(5), 887–904.

Pellegrini, A. D. (2006). The development and function of rough-and-tumble play in childhood and adolescence: A sexual selection theory perspective. In A. Göncü, & S. Gaskins (Eds.), *Play and development: Evolutionary, sociocultural, and functional perspectives. The Jean Piaget Symposium Series* (pp. 77–98). Mahwah, NJ: Lawrence Erlbaum Associates Publishers.

Pellegrini, A. D., Long, J. D., Roseth, C. J., Bohn, C. M., & Van Ryzin, M. (2007a). A short-term longitudinal study of preschoolers' (homo sapiens) sex segregation: The role of physical activity, sex, and time. *Journal of Comparative Psychology, 121*(3), 282–289.

Pellegrini, A. D., & Smith, P. K. (Eds.). (2005). The nature of play: Great apes and humans. New York, NY: Guilford Press.

Perala-Littunen, S. (2007). Gender equality or primacy of the mother? Ambivalent descriptions of good parents. *Journal of Marriage and Family, 69*(2), 341–351.

Pérez-Edgar, K., Bar-Haim, Y., McDermott, J. M., Chronis-Tuscano, A., Pine, D. S., & Fox, N. A. (2010a). Attention biases to threat and behavioral inhibition in early childhood shape adolescent social withdrawal. *Emotion, 10,* 349–357.

Pérez-Edgar, K., McDermott, J. N., Korelitz, K., Degnan, K. A., Curby, T. W., Pine, D. S., & Fox, N. A. (2010b). Patterns of sustained attention in infancy shape the developmental trajectory of social behavior from toddlerhood through adolescence. *Developmental Psychology, 46*(6), 1723–1730.

Perrig-Chiello, P., & Hutchison, S. (2010). Family caregivers of elderly persons: A differential perspective on stressors, resources, and well-being. *GeroPsych,* 23(4), 195–206.

Perry, W. (1999). *Forms of ethical and intellectual development in the college years: A scheme.* San Francisco: Jossey-Bass.

Peskin, J. (1992). Ruse and representations: On children's ability to conceal information. *Developmental Psychology,* 28, 84–89.

Peters, E., Cillessen, A. H. N., Riksen-Walraven, J. M., & Haselager, G. J. T. (2010). Best friends' preference and popularity: Associations with aggression and prosocial behavior. *International Journal of Behavioral Development,* 34(5), 398–405.

Peterson, B. E. (1998). Case studies of midlife generativity: Analyzing motivation and realization. In D. P. McAdams & E. de St. Aubin (Eds.), *Generativity and adult development: How and why we care for the next generation* (pp. 101–131). Washington, DC: American Psychological Association.

Peterson, B. E., & Duncan, L. E. (2007). Midlife women's generativity and authoritarianism: Marriage, motherhood, and 10 years of aging. *Psychology and Aging,* 22(3), 411–419.

Pevey, C. (2003). Living wills and durable power of attorney for health care. In C. D. Bryant (Ed.), *Handbook of death & dying* (pp. 891–898). Thousand Oaks, CA: Sage.

Pharo, H., Sim, C., Graham, M., Gross, J., & Hayne, H. (2011). Risky business: Executive function, personality, and reckless behavior during adolescence and emerging adulthood. *Behavioral Neuroscience, 125*(6), 970–978.

Phelan, P., Davidson, A. L., & Yu, H. C. (1998). *Adolescents' worlds: Negotiating family, peers, and school.* New York: Teachers College Press.

Phillips, C. D., & Hawes, C. (2005). Care provision in housing with supportive services: The importance of care type, individual characteristics, and care site. *Journal of Applied Gerontology, 24,* 55–67.

Phillips, D. A., & Lowenstein, A. E. (2011). Early care, education and child development. *American Review of Psychology, 62,* 483–500.

Phillips, D. P., Brewer, K. M., & Wadensweiler, P. (2011). Alcohol as a risk factor for sudden infant death syndrome (SIDS). *Addiction, 106*(3), 516–525.

Phillips, J. L., Halcomb, E, J., & Davidson, P. M. (2011). End-of-life care pathways in acute and hospice care: An integrative review. *Journal of Pain and Symptom Management, 41*(5), 940–955.

Phinney, J. S. (2006). Acculturation is not an independent variable: Approaches to studying acculturation as a complex process. In M. H. Bornstein & L. R. Cote (Eds.), *Acculturation and parent-child relationships: Measurement and development* (pp. 79–95). Mahwah, NJ: Lawrence Erlbaum Associates Publishers.

Piaget, J. (1950). *The psychology of intelligence.* Oxford, England: Harcourt.

Piaget, J. (1962). *Play, dreams and imitation in childhood.* New York: Norton. (Original work published 1951)

Piaget, J. (1965). *The moral judgment of the child* (Paperback ed.). New York: Free Press.

Piaget, J. (1971). *The psychology of intelligence.* London: Routledge & Kegan Paul. (Original work published 1950)

Pietropaolo, S., Sun, Y., Li, R., Brana, C., Feldon, J., & Yee, B. K. (2008). The impact of voluntary exercise on mental health in rodents: A neuroplasticity perspective. *Behavioural Brain Research,* 192, 42–60.

Pinker, S. (2011). *The better angels of our nature: Why violence has declined*. New York: Viking.

Pinquart, M., & Schindler, I. (2007). Changes of life satisfaction in the transition to retirement: A latent-class approach. *Psychology and Aging, 22(3)*, 442–455.

Pitkanen, T., Kokko, K., Lyyra, A., & Pulkkinen, L. (2008). A developmental approach to alcohol drinking behaviour in adulthood: A follow-up study from age 8 to 42. *Addiction, 103* (Suppl. 1), 48–68.

Pitkanen, T., Lyyra, A. L., & Pulkkinen, L. (2005). Age of onset of drinking and the use of alcohol in adulthood: A follow-up study from age 8–42 for females and males. *Addiction, 100*, 652–661.

Pitrou, I., Shojaei, T., Wazana, A., Gilbert, F., & Kovess-Masféty, V. (2010). Child overweight, associated psychopathology, and social functioning: A French school-based survey in 6- to 11-year-old children. *Obesity, 18*(4), 809–817.

Pittau, M. G., Zelli, R., & Gelman, A. (2010). Economic disparities and life satisfaction in European regions. *Social Indicators Research, 96*, 339–361.

Pitzer, L. M., & Fingerman, K. L. (2010). Psychosocial resources and associations between childhood physical abuse and adult well-being. *Journals of Gerontology: Psychological Sciences, 65B*(4), 425–433.

Pleau, R. L. (2010). Gender differences in postretirement employment. *Research on Aging*, 32(3), 267–303.

Plomin, R., & Bergeman, C. S. (1991). The nature of nurture: Genetic influence on "environmental" measures. *Behavioral and Brain Sciences, 14*, 373–427.

Plomin, R., DeFries, J. C., Craig, I. W., & McGuffin, P. (2003). Behavioral genomics. In R. Plomin, J. C. DeFries, I. W. Craig, & P. McGuffin (Eds.), *Behavioral genetics in the postgenomic era* (pp. 531–540). Washington, DC: American Psychological Association.

Plomin, R., & Spinath, F. M. (2004). Intelligence: Genetics, genes, and genomics. *Journal of Personality and Social Psychology, 86*, 112–129.

Pluess, M., & Belsky, J. (2010). Differential susceptibility to parenting and quality child care. *Developmental Psychology, 46*(2), 379–390.

Pluess, M., & Belsky, J. (2011). Prenatal programming of postnatal plasticity? *Development and Psychopathology*, 23(1), 29–38.

Pogrebin, L. C. (1996). *Getting over getting older: An intimate journey*. Boston: Little, Brown.

Poirier, F. E., & Smith, E. O. (1974). Socializing functions of primate play. *American Zoologist, 14*, 275–287.

Pollak, S. D., Nelson, C. A., Schlaak, M. F., Roeber, B. J., Wewerka, S. S., Wiik, K. L., … Gunnar, M. R. (2010). Neurodevelopmental effects of early deprivation in postinstitutionalized children. *Child Development, 81*(1), 224–236.

Poortman, A. R., & Seltzer, J. A. (2007). Parents' expectations about childrearing after divorce: Does anticipating difficulty deter divorce? *Journal of Marriage and Family, 69*(1), 254–269.

Porfeli, E. J., & Mortimer, J. T. (2010). Intrinsic work value-reward dissonance and work satisfaction during young adulthood. *Journal of Vocational Behavior, 76*, 507–519.

Potter, D. (2010). Psychosocial well-being and the relationship between divorce and children's academic achievement. *Journal of Marriage and Family, 72*, 933–946.

Potts, M., Prata, N., & Sahin-Hodoglugil, N. N. (2010). Maternal mortality: One death every 7 min. *The Lancet*, 375(9728), 1762–1763.

Poulin, F., & Chan, A. (2010). Friendship stability and change in childhood and adolescence. *Developmental Review*, 30(3), 257–272.

Poulin, M. J., Brown, S. L., Ubel, P. A., Smith, D. M., Jankovic, A., & Langa, K. M. (2010). Does a helping hand mean a heavy heart? Helping behavior and well-being among spouse caregivers. *Psychology and Aging, 25*(1), 108–117.

Poulin, M., & Silver, R. (2008). World benevolence beliefs and well being across the lifespan. *Psychology and Aging, 23*, 19.

Prakash, K., & Coplan, R. J. (2007). Socioemotional characteristics and school adjustment of socially withdrawn children in India. *International Journal of Behavioral Development, 31*(2), 123–132.

Pressler, K. A., & Ferraro, K. F. (2010). Assistive device use as a dynamic acquisition process in later life. *The Gerontologist, 50*(3), 371–381.

Preston, S. H. (1991). *Fatal years: Child mortality in late nineteenth-century America*. Princeton, NJ: Princeton University Press.

Prevost, S. S., & Wallace, J. B. (2009). Dying in institutions. In J. L. Werth, & D. Blevins (Eds.), *Decision making near the end-of-life: Issues, developments, and future directions. Series in death, dying and bereavement* (pp. 189–208). New York: Routledge/Taylor & Francis Group.

Prins, P. M., Dovis, S., Ponsioen, A., ten Brink, E., & van der Oord, S. (2011). Does computerized working memory training with game elements enhance motivation and training efficacy in children with ADHD? *Cyberpsychology, Behavior, and Social Networking, 14*(3), 115–122.

Prinstein, M. J., Heilbron, N., Guerry, J. D., Franklin, J. C., Rancourt, D., Simon, V., & Spirito, A. (2010). Peer influence and nonsuicidal self injury: Longitudinal results in community and clinically-referred adolescent samples. *Journal of Abnormal Child Psychology*, 38, 669–682.

Prinstein, M. J., & La Greca, A. M. (2002). Peer crowd affiliation and internalizing distress in childhood and adolescence: A longitudinal follow-back study. *Journal of Research on Adolescence, 12*, 325–351.

Pruett, M. K., Insabella, G. M., & Gustafson, K. (2005). The collaborative divorce project: A court-based intervention for separating parents with young children. *Family Court Review, 43*, 38–51.

Pruis, T. A., & Janowsky, J. S. (2010). Assessment of body image in younger and older women. *Journal of General Psychology, 137*(3), 225–238.

Pryor, J. H., Hurtado, S., SeAngelo, L., Blake, L. P., & Tran, S. (2011). The American freshman: National norms Fall 2010. *Higher Education Research Institute*, 1–4.

Puhl, R. M., & Heuer, C. A. (2010). Obesity stigma: Important considerations for public health. *American Journal of Public Health, 100*(6), 1019–1028.

Puhl, R. M., & Latner, J. D. (2007). Stigma, obesity, and the health of the nation's children. *Psychological Bulletin, 133*(4), 557–580.

Pungello, E. P., Kainz, K., Burchinal, M., Wasik, B. H., Sparling, J. J., Ramey, C. T., & Campbell, F. A. (2010). Early educational intervention, early cumulative risk, and the early home environment as predictors of young adult outcomes within a high-risk sample. *Child Development, 81*(1), 410–426.

Pushkar, D., Chaikelson, J., Conway, M., Etezadi, J., Giannopolous, C., Li, K., & Wrosch, C. (2010). Testing continuity and activity variables as predictors of positive and negative affect in retirement. *Journals of Gerontology: Psychological Sciences, 65B*(1), 42–49.

Putallaz, M., Grimes, C. L., Foster, K. J., Kupersmidt, J. B., Coie, J. D., & Dearing, K. (2007). Overt and relational aggression and victimization: Multiple perspectives within the school setting. *Journal of School Psychology, 45*, 523–547.

Rabin, J. S., Gilboa, A., Stuss, D. T., Mar, R. A., & Rosenbaum, R. S. (2010). Common and unique neural correlates of autobiographical memory and theory of mind. *Journal of Cognitive Neuroscience, 22*(6), 1095–1111.

Rabins, P. V. (2011, April). Memory. *The John Hopkins White Papers.* 48

Rack, J. J., Burleson, B. R., Bodie, G. D., Holstrom, A. J., & Servaty-Seib, H. (2008). Bereaved adults' evaluations of grief management messages: Effects of message person centeredness, recipient individual differences, and contextual factors. *Death Studies, 32*, 399–427.

Radford, A. W., Wheeless, S. C., Shepherd, B., & Hunt-White, T. (2010). Persistence and attainment of 2003–04 beginning postsecondary students: After 6 years—First look. *National Center for Education Statistics, 151*, 1–20.

Rahman, A., Iqbal, Z., & Harrington, R. (2003). Life events, social support and depression in childbirth: Perspectives from a rural community in the developing world. *Psychological Medicine, 33*, 1161–1167.

Rahman, A. N., & Schnelle, J. F. (2008). The nursing home culture-change movement: Recent past, present, and future directions for research. *The Gerontologist, 48*(2), 142–148.

Ramsay, S. M., & Santella, R. M. (2011). The definition of life: A survey of obstetricians and neonatologists in New York City hospitals regarding extremely premature births. *Maternal and Child Health Journal*, 15, 446–452.

Rando, T. A. (1992–1993). The increasing prevalence of complicated mourning: The onslaught is just beginning. *Omega: Journal of Death and Dying, 26*, 43–59.

Rautava, L., Anderson, S., Gissler, M., Hallman, M., Häkkinen, U., Korvenranta, E., ... Lehtonen, L. (2010). Development and behaviour of 5-year-old very low birthweight infants [Electronic version]. *European Child & Adolescent Psychiatry, 19*(8). 669–677.

Raymo, J. M., Warren, J. R., Sweeney, M. M., Hauser, R. M., & Ho, J. (2011). Precarious employment, bad jobs, labor unions, and early retirement. *Journals of Gerontology: Social Sciences, 66B*(2), 249–259.

Raz, N., Ghisletta, P., Rodrigue, K. M., Kennedy, K. M., & Lindenberger, U. (2010). Trajectories of brain aging in middle-aged and older adults: Regional and individual differences. *Neuroimage, 51*(2), 501–511.

Redshaw, M., & Hockley, C. (2010). Instiutional processes and individual responses: Women's experiences of care in relation to cesarean birth. *Birth Issues in Prenatal Care,* 37(2), 150–159.

Reese, E., Jack, F., & White, N., (2010). Origins of adolescents' autobiographical memories. *Cognitive Development, 25*, 352–367.

Reichstadt, J., Sengupta, G., Depp, C. A., Palinkas, L. A., & Jeste, D. V. (2010). Older adults' perspective on successful aging: Qualitative interviews. *The American Journal of Geriatric Psychiatry, 18*(7), 567–574.

Reijneveld, S. A., van der Wal, M. F., Brugman, E., Sing, R. A. H., & Verloove-Vanhorick, S. P. (2004). Infant crying and abuse. *Lancet, 364*, 1340–1342.

Reimer, J., Paolitto, D. P., & Hersh, R. H. (1983). *Promoting moral growth: From Piaget to Kohlberg* (2nd ed.). New York: Longman.

Reimer, K. (2003). Committed to caring: Transformation in adolescent moral identity. *Applied Developmental Science, 7*, 129–137.

Reissland, N., & Hopkins, B. (2010). Introduction: Towards a fetal psychology. *Infant and Child Development, 19*, 1–5.

Reissman, C., Aron, A., & Bergen, M. R. (1993). Shared activities and marital satisfaction: Causal direction and self-expansion versus boredom. *Journal of Social and Personal Relationships, 10*, 243–254.

Reitzes, D. C., & Mutran, E. J. (2004). Grandparenthood: Factors influencing frequency of grandparent-grandchildren contact and grandparent role satisfaction. *Journals of Gerontology: Series B: Psychological Sciences and Social Sciences, 59B*, S9-S16.

Reskin, B. (1993). Sex segregation in the workplace. *Annual Review of Sociology, 19*, 241–270.

Reuter-Lorenz, P. A., & Park, D. C. (2010). Human neuroscience and the aging mind: A new look at old problems. *Journals of Gerontology: Psychological Sciences, 65B*(4), 405–415.

Reuter-Lorenz, P. A., & Cappell, K. A. (2008). Neurocognitive aging and the compensation hypothesis. *Current Directions in Psychological Science, 17*(3), 177–182.

Rice, F., Harold, G. T., Bolvin, J., Bree, M., Hay, D. F., & Thapar, A. (2010). The links between prenatal stress and offspring development and psychopathology: Disentangling environmental and inherited influences [Electronic version]. *Psychological Medicine: A Journal of Research in Psychiatry and the Allied Sciences, 40*(2), 335–345.

Ridgway, A., Northup, J., Pellegrin, A., LaRue, R., & Hightsoe, A. (2003). Effects of recess on the classroom behavior of children with and without Attention-Deficit Hyperactivity Disorder. *School Psychology Quarterly, 18*, 253–268.

Riegel, K. F., & Riegel, R. M. (1972). Development, drop, and death. *Developmental Psychology, 6*, 306–319.

Riggs, S. A., Cusimano, A. M., & Benson, K. M. (2010). Childhood emotional abuse and attachment processes in the dyadic adjustment of dating couples. *Journal of Counseling Psychology, 58*(1), 126–138.

Righetti, P., Dell'Avanzo, M., Grigio, M., & Nicolini, U. (2005). Maternal/paternal antenatal attachment and fourth-dimensional ultrasound technique: A preliminary report. *British Journal of Psychology, 96*, 129–137.

Rinehart, M. S., & Kiselica, M. S. (2010). Helping men with the trauma of miscarriage. *Psychotherapy: Theory, Research, Practice, Training, 47*(3), 288–295.

Rivero, M. (2010). Maternal expression of communicative intentions and pragmatic fine tuning in early infancy. *Infant Behavior and Development, 33*, 373–386.

Roberto, C. A., Grilo, C. M., Masheb, R. M., White, M. A. (2010). Binge eating, purging, or both: Eating disorder psychopathology findings from an Internet community survey. *International Journal of Eating Disorders, 43*(8), 724–731.

Roberts, A., & Good, E. (2010). Media images and female body dissatisfaction: The moderating effects of the Five-Factor traits. *Eating Behaviors, 11*(4), 211–216.

Roberts, B. W., Kuncel, N. R., Shiner, R., Caspi, A., & Goldberg, L. R. (2007). The power of personality: The comparative validity of personality traits, socioeconomic status, and cognitive ability for predicting important life outcomes. *Perspectives on Psychological Science, 2,* 313–335.

Roberts, W., Fillmore, M. T., & Milich, R. (2010). Separating automatic and intentional inhibitory mechanisms of attention in adults with attention-deficit/hyperactivity disorder. *Journal of Abnormal Psychology, 120*(1), 223–233.

Robine, J.-M., & Michel, J.-P. (2004). Looking forward to a general theory on population aging. *Journals of Gerontology: Series A: Biological Sciences and Medical Sciences, 59A,* 590–597.

Rodin, J., & Langer, E. J. (1980). Aging labels: The decline of control and the fall of self-esteem. *Journal of Social Issues, 36,* 12–29.

Rodkin, P. C., & Roisman, G. I. (2010). Antecedents and correlates of the popular-aggressive phenomenon in elementary school. *Child Development, 81*(3), 837–850.

Rodrigues, R., & Schmidt, A. E. (2010). Expenditures for long-term care: At the crossroads between family and state. *GeroPsych, 23*(4), 183–193.

Rodriguez, C. M., & Henderson, R. C. (2010). Who spares the rod? Religious orientation, social conformity, and child abuse potential. *Child Abuse & Neglect, 34,* 84–94.

Roenker, D. L., Cissell, G. M., Ball, K. K., Wadley, V. G., & Edwards, J. D. (2003). Speed-of-processing and driving simulator training result in improved driving performance. *Human Factors, 45,* 218–233.

Roffwarg, H. P., Muzio, J. N., & Dement, W. C. (1966, April 29). Ontogenetic development of the human sleep-dream cycle. *Science, 152,* 604–619.

Rogoff, B. (1990). *Apprenticeship in thinking: Cognitive development in social context.* New York: Oxford University Press.

Rogoff, B., Paradise, R., Arauz, R. M., Correa-Chavez, M., & Angelillo, C. (2003). Firsthand learning through intent participation. *Annual Review of Psychology, 54,* 175–203.

Roisman, G. I., Clausell, E., Holland, A., Fortuna, K., & Elieff, C. (2008). Adult romantic relationships as contexts of human development: A multi-method comparison of same-sex couples with opposite-sex dating, engaged and married dyads. *Developmental Psychology, 44*(1), 91–101.

Romano, E., Babchishin, L., Pagani, L. S., & Kohen, D. (2010). School readiness and later achievement: Replication and extension using a nationwide Canadian survey. *Developmental Psychology, 46*(5), 995–1007.

Rorie, M., Gottfredson, D. C., Cross, A., Wilson, D., & Connell, N. M. (2011). Structure and deviancy training in after-school programs. *Journal of Adolescence, 34,* 105–117.

Rose, A. J., & Asher, S. R. (2000). Children's friendships. In C. Hendrick & S. S. Hendrick (Eds.), *Close relationships: A sourcebook* (pp. 47–57). Thousand Oaks, CA: Sage.

Rosenfield, R. L., Lipton, R. B., & Drum, M. L. (2009). Thelarche, pubarche, and menarche attainment in children with normal and elevated body mass index. *Pediatrics, 123,* 84–88.

Roseth, C. J., Pellegrini, A. D., Dupuis, D. N., Bohn, C. M., Hickey, M. C., Hilk, C. L., & Peshkam, A. (2011). Preschoolers' bistrategic resource control, reconciliation, and peer regard. *Social Development, 20*(1), 185–211.

Ross, L. A., Clay, O. J., Edwards, J. D., Ball, K. K., Wadley, V. G., Vance, D. E., … Joyce, J. J. (2009). Do older drivers at-risk for crashes modify their driving over time? *Journals of Gerontology: Psychological Sciences, 64B,* 163–170.

Rothenberg, J. Z., & Gardner, D. S. (2011). Protecting older workers: The failure of the Age Discrimination in Employment Act of 1967. *Journal of Sociology & Social Welfare, 38*(1), 9–30.

Rothermund, K., & Brandtstädter, J. (2003). Depression in later life: Cross-sequential patterns and possible determinants. *Psychology and Aging, 18,* 80–90.

Roussotte, F., Soderberg, L., & Sowell, E. (2010). Structural, metabolic and functional brain abnormalities as a result of prenatal exposure to drugs of abuse: Evidence from neuroimaging. *Neuropsychology Review, 20*(4), 376–397.

Rowe, D. C. (2003). Assessing genotype-environment interactions and correlations in the postgenomic era. In R. Plomin, J. C. DeFries, I. W. Craig, & P. McGuffin (Eds.), *Behavioral genetics in the postgenomic era* (pp. 71–86). Washington, DC: American Psychological Association.

Rowe, G., Hasher, L., & Turcotte, J. (2008). Age differences in visuospatial working memory. *Psychology and Aging, 23*(1), 79–84.

Rowe, J. W., & Kahn, R. L. (1998). *Successful aging.* New York: Pantheon Books.

Rowe, M. L., Levine, S. C., Fisher, J. A., & Goldin-Meadow, S. (2009). Does linguistic input play the same role in language learning for children with and without early brain injury? *Developmental Psychology, 45,* 90–102.

Rowe, R., Maughan, B., Moran, P., Ford, T., Briskman, J., & Goodman, R. (2010). The role of callous and unemotional traits in the diagnosis of conduct disorder. *Journal of Child Psychology and Psychiatry, 51*(6), 688–695.

Royal College of Obstetricians and Gynaecologists [RCOG]. (1999). Alcohol consumption in pregnancy. Retrieved January 25, 2006, from http://www.rcog.org.uk/index.asp?PageI D=509

Rubin, K. H., Bukowski, W. M., & Parker, J. G. (2006). Peer interactions, relationships, and groups. In N. Eisenberg, W. Damon, & R. M. Lerner (Eds.), *Handbook of child psychology, Vol. 3: Social, emotional, and personality development* (6th ed. pp. 571–645). Hoboken, NJ: John Wiley & Sons Inc.

Ruble, D. N., Martin, C., & Berenbaum, S. A. (2006). Gender development. In N. Eisenberg, W. Damon, & R. M. Lerner (Eds.), *Handbook of child psychology, Vol. 3: Social, emotional, and personality development* (6th ed. pp. 858–932). Hoboken, NJ: John Wiley & Sons Inc.

Ruffman, T., Perner, J., Naito, M., Parkin, L., & Clements, W. A. (1998). Older (but not younger) siblings facilitate false belief understanding. *Developmental Psychology, 34,* 161–174.

Rumbaut, R. G. (2008, March). *Divergent destinies: Acculturation, social mobility, and adult transitions among children of Latin American and Asian immigrants.* Presented at 12th Biennial Meeting of Society for Research on Adolescence, Chicago, IL.

Runions, K. C., & Keating, D. P. (2010). Anger and inhibitory control as moderators of children's hostile attributions and aggression. *Journal of Applied Developmental Psychology, 31,* 370–378.

Rusbult, C. E., Kumashiro, M., Kubacka, K. E., & Finkel, E. J. (2009). "The part of me that you bring out": Ideal similarity and the Michelangelo phenomenon. *Journal of Personality and Social Psychology, 96,* 61–82.

Rushton, J. P., & Jensen, A. R. (2005). Thirty years of research on race differences in cognitive ability. *Psychology, Public Policy, and Law, 11,* 235–294.

Ryan-Krause, P. (2011). Attention deficit hyperactivity disorder: Part III. *Journal of Pediatric Health Care, 25*(1), 50–53.

Ryan, J. J., Glass, L. A., & Bartels, J. M. (2010). Stability of the WISC-IV in a sample of elementary and middle school children. *Applied Neuropsychology, 17*(1), 68–72.

Ryan, R. M., Deci, E. L., Grolnick, W. S., & La Guardia, J. G. (2006). The significance of autonomy and autonomy support in psychological development and psychopathology. In D. Cicchetti & D. J. Cohen (Eds.), *Developmental psychopathology, Vol. 1: Theory and method* (2nd ed., pp. 795–849). Hoboken, NJ: John Wiley & Sons Inc.

Rybash, J. M., Hoyer, W. J., & Roodin, P. (1986). *Adult cognition and aging: Developmental changes in processing, knowing, and thinking.* New York: Pergamon Press.

Saarni, C. (1999). *The development of emotional competence.* New York: Guilford Press.

Sabik, N. J., Cole, E. R., & Ward, L. M. (2010). Are all minority women equally buffered from negative body image? intra-ethnic moderators of the buffering hypothesis *Psychology of Women Quarterly, 34(2)*, 139–151.

Saeteren, B., Lindström, U. Å., & Nåden, D. (2010). Latching onto life: living in the area of tension between the possibility of life and the necessity of death. *Journal of Clinical Nursing, 20,* 811–818.

Saewyc, E. M. (2011). Research on adolescent sexual orientation: Development, health disparities, stigma, and resilience. *Journal of Research on Adolescence,* 21(1), 256–272.

Salisbury, A., Law, K., LaGasse, L., & Lester, B. (2003). Maternal-fetal attachment. *Journal of the American Medical Association, 289,* 1701.

Samson, D., & Apperly, I. A. (2010). There is more to mind reading than having theory of mind concepts: New directions in theory of mind research. *Infant and Child Development, 19,* 443–454.

Sánchez, B., Esparza, P., Cölon, Y., & Davis, K. E. (2010). Tryin' to make it during the transition from high school: The role of family obligation attitudes and economic context for Latino-emerging adults. *Journal of Adolescent Research, 25*(6), 858–884.

Sánchez-Villegas, A., Pimenta, A. M., Beunza, J. J., Guillen-Grima, F., Toledo, E., & Martinez-Gonzalez, M. A. (2010). Childhood and young adult overweight/obesity and incidence of depression in the SUN Project. *Obesity, 18*(7), 1443–1448.

Sandler, I. N., Wolchik, S. A., & Ayers, T. S. (2008). Resilience rather than recovery: A contextual framework on adaptation following bereavement. *Death Studies, 32,* 59–73.

Santesso, D. L., Schmidt, L. A., Trainor, L. J. (2007). Frontal brain electrical activity (EEG) and heart rate in response to affective infant-directed (ID) speech in 9-month-old infants. *Brain and Cognition, 65,* 14–21.

Sassler, S., & Miller, A. J. (2011) Class differences in cohabitation processes. *Family Relations, 60(2)*, 163–177.

Sattler, J. M. (2001). *Assessment of children: Cognitive applications* (4th ed.). La Mesa, CA: Jerome M. Sattler.

Savage, C. L., Anthony, J., Lee, R., Kappesser, M. L., & Rose, B. (2007). The culture of pregnancy and infant care in African American women: An ethnographic study. *Journal of Transcultural Nursing, 18*(3), 215–223.

Savin-Williams, R. C. (2001). *Mom, Dad, I'm gay. How families negotiate coming out.* Washington, DC: American Psychological Association.

Savin-Williams, R. C. (2008). Then and now: Recruitment, definition, diversity, and positive attributes of same-sex populations. *Developmental Psychology, 44*(1), 135–138.

Savin-Williams, R. C., & Ream, G. L. (2003). Sex variations in the disclosure to parents of same-sex attractions. *Journal of Family Psychology, 17,* 429–438.

Savishinsky, J. (2004). The volunteer and the Sannyasin: Archetypes of retirement in America and India. *International Journal of Aging & Human Development, 59,* 25–41.

Saxon, S. V., Etten, M., & Perkins, E. A. (2010). *Physical change & aging: A guide for the helping professions* (5th ed.). New York, NY: Springer Publishing Co.

Sayegh, P., & Knight, B. G. (2011). The effects of familism and cultural justification on the mental and physical health of family caregivers. *Journals of Gerontology: Psychological Sciences, 66B*(1), 3–14.

Sayer, L. C., Bianchi, S. M., & Robinson, J. P. (2004). Are parents investing less in children? Trends in mothers' and fathers' time with children. *American Journal of Sociology, 110,* 1–43.

Scales, P. C., Benson, P. L., & Roehlkepartain, E. C. (2011). Adolescent thriving: The role of sparks, relationships, and empowerment. *Journal of Youth and Adolescence, 40(3)*, 263–277.

Scarr, S. (1997). Behavior-genetic and socialization theories of intelligence: Truce and reconciliation. In R. J. Sternberg & E. L. Grigorenko (Eds.), *Intelligence, heredity, and environment* (pp. 3–41). New York: Cambridge University Press.

Schaie, K. W. (1996). Intellectual development in adulthood. In J. E. Birren, K. W. Schaie, R. P. Abeles, M. Gatz, & T. A. Salthouse (Eds.), *Handbook of the psychology of aging* (4th ed., pp. 266–286). San Diego, CA: Academic Press.

Schaie, K. W., Willis, S. L., & Caskie, G. I. L. (2004). The Seattle Longitudinal Study: Relationship between personality and cognition. *Aging, Neuro-psychology, and Cognition, 11,* 304–324.

Schaie, K. W., & Zanjani, F. A. K. (2006). Intellectual development across adulthood. In C. Hoare (Ed.), *Handbook of adult development and learning* (pp. 99–122). New York: Oxford University Press.

Schetter, C. D. (2011). Psychological science on pregnancy: Stress processes, biopsychosocial models, and emerging research issues. *Annual Review of Psychology, 62,* 531–558.

Schilling, O. K., Wahl, H., Horowitz, A., Reinhardt, J. P., & Borner, K. (2011). The adaptation dynamics of chronic functional impairment: What we can learn from older adults with vision loss. *Psychology and Aging, 26*(1), 203–213.

Schirduan, V., & Case, K. (2004). Mindful curriculum leadership for students with attention deficit hyperactivity disorder: Leading in elementary schools by using multiple intelligences theory (SUMIT). *Teachers College Record, 106,* 87–95.

Schlegel, A. (1995). The cultural management of adolescent sexuality. In P. R. Abramson & S. D. Pinkerton (Eds.), *Sexual nature, sexual culture* (pp. 177–194). Chicago: University of Chicago Press.

Schlegel, A., & Barry, H., III. (1991). *Adolescence: An anthropological inquiry.* New York: Free Press.

Schlinger, H. D. (2003). The myth of intelligence. *Psychological Record, 53,* 15–32.

Schmid, G., Schreier, A., Meyer, R., & Wolke, D. (2010). A prospective study in the persistence of infant crying, sleeping and feeding problems and preschool behavior. *Acta Pædiatrica, 99,* 286–290.

Schmid, G., Schreier, A., Meyer, R., & Wolke, D. (2011). Predictors of crying, feeding and sleeping problems: a prospective study. *Child: care, health and development,* 37(4), 493–502.

Schmitt, D. P., Shackelford, T. K., Duntley, J., Tooke, W., Buss, D. M., Fisher,

M. L., Lavellée, M., & Vasey, P. (2002). Is there an early-30s peak in female sexual desire? Cross-sectional evidence from the United States and Canada. *Canadian Journal of Human Sexuality, 11*, 1–18.

Schneidman, E. (Ed.). (1976). *Death: Current perspectives.* Palo Alto, CA: Mayfield.

Scholte, R., Sentse, M., & Granic, I. (2010). Do actions speak louder than words? Classroom attitudes and behavior in relation to bullying in early adolescence. *Journal of Clinical Child & Adolescent Psychology*, 39(6), 789–799.

Schooler, C. (1999). The workplace environment: Measurement, psychological effects, and basic issues. In S. L. Friedman & T. D. Wachs (Eds.), *Measuring environment across the life span: Emerging methods and concepts* (pp. 229–246). Washington, DC: American Psychological Association.

Schooler, C. (2001). The intellectual effects of the demands of the work environment. In R. J. Sternberg & E. L. Grigorenko (Eds.), *Environmental effects on cognitive abilities* (pp. 363–380). Mahwah, NJ: Erlbaum.

Schooler, C., Mulatu, M. S., & Oates, G. (2004). Occupational self-direction, intellectual functioning, and self-directed orientation in older workers: Findings and implications for individuals and societies. *American Journal of Sociology, 110*, 161–197.

Schoon, I., & Duckworth, K. (2010). Leaving school early-and making it: Evidence from two British cohorts. *European Psychologist, 15*(4), 283–292.

Schoppe-Sullivan, S. J., Brown, G. L., Cannon, E. A., Mangelsdorf, S. C., & Sokolowski, M. S. (2008). Maternal gatekeeping, coparenting quality, and fathering behavior in families with infants. *Journal of Family Psychology*, 22(3), 389–398.

Schor, J. (1991). *The overworked American: The unexpected decline of leisure.* New York: Basic Books.

Schreiner, L. A., Noel, P., Andseron, E., & Cantwell, L. (2011). The impact of faculty and staff on high-risk college student persistence. *Journal of College Student Development*, 52(3), 321–338.

Schwartz, A. N., Campos, J. J., & Baisel, E. J. (1973). The visual cliff: Cardiac and behavioral responses on the deep and shallow sides at five and nine months of age. *Journal of Experimental Child Psychology, 15*, 86–99.

Schwartz, C. E., Wright, C. I., Shin, L. M., Kagan, J., & Rauch, S. L. (2003, June 20). Inhibited and uninhibited infants "grown up": Adult amygdalar response to novelty. *Science, 300*, 1952–1953.

Schwartz, D., Tom, S. R., Chang, L., Xu, Y., Duong, M. T., & Kelly, B. M. (2010). Popularity and acceptance as distinct dimensions of social standing for Chinese children in Hong Kong. *Social Development, 19*(4), 681–697.

Schwartz, S. J., Beyers, W., Luyckx, K., Soenens, B., Zamboanga, B. L., Forthun, L. F., & ... Waterman, A. S. (2011). Examining the light and dark sides of emerging adults' identity: A study of identity status differences in positive and negative psychosocial functioning. *Journal of Youth and Adolescence, 40*(7), 839–859.

Scrimsher, S., & Tudge, J. (2003). The teaching/learning relationship in the first years of school: Some revolutionary implications of Vygotsky's theory. *Early Education and Development, 14*, 293–312.

Seale, C. (2009). Legalisation of euthanasia or physician-assisted suicide: survey of doctors' attitudes. *Palliative Medicine*, 23, 205–212.

Sebastian, C., Viding, E., Williams, K. D., & Blakemore, S.-J. (2010). Social brain development and the affective consequences of ostracism in adolescence. *Brain and Cognition*, 72, 134–145.

Seery, M. D., Holman, E. A., & Silver, R. C. (2010). Whatever does not kill us: Cumulative lifetime adversity, vulnerability, and resilience. *Journal of Personality and Social Psychology*, 99(6) 1025–1041.

Seifert, T. A., Pascarella, E. T., Goodman, K. M., Salisbury, M. H., & Blaich, C. F. (2010). Liberal arts colleges and good practices in undegraduate education: Additional evidence. *Journal of College Student Development, 51*(1), 1–22.

Seiffge-Krenke, I. (2010). Predicting the timing of leaving home and related developmental tasks: Parents' and children's perspectives. *Journal of Social and Personal Relationships*, 27(4), 495–518.

Self-Brown, S. R., & Mathews, S. (2003). Effects of classroom structure on student achievement goal orientation. *Journal of Educational Research*, 97, 106–111.

Seligman, M. P. (2011). *Flourish: A visionary new understanding of happiness and well-being.* New York, NY: Free Press.

Sercombe, H. (2010). The gift and the trap: Working the "teen brain" into our concept of youth. *Journal of Adolescent Health*, 25(1), 31–47.

Settersten, R. A., & Ray, B. (2010). What's going on with young people today? The long and twisting path to adulthood. *The Future of Children, 20*(1), 1–21. Retrieved June 2, 2011, from http://futureofchildren.org/futureofchildren/publications/docs/20_01_02.pdf

Shafer, E. F. (2011). Wives' relative wages, husbands' paid work hours, and wives' labor-force exit. *Journal of Marriage and Family*, 73, 250–263.

Shahaeian, A., Peterson, C. C., Slaughter, V., & Wellman, H. M. (2011). Culture and the sequence of steps in theory of mind development. *Developmental Psychology*, 47(5), 1239–1247.

Shariff, M. J. (2011). Navigating assisted death and end-of-life care. *Canadian Medical Association Journal*, 183(6), 643–644.

Sharp, E. S., Reynolds, C. A., Penderson, N. L., & Gatz, M. (2010). Cognitive engagement and cognitive aging: Is openess protective? *Psychology and Aging*, 25(1), 60–73.

Shaywitz, S. E., Morris, R., & Shaywitz, B. A. (2008). The education of dyslexic children from childhood to young adulthood. *Annual Review of Psychology*, 59, 451–475.

Shearer, C. L., Crouter, A. C., & McHale, S. M. (2005). Parents' perceptions of changes in mother-child and father-child relationships during adolescence. *Journal of Adolescent Research, 20*, 662–684.

Shelden, R. G., Tracy, S. K., & Brown, W. B. (1997). *Youth gangs in American society.* Belmont, CA: Wadsworth.

Sheldon, K. M., Cummins, R., & Kamble, S. (2010). Life balance and well-being: Testing a novel conceptual and measurement approach. *Journal of Personality*, 78(4), 1093–1133.

Sheridan, M., Drury, S., McLaughlin, K., & Almas, A. (2010). Early institutionalization: Neurobiological consequences and genetic modifiers. *Neuropsychological Review, 20*, 414–429.

Shernoff, D. J., Csikszentmihalyi, M., Shneider, B., & Shernoff, E. S. (2003). Student engagement in high school classrooms from the perspective of flow theory. *School Psychology Quarterly, 18*, 158–176

Shierholz, H., & Edwards, K.A. (2011). The class of 2011: Young workers face a dire labor market without a safety net. *Economic Policy Institute*, 306, 2–14.

Shih, F., Lin, H., Gau, M., Chen, C., Hsiao, S., Shih, S., Sheu, S. J. (2009). Spiritual needs of Taiwan's older patients with terminal cancer. *Oncology Nursing Forum*, 36, e31–e38.

Shonkoff, J. P., & Phillips, D. A. (2000). Growing up in child care. In J. P. Shonkoff & D. A. Phillips (Eds.), *From neurons to neighborhoods: The science of early childhood development* (pp. 297–327). Washington, DC: National Academy Press.

Sibley, M. H., Pelham, W. E., Molina, B. G., Gnagy, E. M., Waschbusch, D. A., Biswas, A., & ... Karch, K. M. (2011). The delinquency outcomes of boys with ADHD with and without comorbidity. *Journal of Abnormal Child Psychology:* 39(1), 21–32.

Sijtsema, J. J., Ojanen, T., Veenstra, R., Lindenberg, S., Hawley, P. H., & Little, T. D. (2010). Forms and functions of aggression in adolescent friendship selection and influence: A longitudinal social network analysis. *Social Development, 19*(3), 515–534.

Silva, P. J., & Sanders, C. E. (2010). Why are smart people curious? Fluid intelligence, openess to experience, and interest. *Learning and Individual Differences,* 26, 242–245.

Silveira, M. J., Kim, S. H., & Langa, K. M. (2010). Advance directives and outcomes of surrogate decision making before death. *The New England Journal of Medicine*, 362(13), 1211–1218.

Silventoinen, K., Haukka, J., Dunkel, L., Tynelius, P., & Rasmussen, F. (2008). Genetics of pubertal timing and its associations with relative weight in childhood and adult height: The Swedish young male twins study. *Pediatrics, 121*(4), 885–891.

Silverman, J. G., McCauley, H. L., Decker, M. R., Miller, E., Reed, E., & Raj, A. (2011). Coercive forms of sexual risk and associated violence perpetrated by male partners of female adolescents. *Perspectives on Sexual and Reproductive Health*, 43(1), 60–65.

Simmons, R. G., & Blyth, D. A. (1987). *Moving into adolescence: The impact of pubertal change and school context.* Hawthorne, NY: Aldine.

Simon, L. S., Judge, T. A., & Halvorsen-Ganepola, M. D. K. (2010). In good company? A multi-study, multi-level investigation of the effects of coworker relationships on employee well-being. *Journal of Vocational Behavior*, 76, 534–546.

Simons, D. A., & Wurtele, S. K. (2010). Relationships between parents' use of corporal punishment and their children's endorsement of spanking and hitting other children. *Child Abuse & Neglect*, 34, 639–646.

Simonton, D. K. (1997). Creative productivity: A predictive and explanatory model of career trajectories and landmarks. *Psychological Review, 104*, 66–89.

Simonton, D. K. (2002). Longitudinal changes in creativity. In D. K. Simonton (Ed.), *Great psychologists and their times: Scientific insights into psychology's history* (pp. 67–101). Washington, DC: American Psychological Association.

Simonton, D. K. (2007). Creative life cycles in literature: Poets versus novelists or conceptualists versus experimentalists? *Psychology of Aesthetics, Creativity, and the Arts, 1*(3), 133–139.

Simpson, J. A., Collins, W. A., Tran, S., & Hayden, K. C. (2007). Attachment and the experience and expression of emotions in romantic relationships: A developmental perspective. *Journal of Personality and Social Psychology*, 92(2), 355–367.

Singh, G. K., Siahpush, M., Hiatt, R. A., & Timsina, L. R. (2011). Dramatic increases in obesity and overweight prevalence and body mass index anong ethnic-immigrant and social class groups in the United States, 1976–2008. *Journal of Community Health*, 36, 94–110.

Sinnott, J. D. (1989). General systems theory: A rationale for the study of everyday memory. In L. W. Poon, D. C. Rubin, & B. A. Wilson (Eds.), *Everyday cognition in adulthood and late life* (pp. 59–70). New York: Cambridge University Press.

Sinnott, J. D. (2003). Postformal thought and adult development: Living in balance. In J. Demick & C. Andreoletti (Eds.), *Handbook of adult development* (pp. 221–238). New York: Kluwer/Plenum.

Sisk, C. L., & Foster, D. L. (2004). The neural basis of puberty and adolescence. *Nature Neuroscience*, 7, 1040–1042.

Siu, M. W., Cheung, T. Y., Chiu, M. M., Kwok, T. Y., Choi, W. L., Lo, T. K., … Chua, S. E. (2010). The preparedness of Hong Kong medical students towards advance directives and end-of-life issues. *East Asian Archives of Psychiatry*, 20(4), 155–162.

Siu, O., Lu, J., Brough, P., Lu, C., Bakker, A. B., Kalliath, T., … Shi, C. (2010). Role resources and work-family enrichment: The role of work engagement. *Journal of Vocational Behavior*, 77, 470–480.

Sjörs, G. (2010). Treatment decisions for extremely preterm newborns: Beyond gestational age. *Acta Paediatrica*, 99(12), 1761–1762.

Skinner, B. F. (1960). *The behavior of organisms: An experimental analysis.* New York: Appleton-Century-Crofts.

Skinner, B. F. (1974). *About behaviorism.* New York: Knopf.

Slater, A. (2001). Visual perception. In G. Bremner & A. Fogel (Eds.), *Blackwell handbook of infant development* (pp. 5–34). Malden, MA: Blackwell.

Slater, A., Quinn, P.C., Kelly, D.J., Lee, K., Longmore, C.A., McDonald, P.R., et al. (2010). The shaping of the face space in early infancy: Becoming a native face processor. *Child Development Perspectives, 4*(5), 201–211.

Slavin, M. J., Brodaty, H., Kochan, N. A., Trollor, J. N., Draper, B., & Sachdev, P. S. (2010). Prevalence and predictors of "subjective cognitive complaints" in the Sydney memory and ageing study. *The American Journal of Geriatric Psychiatry, 18*(8), 701–710.

Slevec, J., & Tiggemann, M. (2011). Attitudes toward cosmetic surgery in middle-aged women: Body image, aging anxiety, and the media. *Psychology of Women Quarterly*, 35(4), 617–629.

Slobin, D. I. (1972). Children and language: They learn the same way all around the world. *Psychology Today*, 6(2), 71–74, 82.

Small, B. J., Hertzog, C., Hultsch, D. F., & Dixon, R. A. (2003). Stability and change in adult personality over 6 years: Findings from the Victoria Longitudinal Study. *Journals of Gerontology: Series B: Psychological Sciences and Social Sciences, 58B*, P166–P176.

Smart, J., & Hiscock, H. (2007). Early infant crying and sleeping problems: A pilot study of impact on parental wellbeing and parent-endorsed strategies for management. *Journal of Paediatrics and Child Health*, 43, 284–290.

Smetana, J. G., Campione-Barr, N., & Metzger, A. (2006). Adolescent development in interpersonal and societal contexts. *Annual Review of Psychology*, 57, 255–284.

Smetana, J. G., Daddis, C., & Chuang, S. S. (2003). "Clean your room!" A longitudinal investigation of adolescent-parent conflict and conflict resolution in middle-class African American families. *Journal of Adolescent Research, 18*, 631–650.

Smetana, J. G., Kochanska, G., & Chuang, S. (2000). Mothers' conceptions of everyday rules for young toddlers: A longitudinal investigation. *Merrill-Palmer Quarterly, 46*, 391–416.

Smiley, P. A., Coulson, S. L., Greene, J. K., & Bono, K. L. (2010). Performance concern, contingent self-worth, and responses to repeated achievement failure in second graders. *Social Development, 19*(4), 779–798.

Smith, C. O., Levine, D. W., Smith, E. P., Dumas, J., & Prinz, R. J. (2009). A developmental perspective of the relationship of racial-ethnic identity to self-construct, achievement, and behavior in African American children. *Cultural Diversity and Ethnic Minority Psychology, 15*(2), 145–157.

Smith, G. R., Williamson, G. M., Miller, L. S., & Schultz, R. (2011). Depression and quality of informal care: A longitudinal investigation of caregiving stressors. *Psychology and Aging, 15*(3), 385–396.

Smith, J. P., & Ellwood, M. (2011). Feeding patterns and emotional care in breastfed infants. *Social Indicators Research, 101*, 227–231.

Smith, L., & Hough, C. L. (2011). Using death rounds to improve end-of-life education for internal medicine residents. *Journal of Palliative Medicine, 14*(1), 55–58.

Smith, M. E. (1926). An investigation of the development of the sentence and the extent of vocabulary in young children. *University of Iowa Studies: Child Welfare*, 3, 92.

Smith, R. L., Rose, A. J., & Schwartz-Mette, R. A. (2010). Relational and overt aggression in childhood and adolescence: Clarifying mean-level gender differences and associations with peer acceptance. *Social Development, 19*(2), 243–269.

Smith, T. B., & Silva, L. (2011). Ethnic identity and personal well-being of people of color: A meta-analysis. *Journal of Counseling Psychology*, 58(1), 42–60.

Smock, P. J., Manning, W. D., & Porter, M. (2005). "Everything's there except money": How money shapes decisions to marry among cohabitors. *Journal of Marriage and Family, 67*, 680–696.

Smolak, L., & Stein, J. A. (2010). A longitudinal investigation of gender role and muscle building in adolescent boys. *Sex Roles, 63*, 738–746.

Smolucha, L., & Smolucha, F. (1998). The social origins of mind: Post-Piagetian perspectives on pretend play. In O. N. Saracho & B. Spodek (Eds.), *Multiple perspectives on play in early childhood education* (pp. 34–58). Albany, NY: State University of New York Press.

Smyke, A. T., Zeanah, C. H., Nelson, C. A., Fox, N. A., & Guthrie, D. (2010). Placement in foster care enhances quality of attachment among young institutionalized children. *Child Development, 81*(1), 212–223.

Snarey, J. R. (1985). Cross-cultural universality of social-moral development: A critical review of Kohlbergian research. *Psychological Bulletin, 97*, 202–232.

Snyder, L. (1999). *Speaking our minds: Personal reflections from individuals with Alzheimer's*. New York: Freeman.

Social Security Fact Sheet. (2011). *Social Security: Increase in retirement age*. Retrieved July 24, 2011, from http://www.ssa.gov/pressoffice/Inc-Ret-Age

Social Security Online. (2011). *What is the average monthly social security benefit for a retired worker?* Retrieved July 24, 2011, from http://www.ssacusthelp.ssa.gov/app/answers/detail/a_id/13/related/1/session/L2F2LaEvdGltZS8

Soderlund, G., Sikstrom, S., & Smart, A. (2007). Listen to the noise: Noise is beneficial for cognitive performance in ADHD. *Journal of Child Psychology and Psychiatry*, 48(8), 840–847.

Soenens, B., & Vansteenkiste, M. (2010). A theoretical upgrade of the concept of parental psychological control: Proposing new insights on the basis of self-determination theory. *Developmental Review*, 30(1), 74–99.

Son, J., Erno, A., Shea, G., Femia, E. E., Zarit, S. H., & Stephens, M. P. (2007). The caregiver stress process and health outcomes. *Journal of Aging and Health, 19*, 871–887.

Sonuga-Barke, E. J. S., & Halperin, J. M. (2010). Developmental phenotypes and causal pathways in attention deficit/hyperactivity disorder: Potential targets for early intervention? *Journal of Child Psychology & Psychiatry*, 51(4), 368–389.

Soric, M., & Misigoj-Durakovic, M. (2010). Physical activity levels and estimated energy expenditure in overweight and normal-weight 11-year-old children. *Acta Paediatrica, 99*, 244–250.

Sossou, M.-A. (2002). Widowhood practices in West Africa: The silent victims. *International Journal of Social Welfare, 11*, 201–209.

Spafford, M. M., Rudman, D. L., Leipert, D., Klinger, L., & Huot, S. (2010). When self-presentation trumps access: Why older adults with low vision go without low-vision services. *Journal of Applied Gerontology, 26*(5), 579–602.

Spear, L. P. (2008). The psychology of adolescence. In K. K. Kline (Ed.), *Authoritative Communities: The Scientific Cases for Nurturing the Whole Child* (pp. 263–280). New York: Springer-Verlag.

Spense, A. (1989). *The biology of human aging*. Englewood Cliffs, NJ: Prentice Hall.

Spinath, B., & Steinmayr, R. (2008). Longitudinal analysis of intrinsic motivation and competence beliefs: Is there a relation over time? *Child Development, 49*, 1555–1569.

Spivack, J. G., Swietlik, M., Alessandrini, E., & Faith, M. S. (2010). Primary care providers' knowledge, practices, and perceived barriers to the treatment and prevention of childhood obesity. *Obesity, 18*(7), 1341–1347.

Sprecher, S., & Fehr, B. (2010). Dispositional attatchment and relationship-specific attachment as predictors of compassionate love for a partner. *Journal of Social and Personal Relationships*, 28(4), 558–574.

Spronk, K. (2004). Good death and bad death in ancient Israel according to biblical lore. *Social Science & Medicine*, 58, 985–995.

Srivastava, A., Locke, E. A., Judge, T. A., Adams, J. W. (2010). Core self-evaluations as causes of satisfaction: The mediating role of seeking task complexity. *Journal of Vocational Behavior, 77*, 255–265.

Sroufe, L. A. (2000). Early relationships and the development of children. *Infant Mental Health Journal, 21*, 67–74.

Sroufe, L. A., Egeland, B., Carlson, E., & Collins, W. A. (2005). Placing early attachment experiences in developmental context: The Minnesota Longitudinal Study. In K. E. Grossmann, K. Grossmann, & E. Waters (Eds.), *Attachment from infancy to adulthood: The major longitudinal studies* (pp. 48–70). New York: Guilford Press.

Stamatakis, E. E., Zaninotto, P. P., Falaschetti, E. E., Mindell, J. J., & Head, J. J. (2010). Time trends in childhood and adolescent obesity in England from 1995 to 2007 and projections of prevalence to 2015. *Journal of Epidemiology and Community Health, 64*(2), 167–174.

Stamatiadis, N. (1996). Gender effect on the accident patterns of elderly drivers. *Journal of Applied Gerontology, 15*, 8–22.

Stanley, F., Langridge, A., & D'Antoine, H. (2011). Variability in paediatric outcomes within wealthy countries. *Acta Paediatrica, 100*(1), 26–28.

Stanley, S. M., Rhoades, G. K., Amato, P. R., Markman, H. J., & Johnson, C. A. (2010). The timing of cohabitation and engagement: Impact on first and second marriages. *Journal of Marriage and Family*, 72(4), 906–918.

Stanton, C., Ronsman, C., & Baltimore Group on Cesarean. (2008). Recommendations for routine reporting on indications for cesarean delivery in developing countries. *Birth*, 35(3), 204–211.

Stark, R., Bauer, E., Merz, C. J., Zimmermann, M., Reuter, M., Plichta, M. M., … Herrmann, M. J. (2011). ADHD related behaviors are associated with brain activation in the reward system. *Neuropsychologia, 49*, 426–434.

Stattin, H., & Magnusson, D. (1990). *Pubertal maturation in female development.* Hillsdale, NJ: Erlbaum.

Staufenbiel, T., & König, J. (2010). A model for the effects of job insecurity on performance, turnover intention and absenteeism. *Journal of Occupational and Organizational Psychology*, 83, 101–117.

Stavrova, O., Schlösser, T., & Fetchenhauer, D. (2011). Are the unemployed equally unhappy all around the world? The role of the social norms to work and welfare states provision in 28 OECD countries. *Journal of Economic Psychology*, 32, 159–171.

Stebbins, H., & Knitzer, J. (2007). *State early childhood policies*. New York, NY: Columbia University. National Center for Children in Poverty.

Steele, C. M., & Aronson, J. (1995). Stereotype threat and the intellectual test performance of African-Americans. *Journal of Personality and Social Psychology 69(5), 797–811.*

Steele, S., Joseph, R. M., & Tager-Flusberg, H. (2003). Brief report: Developmental change in theory of mind abilities in children with autism. *Journal of Autism and Developmental Disorders*, 33, 461–467.

Stein, J. H., & Reiser, L. W. (1994). A study of White middle-class adolescent boys' responses to "semenarche" (the first ejaculation). *Journal of Youth and Adolescence*, 23, 373–384.

Stein, S. J., & Oler, C. S. (2010). Emotional and legal considerations in divorce and relocation: A call for alternative dispute resolution. *Journal of Individual Psychology*, 66(3), 290–301.

Steinberg, L. (2001). We know some things: Parent-adolescent relationships in retrospect and prospect. *Journal of Research on Adolescence, 11*, 1–19.

Steinberg, L. (2005). Cognitive and affective development in adolescence. *Trends in Cognitive Sciences*, 9, 69–74.

Steinberg, L. (2008). A social neuroscience perspective on adolescent risk-taking. *Developmental Review*, 28, 78–106.

Steinberg, L. (2010). A behavioral scientist looks at the science of adolescent brain development. *Brain and Cognition*, 72, 160–164.

Steinberg, L., Graham, S., O'Brien, L., Woolard, J., Cauffman, E., & Banich, M. (2009). Age differences in future orientation and delay discounting. *Child Development*, 80, 28–44.

Steinberg, L., & Hill, J. P. (1978). Patterns of family interaction as a function of age, the onset of puberty, and formal thinking. *Developmental Psychology*, 14, 683–684.

Sternberg, R. J. (1984). Toward a triarchic theory of human intelligence. *Behavioral and Brain Sciences*, 7, 269–315.

Sternberg, R. J. (1986). A triangular theory of love. *Psychological Review*, 93, 119–135.

Sternberg, R. J. (1988). Triangulating love. In R. J. Sternberg & M. L. Barnes (Eds.), *The psychology of love* (pp. 119–138). New Haven, CT: Yale University Press.

Sternberg, R. J. (1996). *Successful intelligence: How practical and creative intelligence determine success in life.* New York: Simon & Schuster.

Sternberg, R. J. (1997). The triarchic theory of intelligence. In D. P. Flanagan, J. L. Genshaft, & P. L. Harrison (Eds.), *Contemporary intellectual assessment: Theories, tests, and issues* (pp. 92–104). New York: Guilford Press.

Sternberg, R. J. (2004). A triangular theory of love. In H. T. Reis & C. E. Rusbult (Eds.), *Close relationships: Key readings* (pp. 213–227). Philadelphia: Taylor & Francis.

Sternberg, R. J. (2007). Who are the bright children? The cultural context of being and acting intelligent. *Educational Researcher*, 36(3), 148–155.

Sternberg, R. J. (2010). WICS: A new model for school psychology. *School Psychology International*, 31(6), 599–616.

Sternberg, R. J., & Berg, C. A. (1992). *Intellectual development.* New York: Cambridge University Press.

Sternberg, R. J., Grigorenko, E. L., & Bundy, D. A. (2001). The predictive value of IQ. *Merrill-Palmer Quarterly*, 47, 1–41.

Sternberg, R. J., Grigorenko, E. L., & Kidd, K. K. (2005). Intelligence, race, and genetics. *American Psychologist, 60*, 46–59.

Sternberg, R. J., Torff, B., & Grigorenko, E. L. (1998). Teaching for successful intelligence raises school achievement. *Phi Delta Kappan*, 79, 667–669.

Stice, E., Ng, J., & Shaw, H. (2010). Risk factors and prodromal eating pathology. *The Journal of Child Psychology and Psychiatry*, 51(4), 518–525.

Stiles, J., & Jernigan, T. L. (2010). The basics of brain development. *Neuropsychology Review*, 20(4), 327–348.

Stipek, D. J. (1996). Motivation and instruction. In D. C. Berliner & R. C. Calfee (Eds.), *Handbook of educational psychology* (pp. 85–113). New York: Macmillan Library Reference.

Stipek, D. J. (1997). Success in school—For a head start in life. In S. S. Luthar, J. A. Burack, D. Cicchetti, & J. R. Weisz (Eds.), *Developmental psychopathology: Perspectives on adjustment, risk, and disorder* (pp. 75–92). New York: Cambridge University Press.

St. James-Roberts, I. (2007). Helping parents to manage infant crying and sleeping: A review of the evidence and its implications for services. *Child Abuse Review*, 16, 47–69.

Stolzer, J. M. (2010). The risks associated with maternal antidepressant use during the prenatal and postnatal stages of development. *Ethical Human Psychology and Psychiatry*, 12(2), 86–98.

Striegel-Moore, R. H., & Bulik, C. M. (2007). Risk factors for eating disorders. *American Psychologist*, 62(3), 181–198.

Stringer, K. J., & Kerpelman, J. L. (2010). Career identity development in college students: decision making, parental support, and work experience. *Identity: An International Journal of Theory*, 10, 181–200.

Stroebe, M., Schut, H., & Stroebe, W. (2007). Health outcomes of bereavement. *Lancet*, 370, 1960–1973.

Strohmeier, D., Kärnä, A., & Salmivalli, C. (2010). Intrapersonal and interpersonal risk factors for peer victimization in immigrant youth in Finland. *Developmental Psychology*, 47, 248–258.

Stronach, E. P., Toth, S. L., Rogosch, F., Oshri, A., Manly, J. T., & Cicchetti, D. (2011). Child maltreatment, attachment security, and internal representations of mother and mother-child relationships. *Child Maltreatment, 16*, 137–145.

Sturaro, C., van Lier, P. A. C., Cuijpers, P., & Koot, H. M. (2011). The role of peer relationships in the development of early school age externalizing problems. *Child Development, 82*(3), 758–765.

Sturge-Apple, M. L., Davies, P. T., & Cummings, E. M. (2010). Typologies of family functioning and children's adjustment during the early school years. *Child Development, 81*(4), 1320–1335.

Suárez-Orozco, C., Gaytán, F. X., Bang, H. J., Pakes, J., O'Connor, E., & Rhodes, J. (2010). Academic trajectories of newcomer immigrant youth. *Developmental Psychology, 46*(3), 602–618.

Subrahmanyam, K., Greenfield, P. M., & Tynes, B. (2004). Constructing sexuality and identity in an online teen chat room. *Journal of Applied Developmental Psychology. Special Issue: Developing Children, Developing Media: Research from Television to the Internet from the Children's Digital Media Center, 25*, 651–666.

Subramanian, S. V., Elwert, G., & Christakis, N. (2008). Widowhood and mortality among the elderly: The modifying role of neighborhood concentration of widowed individuals. *Social Science & Medicine, 66*(4), 873–884.

Suhail, K., Jamil, N., Oyebode, J., & Ajmal, M. S. (2011). Continuing bonds in bereaved Pakistani Muslims: Effects of culture and religion. *Death Studies, 35*, 22–41.

Sullivan, H. S. (1953). *The interpersonal theory of psychiatry.* New York: Norton.

Sullivan, S. J., Mikels, J. A., & Carstensen, L. L. (2010). You never lose the ages you've been: Affective perspective taking in older adults. *Psychology and Aging, 25*(1), 229–234.

Sun, S. S., Schubert, C. M., Chumlea, W. C., Roche, A. F., Kulin, H. E., Lee, P. A., … Ryan, A. S. (2002). National estimates of the timing of sexual maturation and racial differences among U.S. children. *Pediatrics, 110*, 911–919.

Suomi, S. J. (2004). How gene-environment interactions shape biobehavioral development: Lessons from studies with rhesus monkeys. *Research in Human Development, 1*, 205–222.

Super, C. M., & Harkness, S. (2003). The metaphors of development. *Human Development, 46*, 3–23.

Super, D. E. (1957). *The psychology of careers: An introduction to vocational development.* New York: Harper.

Supercentenarian Research Foundation. (2011). Retrieved August 8, 2011, from http://www.supercentenarian-research-foundation.org

Surra, C. A., & Hughes, D. K. (1997). Commitment processes in accounts of the development of premarital relationships. *Journal of Marriage & the Family, 59*, 5–21.

Surra, C. A., Hughes, D. K., & Jacquet, S. E. (1999). The development of commitment to marriage: A phenomenological approach. In J. M. Adams & W. H. Jones (Eds.), *Handbook of interpersonal commitment and relationship stability* (pp. 125–148). Dordrecht, Netherlands: Kluwer Academic.

Sussman, S., Pokhrel, P., Ashmore, R. D., & Brown, B. B. (2007). Adolescent peer group identification and characteristics: A review of the literature. *Addictive Behaviors, 32*, 1602–1627.

Sutin, A. R., Terracciano, A., Deiana, B., Uda, M., Schlessinger, D., Lakatta, E. G., & Costa, P. T. Jr. (2010). Cholesterol, triglycerides, and the five-factor model of personality. *Biological Psychology, 84*, 186–191.

Svensson, B., Bornehag, C.-G., & Janson, S. (2011). Chronic conditions in children increase the risk for physical abuse—but vary with socio-economic circumstances. *Acta P diatrica, 100*, 407–412.

Svetlova, M., Nichols, S. R., & Brownell, C. A. (2010). Toddlers' prosocial behavior: From instrumental to empathic to altruistic helping. *Child Development, 81*(6), 1814–1827.

Swami, V., Frederick, D. A., Aavik, T., Alcalay, L., Allik, J., Anderson, D., … Zivcic-Becirevic, I. (2010). The attractive female body weight and female body dissatisfaction in 26 countries across 10 world regions: Results of the international body project I. *Personality and Social Psychology Bulletin, 36*(3), 309–325.

Swann, W. B., Chang-Schneider, C., & McClarty, K. L. (2007). Do people's self-views matter? *American Psychologist, 62*(2), 84–94.

Swenson, C., Schaeffer, C. M., Henggeler, S. W., Faldowski, R., & Mayhew, A. (2010). Multisystemic therapy for child abuse and neglect: A randomized effectiveness trial. *Journal of Family Psychology, 24*(4), 497–507.

Swinburn, B. A., & de Silva-Sanigorski, A. M. (2010). Where to from here for preventing childhood obesity: An international perspective. *Obesity, 18*(Suppl. 1), S4–S7.

Syed, A., & Azmitia, M. (2009). Longitudinal trajectories of ethnic identity during the college years. *Journal of Research on Adolescence, 19*(4), 601–624.

Syltevik, L. (2010). Sense and sensibility: Cohabitation in 'cohabitation land.' *The Sociological Review, 58*(3), 444–462.

Symons, D. K. (2010). A review of the practice and science of child custody and access assessment in the United States and Canada. *Professional Psychology: Research and Practice, 41*(3), 267–273.

Tadmor, C. T., Tetlock, P. E., & Peng, K. (2009). Acculturation strategies and integrative complexity: The cognitive implications of biculturalism. *Journal of Cross-Cultural Psychology, 40*, 105–139.

Tambalis, K. D., Panagiotakos, D. B., Kavouras, S. A., Kallistratos, A. A., Moraiti, I. P., Douvis, S. J., … Sidossis, L. S. (2010). Eleven-year prevalence trends of obesity in Greek children: First evidence that prevalence of obesity is leveling off. *Obesity, 18*(1), 161–166.

Tanner, J. L. (2006). Recentering during emerging adulthood: A critical turning point in life span human development. In J. J. Arnett, & J. L. Tanner (Eds.), *Emerging adults in America: Coming of age in the 21st century* (pp. 21–55). Washington, DC: American Psychological Association.

Tanner, J. L., & Arnett, J. J. (2010). Presenting "emerging adulthood": What makes it developmentally distinctive. In J. J. Arnett, M. Kloep, L. B. Hendry, & J. L. Tanner (Eds.), *Debating emerging adulthood: Stage or process?* (pp. 13–30). New York: Oxford University Press.

Tanner, J. M. (1955). *Growth at adolescence.* Oxford, England: Blackwell.

Tanner, J. M. (1978). *Foetus into man: Physical growth from conception to maturity.* Cambridge, MA: Harvard University Press.

Taveras, E. M., Hohman, K. H., Price, S. N., Rifas-Shiman, S. L., Mitchell, K., Gortmaker, S. L., & Gillman, M. W. (2011). Correlates of participation in a pediatric primary care-based obesity prevention intervention. *Obesity, 19*(2), 449–452.

Taylor, C. A., Hamvas, L., & Paris, R. (2011). Perceived instrumentality and normativeness of corporal punishment use among black mothers. *Family Relations, 60*, 60–72.

Taylor, K. J. (2010). Occupational sex composition and the gendered availability of workplace support. *Gender & Society, 24*(2), 189–212.

Taylor, M. G. (2010). Capturing transitions and trajectories: The role of socioeconomic status in later life disability. *Journals of Gerontology: Social Sciences, 65B*(6), 733–743.

Taylor, M. G. (2011). The causal pathway from socioeconomic status to disability trajectories in later life: The importance of mediating mechanisms for onset and accumulation. *Research on Aging, 33*(1), 84–108.

Tedeschi, R. G., & Calhoun, L. G. (2008). Beyond the concept of recovery: Growth and the experience of loss. *Death Studies*, 32(1), 27–39.

Teeri, S., Valimaki, M., Katajisto, J., & Leino-Kilpi, H. (2008). Maintenance of parents' integrity in long-term institutional care. *Nursing Ethics, 15*(4), 523–535.

Teisl, M., Rogosch, F. A., Oshri, A., & Cicchetti, D. (2012). Differential expression of social dominance as a function of age and maltreatment experience. *Developmental Psychology, 48*(2), 575-588.

Terracciano, A., McCrae, R. R., & Costa, P. T. (2010). Intra-individual change in personality stability and age. *Journal of Research in Personality, 44*, 31–37.

Teti, D. M., Kim, B., Mayer, G., & Countermine, M. (2010). Maternal emotional availability at bedtime predicts infant sleep quality. *Journal of Family Psychology, 24*, 307–315.

Thacker, K. S. (2008). Nurses' advocacy behaviors in end-of-life nursing care. *Nursing Ethics, 15*(2), 174–185.

Thai, N. D., Connell, C. M., & Tebes, J. (2010). Substance use among Asian American adolescents: Influence of race, ethnicity, and acculturation in the context of key risk and protective factors. *Asian American Journal of Psychology, 1*(4), 261–274.

Theis, W., & Bleiler, L. (2011). Alzheimer's Association report: 2011 Alzheimer's disease facts and figures. *Alzheimer's & Dementia, 7*, 208–244.

Thiessen, E. D., Hill, E. A., & Saffran, J. R. (2005). Infant-directed speech facilitates word segmentation. *Infancy, 7*, 53–71.

Thivel, D., Isacco, L., Rousset, S., Boirie, Y., Morio, B., Duché, P. (2011). Intensive exercise: A remedy for childhood obesity. *Physiology & Behavior, 102*(2), 132–136.

Thomaes, S., Stegge, H., & Olthof, T. (2007). Externalizing shame responses in children: The role of fragile-positive self-esteem. *British Journal of Developmental Psychology, 25*(4), 559–577.

Thoman, E. B., & Whitney, M. P. (1990). Behavioral states in infants: Individual differences and individual analyses. In J. Colombo & J. W. Fagen (Eds.), *Individual differences in infancy: Reliability, stability, prediction* (pp. 113–135). Hillsdale, NJ: Erlbaum.

Thomas, A., & Chess, S. (1977). *Temperament and development.* Oxford, England: Brunner/Mazel.

Thomas, A., Chess, S., & Birch, H. G. (1968). *Temperament and behavior disorders in children.* Oxford, England: New York University Press.

Thomas, C., Morris, S. M., & Clark, D. (2004). Place of death: Preferences among cancer patients and their carers. *Social Science & Medicine, 58*, 2431–2444.

Thomas, J. R., & French, K. E. (1985). Gender differences across age in motor performance: A meta-analysis. *Psychological Bulletin, 98*, 260–282.

Thomas, S. V., Ajaykumar, B., Sindhu, K., Nair, M. K. C., George, B., & Sarma, P. S. (2008). Motor and mental development of infants exposed to antiepileptic drugs in utero. *Epilepsy & Behavior, 13*, 229–236.

Thompson, E. M., & Morgan, E. M. (2008). "Mostly straight" young women: Variations in sexual behavior and identity development. *Developmental Psychology, 44*(1), 15–21.

Thompson, R. F., & Einstein, F. H. (2010). Epigenetic basis for fetal origins of age-related disease. *Journal of Women's Health, 19*(3), 581–587.

Thomson, E., & Bernhardt, E. (2010). Education, values, and cohabitation in Sweden. *Marriage & Family Review, 46*(1–2), 1–21.

Tokunaga, R. S. (2010). Following you home from school: A critical review and synthesis of research on cyberbullying victimization. *Computers in Human Behavior, 26*, 277–287.

Tomaszczyk, J. C., Fernandes, M. A., & Macleod, C. M. (2008). Personal relevance modulates the positivity bias in recall of emotional pictures in older adults. *Psychonomic Bulletin & Review, 15*(1), 191–196.

Tomlinson, M., Cooper, P., & Murray, L. (2005). The mother-infant relationship and infant attachment in a South African peri-urban settlement. *Child Development, 76*, 1044–1054.

Touchette, E., Henegar, A., Godart, N. T., Pryor, L., Falissard, B., Tremblay, R. E., & Côté, S. M. (2011). Subclinical eating disorders and their comorbidity with mood and anxiety disorders in adolescent girls. *Psychiatry Research, 185*, 185–192.

Triana, M. (2011). A woman's place and a man's duty: How gender role incongruence in one's family can result in home-related spillover discrimination at work. *Journal of Business Psychology, 26*, 71–86.

Triandis, H. C. (1995). *Individualism & collectivism.* Boulder, CO: Westview Press.

Trick, L. M., Toxopeus, R., & Wilson, D. (2010). The effects of visibility conditions, traffic density, and navigational challenge in speed compensation and driving performance in older adults. *Accident Analysis and Prevention, 42*, 1661–1671.

Troll, L. E. (1983). Grandparents: The family watchdog. In T. H. Brubaker (Ed.), *Family relationships in later life* (pp. 63–74). Beverly Hills, CA: Sage.

Trommsdorff, G., Friedlmeier, W., & Mayer, B. (2007). Sympathy, distress, and prosocial behavior of preschool children in four cultures. *International Journal of Behavioral Development, 31*(3), 284–293.

Troop-Gordon, W., Visconti, K. J., & Kuntz, K. J. (2011). Perceived popularity during early adolescence: Links to declining school adjustment among aggressive youth. *The Journal of Early Adolescence, 31*(1), 125–151.

Trzcinski, E., & Holst, E. (2011). Gender differences in subjective well-being in and out of management positions. *Social Indicators Research, 101*(3), 305–479.

Tulving, E. (1985). How many memory systems are there? *American Psychologist, 40*, 385–398.

Turkheimer, E. (2004). Spinach and ice cream: Why social science is so difficult. In L. F. DiLalla (Ed.) *Behavior genetic principles: Perspectives in development, personality, and psychopathology.* Washington, DC: American Psychological Association Press.

Turkheimer, E., Haley, A., Waldron, M., D'Onofrio, B., & Gottesman, I. I. (2003). Socioeconomic status modifies heritability of IQ in young children. *Psychological Science, 14*, 623–628.

Turkington, C., & Alper, M. M. (2001). *The encyclopedia of fertility and infertility.* New York: Facts on File.

Turner, S., & Alborz, A. (2003). Academic attainments of children with Down's syndrome: A longitudinal study. *British Journal of Educational Psychology, 73,* 563–583.

Turra, C. M., & Goldman, N. (2007). Socioeconomic differences in mortality among U.S. adults: Insights into the Hispanic paradox. *Journals of Gerontology, 62B*(3), S184–S192.

Tyler, D. A., & Parker, V. A. (2011). Nursing home culture, teamwork, and culture change. *Journal of Research in Nursing, 16*(1), 37–49.

U.S. Bureau of Labor Statistics (2009). *The Employment Situation.* United States Department of Labor.

U.S. Census Bureau. (2008). *Unmarried and single Americans week.* Washington, DC: U.S. Census Bureau News.

U.S. Department of Commerce. (2007). *Single-parent households showed little variation since 1994, Census Bureau reports.* Washington, DC: U.S. Census Bureau News.

U.S. Department of Commerce. (2008). *Grandparents Day 2008: Sept. 7.* Washington, DC: U.S. Census Bureau News.

U.S. Department of Health and Human Services. (2009). *Summary health statistics for U.S. adults: National health interview study,* Series 10, number 249.

U.S. Department of Labor. (2011). Usual weekly earnings of wage and salary workers first quarter 2011. *Bureau of Labor Statistics: US Department of Labor,* 1–2.

Udry, J. R. (1990). Biosocial models of adolescent problem behaviors. *Social Biology, 37,* 1–10.

Udry, J. R. (2000). Biological limits of gender construction. *American Sociological Review, 65,* 443–457.

Udry, J. R., & Campbell, B. C. (1994). Getting started on sexual behavior. In A. S. Rossi (Ed.), *Sexuality across the life course* (pp. 187–207). Chicago: University of Chicago Press.

Uecker, J. E., Regnerus, M. D. (2010). Bare market: Campus sex ratios, romantic relationships and sexual behavior. *The Sociological Quarterly, 51,* 408–435.

Ueno, K. (2010). Same-sex experience and mental health during the transition between adolescence and young adulthood. *The Sociological Quarterly, 51,* 484–510.

Umberson, D., Pudrovska, T., & Reczek, C. (2010). Parenthood, childlessness, and well-being: A life course perspective. *Journal of Marriage and Family, 72,* 612–629.

UNICEF (United Nations Children's Fund). (2002a). *The state of the world's children 2003.* New York: Author.

UNICEF (United Nations Children's Fund). (2009). *The state of the world's children: maternal and newborn health, 2009.* Retrieve from http://www.unicef.org/publications/index_47127.html. Retrieved April 26, 2012.

United States Department of Agriculture, Economic Research Service. (2010). *Food security in the United States.* Retrieved September 24, 2011, from http://www.ers.usda.gov/Briefing/FoodSecurity

Urban, J. B., Lewin-Bizan, S., & Lerner, R. M. (2010). The role of intentional self regulation, lower neighborhood ecological assets, and activity involvement in youth developmental outcomes. *Journal of Youth and Adolescence, 39,* 783–800.

Vaaler, M. L., Stagg, J., Parks, S. E., Erickson, T., & Castrucci, B. C. (2010). Breast-feeding attitudes and behavior among WIC mothers in Texas. *Journal of Nutrition Education and Behavior, 42*(35), S30–S38.

van Aken, C., Junger, M., Verhoeven, M., van Aken, M. A. G., & Deković, M. (2008). The longitudinal relations between parenting and toddlers' attention problems and aggressive behaviors. *Infant Behavior and Development, 31,* 432–446.

van Geel, M., & Vedder, P. (2011). The role of family obligations and school adjustment in explaining the immigrant paradox. *Journal of Youth and Adolescence, 40,* 187–196.

van Harmelen, A. L., de Jong, P. J., Glashouwer, K. A., Spinhoven, P., … Elzinga, B. M. (2010a). Child abuse and negative explicit and automatic self-associations: The cognitive scars of emotional maltreatment. *Behaviour Research and Therapy, 48,* 486–494.

van Harmelen, A.L., van Tol, M. J., van der Wee, N. J. A., Veltman, D. J., Aleman, A., Spinhoven, P., van Buchem, M. A., Zitman, F. G., Penninx, B. W. J. H., & Elzinga, B. M. (2010b). Reduced medial prefrontal cortex volume in adults reporting childhood emotional maltreatment. *Biological Psychiatry, 68,* 832–838.

van IJzendoorn, M. H., & Sagi, A. (1999). Cross-cultural patterns of attachment: Universal and contextual dimensions. In J. Cassidy & P. R. Shaver (Eds.), *Handbook of attachment: Theory,* research, and clinical applications (pp. 713–734). New York, Guilford Press.

van Wijnen, L. C., Boluijt, P. R., Hoeven-Mulder, H. B., Bemelmans, W. E., & Wendel-Vos, G. (2010). Weight status, psychological health, suicidal thoughts, and suicide attempts in Dutch adolescents: Results from the 2003 E-MOVO project. *Obesity, 18*(5), 1059–1061.

Vandell, D. L., Burchinal, M., Vandergrift, N., Belsky, J., & Steinberg, L. (2010). Do effects of early child care extend to age 15 years? Results from the NICHD Study of Early Child Care and Youth development. *Child Development, 81*(3), 737–756.

Vaughn, L. M., Ireton, C., Geraghty, S. R., Diers, T., Niño, V., Falciglia, G. A., … Mosbaugh, C. (2010). Sociocultural influences on the determinants of breast-feeding by Latina mothers in the Cincinnati area. *Family & Community Health,* 33(4), 318–328.

Vazsonyi, A. T., & Chen, P. (2010). Entry risk into the juvenile justice system: African American, American Indian, Asian American, European American, and Hispanic children and adolescents. *Journal of Child Psychology and Psychiatry, 51*(6), 668–678.

Veenstra, R., Huitsing, G., Dijkstra, J., & Lindenberg, S. (2010). Friday on my mind: The relation of partying with antisocial behavior of early adolescents. The TRAILS Study. *Journal of Research on Adolescence, 20*(2), 420–431.

Vélez, C. E., Wolchik, S. A., Tein, J.-Y., & Sandler, I. (2011). Protecting children from the consequences of divorce: A longitudinal study of the effects of parenting on children's coping processes. *Child Development,* 82(1), 244–257.

Venetsanou, F., & Kambas, A. (2010). Environmental factors affecting preschoolers' motor development. *Early Childhood Education Journal,* 37(4), 319–327.

Verbakel, E., & Jaspers, E. (2010). A comparative study on permissiveness toward euthanasia: Religiosity, slippery slope, autonomy, and death with dignity. *Public Opinion Quarterly, 74*(1), 109–139.

Verhoeven, M., Junger, M., Aken, C., Dekovic, A., & Sken, M. A. G. (2010). Parenting and children's externalizing behavior: Bidirectionality during toddlerhood. *Journal of Applied Developmental Psychology, 31,* 93–105.

Véronneau, M.-H., Vitaro, F., Brendgen M., Dishion, T. J., & Tremblay, R. E. (2010). Transactional analysis of the reciprocal links between peer experiences and academic achievement from middle childhood to early adolescence. *Developmental Psychology, 46*(4), 773–790.

Vianna, E., & Stetsenko, A. (2006). Embracing history through transforming it: Contrasting Piagetian versus Vygotskian (activity) theories of learning and development to expand constructivism within a dialectical view of history. *Theory & Psychology, 16*(1), 81–108.

Vig, E. K., Starks, H., Taylor, J. S., Hopley, E. K., & Fryer-Edwards, K. (2010). Why don't patients enroll in hospice? Can we do anything about it? *Journal of General Internal Medicine, 25*(10), 1009–1019.

Virmani, E.A., & Ontai, L.L. (2010). Supervision and training in child care: Does reflective supervision foster caregiver insightfulness? *Infant Mental Health Journal, 31*(1), 16–32.

Visconti, K. J., & Troop-Gordon, W. (2010). Prospective relations between children's responses to peer victimization and their socioemotional adjustment. *Journal of Applied Developmental Psychology, 31*, 261–272.

Vogel, L. (2011). End-of-life planning framework calls for fewer checklists. *Canadian Medical Association Journal, 183*(1), 33.

von Bothmer, M. I. K., & Fridlund, B. (2005). Gender differences in health habits and in motivation for a healthy lifestyle among Swedish university students. *Nursing & Health Sciences, 7*, 107–118.

von der Lippe, A., Eilertsen, D. E., Hartmann, E., & Killen, K. (2010). The role of maternal attatchment in children's attachment and cognitive executive functioning: A preliminary study. *Attachment & Human Development, 12*(5), 429–444.

von Hippel, W., Henry, J. D., & Matovic, D. (2008). Aging and social satisfaction: Offsetting positive and negative effects. *Psychology and Aging, 23*, 435–439.

Von Raffler-Engel, W. (1994). *The perception of the unborn across the cultures of the world.* Seattle, WA: Hogrefe & Huber.

Votruba-Drzal, E., Maldonado-Carreno, C., Coley, R. L., Li-grining, C. P., & Chase-Lansdale, P. L. (2010). Child care and the development of behavior problems among economically disadvantaged children in middle childhood. *Child Development, 81*(5), 1460–1474.

Vouloumanos, A., Werker, J. F., Hauser, M. D., & Martin, A. (2010). The tuning of human neonates' preference for speech. *Child Development, 81*(2), 517–527.

Vuorela, N., Saha, M.-T., & Salo, M. K. (2010). Parents underestimate their child's overweight. *Acta Paediatrica, 99*(9), 1374–1379.

Vygotsky, L. S. (1962). *Thought and language* (E. Hanfmann & G. Vakar, Eds. & Trans.). New York: MIT Press and Wiley. (Original work published 1934.)

Vygotsky, L. S. (1978). *Mind in society: The development of higher psychological processes* (M. Cole, V. John-Steiner, S. Scribner, & E. Souberman, Eds.). Cambridge, MA: Harvard University Press. (Original work published 1935)

Waasdorp, T. E., Bradshaw, C. P., Duong, J. (2011). The link between parents' perceptions of the school and their responses to school bullying: Variation by child characteristics and the forms of victimization. *Journal of Educational Psychology, 103*(2), 324–335.

Wade, N. G., Johnson, C. V., & Meyer, J. E. (2008). Understanding concerns about interventions to promote forgiveness: A review of the literature. *Psychology Theory, Research, Practice, Training, 45*(1), 88–102.

Wadsworth, B. J. (1996). *Piaget's theory of cognitive and affective development: Foundations of constructivism* (5th ed.). White Plains, NY: Longman.

Wagner, T. (2000). *How schools change: Lessons from three communities revisited* (2nd ed.). New York: RoutledgeFalmer.

Waldinger, R. J., & Schulz, M. S. (2010). What's love got to do with it? Social functioning, perceived health and daily happiness in married octogenarians. *Psychology and Aging, 25*(2), 422–431.

Waldstein, A. (2010). Popular medicine and self-care in a Mexican migrant community: Toward an explanation of an epidemiological paradox. *Medical Anthropology, 29*(1), 71–107.

Walhovd, K. B., Fjell, A. M., Dale, A. M., McEvoy, L. K., Brewer, J., Karow, D. S., Karow, D. S., ... Alzheimer's Disease Neuroimaging Initiative (2010). Multi-modal imaging predicts memory performance in normal aging and cognitive decline. *Neurobiolgy of Agung, 31*, 1107–1121.

Walker, L. J., & Frimer, J. A. (2007). Moral personality of brave and caring exemplars. *Journal of Personality and Social Psychology, 93*(5), 845–860.

Wallerstein, J., & Lewis, J. M. (2007). Sibling outcomes and disparate parenting and step-parenting after divorce: Report from a 10-year longitudinal study. *Psychoanalytic Psychology, 24*, 445–458.

Wallhagen, M. L. (2010). The stigma of hearing loss. *The Gerontologist, 50*(1), 66–75.

Walsh, J. L. (2008, March). *Magazine reading as a longitudinal predictor of your women's sexual norms and behaviors.* Paper presented at 12th Biennial Meeting of Society for Research on Adolescence, Chicago, IL.

Walter, T. (2003, July 24). Historical and cultural variants on the good death. [INI]BMJ, 327,[FFO] 218–220.

Walvoord, E. C. (2010). The timing of puberty: Is it changing? Does it matter? *Journal of Adolescent Health, 47*, 433–439.

Wan, M. W., & Green, J. (2010). Negative and atypical story content themes depicted by children with behaviour problems. *Journal of Child Psychology and Psychiatry, 51*(10), 1125–1131.

Warr, M. (2007). The tangled web: Delinquency, deception, and parental attachment. *Journal of Youth Adolescence, 36*, 607–622.

Warren, C. S., Schoen, A., & Schafer, K. J. (2010). Media internalization and social comparison as predictors of eating pathology among Latino adolescents: The moderating effect of gender and generational status. *Sex Roles, 63*, 712–724.

Waterman, A. S. (1999). Identity, the identity statuses, and identity status development: A contemporary statement. *Developmental Review, 19*, 591–621.

Waterworth, S., & Jorgensen, D. (2010). It's not just about heart failure—voices of older people in transition to dependence and death. *Health and Social Care in the Community, 18*(2), 199–207.

Watson, J. B. (1930). *Behaviorism* (Revised ed.). New York: W. W. Norton.

Watson, J. B. (1998). *Behaviorism.* New Brunswick, NJ: Transaction. (Original work published 1924)

Watson, J. B. (with the assistance of Watson, R. R.). (1972). *Psychological care of infant and child.* New York: Arno Press. (Original work published 1928)

Weber, J. A., & Wong, K. B. (2010). Older adults with vision loss. *Home Health Care Services Quarterly, 29*, 105–119.

Wechsler, D. (1991). *Wechsler intelligence scale for children (WISC-III).* San Antonio, TX: The Psychological Corporation.

Wedding, D., Kohout, J., Mengel, M. B., Ohlemiller, M., Ulione, M., Cook, K., ... Braddock, S. (2007). Psychologists' knowledge and attitudes about fetal alcohol syndrome, fetal alcohol spectrum disorders, and alcohol use during pregnancy. *Professional Psychology: Research and Practice*, 38(2), 208–213.

Wegmann, K. M., & Bowen, G. L. (2010). Strengthening connections between schools and diverse families: A cultural capital perspective. *The Prevention Researcher*, 17(3), 7–10.

Weibel-Orlando, J. (1999). Powwow princess and gospelettes: Growing up in grandmother's world. In M. Schweitzer (Ed.), *Indian grandparenthood* (pp. 181–202). Albuquerque, NM: University of New Mexico Press.

Weisfeld, G. (1997). Puberty rites as clues to the nature of human adolescence. *Cross-Cultural Research: The Journal of Comparative Social Science, 31*, 27–54.

Weiss, C. C., & Baker-Smith, E. C. (2010). Eighth-grade school form and resilience in the transition to high school: A comparison of middle schools and K-8 schools. *Journal of Research on Adolescence, 20*(4), 825–839.

Weitz, R. (2010). Changing the scripts: Midlife women's sexuality in contemporary U.S. film. *Sexuality & Culture, 14*, 17–32.

Wellman, H. M. (1992). *The child's theory of mind.* Cambridge, MA: The MIT Press.

Wells-di Gregorio, S. W. (2009). Family end-of-life decision making. In J. Werth & D. Blevins (Eds.), *Decision making near the end of life: Recent developments and future directions* (pp. 247–280). New York: Routledge. Routledge Publishing.

Wender, P. H., Reimherr, F. W., Marchant, B. K., Sanford, M. E., Czajkowski, L. A., & Tomb, D. A. (2011). A one year trial of methylphenidate in the treatment of ADHD. *Journal of Attention Disorders, 15*(1), 36–45.

Werner, N. E., & Hill, L. G. (2010). Individual and peer group normative beliefs about relational aggression. *Child Development, 81*(3), 826–836.

Werth, B., & Tsiaras, A. (2002). *From conception to birth: A life unfolds.* New York: Doubleday.

Wertz, R. W., & Wertz, D. C. (1989). *Lying-in: A history of childbirth in America* (expanded ed.). New Haven: Yale University Press.

West, R. L., Bagwell, D. K., & Dark-Freudeman, A. (2008). Self-efficacy and memory aging: The impact of a memory intervention based on self-efficacy. *Aging, Neuropsychology, and Cognition, 15*, 302–329.

White, J. (2006). Multiple invalidities. In J. A. Schaler (Ed.), *Howard Gardner under fire: The rebel psychologist faces his critics* (pp. 45–71). Chicago, IL: Open Court Publishing Co.

White, L., & Edwards, J. N. (1990). Emptying the nest and parental wellbeing: An analysis of national panel data. *American Sociological Review, 55*, 235–242.

Whiteman, S. D., McHale, S. M., & Crouter, A. C. (2007). Longitudinal changes in marital relationships: The role of offspring's pubertal development. *Journal of Marriage and Family, 69*(4), 1005–1020.

Whiteman, S. D., McHale, S. M., & Crouter, A. C. (2010). Family relationships from adolescence to early adulthood: Changes in the family system following firstborns' leaving home. *Journal of Research on Adolescence, 21*(2), 461–474.

Whiting, J. B., Smith, D. R., Barnett, T., & Grafsky, E. L. (2007). Overcoming the Cinderella myth: A mixed methods study of successful stepmothers. *Journal of Divorce & Remarriage, 47*(1/2), 95–109.

Whitson, H. E., Cousins, S. W., Burchett, B. M., Hybels, C. F., Pieper, C. F., & Cohen, H. J. (2007). The combined effect of visual impairment and cognitive impairment on disability in older people. *Journal of the American Geriatrics Society, 55*, 885–891.

Whitson, H. E., Landerman, L. R., Newman, A. B., Fried, L. P., Pieper, C. F., & Cohen, H. J. (2010). Chronic medical conditions and the sex-based disparity in disability: The cardiovascular health study. *Journals of Gerontology: Medical Sciences, 65A*(12), 1325–1331.

Wiik, K. L., Loman, M. M., Van Ryzin, M. J., Armstrong, J. M., Essex, M. J., Pollak, S. D., & Gunnar, M. R. (2011). Behavioral and emotional symptoms of post institutionalized children in middle childhood. *Journal of Child Psychology and Psychiatry*, 52(1), 56–63.

Wilkinson-Lee, A. M., Zhang, Q., Nuno, V. L., & Wilhelm, M. S. (2011). Adolescent emotional distress: The role of family obligations and school connectedness. *Journal of Youth and Adolescence, 40*, 221–230.

Wilkinson, R., & Pickett, K. (2009). *The spirit level: why greater equality makes societies stronger.* New York: Bloomsbury Press.

Williams, J. (2008). Working toward a neurobiological account of ADHD: Commentary on Gail Tripp and Jeff Wickens, dopamine transfer deficit. *The Journal of Child Psychology and Psychiatry, 49*, 705–711.

Williamson, R. C., Rinehart, A. D., & Blank, T. O. (1992). *Early retirement: Promises and pitfalls.* New York: Insight Books/Plenum Press.

Willott, S., & Griffin, C. (2004). Redundant men: Constraints on identity change. *Journal of Community & Applied Social Psychology, 14*, 53–69.

Willoughby, T., & Hamza, C. A. (2011). A longitudinal examination of the bidirectional associations among perceived parenting behaviors, adolescent disclosure and problem behavior across the high school years. *Journal of Youth and Adolescence, 40*, 463–478.

Wilson, D. M., Gottfredson, D. C., Cross, A. B., Rorie, M., & Connell, N. (2010). Youth development in after-school leisure activities. *The Journal of Early Adolescence*, 30(5), 668–690.

Wilson, K. G., Chochinov, H. M., McPherson, C. J., Skirko, M. G., Allard, P., Chary, S., … Clinch, J. J. (2007). Desire for euthanasia or physician-assisted suicide in palliative cancer care. *Health Psychology, 26*, 314–323.

Wilson, S. M., Ngige, L. W., & Trollinger, L. J. (2003). Connecting generations: Paths to Maasai and Kamba marriage in Kenya. In R. R. Hamon & B. B. Ingoldsby (Eds.), *Mate selection across cultures* (pp. 95–118). Thousand Oaks, CA: Sage.

Wilson, T., Karimpour, R., & Rodkin, P. C. (2011). African American and European American students' peer groups during early adolescence: Structure, status, and academic achievement. *The Journal of Early Adolescence, 31*(1), 74–98.

Wilson, V. B., Mitchell, S. H., Musser, E. D., Schmitt, C. F., & Nigg, J. T. (2011). Delay discounting of reward in ADHD: application in young children. *Journal of Child Psychology and Psychiatry*, 52(3), 256–264.

Wimmer, H., & Perner, J. (1983). Beliefs about beliefs: Representation and constraining function of wrong beliefs in young children's understanding of deception. *Cognition, 13*, 103–128.

Windsor, T. D., & Anstey, K. J. (2010). Age differences in psychosocial predictors of positive and negative affect: A longitudinal investigation of young, midlife, and older adults. *Psychology and Aging*, 25(3), 641–652.

Windsor, T. D., & Butterworth, P. (2010). Supportive, aversive, ambivalent, and indifferent partner evaluations in midlife and young-old adulthood. *Journals of Gerontology: Psychological Sciences, 65B*(3), 287–295.

Witvliet, M., Olthof, T., Hoeksma, J. B., Goossens, F. A., Smits, M. S. I., & Koot, H. M. (2010). Peer group affiliation of children: The role of perceived popularity, likeability, and behavioral similarity in bullying. *Social Development, 19*(2), 285–303.

Wolchik, S. A., Sandler, I. N., Winslow, E., & Smith-Daniels, V. (2005). Programs for promoting parenting of residential parents: Moving from efficacy to effectiveness. *Family Court Review, 43,* 65–80.

Wolfe, D. A. (2011). Risk factors for child abuse perpetration. In J. W. White, M. P. Koss, & A. E. Kazdin (Eds.), *Violence against women and children, Vol. 1: Mapping the terrain* (pp.31–53). Washington, DC: American Psychological Association.

Wolfe, L. (2004). Should parents speak with a dying child about impending death? *New England Journal of Medicine, 351,* 1251–1253.

Wood, D., Bruner, J. S., & Ross, G. (1976). The role of tutoring in problem solving. *Journal of Child Psychology and Psychiatry, 17,* 89–100.

Wood, W. R., & Williamson, J. B. (2003). Historical changes in the meaning of death in the western tradition. In C. D. Bryant (Ed.), *Handbook of death & dying* (pp. 14–23). Thousand Oaks, CA: Sage.

Wood-Barcalow, N. L., Tylka, T. L., & Augustus-Horvath, C. L. (2010). "But I like my body": Positive body image characteristics and a holistic model for young-adult women. *Body Image, 7,* 106–116.

Woodruff, K., & Lee, B. (2011). Identifying and predicting problem behavior trajectories among pre-school children investigated for child abuse and neglect. *Child Abuse & Neglect, 35*(7), 491–503.

Woods, N. F., Mitchell, E. S., & Julio, K. S. (2010). Sexual desire during the menopausal transition and early postmenopause: Observations from the Seattle Midlife Women's Health Study. *Journal of Women's Health,* 31(7), 440–449.

World Health Organization [WHO]. (2003b). *Kangaroo mother care: A practical guide.* Geneva, Switzerland: Dept. of Reproductive Health and Research, World Health Organization.

Wray-Lake, L., Crouter, A. C., & McHale, S. M. (2010). Developmental patterns in decision-making autonomy across middle childhood and adolescence: European American parents' perspectives. *Child Development, 81*(2), 636–651.

Wright, M. O., & Masten, A. S. (2005). Resilience processes in development: Fostering positive adaptation in the context of adversity. In S. Goldstein, & R. B. Brooks (Eds.), *Handbook of resilience in children* (pp. 17–37). New York, NY: Kluwer Academic/Plenum Publishers.

Wu, C., & Chao, R. K. (2011). Intergenerational cultural dissonance in parent-adolescent relationships among Chinese and European Americans. *Developmental Psychology, 47*(2), 493–508.

Wu, T., Mendola, P., & Buck, G. M. (2002). Ethnic differences in the presence of secondary sex characteristics and menarche among U.S. girls: The Third National Health and Nutrition Examination Survey, 1988–1994. *Pediatrics, 110,* 752–757.

Wymbs, B. T., & Pelham, Jr., W. E. (2010). Child effects on communication between parents of youth with and without attention-deficit/hyperactivity disorder. *Journal of Abnormal Psychology, 119*(2), 366–375.

Xia, Y. R., & Zhou, Z. G. (2003). The transition of courtship, mate selection, and marriage in China. In R. R. Hamon & B. B. Ingoldsby (Eds.), *Mate selection across cultures* (pp. 231–246). Thousand Oaks: Sage.

Yamasaki, J., & Sharf, B. F. (2011). Opting out while fitting in: How residents make sense of assisted living and cope with community life. *Journal of Aging Studies, 25*(1), 13–21.

Yancey, G. A., & Yancey, S. W. (2002). *Just don't marry one: Interracial dating, marriage, and parenting.* Valley Forge, PA: Judson Press.

Yang, C. K., & Hahn, H. M. (2002). Cosleeping in young Korean children. *Journal of Developmental & Behavioral Pediatrics, 23,* 151–157.

Yang, Y., & Lee, L. C. (2010). Dynamics and heterogeneity in the process of human frailty and aging: Evidence from the U.S. older adult population. *Journals of Gerontology: Social Sciences, 65B*(2), 246–255.

Yates, M., & Youniss, J. (1998). Community service and political identity development in adolescence. *Journal of Social Issues, 54,* 495–512.

Yates, T. M., Allison, J. T., & Luthar, S. S. (2008). Nonsuicidal self-injury among "privileged" youths: Longitudinal and cross-sectional approaches to developmental process. *Journal of Counseling and Clinical Psychology, 76*(1), 52–62.

Yeoh, B. H., Eastwood, J., Phung, H., & Woolfenden, S. (2007). Factors influencing breastfeeding rates in southwestern Sydney. *Journal of Paediatrics and Child Health, 43,* 249–255.

Young, L. M., Baltes, B. B., & Pratt, A. K. (2007). Using selection, optimization, and compensation to reduce job/family stressors: Effective when it matters. *Journal of Business and Psychology, 21*(4), 511–539.

Young, S., & Amarasinghe, J. M. (2010). Practitioner review: Non-pharmacological treatments for ADHD: A lifespan approach. *Journal of Child Psychology and Psychiatry, 51*(2), 116–133.

Yu, H. U., & Chan, S. (2010). Nurses' response to death and dying in an intensive care unit—a qualitative study. *Journal of Clinical Nursing, 19,* 1167–1169.

Zaichkowsky, L. D., & Larson, G. A. (1995). Physical, motor, and fitness development in children and adolescents. *Journal of Education, 177,* 55–79.

Zayas, V., Mischel, W., Shoda, Y., & Aber, J. (2011). Roots of adult attachment: Maternal caregiving at 18 months predicts adult peer and partner attachment. *Social Psychological and Personality Science,* 2(3), 289–297.

Zeanah, C. H., Berlin, L. J., & Boris, N. W. (2011). Practitioner review: Clinical applications of attachment theory and research for infants and young children. *Journal of Child Psychology and Psychiatry,* 52(8), 819–833.

Zelinski, E. M., & Kennison, R. F. (2007). Not your parents' test scores: Cohort reduces psychometric aging effects. *Psychology and Aging,* 22(3), 546–557.

Zeskind, P. S., & Lester, B. M. (2001). Analysis of infant crying. In L. T. Singer & P. S. Zeskind (Eds.), *Biobehavioral assessment of the infant* (pp. 149–166). New York: Guilford Press.

Zettergren, P. (2007). Cluster analysis in sociometric research: A pattern-oriented approach to identifying temporally stable peer status groups of girls. *The Journal of Early Adolescence, 27,* 90–114.

Zhan, J.-Y., Wilding, J., Cornish, K., Shao, J., Xie, C.-H., Wang, Y.-H., . . ., Zhao, Z.-Y. (2011). Charting the developmental trajectories of attention and executive function in Chinese school-aged children. *Child Neuropsychology,* 17, 82–95.

Zimmer-Gembeck, M. J., & Helfand, M. (2008). Ten years of longitudinal research on U.S. adolescent sexual behavior: Developmental correlates of sexual intercourse, and the importance of age, gender and ethnic background. *Developmental Review, 28*, 153–224.

Zoccolotti, P., & Friedmann, N. (2010). From dyslexia to dyslexias, from dysgraphia to dysgraphias, from a cause to causes: A look at current research on developmental dyslexia and dysgraphia. *Cortex: A Journal Devoted to the Study of the Nervous System and Behavior, 46*(10), 1211–1215.

Zucker, A. N., Ostrove, J. M., & Stewart, A. J. (2002). College-educated women's personality development in adulthood: Perceptions and age differences. *Psychology and Aging, 17*, 236–244.

Zunzunegui, M., Alvarado, B., Beland, F., & Vissandjee, B. (2009). Explaining health differences between men and women in later life: A cross-city comparison in Latin America and the Caribbean. *Social Science & Medicine, 68*, 235–242.

Name Index

A

B

C

N

O

P

Q

R

S

Subject Index

D

E

S